THEORY AND PRACTICE
OF
FAMILY PSYCHIATRY

THEORY AND PRACTICE
OF
FAMILY PSYCHIATRY

JOHN G. HOWELLS
M.D., D.P.M.

Director, The Institute of Family Psychiatry
Ipswich and East Suffolk Hospital
England

WITH EDITED CONTRIBUTIONS

BRUNNER/MAZEL *Publishers* · New York

INTRODUCTION TO THE AMERICAN EDITION

CLIFFORD J. SAGER
M.D.
Professor of Psychiatry
New York Medical College

Interest in many aspects of the psychiatry of the family developed over some twenty-five years has now matured into a field that encompasses much data, as well as a unique set of theoretical constructs and clinical techniques, and so justifies the appellation of "family psychiatry." A search for therapeutic expediency has become increasingly broadened in clinical scope and supported by findings from anthropology, sociology, small-group psychology, psychiatry and other fields. Always following behind the therapeutic endeavors have come theory and rationale. Much of the accumulated knowledge of family psychiatry and many of its most original contributors are represented in this volume.

It is fitting that there be this American edition of Dr. Howells' book, which was published originally in Great Britain. The volume transcends national barriers and is of vast interest to us in the United States. The author is most generous in making explicit the many American sources that have contributed to the development of his own thinking. He, in turn, feeds back to us by adding his own rich clinical experience and by providing us with his innovative theoretical synthesis of family psychiatry. I have appreciated Dr. Howells' efforts in family psychiatry for many years and have been influenced in the organization of my own clinical services by his considered approach to the field.

The volume is exquisitely thought through and engineered. It captures family psychiatry at the currently crucial point in its history. In the first section Dr. Howells develops his model for a comprehensive theory and practice of family psychiatry. In this part of the text he refers the reader to a selection of articles which have been most influential in developing his own theoretical position. These key articles themselves con-

v

stitute the latter sections of the book. Thus, we are given an original integration of the source material that follows. All the articles are pertinent and many are milestones in the field. Dr. Howells places them in relation to one another as parts of a mosaic instead of leaving us to see them as isolated gems. This unique composition of the book makes it highly informative and stimulating to the reader.

Acceptance of Family Psychiatry

Family psychiatry is currently a somewhat unsystematized mélange of theory and practice whose common denominator consists of regarding the family as the functional unit, instead of the individual. Despite an apparent intellectual comprehension of the significance and worth of the family approach, great resistance to changing their clinical practice exists among those who received their training more than ten years ago and are invested in individual therapeutic approaches. To practice family psychiatry requires a rather thoroughgoing shift in orientation for the behavioral scientist already trained in methods of individual psychiatry—in terms of the gestalt he studies and attempts to change. It does not involve a mere conceptual addition of family factors as determinants of psychopathology, but requires a basic change in orientation. Its concepts of psychological development of the individual, the development of disturbed behavior (who does it disturb?) as well as its methods of treatment are based on an ecological systems approach that is in conflict with other theoretical positions. Behavior and symptoms are viewed as a product of family processes, which have a reciprocal relationship with each family member's intrapsychic dynamics. Processes and changes in the ecological systems rather than insights alone are seen as the major agents for producing change, although techniques for accomplishing this vary greatly from one therapist to the next. The entire family, various combinations of segments of the family or even individual members may be seen in therapy sessions, depending on the needs of the situation and the availability of family members.

Family therapy cannot make claims at present to be more effective than other forms of treatment. Outcome studies, and particularly those on a comparative basis, are still forthcoming, as they are in most other modalities of treatment. Nevertheless, family psychiatry and therapy are being included in the programs of many hospitals, clinics, universities and training centers, and family approaches are currently creating excitement and enthusiasm, winning an ever increasing number of practitioners. This enthusiasm is related to several factors: 1) dissatisfaction with the theoretical basis and the results of other therapeutic approaches; 2) the theoretically attractive concept upon which it is based—namely, that the family is ecologically the most crucial unit determining the development and functioning of the individual and so presents the ideal focus for therapeutic intervention; 3) the personal charisma of leaders in the field; and 4) the fact that the family approach lends itself to community psychiatry. As the basic social unit in the community the family becomes the natural focus for primary and secondary prevention and case finding as well as for treatment. Through the family's needs one is drawn into contact with the other agencies and systems that affect the unit. Prophylactic work goes hand in hand with therapy.

Despite its current wider acceptance, resistance to this approach is strong and only in a few centers is the family orientation taught and practiced as a major psychiatric *modus operandi*. It is the younger people who tend to be attracted to the family approach as are those who are interested in community psychiatry.

Background

To place this volume in proper perspective and to understand its timeliness it is important to bear in mind that family psychiatry's main impetus came, and to a great extent continues to come, from the therapeutic arena. About twenty-five years ago discontent with the theory and outcome of individual therapy, particularly with psychoanalysis and the psychotherapy of children, led several gifted therapists to explore alternative methods of working with the entire family: the marital dyad, parent-child groupings, sibling groupings and extended families. The inquisitiveness, desire to share, and the talents of the therapists who pioneered these approaches have given the field its freshness and sense of excitement. The early major clinical contributions came from child psychiatry and family social work agencies.

By the end of the 1950's the field of family therapy was well launched. It got off to a somewhat skewed start because the interests of most early investigators in the field led them to focus their research on families whose schizophrenic child was the original patient. These studies were based on the then widely accepted hypothesis that the cause of schizophrenia lay somewhere in pathological family dynamics. Thus, the early research work and hypothesis development centered around attempts to elucidate the genesis of schizophrenic symptoms as a result of processes within the family. Although this research was important in developing many of the concepts still used in the field, it tended to bias and limit our thinking in terms of the "schizophrenogenic" family and the needs of the child. Many of these earlier concepts are being questioned today and the scope of family psychiatry is currently broadening. For example, studies are emerging wherein an adult, not a child, is the referred or identified patient. In addition, interest is growing in families presenting a wide range of psychopathology such as depression, alcoholism or drug addiction, delinquency, neurotic behavior or marital difficulty. Such studies are increasing our range of effectiveness and deepening our theoretical understanding of family dynamics and of psychopathology.

Most of the early hypotheses of family processes and therapy leaned heavily on concepts derived from other disciplines. For example, the idea of family homeostasis derives from physiology; concepts of individual adaptation within the family relate directly to psychoanalytic models; the double-bind illustrates a communication context from which the child cannot escape; and concepts of fragmentation of the family come from sociology. Transcultural studies and the search for universals and differences among families of different cultures owe much to anthropology. This rich influx of concepts and models from other fields, while at first stimulating, soon made clear that each described a different part of the elephant and that we had yet to develop our own meaningful models. Semantics appropriate for family psychiatry are yet to be developed as we continue to utilize the languages of our earlier training, which are not adequate to deal with the unique phenomena of family dynamics. There is a great need for theoretical synthesis while at the same time avoiding premature closure and an orthodoxy that would hinder further open exploration.

Dr. Howells' Viewpoint

Dr. Howells has developed a theoretical scheme that includes and fits into place the various observations and hypotheses of other authors, including his own earlier work. His open-ended theory provides us with a theoretical framework which offers a unifying structure and yet avoids closure. We are presented with the winter skeleton of a tree. The starkness and lack of encumbrances of this model encourage the reader to fill out the branches and leaves himself. Thus, it allows for the inclusion and development of a wide variety of approaches.

In his clinical practice Dr. Howells applies his theoretical position in a consistent manner, utilizing family psychiatry in a comprehensive department of psychiatry. In his hospital and out-patient services at Ipswich and East Suffolk Hospital family psychiatry has replaced individual psychiatry as the basic approach used for all cases. As he so ably says, "Taking the family as the unit applies throughout the system of practice—it applies to the referral service, to the systematization of symptomatology, to the procedure for investigation and to the processes of management or treatment."

Dr. Howells' approach is both eminently eclectic in the theoretical dimension and pragmatic in the therapeutic. I most heartily support his approach at this point in our development of a family psychiatry. He views the individual in depth while seeing him reciprocally as a product of, as well as an influence on, his family. In regard to theory Dr. Howells believes that (p. 59): "Family psychiatry does not overlook intrapsychic events and individual procedures; it embraces both. The individual is an element in the family, and all aspects of his structure and functioning must be encompassed." Concerning a basic aspect of the treatment dimension he says (p. 61), "The individuals or part of a family that are most commonly referred should be accepted as an introduction to the family. To insist on the whole family being referred would presuppose a degree of insight from the family and the intermediaries which would not be forthcoming. . . . To insist on such a degree of insight would exclude the most disturbed families, those most in need of help. What little the family offers should be accepted initially, and the service should work to include the rest." These two quotes illustrate the rational flavor of his point of view.

The author offers his ideas as only a first step towards a comprehensive theory. He is quick to point out that the system he suggests is only tentative and is an attempt to provide a framework that may be helpful in further systematization of our growing store of data. Dr. Howells has accomplished this objective most admirably and his concept may well become the theoretical framework on which we will hang our data for some time to come.

Dr. Howells' mature and innovative thinking and experience are crystallized in this volume. It is a beautiful tribute to him and to family psychiatry and a stimulating gift to workers in the field.

November, 1970

CONTENTS

xi

5

THE COMMUNITY INTERACTION DIMENSION

PART THREE

ILLUSTRATIONS OF CLINICAL PRACTICE
Edited by John G. Howells

1

ORGANISATION

2

THE PRESENTING PATIENT

3
CLINICAL SYNDROMES

4
THERAPY

PART ONE

THEORY AND PRACTICE OF FAMILY PSYCHIATRY

by
John G. Howells

I

FAMILY PSYCHIATRY

DEFINITION

Family Psychiatry,* whereby the family is the functional unit, represents a practical and theoretical system for psychiatry.

Individual psychiatry, taking the adult as the functional unit (adult psychiatry), the child as the functional unit (child psychiatry), or the adolescent as the functional unit (adolescent psychiatry)† is obsolete.

Individual psychiatry is replaced by family psychiatry. Taking the family as the unit applies throughout the system of practice—it applies to the referral service, to the systematisation of symptomatology, to the procedures for investigation, and to the processes of management or treatment.

The referral service aims to collect the whole family, either initially or ultimately. The whole family may present at first, but more frequently it is an individual, a dyad, or part of a family. An individual of any age group or clinical category may be accepted at the beginning; the referral may consist of a dyad, e.g. marital partners, or mother and child, or father and child; part of a family may come, e.g. mother and children. The personal element first presenting may or may not be the most sick part of the family. Psychopathology in any element is nearly always an expression of dysfunction in the whole family group. In all circumstances the ideal ultimate aim is the referral of the total family.

Signs of dysfunction may appear at any point, and usually many points, in the family's structure. Attention to individual symptomatology is not enough. Assessment of symptomatology must embrace the whole family.

The procedures of investigation are planned to produce a complete picture of the family's functioning and dysfunctioning, assets and liabilities.

In treatment and management, measures are employed that can impinge on any one point or on many points in the family structure, and

---

* Howells, J. G. 1963. *Family psychiatry*. Oliver & Boyd, Edinburgh.
† Howells, J. G. 1962. The nuclear family as the functional unit in psychiatry. *J. Ment. Sci.*, **108**, 675.

bring benefit to the whole family. In family therapy the aim is to achieve a healthy family.

Family psychiatry in its theoretical system is a revolt from the present tendency to over-concentrate on individual intrapsychic events alone. It restores balance by giving significance also to events outside the individual; the most cogent are within the family, and others lie in society. Thus account is taken of the individual intrapsychic, family and social events. The family is taken as the best functional unit in clinical practice.

Why should the family be the functional unit? The choice is between the individual, the family or society. The family is a sub-system of society, and the individual a sub-system of the family. The first and most important reason for choosing the family relates to its special significance in the emotional life of the individual and society; in most societies it is the unit for child rearing. A child's emotional health or sickness is dependent on the quality of the influence coming from the individuals closest to it in its formative years, usually the other family members. Thus the family has special significance in the emotional life of people. Furthermore, sick young members of sick families are prone as adults to make sick families of their own later on and thus perpetuate the sick unit from generation to generation. The second reason relates to its position; it is midway between the individual and society. The third relates to its size; it is a manageable 'small group' in society. Occasionally the family is not the significant unit in child rearing, e.g. it may be an institution, or the greater family, the clan. Were these anomalies widespread, they would have led to the acceptance of a larger social group as the functional unit and thus to a less manageable systematisation of psychiatric services; it is fortunate that the optimum group for child rearing is a group manageable in psychiatric practice. As an element in the total field of forces in the life space, the family can claim no more significance than other elements, e.g. the individual, or the community or the culture. But in psychiatric practice it is certainly the most meaningful and convenient unit.

Rarely does a sick person not indicate a sick family, and without exception it still means family involvement. Take the case of a sick person joining a family. Immediately the family is involved. The family have accepted him as a member for motives of its own. The family itself may become ill, or it could become the best agent for producing health in him. The family is still the significant unit. Take again one sick member of an otherwise healthy family—amongst apparently healthy family members, a disturbed illegitimate adolescent, who is the consequence of an isolated unfortunate lapse by the mother, and who is rejected as the memory of an unhappy liaison. The rest of the family interrelationships may be sound. The family has just one problem—this adolescent. Yet, the adolescent may be dependent on the family for referral, cannot be understood in isolation from it and cannot be treated without taking account of the family situation. The rule holds good that the family is the functional unit and family psychiatry the procedure of choice.

When, as it is usual, a sick member indicates a sick family, the members of the family are not all sick to the same degree; the interplay of factors producing pathology from past and present life experiences do not strike each family member equally. But, whatever the degree of pathology, there is family involvement, and family psychiatry is the method of choice in its resolution.

What it is Not

The central idea of family psychiatry—the family as the unit in clinical practice—because of its novelty, provokes, as is to be expected, the intellectual and emotional prejudices usual to the acceptance of a new concept. It calls for a shift in conceptualisation. Furthermore, progress implies criticism of previous practice; the advance may be explained away by saying that it has always been practised without the critic understanding its true nature.

A common misconception is to assume that family psychiatry means using the family background of an individual to help that one person. It takes various forms, which can be illustrated from the management of a child patient. Hitherto in the children's field, emphasis has been placed on the intrapsychic functioning of the child, and little prominence given to the present environmental influences. Phantasies have been assumed to be more important than on-going traumata, even in therapy. The parents' involvement in starting and maintaining the child's illness has not been appreciated. The child has been regarded as an isolated sick individual, for whose care the parents require advice and reassurance *in order to help the child*. This is classical, old-time child guidance and *child psychiatry*. Sometimes the involvement of the parents in the child's illness is perceived, but this perception is often limited by concentrating on the mother-child relationship alone—*child and mother psychiatry*. Less often, attention is given to the involvement of both parents in the child's condition. This may lead to adjusting the joint parental attitude or ameliorating the parental illness *in order to help the child—child and parent psychiatry*. An advance from this position sees the child as a part of a family situation, parents and sibs, that requires adjustment *in order to help the child—child and family psychiatry*. But *family psychiatry* sees the child's illness as a part of family illness. It gives no more, but no less, attention to the presenting child in the procedures of investigation than it does to the remaining family members. It aims to produce a healthy family including a healthy child. Throughout, the family, and not the individual, is the functional unit.

Sometimes family psychiatry is thought of as a procedure which studies specific events in the family background which may have given rise to illness in one person. Prominence is given to such events as divorce, "broken home", hospital admission, the mobility of the family, etc. But family psychiatry sees these as incidents in a long, wide, family life experience. Divorce, for instance, may be an attempt to solve the family's problems; it is the end product of a whole group dynamic process, and the reaction of the individual to it has significance only against this far wider background.

Again, family psychiatry may be thought of as a measure which takes account of the effect on the family of mental illness in one family member. But this is but a part of the whole picture. Of course, account must be taken of such matters as the different attitudes towards a sick person in sick and healthy families, the motives for the care of the patient in the family, family attitudes leading to the individual's hospital care, the ability of the family to co-operate in treatment, the contribution of the family in causing the patient's illness; the family may be equally sick, and it may require help in its own right. Understanding will come from the study of the family as a unit. It is not a matter of the patient *and* his family, but of the patient as *part of* his family.

Due to the great interest in the new technique of family group therapy, this is sometimes thought to embrace the whole of family psychiatry. In fact, family group therapy is just one of the many measures employed in family therapy, the treatment of the family. Family therapy, in turn, is just one aspect of the total system of family psychiatry. To practise family group therapy alone is a severe limitation to the practice of family psychiatry.

The quest for the factors responsible for schizophrenia has focused attention on family psychopathology as the possible causal agent. There is such interest in this aspect of family psychopathology that it might be thought to be the whole of family psychiatry. It has led to prominence being given to the management of this one clinical condition in family practice and overlooking the value of family psychiatry in the management of a wide variety of other clinical conditions. Indeed, there is controversy as to the contribution of family psychopathology in schizophrenia and to the efficacy of resolving family psychopathology in its treatment. Whatever contribution family psychiatry has to make in schizophrenia, it has a more certain place in the management of the far commoner and equally destructive condition of emotional disorder, or neurosis.

ADVANTAGES OF FAMILY PSYCHIATRY

Family psychiatry pays attention not only to intrapsychic events, but also brings into prominence extrapsychic events in the family and community environment of the individual. Individual, family and community psychiatry are indivisible. The door is opened to new outlooks, procedures of investigation and methods of treatment.

An outstanding advantage of family psychiatry is the economy of the procedure. The information so carefully garnered to help one member of the family is precisely the information required, with small additions, to assist all the members of the family. Often the same measures of treatment will help the whole family group.

Again, within families there are 'seesaw' movements; as one member of the family improves, so another deteriorates. It is possible to treat one member of the family to the disadvantage of the remainder. What profit to a family if one member improves while the others become liabilities? Such happenings will not be apparent unless the whole family is under attention.

Furthermore, when the co-operation of the whole family is obtained, there are no impediments introduced by absent members who often feel criticised by implication.

At every level of clinical practice, referral, investigation and treatment, many advantages accrue over the traditional individual procedures.

The *referral* service allows for the acceptance of patients of any age group and of any clinical category. The presenting patient may be the least ill. Behind him are equally or more disturbed additional family members. Family psychiatry does not neglect them.

In the procedures of *investigation* much more attention is paid to the stresses bearing on the individual than in traditional procedures. These invariably arise within the intimates of the presenting patient—often within the family. Thus all possible foci of stress are brought into the investigation. It is soon apparent that it is not a matter of individual psychopathology, but a situational psychopathology involving the whole family. This new investigatory approach has been an impetus to the development of new facilities for investigation—new psychometric techniques and the useful family group diagnosis.

The processes of *treatment* are enormously enhanced by accepting the family as the functional unit. New methods of treatment have emerged which are more effective than traditional procedures, and they can be employed when traditional methods are inoperative. Even individual psychotherapy is enhanced if the therapist bears in mind that he is involved in a great deal more than just the individual patient and his psychopathology; if he casts his horizon to the family, his individual techniques are improved. Dyadic procedures are more in use. Family group therapy, sometimes termed conjoint therapy, has emerged as a profitable and promising method of treatment. Vector therapy has at last come into its own; this procedure readjusts the field of forces in the life space to bring relief and benefit to individuals and families. Greater attention to the impact of the community and culture on the family creates opportunities in the field of preventive psychiatry. By producing a healthy family, a healthy platform is developed which will maintain the health of all the family members.

Lastly, a new area for research has emerged. The infant is born and nourished in a group situation; much more attention is given to the evaluation of the group forces bearing on the infant throughout his formative years. Light is thrown, too, on those members of the family who are often neglected—father, siblings, etc. The family is a sub-unit of the community, and increasing attention is given in research to the family's involvement with the community, culture and society. Other areas demanding attention include: the reason behind the referral of a particular individual patient; the family's contribution in the aetiology of clinical conditions; the generation to generation spread of family psychopathology pointing to the familial rather than the hereditary transfer of neurosis; anomalies of family functioning which throw up new areas for investigation (e.g. one healthy member in an otherwise unhealthy family).

In the pages that follow the author asserts that the usual pattern of psychiatric practice should be that of family psychiatry, and he puts forward a system for its practice.

Clinical work has to be based upon a theory of family functioning, a theory which is still incomplete. In many areas knowledge is sparse or absent. Thus the contributions on theory in Part One represent aspirations in seeking knowledge in these areas. An indispensable aspect of theory is to develop a conceptual model of the family; the one put forward here is a simple one and one that will do as a start to our efforts in conceptualisation. Clinical progress in family psychiatry too, while definite, is still at an early stage. More experience and knowledge are required. Thus again, the contributions on clinical practice in Part One represent aspirations to solve the many problems in this area. This Part records progress to date, reveals failure as well as achievement, and points to targets for the future.

II

DIMENSIONS OF THE FAMILY

1. THE FAMILY

DEFINITION

The family, in some form, appears to be universal; at times, it may be diffuse and not easily identified as a unit. The Oxford Dictionary[1] offers the following definitions of the family: (i) 'The body of persons who live in one house or under one head, including parents, children, servants, etc.' (ii) 'The group consisting of parents and their children, whether living together or not; in wider sense, all those who are nearly connected by blood or affinity.' (iii) 'A person's children regarded collectively.' (iv) 'Those descended or claiming descent from a common ancestor.'

The first definition conforms most clearly to modern ideas of the 'nuclear family'. The nuclear family, sometimes termed the 'immediate family', or the 'elementary family', can be defined as a sub-system of the social system, consisting of two adults of different sexes who undertake a parenting role to one or more children. Hereafter, the 'nuclear family' will be referred to as the 'family'. The 'family of orientation' is often used to designate the nuclear family in which a person has, or has had, the status of a child, and the term 'family of procreation' in which a person has, or has had, the status of a parent. When authority is based on a male as head of the family we speak of a patriarchy, and when on a female as a matriarchy.

The term 'extended family' is used to refer to any grouping, related by descent, marriage or adoption, which is broader than the nuclear family and which conforms most closely to the second definition of the Oxford Dictionary. 'Lateral' extension would embrace uncles, aunts, cousins, etc., while 'vertical' extensions would embrace two or more generations.

A family exists for a particular purpose in the social context in which it finds itself, and is shaped by this fact. The unit may be a small or large nuclear family, a nuclear family extended laterally or vertically or both, an extended family large enough to merit the term 'clan', or it may melt into a community that regards itself as the effective unit.

In psychiatry, concern should be with individuals who have emotional significance as a group. This, most commonly, is the family. But a blood

9

tie is of secondary importance to an emotional tie, e.g. a servant given intimate care of the children may have more significance for them than the natural parents. Thus, in clinical practice, the concept of the family may have to be widened to take account of this.

UNIVERSALITY

Murdock[2] expresses it as his view that the family is a basic group in all human cultures. He substantiates this by a study of 250 representative cultures in which he found no exception to his view. This confirms the conclusions of Lowie[3] in an earlier study.

VARIANTS

Attempts to prove the historical development of the family through various forms to the present highly regarded nuclear family have failed. The form of the family is its response to its social background.

An extended family, sometimes termed a 'joint' family, consists of two or more nuclear families—the extension may be lateral, or, more commonly, vertical. Among the Hindus, for example, may be found an extended family consisting of kinsmen over three or four generations, and their wives and offspring. It constitutes a perpetual corporation owning property generation after generation, and not dissolving after the death of every husband. When descent is dependent on the female side of the family it is termed matrilineal, when on the male, patrilineal. In some extended families, where many women may be present, the word meaning mother is used by the child to refer to other women around him as well; thus it is as if the child were brought up by many mothers.

A polygamous family is dependent on plural marriage. There are two or more nuclear families having one married partner in common. In polygyny there is marriage of one man with more than one woman simultaneously. It may be due to economic factors, or as a means of ensuring an heir. By Koranic law a man may have four wives. The Mormons of Utah practised polygyny until 1890. In polyandry one woman is married simultaneously to more than one man. It is usually associated with matrilineal descent and matriarchy. When the co-husbands are brothers, it is known as Adelphic Polyandry. Sometimes the family is informal, the woman being visited by a succession of men and dwelling alone with her children. Amongst the Nayar of Malabar, the women lived together in a joint family of several mothers and their children. Hobhouse, Wheeler and Ginsberg[4] found monogamy in 66 societies, polygamy in 409 societies (polygyny in 378 and polyandry in 31).

Murdock[2] states that, of 192 societies studied, 47 (24%) have normally a nuclear family, 92 (48%) possess some form of extended family, and 53 (28%) have polygamous, but not extended, families.

Many societies have institutions founded to extend the family in time, to avoid its dissolution at the death of one of the spouses. Levirate is a practice by which a widow is inherited by her deceased husband's successor; it is found amongst ancient Hebrews and in parts of Africa. Sororate is a practice by which a wife is replaced by a sister if she dies or is barren. It is still practised by some primitive people today.

Variants have their counterpart in modern society, close examination of which shows the diversity of family forms and that the nuclear family is not universal. These modern variants are of great research interest, and test many of the hypotheses concerning family functioning. Clinical practice tends to be based on an idealised concept of the family, an ideal often coming from personal prejudice, or personal experience of the worker, and usually conforming to the model of the nuclear family. Atypical family formations are not necessarily unhealthy. The real issue is not the structure of the family, but whether the needs of the family members are being met.

FUNCTIONS

There is much agreement amongst authorities on the functions of the family, which are usually taken to be: (i) the satisfaction of the affectional needs of the family members; (ii) the satisfaction of sexual needs by reproduction; (iii) the protection, upbringing and socialisation of children; (iv) the material maintenance of the members of the family by forming an economic unit; (v) other, normally subsidiary, functions that may have a political, ritual or religious connotation. The emphasis given to each function is not only a matter of variation amongst individual families, but is influenced also by class, community and cultural considerations. The family is a flexible unit.

That family members have affectional needs has become clearer as more study was given to personality. Hitherto it was given less prominence, and it is still excluded from some lists of family functions. Man does not live by bread alone. While his educational and social aspirations may be met elsewhere, his affectional needs are satisfied through his intimates, his fellow family members. Their responses make for harmony, or disharmony that may amount to emotional illness. His present experiences in his family of procreation are vital, but no less important is his past life in his family of orientation. And the two are linked.

The family permits satisfaction of sexual needs leading to the procreation of children. Such children are usually of legitimate status, their family affiliation being known, so that they can enjoy the advantages coming from this. In nearly all societies sex within marriage is privileged and protected by taboos and permissions, which vary greatly but aim to foster the right sexual expression for that society. That sex is not the sole factor in marriage and family is suggested by the fact that sexual liaison is frequently allowed without marriage; in Murdock's[5] study of 250 societies, only 54 forbid liaisons between non-relatives. Furthermore, sexual liaison is frequently allowed outside marriage; in the same study, a majority of societies allowed liaison between a married man and his female relatives.

Children result from sexual expression and have to be reared by the family, which appears to offer the best milieu for their upbringing that can be devised in most, but not all, societies. The family supplies the care of two adults—an insurance against the loss of one. The adults are of different sexes, thus allowing adjustment to both sexes. When the child is the product of a profound act of affectional co-operation, it is cherished as an expression of this and protected thereby. The family as the unit for child rearing is not exceptional. Other methods are practised, e.g. communal or the semi-communal upbringing in the *kibbutz*.[6,7] It may be modified or changed in the future. The child has a number of requirements, and, as long as these are met, the method employed can fit the social system. Society protects its children and its methods of rearing and hence the family. Rearing includes physical care, education and socialising.

The family must provide material maintenance for its members—food, clothing, warmth, shelter, protection and recreation. The two adults are complementary—the wife busy in home and child care, while the husband labours to keep them. Nuclear families, or a number of families linked by kinships, may form strong economic units that lead to mutual prosperity. While the parents support the children, so the children may support the aged parents later on. But nature is flexible. As long as the family is maintained it may allow reversal of work roles, or even work by both.

OPTIMUM SIZE OF FAMILY

Little thought seems to have been given to the question of what is the ideal size of the family to carry out its functions. There may be a limit to the capacity of an individual to pay attention to emotional influences. An individual family member may thus be able to respond only to a few others in a given time. If so, research has yet to be definite about this. The smaller the family, the more concentrated the emotional influences from the small number of people involved. If these influences are beneficial, all is well. Should they be adverse, there is no escape. The larger the family, the more dilute the influences, but with the advantage that each individual has a far wider choice in his relationships, and is thus able to acquire those relationships which suit him best.

In child rearing, excessive emphasis is given to the contribution of the mother, important though it may be. The child is in a group situation from the moment of birth, and benefits from this. Definite knowledge on the spacing of children might show what is a manageable load on the parents and to what extent older children can supplement the parental care of the younger children. Usually, a large number of young children is an economic strain on a family, while a large number of older children makes for a strong economic unit.

THE FUTURE OF THE FAMILY

At first, study of the family tended to be an appraisal of its material and economic aspects. Poverty used to be a real problem. With its conquest, more attention was given to matters of child rearing and reproduction. More recently, the family as an affectional unit has become a focus for study.

A number of researchers in industrial countries see a decline in family functioning, others see an improvement. Kluckhohn[8] represents the former view: '... the traditional philosophy of the family has been threatened in recent decades. Both in Europe and in the United States, the function of protection for the aged, the infirm, and the distressed is being taken over more and more by the State. Greatly increased geographical mobility, changed patterns in regard to employment of married women, and other economic developments make it possible to regard this long-established functional continuity as still a constant. Under modern urban conditions, both men and women can enjoy opportunities (which previously were easily accessible only in family life) without surrendering their independence or assuming family responsibilities.' Spiegel, in Chapter XV, can see dire consequences of acculturisation.

On the other hand, Fletcher[9] maintains that in all true respects the family strength has been improved. He states that there is now a far more satisfactory and refined provision for the needs of the family than in the pre-industrial period or in early industrial Britain, when women were inferior and subjected, women and children were frequently exploited within or outside the family, and conditions in the home were deplorably inadequate. He goes on, 'There is little doubt, then, that the essential functions of the family, centred upon sexual relationships, parenthood and homemaking, are far more satisfactory in modern standards than they were in the family of the distant or the recent past.' He states that the position of the family has been strengthened in its non-essential functions, too. For instance, both parents, husband and wife, are now more responsible members of society than they ever were in the past.

Furthermore, the economic functions of the family have improved. The family today has expert advice much more readily available to it. The husband has security of tenure protected by his trade union or professional organisation. The child in the family has far more educational opportunities than ever before, more of his life is ordained by society as a whole, he is healthier, and the handicapped have better care. Recreational opportunities are greater for the whole family.

Similarly, Parsons[10] has argued that despite divorces and related phenomena, Americans recently have been marrying on an unprecedented scale. They have also been having children in increasing numbers, and they have been establishing homes for themselves, as family units, on a very large scale. This, he feels, would not seem to indicate irresponsibility.

Civilisations change their character with time, and modern society is no exception. Industrialisation has brought a decline in the importance of inherited wealth, and with it social mobility as the class structure narrows. There is greater physical mobility with great waves of emigration and immigration. Women earn their own living. Knowledge explodes old superstitions and faiths, and so new morals and ideals take their place. Seguin[11] has given a vivid account of rapid changes which take place in Peru when primitive communities are absorbed into industrialised societies; family structure changes to a more nuclear type of family.

It would be helpful if there were means of estimating, by agreed signs of family disorder, whether a family system was working well or not. Knowledge is lacking, and some of the indices employed are patently unreliable. For instance, is a high divorce rate a sign of health or ill-health? Divorce figures are difficult to interpret. It occurs more frequently in the childless marriages and in the early years of marriage. But marriage may be as much under strain in its later years, parents keeping together for the sake of the children. Does this make for successful child rearing, or is it a danger to it? Is not divorce an attempt to break up an unhealthy unit in order to recreate healthy ones? Similarly, is a high birth-rate a sign of family stability or a sign of family disorganisation? Again, does physical mobility lead to loss of support from the extended family, or is it a gain to be independent from an extended family, should it be malevolent?

Families are resilient. The main functions of the family are so fundamental that, however social circumstances change, means are found to carry them out. Young[12] gives a fascinating account of the movement of families from a long established community in East London to a new estate outside. Child rearing in London was dependent on an extended family system, which made the maternal grandmother the mother's principle aid in the care of the children. Outside London, the mother's principle aid became the previously neglected father. In either event, children received care. Family resilience is highly correlated with family emotional health; thus breakdown at acculturisation may be an index of family ill-health rather than a product of the change.

The family in modern society is considered by Anshen,[13] Bott,[14] Eisenberg,[15] Elmer,[16] Emerson,[17] Folsom,[18] Glick,[19] Goodsell,[20] Howard,[21] Klineberg,[22] Lowie,[23] Parsons,[24] Parsons and Bales,[10] Porot,[25] Waller and Hill,[26] Westermarck,[27] Zimmerman,[28] Zimmerman and Frampton,[29] and Goode.[30]

Some authors discuss the family as a social unit in relation to its psychological problems—Adler,[31] Flugel,[32] a G.A.P. report,[33] Miller,[34] Spiegel and Bell,[35] Winnicott,[36] Hill,[37] Hess and Handel,[38] Opler,[39] Myers and Roberts,[40] Richardson,[41] Pearse and Crockner,[42] and Ackerman.[43]

Concentration on families in primitive societies is found in Benedict,[44] Malinowski,[45] Mead,[46] and Eaton and Weil.[47]

2. CONCEPTUALISATION OF THE FAMILY

INTRODUCTION

Humanity flows through time. The Past reaches the Present and flows on into the Future. This is a dynamic process of which we are a part, and which we perceive from within the process.

Individuals usually coalesce into small loose groups, the families in the time-space continuum. Time passes, and individuals break off from the families to form new families; and these again pass on into time, coalescing and breaking up.

These coalescing groups, the families, need description. They are complex. Categorisation is essential, so that an understandable description can be communicated to others. To be able to encompass them calls for some frame of reference, which should take account of the separate functioning parts of the family and the family as a whole.

Furthermore, the family is an ever-changing, flowing dynamic entity. To grasp change is usually beyond our conceptualisation. Therefore, we freeze the family process at one moment in time, usually our first contact with the family, and describe what we see. We must be careful to add dynamism to this static picture.

Life development is not smooth, nor is human development—hence pain, anguish and incompetence. For the clinician, description is more than a theoretical exercise. For sick families, he needs a conceptual framework that will allow assessments to be made, therapy to be planned and the outcome to be predicted.

Furthermore, a clinician has to pay special attention to the emotional aspects of the family. It must be confessed that emotion and emotional disorder are concepts not easy to define. Emotion is perhaps the best word we have. Attempting more precise definitions in our present state of knowledge may be disadvantageous. Emotional phenomena are real enough. We cannot deny the existence and force of emotion, even if we cannot define it. For the population at large, the difficulty is even greater. They find it difficult to grasp the significance of emotional matters. It may be due to the fact that emotional matters are inherently subtle, or just unfamiliar, or it may be that the failure to grasp, lack of insight, is a quality of a disturbed population.

AN ANALYSIS OF CONCEPTUAL MODELS

Reuben Hill and Hansen,[48] in an important paper, state, 'Conceptual frameworks are elusive and abstract; indeed, some students have found them to be almost ephemeral.' They go on to analyse many studies of conceptual models of the family, from which they identify five conceptual frameworks:

1. *The interactional approach.* In this approach the family is a unity of interacting persons, each occupying a position within the family and having a number of assigned roles. It has focused on the internal aspects of the family, but neglected consideration of the family as an entity in relation to the community.

2. *The structure-function approach.* In this approach the family is viewed as a social system, one of the many components of the complete social system (society). At best, this approach studies the functions which the family performs in society. This framework, to date, has tended to emphasise the statics of structure, and to neglect change and dynamics.

3. *The situational approach.* Situational analysis studies the situation itself, or the individual overt behaviour in response to the situation. Rather than emphasise interaction, like the interactionalists, situationalists turn to the study of the family as a social situation for behaviour. The family is seen as a unit of stimuli acting towards a focal point (e.g. a child).

4. *The institutional approach.* This is strongly allied with historical analysis. Institutionalists emphasise the family as a social unit, in which dindividual and cultural values are of central concern. It is concerned with broad sweeps of time, and not with individual acts, interacts or transacts.

5. *The developmental approach.* Family developmentalists view the family as an arena of interacting personalities, intricately organised internally into paired positions. The approach furnishes an opportunity for the accretion of generalisations about the internal development of families, from their formation in the engagement and wedding to their dissolution in divorce or death.

This important study underlines the difficulty and complexity of the task of conceptualisation. To be satisfactory, a framework must encompass essential elements from the five approaches.

NOSOLOGICAL CLASSIFICATIONS

The dictates of clinical work have led to a number of clinicians attempting working classifications of family structure and functioning. Some of these will now be described. Their usual aim is to arrive at a family diagnosis, so that the pathology of the family can be described in meaningful terms.

Ackerman and Behrens[49] have tentatively identified seven deviant family groups. These, they say, should be compared with the 'true' family group, which is a social unit externally integrated with the community, as are also its individual members. The seven deviant family groups are as follows:

1. *The externally isolated family group.* This shows the characteristics of failure of emotional integration into the community.

2. *The externally integrated family group.* There is active participation with the community or in the community, but this may compensate for a basic failure in the internal life of the family.

3. *The internally unintegrated family group.* There is failure of internal unity with conflict.

4. *The unintended family group.* Here there tends to be a subordination or exclusion of the needs of the child, with egocentric fulfilment of each parent's individual needs.

5. *The immature family group.* There is immaturity of the parents, with dependence on the extended family.

6. *The deviant family group.* Here there is rebellion against community mores. In one type there is internal integration but rebellion against the community, while in the other type there is internal disintegration with rebellion occurring both inside and outside the family.

7. *The disintegrated, or regressed, family group.* This family group is characterised by trends that have the potential of breaking up the group.

Ehrenwald[50] designed an inventory of 30 attitudes and/or traits. These were grouped in ten triads, or clusters of three traits. Analysis of results with a number of families showed the following family constellations: (i) patterns of sharing and co-operation; (ii) patterns of contagion; (iii) complementary patterns; (iv) patterns of resistance and rebellion.

Patterns of sharing and co-operation belong to the well adjusted area of interaction. Patterns of contagion derive from the area of poorly adjusted family interaction, and tend toward the perpetuation of disturbed patterns within the family. Complementary patterns bring up the fact of change into the fluctuating attitudes in a given society. Patterns of resistance and rebellion tend to counteract the trend towards perpetuation of neurotic or disturbed patterns. They may become a major problem to the coherence of the family structure, and lead to strife and dissension. On the other hand, they may carry, within themselves, the seeds of change for the better.

The effects of contagion were described by Ehrenwald in a later paper.[51] The spread by contagion can be both horizontal and vertical. In the latter case it is transmitted from one generation to the next along genealogical pathways. Homonymic types of pathology implies that contagion of clinically identical pathology takes place. Heteronymic contagion implies that dissimilar types of pathology are transmitted. However, against contagion, or the spread of contagion, there are mechanisms of defence within the family. This factor of 'defence' has similarity to Jackson's 'family homeostasis'[52] and Spiegel's[53] 'equilibration' of the family group. These mechanisms of psychosocial defence are comparable in the family to the ego defences of the individual. Ehrenwald suggests that family diagnosis can be based on diagnosis of patterns of interaction prevailing in the family group. This approach was expanded by him in more detail in 1963.[54]

Titchener and Emerson[55] have devised, from a system for individual interview, a family relations inventory, and an observational meeting with the entire family, an experimental typology of families. It arose from a need to know what kinds of children are reared by what kinds of families. The family types were to be differentiated by qualities of five parameters, these being: role allocation and role behaviour, identification processes, closeness and remoteness of associations, communication, and solution of family conflict by establishing family standards. The typology is based upon a central principle, which states that when the family organisation is tight and cohesive there is need for close adherence to family standards explicitly stated, and when emotional conflict is allowed to erupt in the family system the family standards are vague and gain little adherence. The types of families are stationed along points on the continuum between the two extremes just mentioned. The types are as follows.

1. *The protective unit.* The family is observed to stick closely together against external pressure.

2. *The projective unit.* The family is a stage for playing out impulses and interpersonal difficulties. There are few clear indications, but some outright a-social or antisocial behaviour.

3. *The physical unit.* Here custom only has forced the parents to fulfil social requirements.

4. *The dominated unit.* Here one member of the family, usually the most disturbed member, holds an inordinate sway over the others.

5. *The stable unit.* Here there is tendency to immobility and resistance to change.

6. *The experimental unit.* Here the family functions in a mobile and even venturesome manner.

Otto[56] has developed a framework which may enable practitioners to obtain an understanding of a family by considering the family in terms of a number of clearly distinguishable strength dimensions. They are as follows:

1. The ability to provide for the physical, emotional and spiritual needs of the family.

2. The ability to be sensitive to the needs of the family members.

3. The ability to communicate effectively.

4. The ability to provide support, security and encouragement.

5. The ability to initiate and maintain growth, producing relationships and experiences within and without the family.

6. The capacity to maintain and create constructive and responsible community relationships.

7. The ability to grow with and through children.

8. An ability for self help, and the ability to accept help when appropriate.

9. An ability to perform family roles flexibly.

10. Mutual respect for the individuality of family members.

11. The ability to use a crisis, or seemingly injurious experience, as a means of growth.

12. A concern for family unity, loyalty and interfamily co-operation.

Serrano *et al.*[57] recognise that the various types of adolescent disorder may be related to four types of unhealthy family interaction. The types are:

1. Infantile maladjustment in adolescents.
2. Childish maladjustment in adolescents.
3. Juvenile maladjustment in pre-adolescents and adolescents.
4. Pre-adolescent maladjustment in adolescents.

The 'infantile' maladjustment expressed itself in schizophrenia, with autistic behaviour typical of early infancy. The 'childish' maladjustment expressed itself in aggressive behaviour that appeared uncontrollable. The 'juvenile' maladjustment expressed itself in anxious and fearful behaviour. The 'pre-adolescent' maladjustment in adolescents expressed itself in youngsters who demanded the privileges of young adulthood.

Markowitz and Kadis[58] have classified families as being (i) father-centred families, (ii) mother-centred families, (iii) child-centred families and (iv) family-centred families. In the first instance, the family revolves around the father. He has sole importance and constant gratification. In the second, the mother endeavours to be the magical mother. In the third, paramount importance is given to the child and his welfare as giving status to the family. In the last, there is over-emphasis on the importance of the family as a unit, and the individual is sacrificed to the dictates of the family.

Voiland[59] and her colleagues classify families into four main groups—perfectionist, inadequate, egocentric and unsocial.

A Suggested Family Model

A study of the authorities previously mentioned, the requirements of the situation and clinical experience would suggest that a satisfactory conceptual framework must embrace the following:

1. The individual as an amalgam of the physical and mental; his whole functioning in health and disease, at all times of life.

2. Reciprocal interactions in the family involving individuals, dyads, family coalitions and the whole family.

3. The family as a small group with a structure and properties—roles, leadership patterns, qualities, standards, etc.

4. The family as a sub-system of society and endowed with social properties. The family is an entity in a field of forces, and thus there is a transactional process that includes all family elements, the extended family, community and culture.

5. The material structure of the family.

6. The historical development of the family. Thus the time sequence of Past, Present and Future.

7. The family as a unit of change—its dynamism, its flow, the process.

8. Family functioning and dysfunctioning, health and pathology.

9. Flexibility to allow for different sizes, states and conditions.

10. Practicality that allows the framework to be expanded for research, or contracted according to the dictates of the day-to-day work.

Labelling of families as clinical or other categories is to be avoided. Labelling has a disadvantage of concentrating upon one element, which by chance has come into focus, and thus of giving that element disproportionate attention. In individual psychiatry, for instance, such labels as anxiety neurosis, obsessional neurosis, depression, etc. have focused upon the presenting symptom in the individual, and this has led to a situation where the symptom itself is regarded as the illness and scarce attention is given to the rest of the psychopathological processes within the individual. Such labels limit description. It is the whole *process* in individual, family and society which has to be understood and described and then re-patterned to bring health, efficiency and competence into the individual, family and social system.

It is suggested[60, 61] that the above can be satisfied in a 15-dimensional approach to the family. Five dimensions are each described at three consecutive time periods, the Past, the Present and the Future. The five are those of the Individual Dimension, the Relationship Dimension, the Group Properties Dimension, the Material Circumstances Dimension, the Family-Community Interaction Dimension.

Normally, a family description starts with the Present in its five dimensions. To understand the Present in the light of what has gone on before, then requires a description of the Past in five dimensions. Ideally it should be completed with a description of the Future in its five dimensions; in our present stage of knowledge this is only predictable within crude limits, e.g. that a university career is possible, a marriage breakdown likely or financial difficulties a probability.

The analysis of a simple three-member family is taken for illustration.

1. The *individual dimension* can diagrammatically be represented as shown in Fig. 1.

2. But the individual is not a motionless monument. He *relates* all the while within the family group. Father interacts on mother, mother on father, father on the child, and the child on father, mother on the child,

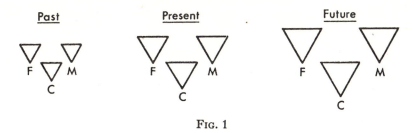

FIG. 1

and the child on the mother. This, then, is a dynamic situation. Minute by minute, hour by hour, day by day, we have the cut and thrust of daily living. This family experience can be seen in the Present, and it also has had a Past, and will inevitably have a Future. The *relationship dimension* is depicted with arrows in Fig. 2.

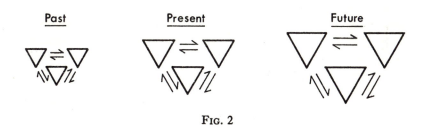

FIG. 2

3. The family members make a small *group*, and thus all that is true about small group dynamics will also be true of the family. This will apply not only now, but has applied in the Past and will apply in the Future. The *group properties dimension* can be diagrammatically represented as shown in Fig. 3.

FIG. 3

4. The family, too, lives in *material circumstances*. They have a house of a certain size in a particular neighbourhood, with a garden or otherwise. They have a certain income, with certain recreational facilities, etc. They keep to a certain diet. The family members have these circumstances now —they differed in the Past, and they will differ again in the Future. The *material circumstances dimension* can be diagrammatically represented, Fig. 4.

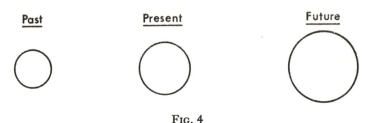

Fig. 4

5. This dynamic group of individuals in its material circumstances *reacts with the community*, and the community in turn reacts with the family. This interaction normally takes place at two levels, the level of the individual and the level of the group.

The individual reacts with the extended family outside, with friends, neighbours, workmates, schoolmates, chance acquaintances, and all these individuals in turn react on the individual in the family. But more than this, the group as a whole reacts with the social system as a whole. In the social system the family is expected to subject itself to the dictates of society. To the family, the social system is symbolised by the term 'they' —'they' being the subtle, intangible community or public opinion. All the while 'they' formulate principles and precepts which are imposed upon the family. 'They' convey what they feel about this or that or other issues through the mass media of communication, the Press, radio, television, etc. All the while, the family is under the scrutiny of 'they', and feels impelled to conform to the standards of 'they'.

This situation applies now, also applied in the Past and will apply again in the Future. The *family-community interaction dimension* can be represented by Fig. 5.

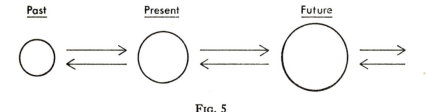

Fig. 5

In Fig. 6 it is now possible to bring together the five dimensions in each of the three time sequences.

Not only is the individual dependent on the past for health, but also for pathology. This is a matter not only of genetic endowment, but also of generation to generation communication, which may determine pathology and the expression of pathology. Thus the family description must include health and pathology in its 15 dimensions.

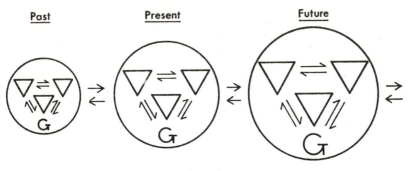

FIG. 6

Family description should thus be based upon 15 dimensions encompassing the dynamic flow through time as a healthy and pathological unit. Labels are avoided. The *process* is all important.

The five dimensions will now be considered in more detail and hereinafter they determine the shape of this book.

3. THE INDIVIDUAL DIMENSION

This takes account of the individual members of the family. They may be of any age, from infancy to senium, and of either sex. Each is met in the Present, but has also a Past and is expected to achieve a Future. To attempt a complete assessment of this dimension would cover ground already familiar to the reader, and thus a relevant summary only is presented.

Assessment of the individual in the *Present* covers every aspect of his functioning and dysfunctioning as a social being. It includes such matters as physical characteristics, vocalisation, memory, perception, imagination, motivation, intellectualisation, interests, value systems, family attitudes, social attitudes and emotional behaviour. To all this must be added an account of handicaps, deviations and emotional dysfunctioning. Many charts of individual assessment are available. The complexity of the subject does not allow for final agreement amongst authorities. The subject in general is reviewed by Allport[62] and as it applies to children by Thompson,[63] Carmichael[64] and Mussen.[65]

The evaluation of the individual in the Present is followed by a description of his life in the *Past*. This shows how his endowment has been shaped by his environmental experience from conception to the present. It includes every aspect of his functioning and dysfunctioning as a social being, as mentioned above. The exploration extends from intra-uterine life, through infancy, childhood, adolescence, adulthood and middle age, to old age.

Recent work suggests that the foetus may be influenced by physical and emotional factors in utero—and at times will be in hazard thereby.

The field has been extensively reviewed by Montagu,[66] and by Pasamanick and Knobloch.[67] That emotional changes in the mother may be significant for the state of the infant is suggested by the work of Sontag,[68] who found that maternal emotion or fatigue produces a marked effect on foetal activity, and that very active foeti tend to be light in weight and to show a minimum of fat storage. Some experimental work by Spelt,[69] whose paper is included in this book (Chapter IV), suggests that an infant in utero can be conditioned to vibration; thus it may possibly be conditioned as well to other stimuli from within and without the mother. Stott[70] has adducted evidence for a congenital factor in maladjustment and delinquency.

The developing infant gains from the environment by learning in the widest sense; this can be pictured in psychoanalytical terms, as has been done by Anna Freud.[71] Experiences in the first year have been a special field of study by Spitz.[72] There is no final knowledge on the respective contribution of endowment and environment. The tendency to exaggerate the latter is counteracted by the work of Chess and colleagues.[73] The contributions of Piaget are reviewed by Woodward.[74] That the environment enriches is exemplified by a paper in this book by Greenacre[75] (Chapter V). Infancy passes into childhood; in Chapter VI Money et al.[76] present a striking illustration of the potency of the environment in childhood in shaping human characteristics, in this instance gender sex. The child's needs have been reviewed by Szurek.[77] Childhood passes into adolescence, and the individual grows and matures still shaped by his environment. An illustration of its influence, a perverse influence in this case, is given by Serrano et al.[78] (Chapter VII); and this age group is extensively considered by Hall[79] and Jersild.[80] Adulthood brings the special experiences of courtship, marriage, pregnancy and parenthood. Middle age adds the menopause, a time of maximum occupational responsibility, and the exodus of the children from the family. Old age can bring grandparenthood, retirement, failing powers, loneliness, dependence, and finally death.

Having assessed the individual's personality as seen in the Present, and the contribution of the Past in shaping it, we should now move on to predicting the experience of this individual in the *Future*. This practice is difficult to achieve, except in the most general terms. It may be possible to predict continuing good health or, conversely, a breakdown in health; suitability for particular occupations or careers may be established; the limits set by intellectual status can be outlined; the probable tendency to emotional ill-health or delinquent behaviour may be prognosticated.

Family psychiatry does not deny the importance of the individual dimension, the need for its careful assessment and for improved precision in its evaluation. But the remaining dimensions are seen as being equally important. Because of their comparative neglect, they are given more attention here.

4. THE RELATIONSHIP DIMENSION

The interaction between persons has not received the same degree of attention from psychopathologists as have the intrapersonal processes of the individual. Thus it deserves longer consideration here. Interaction includes consideration of relationships and of communication.

Relationship is the standing of one person to another. In psychological and psychiatric work special attention is given to the kind of feeling between people; a qualitative judgement is involved, e.g. hostile, dependent, etc.

Communication, in the psychological and psychiatric field, is concerned with the process of connection between persons. It includes (i) study of the means for the passage of information, and (ii) the meaning or message passed between persons, i.e. how it is passed and what is passed.

The interaction starts and ends with the persons involved having standing to one another, i.e. a relationship. Persons start with standing to one another, a meaning to be passed is formulated, the meaning is passed through the process of conveyance, the meaning is received, the standing between the persons is altered. Thus three elements are involved, the standing (relationship), the meaning (message), and the process of conveyance.

The term 'relationship' has been used to head this section, because often, in common usage, the term is employed to cover the whole interaction, the standing and the conveyance. In the following discussion the two terms are distinct.

While the standing between individuals and the meanings conveyed between them have received some attention from psychopathologists, although less so than the intrapsychic life of the individual, less attention has been given to the process of conveying meaning between people. Also, there has been even less interest in non-verbal, as against verbal, communication. What follows is an attempt to redress the balance.

COMMUNICATION

Communication denotes conveyance between people. It includes consideration of the meaning, message or information that is conveyed, and the process of conveyance, the apparatus, the channels. It applies in a conveyance between one person and another (e.g. husband and wife), one person and group (e.g. husband and family), group and group (e.g. family and community). Here it is restricted to the first expression, but what is said is relevant to consideration of communication in the family group and later on in family-community interaction.

The purpose of communication is to influence others, to react to the present situation, to gain security by mutual support, and to receive from others all those elements essential to maturation, existence and security.

It can be intrapersonal or interpersonal. The former belongs to the consideration of cybernetics in the individual dimension. Wooldridge[81] and Ashby[82, 83] offer introductions to the subject. Introductions to the general theory of communication will be found in the writings by Crowley *et al.*,[84] on human communication in those by Cherry,[85] on disorders of communication in a symposium,[86] introductions to communication in its application to psychiatry in the valuable writings of Ruesch[87–112] (a synopsis of his views will be found in Chapter VIII), and in the A.P.A. report edited by Watkins and Pasamanick.[113]

Sometimes the communication theory has been employed in trying to explain the whole of human behaviour. Our limited knowledge does not allow us yet to do this from this vantage point. When knowledge of behaviour is infinite, truth will appear the same from many vantage points.

Meaning

Communication is concerned with the emission, transmission and admission of meaning. The meaning conveyed may arise directly from the sender, or he may be the means of indirect communication from others, e.g. father's views of a child may be conveyed to the child through the mother.

The cues, signs and meanings conveyed from one individual to the other may be simple, for example, a smack to a child, or complex, for example, the pathos of a clown. They are sometimes difficult to discern; a slight intonation of voice can, by cultural habit, convey to another person feelings of interest, affection or empathy. There may be reason to suppose that in the infant relationships are more likely to be conveyed by simple cues, involving one of the basic senses, and that in the course of development the cues, or meanings, become more subtle. It is possible that the mere physical handling of the child by a parent can, over a period of time, begin to have special meanings to the infant; we infer that this is so from the case of a child 'playing up' when the mother wishes to go out in the evening, even though the mother seems only to have gone through the usual repertoire of movements.

Signs are representations. A signal is different; it is an arrival. A symbol, e.g. a word, allows conceptualisation by representing an entity. Semeiotics, the science of signs, concerns itself with events in their functions as symbols. Within it there are three fields: (i) syntactics, which is concerned with the relationships of symbols to other symbols; (ii) semantics, which deals with the relations of signs to the events or objects they purport to designate; (iii) pragmatics, which is the science of the relation of signs to their human interpreters. The pragmatic aspects of language interests the psychiatrists most.

Language is but one channel of communication by the use of words, but it is the primary one in human communication. Linguistics studies phonology, which describes the sounds made when people talk, morphology, which describes the grouping of these sounds into syllables, and syntax, the description of the organisation of words and syllables into utterances. None of these fields is concerned with meaning in language, which is the field of semantics.

Signs, symbols, words, messages, often have an added meaning. An intonation may suggest irony, sarcasm or cynicism. The intensity of the communication may give added meaning—a whisper may denote secrecy, a shout, alarm. The timing of messages in communication may have meaning, as may the sequences of messages. Emotion may add meaning to a message and give it a feel all of its own. Words and actions may have a meaning given to them by the total situation, e.g. a silence may be very meaningful in some contexts. Similarly, a social situation imposes meanings, the role of the individual, the rules of the situation, what is expected, e.g. in one context a smack on a child's bottom may be a sign of the greatest hurt and humiliation, in another a sign of play.

Messages may be distorted by the sender, or by the receiver, or by the process of transmission. Expectations, wishful thinking, prejudices play their part in distortion. Again, the recipient tends to give to the words of others the same meaning which they have for him.

The flow of meaning between one person and another may be security-producing, positive, beneficial, constructive, or it may be insecurity-producing, negative, hurtful, threatening and destructive. Meanings passing between individuals have infinite capacity for help or hurt, health or sickness. They have special force when emanating from persons of particular significance to the individual—those persons in his immediate family circle and those around him in his formative years. The essential matter is the meaning given to the signs in terms of the security and self-respect of the recipient. In the past, excessive attention has been given to the intrapsychic events set in train by the admission of meanings at a moment in time. It has been overlooked that communication is a continuous process, e.g. communication between parent and child. Modification of the stressful meanings themselves can resolve situations and bring relief. Resolution is attempted in psychotherapy, when a counteracting relationship is brought into the situation. It is also an aspect of vector therapy which changes the original stressful meaning by changing its character, its direction, the time over which it operates, or its strength.

Process of Communication

The process of communication involves emission, transmission and admission. In sequence there is a stimulus, sensation, percept, memory, thought, motor expression and feedback (which allows opportunity for correction and clarification). Many elements are employed—physical, nervous, humoral and chemical; one form may change into another, e.g.

physical sound into the chemistry of a neuron. Proprioception is concerned with stimuli arising within the individual or the group, enteroception with stimuli arising outside the individual or the group. In communication, in addition to a message, instructions for its interpretation are conveyed; the part of communication which deals with interpretation is termed metacommunication.

We may expect that meaning be conveyed through the five senses (auditory, visual, olfactory, tactile and gustatory), or through extra senses not yet defined, or through the combination of a number of senses.

Hearing and articulation allow the use of sounds which can be used as symbols to conceptualise meaning. Words are frequently used and have generally accepted meanings—allowing subtle, sophisticated expression of meaning unique to man. Semantics is concerned with the study of such meanings in language. Sounds may have meaning without word formation, and some may have an intense, primitive, biological appeal, e.g. a cry of pain.

Visual and manual skill allow pictorial representation of meaning, in writing, drawing, painting, modelling, carving, etc. Words can be articulated and expressed pictorially in writing. This is especially valuable when meaning needs to be conveyed to another not present. Intense meaning can be conveyed at a distance, e.g. a guilt-inducing letter from parent to child.

Touch is probably next in importance in human communication and has tended to be undervalued. It is employed in areas of intense meaning, e.g. the parents' handling of a child, belligerence between persons, sexual expression between couples, and the expression of love through a kiss, hand holding and fondling. Tactile sensation is an amalgam of touch, cold, heat, pressure and vibration.

The olfactory sense is not usually well developed in humans. It finds its greatest usefulness in the selection and tasting of food. It offers pleasure, as in the smell of a rose, or repugnance, as in the fumes of an unventilated room. It can reach great emotional intensity, e.g. the perfume of the beloved one. Man has learned to employ animals with a highly developed olfactory sense, e.g. police dogs in detection.

Taste is the least developed sense in the human, but it plays a major part in the intake and choice of food.

A great deal may be conveyed even by the use of one sense, such as touch. Critchley[114] relates that the old-time post office telegraphists, continually using Morse code, could convey personal characteristics to the receiving telegraphist at great distance. But each sense has its limitations. That meaning is often conveyed through an amalgam of perceptual stimuli is suggested by some work on such a simple creature as the mouse. Barnett,[115] having surveyed the evidence to show that a handled mouse withstood stress better than unhandled controls, goes on to say, 'At first some emphasis was laid, at least by implication, on the need to stroke the stimulated animal, but recently the emphasis has been put more on the mere fact of handling.' The human, more so than the animal, has complex, sophisticated meanings to convey. Thus he usually employs an amalgam of senses, sometimes all at great intensity.

In early infancy touch, sound and taste play a pre-eminent part. Smell may also be operative, but to assess the part it plays is difficult. At one time disproportionate importance was given to the feeding experience in children, and to the breast as the point of communication. It is being realised that the whole waking experience, coinciding with the feeding experience, is of more significance. Vision comes later, and drawing and writing become possible with increasing manual dexterity. The child, like primitive man, makes much use of direct manual expression in drawing. With the advent of abstract ideas, increasing use has to be made of combinations of senses to express their complexity and subtlety.

Much of human communication is verbal, but in recent times increasing study is being devoted to non-verbal communication. Non-verbal communication has been the subject of comment by Ruesch.[98] Broadly speaking, he divides non-verbal forms of communication into three distinct categories.

1. Sign language, which includes all those forms of codification in which words, numbers and punctuation signs have been supplanted by gestures; these vary from the simple gesture of the hitch-hiker to such complete systems as the language of the deaf.
2. Action language, which embraces all movements which are not used exclusively as signals, for example, acts such as walking and drinking. For these not only serve personal needs, but they also constitute statements to those who perceive them.
3. Object language, which comprises all intentional and non-intentional displays of material things, for example, machines, architecture, art objects, the human body.
These objects not only have material substance, but also an object language.

Birdwhistell[116-122] has studied body motion as a form of communication. Empathy, which is an aspect of 'high level' communication, is a subject of the paper by McGough[123] and Frank.[124] Mirsky et al.[125] have studied non-verbal communication in animals as it relates to the communication of affects. Non-verbal communication is also the theme of a book by Meerloo[126] and a review by Berger.[127] Posture in communication has been studied by Scheflen[128]; his interest in the subject was aroused by observations in psychotherapy.

Meanings are continually conveyed between people, but some may not be consciously perceived by the participants, if recent work by Klein and others[129-137] on subliminal perception is correct. This may be of great significance to communication theory, psychotherapy and social psychiatry.

More knowledge is required about the capacity of the individual for communication; there must be limits. A person, subject to hurt for long enough, ceases to cry when the point of exhaustion has been reached. It may explain spontaneous recovery from, for example, depression, when the mechanisms for its expression become exhausted.

Study must pay increasing attention to the time factor in communication. Possibly, rarely, an overwhelming stress acting over a short period of time may have permanent ill effects—the nuclear incident so significant in outmoded psychotherapy. Stress acting over long periods of time may be a commoner situation and have more permanent ill effects. Consideration of learning theory is relevant to this issue.[138,139,140]

In acute and chronic psychosis, the effects of temporary or permanent interruption of brain functioning by physical agents plays havoc with communication. In schizophrenia there may be similar central, intra-cerebral, interruption of communication, and not extracerebral, as is suggested by some psychopathologists.

Communication in Therapy

A relationship of immense importance in psychiatry is that between the therapist and the patient. It is thus natural that, with the advent of communication theory, efforts have been made to look upon the therapeutic process in terms of it. This has value in allowing a more objective attitude towards the processes and results of therapy, and has brought non-verbal communication to the fore. Freud,[141] of course, always gave a central place in his theories to one aspect of communication—the transference situation.

Lewin,[142,143] like many others, has been interested in the non-verbal cues that form a part of the therapeutic relationship. Enelow[144,145] sees lack of identity as characteristic of neurotic disorder, and relates this to defects of communication that have to be overcome by the psychotherapeutic process. He has also dealt with silence as a form of communication, and with procedures for dealing with it.[146] Meares[147] has written on the general question of communication between patient and therapist, with special emphasis on the importance of non-verbal communication. This more objective attitude towards therapy is illustrated by the work of Crisp[148,149] who has attempted, with a transference score, to devise a means of measuring the attitude of some subjects and patients towards doctors. Scheflen[150] has again been objective in his approach to psychotherapy, and sees the process as a reciprocal communication between patient and therapist in which there is a regulation system. Carl Rogers[151] has reviewed some of the contributions which research is making to our knowledge about relationships.

QUALITY OF RELATIONSHIPS

The standing of one person to another, continually altering due to communication, can be described on various parameters—the position in space, in parity of age, in gender role, in economic terms, in physical characteristics, in educational terms, in ethical terms, etc. In psychology and psychiatry, the concern is to describe the standing between them in emotional terms—hence terms such as anxious, dependent, dominating, clinging, over-protective, aggressive, timid, sensitive, encouraging, possessive, guilty, hostile, disliking, ignoring, tolerant, fearful, jealous, affectionate, sulky, irritable, refusing, rebuking, demanding, threatening, punishing, interested, depriving, secretive, rejecting, etc.

A number of terms are usually employed to outline the value and meaning of one person to another. Some variables may be psychologically more fundamental than others, e.g. those that indicate security or insecurity. Sometimes there is a dichotomy into those indicating a positive attitude and those indicating a negative one—an individual can be positive on one parameter but negative on another. Until there is greater knowledge about the essential qualities, and their rank order, in a relationship, the assessments of relationships will be inadequate, and thus there will be small agreement between authorities.

In the meantime, a number of schedules have been devised to assess and describe relationships. In regard to parent-child behaviour, the Fels Parent Behaviour Rating Scales[152] have been widely employed for many years; such procedures are discussed in Chapter XXVII. Ultimately it will be necessary to describe elements capable of description in any relationship, e.g. not only the relationship of man and woman as two persons, but also the special relationship of husband and wife. It is urgent that precision be brought into this field, because the link between one person and another carries those essential elements of meaning that make for health or sickness. It is important to describe the process of relationship as accurately as intrapsychic events, as the two are indivisible. Equal right must be given to intra- and extrapsychic events; the second have suffered comparative neglect.

A complete description of a relationship includes: (i) a description of each individual involved in the relationship, e.g. an element might be 'not normally aggressive'; (ii) a description of the standing of one person to another, e.g. an element might be 'highly aggressive to Mr. X'; (iii) a description of the effects of the relationship on each person involved in it, e.g. an element might be 'greatly anxiety-producing in Mr. X'. An analysis of the second and third descriptions will clearly show the 'meanings' conveyed between two people in a particular situation.

RELATIONSHIPS WITHIN THE FAMILY

The direct person-to-person relationships within the nuclear family are: (i) father-mother and mother-father; (ii) father-child and child-father; (iii) mother-child and child-mother; (iv) child-child. The reciprocal father-child relationships may be a father-son or father-daughter relationship. The reciprocal mother-child relationship may be either a mother-son or mother-daughter relationship. The reciprocal child-child relationship may be brother-brother, sister-sister, or brother-sister. Indirect relationships and those between sub-groups in the family are considered under the heading 'group relationships'.

It is to be noted that each relationship is reciprocal and involves two communications, e.g. husband-wife and wife-husband. The reciprocality of the relationship can be overlooked, e.g. much emphasis may be given to the fact that a mother is disrupting the emotional life of the child, forgetting that the child is also disrupting the emotional life of the mother.

As will be mentioned in the next section when the group is discussed, each individual plays a number of roles in the family and these influence the relationship. The father-mother relationship may be in addition a relationship of person-person, male-female, husband-wife, business associate-business associate. The father-daughter relationship may be in addition person-person, male-female, adult-child.

Some of the relationships in the family have received disproportionate attention—in particular the marital relationship and the mother-child relationship. One of the contributions of family work is to redress the balance. The father-child, or the child-child relationship in a particular set of curcumstances, may be more significant than the others.

Each of the four main relationships will now be given fuller discussion.

The Marital Relationship

Marriage has been defined by Murdock[153] as being 'a complex of customs centring upon the relationship between a sexually associating pair of adults within the family. Marriage defined the manner of establishing and terminating such a relationship, the normative behaviour and reciprocal obligations within it, and the locally accepted restrictions upon its personnel.' Marriage can be formal or informal. Formal means that it has a legal or statutory basis, and informal means no statutory basis. In Rome at the time of Justinian, it was possible for a marriage to last only as long as the partners in it mutually agreed to keep together. The informal living together of man and woman may be just as significant emotionally as the formal arrangement.

The relationship involves a reciprocal interaction, husband-wife and wife-husband. The pair also interact reciprocally in male-female, person-person, father-mother roles.

The purposes of marriage, usually the first step in founding a family, are similar to the purposes of the family—to satisfy affectional needs, sexual gratification, economic co-operation, and the opportunity to have children. But a marriage can exist satisfactorily without the latter.

Marriage as a social institution has been the subject of a vast literature. Howard,[154] Westermarck,[155] Goodsell[156] and Cole[157] cover its historical aspect. Malinowski,[158] Benedict,[159] Mead,[160] Radcliffe-Brown[161] and Evans-Prichard[162] study primitive societies. Ellis,[163] Davis,[164] Seward,[165] Kinsey,[166] Oliven[167] review its sexual aspects. Hamilton[168], Terman *et al.*,[169] and Burgess and Cottrell[170] consider research on prediction of success or failure, and there are innumerable works offering advice on the various aspects of marriage, sex relations and divorce.

Marriage may be monogamous, and in general this is more likely to occur when the normal sex ratio is not disturbed. Polygamy (plural marriage) is commoner than monogamy. Kluckhohn[171] states that monogamy is found in only 66 societies, as against polygyny in 378 and polyandry in 31. Polygyny is the marriage of one man to two or more women. This union may be informal, e.g. in ancient Egypt marriage was no bar to the right to have concubines, who were, however, inferior in status to the legal wife. Polyandry, the marriage of one woman to two or more men, is rare.

The reasons for marriage are many, from a superficial economic arrangement to an intense personal fulfilment. The choice of a partner may be left to chance, e.g. in some Catholic countries a man may marry any girl from an orphanage to fulfil a religious vow. Such marriages can be successful, as both partners may approximate to the norm of the population and be free of adverse motivation. In Scotland, at one time, a chance meeting at a fair was followed by a trial marriage for a year. A marriage may be arranged by the family of a partner, or by the families of both partners; this applied in the past in Britain, and still applies in many countries today. There is a tendency to marry into the same social class and to choose a partner of similar interests. Prestige may be sought through a husband's social position, or a wife's beauty. The need for economic security may weigh heavily in some situations.

The tendency of like to marry like has been supported by a study by Slater and Woodside.[172] They reviewed early work on the assortive mating, and after comparing a group of neurotic soldiers and their wives with a control sample concluded that there is a high degree of similarity, including a neurotic predisposition, between husband and wife. Kreitman[173] was able to demonstrate that assortive mating on the basis of diagnosis occurred to a statistically significant degree. The numbers, however, were small. The expected frequencies of psychiatric illness in married pairs were studied by Penrose[174] and Gregory.[175] Both found that the incidence of married couples where each partner was mentally ill was in the order of eight or nine times the expected value.

Toman[176–181] in his studies drew attention to influences from the past. He tested the following hypothesis. In divorced couples, (a) older siblings married more frequently to older siblings, and younger siblings to younger siblings; (b) a large number of parents come from like-sexed sibling configurations; (c) early loss of family members is more prevalent. The divorced couples showed significantly less sibling rank complementarity, fewer opposite sex siblings in their family constellations and a greater number of early losses of the family members than did the happily married couples. Other things being equal, the underlying assumptions for these hypotheses are: (a) the optimum situation is one in which partners are unlikely to get into conflict over their rights of seniority, etc.; (b) individuals having opposite sex siblings are used to the other sex and have less difficulty in accepting their marriage partner; (c) the death of a parent or a sibling may make an individual slightly more ready to discontinue relationships of his own accord, or to choose in the first place those which would not last.

Similarly, Pond et al.[182] found that unsatisfactory marital adjustment was associated with emotional disturbance in childhood. Furthermore, neuroticism in husbands and wives was significantly correlated, a finding supported by Hare and Shaw.[183] The paper presented some evidence to suggest that marriage relationships reflect the childhood experiences of the couple.

Subtle, but powerful, emotional influences may also be at work in partner selection. An individual gathers from his family and his life experience an image of the ideal partner; when image and reality coincide there is 'love at first sight'. Furthermore, in the partner may be attractive reflections of an idealised father or mother, or sibling, or previous wife. Behind the choice of a husband or of a wife there may be the dictates of a father or of a mother, or of both, determining what kind of marriage is acceptable to them; rebellion against the expected dictates can play a part equally important. The partner may satisfy an emotional need for security, affection, parenting, domination or subjection, or pity.

There are correlates with successful marital relationships—absence of neurosis, common interests, unselfishness, shared targets, an ability to be realistic and to adjust to new situations, emotional satisfaction, sexual satisfaction, shared social class, shared economic ambitions, shared satisfaction in children, an ability to tolerate differences, to share responsibility, to mix with others and to be in harmony with the extended family on both sides. Most of these factors are correlated with emotional stability.

Marriages may break down. In the United States of America the divorce rate is approximately one divorce for every three to four marriages. Some marriages do not break down, despite marital disharmony of severe degree; partners keep together in unhappiness and conflict, which can lead to severe physical and emotional ill-health and to the ultimate destruction of both in suicide or homicide. It might well be asked, 'Why is it that some marriages do not break up?' There is no single answer. Partners may keep together due to economic need, e.g. a mother with many dependent children, for 'the sake of the children', because the fears of life outside marriage are greater than the anxiety within, or because the loss of personal prestige might be too great, or religious beliefs might make divorce impossible, or because of some basic needs which are met despite the heavy emotional cost. Some make their escape only to remarry a new partner in the image of the last, and so involve themselves once again in a futile struggle.

A marriage, being the most intimate form of shared life, is the strictest test of the ability to sustain an emotional relationship with another person. Thus marriage breakdown is highly correlated with neuroticism; the quality of the sexual relationship being the most reliable guide to the quality of the marital relationship. An emotionally stable partner is usually able to sustain a partner with neuroticism of a severe degree. Two neurotic partners rarely find satisfaction, though for reasons previously mentioned they may stay together.

A marriage may break down because the original reason for it, superficial or fundamental, may have gone. A more desirable partner to fulfil the emotional needs, or the dictates of the image of the ideal partner, may appear. Conflict with the partner who represents a disliked father, mother, sibling or idea may reach a point when life together is impossible. Children may change the family dynamics and produce intense rivalry in a partner. Light is thrown on marital tension in the contribution by Dicks (Chapter IX).

Marital stress reveals itself in four groups of symptoms: (i) those indicative of incompatibility, e.g. quarrelling, physical violence, etc.; (ii) those indicative of sexual disharmony, e.g. frigidity; (iii) those indicative of emotional illness, e.g. psychosomatic symptoms, depression; (iv) those indicative of schizophrenia. Psychosis in a partner is well tolerated unless a paranoid system involves the other partner, and leads to suspicion and strife. Howells[184] showed that, of 40 persons presenting at a marital problem clinic, 23 people were in the category of incompatibility, seven people showed sexual disharmony, eight people exhibited signs of emotional illness and two people suffered from schizophrenia.

Divorce is the subject of a considerable literature.[185, 186, 187]

Parent-Child Relationships

Two main relationships are included in this category—father-child and mother-child. Each is reciprocal. Each can be either a reciprocal relationship with a male or female child. The pair can also interact reciprocally in adult-child, male-female, male-male or female-female relationships.

Children may result from design or accident. If by accident, they may still be accepted and loved, but the chance of rejection is greater. Planned children have a greater chance of acceptance, but some may still be rejected. There are degrees of acceptance, just as there are degrees of rejection. An illegitimate child may be fully accepted, but due to the likely adverse circumstances surrounding his birth he has a greater chance of rejection than a child conceived in a legal union. Children may be wanted to satisfy biological demands, they may be an expression of mutual appreciation by the parents. In other situations the children are an economic necessity, especially male children. Children may be conceived in a whole host of circumstances less favourable to their future acceptance, e.g. they may be an attempt to repair a failing marriage, or an effort to bring relief to a neurotic parent, or a means of making the wife dependent on the husband, or a substitute for a lost parent or husband or sibling or child, or a means of emotional gratification to the mother who may then discard the child when it becomes demanding, or they may be wanted as a support in old age, or as a social requirement, or as a duty in the light of religious ideals.

The meaning given to the child in the emotional life of the parent is of paramount importance in determining the attitude of the parent to child. The meaning is not constant, but fluctuates with the life experience of the parents and can vary from extreme rejection to joyful acceptance, or vice versa. The meaning starts at conception, is reinforced in the mother when movement of the child in utero is experienced, and again at the child's birth. Usually the child is imbued with strong identification with the loved or unloved partner. In addition, it is invested with feelings associated with other intimate figures in the life of the parent—grandparents, siblings and friends. At birth it often becomes the most highly prized object in the life of the parents and thus an object for anxiety, should they be anxious.

The child's own attitude to a parent is not only a reflection of the parent's attitude. A child is nourished by a group situation, and his reaction may be dictated in part by this, e.g. an angry mother does not necessarily provoke anger in a child, as the child may imitate his tolerant father in responding to his mother with tolerance.

The sex gender of the child may be a factor in the meaning given to it by the parent. For economic reasons, family tradition or the emotional requirements of the parent, a son may be preferred. The child is also invested by the parent with the feelings dictated by previous life experience in relation to its gender. Parental attitudes may be latent until the child's gender role becomes more evident in adolescence.

The mother-child relationship has been the subject of intense study. One such study is presented by Szasz in Chapter X of this volume. The child-mother relationship has been less closely studied, no doubt partly because the child does not engage in scientific enquiry and, furthermore, especially in infancy, he cannot share his experiences easily with an adult. One of the dangerous assumptions often made is that the child experiences as an adult. Many of the studies have accumulated into volumes.[188-197]

The father-child relationship has, in comparison to the mother-child relationship, suffered some neglect. Yet, from conception, the father is a vital element in the life of the child, supporting the mother, determining her attitude to the child and frequently playing a direct part in its day-to-day upbringing from the time of birth. In most societies child care in infancy is a matter left almost exclusively to the mother, but this practice is not invariable, e.g. in Polynesian society it is not adhered to, as Margaret Mead found when observing the family in New Guinea.[198] Even in Western civilisation the father often shares in the upbringing of the child, as it was shown by Newson and Newson[199] in their study of infant care. Again, in Great Britain, which is predominantly a bottle-feeding culture,[200] from three months after the child's birth the father may share in the child's feeding experience. A number of studies have now taken place on the father-child relationship, Aberle and Naegels,[201] Bach,[202] Block,[203] Mueller,[204] Peterson *et al.*,[205] Sears *et al.*,[206] Stolz *et al.*,[207] Nash,[208] Grunebaum and Strean,[209] Tasch[210] and English.[211]

Fathering and mothering (parenting) are often assumed to be different entities. Yet both parents, mother and father, are the product of an intimate emotional experience with their own parents of both sexes; they must absorb elements from both. That there are some differences between mothering and fathering is self-evident, but the similarities are much greater. There is no exact knowledge on this issue, but it may be proved that the similarities greatly outnumber the differences. Likewise, adequate substitute parenting may have more similarities than differences to adequate natural parenting. In some circumstances adequate substitute parenting may even outweigh inadequate natural parenting.

The parent-child relationship is recognised as being of vital importance to the satisfactory nurturing of the child. Not only are the child's physical needs largely dependent on it, but so is its intellectual life, its character and the formation of its ideals. Of predominant interest to family psychiatry is the fact that the emotional influences determining emotional health or illness spring mostly from this relationship. Thus the parent-child relationship is strongly echoed in the child's later person-person, adult-adult, husband-wife, father-mother and parent-child relationships.

Conversely, the child has importance to the life experiences of the parent; the child-parent relationship is equally important. A child, in the parents' eyes, often represents the partner and other loved figures. It allows an expression of creativeness in living form, the fascination of growth in its multitudinous aspects, the intimacy of a responding being, the vicarious delight of the child's achievements and the satisfaction of social approval.

Child-child Relationship

This reciprocal relationship may be brother-brother, sister-sister, or brother-sister. This relationship, too, has suffered comparative neglect by psychopathologists, but this has been remedied to some extent by such studies as Brim,[212] Hilgard,[213] Koch[214-220] and Sperling.[221] A child may spend a long period in day-to-day contact with its siblings. In some circumstances it may spend a longer period with a child of near age than with the parents. In some situations in civilised communities,[222] and as a matter of custom in some primitive communities[223] the child may be brought up by its older siblings, child relatives or child friends.

The child-child relationship is usually harmonious and adds to the emotional and social life of each, but it can be strained by a number of factors. Disparity of age can be a strain. There is much to suggest that if the disparity is one to two years, the children develop little rivalry and regard themselves as a pair not far removed from a twin relationship. A disparity in age of from two to five years appears to produce the increasing opportunity for rivalry, while a longer gap reduces rivalry, as presumably the older sibling is too secure to feel threatened by the younger. Unwise parental management, thrusting a new infant on the child without warning, over-protecting a sibling, not allowing participation by the older and giving heavier punishment to the older, may set up hostility between siblings. Furthermore, one sibling, for reasons significant in the emotional life of the parent, may be preferred to another and again set up rivalry. If rivalry is dictated by parental attitude, then the sibling-sibling relationship tends to be worse in their presence. An illustration of study of disharmonious sibling-sibling relationships is that by Levy found in Chapter XI of this volume.

Sex differences in siblings can enrich the life experience of each. A boy acquires certain attitudes towards females from his sister as well as from his mother—and frequently from the female friends of his sister. Similarly, a girl acquires certain attitudes towards males from her brother. Equally, a perverse sibling relationship has ill effects on attitudes to the opposite sex. Thus sibling relationships make a contribution to the 'idealised' picture of the opposite sex, to choice of partner, to relationships with partners in marriage and again to attitudes to own children.

TIME SEQUENCE

Always in consideration of relationships it must be remembered that the relationship we see in the Present has also a Past. The reciprocal father-mother relationship began at courtship, passed through a honeymoon, marriage, a period without children, and parenting, and ended as grandparenting. Elements in the relationship may have become fixed with time. The reciprocal child-parent relationship is usually of shorter duration than the relationship between parents. The reciprocal child-child relationships are usually even shorter. The importance of the process through time can be exemplified by considering the significance of aetiological factors in the development of childhood neurosis. In the past much attention was given to one traumatic event in precipitating emotional disorder. For instance, a violent incident between parent and children on a particular day may be regarded as causal. But more significant than one single incident is the continuous relationship through time with a parent liable to violence. Again, the break up of a family, with loss of parents, may be regarded as causal. But more significant are the ongoing relationships of the child in a family so disruptive that it broke up.

Present relationships flow into the Future. Expectations about the future may influence parent interaction. The reciprocal father-mother relationship is likely to have the longest future, and both the reciprocal parent-child and child-child relationships are likely to be attenuated with time.

5. THE GROUP PROPERTIES DIMENSION

The family is a small group of people, and therefore everything that applies to small group structure and dynamics must apply also to the family. A group is more than a sum of its parts, it is a functioning subsystem of society, with an identity and properties of its own.

While the family has characteristics in common with all other small groups, it has also special characteristics of its own.

1. It is made up of a diverse group of individuals—males and females, adults, adolescents, and children of either sex, whose age range may span two or three generations.

2. The relationships within the family are more intense than in any other group of society. Hence their significance for health or illness.

3. The family normally has a long collective history. Its life is a continuous flow from the distant Past, into the Present, and on to the Future.

4. The family has certain distinct properties; it normally shares one language, one religion, one social class, one house and one income.

5. It has special functions—providing as it does for the affectional needs and the economic requirements of its members, for the sexual satisfaction of the marital couple, and the procreation and upbringing of children.

6. It is a fundamental sub-system of society, and it is recognised as such.

Recent years have seen an increasing interest in the study of groups in all sections of society—industry, education, youth activities, agriculture, voluntary societies, religion, hospitals, fighting services, etc. The subject has received a general review by Cartwright and Zander,[224] and there is an analysis of interaction in groups by Bales.[225, 226] Research on the study of small groups was reviewed by Strodtbeck[227] in an issue of the *American Sociological Review*, which collected together 14 papers on this subject. At the time of this review Strodtbeck reported that the rate of production of small groups bibliographic items was three per week.

In *Bibliography of small group research*,[228] Strodtbeck and Hare show 1407 items on small group research. Hare, Borgatta and Bales[229] published a further collection on small group dynamics in 1955. Roseborough,[230]

Argyle,[231] Phillips[232] and Lindzey[233] also review the subject of small groups. Taylor[234, 235] has considered the therapeutic group as a small group. Group psychology was not overlooked by Freud.[236] Cartwright and Zander offer caution: 'Group dynamics is a relatively young field, and it displays the characteristics of youth. It is experiencing rapid growth and seeking a sense of identity. The issues within the field can be better understood if viewed in this perspective.' One aspect of small group dynamics is the subject of discussion by Shaw in Chapter XII of this volume.

The family is the most obviously important small group, and yet has been comparatively neglected. Cottrell and Foote[237] have studied interpersonal competence amongst family members. Mills[238] reported that three-person groups tend to segregate into a pair and a third party. Strodtbeck[239, 240] in the first paper explored some of Mills' findings in relation to the family group; there were certain differences between the family group and the non-family small group. Ehrenwald, in Chapter XVI, describes family group functions in terms of four major patterns of interaction: (i) patterns of sharing; (ii) patterns of resistance and rebellion; (iii) complementary patterns; and (iv) patterns of contagion.

DESCRIPTION OF THE GROUP

Authorities are not agreed about the description of the personality; even less agreement is to be expected about the description of a group of interacting personalities, embracing structure and function. Krech and Crutchfield[241] suggest the following criteria for a social group. '(a) All members must exist as a group in the psychological field of each individual, i.e. be perceived and reacted to as a group. (b) The various members must be in dynamic interaction with one another.' Titchener et al.[242] regard each family as having a 'style' of its own. The 'style' is determined by a number of 'patterns' that make up its formal properties. There are four large patterns: (i) 'communication' includes cognitive and affective functions and an evaluation of the freedom of expression; (ii) 'organisation' in this framework is the most general of patterns, referring to hierarchy, cohesiveness, structuring, or institutionalising of functions, relations between intrasystemic structures, rigidity and flexibility, and differentiation of roles and sub-systems in family or personality; (iii) 'control' refers to stabilising functions, and subsumes the explicitness, automaticity, consistency, effectiveness and source of these mechanisms; (iv) 'perception' is of members by members, of the system as a whole, by the system of the environment, and so forth. This pattern includes evaluations of sensitivity, scotoma, inhibition and filtering. The sense of identity is a special sub-category of the larger pattern of perception. Once the 'style' of a family is understood, it is then possible to predict the adaptive process of that family to any situation, and also to see how it influences individual personalities. 'Style' may have something in common with the 'double bind' of Bateson and Jackson, the 'pseudo-mutuality' of Wynne, and the perception anomalies of Lidz and the Yale Group. It may be valuable to describe the 'style', or perhaps 'styles', and such related properties, but such descriptions still fall short of a complete picture of the group process.

Hess and Handel[243] see the family described by five essential processes: (i) establishing a pattern of separativeness and connectedness; (ii) establishing a satisfactory congruence of images through the exchange of suitable testimony; (iii) evaluating modes of interaction into central family concerns or themes; (iv) establishing the boundaries of the family's world of experience; (v) dealing with significant biosocial issues of family life; as in the family's disposition to evolve definitions of male and female and of older and younger.

Cartwright and Zander[224] favour the description of a small group by a number of properties. 'Among the properties most often employed are the following: size (number of members), amount of physical interaction among members, degree of intimacy, level of solidarity, locus of control of group activities, extent of formalisation of rules governing relations among members, and tendency of members to react to one another as individual persons, or as occupants of roles.' Here this approach will be followed, and the family as a small group will be discussed in terms of its structure, group interaction and communication, roles, cohesion and general characteristics.

STRUCTURE

The elementary family group usually consists of two parents and one or more children. The group has male and female members amongst its adults and its children. Family members may be of any age, from infancy to senium. The family group may be formal, with a legalised marriage between the parents, or informal. To the elementary family may be added (a) relations, such as grandparents, siblings of parents, cousins of the children, etc., (b) others, such as servants, lodgers, governesses, nannies, etc. Some significance has been given to the ordinal position of children in the family; it has been argued, for instance, that some positions make the child more vulnerable to emotional breakdown. Bossard and Boll[244] have defined roles in large families associated with ordinal position.

Group Transaction

As the member of a group, a family member finds himself involved in a complex pattern of interactions within it. He is, in fact, an element in a field of forces. Furthermore, he and his family are involved in a complex pattern of interactions with the community outside the family. The term transaction now becomes relevant. The study of fields of forces, vector psychology, was an interest of psychologists in the 1930s, but it has since suffered comparative neglect. Kurt Lewin[245, 246, 247] was the leader of a movement which had a great deal to say in its 'field theory' about the organisation of society. The work of Lewin was not specifically applied to the family group. The family, however, is a sub-system of society, and considerations of vector psychology are relevant to it. Thus a brief digression will be made to consider vector psychology, before relevant aspects of it are applied to the family group.

Kurt Lewin[245] held that mathematics and Galilean physics were the basis of dynamic psychology—even social psychology. A central view in his philosophy was that the context, or situation, in which the behaviour occurred was as important as the object: 'Only by the concrete whole which comprises the object and the situation are the vectors which determine the dynamics of the event defined.' The vector is a directed quantity and, as such, force is a vector. In psychology the concern is with emotional forces. Thus vector psychology can be defined as 'a representation of the play of the various tensions and forces within the life space'. The ultimate vectors are determined by both the object and the situation in which it lies. The internal vectors in the object are not to be neglected, e.g. the relationship of a part to the whole. The object can be the individual. Lewin was also concerned with valence—the demand value of a stimulus. 'With all these, however, there remain certain critical properties of the psychobiological environment still undescribed. Objects are not neutral to the child, but have an immediate psychological effect on its behaviour. Many things attract the child to eating, others to climbing, to grasping, to manipulation, to sucking, to raging at them, etc. These imperative environmental facts—we shall call them valences (*Aufforderungscharaktere*)—determine the direction of the behaviour. Particularly from the standpoint of dynamics, the valences, their kind (sign), strength and distribution, must be regarded as among the most important properties of the environment.'

Vector psychology is a useful corrective to dynamic individual psychiatry, which rests on vague definition of elements and speculative ideas of processes. It can be applied to the individual, to society and now to the family. Within the individual its concepts might be applied to memory, perception, thought and motivation, e.g. recall in memory might be described in terms of the valence or demand value or meaninglessness of the message to be recalled. Here, by an amalgamation of Lewin's views, Gestalt psychology, cybernetics and communication theory, it might be possible to construct a model of the internal mental processes of an individual just as useful, dynamic and meaningful as that of the dynamic psychopathologists.

One can proceed from the individual, with his internal vector qualities, to the group, with its external (to the individual) qualities, to the community and its external (to the group) qualities, to the culture and its external (to community) qualities. All four are significant, but there may be some ordinal position of importance to the individual and especially to individual psychopathology—perhaps in the order just given.

Vector psychology may have its limitations. The procedures of physics, concerned as they are with the handling of quantities, may fall short when qualities have to be considered.

A family is a field of forces, and thus some of the concepts of vector psychology, mathematics and physics may apply to it. Within the family can be identified a number of interactions making up a complex transaction. The possible interactions may be summarised as follows:

Individual $\rightleftarrows$ Individual
Individual $\rightleftarrows$ Dyad, i.e. triadic interaction
Individual $\rightleftarrows$ Coalition of family members, i.e. part of a family
Individual $\rightleftarrows$ Whole family
Dyad $\rightleftarrows$ Dyad, i.e. tetradic interaction
Dyad $\rightleftarrows$ Coalition
Dyad $\rightleftarrows$ Whole family
Coalition $\rightleftarrows$ Coalition
Coalition $\rightleftarrows$ Whole family

The dyads, triads, tetrads, coalitions in the family vary greatly. Examples would be a parental constellation of father and mother making a dyad interacting with the child; this, as much as the mother-child relationship, can have a powerful influence on the personality of the child (see Markowitz and Kadis,[248] Vogel[249]). A dyad can consist of two female members of the family, mother and daughter, who interact with a male, father. The mother and maternal grandmother may form a constellation dependent on blood tie and interact with father. It must be noted that each interaction is reciprocal. Furthermore, in addition to direct influences, account must be taken of indirect influences, e.g. father may have mother as his agent in inflicting trauma on his child. Again, any element in interaction with another may simultaneously be interacting with a third or more elements. The complexity of the possible interactions is explained by Henry and Warson in an important contribution to this volume, Chapter XIII.

Relevant to group interaction is, of course, communication theory— the conveyance of meaning between elements in the family is discussed in Section 4. Thus it will not receive further consideration here.

Roles

Individuals in the community are allocated parts to play; this also applies within the family. Moreno[250] has defined the role as 'the actual and tangible forms which the self takes'. Spiegel[251] has defined a role as 'a goal-directed pattern or sequence of acts tailored by the cultural process for the transactions a person may carry out in a social group or situation'. In his paper, Chapter XV in this volume, he describes three types of roles, formal, informal and fictive. These can be explicit and easily defined, or implicit and acknowledged with difficulty. Some of the important roles in the family are mother, father, son and daughter. But each person takes on many other roles—father is man, bread-winner, husband, teacher, disciplinarian, etc.; mother is woman, housekeeper, wife, neighbour, etc.; son is child, male, pupil, someone's cousin, etc. The child's role as determined by the family has been considered by Allen.[252] Roles can be changed, e.g. the baby is fed by father instead of mother. Roles can be reversed, e.g. in the previous example mother takes on father's duties. There can be conflict over roles. Role theory has yet much to contribute to the understanding of family dynamics.

Linked with roles are other family properties. The role of leader is paramount. The leader may be consistent and apply to all situations; more commonly the role playing varies with the situation, e.g. in the home father may be leader but give way to his wife in a social situation. Furthermore, leadership may be overt or covert. Linked to leadership is decision making (see Schlesinger[253]). This may be the prerogative of the leader, or of a dyad, such as the parents, or of a coalition, such as the adults, or of the whole family. Some members of the family are humble, the supplicants; some are even scapegoats (Ackerman,[254] Vogel and Bell[255]).

Cohesion

The family has motivation as a group, but individuals and coalitions may have conflicting motivations and different goals. Thus there may be solidarity in the family group, with co-operating and a consensus of opinion, or there may be alignments leading to splits, competition and no consensus of opinion. There may be struggles for power.

CHARACTERISTICS

Society has values which it cherishes, and these are usually adopted by the family. But sometimes the family may adopt a different set of values from the community and be at variance with it. To some extent a family may be labelled by its values, e.g. a generous family, a law-abiding family, a delinquent family, etc. The family may also adopt collective attitudes to matters before it; it may determine its behaviour by its own codes. Some of its beliefs may have the force of myths (see Ferreira, Chapter XIV). It may have ritual and mannerisms all its own. Lastly, the family has its own activities, divisions of labour and way of life.

TIME SEQUENCE

Account was taken previously of the historical aspects of the individual and of the relationship; the historical aspects of the family group are equally important. The group will usually have existed together for a span of time in the Past, and will move from the Present into the Future. Members of a family have sprung from families of orientation in the distant Past and from them have acquired properties—values, attitudes, beliefs, myths, roles, codes, illnesses and symptoms. (See Mendell and Fisher in Chapter XVII, and Henry,[256] Wardle,[257] and Ehrenwald.[258])

6. THE MATERIAL CIRCUMSTANCES DIMENSION

In many areas of the world the physical and material needs of the family have yet to be fully met. There are also many areas where they are over-met—as if the quest for material satisfaction went on under its own momentum despite satiation. Due to the intangibility of emotional phenomena, man beset by disharmony, dysfunction and unhappiness assumes that the solutions still lie in the tangible, understandable, material sphere. Thus material comfort becomes an end in itself; disillusionment results, but the quest continues. Man realises that he does not live by bread alone, but matters of the mind and spirit have been hitherto difficult to grasp. Material want can lead to dysfunction; emotional want can lead to dysfunction and material poverty. Thus there is an interplay of physical and emotional phenomena. Physical needs will first be discussed. The chapter will close with a demonstration of the impact of emotional phenomena on physical conditions.

HOME ACTIVITIES

These are determined by the background, geographical, cultural and social, in which the family functions.

The family needs protection against the elements—wind, rain, sun and cold. This protection must be available to all age groups. Climate fashions the mode of this. In hot countries the minimum of indoor accommodation is required, as the family spends much of the time out of doors. Great heat dictates shade. A combination of wind and cold results in an igloo. Great wind forces families underground.

The preparation of food normally involves cooking—another home activity. At home, too, the sick must be nursed; the sick and hurt make for the home, which means protection, care and sleep. Recreation is a family activity, much of which, especially for the young, takes place at home. Allied to play is learning; additional to any formal educational system, a child learns especially from the parents. In primitive communities the learning enables the children to follow the occupation of the adults.

Lesser activities in the home include attention to personal hygiene, the making, repairing and washing of clothes, the cleaning of the house and the storage of goods.

Some activities turn around the care of children—feeding, bathing, playing, occupying, protecting and nursing them. In most societies the care of children is a group activity, with all members participating, but the mother is usually the leader, especially with infants, supported by the husband, by the grandparents and by the child's siblings. Exact knowledge as to the time spent by each family member in child rearing is rarely available in any community. Exclusive care of children by the mother is a rarity.

Families vary in the time allotted to each task, e.g. when food and other necessities are plentiful and easily obtained, more time is available for relaxation; in farming communities there are times demanding intense activity, generally followed by slack periods; in civilised areas the hospitals will take over the care of the very sick, and the schools will relieve parents of their children for part of the day. In wealthy areas the machine has made tasks, such as cleaning, washing and cooking, easier and less time consuming; this is especially so where the standard of living has been raised for all income groups, and thus servants have become scarce.

PHYSICAL NEEDS

A family cannot function without support from the community, and, indeed, the modern family enquires about facilities before moving into an area. Shops easily reached are essential to the housewife, and a considerable part of her time will be spent in them. Banking, hairdressing, garage, postal and laundry facilities are all needed by the family. There will be also a demand for a place of worship, with all its extra activities. Schools have to be accessible, as well as recreational facilities for children, playground and playing fields. Adults are prepared to travel to satisfy their need for entertainment; theatres, cinemas, concert halls, clubs, restaurants, etc. all contribute to the relaxation of the family. The car plays an increasing part in the family's way of life, thus the family can enjoy outings to places of interest or recreation with greater ease than in the past.

The family base is its dwelling, which usually requires two main areas—a living area and a sleeping area. It may vary greatly in size and sophistication, from a simple hut to a caravan, a flat, a house, or a many-roomed mansion.

The accommodation should be adequate for the size of the family. Paradoxically, the greater the number of children, the less able are the parents to afford adequate accommodation, as was proved by a survey of 1000 families[259] in an urban area in Great Britain, which showed that families with young children lived in smaller dwellings with fewer amenities. In the families studied, 56·8% of the households lived in three rooms or less; 59·6% lived in 'flats' or 'rooms'. In a previous survey[260] the same investigation team found that accommodation was often very deficient, e.g. one in nine families was overcrowded (one person in three, if each member of the family was counted as an individual); one house in seven was structurally inadequate. Plant[261] has studied the effects of living space on the development of the child's personality. Bossard[262] has evolved a spatial index for family interaction for relating floor space to interrelationship within the household. The material circumstances prevalent in newly formed Copenhagen families is discussed by Kirsten Auken in Chapter XVIII.

In the dwelling the family needs certain obvious facilities, like water, a source of artificial power, electric or gas, for light and warmth and for cooking. Other requirements include furniture and utensils, toys and books. A radio and television set are both found nowadays, even when many other essentials might be absent. Little study has been given to the effect of colour in the home; the use of colour probably reflects the family's personality. A neglected subject, until the coming of the aeroplane, was the effect of noise on the family: harsh noises are distracting and irritating; but many people find continuous music from a radio a desirable accompaniment to family life. A garden, for pleasure or food production, is usually annexed to the house in rural or semi-rural areas. In the absence of a garden, children play either in the street or in the nearest organised playground.

In many parts of the world food does not reach families in quantities sufficient to their needs—this despite the surplus of certain products existing in some countries. Often, when adequate in amount, the food is badly balanced. In the study of an urban area already referred to,[259] 6·5% of the children were badly fed—food being either deficient in amount or in quality. Water is as essential as food; in some areas supplies can be spasmodic and meagre.

Clothing is required for protection from the elements, and when this need has been met surplus effort goes into making it decorative; in areas of great wealth, clothing has become highly sophisticated. Renbourn[263, 264] has recently revealed many aspects of clothing. The Newcastle study[260] showed that, in the families studied, 4·6% of the children were inadequately clad.

Transport has become mechanised in industrial nations. The mule and horse have given place to bicycle, motor cycle and car; in some areas it is commonplace for a family to have at least two cars.

Some families move as a group. The great majority, however, move little in the course of a lifetime. But a high measure of industrialisation has brought a new phenomenon in some countries, e.g. the United States, where families, continually improving themselves, move about a great deal.

The whole family's material state is usually directly proportioned to the income provided by the work of the husband alone, or by that of the husband and other family members. In a minority of cases this is not so. The income may be unequally distributed between the family members, and this may lead to what is termed 'secondary poverty' (see Chapter XIX by M. Young). Furthermore, the income may be inefficiently deployed, a characteristic of problem families to be discussed later.

MATERIAL NEEDS AND EMOTIONAL HEALTH

Physical health can clearly be influenced by material surroundings. Lack of warmth, water or food can threaten life. Lack of cleanliness leads to disease; overcrowding promotes the spread of infection; lack of sleep predisposes to ill-health. Dietary deficiencies are linked to well recognised deficiency diseases. Hare and Shaw[265] found that rates of physical and mental ill-health increased with family size.

Mental health can also suffer. Acute and sub-acute toxic confusional states may result from dietary deficiencies, impure water, and from poisoning by lead toys. These cases are clear-cut. But what are the effects of adverse conditions on emotional health? Poor conditions make, for instance, care of the child more difficult and lead to tiredness, which in turn causes irritability. Children sleep less readily when there is much noise. One living room does not allow the possibility of escape when tensions arise; it also does not allow study or play to be separated from the main family activities. In overcrowded conditions parental quarrels cannot be hidden from the children. Lack of outdoor play facilities adds to the overcrowding. Inadequate diet results in listlessness and irritability. Families lose status in the clan and in the community when their conditions are bad. Lack of privacy for the parents in sexual activities may lead to the frustration of abstinence, or expose the children to the witnessing of sexual intimacies.

Grootenboer[266] sees a relationship between poor housing and poor emotional health of children. Williamson[267] correlates income and marital adjustment. Michael[268] notes how economic states are related to adjustment of adults. But do poor material standards cause emotional illness, or are they a product of it? The Baltimore study,[269-273] reported in Chapter XX, follows up families after their housing is upgraded. On some variables there was an improvement. On the psychological state variable there was no difference between those who were moved and those who stayed in poor housing (control group). Also, some families in the control group did move by their own initiative; for them the improvement in adjustment was commensurate with the extent of the upgrading in housing. But, naturally, the better adjusted families make the biggest step upwards; thus those with the better housing were the better adjusted. Again, if poor conditions are inevitable, they are better tolerated by well adjusted families—in the 1000-families study the authors state, 'In spite of all the difficulties of housing . . . the great majority of mothers coped well with their families.'

EMOTIONAL HEALTH AND MATERIAL REQUIREMENTS

Of great interest are highly pathological families. Mechanisms which are nebulous in a healthy family becomes starkly clear in highly pathological families. Thus such families are of great research interest; indeed, just as physiology learns greatly from the study of pathology, so family psychology gains from the study of family psychopathology. These families, failures in society, are often termed problem, multiple-handicapped or hard-core families. The titles highlight frustration of society in dealing with them. They are called 'problem', denoting that society fails to solve their difficulties, however advantageous the circumstances with which it surrounds these families; 'multiple-handicapped', denoting the variety and multitude of handicaps; some of society's greatest social problems are cradled in these families—child neglect, delinquency, alcoholism, divorce, sloth, poor work records, etc.; 'hard-core', denoting how resistant they are to all the many remedial measures now available to social agencies.

A seven-year-long study on problem families has been conducted in England at the Institute of Family Psychiatry of the General Hospital in Ipswich. The material of the investigation is now under analysis, and some of the findings are reported in Chapter XXI. However, one of the clear findings of this investigation was the magnitude of emotional illness in the members of such families. Not only was there severe emotional illness in family members and in the family as a whole, but it was also clear that the pathology inevitably led to the family's social difficulties. 'Social' difficulties are often thought to arise from some material or moral deficiency. It is overlooked that these 'social' difficulties are personal difficulties produced by emotional illness. It follows that the solution to the emotional difficulties lies in emotional measures—hence the futility of material effort and moral stricture; emotional difficulties have their own emotional antidotes.

Once it is accepted that the core of the matter is in the severe degree of emotional instability, it is possible to redefine the problem family as 'a family showing among its members emotional instability of such a degree that it leads to behaviour which is socially harmful'. Study can now embrace all income groups, and it will be seen that problem families are not found in the lower income groups only. Furthermore, observation can include more manifestations than those in which social agencies are usually interested; it will be seen that many families are in dire distress, although not manifesting those signs usually denoting social failure. A family may, for example, isolate itself, be a problem family, and yet not show the usual social signs. Again, a family may denote its pathology by a ruthless drive in one sphere of activity that may even bring social acclaim, e.g. economic success. Or, again, interest in religious matters may be pursued with a rigidity which may exclude normal feeling.

In the bibliography will be found a selection of entries[274-425] from the reference file of the investigation in problem families at the Institute of Family Psychiatry, Ipswich.

TIME SEQUENCE

A family's material state changes over time. Normally there is a steady improvement until late middle age, with a falling standard as old age is reached. But there is much variation amongst families, and often much fluctuation in an individual family—some of these ups and downs reflect the emotional vicissitudes experienced by the family on its way from the Past, to the Present and on into the Future.

7. THE DIMENSION OF FAMILY-COMMUNITY INTERACTION

This dimension encompasses more than the title suggests. *Neighbourhood* is that part of the social system closest to the family. The body of people living in the same area is termed '*the community*'. Beyond the community in the social system is the *culture*—a large body of people with shared values and meanings. Humanity makes up the total social system, or *society*. Thus this dimension is concerned with the interaction of the family with the total social system, embracing family-neighbourhood, family-community, family-culture and family-social system interaction. The term 'family-community interaction' is adopted for convenience.

STRUCTURE OF THE SOCIAL SYSTEM

The study of the development of parts or the whole of the social system is the concern of historians. The study of the functioning of society is undertaken by sociologists. Much is being learned about the basic functioning and structure of society by the study of primitive communities by the social anthropologists. Cultural anthropology is now often distinguished from social anthropology. It deals with cultural systems rather than with social ones; with the relations, that is, between items of culture, sometimes called 'culture traits', rather than with the relations between persons. Introductions to the understanding of the social system are by Kluckhohn and Murray,[426] Kardiner and Linton,[427] Frank, [428] Parsons[429] and Levy.[430] Contributions in social anthropology are by Evans-Prichard,[431] Radcliffe-Brown[432] and Malinowski.[433]

Social Roles

As an individual has a standing or place in a family, so he has one given him in society. Within the family he may be husband and father; in society he has many more roles—man, consumer, citizen, thief, saint, etc.

Some of these are dependent upon groupings in society, e.g. snob based on class, baker based on occupation, pupil based on education, priest based on religion, voter based on political affiliation, consumer based on the economy, thief based on the legislation, etc. Roles are allotted by others: thus there is a giver as well as a recipient, and without the giver there is no role. Thus role acting or playing is a determinant of interaction between the giver and the recipient.

An individual may be asked to enact one or more roles simultaneously, and these roles may be in conflict with one another. Spiegel[434] has given a central place to the results of this conflict in the aetiology of mental illness. Roles may be ascribed (e.g. by age or sex), may be achieved (e.g. head teacher), may be adopted (e.g. leader) or may be assumed (e.g. a part in a play). Roles may be modified, e.g. leader becomes a follower; or reversed, e.g. father undertakes mothering.

Social Classes

This ranking of individuals and families in society is often on a three-point scale—upper (aristocracy), middle (professional) and lower (working) classes. Hereditary, economic, occupational and religious factors operate in determining the class to which an individual belongs. In some societies the middle, or professional, class hardly exists. In a few societies differences between classes may be hardly noticeable, while in others the differences are very marked, e.g. in feudal societies. Class differentiation can change with time. Social class can exert considerable pressures on the behaviour and values of an individual belonging to it, e.g. on the child-rearing practices.[435]

Income Groups

These may conform closely to social classes; but there are exceptions, e.g. aristocracy may, due to death duties and other reasons become poor but still maintain a prestige position in society. The working class may acquire wealth and a high standard of living but still have a low prestige value in some societies. It is usual, however, for income groupings to be closely related to occupational grouping, e.g. a labourer the world over is in a low economic group; a lawyer usually acquires at least a middle or upper middle economic grouping. Income influences standard of living —housing, education, leisure and health.

Social Values

These constitute the principles, standards, beliefs and mores of society, and collectively make up its disposition, or ethos. These values are acquired by groups, families and individuals within society by the processes of learning—suggestion, imitation, reasoning and conditioning. There is a great social 'pressure' on everybody to conform to the accepted value systems of the community. Failure to conform leads to banishment, disciplinary action, loss of prestige and loss of security. To conform brings appreciation, prestige and security. When the values are wrong, it takes nonconforming pioneers to persuade people to alter them and to demonstrate and institute new values. A society changes its values with extreme reluctance. Kluckhohn[436] has defined a value orientation as 'a generalised and organised conception, influencing behaviour, of nature, of man's place in it, of man's relation to man, and of the desirable and non-desirable as they relate to man-environment and interhuman relations'. A G.A.P. report[437] classified values into given groups—human-nature orientation, man-nature orientation, time orientation, activity orientation and relational orientation. Some of the major values of society are expressed as its religion. Some take on the character of myths.

Social Control

For the general well-being, society enforces certain standards on its members. The strongest control is subtle—the suggestion of the group, threat of loss of appreciation and prestige, the paths of least resistance, the introjection of authority as a father figure, the pressures of class, economic groups, the clan, etc. Furthermore, nature exerts its own discipline—not to wear clothes in a cold climate leads to suffering or death. Society exerts explicit control through formal legal codes; these are normally the 'will of the people', and change with varying conditions and the acquisition of knowledge. There is informal control, through religious standards, conventions, customs and traditions. Allied to control is leadership. This may be based on religion, education, income or class. Sometimes control is by a combination of class and heredity—the Establishment. Leadership may be dictatorial or democratic. Sometimes it is an activity of a group, e.g. the clergy, or a trade union or an elected town council. These groups in turn have their leaders. Harris[438] discusses the emergence of leaders in a small town. Leadership is linked to power—the share of the individual or group is shaping activity or policy in society.

Social Mobility

Industrialisation, wealth, wars and mechanical means of transport have led to accelerating social mobility. People leave rural areas for the higher standards of living of industrialised areas. Wars can lead to the mass exodus of people. Wealth encourages travel. The car, railways, ships and air transport make movement an easy process. The future, it can be confidently predicted, will bring greater mobility and thus more mixing of peoples. Much may be lost and gained by mobility: loss in terms of giving up support of relatives and friends, isolation, the clash of cultural roles and values, the problems of language; gain in terms of escape from traumatic relatives and friends, emergence from isolation, and new and better values. Much has yet to be understood about migration. This is sometimes the prerogative of the healthy, stable, balanced and enterprising. Sometimes it constitutes the escape of the unstable and the weak, who reap another disillusionment in their new community. Failure of integration may not be the fault of the selection but of the individual. Usually the healthy individual has a remarkable capacity for adjustment.

Social Groupings

There are many social groupings, and they are dependent on a number of factors, e.g. politics—Communist, Socialist, Republican, Conservative, etc.; education—day school, boarding-school, university, etc.; religion—Baptist, Roman Catholic, Hindu, etc.; occupation—teacher, clergyman, tailor, etc. An individual may belong to a number of social groupings, e.g. Republican teacher, a graduate who is a practising Buddhist. Each group has its leaders, conventions, practices and standards, and imposes roles on its members.

Function

Allied to the structure of society is its function, and one may dictate the other. A family may gain protection from the community, either against the ill effects of another family or of another community. Individuals and families need the satisfaction and security of identifying with units larger than themselves. Furthermore, a community furthers economic production: much can be achieved which is impossible in smaller units; specialisation is assisted. Again, society makes it possible to pool services and facilities. For example, goods can be supplied through a market system possible only on a large scale, a church can cater for a number of families and, again, a school for a large number of children. Biologically, marriage is possible outside the family or clan. The individual and family profit from the collective wisdom of a larger group, and from values and customs passed down the generations over time.

INTERACTION

Interactions occur within the large group of the community, as within the small group of the family. All these interactions are reciprocal. They are:

Individual family member—Society
Dyad in family—Society
Coalition in family—Society
Family—Society

Units in society are the individual, the near group of the neighbourhood, the area group of the community, the large remote group of the culture and the total social system. Some of the groupings in society may be special groups, e.g. religious, school or work groups. Within society there are blood ties with the individual and family—the close group of the extended family, the near group of the clan, the larger group of the race. As in the family, there may be a large number of simultaneous interactions. Furthermore, some of the interactions come from indirect influences, one group influences another, which in turn influences a third.

As within the family, every interaction elsewhere involves a standing between the two entities involved in the interaction, i.e. a relationship which can have a feeling tone and be described by its characteristics, e.g. one group has a whole set of attitudes, views and emotions towards another group.

Involved in the interaction is communication—meanings are conveyed through the channels of communication. Thus all that has been said about communication in the chapter on relationships applies also to the family-community interaction.

Again, it is convenient to think about society in terms of fields of forces. This matter has already been discussed under the heading of The Group Properties Dimension. Lewin formulated his field theory about society, and his writings are collected in two volumes.[439, 440] Sociologists often prefer to talk of the field of transaction. Spiegel[434] defines this as 'a matrix of interpenetrating systems within which can be discerned foci of organisation'. The transactional approach denotes a whole web, pattern or matrix of activity. The interactional approach denotes activity between two organised bodies. The transactional approach is the better representation of events within the family group, or society.

The interaction of an individual family member, a dyad, a coalition, or the whole family with the individual members of the community involves relationships with members of the extended family, neighbours, friends, workmates, schoolmates and chance acquaintances. *Relatives* have a potent influence—even from a distance. *Friends* can exert strong influences, especially when they are neighbours; depending upon the degree of intimacy and the length of contact, they can have an influence as powerful as that of relatives. *Neighbours* have a role not only as intimates, but also as a reflection of neighbourhood opinion. *Schoolmates* and *teachers* are normally in touch with the individual schoolchild for one-third of his waking life. A *work* situation for male or female can be harmonious or traumatic, depending on the relationships involved. *Casual acquaintances* are many. Trauma, if it occurs, is more likely to be due to a marked impact working over a short period. Chance acquaintances are often accepted as being the mouthpieces of collective community opinion. All these interactions are reciprocal.

Any element in the family can interact with any group of society—

neighbourhood, community, culture, or special groupings. Each in turn interacts with the family. 'They' is a term which represents the subtle, intangible, ever present, collective public or social opinion. Communication media, like newspapers, radio and television, all try, with varying degrees of distortion, to convey this opinion to people at large. The family feels under the scrutiny of 'they', it is conscious of the standards expected by 'they', and it tends to be insecure if not attuned to 'they'. Community pressure on the family is illustrated by Ross and Bruner,[441] and by Margaret Mead in Chapter XXIV. Cultural pressure on families is the theme of Diaz-Guerrero's paper in Chapter XXV, and of Geertz.[442]

Three of the interactions between family and society meet further consideration—those being with extended family, workmates and school-mates.

The family's interaction may be with its *extended family* in vertical extension to an older or younger generation, or in its lateral extension to siblings. There may be both. The group may be large enough to merit the term clan or tribe. Relatives harbour the collective opinion of 'the family'. By right, they have an intimacy with the individual which is denied to others. They may be in lifelong contact with the family, and previous traumata may be reinforced by present actions. Lancaster[443] studies some of the problems associated with the study of kin ties, Radcliffe-Brown[444] analyses kinship systems, and Albrecht[445] has considered the interaction between the aged and their children. In Chapter XXII Bell illustrates the different interactions of disturbed and well families with the extended family.

Members of the family spend a considerable portion of their waking life as adults in a *work* situation. This is again a transactional field. Interactions include management-foreman, foreman-man and man-mate. To produce harmony in these interactions makes for less stress, lower sickness rate and greater productivity. Mothers can profit from going out to work. This practice has always been customary in some areas, and there is no evidence to suggest that it causes any increase in emotional illness or delinquency. The alleged ill effects on the children of mothers going out to work have been greatly exaggerated. Mothers usually take care to protect their children during separation. Indeed, the very disturbed mother brings profit to herself and the child by attenuating the dis- harmony between them by going out to work. The child profits if given good substitute care, and the mother profits by relief from a traumatic situation, by mixing with others, and by gaining encouragement from succeeding at her work. She is likely to be a better mother because of the work experience. A careful review of the literature on mothers at work is made by Maccoby.[446]

Important interactions in the *school* transactional system are head-teacher-teacher, teacher-parent, teacher-child, and child-schoolmate. The teacher is a key figure. To produce harmony in these interactions can compensate the child for any deficiency at home, widen his emotional experience, strengthen his emotional state, and improve his achievement. Relevant studies are by Wilson,[447] Castle,[448] Golan,[449] McCleary,[450] Ojemann et al.,[451] Muuss,[452] and Snider.[453] The school situation is the subject of Chapter XXIII in this book.

FAMILY-SOCIETY INTERACTION AND HEALTH

Society has concentrated on the eradication of the obvious problems of physical ill-health. It can readily see the involvement of social factors in the aetiology of physical illnesses; periodic reminders come in the form of epidemics that handicap large sections of the population. As readily, it has taken large-scale social action against ill-health, usually by creating some national statutory or voluntary health service.

Mental disorder has received less attention, and again concentration has been on the more obvious conditions of psychosis and mental retardation. Emotional disorder has suffered comparative neglect.

Society recognises another set of problems, termed 'social problems'— child neglect, divorce, suicide, illegitimacy, promiscuity, alcoholism, delinquency. Being 'social', they are thought to be appropriate material for study by epidemiology. Social measures are often advocated for their relief—legal reform, economic measures, ethical prompting. Increasingly it is being realised that these so-called 'social' problems are emotional problems, and an index of disharmony in the emotional substratum of individual, family and society. These are matters to be discussed later, under Social Psychiatry.

TIME SEQUENCE

As with every other dimension of the family, family-community interaction has a history. The mode of the present interaction may be explicable only in terms of past interactions. For instance, co-operation or non-co-operation with authority may be flavoured by the parental attitudes to authority in the family of orientation. The combined experiences in the Past and in the Present may determine the nature of interactions in the Future.

III

CLINICAL PRACTICE OF FAMILY PSYCHIATRY

1. GENERAL

Individuals are concerned for themselves and thus come as individuals for help. The therapist pays attention to what comes his way and again concentrates on the individual. The orbit of observation may extend beyond the individual to a dyadic relationship, or, less often, to the family and society. But knowledge of relationships, of the family, and of society are still employed in individual psychiatry to help the individual only. Individual psychiatry sees the individual as the unit in clinical practice.

Humanity flowing in a stream from the Past, through the Present into the Future, might appear at first glance to be made up of a multitude of individuals. Closer observation, however, shows that they coalesce into groups. These groups, the families, expand, individuals split off and new groups are formed. But for the coalescing groups, the families, the flow of humanity would stop. Through these groups humanity propagates itself, and nurtures and trains its new members. Hence the family is the most significant unit in society. In his life span the individual normally experiences two groups, his family of origin as a child, and his family of adoption later. Such groups, family groups, are so tightly formed and have such a continuous history as to claim to be the basis on which society is built.

Family psychiatry abandons the individual as the unit and adopts the family instead. In the author's system for the practice of psychiatry, the family is the unit in referral, in the systematisation of symptomatology, in the procedures of investigation and in the processes of therapy. The loyalty throughout is to the family; the aim is to produce a harmonious, healthy, adjusted family.

Interest in the family and its psychiatry does not always coincide with family psychiatry. Attention may be given to one aspect of the family: the mechanisms by which it produces ill-health in its individual members; one of its relationships, such as the marital, or the child-parent relationship; the family as an economic unit in society; family roles and health; the family as the origin of social problems; the family as the protector of the mentally ill; the impact of illness on the family; the family in pschoanalytical terms; the family group in the treatment of the psychotic, etc. Thus knowledge concerning family functioning and dysfunctioning originates from many points. Emphasis is inevitably uneven. Much has yet to be known. However, the stage has been reached when it may be possible to marshal into a tentative framework knowledge about the family relevant to family psychiatry, a theoretical basis, and to outline a system for the practice of family psychiatry. The former is the aim of Chapter II, the latter is the aim of this chapter.

Like the 'individual psychiatrist', the family psychiatrist is dependent upon the findings of the basic scientists, but in addition he must absorb the relevant work of sociologists, social workers, developmental, experimental, industrial, cultural and social psychologists, cultural and social anthropologists, ethnographers and historians. Reference will be made elsewhere to some of the significant contributions in these fields.

Clinical contributions to the psychiatry of the family have come from many countries and include: in U.S.A., Ackerman[43, 49, 254, 562, 758, 765, 775, 780, 789-838] in New York (outstanding contributions on the correlation of the dynamic psychological processes of individual behaviour with family behaviour, family group therapy, psychoanalytical aspects of the family); Bateson and Jackson and their colleagues[52, 456, 563-632, 779, 839-874, 920] at Palo Alto (the aetiology of schizophrenia, family group therapy, family organisation); J. E. Bell[755, 878-885] (family group therapy); Norman Bell[255, 483, 989] at Harvard (family and society, family organisation); Boszormenyi-Nagy and Framo and colleagues[634, 757, 763, 909, 910, 913] in Philadelphia (family treatment of schizophrenia); Bowen[516-520, 756, 782, 784, 785, 786] in Washington (pioneer work on family group therapy, psychoanalytical aspects of the family and psychosis in relation to the family); Ehrenwald[50, 51, 54, 258, 770] (family organisation); Epstein[502, 503, 946] in Montreal (child and family psychiatry, family therapy); Grotjahn[767, 936, 937, 983] at Los Angeles (psychoanalytical aspects of the family); Ferreira[650, 656, 893-906, 986] in California (family myth and family organisation); Henry[256, 491] at St. Louis (family structure and the transmission of neurosis); Lidz, Fleck and their colleagues[534-559, 773, 886-891] at Yale (aetiology of schizophrenia, family therapy of psychosis, family organisation); MacGregor, Serrano and their colleagues[57, 78, 762, 944] at Galveston (family therapy and adolescence, multiple impact therapy); Mendell and Fisher[490, 787] (multi-generation family patterns); Midelfort[768] (family treatment of schizophrenia); Spiegel[53, 251, 434, 560, 561, 989] at Harvard (family roles, culture and psychosis); Titchener[55, 242, 454] (family organisation and psychosomatic process); Wynne[526-533, 754, 875, 877] at Bethesda (aetiology and family therapy of psychosis).

In Europe, Alanen[633, 671] in Helsinki (family group therapy and aetiology of psychosis); Davis[636, 637, 718, 726] in Bristol (the Oedipus complex and schizophrenia); Delay and Deniker[649] in Paris (families of schizophrenics); Flugel[32] (classic work on psychoanalysis and the family);

Howells[60, 61, 184, 330–333, 459, 1013] at Ipswich (systematisation of clinical practice into family psychiatry, theoretical dimensions of the family, vector psychiatry, vector therapy, family relations indicator, salutiferous community); Knobloch[938, 939, 940] in Prague (family therapy); Laing[638–645] in London (aetiology of psychosis, family organisation); Scott[479, 635] in London (aetiology of schizophrenia); and Vassiliou and Vassiliou[1056–1060] in Athens (family structure, family and community).

The theme common to all the contributions is a revolt from considering intrapsychic events alone. Interactions and transactions outside the individual are given their due place.

Interest in the psychiatry of the family having started at many points has sometimes remained at those points. In particular, disproportionate attention has been given to two aspects—psychosis in relation to family dynamics, and family group therapy. Family psychiatry for the author is the only way to practise psychiatry, and should embrace all clinical activity–referral, symptomatology, investigation and treatment, and all clinical categories.

Family psychiatry does not overlook intrapsychic events and individual procedures; it embraces both. The individual is an element in the family, and all aspects of his structure and functioning must be encompassed. He gains new significance when seen against the background of family and society. Individual procedures of referral, investigation and treatment are elements in the system of family psychiatry, but, again, given new significance when related to the whole.

Family psychiatry does not impose a rigid conformity in interpreting phenomena, e.g. the Freudian, Jungian systems can be retained by their adherents. But, by revealing a larger canvas, it exposes traditional views to a new scrutiny. Re-evaluation may lead to new philosophies which can be embraced as readily in family psychiatry. Nor does it limit psychiatric practice to one clinical syndrome. All are embraced—delinquency, psychopathy, psychosomatic disease, neurosis, psychosis and mental retardation. The core of the system, the essential principle, is that the family is always the functional unit. Thus any existing psychiatric service, whatever its case material, system, facilities, location or philosophy, is capable of adaption to and gaining from family psychiatry.

The sick individual, sick family and sick society are indivisible. All elements of the field of forces in the life space have equal significance as phenomena, but, due to special factors in clinical psychiatric practice, the sick family is the best vantage point from which to work, and ignores neither the individual nor the society. It might be thought that society is only sick in the sense that it contains a number of sick people. It is more correct to say that society itself is sick and therefore must contain a number of sick individuals. Forces within society at the moment are arranged in a pattern that provokes emotional ill-health, and this flows from one generation to the next. Society carries within it the capacity for health, because its field of forces carry the potential for rearrangement. This fact makes clinical endeavour worth while. Progress can be made only at the speed with which knowledge develops. But every clinical effort carries the prospect of new insight; research and clinical work go hand in hand.

The clinician has as his endeavour the production of health. In family psychiatry the goal is a healthy family, with, of course, healthy individuals, a task always limited by the fact that social ill-health pulls the family towards conformity to its norms. Over the generations small gains in the rearrangement of the vectors have a cumulative effect. Gains can be made at individual, family and social levels, and the process is indivisible. For the present, the family is the vantage point, as it is difficult to conceptualise and handle the whole of society. Later, family psychiatry may be the spring-board to *vector psychiatry*, the large-scale rearrangement of emotional vectors in society to the production of health in individual, family and society itself. Vector psychiatry includes analyses of intra- and extrapsychic vectors and application of vector change in treatment and health promotion.

Much thought and print has been expended in attempting to define health. It is easier to feel it than to define it. Its correlates are easier to delimit and describe—emotional and physical well-being, the capacity to adjust to life stresses, the ability to co-operate with others, unselfish actions born of security, efficiency and productivity. All these indicate harmonious functioning in the individual—what he feels is the comfortable state of 'being happy'. Most definitions of health are in terms of the individual; it may be more realistic to attempt a definition in terms of society, which ultimately dictates the state of its elements, such as individuals within it. Health and 'normal' behaviour must not be confused. The normal, usual, statistically average state of emotional functioning in society is far from 'health'. With each succeeding generation it is hoped that the norm will increasingly approximate to health—a state of affairs slowly and hardly achieved in the field of physical health.

2. ORGANISATION

Every psychiatric service should be a family psychiatric service, accepting the family as the functional unit. Some general observations are offered here on the organisation of a family psychiatric service. In Chapter XXVI will be found a model of such a service. Both out-patient and in-patient services should be based on the family as the unit.

Psychiatric services based on the individual as the functional unit are capable of alteration to one based on the family. The starting point is unimportant. Some services are already in varying stages of development —child and parent psychiatry, adult and family psychiatry, child and family psychiatry, marriage and family psychiatry clinics, etc. Additional intake clinics can allow more aspects of the family to be embraced; beyond the special intake clinics is a common system for the exploration and resolution of family psychopathology.

The family psychiatric service must establish a *referral system* through which the family can seek help. In some countries the contact is a direct one from family to service with no intermediary agency. In others, an intermediary, family doctor, family specialist, family nurse, polyclinic, family social worker, welfare agency, etc., directs the family or its members for help. In either event, family or intermediaries must know the procedures of referral.

Even the best intermediaries do not often recognise that psychopathology belongs to the family as a whole, and therefore rarely refer it as a unit. The individuals or part of a family that are most commonly referred should be accepted as an introduction to the family. To insist on the whole family being referred would presuppose a degree of insight from the family and the intermediaries which would not be forthcoming. Insight is correlated with degree of disturbance. To insist on such a degree of insight would exclude the most disturbed families, those most in need of help. What little the family offers should be accepted initially, and the service should work to include the rest.

Signs of pathology can arise at any facet of the family group—in any of its dimensions—in the individual, in the relationships, in its group processes, in its material circumstances and in its social interactions. Thus intake clinics can be based on any one, or on all, dimensions. *Individuals* naturally concentrate on their own discomfort and tend to seek help themselves; agencies make use of this ready referral. Thus a referral service can be based on the individual, with intake clinics for all age groups—child, adolescent, adult and geriatric. A referral service could also concentrate on *relationships*, e.g. the marital, parent-child or sibling-sibling. In practice, the last two are usually associated with a children's intake clinic; it may be useful to establish a marital problems intake clinic to gather in marital problems, a common feature of disturbed families. Establishing an intake clinic for the *family group* is valuable; with increasing understanding of family psychopathology this will become, in time, the method of choice; it must never, however, be inferred that only the group as a whole will be accepted by the service. Intake clinics based on poor *material circumstances* are already a feature of countries with well developed welfare systems. In advanced countries problem, or hard-core, families find their way to such clinics. If the psychopathological nature of their disability is accepted, in future they will be referred to family group intake clinics. *Family-community* interaction may break down at many points, engendering problems which require clinics to cope with them, e.g. delinquency clinics.

Not only may a family show signs of disruption in any dimension, but it may also present with varying types of psychopathology—neurosis, psychosomatic symptoms, delinquency, psychosis. Thus the family or the intermediary must acknowledge that any such manifestation anywhere in the family is accepted as a good reason for referral to the family psychiatric service. This service could base its intake clinics on clinical categories, instead of on signs of pathology in family dimensions.

It matters little which way the service organises its *intake clinics*—on family dimensions, on clinical categories or on age groups—as long as all concerned understand that the aim is to establish a point of contact with the family and, from that, work for the involvement of the whole family. In large services it may be convenient to arrange some degree of specialisation at this point, e.g. some personnel may have special experience in the difficult diagnosis of childhood illnesses and be able to make a special contribution to a children's intake clinic. Again, some clinicians will have special experience of psychosis and make a special contribution to a psychosis clinic. Even small units will find it useful to separate patients with 'process' psychosis from the remainder and to have special clinics for them. But once the intake procedure is over, all clinical workers become specialists in family psychiatry.

The purpose of investigation is to obtain a clear picture of the working of the whole family, its assets and its liabilities, in the historical sequence of the Past, the Present and the Future. In clinical practice there is a tendency to concentrate on pathology and overlook the assets, the mobilisation of which can be so valuable in therapy. Ideally this picture should be obtained by having the whole family to study. In practice, the clinician may have to work with one individual, or a dyad or part of a family. At one extreme the family group may present at the first visit, at the other extreme the family group will never appear as a whole. It may take weeks, sometimes months, and even years, to obtain the co-operation of the whole family.

The procedures of *investigation* should be flexible, to take advantage of any possible avenue of exploration. The approach to the family may be through interview of an individual, dyad or family group. Interview techniques can be supplemented by questionnaires to collect facts about particular aspects of the family, by charts to conceptualise information, and by special techniques of examination. The latter include examination of physical and mental states of members of the family. Clinical psychologists are developing new techniques for family assessment, and these are reviewed in Chapter XXVII. At the conclusion of the investigation of any individual and his or her family, the question must be asked, 'Are the handicaps observed a matter of psychopathology?' An affirmative answer means a task for the family psychiatric service. If the answer is in the negative, the problem is referred to the appropriate agency. At times the answer suggests emotional and other handicaps, and thus calls for a collaborative effort between the family psychiatric service and other agencies. Information collected on the family is recorded in such a way (e.g. under the five dimensions) as to demonstrate the harmonious functioning and dysfunctioning of the family group. The contribution from the Past is carried to the Present and on into the Future.

Much is to be gained from a rapid diagnostic service. Delay at this stage holds up the non-psychiatric agencies who, given a diagnostic formulation, may themselves be able to undertake the management of the family.

As has been mentioned above, the family may be interviewed as a group—family group diagnosis. This promising new technique allows a first-hand, vivid demonstration of family dynamics and should be a matter of invariable routine whenever a part or the whole of the family is accessible. Family group diagnosis must not be confused with family group therapy; what passes for the latter is often the former. One can lead to the other, they may co-exist, but they are still separate operations.

Titchener and Golden[454] have used the 'revealed differences' technique in association with the family group. Each member of the group expresses a number of opinions on various aspects of their family life. All the replies are returned to all the members—thus revealing their differences, which they are invited to discuss. Elbert et al.[455] use a family interaction apperception test in association with a group task which the members undertake together.

Much thought has been given at the Mental Research Institute, Palo Alto, to the analysis of tape-recorded material. Jackson, Riskin and Satir,[456] describe the analysis of a 'blind' tape, and Riskin[457] later describes scales developed in order to make 'blind' interpretations of recordings of family interaction. He believes that the results suggest that it is possible to make clinically meaningful and accurate descriptions of the whole family based on the coded speeches without focusing on the content. Watzlawick[458] published 36 examples from tape-recordings of conjoint family sessions and analysed their content.

Family diagnosis classifications arrived at by clinicians from the study of families have been described by Ackerman and Behrens,[49] Ehrenwald,[50, 51, 54] Titchener and Emerson,[55] Otto,[56] Serrano et al.,[57] Markowitz and Kadis,[58] and Voiland.[59]

The purpose of *treatment* is to produce a harmoniously functioning, healthy family group. Individual psychiatry aims at a healthy individual. As has been said already, this aim can lead to ill-health for others by alteration in the family dynamics. Furthermore, a healthy family unit guarantees the health of individual members. A full result may not be achieved, but any gain in family improvement takes the society further than mere improvement in individuals. A flexible approach to family therapy embraces certain forms of family psychotherapy such as individual psychotherapy, dyadic therapy and family group therapy. In addition to family psychotherapy, family therapy includes vector therapy—a technique aimed at changing the field of forces in the life space of the family to bring advantage to it. Lastly, in a long term and on a large scale, the community can promote emotional health in the family.

Family therapy embraces all therapeutic procedures to assist the family. Family group therapy, it will be noted, is but one technique of family psychotherapy, which in turn is only one element of family therapy. This observation is worth making, as so much therapeutic work on the family is limited by using family group therapy alone; its exclusive use greatly limits the effectiveness of therapy.

That the family, rather than the individual, is the focus of clinical endeavour has repercussions on *facilities*. The family psychiatric service must be accessible to families. Where it serves a community without discrimination of class or income, it should serve a population small enough for it to be identified as a community and for the psychiatric service to know and collaborate with the many family and community welfare agencies. This population should rarely be over a quarter of a million people, and smaller units may be even more effective.

In large units intake clinics may have a separate physical existence. In smaller units intake clinics need only exist on paper, the same physical facilities being used for all clinics, i.e. separate clinics are merely reminders to referral agencies of the nature of the material accepted. In time, virtually all psychiatric problems will be referred as a family problem. After the acceptance of the presenting problem, individual or family, all the many facilities for investigation and treatment can be shared by the personnel working on families. The facilities include rooms for individual and family interviewing and therapy, domiciliary care, physical examination of individuals, physical methods of treatment, psychometrics of individual and family, day hospital and club activities, evening clinics, play procedures, in-patient care of all clinical categories, a dispensary for drugs, and special techniques such as EEG, radiological, pathological, and medical photography. A consultation service can be supplied by allied medical departments.

A reception/waiting room is provided for patients of all ages. A separate waiting area for children in the form of play room, or play garden, adds to the comfort of the family. Some interview rooms must be large enough to accommodate family groups—and ordinary group activities. Teaching can be enhanced by the provision of two-way screens, closed circuit television and seminar rooms. The right use of design, colour, light and furniture can produce a building acceptable to families, and the right blend of the domestic and the functional.

All record keeping must be based on the family unit. Various methods can be devised to give a continuous and cumulative family profile; at the least, the records of individual family members can be kept together.

The focus of all staff activity is a family. Each family demands a team effort. Work roles must be assigned and effort co-ordinated. Formal or informal means can be devised for the purpose. Unproductive talk should be reduced to a minimum, and is reduced to a minimum when staff are experienced. Large formal case conferences are best utilised for teaching and have only a small part to play in routine clinical work. Once responsibility for a family is accepted by a clinical team, the same team should have control of the family's in-patient care too, should this be required.

Few units have sufficient resources for the number of families referred. Thus, to allow families to pass without delay from investigation to treatment calls for a selection of families for treatment. Selection is usually unavoidable. To allow a long waiting list to accumulate does not permit any more families to be treated with the resources available; it hampers the optimum employment of the facilities available and delays the desirable rapid transfer from investigation to treatment.

3. THE PRESENTING PATIENT

The family is sick as a whole; yet it rarely presents at a psychiatric service as a complete unit. An individual may be referred as the 'presenting' patient, the 'propositus', the 'indicating' patient, the 'identified' patient or the 'manifest' patient. What determines that a fragment of the family is sent for treatment rather than the whole? The understanding of the mechanisms concerned with the referral of one member throws light on the correct arrangement of referral agencies and the organisation of the psychiatric service. It exposes important aspects of the psychodynamics of the family. It underlines the central thesis of family psychiatry—that the family is a social unit specially meaningful for psychiatry.

Some of the mechanisms determining the ascertainment of a fragment of the family will be briefly reviewed.

ORGANISATION OF SERVICES

Should the psychiatric service in a certain area be based on adults or children or adolescents, then only that particular age group finds its way to the service, whilst equally, or more, disturbed members of the family cannot be seen because they are in a different age group. Thus the shape of the service determines who comes from the family.

Referral agencies tend to have special interests and attract family members falling within their speciality. The family doctor, for instance, concerns himself with individuals with physical problems; this explains why two out of three emotionally ill patients in general practice present with psychosomatic problems.[459] A social agency specialising in social and welfare problems sends those problems. Should the school be the referral channel for children, it will give special attention to problems of discipline and scholastic failure. Thus the special interests of an agency determine whom they see and refer to a psychiatric service.

Sometimes the individual or family tends to produce symptoms which will demand attention by a referral agency. When a medical practitioner, for instance, concentrates exclusively on physical symptoms, his patients, to gain his attention, must have physical symptomatology. Should such symptoms already be present in a family member, he will consult his doctor because of them and will become the family member ascertained. In such a situation there is pressure to produce a physical symptom—and, if possible, one of special interest to the practitioner or the psychiatric service. For example, much attention was given some years ago by the psychiatric service to amnesia; it was held that it was possible for un-conscious acts beyond the patient's control to take place in this state. Many cases of so-called amnesia were reported, but, when psychiatric opinion about responsibility in states of amnesia changed, this symptom became less fashionable.

The State of the Family Dynamics

This varies from moment to moment in the life history of the family, as the following clinical example illustrates.

Some time ago, a woman aged 40 presented in the Ear, Nose and Throat Department of a general hospital, complaining that her nose was blocked. She was carefully examined. No blockage was found. She was sent away with some nose drops. Within two weeks she returned, still complaining that her nose was blocked. She was re-examined. No blockage was found, and she was sent away with more drops, no doubt of a different colour. Within another two weeks she presented again, still complaining that her nose was blocked. This time, the ear, nose and throat surgeon said, 'There must be something worrying you, Mrs. X.' She replied, 'You would be worried too, if you had a husband like mine.' To which he was quick to retort, 'You must have a marital problem. I shall send you to the Marital Problems Clinic at the Institute of Family Psychiatry.' Over the course of weeks her recital of her husband's mis-demeanours was listened to. Whilst this was done, the husband's condition deteriorated, and he was admitted to a neighbouring mental hospital as a suicidal risk with marked depression. The wife regularly visited her husband in the mental hospital. *Rapprochement*, to some extent, took place, and the husband's condition improved. The mental hospital authorities suggested that since the wife already attended the Institute of Family Psychiatry, after his discharge it might be reasonable for the husband to follow suit. He was accepted by the Adult In-take Clinic and commenced attendance at the Institute of Family Psychiatry. Within a month, one of the hospital's physicians telephoned to say that an 18-year-old youth had been admitted to the Medical Department with threatened perforation of the stomach. He felt there was a big stress factor in the boy's condition. Furthermore, he understood that the father and mother were already attending the Institute of Family Psychiatry. Could the son also be accepted? He came to the Institute of Family Psychiatry via its Adolescent In-take Clinic. Thus all three members of one family were now attending one department.

Briefly, the family psychodynamic picture showed a nagging hyper-anxious wife locked in perpetual strife with her husband. The husband avoided conflict as much as possible by outside activities. The local clergyman befriended him, and at times the husband felt strong enough to retaliate against his wife. Then she developed psychosomatic symptoms, the last being the blocked nose. At moments of peace between husband and wife, she turned her attention to her son—and his stomach ulcer gave pain. The husband's hospital admission brought peace between husband and wife—and so the son became ill.

This fragment of clinical history illustrates the 'seesaw' movement in families. As the wife was supported in the initial investigation, so the husband deteriorated and became depressed. When the husband was supported by his friend, so the wife deteriorated and showed psychosomatic manifestations. *Rapprochement* between husband and wife caused the son to deteriorate and to be referred with acute psychosomatic symptoms.

Thus in families there are 'seesaw' movements. The person 'down' at a moment in time is likely to be the propositus. At the conclusion of a brilliant survey of the exclusive treatment of a child patient, a therapist observed that, at conclusion of the child's treatment, the mother had become severely depressed and was now the inmate of a mental hospital! The dynamics of the family had changed to the mother's disadvantage, and she had become the propositus. Burgum[460] relates the adverse effect of treatment on a father. Lindemann[461] found that attacks of ulcerative colitis coincided with changes in the well-being of other relatives. In Chapter L of this volume Kohl draws attention to the effects on one marital partner of the treatment to another. Mittleman[462] and, again, Rosen,[463] refer to the reciprocal patterns in families produced in psychoanalytical treatment. Chance[464] considers the measurement of changes in families during the treatment of a child.

Vulnerability of a Family Member

One family member may be so placed as to be specially vulnerable to stresses within the family. More than this, these family members may have constellations of personality characteristics which make them vulnerable to a particular stress. In addition, ordinal position, sex gender or age may be important for vulnerability.

A child may be the only child, the first, second, next youngest and youngest. Since the speculations of Adler[465] much attention has been given to the significance of a child's ordinal position in the family. Bossard and Boll[466] have been able to define a number of roles associated with the ordinal position of a child in a large family. In Chapter XXVIII Lasko studies parent behaviour to first and second children. Generally the studies are contradictory. Sewall,[467] and Wile and Jones,[468] for instance, find that birth order is not important. Norton[469] found that higher birth orders are more neurotic, but some investigators have found the oldest child less neurotic. Fisher and Hayes,[470] again, found that if there are three children or more the oldest and the youngest are the most maladjusted. Rosenow and Whyte,[471] on the other hand, found that in the three-children family the second child is more often treated in psychiatric clinics than the third.

Some investigators have associated ordinal position with the nature of the presenting symptom. Mowrer[472] found that alcoholism is commonest in the oldest and 'socially' next-to-youngest (that is, though in fact the youngest, another sibling is treated as the youngest) sibling positions. Kingsley and Reynolds[473] found that psychosomatic symptoms differ according to ordinal position; only children have many gastro-intestinal upsets, skin disorders, feeding disturbances, constipation, asthma and allergies; first children frequently suffer from constipation and feeding disorders; respiratory and ear infections, tonsilitis, diarrhoea, accidents and enuresis are most common in second children.

Although the investigations on ordinal position appear contradictory, when groups are studied, the child's ordinal position in a particular family may yet be highly significant, but understandable only in that unique set of circumstances.

The sex of a child may lead to vulnerability. In families there may be a tendency for parents to reject one gender whilst accepting the other. Again, this may only become apparent when evaluated as part of the psychodynamics of a particular family. Sex may be a factor in determining the attitudes of siblings—as shown by the extensive studies of Koch.[474] Schmuck combines ordinal position and sex of sibling in a study reported in Chapter XXIX.

The age of a family member may be the cause of vulnerability. The writer has observed that in some problem families a mother may pay a child a great deal of attention for the first two years, because of her own needs for an emotional 'lollipop'. At the age of two or three, as the child makes demands on the mother, he is rejected and another infant sought. Thus at an early age the child is accepted, later rejected. Similarly, parents talk of difficulties in acceptance of and in relating to their offspring when they are children or adolescents. Old age is anathema to some families.

ANNIVERSARY REACTIONS

Individuals may not fall ill with equal regularity throughout the year. There are peak periods, e.g. Fowler[475] reports a higher incidence of suicide amongst the Mormons of Salt Lake City at Christmas. This is probably not unique to Salt Lake City. Not only may there be dates, seasons, months of significance to whole populations, but also to individuals. Furthermore, the individual breakdown may reflect a family's association with that moment in time. The significance of the time may not be apparent to an onlooker, as it has meaning only in terms of the life experience of a particular individual or family. It may relate to a great variety of stresses in the past. Hilgard and Newman discuss the subject in Chapter XXXI. Other contributions are by Hilgard,[476] Berliner,[477] Bresler[478] and Scott.[479]

FAMILY MOTIVATION

The family may make use of an individual family member; it can punish a member by sending him for psychiatric treatment, can express guilt through him, and use him in a crisis as a means for getting assistance.

Serrano *et al.* speculate in Chapter VII how the adolescent's primary role in the family is a stabilising factor, i.e. the adolescent internalises or externalises parental conflicts. The neurotic equilibrium of the family is broken when the adolescent's behaviour becomes unendurable to himself, the family and/or society. This creates a crisis and then an appeal for help. Suicide or a suicidal gesture by adolescents may also be a cry for help to the family, as these symptoms may be the only symptom-language understandable by their families (see Stengel and Cook).[480]

Of the many motivations setting in motion family dynamics, some of the most intriguing are those causing the role of scapegoat to be given to a family member. The member becomes the 'butt' for the family. A mother, for example, may imply to her children, 'Things go wrong so much because of the feeble father you have.' The scapegoat is a matter of comment by Ackerman in Chapter XXX, and elsewhere by Frazer,[481] Eissler,[482] Vogel and Bell,[483] Russell and Sambhi.[484]

Frazer observes that the evil of which a man seeks to rid himself need not be transferred to a person; it may equally well be transferred to an animal or a thing. In great emergencies the sins of the Rajah of Manipur used to be transferred to somebody else, usually to a criminal, who earned his pardon by his vicarious sufferings. On his accession, a new king of Uganda used to wound a man and send him away as a scapegoat to Bunyoro to carry away any uncleanness that might be attached to the King or the Queen. Again, men sometimes play the part of scapegoat by diverting to themselves the evils threatening others. Animals, Frazer relates, are often employed as a vehicle for carrying a way or transferring the evil. When a Moor has a headache he will sometimes take a lamb or a goat and beat it till it falls down, believing that the headache will thus be transferred to the animal. Sometimes in the case of sickness, the malady is transferred to an effigy as a preliminary to passing it on to another human being. In this last case the thing is often only a vehicle to convey the trouble to the first person who touches it.

Frazer believes that similar means have been adopted to free a whole community from diverse evils afflicting it. Such attempts to dismiss with one act the accumulated sorrows of a people are by no means rare or exceptional; on the contrary, they have been made in many lands, and from being occasional they tend to become periodic and annual. Public attempts to expel the accumulated ills of a whole community may be divided into two classes, according to whether the expelled evils are immaterial and invisible, or embodied in a material vehicle or scapegoat. The former may be called the direct or immediate expulsion of evils; the latter the indirect or mediate expulsion, or the expulsion by scapegoat. Often the scapegoating vehicle which carries away the collected demons or ills of a whole community is an animal. But a human being may also be the scapegoat upon whom the sins of the people are periodically laid. At Onitsha, on the Niger, two human beings used to be sacrificed annually to take away the sins of the land. Both ancient Rome and ancient Greece were familiar with the use of a human scapegoat.

Frazer also found that the accumulated misfortunes and sins of a whole people are sometimes laid upon the dying god, who is supposed to bear them away for ever, leaving the people innocent and happy. The notion that we can transfer our guilt and sufferings to some other being who will bear them for us is familiar to the savage mind. It arises from a very obvious confusion between the physical and the mental, between the material and the immaterial. Because it is possible to shift a load of wood, stones, or what not, from our own back to the back of another, the savage fancies that it is equally possible to shift the burden of his pains and sorrows to another, who will suffer them in his stead.

COMMUNICATED SYMPTOMATOLOGY

Two or more individuals in a family may share common symptomatology to such an extent that they will be referred together to a psychiatric service. The members may be beset by a common stress, as in the case of two elderly sisters who had lived closely together for many years and who, on hearing that their house was to be sold, walked quietly into the sea, hand in hand, and drowned together. The members of a coalition may borrow symptomatology from one another by imitation or suggestion. A paranoid person can persuade another of a common enemy and draw him into his delusional system.

This manifestation is common in neurotic patients. In psychotic patients it is termed communication insanity, induced insanity, or *folie à deux*. In Chapter XXXIII, Waltzer describes *folie à douze*. Greenberg, Hunter and MacAlpine[485] claim that Sir Kenelm Digby first described the condition known as *folie à deux* in 1658, about 200 years before Baillarger

(1860) and Lasegue and Falret (1897) in France, and Berlyn (1819) in Germany. Lasegue and Falret's paper[486] has recently been translated by Michaud[487] and ends with a useful bibliography. Recent reviews of the condition includes those by Gralnick[488] and Rioux.[489]

Folie à deux should be a fruitful field of enquiry for the family psychopathologist. Some of the earlier papers on closer scrutiny appear to be descriptions of communicated and induced conditions in neurotics. These papers abound with accounts of family mental mechanisms.

ATTENTION-GIVING SYMPTOMS

From time to time a member of a family will manifest symptoms which are striking, call attention to themselves or have considerable 'nuisance value'. Thus another family member, the family or a community agency will seek his referral. Some examples of striking symptoms are tics, speech disorders, hysterical symptoms and skin conditions. A child with encopresis, enuresis or awkward behaviour will quickly come to attention, while an equally disturbed, but apathetic, listless, depressed child may be overlooked.

REFERRAL AS A SIGN OF HEALTH

Insight into one's own emotional state is found to be inversely proportional to the degree of the disturbance. Thus highly disturbed family members avoid, 'can see no point in', or obstruct referral to psychiatric services. Less disturbed family members, on the other hand, can 'see the point' and come as the family's representative. Paradoxically, individual psychiatry can lead to concentration of effort on the least disturbed in the family.

4. CLINICAL SYNDROMES

Clinical syndromes in psychiatry should be regarded as expressions of family psychopathology. This is strikingly true of emotional disorder. Some would claim the same position for psychosis; at the least the family influences it, and psychosis in time has repercussions on the family. Mental retardation must certainly be considered in the context of the family.

For the purposes of this chapter the psychiatric field is divided into three parts—emotional illness, psychosis and mental retardation. Psychosis is subdivided into organic psychosis (acute and chronic) and functional psychosis (schizophrenia and manic-depression).

EMOTIONAL ILLNESS

Development of Symptomatology

An emotional symptom is always the expression of the psychopathology of the whole family. Symptomatology for which obscure and symbolic explanations have been given becomes startlingly comprehensible when seen in the context of the family. The following example will help to make this clear. A boy of 12 suffers from anorexia; for the first few years of his life he was brought up by two grandmothers who lived with his family. The maternal grandmother was permissive and did not believe that a child should be forced to eat. The other held as firmly that a child should eat what was put before it. The strict grandmother forced the child to rebel against her, the other grandmother offered him a way to express his rebellion. So the child refused to eat. When the strict paternal grandmother left the family, her son, the boy's father, inherited her role and tried to force the child to eat the food he did not like. Thus his symptoms continued. A family creates the emotional stress, the emotional disorder and the particular manifestation of the disorder—the choice of symptoms.

The instance just related concerns a symptom, a manifestation of dysfunction, in an individual. But, as surely, symptoms can show at any facet of the family. By tradition, interest has been focused on the individual. Stress may arise in the family in any of its dimensions and at any point in a dimension. As clouds gather in the sky due to a complex of variables, so do stresses within the family. Thus symptomatology can appear in any or all of the five dimensions of the family—the individual, the relationship, the group, the material circumstances and the family-community interaction. Careful examination may show that they invariably appear in all. It should not be overlooked that the family-community dimension is a frequent source of stress, and least under the control of the family. However, a family group may not manifest dysfunction equally throughout its system. One dimension, or one aspect of it, may show disproportionate dysfunction due to the 'set' of the emotional events at that time.

It is usual to subdivide emotional disorder in the individual into certain clinical categories—anxiety states, obsessional, hysterical states, etc. This practice has grave weaknesses. It pays attention to the presenting symptom, often elevates this to the status of a disease, and limits the description of the process. The process is all important and cannot be covered by one or many labels. Each process is made up of such a combination of circumstances as to be unique to itself.

It is still useful to classify symptoms into groups. One such grouping places the symptom in one of three clusters—psychosomatic, affective and behavioural. This would apply to any emotional expression throughout the family, i.e. in any dimension. It can be exemplified by consideration of an individual—say, a child of three. Should this sensitive organism be placed in a position of stress, e.g. by shouting at him, it will be seen that, in general, there are three clusters of reactions. Firstly, the child will show psychosomatic changes—a fast pulse, accelerated heart rate, a pale and moist skin, and, should the shock be great enough, may pass water on to the floor. Furthermore, the child shows affective responses—he is fearful and yet angry. Lastly, his behaviour may change—he may cringe away or take retaliatory measures, such as shouting back or kicking the offender. The three clusters constitute a useful way of grouping symptoms. But it will be noticed that an emotional reaction or disorder is never monosymptomatic. Symptoms are multiple and usually appear in all three clusters.

The choice of symptom is a reflection of family dysfunctioning. The individual's choice is dictated by his life experience in the family, e.g. an angry family evokes anger in a child. The choice of expression in a relationship is similarly determined, e.g. physical hostility may be taboo and verbal hostility alone possible. The material changes in the family can take place only within the limits set by its condition. Group manifestations are a family expression, e.g. sulking may be an expression of hostility in a particular family. The community interaction may determine symptomatology, e.g. that fear be controlled by obsessional ritual or that sexual taboos be imposed. Again, gastric ulceration is a common symptom in Western civilisation but not in primitive communities. Not only do present events dictate choice of symptomatology, but so do those from the past. Mendell and Fisher, in Chapter XVII and in another paper,[490] follow neurotic behaviour through the generations. Henry[491] sees neurotic behaviour. determined by generation to generation transmission. Hilgard[492] talks of 'social heredity'. Every symptom has to be understood as a manifestation of past or present family dysfunction, or as a resultant of both.

Locus of Symptomatology

Each dimension will be briefly considered as it manifests symptoms in the three groupings of psychosomatic, affective and behavioural.

Dimension of the individual. In the dimension of the individual each family member usually shows symptomatology. Naturally this will not be exposed if examination concentrates on one person alone and overlooks the remainder of the family. But each individual does not show psychopathology of the same kind, nor to the same degree. The relationship of an individual's symptom to the family system is considered by Satir in Chapter XXXIII.

Changes in *physical* state due to emotional stress (psychosomatic symptoms) occur at all ages and in any body system. Feeding problems in infants, enuresis and encopresis in children, migraine in adolescents, dysmenorrhoea in women, gastric ulceration in men and bronchitis in the aged are just a few symptoms picked at random.

In Chapter XXXIV Meyer and Haggerty consider streptococcal infection as a reaction to family stress. In Chapter XXXV Serrano and Wilson show how the brain damaged child reacts to the family pattern of behaviour. In Chapter XXXVI Downing *et al.* illustrate the family psychodynamic factor in Gilles de la Tourette's syndrome. Titchener *et al.*, in Chapter XXXVII, see ulcerative colitis as the product of a mother-child relationship which is dictated by family dynamics. Weblin[493] appraises asthma as a family manifestation, and family therapy as an avenue of research and therapy. Breese and Disney[494] consider strepto-coccal infections in family groups. Jordan[495] is concerned with the effects of a disabled child on the life adjustment of its family. The family as an epidemiological unit is considered by Kempe *et al.*[496] and in the Harvard symposium of 1964.[497] The teaching of family care in the medical field is the subject of papers by Meyer,[498] Haynes,[499] and White.[500]

Again, changes in *affect* occur in all age groups. Apathy in infants, timidity in children, anxiety in adolescents, reactive depression in adults, hypochondriasis in the aged: these are a few of the many manifestations which may be observed. Suicide as an aspect of family disorganisation is studied by Tuckman and Youngman in Chapter XXXVIII. A statistical study by Ingham[501] indicates that intrafamily conflicts are important con-comitants of affective symptoms.

Changes in *behaviour* occur also in all age groups. Excessive crying in infants, temper tantrums and destructive behaviour in children, delin-quency in adolescents and antisocial acts in adults are again some random examples. Thus psychopathic states exhibiting antisocial actions belong to the cluster of changes in behaviour. Sargent, in Chapter XXXIX, shows how a homicidal child may be acting as the unwitting agent of the family. Emotional disturbances in individuals, especially children, are increasingly being considered in the context of the family. Attention is directed to the work of Epstein,[502, 503] Reidy,[504, 505] Sobel and Koff,[506] Drechsler and Shapiro,[507] Tyler and Henshaw,[508] Charny[509] and Starr.[510]

Dimension of the relationship. Each relationship will usually show dis-harmony. Naturally this will not be seen unless each relationship is examined, e.g. the mother-child relationship often comes under far greater scrutiny than the father-child relationship; the marital relationship also receives a fair degree of attention—but not always from the psychiatric service. Each relationship will not show psychopathology of the same kind, nor to the same degree.

A disturbed relationship may give rise to any symptom in the three clusters of physical, affective or behaviour change mentioned above, in individuals of the partnership, e.g. a rash or an obsession or violent be-haviour in the partners of the husband-wife relationship. Sometimes the symptomatology is shared by both partners, e.g. impotence in both (a psychosomatic reaction); joint depression, suicide or *folie à deux* (affective changes), or overt quarrelling (a change of behaviour). Furthermore, some symptoms tend to be associated with a particular relationship, e.g. a malrelationship between husband and wife is often responsible for ejaculation praecox, dysparunia, impotence and frigidity.

The symptomatology springing from relationships—marital, parent-child and child-child—are the subject of a considerable literature. Rarely, however, are they seen in the light of family psychopathology.

The group dimension. Symptomatology in the group dimension manifests itself in a pattern common to the whole family. Families may be given to types of physical disability, e.g. accident proneness, stomach disorder or speech disturbances. They manifest affective changes as a group, e.g. tension, panic, irritability, boredom, apathy. The family's pattern of behaviour is shared by all its members, e.g. intolerance, quarrelling, lack of cohesion, exploitation of neighbours. Langsley[511] describes a family group's handling of premature death.

Dimension of material circumstances. Family dysfunction frequently manifests itself in the dimension of material circumstances, e.g. poverty despite an adequate income; sloth resulting from apathy and disinterest; low income due to lack of application; loss of employment as a reaction to family emotional crises. It is fortuitous that adverse material circumstances are the manifestations that arouse attention in referral agencies, rather than individual, relationship or group disharmony. Most often these manifestations come to the attention of social agencies. But selection factors operate, as an agency may have a special function, e.g. a housing agency may ascertain sloth but overlook employment failure, or an agency may serve lower income groups only, and child neglect may be overlooked in a higher income group. Family pathology manifesting itself in material breakdown is best studied in the literature about problem families (see Chapter XXI).

Dimension of family-community interaction. In the dimension of family-community interaction signs of dysfunction may arise at the three points of contact: individual-community interaction, e.g. stealing outside the home by a child; dyad-community interaction, e.g. parents' refusal to send a child to school; or family group-community interaction, e.g. quarrelling with the neighbours. Manifestations may be affective, e.g. *folie à famille*, physical, e.g. family anorexia, or behavioural, e.g. collective antisocial acts. Malmquist[512] sees school phobia as a problem in family neurosis.

PSYCHOSIS

Psychosis, or insanity, strictly defined means 'a condition of the mind'. It is still an open question whether this condition is one of the mind rather than of the cerebrum. By common usage, the term psychosis has come to be used for abnormal states of mind with well described symptomatology, some of which is of unknown aetiology. These states of insanity include organic psychosis (acute and chronic) and functional psychosis (manic-depressive psychosis and schizophrenia).

Of organic psychosis as a family disorder, the literature is silent. Manic-depressive psychosis has passing mention. Schizophrenia in relation to family psychopathology, on the other hand, has had massive coverage; nearly half the literature on the psychiatry of the family deals with it. This is excessive and disproportionate.

A family psychiatric service concerned only with schizophrenia covers only a small part of the whole field. Pemberton,[513] found that, of patients suffering from mental illness in his general practice, 93·6% presented with neurosis, 6·1% with psychosis. On the assumption that 30% of individuals attend a general practitioner with mental illness,[514] only approximately 2% of his total patients are psychotic. Psychosis covers a number of conditions, senile dementia, manic-depressive psychosis and schizophrenia. Thus the percentage of schizophrenia may be as small as 0·5%. That this is so, is suggested in the study by Kessell,[515] who in a general practice found only three psychotic patients. A wider definition, as employed, for instance, in the United States, might embrace 10% of the population—still much the smaller part of the 30%.

Organic psychosis, a term covering such conditions as the delirious states, toxic states, drug intoxication and the chronic states of dementia, should certainly be linked with family pathology. For instance, alcoholism and drug addiction, which lead to acute organic states, are truly comprehensible only as manifestations of family pathology; concentration on the offending addict leads to the intolerable family dynamics from which he suffers to go unassessed; his treatment in isolation is largely futile. Rarely is the agony of family life so manifest as in these conditions—should the observer care to look at the family. Dementia, a handicap as serious as schizophrenia, can also be aggravated by wrong family attention and can in turn be a burden to the family.

Manic-depressive psychosis, one of the functional psychoses, has received some small attention in the literature. Depressive psychotic states should not be confused with reactive neurotic depression, which is much more frequent in the population at large. In this chapter reactive depression is considered under emotional disorder. The stress to which the depression is reactive may be easily overlooked, assumed absent, and an unwarranted diagnosis of psychotic depression made, which will thus expand its statistical significance. Finley and Wilson consider some of the characteristics of the family of manic-depressives in Chapter XLIV.

The bulk of this section must be devoted to a brief appraisal of the flood of literature on schizophrenia in relation to family psychopathology. It must be emphasised that, while he is forced to give disproportionate attention to it, the writer does not share in the implied importance of this clinical category. Emotional disorder is a far commoner condition; it is not a minor illness, it can have drastic and dramatic repercussions on the life of the individual and the family, and can, and does, lead to death in a significant number of people each year; in the United Kingdom 30,000 people attempt suicide every year and 5000 succeed. Furthermore, emotional disorder is so interwoven with the matrix of the family as to be the condition reflecting its psychopathology most sensitively and responding most clearly to beneficial changes in its dynamics.

Schizophrenia and Family Psychopathology

To review in detail the many papers devoted to this subject would require a volume in itself. Thus it is intended to concentrate on initiators in this field and to refer briefly to other important contributors as well. After a broad coverage, the work will be evaluated as a contribution to family psychiatry.

Bowen. Bowen[516] has been admirably clear in stating his views about the family concept of schizophrenia. These are worth outlining in some detail.

Bowen's view, that the schizophrenic psychosis of a patient is a symptom manifesting an acute process involving the entire family, arose from clinical research over three and a half years in which schizophrenic patients and their parents lived together in a psychiatric ward at the National Institute of Mental Health, Bethesda, U.S.A. The family unit is regarded as a single organism, and the patient is seen as that part of the family organism through which the overt symptoms of psychosis are expressed.

The initial focus of the study, started in 1954, was on the mother-patient relationship. At this point there was increasing evidence that the mother was an intimate part of the patient's problems, that the mother-patient relationship was a dependent fragment of the larger family problem, and that the father played an important part in it. At the end of the first year the hypothesis was extended to regard the psychosis in the patient as a symptom of the total family problem. This coincided with developing 'family psychotherapy' as a new plan of psychotherapy.

Bowen has come to regard schizophrenia as a process which requires three or more generations to develop. The grandparents are relatively mature, but their combined immaturities are acquired by the one child who is most attached to the mother. When this child marries a spouse with an equal degree of immaturity, and when the same process repeats itself in the third generation, it results in a child, the patient, with a high degree of immaturity.

A constant finding in his families was a marked emotional distance between the parents. Bowen referred to this as 'emotional divorce'. In all the families the parents have definite patterns of functioning in the 'emotional divorce' situations. Both parents are equally immature. One denies the immaturity, and functions with a façade of over-adequacy. The other accentuates the immaturity, and functions with a façade of inadequacy. There are some constantly recurring situations which accompany the over-adequate-inadequate reciprocity. One is the 'domination-submission' issue. On personal issues, especially decisions that affect both parents, the one who makes the decision becomes the over-adequate one and the other becomes the inadequate one.

One of the outstanding characteristics of the family is the inability of the parents to make decisions. The decision to have a child is the most difficult of all decisions in these families. For the mother, the pregnancy becomes a constant frustration between 'promise of fulfilment' and a 'threat that it could never be true'. A significant shift in the husband-wife relationship begins when the wife first knows that she is pregnant. At this point she becomes more emotionally invested in the unborn child than in the husband.

At the birth of the child the mother is securely in the over-adequate position to another human being, this human being belonging to her and realistically helpless. She can now control her own immaturity by caring for the immaturity of another—the child. The mother-child relationship is the most active and intense relationship in the family. The term 'intense' describes an ambivalent relationship in which the thoughts of both, whether positive or negative, are largely invested in each other. The mother makes two main demands on the patient, the more forcible of which is the emotional demand that the patient remain helpless. This is conveyed in subtle, forceful ways which are out of conscious awareness. The other is the overt, verbalised, 'hammered home' demand that the patient become a gifted and mature person. Bowen thinks of two levels of process between the mother and the patient. Much of the emotional demand that the patient remain a child is conveyed on an action level and out of conscious awareness of either mother or patient. The verbal level is usually a direct contradiction to the action level. In this reciprocal functioning, Bowen sees similarities between it and Wynne's 'pseudo-mutuality' and Jackson's 'complementarity'.

Prominent features of every mother-patient relationship in these cases are the mother's worries, doubts and concerns about the patient. These are a continuation of the mother's over-investment that began before the child was born. The subjects of the mother's over-concern about the patient and the focus of her 'picking on the patient' are the same as her own feelings of inadequacy about herself. The term 'projection' refers to the most all-pervasive mechanism in the mother-child relationship. It has been used constantly by the mother of every patient in her relationship with him. According to Bowen's thinking, the mother can function more adequately by ascribing to her child certain aspects of herself, which the child accepts. This is of crucial importance in the area of the mother's immaturity. The mother then 'mothers' the helplessness in the child (her own projected feelings) with her adequate self, thus a situation that begins as *a feeling in the mother becomes a reality in the child*.

Bowen proceeds to throw light on the mechanisms of symptom formation. The 'projection' occurs also on the levels of physical illness. This is a mechanism in which the soma of one person reciprocates with the psyche of another person. An anxiety in one person becomes a physical illness in another. The somatic reciprocation often includes definite physical pathology. A striking series of such reciprocations occur in a mother in response to a rapid improvement in a regressed patient. Within a few hours of each significant change in the patient, the mother develops a physical illness of several days' duration. Thus Bowen throws light again on reciprocal illness in the family, the 'seesaw' movement.

The child, Bowen believes, is involved in the same two levels of process as the mother, except that the mother actively initiates her emotional and verbal demands, and the child is more involved in responding to the mother's demands than in initiating his own. In this process, Bowen can see similarity with Bateson's 'double bind' hypothesis. The response of the patient to the mother's demands varies with the degree of functional helplessness of the patient, and the functional strength of the mother. A very helpless and regressed patient will comply immediately to emotional demands and pay little attention to verbal demands. The compliance of an inadequate patient to the mother's emotional demands is almost instantaneous. The patient lives his life as though the mother would die without his 'help', and if the mother died then he would die too. The child makes his emotional and verbal demands on the mother by exploiting the helpless, pitiful position.

All Bowen's research families have followed the basic pattern of overadequate mother, helpless patient and peripherally attached father. Bowen leans strongly to the belief that the essential process is confined to the father, mother, patient triad, rather than to the whole family.

When the child's self is devoted to 'being for the mother', Bowen holds that he loses the capacity of 'being for himself'. He stresses the function of 'being helpless', rather than the fixed 'is helpless' viewpoint. The process in which the child begins to 'be for the mother' results in an arrest in its psychological growth. It can now be seen how, in Bowen's view, the acute psychosis develops. The rapid growth of the child at adolescence interferes with the functioning equlibrium of the interdependent triad. There is an increasing anxiety in all three members. The adolescent period is one in which the growth process repeatedly upsets the equilibrium, and the emotional process attempts to restore it. The conscious verbal expressions demand that the child be more grown up. The child's course from adolescence to the acute psychosis is one in which he changes from a helpless child to a poorly functioning adult, to a helpless patient. Once free of the mother, he faces outside relationships without a self of his own. The psychosis represents an unsuccessful attempt to adapt the severe psychological impairment to the demands of adult functioning. It represents a disruption of the symbiotic attachment to the mother and a collapse of the long-term interdependent father-mother-patient triad.

The patient need not develop a psychosis. Bowen believes that unresolved, symbiotic attachments to the mother vary from the very mild to the very intense, that the mild one causes little impairment, and that schizophrenic psychosis develops among those with the most intense, unresolved attachment. There are a number of ways in which the individual in an intense attachment may find some solution to his dilemma. Certain individuals are able to replace the original mother with a mother substititute. The functional helplessness may find expression in somatic illness. The person with a character neurosis uses a flight mechanism to deal with the helplessness. The patients in Bowen's families attempted to find distant relationships. The psychotic collapse is seen as an effort at resolution that failed.

Bowen's work also led to formulations about the therapy of the schizophrenics. It could be seen that when father was encouraged to be less inadequate and to be a husband in a fuller sense, then the 'emotional divorce' disappeared and the patient lost the symbiotic relationship with the mother. The closer emotionally the parents were to one another, the greater the patient's improvement.

In addition to the above important contribution, Bowen has developed elsewhere[517–520] views about special aspects of the family. His collaborators Dysinger[521–523] and Brodey[524, 525] have elaborated on the work.

Wynne. Wynne and his collaborators[526–533] have continued the work on families at the National Institute of Mental Health. These workers have concentrated mainly on schizophrenic illness in which the onset of psychosis occurred acutely in late adolescence or early adulthood. They feel that the striving for relatedness to other human beings may be regarded as a primary feature of the human situation. Another key feature is that every human being strives consciously and unconsciously, in a lifelong process, to develop a sense of personal identity. They consider that the universal necessity for dealing with both the problems of relation and identity leads to three main solutions. These are (i) mutuality, (ii) non-mutuality, and (iii) pseudo-mutuality.

Each person brings to the relations of genuine *mutuality* a sense of his own meaningful, positively valued identity, and, out of experience of participation together, mutual recognition of identity develops, including a growing recognition of each other's potentialities and capacities.

Many interpersonal relations are not characterised by either mutuality or pseudo-mutuality, but by *non-mutuality*. The interchange of customer and sales clerk, for example, does not ordinarily involve, beyond the purchase of merchandise, a strong investment in excluding noncomplementarity or in exploring what the relationship has to offer to either person.

Pseudo-mutuality is a miscarried 'solution' of widespread occurrence. This kind of relatedness, in an especially intense and enduring form, contributes significantly to the family experience of people who later, if other factors are also present, develop acute schizophrenic episodes. In pseudo-mutuality emotional investment is directed more towards maintaining the sense of reciprocal fulfilment of expectations, than towards accurately perceiving changing expectations. The relation which persists cannot be given up, except under very dire or special circumstances, nor be allowed to develop or expand. Thus the pseudo-mutual relation involves a characteristic dilemma: divergence is permitted as leading to disruption of the relation, and therefore must be avoided; but if divergence is avoided, growth of the relation is impossible.

Wynne and his co-workers believed that, within the family of persons who later developed acute schizophrenic episodes, those relations which are openly acknowledged as acceptable have a quality of intense and enduring pseudo-mutuality. In these families the predominant pre-psychotic picture is a fixed organisation of a limited number of engulfing roles. Such a family role structure may already be forming in the phantasy life of the parents before the birth of the child, who sometimes is expected to fill some kind of void in the parents' life. Thus these workers believe that noncomplementarity has a more intense and enduring threat in the families of schizophrenics than it has in other families in which pseudo-mutuality may also appear. They also think that, in the families of potential schizophrenics, the intensity and duration of pseudo-mutuality has led to the development of a particular variety of shared family mechanisms by which deviations from the family role structure are excluded from recognition or are delusionally reinterpreted. The individual family member is not allowed to differentiate his personal identity either within or outside the family role structure.

Normally shared cultural mechanisms and codes facilitate the selection of those aspects of communication to which attention should be paid. In contrast, in schizophrenic relations, the shared mechanisms facilitate a failure in selection of meaning. It is not simply that divergence is kept out of awareness, but rather that the discriminative perception of those events which might specifically constitute divergence is aborted and blurred. At this point, the views of Wynne and his colleagues show similarities to the perceptual anomalies referred to by Bateson and his collaborators as the 'double bind' situation.

Pseudo-mutuality must be maintained at all costs. This leads to the maintenance of stereotyped roles in the families of schizophrenics. These roles constrict identity development and contribute to serious crises, including psychosis. This is the subject of a later paper.[527]

The potential schizophrenic, Wynne and his colleagues believe, develops considerable skill and an immense positive investment in fulfilling family complementarity and in saving the family, as well as himself, from the panic of disillusion. However, as he approaches chronological adulthood, with the shift or loss of family figures, and exposure to new outside relations more seductive or coercive than earlier ones, there comes a time when he can no longer superimpose the family identity upon his ego identity. Acute schizophrenic panic or disorganisation seem to represent an identity crisis in the face of overwhelming guilt and anxiety attendant upon moving out of a particular kind of family role structure. Later, pseudomutuality is re-established, in a chronic state, at a greater psychological distance from the family members, with an increasing guilt and anxiety over subsequent moves towards differentiation, and with heightened autism, loneliness and emptiness of experience. The psychotic episode as a whole represents a miscarried attempt at attaining individuality. He succeeds in attaining independence in some ways, only by withdrawal. In addition, the overt psychosis may have a covert function of giving expression to the family's collective, although disassociated, desires for individuality.

In their original work, Wynne and his colleagues formulated a hypothesis which has been the spring-board for present research. They believed that the fragmentation of experience, the identity diffusion, the disturbed modes of perception and communication, and certain other characteristics of the acute reactive schizophrenic personality structure are, to a significant extent, derived by processes of internalisation from characteristics of the family social organisation. Thus they have gone on to study the links between family patterns of thought disorder in schizophrenia. They believe, after a number of systematic studies, that it is possible to differentiate individual forms of thinking and to predict the form of thinking that will develop from the patterns of perceiving, relating and communication within the family. This work is described in a series of four papers.[528-531] The first of these papers, in which the workers discuss their formulation, can be found in Chapter XLIII.

Through the use of projective techniques, these workers have been able to predict the form of thinking and the degree of disorganisation of each patient's offspring from the tests of *other* members of his family, and to match blindly patients and their families. The workers have evolved a classification of schizophrenic disorders which is based upon thought disorder. This classification provides a means of discriminating along two continua, among varieties of schizophrenic and paranoid thinking. They define thought disorder as including not only forms of thinking which are disrupted or *fragmented* by primary process phenomena, but also by quieter, less bizarre, *amorphous* forms of thinking. In their formulation the amorphous-thinking schizophrenics have a schizophrenic thought disorder of an especially ominous type.

In another investigation Singer and Wynne[532] have differentiated characteristics of parents of childhood schizophrenics, childhood neurotics and young adult schizophrenics. This was done through the analysis of the Thematic Apperception Test and the Rorschach. The parents of 20 autistic children were primarily differentiated at the statistical significant level of accuracy from sociologically matched parents of neurotic children. The parents of the neurotic children, half withdrawn and half aggressive, were in turn successfully differentiated into these two groups on the basis of the parental projective tests. The results showed that the disaffiliative tendencies of the parents of the autistic young children were especially significant, while the parents of patients whose schizophrenia did not become overt until late adolescence or young adulthood appeared to let relationships develop that distorted and impaired the focusing of attention and the acquisition of clear meanings. The parents of the acting-out children in this series were active and energetic in these relationships, though often with various disturbed moods and impulses, and were relatively well defined and clear in their percepts. Parents of a group of withdrawn neurotic children showed especially sadness, together with serious strivings to maintain relationships. Morris and Wynne match styles of parental communication and schizophrenic offspring in another paper.[533]

Lidz et al. Lidz, Fleck, Cornelison and their Yale colleagues have also been responsible for a number of important studies concerning anomalies in patterns of behaviour in the families of schizophrenics. Lidz[534–556] began his interests in the families of schizophrenics in 1949. He studied the histories of 50 patients, and found that in only five cases out of the 50 could the patient be considered to have been raised in a reasonably favourable home, which contained two stable and compatible parents until the patient was 18 years old. The large majority were impeded by multiple deleterious influences, which were chronically present or frequently recurrent. The paternal influence, according to this gross evaluation, was harmful as frequently as the maternal. In 1952 Lidz commenced a series of investigations on the families of 17 patients. These studies are collected together in a recent volume.[557]

Fleck[558] gave a progress report in 1960. By then the workers had found that the study of their families shed much light on many schizophrenic manifestations, and that aspects of the parental personalities, and of intrafamilial behaviour of all members, determine much of what they consider characteristic or pathognomonic of schizophrenia.

Some of the characteristic forms of family dysfunction related to schizophrenic manifestations that the workers observed were:

1. Failure to form a nuclear family, in that one or both parents remain primarily attached to one of his or her parents or siblings.

2. Family schisms due to parental strife and lack of role reciprocity.

3. Family skews, when one dyadic relationship within it dominates family life at the expense of the needs of other members.

4. Blurring of generation lines in the family, e.g. (a) when one parent competes with children in skewed families; (b) when one parent establishes a special bond with a child, giving substance to the schizophrenic's claim that he or she is more important to the parent than the spouse; and (c) when continued erotisation of a parent-child relationship occurs.

5. Pervasion of the entire family atmosphere with irrational, usually paranoid, ideation.

6. Persistence of conscious incestuous preoccupation and behaviour within the group.

7. Socio-cultural isolation of the family as a concomitant of the six preceding conditions.

8. Failure to educate towards, and facilitate emancipation of, the offspring from the family, a further consequence of points 1 to 5.

9. Handicapping of a child in achieving sexual identity and maturity by the parents' uncertainty over their own sex roles.

10. Presentation to a child of prototypes for identification that are ir-reconcilable in a necessary process of consolidating his own personality.

Further findings in these families were that the siblings who were of the same sex as the patient were clearly more disturbed as a group than the siblings of the opposite sex. The paper discussing these findings is presented in Chapter XLII of this volume. This led to an examination of the data on the family pathology of the 17 schizophrenic patients according to their sex. The workers found that schizophrenic males often come from skewed families with passive, ineffectual fathers and disturbed, en-gulfing mothers; whereas schizophrenic girls typically grew up in schism-atic families with narcissistic fathers, who were often paranoid and who, while seductive of their daughter, were disparaging of women, and with mothers who were unemphatic and emotionally distant.

More recently, Lidz[559] has reviewed some of the findings from the families of schizophrenic patients to families generally. In lectures given at Tulane University he examined the thesis that the isolated nuclear family, despite its paucity of stabilising forces, is better suited for pre-paring its children to live in a society that is rapidly changing its adaptive techniques than are families with extended kinships systems. The in-stability of the isolated nuclear family can, however, reach such propor-tions as to be unable to provide sufficient structuring, security and satis-faction for its members. In his second lecture Lidz proposed that the essential dynamic structure of the family rests upon the parents' ability to form a coalition, maintain boundaries between the generations, and adhere to their appropriate sex-linked roles. Failure to meet these few requisites leads to distortion of the ego structuring of their children. In the last lecture he focuses specifically on the transmission of linguistic meanings. A grasp of the complexities of the acquisition of language and logic by the child suggested the possibility that schizophrenic patients received a faulty and confused grounding in linguistic meanings, as well as in other instrumental techniques, and that both limited their adaptive capacities and permitted them to escape from insoluble conflict, or irre-concilable contradictions, by abandoning the meaning system of their culture. Our children obtain their fundamental training in meanings and logic within the family, and, as irreconcilable conflicts also usually have their roots within the family, it appears essential to scrutinise the family environment in which schizophrenic patients grow up. Investigations have shown that such patients have invariably been raised in seriously disturbed families, which almost always contain at least one unusually disturbed parent. Lidz concluded that it is a tenable hypothesis that schizophrenia is a type of maladaption and malintegration due to deficiences in acquired instrumental techniques in ego structuring, rather than the cause of some process which disrupts the integrative capacity of the brain.

Spiegel. Spiegel[560, 561] has paid much attention to the social roles within families, imposed by the culture. A further contribution by him is found in Chapter XV. The acculturation process may lead to strain in the family role systems. Role conflict calls forth re-equilibrating processes, either role modification or role distortion. Role distortion is associated with the appearance of symptoms of psychopathology in family members, including psychosis. In an adult, if the role distortion ceases to operate the symptoms may disappear. However, if in a child the role distortion operates over a long period of time, the deformation of the underlying personality may be permanent.

Ackerman. Ackerman[562] considers the whole spectrum of abnormal mental functioning, including schizophrenia. This latter he links with role playing. Rapid shifts of role, influenced by group stimuli, are often seen. At one pole there is an identification of the self image with the deep bodily surging, unintegrated with the influence of social contacts. And in contrasting group situations there is an identification of the self image with the presumed constraining and hostile, menacing aspects of the surrounding environment, activating the urge to deny the body altogether. The schizophrenic, Ackerman believes, is characteristically apprehensive of loss or destruction of self. If he identifies himself with his bodily drives, he tends to renounce social participation for fear of his own destructive powers, or for fear of being injured through the exposure of his body to retaliatory attack. This renunciation is one kind of destruction of self. On the other hand, if the schizophrenic denies his body and identifies himself with the hostile elements of his environment, he again renounces social participation because of his intense hostile feeling towards other persons, whom he blames for the required sacrifices of the vital pleasures of his body. This is again a kind of destruction of self. The schizophrenic's preoccupation with the threat of destruction evoked by closeness to other persons induces withdrawal and resistance to social participation.

Ackerman illustrates this by referring to schizophrenics who automatically assume the mannerisms of the persons by whom they are surrounded—a phase of their uncontrolled obedience to social pressure. Or they may show a bizarre pattern of opposition to these same influences. In any case, in some schizophrenic individuals one does see remarkable shifts in adaptive behaviour, with lightning transitions in role stimulated by the patient's awareness of the hostile or sympathetic climate of the personal environment. Ackerman believes that adolescence is important as the phase in which schizophrenia can be precipitated. The fragility of the personality, the weakness of the repression, the inefficiency of defences, the closeness to basic drives tend strongly to push into an overt state any latent schizophrenic trends that exist.

Palo Alto Group. In 1952 a group of workers commenced a research project at Palo Alto which terminated ten years later, in 1962. The original formulation is reproduced in Chapter XL. From this work, one element, the 'double bind' hypothesis, has received a great deal of attention. But the workers themselves, however, regard it as part of a general communicational approach to a wide range of human behaviour including schizophrenia.[563-632] They are particularly concerned with the incongruity in communication. In addition, work led to formulations on family organisation and dynamics, therapy, hypnosis and communication, and other matters.

In the original formulation, reproduced in Chapter XL, there were four elements. Haley held that symptoms of schizophrenia were suggestive of an inability to discriminate the Logical Types—a part of communication theory. Bateson added the notion of the 'double bind' hypothesis. Jackson contributed his ideas on 'family homeostasis'—a constancy of the internal environment maintained by an interplay of dynamic forces. Analogies between hypnosis and schizophrenia were added by Weakland and Haley.

It may be useful to repeat here the definition of a 'double bind' from the original paper:

The necessary ingredients for a double bind situation, as we see it, are:

1. *Two or more persons.* Of these, we designate one, for purposes of our definition, as the 'victim'. We do not assume that the double bind is inflicted by the mother alone, but that it may be done either by mother alone or by some combination of mother, father and/or siblings.

2. *Repeated experience.* We assume that the double bind is a recurrent theme in the experience of the victim. Our hypothesis does not invoke a single traumatic experience, but such repeated experience that the double bind structure comes to be an habitual expectation.

3. *A primary negative injunction.* This may have either of two forms: (a) 'Do not do so and so, or I will punish you', (b) 'If you do not do so and so, I will punish you'. Here we select a context of learning based on avoidance of punishment rather than a context of reward seeking. There is perhaps no formal reason for this selection. We assume that the punishment may be either the withdrawal of love or the experience of hate or anger or—most devastating—the kind of abandonment that results from the parent's expression of extreme helplessness. (Our concept of punishment is being refined at present. It appears to us to involve perceptual experience in a way that cannot be encompassed by the notion of 'trauma'.)

4. *A secondary injunction conflicting with the first at a more abstract level, and like the first enforced by punishments or signals which threaten survival.* This secondary injunction is more difficult to describe than the primary for two reasons. First, the secondary injunction is commonly communicated to the child by nonverbal means. Posture, gesture, tone of voice, meaningful action, and the implications

concealed in verbal comment may all be used to convey this more abstract message. Second, the secondary injunction may impinge upon any element of the primary prohibition. Verbalisation of the secondary injunction may, therefore, include a wide variety of forms; for example, 'Do not see this as punishment'; 'Do not see me as the punishing agent'; 'Do not submit to my prohibitions'; 'Do not think of what you must not do'; 'Do not question my love, of which the primary prohibition is (or is not) an example'; and so on. Other examples become possible when the double bind is inflicted not by one individual but by two. For example, one parent may negate at a more abstract level the injunctions of the other.

5. *A tertiary negative injunction prohibiting the victim from escaping from the field.* In a formal sense, it is perhaps unnecessary to list this injunction as a separate item since the reinforcement at the other two levels involves a threat to survival, and if the double binds are imposed during infancy, escape is naturally impossible. However, it seems that in some cases the escape from the field is made impossible by certain devices which are not purely negative, e.g. capricious promises of love, and the like.

6. Finally, the complete set of ingredients is no longer necessary when the victim has learned to perceive his universe in double bind patterns. Almost any part of a double bind sequence may then be sufficient to precipitate panic or rage. The pattern of conflicting injunctions may even be taken over by hallucinatory voices.

The workers conceive the family situation of the schizophrenic as follows:

1. A child whose mother becomes anxious and withdraws if the child responds to her as a loving mother. That is, the child's very existence has a special meaning to the mother which arouses her anxiety and hostility when she is in danger of intimate contact with the child.

2. A mother to whom feelings of anxiety and hostility towards the child are not acceptable, and whose ways of denying them is to express overt loving behaviour to persuade the child to respond to her as a loving mother and to withdraw from him if he does not. 'Loving behaviour' does not necessarily imply 'affection'; it can, for example, be set in a framework of doing the proper thing, instilling 'goodness', and the like.

3. The absence of anyone in the family, such as the strong and insightful father, who can intervene in the relationship between the mother and child and support the child in the face of the contradictions involved.

In this situation, the mother of a schizophrenic will be simultaneously expressing two orders of message. To put it in another way, if the mother begins to feel affectionate and close to her child, she begins to feel endangered and must withdraw from him; but she cannot accept this hostile act, and to deny it must simulate affection and closeness with the child. The child must not discriminate accurately between orders of message, in this case the difference between the expression of simulated feelings (one Logical Type) and real feelings (another Logical Type). As a result, the child must systematically distort his percept of metacommunicative signals. It is essential to appreciate that the double bind situation is responsible for the inner conflicts of Logical Typing.

The workers give an example. The mother might say, 'Go to bed, you're very tired. I want you to get your sleep.' This overtly loving statement is intended to deny a feeling which could be verbalised as, 'Get out of my sight because I'm sick of you.' This means that the child must deceive himself about his own internal state in order to support mother in her deception. To survive with her, he must falsely discriminate his own internal messages, thus upsetting the Logical Typing, as well as falsely discriminate the messages of others. The child is punished for discriminating accurately what the mother is expressing, and he is punished for discriminating inaccurately—he is caught in a double bind. It is hypothesised that a child continually subjected to this situation develops a psychosis. A psychosis seems a way of dealing with double bind situations to overcome their inhibiting and controlling effect.

At first the double bind was studied in relation to a two-party situation, but was later extended to involve a three-party case, mother, father and child. The parents of a schizophrenic child formed a special triadic system in the larger family unit. Psychotic behaviour is seen as an attempt to adapt to double bind situations. Psychotic behaviour was seen as a sequence of messages which infringed a set of prohibitions which were qualified as not infringing them. The only way an individual could achieve this was by qualifying incongruently all levels of his communication. At a later stage interest of the workers focused on the many manifestations of incongruent communication in the family.

At the end of ten years of research the group agreed on a statement about the double bind.[584]

1. The double bind is a class of sequences which appear when phenomena are examined with a concept of levels of communication.

2. In schizophrenia the double bind is a necessary but not sufficient condition in explaining aetiology and, conversely, is an inevitable by-product of schizophrenic communication.

3. Empirical study and theoretical description of individuals and families should, for this type of analysis, emphasise observable communication, behaviour, and relationship contexts rather than focusing upon the perception or affective states of individuals.

4. The most useful way to phrase double bind description is not in terms of a binder and a victim, but in terms of people caught up in an ongoing system which produces conflicting definitions of the relationship and consequent subjective distress. In its attempts to deal with the complexities of multi-level patterns in human communications systems, the research group prefers an emphasis upon circular systems of interpersonal relations to a more conventional emphasis upon the behaviour of individuals alone or single sequences in the interaction.

In Chapter XLI is found a review and reassessment of the double bind hypothesis by a recent collaborator of the Palo Alto workers.

Further views. Some of the more recent, but no less important, views on the family process in relation to schizophrenia will be more briefly reviewed.

Alanen[633] links pseudomutuality, in the sense of Wynne, with the double bind hypothesis.

Boszormenyi-Nagy[634] considers the problems and mechanisms of close family relationships, the total interactional field of the family, with special emphasis on the determining influence exerted on a schizophrenic patient by the unconscious motivations of other family members. He examines the hypothesis that schizophrenic personality development may in part be perpetuated by reciprocal need complementarities between parents and offspring. His observations are based on the study and intensive psycho-therapy of young schizophrenic females, with family therapy in ten cases. In these ten cases, it seemed that the patient was considered sick either because she conformed blindly to her parents' deepest expectations of her, or because she rebelled against them.

Boszormenyi-Nagy believes that it is usually possible to deduce from the parents' reactions to a schizophrenic patient's attempts at separation from them, that they have a great destructive possessiveness and need for symbiotic relatedness to the patient. The parents often seem to be avoid-ing repetition of the pain of an early loss. Unsatisfied with each other, they bind the child to them, and even parentify him. The willingness of the child to surrender his own autonomous life goals can be accounted for by dynamic forces originating in a specifically thwarted super-ego struc-ture. The parent unconsciously shapes the child's early internalised value orientation according to his own symbiotic needs. He directs his most important moral injunctions not primarily towards destructive or sexual impulses, but towards any attempt at increased autonomy. He does not condemn sexual impulses *per se*, but, rather, erotic relationships outside the family. Once the pre-schizophrenic child has developed the counter-autonomous super-ego structure, he reacts at the most simple trigger signal with painful and perplexing feelings of guilt over any semblance of emancipation. In establishing this pathological split between aspirations toward autonomy and symbiosis, the parent must first have used a 'double bind' type of communication. Later, when the patient's own motivational forces lead to resistance against autonomy, the parent's communication may represent only a comment on the patient's impotent internal situation. According to the author, this hypothesis of intrafamilial need comple-mentarity as a psychogenic factor in maintaining schizophrenia is not meant to supersede or exclude other known explanations. However, he feels that more attention should be paid to the needs of patients' parents as influences in super-ego formation.

Scott and Ashworth[635] conceive a 'shadow of insanity' which goes to form the attitude by which one member of the family sees and treats another as mad. The behaviour of the person seen as mad is one deter-minant of the attitude. But the shadow is also fed by potent sources beyond the parents' immediate perception of the patient: sources from the past and from the current social field. In so far as those sources, other than immediate perception, determine the shadow attitude, we may say that one person confers a mad identity on another.

Russell Davis[636, 637] carefully reviews the conflicts of the Oedipus complex which might contribute to the aetiology of schizophrenia. He finds that significant elements are a poor relationship between mother and father, or failure of identification with the father, and an abnormal relationship between mother and son. He gives significance to the period when the child is between 10 and 16 years old.

Laing,[638-645] in his work on the families of schizophrenics, amalgamates the influence of existentialism with psychoanalysis and psychiatry. He regards schizophrenia as a social creation and the outcome of what goes on in the family. The symptoms are 'a strategy invented by the person in order to live in what to him has come to be an unlivable situation.' In these family systems liable to produce schizophrenics, 'mystification' is to be found. 'By mystification is meant the *act* of mystifying and the *state* of being mystified.' The *act* of mystifying is to befuddle, cloud and obscure whatever is going on. The *state* of mystification is a feeling of being muddled or confused. The prime function of mystification is to maintain the *status quo*. Laing sees some affinity between his views and those of Lidz, Wynne, and Jackson and Bateson. With collaborators, he is developing an Interpersonal Perception Method for studying dyadic relationships. His concepts have been employed in therapy and good results claimed. Carstairs,[646] however, claims similar results, and maintains that the work of Laing and his own indicate the non-specific response on the part of schizophrenics to an increased amount of personal attention.

Beckett *et al.*[647, 648] studied exogenous trauma in the genesis of schizophrenia. They uncovered a severe untrafamilial pathology with the use of denial and defence mechanisms which led to the obstruction of ego differentiation.

Like the above workers, Delay *et al.*[649] consider the family as a whole in relation to schizophrenia. Ferreira[650] has reviewed the aetiology of schizophrenia.

A number of contributors have paid attention to special aspects of the family process in relation to schizophrenia—Kim[651] (speech intrusion), Rosenbaum[652] (counterpart of schizophrenic in his family), Speck,[653] (transfer phenomena), Yi-Chuang Lu[654, 655] (comparisons of schizophrenics and non-schizophrenic siblings) and Ferreira[656] (language). Two studies have compared the families of schizophrenics with the families of other clinical groups—Sharp,[657] Stabenau *et al.*[658]

All the work discussed above has been concerned with family process as it relates to schizophrenia. The purist regards any other approach as outmoded. However, we cannot overlook a number of studies concerned with relationships within the family—parent-schizophrenic, mother-schizophrenic and father-schizophrenic.

Parent-schizophrenic. Conclusions drawn from parent-schizophrenic studies are contradictory, as is illustrated by consideration of some of the studies. Ellison and Hamilton[659] found the mothers over-protective and the fathers over-aggressive. Johnson et al.[648] found physical assault of children by the parents. Wahl found[660, 661] the loss of a parent in childhood or adolescence. Reichard and Tillman[662] described overtly or covertly rejecting mothers and domineering fathers. The work of Tietze,[663] Gerard and Siegel,[664] and Kasanin et al.[665] supported the notion of dominant mothers and passive fathers. Caputo[666] investigated this last possibility and found that it required qualification; he found a hostile atmosphere in the homes of schizophrenics and that both parents contributed to it. Prout and White[667] compared the parents of schizophrenics and those of normal males, and found no significant difference between them. Rogler and Hollingshead[668] found that experiences in the childhood and adolescence of schizophrenic persons do not differ noticeably from those of people who are not afflicted by the illness.

Mother-schizophrenic. Studies of the mother-patient interaction have not brought universal agreement as to its characteristics. Fromm-Reichmann[669] refers to the coldness and rejection of the 'schizophrenogenic mother'. Cheek's recent study[670] tended to support this. Alanen[671] noted that the mother tends to be closer to the schizophrenic son than to her other children, and 'possessively protects' him; with their schizophrenic daughters the mothers tended to be aloof. Hill[672] conceived of a mother-child symbiosis which developed into a pathological interdependence that did not allow growth. Limentani[673] and Lyketsos[674] have considered the symbiotic relationship pattern. Searles[675, 676] refers to the pathological symbiotic tic of mother and child. Beavers et al.[677] report a difference between the mothers of schizophrenics and non-schizophrenics on three elements in an interview. Zuckerman et al.[678] compared the mothers of schizophrenics and normals, and in only one out of 23 comparisons was there a significant difference—and this they put down to chance. It might have been expected that psychotic mothers would affect the adjustment of their children. Gardner's[679] and Preston's[680] findings are contrary to this expectation.

Father-schizophrenic. The father-schizophrenic relationship has received less attention in the literature. The small amount of literature produced on this relationship is contradictory—some describe it as passive and ineffectual, others as harsh and dominating—this observed in a recent review by Cheek.[681]

Age group. Some work has concentrated on the age group at which pathological processes are likely to lead to schizophrenia. Foudraine, in an able review,[682] considers the material relevant to schizophrenia in childhood in the literature produced up to 1960. Since then there have been contributions by Waring,[683] McCord et al.,[684] Becker,[685] and a series of interesting papers on childhood loss by Hilgard et al.[686–690] Early adolescence has been given significance by Russel Davis.[636, 637]

Child Psychosis

All the above work refers to adult schizophrenia. Naturally much attention has been given to the family background and family relationships of child psychotics. Kanner's views[691] on the parents of the autistic child require no elaboration. Goldfarb's views[692] on parental perplexity are recently linked to his management of schizophrenic children. The subject has been reviewed by O'Gorman[693] and again by Bender.[694]

Community Care

The schizophrenic who is institutionalised comes from, and is returned to, his home. His care and the impact he has on his family has been the subject of a number of studies—Brown et al.,[695-698] Grad,[699] Goldberg,[700] Deyking,[701] Evans et al.[702] and Cheek.[703] Rogler and Hollingshead[668] found that the impact of schizophrenia on the family depends on the sex of the person afflicted. Faris and Dunham[704] and Hare[705] have observed that city areas in which social isolation is most marked are rich sources of schizophrenic patients; it may be that schizophrenic patients drift to such areas.

Appraisal of Schizophrenia in Relation to Family Psychopathology

Schizophrenia is a grave, if uncommon, disease. It is a dramatic disease, presenting the most intriguing complex of signs and symptoms in the whole of Medicine. Family psychopathology in relation to it was one of the unexplored territories. Once this notion was abroad, the quest was on in earnest. Enough effort has not been expended to allow sober reflection, which it is hoped is fair and reasonable.

1. *Family or individual?* This is the essential question. Does the manifest pathology lie in the family or in the individual? The workers previously mentioned see processes at work in the family that distort communication, perception and meaning. An equally large group of workers, e.g. McGhie and Chapman,[706,707,708] see distortions resulting from interference with the intracerebral organic machinery of thought and communication. Such distortions are observed in organic brain lesions, dementia, acute toxic delirious states and the model psychoses. Thinking in metaphor, for example, can be a defence from the intrusions of fellow family members, or result from organic perceptual difficulties. Two other views are possible as explanations of the perceptual anomalies. Firstly, that an underlying constitutional weakness is released by emotional stress emanating from the family. Secondly, that an existing constitutional weakness in a family member provokes a family reaction which may be harmful, but need not necessarily be so; the important and careful study of Pollin et al.[709] on identical twins may support this view.

These possibilities need further exploration. An admirable review of possible aetiologies of schizophrenia is found in Rosenthal.[710]

2. *Is schizophrenia under study?* This is a crucial question. Visitors from Europe and the U.S.A. attending clinics in the other's area must be impressed with the wide differences in establishing criteria for the diagnosis of schizophrenia. To the writer, the careful criteria for the diagnosis of schizophrenia, based on Kraepelin[711] and Bleuler,[712] would be met only by a fraction of the patients seen under treatment as schizophrenics in family orientated centres in the United States; the remainder, though having a severe degree of pathology, appear to be severely emotionally ill, but not schizophrenic. Thus, should this view be held, the findings of studies on these patients would be relevant to emotional illness, but not to schizophrenia. Reference has already been made to the low incidence of schizophrenia found by English studies.[513, 514, 515] Langfeldt[713] has suggested a solution by using the term 'process' psychosis to cover the organic endogenous type, and 'non-process' to cover the remainder. Stephens and Astrup[714, 715] found that the former had a poor prognosis, and that the outcome depended on diagnosis and not therapy. It is essential to have agreement about the criteria for the diagnosis of schizophrenia before findings can be compared and deductions drawn from the studies.

3. *Is the family psychopathology coincidental?* Should the English epidemiological studies be correct, approximately a third of the population are significantly emotionally disturbed. Should schizophrenics come from a representative group of families of the population at large, then, in a third of the families of schizophrenics, family psychopathology will be found by chance alone. Furthermore, disturbed families are less likely to cope with schizophrenic members, and thus schizophrenics will present from such families in greater numbers, i.e. a selection factor may also be operating.

4. *Are the identified family mechanisms widespread?* It may be that the psychopathological mechanisms described in the families of schizophrenics may also be found in non-schizophrenic families. Emotional divorce, over-inadequacy, projection, pseudomutuality, family schisms, family skews, socio-cultural ideation, distortion of meaning, the double bind, incongruent communication, mystification are elements found in non-schizophrenic families. Control studies will say to what extent. Experience with problem families, as described by Howells in Chapter XXI, would suggest that all pathological mechanisms are more manifest in severely disturbed families—but do not necessarily give rise to schizophrenia.

5. *Does the psychopathology cause schizophrenia?* To establish that anomalies of psychopathology exist in the families of schizophrenics is not enough. A direct link must be established between the anomaly and schizophrenia. As has been said in (3), the anomaly may be coincidental.

6. *Result or cause?* Whilst, on one hand, it can be argued that the family psychopathology has causal significance for schizophrenia, it can

also be held that the schizophrenia causes family psychopathology. It would be strange if such a severe and perplexing disorder did not have some effect on the family state; this must be specially true of childhood psychosis, where one sees the sad disappointment and puzzlement of a mother at the lack of response from her child.

7. *Are other problems raised?* A number are: (a) Why does schizophrenia appear in late adolescence, although family trauma has been bearing on a sensitive organism for a number of years? Some answers are offered. Bowen sees it as a clash of strength between child and parent in adolescence. Wynne sees it as a matter of different processes: 'disaffiliation' in childhood psychosis and distortion of meaning in adult schizophrenia. Ackerman enumerates a number of special factors in adolescence. But other possibilities remain, which are not incompatible with an organic aetiology; many physical conditions are tied to an age of onset. (b) If the psychopathological anomalies are not over-simplified, many other possibilities could be entertained. (c) Although there is agreement between some workers, there are also contradictions. (d) The greater number of hypotheses to explain any phenomenon, the greater the probability of them all being incorrect. (e) Are not the views obscure at times and this lack of clarity dictated by confusion? Over-intellectualisation may have the appeal of mysticism, but carries the danger of being dismissed as a defence for ignorance. (f) Why is only one person in the family schizophrenic? It might be reasonable to argue that the dynamics focus adversely on him. However, other possibilities remain. (g) Why does the family member develop schizophrenia rather than another illness? Again it might be reasonable to argue that the family dynamics are so fashioned for him as to cause schizophrenia. But other possibilities remain.

8. *Are the studies wasted?* There is no difficulty in answering with an emphatic negative. Despite their present inconclusive nature, the studies undertaken up to date may be the spring-board for further conclusive research. Should it even be established, according to the views of the writer, that the patients under study are not schizophrenics, a great deal will have been learnt from these painstaking and ingenious studies about the psychopathology of emotionally disturbed individuals and families.

MENTAL RETARDATION

Much less attention has been given to mental retardation than to schizophrenia in relation to the family. Mental retardation is at least as important, as it impinges on the aetiology of mental defect, on the effect of retardation on the family, on institutional care for the retarded, and on management of the retarded.

Mental retardation is not only a matter of genetics, although there is a correlation between the intelligence of parents and that of their offspring.[716] Tizard and Grad[717] have considered the families of the retarded. Social factors in aetiology, including the home, are discussed by Davis,[718] Kirman,[719, 720] Berg,[721] Gibson and Butler.[722] Bourne[723] has shown how adverse home influences lead to pseudo-feeblemindedness, which he terms 'protophrenia'. Lack of stimulation, as the cause of retardation, has been reviewed by Casler,[724] and deprivation by Spitz.[725] Davis[726] has paid particular attention to the matter of the retarded child. Emotional disturbance produced in a child by family psychopathology can have an adverse effect on his intellectual functioning, school performance and success at work. Lack of interest on the part of parents produces a poor school performance. Excessive pressure, on the other hand, due to a number of pathological mechanisms in parents, can also heighten school performance. Stein and Susser have considered cultural factors. In Chapter XLV, they identify dysmorphic families who produce disadvantages for dull children.

A number of elements in the families of the retarded have been the subject of a report by Farber and Jenne[727-732]; they point our how, regardless of birth order, the retarded child assumes the role of the youngest, and they discuss the effects of marital relationship on the couple's retarded child and the effects of institutional care on the family. Sarason[733] gives an excellent account of the psychological aspects of mental defect.

Not only do families contribute to retardation, but they also react to it; this is the subject of comment by some of the above workers.

Furthermore, the state of the family is an important factor in seeking institutional care. The more disturbed the family, the lower its toleration of difficulty, and therefore the more likely its appeal for institutional care. Stein and Susser, in Chapter XLV, show how this operates in dysmorphic families. Thus socialisation of the retarded in institutions should include giving to the child the family and parental care, hitherto absent in his life. Should the child's emotional state, and hence socialisation, improve, care must be taken not to return him to the previously adverse home, unless the dynamics within it have changed in his favour. Thus, substitute home care may be desirable.

Families with retarded members can be helped by counselling—a subject discussed by a symposium,[734] Drewry,[735] Stang[736] and Hesselberg-Meyer.[737] Goldberg[738] pays special attention to the need to counsel the whole family.

5. FAMILY THERAPY

INTRODUCTION

In therapy, as in all other aspects of family psychiatry, the family is the unit. The purpose of treatment is to produce a healthy family unit. This end is achieved by a variety of means deployed to improve the family unit. Treatment may include a number of family members simultaneously, or the family as a whole.

It may be helpful to define some of the terms in common use. *Family therapy* includes all procedures for the treatment of the family, in all its dimensions. It is convenient to consider it under three main categories: (1) family psychotherapy, (2) vector therapy, (3) social psychiatry.

1. *Family psychotherapy* means treatment of the psyche, individual or family; psychoanalysis is a special form of psychotherapy based on principles devised by Freud. Family psychotherapy can be practised with an individual (*individual therapy*), a dyad (*dyadic therapy* or joint therapy), a whole family (*family group therapy* or conjoint family therapy), a number of families treated together (*multiple family therapy*), and a non-family group (*group therapy*). *Multiple impact psychotherapy* describes an intensive approach developed by the Galveston group of workers and discussed in Chapter XLIX.

2. *Vector therapy* is concerned with effecting changes in the pattern of the emotional forces within the life space of the family, within and without the family, to bring improvement to the family. It is considered here, in Chapter XXVI and in Chapter LI.

3. *Social psychiatry* uses community procedures for the adjustment of the individual and the family.

It must be emphasised that family group therapy is but one procedure of family psychotherapy, which in turn is only one part of family therapy. To use family group therapy alone is to seriously limit the treatment of the family.

Psychotherapy, vector therapy and community psychiatry are complementary, and the most effective family therapy employs all these procedures simultaneously. The therapeutic needs at a given moment can be met by a flexible approach ready to utilise whatever is appropriate. Thus individual or group psychotherapeutic procedures may be employed together. Family psychotherapy and vector therapy, or family psychotherapy and community psychiatry, may be applied simultaneously. Whenever possible, the whole family must be involved in the treatment process. This does not mean the employment of family group therapy alone, but applies to all the therapies appropriate to the task at that time. Treatment may have to proceed with an individual, or with only a part of a family; this may be so because of inability to involve the whole family, or because of the dictates of the treatment situation at that moment. But if only a part of a family is under treatment, the rest of the family is not overlooked, and the aim does not change; to adjust the whole family is still the target.

Treatment need not wait until the whole family group presents itself. Some help can be offered to those who are available, and the opportunity to involve the rest of the family may come later.

Family diagnosis should not be confused with family therapy. Nor should family group diagnosis be confused with family group therapy. The former may lead to clarification of family dynamics, but is not necessarily a therapeutic process. Information is valuable, but full use of it will be made only later—in therapy.

In addition to the treatment procedures mentioned above, physical methods of treatment have a place as adjuncts.

Treatment may be based on an out-patient setting, an in-patient unit or the home. Thus, with the in-patient, whether accompanied by his family or not, no evaluation is made or procedure undertaken without relating it to the context of his family. This does not mean that the individual must always remain in contact with his family. His particular need may be to escape from it; this manipulation will be undertaken more effectively if evaluated in terms of the total situation of his family. It leads to a flexible use of in-patient facilities—sometimes for an individual, a dyad, a part or the whole of the family. The admission procedures involve a family evaluation, as do the ward regime and discharge procedures. The out-patient and in-patient management should be a continuous whole. Members of the family are not mere 'visitors'; they are participants in the clinical process.

Few units are so well staffed as to be able to apply family therapy to all their families. Thus selection becomes necessary. In general, units deploy their facilities to give optimum value. So, therefore, the families selected are those with a degree of disturbance likely to respond, in a reasonable period of time, to the treatment offered by the facilities available. Families with young children have young parents; young parents have not been emotionally ill as long as older people, and thus respond more readily to treatment. The younger the children when the family is stabilised, the more they profit. The number of children in the family is a factor in selection; the greater their number, the greater the benefit that will accrue to society by improving their emotional health. In all families, whatever the degree of disturbance, efforts should always be made to bring relief to the children, the coming generation.

A routine follow-up contact with the family can reinforce previous procedures, offer continuing support, and may, with the detachment of time, allow a realisitic appraisal of the extent and technique of clinical effort.

Family therapy is not exclusively a clinic activity. Liaison with a host of family health and welfare agencies can enhance the scope and effectiveness of therapy.

FAMILY PSYCHOTHERAPY

This includes the procedures of individual, dyadic, family group, multiple family group and group therapy.

Psychotherapy usually takes place in an out-patient clinic. Few clinics offer a service in the family's home. It is held by some that therapy in the clinic is a less artificial situation than therapy in the home, where it creates embarrassment to the family by provoking the interest of the neighbours, and where distractions are many. Others claim that the home, as the family's natural setting, is more revealing, that it is easier to collect family members together there, and that it offers less distractions than a clinic. Therapists feel safer in their own clinic setting and claim that it offers a controlled environment, which makes diagnosis easier. Probably the main determining factor in choice of setting is the time factor; it saves therapeutic time to bring the family to the clinic. Speck discusses home treatment in Chapter XLVIII. There are further contributions by Speck,[739] Friedman,[740] Fisch[741] and Nielsen.[742]

Some have experimented with admitting whole families into hospital— examples being the work of Bowen, Wynne and Pollin at the National Institute for Mental Health, U.S.A. Bowen describes his work in Chapter XLVI. In England, Baker et al.[743] and Glasser[744] have admitted mothers and children, as described in Chapter LII by Main; in some hospitals whole families are now admitted. Sometimes the presenting patient alone is admitted, but his family joins him in hospital for day treatment; such experiments are now being widely followed.

Individual therapy, of any type, can be embraced by family psychiatry according to the experience and inclination of the therapist and the requirements of the patient. It can be of any duration, from lengthy psychoanalysis to brief psychotherapy (see Castelnuovo-Tedesco).[745] When only one member of the family has attended, individual therapy has to be employed. However, it may also be the treatment of choice for one or more family members at that time in management. Or it may be supplementary to dyadic or family group therapy. Facilities will be required for all age groups, child, adolescent and adult. Child therapy usually calls for special facilities and for therapists trained for this age group.

Dyadic therapy involves two family members and the therapist or therapists. The commonest dyad is the marital. Marital therapy is now an accepted part of psychiatric practice, and a vast literature is concerned with it. Kohl, in Chapter L, throws light on the "seesaw" movements of the partners in therapy. Starting-off points into the literature are Nash et al.,[746] Brill[747] and Eisenstein.[748] Dicks reports his special experience in Chapter IX. Dyadic therapy can proceed with any couple—two children, mother and child, or father and child. It may be supplementary to other methods of therapy, or it may be the method of choice at that stage of treatment. Any school of thought in therapy can be encompassed within the framework of family psychiatry.

In family group therapy, the family group is treated together. It is a welcome, if unassessed, new procedure in therapy. However, it has sometimes been given disproportionate prominence, leading to other procedures being overlooked. Perforce, due to the large accumulation of literature about it, family group therapy must be given special attention later.

In multiple family therapy one or many (even over 100) families are treated together. Naturally it is less easy to be precise in the manipulation of each family's dynamics among so many. Thus it is best employed in supportive therapy over situations common to many families. Such a large group can employ powerful suggestion. Its employment in a hospital setting is the subject of contributions by Laqueur et al.[749, 750]

Group therapy treats together a number of individuals from different families. Groups may be male, female or mixed. They may be of any age group—children, adolescents and adults. They may meet formally for intensive therapy, or informally in a club setting. One or more therapists may be employed, and the clinical material is interpreted according to the school of thought of the therapists.

Follow-up studies of family psychotherapy are superficial or non-existent. Problems of evaluation which are considerable in individual psychotherapy, are even greater in family psychotherapy. Much of family psycotherapy amounts to the evaluation of family dynamics without any clear benefit to the family. However, careful research could show that family group therapy is not only the most potent form of group therapy, but also one with advantages over individual therapy. The need for research is evident.

Family Group Therapy

This is a procedure for the treatment of a family through a family group experience with one or more therapists. It has elements in common with group therapy and individual therapy, but also differences from both.

The family group has a strong identity which reaches from the Past and extends into the Future. It existed as a group before therapy, and will go on after it. It is a heterogenic group of both sexes and of all age groups. It is subject to strong influences from the extended family group. Its members have learnt rigid patterns of behaviour in relation to one another. Each member of the family has strong meaning for the others. Powerful emotions can be aroused in it, for good or ill. Yet the family group has features in common with any small group, and thus its therapy has some elements in common with group therapy. The relationship between family group therapy and group therapy is the subject of contributions by Handlon and Parloff.[751, 752]

Family group therapy has also features in common with individual therapy—for example, transference, counter-transference, resistance, affective changes and catharsis. But in family group therapy the number of relationships is greater, and the therapist is part of a web of communication. Ackerman[753] considers psychoanalysis in relation to family group therapy.

Family group therapy is the procedure of choice for any emotional disturbance. Its biggest limitation is that not all the family members may be at a stage, in their relationship with the psychiatric service, where they can agree to attend. Problems of transference may militate against a group coming as a whole; an experienced family therapist can, however, over-come most of these problems. The effectiveness of this form of therapy is dependent on a number of factors. The less the degree of family dis-turbance, the more rewarding, naturally, is the therapy; with our present knowledge, even the best therapists may have difficulty in resolving a severe degree of family emotional disorder. Problems of the Present resolve very satisfactorily; problems with deep roots in the Past are re-sistant. A high degree of disturbance in one family member may be an indication for the time-saving procedure of individual therapy; but family therapy would be as effective, as the remaining near-healthy mem-bers can be mobilised as assets in therapy. Family group therapy is a particularly valuable technique in conjunction with vector therapy, even in the most resistant families, insight can develop to the point when the family can accept adjustment which will change the intra- and extra-family dynamics to their favour. Equally good results can be obtained with all other clinical categories, including the psychopath, the alcoholic and those with severe anomalies. In general, the younger the family members, the more effective the therapy. In the writer's experience, family group therapy is not a profitable procedure for 'process' schizophrenia. Wynne[754] has expressed his views on indications for family group therapy.

It is not always clear what constitutes a family group. The family group in therapy should consist of those who are involved together in an emotionally significant way. Thus the functional rather than the physical group is important, e.g. in a particular set of circumstances a lodger may be a more important father figure for the family than a husband; a nanny may be a more important mother figure than the natural mother. Thus, added to the nuclear family, there may be grandparents, siblings, neigh-bours, friends, servants, etc. Always, the approach should be flexible—in the course of therapy the group may need to shrink or to expand.

Another matter of organisation is that concerning the choice of em-ploying one therapist or several. Sometimes economies dictate the choice of one only. At first, therapists new to the field have difficulty in shifting loyalty from one person to a group. Yet, all have had experience of such a loyalty within their own families; such a shift is possible once the group idea is grasped and habit given time to work. The handling of group loyalty is one of the skills necessary to a family therapist. Having a number of therapists carries the danger of each forming an attachment to an individual family member and setting up rivalries. On the other hand, if more therapists are introduced more dilution is obtained of family disturbance. The greatest problem in having multiple therapists is main-taining adequate communication between them; the difficulties are con-siderable. It has been argued that a number of therapists are collectively wiser and more skilled. But an experienced individual therapist should have the skill to manage alone, and is usually of one mind. The therapist is not only convener, chairman and catalyst, but by his presence he also dilutes the family pathology, acts as an expression of healthy outside opinion, uses his skills as a therapist and benefits the group through the use of his relationship. Some matters of technique and organisation are discussed by Bowen in Chapter XLVI, and Bell in Chapter XLVII, and Howells in Chapter XXVI. Further contributions are by Bell,[755] Bowen[756] and Framo.[757] Ackerman and Franklin[758] offer a verbatim transcript of an entire family group session. Watzlawick[759] has produced a two-hour tape-recording with accompanying text.

The literature on family group therapy is considerable. Most of it is devoted to the treatment of schizophrenia by means of family group procedures. The papers about it, together with the papers on family process in relation to schizophrenia, constitute probably two-thirds of the literature on the psychiatry of the family. Many of the papers are concerned with the management of a 'primary' adolescent family member through a family group; to the author, this does not constitute family therapy, as the aim should be to improve not one person only, but the whole family unit. This has come about because family groups with an adolescent member are easier to manage than those with children. Furthermore, schizophrenics emerge in considerable numbers in adolescence.

Books on the subject of family group therapy are by Chance,[760] Satir,[761] MacGregor et al.,[762] Boszormenyi-Nagy and Framo,[763] Abrahams and Varon,[764] Ackerman et al.,[765] Haley,[766] Grotjahn,[767] Midelfort,[768] Zuk,[769] Ehrenwald,[770] Brody and Redlich,[771] and Liebman.[772]

Family group therapy has been reviewed by Fleck,[773] Rubinstein,[774] Ackerman,[775, 780] Haley,[776, 777, 778] Jackson and Satir,[779] and Parloff.[781]

Significant contributions have been made by many authors.[782–944] In the files of the Institute of Family Psychiatry, Ipswich, are records of a number of additional contributions.[945–986]

VECTOR THERAPY

Constant efforts to produce harmony in the intrapsychic life of the individual by re-alignments within it have been made over the last 70 years. The emotional force brought to bear has been that of the therapist. Family psychiatry, selecting the family as a unit, reveals the individual as being in a field of forces within the family, which in turn is in the wider field of forces of society. Within these fields there are potent forces, continually bearing, for good or ill, on individuals and on families. These forces, if positive, can be deployed in therapy, but have to be counterbalanced, or removed should they be negative. The purpose of vector therapy is to readjust the pattern of emotional forces in the life space to bring relief and benefit to individuals and families.

Psychotherapy, individual or group, is a difficult art. Good results are not easy to obtain. Even in situations when psychotherapy is effective, the lack of resources limits its value. Results are difficult to assess;

methodologically satisfactory surveys are seldom encouraging.[987, 988] In the present state of knowledge it is understandable that precision should be lacking. Yet, the prestige of pschotherapy is high. Patients need emotional contact, relish hope, and are even less able than clinical workers to evaluate results. The appeal of psychotherapy to the therapist is high, as it represents direct personal help to the patient. When an investment is large enough, there is an unacknowledged conspiracy of uncritical acceptance. Resources which would be more effective in vector therapy are deployed in the psychotherapeutic quest. Even some social workers desert their field in favour of psychotherapy. Yet, in the social field, by the use of vector therapy, the special skills of the social worker could revitalise the therapy of the emotionally ill. Psychotherapy has its place but not the right to its present manpower.

Exact assessment of family dynamics is now a reality. The social worker, using interview techniques, can aim at targets different from psychotherapy—effecting rapport with the family, developing insight in the family, prompting the family to action causing change in their favour in the field of forces, and deploying those family agencies which can help to produce and sustain the changes. Liaison between a family psychiatry service and community agencies becomes all important.

Definition of Vector Therapy

A vector denotes a quantity which has direction. Force, including emotional force, is a quantity with direction and therefore can be represented by a vector. Furthermore, as direction is a property of a vector and direction implies movement, it results in a dynamic situation. *Vector therapy effects a change of the emotional forces within the life space to bring improvement to the individual or family within the life space.*

The forces in the life space can be thought of in terms of fields of force. These fields of force are (a) within the individual, (b) outside the individual and within the family, (c) outside the individual and the family and within the community, (d) outside the individual, family and community and within the culture.

Vector therapy can involve:

1. A change in the magnitude of the emotional force, e.g. father's aggression may be diminished.

2. A change in the direction of the emotional force with no change in its magnitude, e.g. father abuses mother instead of child.

3. A change in the length of time during which the emotional force operates, e.g. father works away from home, spends less time at home and his aggression has less duration.

4. A change in the quality of the emotional force when one force replaces another, e.g. father treats his son with kindness instead of with aggression.

To effect these changes, the sources of the emotional forces may have to be moved, e.g. by father going out to work; or the object of the forces may have to move, e.g. the child goes to a boarding school to avoid father's aggression.

Vector therapy not only nullifies the effect of *past* traumata, but also, by producing optimum conditions for emotional growth now, it prevents traumata in the *present*.

Terms borrowed from physics, however, are bound to have some limitation when applied in the field of psychology, where more intangible elements are at work. For example, in physics qualities are not mixed. But we must take account of mixed qualities in psychology. If, with equal force, the father shouts at a child and mother soothes the child, the child does not remain neutral—he avoids his father and clings to his mother, i.e. he does not behave along the resultant of these forces, since the two qualities cannot be compounded.

Comparison with Psychotherapy

An individual moving in time through his life space encounters emotional influences that help to make him an integrated healthy person, but in varying degrees he may meet adverse emotional influences that make for disintegration and ill-health. In either event, account has to be taken of the quality of the influence, its force, its direction and the time during which it operates.

Faced with a disintegrated individual, reintegration is possible by mobilising a set of influences in the present that may still nullify the effects of the previous adverse influences. This can be done (a) by the mobilisation of intense, precise, beneficial emotional influences from a therapist acting over a short period of time in the interview situation, i.e. by psychotherapy; or (b) by mobilising less intense emotional influences of a general nature known to be beneficial over a long period of time outside the interview, i.e. by vector therapy. Thus, for example, a child disintegrated by being deprived of the right kind of care, instead of being subjected to psychotherapy, is placed in a foster home selected for its ability to provide the right care. In the latter case, benefit comes from a new set of beneficial vectors able to act over a long period of time.

Comparisons between psychotherapy and vector therapy are shown below.

Features	Psychotherapy	Vector Therapy
Direction	Precise	General
Strength	Intense	Less intense
Duration	Short period	Long period
Place	Interview	Extra-interview
Field of forces	Largely within individual	Largely without individual

In a given instance, intra- and extra-interview procedures can be employed together, i.e. psychotherapy and vector therapy are complementary. As an example at a simple level, consider the young infant of a highly anxious, ill-adjusted mother, put to the breast and, because of the disharmonious influence from mother, being unable to feed. Direct psychotherapy might effect a change in the mother's personality, so that in time she may be able to mother her infant adequately. The situation can also be broken into by a simple rearrangement of the people who provide the emotional influences playing on the child in the feeding situation. The stable young father who stands by little imagines that he has a part to play in the feeding situation; but by placing the infant on the bottle, and allowing the well-adjusted father to feed him, the infant can have a happy and satisfying feeding experience. By the use of vector therapy a change of forces has been effected and a disharmonious situation has become harmonious. Psychotherapy is worth while for the mother as a long-term project. The infant is best served by the immediate satisfying relationship in the arms of his father. Thus both psychotherapy and vector therapy have a part to play; they are complementary.

The Sources of Emotional Influences

Vector therapy is concerned with emotional forces which must spring from a personal source and which are directed at a personal object. It may be useful to list the personal sources of emotional influences which play upon an individual family member.

1. Influences from within the individual.
2. Influences springing from outside the individual and within the family, as follows: (a) from one individual; (b) from family members who may form a coalition with common features, such as the female members of the family together, or the parents together, or the paternal or maternal relatives together, or the children; (c) from the family group as a whole.
3. Influences outside the individual and family and within the community, as follows: (a) individuals in the community (these may be enumerated as—relatives, friends, neighbours, schoolmates and teachers, workmates, and casual acquaintances); (b) collective community influences.
4. Influences from outside the individual, family and community and within the culture. Cultural pressure exerts powerful control over the major values. Communication media like newspapers, radio, television and national organisations convey these values to people at large.

The Application of Vector Therapy

To be effective, a number of general considerations have to be borne in mind when practising vector therapy.

There must be a reliable *appraisal* of what is going on within the family. By using family group diagnosis, supplemented by individual methods of investigation, it should be possible to achieve an accurate picture of the family situation in its five dimensions. Unless this picture is accurate, the forces will be incorrectly adjusted and a poor therapeutic result obtained.

An individual and his family must *co-operate* with insight. Insight springs from understanding. This may be induced by individual, dyadic or family group sessions.

Again, the manipulation of forces is concerned with changing the emotional rather than the material events within the family. *Emotional prescriptions* are required for emotional ills.

Also, just as damage to the personality is produced by negative influences working over a period of time, so it becomes necessary for reparative work to allow *time* for the positive influences to bring results.

Furthermore, therapy should not concentrate on any one member of the family, but should aim at helping the *whole family*. The maximum benefit comes from the utilisation of services for all family members at the same time—a total front programme.

But, as *childhood* is the period of maximum personality development, it is obvious that special attention, if not priority, will be given in vector therapy to the early age groups.

Forces bearing on family members may sometimes be changed within the family without separating the individual member from the family. At other times, partial *separation* may be required, e.g. day foster care, day hospital care. Sometimes semi-permanent or permanent separation may be essential, e.g. foster care, adoption, or boarding school care. The most skilful use of vector therapy may occasionally allow a family to fragment and, subsequently, result in new and better families being formed from the fragments. This matter is illustrated in Chapter L.

To effect vector therapy calls for organised *facilities*, i.e. a service to supply its requirements. For example, to advise nursery or day foster care for an infant is of no avail unless these facilities exist. This matter now calls for further comment.

Organised Facilities to Support Vector Therapy

It will be clear that many of the facilities required for undertaking this work with families are at present not available in the community, and new services will have to be planned. Community health services are, by and large, designed to help the physically ill, the psychotic, the retarded, but not the emotionally ill.

In the past, too, social services have tended to be ineffective for a number of reasons. It was insufficiently realised that a 'social problem' was invariably a personal problem that would respond only to emotional and not material help. Furthermore, measures for the analysis of family dynamics were crude; thus help was applied in the dark. To add to the difficulties, facilities were inadequate. The social worker, through vector therapy, is the main agent of change and now has a promising approach for exploitation.

Facilities must supply treatment in emotional terms to satisfy an emotional need. It is fundamental to vector therapy that facilities compensate for, or improve, bad personal relationships. The most important therapeutic agent available in the community is a relationship between a well-adjusted individual and another. Thus it is necessary to mobilise those who are emotionally healthy at the points where they can be of maximum assistance to the unhealthy. The strong must help the weak. At some of these vantage points are found such people as nannies, home help workers, day foster mothers, staffs of day nurseries, staffs of residential nurseries, house parents in children's homes, staffs of special institutions for the deprived and maladjusted, workers for the handicapped, teachers, welfare workers, doctors, nurses, executives in all walks of life. To bring the right people to the right place may necessitate a re-allocation of rewards and prestige.

Much advantage comes from one all-purpose worker being responsible for the day-to-day continuous support of families. But such a diversity of special facilities can be used to the best advantage only if the specialist workers are available to support the all-purpose worker. The all-purpose worker must have experience of physical and emotional ill-health, as these conditions are indivisible. Specialist personnel will include health and social workers.

Facilities must exist for children, adolescents, adults and the aged, for all social groups, for all religious denominations, and for the single and the married. Facilities must give seven-days-a-week cover.

To effect a change of emotional forces, a large number of facilities are called upon, even in just one family. For example, in one family the following facilities were employed:

1. Duration of contact between a violent father and his son was reduced by father becoming a night worker.

2. More beneficial male influence came from encouraging the boy to spend time with his uncle, the pleasant mother's well-adjusted brother.

3. The family moved nearer the well-adjusted maternal grandparents and away from the interfering, dominating paternal grandparents, bringing much relief and support to the mother and allowing the boy to spend time with the grandparents—again to his advantage.

4. The boy reacted badly to a strict school teacher, thus a change of school, bringing a more benevolent teacher, was effected.

5. Father mismanaged his men at work, and they retaliated. He was given a job of equal status but not involving man management—with benefit to himself, the factory and his family. At the same time, father

received individual psychotherapy at a late afternoon appointment.

But very violent middle-aged men do not change quickly, if ever. While they change, families require help in the interim.

The use of vector therapy calls for skill and experience. A correct appraisal is paramount. Patiently, by individual and family group procedures, insight must be imparted and co-operation won. Targets are set. Facilities may have to be manufactured or the nearest substitute employed. Given facilities, insight in its organisers may be hard, or never, won. Often the workers are driven to playing a waiting game for weeks, or months—the facilities are there, but the family has yet to see the benefit that would come from using them until an incident exposes their value. The complete fulfilment of aims is never achieved in any field. In this field the results are encouraging and sometimes spectacular. Benefit will accrue with each succeeding generation. Vector therapy can be employed with psychotherapy, and at times when psychotherapy is unavailing or unavailable.

Dozens of facilities are utilised to effect changes in emotional influences bearing on individuals and families. Some random examples are: work placements, therapeutic clubs, special day schools, day hospital care, family planning, home help service, the 'good neighbour' policy, work for mothers, convalescence, sheltered employment, night hospitals, social centres, flats for the aged, foster home placement, day foster care, special residential facilities for the deprived and delinquent, etc.

SOCIAL PSYCHIATRY

The family is a sub-system of the community, of the culture and of society. In recent years increasing attention is being paid to the way the community, culture and society impinge on psychiatry. Social psychiatry is concerned with society as a whole, cultural psychiatry with a part of society—a culture—and community psychiatry with a smaller group, e.g. neighbourhood or institutional group.

Bell and Spiegel[989] trace the history of the term *social psychiatry* from its original usage by Southard.[990] They favour the definition given by Rennie[991]:

Social psychiatry is concerned not only with facts of prevalence and incidence, it searches more deeply into the possible significance of social and cultural factors in the aetiology and dynamics of mental disorder. . . . Social psychiatry, by our definition, seeks to determine the significant facts in family and society which affect adaption (or which can be clearly defined as of aetiological importance) as revealed through the studies of individuals or groups functioning in their natural setting. It concerns itself not only with the mentally ill, but with the problems of adjustment of all persons in society toward a better understanding of how people adapt and what forces tend to damage or enhance their adaptive capacities. . . . Social psychiatry is aetiological in its aim, but its point of attack is the whole framework of contemporary living.

This definition contains the four elements quoted as significant by Ruesch,[992] the study of social functions, relating social condition to disorders of behaviour, the therapy of patients through social management and the prevention of mental ill-health.

Wittkower and Rin[993, 994] state that *cultural psychiatry* is concerned with the cultural aspects of aetiology, frequency and nature of mental illness, and the care and after-care of the mentally ill within the confines of a given cultural unit. *Transcultural psychiatry*, they say, is an extension of cultural psychiatry, the term denoting that the vista of the scientific observer extends beyond the scope of one cultural unit only, whereas the term *cross-cultural* is applied to comparative and contrasting aspects of psychiatry in given areas. The influence of culture on mental illness is the subject of contributions by Linton,[995] Montagu,[996] Agnew,[997] and Leighton and Hughes.[998]

Ruesch[992] has defined *community psychiatry* as a complicated set of operations which are aimed at changing the attitudes and tolerance limits of a given group to insure the best treatment of their sick members.

Illustrations will be given of the application of the four elements in the definitions of social psychiatry by Rennie and Ruesch above.

1. *The study* of social functions is illustrated by the work of Hollingshead and Redlich[999]; in their findings, the incidence of mental disorder appears to vary inversely with the social status of the individual, and whether or not a patient receives psychiatric treatment depends on his place in the class structure.

2. *The relation of social conditions* to illness is illustrated by the work of Myers and Roberts[1000] on some of the material of Hollingshead and Redlich, the study showing that socio-economic stress tends not only to cause psychological disorder, but also to affect its symptomatology. Susser and Watson[1001] discuss society as it affects medicine.

3. *The therapy of patients* through social managment calls for lengthier treatment, as it is the aspect of social psychiatry which receives most enthusiastic support from psychiatrists.

Much attention has been paid to the 'therapeutic community',[1002, 1003,] [1004] 'milieu therapy', 'administrative psychiatry',[1005, 1006] all terms referring to the management of patients in mental institutions. These developments are a welcome modern echo of the work of Pinel in the last century in France, and Tuke in the United Kingdom, and of many other humane administrators in the intervening years. Yet, curiously, in many hospitals an 'intellectualisation' of everyday management of good relationships had to take place before patients could be elevated to the same plane of human dignity as their custodians. The psychology of man management had an accepted place in industry, for instance, long before it found its way into mental institutions. It seemed that the experts on human relations had dragged their feet in the application of their own doctrines. But, in many institutions psychiatrists were alienists, concerned with the medical care of the mentally ill, and not experts in human relations. Psychodynamic principles were foreign to them. Thus old truths on the management of people had to be modernised and intellectualised before they could become acceptable.

Some interpreted social psychiatry to be the after-care of patients in the community following discharge from institutional care. Help was offered to families to maintain their sick members. Linked with this were efforts to prevent the institutionalisation of the sick. Thus day care facilities were set up—day hospitals, training institutions for the retarded, rehabilitation centres, sheltered workshops and night hospitals. Out-patient clinics were established outside mental institutions in the community, e.g. the Worthing experiment,[1007] and at general hospitals, e.g. the Oldham experiment.[1008] Hospitals and local authorities joined together in a common scheme, e.g. in the Nottingham experiment.[1009] A thoughtfully planned after-care programme is that by Cumming and Cumming.[1010] They do not regard the family as a necessarily sound therapeutic instrument. They point to the work of Brown,[1011] in collaboration with Carstairs, which showed that chronic schizophrenics did better in the lodging houses and the homes of siblings than in their own homes, and also did better if their mothers worked. Freeman and Simmons[1012] made similar findings. The Cummings plan their after-care programme bearing the above in mind.

For the emotionally ill, rather than for the psychotics, the principles of vector therapy apply; a host of community agencies can change the adverse vectors to bring relief and improvement in emotionally ill individuals and families.

4. Over *the prevention of mental disorder* there is less clarity. Many of the schemes for the prevention of illness, on closer examination, prove to be measures for treating patients in the community. A preventive programme should concern itself with the healthy and not with the sick.

Most countries devise schemes for teaching mental hygiene. Unfortunately, the knowledge on which good teaching should be based is often absent. The foundation of good health is laid down for the individual during his early years, which are usually spent within his family. Only recently is research moving into the right area. In the early stages, as could be expected, extraordinary mistakes of emphasis were made: e.g. preoccupation with the breast-feeding experience instead of the infant's whole waking experience; an almost total absence of interest in fathering; unchecked hypotheses about the child's sexual life; separation regarded as synonymous with deprivation, and the 'natural home better than any other home' philosophy. False propaganda does harm. Much of the propaganda handed out during 'mental health days and weeks' is ill conceived. Little attention is paid to the meanings conveyed to the public, e.g. the impression is often given that the mentally sick are highly peculiar and extraordinary. While this may attract some monetary help for these unfortunates, it also perpetuates the fear of mental illness. The terms 'insanity' and 'emotional disorder' are not clearly differentiated or understood by the public. Furthermore, it causes the emotionally ill to be reluctant to seek help, lest they be classed with such peculiar and extraordinary patients. Sometimes the emotional needs of the propagandists militate against a healthy approach.

Sometimes health promotion makes a more positive appeal than the prevention of ill-health. The concept of the salutiferous (health promoting) community[1013] is based on the idea that the whole emotional stratum of society should promote healthy emotional living. It is an aspect of vector psychiatry. The family should lie in a field of forces conducive to its well-being. Thus, following an examination of the field of forces, a re-patterning of the forces takes place, which will encourage optimum conditions for emotional health. The programme calls for an examination of every aspect of social functioning, its standards, roles, institutions, organisation and aims. Every one of its multitudinous facets should be examined to assess its value in promoting emotional health. Those which are conducive to health should be retained; those which are antagonistic to health should be changed. The concentration is not on a sick person, the patient, but on the emotional self-improvement of the whole society.

6. THE FUTURE

The development of family psychiatry, this new clinical approach based on the family, will demand further research effort and training programmes planned to bring without delay the new findings to the attention of the appropriate professional workers.

RESEARCH

Research in family psychiatry has its own particular problems, in addition to the obstructions usually met by research in the general field. Nevertheless, worthwhile achievements are possible.

Obstructions to Effective Research in Psychiatry

The field of psychopathology has its own special difficulties for the research worker. Entities are subtle and intangible. There is no definite basic knowledge of what is 'normal' to act as a comparison for the 'abnormal', in the way that there is physiology on which to base pathology in the field of physical medicine.

The *thought processes* of the researcher himself can distort accurate observation, and prejudice the interpretation of facts. An orphan who later becomes a researcher may decry family rearing, or, conversely, give it excessive importance. Again, mother-rejected adults find it difficult to accept any minimising of the uniqueness of the mother; the rejected are dependent on an illusionary rather than a real mother experience. Such biases must be borne in mind in the selection of research workers and the assessments of their findings.

There must be carefully defined *criteria* for the diagnosis of clinical conditions, for judging mental changes and for assessing an improvement, a cure, or a satisfactory outcome. In practice, these requirements are difficult to satisfy. The subject of criteria was thoroughly reviewed by Pert and Simon.[1014] As has already been mentioned in an earlier section, a failure to define neurosis and 'process' psychosis, for example, invalidates many investigations. Confusion is partly due to the fact that symptoms may be common to both conditions. However, in any field of medicine, diagnosis based on symptomatology may show superficial resemblance between disease entities, but this is an insufficient reason for not distinguishing between them. Even in the absence of final knowledge, there are more good reasons for regarding emotional disorder and 'process' psychosis as different disease entities than for regarding them as similar disease entities. Support for this point of view comes from studies such as those by Trouton and Maxwell,[1015] and again by Eysenck.[1016] It is fair to say that in some situations more is lost than gained by defining concepts too closely. We may confine rather than define. For example, elements may be taken out of the concept 'love' and regarded as representing the whole of it, thus severely limiting its meaning.

In the absence of knowledge, *jargon* flourishes. This often becomes meaningless, and makes communication difficult. Richard Asher,[1017] in his Lettsomian lectures of 1959, recalls that Professor Penton advised him that, if he wanted to get something really clear in his mind, he should go home and try to explain it to his landlady's daughter. His point was that, when perfect understanding has been achieved, it can always be expressed in very simple terms, and that the process of so reducing it is helpful. When an idea is expressed in 'landlady's daughter' terms, its wisdom or its folly become obvious. Allied to jargon is intellectualisation, which, in the guise of knowledge, obscures truth and allows ignorance to go undetected. Hazlitt[1018] eloquently expressed himself on the ignorance of the learned.

Too much reliance is given to *anecdote and speculation*. The very lucidity of the psychoanalytical account of emotional and instinctual development given by Anna Freud[1019] makes deficiencies clearer. An unbiased observer may doubt the validity of many statements. Behaviour described may happen sometimes, but is it part of the normal phases of development? Accurate statistical studies alone will tell.

Undue weight may be given to *authorities* leading to uncritical acceptance of their views. The evaluation of a person should be divorced from the evaluation of his ideas, otherwise creeds and cults develop, and, as T. H. Huxley has said, 'Science commits suicide when it adopts a creed.' Steinbeck[1020] puts it more picturesquely: 'It has seemed sometimes that the little men in scientific work assumed the awe-fullness of a priesthood to hide their deficiencies ... as the priesthoods of all cults have, with secret or unfamiliar languages and symbols.'

The research worker is unlikely to formulate a useful hypothesis unless he is *knowledgeable about the field of study*. An example of this would be the formulation of Krynauw[1021] on the beneficial effects of hemispherectomy, in which he claimed that hemispherectomy improved the child's intelligence. His hypothesis was invalidated by the fact that in the investigations, because of his inexperience in the field of psychometrics, he had not allowed for the effect of practice and re-practice on psychological tests.

Too many researches are so conducted that they result in mere statistical correlations, rather than reveal the *causality of relationships*. Correlation does not prove causation. Examples of this will be found in much of contemporary large-scale research on delinquency.

There is a tendency to overlook the fact that the material studied may be *selected material*, and this is particularly true of material studied at teaching hospitals. There is much to be said for using the research resources of the university at the periphery of the medical services. Individuals must be identified, their co-operation won, to encourage them to express the true state of affairs. The capacity of the researcher in psychiatry to produce true rapport is crucial.

A common fallacy is to assume that *samples* of the population at large are healthy groups. In fact, as has been seen in the St. Louis study,[1022] even the control group may contain a large number of unhealthy people. By comparing a random sample of the population at large with a clinic group, the investigator merely compares a diseased group with a group which is less diseased.

The selection of *control groups* presents many difficulties. Patients who are not receiving treatment are rarely willing to attend for investigation. A group which has been investigated for diagnosis will not be a valid control group, since some therapy is often applied during the course of investigation. Furthermore, it is not possible to deny treatment to a patient. It has been suggested that the 'defector group', i.e. those patients who fail to attend for treatment, could be used as control. These patients, however, are unlikely to be truly representative of the original group.

Control groups are often employed for evaluating therapy by comparing matched groups, one treated and the other untreated. Instead of selecting two matched groups, which subsequently receive different therapies, an attempt is sometimes made to select and compare groups of patients who have already received different types of treatment. It is extremely difficult to make these comparisons in retrospect, since, in clinical practice, certain types of patients tend to receive certain treatments, and so the groups selected in this way are not matched. But it is possible for a group receiving one particular form of therapy to act as its own control. The result of therapy for that group may then be assessed by discovering which type of symptom or patient, or which sex or age group, responded best to that form of treatment. This method indicates to some extent which type of patient benefits most from a particular form of treatment. But, with this method, it is not possible to compare the relative values of different treatments.

In any psychological situation there are many *variables*. These variables are difficult to control, e.g. the value of different therapies may be estimated by comparing the differential responses of two homogenous groups of patients. It must be established that the two groups which are being compared differ only in the fact that one receives a specific form of therapy and the other does not. A large number of factors have to be matched between these groups. They must be alike in respect of sex, age, intelligence, duration of the illness, form and severity of the illness, and they must all have been treated under the same conditions, with the same staff and in the same location.

Follow-up studies are employed to relate the state of a patient at one moment in time to the efforts of a clinic some time before. They may be compared to a post-mortem examination, and they have their own special difficulties. The original aim of the treatment must be known before its effect can be evaluated at the follow-up. Other factors may have been operating since therapy began, and these may have caused either an improvement or a relapse. The same criteria must be observed by the same observers at the end of treatment and at the follow-up. Any improvements noted may be due to treatment, or to chance factors coinciding with therapy, or to chance factors since therapy. The standards adopted must be objective throughout; subjective impressions of psychiatric patients are likely to be misleading. The ideal investigation is one which has been carefully planned and carried out by a skilled research team, and should satisfy the most rigorous experimental standards. Investigations should be prefaced by pilot studies to define the variables.

To add to the difficulties, some patients tend to *improve spontaneously*. Little is known about the restitution factors which are operating. Furthermore, there are beneficial elements common to all treatments, as has been shown by the investigations on the placebo response.[1023]

Lastly, there is a reluctance to undertake *negative investigations* likely to disprove strongly held views—an essential operation if many of the existing speculations are to be tested. With the facilities existing at the time, Freud could not proceed in any other way than by speculation. His followers have added untested speculation to untested speculation, with the result that our clinical practice may be far from the truth. If judged by the minute analysis of events, psychopathology of the future may be as 'deep' as psychoanalysis, but will be based upon the findings of carefully conducted research. Science and psychoanalysis was the subject of comment by Freud[1024] himself, and by Hartmann,[1025] Ellis,[1026] Fiegl,[1027] Frenkel-Brunswik,[1028] Hartmann and Loewenstein,[1029] Kris[1030] and Rapaport.[1031]

Research in Family Psychiatry

Here are to be found all the problems attendant on research in individual psychiatry, together with the problems particular to this field.

The unit, the family, is larger and more complex. It has many elements, whether facets, aspects, parameters, qualities, levels or divisions. Happenings are often the resultant of many vectors. To identify and control variables is a considerable task. Furthermore, this unit is in continuous change as it flows through time. The observer may be a part of the field which he observes and change with it.

The complexity of the family sets problems in conceptualisation. A framework is essential for marshalling data, making deductions in a logical sequence, setting up and testing hypotheses, and investigating in a meaningful sequence. There is no final answer. A simple, flexible model must first be constructed, capable of adaption by knowledge. The crucial matter is not the initial model, but the flexibility to change it.

Research in family psychiatry is over a wider field; the individual and his intrapsychic life, important though it is, has to be supplemented by research on relationships, communication, group activities, and community, cultural and social functioning. Fields of endeavour include: cybernetics, communication theory, psychology (developmental, experimental, physiological, clinical and social), neurophysiology, psychopathology, group dynamics, ethology, anthropology (cultural and social), neurology, psychiatry, cultural psychiatry (transcultural and cross-cultural) and social psychiatry. Teamwork embraces many disciplines and brings its own problems of communication. These can sometimes be met by clinical research personnel taking an interest in special fields, or, more commonly, by the specialist research workers moving into the clinical situation and working alongside clinical research workers. 'Pure' research outside the clinical field can be highly relevant. But, at best, arrangements for assessing and communicating to clinical workers relevant material from such research are as yet in an imperfect state.

This challenging situation has provoked much valuable comment. Family research efforts have been reviewed by Hill,[1032, 1033] Hill et al.,[1034] Burgess,[1035] Cottrell,[1036] Dager,[1037] Ehrmann,[1038] Nimkroff,[1039] Nye[1040] and Walters.[1041] Hoffman and Lippitt[1042] consider aspects of family research as they relate to child behaviour. Meissner[1043] reviews research findings on various parameters of the pathological family.

Methodology, of course, is a primary consideration. Hill[1044] evaluates conceptual frameworks, and proceeds to point out the advantages and disadvantages of longitudinal research and its alternatives. Haley[1045] expresses views on types of family research. Levinger[1046] points to advantages of combining observations and subjective report in family research. Blood[1047] considers observational methods, and Rabkin[1048] considers methodologies for family research, with stress on the value of research based on a child's eye view of the family.

Clinical workers have concentrated on family psychopathology as a research area. Lidz[1049] traces the history of psychoanalytical interest in the family, its limitations, and the need for rethinking and reorganising. Parsons[1050] and Hartmann[1051] relate psychoanalysis to sociology. Framo[1052] points to the inadequacy of research which does not take account of hidden emotional motivation and mechanisms in the family. Riskin[1053] describes how the Palo Alto group of workers find that accepting the family as a dynamic system with homeostatic mechanisms to maintain its equilibrium can reveal its underlying mechanisms, if its communication patterns are studied. Jackson[1054] has developed the significance of these ideas in the study of family process. Weakland[1055] advocates family therapy as a special area of research in interaction, communication patterns, exploration of symptomatology, family homeostasia, and for the evaluation of results. Vassiliou and Vassiliou et al.[1056–1060] have deployed ingenious methods to study transaction in Greek families.

The problems encountered in psychiatric and family research are formidable, but they are not insurmountable. Indeed, without the challenge we would be robbed of an intriguing and fascinating quest—perhaps the most significant for human prosperity. The task is no different from those facing workers in other fields. We must rid ourselves of preconceptions, embrace the scientific method, accumulate resources and spend adequate time on the task. There are new assets available to us—the scientific method is well tried, knowledge can be stored more readily, and analysed mechanically.

In addition, the family approach has intrinsic merits. It presents a truer picture of the life situation than does an individual approach. Individuals are seen, for instance, as units in a group; one relationship, say, the mother-child, is not given more prominence than another, say, the father-child; the transference of patterns of behaviour from one generation to another is clarified; the pressures of community, culture and society are not overlooked.

Research should not be conducted cross-sectionally or longitudinally, at one level or another, on healthy or unhealthy family, intra- or extra-psychically—it should be conducted at all points of the family framework. A flexible conceptual framework will allow the synthesisers to build new patterns of knowledge, to adjust them and readjust until no change is possible and final truth is achieved.

Research must proceed at many points and by multiple small steps. Already, significant advances have been made, and a few will be selected for illustration.

Valuable initial findings can be made from the study of an individual case, by observing what changes are directly linked to a particular event and which of them can be predicted to occur when the event is repeated. Experimentation and statistical analysis can follow. An example of a valuable clinical investigation is that by Dekker and Groen,[1061] who were able to produce, in the laboratory, psychogenic attacks of asthma in asthmatic subjects. Emotional stimuli were selected from the histories of the patients; the patients were faced with these stimuli, and attacks of asthma provoked. The relevance of such experiments to the mechanics of psychosomatic symptoms is self-evident.

Social, ethnological and epidemiological studies are also of value. In the social field, one might turn to the Newcastle survey[1062] of a thousand families. This survey shows that only just over half the infants in Newcastle are wholly breast-fed at the end of one month, only one-third at the end of three months, and only one-fifth reach the end of the sixth month without being given a bottle feed. It would seem that we live in a bottle-feeding, rather than a breast-feeding, culture. Of greatest interest, too, in the social field, are the various studies of the community up-bringing of children in the *kibbutzim* in Israel, which have been reviewed by Miller.[1063]

From the ethnological field, anthropologists have interesting things to say about child-rearing practices. In not all communities is the child cared for by the mother. In some of them the care is given by the father (Mead),[1064] in others by the older child (Mead and MacGregor)[1065] and in yet others by relations and friends (Layton and Kluckhohn).[1066] Margaret Mead[1067] concludes in this context, 'Anthropological evidence gives no support at present to the value of such an exaggeration of the tie between mother and child. On the contrary, cross-culture study suggests that adjustment is most facilitated if the child is cared for by many warm, friendly people.' This should induce a more flexible attitude in child rearing.

In the epidemiological field, surveys of the incidence of neurosis in general practice have shown, in a striking way, that emotional disorder in the community is a far more common problem than has hitherto been supposed. The corollary is that the family doctor should be trained and utilised to combat emotional disorders.

Ethology also has some lessons for us, whether its field of operation is in nature, in the laboratory or in the family. I will point in turn to examples of each. Hebb[1068] quotes instances of dogs reared in isolation, who, when released, showed a naïve behaviour, reminiscent of the over-protected and deprived children of restricting parents and of the pseudo-retardation of institutionalised children. In nature, the study of the life of the emperor penguins shows that the infant is reared and protected in the pouch of the father penguin, and at a later date is reared in a day nursery. The most obvious lesson to be learnt is that nature is plastic in its adjustment to situations. Mothering, fathering and parenting are less important than the need to succour the young. Almost any thesis can be supported by analogies from animal behaviour, but one should be careful to look for processes in animals that are homologous and not merely analogous with man. It may then be possible to identify common basic processes.

The field of child development, as would be expected, yields knowledge relevant to child and adult psychopathology. In this field, Piaget's work is of great importance. His theory[1069] of stages in the development of concepts states that they have direct bearing upon the child's appreciation of emotional events around him, and of the impact which these events make upon his personality. If, for instance, as Piaget maintains, an infant under nine months cannot recognise his mother as a human being, it is difficult to see how he can have strong emotions and preferences for her in particular. Of equal importance is knowledge of the child's capacity for memory at this age, and especially of his retentiveness. Equally fundamental is the application of learning theory to personality development.

The fields of genetics, physiology and physiological psychology may be remote, yet they too may help us to establish base lines. It is a commonplace that the less accurate the knowledge we have about the causality of a piece of behaviour, the more likely we are to adduce inheritance as its explanation. We hear on all sides, 'Just like his cousin'; 'His father was just like him'. While the public accepts readily the communication of infections, it is less ready to see that emotional processes are just as communicable. Neurosis is not a genetic disorder, but it is frequently a familial one. Genetical research is moving into this area.

A valuable base line is provided by the studies on reflex activity in the newborn and in the infant; they are applicable to the early assessment of development in the child. We are indebted to the National Spastic Society[1070] for a recent publication on this subject. Mention should be made also of the work of Penfield and Roberts,[1071] who claim to show that the left hemisphere is always the dominant hemisphere for speech function, whether the person is left- or right-handed. As a result of their findings, a good many formulations will come tumbling to the ground.

TRAINING

Training programmes should be organised separately for each group of workers, according to the amount of knowledge in family psychiatry required by that group. One group consists of the professional clinical workers most intimately concerned with family psychiatry as a speciality—psychiatrists, clinical psychologists, psychiatric social workers, occupational therapists, etc. Another group requires that approximately half their training should be devoted to family functioning and dysfunctioning

—family doctors, family social workers, family nurses, and those organising substitute family care for children. A large number of other professional groups need a general knowledge of the subject, e.g. teachers, specialist doctors, clergy, school medical officers, midwives, medical students, nurses, personnel managers, youth employment officers, etc.

Clinical workers who intend to specialise in this field should be trained in·departments adopting a total family approach. A generic theoretical course, supplemented by separate specialist training for each professional group, is an economic procedure. An exclusively theoretical programme is not conducive to maintaining interest. Direct clinical work under supervision must run parallel; a small number of families, or even one family, studied in depth is more instructive than a nodding acquaintance with many. Taped interviews, two-way screens, closed circuit television, films all supplement, but do not replace, direct clinical work. Free discussion should replace formal lecturing. A library of books, papers and pamphlets should be available, together with a cumulative bibliography on family psychiatry. Trainees should be allowed to see the individual and the family against the background of the community and society.

Direct propaganda to the public should be a matter of extreme care, until knowledge is well established. The first task is to train key personnel, and they will, in turn, communicate relevant knowledge to the public at large.

CONCLUSION

Humanity flows through time, and its dysfunctioning is experienced as anguish in the individual, discord in the family and 'social problems' in society. The problem of the material contribution to dysfunction has approached solubility. The emotional contribution is emerging as the next challenge. There is a limit to what society can spend at any time in self-improvement. But the resources available must be increasingly invested in the emotional area. Over the generations, knowledge will make it possible to readjust the patterns of functioning in the continuous field of society, family and individual, so as to bring happiness, relaxation and contentment.

REFERENCES

For the convenience of the reader the references are in the same order as they appear in the text and grouped to correspond to sections in the text. In a few instances, perforce, references are repeated.

II. DIMENSIONS OF THE FAMILY

1. *The Family*

1. 1944. *The Shorter Oxford English Dictionary*, 3rd ed. Oxford Univ. Press, London.
2. MURDOCK, G. P. 1960. The universality of the nuclear family. In BELL, N. W., and VOGEL, E. F. (eds.) *The family*. Free Press, Glencoe, Ill.
3. LOWIE, R. N. 1920. *Primitive society*. New York.
4. HOBHOUSE, WHEELER, and GINSBERG. Quoted by BELL, N. W., and VOGEL, E. F. (eds.) in *The family*. Free Press, Glencoe, Ill.
5. MURDOCK, G. P. 1949. *Social structure*. Macmillan, New York.
6. SPIRO, M. E. 1965. *Kibbutz : Venture in Utopia*. Harvard Univ. Press, Cambridge, Mass.
7. SPIRO, M. E. 1958. *Children of the kibbutz*. Harvard Univ. Press, Cambridge, Mass.
8. KLUCKHOHN, C. 1949. *The family in a democratic society*. Columbia Univ. Press, New York.
9. FLETCHER, R. 1962. *The family and marriage*. Penguin Books, London.
10. PARSONS, T., and BALES, R. F. 1955. *Family : Socialization and interaction process*. Free Press, Glencoe, Ill.
11. SEGUIN, C. A. 1964. The theory and practice of psychiatry in Peru. *Am. J. Psychother.*, **18**, 188.
12. YOUNG, M., and WILMOTT, P. 1957. *Family and kinships in East London*. Macmillan, London.
13. ANSHEN, R. 1949. *The family, its functions and destiny*. Harper, New York.
14. BOTT, E. 1957. *Family and social network*. Tavistock Publications, London.
15. EISENBERG, L. 1960. The family in the mid-twentieth century. *The social welfare forum* 1960. Columbia Univ. Press, New York.
16. ELMER, M. C. 1945. *Sociology of the family*. Ginn, London.
17. EMERSON, G. 1949. *The family in a democratic society*. Columbia Univ. Press, New York.
18. FOLSOM, J. K. 1943. *The family and democratic society*. Wiley, New York.
19. GLICK, P. C. 1957. *American families*. Wiley, New York.
20. GOODSELL, W. 1934. *A history of marriage and the family*, revised ed. Macmillan, New York.
21. HOWARD, G. E. 1904. *History of matrimonial institutions*. Univ. of Chicago Press, Chicago.
22. KLINEBERG, O. 1954. *Social psychology*. Holt, New York.
23. LOWIE, R. N. 1920. *Primitive society*. New York.

24. PARSONS, T. 1951. *The social system.* Free Press, Glencoe, Ill.
25. POROT, M. 1954. *L'enfant et les relations familiales.* Presses Univ. de France, Paris.
26. WALLER, W., and HILL, R. 1951. *The family: A dynamic interpretation.* Dryden Press, New York.
27. WESTERMARCK, E. A. 1921. *A history of human marriage.* Macmillan, New York.
28. ZIMMERMAN, C. C. 1947. *Family and civilization.* Harper, New York.
29. ZIMMERMAN, C. C., and FRAMPTON, M. E. 1935. *Family and society.* Van Nostrand, New York.
30. GOODE, W. J. 1963. *World revolution and family patterns.* Free Press, Glencoe, Ill.
31. ADLER, A. 1952. (RADIN, P., trans.) *The practice and theory of individual psychology.* Humanities Press, New York.
32. FLUGEL, J. C. 1931. *The psychoanalytic study of the family,* 4th ed. Hogarth Press, London.
33. GROUP FOR THE ADVANCEMENT OF PSYCHIATRY. 1954. *Integration and Conflict in Family Behaviour.* Report No. 27.
34. MILLER, E. 1938. *The generations.*
35. SPIEGEL, J. P., and BELL, N. W. 1959. The family of the psychiatric patient. Chapter 5 in ARIETI, S. (ed.) *American handbook of psychiatry.* Basic Books, New York.
36. WINNICOTT, O. W. 1965. *The family and individual development.* Tavistock Publications, London.
37. HILL, R. 1949. *Families under stress.* Harper, New York.
38. HESS, R. D., and HANDEL, —. 1959. *Family worlds: A psychosocial approach to family life.* Univ. of Chicago Press, Chicago.
39. OPLER, M. K. 1956. *Culture, psychiatry and human values.* Thomas, Springfield, Ill.
40. MYERS, J. K., and ROBERTS, B. H. 1959. *Family and class dynamics in mental illness.* Wiley, New York.
41. RICHARDSON, H. B. 1948. *Patients have families.* Commonwealth Fund, New York.
42. PEARSE, I., and CROCKNER, L. H. 1944. *The Peckham experiment.* Allen & Unwin, London.
43. ACKERMAN, N. W. 1958. *The psychodynamics of family life.* Basic Books, New York.
44. BENEDICT, R. 1946. *Patterns of culture.* Penguin Books, London.
45. MALINOWSKI, B. 1929. *The sexual life of savages.* Halcyon House, New York.
46. MEAD, M. 1935. *Sex and temperament in the primitive societies.* Morrow, New York.
47. EATON, J. W., and WEIL, R. J. 1955. *Culture and mental disorder.* Free Press, Glencoe, Ill.

2. Conceptualisation of the Family

48. HILL, R., and HANSEN, D. A. 1960. The identification of conceptual frameworks utilized in family study. *Marriage fam. living,* **22**, 299.
49. ACKERMAN, N. W., and BEHRENS, M. L. 1956. A study of family diagnosis. *Am. J. Orthopsychiat.,* **26**, 66.
50. EHRENWALD, J. 1958. Neurotic interaction and patterns of pseudo-heredity in the family. *Am. J. Psychiat.,* **115**, 134.
51. EHRENWALD, J. 1960. Neurosis in the family—A study of psychiatric epidemiology. *Archs gen. Psychiat.,* **3**, 232.

52. JACKSON, D. D. 1959. Family interaction, family homeostasis, and some implications for conjoint family psychotherapy. In MASSERMAN, J. (ed.) *Individual and family dynamics*. Grune & Stratton, New York.

53. SPIEGEL. J. P. 1960. The resolution of role conflict within the family. In BELL, N. W., and VOGEL, E. F. (eds.) *The family*. Free Press, Glencoe, Ill.

54. EHRENWALD, J. 1963. *Neurosis in the family, and patterns of psychosocial defense*. Hoeber, New York.

55. TITCHENER, J., and EMERSON, R. 1958. Some methods for the study of family interaction in personality development. *Psychiat. Res. Rep.* No. 10, 72.

56. OTTO, H. A. 1963. The production of criteria for assessing family strength. *Family Process*, **2**, 329.

57. SERRANO, A. C., McDANALD, E. C., GOOLISHIAN, H. A., MacGREGOR, R., and RITCHIE, A. M. 1962. Adolescent maladjustment and family dynamics. *Am. J. Psychiat.*, **118**, 897. [Reprinted in this collection as No. VII.]

58. MARKOWITZ, M., and KADIS, A. L. 1964. Parental interaction as a determining factor in social growth of the individual in the family. *Int. J. soc. Psychiat.*, Congress Issue.

59. VOILAND, A., *et al.* 1962. *Family case work of diagnosis*. Columbia Univ. Press, New York.

60. HOWELLS, J. G. 1963. *Family psychiatry*. Oliver & Boyd, Edinburgh.

61. HOWELLS, J. G. 1962. The nuclear family as the functional unit in psychiatry. *J. ment. Sci.*, **108**, 675.

3. *The Individual Dimension*

62. ALLPORT, G. 1963. *Pattern and growth in personality*. Holt, Rinehart & Winston, London.

63. THOMPSON, G. G. 1962. *Child psychology*, 2nd ed. Houghton Mifflin, Boston.

64. CARMICHAEL, L. (ed.). 1954. *Manual of child psychology*, 2nd ed. Wiley, New York.

65. MUSSEN, P. H. (ed.). 1960. *Handbook of research methods in child development*. Wiley, New York.

66. MONTAGU, M. F. ASHLEY. 1962. *Pre-natal influences*. Charles C. Thomas, New York.

67. PASAMANICK, B., and KNOBLOCH, H. 1961. Complications of pregnancy: Climate and foetal damage. In CAPLAN, G. (ed.) *Prevention of mental disorder in children*, p. 87. Basic Books, New York.

68. SONTAG, L. W. 1941. The significance of foetal environmental differences. *Am. J. Obstet. Gynec.*, **42**, 996.

69. SPELT, D. K. 1948. The conditioning of the human fetus *in utero*. *J. exp. Psychol.*, **38**, 338. [Reprinted in this collection as No. IV.]

70. STOTT, D. H. 1962. Evidence for a congenital factor in maladjustment and delinquency. *Am. J. Psychiat.*, **118**, 781.

71. FREUD, A. 1966. *Normality and pathology in childhood*. Hogarth Press, London.

72. SPITZ, R. A. 1965. *The first year of life*. International Univ. Press, New York.

73. THOMAS, A., BIRCH, H. G., CHESS, S., and ROBBINS, L. C. 1961. Individuality in responses of children to similar environmental situations. *Am. J. Psychiat.*, **117**, 798.

74. WOODWARD, M. 1965. Piaget's theory. In HOWELLS, J. G. (ed.) *Modern perspectives in child psychiatry*. Oliver & Boyd, Edinburgh.

75. GREENACRE, P. 1960. Considerations regarding the parent-infant relationship. *Int. J. Psycho-Analysis*, **41**, 571. [Reprinted in this collection as No. V.]
76. MONEY, J., HAMPSON, J. G., and HAMPSON, J. L. 1955. An examination of some basic sexual concepts: The evidence of human hermaphroditism. *Bull. Johns Hopkins Hosp.*, **97**, 301. [Reprinted in this collection as No. VI.]
77. SZUREK, S. The child's needs for his emotional health. In HOWELLS, J. G. (ed.) *Modern perspectives in international child psychiatry*. Oliver & Boyd, Edinburgh. In press.
78. SERRANO, A. C., McDANALD, E. C., GOOLISHIAN, H. A., MACGREGOR, R., and RITCHIE, A. M. 1962. Adolescent maladjustment and family dynamics. *Am. J. Psychiat.*, **118**, 897. [Reprinted in this collection as No. VII.]
79. HALL, G. S. 1904. *Adolescence*, 2 vols. Appleton-Century, New York.
80. JERSILD, A. T. 1955. *Psychology of adolescence*. Macmillan, New York.

4. The Relationship Dimension

81. WOOLDRIDGE, D. E. 1963. *The machinery of the brain*. McGraw-Hill, New York.
82. ASHBY, W. R. 1958. *Introduction to cybernetics*. Chapman & Hall, London.
83. ASHBY, W. R. 1960. *Design for a brain*. Chapman & Hall, London.
84. CROWLEY, T. H., HARRIS, C. W., MILLER, G. A., PIERCE, J. R., and RUNYON. 1962. *Modern communications*. Columbia Univ. Press, New York.
85. CHERRY, C. 1957. *On human communication*. Wiley, New York.
86. PIERCE, J. R. 1964. The relevance of communication theory to disorders of communication, in *Disorders of communication*. Williams & Wilkins, Baltimore.
87. RUESCH, J. 1953. The Interpersonal communication of anxiety, in *Symposium on stress*, p. 154. Walter Reed Army Medical Center, Government Printing Office.
88. RUESCH, J., and BATESON, G. 1951. *Communication: The social matrix of psychiatry*. Norton, New York.
89. RUESCH, J. 1953. Social factors in therapy. In *Psychiatric treatment*, pp. 59-93. Proc. Assoc. for Research in Nervous and Mental Disease. Williams & Wilkins, Baltimore.
90. RUESCH, J., and PRESTWOOD, A. R. 1950. Communication and bodily disease: A study of vasospastic conditions. In *Life stress and bodily disease*. Williams & Wilkins, Baltimore.
91. RUESCH, J., BLOCK, J., and BENNETT, L. 1953. The assessment of communication: I. A method for the analysis of social interaction. *J. Psychol.*, **35**, 59.
92. RUESCH, J., and BATESON, G. 1949. Structure and process in social relations. *Psychiatry*, **12**, 105.
93. RUESCH, J. 1951. Part and whole. *Dialectica*, **5**, 99.
94. RUESCH, J., and PRESTWOOD, A. R. 1950. Interaction processes and personal codification. *J. Personality*, **18**, 391.
95. RUESCH, J. 1949. Experiments in psychotherapy: II. Individual social techniques. *J. soc. Psychol.*, **29**, 3.
96. RUESCH, J. 1953. Social technique, social status and social change in illness. In KLUCKHOHN, C., MURRAY, H. A., and SCHNEIDER, D. M. (eds.) *Personality in nature, society and culture*, 2nd ed., pp. 123-136. Knopf, New York.
97. RUESCH, J. 1956. Psychiatry and the challenge of communication. *Psychiatry*, **17**, 1.

98. RUESCH, J. 1955. Nonverbal language and therapy. *Psychiatry*, **18**, 323.
99. RUESCH, J. 1952. The therapeutic process from the point of view of communication theory. *Am. J. Orthopsychiat.*, **22**, 690.
100. RUESCH, J. 1964. Clinical science and communication theory. *Disorders of communication*, **42**, 247.
101. RUESCH, J. 1956. The observer and the observed. In GRINKER, R. R. (ed.) *Toward a unified theory of human behavior*. Basic Books, New York.
102. RUESCH, J. 1957. *Disturbed communication*. Norton, New York.
103. RUESCH, J. 1961. *Therapeutic communication*. Norton, New York.
104. RUESCH, J. 1962. Declining clinical tradition. *J. Am. med. Ass.*, **182**, 110.
105. RUESCH, J. 1962. Human communication and the psychiatrist. *Am. J. Psychiat.*, **118**, 881.
106. RUESCH, J. 1960. *Am. J. Psychother.*, **14**, 250.
107. RUESCH, J. 1959. General theory of communication. In ARIETI, S. (ed.) *American handbook of psychiatry*, Vol. I. Basic Books, New York.
108. RUESCH, J., and KEES, W. 1956. *Nonverbal communication: Notes on the visual perception of human relations*. Univ. of California Press, Berkeley and Los Angeles.
109. RUESCH, J. 1953. Synopsis of the theory of communication. *Psychiatry*, **16**, 215.
110. RUESCH, J. 1948. The infantile personality: The core problem of psychosomatic medicine. *Psychosom. Med.*, **10**, 134.
111. RUESCH, J., and KEES, W. 1954. *Children in groups*. 16 mm. sound film, running time about 25 min. The Langley Porter Clinic, San Francisco.
112. RUESCH, J., and PRESTWOOD, A. R. 1949. Anxiety: Its initiation, communication and interpersonal management. *Archs Neurol. Psychiat.*, **62**, 527.
113. WATKINS, C., and PASAMANICK, B. (eds.) 1961. *Problems of communication*. American Psychiatric Association, Washington, D.C.
114. CRITCHLEY, M. 1942. Aphasic disorders of signalling. *J. Mt Sinai Hosp.*, **9**, 363.
115. BARNET, S. A. 1961. Behaviour and needs of infant mammals. *Lancet*, i, 1067.
116. BIRDWHISTELL, R. 1959. Contribution of linguistic-kinesic studies to the understanding of schizophrenia. In AUERBACK, A. (ed.) *Schizophrenia*. Ronald Press, New York.
117. BIRDWHISTELL, R. 1957. *Implications of recent developments in communication research for evolutionary theory*. Presented at Georgetown Conference.
118. BIRDWHISTELL, R. 1962. *An approach to communication*. Presented at meeting of American Orthopsychiatric Association, April 24.
119. BIRDWHISTELL, R. 1959. *The frames in the communication process*. Presented at annual scientific assembly of American Society of Clinical Hypnosis, October 10.
120. BIRDWHISTELL, R. 1960. *Kinesics analysis in the investigation of the emotions*. Presented at meeting of American Association for the Advancement of Science, December 29.
121. BIRDWHISTELL, R. 1957. *Kinesics in the context of motor habits*. Presented at meeting of American Anthropological Association, December 28.
122. BIRDWHISTELL, R. 1956. *Introduction to kinesics*. Univ. of Louisville Press, Louisville.
123. McGOUGH, W. E. 1964. The importance of empathic communication in anthropological research. *Int. J. soc. Psychiat.*, Special Edition No. 1.
124. FRANK, J. 1961. Communication and empathy. *Proceedings of the Third World Congress of Psychiatry*.

125. MIRSKY, I. A., *et al.* 1961. The communication of affects. *Proceedings of the Third World Congress of Psychiatry.*
126. MEERLOO, J. A. M. 1964. *Unobtrusive communication.* Van Gorcum, Assen, Netherlands.
127. BERGER, M. M. 1964. Some implications of nonverbal communication in psychotherapy, medical practice, family relations and life in general. *Int. J. soc. Psychiat.*, Congress Issue.
128. SCHEFLEN, A. E. 1964. The significance of posture in communication systems. *Psychiatry*, **27**, 316.
129. KLEIN, G. S. 1959. Consciousness in psychoanalytic theory: Some implications for current research in perception. *J. Am. psychoanal. Ass.*, **7**, 5.
130. KLEIN, G. S. 1959. On subliminal activation. *J. nerv. ment. Dis.*, **128**, 293.
131. KLEIN, G. S., and HOLT, R. R. 1960. Problems and issues in current studies of subliminal activation. In PENTMAN, J. G., and HARTLEY, E. L. (eds.) *Festschrift for Gardner Murphy.* Harper, New York.
132. PINE, F. 1960. Incidental stimulation: A study of preconscious transformation. *J. abnorm. soc. Psychol.*, **60**, 68.
133. TAUBER, S., and GREEN, M. R. 1959. *Prelogical experience—An inquiry into dreams and other creative processes.* Basic Books, New York.
134. FISHER, C., and PAUL, I. H. 1959. The effect of subliminal visual stimulation on images and dreams: A validation study. *J. Am. psychoanal. Ass.*, **7**, 35.
135. KLEIN, G. S., SPENCE, D. P., HOLT, R. R., and GOUREVITCH, S. 1958. Cognition without awareness: Subliminal influences upon conscious thought. *J. abnorm. soc. Psychol.*, **57**, 255.
136. FREUD, S. 1912. Recommendations for physicians on the psycho-analytic method of treatment. *Collected Papers*, Vol. 2, p. 323. Hogarth, London, 1959.
137. REIK, T. 1948. *Listening with the third ear.* Farrar, Straus, New York.
138. WOLPE, J. Learning theory. In HOWELLS, J. G. (ed.) *Modern perspectives in world psychiatry.* Oliver & Boyd, Edinburgh. In Press.
139. EYSENCK, H. J. (ed.). 1960. *Behaviour therapy and the neuroses.* Pergamon Press, Oxford.
140. EYSENCK, H. J., and RACHMAN, S. J. 1965. The application of learning theory to child psychiatry. In HOWELLS, J. G. (ed.) *Modern perspectives in child psychiatry.* Oliver & Boyd, Edinburgh.
141. FREUD, S. The dynamics of the transference. *Standard edition of the complete psychological works of Sigmund Freud*, Vol. XII. Hogarth Press, London, 1958.
142. LEWIN, K. K. 1965. Nonverbal cues and transference. *Archs gen. Psychiat.*, **12**, 391.
143. LEWIN, K. K. 1936. *Principles of topological psychology.* McGraw-Hill, New York.
144. ENELOW, A. J. 1964. Identity and communication. *Am. J. Psychother.*, **18**, 649.
145. ENELOW, A. J., and ADLER, L. M. 1965. The 'here and now' as the focus of psychotherapy. *Sci. Psychoanal.*, **8**, 208.
146. ENELOW, A. J. 1960. The silent patient. *Psychiatry*, **23**, 153.
147. MEARES, A. 1960. Communication with the patient. *Lancet*, i, 664.
148. CRISP, A. H. 1964. An attempt to measure an aspect of 'transference'. *Br. J. med. Psychol.*, **37**, 17.
149. CRISP, A. H. 1964. Development and application of a measure of 'transference'. *J. psychosom. Res.*, **8**, 327.
150. SCHEFLEN, A. E. 1963. Communication and regulation in psychotherapy. *Psychiatry*, **26**, 126.

151. ROGERS, C. R. 1962. Characteristics of a helping relationship. *Canada's ment. Hlth*, Supplement No. 27.

152. BALDWIN, A. L., KALHORN, J., and BREESE, F. H. 1949. The appraisal of parent behaviour. *Psychol. Monogr.*, **63**, No. 4.

153. MURDOCK, G. P. 1960. The universality of the nuclear family. In BELL, N. W., and VOGEL, E. F. (eds.) *The family*. Free Press, Glencoe, Ill.

154. HOWARD, G. E. 1904. *History of matrimonial institutions*. Univ. of Chicago Press, Chicago.

155. WESTERMARCK, E. A. 1921. *History of human marriage*. Macmillan, London.

156. GOODSELL, W. 1934. *A history of marriage and the family*, revised ed. Macmillan, London.

157. COLE, M. 1939. *Marriage past and present.*

158. MALINOWSKI, B. 1929. *The sexual life of savages*. Halcyon House, New York.

159. BENEDICT, R. 1946. *Patterns of culture*. Penguin Books, London.

160. MEAD, M. 1950. *Male and female*. Penguin Books, London.

161. RADCLIFFE-BROWN, A. R., and FORDE, D. (eds.). 1950. *African systems of kinship and marriage*. Oxford Univ. Press, London.

162. EVANS-PRICHARD, E. E. 1951. *Kinship and marriage among the Nuer*. Oxford Univ. Press, London.

163. ELLIS, H. 1935. *Psychology of sex*. Emerson.

164. DAVIS, K. B. 1929. *Factors in the sex life of twenty-two hundred women*. Harper, New York.

165. SEWARD, G. H. 1946. *Sex and the social order*. McGraw-Hill, New York.

166. KINSEY, A. C., POMEROY, W. B., and MARTIN, C. E. 1948. *Sexual behaviour in the human male*. Saunders, New York.

167. OLIVEN, J. F. 1965. *Sexual hygiene and pathology*. Pitman, London.

168. HAMILTON, G. V. 1948. *A research in marriage*. Lear.

169. TERMAN, L. M., *et al.* 1938. *Psychological factors in marital happiness*. McGraw-Hill, New York.

170. BURGESS, W. W., and COTTRELL, L. S., Jr. 1939. *Predicting success and failure in marriage*. Prentice-Hall, New York.

171. KLUCKHOHN, C. 1949. *Family in a democratic society*. Columbia Univ. Press, New York.

172. SLATER, E., and WOODSIDE, M. 1951. *Patterns of marriage*. Cassell, London.

173. KREITMAN, N. 1962. Mental disorder in married couples. *J. ment. Sci.*, **108**, 438.

174. PENROSE, L. 1944. Quoted by KREITMAN in *Psychiat. Q.*, Supplement No. 18, 161.

175. GREGORY, I. 1959. Husbands and wives admitted to mental hospital. *J. ment. Sci.*, **105**, 457.

176. TOMAN, W. 1959. Family constellation as a basic personality determinant. *J. indiv. Psychol.*, **15**, 199.

177. TOMAN, W. 1960. *Introduction to psychoanalytic theory of motivation*. Pergamon Press, Oxford.

178. TOMAN, W. 1960. Haupttypen der Familienkonstellation. *Psychol. Rdsch.*, **11**, 273.

179. TOMAN, W. 1961. *Family constellation: Theory and practice of a psychological game*. Springer, New York.

180. TOMAN, W., and GRAY, B. 1961. Family constellations of 'normal' and 'disturbed' marriages: An empirical study. *J. indiv. Psychol.*, **17**, 93.

181. TOMAN, W. 1962. Family constellations of the partners in divorced and married couples. *J. indiv. Psychol.*, **18**, 48.

182. POND, D. A., RYLE, A., and HAMILTON, M. 1963. Marriage and neurosis in a working class population. *Br. J. Psychiat.*, **109**, 592.

183. HARE, E. H., and SHAW, G. K. 1965. A study in family health: 2. A comparison of the health of father, mother and children. *Br. J. Psychiat.*, **111**, 467.

184. HOWELLS, J. G. 1963. *Family psychiatry*, p. 31. Oliver & Boyd, Edinburgh.

185. LICHTENBERGER, J. P. 1931. *Divorce: A social interpretation.* McGraw-Hill, New York.

186. MOWRER, E. R. 1928. *Family disorganization.* Univ. of Chicago Press, Chicago.

187. WALLER, W. 1930. *The old love and the new, divorce and readjustment.* Liveright, New York.

188. WHITING, J. W. M., and CHILD, I. L. 1953. *Child training and personality —A cross cultural study.* Yale Univ. Press, New Haven.

189. FOSS, B. M. (ed.). 1961. *Determinants of infant behaviour.* Methuen, London.

190. FOSS, B. M. (ed.). 1963. *Determinants of infant behaviour*, II. Methuen, London.

191. FOSS, B. M. (ed.). 1965. *Determinants of infant behaviour*, III. Methuen, London.

192. SODDY, K. 1955. *Mental health and infant development.* Vol. I. *Papers and discussions.* Routledge & Kegan Paul, London.

193. SODDY, K. 1955. *Mental health and infant development.* Vol. II. *Case histories.* Routledge & Kegan Paul, London.

194. TANNER, J. M., and INHELDER, B. 1956. *Discussions on child development.* Tavistock Publications, London.

195. TANNER, J. M., and INHELDER, B. 1956. *Discussions on child development*, Vol. 2. Tavistock Publications, London.

196. TANNER, J. M., and INHELDER, B. 1958. *Discussions on child development*, Vol. 3. Tavistock Publications, London.

197. TANNER, J. M., and INHELDER, B. 1960. *Discussions on child development*, Vol. 4. Tavistock Publications, London.

198. MEAD, M. 1954. *Growing up in New Guinea.* Penguin Books, London.

199. NEWSON, J., and NEWSON, E. 1963. *Infant care in an urban community.* Allen & Unwin, London.

200. SPENCE, J., WALTON, W. S., MILLER, F. J. W., and COURT, S. D. M. 1954. *A thousand families in Newcastle upon Tyne.* Oxford Univ. Press, London.

201. ABERLE, D. F., and NAEGELS, K. D. 1952. Middle-class fathers' occupational role and attitudes toward children. *Am. J. Orthopsychiat.*, **22**, 366.

202. BACH, G. R. 1946. Father-fantasies and father-typing in father-separated children. *Child Dev.*, **17**, 63.

203. BLOCK, J. 1955. Personality characteristics associated with fathers' attitudes toward child-rearing. *Child Dev.*, **26**, 41.

204. MUELLER, D. D. 1945. Paternal domination: Its influence on child guidance results. *Smith Coll. Stud. soc. Work*, **15**, 184.

205. PETERSON, D. R., BECKER, W. C., HELLMER, L. A., SHOEMAKER, D. J., and QUAY, H. C. 1959. Parental attitudes and child adjustment. *Child Dev.*, **10**, 119.

206. SEARS, R. R., PINTLER, M. H., and SEARS, P. S. 1946. Effect of father separation on preschool children's doll play aggression. *Child Dev.*, **17**, 219.

207. STOLZ, L. M., *et al.* 1954. *Father relations of war-born children.* Stanford Univ. Press, Stanford, Calif.

208. Nash, J. 1965. The father in contemporary culture and current psychological literature. *Child Dev.*, **36**, 261.

209. Grunebaum, H. V., and Strean, H. S. 1964. Some considerations of the therapeutic neglect of fathers in child guidance. *J. Child Psychol. Psychiat.*, **5**, 241.

210. Tasch, R. J. 1951. The role of the father in the family. *J. exp. Educ.*, **20**, 319.

211. English, O. S. 1954. The psychological role of the father in the family. *Soc. Casewk*, **35**, 323.

212. Brim, O. G., Jr. 1958. Family structure and sex role learning by children: A further analysis of Helen Koch's data. *Sociometry*, **21**, 1.

213. Hilgard, J. R. 1951. Sibling rivalry and social heredity. *Psychiatry*, **14**, 375.

214. Koch, H. L. 1955. Some personality correlates of sex, sibling position and sex of sibling among five and six year old children. *Genet. Psychol. Monogr.*, **52**, 3.

215. Koch, H. L. 1955. The relation of certain family constellation characteristics end attitudes of children towards adults. *Child Dev.*, **26**, 13.

216. Koch, H. L. 1956. Attitudes of young children toward their peers as related to certain characteristics of their siblings. *Psychol. Monogr.*, **70**, No. 19.

217. Koch, H. L. 1956. Children's work attitudes and sibling characteristics. *Child Dev.*, **27**, 289.

218. Koch, H. L. 1956. Sissiness and tomboyishness in relation to sibling characteristics. *J. genet. Psychol.*, **88**, 231.

219. Koch, H. L. 1956. Some emotional attitudes of the young child in relation to characteristics of his siblings. *Child Dev.*, **27**, 393.

220. Koch, H. L. 1957. The relation in young children between characteristics of their playmates and certain attributes of their siblings. *Child Dev.*, **28**, 175.

221. Sperling, O. E. 1954. An imaginary companion representing a pre-state of the super-ego. *Psychoanal. Study Child*, **9**, 252.

222. Neiser, E. G. 1957. *The eldest child.* Harper, New York.

223. Mead, M. 1954. Some theoretical considerations on the problem of mother-child separation. *Am. J. Orthopsychiat.*, **24**, 471.

5. *The Group Properties Dimension*

224. Cartwright, D., and Zander, A. 1960. *Group dynamics. Research and theory.* Tavistock Publications, London.

225. Bales, R. F. 1950. *Interaction process analysis.* Addison-Wesley, Cambridge, Mass.

226. Bales, R. F. 1959. Small group theory and research. Chapter 13 in *Sociology today.* Basic Books, New York.

227. Strodtbeck, F. L. 1954. The case for the study of small groups. *Am. sociol. Rev.*, **19**, 651.

228. Strodtbeck, F. L., and Hare, A. P. 1954. Bibliography of small group research, 1900-1953. *Sociometry*, **17**, 107.

229. Hare, A. P., Borgatta, E. F., and Bales, R. F. 1955. *Small groups : Studies in social interaction.* Knopf, New York.

230. Roseborough, M. E. 1953. Experimental studies of small groups. *Psychol. Bull.*, **50**, 275.

231. ARGYLE, M. 1952. Methods of studying small social groups. *Br. J. Psychol.*, **43**, 269.
232. PHILLIPS, M. 1965. *Small social groups in England*. Methuen, London.
233. LINDZEY, G. (ed.). 1954. *Handbook of social psychology*. Addison-Wesley, Cambridge, Mass.
234. TAYLOR, F. K. 1954. The three-dimensional basis of emotional interactions in small groups. *Hum. Relat.*, **7**, 441.
235. TAYLOR, F. K. 1955. The three-dimensional basis of emotional interactions in small groups. *Hum. Relat.*, **8**, 3.
236. FREUD, S. 1922. *Group psychology and the analysis of the ego*. Hogarth, London.
237. COTTRELL, L., and FOOTE, N. N. *New directions for research in the family at Chicago*. Univ. of Chicago Press, Chicago.
238. MILLS, T. M. 1953. Power relations in three-person families. *Am. sociol. Rev.*, **18**, 351.
239. STRODTBECK, F. L. 1954. The family as a three-person group. *Am. sociol. Rev.*, **19**, 23.
240. STRODTBECK, F. L. 1951. Husband and wife interaction over revealed differences. *Am. sociol. Rev.*, **16**, 468.
241. KRECH, D., and CRUTCHFIELD, R. 1948. *Theory and problems of social psychology*. McGraw-Hill, New York.
242. TITCHENER, J. L., *et al.* 1963. Family transaction and derivation of individuality. *Family Process*, **2**, 95.
243. HESS, R. D., and HANDEL, G. 1959. *Family worlds : A psychosocial approach to family life*. Univ. of Chicago Press, Chicago.
244. BOSSARD, J. H. S., and BOLL, E. S. 1955. Personality roles in the large family. *Child Dev.*, **26**, 71.
245. LEWIN, K. 1935. *A dynamic theory of personality*. McGraw-Hill, New York.
246. LEWIN, K. 1952. *Field theory in social science*. Tavistock Publications, London.
247. LEWIN, K. 1936. *Principles of topological psychology*. McGraw-Hill, New York.
248. MARKOWITZ, M., and KADIS, A. L. 1964. Parental interaction as a determining factor in social growth of the individual in the family. *Int. J. soc. Psychiat.*, Congress Issue.
249. VOGEL, E. F. 1960. The marital relationship of parents of emotionally disturbed children. *Psychiatry*, **23**, 1.
250. MORENO, J. L. 1961. The role concept, a bridge between psychiatry and sociology. *Am. J. Psychiat.*, **118**, 518.
251. SPIEGEL, J. P. 1957. The resolution of role conflict within the family. *Psychiatry*, **20**, 1.
252. ALLEN, F. H. 1942. Dynamics of roles as determined by the family. *Am. J. Orthopsychiat.*, **12**, 127.
253. SCHLESINGER, B. 1962. A survey of methods used to study decision making in the family. *Fam. Life Coordinator*, **11**, 8.
254. ACKERMAN, N. W. 1964. Prejudicial scapegoating and neutralizing forces in the family group. *Int. J. soc. Psychiat.*, **2**, 90. [Reprinted in this collection as No. XXX.]
255. VOGEL, E. F., and BELL, N. W. 1960. The emotionally disturbed child as the family scapegoat. In BELL, N. W., and VOGEL, E. F. (eds.) *The family*. Free Press, Glencoe, Ill.
256. HENRY, J. 1951. Family structure and the transmission of neurotic behavior. *Am. J. Orthopsychiat.*, **21**, 800.

257. WARDLE, C. J. 1961. Two generations of broken homes in the genesis of conduct and behaviour disorders in childhood. *Br. med. J.*, ii, 349.
258. EHRENWALD, J. 1958. Neurotic interaction and patterns of pseudo-heredity in the family. *Am. J. Psychiat.*, 115, 134.

6. *The Material Circumstances Dimension*

259. MILLER, F. J. W., COURT, S. D. M., WALTON, W. S., and KNOX, E. G. 1960. *Growing up in Newcastle upon Tyne*. Oxford Univ. Press, London.
260. SPENCE, J., WALTON, W. S., MILLER, F. J. W., and COURT, S. D. M. 1954. *A thousand families in Newcastle upon Tyne*. Oxford Univ. Press, London.
261. PLANT, J. S. 1960. Family living space and personality development. In BELL, N. W., and VOGEL, E. F. (eds.) *The family*. Free Press, Glencoe, Ill.
262. BOSSARD, J. H. S. 1951. A spatial index for family interaction. *Am. sociol. Rev.*, 16, 243.
263. RENBOURN, E. T. 1964. Clothing: Physiology, hygiene and psychological aspects, Part I. *Curr. Med. & Drugs*, 4, 3.
264. RENBOURN, E. T. 1964. Clothing: Physiology, hygiene and psychological aspects, Part II. *Curr. Med. & Drugs*, 5, 3.
265. HARE, E. H., and SHAW, G. K. 1965. A study in family health: 1. Health in relation to family size. *Br. J. Psychiat.*, 111, 461.
266. GROOTENBOER, E. A. 1962. The relation of housing to behaviour disorder. *Am. J. Psychiat.*, 119, 469.
267. WILLIAMSON, R. C. 1952. Economic factors in marital adjustment. *Marriage Fam. Living*, 14, 198.
268. MICHAEL, S. T. 1960. Social attitudes, socio-economic status and psychiatric symptoms. *Acta psychiat. neurol. scand.*, 35, 509.
269. HOPKINS, C. E., WALKLEY, R. P., WILNER, D. M., and GOLD, T. T. 1963. Intrafamily correlation and its significance in the interpretation of sample surveys. *Am. J. publ. Hlth*, 53, 1112.
270. WILNER, D. M., and WALKLEY, R. P. 1959. *Housing environment and mental health. Epidemiology of Mental Disorder.* Am. Ass. for the Advancement of Science, Washington.
271. WILNER, D. M., WALKLEY, R. P., WILLIAMS, H., and TAYBACK, M. 1960. The Baltimore study of the effects of housing on health. *Baltimore Hlth News*, 37, 45.
272. WILNER, D. M., WALKLEY, R. P., SCHRAM, J. M., PINKERTON, T. C., and TAYBACK, M. 1960. Housing as an environmental factor in mental health: The Johns Hopkins longitudinal study. *Am. J. Publ. Hlth*, 50, 55. [Reprinted in this collection as No. XX.]
273. WILNER, D. M., WALKLEY, R. P., and TAYBACK, M. 1956. How does the quality of housing affect health and family adjustment? *Am. J. publ. Hlth*, 46, 736.

Problem Families

274. ANDREWS, B., and COOKSON, J. S. 1952. Problem families—A practical approach. *Med. Offr*, 88, 118.
275. ANDRY, R. 1960. *Delinquency and parental pathology*. Methuen, London.
276. ASHTON, T. C. 1956. Problem families and their household budgets. *Eugen. Rev.*, 48, 95.
277. AYRES, B. 1957. *Analysis of central registration bureau data on 100 family centered project families*. Family Centered Project, Greater St. Paul United Fund & Councils, Inc., St. Paul, Minn.

278. Ayres, B. 1959. *Study of public assistance costs in family centered project families from 1953 to 1958.* Family Centered Project, Greater St. Paul United Fund & Councils, Inc., St. Paul, Minn.
279. Ayres, B. 1961. *Economic dependency in F C P families.* Family Centered Project, Greater St. Paul United Fund & Councils, Inc., St. Paul, Minn.
280. Baldamus, W., and Timms, N. 1955. The problem family—A sociological approach. *Br. J. Sociol.*, 6, 318.
281. Barclay, I. 1951. Problem families. *Social Service*, 25, 62.
282. 1964. Biological aspects of social problems—A symposium. *Lancet*, ii, 856.
283. Birt, C. J. 1956. Family centered project of St. Paul. *Social Work*, 1, No. 4.
284. Birt, C. J. 1962. *A community approach to social dependency.* Family Centered Project, Greater St. Paul United Fund & Councils, Inc., St. Paul, Minn.
285. Birt, C. J. 1963. *The A B C's—A new direction in community welfare planning.* Family Centered Project, Greater St. Paul United Fund & Councils, Inc., St. Paul, Minn.
286. 1964. Birth control for problem parents. (Annotations.) *Lancet*, ii, 1111.
287. Black, R. O. 1950. The problem family: A new approach to its reformation. *Nurs. Mirror*, 90, 519.
288. Blacker, C. P. (ed.) 1937. *A social problem group?* Oxford Univ. Press, London.
289. Blacker, C. P. 1946. Social problem families in the limelight. *Eugen. Rev.*, 38, 117.
290. Blacker, C. P. (chairman), Problem Families Committee. 1948. *Problem families: Six pilot enquiries.* Eugenics Society, London.
291. Blacker, C. P. (ed.). 1952. *Problem families: Five enquiries.* Eugenics Society, London.
292. Bodman, F. 1958. Personal factors in the problem family. *Case Conference*, 5, 99.
293. Brockington, C. F. 1946. 'Homelessness in children'. Causes and prevention. An analysis of unparented children in three English counties. *Lancet*, i, 933.
294. Brockington, C. F. 1947. Problem families. *Med. Offr*, 77, 75.
295. Brockington, C. F. 1949. Problem families. *Jl R. Inst. publ. Hlth Hyg.*, 12, 9.
296. Brockington, C. F. *Problem families.* Occasional Papers No. 2, British Social Hygiene Council.
297. Brockington, C. F., and Steinz. 1958. Correspondence: Problem families. *Lancet*, ii, 319.
298. Buell, B., and Associates. 1945. *Community planning for human services.* Columbia Univ. Press, New York.
299. Burgess, E. W. 1954. Economic, cultural and social factors in family breakdown. *Am. J. Orthopsychiat.*, 24, 462.
300. Burgess, E. W., and Locke, H. J. 1945. *The family.* American Book Co., Chicago.
301. Burgess, I. L. 1954. Homeless families in the Netherlands. *Case Conference*, 1, 20.
302. Burn, J. L. 1952. The problem of the child neglected in his own home. *Jl R. sanit. Inst.*, 72, 326.
303. Cargill, W. P. 1951. Problem families. *Nurs. Times*, 47, 412.
304. Cavenagh, W. E., Ratcliffe, T. A., Rankin, T. G., and Philp, A. F. 1958. *The problem family.* Four lectures. Inst. for the Study and Treatment of Delinquency, London.

305. CHOPE, H. B., and BLACKFORD, L. 1963. The chronic problem family. *Am. J. Orthopsychiat.*, **33**, 462.

306. COMMUNITY RESEARCH ASSOCIATES INC. 1953. *Classifications of disorganized families for use in family-orientated diagnosis and treatment.* Community Research Association Inc., New York.

307. COMPTON, B. 1961. *The story of the family centered project.* Family Centered Project, Greater St. Paul United Fund & Councils, Inc., St. Paul, Minn.

308. CONNECTICUT PUBLIC WELFARE COUNCIL. 1947. *Report by the Public Welfare Committee on the needs of neglected and delinquent children to the General Assembly.* Public Welfare Council, Conn.

309. COUNCIL OF SOCIAL SERVICE. 1960. *Forgotten men. A study of a common lodging house.* Council of Social Service, London.

310. ELKAN, I. 1956. Interviews with neglectful parents. *Br. J. psychiat. Soc. Wk*, **3**, No. 3.

311. FAMILY SERVICE UNITS. *An experiment in social rehabilitation.* Family Service Units, London.

312. FISHER, M. 1956. Helping 'problem families': The place of family planning. *Fam. Planning*, **5**, No. 1.

313. FISHER, M., and RODGER, D. 1956. Overburdened families. *Fam. Planning*, **5**, No. 1.

314. FORD, P., THOMAS, C. J., and ASHTON, E. T. 1955. *Problem families: Fourth report of the Southampton survey.* Basil Blackwell, Oxford.

315. FORDER, A. 1950. Problem families and their treatment. *J. ind. soc. Order Comm. of the Society of Friends*, **7**, No. 4.

316. GEISMAR, L. L. 1956. *Reflections on the problems of a central group in the family centered project.* Family Centered Project, Greater St. Paul United Fund & Councils, Inc., St. Paul, Minn.

317. GEISMAR, L. L. 1957. *Family centered project.* Family Centered Project, Greater St. Paul United Fund & Councils, Inc., St. Paul, Minn.

318. GEISMAR, L. L., and AYRES, B. 1956. *Report on study of closed cases.* Family Centered Project, Greater St. Paul United Fund & Councils, Inc., St. Paul, Minn.

319. GEISMAR, L. L., and AYRES, B. 1958. *Families in trouble.* Family Centered Project, Greater St. Paul United Fund & Councils Inc., St. Paul, Minn.

320. GEISMAR, L. L., and AYRES, B. 1959. A method of evaluating the social functioning of families under treatment. *Social Work*, **4**, 102.

321. GEISMAR, L. L., and AYRES, B. 1959. *Patterns of change in problem families.* Family Centered Project, Greater St. Paul United Fund & Councils, Inc., St. Paul, Minn.

322. GEISMAR, L. L., and AYRES, B. 1960. *Measuring family functioning. A manual on a method for evaluating the social functioning of disorganized families.* Family Centered Project, Greater St. Paul United Fund & Councils, Inc., Minn.

323. HEYWOOD, J. S. 1954. Homeless families. *Case Conference*, **1**, 19.

324. HILL, R. 1958. Social stress on the family: Generic features of families under stress. *Soc. Casewk*, **39**, No. 2-3.

325. HINCHCLIFFE, B. R. 1953. Review of 'problem families: Five enquiries'. *Br. J. Sociol.*, **4**, 98.

326. HOBMAN, D. L. 1953. Re-education for problem families in Holland. *Q. Rev.*, No. 595, 62.

327. HOEY, R. A. 1951. Social problem families. *Med. Offr*, **84**, 165.

328. HOFFMAN, W. 1960. *Community planning for services to the multi-problem*

families. Family Centered Project, Greater St. Paul United Fund & Councils, Inc., St. Paul, Minn.

329. HOWARTH, E. 1953. Definition and diagnosis of the social problem family. *Social Work*, **10**, 765.

330. HOWELLS, J. G. 1956. Ill-health and worry: The psychopathology of a problem family. *R. Soc. Promot. Hlth. J.*, **76**, 231.

331. HOWELLS, J. G. 1956. Psychopathology of a problem family. *Med. Wld, Lond.*, **85**, 243.

332. HOWELLS, J. G., and DAVIES, M. 1957. The intelligence of children in problem families. *Med. Offr*, **96**, 193.

333. HOWELLS, J. G. 1966. The psychopathogenesis of hard-core families. *Am. J. Psychiat.*, **122**, 1159. [Reprinted in this collection as No. XXI.]

334. HOWSE, H. J. 1958. Practical approach to problem families. *Med. Wld, Lond.*, **88**, 257.

335. HUBERT, W. H. DE B. 1937. *A social problem group?* Oxford Univ. Press, London.

336. IRVINE, E. E. 1954. Research into problem families. *Br. J. Psychiat. Soc. Wk*, **9**, 24.

337. JONES, D. G. 1945. The social problem group; Poverty and subnormality of intelligence. *Can. Bar Rev.*, March.

338. JONES, D. M. 1950. Family service units for problem families. *Eugen. Rev.*, **41**, 171.

339. JONES, D. M. 1956. Development of family service units. *Soc. Welf.*, **9**, 201.

340. JONES, D. M. 1956. An intensive casework service for problem families. *R. Soc. Promot. Hlth. J.*, **76**, 285.

341. JONES, K. 1956. Correspondence: Neglectful mothers. *Br. med. J.*, i, 397.

342. LIDBETTER, E. J. 1932. The social problem group. *Eugen. Rev.*, **24**, 7.

343. LIDBETTER, E. J. 1933. *Heredity and the social problem group*, Vol. 1. Edward Arnold, London.

344. 1965. Limiting problem parenthood. (Annotations.) *Lancet*, ii, 278.

345. LIPPMAN, H. S. 1954. Emotional factors in family breakdown. *Am. J. Orthopsychiat.*, **24**, 445.

346. MALMQUIST, C. P. 1965. Psychiatric perspectives of the socially disadvantaged child. *Comp. Psychiat.*, **6**, 176.

347. MANCHESTER AND SALFORD COUNCIL OF SOCIAL SERVICE. 1946. Problem families. Report of conference. *Soc. Welf.*, **6**, 221.

348. MARTIN, A. E. 1944. Child neglect. A problem of social administration. *Publ. Admin.*, **22**, 105.

349. MARTIN, A. E. 1944. *The care of neglected children.* Special report to the Leicestershire County Council.

350. MEYRICK, E. B. 1957. Problem families; Their discovery and rehabilitation. *R. Soc. Promot. Hlth J.*, **77**, 100.

351. MILLER, F. J. W., COURT, S. D. M., WALTON, W. S., and KNOX, E. G. 1960. *Growing up in Newcastle upon Tyne.* Oxford Univ. Press, London.

352. MORGAN, D. 1965. The acceptance by problem parents in Southampton of a domiciliary birth control service. *Med. Offr*, **113**, 221.

353. MOSHINSKY, P. 1939. Housing a-social families in Holland. *Eugen. Rev.*, **31**, 171.

354. McDONAGH, V. P., MYERS, F. H., WALKER, F. H., and HALLAS, W. A. 1955. Towards the eradication of the problem family: A symposium. *Jl R. sanit. Inst.*, **73**, 92.

355. OVERTON, A. 1953. Serving families who 'don't want help'. *Soc. Casewk*, **34**, No. 7.

356. OVERTON, A., TINKER, K. H., and ASSOCIATES. 1957. *Casework notebook.* Family Centered Project, Greater St. Paul United Fund & Councils, Inc., St. Paul, Minn.

357. PATERSON, M. T. 1960. An experiment in the rehabilitation of problem families. *Publ. Hlth,* **74**, 467.

358. PEBERDY, M. 1965. Fertility control for problem parents. *Med. Offr,* **113**, 219.

359. PEEL, J., and SCHENK, F. 1965. Domiciliary birth control; A new dimension in negative eugenics. *Eugen. Rev.,* **57**, 67.

360. PHILP, A. F. 1963. Family failure. *A study of 129 families with multiple problems.* Faber & Faber, London.

361. PHILP, A. F., and TIMMS, N. 1957. *The Problem of the problem family.* Family Service Units, London.

362. 1946. Problem families. *Lancet,* i, 928.

363. 1956. Problem families. *Br. med. J.,* i, 103.

364. 1963. Problem families. (Annotations.) *Lancet,* i, 370.

365. QUERIDO, A. 1946. Problem family in the Netherlands. *Med. Offr,* **75**, 193.

366. RANKIN, T. G. 1956. Problem families. *Case Conference,* **3**, 95.

367. RANKIN, T. G. 1958. *The problem family.* Inst. for the Study and Treatment of Delinquency, London.

368. RATCLIFFE, T. A. 1958. *The problem family.* Inst. for the Study and Treatment of Delinquency, London.

369. 1955. Rehabilitating the problem family. *Lancet,* ii, 878.

370. RICHARDSON, M. 1950. Correspondence. *Social Work,* **7**, 425.

371. ROBINSON, E. 1955. Potential problem families. *Woman Hlth Offr,* **28**, 76.

372. RODGER, D. 1965. *The aims, work and practice of family service units with special reference to the Sheffield unit. A guide for social workers.* Family Service Units, London.

373. SAVAGE, S. W. 1946. Intelligence and infant mortality in problem families. *Br. med. J.,* **1**, 86.

374. SAVAGE, S. W. 1946. Rehabilitation of problem families. *Med. Offr,* **75**, 252.

375. SAVAGE, S. W. 1946. Rehabilitation of problem families. *Jl R. sanit. Inst.,* **66**, 337.

376. SCOTT, J. A. 1958. Problem families—London survey. *Lancet,* i, 204.

377. 1966. Social salvage. (Leading article.) *Br. med. J.,* **1**, 121.

378. SELANDER, A. 1966. Hope for troubled families. *Canada's ment. Hlth,* **14**, 17.

379. SHAW, L. A. 1947. The problem of the problem family. *The Seekers,* November.

380. SHERIDAN, M. D. 1955. The training of neglectful and unsatisfactory mothers. *R. Soc. Promot. Hlth. J.,* **75**, 466.

381. SHERIDAN, M. D. 1955. The rehabilitation of unsatisfactory families in the Netherlands: I. The Zuidplein experiment at Rotterdam. *Publ. Hlth,* **69**, 62.

382. SHERIDAN, M. D. 1956. The rehabilitation of unsatisfactory families in the Netherlands: II. Re-education centres at Zuidplein. *Publ. Hlth,* **69**, 80.

383. SHERIDAN, M. D. 1956. The intelligence of 100 neglectful mothers. *Br. med. J.,* i, 91.

384. SHERIDAN, M. D. 1956. The Zuidplein experiment. *Med. Wld, Lond.,* **85**, 248.

385. SHERIDAN, M. D. 1959. Neglectful mothers. *Lancet,* i, 722.

386. SPENCE, J., WALTON, W. S., MILLER, F. J. W., and COURT, S. D. M. 1954. *A thousand families in Newcastle upon Tyne,* Chapter XXIV, p. 146. Oxford Univ. Press, London.

387. SPURGIN, C. 1952. Problem families in Holland. *Magistrate*, **9**, 251.
388. SPURGIN, C. 1954. Problem families in Holland. *Probation*, **7**, 37
389. SPURGIN, F. C. 1956. Correspondence: Neglectful mothers. *Br. med. J.*, i, 397.
390. STALLYBRASS, C. O. 1946. Problem families. *Med. Offr*, **75**, 89.
391. STALLYBRASS, C. O. 1947. Problem families. *Social Work*, **4**, 30.
392. STEPHENS, T. 1944. Sixty-two problem families. *Soc. Welf.*, **5**, 324.
393. STEPHENS, T. (ed.). 1945. *Problem families: An experiment in social rehabilitation.* Pacifist Service Units, London.
394. STEPHENS, T. 1947. *Problem families: An experiment in social rehabilitation.* Pacifist Service Units, London.
395. STEVENSON, A. C. 1950. Recent advances in social medicine. Chapter VI in *Problem families.* J. & A. Churchill, London.
396. TIMMS, N. 1953. Problem families in England. *Almoner*, **6**, 180.
397. TIMMS, N. 1954. The problem family: Some administrative considerations. *Publ. Admin.*, **32**, 236.
398. TIMMS, N. 1954. Problem family supporters. *Case Conference*, **1**, 28.
399. TIMMS, N. 1956. Social standards and the problem family. *Case Conference*, **2**, 2.
400. TINKER, K. H. 1957. *Let's look at our failures.* Family Centered Project, Greater St. Paul United Fund & Councils, Inc., St. Paul, Minn.
401. TINKER, K. H. 1959. *Patterns of family centered treatment: A descriptive study of 30 F C P closed cases.* Family Centered Project, Greater St. Paul United Fund & Councils, Inc., St. Paul, Minn.
402. TOMLINSON, C. G. 1946. *Families in trouble. An enquiry into problem families in Luton.* Gibbs, Bamford, Luton.
403. TONGE, W. L. 1955. The neuresthenic psychopath. *Br. med. J.*, i, 1066.
404. TOWNSEND, P. 1955. Measuring poverty. *Br. J. Sociol.*, **5**, 130.
405. VENNEMA, A. 1962. The hard-core family. *McGill med. J.*, **31**, 79.
406. VARIOUS AUTHORS. 1953. Symposium on towards eradication of problem family. *Jl R. sanit. Inst.*, **73**, 92.
407. WHALE, M. 1954. Problem families: The case for social casework. *Social Work*, **11**, 881.
408. WHARMBY, J. M. 1952. Housing the problem family. *Municipal J.*, **60**, 226.
409. WILLIAMS, H. G. M. 1955. Rehabilitation of problem families. *Am. J. Publ. Hlth*, **45**, 990.
410. WILLIAMS, H. G. M. 1956. Problem families in Southampton. *Eugen. Rev.*, **47**, 217.
411. WILSON, H. 1962. *Delinquency and child neglect.* Allen & Unwin, London.
412. WILSON, H. C. 1959. Problem families and the concept of immaturity. *Case Conference*, **6**, 115.
413. WILSON, H. C. 1958. Juvenile delinquency in problem families in Cardiff. *Br. J. Delinq.*, **9**, 94.
414. WILSON, J. G. 1950. Sixty-five studies in poverty, a way towards progress. *Municipal J.*, **58**, 1557.
415. WOFINDEN, R. C. 1944. Problem families. *Publ. Hlth*, **57**, 136.
416. WOFINDEN, R. C. 1946. Problem families. *Eugen. Rev.*, **38**, 127.
417. WOFINDEN, R. C. 1947. Homeless children: A survey of children in scattered homes, Rotherham. *Med. Offr.*, **77**, 185.
418. WOFINDEN, R. C. 1950. *Problem families in Bristol.* Eugenics Society, and Cassell, London.
419. WOFINDEN, R. C. 1951. *Problem families in Bristol. Occasional papers on eugenics.* Cassell, London.
420. WOFINDEN, R. C. 1955. Unsatisfactory families. *Housing*, **17**, 67.

421. WOFINDEN, R. C. 1955. Unsatisfactory families. *Med. Offr*, **94**, 384.
422. WOFINDEN, R. C. 1961. The changing pattern of medico-social service in the home in Bristol. *Publ. Hlth*, **75**, 304.
423. WOMEN'S GROUP ON PUBLIC WELFARE. 1948. *The neglected child and his family*. Oxford Univ. Press, London.
424. WRIGHT, C. H. 1955. Problem families. *Med. Offr*, **94**, 381.
425. WRIGHT, C. H. 1955. Annual Report on the Health of the City of Sheffield.

7. *The Dimension of Family-Community Interaction*

426. KLUCKHOHN, C., and MURRAY, H. A. 1949. *Personality in nature, society and culture*. Knopf, New York.
427. KARDINER, A., and LINTON, R. 1939. *The individual and his society*. Columbia Univ. Press, New York.
428. FRANK, L. K. 1948. *Personality and culture: The psychocultural approach*. Hinds & Eldridge, New York.
429. PARSONS, T. 1951. *The social system*. Free Press, Glencoe, Ill.
430. LEVY, M. J. 1952. *The structure of society*. Princeton Univ. Press, Princeton.
431. EVANS-PRICHARD, E. E. 1951. *Social anthropology*. Cohen & West, London.
432. RADCLIFFE-BROWN, A. R. 1922. *The Andaman Islanders*. Cambridge Univ. Press, Cambridge.
433. MALINOWSKI, B. 1922. *Argonauts of the Western Pacific. Studies in economic and political science*. Routledge, London.
434. SPIEGEL, J. P. 1957. The resolution of role conflict within the family. *Psychiatry*, **20**, 1.
435. WATERS, E., and CRANDALL, V. J. 1964. Social class and observed maternal behaviour from 1940 to 1960. *Child Dev.*, **35**, 1021.
436. KLUCKHOHN, C. 1951. Values and value orientations. In PARSONS, T., and SHILS, E. A. (eds.) *Toward a general theory of action*. Harvard Univ. Press, Cambridge, Mass.
437. 1954. *Integration and conflict in family behavior*. Report No. 27, Group for the Advancement of Psychiatry, New York.
438. HARRIS, R. 1961. The selection of leaders in Ballybeg, Northern Ireland. *Soc. Rev.*, **9**, 137.
439. LEWIN, K. 1950. *Field theory in social science*. Tavistock Publications, London.
440. LEWIN, K. 1948. *Resolving social conflicts*. Harper, New York.
441. ROSS, A. O., and BRUNER, E. M. 1963. Family interaction at two levels of acculturation in Sumatra. *Am. J. Orthopsychiat.*, **33**, 51.
442. GEERTZ, H. 1959. The vocabulary of emotion. *Psychiatry*, **22**, 225.
443. LANCASTER, L. 1961. Some conceptual problems in the study of family and kin ties in the British Isles. *Br. J. Sociol.*, **12**, 317.
444. RADCLIFFE-BROWN, A. R. 1960. Introduction to the analysis of kinship systems. Chapter 18 in BELL, N. W., and VOGEL, E. F. (eds.) *The family*. Free Press, Glencoe, Ill.
445. ALBRECHT, R. 1953. Relationships of older people with their own parents. *Marriage Fam. Living*, November, 296.
446. MACCOBY, E. E. 1960. Effects upon children of their mother's outside employment. Chapter 41 in BELL, N. W., and VOGEL, E. F. (eds.) *The family*. Free Press, Glencoe, Ill.
447. WILSON, B. R. 1962. The teacher's role—A sociological analysis. *Br. J. Sociol.*, **13**, 15.

448. CASTLE, M. 1954. Institution and non-institution children at school. *Hum. Relat.*, **7**, 349.

449. GOLAN, S. 1959. Collective education in the kibbutz. *Psychiatry*, **22**, 167.

450. McCLEARY, R. D. 1964. The role of the school in a new blighted area. *Int. J. soc. Psychiat.*, Special Ed. No. 2, 28.

451. OJEMANN, R. H., LEVITT, E. E., LYLE, W. H., Jr., and WHITESIDE, M. G. 1955. The effects of a 'casual' teacher-training program and certain curricular changes on grade school children. *J. Exp. Educ.*, **24**, 95.

452. MUUSS, R. E. 1960. The relationship between 'causal' orientation, anxiety, and insecurity in elementary school children. *J. educ. Psychol.*, **51**, 122.

453. SNIDER, B. C. F. 1957. Relation of growth in causal orientation to insecurity in elementary school children. *Psychol. Rep.*, **3**, 631.

III. CLINICAL PRACTICE

2. *Organisation*

454. TITCHENER, J. L., and GOLDEN, M. 1963. Prediction of therapeutic themes from observation of family interaction evoked by the 'revealed differences' technique. *J. nerv. ment. Dis.*, **136**, 464.

455. ELBERT, S., ROSMAN, B., MINUCHIN, S., and GUERNEY, B. 1964. A method for the clinical study of family interaction. *Am. J. Orthopsychiat.*, **34**, 885.

456. JACKSON, D. D., RISKIN, J., and SATIR, V. 1961. A method of analysis of a family interview. *Archs gen. Psychiat.*, **5**, 321.

457. RISKIN, J. 1964. Family interaction scales. *Archs gen. Psychiat.*, **11**, 484.

458. WATZLAWICK, P. 1964. *An anthology of human communication.* Text and tape. Science and Behavior Books, Palo Alto, Calif.

3. *The Presenting Patient*

459. HOWELLS, J. G. 1962. Family psychiatry and the family doctor. *Practitioner*, **188**, 370.

460. BURGUM, M. 1942. The father gets worse: A child guidance problem. *Am. J. Orthopsychiat.*, **22**, 474.

461. LINDEMANN, E. 1950. Modification in the cause of ulcerative colitis in relationship to changes in life situations and reaction patterns. In *Life stress and bodily disease.* P.R.N.M.D., **29**, 706.

462. MITTLEMAN, B. 1956. Analysis of reciprocal neurotic patterns in family relationships. In EISENSTEIN, V. W. (ed.) *Neurotic interaction in marriage.* Basic Books, New York.

463. ROSEN, V. H. 1956. Changes in family equilibrium through psychoanalytic treatment. In EINSTEIN, V. W. (ed.) *Neurotic interaction in marriage*, Basic Books, New York.

464. CHANCE, E. 1955. Measuring the potential interplay of forces within the family during treatment. *Child Dev.*, **26**, 241.

465. ADLER, A. (LINTON and VAUGHAN, trans.). 1945. *Social interest. A challenge to mankind.* Faber & Faber, London.

466. BOSSARD, J. H. S., and BOLL, E. S. 1955. Personality roles in a large family. *Child Dev.*, **26**, 71.

467. SEWALL, M. 1930. Two studies in sibling rivalry. I. Some causes of jealousy in young children. *Smith Coll. Stud. soc. Work*, **1**, 6.

468. WILE, I. S., and JONES, A. B. 1937. Ordinal position and the behaviour disorders of young children. *J. genet. Psychol.*, **51**, 61.

469. NORTON, A. 1952. Incidence of neurosis related to maternal age and birth order. *Br. J. soc. Med.*, **6**, 253.

470. FISHER, W., and HAYES, S. P. 1941. Maladjustment in college, predicted by Bernreuter inventory scores and family position. *J. appl. Psychol.*, **25**, 86.

471. ROSENOW, C., and WHYTE, A. H. 1931. The ordinal position of problem children. *Am. J. Orthopsychiat.*, **1**, 430.

472. MOWRER, H. R. 1941. Alcoholism and the family. *J. Crim. Psychopath.* **3**, 90.

473. KINGSLEY, A., and REYNOLDS, E. L. 1949. The relation of illness patterns in children to ordinal position in the family. *J. Pediat.*, **35**, 17.

474. KOCH, H. L. 1956. Attitudes of young children toward their peers as related to certain characteristics of their siblings. *Psychol. Monogr.*, **70**, No. 19.

475. FOWLER, H. B. Personal communication.

476. HILGARD, J. R. 1953. Anniversary reactions in parents precipitated by children. *Psychiatry*, **16**, 73.

477. BERLINER, B. 1938. The psychogenesis of a fatal organic disease. *Psychoanal. Q.*, **7**, 368.

478. BRESLER, B. 1956. Ulcerative colitis as an anniversary symptom. *Psychoanal. Rev.*, **43**, 381.

479. SCOTT, W. C. M. 1955. A psychoanalytic concept of the origin of depression. In KLEIN, HILMAN, and MONEY-KYRLE (eds.) *New directions in psycho-analysis*. Basic Books, New York.

480. STENGEL, E., and COOK, N. G. 1958. *Attempted suicide*. Maudsley Monographs No. 4. Chapman & Hall, London.

481. FRAZER, J. G. 1927. *The golden bough*, abridged ed. Macmillan, New York.

482. EISSLER, R. S. 1949. Scapegoats of society. In EISSLER, K. R. (ed.) *Search-lights on delinquents*. International Univ. Press, New York.

483. VOGEL, E. F., and BELL, N. W. 1960. The emotionally disturbed child as a family scapegoat. In BELL, N. W., and VOGEL, E. F. (eds.) *The family*. Free Press, Glencoe, Ill.

484. RUSSELL, A., and SAMBHI, M. 1962. Intrafamilial aggressive patterns. *Can. med. Ass. J.*, **86**, 977.

485. GREENBERG, H. P., HUNTER, R. A., and MACALPINE, I. 1956. Sir Kenelm Digby on '*Folie à deux*'. *Br. J. med. Psychol.*, **29**, 294.

486. LASEGUE, C., and FALRET, J. 1877. *La folie à deux (ou 'folie communiquée')*. *Annls méd.-psychol.*, **18**, 321.

487. MICHAUD, R. 1964. *La folie à deux. Am. J. Psychiat.*, **121**.

488. GRALNICK, A. 1942. *Folie à deux* : A review of one hundred and three cases and the entire English literature. Part I. *Psychiat. Q.*, **16**, 230. Part II. Ibid., **16**, 491.

489. RIOUX, B. 1963. A review of *folie à deux. Psychiat. Q.*, **37**, 405.

4. *Clinical Syndromes*

Emotional Illness

490. FISHER, S., and MENDELL, D. 1956. The communication of neurotic patterns over two or three generations. *Psychiatry*, **19**, 41.

491. HENRY, J. 1951. Family structure and the transmission of neurotic behavior. *Am. J. Psychiat.*, **21**, 800.

492. HILGARD, J. 1951. Sibling rivalry and social heredity. *Psychiatry*, **14**, 375.

493. WEBLIN, J. E. 1963. Psychogenesis in asthma. *Br. J. med. Psychol.*, **36**, 211.

494. BREESE, B. B., and DISNEY, F. A. 1956. The spread of streptococcal infections in family groups. *Pediatrics*, **17**, 834.

495. JORDAN, T. E. 1965. The family aspects of physical disability in children. *Child Fam.*, **4**, 78.

496. KEMPE, C. H., WISHIK, S. M., HAGGERTY, R. J., SHAW, E., SHANK, R. E., WHEELER, W., MILLER, R. and CHILDS B. 1965. Family epidemiology. *Pediatrics*, **35**, 856.

497. GIBNEY, H. H. (ed.). 1964. *The family and the doctor.* Proceedings of Harvard Symposium Massachusetts.

498. MEYER, R. J. 1963. *A report of a family care program in medical school.* Presented at the Third Institute on Co-ordinated Home Care.

499. HAYNES, M. A. 1960. An approach to the teaching of family care. *J. Am. med. Ass.*, **173**, 1340.

500. WHITE, K. L. 1963. Family medicine, academic medicine and the university's responsibility. *J. Am. med. Ass.*, **185**, 192.

501. INGHAM, H. V. 1949. A statistical study of family relationships in psychoneurosis. *Am. J. Psychiat.*, **106**, 91.

502. EPSTEIN, N. B. 1961. Treatment of the emotionally disturbed pre-school child: A family approach. *Can. med. Ass. J.*, **85**, 937.

503. EPSTEIN, N. B. 1962. New developments in child and family treatment. *Canada's ment. Hlth*, October Supplement No. 31.

504. REIDY, J. J. 1961. *Family participation in psychiatric treatment of children. Mental health and social welfare.* Columbia Univ. Press, New York.

505. REIDY, J. J. 1960. The emotionally disturbed child; problems within the family. *Sth. med. J.*, **53**, 1127.

506. SOBEL, R., and KOFF, C. 1962. Emotional disturbance is a family affair. *Child Fam.*, **1**, 59.

507. DRECHSLER, R. J., and SHAPIRO, M. I. 1961. A procedure for direct observation of family interaction in a child guidance clinic. *Psychiatry*, **24**, 163.

508. TYLER, E. A., and HENSHAW, P. 1962. Family group intake by a child guidance clinic team. *Archs gen. Psychiat.*, **6**, 214.

509. CHARNY, E. W. 1962. Family interviews in redefining a 'sick' child's role in the family problem. *Psychol. Rep.*, **10**, 577.

510. STARR, P. H. 1957. Comprehensive clinic practices in the child guidance unit. *Ment. Hyg.*, **41**, 44.

511. LANGSLEY, D. G. 1961. Psychology of a doomed family. *Am. J. Psychother.*, **15**, 531.

512. MALMQUIST, C. P. 1965. School phobia—A problem in family neurosis. *J. Am. Acad. child Psychiat.*, **4**, 293.

Psychosis

513. PEMBERTON, J. 1949. Illness in general practice. *Br. med. J.*, **1**, 306.

514. COUNCIL OF THE COLLEGE OF GENERAL PRACTITIONERS. 1958. Working party report. *Br. med. J.*, ii, 585.

515. KESSELL, W. I. N. 1960. Psychiatric morbidity in a London general practice. *Br. J. prev. soc. Med.*, **14**, 16.

516. BOWEN, M. 1960. *A family concept of schizophrenia. The etiology of schizophrenia.* Basic Books, New York.

517. BOWEN, M. 1957. *Family participation in schizophrenia.* Paper presented at Annual Meeting, Am. Psychiat. Ass., Chicago, May, 1957.

518. BOWEN, M. 1959. Family relationships in schizophrenia. In AUERBACK (ed.) *Schizophrenia—An integrated approach.* Ronald Press, New York.

519. BOWEN, M. DYSINGER, R. H., and BASAMANIA, B. 1958. *The role of the father in families with a schizophrenic patient.* Paper presented at 114th Annual Meeting of Am. Psychiat. Ass., San Francisco.

520. Bowen, M., Dysinger, R. H., Brodey, W. M., and Basamania, B. 1957. *Study and treatment of five hospitalized family groups each with a psychotic member.* Paper presented at Annual Meeting of Am. Orthopsychiat. Ass., Chicago.

521. Dysinger, R. H., and Bowen, M. 1959. Problems for medical practice presented by families with a schizophrenic member. *Am. J. Psychiat.,* **116**, 514.

522. Dysinger, R. H. 1961. The family as the unit of study and treatment. *Am. J. Orthopsychiat.,* **31**, 61.

523. Dysinger, R. H. *A study of relationship changes before onset of abruptly beginning schizophrenic psychosis.* Unpublished material.

524. Brodey, W. M. 1959. Some family operations and schizophrenia. *Archs gen. Psychiat.,* **1**, 379.

525. Brodey, W. M., and Hayden, M. 1957. Intrateam reactions: Their relation to the conflicts of the family in treatment. *Am. J. Orthopsychiat.,* **27**, 349.

526. Wynne, L. C., Ryckoff, I. M., Day, J., and Hirsch, S. I. 1958. Pseudo-mutuality in the family relations of schizophrenics. *Psychiatry,* **21**, 205.

527. Ryckoff, I., Day, J., and Wynne, L. C. 1959. Maintenance of stereotyped roles in the families of schizophrenics. *Archs gen. Psychiat.,* **1**, 93.

528. Wynne, L. C., and Singer, M. T. 1963. Thought disorder and family relations of schizophrenics. I. A research strategy. *Archs gen. Psychiat.,* **9**, 191. [Reprinted in this collection as No. XLIII.]

529. Wynne, L. C., and Singer, M. T. 1963. Thought disorder and family relations of schizophrenics. II. A classification of forms of thinking. *Archs gen. Psychiat.,* **9**, 199.

530. Singer, M. T., and Wynne, L. C. 1965. Thought disorder and family relations of schizophrenics. III. Methodology using projective techniques. *Archs gen. Psychiat.,* **12**, 187.

531. Singer, M. T., and Wynne, L. C. 1965. Thought disorder and family relations of schizophrenics. IV. Results and implications. *Archs gen. Psychiat.,* **12**, 201.

532. Singer, M. T., and Wynne, L. C. 1963. Differentiating characteristics of parents of childhood schizophrenics, childhood neurotics and young adult schizophrenics. *Am. J. Psychiat.,* **120**, 234.

533. Morris, G. O., and Wynne, L. C. 1965. Schizophrenic offspring and styles of parental communication. *Psychiatry,* **28**, 19.

534. Lidz, R. W., and Lidz, T. 1949. The family environment of schizophrenic patients. *Am. J. Psychiat.,* **106**, 332.

535. Lidz, R. W., and Lidz, T. 1952. Therapeutic considerations arising from the intense symbiotic needs of schizophrenic patients. In Brody, E. B., and Redlich, F. C. (eds.) *Psychotherapy with schizophrenics.* International Univ. Press, New York.

536. Lidz, T. 1958. Schizophrenia and the family. *Psychiatry,* **21**, 21.

537. Cornelison, A. 1960. Casework interviewing as a research technique in a study of families of schizophrenic patients. *Ment. Hyg.,* **44**, 551.

538. Lidz, T., Cornelison, A., Fleck, S., and Terry, D. 1957. The intra-familial environment of the schizophrenic patient: I. The father. *Psychiatry,* **20**, 329.

539. Fleck, S., Cornelison, A., Norton, N., and Lidz, T. 1957. The intra-familial environment of the schizophrenic patient: III. Interaction between hospital staff and families. *Psychiatry,* **20**, 343.

540. Lidz, T., Cornelison, A., Fleck, S., and Terry, D. 1958. The intra-familial environment of schizophrenic patients: II. Marital schism and marital skew. *Am. J. Psychiat.,* **114**, 241.

541. LIDZ, T., FLECK, S., CORNELISON, A., and TERRY, D. 1958. The intra-familial environment of the schizophrenic patient: IV. Parental person-alities and family interaction. *Am. J. Orthopsychiat.*, **28**, 764.

542. FLECK, S., FREEDMAN, D. X., CORNELISON, A., LIDZ, T., and TERRY, D. 1966. The understanding of symptomatology through the study of family interaction. Chapter IX in *Schizophrenia and the family*. International Univ. Press, New York.

543. LIDZ, T., CORNELISON, A., TERRY, D., and FLECK, S. 1958. Intrafamilial environment of the schizophrenic patient. VI. The transmission of ir-rationality. *Archs Neurol. Psychiat.*, **79**, 305.

544. SOHLER, D. T., HOLZBERG, J., FLECK, S., CORNELISON, A., KAY, E., and LIDZ, T. 1957. The prediction of family interaction from a battery of projective tests. *J. proj. Techniques*, **21**, 199.

545. LIDZ, T., SCHAFER, S., FLECK, S., CORNELISON, A., and TERRY, D. 1962. Ego differentiation and schizophrenic symptom formation in identical twins. *J. Am. psychoanal. Ass.*, **10**, 74.

546. FLECK, S., LIDZ, T., CORNELISON, A., SCHAFER, S., and TERRY, D. 1959. The intrafamilial environment of the schizophrenic patient: Incestuous and homosexual problems. In MASSERMAN, J. (ed.) *Individual and familial dynamics*. Grune & Stratton, New York.

547. LIDZ, T., FLECK, S., ALANEN, Y., and CORNELISON, A. 1963. Schizophrenic patients and their siblings. *Psychiatry*, **26**, 1. [Reprinted in this collection as No. XLII.]

548. FLECK. S., LIDZ T. and CORNELISON, A. 1963. Comparison of parent-child relationships of male and female schizophrenic patients. *Archs gen. Psychiat.* **8**, 1.

549. FLECK, S. 1962. Psychiatric hospitalization as a family experience. *Spec. Treat. Situations*, **1**, 29.

550. LIDZ, T., CORNELISON, A., SINGER, M. T., SCHAFER, S., and FLECK, S. 1966. The mothers of schizophrenic patients. In *Schizophrenia and the family*. International Univ. Press, New York.

551. LIDZ, T., CORNELISON, A., and FLECK, S. 1966. The limitation of extra-. familial socialization. In *Schizophrenia and the family*. International Univ. Press, New York.

552. LIDZ, T. 1962. The relevance of family studies to psychoanalytic theory. *J. nerv. ment. Dis.*, **135**, 105.

553. LIDZ, T., and FLECK, S. 1965. *Family studies and a theory of schizophrenia. The American family in crisis*. Forest Hosp. Publications, Des Plaines, Ill.

554. LIDZ, T., WILD, C., SCHAFER, S., ROSMAN, B., and FLECK, S. 1963. Thought disorders in the parents of schizophrenic patients: A study utilizing the object sorting test. *J. Psychiat. Res.*, **1**, 193.

555. ROSMAN, B., WILD, C., RICCI, J., FLECK, S., and LIDZ, T. 1964. Thought disorders in the parents of schizophrenic patients: A further study utilizing the object sorting test. *J. psychiat. Res.*, **2**, 211.

556. LIDZ, T., and FLECK, S. 1960. Schizophrenia, human integration and the role of the family. In JACKSON, D. (ed.) *Etiology of schizophrenia*. Basic Books, New York.

557. LIDZ, T., FLECK, S., and CORNELISON, A. R. 1966. *Schizophrenia and the family*. International Univ. Press, New York.

558. FLECK, S. Family dynamics and origin of schizophrenia. 1960. *Psychosom. Med.*, **22**, 333.

559. LIDZ, T. 1964. *The family and human adaptation*. Hogarth, London.

560. SPIEGEL, J. P., and BELL, N. W. 1959. The family of the psychiatric patient.

In ARIETI, S. (ed.) *The handbook of American psychiatry.* Basic Books, New York.

561. SPIEGEL, J. P. 1964. Conflicting formal and informal roles in newly acculturated families. In RIOCH, D. M. (ed.) *Disorders of communication,* Vol. XLII. Ass. for Res. in Nervous & Mental Disease, New York.

562. ACKERMAN, N. W. 1958. *The psychodynamics of family life.* Basic Books, New York.

563. BATESON, G. 1955. A theory of play and fantasy. *Psychiat. Res. Rep.,* 2 39-51.

564. BATESON, G. 1956. The message 'This is play'. In *Second Conference on Group Processes.* Josiah Macy Jr. Fnd., New York.

565. BATESON, G., JACKSON, D. D., HALEY, J., and WEAKLAND, J. H. 1956. Toward a theory of schizophrenia. *Behavl Sci.,* 1, 251-264.

566. BATESON, G. 1958. Language and psychotherapy, Frieda Fromm-Reichmann's last project. *Psychiatry,* 21, 96-100.

567. BATESON, G. 1958. *Naven,* 2nd ed. with new chapter. Stanford Univ. Press, Stanford, Calif.

568. BATESON, G. 1958. Schizophrenic distortion of communication. In WHITAKER, C. (ed.) *Psychotherapy of chronic schizophrenic patients.* Little, Brown & Co., Boston.

569. BATESON, G. 1958. Analysis of group therapy in an admission ward. In WILMER, H. A. (ed.) *Social psychiatry in action.* Thomas, Springfield, Ill.

570. BATESON, G. 1959. Anthropological theories. *Science,* 129, 334-349.

571. BATESON, G. 1959. Panel review. In MASSERMAN, J. H. (ed.) *Individual and familial dynamics.* Grune & Stratton, New York.

572. BATESON, G. 1959. Cultural problems posed by a study of schizophrenic process. In AUERBACK, A. (ed.) *Schizophrenia, an integrated approach.* A. P. A. Symposium 1958. Ronald Press, New York.

573. BATESON, G. 1958. *The new conceptual frames for behavioral research.* Proceedings of the Sixth Annual Psychiatric Institute, Princeton.

574. BATESON, G. 1960. Minimal requirements for a theory of schizophrenia. *Archs gen. Psychiat.,* 2, 477-491.

575. BATESON, G. 1960. The group dynamics of schizophrenia. In APPLEBY, L., SCHER, J. M., and CUMMING, J. (eds.) *Chronic schizophrenia : Explorations in theory and treatment.* Free Press, Glencoe, Ill.

576. BATESON, G. 1960. Discussion of Families of schizophrenic and of well children; method, concepts and some results, by Samuel J. Beck. *Am. J. Psychiat.,* 30, 263-266.

577. BATESON, G. 1961. The biosocial integration of behavior in the schizophrenic family, and The challenge of research in family Diagnosis and Therapy. Summary of panel discussion: I. Formal research in family structure. In ACKERMAN, N. W., BEATMAN, F. L., and SANFORD, S. (eds.) *Exploring the base for family therapy.* Family Service Assoc., New York.

578. BATESON, G. (ed.). 1961. *Perceval's narrative, a patient's account of his psychosis,* 1830-1832. Stanford Univ. Press, Stanford, Calif.

579. BATESON, G. Structure and the genesis of relationship, Frieda Fromm-Reichmann Memorial Lecture. *Psychiatry.* (In press.)

580. BATESON, G. 1962. Exchange of information about patterns of human behavior. *Symposium on information storage and neural control.* Houston, Texas. (In press.)

581. BATESON, G. 1962. Communication theories in relation to the etiology of the neuroses. *Symposium on the etiology of the neuroses.* Society of Medical Psychoanalysis, New York. (In press.)

582. BATESON, G. 1962. Problems of credibility and congruence in applying

computational methods to problems of peace, delivered at the Spring Joint Computer Conference, American Federation of Information Processing Societies, San Francisco.

583. BATESON, G. The prisoner's dilemma and the schizophrenic family. (To be published.)

584. BATESON, G., JACKSON, D. D., HALEY, J., and WEAKLAND, J. H. 1963. A note on the double blind—1962. *Family Process*, **2**, 154.

585. ERICKSON, M. H., HALEY, J., and WEAKLAND, J. H. 1959. A transcript of a trance induction with commentary. *Am. J. clin. Hyp.*, **2**, 49-84.

586. FRY, W. F. 1958. The use of ataractic agents. *Calif. Med.*, **98**, 309-313.

587. FRY, W. F. 1959. Destructive behavior on hospital wards. *Psychiat. Q.*, Supplement No. 33, Part 2, 197-231.

588. FRY, W. F., and HEERSEMA, P. 1963. Conjoint family therapy: A new dimension in psychotherapy. In *Topic. Prob. Psychother.*, Vol. 4, pp. 147-153. Karger, Basel and New York.

589. FRY, W. F. 1962. The schizophrenogenic who? *Psychoan. psychoan. Rev.*, **49**, 68-73.

590. FRY, W. F. 1962. The marital context of an anxiety syndrome. *Family Process*, **1**, 245-252.

591. FRY, W. F. *Sweet madness: A study of humor.* Pacific Books, Palo Alto, Calif. (In press.)

592. HALEY, J. 1955. Paradoxes in play, fantasy, and psychotherapy. *Psychiat. Res. Rep.*, **2**, 52-58.

593. HALEY, J. 1958. The art of psychoanalysis. *Psychiat. Res. Rep.*, **15**, 190-200.

594. HALEY, J. 1958. An interactional explanation of hypnosis. *Am. J. clin. Hyp.*, **1**, 41-57.

595. HALEY, J. 1959. Control in psychoanalytic psychotherapy. *Progress in Psychotherapy*, Vol. 4, pp. 48-65. Grune & Stratton, New York.

596. HALEY, J. 1959. An interactional description of schizophrenia. *Psychiatry*, **22**, 321-332.

597. HALEY, J. 1959. The family of the schizophrenic: A model system. *Am. J. nerv. ment. Dis.*, **129**, 357-374.

598. HALEY, J. 1960. Observation of the family of the schizophrenic. *Am. J. Orthopsychiat.*, **30**, 460-467.

599. HALEY, J. 1960. Control of fear with hypnosis. *Am. J. clin. Hyp.*, **2**, 109-115.

600. HALEY, J. 1961. Control in brief psychotherapy. *Archs gen. Psychiat.*, **4**, 139-153.

601. HALEY, J. 1961. Control in the psychotherapy of schizophrenics. *Archs gen. Psychiat.*, **5**, 340-353.

602. HALEY, J. 1962. Whither family therapy? *Family Process*, **1**, 69-100.

603. HALEY, J. 1962. Family experiments: A new type of experimentation. *Family Process*, **1**, 265-293.

604. HALEY, J. Marriage therapy. *Archs gen. Psychiat.* (In press).

605. HALEY, J. *Strategies of psychotherapy.* Grune & Stratton, New York. (In press.)

606. JACKSON, D. D. 1956. Countertransference and psychotherapy. In FROMM-REICHMAN, F. and MORENO, J. L. (eds.) *Progress in psychotherapy* Vol. 1 pp. 234-238. Grune & Stratton, New York.

607. JACKSON. D. D. 1957. A note on the importance of trauma in the genesis of schizophrenia. *Psychiatry*, **20**, 181-184.

608. JACKSON, D. D. 1957. The psychiatrist in the medical clinic. *Bull. Am. Ass. med. Clinics*, **6**, 94-98.

609. JACKSON, D. D. 1957. The question of family homeostasis. *Psychiat. Q.*, Supplement No. 31, Part 1, 79-90.

610. JACKSON, D. D. 1957. Theories of suicide. In SCHNEIDMAN, E., and FARBEROW, N. (eds.) *Clues to suicide.* McGraw-Hill, New York.

611. JACKSON, D. D. 1958. The family and sexuality. In WHITAKER, C. (ed.) *The psychotherapy of chronic schizophrenic patients.* Little, Brown & Co., Boston.

612. JACKSON, D. D. 1958. Guilt and the control of pleasure in schizoid personalities. *Br. J. med. Psychol.,* **31**, 124-130.

613. JACKSON, D. D., BLOCK, J., BLOCK, J., and PATTERSON, V. 1958. Psychiatrists' conceptions of the schizophrenogenic parent. *Archs Neurol. Psychiat.,* **79**, 448-459.

614. JACKSON, D. D. 1959. Family interaction, family homeostasis and some implications for conjoint family psychotherapy. In MASSERMAN, J. (ed.) *Individual and familial dynamics.* Grune & Stratton, New York.

615. JACKSON, D. D. 1959. The managing of acting out in a borderline personality. In BURTON, A. (ed.) *Case studies in counseling and psychotherapy.* Prentice-Hall, New York.

616. JACKSON, D. D., and WEAKLAND, J. H. 1959. Schizophrenic symptoms and family interaction. *Archs gen. Psychiat.,* **1**, 618-621.

617. JACKSON, D. D. (ed.) 1960. *The etiology of schizophrenia.* Basic Books, New York.

618. JACKSON, D. D. 1961. The monad, the dyad, and the family therapy of schizophrenics. In BURTON, A. (ed.) *Psychotherapy of the psychoses.* Basic Books, New York.

619. JACKSON, D. D., SATIR, V., and RISKIN, J. 1961. A method of analysis of a family interview. *Archs gen. Psychiat.,* **5**, 321-339.

620. JACKSON, D. D., and SATIR, V. 1961. Family diagnosis and family therapy. In ACKERMAN, N., BEATMAN, F., and SHERMAN, S. (eds.) *Exploring the base for family therapy.* Family Service Ass. of America, New York.

621. JACKSON, D. D., and WEAKLAND, J. H. 1961. Conjoint family therapy, some considerations on theory, technique, and results. *Psychiatry,* **24**, 30-45.

622. JACKSON, D. D. 1962. Action for mental illness—What kind? *Stanford med. Bull.,* **20**, 77-80.

623. JACKSON, D. D. 1962. 'Interactional psychotherapy' and 'Family therapy in the family of the schizophrenic'. In STEIN, M. I. (ed.) *Contemporary psychotherapies.* Free Press, Glencoe, Ill.

624. JACKSON, D. D. 1962. Psychoanalytic education in the communication processes. In MASSERMAN, J. (ed.) *Science and psychoanalysis.* Grune & Stratton, New York.

625. JACKSON, D. D., and HALEY, J. Transference revisited. (To be published.)

626. JACKSON, D. D., and WATZLAWICK, P. The acute psychosis as a manifestation of growth experience. *A.P.A. Res. Rep.* (In press.)

627. WEAKLAND, J. H., and JACKSON, D. D. 1958. Patient and therapist observations on the circumstances of a schizophrenic episode. *Archs Neurol. Psychiat.,* **79**, 554-574.

628. WEAKLAND, J. H. 1960. The double-bind hypothesis of schizophrenia and three-party interaction. In JACKSON, D. D. (ed.) *The etiology of schizophrenia.* Basic Books, New York.

629. WEAKLAND, J. H. 1961. The essence of anthropological education. *Am. Anthrop.,* **63**, 1094-1097.

630. WEAKLAND, J. H. 1961. Review of E. H. Schein, I. Schnier and C. H. Barker, *Coercive Persuasion,* Norton, New York, 1961. *J. Asian Studies,* **21**, 84-86.

631. WEAKLAND, J. H. 1962. Family therapy as a research arena. *Family Process,* **1**, 63-68.

632. WEAKLAND, J. H., and FRY, W. F. 1962. Letters of mothers of schizophrenics. *Am. J. Orthopsychiat.*, **32**, 604-623.

633. ALANEN, Y. 1960. Some thoughts on schizophrenia and ego development
in the light of family investigations. *Archs gen. Psychiat.*, **3**, 650.

634. BOSZORMENYI-NAGY, I. 1962. The concept of schizophrenia from the
perspective of family treatment. *Family Process*, **1**, 103.

635. SCOTT, R. D., and ASHWORTH, P. L. 1965. The 'axis value' and the transfer
of psychosis. *Br. J. med. Psychol.*, **38**, 97.

636. DAVIS, D. R. 1961. The family triangle in schizophrenia. *Br. J. med.
Psychol.*, **34**, 53.

637. DAVIS, D. R. 1964. Family processes in mental illness. *Lancet*, i, 731.

638. LAING, R. D. 1961. *The divided self.* Tavistock Publications, London;
Quadrangle Press, Chicago.

639. LAING, R. D. 1962. *The self and other.* Tavistock Publications, London;
Quadrangle Press, Chicago.

640. LAING, R. D. 1962. Series and nexus in the family. *New Left Rev.*, **15**,
May-June.

641. LAING, R. D., and COOPER, R. D. 1964. *Reason and violence. A decade of
Sartre's philosophy*—1950-1960. Tavistock Publications, London; Humanities Press, New York.

642. LAING, R. D., and ESTERSON, A. 1964. *Sanity, madness and the family.*
Vol. 1. *Families of schizophrenics.* Tavistock Publications, London; Basic
Books, New York.

643. LAING, R. D. 1965. Mystification, confusion and conflict. In BOSZORMENYI-
NAGY, I., and FRAMO, J. L. (eds.) *Intensive family therapy.* Harper and
Row, New York.

644. LAING, R. D., PHILLIPSON, H., and LEE, A. R. 1966. *Interpersonal perception.*
Tavistock Publications, London.

645. ESTERSON, A., COOPER, D. G., and LAING, R. D. 1965. Results of family-
orientated therapy with hospitalized schizophrenics. *Br. med. J.*, ii, 1462.

646. CARSTAIRS, G. M. 1966. Family-orientated therapy with hospitalized
schizophrenics. Correspondence. *Br. med. J.*, i, 49.

647. BECKETT, P. G. S., *et al.* 1956. The significance of exogenous traumata in
the genesis of schizophrenia. *Psychiatry*, **19**, 137.

648. JOHNSON, A. M., GRIFFIN, M. E., WATSON, J., and BECKETT, P. S. 1956.
Studies in schizophrenia at Mayo Clinic. *Psychiatry*, **19**, 143.

649. DELAY, J., DENIKER, P., and GREEN, A. 1957. Le milieu familial des schizophrenics. *Encéphale*, **46**, 189.

650. FERREIRA, A. J. 1961. The etiology of schizophrenia: A review. *Calif.
Med.*, **94**, 369.

651. KIM, K. 1964. *Study of emotion in family transactions of schizophrenics—
Speech intrusion and interpersonal anxiety.* Paper presented at annual
meeting of American Psychiatric Association.

652. ROSENBAUM, C. P. 1961. Patient-family similarities in schizophrenia.
Archs gen. Psychiat., **5**, 120.

653. SPECK, R. V. 1965. The transfer of illness phenomenon in schizophrenic
families. In FRIEDMAN, A. S., *et al. Psychotherapy of the whole family.*
Springer, New York.

654. LU, Y. C. 1962. Contradictory parental expectations in schizophrenia.
Archs gen. Psychiat., **6**, 219.

655. LU, Y. C. 1961. Mother-child role relations in schizophrenia. *Psychiatry*,
24, 133.

656. FERREIRA, A. J. 1960. The semantics of the context of the schizophrenic's
language. *Archs gen. Psychiat.*, **3**, 128.

657. SHARP, V. H., GLASNER, S., LEDERMAN, I. I., and WOLFE, S. 1964. Socio-paths and schizophrenics—A comparison of family interactions. *Psychiatry*, **27**, 127.

658. STABENAU, J. R., TUPIN, J. T., WERNER, M., and POLLIN, W. 1965. A comparative study of families of schizophrenics, delinquents and normals. *Psychiatry*, **28**, 45.

659. ELLISON, E. A., and HAMILTON, D. M. 1949. Hospital treatment of dementia precox. *Am. J. Psychiat.*, **106**, 454.

660. WAHL, C. W. 1954. Some antecedent factors in family histories of schizophrenics. *Am. J. Psychiat.*, **110**, 668.

661. WAHL, C. W. 1956. Some antecedent factors in the family histories of schizophrenics in the U.S. Navy. *Am. J. Psychiat.*, **113**, 201.

662. REICHARD, S., and TILLMAN, C. 1950. Patterns of parent-child relationships in schizophrenia. *Psychiatry*, **13**, 247.

663. TIETZE, T. 1949. A study of the mothers of schizophrenic patients. *Psychiatry*, **12**, 55.

664. GERARD, D. L., and SIEGEL, J. 1950. The family background of schizophrenia. *Psychiat. Q.*, **24**, 47.

665. KASANIN, J., KNIGHT, E., and SAGE, P. 1934. The parent-child relationship in schizophrenia. *J. nerv. ment. Dis.*, **79** 249.

666. CAPUTO, D. V. 1963. The parents of the schizophrenic. *Family Process*, **2**, 339.

667. PROUT, C. T., and WHITE, M. A. 1950. A controlled study of personality relationships in mothers of schizophrenic male patients. *Am. J. Psychiat.*, **107**, 251.

668. ROGLER, L. H., and HOLLINGSHEAD, A. B. 1965. *Trapped: Families and schizophrenia*. Wiley, New York.

669. FROMM-REICHMANN, F. 1948. Notes on the development of treatment of schizophrenics by psychoanalytic psychotherapy. *Psychiatry*, **11**, 263.

670. CHEEK, F. E. 1964. The 'schizophrenogenic mother' in word and deed. *Family Process*, **3**, 155.

671. ALANEN, Y. O. 1958. The mothers of schizophrenic patients. *Acta psychiat. scand.*, **124**, 1.

672. HILL, L. B. 1955. *Psychotherapeutic intervention in schizophrenia*. Univ. of Chicago Press, Chicago.

673. LIMENTANI, D. 1956. Symbiotic identification in schizophrenia. *Psychiatry*, **19**, 231.

674. LYKETSOS, G. C. 1959. On the formation of mother-daughter symbiotic relationship patterns in schizophrenia. *Psychiatry*, **22**, 161.

675. SEARLES, H. F. 1958. Positive feelings in the relationship between the schizophrenic and his mother. *Int. J. Psycho-Analysis*, **39**, 569.

676. SEARLES, H. F. 1959. The effort to drive the other person crazy. *Br. J. med. Psychol.*, **32**, 1.

677. BEAVERS, W. R., BLUMBERG, S., TIMKIN, K. R., and WEINER, M. F. 1965. Communication patterns of mothers of schizophrenics. *Family Process*, **4**, 95.

678. ZUCKERMAN, M., OLTEAN, M., and MONASHKIN, I. 1958. The parental attitudes of mothers of schizophrenics. *J. consult. Psychol.*, **22**, No. 4.

679. GARDNER, N. H. 1949. The later adjustment of children born in a mental hospital to psychotic mothers. *Smith Coll. Stud. soc. Work*, **19**, 137.

680. PRESTON, G. H., and ANTIN, R. 1932. A study of children of psychotic parents. *Am. J. Orthopsychiat.*, **2**, 231.

681. CHEEK, F. E. 1965. The father of the schizophrenic. *Archs gen. Psychiat.*, **13**, 336.

682. FOUDRAINE, J. 1961. Schizophrenia and the family. A survey of the litera-
     ture 1956-1960 on the etiology of schizophrenia. *Acta psychother.*, **9**, 82.
683. WARING, M., and RICKS, D. 1965. Family patterns of children who became
     adult schizophrenics. *J. nerv. ment. Dis.*, **140**, 351.
684. McCORD, W., PORTA, J., and McCORD, J. 1962. The familial genesis of
     psychoses. *Psychiatry*, **25**, 60.
685. BECKER, E. 1964. Infant development and schizophrenia: New theoretical
     perspectives. *Int. J. soc. Psychiat.*, Special ed. 1, 1.
686. HILGARD, J. R., NEWMAN, M. F., and FISK, F. 1960. Strength of adult ego
     following childhood bereavement. *Am. J. Orthopsychiat.*, **30**, 788.
687. HILGARD, J. R., and NEWMAN, M. F. 1963. Early parental deprivation in
     schizophrenia and alcoholism. *Am. J. Orthopsychiat.*, **33**, 409.
688. HILGARD, J. R., and NEWMAN, M. F. 1963. Parental loss by death in child-
     hood as an etiological factor among schizophrenic and alcoholic patients
     compared with a non-patient community sample. *J. nerv. ment. Dis.*,
     137, 14.
689. HILGARD, J. R., and NEWMAN, M. F. 1961. Evidence for functional genesis
     in mental illness: Schizophrenia, depressive psychoses and psychoneuroses.
     J. nerv. ment. Dis., **132**, 3.
690. HILGARD, J. R., and FISK, F. 1960. Disruption of adult ego identity as
     related to childhood loss of a mother through hospitalization for psychosis.
     J. nerv. ment. Dis., **131**, 47.
691. KANNER, L. 1949. Problems of nosology and psychodynamics of early
     infantile autism. *Am. J. Orthopsychiat.*, **19**, 416.
692. GOLDFARB, W. The therapeutic management of schizophrenic children. In
     HOWELLS, J. G. (ed.) *Modern perspectives in international child psychiatry*,
     Oliver & Boyd, Edinburgh. (In press.)
693. O'GORMAN, G. 1965. The psychosis of childhood. In Howells, J. G. (ed.)
     Modern perspectives in child psychiatry. Oliver & Boyd, Edinburgh.
694. BENDER, L. The nature of childhood psychosis. In HOWELLS, J. G. (ed.)
     Modern perspectives in international child psychiatry. Oliver & Boyd,
     Edinburgh. (In press.)
695. BROWN, G. W., CARSTAIRS, G. M., and TOPPING, G. 1958. Post hospital
     adjustment of chronic mental patients. *Lancet*, ii, 685.
696. BROWN, G. W. 1959. Experiences of discharged chronic schizophrenic
     patients in various types of living groups. *Millbank mem. Fund Q.*, **37**, 105.
697. BROWN, G. W., MONCK, E. M., CARSTAIRS, G. M., and WING, J. K. 1962.
     Influence of family life on the course of schizophrenic illness. *Br. J. prev.
     soc. Med.*, **16**, 55.
698. BROWN, G. W. 1966. Measuring the impact of mental illness on the family.
     Proc. R. Soc. Med., **59**, 18.
699. GRAD, J., and SAINSBURY, P. 1966. Problems of caring for the mentally ill at
     home. *Proc. R. Soc. Med.*, **59**, 20.
700. GOLDBERG, E. M. 1960. Parents and psychotic sons. *Br. J. psychiat. soc.
     Wk*, **5**, 1.
701. DEYKING, E. 1961. The re-integration of the chronic schizophrenic patient
     discharged to his family and community as perceived by the family. *Ment.
     Hyg.*, **45**, 235.
702. EVANS, A. S., BULLARD, D. M., and SOLOMON, M. H. 1961. The family as
     a potential resource in the rehabilitation of the chronic schizophrenic
     patient: A study of 60 patients and their families. *Am. J. Psychiat.*, **117**,
     1075.
703. CHEEK, F. E. 1965. Family interaction patterns and convalescent adjust-
     ment of the schizophrenic. *Archs gen. Psychiat.*, **13**, 138.

704. FARIS, R. E. L., and DUNHAM, H. W. 1939. *Mental disorders in urban areas.* University of Chicago Press, Chicago.

705. HARE, E. H. 1956. Family setting and the urban distribution of schizophrenia. *J. ment. Sci.*, **102**, 753.

706. McGHIE, A., and CHAPMAN, J. 1961. Disorders of attention and perception in early schizophrenia. *Br. J. med. Psychol.*, **34**, 103.

707. CHAPMAN, J., and McGHIE, A. 1962. A comparative study of dysfunction in schizophrenia. *J. ment. Sci.*, **108**, 487.

708. McGHIE, A., CHAPMAN, J., and LAWSON, J. S. 1964. Disturbances in selective attention in schizophrenia. *Proc. R. Soc. Med.*, **57**, 419.

709. POLLIN, W., STABENAU, J. R., and TUPIN, J. 1965. Family studies with identical twins discordant for schizophrenia. *Psychiatry*, **28**, 60.

710. ROSENTHAL, D. (ed.). 1963. *The Genain quadruplets.* Basic Books, New York.

711. KRAEPELIN, E. 1899. Zur Diagnose und Prognose der Dementia Praecox. *Allg. Z. Psychiat.*, **56**, 254.

712. BLEULER, R. 1911. Dementia Praecox oder Gruppe der Schizophrenein. In ASCHAFFENBERG, G. (ed.) *Handbuch der Psychiatrie.* Leipzig und Wien.

713. LANGFELDT, G. 1937. *The prognosis in schizophrenia and the factors influencing the course of the disease: A katamnestic study, including individual re-examination in 1936.* Oxford Univ. Press, London.

714. STEPHENS, J. H., and ASTRUP, C. 1963. Prognosis in 'process' and 'non-process' schizophrenia. *Am. J. Psychiat.*, **119**, 945.

715. STEPHENS, J. H., and ASTRUP, C. 1965. Treatment outcome in 'process' and 'non-process' schizophrenics treated by 'A' and 'B' types of therapists. *J. nerv. ment. Dis.*, **140**, 449.

Mental Retardation

716. PENROSE, L. S. 1963. *The biology of mental defect*, revised ed. Sidgwick & Jackson, London.

717. TIZARD, J., and GRAD, J. C. 1961. *The mentally handicapped and their families. A social survey.* Maudsley Monograph No. 7. Oxford Univ. Press, London.

718. DAVIS, D. R. 1958. Nurture and mental development. In GARDNER, D. (ed.) *Recent advances in paediatrics.* J. & A. Churchill, London.

719. KIRMAN, B. H. 1959. Some social consideration, discussion on the etiology of mental defect. *Proc. R. Soc. Med.*, **52**, 787.

720. KIRMAN, B. H. 1958. Early disturbance of behaviour in relation to mental defect. *Br. med. J.*, ii, 1215.

721. BERG, J. M. 1959. Some pathological factors. Discussion on the etiology of mental defect. *Proc. R. Soc. Med.*, **52**, 789.

722. GIBSON, D., and BUTLER, A. J. 1954. Culture as a possible contributor to feeblemindedness. *Am. J. ment. Defic.*, **58**, 490.

723. BOURNE, H. 1955. Protophrenia: A study of perverted rearing and mental dwarfism. *Lancet*, ii, 1156.

724. CASLER, L. 1961. Maternal deprivation: A critical review of the literature. *Monogr. Soc. Res. Child Dev.*, **26**, No. 2.

725. SPITZ, R. A. 1965. *The first year of life.* International Univ. Press, New York.

726. DAVIS, D. R. 1961. A disorder theory of mental retardation. *J. ment. subnormal.*, **1**, 13.

727. FARBER, B., and JENNE, W. C. 1963. Family organization and parent-child communication: Parents and siblings of a retarded child. *Monogr. Soc. Res. Child Dev.*, **28**, No. 7.

728. FARBER, B. 1959. Effects of a severely mentally retarded child on family integration. *Monogr. Soc. Res. Child Dev.*, **24**, No. 2.
729. FARBER, B. 1960. Family organization and crisis: Maintenance of integration in families with a severely mentally retarded child. *Monogr. Soc. Res. Child Dev.*, **25**, No. 1.
730. FARBER, B. 1960. Perception of crisis and related variables in the impact of a retarded child on the mother. *J. Hlth, hum. Behav.*, **1**, 108.
731. FARBER, B. 1962. Marital integration as a factor in parent-child relations. *Child Dev.*, **33**, 1.
732. FARBER, B., JENNE, W. C., and TOIGO, R. 1960. Family crisis and the decision to institutionalize the retarded child. *Res. Monogr. NEA Council Except. Child*, Series A, No. 1.
733. SARASON, S. B. 1959. *Psychological problems in mental deficiency*, 3rd ed. Harper, New York.
734. 1953. Symposium: Counselling the mentally retarded and their parents. *J. clin. Psychol.*, April.
735. DREWRY, H. 1953. Information for parents of mentally retarded children in New York City. *Am. J. ment. Defic.*, **57**, 495.
736. STANG, F. 1957. Parent guidance and the mentally retarded child. *Publ. Hlth*, **71**, No. 6.
737. HESSELBERG-MEYER, G. 1959. *Social work with subnormal children and their families*. W H O seminar on the mental health of the subnormal child, Milan.
738. GOLDBERG, B. 1962. Family psychiatry and the retarded child. *Can. psychiat. Ass. J.*, **7**, 140.

5. *Family Therapy*

General

739. SPECK, R. V. 1964. The home setting for family treatment. *Int. J. soc. Psychiat.*, Special ed, No. 2, 54.
740. FRIEDMAN, A. S. 1962. Family therapy as conducted in the home. *Family Process*, **1**, 132.
741. FISCH, R. 1964. Home visits in a private psychiatric practice. *Family Process*, **3**, 114.
742. NIELSEN, J. 1963. Home visits by psychiatrists. *Comp. Psychiat.*, **4**, 442.
743. BAKER, A. A., MORRISON, M., GAME, J. A., and THORPE, J. G. 1961. Admitting schizophrenic mothers with their babies. *Lancet*, ii, 237.
744. GLASSER, Y. I. M. 1962. A unit for mothers and babies in a psychiatric hospital. *J. Child Psychol. Psychiat.*, **3**, 53.
745. CASTELNUOVO-TEDESCO, P. 1965. *The twenty-minute hour*. Little, Brown & Co., Boston.
746. NASH, E. M., JESSNER, L., and ABSE, D. W. (eds.). 1964. *Marriage counselling in medical practice*. Oxford Univ. Press, London.
747. BRILL, N. Q. 1964. Emotional problems of marriage. *Int. J. soc. Psychiat.*, Special ed, No. 2, 61.
748. EISENSTEIN, V. W. (ed.). 1956. *Neurotic interaction in marriage*. Basic Books, New York.
749. LAQUEUR, H. P., LA BURT, H. A., and MORONG, E. 1964. Multiple family therapy: Further developments. *Int. J. soc. Psychiat.*, Special ed. No. 2, 70.
750. LAQUEUR, H. P., LA BURT, A. B., and MORONG, E. 1964. Multiple family therapy. In MASSERMAN, J. H. (ed.) *Current psychiatric therapies*, Vol. IV. Grune & Stratton, New York.
751. HANDLON, J. H., and PARLOFF, M. B. 1962. The treatment of patient and

family as a group: Is it group psychotherapy? *Int. J. group Psychother.*, **12**, 132.

752. HANDLON, J. H., and PARLOFF, M. B. Comparisons between family treatment and group therapy.

753. ACKERMAN, N. W. 1962. Family psychotherapy and psychoanalysis; The implication of difference. *Family Process* **1**, 30.

754. WYNNE, L. C. 1965. Some indications and contraindications for exploratory family therapy. In BOSZORMENYI-NAGY, I., and FRAMO, J. L. (eds.) *Intensive family therapy*. Harper & Row, New York.

755. BELL, J. E. 1961. Family group therapy. *Publ. Hlth. Monogr.*, No. 64.

756. BOWEN, M. 1965. Family psychotherapy with schizophrenia in the hospital and in private practice. In BOSZORMENYI-NAGY, I., and FRAMO, J. L. (eds.) *Intensive family therapy*. Harper & Row, New York.

757. FRAMO, J. L. 1965. Rationale and techniques of Intensive Family Therapy. In BOSZORMEYI-NAGY, I., and FRAMO, J. L. (eds.) *Intensive family therapy*. Harper & Row, New York,

758. ACKERMAN, N. W., and FRANKLIN, P. F. 1965. Family dynamics and the reversibility of delusional formation: A case study in family therapy. In BOSZORMENYI-NAGY, I., and FRAMO, J. L. (eds.) *Intensive family therapy*. Harper & Row, New York.

759. WATZLAWICK, P. 1964. *An anthology of human communication.* Science and Behavior Books, Palo Alto, Calif.

Books

760. CHANCE, E. 1959. *Families in treatment.* Basic Books, New York.

761. SATIR, V. M. 1964. *Conjoint family therapy.* Science and Behavior Books, Palo Alto, Calif.

762. MACGREGOR, R., RITCHIE, A. M., SERRANO, A. C., and SCHUSTER, F. P. Jr. 1964. *Multiple impact therapy with families.* McGraw-Hill, New York.

763. BOSZORMENYI-NAGY, I., and FRAMO, J. L. (eds.). 1965. *Intensive family therapy.* Harper & Row, New York.

764. ABRAHAMS, J., and VARON, E. 1953. *Maternal dependency and schizophrenia: Mothers and daughters in a therapeutic group.* International Univ. Press, New York.

765. ACKERMAN, N. W., BEATMAN, F., and SHERMAN, S. N. (eds.). 1961. *Exploring the base for family therapy.* Family Service Ass. of America, New York.

766. HALEY, J. 1963. *Strategies of psychotherapy.* Grune & Stratton, New York.

767. GROTJAHN, M. 1960. *Psychoanalysis and family neurosis.* Norton, New York.

768. MIDELFORT, C. F. 1957. *The family in psychotherapy.* Blakiston, New York.

769. ZUK, G. H. *Pathogenic social systems and family therapy.* Science and Behavior Books, Palo Alto, Calif. (In press.)

770. EHRENWALD, J. 1963. *Neurosis in the family and patterns of psychosocial defense.* Harper & Row, New York.

771. BRODY, E. B., and REDLICH, F. C. 1952. *Psychotherapy with schizophrenics.* International Univ. Press, New York.

772. LIEBMAN, S. (ed.). 1959. *Emotional forces in the family.* Lippincott, Philadelphia.

Reviews

773. FLECK, S. 1963. Psychotherapy of families of hospitalized patients. In MASSERMAN, J. H. (ed.) *Current psychiatric therapies*, Vol. III. Grune & Stratton, New York.

774. RUBINSTEIN, D. 1965. Family therapy. In SPIEGEL, E. A. (ed.) *Progress in neurology and psychiatry*, Vol. XX. Grune & Stratton, New York.

775. ACKERMAN, N. W. 1966. Family therapy. In ARIETI, S. (ed.) *American handbook of psychiatry*, Vol. III. Basic Books, New York.

776. HALEY, J. 1959. Family of the schizophrenic: A model system. *J. nerv. ment. Dis.*, **129**, 357.

777. HALEY, J. 1962. Whither family therapy? *Family Process*, **1**, 69.

778. HALEY, J. 1962. Family experiments: A new type of experimentation. *Family Process*, **1**, 265.

779. JACKSON. D. D., and SATIR, V. 1961. A review of psychiatric development in family diagnosis and family therapy. In ACKERMAN, N. W., BEATMAN, F., and SHERMAN, S. N. (eds.) *Exploring the base for family therapy*. Family Service Ass. of America, New York.

780. ACKERMAN, N. W. 1960. Family-focused therapy of schizophrenia. In SCHER, S. C., and DAVIS, H. R. (eds.) *Out-patient treatment of schizophrenia*. Grune & Stratton, New York.

781. PARLOFF, M. B. 1961. The family in psychotherapy. *Archs gen. Psychiat.*, **4**, 445.

Other Significant Contributions on Family Group Therapy

782. BOWEN, M. 1961. Family psychotherapy. *Am. J. Orthopsychiat.*, **31**, 41.

783. BRODEY, W. M., and HAYDEN, M. 1957. Intrateam reactions: Their relation to the conflicts of the family in treatment. *Am. J. Orthopsychiat.*, **27**, 349.

784. BOWEN, M. 1965. Family psychotherapy with schizophrenia in the hospital and in private practice. In BOSZORMENYI-NAGY, I., and FRAMO, J. L. (eds.) *Intensive family therapy*. Harper & Row, New York.

785. BOWEN, M. 1959. Family relationships in schizophrenia. In AUERBACK, A. (ed.) *Schizophrenia—An integrate approach*. Ronald Press, New York.

786. BOWEN, M., DYSINGER, R. H., BRODEY, W. M., and BASAMANIA, B. 1957. *Study and treatment of five hospitalized families each with a psychotic family member*. Read at annual meeting of American Orthopsychiatric Association. Chicago, March.

787. MENDELL, D., and FISHER, S. 1958. A multi-generation approach to treatment of psychopathology. *J. nerv. ment. Dis.*, **126**, 523.

788. SONNE, J., and SPECK, R. 1961. *Resistances in family therapy of schizophrenia in the home*. Read at Conference on 'Schizophrenia and the family', Temple Univ., Philadelphia, March.

789. ACKERMAN, N. W. 1937. The family as a social and emotional unit. *Bull. Kans. ment. hyg. Soc.*, **12**, No. 2.

790. ACKERMAN, N. W., and SOBEL, R. 1950. Family diagnosis: An approach to the pre-school child. *Am. J. Orthopsychiat.*, **10**, No. 4.

791. ACKERMAN, N. W. 1951. Group Dynamics: 1. Social role and total personality. *Am. J. Orthopsychiat.*, **21**, 1.

792. ACKERMAN, N. W. 1950. Cultural factor in psychoanalytic therapy. *Bull. Am. Psychoanal. Ass.*, **7**, No. 4.

793. ACKERMAN, N. W. 1953. Selected problems in supervised analysis. *Psychiatry*, **16**, No. 3.

794. ACKERMAN, N. W. 1954. The diagnosis of neurotic marital interaction. *Soc. Casewk*, **35**, 139.

795. ACKERMAN, N. W. 1954. Some structural problems in the relations of psychoanalysis and group psychotherapy. *Int. J. group Psychother.*, **4**, No. 2.

796. ACKERMAN, N. W. 1954. Interpersonal disturbances in the family: A frame of reference for psychotherapy. *Psychiatry*, **17**, No. 4.

797. ACKERMAN, N. W. 1955. Group psychotherapy with a mixed group of adolescents. *Int. J. group Psychother.*, **5**, No. 3.

798. ACKERMAN, N. W., and BEHRENS, M. L. 1956. The home visit as an aid in family diagnosis and therapy. *Soc. Casewk*, January.

799. ACKERMAN, N. W., and BEHRENS, M. L. 1956. A study of family diagnosis. *Am. J. Orthopsychiat.*, **26**, No. 1.

800. ACKERMAN, N. W. 1956. Disturbances of mothering and criteria for treatment. *Am. J. Orthopsychiat.*, **26**, No. 2.

801. ACKERMAN, N. W. 1956. Goals in therapy: A symposium. *Am. J. Psychoanal.*, **16**, No. 1.

802. ACKERMAN, N. W. 1957. The family group and family therapy. *Int. J. Sociometry*, **1**, No. 1.

803. ACKERMAN, N. W. 1957. The family group and family therapy. *Int. J. Sociometry*, **1**, Nos. 2 & 3.

804. ACKERMAN, N. W. 1957. A changing conception of personality. *Am. J. Psychoanal.*, **17**, No. 1.

805. ACKERMAN, N. W. 1957. The principles of shared responsibility for child rearing. *Int. J. Soc. Psychiat.*, **2**, No. 4.

806. ACKERMAN, N. W. 1957. An orientation to psychiatric research on the family. *Marriage Fam. Living*, **19**, No. 1.

807. ACKERMAN, N. W. 1957. Mental health and the family in the current world crisis. *J. Jewish Communal Service*, **34**, No. 1.

808. ACKERMAN, N. W. 1957. Five issues in group psychotherapy. *Rev. diagnos. Psychol. personal. Explor.*, **5**, 167-176.

809. ACKERMAN, N. W. 1958. Toward an integrative therapy of the family. *Am. J. Psychiat.*, **114**, No. 8.

810. ACKERMAN, N. W., with BEATMAN, F. L., and SHERMAN, S. N. 1958. Concepts of family striving and family distress: The contributions of M. Robert Gomberg. *Soc. Casewk*, July.

811. ACKERMAN, N. W. 1959. Transference and counter-transference. *Psychoanal. psychoanal. Rev.*, **46**, No. 3.

812. ACKERMAN, N. W. 1959. Theory of family dynamics. *Psychoanal. psychoanal. Rev.*, **46**, No. 4.

813. ACKERMAN, N. W. 1962. Family psychotherapy and psychoanalysis: The implications of difference. *Family Process*, **1**, No. 1.

814. ACKERMAN, N. W. 1963. Child and family psychiatry today: A new look at some problems. *Ment. Hyg.*, **47**, No. 4.

815. ACKERMAN, N. W. 1963. *The family as a unit in mental health.* Proc. Third World Congress of Psychiatry, Toronto.

816. ACKERMAN, N. W. 1964. The family in crisis. *Bull. N. Y. Acad. Med.*, **40**, No. 3.

817. ACKERMAN, N. W. 1965. Non-verbal cues and re-enactment of conflict in family therapy. *Family Process*, **4**, No. 1.

818. ACKERMAN, N. W. 1955. Child and family psychopathy: Problems of correlation. In HOCH, and ZUBIN (eds.) *Psychopathology of childhood.* Grune & Stratton, New York.

819. ACKERMAN, N. W. 1956. Interlocking pathology in family relationships. In REDO, and DANIELS (eds.) *Changing conceptions of psychoanalytic medicine.* Grune & Stratton, New York.

820. ACKERMAN, N. W. Psychological dynamics of the 'Familial organism'. In GERSON, I. (ed.) *The family—A focal point in health education.* New York Academy of Medicine.

821. ACKERMAN, N. W. 1958. Behavioral disturbances in contemporary society.

In GALDSTON, I. (ed.) *The family in contemporary society.* International Univ. Press, New York.

822. ACKERMAN, N. W., and BEHRENS, M. L. 1958. The family group and family therapy. In MASSERMAN, J. (ed.) *Progress in psychotherapy*, Vol. III, Part 3. Grune & Stratton, New York.

823. ACKERMAN, N. W. 1959. The psychoanalytic approach to family. In MASSERMAN, J. (ed.) *Science and Psychoanalysis—Individual and family dynamics*, Vol. II. Grune & Stratton, New York.

824. ACKERMAN, N. W. 1959. (With LAKOS, M. H.) Treatment of a child and family, in *Case studies in counseling and psychotherapy.* Prentice-Hall, New York.

825. ACKERMAN, N. W. 1959. In STANDAL, S. W., and CORSINI, R. J. (eds.) *Critical incidents in psychotherapy.* Prentice-Hall, New York.

826. ACKERMAN, N. W. 1959. The adolescent. In *Social problems.* Row, Peterson, Evanston, Ill.

827. ACKERMAN, N. W. 1959. Discussion: Selection of schizophrenic patients for office practice. In RIFKIN, A. N. (ed.) *Schizophrenia in psychoanalytic practice.* Grune & Stratton, New York.

828. ACKERMAN, N. W. 1959. The emotional impact of in-laws and relatives. In LIEBMAN, S. (ed.) *Emotional forces in the family.* Lippincott, Philadelphia.

829. ACKERMAN, N. W. 1960. Family-focused therapy of schizophrenia. In *The out-patient treatment of schizophrenia.* Grune & Stratton, New York.

830. ACKERMAN, N. W. 1961. Psychotherapy with the family group. In MASSERMAN, J. (ed.) *Science and psychoanalysis*, Vol. IV. Grune & Stratton, New York.

831. ACKERMAN, N. W. 1961. Preventive implications of family research. In CAPLAN, G. (ed.) *Prevention of mental disorders in childhood.* Basic Books, New York.

832. ACKERMAN, N. W. 1961. The emergency of family psychotherapy on the present scene. In STEIN, M. I. (ed.) *Contemporary psychotherapies.* Free Press, Glencoe, Ill.

833. ACKERMAN, N. W. 1961. The schizophrenic patient and his family relationships—A conceptual basis for family-focused therapy of schizophrenia. In GREENBLATT, D., LEVENSON, D., and KLERMAN, G. (eds.) *Mental patients in transition.* Charles C. Thomas, New York.

834. ACKERMAN, N. W. (with RICHARDSON, H. B.). 1963. Psychotherapy for the general practitioner. In LIEF, LIEF, and LIEF (eds.) *Psychological basis of medical practice.* Harper & Row, New York.

835. ACKERMAN, N. W. 1964. Adolescent struggle as protest. In *Man and civilization: The family's search for survival.* McGraw-Hill, New York.

836. ACKERMAN, N. W. 1963. Family psychotherapy. In *Encyclopedia of mental health*, Vol. 2. Franklin Watts.

837. ACKERMAN, N. W. The family approach to marital disorders. In GREENE B. L. (ed.) *The psychotherapies of marital disharmony.*

838. ACKERMAN, N. W., and FRANKLIN, P. F. 1965. Family dynamics and the reversibility of delusional formation: A case study in family therapy. In BOSZORMENYI-NAGY and FRAMO (eds.) *Intensive family therapy.* Harper & Row, New York.

839. BATESON, G., JACKSON, D. D., HALEY, J., WEAKLAND, J. H. 1963. A note on the double bind—1962. *Family Process*, **2**, 154.

840. JACKSON, D. 1953. Psychotherapy for schizophrenia. *Scient. Am.*, **188**, 58.

841. JACKSON, D. 1954. Office treatment of ambulatory schizophrenics. *Calif. Med.*, **81**, 263.

842. JACKSON, D. 1954. Some factors influencing the Oedipus complex. *Psychoanal. Q.*, **23**, 566.
843. JACKSON, D. 1955. The therapist's personality in the psychotherapy of schizophrenics. *Archs Neurol. Psychiat.*, **74**, 292.
844. JACKSON, D. 1956. Counter-transference and psychotherapy. In FROMM-REICHMAN, F., and MORENO, J. L. (eds.) *Progress in psychotherapy*, Vol. 1. Grune & Stratton, New York.
845. JACKSON, D. 1957. The question of family homeostasis. *Psychiat. Q.*, **31**, 79.
846. JACKSON, D. 1959. Family interaction, family homeostasis and some implications for conjoint family psychotherapy. In MASSERMAN, J. (ed.) *Individual and familial dynamics*. Grune & Stratton, New York.
847. JACKSON, D. (ed.). 1960. *The etiology of schizophrenia*. Basic Books, New York.
848. JACKSON, D. (ed.). 1960. A critique of the literature on the genetics of schizophrenia. In *The etiology of schizophrenia*. Basic Books, New York.
849. JACKSON, D. 1961. The monad, the dyad, and the family therapy of schizophrenics. In BURTON, A. (ed.) *Psychotherapy of the psychoses*. Basic Books, New York.
850. JACKSON, D. 1962. Family therapy in the family of the schizophrenic. In STEIN, M. I. (ed.) *Contemporary psychotherapies*, pp. 272-287. Free Press, Glencoe, Ill.
851. JACKSON, D. 1962. Interactional psychotherapy. In STEIN, M. I. (ed.) *Contemporary psychotherapies*, pp. 256-271. Free Press, Glencoe, Ill.
852. JACKSON, D. 1962. Schizophrenia. *Scient. Am.*, **207**, 65-74.
853. JACKSON, D. 1964. *Myths of madness*. Macmillan, New York.
854. JACKSON, D. 1965. The study of the family. *Family Process*, **4**, 1-20.
855. JACKSON, D. 1965. Family rules; the marital *quid pro quo*. *Archs gen. Psychiat.*, **12**, 589-594.
856. JACKSON, D. 1965. Conjoint family therapy. *Mod. Med.*, 173-198.
857. JACKSON, D., and CRAMMER, L. 1964. Schizophrenia: An adaptation to a socially pathogenic context. *Issues curr. med. Pract.*, **1**, No. 8.
858. JACKSON, D., and KANTOR, R. 1962. Some assumptions in recent research on schizophrenia. *J. nerv. ment. Dis.*, **135**, 36-43.
859. JACKSON, D., KNUPFER, G., and KRIEGER, G. 1959. Personality differences between more or less competent psychotherapists as a function of criteria of competence. *J. nerv. ment. Dis.*, **129**, 375-384.
860. JACKSON, D., OREMLAND, J., KRIEGER, G., and BLAZEJACK, R. 1958. Factors affecting results in psychotherapy. *Dis. nerv. Syst.*, **19**, 289-294.
861. JACKSON, D., RISKIN, J., and SATIR, V. 1961. A method of analysis of a family interview. *Archs gen. Psychiat.*, **5**, 321-339.
862. JACKSON, D., and SATIR, V. 1961. Family diagnosis and family therapy. In ACKERMAN, N., BEATMAN, F., and SHERMAN, S. (eds.) *Exploring the base for family Therapy*. Family Service Ass. of America, New York.
863. JACKSON, D., and WEAKLAND, J. 1961. Conjoint family therapy, some considerations on theory, technique and results. *Psychiat.*, **24**, 30-45.
864. JACKSON, D., and YALOM, I. 1964. Of family homeostasis and patient change. In MASSERMAN, J. (ed.) *Current psychiatric therapies*, Vol. 4. Grune & Stratton, New York.
865. BLOCK, JEANNE, and PATTERSON, V., BLOCK, J., and JACKSON, D. 1958. A study of the parents of schizophrenic and neurotic children. *Psychiatry*, **21**, 387-397.
866. WEAKLAND, J., and JACKSON, D. 1958. Patient and therapist observations

on the circumstances of a schizophrenic episode. *Archs Neurol. Psychiat.*, **79**, 554-574.

867. SATIR, V. 1963. Schizophrenia and family therapy. In *Social work practice.* Columbia Univ. Press, New York.

868. SATIR, V. 1963. The quest for survival. *Acta psychother.* **11**.

869. SATIR, V. 1965. Conjoint marital therapy. In GREENE, B. L. (ed.) *The psychotherapies of marital disharmony.* Free Press, Glencoe, Ill.

870. SATIR, V. 1965. The family as a treatment unit, *Confinia psychiat.*, **8**.

871. SATIR, V. 1965. Conjoint family therapy. In *The American family in crisis*, Vol. III. Forest Hosp. Publications, Des Plaines, Ill.

872. SATIR, V. 1965. Communication as a tool for understanding and changing behavior. In *Human growth and diversity*, Proceedings of 16th Annual Conference of Calif. Assoc. of School Psychologists and Psychometrists.

873. HALEY, J. 1963. Marriage therapy. *Archs gen. Psychiat.*, **8**, 213.

874. HALEY, J. 1961. Control on psychotherapy with schizophrenics. *Archs gen. Psychiat.*, **5**, 340.

875. WYNNE, L. C. 1961. The study of intrafamilial alignments and splits in exploratory family therapy. In ACKERMAN, N. W., BEATMAN, F. L., and SHERMAN, S. N. (eds.) *Exploring the base for family therapy.* Family Service Ass. of America, New York.

876. SCHAFFER, L., WYNNE, L. C., DAY, J., RYCKOFF, I. M., and HALPERIN, A. 1962. On the nature and sources of the psychiatrist's experience with the family of the schizophrenic. *Psychiatry*, **25**, 32.

877. WYNNE, L. C. 1964. *Some guidelines for exploratory family therapy.* Third International Symposium Psychother. Schizophrenia, Lusanne, p. 24.

878. BELL, J. E. 1953. Family group therapy as a treatment method. *Am. J. Psychol.*, **8**, 515.

879. BELL, J. E. 1955. *The nature of social depreciation and of defenses against being adjudged: A study of the cerebral palsied child in his family.* (Mimeo.) Ass. for the Aid of Crippled Children.

880. BELL, J. E. 1962. Recent advances in family group therapy. *J. Child Psychol. Psychiat.*, **3**, 1.

881. BELL, J. E. 1963. A theoretical position for family group therapy. *Family Process*, **2**, 1.

882. BELL, J. E. 1964. The family group therapist: An agent of change. *Int. J. group Psychother.*, **14**, 72.

883. BELL, J. E. 1961. Family group therapy. *Publ. Hlth Monogr.*

884. BELL, J. E. 1961. Counseling with families. *Ment. Hlth Res. Inst. Bull.*, **3**, 31.

885. BELL, J. E. Contrasts in diagnosis and treatment processes in marital counseling: Some comparisons between individual and joint treatment. In AIDMAN, T. (ed.) *Marital counseling* (tent. title). (In press.)

886. LIDZ, T. 1963. *The family and human adaptation.* International Univ. Press, New York.

887. LIDZ, T., and FLECK, S. 1960. Schizophrenia, human integration and the role of the family. In JACKSON, D. (ed.) *Etiology of schizophrenia.* Basic Books, New York.

888. LIDZ, R. W., and LIDZ, T. 1952. Therapeutic considerations arising from the intense symbiotic needs of schizophrenic patients. In BRODY, E., and REDLICH, F. (eds.) *Psychotherapy with schizophrenics.* International Univ. Press, New York.

889. FLECK, S. 1965. Some general and specific indications for family therapy. *Confinia psychiat.*, **8**, 27.

890. FLECK, S. 1962. Residential treatment of young schizophrenic patients. *Conn. Med.*, **26**, 369.

891. FLECK, S. 1963. Psychiatric hospitalization as a family experience. *Acta psychiat. scand.*, **39**, 260.

892. STANTON, A. H. 1961. Milieu therapy and the development of insight. *Psychiatry*, **24**, 19.

893. FERREIRA, A. J. 1959. Psychotherapy with severely regressed schizophrenics. A report of two cases. *Psychiat. Q.*, **33**, 664.

894. FERREIRA, A. J. 1964. The intimacy need in psychotherapy. *Am. J. Psychoanal.*, **24**, 190.

895. FERREIRA, A. J. 1961. Empathy and the bridge-function of the ego. *J. Am. psychoanal. Ass.*, **9**, 91.

896. FERREIRA, A. J. 1964. The intimacy need in psychotherapy. Presented at Fifth Internat. Congress for Psychotherapy, Vienna, August 1961. *Am. J. Psychoanal.*, **24**, 190.

897. FERREIRA, A. J. 1963. Decision-making in normal and pathologic families: A study. *Archs gen. Psychiat.*, **8**, 68.

898. FERREIRA, A. J. 1963. Rejection and expectancy of rejection in normal and pathological families. *Family Process*, **2**, 235.

899. FERREIRA, A. J. 1964. On silence. *Am. J. Psychother.*, **18**, 109.

900. FERREIRA, A. J. 1964. Interpersonal perceptivity among family members. *Am. J. Orthopsychiat.*, **34**, 67.

901. FERREIRA, A. J. (with WINTER, W. D., and OLSON, J. D.). 1965. Story sequence analysis of family TATs. *J. proj. Techniques*, **29**, 392.

902. FERREIRA, A. J. 1965. Family myths: covert rules of the relationship. Presented at the Sixth Internat. Congress of Psychotherapy, London, 1964. *Confinia Psychiat.*, **8**, 15.

903. FERREIRA, A. J. (with WINTER, W. D.). 1965. Family interaction and decision-making. *Archs gen. Psychiat.*, **13**, 214.

904. FERREIRA, A. J., WINTER, W. D., and POINDEXTER, E. J. Some interactional variables in normal and abnormal families. *Family Process*. (In press.)

905. FERREIRA, A. J., and WINTER, W. D. Stability of interactional variables in family decision-making. *Archs gen. Psychiat.* (In press.)

906. FERREIRA, A. J. (with WINTER, W. D., and OLSON, J. D.). Hostility themes in family TAT. *J. proj. Techniques.* (In press.)

907. ZUK, G. H., and RUBINSTEIN, J. D. 1965. A review of concepts in the study and treatment of families of schizophrenics. In BOSZORMENYI-NAGY, I., and FRAMO, J. L. (eds.) *Intensive family therapy*. Harper & Row, New York.

908. BAUER, I. L., and GUREVITCH, S. 1952. Group therapy with parents of schizophrenic children. *Int. group Psychother.*, **2**, 344.

909. BOSZORMENYI-NAGY, I. 1962. The concept of schizophrenic from the perspective of family treatment. *Family Process*, **1**, 103.

910. BOSZORMENYI-NAGY, I., and FRAMO, J. L. 1962. Family concept of hospital treatment of schizophrenia. In MASSERMAN, J. (ed.) *Current psychiatric therapies*, Vol. 2. Grune & Stratton, New York.

911. CARROLL, E. J. 1960. Treatment of the family as a unit. *Penn. med. J.*, **63**, 57.

912. CUTTER, A. V., and HALLOWITZ, D. 1962. Different approaches to treatment of the child and the parents. *Am. J. Orthopsychiat.*, **32**, 152.

913. FRAMO, J. L. 1962. Theory of the technique of family treatment of schizophrenia. *Family Process*, **1**, 119,

914. FRIEDMAN, A. 1962. Family therapy as conducted in the home. *Family Process*, **1**, 132.

915. FROMM-REICHMANN, F. 1948. Notes on the development of schizophrenia by psychoanalytic psychotherapy. *Psychiatry*, **11**, 267.
916. GOOLISHIAN, H. A. 1962. A brief psychotherapy program for disturbed adolescents. *Am. J. Orthopsychiat.*, **32**, 142.
917. GUNTRIP, H. 1960. Ego-weakness and the hard core of the problem of psychotherapy. *Br. J. med. Psychol.*, **33**, 163.
918. HANDLON, J. H., and PARLOFF, M. B. 1962. Treatment of patient and family as a group. Is it group therapy? *Int. J. group Psychother.*, **12**, 132.
919. HAYWARD, M. L. 1961. Psychotherapy based on the primary process. *Am. J. Psychother.*, **15**, 419.
920. JACKSON, J. 1962. A family group therapy technique for a stalemate in individual treatment. *Int. J. group Psychother.*, **12**, 164.
921. KIRBY, K. and PRIESTMAN, S. 1957. Values of a daughter (schizophrenic) and mother therapy group. *Int. J. group Psychother.*, **7**, 281.
922. GRALNICK, A. 1963. Conjoint family therapy: Its role in rehabilitation of the inpatient and family. *J. nerv. ment. Dis.*, **136**, 500.
923. GRALNICK, A. 1959. The family in psychotherapy. In MASSERMANN, J. H. (ed.) *Individual and family dynamics*. Grune & Stratton, New York.
924. GRALNICK, A. 1959. Changing relation of the patient, family and practising psychiatrist to the therapeutic community. In DENBER, H. C. B., *et al.* (eds.) *Research conference on therapeutic community*. Charles C. Thomas, New York.
925. GRALNICK, A., and D'ELIA, F. 1961. Role of the patient in the therapeutic community: Patient-participation. *Am. J. Psychother.*, **15**, 63.
926. GRALNICK, A. 1959. Relation of the family to a psychotherapeutic inpatient programme. *Int. J. soc. Psychiat.*, **5**, 131.
927. RABINER, E. L., MOLINSKI, H., and GRALNICK, A. 1962. Conjoint family therapy in the inpatient setting. *Am. J. Psychother.*, **16**, 618.
928. SILVERBERG, J. W., D'ELIA, F., RABINER, E. L., and GRALNICK, A. 1964. The implementation of psychoanalytic concepts in hospital practice. *Sci. Psychoanal.*, **7**; Grune & Stratton, New York.
929. RABINER, E. L., GOMEZ, E., and GRALNICK, A. 1964. The therapeutic community as an insight catalyst. *Am. J. Psychother.*, **18**, 244.
930. GRALNICK, A. 1962. Family psychotherapy: General and specific considerations. *Am. J. Orthopsychiat.*, **32**, 515.
931. GRALNICK, A., and LIND, A. 1963. Integration of the social group worker and psychiatrist in the psychiatric hospital. Read at Meeting of A.P.A., St. Louis.
932. GREENHILL, M. H., GRALNICK, A., DUNCAN, R. H., YEMEZ, R., and TURKER, F. 1966. Considerations in evaluating the results of psychotherapy with 500 Inpatients. *Am. J. Psychother.*, **20**, 58.
933. GRALNICK, A., and SCHWEEN, P. H. 1966. Family therapy. *Psychiat. Res. Rep.* No. 20.
934. SONNE, J. C., SPECK, R. V., and JUNGRIS, J. E. 1962. The absent-member maneuver as a resistance in family therapy of schizophrenia. *Family Process*, **1**, 44.
935. SPECK, R. V. 1965. Some specific therapeutic techniques with schizophrenic families, in *Psychotherapy of the whole family*. Springer, New York.
936. GROTJAHN, M. 1959. Analytic family therapy: A survey of trends in research and practice. In MASSERMANN, J. H. (ed.) *Individual and familial dynamics*. Grune & Stratton, New York.
937. GROTJAHN, M. 1960. *Psychoanalysis and the family neurosis*. Norton, New York.
938. KNOBLOCH, F. 1965. Family psychotherapy. *Psychother. Psychosom.*, **13**, 155.

939. KNOBLOCH, F. Psychotherapy in terms of small group therapy.
940. KNOBLOCH, F., and SOFRNOVA, M. 1954. Family psychotherapy. Part I. Notes on the technique of family psychotherapy. *Neurologie Psychiat. česka*, **17**, 217.
941. RITCHIE, A. 1960. Multiple impact therapy: An experiment. *Social Work*, July, 16.
942. GOOLISHIAN, H. A. 1962. A brief psychotherapy program for disturbed adolescents. *Am. J. Orthopsychiat.*, **32**, 142.
943. SCHUSTER, F. P. 1959. Summary description of multiple impact psychotherapy. *Tex. Rep. Biol. Med.*, **17**, 426.
944. MACGREGOR, R. M. 1962. Multiple impact psychotherapy with families. *Family Process*, **1**, 15.

Additional Contributions

945. RAKOFF, V. 1965. Training in family psychiatry. *Can. psychiat. Ass. J.*, **10**, 206.
946. EPSTEIN, N. B., SIGAL, J. J., and RAKOFF, V. 1966. Some issues in family therapy. *Laval méd.*, **37**, 146.
947. ZUK, G. H. 1965. On the pathology of silencing strategies. *Family Process*, **4**, 32.
948. ZUK, G. H. On silence and babbling in family psychotherapy with schizophrenics.
949. ZUK, G. H. On the meaning of laughter in family psychotherapy with schizophrenics.
950. MINUCHIN, S. 1965. Conflict resolution family therapy. *Psychiatry*, **28**, 278.
951. REIDY, J. J. 1962. An approach to family-centred treatment in a state institution. *Am. J. Orthopsychiat.*, **32**, 133.
952. BODDIE, C. A., and CUMMINGS, J. E. 1962. *An experiment with conjoint group therapy in a child guidance clinic.* Paper presented at annual meeting of American Psychiatric Association.
953. MITCHELL, C. B. 1960. The use of family sessions in the diagnosis and treatment of disturbances in children. *Soc. Casewk*, June.
954. BODDIE, C. A., and CUMMINGS, J. E. An experiment with conjoint group therapy in a child guidance clinic.
955. THARP, R. G., and OTIS, G. D. 1965. *Toward a theory for therapeutic intervention in families.* Western Psychological Association, Honolulu, Hawaii.
956. THARP, R. G. 1965. Marriage roles, child development and family treatment. *Am. J. Orthopsychiat.*, **35**, 531.
957. GLASSER, P. H. 1963. Changes in family equilibrium during psychotherapy. *Family Process*, **2**, 245.
958. GROSSER, G. H. 1964. Ethical issues in family group therapy. *Am. J. Orthopsychiat.*, **34**, 875.
959. CAREK, D. J., and WATSON, A. S. 1964. Treatment of a family involved in fratricide. *Archs gen. Psychiat.*, **11**, 533.
960. SHELLOW, R. S., BROWN, B. S., and OSBERG, J. W. 1963. Family group therapy in retrospect: Four years and sixty families. *Family Process*, **2**, 52.
961. HARMS, E. 1964. A socio-genetic concept of family therapy. *Acta psychother.*, **12**, 53.
962. SAMUELS, A. S. 1964. Use of group balance as a therapeutic technique. *Archs gen. Psychiat.*, **11**, 411.
963. COHEN, R. L., CHARNY, I. W., LEMBKE, P. 1964. Parental expectations as a force in treatment. *Archs gen. Psychiat.*, **4**, 471.
964. GREENBERG, I. M., GLICK, I., MATCH, S., and RIBACK, S. S. 1964. Family Therapy: Indications and rationale. *Archs gen. Psychiat.*, **10**, 7.

965. WREN, W. W. 1964. *The use of family therapy in a community clinic.* Paper presented at Sixth International Congress on Psychotherapy, London.
966. HAAS, A. Simultaneous relationship therapy.
967. LIEBERMANN, L. P. 1957. Joint-interview technique: An experiment in group therapy. *Br. J. med. Psychol.*, **30**, 202.
968. KAFFMAN, M. 1963. Short term family therapy. *Family Process*, **2**, 216.
969. THORMAN, G. Family therapy—Help for troubled families. *Publ. Affairs Pamphlet* No. 356.
970. FREEMAN, V. J. 1964. Differentiation on 'unit' family therapy approaches prominent in the United States. *Int. J. soc. Psychiat.*, Special ed. No. 2, 35.
971. BLAIR, A. 1961. Family Counselling: A new way to treat individual problems. *Parents' Mag.*, October.
972. CARUSO, G. J. 1963. Family orientated psychotherapy, A review. *J. La. St. med. Soc.*, **115**, 312.
973. NORTON, N. M., DETRE, T. P., and JARECKI, H. G. 1963. Psychiatric services in general hospitals: A family orientated redefinition. *J. nerv. ment. Dis.*, **136**, 475.
974. PARLOFF, M. B. 1961. The family in psychotherapy. *Archs gen. Psychiat.*, **4**, 445.
975. OTTO, H. A. 1966. Treatment and family strengths. *Canada's ment. Hlth*, **14**, 1.
976. BLINDER, M. G., COLMAN, A. D., CURRY, A. E., and KESSLER, D. R. 1965. 'MCFT': Simultaneous treatment of several families. *Am. J. Psychother.*, **19**, 559.
977. CURRY, A. E. 1965. Therapeutic management of multiple family groups. *Int. J. group Psychother.*, **15**, 90.
978. LEHRMAN, N. S. 1963. The joint interview: An aid to psychotherapy and family stability. *Am. J. Psychother.*, **17**, 83.
979. GUERNEY, B. Analysis of interpersonal relationships as an aid to understanding family dynamics: A case report.
980. BERGE, A. 1965. Psychotherapy of the family group. *Rev. Neuropsychiat. Infant.*, **13**, 651.
981. KOHL, R. N. 1962. Pathological reactions of marital partners to improvement of patients. *Am. J. Psychiat.*, **118**, 1036.
982. FRIEDMAN, A. S. 1964. The 'well' sibling in the 'sick' family: A contradiction. *Int. J. soc. Psychiat.*, Special ed. No. 2, 47.
983. GROTJAHN, M. 1960. *Psychoanalysis and the family neurosis.* Norton, New York.
984. SINGLETON, G. Comments on Murray Bowen's concept of 'Undifferentiated ego mass'.
985. SLATER, V. L., and MILLEDGE, E. Family involvement in mental illness.
986. FERREIRA, A. J. 1960. The 'double bind' and delinquent behavior. *Archs gen. Psychiat.*, **3**, 359.

Vector Therapy

987. EYSENCK, H. J. 1964. Critical review of the effects of psychotherapy. *Int. J. Psychiat.*, **1**, 99.
988. BRILL, N. Q. 1964. The economics of psychotherapy. *Int. J. soc. Psychiat.*, Special ed. No. 3, 24.

Social Psychiatry

989. BELL, N. W., and SPIEGEL, J. P. 1966. Social psychiatry. *Archs gen. Psychiat.*, **14**, 337.

990. SOUTHARD, E. E. 1917. Alienists and psychiatrists. *Ment. Hyg.*, **1**, 567.
991. RENNIE, T. A. C. 1955. Social psychiatry—A definition. *Int. J. soc. Psychiat.* **1**, 5.
992. RUESCH, J. 1965. Social psychiatry. *Archs gen. Psychiat.*, **12**, 501.
993. WITTKOWER, E. D., and RIN, H. 1965. Transcultural psychiatry. *Archs gen. Psychiat.*, **13**, 387.
994. WITTKOWER, E. D. Transcultural psychiatry. In HOWELLS, J. G. (ed.) *Modern perspectives in world psychiatry.* Oliver & Boyd, Edinburgh. (In press.)
995. LINTON, R. 1956. *Culture and mental disorders.* Thomas, Springfield, Ill.
996. MONTAGU, A. 1961. Culture and mental illness. *Am. J. Psychiat.*, **117**, 15.
997. AGNEW, P. C. 1961. Culture deprivation and mental illness. *Q. Bull.*, **35**, 54.
998. LEIGHTON, A. H., and HUGHES, J. 1959. Cultures as causative of mental disorder. In *Causes of mental disorders : A review on epidemiological knowledge.* New York.
999. HOLLINGSHEAD, A. B., and REDLICH, F. C. 1958. *Social class and mental illness : A community study.* Wiley, New York.
1000. MYERS, J. K., and ROBERTS, B. H. 1964. *Family and class dynamics in mental illness.* Wiley, New York.
1001. SUSSER, M. W., and WATSON, W. 1962. *Sociology in medicine.* Oxford Univ. Press, London.
1002. JONES, M., *et al.* 1952. *Social psychiatry.* Tavistock Publications, London.
1003. JONES, M. Community psychiatry. In HOWELLS, J. G. (ed.) *Modern perspectives in world psychiatry.* Oliver & Boyd, Edinburgh. (In press.)
1004. RAPOPORT, R. N. 1960. *Community as doctor, new perspectives on a therapeutic community.* Tavistock Publications, London.
1005. CLARK, D. H. 1963. Administrative psychiatry, 1942-1962. *Br. J. Psychiat.*, **109**, 178.
1006. CLARK, D. H. 1964. *Administrative therapy : The role of the doctor in the therapeutic community.* Tavistock Publications, London.
1007. CARSE, J., PANTON, N. E., and WATT, A., 1958. A district mental health service. The Worthing experiment. *Lancet*, i, 39.
1008. FREEMAN, H. L. 1960. Oldham and District psychiatric service. *Lancet*, i, 218.
1009. MACMILLAN, D. 1958. Community treatment of mental disease. *Lancet*, ii, 201.
1010. CUMMING, J., and CUMMING, E. 1962. *Ego and milieu.* Atherton, New York.
1011. BROWN, G. W. 1959. Experiences of discharged chronic schizophrenic patients in various types of living group. *Millbank mem. Fund. Q.*, **37**, 105.
1012. FREEMAN, H. E., and SIMMONS, O. G. 1958. Mental patients in the community: Family settings and performance levels. *Am. sociol. Rev.*, **23**, 147.
1013. HOWELLS, J. G. 1963. *Family psychiatry.* Oliver & Boyd, Edinburgh.

6. *The Future*

Research

1014. PERL, R. E., and SIMON, A. J. 1942. Criteria of success and failure in child guidance. *Am. J. Orthopsychiat.*, **12**, 642-658.
1015. TROUTON, D. S., and MAXWELL, A. E. 1956. The relation between neurosis

and psychosis—An analysis of symptoms and past history of 819 psychotics and neurotics. *J. ment. Sci.*, **102**, 1.

1016. EYSENCK, S. B. G. 1956. Neurosis and psychosis: An experimental analysis. *J. Ment. Sci.*, **102**, 517.

1017. ASHER, R. 1959. Lettsomian lectures.

1018. HAZLITT, W. *Table Talk*, 1821-2, 1824, Dent, London.

1019. FREUD, A. In ELLIS, R. W. B. (ed.) 1966. *Child health and development.* 4th ed. Churchill, London.

1020. STEINBECK, J. 1958. About Ed Ricketts. In *The log from the Sea of Cortez.* Heinemann, London.

1021. KRYNAUW, R. A. 1950. Infantile hemiplegia treated by removal of one cerebral hemisphere. *J. Neurol. Neurosurg. Psychiat.*, **13**, 243.

1022. O'NEAL, P., and ROBINS, L. N. 1958. The relation of childhood behavior problems to adult psychiatric status: A 30-year follow-up study of 150 subjects. *Am. J. Psychiat.*, **114**, 961.

1023. SHAPIRO, A. The placebo response. In HOWELLS, J. G. (ed.) *Modern perspectives in world psychiatry.* Oliver & Boyd, Edinburgh. (In press.)

1024. FREUD, S. 1887-1902. Project for a scientific psychology, in *The origins of psychoanalysis.* Basic Books, New York, 1954.

1025. HARTMANN, H. 1958. Comments on the scientific aspects of psychoanalysis. *Psychoanal. Study Child*, **13**.

1026. ELLIS, A. 1956. An operational reformulation of some of the basic principles of psychoanalysis. In FEIGL, H., and SCRIVEN, M. (eds.) *The foundations of science and the concepts of psychology and psychoanalysis.* Univ. of Minnesota Press, Minneapolis.

1027. FIEGL, H. 1949. Some remarks on the meaning of scientific explanation. In FEIGL, H., and SELLARS, W. (eds.) *Readings in philosophical analysis.* Appleton-Century, New York.

1028. FRENKEL-BRUNSWIK, E. 1954. Psychoanalysis and the unity of science. *Proc. Am. Acad. Sci.*, **80**.

1029. HARTMANN, H., and LOEWENSTEIN, R. M. 1947. The function of theory in psychoanalysis. In LOEWENSTEIN, R. M. (ed.) *Drives, affects, behavior.* International Univ. Press, New York.

1030. KRIS, E. 1947. The nature of psychoanalytic propositions and their validation. In HOOK, S. K., and KONWITZ, M. R. (eds.) *Freedom and experience.* Cornell Univ. Press, Ithaca.

1031. RAPAPORT, D. 1958. The structure of psychoanalytic theory. (A systematising attempt). In KOCH, S. (ed.) *Psychology : A study of science.* McGraw-Hill, New York.

Research in Family Psychiatry

1032. HILL, R. 1951. Review of current research on marriage and the family. *Am. sociol. Rev.*, **16**, 694.

1033. HILL, R. 1958. Sociology of marriage and family behavior, 1945-1956. *Curr. Sociol.*, **7**, 1.

1034. HILL, R., FOOTE, N., MANGUS, H. R., POLAK, O., and LESLIE, G. 1957. Appraising progress in research. *Marriage Fam. Living*, **19**, 59.

1035. BURGESS, E. 1947. The family and sociological research. *Sociol. Forces*, **26**, 1-6.

1036. COTTRELL, L. S. 1948. The present status and future orientation of research on the family. *Am. sociol. Rev.*, **13**, 123.

1037. DAGER, E. Z. 1959. A review of family research in 1958. *Marriage Fam. Living*, **21**, 287.

1038. EHRMANN, W. 1957. A review of family research in 1956. *Marriage Fam. Living*, **19**, 279.

1039. NIMKROFF, M. F. 1948. Trends in family research. *Am. J. Sociol.*, **53**, 477.

1040. NYE, F. I., and BAYER, A. E. 1963. Some recent trends in family research. *Social Forces*, **41**, 290.

1041. WALTERS, J. 1962. A review of family research in 1959, 1960 and 1961. *Marriage Fam. Living*, **24**, 158.

1042. HOFFMAN, L. W., and LIPPITT, R. 1960. The measurement of family life variables. In MUSSEN, P. H. (ed.) *Handbook of research methods in child development*. Wiley, New York.

1043. MEISSNER, W. W. 1964. Thinking about the family—Psychiatric aspects. *Family Process*, **3**, 1.

1044. HILL, R. 1964. Methodological issues in family development research. *Family Process*, **3**, 186.

1045. HALEY, J. 1964. Research on family patterns: An instrument measurement. *Family Process*, **3**, 41.

1046. LEVINGER, G. 1963. Supplementary methods in family research. *Family Process*, **2**, 357.

1047. BLOOD, R. O. 1958. The use of observational methods in family research. *Marriage Fam. Living*, **20**, 47.

1048. RABKIN, L. Y. 1965. The patient's family: Research methods. *Family Process*, **4**, 105.

1049. LIDZ, T. 1962. The relevance of family studies to psychoanalytic theory. *J. nerv. ment. Dis.*, **135**, 105.

1050. PARSONS, T. 1953. The superego and the theory of social systems. In PARSONS, T., BALES, R., and SHILS, E. (eds.) *Working papers in the theory of action*. Free Press, Glencoe, Ill.

1051. HARTMANN, H. 1950. The application of psychoanalytic concepts to social science. *Psychoanal. Q.*, **19**, 385.

1052. FRAMO, J. L. 1965. Systematic research on family dynamics. In BOSZOR-MENYI-NAGY, I., and FRAMO, J. L. (eds.) *Intensive family therapy*. Harper, New York.

1053. RISKIN, J. 1963. Methodology for studying family interaction. *Archs gen. Psychiat.*, **8**, 343.

1054. JACKSON, D. D. 1965. The study of the family. *Family Process*, **4**, 1.

1055. WEAKLAND, J. H. 1962. Family therapy as a research arena. *Family Process*, **1**, 63.

1056. VASSILIOU, G., and VASSILIOU, V. 1965. Attitudes of the Athenian public towards mental illness. *Int. ment. Hlth Res. Newsletter*, **7**, No. 2.

1057. VASSILIOU, V., and VASSILIOU, G. 1965. *Detecting changes during psychotherapy—A pilot study*. Presented at the First Research Conference of the Association of Greek Psychologists, Athens.

1058. VASSILIOU, V., and VASSILIOU, G. 1965. *On the semantics of 'Philotimo'*. Presented at the First Research Conference of the Association of Greek Psychologists, Athens.

1059. GEORGAS, J., and LEOUSSI, L. 1965. *Development of normative Rorschach patterns on 7-year-old Greek students*. Presented at the First Research Conference of the Association of Greek Psychologists, Athens.

1060. TENEZAKI, M., and VASSILIOU, V. 1965. *Fears and expectations of Athenians concerning Greece—First results from the application of Cantril's self-anchoring scale on a representative sample of Athenians*. Presented at the First Research Conference of the Association of Greek Psychologists, Athens.

1061. DEKKER, E., and GROEN, J. 1956. Reproducible psychogenic attacks of asthma. *J. psychosom. Res.*, **1**, 58.
1062. SPENCE, J., WALTON, W. S., MILLER, F. J. W., and COURT, S. D. M. 1954. *A thousand families in Newcastle upon Tyne*. Oxford Univ. Press, London.
1063. MILLER, L. Child rearing in the kibbutz. In HOWELLS, J. G. (ed.) *Modern perspectives in international child psychiatry*. Oliver & Boyd, Edinburgh. (In press.)
1064. MEAD, M. 1935. *Sex and temperament in three primitive societies*. Morrow, New York.
1065. MEAD, M., and MACGREGOR, G. M. C. 1951. *Growth and culture*. Putnams, New York.
1066. LAYTON, D., and KLUCKHOHN, C. 1947. *Children of the people*. Harvard Univ. Press, Cambridge, Mass.
1067. MEAD, M. 1954. Some theoretical considerations on the problem of mother-child separation. *Am. J. Orthopsychiat.*, **24**, 471.
1068. HEBB, D. O. 1958. The mammal and his environment. In REED, C. F., *et al.* (eds.) *Psychopathology*. Harvard Univ. Press, Cambridge, Mass.
1069. WOODWARD, M. 1965. Piaget's theory. In HOWELLS, J. G. (ed.) *Modern perspectives in child psychiatry*. Oliver & Boyd, Edinburgh.
1070. ANDRE-THOMAS, *et al.* 1960. *The neurological examination of the infant*. National Spastic Society.
1071. PENFIELD, W., and ROBERTS, L. 1959. *Speech and brain mechanism*. Princeton Univ. Press, Princeton.

PART TWO

ILLUSTRATIONS OF THE DIMENSIONS OF THE FAMILY

Edited by
John G. Howells

1. THE INDIVIDUAL DIMENSION

2. THE RELATIONSHIP DIMENSION

3. THE GROUP PROPERTIES DIMENSION

4. THE MATERIAL CIRCUMSTANCES DIMENSION

5. THE COMMUNITY INTERACTION DIMENSION

1

THE INDIVIDUAL DIMENSION

This dimension encompasses the individual's life experience in the Past, his functioning in the Present, and what is predictable about his behaviour in the Future.

From the many elements in the time sequence of Past, Present and Future in the history of the individual, the following illustrations have been selected:

> Intra-uterine experiences
> Infancy
> Childhood
> Adolescence

IV

THE CONDITIONING OF THE HUMAN
FETUS *IN UTERO**

The individual's intra-uterine experiences as a factor in shaping his personality are often overlooked. In this paper the author gives evidence of the reaction of the foetus to stimuli external to the mother.

It is commonly recognized that environmental factors influence the organism from the moment of fertilization, but experimental studies of their effects on the behavior of mammalian fetuses have usually disturbed the fetal environment severely. The possibility that conditioned response technique provides a method which would eliminate resort to surgery has long been seen. Successful conditioning of young infants[2, 3, 6, 7, 8, 10] and of sub-human mammals in which neural structures had been damaged[1, 11, 12, 13] indicated that lack of cortical development in the fetus presented no problem. Ray[15] made the first attempt, using the previously reported fetal response to loud sound[4, 14] which he sought to condition to a vibrotactile stimulation applied to the maternal abdomen. Although results on this single case were inconclusive, his use of individual receiving tambours, taped to the maternal abdomen over the fetus, eliminated

* This study was conducted, under the direction of Dr. J. F. Dashiell, in partial fulfillment of the requirements for the doctoral degree at the University of North Carolina. I am indebted to The Watts Hospital, Durham, North Carolina, and to Dr. R. A. Ross, Chief of Obstetrical Department there, for generous cooperation. My greatest debt is to Elizabeth P. Spelt, who contributed to every phase of the work, including the arduous analysis of hundreds of feet of kymograph records. The costs of the research were met by a series of grants from the Smith Research Fund of the University of North Carolina Graduate School.

Reprinted from THE JOURNAL OF EXPERIMENTAL PSYCHOLOGY, Vol. 38, June 1948, pp. 338-346.

much distortion of records by maternal breathing. This study was suggested by Ray's work and resembles his in general procedure.

APPARATUS

The source of noise (US) was a box $29\frac{3}{4}$ in. square, $10\frac{5}{8}$ in. deep, made of $\frac{1}{2}$ in. pine stock. It stood on one side, surmounted by a metal framework which carried an oak clapper five in. wide, $22\frac{1}{2}$ in. long, and one in. thick. Pivoted one in. from the top, the clapper had a narrow steel handle nine in. long. A steel spring ran from each edge of this handle to the supporting framework, so that a pull of some eight pounds was necessary to raise the clapper, through an arc of 85°, to the stop which limited its excursion. When released the clapper struck the face of the box sharply, closing a circuit through a dry cell and signal marker. On top of the box were mounted all the controls for E's use.

Vibrotactile stimulation (CS) was provided by an ordinary doorbell, with the gong removed, the striker bent outward at an angle of 90° to its original position, and the interrupter soldered shut. The striker vibrated strongly but almost silently in response to four volts of 60-cycle A.C. This stimulator, fastened to a block of wood, was held in an adjustable metal clamp at the end of a movable support affixed to the side of the bed in which the Ss lay. Thus, the striker could be made to vibrate perpendicularly to the surface of any part of the abdomen. A dual key controlled the transformer-stimulator circuit and a dry cell-signal marker circuit.

Fetal movements were recorded by means of three pairs of 50-mm. receiving tambours taped to the maternal abdomen, each pair connected to a one-inch recording tambour. The method of placing the tambours is described below.

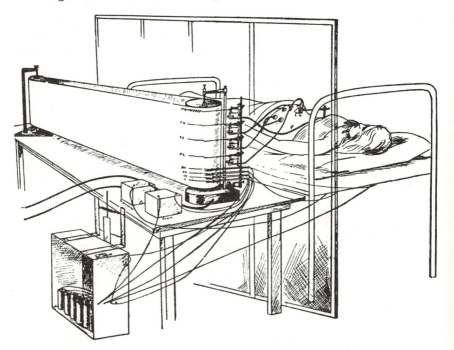

FIG. 1. Sketch of apparatus arrangement for fetal conditioning study.

S operated a signal marker whenever she felt fetal movement by pressing a push button which she held in her hand. A Manning pneumograph[16] connected to a one-in. recording tambour supplied records of maternal breathing. An electric clock and signal marker provided a time line marked in intervals of five sec.

All recording devices were vertically moving ink-writers which bore upon an electrically driven long-paper kymograph. The kymograph, apparatus controls, and *E* were screened from *S*'s view when she lay in bed, as indicated in Fig. 1.

Subjects and Procedure

Except for three non-pregnant control *S*s and one of the pregnant *S*s, all 16 *S*s were selected from patients attending the obstetrical clinic of an urban hospital. All but two were past the seventh calendar month of gestation. Only patients whose histories were free from evidence of pathology during pregnancy were considered, and only those willing to participate actually served as *S*s. Not that *S*s knew they were taking part in an experiment, for the word was scrupulously avoided by everyone who dealt with them. *S*s were told that since confinement was approaching and since their progress thus far had been excellent, the staff wanted some 'special information' to be obtained from X-ray pictures and from records of fetal movements to be made twice daily for 10 days or two weeks. They were told that no cost was involved, and that they would be guaranteed free care in the hospital's obstetrical ward when they came to term. Since the hospital was sufficiently crowded to admit only a fraction of the group attending the clinic, certainty of admission was an important reward. It was made quite clear, however, that they were free to decline without jeopardizing the normal chance of admission, for no record was made of their decision on the clinic card. A few of those interviewed did so decline.

After appointments for subsequent admission to the hospital had been arranged, each *S* went to the radiological department, where two X-ray pictures of the abdomen were made: an anteroposterior view and a lateral view. These plates and the radiologist's report were available well in advance of the admission time for each *S*.

Each pregnant *S* entered the obstetrical ward on the day of her appointment as a regular patient, and was required to rest in bed for at least a half-day before the first experimental period. When she went to the experimental room for the first time, the operation of the instruments was superficially explained, but no insight into the problem was provided, nor did any *S* ever have an opportunity to examine the records until after her last session. Even then no information beyond the original statements made in the first interview was offered, less the study become a matter of ward gossip.

Before each experimental period the assisting nurse applied the pneumograph to *S*'s chest and put her to bed. In an effort to record fetal movements as adequately as possible, the data from X-rays, external manual examination, and fetal heart sounds were employed to determine the position of the fetus. One pair of receiving tambours was taped to the abdomen over the fetal head, another over the fetal arms, and the third over fetal legs.* It was never supposed, however, that selective records were thus obtained, or that movements recorded from one area had different significance from movements recorded elsewhere. Next, the vibrotactile stimulator was adjusted at some convenient spot on the abdomen,

---

* In 12 of 13 cases the fetus was in cephalic presentation at the time of X-ray; in 10 of 13 cases, the fetal back was to the left, with the head usually in the left occiput anterior position.

although its location varied for every S from time to time. Then S took the push button with which she indicated that she felt fetal movement. Finally, E connected the abdominal tambours and the pneumograph to the recording apparatus, and started the clock and kymograph.

Procedure during the first experimental periods varied slightly for different Ss. Most Ss had two sessions daily, lasting from 30 to 75 min. each, depending largely on S's comfort. Three Ss in the experimental group (Group I, nos. 10, 12, 15) received 8-16 successive US, followed by 3-10 successive unreinforced CS (five sec. each) as a control for the possibility of pseudo-conditioning. The other Ss in Group I (nos. 16, 17) received 5-15 successive unreinforced CS without prior US. Actually, only three CS were needed to demonstrate the indifference of the vibrotactile stimulus, since it never elicited a response, without reinforcement, after three successive failures. Ss were warned about the noise on the first trial or two, but very few were startled, even on the first day.

Conditioning procedure involved presentation of CS for five sec., terminated by the loud noise (US). Since Ray had shown that successful stimulation of the fetus induces a 'refractory period' lasting some four min., the principle of separating successive stimulations by intervals of somewhat greater length was followed, except on one or two occasions when the validity of the principle was checked.

Special control groups were treated somewhat differently. Thus, Group II consisted of six Ss (nos. 1, 3, 4, 8, 9, 14) with whom the CS alone was tested for indifference during the last two months of pregnancy. Group III included three non-pregnant Ss (nos. 19, 20, 21) each of whom served for two 'conditioning' periods. In Group IV were two Ss (nos. 5, 18) with whom the effect of fetal age on the response to sound (US) alone was investigated by beginning presentation in the seventh month of gestation.

RESULTS

Group I. Two Ss in this group had displayed indications that the conditioning procedure had been effective, when the experiment was interrupted by labor. S-10 during the first four sessions received 16 successive US followed by 10 successive CS. Although the fetus responded regularly to the noise, the vibrotactile stimulus was ineffective. By the eighth session three successive responses to CS alone appeared, but labor began the following day. Similarly, with S-17 three successive responses to CS alone appeared by the eighth session, but the onset of labor precluded further experimenting.

Results with the other three Ss in Group I will be presented in greater detail. Records of S-16 showed the first fetal response to CS alone after 21 paired stimulations, and others appeared at intervals until in the sixth session, after 59 reinforced presentations, a series of seven successive CRs occurred. At the beginning of the seventh session the next morning, and with no reinforcement, four more CRs were elicited, followed by irregularly spaced responses as experimental extinction developed. There was no indication of recovery of the response the following day, although US was still effective. These data are summarized in Table 1.

S-15 received 10 successive US followed by three successive CS during the first two sessions. As before, the noise was effective, the vibro-

TABLE 1

Results from Subject 16. Trial numbers in italics indicate unreinforced presentations of the conditioned stimulus; all others are paired presentations. Letters in the Resp. column show which recording systems revealed the response: H—fetal head; A—fetal arms; L—fetal legs; M—maternal signal. This S had only one experimental period per day; the interval between successive days is indicated by the dashes.

Trial	Resp.	Trial	Resp.	Trial	Resp.	Trial	Resp.	Trial	Resp.
14	LM	32	HALM	50	HA M	67	H LM	84	
15	LM	33	HALM	-----	-----	68	H	85	
16	H LM	34	HALM	51	ALM	69	H M	86	H M
17	H LM	35	LM	52	H M	70	HALM	87	
18	LM	*36*	LM	53	LM	71	HALM	88	HALM
19	H LM	37	ALM	54	ALM	72	H	89	
20	ALM	-----	-----	55	HALM	*73*	HALM	90	
21	LM	38	H LM	56	M	*74*	ALM	91	H LM
22	M	39	H LM	57	LM	*75*	HALM	92	
23	H LM	40	H LM	58	ALM	*76*	HALM	93	
24	HALM	*41*	H LM	59	HALM	*77*	HALM	94	
-----	-----	*42*		60	ALM	*78*	HALM	95	
25	LM	43	ALM	*61*		*79*	HALM	-----	-----
26	A M	44	HA M	*62*	ALM	-----	-----	96	
27	ALM	45	H M	-----	-----	*80*	A M	97	
28	ALM	46	HALM	63	H M	*81*	H LM	98	
29	H LM	47	HALM	64	H M	*82*	HALM	99	HALM
30	HALM	*48*	A M	65	H LM	*83*	H M	100	
31		*49*		66	HALM				

tactile stimulus ineffective. The first response to CS alone occurred in the sixth session after 16 paired stimulations. Others occurred irregularly, but since this S was still in the eighth month of gestation, she was allowed to leave the hospital at her own request after the eleventh session. She returned two weeks later and the experiment was resumed. The CS alone was ineffective, but after 31 reinforcements six successive CRs appeared, followed by experimental extinction. With 12 more reinforcements the CR was reinstated at the end of the session. The data obtained after S's return are summarized in Table 2.

S-12 was perhaps the most interesting of the group, because of the extensive study of the CR which was possible. During her first two sessions, eight successive US were followed by four successive CS which were ineffective. The earliest response to CS alone came in the seventh session after 21 paired stimulations, when on two successive trials (Table 3, nos. 27-28) CRs occurred. Three more CRs were obtained at the beginning of the ninth (nos. 40-44). When four successive CS produced no direct record of fetal response (nos. 55-58), S was permitted a 24-hour rest period to see whether spontaneous recovery would develop. That such recovery occurred is evident. Eleven successive CS alone produced six clear reactions in the fetal records and on two other trials the maternal signal was pressed (cf. Table 3, trials 59-69). The response was then extinguished again, although the fetus still responded to the noise. S was then discharged, but returned to the hospital 18 days later as a result of false labor. Hence it was possible to resume experimental work exactly

TABLE 2

Results from Subject 15. Trial numbers in italics indicate unreinforced presentations of the conditioned stimulus; all others are paired presentations. Letters in the Resp. column show which recording systems revealed the response: H—fetal head; A—fetal arms; L—fetal legs; M—maternal signal. Intervals between sessions on a single day are shown by asterisks, between sessions on successive days by dashes.

Trial	Resp.	Trial	Resp.	Trial	Resp.	Trial	Resp.	Trial	Resp.
72		86	AL	98	A	111	ALM	124	LM
73	HALM	-----	-----	99	HA	112	HALM	*****	*****
74	L	87		100	A	113	HALM	125	
75		88	HAL	101		114	HALM	126	L
76		89	L	102	HALM	115	HALM	127	L
77	ALM	90		103	HALM	116	HALM	128	
78		91	HA	104	L	*****	*****	129	ALM
79		92	HA M	105	HALM	117	AL	130	LM
*****	*****	93	HALM	-----	-----	118	L	131	ALM
80		94	HALM	106	LM	119		132	ALM
81		95	HA M	107	AL	120		133	
82	ALM	*****	*****	108		121		134	M
83	L	96	LM	109	L	122	L	135	
84	L	97	L	110	HA	123	HAL	136	LM
85	HALM								

three weeks after the last previous session. In the next two periods, CS was presented alone 12 times in succession; seven of the first nine stimuli were effective, showing retention of the response over this interval, while the last three were ineffective. On the next day only two CRs were elicited in eight trials, and S was again discharged. She returned 13 days later, when X-rays showed that the fetus was probably past term, but it was possible to run one more experimental session before labor was medically induced. There was no response to CS alone although the two stimuli together were effective. These data appear in Table II3.

Group II. This group included six Ss, all in the late eighth or the ninth month of pregnancy, with whom the CS alone was tested to discover whether it became effective simply as a result of advancing fetal maturity. Although each S received 4-7 unreinforced vibrotactile stimuli, none of the 32 trials elicited a response.

Group III. In this group were three non-pregnant Ss, members of the hospital's staff, each of whom served for two standard experimental periods. Presentation of the two stimuli in varying combinations, for 16-23 trials per S during the two sessions, yielded no records remotely resembling those obtained with pregnant Ss.

Group IV. This group consisted of two Ss whose records indicated that the US used (noise) was ineffective before the eighth calendar month of gestation. S-5, in whom gestation had progressed to the latter part of the seventh month was exposed to 39 successive US. On only one occasion did the records show what might have been a fetal response. On eight other trials the maternal signal appeared without evidence of movement in the fetal records.

TABLE 3

Results from Subject 12. Trial numbers in italics indicate unreinforced presentations of the conditioned stimulus alone; all others are paired presentations except no. 91, which was the sound alone. Letters in the Resp. column show which recording systems revealed the response: H—fetal head; A—fetal arms; L—fetal legs; M—maternal signal. Intervals between sessions on a single day are shown by asterisks, between intervals on successive days by dashes. Longer intervals are specifically stated.

Trial	Resp.	Trial	Resp.	Trial	Resp.	Trial	Resp.	Trial	Resp.
22	M	41	LM	58		77		95	
23	L	-----	-----	-----	-----	78		96	
24	A	42	LM	59	M	Three weeks'		97	ALM
25	LM	43	L	60	ALM	interval		98	LM
26	LM	44	LM	61		79		*****	*****
-----	-----	45		62	LM	80	AL	99	HAL
27	ALM	46		63		81	L	100	AL
28	A M	47		64	ALM	82	L	101	HAL
29	M	48		65	L	83		102	L
30	A M	*****	*****	66	M	84	ALM	103	
31	ALM	49		67	LM	85	LM	104	L
32	L	50	ALM	*****	*****	86	LM	105	
33	ALM	51	M	68	ALM	87	A	106	L
*****	*****	52	LM	69	ALM	88		107	
34	LM	53	ALM	70		89		13 days' interval	
35	LM	54	LM	71		90		108	
36	LM	-----	-----	72		91	LM	109	
37		55	M	73		-----	-----	110	
38	L	56		74		92		111	
39	LM	57		75	ALM	93	LM	112	HALM
40	ALM			76	LM	94		113	AL

S-18 was tested at intervals from the middle of the seventh month to the middle of the eighth. During the seventh month 60 US yielded no indication of movement, either in the fetal or the maternal records. During the eighth month the US was presented four times during the first week, with the maternal signal indicating fetal movement unsupported by the direct records. In the third week, seven stimuli produced three definite fetal reactions and one indicated by the maternal signal only.

DISCUSSION

At present no experimental procedure will permit one to test Holt's thesis[5] (pp. 37-43) that intra-uterine conditioning accounts for certain of the behavioral characteristics of the human neonate. On the other hand, it is clear that the human fetus can be conditioned experimentally during the last two months of pregnancy. The records, of course, cannot be expected to yield data on comparative motility of fetal head, arms, and legs. The placement of the fetal body during the last weeks of gestation and the limitations imposed by recording only from the abdominal surface preclude such interpretation. Furthermore, it is impossible to derive precise quantitative values for latency, duration, or extent of response, for much the same reasons. Actually, examination of the records indicates that responses to paired stimuli have shorter latencies than do CRs, but the distributions overlap. In the same way, although both sharp, quick responses and slower, longer lasting movements appear, it has not been possible to attach any significance to the difference.

If these records do not permit analysis of the sort mentioned, they are, none the less, not greatly distorted by such factors as maternal breathing and gross bodily movement. When such distortion does occur, as the

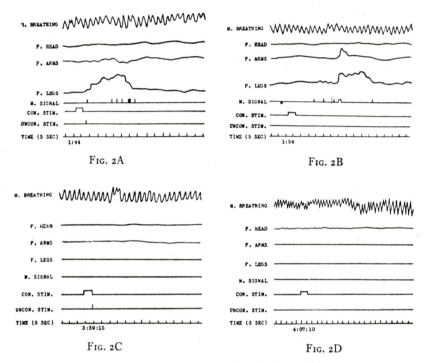

FIG. 2A

FIG. 2B

FIG. 2C

FIG. 2D

FIG. 2. Sample kymograph records from fetal conditioning study. A, showing response to both stimuli, and B, showing response to CS, obtained from same *S*. C is a record from a non-pregnant control *S*. D shows result of applying CS alone in late pregnancy without previous conditioning trials.

result of a deep sigh for example, it can be readily detected because all three fetal curves move in the same direction simultaneously, and the irregularity appears in the maternal breathing curve as well. This is never true of fetal responses, and the fact is obviously of importance in reading the curves.

The amount of agreement between the direct records and the maternal signal indicating perceived fetal movement is significant. As a measure of the degree of correspondence, a bi-serial *r* was computed, based upon the number of fetal curves (0-3) in which a given response appeared, and upon its presence or absence in the maternally made record. For 529 stimulations of the 13 pregnant *S*s, $r_{bis} = \cdot784$, $\sigma_r = \cdot017$.

Obviously, further study of more Ss is to be desired. Analysis of the effective unconditioned stimuli which may be used, of the length of retention which may be obtained, and of the age at which sensitivity to auditory stimuli develops would be profitable. In this last connection, it may be significant that Langworthy[9] found fibers of the cochlear branch of the eighth cranial nerve much more lightly myelinated in a seven months fetus than in the eight months old specimen which he examined. It will be recalled that in our two Ss who served during the seventh month of pregnancy, the noise was almost completely ineffective as a stimulus to fetal movement. There are, then, enough problems still deserving investigation to justify further study of the fetal conditioned reaction.

SUMMARY

Utilizing a vibrotactile CS and a loud noise as US, it was possible to establish a CR in the human fetus *in utero* during the last two months of gestation. Some 15-20 paired stimulations were required to establish the response to the point at which one could anticipate three or four successive responses to CS alone, but additional practice made possible as many as 11 successive CRs. Experimental extinction, spontaneous recovery, and retention of the response over a three weeks' interval were demonstrated, as well as a significant degree of agreement between direct records of fetal movements and maternal report of perception of fetal movement.

REFERENCES

1. BROGDEN, W. J., and GANTT, W. H. 1937. Cerebellar conditioned reflexes. *Am. J. Physiol.*, **119**, 277-278.
2. DENISOVA, M. P., and FIGURIN, N. L. 1929. The problem of the first associated food reflexes in infants. *Vop. genet. Refl. Pedol. Mladench.*, **1**, 81-88. (See *Archs Psychol.*, 1933, **23**, 73-75.)
3. FIGURIN, N. L., and DENISOVA, M. P. 1929. The physiology of the differentiation of external stimuli. Based upon experimental data on the formation of differentiation in infants under one year. *Vop. genet. Refl. Pedol. Mladench.*, **1**, 131-165. (See *Archs Psychol.*, 1933, **23**, 75-76.)
4. FORBES, H. S., and FORBES, H. B. 1927. Fetal sense reactions: Hearing. *J. comp. Psychol.*, **7**, 353-355.
5. HOLT, E. B. 1931. *Animal drive and the learning process*. Holt, New York.
6. JONES, H. E. 1930. The retention of conditioned emotional reactions in infancy. *J. genet. Psychol.*, **37**, 485-498.
7. KANTROW, R. W. 1937. An investigation of conditioned feeding responses and concomitant adaptive behavior in young infants. *Univ. Iowa Stud. Child Welf.*, **13**, No. 3.
8. KASATKIN, N. I., and LEVIKOVA, A. M. 1935. On the development of early conditioned reflexes and differentiation of auditory stimuli in infants. *J. exp. Psychol.*, **18**, 1-19.

9. LANGWORTHY, O. R. Development of behavior patterns and myelinization of the nervous system in the human fetus and infant. *Carnegie Inst. Publ.*, No. 443, 1-57.

10. LEVIKOVA, A. M., and NEVYMAKOVA, G. A. 1929. The problem of the formation and differentiation of associated reflexes to auditory stimuli in infants. *Vop. genet. Refl. Pedol. Mladench.*, **1**, 89-105. (See *Archs Psychol.*, 1933, **23**, 77-78.)

11. LIGHT, J. S., and GANTT, W. H. 1936. Essential part of reflex arc for establishment of conditioned reflex. Formation of conditioned reflex after exclusion of motor peripheral end. *J. comp. Psychol.*, **21**, 19-36.

12. MARQUIS, D. G., and HILGARD, E. R. 1936. Conditioned lid responses to light in dogs after removal of the visual cortex. *J. comp. Psychol.*, **22**, 157-178.

13. MARQUIS, D. G., and HILGARD, E. R. 1937. Conditioned responses to light in monkeys after removal of the occipital lobes. *Brain*, **60**, 1-12.

14. PEIPER, A. 1925. Sinnesempfindungen des Kindes vor seiner Geburt. *Z. Kinderheilk.*, **29**, 236-241.

15. RAY, W. S. 1932. A preliminary study of fetal conditioning. *Child Dev.*, **3**, 173-177.

16. SPELT, D. K. 1939. The Manning pneumograph. *Am. J. Psychol.*, **52**, 116.

V

CONSIDERATIONS REGARDING THE
PARENT-INFANT RELATIONSHIP

PHYLLIS GREENACRE

*It is generally accepted that infancy is a period of
profound significance for the developing personality.
This paper discusses those intimate relationships, of
great importance, between the parent (mother and
father) and the child.*

INTRODUCTION

The subject 'The Theory of Parent-Infant Relationship,' assigned for the
papers shared by Dr Winnicott and me for discussion at the International
Congress in 1961, is a broadly inclusive one. It is my understanding that
the Committee designing the programme intended that these papers
should not merely give a résumé of generally accepted theory of parent-
child relationship in very early childhood, but should deal especially with
those aspects of the subject to which the authors have devoted special investigative attention and concerning which they have developed points of
view expanding, elaborating, or even diverging from theories already
widely accepted. I have therefore entitled this paper 'Considerations Regarding the Infant-Parent Relationship'. This assignment is a pleasing
one since it presents the opportunity and the obligation to consolidate and
clarify work on certain problems of infantile development which have preoccupied me throughout all of the years of my psycho-analytic practice.

It is necessary, too, to define our subject further. The term *infant* may
be variously used. From the angle of the law, an infant is a person below
the age of full maturity—generally fixed in our Western countries at 21.*

* This definition of maturity and infancy actually closely coincides with linear
skeletal growth measurement, in the male. The fixing of the end of infancy at 18 in the
female is also in accord with these biological growth statistics.

Reprinted from THE INTERNATIONAL JOURNAL OF PSYCHO-ANALYSIS,
Vol. 41, Part 6, 1960, pp. 571-584.

The implication here is that the span of physical growth is definitely fulfilled by this time and that the mental capacity for full individual responsibility has correspondingly developed. In pediatric and general medical
practice, the term *infant* is often used for the child who cannot yet walk.
After this he becomes a toddler. Here then it designates approximately
the first year or 18 months after birth. In certain educational groups, the
infant is the child who may attend infant schools or not yet be in school
at all. The distinction then corresponds in time to the oedipal period,
the resolution of which gives an additional push of independence and ex-
pands the child's activity so markedly beyond the home and family circle.
When in psycho-analysis we speak of the infantile neurosis, we generally
also include the time through the oedipal period. Our Programme Committee, however, designated the period to be discussed now as comprising
the first two years after birth. This corresponds to the stage of fairly
adequate establishment of the skills of walking and talking and of the initial
capacity for secondary process thinking. It is of especial interest as it
includes the inception and early stages of ego development.

What seems conspicuous and significant here is that in whatever way
the term *infancy* is defined, its limit appears to be marked by maturational
attainments involving some definite independence from the mother or
from both parents. It is indeed with physical maturational factors* reaching meaningful stages in body structure, form, and function that this
paper will concern itself; to examine the interplay of these with the parent-
infant relationship and the accompanying effect on the psychic development of the infant. In his book *Ego Psychology and the Problem of Adaptation*[21] Hartmann points clearly and repeatedly to the influence of biological
maturational processes and stages on ego development: and in conjunction
with ego function, on the reality adaptation of the total personality throughout life.

It is a temptation to quote liberally here, since the book contains a discussion, rich in its suggestions, concerning the intrinsic interrelation
between biological factors and psycho-analytic findings and theories.
While Hartmann considers that the examination of biological growth
processes does not, strictly speaking, belong within the field of psycho-
analysis, he emphasizes that nonetheless some thought must be given to
them in understanding fully the significance of psycho-analysis for education, sociology, and mental hygiene, difficult as these fields are to delimit
and define. As he mentions (p. 4), already in 1936 Anna Freud in *The*

---

* The terms *growth*, *development*, and *maturation* have been variously used by investigators. In general, *growth* has the connotation of increase in volume or weight;
development may include this but emphasizes rather increase in elaboration of structure
and/or functioning; whereas *maturation* stresses development in the direction of an
optimal functional state. Since these terms have been used with such a degree of overlap
in their meanings, to attempt to use them with a precise discrimination might be more
confusing than clarifying. I am therefore following the decision of H. V. Meredith who
reviewed the literature in 1945,[32] and using them interchangeably.

Ego and the Mechanisms of Defence[4] (pp. 4-5) had defined the task of psycho-analysis as the attainment of 'the fullest possible knowledge of all the institutions (id, ego, and superego), of which we believe the psychic personality to be constituted and to learn what are their relations to one another *and to the outside world*' (italics mine). Utilizing this, Hartmann adds, first, that it is possible however that psycho-analysis may be expected to furnish or become a general developmental psychology; and second, if and when this occurs, it must involve the study and appreciation of areas outside of the neuroses with which we habitually concern ourselves. He believes that an anticipation of this kind was entertained by Freud in the early years of his work when he referred repeatedly to the biological and physiological substructure of psycho-logical phenomena, and it may again have been in his mind at the time of his writing 'Analysis Terminable and Interminable' (1937).[7] 'After all,' Hartmann says, 'mental development is not simply the outcome of the struggle with instinctual drives, with love objects, with the superego and so on. . . . We have reason to assume that this development is served by apparatuses which function from the beginning of life. . . . Memory, associations, and so on, are functions which cannot possibly be derived from the ego's relationship to instinctual drives or love objects, but are rather prerequisites of our conception of these and their development' (p. 15).

It is possible that the tendency rigidly to restrict the field of psychoanalysis to meta-psychology in consideration of the established mental institutions was strengthened not only by the fact that psycho-analysis developed largely as a therapeutic method dealing essentially with pathological conditions, and the theory was influenced greatly by clinical investigations; but further, since the need to keep psycho-analytic treatment clear of other adjunct therapies is an essential one the vision of theory may have followed suit. Latterly the need to reaffirm strict boundaries of the preserve of psycho-analysis has resulted from its very popularity with the attendant danger of its dilution or degradation by those workers in our own and adjacent fields who enthusiastically embrace it without sufficient training in psycho-analysis itself and therefore sometimes work without adequate discrimination.

At any rate, if psycho-analysis is to develop a general psychological theory, as seems probable from an expansion of interest in the science of psycho-analysis itself, as well as from its inherent growth in its practical applications, then concern with related problems of biological development inevitably has a place. Stated even more specifically, the objection can no longer be raised that 'all of these problems are outside the field of psychoanalysis . . . if we seriously intend to develop the ego psychology begun by Freud, and if we want to investigate those functions of the ego which cannot be derived from the instinctual drives. These functions belong to the realm (of) . . . the autonomous ego development. It is obvious that these apparatuses, somatic and mental, influence the development and the functions of the ego which uses them: ... that these apparatuses constitute one of the *roots* (italics mine) of the ego' (Hartmann, p. 101).

THE SCOPE OF THIS PAPER

It is the purpose of this paper to indicate my conceptions concerning the mutual impact in the infant of maturational forces and the parental influences, predominantly those of the mother, during the first two years after birth. The special focus is on the development of the ego. I have long been impressed from a phenomenological angle with the appearance of certain stages, one might say nodes, of striving and of capacity for independent activity in the young child. Futher these seemed to be in a close time relationship to definite stages of physical maturation: periods at which physical attainments, only recently impossible or uncertain, 'clicked'. The young infant then appeared to have a *feeling of gratification* in the achievement with subsequent increase in ease (a kind of physical confidence) apparent in the readiness and firmness of the do-it-again attitude of expectancy.* When one uses the term *striving*, as I have, it might seem to imply already the self-direction of a developed ego. What I am talking of is certainly on the borderland of ego development, but seems to me to be an expression of a maturation pressure to act or to move in a certain fashion, according to the unfolding of innate growth patterns, and to form the body groundwork of autonomous ego expansions.

It is easy to be misled in interpretations of such observations by the subjective elements in the observer. Medawar remarks, 'Everybody recognizes that there are indeed profound similarities between the behaviour of man and animals, but biologists and laymen think about them in entirely different ways. When laymen see mice nursing and cherishing their young, their first thought is, "How like human beings they are, after all!" The biologist (at all events when he is on duty) thinks, "How mouse-like after all are men!" '[31] I have always felt cautious about extrapolating from observations of animal behaviour and making interpretations on the basis of its similarity to human behaviour. My use of a *biological* point of view has rather to do with efforts to understand developmental stages and problems in the human being from the angle of general biological principles, especially those having to do with growth and maturation.

I myself have never been a systematic direct observer of young children; many direct observations have been casual and involved with a personal relationship as well. I have however attempted to use the work of others (psychologists and pediatricians) especially concerning physical and behavioural maturation stages in infancy. This has been supple-

* This reminds one strongly of Hartmann's statement that the pleasure of the developing ego functions is an essential in the acceptance of reality.[22]

mented by the work of psycho-analyst colleagues, especially of those with wide clinical and theoretical interests. Primarily my own interest was stimulated early by Freud's 'Three Essays on Sexuality'[8] in which he clearly saw the libidinal phase development as based on physical growth stages, and later repeatedly emphasized the constitutional elements in the source and intensity of instinctual drives.

CHARACTERISTICS OF GROWTH

Biological growth has certain general characteristics important for our understanding of the interrelation of mental and physical progress in the infant: *first*, it has a high degree of autonomy in its patterning: *second*, with some exceptions and variations it tends to progress in a cephalo-caudal direction; *third*, the younger the organism, the greater the rate of growth (size, weight, and progressive differentiation); *fourth*, it proceeds with a reciprocal interweaving of development of related counteracting functions of neuromotor systems (e.g. extensor and flexor muscular capabilities), evident in periodic shifting of dominance of the component functions or systems with a progressive modulation and integration of resultant activity; *fifth*, it is subject to progressive fluctuations culminating in more stable conditions and responses; this has already been referred to as the tendency to reach stages or nodes before new directions of growth; *sixth*, in general it progresses according to an overall principle of individuation—i.e. development always involves a response of the organism as a whole and growth of any of its component parts or systems does not readily get markedly out of bounds. This response of the total organism, however, does not preclude a real uniqueness of the individual in specific details on a constitutional basis.[12]

The homeostatic organization of the individual is not as stable or efficient in infancy, however, as it is in later life. This principle of life seems to gain superior strength after the big increments and fluctuations of growth are past. In infancy the neonatal period (two to four weeks after birth) has an extremely high mortality rate, due probably to the inability of the newborn to adapt readily to the experience of birth, and especially to the changed environment. After the first two years of infantile life, the ego certainly plays an important role in synthesizing and integrating the various aspects of any given experience, whatever its nature (Nunberg).[34, 35] But this integrative tendency in the organism, which is related, possibly in an organic way, to the later homeostatic principle, exists in some degree even in the time before and during the early development of the ego, when experience does not involve any appreciable degree of true object relationship.

Perhaps at no stage is the autonomous character of the maturation processes so clear as in intrauterine life, where it is coupled, however, with an essential dependence of the embryo or foetus on the mother for life itself. Indeed without this complete maternal protective envelope and passively supplied nutrition the very young embryo could not increase in size and complexity because of the inevitable exorbitant need for sustenance simply to maintain its body heat, owing to the relatively high ratio of body surface to volume.[31]

Ideas of the influence of the mother on the unborn have varied greatly from the old superstitious beliefs in prenatal marking by the attitudes and specific experiences of the mother to a concept of intrauterine life, also derived from fantasy, as completely exempt from any disturbing maternal influence. Our knowledge is still incomplete. But it seems significant that in general severe disturbance in the mother may, according to its nature, affect the nutrition and size of the foetus, or conceivably promote a heightened reactivity to certain stimulations. But it does not ordinarily interfere otherwise with the fetal growth patterns. It is evident however that there are epochs of intrauterine growth with acceleration of growth in size as well as in structural changes which are relatively greater than those occurring after birth. And there are special periods of vulnerability when external influences may have a catastrophic effect.[33]* But in general the progress of development in size and form is steadfastly determined by endogenous rather than exogenous stimulations. Gilbert describes the anomalies of development as misfortunes of growth at critical stages.[14] It is interesting too in connexion with the autonomous patterning of growth that the growth tendency in weight of premature babies after birth conforms to that of foetuses of the same size and age rather than to that of full term babies of the same chronological age, computed from the date of birth (Scammon 1922).[37]

The tendency of maturation to extend in a cephalocaudal direction is of importance in the concept of early determinants in ego development. It means that the maturation of the special senses, olfaction, vision, and hearing as well as the neuromuscular patterning of mouth activity is proportionately farther along at an early age than is that having to do with the movements of the hands and feet, or even of the trunk. Thus most observers find that focussing of the eyes occurs before, and is instrumental in furthering, controlled movements of the hand and lower arm. Earlier the arms, and the legs tend to react as wholes, the impulses to action arising mainly from the shoulder and the pelvic girdles. As maturity advances, mobility asserts itself at the elbow and the wrist joints and at the knee and the ankle joints. From about four months on, the elbows and digits participate in reaching movements with increasing effectiveness until at nine or ten months they approximate to the shoulder effectiveness (Halverson).[20] But at four months, the eye muscles have already attained

* The first three months of pregnancy, when organogenesis is proceeding rapidly, is a period of special susceptibility to influence from maternal illness, notably rubella. The second three months (4-5-6 mos.) is much safer, and the third trimester again somewhat hazardous. Nelson's *Textbook of Pediatrics*, p. 27.

a fair degree of focussing. There is thus a definite time lag in the developing of controlled movements in forearm and hands behind that of visual movement and focussing. Even more striking is the disparity in time development of the control of movement at the two ends of the gastrointestinal tract. The movements of the mouth are well developed at birth, whereas control of the lower bowel is not attained for many months. This is so much an analytic truism that its implications as part of the sequential growth pattern may be readily overlooked. The question of the significance of the cephalocaudal maturational direction tendency will be discussed again in connexion with the development of the body ego.

THE BODY EGO

Hoffer's papers[27, 28, 29] on the development of the body ego (1949-1950) offer an excellent starting-point for this discussion. On the general foundation of the conception put forward by Hartmann, Kris, and Loewenstein[23] that both ego and id arise from an undifferentiated state, rather than Freud's earlier formulation of the ego becoming differentiated from the id (1927),[9] and that the first and most fundamental step leading to ego differentiation 'concerns the ability of the infant to distinguish between the self and the world around him', Hoffer proceeds to examine the possible ways in which the separation of the body self from 'the other' (anything in the outer world) may occur.

Freud had spoken of internal perceptions, more fundamental and more elementary than the external ones to which the infant also responds, that is, the response of the body to itself and to the internal organs, with changing states of tension and relaxation. It would seem then that these might form a kind of central core of dim body awareness. If it is correct that the body states giving rise to these perceptions are by no means completely chaotic but are already knit together in some ways by the internal patterning of ontogenetic development, this quasi-organization in itself would contribute to the 'coreness' of the primitive body image at its inception; and the problem of separateness would become largely focussed on the surface of the body,* and on the awareness of especially those functions involved in perceptions of contact of varying intensities.†

* I have had the idea that the process of birth itself is the first great agent in preparing for awareness of separation; that this occurs through the considerable pressure impact on and stimulation of the infant's body surface during birth and especially by the marked changes in pressure and thermal conditions surrounding the infant in his transfer from intramural to extramural life.[16]

† It is interesting in this connexion that the subcutaneous tissue tends to increase rapidly in thickness during the first nine months after birth, while growth of the body as a whole is decelerating. Thereafter it tends to diminish, so that by five years it is approximately half as thick as at nine months (Nelson's *Textbook of Pediatrics*, p. 15).[33] It is possible that this is part of a response to the need for heat conservation during a period in which growth, although decelerating, is still disproportionately great for the conditions of the external environment. A similar increase in subcutaneous tissue occurs in prepubescence and decreases again when the general growth impulse diminishes. In con-

Touch is obviously important in the determination of the self from the non-self—of the body from the environment. Through it are mediated any perceptions of differences in temperature, texture, moistness, and many other subtle changes in kinaesthetic vibratory sensations and pressures, differences which gradually build up to some sense of degrees of separateness or of aloneness. Hoffer states that the special importance of touch in the development of the body ego lies in the fact that touching one's own body elicits two sensations of the same quality, and that as these areas with similar sensory responses become gradually united or confluent, an important step in the delimitation of the body from the outer world is achieved. But I would add that touch may also be a potent conveyor of the opposite—i.e. make for a sense of oneness with the other, or not-self, if the 'other' is or approximates to the warm body of the mother or nurse. There is then a relatively small degree of difference in temperature, texture, smell, resilience, etc. (compared for instance with such qualities of inanimate objects, and the difference is one to which the infant has already become acclimatized.

The transitional object itself described by Winnicott[41] is a monument to the need for this contact with the mother's body, which is so touchingly expressed in the infant's insistent preference for object which is lasting, soft, pliable, warm to the touch, but especially in the demand that it remain saturated with body odours. While the comfortable and familiar smelliness of the chosen transitional object is actually derived from the infant's own body, the fact that the object is usually pressed against the face close to the nose probably indicates how well it substitutes for the mother's breast or soft neck. It is virtually impossible for the infant to use any part of his own body for as good a simulation of the breast. His attempts with fingers and toes may be incompletely satisfying because of the lack of softness of the digits and their difference in configuration from the mounds and hollows of the maternal body.

It seems to me that vision is not only an adjunct but an indispensable one in establishing the confluence of the body surface and promoting awareness of delimitation of the self from the non-self. 'Touching' and taking in of the various body parts with the eyes (vision) helps in drawing the body together, into a central image beyond the level of mere immediate sensory awareness. Further the very functioning of visual perception in a focussed way (which is possible at an early stage in accordance with the cephalocaudal principle of maturation), as different from the reciprocal contacts between body parts by cutaneous touch, may offer a kind of nuclear beginning to an ego development at a mental level.* It is a self-

nexion with the fitting together of these various media of growth impulses it is interesting that this first post-birth increase in subcutaneous tissue diminishes at a time when peripheral locomotor activity (crawling, attempts at walking, and muscular play) has definitely entered a new phase.

* Gesell remarks: 'The eyes take the lead in the conquest of and manipulations of space. The baby takes hold of the physical world ocularly long before he can grasp it

observing function which gains significance as it combines with and oversees the self-perception of touch to form some kind of image of much of the body self, and to separate it from other objects, both animate and inanimate.

In Hoffer's papers he further traces the integration of the hand-mouth activity which emerges with increasing capacity for direction and control during the third and fourth months (10-16 weeks). He considers that (i) appearance of pleasure, (ii) the probable functioning of memory evident in the consistent use of definite patterns of finger and hand sucking, (iii) the possible existence of reality testing in the discarding of other objects offered, and (iv) the considerable control by the infant of his own need satisfaction through finger sucking—all of these developments indicate a definite ego beginning. I would agree fundamentally with all this, except that I would give a much more significantly important place to vision in the establishment of this organized control.

Certainly the pervasive and powerful influence of vision is soon apparent when the infant begins to indicate choice through his head movements (Spitz).[39] The *no* makes a refusal through a direct turning of the head to the side to dispose of the undesired stimulating object by removing it from vision; whereas the *yes* through up and down movement permits it to remain in the range of focus and be affirmed again and again. Thus the *no* seems related to an unsuccessful form of the negative hallucination which through its externalization gains the secondary force of communication. But the contrast between the affirmative and the negative is determined in large measure by the bilaterality of the eyes.

MATURATION, PLEASURE IN FUNCTIONING, AND THE BEGINNING OF AGGRESSION

For a long time it has seemed to me that we must look for the primordial origins of aggressions as well as of libidinal pleasure in the early processes of maturation. It may even be that aggression and bodily satisfaction are at times overlapping aspects of growth itself, i.e., satisfaction in the period before earliest inception of the ego or the establishment of any appreciable degree of object relationship. This is the period, especially of intrauterine life and the first weeks after birth, when the physical activity of the organism consists very largely of the multiplication of the cellular elements and their differentiation and organization into different organ systems. Even the active functioning of the different organs is generally much below that which will develop in later infancy and childhood. While the physical apparatuses are being perfected, the rate of growth in volume, weight, and complexity or organization is stupendous. If this were to continue unabated after the first three months of pregnancy, when organo-

manually. He can pick up a pellet 7 mm. in diameter fully 20 weeks before he picks it up with his fingers.' 'Ontogenesis of Infant Behavior'.[12]

genesis has been completed, all other life would soon be crowded out. But such growth paradoxically can occur only when the organism is in a relatively helpless state, and is primarily a growing rather than a going concern. After the third month of foetal life, independently active functioning begins to become apparent. The mother feels movements of the fetal extremities as kicks and pushes.* Growth, in the sense of increment, is diminished, although still prodigious compared to what it will be by the postnatal time when these kicking movements have begun to be used for crawling or early attempts at walking, or later when kicking is utilized as a hostility directed against the object.

The question of any *rudimentary pleasure in functioning* must here be raised, as well as its corollary, the way in which this leads over to or is connected with later *ego pleasure* in functioning I have already referred to Hartmann's statement that the pleasure of developing ego functions is an essential in the acceptance of reality; and to Hoffer's conception that the appearance of pleasure in the functioning of the hand-mouth movements is one of the criteria of beginning ego formation (at a mental level). I have mentioned the appearance of infantile gratification in achievement, for example in the beginning of walking. These references are all to behaviour at the very beginning or in the early stages of psychological ego development.

In prenatal and neonatal periods, however, there can only be a very primitive and basic form of narcissism. In Freud's early paper on narcissism[10] he refers to the 'narcissistic libido of the foetus', and again to the 'libidinal complement to the egoism of the instinct of self-preservation, a measure of which may justifiably be attributed to every living creature'. In the chapter on the Analysis of Anxiety, in *The Problem of Anxiety*[11] he expresses the belief that the foetus at birth cannot be aware of anything beyond a gross disturbance in the economy of its narcissistic libido resulting from the 'pressure of large amounts of excitation giving rise to novel sensations of unpleasure: numerous organs enforce increased cathexis in their behalf, as it were a prelude to the object cathexis soon to be initiated. . . .' (pp. 96, 97, 102).†

With these considerations in mind one may ask whether this early form of narcissism may not be described as the libidinal investment of growth, before independent life is at all possible. The further question arises whether the conception of unpleasure may not have its counterpart in an early form of pleasure: a prelude, perhaps little more than a relative

---

* The foetal heart has begun to beat in the first month. Corner puts these facts very picturesquely: '. . . the months before birth are in their way the most eventful part of life and we spend them at a rapid pace. At the beginning the body consists of one cell; by the time of birth, it has two hundred billion cells. . . . You had the beginnings of a brain before you had hands, and of arms before legs; you developed muscles and nerves and began your struggle' ([3] Chap. 1, 'The Embryo as Germ and as Archive').

† In early papers on 'The Biological Economy of Birth' and 'The Predisposition to Anxiety', Part I, I have made some attempts to discuss the theoretical implications of this concept of foetal narcissism.[16, 17]

resting stage of ease with diminished tension, a slight plateau in development such is as conceivably indicated at about the 3rd to 4th month of pregnancy, before the initiation of a new phase or a new form of activity occurs. It is important, however, that the diminished tension is not due to an arrest in activity but rather to a smoothness in performance of recently acquired activity. In infancy one sees such periods, I believe, around the 4th or 5th months and again around the 15th to 16th month, in relation to specific functional achievements. At these more general stages or nodes of development, there is a suggestion of well-being and of the fitting together and 'clicking' of interrelated activities with a temporary relief from the urgency of old pressures. New maturational drives may be felt then as pleasant stimulation rather than experienced yet as uncomfortable accumulations of tension. At such times, it would seem as though in the endless interweaving processes of growth, a fundamental part of the pattern has emerged more clearly.

What then are the antecedent stages in the development of aggression? But first, how shall we define or describe it? It is for the most part agreed that there are two sets of instinctual drives—the sexual and the aggressive drives. From a biological angle, these may be considered to be largely in the service of the continuation of the species and of the individual respectively. But from the angle of the individual life adaptation, obviously they cannot be reduced only to these terms. On the other hand, I find it helpful not to disregard completely the implications of the biological beginnings of activity even when trying to understand it at a psychological level. It may be for this reason that it is more difficult for me to grasp clearly the article on the theory of aggression by Hartmann, Kris, and Loewenstein (1949),[24] than Hartmann's discussion of ego psychology and the problem of adaptation[21] or his article on the psycho-analytic theory of the ego.[22] In the first of these, any real consideration of the biological has been pretty much tidied out of the discussion in the interest of avoiding possibly murky speculation.

Hartmann, Kris, and Loewenstein speak of 'impulses of an aggressive nature, manifestations of destructiveness or *cruelty*' (italics mine). One is aware that with the addition of the term cruelty an animate object is implied, for cruelty involves suffering of another. Aggression at this level then can occur only with an established ego and the development of appreciable object relationship. I would prefer to consider aggressive instinctual drives first simply as destructive drives, or before the dawn of the ego and object relationship, to consider them as biological assertiveness, a manifestation of processes of growth.

If aggression is an instinctual drive, it must be potentially present in some degree of primitive organization before the development of the ego. It seems that the earliest form of aggression exists in the great expansion and evolution of the newly fertilized ovum. In some unicellular organisms it is manifested in the pseudopodal activity by which the organism reaches out and envelops particles with which it comes in contact. In this simple form, aggression is a *going at* or *towards*, an *approaching* as the derivation of the word implies. In the fertilized ovum there is a marked increase in activity and an awesomely rapid increase in size, complexity, and organization after implantation in the uterine wall. Already a peculiar biological partnership has been set up between embryo and host, in which the partners are continuously more intimately together and more separate than in any other relationship in life.

But my point here is that since the embryo and its maternal host are now obligatorily a combined concern, in which the mother's body is the nutrition gatherer for the embryo and the supply is lavish, this energy of the primordial aggression is not needed for the attainment of nutrition and can be utilized in biological creativeness in the building up and the functional differentiation of the organs. Thus the mother's body has taken over almost completely the satisfaction of embryonic destructive drives. If we accept at all the biological conception of ontogeny repeating phylogeny we are confronted with the extraordinary situation of this energy going into a life, in a sense apart from the embryonic environment (the uterine cavity) which is, however, a reliving of the reactions to all the environments of aeons past. This is a feat which is almost beyond our true comprehension. It is not that the assertive drive is turned inward against the organism, as we might later conceive it to be, in an established organism, when it then becomes self-destructive, but it is still in a sense an outward drive in which the environments of the past are internalized as part of the process of developing organization, in an unbelievably condensed recapitulation. Once this cycle has been completed and the foetus has caught up with time, then such an enforced passivity might endanger rather than promote the development of the organism. Is this turning of the energy into the work of organizational growth a change in the nature of the energy?

When the period of the first three months of organogenic growth is past, and the nervous and muscular systems are sufficiently well developed, the energy begins to be peripherally directed again and movements of the extremities occur. The mother 'feels life' in the fourth month. Even earlier movements can be elicited by specific stimulations in embryos removed from the body, but by the fourth month they seem to occur regularly owing to the reaching of some kind of integration point of the functional processes going on in connexion with the autonomously interweaving undertakings of maturation. During the later months of pregnancy there is an increasing amount of peripherally directed activity.

After birth the infant must begin to fend even more for himself, taking the nourishment aggressively from his mother through nursing, rather than receiving it passively through his blood stream. But it is at the times of the auspicious harmonizing of related functions, the arrival at a fairly smooth meshing of these functions to reach a more complex economizing activity, that the body ego develops and contributes to the beginning mental ego. I would refer here again to Hartmann's statement, 'These apparatuses, somatic and mental, influence the development and functions of the ego which uses them—that these apparatuses constitute one of the roots of the ego.'[21] This is in keeping too with Freud's early statement that pleasure tended to be linked with the self and unpleasure with the outside-the-self. It is also related to the concept of Hartmann, Kris, and Loewenstein,[23] who say 'Every step in the formation of the object corresponds to a phase in psychic differentiation. That differentiation itself is determined by the *maturation* of the apparatus, which later comes under the control of the ego, and by the experiences which structure the psychic apparatus. Hence both processes, differentiation of psychic structure and relation of the self to external objects are interdependent' (p. 27). Again, 'The formation of the ego can in part be described as a learning process, which supplements the growth of the apparatus of the ego. The gratification of demands stemming from instinctual drives is guaranteed by learning' (p. 13). What I have been considering is the prelude to this, the biologically autonomous beginnings, which have been described as belonging to the no-man's-land between biology and psychology (Hoffer).[29] It is probably important that in prenatal life there is the beginning of a brain before there are hands.

But we are now confronted with the question of the fate both of the raw aggression of infancy and of the concomitant pleasure in functioning which seem so important in the formation of the ego and later are utilized by it. This brings us to the next division of this paper.

THE PARENT-INFANT RELATIONSHIP AND MATURATION

'The children most physically endangered by the present state of affairs [i.e. conditions of disrupted family life under war conditions in London] are those up to two years of age. It is easy to understand that infants simply cannot live in a state of emergency. . . . Development demands its own conditions, irrespective of war and peace or all other happenings in the outer world' (Freud-Burlingham Reports).[6]

During the first two years after birth, one of the main tasks of the infant undoubtedly has to do with making a sound separation from the mother and the commencement of an individual existence, with the later establishment of the sense of reality, of early object relationship, the beginning of secondary process thinking, and the first stages of the sense of identity, in conjunction with, interdependent with and under the mediation of the young ego.

The infant begins by having to work for a living in nursing and continues by taking over gradually and with the mother's co-operation the other concerns of his body life. The pleasure in and control of the satisfaction of his bodily demands and functions—his pregenital sexual life—proceeds according to rather well marked phases, determined by maturational development associated with the different body zones involved. It is not necessary for the focus of this paper to recapitulate much concerning early libidinal phase development which was one of the cornerstones of Freud's early observations and the beginning of analytic theory. I shall pay more attention now to thoughts concerning the evolution of the early ego. There are certain comparisons, interrelations and contrasts between ego and libido developments.* But this will be referred to again somewhat later.

During the early part of this period it is obvious that the mother or her substitute is the exclusively important person in the infant's life. The father may play a role as a substitute for the mother but his more muscular body is a less acceptable cushion than is that of a nurse or other female helper. This is especially true during the undifferentiated phase, immediately succeeding the neonatal lethargy and extending into the greater part of the first year.

By the time of birth the sensitivity of the body surface is well developed in the mouth area especially, where skin and mucous membrane responses are active and the neuromuscular pattern for sucking is well established. But in addition to the hunger needs, the contact with the mother's body to supply warmth and exercise through its motion is essential, as the work of Spitz[38] and others[1, 2, 36] has specifically demonstrated. It is probable that the rhythm of the maternal movements associated with body warmth offers the infant a partial reinstatement of prenatal conditions and helps bridge over the transition from intramural to extramural life. With the infant a little more advanced or in an alert awake state rather than a sleepy one, the body contact with the mother may offer stimulation and a degree of toning up of peripheral muscles which helps in their functional maturing. Naturally then the ease and freedom from tensions with which the mother accepts these reciprocal activities contributes much to the well-being of the infant.

This fluctuation between oneness with the mother and separateness from her either through temporary loss of contact with her or through the experiencing of strong own-body sensations different from what have been experienced in contact with her seems very important, as it furnishes the beginning of what will become a psychological separation as well.† While it is believed that the awareness of the boundary between maternal

* See papers of Hartmann, and Hartmann, Kris, and Loewenstein already mentioned, and Hartmann in 'Comments on the Psychoanalytic Theory of the Ego'.[22]

† On the basis of clinical psycho-analytic observations, I have thought that infants who slept habitually in bed with their parents were stimulated by primal scene activity and took on through vision, hearing, and kinaesthetic sensory responses the excitement of the motility, incorporating it into general body excitability. Naturally in cases of this kind, frequently the repeated exposure to the primal scene goes on throughout a long span of time in infancy. It is not easy then to determine what is incorporated from the first months and how much it adds to the intensity of responses to exposures of a later

and own body experience is at first non-existent or very dim and then uncertain, it is evident that there is a gradual increase in the appreciation of differences.

By the end of the first six months, there is the appearance of actively asserted pressure *against* the mother as part of the growing maturational separateness. Specifically during the fourth to sixth months, it is very common to see an infant jump up and down while being held by the mother while she remains seated. As the baby pushes in a somewhat bouncing motion with his feet against her thighs or abdomen, he shows unmistakable signs of pleasure with gurgling and laughing. His activity involves ability to extend the legs and the trunk as well in rhythmic co-ordinated movements, with a much more powerful thrust than he has been able previously to command. The appearance of signs of some degree of gratification is convincing. This behaviour occurs after the extraocular muscles have matured and movements of the eye are fairly well controlled. Ordinarily then the infant is in visual contact with the face of the mother as he thus dances against her body. Earlier too, he has been wont to touch her breast and then her face with his hand in a fumbling way, but generally without much force. It is my belief that this forceful pressing or pushing activity is part of a definite phase resulting from favourable maturational development and a meshing of related functional activities to permit this new step, with some inner feeling of exhilaration and bodily confidence. It is comparable to what Hoffer described between hand to mouth and finger selection for sucking in his paper on the 'Development of the Body Ego'.[27] But at this stage there is a correlation of activity of the legs, arms, and trunk, involving also vision—with the appearance of the very beginning of object relationship to the mother. The physical aggression in this behaviour is striking even though one cannot think in terms of motivation, but rather of a degree of biologically autonomous againstness, which combines with and may be augmented by the mother's tendency to respond with reciprocal motion. In this activity there may be an increasing sense of physical power and of the ability to initiate motor activity and to control it to a degree. There may also be a certain amount of reality testing in the rhythmic quality of back-and-forthness, reminding us of the throwing of the ball (which will occur later) and the pleasure of having it returned, or of the peek-a-boo game. Furthermore, the relationship to the object (the mother) is generally maintained through vision, throughout the play. A little later babies do not need the mother's co-

period. Certainly young infants react markedly and in highly individual ways to both motion and sound.

On the other hand, early deprivation of stimulation from body contact and from being handled may have serious consequences. It is well known now that babies treated by routine mass methods, as in some foundling hospitals, suffer severely in physical health as well as in their emotional development. The deficiency in bottle feeding as a substitute for breast feeding may be largely in the loss of the exercise of being handled and of the stimulation of body contact. This is especially true where bottles are propped and only the mouth and cheeks are active in the feeding.

operation and will go through these alternately bending and straightening up motions while hanging on to a crib side or a chair.

According to my observations, partly direct but casual ones in caring for children, and in part through reconstructions in working with adult patients, there are also later stages of body maturation and awareness linked with phases of ego development. One occurs at about the fifteenth to sixteenth month or so and seems to be associated with the accomplishment of walking. A later one is associated with the period of the phallic phase.* In both of these there is certainly a component pleasure of skin, muscle, and kinaesthetic erotism; further the genital contribution to the total body exhilaration is most apparent in the phallic phase. This, however, is beyond the limits set for this paper. But the pleasure has also an element of reaction to integration, organization, and mastery, which show in an attitude of confidence and assurance in repetition.† It is experienced in connexion with executive activities which predominantly involve a reaction to and on the environment, rather than a primary focus on control of bodily functions, as is the case in the activities of the special erogenous zones in the libidinal phase development. Still there is much in common and a certain amount of interrelation between the patterning of the aggressive instinctual drives and that of the sexual ones.

In the development of control of both sets of instinctual drives the attitude of the infant's partner, the mother, is of paramount importance. We are familiar with the fact that attention to self-demand in feeding and to the use of trial situations in toilet training seems to be helpful in selecting of *timing* for the regulation of schedules both for feeding and toilet training. This is then in accordance with the maturational readiness of the infant to respond adequately and with a minimum of strain. Essentially this means the appreciation of the baby as a developing organism rather than as a miniature adult, and may indicate a developed object relationship rather than a narcissistic one on the part of the parent towards the infant. It is also a matter of clinical experience that great distortion in the timing of the management of libidinal phase activities together with the accompanying disturbance in infant-mother relationship tends to promote a fixation on the special erogenous zone. Some increase in ambivalence and the provocation of conflictual aggression with consequent defence formation then occurs.

According to my conception somewhat comparable conditions may arise from an inadequate cooperation between mother and infant, if she fails to accept and respond to the maturation needs of the infant's aggressive drives, as these emerge into new constellations of organized activities. Disturbances seem to arise especially with respect to her failure to accept

---

* I have mentioned these elsewhere chiefly in connexion with disturbance of their development in the perversions.[11] Lowenstein also has noted the possible relation between these last two periods (that at about sixteen months and that at four years) with respect to ego development.[31]

† Compare Hendrick's conception of an instinct of mastery.[25, 26]

the infant's growing separation from her, or to see readily enough the spurts of aggressive behaviour as part of growing motor executive abilities rather than as simply increasing destructive urges threatening to the infant and to the property around him. In such instances, by curbing the child excessively either with actual physical restraint or with constantly anxious responses to his activity, she prevents the optimal utilization of the energy of the aggressive drives in the biologically creative formation of new body skills. This further interferes with the attendant pleasurable gratifications and promotion of body ego and early mental ego development. Instead there is then an increment in the destructive or cruel aggressive drives. Object relationship is impeded and turned in a hostile direction, in reaction to the interference with the maturation pressures. In attitudes of anxious restrictiveness the mother may then promote exactly what she has thought she wished to guard against, viz. outbursts of destructive temper and some constriction of learning.* Marked and consistent interference of this kind may result in impairment of sound ego development. Conversely an optimal empathic response to and support of the infant's developmental needs by the mother will result in utilization of a suitable portion of aggressive energy in constructive enterprise with attendant gratification. This situation strengthens ego development and promotes functions which are later the concern of the well developed ego.†

This seems to me a paradigm of that part of character structure in which the ego is able to 'neutralize' an amount of aggressive energy and use it in constructive service, first in the organization of body motility and later in the attainment of more elaborated skills of use in social relationships. This is in contrast, on the one hand to the almost exclusive abandonment to the gratification of aggressive discharge with a minimal ability to check impulses and, on the other, to the control of aggression in compulsive reaction formation with the development of strong competitive drives, conditions which may follow poor maternal handling. In the latter case the choice of activity for development of skill may be socially

---

* In connexion with the infantile reaction to restraint, J. H. Taylor, an experimental observer, concluded that infant responses to restraint (after the first few weeks) depend not so much on the external stimulus as upon an *internal* condition. Consequently the evaluation of observations in terms of external stimulus and overt behaviour may give rise to erroneous conclusions.[41]

F. Goodenough, studying temper outbursts in early childhood, found that shows of temper in the first year occurred mostly in connexion with routine care such as dressing and bathing. By two years, however, temper outbursts occurred largely in connexion with conflict with the mother over establishment of routine habits and about equally in conflict with her over authority in matters not directly connected with habit training. These were early studies, when pediatric advice generally was in the direction of early 'habit training' rather than fitting this to the maturational needs of the infant.[15]

† The acceptance of the aggressive pressures and assertiveness of the infant does not mean, however, a complete permissiveness and lack of any restrictions, as has sometimes been attempted by 'progressive' parents. For a discussion of these aspects of the situation see A. Freud.[4]

acceptable. But the aim of the aggressive drive is still primarily a gratification of the sadism through 'beating out' the other in competition. The apparent ego strength is then more a matter of durability, maintained at the expense of flexibility and of primary enjoyment in fruition of the skill itself. In the end, the sadism, with its attendant conflicts, may then invade or constrict other areas of character development.

THE SENSE OF IDENTITY AND EARLY IDENTIFICATIONS IN INFANCY

So far, this discussion has been concerned largely with the development of the first year of life, the dependence on the mother and the increasing separation from her, owing to the maturation processes feeding infantile autonomy. The second year of life is psychologically infinitely more complex. In the first year the attachment to the mother has been established largely on the basis of her being a need-fulfilling person; 'in the second year, the child loves her as a separate person' (Freud and Burlingham Reports, p. 49).[6] Already after the first months of the first year and well established in the second year, is the infant's reaction to the father, which seems rarely as intense as it is towards the mother, probably owing to the lesser constancy and bodily intimacy of the contact. By this time, however, the infant may well respond to the more vigorous play of some fathers, and differentiate quite clearly his expectations as to what may be obtained in this respect from each parent. The father's place is increasingly important and complex.

The accomplishment of walking, ordinarily around 15-16 months, seems to be the definite crossing of a threshold of development and contributes, through its combination of rhythm and space, to an early stage of organization of secondary process thinking, with a strengthening of the sense of time, and of sequence. With walking there is an enlargement of the capacity of re-visiting and re-experiencing exploratory activities, which in turn lends support to the developing sense of reality, and to the very beginning of associations which will lead in the direction of awareness of consequences and reasoning. Extravertive behaviour—throwing or casting toys out, pushing chairs and small objects around—is increased; sensory experiences are multiplied and may be increasingly experienced on the infant's own initiative. I have several times watched infants at this stage (when walking can be achieved with confidence) in their delighted exploration of a wide variety of sensory experiences in a garden: smelling the flowers, patting them, feeling the texture of stones, gravel, sand; listening to the sounds of a fountain with a kind of sophisticated attention. Walking has permitted an enormous increase in the infant's world under his own relative control.

Simultaneous with this awareness of the outer world is an increasing awareness of his own body and body functions. The infant begins to pay attention to his own urinary puddles, after they have occurred, but does not show by sound or gesture a differentiation between urination and bowel movement. During the next few months there is ordinarily an increasing strength of sphincter control and regularity of rhythm; and by a year and a half or so he may communicate his excretory needs before he sees the products[13] (pp. 33-34). Greater precision of observation of his own body and the bodies of others develops, and by the end of the second year there is an awareness of similarities and differences between the self and others, with respect to body parts and their representatives in clothing, and the expression of preferences and distastes. All this is part of the growing sense of identity and individuality, such that by the end of the next year (at 3) the young child regularly knows and can verbalize his name, his sex, and the basic facts of his family orientation.[13]

There is some indication that in the first year after birth, and especially after the fourth or fifth month, the infant shows a fluctuating primitive identification alternating with a progressively increasing depth of separateness from the objects around him. This is based on his helplessness and his functioning actually as a part of and at the mercy of others and the capacity and constancy of the mother as a need-fulfilling agent. This primitive identification is thus quite different from identification, as we understand it, after the establishment of the ego, when it may be a passive, fated identification through awareness of likeness to another individual, or an active one in the wish to be or become so in form or functioning. Already sexual differences are noted, in accordance with the opportunities for observation; other differences, such as hair texture and colour, are commonly noticed.

By the sixth month after birth there is a quasi-automatic responsiveness in smiling, and the taking over through vision and body contact of the moods and tensions of others in the environment. This responsiveness gradually becomes a more complex imitativeness. By the end of the first year, an infant may go through motions imitating an adult lighting a cigarette or doing some other special task (Gesell).[13] It is doubtful whether this is an identification in the sense of a strong wish to be like another special person, such as might be clear a year later. It seems rather that it is a transitional stage between primitive identification and the more purposeful object identification which is just beginning. It may partake of the wish to try out whatever is seen in activity and be in part a motor exploration. But during the latter half of the second year, quite complicated imitations are attempted, expressing the wish to become or to recall the imitated person.

Certain characteristics of states of primitive identification have impressed me through clinical observations, though I am by no means sure that others would agree with them. While this identification belongs to the stage of incomplete differentiation between the self and the other, and is superseded in importance by object-related identifications after the establishment of the ego and the sense of self, still it seems never to be completely abandoned. It can be and generally is repeatedly reactivated under special conditions of later life. It seems to me to be the basic nucleus of empathy and possibly one of the essential ingredients of the matrix from which transference reactions develop. Further it may throughout life be powerfully activated by contact with intense moods of others which then become highly communicable. This is especially true in group situations involving states of emotional excitement and may become an important factor in group irrationalities, such as riots and states of religious excitement.

It has also seemed to me that prolonged and unrelieved contact of an infant (during the first year or year and a half after birth) with another individual, usually another child, leaves a permanent effect of diminished differentiation of the self from the other, and consequently weakens and confuses the sense of identity, producing an effect somewhat simulating twinning.[19] I have especially noticed this in certain perversions, where it seemed to contribute, along with other factors, to the uncertain sexual identity.

CONCLUDING REMARKS

In the time at my disposal for the preparation of this paper and in consideration of the reader's span of endurance, I found it not feasible to cover the subject of the *Theory of the Parent-Infant Relationship in the First Two Years* in its entirety. I have therefore limited myself to a discussion of selected problems of development within this broad framework. I have chosen those aspects of the parent-infant relationship which are especially constellated around and by the maturational forces in the infant. Here again, I have had to establish some further limits and have focussed almost exclusively on the biological beginnings of aggression as it is involved in skeletal muscle maturation, and the relation of this to the development of the ego.

I conceive of maturation as proceeding by certain stages according to general principles of growth. These stages are marked by periods of special activity accomplishment (organic learning) and are accompanied by the appearance of pleasure. The first postnatal stage of this kind seems to appear at about five months and marks the first clear separation from the mother which is under the infant's control; and is followed by the definite emergence of the beginning mental ego. Thus there is a contrast to the earlier development arising from purely biologically determined forces in the infant, supplemented by maternal contact and care. Throughout this period of early ego emergence, the mother (or her substitute) is the partner to the infant in responsiveness to his functional attainments. Her attitude is highly important in determining how much the innate aggressive instinctual drive may be augmented by frustration at these critical periods—or the opposite—the development of gratifying and ego-strengthening realization of accomplishment.

The development of the libidinal phases has been but scantily dealt with as it has been rather thoroughly described elsewhere. There is the serious omission, however, of the contribution of oral aggression as evident in crying, biting, and the development of speech. It is of some interest, for example, that biting of the mother's nipples associated with the eruption of teeth coincides in time with the five-month period of maturation in skeletal muscle activity, and that crying seems to change from an undifferentiated type of discharge to a more specific and somewhat controlled one in the same era. The emergence of patterns of essentially visceral muscle activity with an interplay with skeletal muscle in gesture as part of communication, forms an integral part of early aggression. Certain early forms of excretory aggression might merit consideration here, although the intensity of their influence belongs more to the period between 12 and 36 months.

The developments of the second year after birth (especially the period of 18 to 24 months) having to do with the establishment of secondary process thinking, memory, the sense of reality, identifications, and the sense of identity are only briefly sketched. The consummation of speech belongs to this period also. One is impressed with the flowering of the complexities and subtleties of the infant's development after the second period of maturational achievement which I have described as occurring at about 15 to 16 months, with the accomplishment of walking.

I trust that I may be pardoned the omissions and inadequate treatment of some parts of this broad subject, with the hope to remedy these in further studies in the future.

REFERENCES

1. BAKWIN, H. 1942. Loneliness in infants. *Am. J. Dis. Child.*, **63**, 30-40.
2. BRODY, S. 1956. *Patterns of mothering.* International Univ. Press, New York.
3. CORNER, G. W. 1944. *Ourselves unborn. Natural history of the human embryo.* Yale Univ. Press, New Haven.
4. FREUD, A. 1936. *The ego and the mechanisms of defence.* Hogarth, London, 1937.
5. FREUD, A., and BURLINGHAM, D. 1943. *Infants without families.* Allen & Unwin, London; International Univ. Press, New York, 1944.
6. FREUD, A., and BURLINGHAM, D. 1943. *War and children*, pp. 49, 98. Medical War Books, New York.
7. FREUD, S. 1937. Analysis terminable and interminable. *C.P.*, **5**.
8. FREUD, S. 1905. Three essays on the theory of sexuality. *S.E.*, **7**.
9. FREUD, S. 1923. *The ego and the id.* Hogarth, London, 1927.
10. FREUD, S. 1914. On narcissism. *C.P.*, **4**.
11. FREUD, S. 1926. *The problem of anxiety.* Norton, New York, 1936.
12. GESELL, A. 1946, 1954. Ontogenesis of infant behavior. In CARMICHAEL, *organic growth and transformation*, pp. 110-114. Constable, Edinburgh.

13. GESELL, A. 1940. *The first five years of life,* pp. 29-50. Harper, New York.
14. GILBERT, M. S. 1938. *Biography of the unborn.* Williams & Wilkins, Baltimore.
15. GOODENOUGH, F. L. 1931. Anger in young children. *Univ. Minn. Child Welf. Monogr.,* No. 9.
16. GREENACRE, P. 1945. Biological economy of birth. *Psychoanal. Study Child,* **1**.
17. GREENACRE, P. 1941. Predisposition to anxiety, Part I. *Psychoanal. Q.,* **10**.
18. GREENACRE, P. 1953. Certain relationships between fetishism and the faulty development of the body image. *Psychoanal. Study Child,* **8**.
19. GREENACRE, P. 1958. Early physical determinants in the development of the sense of identity. *J. Am. Psychoanal. Ass.,* **6**.
20. HALVERSON, H. M. 1933. The acquisition of skill in infancy. *J. genet. Psychol.,* **43**.
21. HARTMANN, H. 1958. *Ego psychology and the problem of adaptation.* Imago, London; International Univ. Press, New York.
22. HARTMANN, H. 1950. Comments on the psychoanalytic theory of the ego. *Psychoanal. Study Child,* **5**, 74-95.
23. HARTMANN, H., KRIS, E., and LOEWENSTEIN, R. M. 1946. Comments on the formation of psychic structure. *Psychoanal. Study Child,* **2**, 11-39.
24. HARTMANN, H., KRIS, E., and LOEWENSTEIN, R. M. 1949. Notes on the theory of aggression. *Psychoanal. Study Child,* **3-4**.
25. HENDRICK, I. 1942. Instinct and the ego during infancy. *Psychoanal. Q.,* **11**.
26. HENDRICK, I. 1943. Discussion of the instinct to master. *Psychoanal. Q.,* **12**.
27. HOFFER, W. 1940. Development of the body ego. *Psychoanal. Study Child,* **5**.
28. HOFFER, W. 1949. Mouth, hand and ego integration. *Psychoanal. Study Child,* **3-4**.
29. HOFFER, W. 1950. Oral aggressiveness and ego development. *Int. J. Psycho-Analysis,* **31**.
30. LOEWENSTEIN, R. M. 1950. Conflict and autonomous ego development during the phallic phase. *Psychoanal. Study Child,* **5**.
31. MEDAWAR, P. B. 1957. The uniqueness of the individual. In *The pattern of Manual of child psychology.* Wiley, New York.
32. MEREDITH, H. V. 1945. Toward a working concept of growth. *Am. J. Orthod. Oral Surg.,* **31**, 440-458.
33. NELSON. *Textbook of pediatrics,* 6th ed. Saunders, New York.
34. NUNBERG, H. 1937. *Practice and theory of psychoanalysis,* pp. 165-170. International Univ. Press, New York, 1955.
35. NUNBERG, H. 1931. The synthetic function of the ego. *Int. J. Psycho-Analysis,* **12**.
36. RIBBLE, MARGARET. 1943. *The rights of infants.* Columbia Univ. Press, New York.
37. SCAMMON, R. E. 1922. On the weight increments of premature infants compared with those of the same gestation age and those of full term children. *Proc. Soc. exp. Biol., N.Y.,* **19**.
38. SPITZ, R. A. 1945. Hospitalism. *Psychoanal. Study Child,* **1**, 53-73.
39. SPITZ, R. A. 1957. *No and yes.* International Univ. Press, New York.
40. TAYLOR, J. H. 1934. Innate emotional responses in infants. *Ohio Univ. Stud. Psychol.,* **12**, 69-81.
41. WINNICOTT, D. W. 1953. Transitional objects and transitional phenomena. *Int. J. Psycho-Analysis,* **34**.

VI

AN EXAMINATION OF SOME BASIC SEXUAL CONCEPTS: THE EVIDENCE OF HUMAN HERMAPHRODITISM

JOHN MONEY, JOAN G. HAMPSON AND JOHN L. HAMPSON

Childhood experiences shape the personality. A striking illustration of this is parental assignment of sex determining gender role.

INTRODUCTION

Despite advancement of knowledge in embryology and endocrinology' most people have continued to make an absolute dichotomy between male and female—a dichotomy as seemingly axiomatic as the distinction of day from night, black from white. In psychology and psychiatry, this dichotomy is represented in the conception of predominant masculinity or feminity of the sexual instinct or drive.

A comprehensive theory of instinctive sexuality was first expounded to a medical audience by Freud at the beginning of the present century.[1] Developing and expanding earlier instinctive theories, Freud utilized, inter alia, the conception of innate bisexuality, namely, that instinctive masculinity and instinctive feminity are present in all members of the human species, but in differing proportions.

Freud construed his theory of innate and constitutional psychic bisexuality on the basis of embryological evidence of an hermaphroditic phase in human embryonic differentiation, and on the basis of anatomical evidence in congenital hermaphroditism itself. At a later date, he adduced the evidence of early experiments in endocrinology concerning hormonal reversal of sex in animals as a further support for his bisexual theory.

In an endeavor to ascertain if new and additional information relevant

Reprinted from BULLETIN OF THE JOHNS HOPKINS HOSPITAL, Vol. 97, No. 4, October 1955, pp. 301-319.

to psychologic theory of sexuality might be obtained from the study of hermaphroditism, the authors have, for the past four years, systematically been making psychologic studies of hermaphroditic patients. The work has been done in close cooperation with Dr. Lawson Wilkins who has been responsible for diagnostic, endocrine and other medical studies of the majority of the patients.

The sexual incongruities which occur in hermaphroditism involve divers contradictions, singly or in combination, between six variables of sex. These six variables are:

1. Assigned sex and sex of rearing;
2. External genital morphology;
3. Internal accessory reproductive structures;
4. Hormonal sex and secondary sexual characteristics;
5. Gonadal sex;
6. Chromosomal sex.

Patients showing various combinations and permutations of these six sexual variables may be appraised with respect to a seventh variable:

7. Gender role and orientation as male or female, established while growing up.*

Thus one is enabled to ascertain something of the relative importance of each of the six variables in relation to the seventh.

Patients in whom ambisexual contradictions exist include seven subgroups in the traditional diagnostic category of hermaphroditism,[2, 3] and a group traditionally diagnosed as ovarian agenesis but now more accurately named gonadal agenesis, or dysgenesis, since the chromosomal pattern is male[4,5] (Table 1). We have studied 76 patients in all.

CHROMOSOMAL SEX

Barr's technique of chromosomal sex determination from skin biopsies has, since January 1954, revealed the chromosomal sex of some of our patients.[7,8]† Though it is too early to make a final definitive statement, it appears reasonably likely that, among the eight varieties of ambisexual development, a female chromosomal pattern is always present in varieties 1 and 2, and a male chromosomal pattern in varieties 6, 7, and 8. It happens

* By the term, gender role, we mean all those things that a person says or does to disclose himself or herself as having the status of boy or man, girl or woman, respectively. It includes, but is not restricted to sexuality in the sense of eroticism. Gender role is appraised in relation to the following: general mannerisms, deportment and demeanour; play preferences and recreational interests; spontaneous topics of talk in unprompted conversation and casual comment; content of dreams, daydreams and fantasies; replies to oblique inquiries and projective tests; evidence of erotic practices and, finally, the person's own replies to direct inquiry.

† Chromosomal sex determinations were done by Dr. M. L. Barr and Dr. K. L. Moore at the University of Western Ontario.

TABLE 1

*Varieties of Somatic Ambisexual Development**

1. Congenitally hyperadrenocortical female	42
2. Female, with well differentiated phallus, normal ovaries and normal internal reproductive structures	2
3. True hermaphroditism	1
4. Male, with unarrested mullerian differentiation:	
(a) with normal penis and one or both testes cryptorchid	0
(b) hypospadiac and cryptorchid	3
5. Gonadal agenesis (dysgenesis), with simulant female infantile body morphology and male chromosomes	11
6. Simulant female, with testes, blind vagina, mullerian vestiges and breasts	3
7. Cryptorchid male hypospadiac, with breasts at puberty:	
(a) with urogenital sinus	1
(b) with blind vaginal pouch	0
8. Cryptorchid male hypospadiac:	
(a) with urogenital sinus	11
(b) with blind vaginal pouch	2
	—
	76

* For the purposes of this classification, the criterion of male and female is gonadal. The classification is based on the study of over 300 cases in the literature, in English, of the last half century.[6] Within each category, patients resemble one another closely enough to be strictly comparable as somatic units for the purpose of psychologic study.

that eight true hermaphrodites so far reported on have had a female, and four a male chromosomal pattern. The chromosomal sex of males in whom mullerian differentiation is relatively unarrested has yet to be elucidated. Gonadal agenesis (dysgenesis) may occur either in chromosomal males or chromosomal females who, in all other respects, are identically feminine.

In the interests of precision, only those patients from whom skin biopsies have been taken, and the chromosomal sex actually determined, are included in Table 2. The 19 cases listed in this table are those in which there was a contradiction between chromosomal sex and the sex

TABLE 2

Chromosomes and Rearing Contradictory
(19 cases)

Chromosomes	Gonads	Endogenous hormonal sex	Internal accessory organs	External genital Morphology	Assigned sex and rearing	Gender role	Type of ambisexual development
♂	none	none	♀	♀	11 ♀	11 ♀	gonadal agenesis (dysgenesis)
♂	♂	1 ♀ 2 juv.	vestigial	♀	3 ♀	3 ♀	simulant female
♂	♂	1 ♂ 3 juv.	vestigial	⚥	4 ♀	4 ♀	cryptorchid male hypospadiac
♀	♀ left ♂ right	⚥	⚥	⚥	1 ♂	1 ♂	true hermaphroditism

of assignment and rearing. In every instance, the person established a gender role and orientation consistent with assigned sex and rearing, and inconsistent with chromosomal sex. Thus, it is convincingly clear that gender role and orientation as male or female evidenced itself independently of chromosomal sex, but in close conformity with assigned sex and rearing.

GONADAL SEX

Among the 76 patients, there were 20 in whom a contradiction was found between gonadal sex and the sex of assignment and rearing (Table 3). All but 3 of these 20 disclosed themselves in a gender role fully concordant with their rearing. Gonadal structure *per se* proved a most unreliable prognosticator of a person's gender role and orientation as man or woman, boy or girl. By contrast, assigned sex and rearing proved a most reliable one.

TABLE 3

Gonads and Rearing Contradictory
(20 cases)

Gonads	Chromosomes	Endogenous hormonal sex	Internal accessory organs	External genital morphology	Assigned sex and rearing	Gender role	Type of ambisexual development
♀	♀	♀	♀	⚥	2 ♂	2 ♂	female with phallus and avagenesis
♀	♀	♂	♀	⚥	4 ♂	4 ♂	hyperadrenocortical female
♂	?	1 ♂ 2 juv.	⚥	⚥	3 ♀	3 ♀	male with unarrested mullerian differentiation
♂	♂	1 ♀ 2 juv.	vestigial	♀	3 ♀	3 ♀	simulant female
♂	♂	4 ♂ 4 juv.	vestigial	⚥	8 ♀	5 ♀ 1 ♀ → ♂ 2 ♂	cryptorchid male hypospadiac

HORMONAL SEX

To consider now the relationship between hormonal sex and gender role: hormonal sex must be distinguished from gonadal structure, for ovaries do not always make estrogens, nor testicles androgens. The ovaries of hyperadrenocortical female pseudohermaphrodites are inert, and though their adrenals produce an excess of estrogens as well as of androgens, androgenic activity dominates and the body is excessively virilized. The testes of male pseudohermaphrodites of the simulant female variety produce estrogens which feminize the body.

Table 4 summarizes the data on the 27 patients who went through and beyond a puberty—or, in the case of hyperadrenocorticism, a precocious puberty-equivalent—in which hormonal influences produced a secondary sexual development contradictory of the sex in which they were living. Subsequently the contradiction was corrected with hormonal therapy and, where indicated, with plastic surgery. Psychologic data were gathered before treatment, when possible, otherwise retrospectively.

TABLE 4

Hormonal Sex and Rearing Contradictory
(27 postpubertal cases)

Endogenous hormonal sex	Chromosomes	Gonads	Internal accessory organs	External genital morphology	Assigned sex and rearing	Gender role	Type of ambisexual development
♀	♀	♀	♀	♂	2 ♂	2 ♂	female with phallus and avagenesis
♀	♂	♂	vestigial	♀	1 ♂	1 ♂	cryptorchid male hypospadiac with breasts
⚥	♀	⚥	⚥	⚥	1 ♂	1 ♂	true hermaphroditism
♂	♀	♀	♀	⚥	18 ♀	17 ♀ / 1 ⚥	hyperadrenocortical female
♂	?	♂	⚥	⚥	1 ♀	1 ♀	male with unarrested mullerian differentiation
♂	♂	♂	vestigial	⚥	4 ♀	1 ♀ / 1 ♀ → ♂ / 2 ⚥	cryptorchid male hypospadiac

Of the 27 people whose hormonal functioning and secondary sexual body morphology contradicted their assigned sex and rearing, only 4 became ambivalent with respect to gender role as male or female. All four had been reared as girls. One, acting on his own initiative, began living as a man from the age of sixteen onward. The other three, while living as women, showed some degree of bisexual inclination. These four patients do not, in themselves, offer any convincing evidence of hormonal sex as a causal agent in the establishment of maleness or femaleness of gender role: the patient who lived as a man declined testosterone substitution treatment after surgical castration for malignancy, and the three who lived as women had been thoroughly feminized on estrogen substitution treatment. Moreover, the other 23 of the 27 patients established a gender role consistent with their assigned sex and rearing, despite the embarrassment and worry occasioned by hormonal contradictions. Like gonadal sex, hormonal sex *per se* proved a most unreliable prognosticator of a person's gender role and orientation as man or woman, boy or girl.

INTERNAL ACCESSORY ORGANS

Since the uterus is the organ of menstruation, and the prostate the major organ of seminal fluid secretion, it is necessary to compare maleness or femaleness of gender role with internal reproductive equipment. There were 17 cases in whom assigned sex and rearing was inconsistent with predominant male or female structures internally (Table 5). Gender role agreed with rearing in 14 of these 17. The 3 remaining were the same three individuals as deviated in Tables 3 and 4.

TABLE 5

Internal Accessory Organs and Rearing Contradictory
(18 cases)

Internal accessory organs	Chromosomes	Gonads	Endogenous hormonal sex	External genital morphology	Assigned sex and rearing	Gender role	Type of ambisexual development
♀ > ♂	♀	♀	♀	♂	2 ♂	2 ♂	female with phallus and ovogenesis
♀ > ♂	♀	♀	♂	♂	4 ♂	4 ♂	cortical female hyperadreno-
♂ > ♀ vestigial	♂	♂	1 ♀ 2 juv.	♀	3 ♀	3 ♀	simulant female
♂ > ♀ vestigial	♂	♂	4 ♂ 4 juv.	♂	8 ♀	5 ♀ 1 ♀ → ♂ 2 ♂	cryptorchid male hypospadiac
⚥	♀	⚥	⚥	⚥	1 ♂	1 ♂	true hermaphroditism

In estimating the significance of the comparison in Table 5, one must bear in mind that only rarely in hermaphroditism does either the uterus or the prostate reach full functional maturity, without medical intervention. Of the 17 cases, there were only 3 for whom this statement did not hold: though all three had a functional uterus, they had been reared as boys and had a thoroughly masculine gender role and outlook. So far as the evidence goes, there is no reason to suspect a correlation between internal accessory organs and maleness or femaleness of gender role.

EXTERNAL GENITAL APPEARANCE

It goes without saying that the external genitals are the sign from which parents and others take their cue in assigning a sexual status to a neonate and in rearing him thereafter, and the sign, above all others, which gives a growing child assuredness of his or her gender. Nonetheless, it is possible for an hermaphrodite to establish a gender role fully concordant with assigned sex and rearing, despite a paradoxical appearance of the external genitals.

TABLE 6

External Genital Appearance and Rearing Contradictory
(23 cases)

Predominant external genital appearance	Chromosomes	Gonads	Endogenous hormonal sex	Internal accessory organs	Assigned sex and rearing	Gender role	Type of ambisexual development
♂	♀	♀	♂	♀	15 ♀	15 ♀	hyperadrenocortical female
♂	?	♂	1 ♂ 1 juv.	♀	2 ♀	2 ♀	male with unarrested mullerian differentiation
2 ♀ 3 ♂	2 ♂ 3 ♂	2 ♂ 3 ♂	2 juv. 2 ♂ 1 juv.	2 vestigial 3 vestigial	2 ♂ 3 ♀	2 ♂ 1 ♀ → ♂ ·2 ♀	cryptorchid male hypospadiac
♀	♂	♂	♀	vestigial	1 ♂	1 ♂	cryptorchid male hypospadiac with breasts

There were 23 among our 76 patients who, at the time they were studied had lived for more than two-thirds of their lives with a contradiction between external genital morphology and assigned sex (Table 6). For one reason or another, they did not receive surgical correction of their genital deformity in infancy, but lived with a contradictory genital appearance for at least five and for as many as forty-seven years. In all but one instance, the person had succeeded in coming to terms with his, or her anomaly, and had a gender role and orientation wholly consistent with assigned sex and rearing.

It is not contended that these people encountered no difficulties in their lives. On the contrary, there was considerable evidence that visible genital anomalies occasioned much anguish and distress. Distress was greatest in those patients whose external genital morphology flagrantly contradicted, without hope of surgical correction, the sex in which they had grown up and established, indelibly, their gender role and orientation as boy or girl, man or woman. Distress was also quite marked in patients who had been left in perplexed confusion about the sex to which they belonged, in consequence either of parental or medical indecision, or of insinuations from age-mates that they were half boy, half girl. Uniformly, the patients were psychologically benefited by corrective plastic surgery, when it was possible, to rehabilitate them in the sex of assignment and rearing. Only one patient failed to take advantage of plastic surgery. Instructively enough, he was the person who, on his own initiative, changed his birth certificate and began living as a man from the age of sixteen onward. He was unable to summon up enough courage to have his genitals masculinized.

It is relevant to note in passing that psychotic symptoms in all of the patients were conspicuous by their absence. In remarkably few instances, evidence of neurotic symptomatology was apparent. In some, but by no means all patients, feelings of bashfulness, shame and oddity were to the fore, and they had great initial diffidence in talking about themselves.

ASSIGNED SEX AND REARING

Chromosomal sex, gonadal sex, hormonal sex, internal accessory reproductive organs and external genital morphology—each of these five variables of sex has passed successively in review and has been compared first with assigned sex and rearing and, second, with the gender role and orientation as boy or girl, man or woman, which the person established while growing up. In only 4 cases among 76 was any inconsistency between rearing and gender role observed, despite the many inconsistencies between these two and the other five variables of sex.

Evidently there is a very close connection between, on the one hand, the sex to which an individual is assigned, and thenceforth reassigned in a myriad subtle ways in the course of being reared day by day, and, on the other hand, the establishment of gender role and orientation as male or female.

GENDER ROLE AND ORIENTATION

In the light of hermaphroditic evidence, it is no longer possible to attribute psychologic maleness or femaleness to chromosomal, gonadal or hormonal origins, nor to morphological sex differences of either the internal accessory reproductive organs or the external genitalia. Conceivably, of course, instinctive masculinity or feminity may be attributed to some other innate bodily origin. For example, Krafft-Ebing[9] among others has suggested special brain centers. There is, however no support for such a conjecture when, as may happen in hermaphroditism, among individuals of identical diagnosis, some have been reared as boys, some as girls (Table 7).

There are 55 cases represented in Table 7, including the only 4 in the whole series of 76 in whom ambivalence of gender role was found. The four had been reared as girls. Among the 51 remaining, 42 reared as girls

TABLE 7

Male and Female Assigned Sex in Patients with Same Diagnosis
(55 cases)

Assigned sex and rearing	Gender role	Type of ambisexual development
38 ♀ 4 ♂	37 ♀, 1 ♂ 4 ♂	hyperadrenocortical female
8 ♀ 5 ♂	5 ♀, 1 ♀ → ♂, 2 ♂ 5 ♂	cryptorchid male hypospadiac

had established a feminine gender role and orientation, while 9 reared as boys had established a masculine gender role and orientation.

From the sum total of hermaphroditic evidence, the conclusion that emerges is that sexual behavior and orientation as male or female does not have an innate, instinctive basis.

In place of a theory of instinctive masculinity or femininity which is innate, the evidence of hermaphroditism lends support to a conception that, psychologically, sexuality is undifferentiated at birth and that it becomes differentiated as masculine or feminine in the course of the various experiences of growing up.

Those who find the concept of instinct or drive congenial may choose to say that there is a sexual instinct or drive that is undifferentiated and genderless at birth. In that case, sexual drive is neither male nor female to begin with, and it can be assumed to have no other somatic anchorage than in the erotically sensitive areas of the body. So limited, sexual drive becomes a special example of a kinaesthetic or haptic drive—an urge to touch and be touched, an urge for bodily contact.

Those who find the concept of drive uncongenial may choose simply, to say that in the human species there are erotically sensitive areas of the body, especially the genital organs, and that these areas are sometimes stimulated and used by oneself or another person. In the course of growing up, a person's sexual organ sensations become associated with a gender role and orientation as male or female which becomes established through innumerable experiences encountered and transacted.

Our studies of hermaphroditism have pointed very strongly to the significance of life experiences encountered and transacted in the establishment of gender role and orientation. This statement is not an endorsement of a simple-minded theory of social and environmental determinism. Experiences are transacted as well as encountered—conjunction of the two terms is imperative—and encounters do not automatically dictate predictable transactions. There is ample place for novelty and the unexpected in cerebral and cognitional processes in human beings.

Novelty and unexpectedness notwithstanding, cerebral and cognitional processes are not infinitely modifiable. The observation that gender role is established in the course of growing up should not lead one to the hasty conclusion that gender role is easily modifiable. Quite the contrary! The evidence from examples of change or reassignment of sex in hermaphroditism, not to be presented here in detail, indicates that gender role becomes not only established, but also indelibly imprinted. Though gender imprinting begins by the first birthday, the critical period is reached by about the age of eighteen months. By the age of two and one-half years, gender role is already well established.

One may liken the establishment of a gender role through encounters and transactions to the establishment of a native language. Once imprinted, a person's native language may fall into disuse and be supplanted by another, but is never entirely eradicated. So also a gender role may be changed or, resembling native bilingualism, may be ambiguous, but it may also become so indelibly engraved that not even flagrant contradictions of body functioning and morphology may displace it.

CASE ILLUSTRATION

The following illustrative case has been chosen because it shows convincingly how gender role and orientation may be fully concordant with the sex of assignment and rearing, despite extreme contradiction of the other five variables of sex.

Introductory data: The patient was twenty-four years old and married at the time of psychologic study. He had lived all of his life as a male. Except for a small hypospadiac phallus and fused, empty labioscrotum, he was found to be anatomically and physiologically female when, at the age of eleven and one-half years, he entered a hospital because his breasts had begun to enlarge and his body had grown increasingly feminine in contour. His genital abnormality, of which there was no known familial incidence, had been known to exist since birth. The penis had not enlarged significantly with the onset of puberty. Its glans was completely hidden by wrinkles of foreskin. Although the urethral orifice was located at the base instead of the tip of the penile shaft, the boy was able to stand to urinate. Testicles could not be palpated. The scrotum was contracted and not in the least pendulous.

Exploratory laparotomy revealed a uterus, fallopian tubes, bilateral parovarian cysts, and two cystic gonads in the position of ovaries. The uterus did not connect with a normal vagina, but appeared to open into the upper urethra. No organs of the male reproductive system were discerned internally. The uterus, tubes and gonads were removed, especially as the parents thought their child should remain a boy. Only two sections of the gonads were examined microscopically. They revealed ovarian structure, with primordial follicles containing ova, a few intermediate forms of developing graafin follicles, and several large cyst-like structures lined with granulosa cells.

Postoperatively, male hormone therapy was instituted and continued regularly thereafter. When the patient was twenty-one, therapy was withheld for about nine months on a trial basis, with a result that he felt weak and easily fatigued. Two years later, in preparation for marriage, he underwent plastic surgery in order to transpose and straighten the penis. At this time he appeared quite masculine in stature, though the breasts had remained slightly enlarged. Facial hair required shaving every second or third day. The pubic hair was masculine in distribution and the voice deep. A small, soft prostate was palpable.

First impression: "At first sight and throughout the first meeting with this man, I kept thinking that nothing in his general appearance, manner or conversation betrayed a single hint of the information filed away in his medical record. He would pass anywhere as the advanced graduate student that he was. So much was he a young man, indeed, that I wondered briefly if it might be best to leave well enough alone and not risk stirring up doubts and forebodings. He quickly grasped the purpose of psychological research study, however, and readily consented to cooperate."

Interviews: At all times the man talked fluently and spontaneously, unperturbed by recording apparatus, with no signs of withholding information through embarrassment. He had been told that utmost discretion would be used in concealing his identity—which was an imperative expediency in view of his educational affiliations and associations—and that he would be able to censor the manuscript of the case report before its circulation or publication. Most of the interviews and tests were completed within a single week, with only one examiner, over a period of about fifteen hours. After that there were a few meetings, including two or three informal visits with the man and his wife during the ensuing two years, and a few written notes for another two years.

Family: Both the mother and the father were university graduates. Through their own efforts and achievements they had earned considerable social standing in the community in which they reared their family of three. The patient had two brothers, three years and fourteen years his junior. The family kept together as a quite closely knit unit. Judging from the patient's memories, comments and anecdotes, he was not idealizing when he said: "I think that my relationship with my family, although rocky in spots, has been very happy. I'm devoted to them all. . . ." He and his wife returned home for occasional visits.

Thumbnail self-sketch: "Well, I suppose I'm not an unattractive person for most people. I'm generally optimistic, I think. Probably a little on the lazy side when all is said and done. I probably don't work as hard as I ought to work. I have a pretty good head. It isn't the best head in the world, but it's better than average, and I'm really content with it even though I sometimes wish it were better. I think it's good enough and thank God for what I've got. I expect I'll in my own time do a decent job of living. I don't expect to be much better than average. I expect that I'm sort of average, average good, a little higher than average, in about everything. Average good, in the moral sense, average intelligent, average ambitious, and so on. And that my life will pretty much follow out what—this general route that's kind of set for me, by what I am. I'll do all right. I expect that I can have some pretty rugged things happen to me and it won't jar my general optimism too much. A lot of things I can think of I wouldn't like to have happen, but even so I imagine I'll get along all right no matter what happens because I manage to—for the reason that I am what I am and it has contributed to my average or slightly above average intelligence and so on and so forth, I am able to slough off a lot of stuff better than not. I don't think I'm too dangerously supersensitive or anything of that sort. I imagine I'll belong in the division of perfectly pleasant and not unuseful existence; I hope I'll be be able to raise a batch of children that will be as happy as I think I'll be."

Day-to-day routines: At the time of the interviews, the man was well advanced toward obtaining a doctorate in one of the aesthetic disciplines. During the academic year he worked not only at his own studies, but also as a part-time instructor. Whether in the applied, historical or theoretical branches of his field, his accomplishment and achievement had been recognized as outstanding.

There were times, however, when he was not satisfied that he was concentrating on his work sufficiently. "I am ambivalent," he said, "about working harder and taking life easy. I don't expect to be much better than average; I have always been rather modest about my ambitions and expect it is founded on a certain amount of slothfulness. I probably don't work as hard as I ought to work."

The slothfulness or taking life easy, as he called it, appeared in different guises. For example, he was as he said rather modest in his expressed ambitions for a career, contented to aim at a sure target rather than gamble for a great prize. Again, his account of the course of a typical day gave supportive evidence of a dilatory tendency, one very common in students, namely putting off assignments until the very last minute. The time thus gained was spent with his wife, or at some extracurricular study, or talking with and entertaining friends who might call. Fellow students were frequent callers, as the couple occupied an apartment near the college.

Easy-goingness was also apparent in the infrequency with which the man became agitated, irritated or angry. "I don't know that I've been really angry since I was a little boy," he declared. "Really right down at the guts angry I don't think I've been for a long, long time. I was considerably annoyed last year when one guy wouldn't give me $100 when I wanted it. But anger is kind of exhausting and I tend to avoid it if I possibly can."

It was not that the man was timid or self-effacing, nor a social isolate. While growing up he had always shared some interests with friends of his own age, especially his brother. "But I didn't make friends very easily," he said of grade school days. "And I wasn't a sportsman at all and I frequently got kind of kicked around because I didn't know how to hit a ball with a bat and that sort of thing. . . . But I never felt that life was giving me the blunt end of the stick." He avoided competitive team sports and gymnasium classes because of his genital condition, but joined various other school groups and clubs.

Before leaving high school, he had begun attending a summer colony workshop. There he made many lasting friendships, and there he later met his wife. His first trip abroad had been in childhood with his family, since which there had been others, including one with his wife.

Religious teaching and Sunday school attendance had not been part of the man's childhood experience. Not until college years did he give serious thought to religious, along with philosophical matters. After he met his wife who was devoutly Catholic, he found "Christianity started to make sense, perhaps because she had impressive, implicit faith, and good sense too. I overcame my family-derived horror of Catholicism," but he was far from dogmatic about his personal credo. With his wife he was a regular church attender.

Intelligence test: Wechsler-Bellevue Intelligence Scale results were as follows: verbal IQ 144; nonverbal IQ 133; full IQ 143. A high standard of accuracy was maintained on each subtest. The overall rating was at the level of very superior.

Somatic growth and appearance: After surgical arrestment of pubertal feminization, virilization was induced and maintained by substitution treatment with androgens. The young man had a straightforward understanding of these medical facts, as will become apparent in the following.

Sexuality: "As far back as I can recall, I was always aware of having a genital peculiarity. In our household we were always free and easy about nudity, so I knew I was different from my father and brother." But in the early years of childhood, "it just seemed that men were the superior sex and they had a better thing to pee with."

That the urinary implications of the anomaly were of major import initially was indicated by the first response to the request for earliest memories: "I remember myself squirting the hose. I think I squirted my father in the process. And it was lots of fun." This memory, dating from the age of two, had been reinforced from a photograph taken on the occasion; "and yet, when I look at it, it kind of brings me back, you know, that wonderful feeling of power you have when you're watering something! Well, it kind of brings back something of being a master in your own domain as you squirt this blasted hose around."

Also remembered were a couple of early childhood incidents when the boy and some playmates set up secret urine receptacles behind a garage and in the basement. There were "peeing contests" on a few occasions, including one in which the little boys were amazed to find that a little girl was able to meet a challenge and "pee into a glass."

Sometimes experimentation became more frankly sexual, as when a small group of boys tried to stick assorted items into their orifices; but there were no mutual explorations. While still a young child, the boy learned not to expose himself, regardless of what the others did. His mother, who was less embarrassed by his anomaly than his father, had always talked to him, explaining that he was different from other boys and had special reason not to get into sex play.

"I took more care as I became more aware of the unconscious meannesses of children," he said, "and I got so that I could go to the toilet almost anywhere and manage it so that no one would see." Only once, in high school, did a boy who presumably had participated in infantile sex play make an oblique reference to his friend's genital anomaly. It was in connection with exemption from gymnasium classes. "I said: 'Oh that cleared up a long time ago,' and closed the subject as quickly as I could, but was really quite upset." One or two close contemporary friends were thought to have vague suspicions "that something is wrong." But apart from medical people, wife and family, "nobody else knows as far as I know; and I wouldn't like anybody else to know. I still have a fear that I would be made fun of, and that it would be talked about."

Sex was not a matter for harsh discipline or secrecy in the family. "I knew very early, about six or so, about the process of birth, about the kittens the cat had and where babies come from. It wasn't untill I was in the ninth grade that boys told me about the sexual act. I didn't believe it though, and didn't quite dare ask my father. I finally did," but did not get a direct answer, and was eventually convinced from discussions with contemporaries and from comprehensive reading.

"Of course about then it began to dawn on me that I was singularly unequipped; and from then on it became a more acute worry, although it never bothered me very much. But I was aware of it. Other boys had talked about masturbation which I had never thought of up until that time. I had a hell of a time. I experimented for a year before I found out what was necessary, because the kids I knew used the term jerk off or pull off and I didn't know what physically you did. And I didn't realize you were supposed to have an erection to do this. Then I masturbated more or less continuously until I got married. But I never thought it was right; it seems wrong that you should use your head to get out of a trouble which is by the direct route of logic in nature unnatural."

At the age of eleven "to my great horror I discovered that I had breasts beginning to develop. This seemed quite a calamity. And it was from that time, after the exploratory operation, that I knew I would never have any children, and that was a kind of continual bother. Mother was quite sure that I would never marry;" and was very upset when, with the first serious love affair at nineteen "I said I was damn well going to get married, somehow. Even at sixteen I was thinking about it. Probably because I'd been told I couldn't ever get married anyway. And I had great moral difficulties because I was undecided as to whether I should marry this girl and whether I was going to give some girl a raw deal. Dad was more reticent about it, not knowing quite what to say; and my doctor didn't want to commit himself. But I went ahead anyway.

"In a sense my life has centered around this problem of getting married in that I have always wanted to get married. It's been one of the things that I was going to do, if it was humanly possible. That has been a controlling factor and a challenge all the way along, from some of my earliest memories. Patsy Jane, I can remember when we moved, I kissed her goodbye and took her pictures. I must have been about seven. And then I had a girl friend after that, who continued to write to me." At high school there were the jealousies and rivalries over girl friends; the love notes; "the big fuss about who would dance with whom at dancing school;" the party games of post office; "and, if you were very lucky, the concession of a kiss." In the early college years there was the first serious affair "with Dorothy. And then the girl who is now my wife."

Of the findings at the exploratory operation "I still haven't got the whole works. I still don't know everything about it. But I've gathered that there'd been some kind of female apparatus in there by mistake and that it had been taken out. I also knew that they were looking for testes; and didn't find them. I guess they found a couple of ovaries or something too. That's about all I know about it."

Some weeks later the man did recall in a casual conversation that he had, at the age of eleven, been asked if he wanted to be a girl. The idea had had no appeal. This knowledge, together with the evidence of enlarged breasts, apparently had more significance than that manifested in conscious awareness, witness the following passage of free association: "We ranged in size the same way as we ranged in age. And nobody could ever figure is out when we were on these trips together. They always thought we were some god-forsaken kind of damned pervert bunch. Nobody, obviously I was, I couldn't be the daughter or, or the son or, or Chloe wasn't Homer's daughter and he as', she couldn't be his wife very easily, and I wa', nobody could figure my relationship to; we even considered scratching the name of the institution off the side of the station wagon."

For the most part, however, the ambiguity of sexual status had been well thought out. Only once, in late childhood had there been "some experimenting with my brother, but we were pretty thoroughly frustrated and disgusted and gave that up as a bad job." It was during the college freshman year that the issue came really into focus. "I got to know vaguely of things about drinking; and some of the queer flabs around." One acquaintance "travelled with a weird group of avant garde writers and knew an awful lot of the fairies around." A couple of homosexual guys in the dormitory committed suicide.

"One night a guy came up into my room when I was lamenting about women —I hadn't heard from Dorothy for some time—and looked at me and said: 'Say well, have you ever thought of trying anything else?' And gee, I about vomited on the spot, not knowing whether this was an offer or what. I began to think that maybe other people thought I was funny or something."

Sex was in mind frequently, "and I would think about all kinds of sex, what kinds there were, and then I would wonder if I was safe or not. Whether I would find myself liking it too much or something. Yet, if I ever started making any image of homosexuality, I could never get myself into it. It was always other people. Yet I could always think of myself as a possibility for the game. Physically I might have been the best bet in college for some joker. I presumed that some men might find me rather appealing because, well, I'm not a terribly hairy person, and my femininity, in other words, those things about me which are less masculine, less pronouncedly masculine.

"I was much concerned with my breasts at that time. Now I don't care about them, although I am careful how I dress. But at that time people did say things about them. That's something I hadn't thought of, but that might have had quite a lot to do with it. You see I had this tendency to be very conscious, or subconsciously aware of my breasts; and I suppose I always did make some kind of female association there.

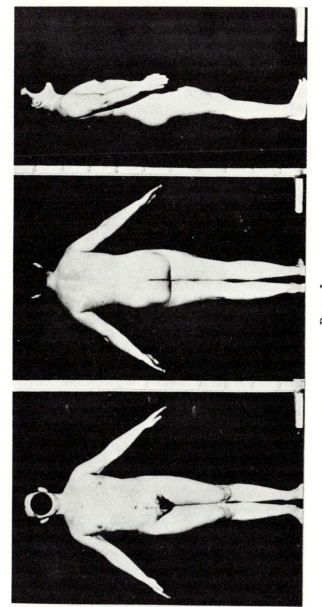

PLATE I

"During all this time I was well into this affair with Dorothy; in which I knew consciously and rationally that I had every reason for feeling that I was perfectly okay because I knew perfectly well that I was attracted to women. I had been sneaking out against family opposition, and flying over to spend the weekend with her. And one of my great undergraduate experiences was sleeping all night in the same bed with her. It was strictly a dry run, but it was great sport.

"The guys at school were all big talkers about women and I let it be known that I'd been a heller when I was in high school—which of course is very far from true—and was now going steady. There were some very vigorous parties, especially at the summer school resort, but I never had any affairs. I would like to have been around raising cain, but in addition to what vague moral feelings I had about it I knew damn well I couldn't. I was very lucky to have any instincts in that direction, I guess. I was taking testosterone; if I wasn't I don't think I would have given a hoot for anybody. I was also in a sense fortunate in falling in with a crowd that was all straight too. I don't think with my particular background I ever would have been very sympathetic to the fairy groups. It was too black and white like that, my family tradition, although there had never been anything very specific about it. I was lucky to be with a gang that were overtly sex happy and spending a lot of time running around finding it."

The resolution of sexual uncertainties was neatly illustrated in a dream, the only one which he could recall. It was dreamed nearly two years earlier, when he and two fellow instructors from the summer school had visited a man whom they thought homosexual. "I dreamed that I was in a church eating supper—stuffed cabbage leaves or something. Rae was with me and we were sitting with strangers at a table in front of the sanctuary. Homer and Chloe were at a table within the sanctuary. The altar was off in the transept. I looked up and in the first pew was this fairy wearing pearl earrings, lipstick and henna in his hair. He was with someone who looked like his mother and was grinning kind of silly. I laughed and went up and told Homer and Chloe to look at him. I came back and was concerned that Rae wasn't eating anything, so we went somewhere else and had supper together. It was a very happy dream. My big problems were resolved. Chloe and I figured it out. I wasn't a fairy because I was with Rae and was able to laugh at this other guy. And I was still able to talk to Chloe and Homer who were my friends, but who wonder about my marrying a Catholic girl and my feelings about Catholicism. And although Rae wasn't quite happy we went somewhere else and were very happy. I remember thinking kind of guiltily that she wasn't eating, because I was enjoying myself tremendously."

"Rae and I had a devil of a time trying to find out whether it was really all right for us to get married. We worried through that. We figured if we could get through that we could get through anything. So I think we can. Gee that was awful. Well, anyhow, we talked to my doctor and he said he thought it would be okay; and we talked to the Church and they said it was okay and so, with many a prayer, we took the giant step and got ourselves engaged and decided it was foolish to wait after you were engaged, and so we got married. At this point we feel, typically, that we're the luckiest people in the world."

Before being married he underwent a plastic repair of the genitalia so that the penis was more advantageously placed for coitus. "And Rae and I make out very well now, of course we're still just married, but it's a rough day when we don't get to bed at least once. And I consider that pretty normal for the first six months of married life. I've never felt that I was particularly abnormal in respect to the strength of libido, but that I seem to fit in the middle somewhere."

Since the age of twelve he had taken testosterone regularly except for one period of several months during which he felt a lack of energy and "probably a little bit of diminution of libido, but not enough to really worry about. I wasn't conscious of being completely apathetic." Ordinarily, there is plenty of erotic sensation localized in the penis. It erects very automatically. "In fact there was one time when I first started taking testosterone when I just needed to move and uff!—there she was, from the friction of my pants."·

There is minimal fluid discharge at ejaculation, "but I have the sensation of ejaculation; I'm quite sure it's the same sensation. It may be greater or lesser intensity, I don't know. At any rate it's entirely satisfying. Of course we have had to experiment quite a bit, to find the best ways for Rae always to have an orgasm," since the erect penis is only about two inches long. "If she doesn't that makes me very unhappy."

A spontaneous gaiety in their marriage was clearly reflected in a passage of free association: "And we had good fun in bed the other day; gee it must have been two hours. We've felt good ever since." At this point he paused, checked himself, awakened from somnolence, laughed and said he had been thinking about examining his wife and of the day when she may get ambitious enough for fellatio in love making. "Rae's awfully nice. She's really awfully nice. I love her a great deal."

The blank-card story of the Thematic Apperception Test evoked a portrayal of family life around the meal table with the children whom they both took for granted they would rear. A family by adoption was, at that time, uppermost in mind, although the possibility of artificial insemination was not excluded. Some years later, the moral issues of artificial insemination having been thoroughly threshed out, the wife became pregnant and gave birth to a child.

PSYCHOLOGICAL APPRAISAL

To all who knew him, it was perfectly obvious that this man had achieved conspicuous, all-round success in coping with life. Only those who knew his medical record knew of the odds against him. To the world at large he gave no sign of having had to surmount the tremendous obstacles imposed by the contradictions of his genital anomaly. He passed simply as an ordinary male college graduate—one of the more stable and well-adjusted.

The challenge to overcome genital defections was pervasive and of long standing: the man said so directly, as well as in unpremeditated sayings and test responses. In early childhood there had been peeing contests; at puberty a total lack of appeal in the idea of changing to live as a girl; in the teens a nagging uncertainty about genital mechanics but a determined resolution to get married; and finally plastic surgery of the genitalia and an erotically successful marriage.

For all its pre-eminence, sexuality did not blot out all else. Academically the man had always made superior achievement. Yet he disparaged himself as being slothful and lazy, and wondered if he might "fall down on the score of lack of penetrating enough intelligence." He spoke of daydream rivalries with a colleague "who is infinitely quicker in mind than I am, which irks me no end."

It seemed possible that the red-hot fire of this man's endeavor had burned in the service of psychosexual problems, and that it might not glow so intensely in the service of work and aesthetic creativeness. Allowing that one must speculate and not be sure in these matters, it also seemed that the kind of logical, systematic literalness requisite for solving psychosexual problems was incompatible with the flashy erraticness of creative insight, penetrating intelligence and a quick mind.

In discussing personal sexual matters, the man exhibited an astonishing degree of empirical detachment and logical reasoning. He had an accurate fund of information about himself which, presumably, had helped him to look at his own case with detachment. He had not been kept in the dark without answers to questions. He had not been obliged to jump to conclusions, putting two and two together for himself.

Judging from Rorschach and Thematic Apperception Test responses, he was the sort of person whose attention kept pretty well anchored to clear outlines in perceptual experience. He didn't venture too far with confabulation and make-believe. He described and analysed instead. As most people would say, he was very realistic.

Fantasies and personal myths and symbol did not appear to occupy much of a place in the economy of his mental life. It would be brash to theorize about castration, Oedipus or other complexes, on the basis of evidence collected. Suffice it that the man said enough about his childhood relationship with his mother for the Oedipal attachment considered normal in boys to be attributed to him also, his somatic status notwithstanding. It was not an exaggerated or prolonged attachment. Eventually it gave way to a concern with girl friend relationships and marriage and with the anatomical problem of adequacy in intercourse.

Erotically, there is not a single doubt about the man's masculine orientation though, for those who seriously measure masculinity with a yardstick of pugnacity and aggressiveness, he will not get full marks. He rated himself as being a person slow to anger. His general behavior and demeanor confirmed his estimate.

This slowness to anger was a lack of aggressiveness in the narrow sense of belligerence. It did not include a lack of confidence and initiative making for tentativeness and hesitancy. It was an absence of attack but not of mastery. It was the substitution of strategy for disorganized fighting. At times it was also removal of oneself from provocateurs so that aggression was not aroused.

Though slow to anger, the man was not, then, inhibited and helpless. His control and restraint did not in this or any other context run to excesses; it was temperate and moderate. Thus vigilance was exercised lest the legitimate secret of his anomaly become public, but the secret was openly and frankly discussed under appropriate circumstances. The quality of vigilance and cautious moderation tempered most of his doings in life. His ambitions were modest, he said, and in fact they were, for he had talent and intelligence which would have justified even grandiose aspirations.

All in all, beyond every possible doubt, this person was psychologically a man. He was fortified with a diplomatic arrogance which adjusted to the human demands of the occasion, yet enabled him to choose and select his standards rather than run with the herd. He was meeting life most successfully without any suspicion of psychopathology. There was every reason to believe that he would continue to do so. His life is an eloquent and incisive testimony to the stamina of human personality.

SUMMARY

Seventy-six hermaphroditic patients manifesting somatic ambisexual anomalies were studied psychologically and their gender role and orientation appraised. Gender role and orientation was compared with the sex of assignment and rearing, and with each of five other variables of sex, namely, chromosomal sex, gonadal sex, hormonal sex, internal reproductive organs, and external genitalia. Gender role and orientation was found to be congruous with the sex of assignment and rearing in 72 of the 76 patients, despite contradiction between this pair of variables and one or more of the other five. It was concluded that the sex of assignment and rearing was better than any other variable as a prognosticator of the gender role and orientation established by the patients in this group. The bearing of this finding on instinct theory in psychology and psychiatry was examined. A case report was given to illustrate how gender role and orientation may be fully concordant with the sex of assignment and rearing, despite extreme contradiction of the other five variables of sex.

REFERENCES

1. FREUD, S. 1953. Three essays on sexuality. *The standard edition of the complete psychological works of Sigmund Freud*, Vol. VII. Hogarth, London. See especially the first essay.
2. MONEY, J., HAMPSON, J. G., and HAMPSON, J. L. 1955. Hermaphroditism: Recommendations concerning assignment of sex, change of sex, and psychologic management. *Bull. Johns Hopkins Hosp.*, 97, 284.
3. WILKINS, L., *et al.* Hermaphroditism: Classification, diagnosis, selection of sex, and treatment. *Pediatrics.* In press.
4. HAMPSON, J. L., HAMPSON, J. G., and MONEY, J. 1955. The syndrome of gonadal agenesis (ovarian agenesis) and male chromosomal pattern in girls and women: Psychologic studies. *Bull. Johns Hopkins Hosp.*, 97, 207.
5. GRUMBACH, M. M., VAN WYK, J. J., and WILKINS, L. 1955. Gonadal dysgenesis, ovarian agenesis, male pseudohermaphroditism: Bearings on theories of human sex differentiation. Read at the 37th annual meeting of The Endocrine Society, 2 June. *J. clin. Endocr. Metab.* In press.
6. MONEY, J. 1952. *Hermaphroditism: An inquiry into the nature of a human paradox.* Unpublished doctoral thesis, Harvard University Library.
7. MOORE, K. L., GRAHAM, M. A., and BARR, M. L. 1953. The detection of chromosomal sex in hermaphrodites from a skin biopsy. *Surgery Gynec. Obstet.*, 96, 641.
8. BARR, M. L. 1954. An interim note on the application of the skin biopsy test of chromosomal sex to hermaphrodites. *Surgery Gynec. Obstet.*, 92, 184.
9. KRAFFT-EBING, R. VON. 1930. *Psychopathia sexualis*, 7th ed. F. A. Davis Co., Philadelphia.

VII

ADOLESCENT MALADJUSTMENT AND FAMILY DYNAMICS

ALBERTO C. SERRANO, EUGENE C. McDANALD,
HAROLD A. GOOLISHIAN, ROBERT MacGREGOR,
AND AGNES M. RITCHIE

*Passing through adolescence, the individual is not immune
from formative influences within the family. Clinical
work demonstrates how adolescent behaviour is a product
of family patterns interaction.*

The staff of the Youth Development Project, a psychiatric outpatient clinic for adolescents and part of the department of psychiatry and neurology at the University of Texas Medical Branch has been studying for more than three years, a brief, intensive family centered psychotherapy program called Multiple Impact Therapy. In this treatment procedure, family groups, mobilized around the emotional disturbance of an adolescent, have been seen by an interdisciplinary team.

The treatment aspects of the method were described by Dr Schuster to this audience two years ago. The results are now being evaluated and prepared for publication.

The purpose of this presentation is to point up what we have learned about the dynamics of the 63 disturbed adolescents and their families. It is our impression that our patients fall into four diagnostic categories, and that there are four types of family interaction, each associated with one of the four types of adolescent disturbance.

The categories of maladjustment in adolescence approximate in their description Sullivan's[1] and Erickson's[2] conceptions of what happens to an individual when specific developmental tasks are not completed at the appropriate stages of growth.

Reprinted by special permission of the American Psychiatric Association from
THE AMERICAN JOURNAL OF PSYCHIATRY, Vol. 118, No. 10, April 1962,
pp. 897-901.

These categories are: the infantile maladjustment reaction in adolescence; the childish maladjustment reaction in adolescence; the juvenile maladjustment reaction in adolescence; and the preadolescent maladjustment reaction in adolescence. These types are supported by studies of the developmental histories, clinical observations and psychological testing of the disturbed adolescents in our series.

INFANTILE MALADJUSTMENT REACTION IN ADOLESCENCE

This first category includes six schizophrenic youngsters ranging in age from 14 to 17. The small size of our sample precludes any specific contribution to the dynamic theory of schizophrenia, but our findings are similar to those of other investigators in the field.[1,3,4]

These youngsters live in an autistic fashion typical of early infancy. They appear dedicated to maintaining a symbiotic relationship with "the mothering one." Their socialization is extremely limited and makes no sense to their peers. They relate as though peers were objects or spectators. They are indifferent toward authority and education. Their individuality seems to have been sacrificed for the illusion of being omnipotent masters in their fantasy world.

Puberty changes intensify their being perceived more clearly as deviant members of their group. Although they seem to trust no one, including themselves, they deal with their uncertainty by occupying themselves in keeping an adult happy, sad, or otherwise emotionally involved. This is a full time preoccupation that appears to have interfered with their emotional growth.

One of the striking facts about the families of these adolescents, although not unique to this group except in terms of severity, was the contrast between the overt and covert patterns of parental leadership. The parents seemed on the surface to function according to the imperatives of our culture. Typically, the fathers appeared to function as moderately successful breadwinners, while the mothers appeared to be in a relatively passive position as homemakers. At a covert level it was typical for one of the parents to accept his own exclusion, avoiding leadership, while the other parent functions subtly in a dominant position.

All of these couples were unhappy and had been so most of their lives. They were mistrustful of themselves and of others. They became disillusioned with one another early in their marriage after each found the spouse was not the kind of person that could make up for the unhappiness of the past. Their life-long frustration and hostility were continually reinforced in the marriage relation but remained concealed except for occasional outbursts over irrelevant issues.[6] As has been observed in families of schizophrenics, by Lidz[5] and others,[7] they showed no capacity for flexible cooperation.

One of the children born in this climate of parental emotional divorce, became engaged in a prolonged and consuming symbiotic relationship with the more aggressive and needy parent. Though rejecting and over-protective, the mothering parent seemed to have been allowed by the weaker spouse to mould and coerce the child in a way that granted total control. Thus symbiosis appeared to have been the only working solution for a child in this situation. The selection of a particular child to occupy this position seemed related to various factors such as response of the family to the birth of a child of a certain sex or appearance, environmental stress, sibling position, illness, physical handicap, or constitution. These findings are similar to those described by Vogel and Bell[8] on the selection of a family scapegoat.

When the emotional needs of the mothering one were met by the schizophrenic child, one or more of the siblings seemed to have been thereby saved from a similar fate and to have acquired instead the conventional values of the family. This so-called "well sibling," by being dependable, seemed able to achieve a working adjustment inside and outside the family. He did not, like his sick sibling, get involved in a double binding relationship with the dominant parent, but formed a close relationship with the weaker and excluded parent, who apparently had a more positive influence on him.

Crises brought these families to seek professional help for their sick child after his infantile behavior became unbearable to them or society or when the youngster became overtly psychotic after failure to adjust to the increasing demands of reality.

These families in their initial encounter with the team were highly resistive to altering their communication patterns but were interested in extruding the "sick member" or in having him labeled as defective, homosexual, or hopeless.

CHILDISH MALADJUSTMENT REACTION IN ADOLESCENCE

This second category was represented by 20 boys and 1 girl, referred for aggressive behavior that appeared uncontrollable. Their acting-out behavior was manifested by temper tantrums, threats, destruction of property, truancy, car theft, running away from home, and failing at all adult sponsored projects. They troubled their parents and the community with their arrogance and negativism, their anti-learning attitude, their low tolerance for frustration, and the tendency to get themselves in trouble in an impulsive way that made the responsible adults ashamed and sorry. They seemed to live out a power fantasy calculated to make others hate them. Although dynamically similar in many respects to the infantile adolescents, this type of youth appeared mostly engaged in a struggle for autonomy that his parents seemed emotionally unable to grant. Having specialized in manipulating adults, these young persons failed to make affective contact with their peers and made little sense to them. This made it necessary to avoid situations with peers that might validate their feeling of impotence as individuals. They associated with peers of both sexes only when they could impose their own terms and thereby avoid competition; more typically they associated with younger or older youths. As puberty progressed, the childish behavior became more obvious and seemed to lose its charm to the mothering ones, who after years of believing or acting as though child rearing was their exclusive responsibility, decided to give up that role, and this increased the child's efforts to remain important. While in the infantile adolescent group the mothering parent was successful and satisfied in maintaining the symbiotic relationship with the sick one, in the childish adolescent group dependence on the child by the mothering ones gradually declined and this was experienced by the adolescent as rejection. His solution then became a desperate attempt to hold on to the mothering one by increasing the nuisance value of his childish behavior.

The family matrix of the childish adolescents showed a high degree of imbalance in leadership in the home. Their fathers had more ego strength and appeared to be more capable of leadership in most instances. Most of these 21 fathers began their participation in the life of the family after the mother-child relationship had developed during the fathers' absence. The fathers were all dealt with by the children as though they were intruders. They were or became reluctant to exercise authority. As a rule they functioned in a passive-aggressive way and permitted their wives, who needed their support, to fall flat on their faces in their efforts to control the children. These parents had feelings of unworthiness, inferiority, self-doubt, and were afraid of showing their hostility overtly. These fathers too became non-participant observers whose observations tended to be disqualified by the family as a whole.

In a majority of our cases, the childish adolescent was the oldest of several siblings. He was regarded as undependable and tended to lose his birthright to a more dutiful conforming younger sibling. The childish adolescent patients were usually referred as a result of a crisis situation at about age 15. Their families brought them to the clinic asking for advice on how to curb the annoying behavior of their child. These were situations that brought a heretofore excluded father more meaningfully into family relations concerning the nominal patient. While initially the parents were highly resistive to focusing on anything but how to alter the child's behavior, the interest of the team in helping them to achieve satisfaction as parents within the framework of their personal limitations brought a rapid reduction in their resistance to self-study.

JUVENILE MALADJUSTMENT REACTION IN ADOLESCENCE

This third category included 13 boys and 3 girls who were anxious and fearful. They presented a variety of somatic symptoms such as headaches and gastrointestinal disturbances as well as other neurotic traits. Their average age was about 12. They seemed intimidated by parental authority. Their problems appeared to be related to fear of initiative and to guilt.[6]

Most of these anxious children participated in groups composed of their age mates, but their worries about competition kept them from being intimately involved. They seemed to learn well according to national achievement test standards, but often had poor marks. They had internalized patterns of conformity similar to those of over-conscientious adults. Their presenting problems were tics, annoying habits, poor attention, somatic symptoms, and phobias.

Occasional delinquent acts of a neurotic sort seemed to invite the intervention of authority, which resulted in their being regarded as maladjusted rather than mean. These neurotic adolescents in our series came from homes in which the parents were strongly competitive for authority, each claiming that he had the right idea about the proper raising of the children. Most of the fathers took an aggressive position manifested by authoritarian and hypercritical attitudes,[12] that ostensibly covered over feelings of inferiority, doubts about their identity and fear of intimacy. The mothers had basic conflicts similar to the fathers', and were habitually on the defensive in response to the husbands' repeated unfavorable reflexions on their ability to function in the mothering role. In most cases these parents quarrelled frequently and openly in the children's presence about inconsequential details of child rearing.

The relation of the fathers to these adolescents was rarely so direct as to allow them to vie openly for the maternal role. It appeared that what the fathers demanded of their wives for the children was very much like what they wanted for themselves, yet because of their lack of awareness of dependency on their wives, they failed to consciously perceive the children as rivals. The maladjusted juveniles behaved in oedipal fashion, acting as though they expected and feared retaliation from the father for the closeness they had with the mother. Intense sibling rivalry characterized these families. As initiative and capability seemed to be punished with criticism and blame, these over-intimidated children usually expressed the feeling that they could not alter their way of relating to others.

Prior to marriage these parents generally had some degree of relatedness to the community. Marriage and the appearance of children were regarded as unhappy interruptions of those rewarding premarital experiences. The fathers, however, had a reputation for being hard to get along with and showed limited adaptability in their vocational life.

Generally the cases were referred by school authorities after they found the neurotic symptoms so disruptive as to justify the exclusion of the children from school. In most of these cases the parents' marriage was at a critical point. Initial cooperation in treatment was high in these families, although it often quickly changed to an expression of ambivalence about their dependency in the manner of the help-rejecting complainer.

PREADOLESCENT MALADJUSTMENT REACTION IN ADOLESCENCE

Our fourth type is represented by a group of teenagers with an average age of 16. These youths were in tune with peer group norms and demanded the privileges of young adulthood. They also demanded recognition of their disregard for the responsibilities that go with those privileges. Their parents reported a fairly recent onset of rebellious and delinquent behavior. In contrast with the guilt-free acting-out of the childish adolescents, who appeared to be struggling for a sham autonomy, this group seemed to have doubts about their identity. They participated with their peers and to a large extent made sense to them, but at one time or another they forfeited their status in the group by getting the group into trouble.

They seemed to exaggerate their bonds and identification with the gang[9] at a time when their age mates start to shape their individual identities. These adolescents had many doubts about their manhood or womanhood. This seemed related to the doubts the parents had about themselves.

These adolescents got in trouble with the school and the community. Their school placement was generally in accord with their mental ability, despite their façade of indolence and frequent difficulties with authority. Actually, this group was ambivalent about authority. Their misbehavior appeared at times almost deliberately calculated to require parental and community disapproval, as well as firmer and more consistent discipline. They showed more anxiety than the childish acting-out adolescents; yet they were more self-confident about their ability to do things. They were interested in social and sexual activities that expressed contempt for their parents' values. At the same time these activities were sponsored by the parents' failure to do anything about their children's misbehavior.[10]

The majority of the fathers appeared in civic life to abound in "goodness." They were active leaders in business. At home, however, they functioned as passive-aggressive critics. The mothers as a whole were self-critical and admitted to feelings of inferiority or past failures. These adolescents were either the oldest or the only child. They resented the freedom of the younger siblings who seemed to them to be more priviledged. Yet they tended to be admired and liked by these younger siblings.

Crises mobilized these families in an attempt to keep in the home the rebellious child whose behavior seemed to endanger his remaining a sick yet vital part of the family. The defiance of school and community made institutional placement a necessity or a possibility.

In treatment these youths were fairly verbal and expressed their complaints and their understanding of the history of their difficulties, without however being willing to compromise their loyalty to and identification with their particular deviant group standards.

The fathers were quite matter-of-fact and cooperative, although unaware of the extent of their involvement in the problem. They appeared to be shrewd observers of their family. Their failure to act on their observations was a surprising discovery to them.

The mothers were self-critical and generally more resistive and guilty in treatment, feeling that the investigation would uncover that they were at the root of the adolescent's difficulties. Both parents had fairly complicated relations in the community but had no projects which they shared.

While they were competitive in their relations with their equals, often as a couple they had worked out a division of labor that unwittingly fostered the weakness of one or the other. Their appreciation of what to take for granted was impressive and involved tacit agreement not to invade established areas of privacy. The few matters openly discussed were quite superficial and tended to be without emotional involvement.

CONCLUSIONS

The various types of adolescent disorder may be related to four types of unhealthy family interaction. The adolescent's primary role in intrafamilial imbalance is to function as a stabilizing factor, that is, he internalizes or externalizes the unresolved, unspoken parental conflicts. The realization of his individual potentials and emotional growth are impaired, inasmuch as they are made secondary to the primary role. The neurotic equilibrium of the family is broken when the adolescent's behavior becomes unendurable to himself, the family and/or society. This precipitates a crisis that tends to mobilize the family to seek some type of help. It is at this time that a clear understanding of adolescent maladjustment and family dynamics becomes most important for diagnostic and therapeutic purposes.[11]

REFERENCES

1. SULLIVAN, H. S. 1953. *The interpersonal theory of psychiatry.* Norton, New York.
2. ERIKSON, E. H. 1959. *Identity and the life cycle.* International Univ. Press, New York.
3. ARIETI, S. 1955. *Interpretation of schizophrenia.* Brunner, New York.
4. JACKSON, D. D. (ed.). 1960. *Etiology of schizophrenia.* Basic Books, New York.
5. LIDZ, et al. 1957. *Am. J. Psychiat.*, **114**, 241.
6. WYNNE, L. C., et al. 1958. *Psychiatry*, **21**, 205.
7. VOGEL, E. F. 1960. *Psychiatry*, **23**, 1.
8. VOGEL, E. F., and BELL, N. W. 1960. *Psychoanalysis*, **47**, Summer.
9. JENKINS, R. L. 1944. *Am. J. Orthopsychiat.*, **14**, January.
10. JOHNSON, ADELAIDE M. 1949. Sanctions for superego lacunae of adolescents, in EISSLER, K. R. (ed.), *Search lights on delinquency.* New Psychoanalytic Studies. International Univ. Press, New York.
11. ACKERMAN, N. W. 1959. *Psychodynamics of family life.* Basic Books, New York.

2

THE RELATIONSHIP DIMENSION

This dimension encompasses an account of all the intimate relationships of each family member in the Past, his relationships in the Present, and what can be predicted about those in the Future.

Of the many elements of the relationships in the time sequence of Past, Present and Future, the following have been selected for illustration:

Theory of communication
Husband-wife relationship
Parent-child relationship
Sibling-sibling relationship

VIII

SYNOPSIS OF THE THEORY OF

HUMAN COMMUNICATION

JURGEN RUESCH

The process by which meaning passes between individuals is now being subjected to scientific enquiry. A synopsis of some of the accumulated knowledge is presented in this paper.

The psychiatrist, who in his therapeutic activities attempts to restore or develop anew the relationship of the patient to self and others, today has several systems to choose from. But inasmuch as he actually uses communication to improve the communication methods of the patient, the development of an appropriate scientific system suitable for the study of intrapersonal and interpersonal communication seems to be a necessary and logical step. The present paper constitutes an attempt to sketch a communication model suitable for the study of the psychiatrist's operations.

The human activity of communication links person to person, individual to group, and smaller social organizations to larger societal structures. Human behavior is obviously influenced by what people think and feel, and it is evident that their transactions and interactions are guided by information acquired in the course of social contact. The scientific model of communication is especially applicable to the study of human relations. Data pertaining to the ways and means by which people exchange messages, to the correction of information through social contact, and to action undertaken as an outgrowth of communication are handled successfully within the scientific model of communication. Conversely, scientists who are not interested in the relationships of human beings or of other biological entities and who are not desirous of studying social forms of

Reprinted by special permission of the William Alanson White Psychiatric Foundation from PSYCHIATRY: JOURNAL FOR THE STUDY OF INTERPERSONAL PROCESSES, Vol. 16, No. 3, August 1953, pp. 215-243.

organization—as, for example, the anatomist or the neuropathologist—will have little use for a scientific model of communication. The communication model is used with success whenever two or more biological or social entities have to be related to each other. Where the scientist has only one entity to contend with, the communication model is less suitable.

Although many scientists will have no opportunity to apply the theory of communication in their particular line of work, all scientists are by necessity concerned, both practically and theoretically, with the fact that scientific observations must be reported to other scientists and perhaps to the public in communicable terms. A deeper understanding of the dual function of the theory of human communication can be gained by considering the assumptions upon which it is built; these assumptions can be divided into the premises generally accepted by modern scientific philosophers[22, 15, 58] concerning the characteristics of naturally occurring events and those which are specifically geared to the scientist's role as a human observer.

PREMISES UNDERLYING THE THEORY OF HUMAN COMMUNICATION

Delineation of the scientific universe. Though it is granted that all events in nature are somewhat related, it is the task of the scientific observer to limit his field of observation. Delineation of the field of observation is not only spatial, or topical, but also temporal, inasmuch as the human being has to express successively what in nature takes place simultaneously. Thus the delineation of the scientific universe is a dialectical device forced upon scientists because of the structural limitations of man's communication instruments. The scientist's observations and reports can only be mediated through the human observer's ways of communication.[54]

Belief in the rational understanding of nature. Were a scientist to believe that he could not understand nature, he would cease to observe, to construct models, and to label himself a scientist. Implicitly, therefore, every scientist assumes that nature can be understood rationally and that from the observation of events some generalizations can be derived which can be stated in either formal or empirical terms. It follows that if the scientist's instruments of observation are not equipped to perceive certain events which occur in nature, no scientific information will be available. Furthermore, the assumption is made that the events observed in nature can be properly reproduced through some device of symbolic representation. When an observation is made which cannot properly be fitted into the scientific model, the scientist becomes aware of a gap in his body of information. In such a case, either he acquires additional information in the hope of supplying the missing link or he changes the characteristics of his system.

Scientific distortions. In addition to the distortions introduced through the use of language systems, there exist the distortions introduced through the selective observations and operations of the observer. Not only does the scientist observe, but he also uses his information for a given purpose which often dictates the format and other characteristics of his model. The scientific distortions which scientists have to contend with are very much like the distortions encountered in map projections in which the three-dimensional globe is represented in Mercator or polyconic projection in two dimensions. Human beings who have observed some complex events in nature have to simplify and condense their data for purposes of recording, thinking, and communicating, in spite of the fact that such an operation introduces new distortions. Therefore, one must assume that all models constructed for the understanding of nature are somewhat simpler than the real events and that only a few functions will be appropriately represented in the system, while others will be highly distorted. However, through the use of multiple systems this error can be somewhat compensated for.[54]

Uncertainty. Certainty in the human being is a function of the completeness of his information. One must assume that there are myriad events which have not been observed as yet and myriad more which never will be known. In present-day theory construction, therefore, provision must be made for information which is not yet available or which never will be available. The area where the as yet unknown information is known to exist has to be bridged by assumptions in order to close the gap. All modern scientific systems have such areas of uncertainty, and the awareness of this uncertainty is the feature which distinguishes scientific systems from some political and religious systems which tend to negate the existence of uncertainty.

Open and closed systems. A system is closed if no material enters or leaves it; it is open if there is import and export and, therefore, change of the components. Living organisms are open systems, remaining constant as a whole though there is a continuous flow of the component materials. This characteristic feature of most biological systems is called a steady state.[69] In addition, vital systems can be distinguished from physical systems through the criterion of equifinality. In most physical systems the final state is determined by the initial conditions, while in biological systems the final state is reached from different initial conditions and in different ways. According to Bertalanffy,[4, 5] open systems which attain a steady state can be said to behave in an equifinal way, and it seems safe to assume that the majority if not all of biological, psychological, and social systems fulfill the criteria of open systems and of equifinality—that is, growth.

Lineal and circular systems. In the nineteenth century, scientists used lineal systems to analyze their observations. Events were linked to events by spacing them in time or by patterning them in space, and in the prevailing theories of causality that which preceded was thought to determine completely that which followed. Though today scientists still have to maintain that cause and effect have to follow each other in time, they have become careful in making statements about causality.[8] Present-day scientific systems used in biology and social science have in common the characteristics of being circular, of having self-corrective devices, of being able to establish vicious circles, of having purposive or seeking aspects, of maximizing or minimizing certain features—in brief, of reacting with adaptive and predictive responses bearing upon maintenance of a steady state at a fairly high level of orderliness.[68] In such systems, part functions are always functions of the system as a whole, and the chains of causation are at least circular, and sometimes even more complex.

Class theory and field theory. In the traditional, class-theoretical, Aristotelian approach, an event was grouped with other events into classes dominated by similar characteristics. The establishment of a class of events was determined by the question of regularity in terms of frequency of recurrence, and therefore the individual case had no place in Aristotelian thinking.

In the present-day, field-theoretical, Galilean approach,[32, 34] events are studied with respect to the field in which they take place, and an attempt is made to specify the conditions under which an event might occur. Functions are conceived as forces; as a result value concepts, dichotomies, and other old-fashioned alternatives have gradually disappeared. Inasmuch as the laws in the field-theoretical approach are not based on class characteristics but upon the relationship between an object and its field, similar principles can be applied to a single case also. While in the traditional class-theoretical approach the characteristics of an object were completely determined in advance, in the field-theoretical approach the characteristics and dynamics of an object are determined by its relationship to the surroundings. In social science, the field-theoretical approach is more to the point than the class-theoretical approach because all human beings are surrounded by an environment and all scientific observations have to be made from some position located in the environment.

Representativeness of observation. Every scientist makes the silent assumption that his sense organs and evaluative functions are capable of encompassing that which he anticipates observing and that his instruments of observation really do observe or measure that which he purports to measure.[9] A scientist usually assumes that his observational indices or measurements are as representative as possible of the functions he wishes to study. Erroneous conclusions are reached if his instruments and gadgets record incidental events which are not characteristic of the functions to be observed, or if his direct observational cues are indistinct.

Operational approach. Science, as Stevens[62] puts it, consists of a set of empirical propositions agreed upon by the members of society. Therefore only those propositions which are based upon public and repeatable operations lend themselves for discussion or agreement and disagreement, and only that type of operation can be admitted to the body of science. This approach, which has been labeled *operationism*, insists upon operational definitions of variables and of operations with data; it obviates meaningless concepts such as intuition and dispenses with demons and other devices which attribute unobservable properties to the events under observation. While operationism has long since found its place in physical science, it still is a subject of debate in the social sciences. The author believes, however, that the operational approach as set forth in a model of communication can be applied to the study of intrapersonal, interpersonal, and group phenomena and to large scale social events.[54]

Variables and frames of reference. For obvious practical reasons, the scientist must limit his observations in time and in space and concentrate upon the observation of a few relevant functions. In so doing, he must assume that the functions he studies will vary (variables),[11] while other functions which serve as points of orientation will remain relatively stable and unchanged (frame of reference).[10] Though it must be granted that change is a universal aspect of life, nonetheless functions undergo transformations at different rates; this fact is made use of in science since those functions with a slower rate of change are taken as frames of reference for those with a faster rate of change. Thus the scientist has to assume that during the period of observation and measurement the function under observation does not change.

Within the system that a scientist uses to understand events in nature, the term "variable" can be defined as a symbol standing for a class of events which, under different conditions, have variable quantity and direction. The term "frame of reference" then refers to those symbols which stand for a class of events which, under these given conditions, do not have significant variation in quantity or direction.

Structure and process. An observer can arrange information in various ways. Use of spatial coordinates and disregard for temporal coordinates results in structural assessment, while maximization of temporal coordinates leads to the consideration of process.[54] When data at Time I are compared to data at Time II and then are related in such a way that inferences can be made about the change which has occurred, one speaks of process. At any one moment, scientists have the choice of considering complex spatial patterns (structure) and ignoring time, or of considering complex changes in time (process) and ignoring spatial arrangements— both notions being complementary to each other.[53] In any scientific system, distortions will come about from condensing either spatial or temporal events—that is, from regarding events in space as though they occurred in one place or regarding events in time as though they were not subject to change. And the adequacy of a particular scientific system will depend essentially upon what distortions it introduces.

Part and whole. In present scientific systems it is assumed that change in a part involves a change in the whole and that a change in the whole involves a change in the parts. In any system, therefore, it is very important that the relationship between part components and whole be stated in terms of symbols and concepts which are characteristic of the system. It is awkward to mix concepts derived from chemistry with those that originate in evolutionary theory or to combine statements about an individual with statements about culture. In order to avoid these difficulties, a system has to be used which includes a variety of dimensions—for example, the system of communication.[49]

Causality and determinism. In order to understand nature, scientists distinguish between cause and effect. One event occurring in a time-space continuum is labeled "cause" and another is labeled "effect" if the occurrence of the effect is dependent upon the occurrence of the cause.[8] An event which has been defined in terms of one scientific universe cannot be the cause of another event which has been defined in terms of another scientific universe. Causes and effects, therefore, have to be formulated within the same frame of reference. When events are formulated in different frames of reference, the scientist can only speak about coexistence, correlation, and perhaps interdependence; on the basis of such relationships he can predict predetermined situations.

Assumed reality and perceived reality. In science a distinction is made between what is perceived in nature and what is believed to exist in reality. This distinction is useful in the field of physical sciences because subsequent experimentation may lead to a reproduction of natural events and hence to a check of the accuracy and completeness of the data and of the scientific model. However, difficulties arise when this distinction is applied to the field of social science. By definition, social science is concerned with what human beings do. Man-induced action presumes perception, and social reality is a function of perception. In the field of human communication, therefore, it has become a necessity to part with traditions of physical science. Social transactions engaged in by people cannot be treated as such but have to be viewed through the eyes and ears of a human observer. Since it is impossible to determine what part of a given scientific report on social events is based on the bias of the observer and what part is traceable to the characteristics of the observed events, it is preferable to abandon the distinction between assumed and perceived reality and to deal exclusively with the perceived reality.[54]

The social context of scientific observation. Every scientist lives in a social matrix,[54] and the questions he raises reflect the social and scientific philosophies of his time. It is impossible for others to interpret an observer's report unless some statements are available about the matrix or the field in which the observations were made. Statements about the social situation or the context in which an investigation was undertaken usually are helpful in understanding the bias introduced by personal factors, by membership in a professional discipline, or by exposure to large-scale social events.

The social situation as a new entity of study. Though any human being or animal is, biologically speaking, a natural and practical entity, it does not follow that the human being or the animal is a useful scientific entity. To study one ant in a glass jar will tell little, if anything, about the ant's relation to other ants or about the social organization of ants as a whole. In communication theory, therefore, the unit of study is the social situation which is defined by the network of communication in which the individual is participating. Without an observer there is no scientific information. Therefore information as to social events can only be gathered in a social situation in which at least two people participate.

The relationship between observer and observed. If the characteristics of the observer are of the same magnitude as those of the phenomena studied, the observer must be supposed to influence the processes under observation as well as to be affected himself by the ongoing events.[68] In this case, the observer becomes a part of the system and his report will be subjectively colored. This characteristic dilemma of the social sciences is based upon the fact that the properties of human observers are almost identical with the properties of the objects of observation—namely, people. In the physical sciences, in contrast, the properties of the observer are usually very different from those of the observed; hence the observer is likely to remain relatively outside of the system that he is studying and his report will be more objective.

In communication theory, therefore, speculations as to the nature of the observed events are replaced by a consideration of the idiosyncratic picture which the human observer possesses. Any scientific system used for the study of social events must provide a place for data relating to the human observer so that his report can be evaluated by others who either observe the same events or observe the first observer and then re-evaluate his report. At times this observation by an alter-observer can be replaced by self-observation.[54]

Complementarity of information. Heisenberg[29] states in his principle of indeterminacy that the velocity and the position of a physical particle can never be completely ascertained at the same instant. Switching the universe of discourse from that of wave mechanics to that of communication, one finds that a similar principle applies. At any one moment, the observer can look at an event from one position only. By the time he alters his position, his focus of interest, or his attitude, or by the time he poses the question he wishes to ask, the event may already have changed. These circumstances force us to recognize a novel relationship, conveniently termed "complementarity,"[7] between empirical findings obtained under differing conditions. In the field of communication examples of such complementarity of information are: concern with others or concern with the self (intro- and extero-functions), the view from inside out or from outside in (participation and observation), concern with the present or with the past (diachronic and synchronic statements), and consideration of spatial or of temporal coordinates (structure and process).

The problem of complementarity of information owes its existence to the inability of the human observer to observe more than a few things at a time. One must assume that conscious awareness is limited to a single pattern or cluster of events, and that if the observer wishes to focus simultaneously upon other features he cannot do so without blurring the previous pattern. The more successful the observer is in isolating an event and the more distinct the perceptual cues become, the more specific is the information he gains; but the more he concentrates upon details, the less he learns about the relatedness of this to other events. Conversely, the more inclusive the report is, the more information the observer gains about relationships, although he loses information about details. This peculiar problem bearing upon the nature of human observation probably is responsible for the problem of polarity. The scientist is aware that when he focuses upon one thing he must have at that very moment in his field of awareness a label for all those things he is not considering. This particular problem is considered best in terms of the theory of values, which subject has been expanded elsewhere.[54]

The transactional point of view. Dewey and Bentley[18] have in masterful words summarized three positions encountered in psychological theory. They distinguish the following levels of organization on which scientific inquiry can proceed: (1) self-action, in which things are viewed as acting under their own powers; (2) inter-action, in which thing is balanced against thing in causal interconnection; (3) trans-action, in which systems of description and naming are employed to deal with aspects and phases of action without final attribution to "elements" or other presumptively detachable or independent "entities," "essences," or "realities," and without isolation of presumptively detachable "relations" from such detachable "elements." In present-day psychiatric and psychological theory —and this includes the outline of communication presented in this paper— the transactional point of view has been generally accepted.

The multiple meaning of the term "communication." The term "communication" refers on the one hand to a ubiquitous activity engaged in by all human beings and on the other hand to a scientific procedure designed to gather data about the way people behave. In one instance, communication refers to that which is assumed to exist in reality quite independent of the actions of an identified human observer, and in another instance it refers to the processes of communication which the observer must use when observing, experimenting, and eventually making his scientific reports.

While in the physical sciences the human observer uses communication to report scientific facts and theories pertaining to the material world, in the social sciences the processes of communication are used to investigate communication itself. How this difficulty can be managed will be discussed in the next section.

THE ELEMENTS OF COMMUNICATION THEORY

The terms social situation, status, roles, rules, and social techniques refer to theoretical constructs used in the understanding of social action.[45, 46, 47] Underlying these constructs is the assumption that during the period of observation events will not change and roles or social situations will remain stable. The purpose of introducing into communication theory some of the sociological concepts is to create a bridge between the wider societal framework and the narrower interpersonal framework in which psychologists and psychiatrists operate. These concepts are, of course, not simply borrowed from these other systems; they are translated and specially fitted into the framework of communication.

Cultural and social institutions define the situations in which human beings operate. In the course of the centuries, cultural institutions have arisen pragmatically around the important and repetitious situations of daily life. In cultural terms, rules and laws represent the institutionalized aspects of social action, and roles the personalized aspects. In individual terms, conscience, ideals, and morals represent the institutionalized component, and the sensory-effector system represents the personal and practical aspects. Therefore, on the individual level as well as on the group and cultural levels we have to distinguish between the institutionalized—that is, the formalized and regulated—aspects of social action and the unique, individual, and often spontaneously arising aspects which are contained in the expressions of single persons or groups.

SOCIAL SITUATIONS, STATUS, ROLES, RULES, AND TECHNIQUES

In communication theory, the unit of consideration is the social situation. A social situation is established when people enter into interpersonal communication. For practical purposes, a social situation is thus limited to people who either talk or write to each other, although they may be connected by some other device of communication. In a social situation, the behavior of the participants is organized around a common task which implies the existence of rules, of status assignment, and of role differentiation.

The social situation. The scientific concept of "social situation" is a structural assumption used in understanding a set of social processes which occupy a defined portion of the time-space continuum. Social and cultural institutions usually define the situations; once the individual has identified the label of the situation correctly, he can proceed with the previously established behavior patterns which were designed to cope with such situations.

Scientifically, a complete description of a social situation[57] includes the label and the identifying characteristics; a description of the relevant rules, of the status assignment of the participants, of available rewards, of emotoins which are supposed to be displayed, and of the implementations which are possible; an identification of the goals and the points of departure of social action; and a description of the premises upon which such social action is based. These aspects, when perceived in their entirety by a participant, are closely related to what a psychiatrist calls social reality. With respect to time, it is obvious that any situation evolves from a previous situation and dissolves into a subsequent one.

In daily living, people may refer to a social situation by saying, "I have to attend a meeting," "I am expected for dinner," or "I have to go to a funeral." These words label the situation and delineate for a member of the same social system some aspects of the situation in space and in time and of the behavior which can be expected. To the foreigner, however, such statements mean less because he is unable to fill in from experience the relevant connotations which pertain to this particular social system.

The scientific observer is in a somewhat similar position. Observation alone is rarely satisfactory for the study of social situations. A participant who assumes an active role, with the desire and the ability to communicate, is undoubtedly in a better position to report about events in terms of rules and roles and with reference to those subtle cues which determine the label of the situation than is a rather passive observer who, by definition, remains relatively outside of the main events.

Social situations are frequently identified by signs and signals which originate in the material environment. Architecture, furniture, clothing, *décor*, trade symbols, verbal signs, and name plates can all be employed as cues for the identification of a situation—subject, of course, to modifications introduced through the action of people.

The institutionalized situations found in a modern technical civilization crystallize around a variety of foci: There are situations which bear upon the *interrelationship of family or household members* at home. Here, the labels of the situations are dependent upon activities such as eating, washing, cooking, sleeping, training of children, and relationship to pets and domestic animals.

Again, there are situations which are grouped around the *social and recreational activities* of people; these include entertainment, amusement outside of the home, sports, gang activities of children, membership in clubs and associations, approaches to one's own sex and to the opposite sex, travel, and, last but not least, ceremonials and festivities.

There are a number of situations which bear upon the *occupational life* of people. Some of these define the interrelationship in terms of status— that is, age, seniority, intelligence, skill, or property; others classify people in terms of skill alone. There are terms which differentiate various school grades, which delineate unskilled, semiskilled, and skilled work situations, and which label maintenance, trade, and administrative activities.

Sometimes situations are labeled according to the facilities which people have at their disposal to perform a service. Western Union can transmit telegrams; the Union Pacific can transport goods and people; and the stock exchange is geared to the trading of stocks. One finds standard situations in restaurants, which have space, equipment, and food available for serving their guests; there are situations which have to do with housing, clothing, repair of plumbing, shoe-shining, and the care of the sick in hospitals. Finally, some situations are labeled according to the relationship which characterizes the interaction between government officials and the population; these situations are highly institutionalized and formalized, as evidenced in court procedures, tax collection, or public health measures.

But regardless of how the situation is officially labeled, the individual, if he desires to communicate successfully, has to go beyond the gross identification of the label. The label is only an approximation making it possible for the person to scan his memory for a number of possible behavior patterns which might occur in the immediate future, to establish some general directives, and to set some limits for his expectations. Recognition of the subtleties of the situation is related to the identification of status and roles.

Status and roles. The term "status" has long been used to refer to the position of an individual in the prestige system of society, while the term "role" has been used to designate the sum total of action patterns associated with a particular status. Status is assigned by others, but roles are action patterns learned by an individual in the course of his development. Social scientists, therefore, have been interested in conceptualizing social events[27, 35, 47, 67] in terms of caste, class, and status and role systems, while psychiatrists, with their orientation towards the individual, have tried to conceptualize interpersonal events less in terms of systems than in terms of mutually developed and individualized roles,[1, 43, 57, 63] frequently with a therapeutic purpose in mind.[40]

Language is full of terms which describe status and roles. Terms such as king, slave, notable, and general refer to the position in the prestige scale of society, while terms such as husband, friend, son, lawyer, or physician refer to specialized behavior of individuals within a group. To be precise, the term "role" labels an individual as a participant in an intricate network of human relations. Roles are multipolar phenomena denoting the relationship of one person to one or more other people, or expressing the relatedness of many people to many other people. There is no husband without a wife, no father without a son or daughter, and no tax collector without taxpayers. People identify status and roles in many ways. Uniforms, lapel buttons, and styles of dressing are external marks of identification; manners, gestures, and ways of talking are more intimate marks of identification; personal introductions—"I am so-and-so"—may overtly clarify a role. But regardless of what the criteria are, in practice almost all people use the sum total of cues and clues present, including the sensations which arise inside their own organism.

In daily life, role and status are the keys to the interpretation of messages. One talks differently and about different things when one is questioned by a judge than when one buys a vacuum cleaner from a salesman. With the help of roles, people are able to address each other without being personally acquainted; a sick person may ask for a physician, and a person in need of protection may call for a policeman although in both cases the principals have probably not met before.

The role and the status of receivers and senders in a network of communication indicate to the participants how a message ought to be interpreted. For example, a person who enters a used car lot as a prospective buyer is treated differently and his words are weighted and interpreted differently than if he had identified himself as a seller who wished to get rid of his jalopy. In communication theory, therefore, roles have a double function: they identify the participants; and they represent silent messages about communication which constitute instructions of the receiver to the sender about the way he should be addressed and from the sender to the receiver about the way his message ought to be interpreted.

Once a participant has, consciously or unconsciously, identified the role which he is likely to assume, he will, in the course of communication, raise a number of questions which will give him further information about the details of the role he is about to engage in—questions pertaining to the initiation of activity and to active or passive participation, and questions of prestige, intimacy, and similarity. Furthermore, he will inquire whether these roles are of short- or long-term duration, whether they can be altered or whether, once engaged in, they remain stable over a period of time. He will be interested in whether his assuming a role will result in social contact with others, whether it will involve the execution of stereotyped functions, as in the work of a bookkeeper, or of varied functions, as in the job of the trouble-shooter. He will inquire into whether or not his role will force him to adapt to others, to control others, to mediate between others, or to complement the function of others. And finally, if he is searching for roles analogous to family situations, he may wonder whether a role is parental, filial, mate-like, or sibling-like. And he may explore whether the role deals with exchange of information, with trade, with cooperation, with competition, or with a variety of these functions.

Rules. Much has been written about the nature of laws and rules.[14] The laws of natural science, if valid at all, cannot be violated. If anyone could in the least depart from such a law, it then would be proved false as a scientific or universal law. But it is of the very essence that legal rules, customs, and traditions are violable and that sanctions are provided for their violation. They do not state what always is, but attempt to decide what ought to be. In any society one often finds conflicting usages and customs, so that specific rules are enacted by the legislatures; and these rules are elaborated upon by courts and enforced by the state. Rules are normative devices, established by people to create social order and to avoid conflict and chaos. Natural laws, on the other hand, reflect some inherent properties of nature, as conceived by scientists.[16]

In daily life, each social situation is governed by written or unwritten rules; they instruct the participants about the procedure—that is, the "what," the "when," and the "where." Rules contain directives for the participants and frequently are restrictive. In everyday communication rules control the flow of messages; they indicate who may talk to whom, prescribe the form in which messages must be presented, and specify how long someone may talk and what not to say. The rules of communication have been laid down in written language for many institutionalized situations: for example, procedures in courts of law, civil service reports, military communications, and the etiquette of state receptions. Less formal, but nonetheless rather binding, are the rules of custom which prescribe the behavior at funerals, marriage ceremonies, initiations, and celebrations.

Perhaps the most precisely defined rules are those which apply to games such as bridge or poker, football or baseball. Such rules usually specify the following: a description of the game including its label and purpose; the time duration of the game; the place of the game and the facilities and equipment necessary; the distribution of status and roles during the game; the rewards for playing or winning the game; the sanctions for violation of rules; the provisions for ending the game prematurely, for dealing with outside interference, for change of rules, and finally for abolishing the game and disbanding the players.

This analysis can without difficulty be applied to daily life situations, if one substitutes the word "social situation" for "game." Most of our social situations are little games with a variety of rules which the participants have to learn if they wish to survive. Von Neumann and Morgenstern[44] have successfully applied the game model to an analysis of economic behaviour, and there is no doubt that such a model is most relevant to communicative behavior. All human relations and communication systems are governed by rules; these are either handed down from generation to generation or newly created by mutual consent or by forceful imposition. A great deal of time is spent at home or in school in teaching the rules governing communication in social situations; and those who openly defy these rules land either in jail or in mental institutions.

Social techniques. Constructs such as situation, rules, status, and roles do not suffice to encompass all the subtleties of communication. For example, there is no doubt that there are different kinds of fathers who have different effects upon their children, in spite of the fact that they have identical roles and observe similar rules. Thus a scientist can report in words about the social situation, rules, and roles that he has observed, but he is unable to do justice to the subtleties of social action, for words are not satisfactory to completely describe social events. In the past, different disciplines have suggested a variety of schemes to encompass these more subtle aspects of social action. In psychoanalytic theory, for instance, the attempt is made to explain nonverbal actions of people and interaction with the surroundings by focusing upon the bodily orifices. By adoption of the analogy of food intake and elimination, terms such as anal and oral are used to denote the varieties of social approaches employed by individuals. Specifically, Alexander in his vector theory, Erikson in his enunciation of modalities, and Fromm in his basic orientations[2, 19, 25] have elaborated on Freud's earlier theories bearing upon the erogenic zones of the body. Such formulations have some shortcomings, however, in that social approaches are never the function of only one person. An overly dependent, oral character, for example, must find someone to be dependent upon. The dependent and the dependee thus form one unit.

In modern communication theory, then, such social approaches are described as multipolar phenomena determined by at least two, if not more, people. I have labeled the network of these subtle, essentially nonverbal social actions between people as "social techniques."[48] Though the term "social technique" to my knowledge was coined only recently, by Tolmann,[66] the evolution of the concept of social technique dates back to ancient poets and philosophers. Machiavelli,[37] for example, described the procedures of diplomacy, with emphasis upon ruling and domination, and the effects to be achieved from these. Novelists such as Cervantes, Goethe, and Zola describe exquisitely the social techniques and transactions of a Don Quixote, a Werther, or a Nana; but the social scientists of their time were still concerned with concepts which considered the person as a self-contained and isolated entity. Only in recent years especially under the influence of Lewin, Parsons, and Sullivan,[33, 46, 63] have the transactional approach[18] and the observation of effects been stressed.

The methods of manipulation, operation, social engineering, and social technique can only be reported by a person who is a participant. The manifest content of the messages contains few if any clues about the nature of such techniques so that only an actual participant can gauge, from the wear and tear which he experiences, the influences to which he has been subjected. Frequently a person may be unaware of his own manipulative tendencies, and only after another person calls attention to what is going on can the full extent of the operation be assessed. Social transactions frequently make use of nonverbal means of communication, and a variety of action signals are combined into intricate patterns of social action.[57] Context, action sequence, timing, and intensity are skillfully used by the participants to influence each other. People who are manipulators are extremely sensitive to the responses achieved in the listener, and their procedure cannot be characterized by what they say or by how they say it, but primarily by their persistently adaptive mercurialness. To attempt to characterize these rapid changes is difficult, but a descriptive classification may conveniently start with their purpose—that is, the anticipated effects which manipulators want to achieve.

From a descriptive point of view, I would like to mention first those techniques which can be labeled *interpersonal tactics*; they are employed to establish new or to alter existing relationships. Designed to bring about a change in role distribution (for example, the techniques of social climbing[52] and decline), interpersonal tactics are used for the purpose of approach (for example, the "pick-up" technique of young men), detachment (for example, the techniques of detachment from the parents), or annihilation (for example, the technique of warfare). These techniques not only characterize individuals but often are typical for the activities of groups of people. The techniques of revolutionaries (Fascists, Nazis, Communists, and anarchists) as well as the techniques of propaganda,[60] when successful bring about changes in role distribution, status, and the observation of rules.

Another type of technique is geared to the *maintenance of relationships* that already exist. On a group level the techniques of the government in power, and on a family level the techniques of domineering parents are designed to maintain the status quo. On an interpersonal level, these approaches can conveniently be grouped around the topics of intimacy, prestige, identity, and family role. In orde to maintain distance, for example, an individual may remain aloof, may prevent people from gathering much information about him, and may always be choosey about friends and groups he comes in contact with. He may become aggressive, punitive, or rejecting, or he may freeze other people when they trespass his privately set boundaries. In contrast, there are the techniques which are designed to maintain a feeling of intimacy with others; sharing a common purpose or common information, doing the same things, and conforming in thought and belief serve the purpose of getting closer.

The methods for maintaining prestige and superiority[48] and those designed to insure self-abasement are well known. To maintain superiority, a person does not seek a common meeting ground with others but, on the contrary, surrounds himself with people who in every respect feel inferior to him.

Finally, there are the techniques related to the *maintenance or clarification of identity*.[48] Actions which stress similarity involve copying and imitation—for example, the boy who acts like his father. Actions which stress the difference between people involve confrontation, negativism, and independence—for example, the actions of boys and girls who, when dating, dress up and emphasize their difference to increase their attractiveness.

So far, I have pointed to some of the characteristics of social techniques. Now I should like to discuss the denotative devices that are used to describe actions and techniques in terms of verbal language. Language cannot do justice to the subtle differences in social techniques; although the English language is particularly rich in verbs and terms referring to action,[38] it cannot encompass fully that which is actually experienced.

But the study of verbs reflects somewhat the variety of social techniques which have been observed. Not all of these verbs denote interpersonal transactions; some terms denote the actions of single individuals irrespective of others, and other terms refer to the interaction of two or more people. It is well to remember that interaction verbs silently imply the presence of several people, even if grammatically the verb is related to one subject only. The peculiarities of language often necessitate a discrepancy between strict semantic meaning and pragmatic interpretation. But a review of the words suggesting the various modes of participation will give the reader an impression of the varieties of social transactions.

The term *approach*[48] denotes actions which are designed to bring people closer to each other; they are characterized by display of friendliness and absence of threat. The word approach refers to a truly interpersonal process: it presupposes initiative on the part of one person and readiness to respond on the part of the other person.

Preservation of existing relationships is achieved through providing satisfaction of the other person's needs, threatening reprisals for eventual dissolution, or perhaps exaggerating the consequences of an eventual separation. Most existing verbs refer to a change of relationships. *Cooperation* is perhaps the only term which can be appropriately used to denote actions which keep things going and maintain relationships.

The term *detachment* refers to social situations and interpersonal relations in which a dissolution of an existing relationship becomes necessary. By this technique, a person may withdraw the inherent gratifications in a situation and increase the frustrations of others. The same purpose can be achieved by threat or by isolating oneself from others.

If approach, preservation, and detachment refer to the over-all effect which a person can achieve with a technique, there are also more specific terms which denote the way such a change has been brought about. *Intake* denotes an increase or gain, either in food and beverages or in information.[26] *Annihilation*[57] refers to the reduction of interference. *Retention*[19] refers to exclusive possession and withholding of substances or information. *Elimination*,[19] or *riddance*, refers to the treatment of people or things as if they were waste material. *Avoidance*[19] designates the diminution of contact with other persons or things. *Marketing*,[19] or *exchange*, denotes the simultaneous intake and output—that is, exchange—of materials or information with other people. *Attracting*,[57] *showing off*, or *displaying* reflects all those actions which imply a signaling for attention. *Play*[57] denotes the rehearsal of actions with the mutual understanding that whatever the outcome of the situation may be, the results are not going to have serious consequences. *Exploration*[57] is concerned with the penetration of the unknown; going into strange surroundings rather than bringing the strange surroundings to the self is characteristic of this approach. *Intrusion*[19] denotes the forceful thrust of a person upon another person or organization with the intent to penetrate. *Inception*[19] is the opposite of intrusion; it refers to the envelopment of that which intrudes. *Creation*[57] is concerned with the production of the new or not existing. *Raising*,[57] *developing*, and *letting grow* are words which denote the process by which existing organizations or persons provide an opportunity for the newly created organization or person, and thus gradually give independence to that which is to be raised or developed.

In the theory of human communication, constructs such as social situations, rules, status, roles, and social techniques truly reflect the actions which people have to undertake if they wish to communicate. For both the participant and the theoretician, the social situation defines the matrix and outlines the field in which communication takes place. Rules determine what language is to be spoken, what messages have priority, and who can talk to whom. Status and role identify the human participants engaged in communication and serve as explanatory—that is, metacommunicative—messages; as in the denotation of music, they are the keys which instruct the participants in how to interpret the messages. Social techniques, finally, are a way to describe the intentions of people and the effects they have achieved with social action when action itself is the language in which the messages are coded.

Information, Language, and Codification

Information is probably the most important theoretical construct in communication theory. It refers to the fact that events going on in nature can be represented in other places and at other times. What is represented is obviously not the original event but a system of relationships which closely approximate the original event. Information may be coded outside of the human organism in terms of verbal symbols, objects, drawings and sketches, full- or small-scale models, and in many other forms. Inside the human organism, information is coded probably in terms of nervous and chemical signals. Information held by human beings is made accessible to self by feeling and thinking and to others by means of expressive movements—that is, action, including speech.

Information has a number of highly characteristic properties. It is always selective, much as sensory processes are always selective. The selectivity depends in part upon the structure of the end organs, and in part upon the observer who selects out of the potentially available information that which he is interested in. The observer's personal interest depends upon his purpose at that moment, which in turn is influenced by previous experiences. Focusing, therefore, is an operation which necessarily results in distortions. Simultaneous events have to be perceived successively, and one can only infer that things happen at the same time. Likewise, the evaluation of successive events is telescoped into simultaneous considerations whenever messages are evaluated. That which is magnified stands out; the rest becomes background.

The perceptual-evaluative apparatus of the human being is, for practical purposes, limited to the observation of one aspect of events at any given time. In order to obtain more complete information, the observer has to focus in succession upon different aspects of events. For this purpose, he must assume that perceived events essentially do not change during the period of observation—an assumption which, in the case of human behavior, is highly improbable. At any one moment, the information received through perception of events is rather incomplete. Therefore, it has to be complemented with other pieces of incomplete information derived from additional observations at different times. These limitations of the perceptual-evaluative apparatus of the human being lead to a dialectic problem which one may refer to as the *complementarity of information*.

When an observer is concerned with observing himself, he cannot be concerned with others; if he specializes in transmission, he is less concerned with perception; and if he focuses upon interpersonal events, he cannot be equally concerned with group events. Though we must assume that individual, interpersonal, group, and cultural events occur simultaneously in reality, the human observer must, for dialectic reasons, observe these phenomena in succession. Although, for example, an observer in an interpersonal situation may be concerned at one moment with the assessment of the behavior of another human being, he may at the next instant proceed to observe his own feelings and thoughts; but by the time he really arrives at that observation, the behavior of the other person may have changed. In order to gain a more complete picture of the other person, he therefore must make some assumptions which will stabilize the situation. The observer usually assumes that his self-observations and the observations of the other person occur simultaneously, although he knows that this assumption does not correspond to reality. The complementarity of information—that is, aspects which complement each other but which, at the time they are gathered, are mutually exclusive—is a formidable problem in the majority of human functions.[54] One such dichotomy is the participant and the observer; another pertains to proprio-functions and extero-functions; a third dichotomy is action as implementation and action as language; a fourth is structure and process; and there are many others.

The *complementarity between proprio- and extero-functions* is for the psychiatrist of greatest importance. The proprio-functions refer at all levels of communication to the system in which the observer is an integral part, and the extero-functions refer to those systems in which the observer is not a part. One can distinguish between proprio-perception, -evaluation, and -transmission and extero-perception, -evaluation, and -transmission. Proprioception at the individual level consists of focusing upon stimuli arising inside the organism, evaluating such matters as fatigue, headache, temperature sensations, shame, guilt, or anxiety. Conversely, in exteroception, an individual focuses upon stimuli arising outside of his organism; he observes objects or nature, and the self as seen or heard through his exteroceptive sense organs. In propriotransmission, the messages are directed at internal destinations and are not intended for communication with the outside world; it is a rather unconscious phenomenon involving primarily the smooth muscles. Muscular tension, involuntary movements, and contractions of the smooth muscles of the respiratory, intestinal, and vascular systems are examples of propriotransmission. In exterotransmission, conversely, the message is directed at external destinations, and the transmission is mediated principally through contractions of the striated muscles. It manifests itself in speech, gesture, and in other instrumental actions. Proprioevaluation is undertaken solely for the purpose of internal consumption so that the individual can evaluate feelings of gratification or frustration, make choices, and consider the need for restraining his desire for action. In exteroevaluation, it is the consideration of external events that matters; here the individual can evaluate his impact upon others, his roles, the social situation, and other pertinent factors.

Proprioception at the group level is centered on perceiving events happening in one's own group—for example, a football team in a huddle assesses the state of its own team. In exteroception, the behavior of the other group is observed—for example, a football team perceives the weakness of the other team. In propriotransmission, the activities serve the purpose of conveying a message to other members of the group—for example, a police patrol maintains communication with headquarters. In exterotransmission, the activities are oriented towards other groups—for example, the activities of propaganda and advertising agencies are measured in terms of the reactions of the audience. In proprioevaluation, the state of one's own group is evaluated—for example, an arctic expedition may find it meaningful to assess the state of health of its own group. In exteroevaluation, one group evaluates another group—for example, the Supreme Court reviews a verdict of a lower court, or the executive committee of an organization reviews the actions of another organization.

At the societal level, all participants are almost unaware of being an infinitesimal part of an extensive communication system.. In general, people may be slightly more aware of the existence of these large superpersonal systems when they observe other cultures or when they study the anonymous messages and mass communications within their own culture. Proprioception at the societal level occurs rarely; perhaps it is limited to historians, sociologists, economists, and colonial administrators who study the broad aspects of their own culture. Exteroception is more frequent since observation of the enemy or of other nations is a rather common occurrence. In propriotransmission, the actions of the group are directed towards one's own culture—primarily towards posterity. And in exterotransmission, messages are directed at other cultures—for example, the messages of the white man to what he considers more primitive civilizations. Proprioevaluation considers one's own culture in absolute terms; for example, people decide what sort of constitution they wish to have. In exteroevaluation, other cultures are assessed, especially in times preceding great wars and large-scale social conflicts.

The human being can undertake a number of *operations with information* which will yield additional information. Selection, maximization, amplification, interpolation, extrapolation, suppression, and abstraction are but a few examples. When a person encounters difficulties in action, he resorts to his intellect. With the help of thought, which is born of failure and fulfills an essentially reparatory function, action is analyzed, past events are reconstructed, and future events are anticipated; and opportunity for substitute gratification in fantasy occurs in mediation and self-observation. But not all operations with information constitute a gain for the individual. In abstraction, for example, an observer has to focus upon generalities and has to neglect specific and unique features; indeed, he cares only for the statistical mass effect. In this sense, abstraction is a one-way procedure, since it is impossible to infer the specific events from knowledge of principles. When abstraction and extrapolation are carried too far, when information is not properly weighted and is one-sidedly maximized, catastrophe is around the corner: either the person becomes neurotic or psychotic or the erroneous evaluation of reality prevents his survival.

Operations with information serve the purpose of maintaining the steady state of the communication system. It is obvious that such operations may be fluid or rigid, and true or untrue with reference to reality. In order to encompass the effect upon the system, operations with information may be termed open-end, optimal, and closed-end.

At the personal level, the closed-end functions are exemplified by repetitive, unalterable, persevering, and stereotyped operations involving perception, judgment, and action. The open-end functions are represented by chaotic, unstable, or excessively fluid operations with mutually contradictory frames of reference which are so transient and overlapping that they cannot be utilized. They manifest themselves in the inability to organize or to integrate, the inability to check and countercheck information, and the lack of stabilization in habit formation. Optimal operations with flexible frames of reference range in between the open and closed procedures. Under optimal conditions, perceptive entities such as cues are changed when proven ineffective, evaluation is geared to problem-solving operations, and transmission is concerned with flexible action which is subordinated to the functioning of the whole organism.

One of the most important operations with information is learning, which consists of stabilization of existing functions by renouncing new choices and repeating the old ones. Closed-end functions refer to excessive learning in which adaptation is renounced because of overspecialization, while the open-end procedures refer to the inability to learn and renunciation of the advantages gained by repetitive performance.

In interpersonal communication systems, closed-end operations manifest themselves by rigidity to the extent of endangering the existence of the system: perception is so stereotyped that nothing new can be encompassed; evaluation is logically so consistent that it becomes inconsistent with nature; and transmission is repetitive to the point of boredom. The compulsive neurotic is a pertinent example. Open-end operations, in contrast, are so loosely defined that change becomes too rapid: perceptions are varied and inconsistent; evaluations are contradictory and serve the whims of the moment; and in transmission anything can be said or done. The whole procedure lacks long-term goals and is essentially overadaptive to the point of shiftiness. Optimal operations are flexibly defined according to purpose. That which interpersonally may be seen, judged, or talked about varies and is always subservient to the imminent task, and this includes the notion of disrupting the relationship if it is no longer useful.

In group systems, closed-end operations involve excessive specialization and division of labor. Thus the group, because of its formal organization, finds itself in a precarious equilibrium which is exemplified in bureaucratic and authoritarian practices. The open systems, in contrast, have an excessively loose and undefined group structure. Here we find lack of specialization and fluctuation of role distribution, while the rules are made up or changed with progressive development. Such chaotic or transient systems of communication are characteristic of war-time, emergency, and frontier situations. Finally, under optimal conditions, the group structure is stabilized and varies according to circumstance. Because of the flexible assignment of specialization, corrective mechanisms operate effectively under such conditions.

At the societal level, closed-end operations pertain to rigidly defined roles of groups as they occur, for example, in an old caste society which functions without the buffer effects of a class society. In the open-end systems of operation, roles and rules are loosely defined, and nobody knows precisely what the function of a group is; an example of this kind is found in the culture-contact groups of great harbor cities like Shanghai. Under optimal conditions, then, roles and rules of these groups and the functions of society are flexibly defined. Examples of this type are numerous in the founding years of any nation.

While the concept of information refers to the inside representation of outside events, the concepts of language and *codification* refer to the technical aspects of the recording of such information. Retention of information necessitates some imprints or traces which, when they are known to several people or to the same person at various dates, are referred to as a code.

All *action* can function as language. Any action undertaken by an organism is a statement which, when perceived and understood by other organisms, becomes a message. Messages are conveyed by signals which as they travel along certain pathways can be conceived of as signs.[21] A sign possesses problem-solving properties or cue value for an observer by force of its own structure and because of the attention which is paid to it. A ·reciprocal relationship exists between signs and signals. For example, one must assume that neural impulses in transit are rather uniform and that they probably vary only in time and intensity. The multifariousness of a human being's impressions, therefore, cannot be satisfactorily explained by the variability of nervous signals, but rather by the channeling of these signals into certain network configurations referred to as signs. The relationship between the uniformity of signals and the heterogeneity of signs inside the organism is reversed when one considers the communications network outside of the organism, for in the latter the variability is due to variations in signals. When perception takes place, the multiplicity of signals is translated within the human organism into a multiplicity of signs, which process is reversed when transmission of messages towards the outside becomes necessary.

The principal human code is language. Here it seems profitable to distinguish, with Morris,[41] a number of related disciplines. Semiotics, which is the science of signs, concerns itself with events in their functions as symbols. Within the field of semiotics one finds the field of syntactics, which is concerned with the relationships of symbols to other symbols; the field of semantics, which deals with the relations of signs to the events or objects they purport to designate; and the field of pragmatics, which is the science of the relation of signs to their human interpreters. Psychiatrists are, of course, most interested in the pragmatic aspects of language.

Language, in the narrower sense of the word, denotes the universal properties of events. That which is in common with other events is expressed in words or symbols, the field of mathematics being the supreme example of such relational statements. In order to describe more unique events, language has to list a large number of universal aspects, and through special spatial and temporal arrangements of these factors the more divergent nature of these events is indicated. Thus language in action[28] conveys statements of probability. Really unique events can only be experienced; they can never be described.[31]

When an observer studies a single human being in isolation from others, the nature of codification inside of this individual cannot be explored directly; today, however, it is generally accepted that information is codified in terms of nervous impulses or signals which travel along certain nervous pathways. In addition, information is probably also codified in terms of chemical impulses which are conveyed contiguously from cell to cell and along the humoral pathways.

Codification at the interpersonal level is accessible to observation and experimentation. In its simplest form, a person may point to a thing, an organ, or an action and let it speak for itself. This process may be referred to as ostensive communication. Next in complexity are the action symbols, which can vary from universally understood gestures to highly individualized forms of expression. Finally we have the spoken or written word, mathematics, and all other types of essentially verbal forms of codification.[39]

Although language continues to be the essential form of codification, it loses some of its importance at the group level. Much information is codified in terms of the activities of the organized group. For example, each individual may hold a small piece of information which is entirely useless to him alone; but when he is in contact with a group—be it a football team or a symphony orchestra—the isolated pieces of information fall into place. Some of this information becomes accessible in action only, and one must assume that the codification of this type of information is contained in the group as a whole. Just as a metacarpal bone has little or no information about the organism as a whole, so does an individual have little information about the group. The codification of information is divided among many people, and only when the mosaic is put together does it become significant.

At the cultural and societal level, the codification processes are spread over large geographical areas and a considerable segment of time. The time-binding effect of cultural codifications bridges the gap between generations. Custom and tradition, and particularly language, are handed down through the ages. But the thousands of individuals who contributed towards a culture remain anonymous; for example, the architects and workers who built cathedrals and amphitheatres of the past remain unknown by name. The pyramids of Egypt were built by thousands of unidentified people—a message to posterity codified in stone. In analyzing space-binding codifications, one finds that roles do not refer to individual persons any more but denote the specialized functions of a group within the organized network of society. At this level, one talks, for example, about lawyers, physicians, and farmers rather than about any single individual, and rules then define the interrelatedness of these groups.

In thinking about codification,[54] it is well to remember that these processes are a function of the time and space scales of the system. Large organizations spread their codifications over larger segments of space and time than smaller organizations. And it may well be that many forms of codification have escaped man's attention, either because they are too large or because they are too small in terms of our own human scales of observation.

While verbal language is generally accepted as a common code system in communication, the concept of silent action as codification seems to present some particular difficulties. People commonly assume that information is transmitted in terms of words or gestures; they tend to forget that the direct observation of action, for example, of a man tying his shoelaces or offering his girl friend a cigarette, is perhaps the most important system of interpersonal codification. Words and gestures stand primarily for other events; they have little intrinsic value of their own and therefore are readily regarded as symbols. In contrast, silent actions (exclusive of gesture) always have a potentially twofold function: they are an implementation in their own right, or they may stand for something else, or both. This double meaning of actions introduces great difficulties into the evaluation of nonverbal communication inasmuch as a perceiver can never be quite sure when an action is intended to convey a message and when it is intended for other purposes.

Even at the personal level some information seems to be coded in terms of action. A person cannot learn to play the piano, for example, by reading a book; instead he has to move his muscles if he wishes to get the feeling of it. The same is true of athletes, who actually practice the motions of golf or tennis prior to a competition in order to recall the actions that they are going to need. Apparently some signs are coded in the organism by a network which includes, in addition to the central nervous system component, the effector organs in action.

At the interpersonal level, information is really contained in the interaction between two or more persons; it is elicited by complementary action of several people. Sexual intercourse seems to be the best example of this; each partner possesses part of the information, and the parts, when combined, are complementary in nature, resulting in true interaction of the couple.

At the group level, the information possessed by a specialized team— for example, a bomber crew—is elicited by translating it into action. Each member of the group has a piece of information and proceeds with a piece of action; but this information or action is meaningless unless it is combined into a whole. Group action, therefore, is characterized by the fact that each individual has to cooperate. The success of the group depends upon this cooperation—nobody can do it alone—and the survival of the individual depends in part upon the successful action of the group. The predictability of group action is of a different order of difficulty from the predictability of interpersonal action because as an individual no one is capable of encompassing all the information pertinent for prediction. There is no "group brain."

At the societal level, the connections between action and codification are even less comprehensible. There is no "cultural brain," and the information is scattered over centuries. Predictability is minimal, and nobody is capable of combining in one head all the information that is available. That which large groups do to each other seems to be known more in terms of action than in terms of information; but, nonetheless, the theoretical assumption must be made that information exists which is shared by the members of a society or a cultural group. This knowledge is obviously in part taken over from previous generations who gradually evolved child-raising practices, laws, styles of architecture, techniques of agriculture, and a host of other things which would contribute toward their survival.

In summary, it can be stated that the code systems used by human beings are numerous. They vary from nervous impulses, chemical agents, contraction of muscles, and actions of organisms to social action of aggregates of human beings. Practically any object or action may stand for something else; therefore it is important to discover the instructions which accompany messages, including directions about the code system which is being used.

METACOMMUNICATION

A musician who wishes to play a piece of music which is new to him has to first identify the key and the clef in which the notes are written, for both represent instructions to the player regarding the interpretation of the musical symbols. In direct person-to-person communication without mediation through a musical score the same relationship exists. A person who perceives a message divides it into two parts: one part might be labeled the content of the message; and the other, the instructions. These instructions which refer to the interpretation of the message constitute communications about communication, or "metacommunication."[54]

Both sender and receiver are involved in metacommunication. The sender must bear in mind that it is his task to instruct the receiver, and the receiver in turn has to interpret the instructional messages which accompany the main body of the message. Instructions given by the sender may be explicit or may remain implicit in the situation, and the interpretations made by the receiver may or may not correspond to the intentions of the sender. The sender of a message may give explicit instructions; for example, a person who enters a room and introduces himself as the telephone repair man instructs the other people about his forthcoming actions. Less explicit are the instructions given through the uniforms of policemen, judges, and other officials; when such functionaries speak, they assume that the listener will interpret their words in accordance with the role that they have assumed. In person-to-person communication, a gesture may contain the explanation and the instructions for the interpretation of the words that are being said; or, conversely, words may contain the explanations for a diagram which represents the content. Be that as it may, consciously or unconsciously every sender and every receiver divides the message into two parts—the content, and the instructions.

In many situations, instructions are not given explicitly by the speakers because the assumption is made that the other persons know what they are. These implicit instructions, which people assume need not be expressed because they are shared by all, are termed "values." In any culture, the ways of communication are prescribed by tradition and are taught to the child as he grows up. The signals used to evoke in the listener the appropriate set of assumptions are usually of a nonverbal nature. The intonation of a voice, the way an action sequence is structured, the speed of presentation, and many other subtle patterns may be used as instructions. Furthermore, omissions may serve as a way of giving instructions. If a person does not greet another or does not shake hands when a greeting or handshaking might be expected, the omission may serve as instruction for the interpretation of forthcoming messages. A person who smokes a cigarette lets it be known that he does not smoke a cigar and does not smoke a pipe, and may thereby instruct the visitor not to smoke a cigar. Metacommunicative instructions which are left implicit require that all the participants share the same values if communication is to be successful. The experienced and mature person has a knowledge of all the implications and of all the metacommunicative shadings prevailing in a given culture and subculture.[54] This level of functioning is rarely attainable for the mentally sick patient.

A brief review of the varieties of metacommunication may help the reader to gain a bird's-eye view of the complexity of the problem. Explicit instructions are usually given in written or spoken words—for example, the manuals issued with new pieces of machinery and equipment, or the orders given in a military chain of command. In daily life, in contrast, verbal instructions may not necessarily predominate; roles and the props which identify roles are the most frequently used instructions. Personal identification marks, uniforms, style of dress, hair-do, jewelry, hats, coats, umbrellas, brief cases, shoes, and other belongings of a personal nature and the particular pattern in which they are arranged convey to the perceiver a great many instructions as to how forthcoming messages are to be interpreted. In public life, the uniforms worn by military persons, police officers, and firemen, the gowns worn by professors at commencement exercises, and the robes worn by judges in court remain the most specific reminders of the roles that these persons have assumed. Sometimes it is the situational props rather than the personal equipment which instruct the participants in how to send and how to receive messages. Accordingly, messages in a church will be given and interpreted differently from the same messages spoken on the dance floor, in an office building, or in the sports arena.

Posture, facial expression, and gesture, as well as movement of the body, convey another set of instructions. An erect or submissive posture, the deliberately formal or informal posture, the military bearing, or the stiff-necked attitude convey distinct instructions. Facial expressions and gestures refer primarily to the emotional state of the person, and these, combined with the posture, may transmit to the receiver the pompous, grave, and solemn attitude of a judge or the pugnaciousness of a prize fighter. The hurried movements of the person who is trying to catch a train, the relaxed movements of a person sunning himself on the bench in the park, the threatening movements of an angry person, the signs of greeting and farewell, and the gestures of seduction and insistence all accompany verbal or nonverbal messages in forms of instructions. Sometimes the metacommunicative messages are contained in the structure of a statement which enables the perceiver to identify from the way things are said that the speaker is a salesman or a psychiatrist, a policeman or a delivery boy. The structure of a sentence, the emphasis and the twist given, may thus betray purposely or unconsciously the intentions of the speaker.

The rules inherent in a situation likewise determine the flow of messages and constitute metacommunicative, instructions. As part of the general value system, everybody knows how to behave in a committee meeting or on the football field, in the movies or at a funeral. However, in person-to-person communication the complexity is increased by all those statements which are designed to indicate that a change of rules, of values, and of roles has taken place. For example, the psychiatrist, though being a therapist, assumes various roles as a result of a mutual understanding between him and the patient. Likewise the district attorney, the clergyman, and the policeman assume subsidiary roles within the over-all role. After a committee meeting, for example, some of the men may gather together in an informal way to have a drink; and since the official ceremony is terminated, different roles and rules apply. In person-to-person conversation, people may first talk to each other in the roles of buyer and seller, then converse as man and woman, and finally proceed to their roles as fellow members in an orchestra—all of these changes embracing a time period of only a few seconds. Instructions may also be contained in the way a sequence of messages is presented, the contrasts that are chosen, the omissions that are made, the intensities that are used—in brief, they are contained in the complexities of the pattern itself.

Upon initial contact in a new situation with strange people, the first thing that happens is a mutual exploration of each other's methods of metacommunication. An astute person explores another person in order to find out what sort of codes, rules, and roles the other person embraces so that the forthcoming messages may be correctly transmitted as well as interpreted. Meeting new people means learning new ways of metacommunication, while meeting old friends usually means adhering to a more stabilized form of metacommunication.[54]

FEEDBACK AND CORRECTION

In daily language the word "statement" refers to an expressive action of an individual, or essentially to the fact that something has been transmitted. The term "message" refers to statements which have been interpreted, in which the intention of the sender to achieve a desired result is implicitly acknowledged. Whenever the intention of the sender coincides with the result achieved in the receiver, then the message has been understood. It is well to remember that the receiver can only infer the intentions of the sender, and the sender can only observe the reactions elicited in the receiver. There always remains an element of uncertainty, although, through correction, the uncertainty can be narrowed down practically to the point of elimination.

In the process of transmitting a message, a number of unintentional signals will arise which are likely to blur the message. Communication engineers refer to the signals which are added in the course of transmission but which were not intended by the sender as "noise." These unwanted additions are due to the external circumstances beyond the control of sender or receiver. In human communication, where the channels of transmission are not distinctly separated as in communication engineering, there is an additional source of distortion which depends upon the background against which a message is delivered. The sender, for example, may be totally unaware of other stimuli reaching the receiver which in turn will distort—maximize or minimize—the message which he is about to send. The art of human communication, therefore, consists in presenting a message in such a way that it will stand out and contrast with the other stimuli which the receiver may perceive. If such contrast is achieved, the chances for successful transmission of the message are greatly enhanced. In daily life, this process is frequently referred to as control, since it is concerned with the elimination of unintentional messages on the part of the sender, and with an isolation of the message on the part of the receiver.

Human communication consists of receiving, transmitting, and replying to other people's messages. If a person intends to communicate and his intention is acknowledged by another person, this very acknowledgment produces a sensation of relief in the sender. If, in addition, the sender has the feeling that the message has been correctly understood, the relief becomes more intense and can be likened to a feeling of gratification or pleasure.

Acknowledgment of messages can be either positive, negative, tangential, or absent. "Yes" and "no" are almost equally satisfactory, while tangential acknowledgment or absence of any acknowledgment produces marked frustration. "Yes, I have understood" is gratifying. "No, I have not understood" indicates at least the readiness of the other person to proceed with understanding. In tangential acknowledgment, the intentional message of the sender is not responded to, but another unintentional message is acknowledged. For example, if a child joyously runs to the mother to show her a flower and his mother responds by saying, "Wash your hands—they are dirty!," she responds to an unintentional statement of the child which was expressed in his dirty hands. The intent to communicate, the showing of the flower, and the desire for a response were disavowed. Repeated experiences of this type kill the intent of the child to communicate or to share information. Thus such a child may never learn to match the actual effect of his message with the anticipated results, and the basis for correction of information may be destroyed. If adults do not even respond with tangential acknowledgments but ignore the child, the child will learn to withdraw and seek the management of his frustration by means other than communication. In human communication there exists a series of situations which range from gratifying communication to frustrating communication, which in daily language is labeled "rejection"; they might be arranged as follows in order of increasing frustration: (a) acknowledgment of a message including acknowledgment of the intent and the content; (b) acknowledgment of the intent but not of the content; (c) lack of acknowledgment of both intent and content, but acknowledgment of an incidental statement which was not intended; (d) lack of acknowledgment of intent, content, and other statements.

In a two-person system, feedback and correction of information constitute the most important interpersonal experience. When person A emits a message, person B usually replies by adding, subtracting, compensating, attenuating, or by reinforcing one part of the message or another. The effect produced on B is thus fed back to the first person, and in a continuous process messages travel forth and back until the intent of the sender and the effect achieved in the receiver have been clarified. Either the correspondence of certain information can be established between sender and receiver, or areas of disagreement can be delineated; and if both persons know the areas of disagreement, they have achieved communication. It is well to remember that all the information a person possesses about himself is derived from others. His impression of the impact he has upon others is what makes up the picture of himself; unless a person is in constant communicative exchange with others, his information becomes antiquated, and his chance of survival is lessened.

In a given situation, a person may or may not be able to tolerate correction, depending upon the intensity or the amount of correction. Too much correction at once will overwhelm the sender and will lead to a total refusal of that correction; too small a correction will induce him to overlook the differences. Correction thus has to be properly timed and quantified. The increments have to be such as to correspond to the particular tolerance for change. Correction, or learning, is a problem which has fascinated the psychologists for a long time;[42] while the learning theorists divided their correction into two types—problem-solving on the basis of trial-and-error, and the kind of learning known as conditioning— no such distinction is necessary in communication theory. It is always the perception of an effect achieved, either in others or in oneself, which is subject to correction and feedback. The varieties of feedback have been extensively described by Wiener and the communications engineers.[21, 23, 68]

In summarizing the concepts of feedback and correction, it is important to remember that the process in which correction of information occurs within a system and then is fed back to the control center is characteristic of animals, individual human beings, human society, and some machines. This introduction of corrections based upon the considerations of effects, both in humans and in machines, makes this type of organization superior to those systems which are not characterized by corrective mechanisms. The difference between mental health and illness lies in the appropriate functioning of these feed-back mechanisms.

THE COMMUNICATION MODEL IN OPERATION

The subject matter of communication has been treated by Shannon and Weaver[59] at three levels of complexity: at the technical level they have been concerned with the machinery itself as well as with the problems arising in connection with the accurate transmission of symbols; at the semantic level, they have added to the already existing technical considerations the issue of whether the transmitted symbols really convey the desired meaning; and at the effectiveness level, they inquire into the additional question of impact and effect. The technical problems of communication really are the concern of engineers in the fields of biology, medicine, physiology, electronics, and biochemistry.[3, 68] People in these fields are concerned with the study, the maintenance, and the repair of the communications machinery and network. Semantics, or the attempt to relate signs and symbols to actual events, is the subject matter of philology and philosophy.[28, 41] The effectiveness problem, however, belongs to the psychiatrist who endeavors to study and to report those conditions which impede effective behavior following the receipt of a message.[54] And on a wider scale this is the true concern of any administrator and executive. Let us now consider those operations which are of particular interest to the psychiatrist.

First, a word about the term "communication" which, as it is used in this paper, includes all procedures by which one mind may affect another.[59] Though the spoken word is the principle medium of human communication, all actions of human beings have to be viewed as potential sources of messages. An action becomes a message when it is perceived, either by the self or by other people. In other words, signals in transit become messages when there is a receiver which, at the destination, can evaluate the meaning of these signals. Such a definition includes communication between human beings and animals, as well as between animals. As a matter of fact, all biological organisms, including plants, receive, evaluate, and send messages. In brief, *communication is an organizing principle of nature*.

A communication system is delineated in space by the network in which a given message travels from its origin to its destination. Thus, neither the nature of the message nor the manner of transmission defines the unit of study. It does not matter whether a message is embodied in a pamphlet distributed by a government agency, whether it is transmitted by the human voice, or whether it travels along neural pathways or through the bloodstream. What matters is the fact that information has been transmitted from one point to another, thus defining the segment of the universe which is to be studied.

Communication connects the various parts within one organism and links this organism to other organisms. The use of the term "organism" implies, of course, that a line of demarcation exists which separates one organism from the other. Likewise, it is necessary to assume that an organism can only act as an entity if a line or demarcation exists within the organism itself, separating the center from the periphery. Therefore, each organism can be conceived of as possessing an inner and an outer surface or boundary. At the outer line of demarcation, the signals received are transformed into impulses of a kind that can travel within the organism. Conversely, when impulses leave the organism they are transformed into signals which can reach other organisms. At the inner line of demarcation, signals originating in the organism itself are transformed in such a way that they can be combined with the signals originating outside, so that coordinated action becomes possible. In other words, every biological organism or society of organisms is characterized by the fact that outside and inside events are suitably represented.

But the complexity of such representation and the type of interconnection between the component parts are functions of the magnitude of the communication system in question. Thus a human observer can focus upon communication at various *levels of complexity*, but, inasmuch as the characteristics of his perceptual apparatus remain the same, the individual details will appear in greater or smaller magnification.[54] The greater the number of people who are considered, the less the individual details are perceived. Because of the constant and limited perceptual capacity of the human being, the problem of identity of particles exists. It is obvious that there is so much information available about any one human being that he can be identified. When hundreds or thousands are observed, they begin to look alike and seem to lose their identity. At the personal and interpersonal levels, one deals with identified people and problems; at the societal level, one deals with statistical mass phenomena.

The reader will best understand this conceptual model of communication by remembering that the perceptual capacity of an observer is fixed —that is, the observer either can see one human being in great detail or can perceive a large number of people in little detail. Out of the continuum of communication networks which range from parts of one person to many hundred thousands of people I have arbitrarily selected four types of network—four levels of complexity, as it were—and I have named these personal, interpersonal, group, and societal.

At the personal level, the focus of the observer is limited to his person, and the various functions of communication are found within the self. At the interpersonal level, the perceptual field is occupied by the observer and another person. At the group level, he is one of many people. And at the cultural level he is an infinitesimal part of one of many groups. With increasing complexity, the importance of the individual diminishes, and at the higher levels one person becomes only a small element in the function of communication. The focus of the human observer is not fixed; rather it has to be viewed as a fluctuating or oscillating phenomenon in which he takes quick glances at various levels and at various functions from various positions. Communication is an extremely dynamic phenomenon with a rapid rate of change in both that which is observed and the position from which the observation is made.

The psychiatrist usually operates either at the interpersonal or at the group level. When dealing with an individual patient, he explores the examinee's communication system at the interpersonal level; here, with an active exchange back and forth, he can make direct observation. However, if the psychiatrist makes statements about what goes on inside of the other person, in so doing he changes his position as an observer; he now operates neither at the interpersonal level nor at the group level, but he assumes that he is a self-observer inside the patient. Sometimes the psychiatrist operates as a group expert. He then makes observations within a group and makes inferences about how a patient would behave if he were alone, in a twosome situation, or acting as a member of society at large. It is well to remember that only communication at the interpersonal or group level can be observed and experienced directly. All statements made and found in the literature about behavior at the societal level and behavior at the personal level (the patient alone with himself) are statements which have been inferred from direct observation.

All biological organisms and social organizations are characterized by the ability to communicate. Every communication system must have at least two units, each equipped with the ability to perceive, evaluate, and transmit messages. A system composed of two units can be relatively self-contained and independent of other units. A biological organism is usually a single unit and dependent for communication upon other units. Within a social system, circumstances frequently force an organism to specialize in one or another function which then is developed to perfection. As long as the system exists the individual will function properly; but if the communication system breaks down, such highly specialized individuals are ill-adapted to survive. As a matter of fact, the more an organism masters all functions of communication, the better it will be able to survive. Mature people are characterized by a harmonious integration of the three functions of communication while retaining their ability to switch their specialization within the larger organization.

In describing the *functions of communication*, a simplified version of a two-person communication system may be used as an example. Starting with the description of the processes of exteroception of person A, three sets of stimuli can be distinguished: the first set derives from objects and events other than persons; the second set derives from actions of any other person; and the third set derives from the actions of A which are seen or heard by him through his own exteroceptors. These three sets of stimuli reach A's sense organs; there, the acoustic, visual, olfactory, gustatory, tactile, thermal, pain, and vibratory stimuli are transformed into nervous and perhaps chemical impulses which then travel within the organism along nervous and humoral pathways. After the signals have been transformed within the receiver, they are then transmitted to the communication center where they are joined by impulses which arise in the organism itself; proprioceptive signals arise in the sensory end organs and the muscles, serving to inform the communication center about the state of the organism. Combined exteroceptive and proprioceptive input then impinges upon the memory which consists of traces of past events which have left their imprints in the organism—probably in the form of nervous impulses which circulate within the communication center itself.

The processes of perception, therefore, have three roots—exteroception, proprioception, and recollection of past events.[6,54] These combined impulses are then subjected to a complicated series of operations within the communication center which results in the evaluation of what has been perceived. Person A then can be said to possess information about the social situation, about himself, and about others. At the same time that these events take place in A, similar processes may occur in person B. Whether A and B are able to successfully communicate with each other will depend upon each one's ability to transmit messages.

Efferent impulses, being the result of complicated operations with the information on hand, are intended to transmit messages to the outside world (exterotransmission) and to other stations of the body (propriotransmission) so that coordinated action becomes possible. Once the impulses have reached the transmitter, they are transformed into muscular contractions and glandular activities; at that moment, information is transformed into action. This action has communicative aspects for the recipients as well as for the person who emits the original statement.

A statement emitted by A can be picked up by B; and after it has passed through the organism of B, the transmitter of B will broadcast the response to A. A statement becomes a message when a receiver interprets it. Persons A and B must be viewed as one system in which messages circulate and oscillate forth and back innumerable times. Inasmuch as A knows the content of his original statement, B's reply gives him a chance to evaluate whether B has interpreted the message the way he originally intended. If that is the case, the gradual interchange of information and successive correction leads to the establishment of correspondence of information between A and B, which state might be called "understanding."

An interesting point arises when one attempts to draw a line between the communication machinery and the surroundings. Such a boundary does not coincide with the surface of the body. As a matter of fact, people have fluctuating views about where such a boundary is located. The first view which a person may have of himself is from the vantage point of an outside observer. Here, he perceives himself as part of a social situation and views himself as being part of the environment. In a second perspective, from an internal point of observation, the private "self" is located away from the surface of the body and is endowed with a sentiment of privacy, the content of which is rarely revealed in public. In communication theory, these two views can be represented by a line separating the transmitter and receiver of a person from the communication center. The human body, which shelters the communication instruments, is visible to the outside world as well as to the self, but the communication center is not. That such a division has not merely a theoretical importance is revealed in the course of psychotherapy. After all, one of the tasks of therapy is to reduce the importance of this boundary in an attempt to equate the individual's private view of himself with that of outside observers.

When several people organize their activities around a common task or purpose, a group is born. The observer who wishes to study the *communication system of a group* ought to participate in its activities, because little can he learn by mere observation. However, the participation method suitable for the interpersonal level—that is, the introjection of information into the system with the intent of allowing it to circulate until it returns to the sender who then registers the distortions and hence obtains a picture of the other person—rarely is satisfactory at the group level. This is because the group network may be so ramified and extended that the information introjected by the observer disappears from sight and never returns to him. What, then, are the methods which a scientist can use at this level? In addition to ordinary observation, he can trace the pathways along which messages travel. By and large, the average observer is so busy watching the content of messages that he neglects to focus upon the pathways; the student of group behavior, therefore, does well to emphasize these technical characteristics more than the content. Such a procedure is permissible inasmuch as the content of messages is subordinated to the task of the group, and the task is likely to be defined and to remain stable for longer periods of time.

Whenever a group convenes, usually one or more persons begin by making statements; these may be verbal or gestural, or they may be expressed in some activity. The other members of the group tend to reply to initial statements or to make additional statements. By following the events forth and back, the scientist learns which statements are replied to and interpreted, how they are interpreted, and how such interpretation furthers or impedes the task of the group. By tracing the flow of messages, he is then able to discover the assumptions which the group makes and the discrepancies which exist in the assumptions made by the various members.

In *the assessment of a communication system*, the scientific observer may raise the following questions:

(1) *What are the limitations and the context of communication as seen by the consensus of observers?* If properly answered, this question will yield information about the physical and social reality in which the exchange of messages takes place; and information on the label of the social situation, the levels and the functions of communication called for, the rules to be observed, the roles to be assumed, the channels to be used, and the meta-communicative instructions to be given.

(2) *Who is saying it?* Information about the source of the message can be gained by an analysis of the physical condition of the sender, his idiosyncratic view of his social reality, the levels and functions of communication he uses, the information he possesses, and the language, coding devices, and transmission channels he employs.

(3) *To whom is it said?* The analysis of the destination of the message —the receiver or audience analysis—starts with an inquiry into the physical condition of the receiver and his views about the social reality which he perceives. It is followed by an analysis of the levels and functions of communication, of the information available at the destination before receipt of the message, and of the language, the decoding devices, and the channels used at the destination for perceiving, evaluating, and responding to the message.

(4) *What is said?* Content can be operationally defined as the comparison of the intent of the sender with the interpretation of the receiver; the discrepancies observed form the basis for the identification of the events to which the message referred.

(5) *What media of communication are used?* This question is aimed at an analysis of the channels and symbolization systems used. Participants and observers study separately the perception and transmission channels employed, compare the input with the output, study the stations of transformation of information, the loss of information incurred in such a transformation, the symbolization systems used, and the way in which the various sensory modalities are combined.

(6) *How is it being said?* An answer to this question yields information about the ways of metacommunication. Analysis of the roles assumed, the rules used, the specific instructions given, the interpretations made, as well as an analysis of the quantitative aspects of communication, furnishes information about the metacommunicative cues used.

(7) *What is the result of the exchange of messages?* This question is geared to analyze the correction of the information at the source and at the destination of the message, and the action which was undertaken at the source as well as at the destination subsequent to the exchange of information. Finally, one should be able to analyze the effects which action has had upon the existing communication system, its influence upon the

steady state, and the possible reversible or irreversible changes which have been introduced.

Communication is a young science, and the experimental designs and observational methods used to implement the assessment of communication in an attempt to answer the above questions are still limited in number. So far, only a few topics have been elaborated: redundancy in language;[59] the distinctive features of speech;[30] other characteristics of language;[39] social perception;[6] the timing characteristics of interaction[13] and the verbal assessment of interaction;[55] the effects of social communication in a group,[12, 20] and particularly in staff interaction;[61, 64] decision-making;[17] psychiatric interviewing.[50, 51, 56] Help in the understanding of communication in the animal world has come from biologists such as von Frisch, Lorenz, and Tinbergen.[24, 36, 65]

SUMMARY

A recapitulation of the highlights of the theory of human communication embraces the following points:

Communication is an organizing principle of nature inasmuch as all biological and social organizations are characterized by the need and the ability to communicate. The basic functions of communication are reception, evaluation, transmission, and conduction. These functions may be located in one and the same organism or may be divided among many organisms. The unit of scientific inquiry is the social situation which is established as soon as at least two, if not more, organisms or organizations have engaged in communication.

The communication apparatus of man has to be viewed as a functional entity and not as a conglomeration of organs. It is composed of: sense organs, the receiver; effector organs, the sender; and the communication center—that is, the place of origin, destination, and retention of messages. The remaining parts of the body, which are channels of conduction, are devoted to the sheltering and the upkeep of the communication machinery.

The functions of communication are to maintain contact with other biological beings and to avoid isolation—a tendency which is basic and inborn—to receive and transmit messages and to retain information, to reconstruct the past and to anticipate future events, to perform operations with the existing information for the purpose of deriving new aspects which were not directly perceived, to initiate and modify physiological processes within the body, and to influence and direct other people and external events.

Interpersonal communication is characterized by the presence of expressive acts on the part of one or more persons, the conscious or unconscious perception of such expressive actions by other persons, and the return observation that such expressive actions have been perceived by others. The awareness of having been perceived is the event which signals the establishment of an interpersonal network. Intrapersonal communication, then, becomes a special case of interpersonal communication. An imaginary entity made up of condensed traces of past experiences represents within one person the missing outside person.

In group communication, each person fulfills, temporarily or permanently, a specialized function within the network of the group. Correction of information still is possible; but because of the extent of the network, correction is frequently delayed. Messages have to converge on or emerge from the communication center, and this circumstance has some peculiar implications. Incoming messages must be abstracted and condensed because of the limited capacity of the perception-evaluation machinery; outgoing messages are addressed to a great many people and therefore cannot apply to any one person in particular too well. Group communication, therefore, is more limited than interpersonal communication.

Communication at the societal level is characterized by mass communication through media such as the radio, television, movies, or the press. When exposed to such mass communications, an individual is likely to feel, on the one hand, that he is a participant in a larger superpersonal system and, on the other hand, that he is unable to delineate the system. This contradiction is brought about by the fact that in mass communications the originators and the recipients of messages are so numerous that they usually remain anonymous. Therefore, under such conditions the individual is able neither to observe the effect of his own messages upon others nor to communicate his personal reactions to a message originating from committees, organizations, or institutions. Cause and effect become blurred; correction and self-correction become delayed in time and removed in space, and if correction finally occurs it is often no longer relevant.

The limitations of man's communications are determined by the capacity of his intraorganismic network, the selectivity of his receivers, and the skill of his effector organs. The number of incoming and outgoing signals as well as the signals that can be transmitted within the organism are limited. Beyond a certain maximum, an increase in number of messages in transit leads to a jamming of the network, and so to a decrease in the number of messages which reach their appropriate destinations. This state is commonly referred to as anxiety. The sharing of anxiety with nonanxious or nonthreatening individuals by means of communication becomes an efficient device for tolerating the impact of interference.

Communication facilitates specialization, differentiation, and maturation of the individual. In the process of maturation, reliance upon protective and corrective actions of others is gradually replaced by interdependence with peers in terms of communication. Instead of looking to elders for guidance, the adult person seeks information from contemporaries on how best to solve a problem. Exchange of information is substituted for bodily protection, and action of self replaces actions of others. Successful communication with self and with others implies correction of stored-up information. In such an ongoing process, up-to-date information about self, the world, and the relationship of self to the world is likely to increase the individual's chances of mastery. Successful communication at all levels, characterized by a sensation of pleasure in the individual, is the backbone of mental health.

REFERENCES

1. ACKERMAN, N. W. 1951. 'Social role' and total personality. *Am. J. Orthopsychiat.*, **21**, 1-7.
2. ALEXANDER, F. 1935. The logic of emotions and its dynamic background. *Int. J. Psycho-Analysis*, **16**, 399-413.
3. ASHBY, W. R. 1952. *Design for a brain.* Wiley, New York.
4. BERTALANFFY, L. VON. 1950. The theory of open systems in physics and biology. *Science*, **3**, 23-29.
5. BERTALANFFY, L. VON. 1952. *Problems of life: An evaluation of modern biological thought.* Wiley, New York.
6. BLAKE, R. R., and RAMSEY, G. V. (eds.). 1951. *Perception: An approach to personality.* Ronald Press, New York.
7. BOHR, N. 1948. On the notions of causality and complementarity. *Dialectica*, **2**, 312-319.
8. BORN, M. 1948. *Natural philosophy of cause and chance.* Oxford Univ. Press, London.
9. BRUNSWIK, E. 1951. *Systematic and representative design of psychological experiments.* Univ. of California Press, Berkeley and Los Angeles.
10. BRUNSWICK, E. 1952. The conceptual framework of psychology. *International Encyclopedia Unified Science*, Vol. 1, No. 10. Univ. of Chicago Press, Chicago.
11. CANTRIL, H., AMES, A., HASTORF, A. H., and ITTELSON, W. H. 1949. Psychology and scientific research: I. The nature of scientific inquiry; II. Scientific inquiry and scientific method; III. The transactional view in psychological research. *Science*, **110**, 461-464, 491-497, 517-522.
12. CARTWRIGHT, D., and ZANDER, A. (eds.). 1953. *Group dynamics: Research and theory.* Row, Peterson, Evanston, Ill.
13. CHAPPLE, E. D. 1940. Measuring human relations: An introduction to the study of the interaction of individuals. *Genet. Psychol. Monogr.*, **22**, 3-147.
14. COHEN, M. R. 1933. *Law and the social order.* Harcourt, Brace, New York.
15. COLLINGWOOD, R. G. 1945. *The idea of nature.* Clarendon Press, Oxford.
16. CONANT, J. B. 1951. *Science and common sense.* Yale Univ. Press, New Haven.
17. DEUTSCH, K. W. 1952. Communication theory and social science. *Am. J. Orthopsychiat.*, **22**, 469-483.
18. DEWEY, J., and BENTLEY, A. F. 1949. *Knowing and the known.* Beacon Press, Boston.
19. ERIKSON, E. H. 1950. *Childhood and society.* Norton, New York.
20. FESTINGER, L., *et al.* 1952. *Theory and experiment in social communication.* Ann Arbor Research Center for Group Dynamics, Inst. for Soc. Research, Univ. of Michigan.

21. FOERSTER, H. VON. (ed.). 1950, 1951, 1952. *Cybernetics: Circular, causal and feedback mechanisms in biological and social systems.* (Transactions 6th, 7th and 8th Conferences.) Josiah Macy, Jr. Foundation, New York.
22. FRANK, L. K. 1951. *Nature and human nature.* Rutgers Univ. Press, New Brunswick, N.J.
23. FRANK, L. K., HUTCHINSON, G. E., LIVINGSTON, W. K., McCULLOCH, W. S., and WIENER, N. 1948. Teleological mechanisms. *Ann. N.Y. Acad. Sci.,* 50, 187-278.
24. FRISCH, K. VON. 1950. *Bees, their vision, chemical senses, and language.* Cornell Univ. Press, Ithaca.
25. FROMM, E. 1947. *Man for himself.* Rinehart, New York.
26. GRINKER, R. R. 1953. *Psychosomatic research.* Norton, New York.
27. HARTLEY, E. L., and HARTLEY, R. E. 1952. *Fundamentals of social psychology.* Knopf, New York.
28. HAYAKAWA, S. I. 1949. *Language in thought and action.* Harcourt, Brace, New York.
29. HEISENBERG, W. 1930. (ECKART, C., and HOYT, F. C., trans.) *The physical principles of the quantum theory.* Univ. of Chicago Press, Chicago.
30. JAKOBSON, R., FANT, C. G. M., and HALLE, M. 1952. *Preliminaries to speech analysis.* (Technical Report No. 13.) Acoustic Laboratory, Mass. Inst. Tech., Cambridge, Mass.
31. JOHNSON, W. 1946. *People in quandaries.* Harper, New York.
32. KORZYBSKI, A. 1948. *Science and sanity.* International Non-Aristotelian Library Pub. Co., Lakeville, Conn.
33. LEWIN, K. 1935. *A dynamic theory of personality.* McGraw-Hill, New York.
34. LEWIN, K. 1951. *Field theory in social sciences.* Harper, New York.
35. LINTON, R. 1945. *The cultural background of personality.* Appleton-Century, New York.
36. LORENZ, K. 1952. *King Solomon's ring.* Crowell, New York.
37. MACHIAVELLI, N. 1940. *The Prince* and *The discourses.* Modern Library, New York.
38. MADARIAGA, S. DE. 1928. *Englishmen, Frenchmen, Spaniards.* Oxford Univ. Press, London.
39. MILLER, G. A. 1951. *Language and communication.* McGraw-Hill, New York.
40. MORENO, J. L. 1946. *Psychodrama,* Vol. 1. Beacon House, New York.
41. MORRIS, C. W. 1946. *Signs, language, and behavior.* Prentice-Hall, New York.
42. MOWRER, O. H. 1950. *Learning theory and personality dynamics.* Ronald Press, New York.
43. MULLAHY, P. (ed.). 1952. *The contributions of Harry Stack Sullivan: A symposium on interpersonal theory in psychiatry and social science.* Hermitage House, New York.
44. NEUMANN, J. VON, and MORGENSTERN, O. 1944. *Theory of games and economic behavior.* Princeton Univ. Press, Princeton, N.J.
45. PARSONS, T. 1949. *Essays in sociological theory, pure and applied.* Free Press, Glencoe, Ill.
46. PARSONS, T. 1951. *The social system.* Free Press, Glencoe, Ill.
47. PARSONS, T., and SHILS, E. A. (eds.). 1951. *Toward a general theory of action.* Harvard Univ. Press, Cambridge, Mass.
48. RUESCH, J. 1949. Experiments in psychotherapy: II. Individual social techniques. *J. soc. Psychol.,* 29, 3-28.
49. RUESCH, J. 1951. Part and whole. *Dialectica,* 5, 99-125.
50. RUESCH, J. 1952. The therapeutic process from the point of view of communication theory. *Am. J. Orthopsychiat.,* 22, 690-700.
51. RUESCH, J. 1953. *The interpersonal communication of anxiety.* Paper presented

at the Symposium on Stress, Army Medical Service Graduate School, Walter Reed Army Medical Center, March.

52. RUESCH, J. 1953. Social techniques, social status, and social change in illness. In KLUCKHOHN, C., MURRAY, H. A., and SCHNEIDER, D. M. (eds.) *Personality in nature, society, and culture*, 2nd ed. Knopf, New York.

53. RUESCH, J., and BATESON, G. 1949. Structure and process in social relations. *Psychiatry*, **12**, 105-124.

54. RUESCH, J., and BATESON, G. 1951. *Communication: The social matrix of psychiatry*. Norton, New York.

55. RUESCH, J., BLOCK, J., and BENNETT, L. 1953. The assessment of communication: I. A method for the analysis of social interaction. *J. Psychol.*, **35**, 59-80.

56. RUESCH, J., and PRESTWOOD, A. R. 1949. Anxiety: Its initiation, communication, and interpersonal management. *Archs Neurol. Psychiat.*, **62**, 527-550.

57. RUESCH, J., and PRESTWOOD, A. R. 1950. Interaction processes and personal codification. *J. Personality*, **18**, 391-430.

58. RUSSELL, B. 1948. *Human knowledge, its scope and limits*. Simon & Schuster, New York.

59. SHANNON, C. E., and WEAVER, W. 1949. *The mathematical theory of communication*. Univ. of Illinois Press, Urbana.

60. SMITH, B. L., LASSWELL, H. D., and CASEY, R. D. 1946. *Propaganda, communication, and public opinion*. Princeton Univ. Press, Princeton, N.J.

61. STANTON, A. H., and SCHWARTZ, M. S. 1949. The management of a type of institutional participation in mental illness. *Psychiatry*, **12**, 13-26.

62. STEVENS, S. S. 1939. Psychology and the science of science. *Psychol. Bull.*, **36**, 221-263.

63. SULLIVAN, H. S. 1947. *Conceptions of modern psychiatry*. William Alanson White Psychiatric Foundation, Inc., Washington, D.C.

64. SZUREK, S. A. 1947. Dynamics of staff interaction in hospital psychiatric treatment of children. *Am. J. Orthopsychiat.*, **17**, 652-664.

65. TINBERGEN, N. 1951. *Study of instinct*. Oxford Univ. Press, New York.

66. TOLMAN, E. C. 1942. *Drives toward war*. Appleton-Century, New York.

67. WARNER, W. L., MEEKER, M., and EELLS, K. 1949. *Social class in America*. Science Research Assoc., Chicago.

68. WIENER, N. 1948. *Cybernetics, or control and communication in the animal and the machine*. Wiley, New York.

69. WOODGER, J. H. 1952. *Biology and language: An introduction to the methodology of the biological sciences, including medicine*. Cambridge Univ. Press, London.

IX

EXPERIENCES WITH MARITAL TENSIONS
SEEN IN THE PSYCHOLOGICAL CLINIC

HENRY V. DICKS

The marital relationship has been the subject of close study by many disciplines. In this paper a clinician puts forward tentative formulations to explain pathological marital relationships.

This paper outlines some recent work of a diagnostic and exploratory character done as part of the clinical services in the Adult Department of the Tavistock Clinic with a series of married couples whose main reasons for seeking help were various forms of marital disharmony or maladjustment. It is in the nature of a preliminary communication presenting the scope, the sample, the methods of study and some tentative generalizations on the dynamics of the interpersonal relations observed.

The motives which prompted Dr Mary C. Luff and the writer to undertake the pilot study herein described were both those of clinical and of theoretical interest.

Considering that therapeutic intervention in marriage trouble is now an established part of many medical and social services of this country, it may seem at first sight surprising how little systematic clinical or scientific attention the subject has received as compared with, say, child guidance, educational psychology, delinquency, industrial relations and other fields of applied psychology dealing with the problems of personality and interpersonal relations. It is permissible to assert that the practice of marital counselling, conciliation, etc., has remained, technically, on a level of *ad hoc* empiricism, and is lacking a clearly formulated

Reprinted from THE BRITISH JOURNAL OF MEDICAL PSYCHOLOGY, Vol. 26, Parts 3 & 4, 1953, pp. 181-196.

conceptual basis related to accepted theory.* In the face of mounting demands for 'expert' help with the more difficult type of cases referred to us by family doctors, social case work agencies and the Probation service, we soon realized that we had no firm basis for appraising the diagnosis, prognosis or specific methods of technical psychotherapeutic help *for the marriage as the sick entity*. The present paper is a first attempt to communicate some of our experience in trying to master the practical tasks of assessment of the forces involved in the marital tension, to render help, and to move towards describing the phenomena in terms of the interaction process.

The married pair (with or without children) constitutes the ultimate unit of social structure through whom the continuity and the changes in the culture are transmitted. It is also the final social unit on which the waves of all social disturbance break (see Dicks, 1947). The quality of this relationship in which the vast majority of human beings at one time participate largely determines the formation of personality for the next generation, and thus to no small extent influences the psychological climate of the future in all other social fields. Some understanding, therefore, of the causes of marital stress which has reached the 'clinical' level of intensity is likely to be a basis for rewarding mental hygiene action in perhaps preventing troubles in the other areas in which the married pair participate as parents, workers, and so forth.

In the wider perspective, with which this paper cannot hope to deal, the marital relationship offers a uniquely valuable field for the study of 'personality in action'. It is that human situation in which the personality structure is most fully challenged, and object relations can be seen, as it were, most nakedly displayed. Not even the trials of war show up the adequacy or insufficiency of maturity and of capacity for sustaining meaningful and satisfying human relations so clearly as marriage and its stresses. People will fail in marriage when they are apparently well adapted in all other social roles. Study of marriage breakdown is thus a potentially rich mine of insights into personality; into the roots of love and hate in society; into the very matrix of social behaviour.

Much has been published on the sociology of marriage, dealing with demography, economic and social status and background, kinship data and many other interesting observations. The present study has gathered such data and recognizes their relevance. But instead of making these the focus of the observations, it has tried to concentrate attention on the psychological forces of the actual relationship between the two persons who have been influenced by all these antecedents and present field pressures from inside and outside their personalities. It is hoped that in

---

* These remarks are not to be interpreted as a disparagement of the sincere and often successful work of marriage counselling agencies. They are rather a criticism of the lack of research by our own professions.

this way depth may be added to the more extensive kind of social survey as exemplified by the recent work of Slater & Woodhead (1951).

THE SAMPLE

The observations in this paper are based on work with seventy couples, of whom three were living as man and wife without formal marriage ties and two were engaged, while the rest were legally married.

Excluded—perhaps without good reason—are those in whom one or other partner was found on first contact to be suffering from gross psychotic or psychoneurotic disorder. In other respects the sample is unselected by us except that some overtly felt marital stress formed the reason for seeking help at the Clinic. Such stress, by our definition, included symptoms of sexual impotence or frigidity in the marital situation.

Many of the couples decided from the first to seek advice jointly. In others, especially the impotent ones, one presented as the afflicted partner, in which case we ourselves drew the other spouse into the picture, with varying degrees of willingness and co-operation on their part.

The sources of referral were the parties themselves, or their family doctors, other psychiatric clinics, and social case work agencies (including one or two from the Probation service). The common factor was that the problem was felt to be beyond the scope of the referring agents. Thus it will be seen that the sample, though unselected at the Clinic, is a rather special one. It consisted almost wholly of couples who either still wished for a continuation of their marriage with better feelings towards one another, or who at least wanted to clarify their own motives and consciences prior to ending their marriage as decently as possible. They were also 'difficult' in that the simpler approaches had been tried without benefit.

The sample, further, was biased towards the middle-class *intelligentsia*, and contained perhaps a larger proportion of Jewish couples than the norm for the population of the United Kingdom. The lowest social strata of our community were not represented. The length of marriage ranged from one to two years to people with grown-up families, with an average of six to eight years.

While we had excluded from our series in this study those who had prima facie psychiatric disorders, we soon discovered that on closer clinical scrutiny a sizeable proportion of the people in our series suffered from more or less serious, though hitherto unrecognized, psychiatric conditions usually falling under the category of character disorders. Such cases were sent on for treatment in the ordinary way if they so wished and if it was felt that this would be helpful to them as individuals after the stage of diagnostic investigation of the couple.

This paper is concerned, therefore, with observations on a group of married couples in whom varying degrees of behaviour disorder were manifested mainly in relation to their present partners, and who outside the marital relationship had been reasonably or highly successfully functioning personalities. Evidently there was something to be discovered about behaviour towards the partner in the marital role which had passed muster outside, though the trends could sometimes be inferred from data in the pre-marital history (including that of previous marriages), or in the behaviour data outside the marriage.

METHODS OF STUDY

Our fundamental theoretical assumption is that a marital relationship (like any other) is a resultant of the interaction of forces inherent in two personalities with a long history, fashioned out of participation in past object relationships, needs and pressures, from the cradle onwards, in the complex fields of their individual and social past. These histories, together with a clinical profile of the present individual personality, provide the essential clues to the present structuring of their need systems, their values and their role-expectations. Thus, our first step is individual interviewing at sufficient depth to enable us to assess each individual's personality, with special emphasis on attitudes to married life and co-operation to children and parenthood, and thus on the level of object relations of which they are capable. Dr Luff has usually interviewed the wife, and the writer the husband. We think it wise to have for each party one doctor who, so to speak, knows their side of the case well. These individual interviews have frequently, where appropriate and possible, been supplemented by both cognitive and projection tests, usually the Hartford Shipley Scale and a Rorschach and/or Thematic Apperception Test (Phillipson modification).*

The next methodological step, perhaps of special interest for this study, has been to hold joint sessions of the two doctors with the two spouses. Such sessions usually last around two hours, and are sometimes repeated on one or, more rarely, several occasions. Our attitude in these interviews is that of relatively passive observers, the situation being allowed to develop spontaneously, but with interpretations and clarifying remarks being offered as and when that seems wise. The setting of the joint session has thus been exploratory and diagnostic, but also motivated on both sides by the therapeutic aim of making the emerging material available for the parties to understand and work through. We have endeavoured to gain and communicate insights about what each partner's difficult behaviour is intended to convey or do to the other, and out of what past or present experiences and impulsions that behaviour was fashioned. As a therapeutic technique we have attempted to replace the time-honoured method of advice and exhortation by one of clarification; as it were,

---

* For these valuable supplementary data we have been indebted first to Mr Herbert Phillipson and Mr Gerald Staunton, but now more especially to Mr John Boreham.

saying to the parties, 'You see now that you are behaving towards your partner in such-and-such ways because of such-and-such needs in yourself' in the presence of the spouse. Any demands by the parties to be told what to do or to place the burden of advice or decision on our shoulders have been interpreted and referred back to the clients. Often such an interpretation of dependence has been the starting-point of insight.

The phenomena observed are naturally very complex and rich in content, the full recording of which is not as yet adequate, and which can only be sketched in very vague outline for the reader. It may be said that the typical situation develops somewhat as follows: one or other of the spouses (often the wife 'by courtesy') states their complaints about their husband or wife, which may be a rehash of, or at times significantly different from, their original statements at individual interview. There may follow the exposition of the counter-statement by the second spouse. As a rule these are sedate speeches with good control of feelings, but often one may at this stage begin to see the tensions rising, as by fidgeting, blushing, interruptions and rebuttals, with glances at the doctors conveying such meanings as 'You see what I am up against', contempt, real distress or amused incredulity.

There may now follow a phase of silence or direct appeal to us to give advice, dealt with as already stated. Points of such behaviour, or of the attitudes revealed are now commented on by us; as for example: 'We notice that you, Mrs X., feel your silences, which you fall into, to be a sort of hopeless despair at not making your husband understand; he, on the other hand, as you have heard, feels they are a way of punishing him', etc. Or, in another development of the situation: 'We have heard you both interpreting your reactions to all these trivial incidents, as you call them, in two quite different ways. Let us try and see why you feel it to be so important to score off each other in this way', etc. These attempts to focus the discussion on somewhat deeper levels might be followed by resistances, often in the form of each spouse bringing more material and detail to support their own point of view.

Somewhere at this point the mutual heaping of charge upon charge often results in a switch from addressing the doctors to direct conversation between the spouses. This is perhaps the most important part for the observers and yields the richest insights for subsequent clarifying and interpretative comments which can on strength of less inhibited behaviour be made about what is happening between the parties 'here and now'. With the individual case histories in mind one can frequently interpret fairly quickly and obtain a relief of tension and a consent to the interpretation at feeling level from one or both parties. While we often interpret to one party while the other listens, and then shift our comments on to the second party, it is probably better to reserve such interventions by the psychiatrists until a piece of 'interaction' is clear and can be put to them as such. For example: 'Listening to you, it sounds as if you are both terribly afraid of letting your love feelings come out towards each other. You, Mr X., from what you have told us (facts and phantasies (a), (b), (c)) are clearly looking upon taking the initiative in saying nice things to your wife as a kind of weak, childish yielding for which you have felt you would be laughed at and which is out of keeping with the whole way you were brought up to regard a man's role; therefore it seems to you that in showing this weakness you are delivering yourself up to this woman's power, etc. Instead you carp at her to try and make her think you are very strong. You, Mrs X., not realizing what has held your husband back, interpret his behaviour as in some way disapproving of you, and so you have despaired of getting the loving advance out of him. He makes you feel angry and depressed, and you punish him by going cold on him, etc. He seems more like a threatening kind of authority than the nice man you wanted to make love to you. Yet you can both see now how you have aroused in each other these old fears and hates of being rejected which you had experienced (points of history (d), (e), (f)). So you now fence for positions to show one another that you don't need the other, etc.'

This type of interpretation may be as simple as the above or more complex, bringing in other aspects such as guilt and aggression as the case seems to demand. It is often a case of more piecemeal interpretations in which the insights of the observers valuably supplement each other, both in language chosen and in adding or in clarifying meanings. In a number of cases we do not reach this level at all. By a kind of unspoken consensus which develops among fellow-workers it emerges that the attitudes of the parties would make such intervention useless as a mere piece of intellectual communication. A kind of 'leave well alone' sense warns us to refrain.

The reaction of the parties to interpretation, their own capacity for insight, their emotional genuineness and warmth show up very clearly in these situations. It is often after an interpretation of the above-cited type that material relating to intimate sexual life becomes available and hitherto unrevealed facts and memories emerge, often as spontaneous bits of personal history which the other spouse may greet with a surprised 'Why have you never told me?'—in sympathy or in anger. These are again used in amplification of the interpretative comments.

Enough has perhaps been said to show the technique employed and the nature of the material which is observed and dealt with.

'Action paragraphs' usually emerge towards the end of a joint session. If the influence of social factors, e.g. housing problems, home help, etc., is large enough to warrant our intervention, arrangements are made for referral to sources of likely aid. A spouse who had hitherto regarded himself or herself as the 'normal' victim of the other's troublesome behaviour may ask for treatment. Both parties may wish to come again, or else 'wait and see' the working out of the new viewpoints which the session has brought. Lastly, a fair number will go away with little if any lightening of their problems. From these people one usually gets the most profuse expressions of gratitude for having failed to disturb the status quo.

Second and subsequent joint sessions may or may not proceed in much the same way, with perhaps greater frankness. We have not so far had experience of carrying joint sessions with a given couple on over a prolonged series of interviews. Rather have we tended to see the spouses again separately in the belief that such things as face-saving, aggressive phantasies or intimate past sexual history which might have to be dealt with as part of the aftermath of joint sessions, would be worked through more easily in individual interviews. Or, as already stated, one or both partners are referred to the regular treatment services of the Clinic, not necessarily by one of us. The aim of such therapy would then be the usual one in analytic types of psychotherapy, i.e. of endeavouring to change the individual's deep attitudes towards the object by reality testing in the treatment situation.

SOME GENERALIZATIONS FROM THE FINDINGS

In an endeavour to abstract general propositions from the rich material of this study, use has been made of the individual case records (including test findings), and especially of the observations on each partner and their relation to one another in the joint interview. At the simplest level, we have compared a number of our recorded social variables with variables in the respective spouses, throughout the series, without very interesting results. The outstanding recurrent finding along these lines is one already noted by most writers on the subject: the frequency of unhappy or disrupted family backgrounds in the past histories of these couples. At another level we have made judgements about the general adaptation and maturity of these people's object-relations as projected upon the canvas of their married life as well as outside it. These would include capacity for libidinal gratification; attitudes of activity or passivity in social and sex roles; levels and intensity of aggressivity and its fate in terms of defence mechanisms, acting out and so forth.

We have noted something also on the lines of areas of co-operation and decision-making by the couple in the hope of arriving at a 'rating' of the closeness of the bonds uniting the spouses within their marital 'field'.

These levels of analysis, taken by themselves however, seemed to suffer from the disadvantage that they either picked out relatively 'static' factors, or that they remained to some extent external to the essential interaction process. The special task the project set itself was to follow the process of dovetailing of those partial aspects into a meaningful whole, i.e. the satisfactions or dissatisfactions which role distribution, dominance or submission and the like were giving to the partners in their mutual relationship. It seemed as if it mattered little, for example, who administered the money or did the washing up, as compared to the interpretation which each partner put upon these social functions or their omission under the pressure of their conscious or unconscious feelings about the other. Any such detail in role distribution could become a peg on which to hang their feelings once these had become disturbed.

In one sense, all the past and present history and stress antecedent or peripheral to the marital relationship has converged to determine these feelings and even the choice of the spouse upon whom they become focused. We cannot think of marriage as a field immune from the 'outside world'. In another sense, it is an easy temptation to describe the marital relationship as if it were the product of nothing but a string of such social variables or vectors impelling each partner and impinging on the other with his bundle of vectors. This would be to forget that the marital relation is a unit *sui generis* whose social-cultural task is the forging of an integrate, different from the sum of its parts, by the means of a satisfying interaction. The general propositions which follow will be concerned with the hindrances to the making of this integrate, so that perhaps we may later be able to give more precision and clarity to the description and prediction of the ingredients of marital success.

(1) *The importance of role expectations*

Perhaps the most unequivocal and generally valid proposition that can be derived from our clinical observations on disturbed marriages is the following:

Many tensions and misunderstandings between partners seem to result from the disappointment which one or both of them feel and resent, that the other fails to play the role of spouse after the manner of some stereotype or figure in their fantasy world.

We learn that people frequently love and marry not real persons, but that they in varying degree distort the reality by investing their objects with qualities derived from past significant psychological objects, among whom parents of the opposite or even the same sex are common. It will be said that this means no more than that immature persons without good emotional reality sense are apt to make up the numbers of the unhappily married; that this proposition is only a restatement of the old notion of neurotic object-choice.

There are, however, new elements in this way of restatement. First, the factor of role expectation. We have no reason to think that neurotic object-choice in the sense of partial idealization or other distortion of reality of the partner's personality is limited to the unhappy. It is a question rather of the closeness of fit between what the partners expect of each other's behaviour (what they 'project' into each other) and the actual personality and behaviour towards each other or in their role. Readers must know of many marriages in which grossly neurotic personalities have made matches which have brought them lasting satisfaction of their 'immature' needs through a good fit or dovetailing with complementary needs in the partner; at times through an adaptation of one or both to meet the partner's need, even if this meant some degree of denial mechanism or splitting in their own personalities. It is the lack of fit, and the intolerance in the partner(s) of such disappointment which seems to lead to misunderstanding and resentment expressed in the symptoms of stress, neurotic or 'acted out'. Secondly, this reformulation of a well-known finding in medical psychology covers all the phenomena of culture distance in the sociological sense. Ethnic, religious, class or educational patterns no less than the more idiosyncratic family cultures of the husband and wife can be included. The partner fails to do and say things which the spouse had tacitly and confidently expected from his now internalized deeper value patterns of how wives or husbands should behave or speak.

(a) In the simplest cases this expectation may be fairly conscious.

Case 1. Thus, in the case of Mr and Mrs H., the husband came from a family in which the policeman-father had in a kindly but gruff way dominated the mother and children. His wife came from a matriarchy with a cowed compliant father, and had until her not very young marriage been accustomed to the freedom of a business girl as well as to the free expression of feelings. The marriage was threatened by the husband's discovery that his rather heavily avuncular attempts at kindly discipline of his wife produced not compliance but a violent mixture of hysterical fireworks and baleful sulking. The wife resorted to this form of attack by reviving her pattern of dealing with her dominant mother when she found that her husband did not play his role in the way her father had done.

The parties had little difficulty in accepting the interpretation of their behaviour towards each other in terms of their respective parental role-expectations. He was of obsessional, she of hysterical personality structure. Neither had been psychiatrically ill apart from their current marital difficulties in which neither would yield any ground.

It can be said that they had picked each other in the belief that each expected to find the other an easy conformer to the pattern of their respective parents of the opposite sex, while also expecting to play their own marital role by identification with the way they had seen their own parents of the same sex perform theirs.

Thus we may say that there is a group of marital problems in which the basic disturbance seems to lie in a direct disappointment, on one side or on both, with the fantasied but absent likeness of the partner to a good and compliant parent image. In the absence of this unalloyed conformity, resentment and its corollaries break surface, disclosing the deeper ambivalence towards the earlier object now transferred to the spouse and visited upon him or her with the earlier but now childish resources for revenge or for courting favours. Forbidding, rejecting qualities are attributed to the partner, and, since the partner is so frequently also unconsciously involved in reciprocal collusion (as in the above case), he or she obligingly reacts. Projection and paranoid attack ultimately make their fantasies come true.

(b) Things are not often as simple as the situation just described. More frequently, the object-choice by an expected similarity to a past object is deeply unconscious and is consciously denied. In such cases we may speak of choice of mate by *contrast* to an ambivalently invested object, at least so far as the time of courtship is concerned. We observe several different outcomes. The first is that the need for the qualities of the parental figure, though denied, nevertheless asserts itself and causes ambivalent behaviour illustrative of the disappointed role expectation.

Of this variety the following is an example:

Case 2. A youngish couple came on account of incessant quarrels over details of running the home and feeling overwhelmed by the weight of domestic chores, though their home was a small suburban house with one child. It transpired that the wife was driven to nagging her husband because he would not take any responsibility but insisted 'as his right' on spending nearly all his spare time in tinkering with his radio and his car. When he did help, it was to make heavy weather of it with a martyred air. This was his way of punishing his wife for making demands on him. His unconscious attitude to her was one of comparing her all the time to his very efficient, spoiling and indulgent mother who expected 'no return' from her favoured son. Any woman who made demands received the sadistic revenge of his ambivalence typical of a mother-tied boy. This masqueraded under the cloak of a sense of self-sacrifice, constant tiredness and futile obsessional attempts at planning all their activities, including their expenditure on pleasure. His wife's reaction increased his image of her as a devouring mother figure who must be frustrated at all costs, and stimulated greater efforts to maintain his omnipotent dependence and obstructive passivity. She was a social striver and a perfectionist who could brook little disorder.

Here was a case where the man was unconsciously expecting a direct continuation of female behaviour along the only heterosexual object-relation he was capable of—that of the omnipotent, indulgent but dangerous mother.

These ties to past object relationships may influence choice of mate even where at conscious level the attraction to one another is by contrast, or apparent contrast. In such a case we may speak of the disappointment or resentment which appears in the relationship when the partner is discovered or felt to be acting out the role in the manner of the rejected parent figure. The expectation was that the spouse would *not* be like the parent object, but is found to be a replica after all. This variant of the disappointed role expectation was brought home to us by

Case 3. A professional man of Scottish Presbyterian antecedents is greatly attracted to and marries a lively young girl of pronounced, fanatical, left-wing tendencies. He has been brought up in a home in which there was a weak and compliant father and a dominating but spoiling mother who ran the house like clockwork. The man is attracted to his 'emancipated' wife because she seems in every way so different from the mother, who was a traditional and religiously puritan martinet who spoilt her menfolk and had rigid ideas on the role of mothers and wives as pillars of home and kitchen. The parties agree that the modern democratic left-wing intellectuals' marriage is one of absolute equality, in which housework, care of children, etc., are shared alike and on a voluntary basis, and in which there shall be freedom for both to pursue their on the whole closely related social and political interests. The wife comes from a family with a very dominating father, against whom she had been in perpetual rebellion, which may have influenced her iconoclastic and revolutionary attitudes. The marriage is threatened because of the increasing sense of annoyance of the husband with his wife for neglecting her domestic duties so frequently, and leaving him the care of the baby, the washing up, etc., not providing a meal when he comes home in the evening while she is out at political meetings. Initially shown by long sulks, this anger has begun to be violently expressed. The wife retaliates by hysterical behaviour, having the general import of denying him even the semblance of dominance over her. The husband's behaviour is determined, as shown by the joint interview, by his need to stand up to what is now seen to be a rather bossy, self-willed woman who comes increasingly to resemble in his mind his dominant mother, and to resist falling into his weak father's role. As he does this so his wife increasingly begins to attribute to him the same patriarchal authoritarian behaviour which she had fought, but no doubt was secretly attracted to, in her father. Thus, whilst the superficial conscious motivations in the object-choice on both sides were a contrast to the parents of the opposite sex, in effect there had been an unconscious compulsion to repeat the parent-child relationship in each case.

It was interesting to note how with the displacement of his mother-figure to his wife the husband's political views had also taken a turn to the Right and thereby caused the rift between them to widen by adding communist contempt for his backsliding to her fury for his ineffectual authoritarianism.

Allowing for great condensation in the description of the case, little doubt could be felt that there was a situation of unconscious collusion in object-choice underlying the attempt on both sides to 'break free' from the oedipal ties, now transferred into the marriage itself. Both partners, in fact, seemed to possess certain traits taken over from the parents which were revealed in the challenge of their marital relation but which were not apparent to each other during courtship when only the desired, longed-for qualities, but not the 'bad' aspects of the parental model, were present to their conscious view.

In yet a third variant of apparent contrast to the past ambivalent object, qualities of the latter may be attributed to the spouse which require a good deal of contribution from fantasy. The partner may be blamed and hated for traits which he or she does not in fact display, but which are projected by the other party into the spouse. Of several similar cases seen, the following will serve to illustrate this point.

Case 4. A highly narcissistic, elegant, self-made 'big city-slicker' barman of 43 presented himself on account of partial impotence. He felt depressed also by the awareness that he had little affection for his wife, that he hated her Cockney accent (he had one himself), and that he made quite absurd demands on her standard of smartness in dress and tidiness in the home, reacting with undue violence when she fell below his insatiable expectations. He was one of a large family of slum parents, with a disorderly father and a kind mother who struggled ineffectually with the poverty and chaos of the home. He had early determined to escape, had risen via West End club jobs to have an appreciation of smart upper class people and their form of living, and was motivated almost entirely by needs for social and financial status.

His wife, chosen as a contrast figure to his mother, was a still pretty, well-groomed former beauty-specialist, now grown plump; warm and easy-going, who did not make any complaint about her husband, as his financial provision and high regard for her own narcissistic needs seemed to satisfy her requirements. Here, the man's compulsion to identify his wife with the slatternly mother of his childhood was based on little reality, but explained his symptoms of marital behaviour. He hated even the normal degree of intimacy and disarray of home life which at once evoked the guiltladen oedipal ambivalence of his childhood.

(c) It will be apparent that the weight of pathology falls now on one, now on the other spouse, and in some cases fairly evenly on both. But even where we can for diagnostic purposes identify the primary disturbance as originating in the personality of one partner, we always have to deal with the reactions of the second one. There are, after all, also normal role expectations which can be disappointed and lead to reactive and defensive behaviour in the 'normal' partner. Apart from lack of fit due to cultural distance, there is the impact of continuing immature demands or inhibitions by one partner which frustrate healthy needs of the other.

It is a moot point whether in fact a mature and healthy person does choose an 'ill' partner, or whether there is not always an unconscious element of collusion or self-deception by denial inherent in these marriages. Flexibility of personality and different rates of maturation are perhaps also involved. The present study cannot answer this question, but strengthens the view that unconscious collusion does exist in all cases. It is a matter of degree of domination by unsolved past-object relations.

The 'healthier' spouse sooner or later ceases to comply with the immature needs of the other as hope of a change for the better fades. Unless there is a parting at this stage, the assailed partner begins to regress towards a defusion of latent ambivalence, and may on examination present a more obvious clinical picture of neurotic disturbance than the basically 'iller' other spouse.

As an example for some of these points the following case may be cited.

Case 5. A foreman of 41 and his wife of 38. The husband had been the illegitimate son of his mother, and had led a Cinderella existence as a barely tolerated member in the home of a rather brutal, former boxer who was his official father whom he repudiated, with futile attempts of his weak indulgent mother to shield him from her punitive husband. The real father had been a 'gentleman' who formed a contrasted figure for identification. His personality was over-conscientious with a great deal of counter-cathexis of aggression; restitutive, and intensely serious. He was attracted to his wife through the latter's foster-mother who befriended him after he ran away from home in adolescent despair. His need was for a gentle, loving mother-figure whom he saw in his wife by extension from her 'Grannie', as she was called.

The wife came from a disrupted home with a psychotic mother. She proved to have had a severe split in her feelings during the courtship, and during the joint interview it dramatically emerged that she had looked upon her saturnine and rather handsome husband as a dark Mephistophelean seducer, dangerous and yet irresistible. She tried to throw him over in favour of a blonde, gentle boy friend. He withdrew for a time. In the end she felt compelled in a fit of conscious vengefulness towards him to seduce him, become pregnant, and insist on marrying him. Since then she spends her time in accusing him of lack of consideration, reticence, and mental cruelty, etc., goading him into counter-action based on his unconscious internalized qualities of his bad authoritarian stepfather. He is aware that he gratifies her image of him by reacting with impulsive violence and sadism towards her, and this leads him to contrition and depression, making him very weak in his dealings with his wife. It was very striking how during the joint interview the wife was denying her own masochistic and aggressive sexual needs and projecting them in the form of sadism into her husband, thus to some extent evoking his own strongly counteracted aggressive tendencies from which he had earlier tried to escape both physically and psychologically.

(2) *The power of past identifications*

The first proposition dealt with projection of past objects into the marital partner. A finding closely related dynamically to this is that

marriage, and often marriage alone, will cause a return in a spouse's own behaviour of a repressed bad internal object, which has been identified with in the past, however hard both partners may have attempted to develop a personal ego-ideal or pattern of behaviour in denial or contrast to that of the bad internalized figure whom they had banished into the unconscious.

This was perhaps especially clear in the husband of case 5, who found himself developing tendencies of an authoritarian patriarchal wife-suppressing kind such as he had introjected from his brutal stepfather, when his whole aspiration had been for a marriage of gentle and rational co-operation and repression of the aggressive father in himself. It is often with great distress that such people find themselves compelled to behave towards their spouses in ways which morally they greatly disapprove of, and which they may or may not recognize as being repetitions of rejected or feared parental behaviour. This proposition would lend support not only to the theory of internal object-relations (see Klein (1948) and Fairbairn (1952)) but also to the related concept of the introjection of learnt behaviour patterns as a factor in the continuity of culture pattern and its resistance to change.

(3) *The partner as the 'other half'*

A third generalization which seems justified by the experiences of this study is the following:

Subjects may persecute in their spouses tendencies which originally attracted them, the partner having been chosen as a representation of lost or repressed aspects of the subject's own personality.

This is a proposition which already commands considerable assent.

Whether in popular parlance under the term 'my better half', or in Jungian terms as the 'anima' or 'animus' projection, there is wide agreement that people tend to seek mates who somehow complement or complete the subject's own personalities. Masculine men are said to marry feminine women and vice versa, as if in search of potentialities not available to the self. Using the same frame of reference as hitherto, one would say that what is here described overlaps only partially with Proposition 1. What is sought and yet ambivalently resented in the partner is not only a parent figure but something of the self's repressed infantile needs in relation to a forbidden or unavailable parent object. The following case may illustrate this point:

Case 6. A young couple, husband aged 28, wife 20, when seen. The husband was a technician who had developed strong and consistent left-wing views which one could not help attributing in part to his unrecognized deep sense of deprivation at the oral level. His history as he gave it was that both his parents had virtually starved to death during the industrial depression after the first war, and he had been lovelessly and very austerely brought up in orphanages, losing contact with his siblings. This was related with great bitterness. Even a kindly later foster-home could do no more than put a veneer of reparative social concern on his fierce sense of emotional insecurity. He was an extremely rational, over-controlled young man, with a rigid and doctrinaire character, with great counter-cathexis of aggression, impulsiveness, romance and all other feelings. He also wanted to make his marriage and the rest of his life an example of rational control and enlightened class-consciousness reasonableness. He had married a very indulged, spontaneous and warm-hearted girl from a different cultural and ethnic background. They were regarded by their friends as a model of happiness. The difficulty which brought them was the wife's inability to have an orgasm, and what both of them guiltily called childish quarrels, provoked by the wife, despite a very great deal of love and sense of being well-suited to each other. They believed in early mental hygiene. The joint interview showed that the wife was full of barely disguised resentment over her husband's rationality and his power to make her feel an uncontrolled, unreasonable child because she escaped from his excessive demand for a planned marital life by frigidity and by occasionally going into violent tempers. The husband was able to demonstrate to our satisfaction, if not to his own, that his alleged rationality concealed a lot of subtle aggression, especially manifested in emotional withholding and as sarcasm and censoriousness, which was a way of persecuting in his wife his own repressed oral demandingness. His wife was quite aware that she would have preferred a straight, tough male to whom she could have responded with gratifying feminine submissiveness and emotional abandon. As it was she was not permitted a baby until the home was paid for, and was expected to be a model of rationality at all times. It also emerged that it was the husband who insisted on consulting us, as to him his wife's emotionality presented a great threat of destruction of their whole relationship.

It was concluded that the greater part of his attraction to his wife lay in her capacity to live and be an expression of his own repressed oral needs. When his wife showed her anger this became an image of his own repressed anger at frustration, while her frustration of him by frigidity roused very great anxiety in him with protestations that he was 'doing everything right' and that he was to all intents a perfect lover. In her frigidity the wife as a gratifying object became threatened by his own unconscious resentment. His scornful rejection of our interpretation about his fear of feeling and of spontaneity was in marked contrast to his (much younger) wife's capacity for insight both of her own and her husband's problems. Her admiration for her husband's powers of control and her sincere regret rather than guilt over her shortcomings were a function of her own lack of a safe, protective father: the latter was one of those quiet, failure-seeking Jewish men who was always in money difficulties. The wife's reaction was to be interpreted more on the lines of disappointed role expectation: the husband's failure to gratify her feminine sexual needs and feelings while fulfilling the requirements of ordered reason and system in life which had been markedly absent in her own background.

Of course, the contrast between seeking a parent figure and seeking a partner who embodies past needs of the subject is not absolute. The needs relate to the object. The above wife was not only 'an Id object' or embodiment of passivity and 'greed' for her husband, but also in part a gratifying, yielding maternal object, the rejection by whom through frigidity caused him distress. Nevertheless, the distinction between these two aspects of disturbance of marital relationship seems valid and worth stressing.

(4) Dominance-submission conflicts

A fourth and obvious generalization is that

marital disharmony is frequently the expression of dominance/submission conflicts rooted in discrepancy between role and unconscious needs.

This proposition is not an independent hypothesis. Rather is it a restatement of factors common to the preceding propositions. The conflict between the demands of the marital role and certain needs for dominance or for passivity in the personality is clearly primarily internal. But, like other conflicts, it may be externalized in the marital relation. We may see in the struggle for ascendancy among a married couple the projection of a bad object (such as a frustrating parent), or denials in one or both of them of their own deeper needs by a process of over-compensation. The partner may be attacked as if he or she were a frustrator in order to justify the subject's own aggressive feelings towards the object, and to ward off guilt at the failure in role fulfilment. Lastly, attack may be used as a method of defence against the bad object felt to be in the partner which would destroy the subject unless forestalled and weakened.

An example of a more or less one-sided operation of all these factors (and few cases present a simple picture of pure single factor dynamics in real life) we can refer back to the behaviour of the wife in case 5.

This was the woman who during the joint interview staggered and exclaimed 'He looks like a devil' about her husband. The subsequent material showed that she had built up a violent defensive over-compensation of dominating her husband by a consistent denial to him of every gratification or comfort and by constant attacks, physical and verbal, charging him with sadism. This was motivated unmistakably by her denial, and projection on him, of her own sado-masochistic sexual needs which had originally led her to seduce him 'to prove how bad he was', and in so doing to be able to castrate and reduce him to a helpless puppet in her hands. If he reacted violently she screamed out her justification of her own fantasies. If he withdrew into himself she was equally able to accuse him of lack of love and co-operativeness. Every opinion he offered was turned into an argument in which she had to win by quoting newspaper authorities at him or finally shouting him down.

This case opens up some typical subcategories in the phenomenology of the dominance-submission struggle within and between the partners. The subdivisions are in terms of whether dominance is exerted by repressing (or suppressing, denying) passivity, or passivity is emphasized as a defence against aggression. In neither case is the attitude successful because of the underlying ambivalence, and because of the complexity of the partner's role expectations.

(a) *Dominance and role.* Under this head fall those cases in whom the assumption of a dominant or aggressive attitude toward the spouse is not what one might call a simple characteristic but is based on the uneasy struggle to keep passive wishes out of consciousness.

In the male such 'bogus-tough' behaviour is often rationalized as appropriate to playing the masculine role in accordance with the cultural stereotype. Owing to the unconscious collusion in object-choice this behaviour is appreciated by the wife, again unconsciously, for what it is. As the result we observe the kind of situation described in cases 1 and 2, of unsuccessful attempts by the husband to assert his dominance and 'rights', terrified to be tender because of his deep fear of being swallowed up or destroyed by his wife if he 'showed weakness'. There are many marriages in which this sadistic form of role playing is successful owing to the wife's need to be dominated, or even to play the long-suffering or placidly acquiescent maternal role *vis-à-vis* such a demanding male, with his dread of tenderness. In this series of cases, the women have, as it were *ex hypothesi*, seen through or been hurt by this type of male dominance because it has not seemed secure or consistent with their role expectation, or because of their own deeper fears and needs.

In the women, shrewish dominance has not infrequently been unconsciously provoked by their ambivalently dependent husbands. We may call such dominant behaviour either reactive or regressive, according to whether we think of the stimulus or of the history of development. Where a wife finds herself deprived of the healthy and secure leadership or partnership of her husband, she will, whether she knows it or not, feel cheated and react by overt or concealed frustration rage as well as by retreat from the full feminine genital position (assuming she had reached it). She will regress, at least in respect of her relation to her husband, towards phallic or anal positions.

In other cases such dominant behaviour is more properly described as primary, and is then based on the well-known factors of dread of the sadistic father figure, or more rarely on the denial of passivity to the mother. In both cases we are, from the sociological point of view, dealing with a refusal to accept, or to continue in, the female role. In the primary cases this refusal is based on exaggerated intrapersonal fantasies of the dangers of passivity or even of co-operation. In the secondary cases it is based on a traumatic reactivation of such fantasies latent in most women.

(b) *Submission and role.* The second variety of difficulty comes close to an obsessional type of defence in which submissiveness and gentleness cover the fear of acting aggressively or destructively towards the ambivalently invested love object, to the point of incapability even of normal degrees of self-assertion or dominance in any situation where the partner and the role would demand it.

Leaving aside the sex life for the moment, the husbands with strong counter-cathexis of aggression are usually the ones who are 'helpless clay' in their wives' hands. Terrified of their woman's reactive dominance as reflecting the bad and destructive aspects both of their mother-figures and of their own repressed feelings, they are unable to see the provocation implicit in the wife's behaviour for the man to show power and assure her that he does possess a potent penis.

Typical behaviour by such husbands is apathy and withdrawal—to the pub or just as often into the work situation or back into the bosom of their families. This passive resistance makes matters worse and is, of course, interpreted by the wives as a withdrawal of love. Sporadic and guilt-laden breakdowns of control and fitful violence in such men are either early symptoms which denote a fairly live relationship; or they are late symptoms betokening a giving up of any attempt to play a loving role according to the valued pattern of the 'parfit genteel knight'—a capitulation to the bad internal forces (cf. the husband in case 5).

Passivity when used as a method of attack by the wife sometimes takes a similar form to that of the male—a 'giving-up' and retreat into non-co-operation. But it is a matter of observation in the group studied that such defensive passivity as a rule has to mobilize hysterical and phobic mechanisms to its aid, which contain both the appeal to be succoured by the husband and the power-through-weakness motive by which he is forced to become a slave.

Both parties, lastly, may use the behaviour of compulsive martyrdom to the domestic chores and compulsive pseudo-co-operation in their respective spheres, which may indeed form the chief overt battleground. The identification of each spouse with the children (if any) as objects of the other's maltreatment and the use made of these small victims as pawns in the struggle for power are too well recognized to need elaboration.

(5) *Repercussions on sex life*

It has been stated earlier that included in the series of cases have been those presenting as sexual failure in one or both partners. Where such failure has existed in both parties from the beginning, experience has shown that there has been very strong unconscious collusion in object-choice. In each case of this kind in our group the couple have come impelled more by cultural and family pressures ('It is time you had children') than by intrapersonal needs. They have also refused further help and gone away content to leave well alone, having adapted themselves to a life of tender platonic co-operation.

Where such failure has been one-sided from the beginning (and yet the marriage has still continued), the impotent party has as a rule felt guilty and consciously eager for treatment. One recalls only one case in which the frigid and dyspareunic wife tried to justify her symptoms on grounds of puritan principles, having married a mentally healthier member of the same strict sect whose carnal needs had overcome his earlier agreement with her uncompromising value systems. It was in this case the husband who felt guilty.

Nevertheless, both parties in a marriage where one partner is sexually incapable or frigid, will react with the defences against regression which their personality structure has fashioned for them—by acting out or by neurotic symptoms—and this largely in response to role expectations, healthy or pathological. This paper does not aim to go into the complex details of the psychopathology of sexual frustration in individuals.

As was said earlier, the focus of our interest was the attempt to gain insight into how married couples affected each other so as to cause tension and bad relationships. In the sphere of **sexual)** relations between the partners this point of view made us look for hypotheses to account for the appearance of disturbances in sexual functioning *where this had already been more or less successfully established.* The point may be expressed as a question: 'What happens to the sexual interest, the genital libido, under the impact of the events this paper has suggested as occurring in the object relations of the spouses?'

In some of the couples the tensions are but episodes which may at least in earlier stages, end in reconciliation and in a great access of tenderness and sexual activity. But even in them the episodes are marked by a conscious diminution or extinction of sex feelings for the partner. The point is that when the marriage is one in which the partners are unable to tolerate ambivalence and split it into its component feelings, the genital libido for each other is thereby greatly weakened. Every couple examined report such disturbances.

Sexual coldness follows closely upon the rift. From the moment when the disappointment of role expectation begins the process, the corollaries become activated, unconsciously influencing the pathways of 'somatic compliance'—the sexual function. It could be said that when the marriage partner becomes fused in fantasy with the idealized and frustrating parent figure the incest-barrier is conjured back to life in relation to them.

(*a*) In the case of *female frigidity* or refusal of coitus we have seen the whole range of defence mechanisms from anxious incest-taboo and hysterical inhibition covering a latent revolt against passivity, masochism and the feminine role, to reaction-formations against highly sadistic pre-genital destructiveness towards the male, oscillating between referral to the subject and to the object.

It has become a common experience to discover by directly stated material from the wife or by the clearest of inferences from her lightly dis-guised attitudes that frigidity and withholding of coitus are hostile and aggressive acts. They are part of the assertion of female power by passivity or martyred acquiescence, making the husband feel guilty or incompetent according to the nuance of the wife's demeanour. In the main this form of female revenge succeeds well: the unconscious collusion in object-choice sees to that.

If the husband becomes aggressive or looks elsewhere for sexual gratification, the wife becomes an aggrieved party in law. If he becomes anxious, withdrawn and impotent with her she has the secret triumph of having castrated him and may well begin to complain of his lack of tenderness towards her.

(b) In the case of *male impotence*, relative or complete, analogous mechanisms occur, although genital functions may have been quite well established in the pre-marital phase—either or both with the present wife and with earlier girl friends or wives.

There seem to be two major attitudes towards the wife which deter-mine such regression—apart from those cases which may have been neurotic all along.

The first is the guilt felt at her squeamishness or modesty or girlish apprehensions during honeymoon trials. There are, needless to say, personality predispositions to such guilt, as well as cultural (role playing) determinants for them. But they start the vicious circle of mutual resent-ment, in the man for being confronted with a living reproach at his more aggressive sexual wishes which may evoke the fantasy equation: wife = frustrating mother. In the woman for having been cheated of the display of virile overcoming of her—the frustration of having the good penis restored to her.

The second is essentially the emergence of a split in the object-rela-tions of the husband, closely related to the first. It is something like the need to deny the sexuality of the wife once she has become such in law, sometimes even before that. She quickly becomes desexualized, idealized, fused with the maternal image in its possessive, restrictive aspect. Her own sexual demands may arouse anxiety and disgust. This state may only declare itself with the arrival of a baby which still further emphasizes the maternal role of the wife and evokes the husband's jealousy. In this feeling there may be components of adolescent or childish revolt against the maternal authority, or an identification with the henpecked weak father, or both. Such feelings are in conflict with the reality demands of some limitation on a man's freedom which he interprets as wounds to his narcissistic status and role needs. Both these may be inflated by the husband into enormous sacrifices: giving up all games, all old associations 'with the boys' of his bachelor days, etc. He feels caged and caught and fears being totally devoured. These are the kinds of things which lend themselves well to rationalizations about the squalid conditions of the home, about difficult economic circumstances militating against successful marriage, and so forth.

(6) *The question of affection*

The emotional situations which were outlined in the foregoing are often accompanied by assertions of feelings of continued affection. The couple, or one or the other, will emphasize that they still love the partner, or at least would be able to love if these unfavourable reactions which cloud their relationship could be cleared away. It is precisely this continuing need for the other which is the surprising feature of some of these cat-and-dog marriages. No doubt at times we may attribute such 'loyalty' to a sense of duty, especially where there are children, or to habit plus social conformity pressures (such as fear of admitting failure publicly or letting down their own values). At other times one senses that there is a genuine relationship, a mutual collusion of clinging to the object. The ambivalent, hostility-soaked relationship represents, as it were, the highest common denominator of object-love of which the given partners are capable with each other. The particular means of communicating their love needs to each other in heavily disguised and oblique ways by sulks, denials and 'representation by the opposite', often conceal a good deal of real libidinal investment in the relationship. In theory at least, and in practice sometimes, this finding provides a basis for interpretative and therapeutic work. We have, so to speak, to decipher the code each partner is using to cover up their conflict-covered libidinal need of the other, and to create their insight into what they really want from each other.

CONCLUSIONS

In this paper I have only attempted to give some preliminary hypotheses in very broad terms on recurring experiences in marital counselling.

I have largely omitted considerations of a more commonly understood kind which we may take as read. These are the social factors: influence of in-laws, economics and housing, or culture-clash, where spouses spring from backgrounds with very different patterns of values, of class and economic behaviour, of tastes, prejudices and taboos. Nor have I been able to touch on marriages doomed from the first because contracted not from affection (however unrealistic) but under some form of stress: a child on the way, the rebound from another affair, or as a desperate remedy for social loneliness. I believe, however, that all these social factors must, in the final analysis, be studied in terms of the meaning they have for the two intrapersonal worlds.

It will be appreciated from the tentative nature of this paper how badly major research programmes are needed to expand and refine the kind of hypotheses herein proposed, to test them out and to relate the social and the psychodynamic aspects to each other. Equally valuable would it be to compare so-called normal marriages with those that require our help overtly. It would be a great advance in knowledge if we could show how the need systems indicated as well as the social pressures and discouragements working against mature and satisfying marital relationships are dealt with and 'buffered' in the happy marriage, where they must occur just as often as in the unhappy. Also important is the comparison of samples such as ours with those who feel their marriage to be a failure and are only bent on legal termination of it.

Nor have I been able to enlarge on the question of therapy. We have entertained extremely modest expectations from the results of the joint interview technique in its present brief form, and this has on the whole been proved the realistic attitude. A small proportion of couples may be said to have benefited by lessening of guilt and tension and by a greater capacity to see their spouses with a little more tolerance and insight, if only temporarily. If the method could be followed through by frequent and long enough series of such interviews I think it could be quite effective in the properly selected case. This would provide a possible model for a technique of remedial work in this important field.

REFERENCES

1. Dicks, H. V. 1947. Principles of mental hygiene. In Harris, N. G. (ed.) *Modern trends in psychological medicine*, pp. 322-325. Butterworth, London.
2. Fairbairn, W. R. D. 1952. *Psycho-analytic studies in personality*. Tavistock Publications, London.
3. Klein, M. 1948. *Contributions to psycho-analysis*. Hogarth, London.
4. Slater, E., and Woodhead, M. 1951. *Patterns of marriage*. Cassell, London.

X

THE COMMUNICATION OF DISTRESS
BETWEEN CHILD AND PARENT

THOMAS S. SZASZ

*Meanings passed from parent to child shape its behaviour.
The cry, a basic sign of distress, is the subject of study in
this paper.*

'No man is an island', said John Donne. And before him, the men who
wrote the Bible observed that 'Man does not live by bread alone.' As the
body requires food for survival, so the soul—or as we would say today,
the social self—requires human contact lest it perish. This contact, arising
in the reciprocal needs of people, is made possible by various techniques
of *communication*. These techniques are of an astounding variety and
range, from simple gestures and body movements to conventional signs
of abstract scientific languages.

In this essay I shall focus on a very basic—perhaps the most basic—
communicative method used by man, namely the communication of distress between child and parent. This is the type of communication with
which everyone of us commences in his own linguistic career. Then, as
parents—or even if we have no children of our own, as adults—we re-
experience the use of this language when our children, or others dependent
on us, 'cry' to us in 'pain'.* This sort of communication then, may be

* Some comments concerning the use of certain key concepts—such as distress, pain,
anxiety, etc.—are in order here. I shall use the word *distress* to refer indiscriminately to
various states of unpleasurable tension. A crying infant, for example, will be spoken of
as being in distress. His distress is often interpreted by the parents as *pain*, and they may
proceed to look for its causes (e.g. open safety pin, hunger). I shall prefer to speak of
pain, however, only in those instances in which the experiencing person conceives of his
distress as a disturbance referable to his own body. Occasionally the word 'pain' (between
quotation marks) will be used when speaking of unpleasant feelings which are akin to
pain, but lack a clear bodily referent. The word *anxiety* will be used to describe distress
pertaining to interpersonal dangers. In this usage I have followed the principles laid
down and discussed in my book, *Pain and Pleasure* (Szasz, 1957).

Reprinted from THE BRITISH JOURNAL OF MEDICAL PSYCHOLOGY,
Vol. 32, Part 3, 1959, pp. 161-170.

considered as the skeleton, so to speak, around which the body of all other, later, communications is built. The structure and function of the linguistic body, that is of communications in general, may be illuminated by studying this core-communication and its effects on later behaviour.

THE PAIR:
CRYING CHILD—SUCCOURING MOTHER

Empirical observations concerning the phenomenology of an infant or child in distress, crying, and his mother, attempting to comfort him, can be made so easily that it would be out of place to treat this subject in detail. Instead of describing this interaction, I shall present a schematized account of the major variations which are encountered. The source of the communication—the speaker, as it were—is the child. He cries, weeps, sobs, shrieks, agonizes, or, in brief, communicates what we regard as a feeling of being in distress, being hurt, being in 'pain', or suffering. What does this message do to its recipient? The listener—particularly if he is the parent who loves the child and is both legally and morally responsible for him—will become anxious, pained, or generally upset. There is, of course, no mystery to this. It is not done by the 'sympathetic magic' of voodoo rituals (which, however, probably mirror this basic human interaction), but simply through communication. People affect each other—and they do so profoundly—by means of messages. In this case, it is through the exposure of one person to witnessing the suffering of another.

Once this communication has occurred, the need arises in the recipient to master the 'pain'. The locus of this 'pain' or discomfort may be placed provisionally either in the infant, or in the parent, or in both. At first it will not matter to what locus the distress is assigned, but later, as we shall see, it will make a difference.

How is this 'pain' or discomfort mitigated or mastered? First, there are the simple manœuvres of feeding the baby, changing him, cuddling him, walking with him, and so forth. If any of these succeed, and the infant stops crying and becomes comfortable, the cycle of tension-and-its-mastery comes to an end. More often than not, these cycles can be terminated satisfactorily. Let us therefore turn without further delay to those instances in which the infant's communications of distress persist over long periods and defy all parental efforts to bring relief. What happens now is that the parents' tension, anxiety and 'pain' begin to mount too. Soon they feel that they can stand it no longer. They experience a panicky feeling of being *overwhelmed by tension*. This is one of the most threatening of human experiences. It matters little whether the fear of being overwhelmed results from the tensions stimulated by a child's crying, one's own sexual excitement, rage, doubt about one's (sexual) identity or whatever. In all of these instances the danger is that the ego (or self) will lose control over its destiny and crumble. This is the crisis which may terminate in a desperate social act, in an acute psychotic break-down, suicide or homicide. Before taking such desperate measures, how-ever, the parents usually resort to one of another of the following manœ-uvres to allay their mounting tension:

(1) If the mother has been taking care of the child, she may decide to leave her task and enlist someone else's aid. The husband, a grandparent, a baby-sitter or someone else, may be called in to help to dilute, as it were, the concentrated toxicity of listening to a crying infant single-handedly.

(2) A physician (paediatrician) may be called to help on the assumption that the child's 'pain' is an indication of illness. This may or may not be the case, but in any event the physician—his personality, advice, treat-ment—may be sought as an emergency buffer which the mother can place between herself and her crying child.

(3) As things grow worse, the parent's (or parent-substitute's) need to stop the baby's crying becomes increasingly desperate. This may lead to such things as letting the baby alone to 'cry himself out' in a distant part of the house, giving him sedatives or narcotics, attacking him physically, or finally even killing him.

(4) Last but not least, parents and others learn to *endure* and *bear* the child's crying and 'pain' without recourse to overt action. They learn to wait.

We are now ready to examine some of the factors which determine which of these solutions is adopted in any one case.

THE PARENTS' DREAD OF THE CHILD'S CRYING AND UNHAPPINESS

In the light of the interaction between parent and child which has been sketched, it is readily understandable that parents are disposed to dread their child's crying. Fundamentally this is no different from the general fear which people have of experiencing injuries and pains. It is the same fear once removed. However, in addition to the directly painful character of this experience for the parent as well as the child, the child's crying threatens the parent from yet another angle. The source of this threat arises from the fact that in all close human relationships which are charac-terized by a high degree of *mutual interdependence*, the suffering and un-happiness of one member assumes a *signal-function* for his partner. This means that his suffering will signify not only that he is hurt or sick (which may or may not be the case) but *also* that his partner is *bad*, for he has failed to gratify his needs! Thus arises the more general idea that in all sorts of human relations one's partner's unhappiness or discomfort signi-fies *the badness of the self*. Once this step has been taken, its corollary follows, namely that one's *self-esteem* may be maintained or augmented by means of making one's partner happy. Making one's self-esteem de-pendent in these ways on the pleasure or pain (comfort or discomfort) of one's partner leads to all sorts of complications in human affairs. I shall only suggest what some of these are.

To the child's insistent crying, which sounds as if he were saying 'I'm so unhappy . . .' the parents' reply is, 'Please, be happy . . .'.

We know that parents will go to great lengths in their efforts to silence a child's painful crying. Less well recognized are their efforts—sometimes going to absurd lengths—*to prevent* such crying. So-called permissive parental behaviour, it has seemed to me, often may be explained along these lines. In other words, parents may be permissive—meaning that they fail to set limits to the child's activity and permit encroachment on their own autonomy—mainly in an effort to avoid punishing the child (except perhaps by so-called discussion). Limiting a child will make him sometimes unhappy, of course, even if only for a brief period of time, and this some parents almost phobically avoid. They seem to aspire to the impossible ideal of raising children *without ever openly hurting them*. They must always be 'good'—their goodness being defined by the avoidance of a clear, point-to-point correspondence between any deliberate act on their part and their child's crying or unhappiness. Once launched on this course, the family is headed from one trouble to another. One frequent outcome is a severe inhibition of self-expression on the part of the child.

This same pattern of the adult's inhibited self-assertion, lest it cause 'pain' to others, may be noted in many other situations. In some of these, it has seemed to be nothing but a new edition of the pattern which has been sketched. I have repeatedly encountered, for instance, a marked reluctance in persons occupying relatively important positions to assert their rights in situations of conflicting interests. In these persons, self-assertion was significantly limited toward those who depended on them, or who occupied a subordinate relation to them. Thus, they found themselves unable to control their junior partners, employees, secretaries and so forth, but experienced no inhibition of their assertiveness with their equals and superiors. Such persons aspire to control their subordinates by setting a good example, but find themselves unable to reprimand them for open breaches of the work-contract. Their behaviour in every way resembles that of the over-permissive parent, and indeed, this is how they treat their children, too. In one of my patients, this went so far that he permitted his co-workers to 'walk all over him'—and still he found himself unable to do anything about it. When we discussed this, his response was to sketch a detailed mental picture of the complications which would result from any other course of action. He imagined that greater self-assertion would only cause distress to others—and that this in turn would lead to their aggression—and so to even more trouble, culminating in a complete dissolution of the relationship. This he was eager to avoid. In fact, he was so eager to avoid this, that time and again he found himself forgetting to state his position when face to face with his adversary, only to remember all the things which he wanted to say as soon as he was alone.

Such behaviour is often ascribed to the person's anger, of which he may not be fully aware. According to this interpretation, self-assertion is curbed because it heralds 'excessive aggression'. This may be true as far as it goes, but is a rather incomplete picture of the situation, for it leaves unanswered what is 'excessive aggression'. And this is just the point. For a person is prone to feel that his self-assertion is too aggressive in one of two circumstances. First, if he really is very angry, and harbours a great deal of pent-up rage. Secondly, if almost any kind of self-assertion, especially when directed toward those who are weaker, will seem to him as 'too much' because of its painful effect on them. It is precisely in this signal function of the distress of others that the danger lies for oneself.

It is evident from this discussion that what may appear like masochistic behaviour to an onlooker may seem like a rational and necessary compromise to the patient. And who is to say who is 'right'? Only by repeated attempts at defining one's autonomy in ways other than this can a person ascertain what the other member of the relationship is able and willing to tolerate. In some instances such attempts will lead to a breakdown of the relationship. In others, they may lead to entirely new kinds of human interchanges. My aim is to emphasize that bearing one's own 'pain' patterned after the early parent-child interaction, may often seem like the easiest—or, as it were, cheapest—way out of the dilemmas with which conflicting human needs and aspirations so often present us. Mothers, especially when harried by their children, will often express this by stating that it is easier to say 'yes' than it is to say 'no'. That this should be so is readily apparent, for it simply means that *our distress* is at least under *our own control*, whereas someone else's is not. Hence, suffering in others exposes us to the threat of uncontrolled, unmasterable tension. The suffering which we deliberately assume—particularly when it is borrowed and does not arise spontaneously from within our own body— while unpleasant enough, is at least secure in its predictability. It holds no surprises. And for the security of 'no surprises', man is often willing to trade his freedom and much of his autonomy.*

THE CHILD'S DREAD OF HIS PARENTS' SUFFERING AND UNHAPPINESS

The parent's fear of his child's unhappiness—signalling as this might his own badness—has its counterpart in the child's fear of his parents'

---

* Leites and Wolfenstein have commented on the obligatoriness of pleasure characteristics of many adult activities in present-day American culture. They noted the connexions between the older, puritan 'goodness morality' and the new ethic of 'fun morality', by laying bare the common ground which they shared, both being techniques of impulse control. Their socio-psychological analysis of this subject (Leites & Wolfenstein, 1950) and my attempts (Szasz, 1957, 1959) to identify and describe the communicative aspects of discomfort and comfort, may be regarded as studies of a single problem from two complementary frames of reference.

suffering and personal disorganization. This reaction may begin as early as the fourth or fifth year, and may become intense by the early teens. The psychological core of this attitude lies in the same signal function of the unhappiness of one's partner as has been described. The child, even more than the adult, is prone to think that if mother is upset he must have caused it. He is ready to assume responsibility and blame for the other's distress.

In addition to the basically egocentric logic of the child, however, the fear of his parent's suffering has other bases. Foremost among these is the bio-social fact that the child is dependent on the parent's integrated behaviour for his own survival and comfort. Hence, he has a pragmatic motive for keeping mother and father in good shape, so to speak. Indeed, this need to keep the parents healthy and happy is similar to the adult's need to keep his body healthy. In both cases, the selves depend on the proper functioning of other systems; in the first instance, on the parent, in the second, on the body.

Thus far we have discussed relatively general factors—that is, factors which exist irrespective of the specific family constellation—which promote development in the child of the disposition to dread his parent's distress. It is evident, however, that certain kinds of parental behaviour facilitate, while others retard, the development and flowering of this disposition.

Masochistic parental behaviour is the stimulus *par excellence* to develop the child's dread of parental anguish. Parental masochism is analogous in this regard, to, say, infantile colic or chronic whininess. Both the persistently whining child and the masochistic parent say in effect: 'I am so unhappy. You *must* do something to make me happy!'

Striking examples of this attitude may be noted in persons, who, as children, experienced clear-cut evidences of a parent's (usually the mother's) vulnerability and weakness. These children learn through experience that it is very dangerous to overload, as it were, this beast of burden—the mother—for if overloaded, she will break down, and they will be carried down to ruination with her. The thing to do, therefore, is to 'be good to mother'. The implication, of course, is that mother is not only weak in her proneness to break down, but also that she does not know how to regulate her own burdens. This task, then, falls to the children. Self-inhibition for them becomes tantamount to security. The following clinical excerpts illustrate the salient features of this process.

This young man was raised in a home in which his mother's inadequacy in the face of various tasks was a constant irritation to his father. It seemed, in retrospect, that his mother was partly childish and weak, but partly quite capable. Some of her behaviour which was thought of as disability appeared to constitute, however, rather effective methods of sabotaging endeavours of which she disapproved. Her revolt against her husband went so far as to include a suicidal attempt, to which he responded with appropriate alarm. The unwritten motto of the family henceforth became: 'Let's keep mother happy.' This did not mean that mother was especially tyrannical, but she did keep her husband—and certainly her child (the patient)—in a state of perpetual alarm concerning her vast potentialities for un-happiness. This child grew up to become an extremely responsible individual. This manifested itself in scrupulous responsibility not only for his own actions, but also in a readiness to assume responsibility properly belonging to others. He was extremely timid in his relations to his mother, fearing even now—when his mother showed no evidence of any personal troubles and to the contrary was con-ducting her life quite well—that he might hurt her by some trivial act. He dis-played a similar attitude toward his superiors. While painful to him, this attitude made him well respected and contributed to his social success.

Another patient was cared for by an over-attentive, domineering mother, and a depreciated but steady father. While the mother was strong most of the time, she occasionally indulged in what seemed—in retrospect, again—like some sort of temper-tantrum. The patient remembered several of these, since they served to focus her fears on what might happen to mother (if she misbehaved, or other-wise brought on such a catastrophe). In one of these attacks, the mother sent her daughter out of the house, pulled down all the shades and lay screaming on the floor in the darkened room. She seemed to recover from this episode without difficulty. (But the patient did not.) In view of her socio-cultural milieu, this behaviour may have been neither unusual nor alarming. To her daughter, how-ever, it meant that 'mother was going crazy'. She grew up with this dread and harboured it without modification as an adult. She entertained similar fears con-cerning her husband.

These clinical excerpts illustrate some of the situations which foster the conviction that self-inhibition and bearing one's own distress may be the lesser of two evils. For the child, it is a greater danger to feel that, because of lack of proper self-control, mother has become ill, went crazy or died. Then he would have to bear the loss of his most important human object and in addition suffer guilt for having committed a horrible crime against her.

SOME SPECIAL INSTANCES OF THE INABILITY TO BEAR THE DISTRESS OF ANOTHER

Let us apply some of the observations and ideas which have been pre-sented to concrete situations. I shall comment briefly on three special problems, the first in medicine, the second in psychiatry and the third in the raising of children. In each, the issue of bearing the distress and suffering of another—and the inability to do so—is crucial for the proper understanding of the communications which are being exchanged.

(1) *The physician's inability to be inactive*

The physician who assumes the care of a chronically ill and actively suffering patient is in a position much like that of a mother who cares for a colicky, whiny, sleepless baby. Both are confronted by a person whose pain they want to relieve or at least alleviate. Both remain persistently unsuccessful in their attempts to achieve this goal.

The physician caught in this dilemma, much like the patient himself, has a choice between bearing the discomfort and 'sitting it out', so to speak, on the one hand, or taking some action, on the other hand. Unfortunately, for both him and his patient, his social contract with the sick is so codified that he tends to be rewarded for unnecessary or even harmful interventions, whereas he receives nothing—or may even be penalized— for judicious waiting. I shall not belabour this point since it is familiar enough to most of us. I only wish to stress an interesting comparison between medicine and jurisprudence which highlights this problem. We are justly proud of our Anglo-Saxon laws according to which it is better to let a thousand guilty men go free than to convict a single innocent one. In medicine we seem to espouse rules which are exactly the opposite. According to these rules—which are largely unverbalized and unwritten— it is better for a physician to employ complicated, dangerous and destructive treatments (or diagnostic measures) a thousand times and fail, than it is to miss using an effective treatment (or test) in a single case in which it would have helped.

These considerations raise questions of medical ethics beyond the scope of this essay. It is clear, however, that medicine—like law, engineering or international relations—must be played according to *some rules*. It behoves us to make these rules explicit. If we fail to do this, we lose the chance to change the rules in those circumstances in which they are unserviceable. I submit that while most of the rules of the 'medical game' fit the needs of acute treatment problems relatively well, they do not adequately serve the requirements of problems of chronic suffering (Szasz, 1958).

(2) *The challenged psychiatrist and his response:*
Suicidal threats and commitment

A typical psychiatric problem which lends itself to analysis along this same line is that of the patient who threatens to kill himself. Needless to say, I shall not go into all of the psychological and social complexities of this subject. Rather I shall focus on only one facet, namely the suicidal threat as a *communication*—a cry—to which the psychiatrist must respond.

The threat of suicide may be regarded as an adult version of crying. Both are communications and imply suffering, pleading, asking for help, saying as it were, 'I am so very unhappy—please do something to make me happy'; both may be aggressive and threatening, too. How such a plea is countered depends largely on the social context in which it occurs. In contemporary American society, medicine is practised in such a way that physicians—and especially psychiatrists—are considered as persons to whom those who suffer may legitimately turn and expect to be helped. In this respect they play a role similar to that of parents vis-à-vis their needy children. The parallel between the roles of healer and parent is, of course, thoroughly familiar and has been widely explored in modern psychiatric and sociologic writings. I wish to point out that in so far as the patient threatening suicide is regarded like a child in relation to his parents, it becomes the profession's (and the psychiatrist's) *responsibility* to prevent this action. If, however, the patient is in fact an adult, the question may be raised as to how the physician can be held responsible? Is the patient not self-responsible? And if we deprive him of the freedom to act in certain ways, are we not also depriving him of some of his adult autonomy and legal rights?

This difficult ethico-medical dilemma has been resolved by taking recourse to demoting the patient threatening suicide to the rank of disenfranchised child. Accordingly, it becomes the physician's responsibility to prevent suicide whenever possible. This can be done generally in only one way, namely by committing the patient, usually against his will, to a mental hospital. This, of course, entails that the patient temporarily loses some of his civil rights. Moreover, even after his release from the hospital, having been committed may cause him severe injury occupationally and socially, and this may last for as long as he lives. The physician on the other hand, is on completely safe ground when he insists on commitment. For popular opinion today demands that in these circumstances the physician act as an *agent of society* and that he carry out its wishes, which is to prevent *openly codified* suicide. The threat of suicide—or its alleged threat—is thus one of the standard psychiatric findings which may be employed if one wishes to commit someone.

It is implicit in these rules that the physician can be held responsible only for suicidal threats which he *interprets* as such. Obviously he cannot be held responsible for suicide when the intention has not been communicated to him. Thus suicides framed, so to speak, as accidents, are generally considered to fall outside the scope of medicine and the rules applicable to it. My point is simply that it is theoretically more accurate —and practically more useful—to regard suicidal threats as communications, rather than as signs or symptoms of an alleged mental illness. If we so regard them, however, we cannot penalize those who are most adept at understanding this 'language'. This would be the case if we were to take seriously the present rules of this 'game', according to which it is the physician's (psychiatrist's) responsibility to prevent suicidal threats from being implemented.

Returning to the analogy between the suicidal threat and the child's painful crying, we may formulate certain conclusions. In many cases of crying, judicious waiting, bearing the tension, constitutes the most rational course of action. This amounts to *action by inaction*. Applying the same principle to the patient who threatens suicide implies that commitment, electric shock or tranquillizers need not be the only reasonable or acceptable psychiatric approaches to this problem.

It was more my intention to raise questions than to answer them, and I shall leave the discussion of the problem of suicide without developing this theme any further. My present aim has been limited to suggesting that the action-oriented attitudes of the standard medical and psychiatric responses to the suicidal patient may better serve the interests of the healers (and of the society whom they represent) than those of the sufferers.

(3) *The parent's inability to tolerate his child's crying*

I have already commented on the general problem of the parent (or parent-surrogate) faced with a crying, tortured child, whose distress he cannot readily relieve. I shall now consider a special instance, namely a parental response which may be paraphrased thus: 'I shall make you happy even if it kills you.' The parent's need for the child to be happy leads, in these circumstances, to an almost uncontrollable urge to make the child *stop acting* unhappy. For, if the child would only stop crying—so the parent thinks—it could be assumed once more that he was contented and happy. This urge to stop the telephone from ringing—that is, the child from crying—may lead to killing the infant. Here is such a case (quoted from the *Syracuse Herald-Journal*, 3 September 1958):

Baby's Death Laid to Dad. (Rochester AP)—A father who says 'I can't stand to hear babies cry' has been charged with first-degree manslaughter in the beating of his two-month-old son. Police said Philip Coax, 24, a factory worker, admitted striking his son, Gordon, but denied that the blows were the cause of death. He brought the baby to a hospital Saturday and told doctors that the boy had fallen out of his crib and strangled in the bed clothes. Coroner's physician Dr Walter A. Riley said a brain concussion caused death.

Occurrences such as this one are reported in the newspapers at frequent intervals. Besides the parents themselves, baby-sitters are sometimes implicated. In either case, the reason or explanation of the offending adult is that he could no longer stand the infant's (or child's) crying. I am aware that psycho-analysts or psychiatrists may interpret this kind of crime as due to the parent's hostility, conscious or otherwise, toward the child. While hostility may have some bearing on such parental behaviour, it can in no way *explain* it. Resentful or angry feelings could be satisfied just as well—in fact even better—by letting the child cry unrelieved, neglecting him, etc. The argument that infanticide of this type may be motivated by 'too much hate', as it were, may be countered further by its opposite, namely, that it is the result of 'too much love'. This argument could be supported by the popular equation of a loving attitude toward another with a sympathetic perception of *his* needs and feelings. From this point of view, excessive responsiveness to the baby's distress would have to be regarded as evidence of 'too much love'. The terms 'love' and 'hate', however, fail to give us the sort of conceptual assistance which we need to describe and explain this phenomenon. It seems to me that more relevant than the disembodied (and religiously-overladen) notions of 'love' and 'hate' is the matter of the adult's tolerance for bearing distress, both his own and that of another. Then, given his low tolerance for bearing tension, the question arises as to how he will seek mastery and relief of tension.*

SOME PRACTICAL CONCLUSIONS

My argument should allow us to draw some practical inferences. What are they? Let me conclude by stating them briefly.

(1) The adult's interaction with a crying child, especially if his own, presents him with a task similar to that which he himself had to master as a child. This is the task of *defining the boundaries* between himself and another person. All children must master the task of differentiating themselves from their parents, first however modestly, and later with the aim of achieving increasing autonomy and 'mature' interdependence. Parents faced with crying children—or doctors faced with suffering patients, lawyers faced with troubled clients, and so forth—all re-experience the same problem in a new form. The adult's task once again becomes that of differentiating himself from his partner in order to achieve a greater separateness.

(2) Only after having achieved this separation and definition of respective identities, is the parent (physician, lawyer, educator, etc.) in a position to consider the problem of his partner in a rational light. Only then can he ask, 'What can I do for the person in distress?', and answer it on the basis of reason *and* compassion, and not simply on the basis of shared suffering. Since serious suffering impairs rational judgement, answers emanating from sympathetically shared suffering are not apt to be of much value. Proper differentiation of the boundaries between helper and sufferer will also permit the development of that *autonomy* on the part of both which is the necessary basis for an *interdependent mutuality*. In this type of relationship, help may be offered or withheld depending on its rationally judged effects, rather than because the helper is emotionally driven to give or to withhold it.

(3) Having achieved sufficient separateness from the child (sufferer), the parent (helper) may find that he is unable to do anything that will relieve the child's 'pain'. This implies that the best that he can do is to *bear* it. But what exactly does this mean? To begin with, it does *not* mean that the parent will have to leave the child, nor that he will be driven to shut off the crying. It means, rather, an *inner restructuring* of the situation in which parent and child find themselves. In large part, this is a cognitive restructuring, for it implies that the problem will now seem different than it appeared when immediate action was necessary.

* The role and significance of social factors—such as poverty, social isolation, lack of education, etc.—as determinants of certain patterns of tension-relief have not been considered in this essay. Yet, the social—in contrast and in addition to the psychological—dimensions of this problem are clearly of great importance. For instance, it is my impression that infanticide of the type discussed above is primarily a lower-class phenomenon; whether this is really so would need to be empirically verified.

This does not mean that the change is purely an intellectual one. On the contrary, as in the case of any cognitive transformation, the change implies a profound alteration of feelings as well. Seeing the problem, and the task, in a new light should permit the parent to *wait* more comfortably than before. The passage of time, instead of being dreaded as the certain carrier of more suffering, will now be regarded as the likely harbinger of a change for the better.

(4) Finally, another conclusion is inherent in this line of thought. It is the realization, that, given a certain (considerable) measure of personal autonomy, and therefore of separateness between people, it becomes quite impossible for anyone to 'make someone (else) happy'. The only person toward whose happiness we can contribute directly is our own. To the happiness of others, as I see it, we can contribute at most indirectly. In other words, we can aspire to avoid making others positively unhappy, which is what we do whenever we actively interfere with their aspirations or particular techniques for mastering problems. We can, moreover, facilitate and encourage autonomous aspirations in all those with whom we come in contact. None of these things, however, will *make* them 'happy'. At best, they may provide the other person with the opportunities for maximal self-realization. It is apparent, then, that viewing the matter in this way makes it necessary to abandon the idea—and the hope—that we have the *power* (the ability, the 'love', etc.) to make someone else happy. Yet, *what we lose, he stands to gain*. So, truly, we can turn defeat into victory. For the ability to become happy now becomes a potentiality that the other person may achieve through his own activities (and not by the 'charity' and 'love' of our 'gifts' to him). The adherence of parents, physicians and others to the seemingly painful role of trying to make others happy may then be understood, perhaps, as being partly due to the step sketched above; namely, to man's reluctance to acknowledge that '*love' does not cure all*! As long as one believes this—and psychoanalysis began to encourage this belief just when the power of Christian religious thought began to wane—all he needs to do is to try to perfect his ability to love. It would seem to me, however—and this is what I wish to emphasize—that the 'scientific reality', so to speak, of human relations is more complicated than the Bible would have it. Man must *actively* work out his relationships with those about him. And in this endeavour a loving attitude is no more than a mere beginning, or a prerequisite. Its possession guarantees harmonious human relationships and a 'good life' no more than does the knowledge of the English language guarantee the ability to write like Shakespeare.

SUMMARY

The thesis that man's social self may be studied best by examining his communicative behaviour is now shared by diverse professional persons interested in increasing our knowledge in the area currently known as be-havioural science. Among all of man's communicative techniques, prob-ably none is more basic—in the dual sense of being earliest and most consequential—than the helpless child's cry and the helpful parent's response to it.

This discussion has been divided into five parts. (1) We began with the crying child and the succouring mother, and noted that the former's distress creates a high level of tension in the latter. This requires various techniques for mastering 'pain'. (2) The parent often comes to dread the child's crying. This outcome is fostered by the parental interpretation that the cry is a sign of his own badness. This inference concerning one's self-esteem leads, further, to the insistent need to make the other person happy. This is sought since the other persons' happiness is now inter-preted as signifying one's own goodness. In other words, if the child 'has fun', it means that the parent has fulfilled his duties and hence need not feel guilty or anxious. (3) A later edition of the same sort of human inter-action is encountered in the frequent dread which children have concern-ing their parents' suffering and unhappiness. (4) Some special cases of the inability to bear the distress of another were presented. Three examples were offered: (a) the physician's inability to remain inactive and tolerate the unremitting suffering of the chronically ill patient; (b) the psychiatrist challenged by the threat of suicide and his response to it, namely commit-ment of the patient; (c) the parent's (or parent-surrogate's) inability to tolerate the child's crying, and his desperate attempt to silence the painful noise by killing the child. All three instances illustrate the overriding importance for the adult of the need to learn to tolerate the distress of another. Failures to learn this result in actions which are labelled helpful by the helper but which are usually experienced and regarded as harmful by the sufferer. (5) Finally, some practical conclusions were offered. Men cling to the seemingly painful and self-defeating idea that if only they would try harder—that is, *if they loved enough*—they could make their loved ones 'happy'. The persistence of this belief was attributed, at least partly, to the hope it offers for mastering *within a person's self* what may well be problems of very much greater complexity, allowing mastery only on a quite different level. I submit that man cannot *make* his fellow man happy, for this is a task on which each man must labour on his own behalf. We can, of course, do much to provide children, students, patients, friends—perhaps everyone with whom we come in contact—with oppor-tunities to acquire those things which will enable them to make good choices and wise decisions. This may range all the way from healing the physically sick to providing education, employment, legal protection, and so forth. Beyond this, the most that we can do—it seems to me—is to avoid making others unhappy, by depriving them of those opportunities for mastery and self-realization without which their only course lies in inviting gratification by exhibiting suffering.

REFERENCES

1. LEITES, N., and WOLFENSTEIN, M. 1950. *Movies. A psychological study.* Free Press, Glencoe, Ill.
2. SZASZ, T. S. 1957. *Pain and pleasure. A study of bodily feelings.* Basic Books, New York; Tavistock Publications, London.
3. SZASZ, T. S. 1958. Scientific method and social role in medicine and psychiatry. *Archs Intern. Med.*, **101**, 228-238.
4. SZASZ, T. S. 1959. Language and pain. In ARIETI, S., *et al.* (eds.). *American handbook of psychiatry*, chap. 49. Basic Books, New York.
5. WOLFENSTEIN, M. 1951. The emergence of fun morality. *J. soc. Issues*, **7**, 15-25.

XI

HOSTILITY PATTERNS

Deviations from the "Unit Act" of Hostility

DAVID M. LEVY

Children react not only to adults, but also to other children within the family. Patterns of aggression often originate from these interactions with siblings.

The sibling rivalry (SR) experiments offer certain special advantages in the study of hostility patterns. The children are placed in identical situations, in the play of the older child and the new baby at the mother's breast. The same play material and the same technics in encouraging and stimulating activity are used. Each child brings his particular experience and personality configuration to bear on a standardized play situation.

In most cases repeated acts of hostility against one or more of the objects in the play can be observed, in a progressive series, ranging from highly inhibited to fully uninhibited forms. Comparison of the numerous patterns, besides careful study of the minutes phase in the changing series of events, should aid in delineating psychodynamics of the hostile act in general and, in particular, its performance in the SR situation.

Every hostile act, as observed in the SR situation, may be considered a true representation, or a deflection from a true representation, of the following: a direct personal assault on a definite social object. Stated in terms of the specific play situation, the "model" act represents the child attacking the baby sibling with its teeth, hands, or feet. It may be represented graphically as in Fig. 1.

Any deviation from this play may be regarded as a modification, or a

Reprinted from THE AMERICAN JOURNAL OF ORTHOPSYCHIATRY Vol. 13, No. 3, July 1943, pp. 441-461.

complexity, of the simple structure of the hostile act. Such modifications are observed at every phase. They are indicated by dashes made at various points in the graph (Fig. 2).

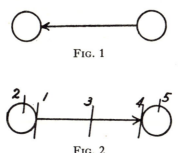

Fig. 1

Fig. 2

Point 1 has reference to the "impulse"; to that phase of the act immediately preceding the release of movement in relation to the object (muscular or verbalization of muscular movement). It is sometimes difficult to differentiate inhibition of the impulse from "getting set," or readiness to act.* When the child says, "I don't know what to do," or "I can't think of anything," though actually, as later events may prove, he does do something, it is still difficult to know whether he held back the impulse to attack, or was merely in the process of orientation, of adjusting to a new situation. In most instances, however, no difficulty is presented; for example, when the child says of himself (or of the doll representing the self) that he doesn't want to do anything to the baby, or punishes the self-doll for wanting to hit the baby, etc.

Point 2 refers to deviations in the use of the self alone as the attacker. The child, for example, may use an animal to attack the baby, may add another child or many children to make the attack, or may ask the examiner to start it ("You do it for me").

Point 3 refers to deviations in the act, after release of movement in relation to the object, before contact with the object has occurred. The deviations at this point represent every variety of avoidance of impact with the object, blocking of movement (withholding attack after making an attacking gesture of slapping, crushing, etc.), or shunting the attack on to other objects.

Point 4 refers to forms of attack and their deviations. The child, for example, instead of assaulting the object, may tease it, abuse it verbally,

* When the play is started in the usual manner, the child is told that the mother has to feed the baby. Clay breasts are put on the mother-doll, the baby is placed in position and encircled by the mother's arms, whereupon the mother is seated in a chair and a doll representing brother or sister is placed near the chair. The child is then told, "Now, this is the game. The brother comes and sees a new baby at the mother's breast. He sees it for the first time. Now what does he do?" (Studies in Sibling Rivalry, Research Monograph No. 2, Am. Orthopsychiatric Assn., 1937.)

distort it, throw objects at it, conceal hostility with evidence of affection, and so on.

Point 5 represents deviations in the object of attack; for example, instead of attacking the baby, the child attacks any other object, including the examiner, or adds other babies, attacking a crowd rather than a single object.

After he attacks the object, the child typically attacks the self, attempts to restore the object, and makes a verbal justification for the hostile act. All varieties of the punishing, restoring, defensive maneuvers have been studied, besides numerous other forms. The absence or distortion of any of the three typical sequelae (punishment, restoration, defense) of the hostile act, are likewise noted. This study is an attempt to illustrate the method of investigation as applied to the SR experiments of a particular patient. The child's phantasy as revealed in known behavior, dreams, drawings, compositions, and the Rorschach test, are investigated and compared with the patterns as manifested in the SR play.

Since the case study is oriented to the particular manifestations revealed in the SR experiment, only those phases of the life history that have special reference to them are depicted. The patient was a boy age 11 years 11 months at the time of referral. His sister, the only other child in the family, was 9 years 5 months old. The presenting problems were disobedient and negativistic behavior, difficulty in making friends, and undue sensitivity to criticism.

At the time of the SR experiment, he was jealous of his sister and fought with her. The fights were more in the nature of verbal spats, with occasional blows. At the same time, he confided in her frequently and asked for her advice. As time went on she assumed more and more a maternal role with him. In spite of the jealousy and quarrelling there was a close and warm attachment.

The experiment was made in the 29th session. It was deferred because he had previously refused to "play with dolls." The standard material, a steel "amputation" mother-doll, a rubber brother-doll, a celluloid baby-doll, and a chair, was used. This time he made a slight protest about "playing with dolls." He criticized the clay breast I made for the mother-doll. He added a second breast, and then fashioned both of them in a more pendulous form.

SIBLING RIVALRY EXPERIMENT

Trial I. Patient: "He gets jealous and runs away. Anyhow I never saw my sister at the breast."

Trial II. Patient: "He's jealous and runs away. Jealous hatred. I get that way often."

Trial III. Patient: "He gets curious, hides behind the door, so nobody can see him when he looks. Anyhow it wouldn't happen. They would never let him in the room."

Trial IV. (Usual stimulus sentence. I said, "Now the play is different. The brother comes in and says, 'That bad, bad baby at my mother's breast.'") Patient: "Brother gets mad. He says, 'You nasty mother, why do you have another baby?' He gets mad." He refused to go on. I encouraged him. He said, "It couldn't really happen." Then, "Well, you asked for it." He crumpled up the baby and put the brother to the breast. He said, "The brother drinks." (Then what happened?) "The mother catches him and gives him a spanking." He illustrated the spanking.

Trial V. He grabbed the baby, threw it away, then took the mother-doll, spanked her and said, "Nasty, nasty mother, for getting another baby. Then the brother goes away and cries. Then the mother sits down and cries and cries. Then the husband comes in and they get after the brother and send him to jail." This he demonstrated in detail.

Trial VI. Patient: "He (the brother) takes the baby away. He goes to the breast. Then the baby has a fight with the brother and the brother was what you're thinking. I'm just copying you. He marries the mother. Then the father comes and says, 'You can't marry my wife,' and beats him up." He illustrated with an imaginary father. He then took the mother apart and when I asked why, he said, "It's not what you're thinking, tearing her limb from limb because she had another baby."

Analysis of SR Experiment with Comments

Trial I. An *escape* reaction. "Anyhow I never saw my sister at the breast," represents a *denial* that the play has reference to his own experience. This, though true, is a type of defense he exploits, as seen later on in the analysis.

Trial II. *Escape.* Repetition of I, omitting the *denial*.

Trial III. *Escape* again. This time by hiding instead of running. The *denial* is in the form of the impossibility of such an occurrence. The fact that the escape reaction (hiding) is used to protect a guilty curiosity of seeing the baby at the breast, implies a sexual curiosity.

Note that though the patient recognizes jealousy of the baby in relation to running away, there is no "mounting" of activity in the first three trials. The play of sexual curiosity in Trial III may have diverted him from the rivalry aspect of the play, or the use of escape reactions may explain the lack of progress, since Trial II is simply a repetition of Trial I.

Trial IV. *Inhibition of impulse.* When the hostile feeling is activated, he releases verbal hostility against the mother, then comes quickly to a halt. As the sequence of the play indicates, he fights off the impulse to attack the baby. His defense against the impulse is in the form of *refusal* (he refused to go on), and *denial* ("It couldn't really happen"—a type of defense used for the third time and implying in this connection that there's no point to the whole thing, so why bother?).

Projection. The remark, "Well, you asked for it," is classified as a projection, though that is probably an elastic use of the term. I did ask for it in the sense that I urged him to go on. I never told him what to do; however, my encouragement ("Go ahead," and "Let the brother do what he wants to") clearly implied that he yield to his impulse in the play. Thereafter the attack followed, implying that the "projection" which involved sanction, facilitated the assault.

A strong assault. Crumpling up the baby is an assault, stronger than a "mild assault," like flicking the baby or dropping it, and weaker than a primitive assault like biting off a part of the baby-doll, or really crushing it with hands or feet. Primitive assaults are seen most commonly at the ages of 3, 4, and 5, after which they become much less frequent.

Regression. He "puts the brother to the breast."

Escape and punishment. "The mother catches him and gives him a spanking." The punishment seems appropriate to the act, as measured against the play of children in this situation. However, my question, "Then what happened?," made for this additional act, since he had come to a halt. Since typically the attack and the regressive behavior, or either, are followed by punishment, I assume that it was left out; further, that it was left out because the fear of punishment was greater in his case than in that of others, unless further sequences of play fail to support such an assumption. *Escape* is inferred from his statement, "The mother catches him."

Trial V. The impulse is quickly released. *Strong assault* on the baby, and a *mild assault* on the mother follow. Then an escape reaction occurs ("The brother goes away") to be followed by tears. The boy's tears may represent *regret* at his action. The mother's constant crying represents *sorrow.* Then *punishment* of a severe type follows, through action of father and mother. The sequelae of the attack are unusually severe. They would be more appropriate to overt destruction of the baby and mother. They are exaggerated in comparison with most of the reactions of children (about 140) who experienced the SR play. The usual punishment for "throwing the baby away" is a spanking, scolding, or a similar act on the brother-doll. It is also unusual for the brother and mother to be in tears.

The assumption in Trial IV is suggested by the play in Trial V. The patient withholds his aggression because his fear of punishment is great. Release of his aggression carries too severe a penalty. Hence the escape reactions in the earlier trials, and the defense against the oncoming push into activity through his *denials* are easily comprehended.

Trial VI. *Mild assault* ("He takes the baby away"). *Regression* ("He goes to the breast"). *Punishment* (a retaliation—"Then the baby has a fight with the brother"). The rivalry play then gives way to the Oedipus play. The punishment for marrying his mother is performed by an imaginary father, rather than a father-doll (as in Trial V). *Assault* on the mother, by amputation, then follows the rivalry play, judging by his denial of what I am "supposed" to be thinking—a *projection.*

As compared with Trial V, the consequences are all toned down. Judging on the basis of other SR plays, the reason may be found in his keeping the assault mild, in using a purely imaginary father rather than the more "realistic" figure-representation, and also in making an attack while at the same time denying its meaning.

The intrusion of the Oedipus situation in the SR play is more likely to be found in the pre-adolescent, hardly at all in the younger groups. It is not usual even at this age level, the rivalry aspect of the relationshup being well maintained. One reason for the mixture may be due to the fact that the SR experiment was made in the 29th interview, and was preceded by a number of sessions in which sexual feelings towards the mother had been revealed.

In the case of this patient, as in many others, playing out a situation is more productive of anxiety, hence a superior form of emotional release, than verbal phantasy. It is worth noting that inhibition of the impulse (at the point of release) occurred but once. The patient was otherwise always ready to respond to the situation in some way or other, if only to escape from it.

"The brother was what you're thinking. I'm just copying you." That is a pattern of defense classified as *denial*, in this case a form of projection. He assumes that I, not he, has the idea that the brother has a sexual impulse toward the mother, and denies that such an idea has any reference to himself.

Now referring back to the "model" act of hostility, we may summarize the patterns as follows:

1. *Impulse.* There is little difficulty in this case at the point of release. One instance of "refusal" at the impulse occurred.

2. *The self.* Evidently he accepts himself as the one who feels "jealous" and has "jealous hatred." When the impulse is activated, he utilizes my sanction as an aid in the attack ("Well, you asked for it," and "I'm just copying you"). Hence there is difficulty in taking responsibility for the self as sole agent.

Simpler forms of this mechanism are seen when the child, instead of attacking on his own, adds figures to represent allies, often brothers and friends, or represents an animal as the attacker. The mechanisms may be paraphrased as follows: "Not just I, all of us together are doing it" (use of allies); "I'm not doing it, he is doing it" (use of animal fairy, witch, etc.); "I'm doing it with your permission" (sanction of grown-up); "I am doing it because you asked me to" (attack disguised as obedience to grown-up). Even young children (age 5) may protect the self as attacker through use of natural forces like winds, volcanoes, or accidents. This mechanism may be paraphrased: "It wasn't my fault, it just happened. I could do nothing about it."

All deviations from the simple assault may be regarded as devices for the protection of the self from the consequences of the act. So far we have dealt with those phases of the act that occur at the point of release and the self as the instrument of attack.

3. *Aim.* Escape reactions occur in five instances. They represent deflections of aim in four. In one instance, an escape follows the assault. The patient presumably feels an impulse to attack and immediately runs away. The impulse is released, so that a relationship to the object takes place, though in the form of escape. The consistency of this reaction—it occurs in five of the six trials—indicates (as determined by comparative studies, besides clinical data) a high degree of anxiety. The highest degree of anxiety overtly manifested under "deviations in direction" is seen in younger children when they actually run out of the playroom. Other mechanisms in this category are "escape into distraction" (typically getting busy with some other form of play), "displacement" (deflecting aim of attack onto other objects), and "inhibited movement" (stopping an attacking gesture after it has started).

4. *Attack.* The attack on the baby was in the form of crumpling it (in IV), throwing it (in V), removing it from the breast without violence (in VI). The strongest attack was in Trial IV (strong assault). It became less and less violent in the trials following.

Attack on the mother was verbal in Trial IV ("You nasty mother"), spanking and verbal in Trial V ("Nasty, nasty mother" etc.), amputation in Trial VI. In contrast with the attack on the baby, the attack on the mother increased in violence with each trial.

The strongest attack, judging by the retaliation, occurred in Trial V when both mother and baby received the strongest combination of violence. Excepting the two verbal attacks, some form of assault was used. None of the deviations of the assault patterns in terms of teasing, attacking from a distance, accidents, illness, operations, traps, stealing the baby's food, etc., were employed. The patient either grappled with the object directly or kept at a distance from it (escape). There is a sort of all-or-none rule in his procedure, implying an impulsive quality. There is a flexibility in the form of his attack. The assault on the baby decreases, that on the mother increases. The attack on the baby starts at the peak and then descends—a reversal of the usual order, and a further indication of impulsive behavior. The attack on the mother, which follows, rises in a more usual manner.

5. *Object.* There is no deviation in the object. The patient does not change it to anything else, nor does he add other objects, so that by attacking a group he is protected from the implied accusation that he is attacking a specific individual.

6. *Sequel.* Sequel is not a well-chosen word to indicate the events following the attack on the object, since it implies that the act is completed. The act usually continues after the attack has been made. The word, sequel, for want of a better word, is used with the understanding that it applies to that phase of the act following attack on the object.

The punishment has already been noted as unduly severe. In Trial V, when punishment appears a second time, it is related to the Oedipus situation. This complication has also been noted previously. Since the mechanisms described for the hostility pattern are generally applicable to any act involving danger to the self, the mechanisms are included as part of the SR play.

Frequently the child punishes the doll representing the self immediately after the attack (and in some cases before the attack is released, as an inhibition to the impulse). In this case the father and mother figures are used to administer the punishment. In Trial IV punishment occurred after I asked, "Then what happened?" It appeared that the act would otherwise have ended. At this point, since the data on the SR experiments have not all been compiled, I may only infer that there is an indication of keen anxiety, consistently found in cases when the punishment is left out. Its severity when it appeared is confirmatory evidence. In Trial VI the punishment was not demonstrated by the use of the figures in the play.

The punishment is glossed over in the story, "Then the father comes and says, 'You can't marry my wife,' and beats him up." That type of defense, a story type of verbalization, is difficult to capture. One can only record as far as possible, the manner of expression. The use of an imaginary father rather than a real father-doll is a help, since by keeping the play in the realm of sheer phantasy, the patient has a strong measure of protection. Another confirmatory datum occurs in Trial IV when he represents the brother as running away after the act, is then caught and punished.

His denials (4 instances) are of the same order. They are his most frequent and intensive form of defense. The expressions are used as follows: "Anyhow I never saw my sister at the breast" (Trial I); "Anyhow it wouldn't happen . . ." (Trial III); "It couldn't really happen" (Trial IV); and "I'm just copying you" (Trial VI). Through such tactics he denies any relation of the play to himself, or to reality, or to anything logical, or to anything that went on in his mind.

The projection mechanisms were used to ascribe the responsibility of the attack to me (Trial IV, "Well, you asked for it"), and a denial that he had any idea of attacking the mother (Trial VI, while amputating the mother-doll, "It's not what you're thinking, tearing her limb from limb because she had another baby"). One of his denials ("The brother was what you're thinking, I'm just copying you") may also be classified as a projection, since thereby he ascribes his own ideas to me.*

Regression occurs in two responses when the brother is restored to the breast from which the baby was taken away. Regressive responses at this

---

* Since all "projection mechanisms," as the term is used in psychiatry, contain a denial and an accusation—an implied denial that the impulse or idea or act belongs to the self, and the direct accusation that they belong to someone else—the differentiation from denial is sometimes difficult. Actually, "projections" are denials in which the thing denied is "projected."

age period are infrequent. Though complicated by the Oedipus play, they represent a strong need for protection as in infancy.

The absence of restoring behavior is noteworthy. It occurs so frequently after any attack that rises above a mild assault that its absence requires consideration. Some children feel the process of restoration before it occurs and say in advance of the attack, "And I won't put it together again." Whatever the explanation of its origin, restoring behavior is a valuable restorative in the equilibrium of the hostile act. The absence of this "constructive" feature is a handicap in the patient's psychic resources in overcoming the anxiety following the attack.

We may summarize the psychodynamic patterns as revealed in the SR play by stating that our patient has a strong aggressive impulse with a tendency to quick release of destructive behavior, withheld from execution because of an intense fear of punishment and disapproval; that in the release of his impulse, at least as manifested in the SR play, there is evidence of strong anxiety shown by frequent "escapes" and "denials." The implication of these mechanisms in terms of his method of defense against the anxiety set off by his aggressive impulse, is that he tries to escape or avoid situations in which there is danger of actual combat. His method of defense against disapproval (an implied accusation) is by deny-

SUMMARY OF THE CLASSIFICATIONS IN THE SR PLAY

I. 1) Escape
   2) Denial
II. 1) Escape
III. 1) Escape
   2) Denial
IV. 1) Inhibition of impulse
   2) Refusal
   3) Denial
   4) Projection
   5) Assault (strong)
   6) Regression
   7) Escape
   8) Punishment
V. 1) Assault (strong)
   2) Assault (mild)
   3) Escape
   4) Punishment
   5) (Regret)
   6) (Sorrow)
VI. 1) Assault (mild)
   2) Regression

   3) Punishment
   4) Assault (strong)
   5) Projection
   6) Denial

Totals

Inhibition of impulse....	1	
Escape................	5	
Denial	4	
Refusal...............	1	
Projection	2	
Assault		
Mild..............	2	
Strong...........	3	
Primitive..........	0	
Punishment...........	3	(+2)
(Regret)		
(Sorrow)		
Regression............	2	
	—	
	23	(+2)

ing that his actions or motives could be interpreted as really implying any evil intention, or having any logic in them at all. The projections in the play imply also a strong tendency to divert blame from himself and attribute it to others. This would, of course, involve much argumentation in which, it is assumed, his aggression would be especially manifested. Judging by the use of "sanction" in releasing his aggression, it is implied that he would utilize the aid of others, and in argument, protect himself by recourse to authority. This implication is consistent also with the regressive behavior in the SR play, indicating infantile dependency, a strong bid for support, yet at the same time competitive struggle for first place.

In terms of the SR situation, we may say that he had not quite relinquished his position as the only child at the time of the play, and that his competitive, jealous behaviour was not yet modified into acceptance. The absence of restoring behaviour would indicate difficulty in developing the accepting phase.

DRAWINGS

Since the patient was facile in drawing sketches, this became a favorite activity during treatment. He produced 85 altogether in about 20 sessions. The method developed into a routine. He would start drawing as many as came to his mind, 3 to 5 per session, in all but a few instances. After he finished, I would ask him to explain what he drew, and then would use them as a basis for his associations. The drawings may be classified as follows.

Landscape (9): They deal directly or by association with violence, death, suicide, destruction, isolation. Titles of these drawings as given by him were: "Forest fire," "Fire," "People falling down a cliffy ledge," "Landscape" (associated with isolation), "Sun and cloud," "Waterfall" (associated with death), "Mountains in snow," "Ships in a storm," "Storm" (associated with death). (See meaning of cliffs and chasms in his Rorschach test.)

Drawings containing animals (14): These are concerned chiefly with the subject of the captor and the prey. In these he identifies himself chiefly with the victim. He associated a cat and dog picture with himself and sister.

Other drawings in this series deal with escape, punishment, fright, curiosity. Titles: "Angry horse left behind," "Panther and prey," "Curious dog," "Frightened rabbit," "Cat and dog," "Eagle, its eggs are stolen," "Eagle and fish," "Dog running from fox," "Fight with a whale," "A duck and a cage" (associated with imprisonment), "Hunter killing an animal," another with the same title, "Fox and chicken," "Knight and dragon" (associated with death).

Drawings of objects (5): In three, the content is violent death (train crashing into a tree, plane on fire, car hitting a rock). The fourth drawing is the "Holy Cross" associated with getting rid of his fears. The fifth is a drawing of a book, associated with his interest in reading.

Drawings of people (57): These deal chiefly with the subjects of crime and heroes. He drew one series of 12, dealing with the exploits of a gangster—his killings and final capture and death. One drawing deals with pirates. The drawings of heroes contain mostly baseball and football players. There are three drawings of suicide and one of a funeral. All the subjects referred to under landscapes, animals and objects are also depicted in this series.

In general, the drawings portray a competitive dog-eat-dog existence, in a world full of danger and violence, in which the patient is struggling along in the form of a helpless abandoned victim, trying to escape from the enemy, driven from pillar to post, finally resorting to suicide; and also, in the form of a great hero, winning the applause of the crowd and vanquishing all his foes.

The drawings help to illuminate his responses to the Rorschach test. The replies of chasms, steep rocks and cliffs, as evidence of anxiety, are confirmed. They represent dangerous forces of nature, chiefly in the form of falling into depths. The Rorschach replies—the dead animals, people wearing masks and the animal with fire shooting out of its mouth— are similar in content to his drawings.

DREAMS

The patient related twenty dreams. In eight, the content was chiefly of killing (4) and crime (4). In one of these, he saved his mother from robbers; in another, dealing with spies and tortures, there is clear indication of sexual activity with his mother's breasts. In one of the murder dreams, his sister is killed; in another she is "symbolically" killed, i.e., two baby carriages appear and only one baby is present.

Five are frank Oedipus dreams in content or by ready association; for example, getting a woman away from her husband, a fight with a man for a woman, a dream in which he falls in love with an older woman, and one dealing with the parents separating. Three concern his more independent sex drive. One is a symbolic coitus (climbing up a ladder with a girl); one, symbolic of some form of sex curiosity; and a third is a direct sex exploration, a dream in which he is kissing a girl. Four dreams (including two already described) contain manifestations of rivalry—with school mates and with his sister, and one is concerned with his offering someone a gift.

Of the twenty dreams, two were repetitions of dreams he had had many times before. They were usually frightening, sometimes nightmarish; for example, a dream of being caught by robbers, and awakening with a cry when he was just about to kill himself or be killed. (The patient said he remembered all his dreams very well, and always used them in his daydreams, turning them around, however, so that he would "best the robbers, catch Public Enemy No. 1," etc., a control, he realized, he could not exert in dreams of the night.)

The second repeated dream was one in which he saved his mother from robbers. In some of these he ran away from her. Then, he said, "she goes with her husband against me." It appears evident that at the time of treatment anxiety engendered by his aggressive impulses was especially activated by the Oedipus situation.

Both dreams and drawings are similar in content; in fact, the same type of associations was yielded by both. The dreams in contrast offered a greater wealth of data in terms of content and associations, and also less concealment. This contrast is true in general. Dreams are more productive of unconscious material, both in younger and older children than are drawings. However, it should be noted that to some of his drawings associations were quite similar and as productive as dreams. In contrast with the drawings, his dreams contained very little landscape, animals or objects. They were almost all of people in some sort of action.

DEFENSE PATTERNS OF THE HOSTILE ACT IN DREAM STRUCTURE*

Repeated dream		*Running away* from robbers.
Dream No.	1	*Hiding* from cops. *Surrender* to cops.
	3	*Accident.* Takes his girl friend up a ladder, about to tell her something, then accidentally falls down. (He was going to do something sexual to her. Accident used as disguised punishment (?) or protection against sexual impulse.)
	5	*Bribery.* Pays his way out of being tortured.
	12	*Use of allies.* In fighting with a boy, he is getting the worst of it, and a girl helps him.
	13	*Hiding and running away.*
	16	*Disappearing.*
	19	*Denial.* Death of his rival changes to "nothing serious."

Of the nine patterns, four are "escapes," one is denial of the "reality" of the act, one probably punishment. Surrender represents passive acceptance. The patterns so far are typical of those in the SR play. The use of bribery to placate the assailant and of an ally to serve him were not used in the SR, though in the latter instance his use of the examiner to aid in the attack is analogous. As in the SR, no restoring devices were used, and the punishment (attacks made upon him) was severe. Rivalry with a boy or with his sister occurred in five of the twenty dreams (6, 7, 12, 18, and 19).

* Exclusive of symbolism.

DEFENSE PATTERNS IN RESPONSE TO ASSOCIATIONS AND INTERPRETATIONS

In Session I, after reviewing his eight drawings I said, "Now let's see what all this has to do with your life." He said, "Bet you can't. Bet you can't" (Rivalry). In Session VI he said he likes to argue. "I am the greatest arguer in the world." He said he can always get satisfaction in his imagination. "In my imagination I can control the world."

In IX, in association to a drawing of a boy stealing bananas, I asked his association to banana. He appeared anxious, ran a pencil over his face, asked what time it was, said, "What good is it to know what banana is?" He then told me what it meant and that he was scared to say it. Then he said, "It's time to go." The secretary knocked at the door to indicate that time was up. He said, "It's about time."

In X, in association with a dream in which it become clear that his description of a woman who was supposed to be his wife fitted his mother closely, he first denied the obvious and then asked, "Do other boys have dreams like this?"

In XII, he told of a dream in which he went up a ladder of lights with a girl, was about to tell her something, then fell down. Then he was in a rich mansion, but it was in school. He started bouncing the ball and then flew into the living room where his mother was. Then he said, "Get this in your head. It was in school and it was a rich mansion. And my mom couldn't be in school. So it's flukey. Now I'll give you three guesses what I was going to say." Later he said, "You can't explain the dream. You can't explain the lights and about the girl and the mother." (Denial of meaning, by argument; use of attack by attempting to dominate— "three guesses," "You can't explain . . ."—as protection against fear of association.)

In XIII, after a typical Oedipus dream, in which he was kidnapped by a man and a woman whom he described and recognized as his mother and father, he said quickly, "I know the whole thing. The mother was my mother and the man was my father, and I wanted to marry her so she turned against me. But what has this money got to do with it?" (Defense by the quick interpretation, as though to say, "Don't tell me, I know, but explain something else." Defense by racing through an interpretation, and distraction.)

When asked the meaning of "going up and down," an item in the dream, he said, "I refuse to tell you. Anyhow it doesn't explain the money." (Refusal and distraction.)

He asked me the meaning of something in the dream and anticipating that I would ask him its meaning, he said, "You know it already, so why waste time." (He wanted a quick interpretation so he could quickly pass to something else—a form of escape.)

Also in XIII, in association to "skushy fatty bulldogs," I repeated,

"Two big skushy fatty things." He said, "Tits, but it's dumb. Why sic them after me? Anyhow why say such vulgar things? Let's get it over with. Anyhow I don't think it's right. I disagree." (Denial of meaning— "It's dumb." Projection—"Why say such vulgar things." Escape— "Let's get it over with.")

At another point in the same session, he denied his own interpretation —the horn of a rhinoceros as penis. He said, "Where did it get blue from? I got you caught there. How do you know it's all true? You got no proof for any of this." (Attack by projection, and denial of meaning.) Of another dream, "The whole thing's nuts. That's clear. Let's get to the other dream." (Escape by racing to the next thing.)

(He was interested in unravelling dream and treated it like a mystery story.) He was very challenging. Said, "Now what does that mean? You're stuck." I admitted it, and then he proceeded good-naturedly. Note the frequent defense—"That wasn't my idea. That was yours."

In XVI, he said after I interpreted his dream, "There, you're stuck again." (Defense by distraction and attack—competition with me.)

XX. "If you try to take away my imagination, I'll stop coming."

In XXI, he said he had three dreams and he solved them all himself. (Competition.)

In XXII, before associating a woman in a dream as his mother, he said, "I know what you're thinking of." (Projection.) Again he associated, and said, "It's nuts."

In XXIV, after my interpretation, he said, "Well, you got that right for once."

In XXVII, he said to me, before making an association, "I can always tell what you're thinking of." Regarding thoughts about birth, he said, "Don't think I think about these things all the time—just once a year." (Defense of rare event.) Then he said, "I know what you're thinking of. Want to guess?" It was coitus with mother. Then he made a face at me; asked, "What time is it?" Then said, "So what! So what! Oh yes, oh yes, oh yes." Regarding masturbation, "I do it once in a blue moon." He picked up a game and looked at it. (Distraction.)

In XXIX the SR experiments were made. After XXX, there was much dropping of defenses, but in XXXII he said, "What do the pictures mean? You're the genius around here." (Competition.)

In XXXIII he said, "I made up my mind never to agree with you." When I replied that he hated to think I could help him, he said, "I know it. I'm the only one who can help me."

In his defense against acceptance of the meaning of the phantasies, whether of dreams or drawings, the patterns were again chiefly in the form of escapes (10 instances) and denials (8 instances). A type of rivalry with the therapist was another frequent form.

The escape patterns were simple indications of a wish to leave, in three instances ("What time is it?" "It's time to go") and "distraction" in two instances (attempting to get my attention away from important to what he regarded as irrelevant material). A more subtle form consisted in "racing" through the "dangerous" associations, landing onto "safe" or presumably innocuous associations (4 instances). After an obvious Oedipus dream, he said quickly, "I know the whole thing. The woman was my mother, and the man was my father, and I wanted to marry her so she turned against me, but what has the money got to do with it?" At another point he made this pattern more obvious by saying, "Let's get it over with." This method was used again when he said about a symbolic sexual act, "You know it already, so why waste time?" and again, when he said quickly of a dream, "That's clear, let's get to the other dream." This "chase" through the dangerous meanings is quite like the escapes in the play, and the frequent running away episodes in the dream.

His denials (8 instances) that the dreams or drawings had meanings which I, or even he, attributed to them, were chiefly in the form of arguing. He would argue that a dream couldn't mean anything because of its inconsistencies, and after an interpretation was made with his help, he would argue that I couldn't explain this or that detail. He would deny meanings by saying they were "flukey" or "dumb" or "nuts." He would even deny his own interpretation by trying to prove it was illogical because of a detail; for example, in the instance of the horn of rhinoceros as a penis. At one point, he said, "I made up my mind never to agree with you."

In spite of the arguments employed to disprove the point that interpretations had any relation to his own feelings or experience, he actually refused to give associations on only one occasion. This occurred in association to the phrase "going up and down" (Dream 6). It clearly had sexual meaning. He said, "I refuse to tell you."

In his arguments he would challenge my ability to solve the meaning of his dreams or drawings. On other occasions his rivalry with me was quite obvious. All the activities in which he challenged my ability or was clearly competitive were classified under rivalry. They occurred frequently (on more than 12 occasions). For example, when asked to see what his drawings had to do with his own experience in life, he said, "Bet you can't. Bet you can't. Bet you can't." He would try to make me guess what his associations were, saying, "I'll give you three guesses." He would challenge me—"You're stuck, you can't explain" this or that. Sometimes he would say, "I know exactly what you're thinking," "Well, you got it right for once. What do the pictures mean, you're the genius around here." On one occasion he said in a competitive manner, "I had three dreams and I solved them all myself."

The competitive relationship with me appeared to serve a number of functions. Besides fulfilling a competitive role, as with his sister, father, and school mates, it served as a defense against anxiety by putting me in the weaker position. He was the one who knew, I was the one who had to guess. He could then decide if I was right. He tried to reverse our roles so that I could not be dangerous to him. Since the main reliance of his aggression was the argument, he held tight to his intellectual weapon, afraid to release it.

The rivalry served also as a distraction. By turning the interpretive phase of the therapy into a contest, he could escape into a kind of play in which we matched wits. Actually it was a play, since the rivalry was a pattern that never really hindered the process of interpretation. It became a kind of ritualistic pattern, preceding his acceptance of the meaning of his phantasy, or a request for my help in solving the problem. The pattern was modified as time went on, but some elements of it were maintained more or less throughout.

Defense patterns in the form of projections occurred in five instances. He criticized me for an interpretation he made himself. After referring to breasts as "tits," he asked me why I said such vulgar things. On those occasions in which he said, "I know what you are thinking," the defense was evidently a projection, if also a form of rivalry.

The "defense of universality" occurred only once. After it appeared obvious that his description of his wife in a dream tallied with his mother, he denied the resemblance, then admitted it, and asked "Do other boys have dreams like this?"

A defense of the opposite variety occurred also on one occasion—the "defense of rareness," a common form in children. He evidently felt guilty in describing the process of birth and said, "Don't think I think about these things all the time—just once a year." (Defense of rarity is similar to the defense of "long ago.")

STORIES AND DAYDREAMS

In his day phantasies there were baseball and football teams in which he remembered the names and characteristics of each player. He phantasied also battles of imaginary nations with names of generals, cities, etc. Usually the names of people were thin disguises for real names. Such phantasies went on for years and occurred at any odd moment during the day. They were responsible for one severe accident in which he was run over by a taxicab, suffered a skull injury, and luckily made a full recovery. The day phantasies dealt chiefly with the subject of rivalry, and involved Oedipus rivalry at the time of treatment.

At the age of 12, he had a serial story in his phantasy concerning a battle between the countries of Kesk and Zelzibar. Movran was the only city of Zelzibar. Whoever captured it would win the battle. Zelzibar was owned by a man named Rocky Smith. To quote the patient, "The people were wild. He couldn't make them do any work so the country couldn't progress. So after he revolutioned, he gave his country to the other country so he could be ruled and protected, although the other country would get a lot of money out of it." Other countries wanted to rule Zelzibar, countries called Young and Inton. One country got into Zelzibar by tunneling through its mountains. He said, "This war lasted two weeks in my imagination—a record!"

Further details had to do with war strategy. The names were definitely related to friends and family and carried through the same plots as in his drawings and dreams.

He wrote numerous stories. They concerned detectives and criminals and boxers. He wrote poems about crimes and similar topics.

RORSCHACH TEST

A formal study of the Rorschach test will not be presented. The responses are recorded for those who wish to study them. They indicate definite evidence of anxiety in an intelligent boy who is introverted and has a rich and very active imagination. The responses seem to confirm especially the content of the drawings. Evidence of anxiety was seen in the black-white and space responses (six)—chiefly chasms, steep rocks and cliffs. There was color shock to Plate IX, followed by response of "rocky chasm."

Rorschach Test. Time: 21 minutes. Age of patient: 11 years, 11 months.

I 1) Two people holding hands (W, except central portion.)
   2) A little kid between them (lower $\frac{2}{3}$ central area.)
II 1) Two people wearing masks, their hands together. They are kneeling down. (W)
   Pause. Encouraged.
   2) (Reversed) Like a cave or chasm and the steep rocks. (W)
III 1) Two people holding a pail.
   2) A forest. (Negro heads are trees, and light gray is the rest of the forest.)
IV 1) (Side) A dead butterfly.
   (Several urns.)
   2) A big animal. Midpart is the tail.
V 1) (Immediately to side position, then straight) Butterfly.
   2) (Reversed) A person standing on his hands. (Mid section.)
VI 1) A skeleton (top $\frac{1}{3}$), and
   2) Left-over skin of a dead animal. (W)
   Pause. Encouraged.
   3) and 4) (Reversed) A chasm and the sun. It looks like a face and the cliffs. (Lower mid streaks, eggs and lateral extension of them, making the bottom central angle.)
   5) (Side) A lake, trees and at the rim and sky all reflected in the lake. (Trees on rim of lake are the whole central streak; the rest of one side is the lake and the other side is the sky.)
VII It looks like a lot of things.
   1) and 2) Indian children sitting on a rock, each pointing (lateral paw) to something he saw.
   3) and 4) Two rocky mountains and waterfall (clasp) running down. (W)
VIII No pause. 1) A wolf. (Lateral pink)
   2) A lady with a colored dress. She's holding two pet animals. They're climbing up her hand. But she has no head. (W)
   3) (Reversed) Like a seat with nobody in it. (W)

IX 1) and 2) (First long pause, 32".) I see a rocky chasm again. There's the rainbow. (Brown area and space; rainbow is the central prongs.)

   3) and 4) (Side) Two jaws of an animal (medial brown profiles) and fire shooting out of its mouth (gray green stalk). It's a dragon, there's its head (green). (W)

X 1) Two people holding up a pole. You can't see their heads because they're bending back.

   2) (Reversed) A rocky ledge (Pink), and

   3) The blue things are men holding a can with food in it, and

   4) That green thing is a tame bird coming down to eat it (low green). (Later said it was a wild bird and they made it tame.)

   5) Spiders (Lateral blue)

   6) A bug (Lateral gray)

There were five responses with content of frightening aspect: (1) Two people wearing masks. (2) A dead butterfly. (3) Skin of a dead animal. (4) Two jaws of an animal with fire shooting out of its mouth. (5) Men hold a can of food and a bird comes and steals it.

CLINICAL DATA

According to the mother, the patient became a feeding problem several months before his sister's birth. He was then two years and a few months old. He refused food unless the maid or mother helped feed him. Previously he had learned to eat nicely without the help or presence of a grown-up. The difficulty lasted for some months and thereafter he was a finicky eater for several years.

When he first saw his baby sister, he said, "She's cute." There was no evidence of jealousy in the early months. When grown-ups came to visit he brought them to see the baby as though to show her off. Later, when his sister was 7 or 8 months of age and could get at his things, he became very angry. He would hurl blocks at her. The baby had to be guarded from his attacks.

(Note that the so-called SR reaction was evident before the baby was born. The SR reaction is primarily to privation or change in terms of care, affection, attention, or to differences in the appearance or routine of the child's familiar world. One of my patients showed the first untoward reaction before the birth of the next baby when a bassinet was placed in his room. The baby may not be perceived as the object of rivalry, if at all, for months or even years especially when the age difference is but two years. This may be so even when SR reactions are not in evidence until after its birth. Note also that the patient's response to the change preceding the birth of his sister was in the form of regression and, as in the SR play, in relation to feeding.)

According to the written observation of a school teacher who visited the home when the patient was three years old, both parents were "strict," though affectionate. As time went on, however, the father became immersed in business difficulties and left the responsibility of rearing the children almost entirely to the mother. At the time of treatment the parental picture was clearly that of an indulgent father who needed strong persuasion to play with his children or assert occasional authority; and a mother, competent, responsible, worrisome and affectionate, though lax in disciplining her son. Certainly he was allowed the privilege of impudent retort and marked freedom of expression. There were occasional tense scenes in which the mother spoke to him severely. She tried to make him fully aware of his bad manners and lack of consideration for others. These unfair "bawlings," according to his version, were especially reserved for him. When the sister tore her shirt, he said to her, "Because you're the favorite, nothing will happen," and added, "She gets all kinds of credit, her beautiful little curls."

After the late infantile period of primitive jealousy, the relationship to his sister became bossy and competitive. At the beginning of the treatment period (age 11 years 11 months to 12 years 0 months) he expressed his criticism of her and his feelings of jealousy quite freely. He often "dreamed" (daydreamed) of victorious competition with her. At that time evidence of affection also had been apparent for some years. A confidential relationship was established. Toward the end of the treatment he spoke about his affection for her and his protective feelings toward her. He confided in her and asked her advice. Her role to him became increasingly maternal, though verbal spats were still occasionally in evidence.

Careful records of his behavior were made on occasion by his teachers, beginning in the nursery school. At 3 years 4 months, a continuous record of his activities was kept for an hour and a half. The record contained twenty-three instances of activity centering on possession of objects. They were mostly protective retorts—"No, all mine," "Don't touch that," "No, you can't have any of these dishes—mine—all my dishes—can't have any." There were several boasts about possessions; for example, "I've got apples home. Yes, I have, and cookies." He made one attempt to snatch an object from another child.

The same record contained five instances of negativistic behavior. One: A child was playing with a suit case; patient kicked it. Two: A child started walking up steps; patient pushed him. Three: A child showed the teacher a picture and said it was a duck; patient said, "No, that's not a duck." Four: A child said, "Dollie's in there." Patient said, "No dollies." Five: A child said, "Asleep, asleep." Patient said, "No, not asleep."

It was noted that he was shy at first and stood behind a door. "He said, no, automatically, to all suggestions, yet he yielded easily." "His attitude was very negative," yet he made approaches to the children.

After five months (age 3 years 11 months), he became more sociable with children and grown-ups in the nursery school, though he was still considered withdrawn as compared with the others, and negativistic. Descriptions of his negativistic behavior and lack of "integration with the group" feature the school notations up to age 10. When he was nine years old, it was noted that he had "hostile" reactions to teachers, that his violence was chiefly in speech, though he would occasionally bump into a teacher and slap her lightly, as though the gesture was not intended to be taken seriously. It was noted also at this time that when visiting with other children in the toy department of a store, he was visibly frightened when a clown came near. In the period of his improved social relationship, he usually made a close friendship with one child.

Through ages 7, 8 and 9, his vivid imagination and creative phantasy were striking. At age 8, several stories he dictated to his teachers were preserved. The first two deal with SR situations. In the first, two parents decided to have a baby. When the baby was five years old, he went to school. "He did not know any children but he killed lots of teachers." Details of the murders were cited. The children thought the boy was so nice they gave him a choice of anything he wanted. The boy said, "I want some soldiers like as I was a king." They were his army. He was the strongest. John, who became his best friend, was next. The army marched past his home. Then he went into his house and told his parents he would never see them again. He went off with his army to the regular American army to fight the English.

In the second story, a boy, a girl, and their father and mother each fell down the stairs, which were made out of paper. The police came and arrested them all. They were next in prison, starving. Then the patient arrived with his army of 20,000 men. They burned the prison and the poor prisoners escaped by jumping out through holes made by fire. "They hung the police up on a string" and then marched back to New York.

(In terms of the SR situation, the response to the new baby in the first story is to ignore her, and attack the mother. The objects of attack, baby and mother, are changed in the story to children and teachers. The competitive struggle is solved by infantile omnipotence, and the parents are punished by his departure—an exploitation of the escape reaction.

(The SR solution in the second story is an attack on the entire family group. The attack, in which he also is included, changed into an accident and, to make doubly sure no evil intent can be charged against him, the stairs are changed into paper. That is similar to his "it-couldn't-really-happen" defense in the SR play. Then the solution, through infantile omnipotence, takes both a restoring and a destructive form, and he is the hero of both actions. The use of an ally, a best friend, in both, may indicate the affectionate phase of his relationship to his sister. His best friend is put in a safe secondary status. The arrest of the entire family, presumably because they fell down the stairs, indicates that the fall represents a punishable act—an attack. It is a frequent disguise, especially in SR play, though not often followed by punishment. It usually serves its purpose of concealment and averts a penalty. The punishment in relation to food is consistent again with food responses in the actual SR and in the SR play. The unusual method of escape, through holes made by fire, is a birth symbol, judging by similar representations in the treatment sessions. The hanging of the policemen, representing in the usual way an attack on the father, indicates a merging of Oedipus and SR phantasy, as in the SR experiments. In the stories written at the time of treatment, this merging is seen more clearly.)

At the ages of 10 and 11, interest in reading and creative writing were noticed. In contrast, he had no interest in arithmetic. His general behavior was recorded as a see-saw of shrinking and boisterous rude behavior. He was unduly sensitive, though he entered all group activities. He had a "genuine friendship" with one boy in the school. He revealed much interest in world affairs and constantly quoted his father in support of his arguments.

When he was 12, a teacher stated that he showed less evidence of absorption in his imaginary world and less anxiety in his school work. He did his own thinking, read only the best books, wrote many stories and painted pictures of Indians, hunting scenes, and animals tearing into each other. He was very friendly with his teachers; was still sensitive and argumentative.

His relationship to boys, as revealed during treatment, confirmed the observations made by his teachers in the nursery school. There the competitive attitude was manifested in a struggle to exclude all others—to push them away from his possessions and to keep them out of his territory. His negativistic retorts to children were presumably designed to deny that any child besides himself had a right to say anything, or could say anything correctly. At the same time, he was trying to remain in some social relationship, and his bids for friendship gave promise that he would in time make a definite alliance. Up to the period of treatment his relationship with boys followed consistently the history of his relationship with his sister (excepting in the first 7 to 8 months of her life). The stages were: 1. Refusal of any form of social acceptance. 2. Acceptance of the presence of the rival, though at a safe distance. 3. Acceptance of social contact on a competitive basis. 4. Close, loyal friendship with a favorite, though maintaining superior status. At the time of treatment he had not yet developed an easy give-and-take relationship. Friends were still rivals, allies in battle, audiences to applaud his exploits, at times even confidantes, but they were never taken for granted simply as friends.

His negativistic retorts in the nursery were traceable later on as arguments in which he just had to win. They became for some years *a modus vivendi*. When pressed for facts, he used the authority of his father; later, also, of myself. He would tell me about the arguments he had at school and ask for information which would demolish his foes.

In his battle of words, he suffered from the intensity of his feelings. He was able to marshal facts well enough in class debates, but in personal arguments he would become too excited to organize his thoughts. As a result, after the battle, he had many phantasies of the things he might have said. The subjects were anything from baseball to world events. Social and political subjects gradually played a more prominent role.

The strong rivalry relating to possessions that first appeared in response to the baby sister and, later on, in the nursery school, was manifested at the time of treatment in his attitude toward money. He watched every penny, complained about the cost of movies, and thought of various projects for making money. At the same time he was extravagant in purchasing gifts. Naturally there were various other influences that helped shape his attitude toward money; however, the consistency of holding on to possessions starting in the rivalry situation, appeared to be an important factor.

In the SR play his patterns measured against the clinical data in this section show the SR dynamics only in terms of their operation at the time of study. It would be impossible to reconstruct directly from the play material the developmental phases of the SR relationship. The SR play reveals in his case, generally, the play of his aggression. It tells how he handles his hostilities. It reveals the strong aggressive tendencies, the fear of release, the quick escape, and fits well into the pattern described by his teachers of initial attack and compliance. The competitive tendencies and argumentation with recourse to authority are easily implied from the SR play. Furthermore, the play, more than the observation of his behavior, reveals clearly his methods of defense against the anxiety set off by the aggressive impulse.

SUMMARY AND CONCLUSIONS

A study of hostility patterns was made by determining, through a standardized play situation, the act of hostility reduced to its simplest form (the "unit act"). The act represents the child assaulting the baby, the attack being followed by punishing, restoring and self-justifying behavior. The various phases of the act and the deviation from its simple structure were investigated. This involved a study of the impulse, i.e., the phase preceding the release of movement in relation to the object; the self, and deviations in the use of the self as attacker; the aim, and deviations in the aim after release of movement in relation to the object before contact with the object had occurred; the assault, and deviations from that form of attack; the object, and deviations in the use of the object as the target of attack. Besides investigating these phases, all deviations from the usual punishing, restoring, and self-justifying behavior were analyzed.

The particular patterns manifested in the play were found to have special characteristics representing general and individual psychodynamics of hostility. The method of investigation was applied in detail to the SR play of a particular patient. When his responses at the various phases of the hostile acts were classified and analyzed, they revealed a regressive trend to the infantile dependent state, and a strong aggressive impulse with a tendency to quick release of destructive behavior, withheld from execution by an intense fear of punishment. This pattern and others were compared with those obtained by analyzing the patient's life history, dreams, drawings, stories, associations during treatment, and the Rorschach test. The material obtained from each of these sources revealed the same mechanisms, though highlighting different aspects.

The content of the drawings revealed especially the competitive and violent struggle for position, the dangers involved in the battle, triumphant victories including death to the enemy, tragic defeats, helpless states, and even suicide. More than any other form, the drawings made use of animals and landscapes.

The defense patterns used in his dreams, revealed in their manifest content, were especially typical of those in the SR play. In both, escape reactions were featured, punishment was unduly severe, and restoring behavior was absent. Only one defense pattern classified as "denial" occurred in the dreams, an instance in which the death of a rival was changed into "nothing serious." "Denials" occurred four times in the SR play. In his defense against acceptance of the meaning of his phantasies, whether of dreams or drawings, the patterns were as in the SR play, chiefly in the form of escapes and denials.

Including all forms, the escapes were seen as: 1) running away, 2) hiding, 3) disappearing, 4) distracting conversation or play, 5) indication of a wish to leave, 6) racing through "dangerous" to irrelevant associations. The denials were seen as: 1) a denial that the phantasy was part of a real experience, 2) or that it could happen, 3) or had any logic in it, or 4) was even his phantasy.

The rivalry aspects of the SR play appeared also in drawings, dreams, written compositions, and in his relationship with the therapist. The phantasy of direct aggression in the form of assault or murder, appeared in SR plays, dreams, drawings, and compositions. Such phantasy appeared more frequently and intensely in the drawings and written compositions than in the dreams and SR play. On the other hand, direct evidence of regressive behavior and of sexual phantasy appeared in the SR play and dreams alone.

Contrasting his dreams, drawings, and SR play, direct release of hostility was most frequent and intense in the drawings, less in the play, least in the dreams. The reverse order occurs in regard to sexual behavior. The patterns of defense against release of sexual or hostile impulses were relatively more frequent in the play and least in the drawings. Since the patterns of defense may be considered as indices of anxiety, we may conclude that all in all his dreams reflected more anxiety than the other media of phantasy; or, put in other words, more protective devices were utilized in his dreams in the attainment of a goal.

A study of the SR reactions, traced through a series of observations made at home, in the nursery school, and grade school, revealed their various developmental phases: 1. Refusal of any form of social acceptance. 2. Acceptance of the presence of the rival, though at a safe distance. 3. Acceptance of social contact on a competitive basis. 4. Close, loyal friendship with a favorite, though maintaining superior status.

The play showed the SR dynamics only in terms of their operation at the time of study. It revealed the methods of defense against the anxiety set off by the aggressive impulse more clearly than the clinical study. It did not reveal the SR relationship in its genetic or developmental phases.

The method of investigation was especially directed to the study of the hostility patterns. Other patterns were considered, when necessary, since dynamic patterns merge. The study of special dynamics which is, of necessity, a deliberately selective process, was aided by utilizing an experimental method, and tracing through the special dynamics in the real and phantasy life of the patient. The experimental play situation enables a certain precision of method and the possibility of new observations otherwise quite elusive.

3

THE GROUP PROPERTIES DIMENSION

This dimension gives an account of the family's functioning as a sub-group of society in the Past and in the Present, and of what can be predicted about it in the Future.

Of the many elements of the family group functioning in the time sequence of Past, Present and Future, the following have been selected for illustration:

Information in small groups
The family as a field of forces
Family myths
Family roles
Family diagnosis
The family through generations

XII

SOME FACTORS INFLUENCING THE USE OF INFORMATION IN SMALL GROUPS

MARVIN E. SHAW

The family is a small group and most of what is known
about small group functioning applies to the family.
The use of information in small groups is the subject of
the research discussed in this paper.

The effective use of information is essential for efficient group functioning. If group members do not apply to the group task the information which each possesses individually, effective group decisions are not possible. Despite the importance of this problem, relatively little research has been done with a view to isolating the variables which affect the use of information in groups.

Perhaps the most directly related work is that of Maier (1950, 1953). He has shown that a leader who knows the correct solution to a problem is more effective in leading a group to that solution than is a leader who has not been given this information by *E*. He also demonstrated that a discussion leader is more effective when he leads the group to participate in solving the problem than when he tries to "sell" the correct solution to the group (Maier, 1953).

A study by Shevitz (1955) has shown that exclusive possession of expert knowledge about a group problem results in a greater number of attempts to lead, and that the effect of such possession is to secure status within his group for an individual and to differentiate him from other group members. Similarly, it has been shown that a person who has more information related to a problem solves the problem more quickly than group members who have more limited information (Gilchrist, Shaw, & Walker, 1954; Shaw, 1954).

The studies cited above dealt exclusively with the effects of differential

Reprinted from PSYCHOLOGICAL REPORTS, Vol. 8, 1961, pp. 187-198.
© 1961 Southern Universities Press.

possession of information; none attempted to deal with variables related to differential usage of such information. Thus the question of what variables influence the use of information in a group is still open. On the basis of evidence gleaned from these studies, however, and on *a priori* grounds, it seems likely that three classes of variables will be related to the effective use of information in groups: (a) the nature of the information, (b) the personality characteristics of the individual who possesses the information, and (c) the personality characteristics of the other members of the group.

With respect to the first of these, it may be expected that the important factors will be the objective probability that the information leads to correct solutions of problems to which it applies, and the subjective probability (the possessor's confidence) that the information will lead to correct solutions of problems to which it applies. Subjective probability may vary directly with objective probability, but it may be that it will depend upon other characteristics of the situation, e.g., the percentage of decisions which permit the application of the information and lead to correct solutions.

With regard to the characteristics of group members, the possibilities are almost unlimited. Obviously, the ability of the possessor will be of great importance, as well as the abilities of the other group members. In the more strictly personality areas, individual prominence tendencies, attitude toward authority, need for achievement, need for recognition, and the like, are promising candidates.

EXPERIMENT I

The primary purpose of this experiment was to study the effects of objective and subjective probability upon the use of information in small groups. Secondarily, a number of personality characteristics were examined to discover possible relations to information usage.

METHOD

Subjects

The 140 Ss were male students at the Massachusetts Institute of Technology. They were divided into 20 groups of three Ss each and 20 groups of four Ss each. Prior to the experimental session in which he served, each S had taken the Concept Mastery Test (CMT) (Terman & Oden, 1947), the F-scale, and the Individual Prominence (IP) scale (Shaw, 1959).

The group task

The task of the groups was to make a series of binary decisions. On a given trial, a design* similar to the one shown in Fig. 1 was projected on a screen that could be seen by all members of the group. As a group, they were required to choose either "1" or "2". The correct choice was determined by a set of rules which were applied in a hierarchical manner. Rule 1 stated that the number on the right is preferred to the one on the left; Rule 2 that the top number is preferred to the bottom one; and Rule 3 that the number in the direction of the greatest number of open spaces is the preferred one. If all rules can be applied, then Rule 3 gives the correct answer. If only Rules 1 and 2 can be applied, then Rule 2 gives the correct answer. Rule 1 gives the correct answer only if neither Rule 2 nor Rule 3 can be applied. In the example given in Fig. 1, Rule 3 cannot be applied since there are as many open spaces in the direction of "1" as in the direction of "2."

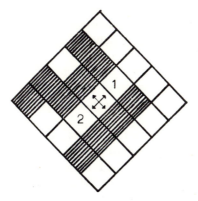

Fig. 1. Example of the five-by-five grid used in connection with the group task.

Experimental design

One person in each group (R) was given one of the three rules without the knowledge of the other group members. On any given trial, the rule given R could either be applied or not, and if it could be applied, it specified either a correct or an incorrect decision.

Four experimental conditions were investigated. In Condition I the rule given R applied to all decisions and always led to the correct decision; in Condition II the rule could be applied to all decisions, but led to the correct one in only 50% of the cases; in Condition III the rule could be applied to only 50% of the decisions, but when it could be applied it always produced the correct decision; and in Condition IV the rule given R could be applied to only 50% of the decisions and when it did apply it indicated the correct decision only 50% of the time.

* This problem was formulated by Mr. Belver Griffiths and suggested to the author by Dr. Alex Bavelas.

Thus the objective probabilities that R knew the correct decision because of his knowledge of one of the three rules were 1.00, .50, and .25 for Conditions I through IV, respectively. On the assumption that the group accepts R's suggestions when his rule applies and operates on a chance basis when it does not, the anticipated percentage of decisions correct would be 100, 50, 75, and 50 for Conditions 1 through IV, respectively. These percentages also hold for R alone; i.e., the corresponding objective probabilities that R will make the correct decision are 1.00, .50, .75, and .50.

Procedure

Five four-person and 5 three-person groups were assigned to each of the four experimental conditions. Ss were brought into the experimental room singly and seated at a round table facing a $6' \times 6'$ projection screen. Before being brought into the experimental room, the person chosen for the R role was given the rule privately and instructed to use it in any way possible to help the group perform well; however, he was not to indicate in any way that he had been given special information by E. Other group members were given no information regarding R's privileged status, and so had no reason to suspect that he differed in any way from others in the group.

When all Ss had been seated, E described the nature of the task and gave an example. The general nature of the rules, including the fact that there were three rules that applied in hierarchical fashion, were also described by E. When he was satisfied that all present understood the task, the first slide was projected on the screen by means of a standard 2×2 Revere projector fitted with a remote control cord. The slide remained on the screen for 2 min. or until the group had reached a decision, whichever was the shorter time. During this period, Ss were encouraged to discuss the decision among themselves freely. When a decision had been reached and recorded, E informed the group as to the correctness of their decision after which the next slide was presented. Each group was required to make 24 decisions.

Records were kept of the number and order of suggestions, the final choice on each trial, and the time required to reach the decision. At the end of the session, all Ss were asked to rate their own satisfaction with the group, their effort relative to the group task, and the amount of their own influence on the final group decision. They were also asked to rank the other group members in order of influence on group decisions. R was asked, in addition, to rate his confidence that the information he possessed would lead to the correct decision, and to estimate the percentage of trials on which he knew the correct answer and the percentage of time the group accepted his suggestion.

RESULTS

In presenting the results we will attempt to answer three general questions: (a) What effect did the variations in the nature of the rule information have upon R's behavior? (b) What effect did these variations have upon group performance? and (c) How were the personality measures related to R's behavior and to group performance? The first two questions relate to the primary purpose of the experiment and the last one to the exploratory phase of the investigation.

R's behavior

The questionnaire rating responses were assigned scores varying from 1 to 5, and these scores were analyzed by analysis of variance techniques. Group size affected R's behavior only with respect to his confidence in the rule which he had been given by E; R had more confidence in the rule ($p < .05$) in the 3-person groups (Mean $= 4.3$) than in the 4-person groups (Mean $= 3.8$). Table 1 gives the mean responses by R to the questionnaire items in the four information conditions with the group size classification omitted. In general, the results agree with common-sense expectations. R had more confidence in the rule ($p < .001$), was better satisfied ($p < .05$), and perceived that he had more influence on the group decision ($p < .001$) when his information always gave the correct decision if it could be applied than when it was correct only 50% of the time. Percentage of time he thought he knew the correct answer and percentage of time he perceived the group as agreeing with his opinion were influenced by both variations in rule application and rule validity ($p < .05$ and $p < .001$, respectively, for both variables). These percentages corresponded fairly closely to actual group performance scores. Information conditions had no effect upon R's rated effort.

TABLE 1

QUESTIONNAIRE RESPONSES BY R IN THE FOUR INFORMATION CONDITIONS

Rule Application:	100%		50%	
Rule Validity:	100%	50%	100%	50%
Confidence in rule	4 9	3.4	4.7	3.4
Satisfaction	4.5	3.4	3.7	3.7
Effort	3.7	3.5	3.8	3.2
Influence	3.9	3.2	3.9	3.0
% knew answer	97.5	52.5	70.0	50.0
% group agreed	90.0	62.5	72.5	65.0

Relative to the average group member, R rated his satisfaction higher only in Condition I ($p < .05$). He perceived himself as having more influence on the group decision than did the average member in both Conditions I and III ($p < .05$), i.e., when his rule was always correct.

During the decision-making process, R did not behave markedly differently from others in the group. His position in the speaking order was not significantly different from chance, nor did he make more suggestions than others in the group. According to observations by E, his contribution to the group decision was unique only in that he suggested the decision required by his rule whenever it could be applied to the task.

Group performance

Group size influenced group performance only with respect to total suggestions by the group; as would be expected, four persons offered more suggestions than did three persons ($p < .001$). In the presentation of means which follows, the group size classification has been ignored.

Table 2 gives the means for percentage of decisions correct in each of the information conditions, and Table 3 gives the results of the analysis of variance applied to these scores. As can be seen from an examination of these tables, both variations in application and validity of R's information were related to group effectiveness. It will be noted also that the percentages of correct decisions correspond very closely to the anticipated values which were based upon the assumption that the group would accept R's suggestion when his rule could be applied and operate at chance level when it could not be applied to the group decision.

TABLE 2

GROUP PERFORMANCE SCORES AS A FUNCTION OF THE NATURE OF R'S INFORMATION

Rule Application:	100%		50%	
Rule Validity:	100%	50%	100%	50%
Mean	92.5	51.7	72.0	54.3
SD	7.1	10.6	6.8	13.8

TABLE 3

ANALYSIS OF VARIANCE OF GROUP PERFORMANCE SCORES FOR THE FOUR INFORMATION CONDITIONS

Source	df	MS	F	p
Rule Application (RA)	1	864.9	7.99	< .01
Rule Validity (RV)	1	8468.1	78.19	< .001
Group Size (S)	1	48.4		
Groups Within	32	108.3		
RA × RV	1	1254.4	11.58	< .01
RA × S	1	28.9		
RV × S	1	52.9		
RA × RV × S	1	1.6		
Total	39			

Mean number of comments by all group members for each of the information conditions is given in Table 4. The significant finding for our question is the significant Rule Application × Rule Validity interaction term ($p < .05$). The group decision required less communication when

R's rule always applied than in other conditions and always gave the correct decision.

TABLE 4

MEAN NUMBER OF COMMENTS PER TRIAL AS A FUNCTION OF
INFORMATION CONDITIONS

Rule Application:	100%		50%	
Rule Validity:	100%	50%	100%	50%
Mean	11.0	19.0	19.1	19.1
SD	7.5	7.8	6.8	8.7

Table 5 shows mean time per decision as a function of the information variations. Time scores were influenced both by variation of rule application ($p < .05$) and by variation of rule validity ($p < .01$). Time required varied inversely with the probability that R's rule would give the correct decision. It is interesting that it required as much time for a decision that was "known" to be correct by R (the applied 50%, correct 100% condition) as for a decision that was strictly a chance proposition. Evidently, R's suggestions were accepted readily by the group only when he was 100% correct!

TABLE 5

MEAN TIME (MIN.) PER DECISION AS A FUNCTION OF INFORMATION CONDITIONS

Rule Application:	100%		50%	
Rule Validity:	100%	50%	100%	50%
Mean	0.73	1.23	1.26	1.49
SD	0.20	0.15	0.15	0.20

Personality and performance

Due to the small number of cases, the findings presented in this section can be considered merely suggestive, at best. For this reason, only crude analyses were undertaken.

It was expected that the personality characteristics both of R and of other group members would be related to R's attempts to use his information and to its effects upon group performance. This means that R's behavior and, hence, its effects on the group, should be determined by his position relative to other group members rather than by his position in the general population. The deviation of R's score on each of the three tests (CMT, F scale, IP scale) from the corresponding mean score of his group was taken as an index of his relative standing in the group. Rank order correlations were computed between this index and measures of R's behavior and estimates of group performance for each of the experimental conditions taken separately. These individual *Rhos* were then averaged to obtain an estimate of the overall relationship.

The CMT is a reasonably good measure of intellectual ability. It is not surprising, therefore, to find that R's CMT index correlated negatively with time to make a decision (average $Rho = -.77$), comments (average $Rho = -.56$), R's rated effort (average $Rho = -.31$), and R's influence rank by others (average $Rho = -.18$); it correlated positively with percentage of total comments made by R (average $Rho = +.40$). Thus the greater R's ability relative to the group, the less time required by the group to make a decision, the fewer comments required by the group (but the greater the proportion made by R), the less effort R felt he expended, and the more influence he was perceived as having on the group decision.

More interesting, perhaps, is the fact that these relationships decreased in strength as R's information led to fewer correct decisions. For example, the correlations between R's CMT index and time to make a decision were $-.90$, $-.65$, $-.17$, and $+.27$ for Conditions I through IV, respectively. Similarly, Rho values for total comments were $-.90$, $-.79$, $+.10$, and $-.05$ for Conditions I through IV, respectively. Thus it appears that R's relative ability has its most pronounced effect in situations in which his information applies most frequently. However, the relationship of his CMT index to group performance was stronger in the conditions in which his information was always correct (average $Rhos$ were $+.73$, $-.40$, $+.71$, and $+.30$ for Conditions I through IV, respectively).

Correlations between R's F index and other measures generally were smaller than corresponding CMT correlations and in the opposite direction. It seems that these relationships are largely accounted for by the negative correlation between intellectual ability and F-scale scores (Cohn, 1952).

The findings relative to R's IP index were generally inconsistent. For example, the correlations between this index and time to make decisions were $-.68$, $-.05$, $+.75$, and $+.20$ for Conditions I through IV, respectively. It was felt that it would be nonsensical to average this set of $Rhos$ since there is no discernible pattern relative to experimental conditions. Relationships between R's IP index and other variables tend to be just as inconsistent. In only one case did a pattern seem to emerge: R's IP index and his rated effort correlated $+.31$, $+.49$, $-.22$, and $-.38$ in the four experimental conditions. One might suppose that the higher R's relative IP the harder he tried when his rule applied to all decisions, whereas the opposite occurred when his information applied to only half the decisions. However, this interpretation stretches the data more than a little.

EXPERIMENT II

The results presented above show clearly that the nature of the information possessed exclusively by one member of a group influences both the possessor's (R's) behavior (ratings, suggestions, etc.) and the performance of the group in making decisions. It is not clear, however, whether these effects on the group's performance are due to group members' acceptance of R's suggestions at all times, or only when he is always correct. A second experiment was designed to determine which of these hypotheses is correct.

Although preliminary work had indicated that little or no learning could be expected during the 24 trials permitted groups, the results of Experiment I indicated that some learning did take place. Therefore, the second experiment also included a control group to determine performance when no group member had been given prior information.

METHOD

The group task and general procedure was the same as in Exp. I. Ss for the second experiment were male undergraduates at the University of Florida. Eight groups of four persons each were run in each of three conditions. Ss were assigned haphazardly to groups and conditions.

The experimental design involved a control and two experimental conditions. In Condition I, R's information could be applied to all decisions and led to the correct decision 75% of the time. The purpose of this condition was to reveal whether the group would accept R's suggestions when these suggestions sometimes failed to lead to the correct decision but were nevertheless better than chance (expected score = 75%). In Condition II, R's information could be applied to $66\frac{2}{3}$% of the decisions and when it did apply it led to the correct decision only $31\frac{1}{4}$% of the time. In this condition, if the group accepts R's suggestions based upon his rule information, the performance of the group should be depressed below chance expectations (expected score = $37\frac{1}{2}$%). Condition III was a control in which no group member had been given any information prior to the experimental session (expected score = 50%).

RESULTS

The results of Exp. II were considered in terms of both R's behavior and group performance.

R's behavior

As in the first experiment, R's behaviour was not significantly different from that of the average group member. He made no more suggestions and rated satisfaction, effort, and influence no higher than did other group members. He rated his confidence in the rule higher in Condition I (Mean = 3.5) than in Condition II (Mean = 3.1) but this difference was not significant. The direction of the difference was the same as that found in Exp. I; i.e., the more frequently the rule gave the correct decision, the greater R's confidence in it.

Group performance

The first finding of interest with respect to group performance was that the control group performed above chance expectations: (Mean per cent correct = 62.5). This suggests that some learning occurred, and means that the objective probabilities should be reconsidered. However, the probabilities based upon this obtained percentage rather than the chance expectation of 50% correct differed only slightly.

The performance scores for the three conditions were significantly different ($p < .05$), the means being 75.5%, 60.4%, and 62.5% for Conditions I through III, respectively. Thus, groups in Condition I (applied 100-correct 75) performed significantly better than did groups in the other two conditions. Those in Condition II (applied $66\frac{2}{3}$-correct $31\frac{1}{4}$) performed no better than did those in Condition III (control).

Groups required fewer comments to make decisions in Condition I than in Condition II ($p < .05$), whereas Conditions II and III did not differ in this respect (means were 8.3, 9.8, and 10.5 for Conditions I through III, respectively). Similarly, mean time per decision was less in Condition I than in other conditions (means were 0.67 min., 1.10 min., and 0.96 min., respectively), although differences were not statistically reliable.

DISCUSSION

The results presented above reveal that the answer to the question regarding which hypothesis is correct is not a simple either-or matter. While it is clearly evident that the group does not accept R's suggestions at all times (if so, the group performance score in Condition II should have been approximately 37% instead of the obtained 60.4%), it is equally clear that it does not reject his suggestions at all times other than when he is 100% correct (if so, the group performance score in Condition I should have been approximately equal to the control's performance of 62.5% rather than the obtained value of 75.5%). Apparently, then, group members accept R's suggestions on some basis other than merely whether or not he is always correct. A tentative explanation for this process is offered in the following section.

GENERAL DISCUSSION

Considering the results from both experiments, there are several interesting relationships worthy of examination. First, we might inquire concerning the relationship between R's confidence in the information he had been given and (a) the objective probability that the information would lead to the correct decision if accepted, and (b) group performance scores. The rank order correlation between R's confidence and objective probability was $+.97$, and that between R's confidence and group performance was +.71. Group performance and objective probability correlated +.80. This suggests that objective probability and subjective probability (confidence) are practically identical and relate closely to group performance. Furthermore, the high positive correlation between the probability that R will suggest the correct decision and the performance of the group indicates that the person who possesses useable information exerts a powerful influence upon group decision-making. How is this accomplished?

In attempting to answer the above question it may be noted that there are two parts of the group which could be affected by the nature of the information possessed by any given member: the information possessor himself and the other group members. It has already been mentioned that an observer was unable to detect any difference in the behavior of R and other group members beyond the simple fact that R suggested the rule answer when the rule applied to the decision. It would appear, then, that the effect occurs among the other group members. Unfortunately the observer was set to look for differences between R and others, rather than for differences between experimental conditions. If such differences existed, they could be identified only by the way they influenced objective behavioral measures. Aside from the differences in ratings of satisfaction, influence, and effort between conditions in which R was always correct and other experimental conditions, the most noticeable differences among conditions were R's estimates of percentage of time the group agreed with his suggestions. As shown in Table 1, these estimates were roughly proportional to the objective probabilities that R's suggestions would be correct. Assuming that R's perceptions of the group's acceptance of his suggestions were accurate and that the group performed as well as the controls on all other trials, performance scores expected in the various experimental conditions were computed. These computed scores correlated +.97 with obtained scores.

If it be accepted that a group member's suggestions will be agreed with by the group in proportion to the validity of such suggestions, the question of how this "probability matching" comes about is still unanswered. It may be that this agreement is artifactual. If problem-solving groups are concerned with eventual 100% success, it follows that their choice distributions should match distributions of correct decisions, as has been suggested in connection with problem solving individuals (Goodnow, 1955). This would mean that the group's decisions (choices) would agree with R's suggestions to the extent that his suggestions agreed with the distribution of correct choices, independently of his influence upon the group process. However, this interpretation does not explain differences in group performance under different experimental conditions.

It seems more likely that subjective probability (confidence) determines how the possessor of information will present his suggestions, which in turn influences how the group responds to him. If so, the procedures followed in the experiments reported here were not sensitive enough to detect these effects. Further research will be required to resolve this issue.

One final point should be mentioned. The greatest discrepancy between expected and obtained scores (discussed above) was in the applied $66\frac{2}{3}\%$-correct $31\frac{1}{4}\%$ situation. In this condition the expected score of 52.1% correct was less than the earned score of 60.4% correct and less than the score of 62.5% correct earned by the control groups. It appears that the group almost completely rejects a member's suggestions when acceptance of them would reduce their performance below chance expectations.

SUMMARY

The purpose of the experiments reported here was to study factors which contribute to the effective use of information in small groups. The general procedure was to provide one group member with exclusive information related to the group task, and observe how this influenced his behavior, his effectiveness in influencing the group, and the group's performance.

In the first experiment, R's information applied to the group task either 100% or 50% of the time, and when it did apply it led to the correct decision either 100% or 50% of the time if accepted by the group. Thus, R's information gave him the correct decision 100%, 50%, 50%, or 25% of the time, depending upon the experimental condition. R's behavior was not markedly different from that of other group members in any of the four conditions; however, he rated his confidence in the information, satisfaction, and perceived influence on the group higher when his information always gave the correct decision than in the other conditions. Group performance scores (percentage of decisions correct) corresponded fairly closely to expectations based upon the assumption that the group would accept R's suggestions when his information applied to the decision and perform at chance level at other times. However, it was noted that the same prediction would obtain if the group accepted R's suggestions only when he was always right and performed at chance levels on other trials. Exp. II attempted to determine which of these two possibilities was the correct one.

The second experiment investigated three experimental conditions: a control condition in which no one had any special information, a condition in which R's information applied to all decisions but led to the correct decision only 75% of the time if accepted, and a condition in which the information applied $66\frac{2}{3}\%$ of the time but led to the correct decision only $31\frac{1}{4}\%$ of the time if accepted by the group. The results suggested that groups do not merely either accept or reject another member's suggestions, but rather accept them in proportion to their correctness. Some possible explanations of this process were given.

REFERENCES

1. COHN, T. S. 1952. Is the F-scale indirect? *J. abnorm. soc. Psychol.*, **47**, 732-739.
2. GILCHRIST, J. C., SHAW, M. E., and WALKER, L. C. 1954. Some effects of unequal distribution of information in a wheel group structure. *J. abnorm. soc. Psychol.*, **49**, 554-556.
3. GOODNOW, J. J. 1955. Determinants of choice-distribution in two-choice situations. *Am. J. Psychol.*, **68**, 106-116.
4. MAIER, N. R. F. 1950. The quality of group decisions as influenced by the discussion leader. *Hum. Relat.*, **3**, 155-174.
5. MAIER, N. R. F. 1953. An experimental test of the effect of training on discussion leadership. *Hum. Relat.*, **6**, 161-173.
6. SHAW, M. E. 1954. Some effects of unequal distribution of information upon group performance in various communication nets. *J. abnorm. soc. Psychol.*, **49**, 547-553.
7. SHAW, M. E. 1959. Some effects of individually prominent behavior upon group effectiveness and member satisfaction. *J. abnorm. soc. Psychol.*, **59**, 382-386.
8. SHEVITZ, R. N. 1955. *Leadership acts: IV. An investigation of the relation between exclusive possession of information and attempts to lead.* Ohio State Univ. Research Foundation, Columbus.
9. TERMAN, L. M., and ODEN, M. H. 1947. *The gifted child grows up*, Vol. IV. *Genetic studies of genius.* Stanford Univ. Press, Stanford, Calif.

XIII

FAMILY STRUCTURE AND
PSYCHIC DEVELOPMENT

JULES HENRY AND SAMUEL WARSON

More attenton has been paid to the individual's intra-psychic processes than to the field of forces in which he stands. The family constitutes a field of forces.

The present effort is a continuation of work begun earlier on systematic elucidation of American culture as it relates to the problem of mental health. An understanding of the relation of culture to mental health must derive from a holistic approach to the problem. Choice of particular factors, such as sexual life or economics, as the point of departure for the understanding of the factors that determine mental health or disease can result only in a particularistic insight. Furthermore, such choice tends to be based on chance, and not on a comprehensive theoretical system. Actually "chance" selections are determined by social events, which bring it about that one aspect of personality should appear important *at the moment*: if it is "the machine" that seals man's fate today, it will be sex tomorrow, and nursing the day after. This is bound to occur where the selection of particular factors as prepotent in personality development derives from "social chance." Hence our proposition is that understanding of the true relation between personality development and culture must include a total, systematic analysis of culture.

Basic Propositions

1. Whatever mechanisms turn out to be dynamic in personality must be conceived of as operating in a *field of forces*. This means that, for

Reprinted from THE AMERICAN JOURNAL OF ORTHOPSYCHIATRY, Vol. 21, No. 1, January 1951, pp. 59-73.

example, the oedipus complex must be conceived as functioning in a *total* situation, and not only with reference to the parents and the child. The oedipus complex is dynamic in a field in which relations between parents and other siblings are forces; in which relations between the other siblings are forces; in which relations between the child and other persons in the home, such as relatives, are forces; and finally, in which society as a whole is a force. All of these bear upon particular children at particular times. Hence understanding of a patient is not possible in terms of one mechanism or set of mechanisms alone. Each one must be referred to the *field*.*

2. The family may be conceived of as a field of forces. It is made up of a complex of interactional systems composed of the individuals in the family. Each one of these systems may, and generally does, have a bearing on the development of personality. The larger the family the larger the number of interactional systems. This relationship may be expressed ideally by the formula $2^n - n - 1$, in which n is the total number of members of the household or family.† This formula tells us that whereas in a family of three, four interrelationships are possible (mother-father, mother-child, father-child, and father-mother and child), in a family of four there are 11 interrelationships, in a family of five there are 26, in a family of six there are 57 such possible relationships and so on. Thus, as the size of the family increases the size of the field and the complexity of the systems increase rapidly. In human society each one of these interactional systems (relationships) has a different emotional quality. The personality of the

---

* This, of course, is a very general scientific problem. It faces us, for example, in our attempt to understand the functioning of *one* hormone, in a system in which many hormonal and other biochemical agents are functioning at the same time. In such situations the scientist is often—and has often been—tempted to reduce the number of variables by overcontrol of the experimental conditions. This leads to oversimplification. Our indebtedness to Kurt Lewin for the concept of "field forces" in psychology will be obvious to students of his work.

† We are indebted to Dr. Thomas L. Downs of the Department of Mathematics of Washington University for help on this problem. It will be recalled that C. R. Carpenter (*A Field Study in Siam of the Behavior and Social Relations of the Gibbon*, Comparative Psychology Monographs, 16: 5, 1940) described the relationship in groups of gibbons by the formula $n(n-1)/2$, the formula for the combinations of n things taken two at a time. This was based on the assumption that infrahuman primate interaction was essentially dyadic. Our formula is based on the fact that human interaction, because of human capacity for manipulation of multidimensional systems, cannot be adequately described by a simple combination formula. Meanwhile the following theoretical consideration must be taken into account: The formula $2^n - n - 1$ does not alone give the total number of possible relationships within even a very small universe (such as a family of six people, for example), for it takes account only of dichotomous systems. Thus, in a universe containing six elements A, B, C, D, E, F, the formula takes account of such systems as A, B; AB, CDEF; ABC, DEF; EF, ABCD, etc., in successive *pairs* of constellations. But such constellations as AB, CD, EF (father and mother as a pair interacting with opposed sibling pairs CD, EF) in which multiple configurations of pairs develop and interact are also possible. In larger universes—larger families—triads, tetrads, etc., will develop and interact. These systems must perforce be added to the ones taken account of by the formula $2^n - n - 1$. The formula to describe this type of configuration, however, has not yet been developed.

individual is conceived by us to be in part the product of these emotionally colored interactional systems, operating through a variety of endopsychic processes.

3. Social structures are relatively permanent systems of interaction or shared activity. In this paper we consider social structure only from the standpoint of interactional systems, leaving the problem of activities for a later study.*

Social structures are of two basic types: 1) *Formal structures.* These have to do with prescribed or juridically determined behavior. The so-called usual type of family in America composed of parents and children is such a structure. It is a relatively permanent complex of interactional systems and its structure and responsibilities are codified in our laws. 2) *Informal structures.* These are relatively permanent but *not* prescribed or juridically supported. In the United States a family consisting of parents, children and grandparents may be relatively permanent, but its structure and responsibilities receive no unitary reflection in law.

In dealing with behavior problems in our culture, these informal structures frequently loom as more important than the formal ones. The formal structure is of importance to the lawyer. It is also of importance to the child, not only because he may live as part of it, but because even though he may never experience a family that embodies the juridical ideal, this ideal may be of significance in forming his attitude toward his own situation. On the other hand, the informal family, the one or ones in which he may actually live, plays a crucial role in shaping his personality.

This introductory paper is concerned with a study of the relationship between family structure in our culture as creating a field of forces, and the development of personality. We discuss one case in detail and attempt some limited generalizations.

The Case of E. N.

E. N. is a girl of eight, the older of two sisters, living with her mother, father, sister and maternal grandmother. She was referred because of tongue sucking. She began sucking her lower lip at three months, later pieces of cloth, food, her thumb, and finally her tongue. Many attempts had been made to stop the sucking; the most recent was an orthodontic appliance. This was unsuccessful and the patient developed a bloody vaginal discharge which her pediatrician said was due to masturbation. The younger sister, age 3, is a persistent thumb sucker, the mother bites hangnails and the maternal uncle is a persistent nail biter.

Although pregnancy and delivery were uneventful, the puerperium was

---

* Activities that belong within the category of structure, but are not clearly interactional systems, are, for example, the prescribed division of labor, as between males and females in some societies; the patterns of restraints, responsibilities, rewards, punishments, etc. These are, in many cases, highly rigid and juridically supported. Hence they rightly belong within the category of "social structure."

complicated by the development of a severe breast infection in the mother and impetigo in the patient. The mother was very ill and unable to take care of her child for four months. During this period the patient was cared for by the grandmother and the grandmother's maid. It was during this time also that there was an episode of colic and the extraneous sucking began. At about one year, after the patient was taken from the bottle, she started screaming at night, was hospitalized for three days, and became markedly withdrawn, with the dropping out of sucking activities for a short time. She was very active and demanding of attention as a small child, and slept poorly except when in the maternal grandmother's room. She was afraid of the dark and strange noises before the age of three, and has had intermittent fears and nightmares since. She is of superior intelligence and made a relatively good school adjustment. Although there were occasional temper tantrums at home, she is well controlled outside and gives the impression of a maturity beyond her years.

The patient's mother is a well-turned-out, youthful-appearing woman with a disarming sophistication. However, lack of emotional maturity was revealed in her attitudes and in her psychosexual development. It became apparent in the treatment situation that the kernel of her personality problems is a hostile dependent relationship to her own mother. Whatever steps toward maturity her first pregnancy may have stimulated (she felt she had enough breast milk for the whole hospital) were probably reversed by the traumatic nature of her post-partum course. She was very ill physically and had a somewhat mutilating breast operation. Following her prolonged separation from the infant she developed a conscious aversion to the child, and avoided the maternal role as much as possible, turning this over to the grandmother. The latter was apparently willing to accept this, although overtly critical of the patient's mother for not taking her share of responsibility in the home. (It is interesting to note, however, that the patient has a similar type of hostile dependent relationship to the grandmother and there is also a close similarity in the grandmother's attitude toward the two.)

The maternal grandfather died of a lingering illness when the mother was seven. Her maternal grandfather (grandmother's father) then assumed responsibility for the family and was quite indulgent with the mother (the patient's mother). The patient's mother has one brother, nine years older, who played the role of an indulgent older brother. The mother has had intermittent "colitis" since the death of her father and has many hypochondriacal preoccupations.

The mother's relationship to the patient has been characterized by excessive pushing of the patient toward independence; hostility provoked by rivalry situations for the father; intolerable of oral activities to the point of using harsh measures to curb them, and guilt after expression of direct hostility, and satisfaction from the patient's exhibitionistic activities.

The father is a moderately successful American business man. While both he and his wife strive to give the impression that he is an "ideal" husband—a good provider, protective, attentive and not demanding—there is abundant evidence of emotional immaturity in all of his family relationships. He was the youngest child of a large family, was submissive, followed the pattern set by his father and entered the father's business. The father figures in both the mother's* and father's families were aggressive, successful, domineering and "patriarchal." The patient's father does not have close relationships with his siblings except in the family business and here the relationships are overtly hostile and dependent. He became interested in the mother when they were in school together and never lost his adolescent romantic approach to her.† He was quite content to move in with the mother-in-law and did not even assume much financial responsibility for the home until this was forced on him by her. He shares his wife's feelings toward her mother, but is more overt in the expression of hostility and more concealed in his dependency.

The motivation for children has never become clear except in its social aspects ("the thing to do"). The children were planned for and the fact that they were both daughters was supposedly acceptable and even desired by the mother. The father has had little active interest in or direct contact with the children and has complied in his wife's attitudes toward them. The seductive nature of his relationship to the patient is evidenced by his interpreting a casual observation by the pediatrician, that she seemed inhibited sexually, as advice to expose himself to her. This he did during the course of treatment by inviting her to have a shower with him. Sadistic feeling was shown on another occasion during the treatment when the father stripped the patient and beat her with a belt. This was on the mother's instigation after the patient had expressed her hostility to the mother more directly.‡

Comparatively little is known of the younger sister. Both parents initially described her as a much more satisfying child, and only later brought out symptoms of fear, enuresis and thumb-sucking. In play activities the patient reveals concern about parental sexual activities also. She substitutes herself for her mother and fantasies death and destruction as the consequence of such activities. Meanwhile confusion about the mother figure was illustrated in the Thematic Apperception Test, where mother and grandmother were interchanged. Her conception of the role of her father is interchangeable with that of a boy friend, and this too has substance in the reality situation.

The grandmother is always described in terms of her good looks, and is well preserved for a woman of 70. She sang on the stage in her youth,

---

    * Bearing in mind that in the mother's family the father figure was the patient's great-grandfather, the mother's grandfather.

    † We are aware that this is a characteristic American sex attitude: the husband should forever remain the boy lover.

    ‡ These acts may have been stimulated because the child was under the care of a male therapist.

and was allegedly a person of great talent and beauty. There was apparently considerable rivalry between her and her sister. The grandmother lived in her father's home after the death of her husband, and never became reconciled to his remarriage after the death of her mother. Although the grandmother was supposedly close to her daughter (patient's mother) the latter preferred the aunt as a confidante. The grandmother exerted a powerful influence on her daughter's choice of husband, and the daughter was jealous because of her husband's interest in the grandmother. (He was apparently seductive with the grandmother initially.) The grandmother functions as housekeeper and baby sitter and is critical of both parents for their failure to take sufficient responsibility in the home and for engaging in many extracurricular activities, which, incidentally, exclude her. She prefers the patient to her sister and attempts to be as controlling with her as with her daughter.

Thus far we present the case history as the traditional constellation of child, mother and father, in terms of behavior patterns and emotional relationships. These have their being, however, in a field of forces created by interactional systems within the family, and which have a peculiar character of their own. They generate a complex of external forces which in their turn enter into and complicate the working out of the basic personality problems of the individuals in the family. On the other hand, these systems are, in great part, the product of the very personality problems the parents and the maternal grandmother bring to the family organization. *Thus the very forces* (personality needs of the parents and grandmother) *that create the peculiar interactional systems we shall analyze act in their turn to complicate the solution of personality problems, and give them a new quality.*

Interactional Systems in the N Family

Since guidance work is child-centered our analysis of the interactional systems will be done from the point of view of the patient, E. This child lives in contact with five major interactional systems,* which we shall call families. The *first* is that of her mother and father without the patient. The mother and father love to go off together and leave the children alone with the grandmother (MM). Thus the record states:

1. Mrs. N fairly glowed as she told of her vacation with father . . . during the first week of August. The two youngsters remained home with the grandmother and the maid.

2. Mother feels that she and father are young† and they should get away from the youngsters now and then.

---

* The formula $2^n - n - 1$ tells us that a considerably larger number of actual interactional systems exist here. For the purpose of this paper we discuss only the five which we consider relevant to our thesis at this point.

† The theme of "youth and beauty" runs like a refrain through the verbalizations of the mother. This characteristic folk attitude of contemporary America is closely related

The presence of the MM in the home permits the M and F to yield to their centrifugal tendencies and fly from the children into their own paradise of youth—without children. This flight is made possible by the existence of the *second* family, that of the MM alone with the children; and this, in turn, has been made possible because of the peculiar role of the MM. The case record gives the following picture of her position in the home:

1. Mother spoke of the children's fondness for MM and admitted that this causes some difficulty because the children look to MM for direction. The children never pay any attention to the maid but will obey the MM. . . . MM does not go out a greal deal . . . just likes to stay home. Mother is out of the home a great deal, taking part in activities. . . .*

2. MM has always sort of run things, the mother said.

This is a vicious cycle, for dominance of MM in the home leads to loss of mother's interest in the home which leads to further dominance of MM, with ensuing further loss of interest by mother. This cycle goes its way regardless of whether we start with the dominance of the MM or the lack of interest of the mother.

The *third* family includes the patient, her sister, and their mother and father. It comes into existence only on those occasions when the four (M, F, children) go out together without the grandmother. That the patient recognizes the existence of such a family constellation appears from her doll play and conversation, for she makes efforts specifically to exclude the grandmother. This third family is in part a reaction to guilt, for it is largely in their efforts to "make things up" to the children for their flights into family I that family III is created by the parents. Thus the mother states:

Mother and father felt very bad about going away on a vacation and leaving the children at home. Mother saw other children at the resort and thought how nice it would be to have the youngsters there. *Then she knew she was just kidding herself* because she and father enjoyed themselves alone. Mother feels that she and father are young and they should get away from the youngsters now and then. She and father decided they would make it up to the youngsters by doing many nice things for them on their return home. . . . Since they have been home they have taken the children to various places to make up to them. Mother does not think she will ever go on another vacation again without the children; *it is really not the thing to do.*† Throughout this interview the mother emphasized how much she

to the other American attitude, "Let us, oh love, be off alone (without the children) so we can be young again and drink of love."

* Thus this middle-class woman finds in the class criterion of conspicuous leisure the channel through which she can escape, with an appearance of "legitimacy," from her unwanted family. In her demonstration of leisure, as well as in her habitually "lacquered" appearance, this mother is an embodiment of Veblen's *Theory of the Leisure Class.*

† Thus folk attitude, while glorifying eternal youth and romantic love-escape from children, wags a finger when it happens, saying "Where are thy children, sinner?"

was doing for and with her daughter, the patient. Thus the third family springs in part from parental guilt at not having been a proper parent, rather than from a full-hearted union in love with the children.

The patient, however, while ministered to more by the grandmother than by the mother, is hostile to her, and wants to be rid of her. The patient's play in therapy illustrates this:

1. In playing house the two girls were given separate beds in another bedroom, and the grandmother was put to bed in the attic, with some spare furniture.

2. In placing the dolls in their sleeping position the patient showed great indecision as to where the grandmother should sleep, associated with some annoyance, which the therapist commented on, saying that grandmothers can be a nuisance sometimes, to which the patient agreed quite heartily. Then the little girl began to cry for her mommy, but the grandmother went to comfort her. But the little girl was almost inconsolable. . . . The grandmother complained about all the noise . . . (later in the same session). Two of the horse dolls . . . turned into robbers who roamed through the house and did immense destruction, but only after the mother had left . . . leaving the grandmother and the two children.

The *fourth* family constellation includes grandmother, mother, father and children. This is the constellation in which interaction is fiercest, where the play of forces is most intense. The patient projected this situation in doll play:

The father, mother and grandmother were placed in chairs. The father was talking to the grandmother; the mother asked what they were talking about and walked over and scolded the father. He went to bed. The older girl came in and whispered something to the grandmother. The mother wanted to know and was grudgingly told. Then the father from upstairs wanted to know what was going on, and was somewhat rebuffed. Then the little girl came down and whispered to the grandmother that the older girl had spent $50 on a pair of shoes.

It is clear from this that the patient has detected that everyone in the family functions in situations that at one time or another exclude her. The complex of multiple families does not provide the basis for *shared social experience*. Hence *each person becomes prey to the forces that attack all.*

One more example will illustrate more fully the dynamics of this family.

Father said that grandmother is an upsetting factor in the home. She is extremely fond of patient and sometimes tries to interfere when patient is reprimanded. . . . Father then said that grandmother is upsetting to mother. She has discontinued all her friendships and goes around only with grandmother's friends. Mother then feels guilty if she goes somewhere in the afternoon without grandmother. Grandmother will stay home and take care of the children and fix dinner, which isn't necessary since the family has a maid. Grandmother throws this up to mother . . . which often results in mother's being in tears, with father and child being in the middle. . . . Grandmother wants the house neat all the time and puts some pressure on mother about this. . . .

The next problem is that of the *fifth* family. It includes only the grandmother, the grandmother's sister, the mother and the mother's brother. This family exists side by side with, and in many respects definitely apart from, the other families. Even when it is not actualized in behavior its psychological persistence has a dynamic power. That is to say, even when no overt interaction takes place between the members, the material existence* of this family can have an effect on the behaviour of the members and those in contact with them. These four people have a pattern of interaction, a body of shared experiences and understandings that is not part of the regular interactional systems of the other families. They have lived many years together, and still visit, correspond and inter-act in such a way as to specifically exclude the father and the children. For example, it is the mother's brother who *really* understands how the mother feels about the grandmother; it is the mother's brother and the grandmother's sister who commune and share burdens when the grand-mother becomes ill. It is the grandmother to whom the mother reads sections of a book about a homosexual. Finally, there is the desperate hostility-dependence relationship between the grandmother and the mother, whose tension pervades the mother's entire existence. Energies and affections the mother devotes to this family (of brother, grandmother and grandmother's sister) are subtracted from her interest in her children and husband. Thus, although the patient has no direct contact with this family as a whole, and is aloof from its interactional system in a direct sense, it does have an *indirect* effect on her.

The diagram (p. 352) depicts the patient's situation. She is the "center" of five sets of forces radiating from the five interactional systems or "families." She herself is part of families II, III and IV and forms part of their interactional systems. Hence she is *directly* affected by them. Families I and V are, both in different senses, tangential to her, yet she feels their effects with varying degrees of indirectness. The single-headed arrows indicate that the action of the system is upon the child without her participation in it. The double-headed arrows indicate that the system acts on the child, but that she also acts upon it. No system is conceived to be without effect upon the child. The separate yet overlapping character of the circles indicates that although each system has its own pattern of interaction and shared experience that is different from the others all the systems affect one another. Ideally, of course, each circle should be shown

---

* In the light of the influence of dead ancestors in China, of the importance of the "old" ancestry in upper-class American families, and of many instances of persisting attachment to the dead, one needs in some cases to take account of the importance of nonmaterial "presences" as well as material ones.

intersecting *all* the other circles, for system V affects system II through the grandmother; system III affects system V through the mother and so on. A diagram illustrating this could be drawn but it would be too complex.

Effect of the selected interactional systems on the patient

In considering the influence of the various family structures on the personality development of the patient, we note a common factor in the personalities she interacts with most. This is the narcissism of the parents and the grandmother. It is this that makes possible the creation of the constellations we have described, and it is this that gives them their strongly competitive emotional atmosphere.

From a psychodynamic point of view the patient is obviously disturbed by feelings which can be related to the oedipus complex. However, the multiple interactions affect the intensity of the patient's oedipal feelings, her problems in adjusting to them, and in working through this stage of her development. In studying the relationships of these feelings to the various family constellations we observe the following:

Family I. Competition is least marked here because the parents are complementary, and can thus gratify their narcissistic needs. However, the fact that the children are physically excluded by the mother stimulates the patient to a more active relationship to the father.

Family II. In this family the grandmother acts as a mother to the patient. The mother, however, is also a child of the grandmother. Hence mother and patient are now like siblings. In this family the patient finds refuge from the hostility of her mother, and finds support in the grandmother for her own feelings of hostility toward the mother. This will enable her to continue in a rivalry situation with the mother, and thus indefinitely postpone the solution of her oedipus complex.

Family III. This family is probably the most disturbing for the patient in that she can observe the romantic interaction of her parents as lovers rather than as parents, while she is still excluded by the competitiveness of the mother. She seeks relief from the excitation through fantasy and autoerotic activity. The reality situation gives too much substance to her oedipal wishes for these to be successfully repressed as unobtainable.

Family IV. In this family, satisfying social relationships and shared experiences should be at their peak, according to cultural conceptions of the family as a cohesive unit. Nevertheless it is precisely here that the disorganizing force of competition is most marked, and the members, instead of finding satisfaction in it, fly from it into their more gratifying private worlds. The effect of family IV on the patient, therefore, is that instead of finding the resolution of some of her problems in it she is driven rather into isolation and fantasy.

Family V. Here the close and relatively gratifying relationship between

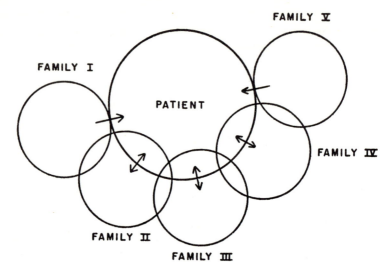

FIG. 1. Diagram illustrating the relationship of the family constellations to the patient and to one another. Family I: M, F. Family II: MM, children. Family III: M, F, children. Family IV: MM, M, F and children. Family V: MM, MM sister, MB, M.

the mother and grandmother has for the patient only the consequence of exclusion from the kind of relationship with a mother figure that would be of help to her in the resolution of oedipal feelings.

To sum up: Merely to look at this case from the standpoint of the eodipus complex leaves unexplored and hence not understood, the enormously complex situation in which it develops and in which the feelings arising from it must be worked out.

Some of the important characteristics of the five family constellations are summarized in Table 1.

Table 1 shows schematically how the constellations function in such a way as to exclude various individuals at different times; to gratify some people and not others. A count of the number of times different individuals appear in each column gives a rough approximation of the state

TABLE 1

INCLUSION-EXCLUSION-GRATIFICATION CONFIGURATION OF THE N FAMILY
EXTENDED ALONG THE MATERNAL LINE*

Family	Included	Excluded	Gratified
I	M and F	MM and children	M and F
II	MM and children	M and F	MM and children
III	M, F and children	MM	M and F
IV	MM, M, F, and children		
V	MM, M, and MB	F and children	MM and M

* The N family means, for purposes of this paper, the individuals related through blood or marriage to the grandmother.

of affairs in the N family: The person who is most often included and gratified is the mother. The persons least gratified are the children. Thus the N family is designed in such a way as to afford the mother the greatest possible gratification. The problem for therapy is: How willing will this mother be to redesign a social configuration that affords her so much gratification? The discovery of the problem of the *social* as distinguished from the *individual* problem is made possible by the analytical method we have employed. Approach to the mother must be not alone in terms of her relationship to her children, but in terms of her whole design for living!

Social and cultural forces as well as personality needs make possible the creation of the constellations we have described and these constellations have helped to make it impossible for the patient to form the identifications that contribute to emotional growth. The differences between representatives of three generations are blotted out by competitiveness arising from narcissistic needs. These can be gratified by the adults to a greater or less degree in the various constellations, but such gratifications are denied the child and as a result her development is blocked.

SUMMARY AND CONCLUSIONS

Evidence has been presented to demonstrate that a household may be described and analyzed as a field of forces whose essential dynamic is derived from systems of interacting persons. These systems may be discovered and counted and their emotional qualities described. In each one of these systems each person in the household functions in a somewhat different way. The exact character of each system is eventually determined by the personality configurations of the individuals. Meanwhile the systems they set up by virtue of their personality configurations react upon them to affect their behavior. The interactional systems operative in complex households are forces that ultimately have an important determining effect on the fate of any endopsychic process. Thus the oedipal conflict, narcissistic needs, or masturbatory fantasies will be worked through not only in terms of parent-child relations, but also in terms of the total field of forces set in motion by the interactional systems that are generated. Hence it is not possible to understand the vicissitudes of child development in terms of simple parent-child or sibling relationships. We must attempt to understand child development in terms of household—or even broader—configurations.

We feel it important to call attention to the relative rigor with which the interactional systems can be determined and counted. This provides a framework of unusual precision within a discipline such as ours, which is relatively imprecise in its determinations. It suggests the possibility of a somewhat more precise approach to the problems of research in psychodynamics. While we recognize the necessary and important role of intuition in interpreting human behavior, we feel at the same time that structural frameworks that give more exact reference fields for analysis can be exceedingly useful as heuristic devices. It is in this sense that we offer this contribution.*

ADDENDUM

Since this paper was written, the January 1950 issue of THE JOURNAL has appeared, containing remarks by Alexander† and Escalona‡ which bear directly on the thesis we have presented. Thus Alexander says, "New knowledge will come from further, more precise study of what may be called the emotional structure of the whole family . . . psychodynamic understanding of the total configuration of the family still wants for further investigations. . . . What we shall need is a kind of chart on which the complex crosscurrents of interpersonal relationship between the different members of the family can be traced in the terms of psychoanalytic dynamics." And Escalona: "The other way of dealing with multiple variables . . . is to think of all the different variables which constitute a given situation as mutually interrelated in such a way as to form a constellation (or pattern, or whole, or gestalt) which will alter the manner in which each of the single variables is related to the phenomenon in question.'

Thus both these scholars foresaw the need for the thing we have attempted in this paper: the more exact description of *family-wide* emotional configurations; and the description of the *total field* of forces of which the given individual is part.

DISCUSSION

BRUNO BETTELHEIM, PH.D. I consider it a privilege to discuss this excellent paper. To my knowledge it is the first application of an interdisciplinary approach, combining social anthropology, gestalt psychology and psychoanalysis, to the problems of a particular patient. Such an approach to the understanding of human behavior seems so fruitful to me that we may expect to see it applied more frequently in the future, and more extensively than it was possible for the authors to do within the time allotted them on this program. It is too bad that they were unable to present more material on their study of the relationship between culture and personality development. I, for one, am looking forward to seeing it presented in much greater detail.

* In general, responsibility for the materials presented here is divided between the authors as follows: Henry, for the interactional analysis and basic propositions; Warson for interpretation of the case history and analysis of the behavior of the patient as referred to the field of forces.

† Franz Alexander in Symposium *Looking Ahead in the Fields of Orthopsychiatric Research*, at the 1949 meetings of the American Orthopsychiatric Association. Am. J. Orthopsychiatry, 20: 1, 1950, p. 77.

‡ S. K. Escalona, *Approaches to a Dynamic Theory of Development*. Round Table, 1949 meetings. Ibid., p. 159.

Like Sir Henry Harcourt-Reilly, the psychiatrist in T. S. Eliot's play, *The Cocktail Party*, the authors felt that

> ... before I treat a patient
> I need to know a good deal more about him
> Than the patient himself can always tell me.
> Indeed, it is often the case that my patients
> Are only pieces of a total situation
> Which I have to explore. The single patient
> Who is ill by himself is rather the exception.

The single patient who is ill by himself is indeed the exception, but to explore the total situation with the patient alone, as the prevalent practice has been in psychoanalysis, is often inadequate for understanding the many strains that originate in the various fields of forces to which the patient is exposed, an understanding which becomes more and more important for helping him with his difficulties as we move from the psychology of the unconscious to that of the ego.

In the case of the child cited by Drs Henry and Warson, as in almost any recent case, the various stresses exercising their impact on the patient had been aggravated by the continuous changes in social mores which have been taking place during the last two generations and which are still going on. In a more stable culture, the various fields of forces in which a child moves—for example, the field of the grandparents or of the parents—are more or less uniform, at least in regard to the cultural mores. Of course, these will always differ with the specific personalities of individual people. But because of the speed with which cultural changes now take place, the demands on the child originating in the fields of the different generations grow less and less compatible. So the child is exposed to the differing if not contradictory mores of grandparents, parents, teachers, all of whom, in addition to the difference in age groups, may have been raised in different cultural settings, such as New England, or the South, or Europe. The child finds himself thrown into an even greater quandary by the forces impinging on him, and the task of integrating all of them into a consistent personality pattern becomes well-nigh impossible.

While it is easy to recognize how a child suffers from having to integrate the pressures originating in five different fields as in the example, I am not sure that we are equally ready to recognize that the child guidance approach, for example, also adds to the number of fields of interaction to which the child is exposed. While it remedies the detriments of the most pressing field, that of the parents, for example, the total situation is also complicated by the addition of new stresses. We must also realize that not even the social worker or the psychiatrist is free of the specific mores of the settings in which he grew up, and particular children are often more responsive to the inner feelings of a therapist than to his overt expression, or the plan of concerted action on which psychiatrist and social worker agree. A psychiatrist, for example, who finds himself in what is now politely called later maturity, may be working as part of a two-man team with a very young social worker. In terms of their personality structures these two may also belong to different cultural fields, and these factors may exercise a disturbing rather than an integrating influence on the child-parent field, unless both are fully aware of the difference between the cultural fields to which they adhere and take it always into account. The need for such an awareness, and for constantly working it through within the therapeutic team, seems to be suggested by this paper, and is further highlighted by a recently published paper on the patients' reactions to stresses originating within the field of the therapists, "Observations on Dissociation as Social Participation," by Stanton and Schwartz (*Psychiatry*, XII: 4, 339-354, 1949).

As may seem natural, I was struck by how closely the findings of Henry and Warson apply to the field of my immediate experience, namely, the work with emotionally disturbed children at the Orthogenic School. In working with these children we often wondered about the relative speed with which we were able to calm down children who had been hyperactive and agitated for years despite various therapeutic efforts. We also wondered about the considerable improvements in other respects which we could often observe within a few weeks after the children's admission to the School. These sudden changes in symptomatic behavior were by no means accompanied by commensurate structural changes in the child's personality. But further study convinced us that sudden changes for the better in symptomatology, unaccompanied as yet by changes in personality, were brought about because at the School we had succeeded in creating a total environment. The School, although different from the old environment of the child—and hence presenting him with a difficult task of adjustment—seemed to have exercised an immediately quieting influence because the child was freed of the impact of the various and often contradictory strains originating in the various fields of forces in which he used to move, such as his home, the school, the group of his peers, the grandparents, and sometimes even the psychiatrist. The very fact that the child was no longer exposed to various fields of forces, that he no longer had to live under their pressure or try to manipulate his personality to conform to emotional demands which were often contradictory, all these exercised a calming influence without too much delay.

Thus the fact that they were now living within a single consistent field of forces had an immediately beneficial impact. Even with the very limited emotional resources of these severely disturbed children, they could now manage to maintain themselves within one particular field of force. Before that, their ability to manage their lives had broken down entirely, when confronted with the task of managing the strains and pressures of several contradictory fields, while they were living in what by tradition we still call a child's home. In view of Drs Henry and Warson's paper perhaps we should no longer call such a conglomeration of pressures converging on one child his home, but would do better to replace the term by saying that the child lives at the center of many fields of forces, where he is a fulcrum of conflicts. It was perhaps these considerations which Freud had in mind when he preferred to treat patients living in a city apart from their families, or at least patients who were not in direct or continuous interaction with the persons closest to them. The present findings thus corroborate Freud's wisdom and intuition.

XIV

FAMILY MYTH AND HOMEOSTASIS

ANTONIO J. FERREIRA

*Each family group has a life of its own and develops its
own myths.*

In the footsteps of Claude Bernard and Cannon, whose emphasis on the
constancy of an internal milieu is well known, Jackson[1] introduced the
concept of "family homeostasis" to denote the observation that the continuous interplay of dynamic forces within the family tends towards the
maintenance of certain forms of equilibrium among family members.
This concept, emphasizing the emotional unity of family relationships,
has been, since, much documented. In fact, in certain circles it has become
acceptable to regard individual symptomatology almost exclusively as a
manifestation of a greater Gestalt: the family. This point of view, apparently shared by an increasingly larger number of therapists and investigators, has markedly changed the direction of psychiatric inquiry and
is being reflected in recent developments in psychotherapy and research.

The purpose of this paper is to investigate some particular aspects of
the family relationship, here to be referred as *family myths*, with a view to
clarify their origin and functional importance as homeostatic mechanisms
in family life. As used here, the term "family myth" refers to a series of
fairly well-integrated beliefs shared by all family members, concerning
each other and their mutual position in the family life, beliefs that go un-
challenged by everyone involved in spite of the reality distortions which
they may conspicuously imply. It should be noticed that although the
family myth is part of the family image, it often differs from the "front"
or social facade that the family as a group attempts to present to outsiders.
Instead the family myth is much a part of the way the family appears to its
members, that is, a part of *the inner image* of the group, an image to which

Reprinted from the ARCHIVES OF GENERAL PSYCHIATRY, Vol. 9, November 1963, pp. 457-463.

all family members contribute and, apparently, strive to preserve. In terms of the family inner image, the family myth refers to the identified roles of its members. It expresses shared convictions about the people and their relationship in the family, convictions to be accepted *a priori* in spite of the flagrant falsification which they may represent. The family myth describes the roles and attributes of family members in their transactions with each other which although false and mirage-like, are accepted by everyone in the family as something sacred and taboo that no one would quite dare to investigate, much less to challenge. The individual family member may know, and often does, that much of that image is false and represents no more than a sort of official party line. But such knowledge, when it exists, is kept so private and concealed that the individual will actually fight against its public revelation, and, by refusing to acknowledge its existence, will do his utmost to keep the family myth intact. For the family myth "explains" the behavior of the individuals in the family while it hides its motives; and often it becomes a formula for actions to be taken at certain defined points in the relationship. The following excerpt illustrates this idea.

Family 1.—The mother in this family constantly "worried" about the daughter's state of health for "she is weak and anemic . . . and anything gets her down . . . she needs a lot of rest . . . gets tired easily." The father, moved by such arguments, was often forced to take off from work to drive the wife and the child (now 16 years old) to the doctor. Though there was no physical evidence of the daughter's weakness, a physician was soon found who went along with the myth. And the inevitable prescription for vitamins or some other pill promptly came to make reasonable everyone's behavior and strengthen the myth. Thus, in its present form, the following sequence of events became typical for this family: Apparently whenever forsaken by the husband, the mother would express preoccupation about the daughter's health, "always so sickly and dependent," and plan an immediate trip to the physician's office. Since in her own and the husband's opinion, the mother was "too nervous to drive," the father, gallantly described as "strong and bothered by nothing . . .," had to risk his job to perform the "duty" of driving the whole family to the doctor. For years the child had accepted well the role of a weak and inferior being, "too young to date, or at any rate, to go to the doctor by herself." "As a matter of fact, my wife already lost all hope that she will ever marry," the father explained, as prelude to stating that he had been contemplating (for time immemorial) to find some extra or better work to supplement the family income and pay the ever increasing doctor's and pharmacy's bills. In this frame of mind psychiatric help had been considered only as a step that they "couldn't afford," not even free of charge, for the father "just couldn't take off from work any more times," the mother was "too nervous to drive," and the daughter was "too young and weak to do that much all by herself." Recently, however, this myth was severely shaken when the daughter unexpectedly announced that she had intentions of going into nurse's training in a not so nearby hospital. The mother immediately got more "nervous." The father took off from work "to drive the wife and daughter to the doctor's" and (again) "to look for a better paying job." And the daughter began fearing that "my mother may be right . . . I don't know if I'll be able to take all of that work . . . particularly the nights . . . I've always tired easily at night . . . my mother says it is foolish for me to even try"; however, "this time I am going to try . . . besides," she added with a fleeting smile, "besides I'll be in a hospital with doctors and people to help me if I get sick or faint or something." Seemingly, this family myth could no longer be maintained, although the mother insisted that one more doctor ought to be consulted: a psychiatrist.

Often, as this family showed, it seems that psychiatric help is sought whenever some important family myth becomes inoperative or at least seriously threatened by developing events. In fact, the rush to a psychiatrist in such situations may constitute a last-ditch attempt to maintain the status quo and re-establish the previous steady state. The family as a whole may then come to expect that the psychiatrist will help them to regain the formula of their relationship, the myth that until now everyone shared and maintained.

The theme of the myth is apparently related to the way in which the family expects "help," psychiatric or otherwise. In this regard it must be observed that the family myth usually emphasizes one of two general themes: (1) the theme of the happiness or (2) the theme of the unhappiness of one or more of the family members. The theme of happiness is apparently aimed at maintaining the status quo by *doing nothing*, i.e., by blocking and obstructing any action (such as psychotherapy) designed to produce changes in the daily living and the relationship; whereas the theme of unhappiness aims instead at *promoting action*, i.e., at doing something that, at least in label, holds the promise of changing, "improving," or "curing" the stated sufferings and ills of the relationship. The distinction between these two general themes seems to have important implications, particularly in terms of the family's motivation for psychotherapy.

Assuming, of course, that the decision to consult a psychiatrist represents an attempt, albeit a last one, to maintain the family homeostasis and regain the steadiness of the relationship, the general *theme of unhappiness* goes with the professed wish that someone will "do something" to help a certain person in distress, usually already identified as the "patient." As a rule, with this theme, the family rejoices at the idea of psychotherapy, that is to say, some action publicly destined to help the "patient." And sometimes, in this way, the procedures of psychotherapy could easily become an integral part of the family myth. For instance, family 1 was attempting to re-establish the myth that the daughter was a weak and sick child who required the constant protection of a mother "unfortunately too nervous" to provide it without the full participation of the "fortunnately strong" father. The psychiatrist was requested, but his attention was directed in advance to an identified "patient" for whom some form of tag or "diagnosis" was undoubtedly expected.

In contrast, the family's *theme of happiness* embodies the plea that the psychiatrist will strengthen the myth that "all is well," and that "there is nothing to worry about." Indeed these families seek the statement that "you don't have any problems to speak of, and your relationship may go on as it has been in the past with no major alteration, one happy and contented family." In this statement, the family hopes to find the necessary ingredients to maintain the status quo; the psychiatric consultation had been sought solely as a means to confirm the "stability" of their relationship and to halt whatever destructive new force or development might have threatened the mythical "bliss" of their life together. The following excerpt illustrates the theme of "happiness" and the role that the psychiatrist may be called upon to play in it.

Family 2.—The father, a 45-year-old engineer, was a "happy man" according to his own description and that of the other family members. He wore a constant smile, wide and grotesque, as if fixed by surgery, like a spasm, reminiscent of Hugo's *l'homme qui rit*. Allegedly, nothing would affect his grinning face, and nothing could alter the optimistic view he had of the present and future of his family. The mother, also in the middle 40's, displayed a marked facial tic which, however, no family member seemed to be able to notice clearly and that she, herself, was ready to explain on the account of being "a bit tired today." The older children, a boy of 15 and a girl of 13, "never had any problems." The psychiatric evaluation came about at the insistence of the school authorities who felt that the youngest boy's frequent absences from classes required further inquiry. Jim (let us call him) was a sad-looking 11-year-old, thin and short for his age, who spoke little but always in a whining tone as if announcing tears that never came. On the surface the school phobia began around the subject of transportation to school. The school bus, according to the mother, came "too early," and the father could not always drive Jim to school without the risk of getting to work "too late." So the mother would have to drive Jim to school, or have him escorted by the older brother or sister. This arrangement worked "very well and very nicely," although on more than a few occasions Jim had to stay home and miss school. Three months after the beginning of classes, however, the situation was altered by Jim's professed refusal to go to school in the morning. He began complaining of morning headaches, of feeling nauseated, and, as the mother put it, "just seemed to have lost a bit of his pep . . . and takes so long even to get dressed . . . as a result, by the time he was ready for school, it would be too late, the bus had long gone, his father had left too, and the other two children had their own things to do. . . ." "Besides," the mother added, "Jim starts crying and looking so sad that I not always have the heart to insist. . . ." To the father this development was no cause for concern, for he remembered that, in his days, he had a little problem like that too although it quickly went away as he became again his "happy self." The family agreed to come for a few sessions of conjoint therapy. During these sessions it was observed that they all seemed to take cues from the father's happy front—all, that is, except Jim whose face, if it correlated with the father's, was in the negative sense of growing in sadness as the father's grew in smiley looks. The father's "happy' disposition was never challenged by anyone. "That's true," the father commented, "I am always happy." "Yes," mother said with not-well-hidden rancor, "he's always smiling, nothing bothers him." "Ya," said the daughter, "Daddy's always happy and cheerful." Although it had become rather obvious that there were things in this family that did not go "well," everyone was enormously reluctant to acknowledge any troubles which might spot the myth of a family nirvana. For instance, the mother's frequent headaches and facial tics were accepted to be only signs of "overwork and nothing else." And the father's coming home and going immediately to bed without saying a word or having dinner was often unnoticed by the family unaware of the fact that he had already arrived. Sexual life had been reduced to "sometimes," and inter-spouse open disagreement to "never." After a few sessions of family therapy, it became quite apparent that this family did not show any inclination to face the many problems they had. Under the supposed leadership of the father, they spend most of the time smiling at each other, disqualifying the rare assertions that one of them might have made, and staring at the therapist with fixed grins as if saying in a sort of nonverbal chorus, "See how happy we are." Despite Jim's sad expression and heavy looks, there could be little doubt that this family was just biding time to quit their ill-fated adventure into a psychiatrist's office. It seemed, therefore, that if some hope of making a dent in this family's pathology was to remain, a more stirring approach ought to be tried and the family myth frontally attacked. So, choosing a time when father had again emphasized his perennial happiness, the therapist gave him a long look and in an assertive, serious tone, wistful and compassionate, stated to his smiling face: "You are a very unhappy man . . . even unhappier than I thought . . . for you even have to hide your un-happiness and disguise it under the mask of a smile and happy-sounding phrases . . . no wonder that often, to me, your smile looks so much more like a squint of pain filled with tears than. . . ." The father's face became profoundly serious. The smile was gone. The mask was off. He did not struggle; he did not argue or even try to answer. For a very heavy second the whole family remained silent and motionless as if transfixed by the therapist's statement. The daughter was the first one to recover and, in a sally against the therapist, stated with increasing conviction and vehemence, "You are wrong about my father and I don't like you any more . . . besides, I like him to smile and be always happy." Glancing at her father she placed her hand on his lap, reassuringly. The father essayed a faint smile that grew a bit larger when the mother joined in. "I do not think you (therapist) are right. My husband has always been a happy person . . . even before we married he had this happy disposition . . . I guess he was born this way . . . some people are, you know. . . ." By this time the father had regained his composure and his smile, "That's true," he said, "I have always been able to see the happy side of things . . . never had any reason to worry or fret about, no problems . . ." The therapist interrupted, "What about Jim's problems?" "Jim does not have any real problems," he answered; and, turning to Jim, he enlarged his steady smile to say, "You are going to start going to school, aren't you?" Jim sank deeper in his chair.

Apparently, as in this family, the myth represents an agreed upon level of compromise from which every family member derives satisfactions, meager perhaps, but not otherwise available. Often the myth becomes the foundation of family life. And it seems that Thomas Mann[2] might have had the family group in mind when he spoke of the myth as "the tireless schema, the pious formula into which life flows when it reproduces its traits out of the unconscious." Thus the myth is supported by all family members who *as a group* are likely to resist any outside attempt to shake or challenge the accepted group image. The situation illustrated by family 2 indicates well what is likely to happen whenever the therapist attempts a frontal attack upon the family myth: The family members are drawn together and, with an unanimity which they rarely display, thrust against the common enemy, *una voce* and with feeling. It is interesting to realize in this regard that, although an individual family member (or members) may be aware of the fantasy nature of a certain aspect of the family inner image, as a member of the group he is quick to adopt a preassigned role and deny the awareness he may otherwise possess. As in H. G. Wells' *The Country of the Blind*—where blindness was at the basis of morality and Bogota's sight made him not a king but a pariah whose "sanity," in the opinion of the local doctors, could only be regained by surgical removal of his eyes—the family myth imposes upon its participants a necessary limitation of insight and awareness. Hence, the family myth modifies the perceptual context of family behavior, as it provides ready-made explanations of the directives and rules that are to govern the relationship. The *economic value* of the family myth is thus apparent. It is indeed an instance of a living cliché, an animated album of family pictures that no one quite dares to erase or throw away, essential as they are to the legitimization and consecration of the ongoing relationship. The subject matter of a family myth may be on the surface focused predominantly on an individual; but the emotional forces that give it cause and maintenance are always of a higher order, that is, involve the whole family system of relationships. With this point of view, a new dimension is added to the classical symptoms of individual psychiatric nosology—the phobia, the compulsion, the obsession, the hysterical attack, the suicidal gesture, and others. Indeed, when considered in terms not of the individual, but of the particular relationship within which they occur, these symptoms become susceptible of a much richer significance and suggest sometimes radically different therapeutic approaches. The following situation illustrates this point.

Family 3.—A "very nervous" young woman sought psychiatric help because she felt about to reach a point where she would be totally incapable of taking care of the house, husband, and two pre-kindergarten children. She was a rather intelligent woman, educated, well read, and sophisticated. Allegedly, many phobias were heavily interfering with her capacities, and she had confined herself to the house to a very great extent. She reported that she was sleeping poorly, had no appetite, and it seemed as if the whole house was about to fall on her. By the time she decided to consult a psychiatrist, she had, of course, been prescribed many pills "in spite of the cost." Her husband, in the middle 30's, was a rather waxy-looking individual, thin and nonassuming, who worked two jobs at once for a total of 16 hours a day in order to maintain the family through the ever increasing medical expense. "Darling," he often said to his wife, whose agitated demeanor frankly contrasted with his over-calm appearance, "if you need psychotherapy then *that* is what you need, the cost won't matter, your health comes first. . . ." He suffered from a gastric ulcer and on more than a few occasions had been advised to seek psychotherapy for himself. However, he considered himself "not so bad as that . . . my wife is the one who needs help." Reportedly their two children were doing all right, although there were indications that they were becoming "a bit nervous." During a psychiatric evaluation of their problems, husband and wife quickly agreed that psychotherapy should not be of the conjoint type; they further agreed that the wife should be the one to go into individual psychotherapy, basing their decision on her flurry of symptoms which seemed, in fact, to be more than necessary justification for such an endeavor. But after a few weeks of individual therapy it became quite apparent that the wife was using therapy in the same way she had used many of her symptoms, i.e., solely as an aggressive gesture against the husband who was thus always kept in a turmoil trying to keep the family going ("the last pharmacy bill was over a hundred dollars"), his two jobs by now indispensable, his ulcer and his run-down appearance and endurance. In this light, it seemed indicated that if the wife was to continue individual therapy, she should either get herself a job to pay for her own therapy or apply for therapy at a public low-fee clinic. However, she refused either idea. And when, at the therapist's insistence, a joint session with the husband was arranged to discuss the over-all situation, she became very insistent that the therapist would prescribe something for her "nerves," for her sleeplessness, for her "fears," and so forth. During the few conjoint sessions that followed, she continued to stress her need for help ("more psychotherapy, or at least some pills to calm me down and let me have a good night's sleep") promptly seconded by her husband's statement that, "Doctor, *she* just can't go on like this." The idea of her going into a state hospital was discussed and also refused on the grounds that "for sure I'd get worse"; and her considerations about a private hospital (it would have played again into her wishes to hit her husband with more medical expenses) were flagrantly beyond their economical reach. In vain the therapist emphasized that her problems and his problems were linked, and needed to be seen as a unit, as a family problem, as a trouble in their relationship and not in her alone. On that, they were most insistent that the therapist had "always been wrong." And the husband would say, "my problems are small and not important . . . if she could recover or be cured there would be little else necessary"; to which the wife would add, most assuredly, "my husband has no problems, it's only me . . . I'm the one who has emotional trouble, not him . . . if I didn't have these things bothering me, my husband would be all right," etc. It was at one of these points that the therapist steered a much different course: With a serious expression, thoughtful and most authoritative, the therapist suddenly announced: "All right, I will prescribe some pills." Both spouses looked very pleased, and for an instant a festive smile bridged husband and wife. The therapist continued: "I will prescribe something which, I am sure, will bring about marked relief. But I will prescribe on one condition: that you will follow my instructions exactly." In solemn silence both spouses agreed. After a brief pause the therapist proceeded: "The way I want these pills to be taken is as follows. . . ." Pointing to the wife, "Every time you feel very nervous . . .," and turning around to point to the husband, "*you* take a pill." Stunned, the husband and the wife went into a burst of laughter, but the therapist's face remained unruffled and serious. "Doctor," the wife finally said, "if we were to do that, my husband would soon be killed with so many pills. . . ." With this comment her laughter grew louder, on a higher register, while the husband could hardly manage a sallow smile that soon dimmed and withered as her merriment continued. The therapist proceeded: "Well, of course, it will be up to you (husband) to decide whether or not you want to take the pill she tells you to take . . . but (to the wife) if he refuses to take the pill, it is likely that your nerves won't improve, and it will be up to you (wife) to insist that he will take the medication for your benefit." And, the therapist concluded: "When it arises, this question of whether or not to take a pill is a matter that you may consider to discuss fully . . . besides (to the husband) the pills are strong, and I recommend that you will not abuse them . . . they could be toxic. . . ." In spite of the couple's attempt to see only humor in the therapist's words, it soon became apparent to them that the recommendation was genuine and that the therapist was ready to make it good with a prescription blank. The laughter subsided. And although they refused the prescription, and further attempted to disqualify the seriousness of the therapist's gesture, it was noticed that, as they departed, they were looking at each other with what appeared to be a new kind of attention. They never sought the therapist's services again, but it was learned that the wife not only did apply for psychotherapy at a public clinic, but also found herself a job while her husband dropped one of his. Reportedly, the phobias, the anxiety, and the sleepless nights decreased or even disappeared; and although she had at times been heard to curse aloud the "heartlessness" of her former therapist, the husband was known to have become less moved by her alleged discomforts and more versatile in his ways of handling family crisis.

Apparently most family myths have their origin in early days of the relationship, i.e., during courtship and the first two or three years of married life, when formulae for "togetherness' are being actively sought and the future of the relationship still looms uncertain. Often times, the birth or the adoption of a child will depend upon formulae such as "a baby will solve marital problems" likely to evolve, later on, into the myth that "we would divorce if it were not for the children. . . ."

The family myth represents nodal, resting points in the relationship. It ascribes roles and prescribes behavior which, in turn, will strengthen and consolidate those roles. Parenthetically we may observe that, in its content, it represents a group departure from reality, a departure that we could call "pathology." But at the same time it constitutes, by its very existence, a fragment of life, a piece of the reality that faces, and thus shapes, the children born into it and the outsiders that brush by.

Seemingly, the family myth is called into play whenever certain tensions reach predetermined thresholds among family members and in some way, real or fantasied, threaten to disrupt ongoing relationships. Then, the family myth functions like the thermostat that is kicked into action by the "temperature" in the family. Like any other homeostatic mechanism, the myth prevents the family system from damaging, perhaps destroying, itself. It has therefore the qualities of any "safety valve," that is, *a survival* value. This is undoubtedly an enormously important function of the family myth and one which must not be overlooked in the course of any form of psychotherapeutic intrusion. For *the family myth is to the relationship what the defense is to the individual.* The myth, like the defense, protects the system against the threat of disintegration and chaos. It tends to maintain and sometimes even to increase the level of organization in the family by establishing patterns that perpetuate themselves with the circularity and self-correction characteristic of any homeostatic mechanism. Like the defense, the family myth represents a sort of compromise among family members, perhaps a way in which every family member derives satisfactions not otherwise available. The defense, in fact, is part of what permits the individual to accept the family myth at face value, that is, without challenge. An important implication is that whenever the myth is shaken by events or circumstances, so are the individual defenses. And conversely, when the individual's defenses are tampered with, so is the system of family myths in which the individual is involved. Thus, to maintain oneself within a given myth, a certain amount of insightlessness is necessary. The struggle to maintain the myth is part of the struggle to maintain the relationship—a relationship that is obviously experienced as vital, and for which, it seems, the child may have no choice in reality, while the parents may have no choice in fantasy. Be that as it may, the circularity of the situation is quite clear. The homeostatic function of the myth imposes the self-reinforcing of the pathology of the individual family members. For instance, a boy (by now in the mid-30's) whose family myth had established that he was, "like mother, dumb and stupid," reminisces in psychotherapy: "I was trying so hard to be what my mother wanted me to be that I actually felt very proud of my dumbness and inability to spell . . . for then she (mother) would laugh at my dumbness, pleased with me, and say that 'I was her son all right,' since, like her, I didn't seem to be able to accomplish much in school or about anything else . . . even today, when in the presence of my parents, I've caught myself trying to behave as if I were dumb!" Another patient makes a similar sort of observation about himself: "In my family it had become generally accepted that I was awkward and uncoordinated . . . and I remember actually bumping myself around the house and behaving clumsily at the table and in the company of my mother's friends as if I were a big chunk of heavy wood . . . my mother used to say that I was too tall, and had no grace at all . . . I well remember exaggerating the swing of my arms and bumping into things, I guess to please my mother and prove her right . . . though somehow she would then always reprimand me for it."

As these examples show, the individual's behavior and the family myth go hand in hand, and the behavior scientist, whether clinically or experimentally inclined, is beginning to appreciate that in many ways the individual and the group (family) are two distinguishable but, in their interreflections, inseparable worlds: the individual as the "all in one," the family as the "one in all." The role that the individual plays is meaningless until and unless viewed in the framework of the relationship. And both points of view, the individual and the relationship, must be kept together, since apparently each represents what the Chinese call a *chien*: a fabled bird with one eye and one wing. Two such birds must unite for flight to be achieved.

REFERENCES

1. JACKSON, D. D. 1957. The question of family homeostasis. *Psychiat. Q.*, **31** (Suppl.), 79-90.
2. MANN, T. 1936. Freud and the future. *Saturday Rev. Lit.*, **14**, 3-4.

XV

CULTURAL STRAIN, FAMILY ROLE PATTERNS, AND INTRAPSYCHIC CONFLICT

JOHN P. SPIEGEL

Each family member has a part to play, assigned to him by the family and its cultural heritage. The given role has potentiality for emotional health or illness.

INTRODUCTION

Considerable evidence has by now accumulated pointing to the intimate relation between individual psychopathology and the interpersonal relations within the family, especially during the crucial, formative years of childhood. At the same time, sociologists and anthropologists have called attention to the great variation in the structure and function of the family in different cultures. These social scientists have also demonstrated that the signs and symptoms of what is called mental health and mental illness vary from society to society, depending upon the cultural orientations of the particular society. What is not known, however, is the way in which variation and conflict in cultural value orientations affect the interpersonal relations within the family from the point of view of harmony and discord. Neither is there any certain knowledge of the connection between discord and harmony in the family and mental health or illness in the family member.

The report which follows presents, in a necessarily schematic way, the tentative findings of this study in the area of cultural value orientations and the value and role conflicts associated with the acculturation process in families, and role conflict in relation to family psychopathology. Family roles are first defined and described.

FAMILY ROLES

For the purposes of the research reported here, a social role is conceived

Original paper. © 1968, John P. Spiegel.

as a concrete pattern of acts structured in accordance with cultural value orientations for the function a person has with his role partners in a social situation. Illustrations will be given of the variation in role structure for the same roles, such as husband and wife, in accordance with varying cultural values. An attempt will also be made to classify all possible inter-personal behaviours in terms of a taxonomy of roles based upon the func-tion of the role. The major divisions of the taxonomic scheme are Formal, Informal, and Fictive Roles. Although these categories are differentiated internally in the scheme, only general illustrations will be given here.

Formal Roles vary on a continuum from more to less general. The more general roles, such as age and sex (old man, young woman), are occupied by all people at all times, and are allocated or distributed among a population on the basis of Ascription. This means merely that no person has much choice or control over these roles. He has to enact them pretty much in accordance with the uniform expectations of his culture. The less general roles, such as occupational or recreational roles, are not subject to such uniform pressures, so that, from the point of view of the culture, a person may or may not take such roles. He may have to take an occupational role, for example, because of economic pressure, but—except under conditions of slavery—he can resign from it, whereas he cannot resign his sex role. Still, if he wishes to take an occupational role, he must go to some trouble to obtain it. Therefore we say that such roles are allocated on the basis of Achievement.

Informal Roles differ from Formal Roles in that they are not so stylized, so visible, and frequently not so easily identified. Although such Formal Roles as Daughter, Chairman and Boy Scout are permitted some latitude and variation in the way they are to be enacted even in the same culture, nevertheless, this latitude is fairly circumscribed. Informal Roles, such as the Fool, the Hero, or the 'Show-off', are much less highly patterned and much more loaded with evaluative attitudes, either positive or nega-tive. They are usually spoken of as character traits; but since they are actually loosely patterned ways of behaving in social situations, they can be treated as roles. This point of view implies that all traits of character—so-called 'character structure'—are acquired through the ordinary prin-ciples of learning and reinforcement. The Informal Roles are learned in childhood and adolescence and are frequently acquired outside of aware-ness, since they are difficult to identify and cannot easily be sorted out through cognitive operations. Since so much of this learning is outside of awareness, it has a compulsive quality. The 'compulsiveness' with which an individual takes his Informal Roles seems paradoxical, because, from the point of view of the culture, there is no need for him to take any of them. For this reason, we say that the Informal Roles are allocated on the basis of Adoption. So far as the rules of society are concerned, the individual may or may not adopt almost any Informal Role.

Fictive Roles are unreal or imaginary and are therefore taken either in jest or in play—as with a child 'playing' Doctor or Nurse—or are the result of a serious defect in reality testing, as in the delusions of a psychotic. Therefore, we say they are allocated on the basis of Assumption, and we sometimes speak of them as Assumed Roles. Because of their function in interpersonal relations, which is that of an avenue of relief from the 'strictness' of reality, the latitude for variation in the way they are patterned is almost unlimited.

In addition to these structural categories, there is one more structural distinction which we have been making and that is the difference between Explicit and Implicit Roles. Explicit Roles occur close to the surface of the interpersonal situation, are easily identified, and are usually acknowledged without too much difficulty by the role partners. For example, a person may say, 'Yes, I know I've been acting like a damn fool,' acknowledging his Informal Role and making it explicit. Implicit Roles tend to occur below the surface of the role transactions, are hidden from the awareness of at least most of the role partners and are acknowledged with difficulty, if at all. Nevertheless, their presence definitely structures the interpersonal situation. The Explicit-Implicit structural variable cuts across all the other structural categories. In other words, any Formal, Informal or Fictive Role may vary on the Explicit-Implicit continuum. It is probably obvious that the unconscious acquisition of Implicit Roles —that is, through learning without awareness—especially when the Implicit Role is incongruous or dysfunctional in the family setting, can contribute significantly to the formation of intrapsychic conflict.

Role Complementarity

As we have said, the structural aspect of roles is based on the various functions which the role provides for in a social situation. Conversely, the functional aspect of roles is dependent upon their structure. This is not circular reasoning, but is based upon a mechanical analogy. Just as gears exist in order to transmit and transform kinetic energy, so the function of gears is based upon their structure—their size, shape, smoothness of interlocking and the like. Just as with gears, the functional adequacy of a role in a social situation is based upon the neatness with which it interlocks with the role of one's partner. Following Parsons,[5] we call this the principle of 'complementarity', and we try to detect those events which establish, maintain or destroy the complementarity. For example, complementarity tends to be destroyed, or markedly reduced, if the value patterning of the roles is so incongruous that they do not fit in with each other.

Role Distortion

'Role Distortion' is composed of two sub-categories and attempts to handle the conflict or discrepancy which has reduced complementarity through a forcible alteration in the roles rather than through a direct confrontation of the origin of the conflict. This results in an avoidance of the underlying conflict rather than a resolution of it. In the first sub-category, called 'Role Induction', the role partners try to induce each other to change their roles in conformity with each other's expectations through a variety of manoeuvres which have only one thing in common—that they circumvent the actual conflict. Such manoeuvres include coercing, coaxing, praising, blaming and masking. If these techniques are successful, a change in the superficial patterning of the role in the direction of increased complementarity occurs, without any change in the underlying incongruity of value orientations or of role commitments. In the second sub-category, called 'Role Dislocation', the role partners attempt to avoid conflict by shifting to each other—or to someone outside the role system—the role which is the seat of conflict. Such exchanges of roles are accomplished through a variety of manoeuvres, often at the implicit level, so that they are extremely difficult to detect at the time they are going on. A large part of psychotherapy consists in detecting who has taken over whose role in the attempt to establish a more congruous relocation or reassignment of the role structure within the family. Relocation cannot take place, however, without the release of anxiety among the family members as the underlying conflict comes to the surface.

THE RESEARCH DESIGN

Three sub-cultural groups were selected in Boston, U.S.A., Irish-Americans, Italian-Americans and 'Old' Americans, from which to choose families for this study. A minor reason for picking these groups was that they existed in abundance in the environs of Boston. The major reason was that they made it possible to contrast the impact of two different versions of the Catholic religion with a Protestant group, representing the dominant religious orientation of the U.S.A. Moreover, it was expected that, because of their variation from the dominant values of the country, Irish-Americans and Italian-Americans would demonstrate, more clearly than would be the case for some other groups, the problems of strain between cultural value orientations in the process of coming to terms with the new environment.

All the families chosen were in the working-class (upper-lower to lower-middle) urban population. There were two reasons for this choice: firstly, they made it possible to hold the class factor constant, so that the variation noted could be said to be predominantly attributable to the ethnic and regional differences; secondly, the effects of upward social mobility as a source of cultural strain could be estimated, and it was expected to obtain evidence for this factor by choosing families which were near the bottom of the class strata but not so far down as to eliminate the possibility of upward striving. The interest in upward mobility was inevitably linked to an interest in the transition between generations. Accordingly, the research design called for Irish-American and Italian-American families, chosen so that the grandparents were born in Southern (Catholic) rural Ireland and in Southern rural Italy, and for 'Old' American families which had been in the United States for at least four generations and were predominantly of Scotch-English stock.

In choosing our families, we divided each of these sub-cultural groups into two sub-groups on the basis of the mental health–mental illness dimension. One-half of all the families selected according to the cultural dimension contained an emotionally disturbed child who had been brought to the out-patient psychiatric clinic at the Children's Medical Center in Boston for diagnosis and treatment. These have been called Group A families. In casual conversation at research meetings they were called 'sick' families, but this was merely a convenience. The second sub-group, Group B families, were chosen on the basis that no family member manifested an overt emotional disturbance. Informally, these were called 'normal' or 'ordinary' families.

Observations have been completed on a sample of 18 families, nine in Group A and nine in Group B. In both these groups three families were Irish-American, three Italian-American and three 'Old' American.

VARIATION IN THE BASIC VALUES OF FAMILY SYSTEMS

In the following discussion it is assumed that the reader is familiar with the essential features of the theory of variation in cultural value orientations as it has been set forth by Florence Kluckhohn[1, 2, 3, 4] in several publications. Therefore, detailed discussion of the theory will be omitted by proceeding directly to its application to a comparison of the modal values of the American Middle-Class family, the Italian Working-Class family, and the Irish Working-Class family.

The configuration of value orientations assigned to the original or native cultures of these three groups are outlined in Table 1. In thinking of these configurations for Italian and Irish families, the reader should bear in mind that these are the value patterns which were observed to be typically brought to the urban environment of the United States from rural Italy and Ireland. They do not, of course, fit every immigrant family from these two countries nor even all those from the same general locale, but a consideration of the variation within a culture can be postponed until the strains arising out of the process of transition to middle-class American values for these families are discussed. At the outset, therefore, we will focus on the goodness of fit and strain in the original value orientations and, at the same time, show how the cultural value orientations are associated with the definition of family role patterns.

In the *American* Middle-Class family, the Individual-Collateral-Lineal

TABLE 1

RELATIONAL ORIENTATION

Orientation	Culture		
	Middle-Class American	Italian-American	Irish-American
Relational	Individual > Collateral > Lineal	Collateral > Lineal > Individual	Lineal > Collateral > Individual
Time	Future > Present > Past	Present > Past > Future	Present > Past > Future (but some indication of an earlier Past > Present > Future)
Man-Nature	Over > Subjugated > With	Subjugated > With > Over	Subjugated > With > Over (doubt about first order here and some doubt that there is a clear-cut first order preference)
Activity	Doing > Being > Being-in-Becoming	Being > Being-in-Becoming > Doing	Being > Being-in-Becoming > Doing
Human Nature	Neutral > Evil > Good shifting from an earlier Evil > Mixed > Good	Mixed Good and Evil predominantly	Most definitely an Evil basic nature with perfectibility desired but problematic

order within the relational orientation is illustrated by the primacy which individualistic goals of each family member have over collective goals in the family.

The autonomy of the husband, wife and children are stressed *vis-à-vis* each other. Each is encouraged to express his feelings and opinions about matters, and, if there is a difference, a majority opinion is solicited to determine the action to be taken. The minority is still vocal in any event, and children are from an early age trained to think, speak and act independently. Husbands and wives co-operate as individuals in running family affairs and in bringing up the children, discussing and arbitrating contested points. The wife, however, is more tied to the collateral family group, while the children are young, than is the husband, and this may make for some strain in their relations, since it does not fit with the egalitarian principle of the same rights for everyone. The individualism requires that the nuclear family live separate from relatives, ready, willing and able to break all ties and move elsewhere if this should be necessary. The amount of independence thus expected of the husband may represent a strain if he should get into difficult financial or personal straits. The second-order collateral position is reserved mainly for recreational roles and crisis situations. Then group goals may take precedence over the individual, lest he be a 'spoil-sport' at a party, or think too much about himself in a crisis. The lineal, hierarchical outlook is in last position, and is neither well understood nor liked. Neither father nor mother should be boss over each other or the children. All should be good companions to each other.

In the *Italian* family, the Collateral-Lineal-Individual ordering is associated with the primacy of the family as a group.

Preservation of the family network is more important than the fate or goals of an individual, and this means the extended family relationships. Individualism (not to be equated with individuality), being in last place, is not well understood and is often feared as showing selfishness, disloyalty, or outright hostility to the family. The children are trained for dependence on family relationships which must be preserved at all costs. Rather than show interest in their opinions, parents tell children in no uncertain terms how they should behave. The second-order lineal position is invoked for critical decisions when the husband becomes the boss and the wife his executive. There is no question about the wife's primary allegiance to home and children, from whom she is seldom parted. She is, in fact, seldom out of the house, and the children are not allowed to roam beyond eyesight or earshot. Travelling from the home is undertaken only for the sake of occasional visiting with relatives or short shopping tours. Marriages are to some extent arranged by the families of the girl and boy concerned. Intense strain is experienced by the spouses if the two families should have a falling out, since the collaterality is bilateral, and neither husband nor wife can claim priority for his or her family.

In the *Irish* family the Lineal-Collateral-Individual pattern is reflected in a strongly hierarchical family structure of dominance and submission in relation to age and sex.

The father is definitely the boss, though he owes subservience to his parents and older relatives if they are still alive. Women are subservient to men in the home, the male members, for example, eating first and being served by the women. Individualism is feared and rejected as showing lack of respect for the authority structure of the family. Collaterality, in second-order position, shows up in the importance put upon the extended family but always in the context of levels of authority. The loss of individual importance is compensated by the help which the individual can expect if he is in trouble, needs a job, etc. from the authorities controlling the family network. However, if this help is not forthcoming—as frequently happens in Ireland due to poor economic and agricultural conditions— then resentment against the system is stimulated. This can either be canalized through emigration—the most frequent solution—or acted out in the role of the typical Irish rebel.

TIME ORIENTATION

With respect to the time orientation, the *American* Middle-Class family is guided by a Future-Present-Past ordering.

Both husband and wife plan far ahead for themselves and their children, hoping that the future will be different from the past—preferably bigger and better. The significance of children is enhanced because youth symbolizes the future, while the ageing is sad because it signifies a running-out of future time. No one wants to be considered old, not even the men, who, though deprived of their wives' advanced cosmetic techniques, nevertheless find ways of appearing youthful. Past time, being in the last position, tends to be ignored. Thus a 'tradition' is considered either quaint or waiting to be replaced with something new, which will undoubtedly be better. History is not interesting in and of itself, but only as it may point the way to the future. Parents pay little attention to their forebears, and their children are not impressed with family lines of descent. Present time, like collaterality for the American Middle-Class family, becomes prominent only in times of crisis and in recreational situations when 'having a good time' means forgetting, temporarily, about the clock, the calendar and the appointment book. Often such forgetting is none too successful without the aid of alcohol, and the 'driven' quality of American family life—the difficulty in relaxing in the present or reminiscing about the past—is one of its principal sources of strain.

In the *Italian* rural family the pattern of orientation to time is Present-Past-Future.

Little change is expected; the past and future are both interpreted in terms of the present. Life is seen as a cycle of familiar events: the seasons, the holidays or fiestas, birth, maturation and death, comedy and tragedy are expected to occur in the same way year in and year out. Therefore there is no need to plan ahead, and children are trained to attune themselves to the natural patterns which always have been and always will be. However, the past is in second-order position, so that for certain purposes, such as biological processes, it is invoked. Ageing, for example, is not considered a mark of decline but of increasing dignity, respect and prestige. Wives age rapidly toward the end of child-bearing, becoming portly and adopting the black garment which signifies that their sexual life is over and that they have something to mourn for—a dead relative, their own youth and beauty and health—and something to claim—the respect, love and consideration of the young. Orientation to the future, which signals preparation for novelty, is ill-understood and regarded as too vague to trouble with. Thus, change of any sort, political, economic or social, is disturbing and likely to be resisted or reinterpreted to fit into what has always been.

In the *Irish* family these orientations to time occurs in the same order, but the constant interpenetration into concrete events of the other value orientations makes for some differences.

There is evidence that, at one time, the past may have been in first-order position. At any rate, although the Irish, like the Italians, do not expect change, they are more likely to invoke the past as sanctioning the present when confronted with the possibility of change. They are also more apt to think back to a time of glory in the past. There are ancestors to be proud of, a history to teach and an ancient language to be relearned. (It is significant that when Mussolini tried to resurrect the glory that was Rome, his efforts met with little success among the Italian rural population.)

Man-nature Orientation

For the man-nature orientation, the *American* Middle-Class pattern, Over-Subjugated-With, indicates the boundless optimism with which all problems are to be attacked.

The first-order position of dominance over the forces of nature governs parents' attitudes toward illness, failure, and fortuitous events in themselves and their children. With enough time and effort (and money!) illness should be cured, failure corrected and bad luck overcome. Nature (or supernature) is seen as something that can be brought around or bought off; the happy ending is to be engineered, the angle found, the gimmick contrived, the know-how located. There is always an expert around the corner. Tragedy ought not to exist, but is given prominence on the front page as a public reminder that we have not yet got complete control. When human control is actually baffled, as with death, then a shift to the second-order subjugated-to-nature is possible. Religious attitudes then determine, but do not quite take up the slack of, the emotional environment of failure. The harmony-with-nature position is little appreciated. Nature is seen as something either to be breached or yielded to, but not as something to be lived with. Thus a strain, felt as guilty responsibility, is experienced by American parents whenever their children become chronically ill and especially when they develop mental illness.

In the *Italian* family, the Subjugated-With-Over positions are consonant with an attitude of near helplessness and dependence toward overwhelming problems.

Fatalism and the tragic attitude take the place of American optimism. Religious rituals and beliefs support the individual in his helplessness in large part. However, the second-order emphasis on the harmony-with-nature position sanctions a shift from religion to magic in certain circumstances. Then the evil eye and other animalistic beliefs bring forth apotropaic practices which reach far back into ancient folk-lore. The mastery-over-nature position is so weak that little understanding of, or confidence in, the use of technical devices or scientific procedures exists.

Although man-nature pattern for the *Irish* family is currently being formulated as similar to the Italian, there is doubt as to the clear-cut first-order preference.

The harmony-with-nature position is so prominent in the rural Irish culture that it appears to function as an alternative to the subjugated position. This prominence is registered as a blurring of distinctions between man and nature, between human actions and animistically conceived (sometimes personified) forces in nature such as the wee folk. This conception of causality favours projection of responsibility for action or, rather, diffusion of responsibility. As a result, family members easily get into violent controversies over who did what, who initiated the action, and who has had to bear the brunt of it. The animistic forces in nature may be responsible for favourable or unfavourable outcomes, just as in Homeric myth Achilles is protected by Athena and killed by Apollo. This blurring of distinctions also creeps into the practice of Catholic ritual and doctrine, although here the weight of the emphasis shifts to the subjugation-to-nature position. At any rate, it seems that the tension between these two positions is correlated with the pronounced tendency among Irish family members to deny personal responsibility and to distort the actual flow of events to such an extent that it is difficult for the outside observer to find out what has actually occurred.

ACTIVITY ORIENTATION

In the activity orientation, the *American* Middle-Class family shows the preference Doing>Being-in-Becoming.

Externally judged performance with accent on accomplishment and achievement is the standard of appraisal for family members in most of their roles. What a person does and what success he has had in doing it applies alike to parents and children. Brothers and sisters are compared with each other on this basis, and also with their age mates at school and in the neighbourhood. Parents compare themselves to other parents from the point of view of their adequacy and competence in bringing up the children. This attitude is, of course, reinforced by the mastery-over-nature position, so that no problems in child-rearing can occur without guilt. The doing preference is so strong that a person is often identified with his occupation, and the first question asked of any newcomer is, 'What does he do?' Being is reserved mainly for recreational roles, when spontaneity and self-expression are the order of the day. Being-in-becoming is regarded as too artistic, impractical or dilettantish to rate high as a personality attribute.

In the *Italian* family Being is in the first-order position, and family members respond to each other primarily in terms of spontaneity, well seasoned with dramatic emphasis.

Behaviour is expressive, emotional and voluble. Anger flares out but is rapidly replaced with tenderness, and sensibilities are not offended by the naked show of feeling. Children, for example, are expected to show violent anger on being controlled, but they are not permitted to be disobedient. Sexuality is always implicit in the contact between the sexes, at whatever age, and is not expected to be controlled so much by the individual. It is rather the collateral group which exerts control, largely by segregation of the sexes and vigilant supervision of all contacts between girls and boys up to marriage. Thus, suppression rather than repression is the mechanism of control of impulse. The second-order position of being-in-becoming is manifested in the strong interest in aesthetic matters—in colour, form, music and kinesthetic experience. The third-order position of doing is associated with a general disinterest in personal achievement, and work for the sake of work. Driving ambition is actually regarded as dangerous unless it can be looked upon as a symbolic achievement of the group, not as an attribute of the individual. Thus, success is permitted to the individual on a representative basis only. Talking about one's personal success and even receiving personal praise (e.g. 'What a beautiful child you have!') are regarded alike as threats to the solidarity of the collateral group and are discouraged.

In the *Irish* family the activity orientation is ordered in the same way but the penetration of the other value orientations makes for some concrete differences.

For example, sexuality as well as other impulses are under the control of the authority structure of the group. In the Italian family impulses can be released if they are undetected, but any member of the collateral system can act as an external control. In the Irish family control has to be exerted by a properly constituted authority. Furthermore, because of the influence of the Evil-and-almost-immutable view of *human nature* which we have not yet discussed, the Irish regard sexuality as much more dangerous than do the Italians, and it is both intensely stimulated and harshly punished. On the other hand, the consumption of alcohol ('a good man's weakness') is not regarded as evil but as convivial. Both impulses are subject to group authoritarian rather than to individual controls, but in the first case with a sadism which favours its clandestine appearance, and, in the second, with a token disapproval which actually encourages its widespread and public use.

HUMAN NATURE ORIENTATION

The human nature orientation is the most complicated of all five orientations to describe, because it is actually a sixfold breakdown. Furthermore, the case is made more complex by the fact that the *American* Middle-Class family is still in a phase of transition from the evil-but-perfectible position of the Puritan heritage to the neutral (neither good nor evil) outlook of contemporary behavioural science. However, for the sake of simplicity, some of this variability is here reduced by describing the interpersonal relations in the American family as if the neutral position were well entrenched, and representative of this group. It should be remembered that this description is merely a hypothesis (as are all the previously mentioned cultural value orientation configurations) which was made on the. basis of a general examination of the culture. Its validity has to be confirmed or refuted on the basis of empirical testing through the use of standardized instruments (such as Florence Kluckhohn *et al.*[4] have used on five cultures in the South-west) and through the detailed study of representative families, which we are now conducting.

The first-order neutral position is expressed in the attitudes of American parents toward their children's misbehaviour.

This is not conceived to be a sign that the child is born evil and has to be taught how to be good. Rather, it is thought to signify that the child is experimenting in a trial and error way, is 'testing the limits' of control, is just showing high spirits, or is temporarily suffering from 'insecurity', or some other interpersonally conceived motive. The idea that the child is essentially neutral at birth, and can become healthy or disturbed as a result of his experiences in the family, adds another contribution to the guilt of the parent if the child fails to measure up. Similarly, the husband and wife will 'tolerate' a great deal of difficult behaviour in each other and in relations outside of the family on the ground that it represents some inner disturbance in equilibrium rather than a basically evil and unaccept-able (nasty or malevolent) impulse. However, the evil-but-perfectible view, whether or not it has moved all the way over to a second-order position, lurks nearby, ever ready to spring into prominence. Strained to the limit of endurance, either through fatigue or prolonged exposure, the parent may suddenly reverse himself and severely condemn behaviour in a child which he has previously accepted with patient and kindly disapproval ('You really shouldn't do that, you know,' becomes 'Cut it out, you nasty little brat'—to be followed by guilt and over-compensatory kindness). The third-order position, that human nature is basically good, is maintained as a theoretical possibility without much substance. Except for the reformer's attitude—that man is born good and becomes evil only as a result of the corrupting influence of society—little credence is given this view in any of the three cultures.

In the *Italian* family the human nature orientation centres on a pre-dominantly mixed (good and evil) position, conceived as subject to some but not too much influence.

Perfectibility is not really expected and is not an issue. Good will show up at some times, evil at others, and one must be constantly prepared for and appreciative of either. It is also considered that they will sort out in different proportions in different people on the basis of inherited propensity. This attitude combines with the collateral basis of impulse control and the subjugated-to-nature orientations to produce a lively appreciation of the possibility of imminent tragedy. An out-break of violence, including homicide, is no surprise, and, while not condoned, neither is it a shock. Considering the large number of children fostered by the collateral system in any one family, it is to be expected that one or two may turn out to be mostly evil, while another may turn out to be mainly good (and therefore destined for the priesthood). No matter how it turns out, the parents are little involved in the outcome. They have either good or bad luck, but that is all.

In the *Irish* family man is conceived to be not only born basically evil, but also capable of little improvement.

However, perfectibility is considered desirable and is wished for, though somewhat wistfully since it is considered to happen so rarely and with so much difficulty. In spite of this (or, perhaps, because of it) it is necessary constantly to stamp out evil, somewhat like Sysiphus, without the expectation that it will do much good. The disposition to evil is intimately connected with sexuality, and this connection extends the Sysiphus analogy. While it is not really possible to stamp out sexuality, it might be better for mankind if it did not exist, and therefore one keeps trying to get rid of it. The more one tries, the more it flourishes. The upshot of all this is a harsh and puritanical family (and religious) emotional en-vironment, relieved only by the ubiquitous comic spirit. Humour substitutes for understanding and acceptance of self and others.

This concludes a thumb-nail sketch of the basic value orientations and the associated role behaviour in the three native cultures studied.

VALUE AND ROLE CONFLICTS ASSOCIATED
WITH THE ACCULTURATION PROCESS

In the foregoing section the value orientations native to rural peasant Italian and Irish families and those characteristic of the American Middle-

Class have been described. When the immigrating family arrives in the U.S.A., it is to the latter set of values that it must adjust, because these are what it means to be an American. The newly arrived family goes through a prolonged period of readjustment and adaption while it is learning how these new values work, what part of them it wishes to adopt, what part of its original set of values it wishes to change. The readjustment is always experienced with some difficulty. In the families studied it was found that the amount of difficulty varied with fortuitous and contingent circumstances—such as the more or less accidental isolation of a particular Italian family from the neighbourhood where most of the other Italians live. However, it also varied with the particular configuration of values (the variation from the modal type) which a family brings to this country. As a result of these two sources of variability interacting with each other, there are great differences in the pace and order of change from family to family. These two factors—differences in the rate and order of change—were found to be closely associated with the degree of interpersonal equilibrium or disequilibrium in the family. Thus they contribute to the distinction between Group A and Group B families.

Despite these elements of variability, there are some general trends which can be discriminated and which distinguish the difficulties in the path of acculturation between the Italian and the Irish families. The difficulties are concerned mainly with the goodness of fit between the modal Italian and Irish values and the American Middle-Class values. For example, simple inspection of Table 1 shows that in four out of the five value orientation categories both the Irish and the Italian families, to conform to the American pattern, have to move from values which are for them in the first-order position to those which are in a third-order position. On the basis of theoretical considerations and also from the empirical experience gained from this study, it can be stated that this is a very difficult shift—much more troublesome than shifting from a third- to a second-order position. This is part of the reason why the *order* of change is so significant to interpersonal equilibrium in the family. A second reason for the importance of order of change is that some orientations are more crucial than others. A third- to first-order shift in the relational orientation for Italian families, for example, is more devastating than a similar shift in the activity orientation. However, we will have to postpone further consideration of the question of order of change until we have examined some of the differential consequences of change in the various categories for Italian and Irish family role structure.

ITALIAN FAMILIES

In discussing the problems incurred in the process of transition for the Italian family, we will consider first the husband-wife roles and then the parent-child roles. In the background at all times will be the more general problem of the alternate cultural definitions of masculinity and femininity in Italian and American society.

Husband-wife roles

Although there are difficulties for both masculine and feminine roles owing to the disjunction between the value positions, in some ways the problems seem more severe and trap-like for the male Italian.

For example, the masculinity of the husband in Italy is signified and supported by the segregation of his domestic roles from his wife's. He does not do women's work. Care of the house, the children and of some household expenses are left to his wife. He works hard to support the evergrowing family, but is not expected to plan for a future career of advancement in a series of jobs. Nor is he expected to be self-reliant and self-controlled for the sake of such ambition. In fact, he rarely discusses his work at home. In addition, there are a whole range of topics which men do not discuss with women because they are women's talk. The masculinity of the male is based not on occupational achievement in the world of men, nor on general verbal and interpersonal skills with women, but on physical action: strength, energy, personal physical attractiveness, and flirtatious interplay which implies that, were it not for the heavy control of the collateral group over his free choice, sexual contact would occur. It may even occur in spite of it; that is, impetuosity and the possibility of escaping group surveillance produce an atmosphere in which anything is possible since the controls are so feebly internalized.

The masculinity of the American Middle-Class husband, on the other hand, is closely tied to interpersonal skills, and to independence, self-reliance and self-control. The trend is in the direction of the man discussing matters of all kinds with his wife and with women in general. There may be personal reasons for verbal reticence, but not cultural reasons. He has to work hard, too, but the emphasis is less on quantity than on quality of work, on clever planning, spotting of opportunities, and the ability to persuade others of his ability. He has to sell himself in the world of man. In the world of women he also talks a great deal about his work, his career and himself in general, as evidence of his masculinity. The specifically sexual aspect of the contact, however, is muted through intense control. The inevitable control in extra-marital relations receives additional support from the man's dependence on and loyalty to his wife. She is the only person on who he is permitted to be dependent, because of the pervasiveness of individualism. At the same time, neither husband nor wife are without ambivalence about the extent of this dependence. As a result, extra-marital sexual contact is likely to arise more as a revolt against the dependence than because of the attractiveness of women, the force of the sexual impulse and the pleasure of satisfying it. When it does arise, it is likely to be accompanied by guilt because of the violation of the internal standard, and the disloyalty to the wife. On this account, temptation may well be warded off by the closeness to the wife, which comes from an increased sharing of the roles in the home.

In the study, the rate at which the Italian male makes the transition from the original cultural definition of the male role to the American varies a great deal. But, if he undertakes the transition at all, he may arrive at a point where the alternate definitions cancel each other out, and he finds it difficult to define his masculinity in any terms. From the point of view of his original values, the American male is feminized because of the excessive sharing of roles with women, and the over-control or suppression of sexual and aggressive displays. From the point of view of American Middle-Class values, the Italian male is child-like, and if he is masculine it is in an over-compensated way. He interacts with women mainly in sexual or dependent ways. He cannot well control himself, he is tied to his parents and his relatives, and he does not know how to accept responsibility—all somewhat feminine or childish qualities. He is trapped in a cultural impasse which can be very difficult to resolve.

Before going on to consider how the impasse can be resolved, one must look at the parallel problems in the feminine role.

The American woman's domestic role is not only a variant one, off the track of the dominant, first-order values, but is in addition quite disjunctive and inconsistently structured. For example, in childhood and adolescence the American girl is trained in the same way and according to much the same values as the male. Both at home and in the schools she is taught the first-order values of future-time planning, doing and individualism. She is on her own from an early age, learning to control her impulses and to take care of herself—both from the point of view of achievement and of sexual contact. These two goals coalesce in the courtship experience, when the girl has, of her own devices, to find the right man to marry and to control pre-marital sexual experience. Whether or not she has been successful and has made the right marriage, she soon has to try to switch her already well-internalized values. For a time after marriage, she may work and plan and save in accordance with these values. After the birth of the first child, however, she is forced into a domestic role, tied to the home and the child and the day-to-day small errands. These mean being tied down to a collateral system, especially after more children appear, and to a present-time existence. In the activity orientation, her training for successful performance is canalized into child-training functions, which she carries out with so much technical to-do—varying along with the latest how-to-do-it manual on the care of children—as to amount to a professionalization of the mother role. For the rest, however, her domestic functions are patterned in accordance with being-in-becoming and being values for which she has not been well trained, and which she only poorly understands. She is supposed to be responsible for the beauty and care of the home and for the intellectual and cultural interests of the family, going to lectures, concerts, clubs of all sorts, and, in general, 'keeping up' with things. These activities, unfortunately, are not fully satisfying to her primary and still first-order internalized values. Thus she tends to be resentful of her husband, who is potentially able to implement these values. If he is reasonably successful at reaching his goals, she is able to gain some vicarious satisfaction, and for this reason—in spite of her resentment—she is apt to keep him under pressure to succeed. Vicarious fulfilment is also available to her through the success of her sons, for which she pushes. But the ambivalence towards her husband remains largely unrelieved by the vicarious gratifications, and it is further increased by the demands for dependent satisfactions which he inevitably puts forth. Finally, it is reinforced by the fact that she remains constantly responsible for controlling her sexual impulses on the basis of the first-order individualism which she cannot implement nor obtain satisfaction for in other ways. Thus the degree of internal frustration is high unless she can obtain some outlet for her basic values through part-time work.

In the Italian family there is no split between the values governing the masculine and feminine roles, even though these roles are highly segregated. Women reflect in marriage the same values which characterize the overall culture. Because of the split in the value patterning of the American wife, however, the path of transition for the Italian woman is different and somewhat easier than it is for the man. This is because the somewhat variant values of the wife's role in the American Middle-Class—present time, collaterality, and being or being-in-becoming—are already those in which she has been trained as an Italian. Nevertheless, the situation is not quite this simple. If she is of the first generation born in this country, then the value training she will have had in school, through the mass media and through contacts with non-Italian age mates will feature the typical American first-order pattern which is so strongly contrasted with the Italian pattern. Therefore, she may have grasped future time, individualism and doing values to a sufficient degree to attempt to manifest some of them in action, during adolescence and during marriage. For example, she may attempt to date boy friends according to the American system, look for a husband apart from her family's rather frantic efforts to arrange a marriage for her, and to test out her ability to control her sexual impulses in unsupervised contacts with boys. These developments almost always produce a strain in the area of sexual behaviour and sexual identity. The Italian girl is trained in collateral and being values in her home—so that impulse control is not well internalized, while impulse stimulation is high. As a result, the free and easy contact with boys in social situations during adolescence, and with men following marriage, usually in the absence of supervision, results in a pervasive sexual stimulation and temptation. This inner situation is then likely to be unconsciously interpreted by the woman herself as being dangerously close to the characteristics of a prostitute. The defence against such a self-picture varies from denial and projection of the promiscuous impulse to others—frequently the husband, or the daughter who is approaching adolescence—to withdrawal accompanied by phobic symptoms, such as the inability to go shopping or even walk down the street alone.

These possible outcomes of the acculturation process indicate that there is, for the Italian-American woman, a sex role trap—an impasse—similar to that which the man faces. On the other hand, the trap is not so pervasive for her as it is for him. As we have stated, in other domestic roles her typical Italian first-order values resemble to some extent those on which American domestic roles are based for the wife. She has usually been well trained to cook, take care of the home and look after the children, and finds these activities congenial and easy for her to carry out with success. As she identifies herself as a successful *American* wife, she begins to put pressure on her spouse to become a successful *American* husband. As a first generation Italian-American, she will have internalized—to be sure, at a superficial level—many of the American values, as we have described above. At least she can talk a good American line, and this line she now hands to her husband. Why doesn't he get a better job, improve his skills, learn to speak with more poise, develop better manners? These things are easy for her to say, since she does not have to undergo as much relearning as he does. The effect upon the husband is to put him in rather an inferior position, squeezing him into the masculine role trap which we have already described.

Parent-child roles

The elements of strain in the husband-wife roles in the Italian-American family are likely to involve the children in very complicated side effects, which we will mention later when we take up the question of role conflict in more detail. However, even in the absence of such side effects, the socialization of the children is likely to run into snags owing to the difference in American and Italian values. The central issue has to do with the tension between Italian collaterality and American individualism.

The *Italian* parents keep their children under close scrutiny to make certain that they do not get into trouble. American individualism, to which the children are exposed outside the home, requires that they be able to take care of themselves in all sorts of situations, and that they be free to roam and to experiment away from the parents' supervision. The Italian parents fight hard against so much freedom, but at the same time they begin to hope that their children, especially the sons, will be able to implement doing and future-time values. They want their children to do well in the American scheme of things, to have good careers and to climb up the class ladder. At the same time, they can do very little to help their children in this, since they have little knowledge of the means to these ends from their own experience. The resulting position of the sons is a difficult one. They are expected to do well, without being given the necessary individualistic freedom to achieve this, and without adequate role models to follow. The strain is most severe for the first sons, who have to function as ice-breakers, making it easier for the younger children. Yet, the strain is not necessarily overwhelming, neither for the children nor for the parents.

Remaining to be discussed is the question of the reduction or avoidance of strain, and the manner in which this question is related to the matter of the order of change in value orientations. In this study, those families which hold the *relational, nature of man* and *man-nature* orientations constant, while attemptng to change the *activity* and *time* orientations, seem to experience the least strain. If the collateral family and neighbourhood system holds together, doing and future-time behaviours can be gradually learned. They can be learned more easily if the planning for a future career takes place in areas which are already familiar to the Italians and in which collaterality is maintained, such as the priesthood, and organized sports and entertainment. However, the professions, such as law and medicine—which have prestige in Italy itself—may also be attempted, the whole extended family pitching in to help financially and in every other way possible. Later, in the generation of the sons who have succeeded in this fashion, the collaterality of the family system may gradually be weakened and shifted to the more American individualism.

In contrast to this gradual and orderly change in values are those families which experience a sudden and initial change in the integrity of the collateral family system from the outset. This may come about through a variety of circumstances, but it is always disturbing. Without the support of the collateral system, the strains in husband-wife and parent-child roles, which have been described above, become severe. Illustrations of the effects of such strain, descriptions of some of the mechanisms by which role conflict is handled, and their relation to symptom formation in the individual, will be described. At present, however, it is possible only to give an impressionistic picture—for the systematic analysis supportive of this statement has yet to be completed—but it seems that orderly change in values, with the preservation of collaterality in the first position, tends to characterize our Group B ('normal') families, while the breakdown of collaterality, with a jumbled and contradictory rearrangement of the other value orientations, seems to be descriptive of the Group A ('sick') families.

IRISH FAMILIES

Although the cultural transition in the Irish-American family brings up many of the same problems facing the Italian-American family, there are also significant differences. Only a few of these differences will be touched upon here. In the native culture of rural Ireland there exists, according to this study, a set of strains generalized to many roles arising from the lack of fit between the first-order positions of present time and lineality, on the one hand, and between lineality and the evil and wellnigh imperfectible orientation towards human nature. These incongruent value orientations will be discussed in a general way first, and then their implications for the roles of men and women will be distinguished.

When the lineal aspect of the *relational* orientation is placed in the first-order position, then the organization of any group is based on the presence of levels of hierarchy dominated by authority figures. When this lineal principle is also combined with a first-order past-time orientation, then the legitimacy of the power exercised by the authority figure is wedded to the right of any particular person to occupy the position of power on the basis of past traditions. A father has always exercised power over his family in the past, and so has the right to demonstrate it in the present. A certain family or clan has always claimed the right of succession to local administrative posts, and, although this may be changed, the weight of tradition tends to perpetuate it. However, a present-time orientation weakens this kind of support emanating from a tradition, while it has no similar weakening effect upon the degree of power exercised by an authority once he has obtained the position of importance. Without the support of a past-time emphasis, both the degree of power exercised by a person in authority and his right to the position appear to be arbitrary, and subject to possible challenge. The greater the disposition to challenge, the more arbitrary and even tyrannical the authority figure may become. The disposition to rebel augments the disposition to tyranny in a process of mutual amplification which may be difficult to contain. Not only in the Irish family but throughout Irish social structure the poor fit between lineality and present time is associated with intensely ambivalent feelings between leaders and followers. The followers desperately need authority figures to tell them what to do, but resent the ones they happen to have. Thus, relations between fathers and sons in Irish families are likely always to be strained. This is one of the reasons why relations between Irish sons and mothers are often idealized, since the father can never be in an unambivalent position.

The incongruity between lineality and a basically evil view of human nature is perhaps even more productive of strain. It is assumed that everyone is born with a strong tendency to sin and that this can only be controlled, if at all, by the most intense and unremitting effort. Furthermore, the individual is held almost completely responsible for the control of his own sinful tendencies. The usual mechanism of external control used among the Irish is that of arousing shame and guilt through blaming and reproaching. The assumption behind such techniques is that the individual should have learned—or, at least, should realize that he should have learned—how to control himself. This is much different from the Italian system, in which the group rather than the individual is responsible for the control of impulses, which, in any event, are not looked upon as so irretrievably wicked. In the Irish interpersonal situation, the incongruity is marked by the fact that, although the individual is supposed to control his *evil* impulses, he is not expected to control or take responsibility for anything else. The lineal principle emphasizes submission to and dependence on authority rather than on oneself. Thus, from the point of view of the personality structure of the individual, the ego is caught in a squeeze play between the strong and inevitably sinful impulses arising in the id, and the harsh morality implanted in the super-ego. The impulse life is perpetually being stimulated by the degree of unpleasant notice given it by external figures. At the same time, the ego is not being effectively trained to control such impulses.

The upshot of such a system for personality training is a pervasive sense of guilt and a disposition to melancholy in the typical Irish character structure. There is, however, one avenue of relief from this oppressive intrapsychic and interpersonal situation, and this is the ubiquitous capacity for denial which develops within the ego. It is associated with the strong second-order position of harmony-with-nature in the *man-nature* orientation. As has been discussed previously, the blurring of causality between man and nature makes it possible to shift responsibility for events from one person to another, or from a person to an animistically conceived natural force. Thus it is common for one person to deny having something which he actually did, if this action should become the stimulus for reproach, either from his own conscience or from someone else. He will say either that it was done by someone else, or by some magical agent or impersonal force such as luck ('the luck of the Irish'). Denial, as the escape from the sense of sin, is, however, only one side of the coin. The other side is confession. Denial and confession constitute mutually augmenting influences. The more a person denies, the more he is pressured to confess. The more he partially (and unconsciously) wishes to confess, the more he overtly denies. Whichever way the process goes, the ego and the super-ego are involved in conspiratorial exchanges. When denial is in effect, the super-ego goes along, illicitly, with the lie, and there is nothing to be guilty about. When confession occurs, the super-ego plays the tyrant to the humiliated ego, thus masking its former defection by an exaggerated display of threat. The resulting remorse is prepayment for the next episode of denial, as well as delayed tribute for the last such episode. These complicated intrapsychic manoeuvres mirror, in large part, the interpersonal exchanges which the individual has actually experienced. They contribute to what can be called a 'swiss cheese' super-ego—strong and resilient in some spots, apparently absent in others.

Husband-wife roles

These general strains have particular effects on the patterning of husband and wife roles.

The husband's training for dependence on authority makes it difficult for him to act as a strong figure in his own home unless he has a secure position in an external chain of authority. But his ambivalence toward authority makes it difficult either to accommodate comfortably towards such a hierarchical structure or to do without it. On the same grounds, it is difficult for him to exert his authority in the home, but he cannot be deprived of it. The most usual solution is that the wife actually becomes the strong figure in the home, while trying to preserve the official picture of her husband as the authority. She rules from behind the throne, so to speak, ignoring, at least in public, her husband's weaknesses. Meanwhile, the husband tends to escape from the strain of this somewhat shaky position in his home—and also from responsibilities—by spending a good deal of time drinking with male cronies at public bars.

The difficulties over impulse control tend to centre specifically on sexual control. For the male, the controls are not really expected to work, no matter how desirable this might be. Ireland has the oldest age at marriage of any European country. The men are apt not to get married until their thirties, and until marriage they are treated as adolescents. The unmarried male is not expected to refrain from sexual experience, but neither is he supposed to have sexual contact with an unmarried girl of good family. Therefore, he must find prostitutes or girls whose reputation has already been tainted. This means that he must 'act out' in any sexual contact the general feeling that sex is a sinful thing. It also means that there is a great temptation, on both sides, to act this out with an unmarried virgin—that is, on the male's part to corrupt the girl, on the girl's part to be corrupted and thus express in action her inner feeling that her sexual impulses are sinful.

The danger in which this places the unmarried girl is great and tends to be handled on all sides by a denial, for as long as possible, of the approach of sexuality in the girl. Whereas prolonged adolescence tends to be emphasized for the male, adolescence tends to be ignored in the female. She is treated as a little girl, who would not be aware of sex, for as long as possible. Then, suddenly, she is ready to be a wife and a mother, and her parents seek to arrange a marriage as quickly as possible. Thus adolescence, which could be a period of sexual experimentation, is treated as if it did not exist for precisely this reason. The fear of the evil consequences of sexual experimentation is compelling, and leads parents to worry excessively that their daughter might be attempting it. The non-recognition of adolescence in the female is an attempt to be rid of this concern. When marriage does finally take place successfully, the marital pair have difficulty establishing a mutually satisfying sexual relationship because of the strong sense that any sexual contact is sinful.

These strains in the masculine and feminine roles in the Irish family undergo a special development in this country when the family begins to adjust to the

American scene. With his training for dependence on a hierarchy, the Irish-American male tends to look for a job in a hierarchical organization. Political organizations, public services such as the Police Force, municipal services of all sorts are naturally available organizations designed for such a need. If he already has a relative in one of these organizations, then the dependence on authority pays off through the ease with which the relative can obtain a job for him. On the other hand, if there has been a break in the chain of authority for a particular individual, then he may become isolated and experience great difficulty obtaining employment. However, even if he is able to maintain his dependence on the authority chain, the strain in the husband-wife roles increases as the wife becomes aware of American values. Learning of the more egalitarian, individualistic structure of husband-wife roles in this country, she becomes less and less willing to submit to his authority and to hide her feelings about his weaknesses. However, she is no more able than he to implement the individualistic orientation in her definition of her role. What occurs is quite the contrary: a reversal of roles. She stops ruling from behind the throne and seizes the throne itself. She is now *the* power in the family. At its most extreme limit, this role reversal assumes the 'Jiggs and Maggie' pattern, with the wife, powerful and sadistic, badgering her poor, weak husband, who is able to protect himself only through a pathetic humour or by temporary flight.

In the area of sexual behaviour, American family patterns, especially those concerned with adolescence, produce increased anxiety for the Irish-American parents. The free dating and the permission for unsupervised sexual contacts characteristic of American adolescents produce a fear often bordering on a conviction that sexual intercourse has or will take place before marriage. In this anxious emotional environment, the Irish-American adolescent girl is strongly tempted to act out her parents' fears, or else is tempted to reject sexual experience altogether. A way to avoid either of these possibilities is, of course, present in the increased opportunity for early marriage in the U.S.A. However, both illegitimate pregnancy and entrance into religious orders are frequent occurrences.

As with the Italian-Americans, the study tried to discern how the order of change in the Irish-American value orientations might be related to the intensity and extent of strain in family role systems. This is not yet clear, because there appears to be so much strain in all the Irish-American families in the sample, both in Group A and Group B. This might be due, of course, to a sampling bias, but at present there is no way of checking on this question, and therefore one must assume that the families in the sample are representatives of the group studied. If this assumption is made, then it would appear that there is so much strain in the original Irish culture, and this culture is so vulnerable and so ill-prepared to deal with the changes which must be encountered from the exposure to American Middle-Class values, that, no matter what the order of change may be, there will be some increase of strain in the family roles as a result of the transitional process. Nevertheless, even though this may be the case, the material studied seems to suggest that this increase in strain can be held to a minimum if the family is able to maintain itself for at least two generations in a supportive lineal network of extended family and community relations and if, at the same time, there is very little attempt to change the first-order positions of present time and being. If this occurs, then the meaning of individualism and a more neutral or mixed interpretation of the human nature value orientation can be slowly learned. As this happens, the intense sense of guilt and shame can be reduced, and the ego's control over impulses can be increased. It seems that not until this occurs can doing and future-time values be implemented, so that the family can accommodate itself comfortably to Middle-Class patterns.

This entire formulation, however, is mainly a conjecture, since the evidence for it in the material observed is so slim. On the whole, the material shows the persistence without much change of lineal and evil orientations alongside premature or pretentious attempts to implement doing and future-time values—attempts that are doomed to failure because the means to these ends are not yet available (and would not fit, if they were available) to the family.

THE RELATION BETWEEN ROLE CONFLICT
AND PSYCHOPATHOLOGY

In the preceding sections evidence has been presented for the development of conflicts in role relationships within the family—conflicts which are associated with a lack of fit or incongruity in the cultural value orientations in accordance with which roles are patterned. The incongruity in values has been traced both to strains existing within the native cultures of Italy and Ireland, and to the acculturation process as it occurs in this country. To conclude, the following is a brief account of the connection between role conflict and the organization of the family, on the one hand, and the psychological health or illness of the individual, on the other.

Interpersonal relations within the family can be described in terms of a theory of the structure and function of social roles which relates behaviour to the organization of cultural values, on the one hand, and to the organization of intrapsychic process, on the other. The issues of psychopathology can be related, through this theoretical approach, to the presence of complementarity or conflict in the basic patterning of the roles.

Role conflict can be traced either to a too great variation in the value orientations leading to a lack of fit in the patterning of roles between role partners, or to discrepancies in the commitment of role partners to their roles. In either event, the presence of conflict evokes homeostatic mechanisms which function to reduce the conflict and restore complementarity in the role patterning.

The homeostatic mechanisms, or re-equilibrating processes, are of two different kinds. The first kind, called Role Modification, consists of efforts by the role partners to face their basic conflicts, find their origins, and settle upon some novel solution through compromise and gradual changes in adjustment. The second, called Role Distortion, consists of various efforts made by a role incumbent to induce his role partners to modify their behaviour to confirm his own expectations, i.e. Role Induction, or to shift his roles so as to achieve greater satisfaction of his expectations, i.e. Role Dislocation. Role Distortion, if successful, avoids the basic conflict in the role system, but the conflict is likely to reappear in a disguised form in another role system.

The greater the intensity of the basic role conflict incorporated into the husband-wife roles at the time the marriage is formed, the greater the likelihood that the Role Distortion, rather than Role Modification, will be used to avoid conflict.

Role Distortion is associated with the appearance of the symptoms of psychopathology in a family member. When it ceases to focus upon a family member, the symptoms may disappear, with or without change in the underlying personality structure. If Role Distortion focuses upon a child in the family over a prolonged period of time, the symptom may become associated with a deformation of the underlying personality structure. When the deformation of the personality has been well established, the symptomatic behaviour may not disappear even though he is no longer involved in a Role Distortion.

In Group B ('normal') families, role conflict is less severe—both intensively and extensively—than in Group A ('sick') families. Conflict, when present, is more likely to invoke Role Modification than Role Distortion, and thus is easier to dispel. The sources of conflict in Group B families, however, are the same as those in Group A families.

REFERENCES

1. KLUCKHOHN, FLORENCE R. 1950. Dominant and substitute profiles of cultural orientations: Their significance for the analysis of social stratification. *Social Forces*, **28**, 276-293.
2. KLUCKHOHN, FLORENCE R. 1953. Dominant and variant value orientations. In KLUCKHOHN, CLYDE, and MURRAY, HENRY A. (eds.) *Personality in nature, society and culture*, 2nd ed., pp. 342-357. Knopf, New York.
3. KLUCKHOHN, FLORENCE R. 1958. Family diagnosis: Variations in the basic values of family systems. *Social Casewk*, **39**, 63.
4. KLUCKHOHN, FLORENCE R., and STRODTBECK, FRED. L. 1961. *Variations in value orientations*. Row, Peterson, Evanston, Ill.
5. PARSONS, T., BALES, R. F., and SHILS, E. A. 1953. *Working papers in the theory of action*. Free Press, Glencoe, Ill.

XVI

FAMILY DIAGNOSIS AND MECHANISMS
OF PSYCHOSOCIAL DEFENSE

JAN EHRENWALD

Much effort has gone into classifying discrete patterns of family functioning. One such schema is described here.

Family diagnosis, in order to be brought up to the standards currently applied to psychiatric diagnosis in the individual, has to proceed in two major steps. First, it must aim at a descriptive, taxonomic delineation of patterns characteristic of a given family constellation. Secondly, it must seek to arrive at a deeper, dynamic, psychosocial understanding of such patterns. In a previous study,[1] I have tried to outline the guiding principles of the first step in such a venture. It is based on an *Inventory of Thirty Traits and Attitudes* contained in a broad spectrum of more or less habitual ways of relating which can be observed in members of a given family group (Table 1). They range from "giving-supportive-affectionate" on the "socially desirable, well-adjusted" end of the scale, to "erratic-eccentric-defective" on the other side. The 30 traits and attitudes, grouped in 10 clusters or triads, are presented to a clinical observer or judge who is asked to state which cluster or triad of interactions is, in his opinion, "most outstanding" or "most characteristic" of the interpersonal relationships, say, between husband and wife, mother and son, father and daughter, sibling and sibling, etc. A simple method of preferential rating or ranking makes the diagrammatic representation of the diverse combinations and permutations of patterns of interaction possible. At the same time it permits a quasi-mathematical treatment of the data arrived at in this way. Two charts drawn along these lines suffice for the diagnostic representation of the interpersonal relationships of one family pair, while according to the formula $n(n-1)$ six charts are needed to do justice to a family of three, 12 charts to a family of four, etc. It should be noted,

Reprinted from FAMILY PROCESS, Vol. 2, No. 1, March 1963, pp. 121-131.

TABLE 1

INVENTORY OF TRAITS AND ATTITUDES

		A Father, mother, spouse		B Child, sibling		
Symb*	1 2 3	symbiotic (early).......... symbiotic (prolonged).... symbiotic (continued).....	1 2 3	same as in A same as in A same as in A		
I	4 5 6	giving.................. supportive.............. affectionate.............	4 5 6	responsive compliant same as in A		
II	7 8 9	cooperative............. permissive.............. indulgent...............	7 8 9	companionable cooperative docile	well adjusted	
III	10 11 12	protective.............. domineering controling... authoritarian...........	10 11 12	independent socially aggressive self-assertive		
IV	13 14 15	competitive............. rejecting, punitive....... hostile, aggressive........	13 14 15	same as in A defiant, rebellious same as in A		
V	16 17 18	clinging................ dependent.............. demanding.............	16 17 18	same as in A same as in A same as in A	poorly adjusted, e.g., neurosis	
VI	19 20 21	rigid................... distrustful.............. inhibited...............	19 20 21	same as in A same as in A same as in A		
VII	22 23 24	cold................... withdrawn.............. autistic.................	22 23 24	fearful same as in A same as in A		
VIII	25 26 27	passive................. submissive.............. masochistic.............	25 26 27	same as in A same as in A same as in A	breakdown or failure, e.g., psychosis	
IX	28 29 30	destructive............. sadistic................. castrating..............	28 29 30	same as in A same as in A explosive		
X	31 32 33	erratic................. eccentric............... defective...............	31 32 33	same as in A same as in A same as in A		
Brk*	34 35 36	absent................. incapacitated........... deceased...............	34 35 36	same as in A same as in A same as in A		

* Symb stands for symbiotic. Brk stands for broken home.

The Interaction Study described in the text is based on a list of 30 traits and attitudes. They are grouped in 10 triads or clusters of three traits. Each triad or cluster of traits and attitudes is marked by the numerals I to X.

furthermore, that by averaging the scores obtained in two or eight or 12 interaction charts, diagrammatic Family Profiles can be arrived at characteristic of an existing family constellation in terms laid down in the Inventory of Traits and Attitudes (Figs. 1 and 2).

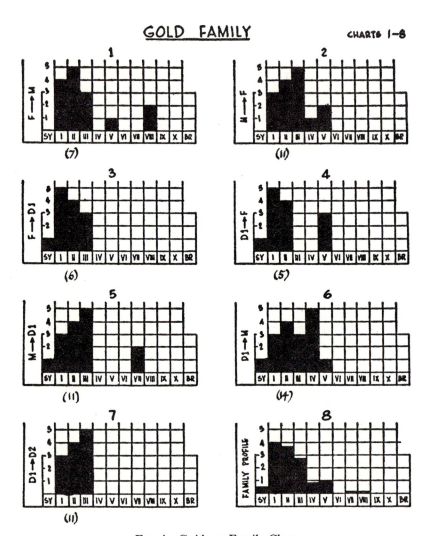

FIG. 1. Guide to Family Charts

Charts 1-16 present the information obtained by using the Inventory of Traits and Attitudes (see Table 1). Each chart represents ratings of attitudes exhibited by one family member in relation to his or her opposite number in the family pair. F → M stands for father in relation to mother, and vice versa. F → D1 stands for father's attitude in relation to the first daughter, etc. In Chart 1 the triad of attitudes designated II in Table 1 and in the chart is rated as 5; that is, the traits "cooperative, permissive, indulgent" are deemed to be father's "most outstanding" attitudes in relation to mother. The number (7) printed under the baseline of the chart indicates that on closer scrutiny "cooperative" is the individual trait "most characteristic" of his attitude toward her (see Table 1).

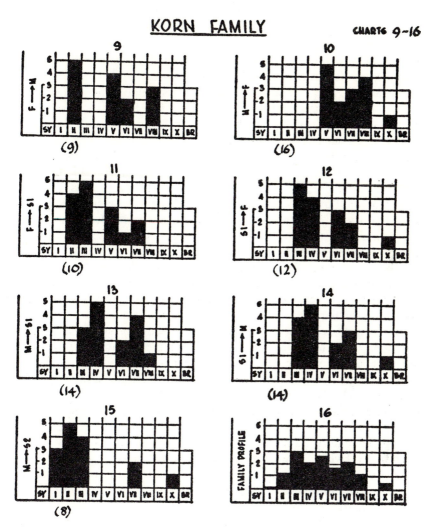

FIG. 2

The number (6) under the baseline stands for "affectionate", the number (14) in Chart 13 stands for "rejecting-punitive", etc. The method of arriving at the Family Profile (Charts 6 and 8) is explained in the text.

Charts 1-8 (the Gold Family) are illustrative of a "well-adjusted" family group. Their heaviest weighting is in the left, "well-adjusted", area of the charts. The Korn family is illustrative of a "maladjusted" family group, with most higher scores in the area of sick interpersonal attitudes (Charts 9-16).

(Table and Charts are from "Neurotic Interaction and Patterns of Pseudo-heredity in the Family," *Am. J. of Psychiat.* 115, 134-142, 1958.)

There is no need in the present context to go into details of the procedure. Be it sufficient to state that four major patterns of interaction between members of a family group have emerged from these studies: (1) Patterns of sharing, (2) patterns of resistance and rebellion, (3) complementary patterns, and (4) patterns of contagion. *Patterns of sharing* are derived from the prevalence of "giving-supportive-affectionate" attitudes in the family group. They presuppose a tendency to cooperation and mutual aid in the interpersonal relationships of all family members. Such attitudes, it should be noted, can be found throughout the animal kingdom, at least as far as intra-species behavior is concerned. They have what biologists describe as positive survival value. Indeed, we have learned from P. Kropotkin, from W. C. Allee,[2] A. Portmann,[3] and other students of animal behavior, that species lacking such propensities for social organization fall by the wayside of the evolutionary process. It is needless to say that the same is true for human society. Viewed from the psychoanalytic angle, patterns of sharing can be described as reaction formations against hostile-aggressive instinctual drives in a given social organization.

Patterns of rebellion and resistance are usually called forth in the younger generation in response to "controlling-authoritative" attitudes in their elders. They are perhaps without precedent in the evolutionary process. Rebellion against a seemingly preordained mode of existence, non-conformist behavior and intellectual dissent are specifically human inventions. This rebellion is best symbolized by the myth of Prometheus who stole the fire from Zeus and, incidentally, cheated him when he smuggled ingredients of inferior quality into his sacrificial offering. Seen from this angle, Prometheus can be described as the mythological precursor of all rebels, heretics and revolutionaries in the western world and, for that matter, of the juvenile delinquent of our time.

Complementary patterns can more readily be traced back to lower evolutionary levels. The pecking order among chickens is a well-known example of dominance and submission in animals. Sado-masochistic patterns are adumbrated by observations described by ethologists in the fallow deer, the iguana, the lava lizard and even in fish and snakes.[4, 5] These workers have called attention to the striking manner in which a weaker animal, facing a stronger opponent of the same species, may come out unharmed from the encounter. After an initial exchange of bites, wolves or dogs assume a posture of submission and surrender. The defeated animal turns its head away, offering its unprotected throat to the fangs of the victor. This gesture, we are told, has an immediate inhibitory effect upon the aggression of the victor and puts an end to the battle. Every dog owner is familiar with similar behavior in the puppy who rolls on his back, exposing his proverbial soft underbelly to his master at the crack of his whip or the raising of his voice. Ethologists do not seem to hesitate to apply the same principle to man. According to K. Lorenz,[4] the normal human being, faced with a victim who throws himself defenseless at his feet, is strongly inhibited from further aggression. In a similar vein, I. Eibl-Eibesfeldt[5] has pointed out that unfettered intra-species fighting is maladaptive, possessed of negative survival value. Thus certain patterns of dominance versus submission, of control versus dependence and full-fledged sado-masochistic patterns in man, show a more than incidental similarity to observations in animals.

A fourth pattern of interaction in the family is the pattern of psychological *contagion*. It is in effect the maladaptive counterpart to patterns of sharing and is responsible for the ominous spread of neurotic disturbances in the family in both the horizontal and in the vertical, i.e., in the same and different generations. Elsewhere[1A] I described in some detail the Obscomp family to illustrate this point. Obscomp is a pseudonym and stands for *obsessive-compulsive*. In this family, observed over a period of 15 years, obsessive-compulsive pathology was present in 13 out of 14 individuals. It was transmitted over four filial generations and associated with a uniform pattern of dominance versus submission or sado-masochistic relationships in virtually all members of the family group. This is what can be described as *homonymic* contagion, transmitted from one generation to the next along genealogical pathways.

It should be noted at this point that despite the existing undercurrents of hostility and repressed aggression characteristic of obsessive-compulsive personalities, there was no overt evidence of rebellion or resistance in this family group. In effect, its very absence may be one of the reasons for the virtually unlimited spread of neurotic contagion in the Obscomp pedigree in both the horizontal and the vertical. It is needless to say, however, that patterns of contagion are not confined to obsessive-compulsive families. They can be observed in families showing a wide variety of psychopathology among its members, ranging from schizophrenic reactions or alcoholism to delinquency, homosexuality and incest.

It is at this point that our proposed descriptive, taxonomic approach to family diagnosis can be used to the best advantage. It suggests that it is not the conventional, Kraepelinian nosological entity which is subject to transmission from one member of the family group to another, but specific clusters or patterns of interpersonal relationships. This observation can in effect be described as the first postulate of psychiatric epidemiology.

It should be noted, furthermore, that mental contagion, viewed in this light, need not necessarily consist of transmission of clinically identical or *homonymic* types of pathology. A compulsive parent may produce an equally compulsive child. Alternatively, the child may rebel against excessive parental control and authority and become a delinquent, a homosexual or a schizophrenic. He may respond in terms of *heteronymic* contagion. These two alternative types of contagion in the family, ranging from neurotic to psychotic or psychosomatic pathology, can be described as the second postulate of psychiatric epidemiology.

A third postulate is concerned with the part played by the time factor in the development of neurotic contagion. It is readily understood that patterns of contagion presuppose the slow, grinding effect of psychological interaction between person and person. All the available evidence indicates that the cumulative effects of neurotic attitudes extending over several generations tend to reinforce their contagious potential. This can be contrasted with the diminishing return of shorter and shorter periods of exposure to such influences in a person's lifetime. Thus, with the notable exception of greater susceptibility to such influences in the early post-natal period, there seems to be a simple linear correlation between duration of exposure and the contagious effect of a specific set of disturbed interpersonal attitudes.

A fourth postulate to which J. Meerloo has recently called attention[6] should be mentioned in passing. This concerns the marked contagious effect of primitive, archaic types of communication in interpersonal relationships.

In the face of this ominous tendency of the pathology to spread in both the horizontal and the vertical, the question of resistance or immunity is evidently of paramount importance. What are the forces that are apt to stem the tide of sick interpersonal attitudes, with their tendency to mutual reinforcement and potentiation? I believe that certain patterns of interaction in the family discussed on a previous page give a tentative answer to this question. A first factor or *mechanism of defense* against the spread of sick attitudes is illustrated by the pattern of sharing, that is, by the "contagious" effect of cooperation and mutual aid in the family. I hinted that mutual aid and cooperation can in effect be described as reaction formations against aggressive, hostile behavior in intra-species relationships. Another significant mechanism of defense against the spread of illness in the family are patterns of resistance and rebellion. Although they may lead to antisocial acting out, to juvenile delinquency, crime, political radicalism, and the like, they may serve as antidotes especially against the homonymic type of contagion in neurotic or psychotic family groups. They also help bring about innovation and cultural change. A third potential antidote is provided by complementary patterns in the family. They are instrumental in maintaining family homeostasis as described by D. Jackson,[7] or what J. P. Spiegel[8] termed "equilibration" of the family group. They help to establish a *modus vivendi* between two disturbed members of a family pair. They may manifest themselves as interlacing or dovetailing neurotic defenses and serve as mutually beneficial compensatory devices cushioning or camouflaging neuroses existing in one or both partners. They thus tend to neutralize neurotic attitudes within a given family pair and to establish an at least pathological level of adjustment. This is best illustrated by sado-masochistic or dominant-submissive patterns; by patterns of dependence versus control, etc.

Viewed in this light, the patterns reviewed here can indeed be described in terms of mechanisms of psychosocial defense. They help to maintain the integration of family life on a functionally viable level—however neurotic individual family members may be. Patterns of psychosocial defense can thus be regarded as teleological or pseudo-teleological regulatory mechanisms resulting from natural selection. Still, they are comparable to ego defenses described by Anna Freud,[9] serving the same purpose in the individual patient. As in the case of integration of individual personality structure, their operation is largely unconscious or automatic, in contrast to the wide variety of conscious devices, legalistic provisions, institutions and other expedients used by society to safeguard its functioning.

The deeply rooted instinct of care for the young; the well nigh universal incest barrier; the injunctions against patricide and matricide; the diverse rituals of courtship and mating observed in most cultures, belong to the same category. Less universal, but of marked interest in the present context as an antidote against the spread of mental contagion along genealogical pathways, is what Karl Abraham[10] described as neurotic exogamy. So is the tendency of homosexuals, of many schizophrenics and severe neurotics to exclude themselves from the demands and opportunities of courtship, marriage and procreation. The tendency characteristic of these individuals to withdraw from social contact, to live as isolates or hermits in self-imposed psychological quarantine, can likewise be described as important mechanisms of psychosocial defense. They protect the individual patient from intolerable stress emanating from his fellows and may save his family and the community from psychological contagion emanating from him.

These few examples of psychosocial defense operating in the family may suffice in the present context. They should go far to show that the study of patterns of interaction in the family along descriptive-taxonomic lines merely prepares the ground for a more significant dynamic or psychosocial evaluation of family processes. The two combined may help to bring our largely empirical approach to family diagnosis up to the standards of currently dynamically-oriented theories of individual behavior and pave the way for rational methods of family therapy.

SUMMARY

Family diagnosis presupposes the availability of well-defined descriptive terms to characterize patterns (and derivative patterns) of interaction within family pairs and in the family as a whole. On the basis of an Inventory of thirty traits and attitudes descriptive of interpersonal habitual relationships in family members, four major patterns of interaction have emerged: (1) patterns of sharing, (2) patterns of resistance and rebellion, (3) complementary patterns and (4) patterns of contagion.

Patterns of sharing are derived from the prevalence of "giving-supportive-affectionate" attitudes in the family. Patterns of resistance and rebellion are usually seen in response to "controlling-authoritative" patterns. They may constitute a break in the continuity, not only of family tradition, but also of neurosis transmitted from one generation to the next. Complementary patterns tend to neutralize neurotic attitudes in a family pair and thus to establish pathological patterns of adjustment. Patterns of contagion result from the prevalence of sick interpersonal relationships in the family. Mental contagion may be homonymic or heteronymic. Its spread is illustrated by study of the Obscomp pedigree extending over 15 years. In this pedigree obsessive-compulsive pathology was present in 13 out of 14 individuals and was transmitted over four filial generations. The Obscomp family is contrasted with family groups in which patterns of resistance, complementarity or heteronymic contagion tend to counteract the unlimited spread of contagion in the family group and in the community at large. Such regulatory patterns are described as mechanisms of psychosocial defense and can be compared with ego defenses in the individual. They are of a seemingly teleological nature, but are presumably due to natural selection operating on the biosocial plane.

More specific examples are patterns of dominance versus submission; sado-masochistic relationships; neurotic exogamy; self-imposed psychological quarantine and celibacy seen in many schizophrenic patients and severe neurotics. Rational family diagnosis must be based on diagnosis of patterns of interaction prevailing in the family group. Rational family therapy should be guided by the proper understanding of prevailing patterns of psychosocial defense.

REFERENCES

1. EHRENWALD, J. 1958. Neurotic interaction and patterns of pseudo-heredity in the family. *Am. J. Psychiat.*, **115**, 134-142.
1A. EHRENWALD, J. 1963. *Neurosis in the family and patterns of psychosocial defense.* Hoeber-Harper & Row, New York.
2. ALLEE, W. C. 1951. *Cooperation among animals with human implications.* Abelard, New York.
3. PORTMANN, A. 1961. *Animals as social beings.* Viking Press, New York.
4. LORENZ, K. Z. 1952. *King Solomon's ring.* Crowell, New York.
5. EIBL-EIBESFELDT, I. 1961. The fighting behavior of animals. *Scient. Am.*, **205**, 112-116.
6. MEERLOO, J. A. M. 1959. Mental Contagion. *Am. J. Psychother.*, **13**, 66-82.
7. JACKSON, D. D. 1959. Family interaction, family homeostasis, and some implications for conjoint family psychotherapy. In MASSERMAN, J. (ed.) *Individual and familial dynamics*, pp. 122-141. Grune & Stratton, New York.
8. SPIEGEL, J. P. 1960. The resolution of role conflict within the family. In BELL, N. W., and VOGEL, E. F. (eds.), *A modern introduction to the family.* Free Press, Glencoe, Ill.

9. FREUD, A. 1946. *The ego and the mechanisms of defense.* International Univ. Press, New York.
10. ABRAHAM, K. 1921. *Ueber Neurotische Exogamie, Klinische Beitraege zur Psychoanalyse.* Inter. Psychoan., Verlag, Wien.

XVII

AN APPROACH TO NEUROTIC BEHAVIOR
IN TERMS OF A THREE GENERATION
FAMILY MODEL

DAVID MENDELL AND SEYMOUR FISHER

The functioning of a family in the Present and in the Future is coloured by the experiences of consecutive generations in the Past.

In a previous paper[4] we described a study of the communication of neurotic behavior patterns within families. This study involved fourteen families of two generations of kin and six families of three generations of kin.* The two generation families included mother, father, and one or more of their children, while the three generation families included in addition either a maternal or paternal grandparent. The various families were studied in the course of evaluating various of their members who had sought treatment from one of the present writers, a psychiatrist. Every family member was intensively interviewed, and usually at least one from each family was seen for individual or group psychotherapy. In addition, the Rorschach Ink Blot Test and the Thematic Apperception Test were administered to each. During the analysis of our data we found that any given family tends to be characterized by a distinguishing theme or problem area. Each family is marked by its somewhat unique struggle with a difficulty common to its members. Each family shares with the others an unusual concern with a given conflict. Thus, one family might be struggling principally with the problem of how to discharge aggressive feelings; another with the problem of controlling exhibitionistic impulses;

* This paper is on substantially increased numbers of cases including families with all 4 grandparents.

Reprinted from THE JOURNAL OF NERVOUS AND MENTAL DISEASE, Vol. 123, No. 2, February 1956, pp. 171-180.

and another with difficulties centering about wishes for unlimited passive gratification. We observed that each family could be classified in terms of its category of struggle. The fact that members of the same family were concerned with a common central problem was quite apparent in the clinical data. However, such overlapping of areas of concern among family members was especially clear in their projective test productions. Members of the same family gave remarkably similar test responses. Indeed, in most instances even the grandparent and grandchild in a given family would produce patterns of fantasy characterized by unusual similarity. We have since discovered that Morris and Nicholas[6] found just such similarity in the Rorschach records of family members whom they evaluated. We should like to emphasize the uniqueness of the data provided by analyzing data from two and three generations of family members. Such data eliminate much of the speculative element in determining the patient's feelings regarding his parental figures, the reality of his fantasies regarding them, and the general tradition in which he grew up.

On the basis of such data and a variety of studies of others[1,7,8] which have pointed up the basically parallel dynamics of members of the same family, we have derived some perspectives concerning neurotic behavior and its treatment. We have found it meaningful to perceive each individual who comes in for psychiatric treatment as a representative of his family group. We conceptualize that individual as having been the member of a group of persons, all of whom were trying in various ways to help themselves and to help the others to deal with some conflictual disturbing issue. When the individual comes to a therapist for help, we assume that he is admitting the failure of his group as an effective milieu in which to find the solution he seeks. Our data suggest that the individual seeking therapeutic help frequently approaches the therapist in protest against the ineffectiveness of the group to which he belongs. But also his behavior may be a response to conscious or unconscious pressures from the group members, all of whom sense their mutual ineffectiveness and desire an outside agent to bolster the group structure. Just as a given patient in a group therapy situation may be stimulated by the total group to express a feeling toward the therapist which the group as a whole cannot express, so may one family member be incited to obtain outside aid for the total group. Thus, when the patient establishes relationship with a therapist, he is in a sense recruiting him to membership in a specific group. It is, of course, well known that when an individual enters into psychotherapy, this has intense repercussions on those in his intimate circle. His relationships with his intimates may change and in turn their relationships with each other may shift. The therapist becomes a significant figure to these intimates and at different levels of reality is a new force which they must reckon with in their responses to each other and particularly toward the "patient". The therapist becomes a special kind of member of that group.

We now have clinical and projective test data which point up the spread of effect resulting from one of the group's members entering into therapy. We find that when patients have been in treatment for an extended period and show significant changes in their behavior and in their projective retest responses, their spouses who have not been directly in treatment also show significant changes in their behavior and projective retest responses. An important implication of our point of view is that actually a therapist is usually treating a group and not an individual. To some degree, the individual who comes for help is a fortuitous choice of the balance of forces in the group at a given time. We have repeatedly observed family groups in which first one member and then another member would find it necessary to obtain psychotherapy. It is not as if one member of a family were sick and the others well. On the contrary, we have found consistently that sick individuals come from sick groups and that as the group structure varies, different members of the group are subjected to shifts in their load of stress and consequently experience varying degrees of discomfort. Implicit in this formulation is the idea that the prognosis for an individual in therapy is to an important degree a function of how the group of which he is a member responds to the entrance of the therapist into the group structure. Does the group accept the therapist and is it able to utilize that which the "patient" gets from the therapist as a means for solving the basic group difficulty? Or does the group seal out the "patient" like a foreign body and refuse to allow him to introduce the therapist into the group structure? We have noted that the concept of individual ego strength is a considerable oversimplification. Each individual's ego strength should be evaluated relative to the support he derives from his intimate group membership. So often, now, we have observed individual patients who look very sick in terms of clinical and psychological test data when they are evaluated as isolated and separate personalities; but who function well within the context of the aid and support derived from their group membership. The work of Doane and his co-workers at McGill[2] has recently pointed up in dramatic fashion how fragile is any individual's ego strength when he is drastically separated from the opportunity for interaction with others. They found that normal individuals subjected to relatively brief periods of drastic isolation from most forms of sensory stimulation develop marked regressive tendencies, e.g., hallucinations and delusions. Ego strength is apparently a highly relative concept and can vary greatly as the individual's life situation changes and as his opportunities for certain kinds of interaction with others change.

In a limited sense, the idea of treating the group in which an individual has membership rather than simply treating the individual alone is already an underlying assumption of the treatment procedure in many child guidance clinics. Frequently in such clinics the problems of the child are attacked by treating not only the child but also his mother and in some instances also his father. The rationale behind this procedure is that the child is still so dependent upon his mother and father and so much controlled by their attitudes that even if he were to change some of his own attitudes in the therapy, he would not be able to express them in action against the resistance of the relatively powerful parental figures. Thus, changes have to be brought about in his family group before he is free to change. There has been little effort expended toward the extension of this principle to adult patients. It has somehow been assumed that the adult patient's relationships with his family group are qualitatively different from those of the child and that these relationships may, by and large, be treated as peripheral to the basic therapist-patient interaction. Our observations indicate that patients who come for treatment are actually in the same dilemma as the child who enters therapy, the difference being only a matter of degree. The adult patient too may find that his efforts to change are paralyzed by the rigidity of his intimates. His own group may block him drastically. It is, of course, also capable of becoming a very helpful facilitative force. This group-oriented concept of the neurotic patient has stimulated one of the writers who is a psychiatrist to use a variety of techniques for involving not only the patient, but his whole family in the therapeutic process. Illustrative of such techniques is the placement of not only the "patient" but also simultaneously of other key members of his family in individual or group psychotherapy. One may cite, as further illustration, a technique which involves the calling together of all family members into formal group meetings where free interaction is encouraged and interpretations are made of some of the patterns characteristic of the group and the relationship of these patterns to the behavior of the "patient".

The whole approach to the patient as the representative of a disturbed group stands in opposition to the atomistic point of view frequently found among those who treat patients psychotherapeutically. Many patients are still viewed as though they were individual units whose goals, prognosis, and illness could be evaluated with only a superficial knowledge of the group matrix in which they live. We are taking the position that each patient should be viewed as a link in a long-term continuing historical process which involves a specific subculture. The patient is a product of group disorganization, and his difficulties may profitably be formulated in terms of the history of the group in which he lives. Various anthropologists, e.g., Jules Henry,[5] have emphasized the importance of such an approach. Similarly, Eric Erikson[3] exemplifies a psychoanalyst who has diligently sought to relate various sorts of pathology that he has observed in the United States to basic historical trends which have characterized the development of this country. Of course, others have also supported this type of approach. But what has been lacking in establishing the value of the approach is specific detailed documentation. It is well to say that the individual patient represents the outcome of certain kinds of group pathology, but it is quite another matter to establish the point with detailed data. It is our main objective in the present paper to present a variety of data concerning the characteristics and interactions of three generations of individuals belonging to a family cluster. Our aim is to show the continuities running through these three generations and to attempt to set up an illustrative model of how long-term group dynamics give rise to the pathology we finally see in the individual "patient".

Our analysis of the three generation family cluster involves two levels of data. First of all, we have intensive individual interviews with each member of this cluster and in two instances the records of individual therapy sessions. Secondly, we have Rorschach and Thematic Apperception data from each member. We will attempt to show how the data from these sources fall into a pattern indicative of a basic trend or continuity.

The family group in question first came under study when a young wife who was pregnant with a second child began to show severe symptoms of depression, feelings of futility, and an increasing inability to care for her husband and first child. The family cluster in which she had membership consisted of seven other persons. She and the others in this cluster may be categorized into three subgroups:

The patient	Patient's father	Patient's husband's father
Her husband	Patient's mother	Patient's husband's mother
Her child		

Before undertaking the analysis of this cluster it would be well to sketch some background facts concerning each subgroup. The patient and her husband have been married five years. They have a son four years of age. The husband has lived in the United States 15 years, having been born in a Jewish family in Poland. He came to the United States at the age of 15. He has one brother and two sisters. He completed the seventh grade in school. Since the age of 15, he has worked with his father and brother in a wholesale meat packing business. The patient herself is from a Jewish family and is an only child. She was born in the United States and completed 12 years of school. She married at the age of 16.

The patient's parents were born in the United States. The mother completed high school, and the father completed six years of school. A good part of the father's work career has been tied up with running a retail grocery store. More recently, he sold his business and is employed as a clerk in a clothing store.

The parents of the patient's husband were both born in Poland. They fled Poland just before the Nazi invasion. They have had little or no formal education. The father was a butcher in Poland. When he came to the United States, he established and now owns a wholesale meat packing company. All of the above-mentioned subgroups live in the same city and have fairly frequent interaction with each other.

In the process of reviewing the large quantity of information that we had concerning these various family members, we attempted to find an over-all conceptual model which would embrace the pattern of struggle of each individual member and at the same time account for the sequence of affairs which culminated in the patient's getting sick enough to seek psychiatric help. We began by considering the present cluster to have originally consisted of two smaller clusters: (1) The patient and her family; (2) The patient's husband and his family. Our analysis of these smaller clusters will be described first.

The data suggest that management of passive fantasies has been one of the main problems with which the patient and her family have been most persistently confronted. They all seem to face life with strong anxiety and to yearn for magical aid which will relieve them of the need to expend any effort on their own. The importance of this problem to them is indicated by a variety of factors. In its acute most obvious form the problem is apparent in the symptomatology of the patient. Her symptoms involve mainly a sense of futility and an inability to expend enough energy to perform her duties as a wife and mother. She simply "gave up". In the case of the mother and father the existence of such a problem is not immediately apparent in terms of their behavior. Just why the problem is not apparent in their overt behavior will become clear at a later point. However, one does have clear indications, in terms of the fantasies evoked from them by the projective tests, that this is a basic conflict area for them. The following is an extract from the psychological report regarding the mother:

"The urge to rest and be passively incorporating is very strong within her. Indeed, as she has gotten older the intensity of her passivity has probably increased—She has fought against passivity all of her life—."

The following is an extract from the psychological report regarding the father:

"He has gone through life with a strained feeling—He feels depleted—He is defending himself against passivity—There are signs that he has strong tendencies toward unrealism and wishful interpretations."

In the Rorschach records of both the father and mother there are numerous references to such passive images as:

"Two animals resting—Someone holding them up."
"Cats—Persians, fat, leaning on something. Rest back. Leaning back."

The patient's projective responses contain similar images. While such passive fantasies are prominent, the outstanding thing about this family subgroup is its style of defense against these fantasies. The mother and father have both fought hard to deny any weakness or passivity in themselves and have often made highly compensatory gestures in the opposite direction. Both have carried considerable responsibility, and in an interview situation they make it clear how much they have done for other people. Their heavy involvement in defending themselves against passivity is also very clear in their projective test responses. Thus, the mother is described in terms of psychological test data as follows:

"She has fought against passivity all of her life and has tried in a compensatory way to be commanding."

The father is similarly referred to as follows.

"He perseverated throughout his test responses on the theme of smallness *vs* bigness. He cannot tolerate the possibility that he is a little man or a weak man. When assailed by doubts about himself, he must quickly do something that is reassuring."

At still another level we may point up the tradition in the family of presenting a strong front by noting that the mother comes from a family in which she was the oldest and had to assume responsibility for raising several of her brothers and sisters when her mother died. In this family setting she was expected to forget her own wishes about taking it easy and to devote all of her energy to her siblings. She said during one interview, "We had to learn to stand on our own feet." As we reconstruct it, when the patient (an only child) was born into this family atmosphere, she represented a new responsibility which must have been a significant threat to the passive wishes of the father and mother. However, they reacted to the threat with their usual denial of any weakness or resentment and set out in a compensatory way to prove they had a generous giving attitude toward the new child. In order to prove their good intent they attempted through the years to relieve this child of all responsibility and persisted in treating it like some helpless pet which must be carefully fed and which could not survive on its own. The patient reflects this attitude on their part when she says during a therapy session: "I can't do things myself. I was always part of a team. My parents were in the grocery business and so I was with them a lot." "I always depend too much on my parents for their judgment—." The patient came to expect that her mother and father would keep her completely supplied without much real effort on her own part. Over-all, one may conceptualize a basic pattern of relationship in this family group which is a function of three variables: 1) A mother and father. with strong passive fantasies who deny such fantasies and defend against them by compensatory activity and giving. By giving they deny that they want primarily to be in the role of the taker. 2) A daughter who imposed a new load upon them, and who in this fashion stirred up their activity-passivity conflicts so much that they had to give to her excessively as a means of denying their underlying wishes to be rid of her. 3) The resulting inability of the daughter to be an independent person and her chronic need to take from them excessively.

The patient's husband and his family constitute the second original family cluster. We also conceive of their most pressing area of struggle and conflict as revolving primarily about issues of passivity. The father and mother are people with poorly-defined ego boundaries who feel secure only to the degree that they are part of a group in which they are on the receiving end of many contributions. One finds in their projective test responses that they frequently picture themselves as being without separate identity and as merged with others. Thus, in the Rorschach the father described a figure which turned out to be something "With legs sticking out. It's mixed up. Like a play on the stage. Like a horse. Dress up. Maybe three or four people inside." That is, this one figure actually consists of three or four people merged together inside of a costume. The mother, too, projects Rorschach responses in which there is an emphasis on fusion with others and indistinctness of ego boundaries. Here is an example:

"Two hearts *melted together*."

At an overt behavioral level this family problem is apparent in the kinds of conflicts which exist between the mother and father. Each emphasizes that the other does not give enough. The mother complains that the father stays at his place of business almost constantly, except to eat and sleep. She feels that he has placed upon her the responsibility for raising the family and for all family affairs aside from those strictly pertaining to the business. She takes a very martyred and long-suffering attitude toward the demands she feels he has made through the years. He, on the contrary, indicates that he has a right to expect his wife to do all the things he asks of her because he has to work so hard at his business. As he sees it, he simply does not have the time to make a living and also to contribute much energy or interest to his family. He expects them to realize this. Incidentally it is interesting in terms of the concept of family continuity that his grandfather is described as a person who was so preoccupied with his own affairs that he sometimes forgot the names and relative ages of his children. In any case, both the mother and father are tremendously unsatisfied people, and they are deeply disappointed in what they are able to get from each other.

The most significant aspect of their dissatisfaction is their unconscious way of coping with it. They both unconsciously assume that parents have a right to call upon their children for the things they cannot get elsewhere. They expect a child to make big contributions to its parents. The mother expresses this fantasy beautifully in a Rorschach image.

"Two babies holding together. Keeping the man and woman together."

In the response she puts babies into the role of maintaining the relationship between two adult figures. She sees a baby as something for whose possession parents compete.

"Looks like a baby in the middle and one wants it and the other one wants it."

At a behavioral level, one finds that the mother and father have both expected exorbitant giving from their son (patient's husband). Thus, the father demanded that the son take an active part in his business at an early age and severely punished him when he tried to take time out for recreational activities. He now expects his son to devote 16 or more hours a day to the business. The son has felt so obligated to the father that for long periods he accepted very minimal wages and put most of his share back into the business. Similarly, the mother has revealed in some of her interview responses that she feels she has let her son down in various ways. She describes her son as having been "hard to raise" and refers to several incidents in which other people took advantage of him and she did not feel strong enough to help him or defend him. She blames her husband for this and indicates that she could not help her son at certain crisis points because her husband demanded that she be responsible for so many other things. Clearly, she senses that she has been very stingy and has given little to him.

One finds a species of confirmation of the validity of the conceptualization about how demanding the mother and father have been of their son in terms of some of his fantasies and behavior. There are indications that he unconsciously thinks of himself as a beast of burden whose duty it is to give of himself to others to the utmost. A Rorschach fantasy he produced conveys this feeling on his part:

"Shape of a camel. Use it in the desert. Carry people across the desert. It's something that other animals couldn't do. It has a reserve of water and carries a big load."

Likewise, in one TAT story he pictures a situation in which a child wants to study and learn, but the parents want the child to plough a field. Perhaps the best sign of his exorbitant giving to his parents is the fact that even though he is now married, he continues to put the major portion of his time, effort, and interest into his father's business. It would appear, then, that the primary interrelationship pattern in this family group is a function of 1) A mother and father who have very intense passive wishes and who feel they have a right to receive much help from their son; 2) A son who responds to the parental expectations and who has learned to fill the role of a giver and self-sacrificer.

The immediate family subgroup of which the patient is now a member was formed when she and her husband left their original respective families in order to get married. Both of their families were struggling with a similar dynamic problem but with opposite modes of defense. In her family the patient was on the receiving end of compensatory giving, whereas her husband had functioned in his family mainly in the role of a giver. The characteristics and development of the new group they formed by their marriage were in a sense predetermined by their previous group memberships. The patient had met her husband while she was attending high school and married him at the age of 16, just after graduating. He was 25 years of age. Her parents protested strongly against the idea of her marrying so young. But actually one finds data which suggest that they were unconsciously exerting strong pressure on her to slacken her demands on them and to give up the role of taker. For example, they proposed that when she graduated from high school, she go on to college or find a job of some sort. She did not wish to go to college, and her only alternative would have been to go forth and find a job. Around this time there occurred an incident which is symbolic of the pressure that was being put upon her by her parents. It was her custom to spend a good deal of time at home amusing herself inside the house. One day her mother locked her out of the house for awhile and told her that she was doing it for her own good, so that she would get some fresh air. When the patient finally announced that she was going to get married, the parents in their typically defensive way made many gestures of protest, but their basic wish to be free of her is obvious.

The patient saw in her husband someone who would permit her to play the role of taker as she had previously acted out in her family. By joining with him she was hoping to reinstitute the kind of group structure in which she was most comfortable, but from which she was being ejected. There were several ways in which he gave promise of permitting her this role. First, there was the fact that he was considerably older than she. Secondly, he profusely pledged to do his best to make her happy. During a therapy session the patient in referring to her husband's courtship said, "He rushed me." However, one may postulate that the most important part of her expectation of him was based on her conscious or unconscious knowledge that he was already functioning as a giver in his family. The precedent has already been set. It is interesting that the patient's husband sought her out for a marriage partner even though she was obviously young and immature and demanding of contributions. From what we know about him and from analogous data derived from other families we have studied, we assume that he sought her out precisely because she was a taker. His previous group membership had been based on giving to others, and in a paradoxical way he finds the giving role most comfortable, despite the various hardships it may involve. One would guess too that even though the marriage clearly involved his having to deal with strong demands from his wife, such demands seemed relatively mild compared to the load placed upon him by his mother and father.

The patient and her husband developed a markedly conflictual relationship from the very beginning of their marriage. Their basic difficulty centered on her complaint that he did not show her enough interest. In her therapy productions the patient refers to him as having been "selfish", "showing little affection", and "taking me for granted". The most apparent and visible cause of his neglect of her was the fact that he put almost all of his waking hours into working in his father's business. When he came home from work, he was tired and had little left over to give to her. It is apparent that what happened was that he was unable to break off his ties of obligation to his original family group, even after making definite commitments to his wife. His membership in his original group was still primary, and he could not adequately play the role of giver in the new grouping. He had to continue to give a large part of himself to his father particularly. The patient defensively made various attempts to re-establish her old relationship pattern with her father and mother and also went so far as to threaten her husband with divorce. But she was unable to mobilize her father and mother into a position sufficiently supportive so that she could safely leave her husband and depend on them. She did stimulate them into a sympathetic supportive attitude, and she recruited some indirect aid from them by influencing them to speak to her husband and to suggest to him that he be more considerate. Apropos of such pressuring of her husband, she said during one therapy session that perhaps she had always expected too much of him.

About a year after the marriage a boy was born. The pregnancy was unplanned, and this event further increased the tension in the group. The patient felt terribly burdened, was depressed, and began to make a variety of new demands of her husband. She particularly focused on the idea of his being more of a father and paying more attention to his son. They had numerous arguments about why he did not play more with his son and do more for him. She felt he left the whole burden of raising the child on her. The entrance of the child into the group meant, then, that he was subjected to even more stringent demands to play a giving role in this group. He experienced this increased pressure as something very painful and responded by withdrawing even further from this grouping and turning his energies more to his original family. The patient as a result redoubled her pressure on her own original family and got considerable new support from her mother and father. Her husband recalls in some of his current interview responses that at that time her parents took over many of her responsibilities. For example, they helped her in numerous ways with the child. With additional help from her family, the patient and her husband and child were able to attain an equilibrium tolerable enough for the three of them to continue to live together. It is striking that during this period the husband's mother and father, true to their defensive style which involves taking rather than giving, held themselves rather aloof and gave little of their time or interest to either the patient or the new child.

When one examines the fantasies of this child, as they appear in projective tests, one is impressed with how accurately they reflect the structure of his family group. This child unconsciously sees the mother figure as someone distant, someone who has gone away and is not available to give help. Despite father's relatively cold attitude, he still unconsciously sees him as a main source of supplies and the strong one. Here is an extract of a description of his relationship with father which is based on projective test material:

"Father appears to him as his only hope. He is trying to deny whatever is negative in his relationship with father and to idealize him as a giver." The child accurately registers the fact that mother is not a giver, but that father is.

The patient's parents gave considerable attention to this child initially as a way of relieving her of responsibility, and the child was well aware of the function of his grandparents in this respect. At times he has made such remarks as the following to his mother:

"Take me to grandmother so you can lie down and rest."

Gradually, the grandparents became very involved with the child and began to focus all their giving on the child and to give less to the patient. This is particularly true of the grandfather who lavishes gifts on the child and treats him as a great favorite. The child seriously diverted from the patient the attention and interest she had previously received from her parents. She felt chronically tense and dissatisfied. Over-all, as one studies the data concerning the patient and her husband and child during the several years following the birth of the child, one can see that at best they were all in a state of uncomfortable tension and barely able to hold together as a group.

Four years after the birth of the first child the patient became pregnant again. This new stress finally upset the equilibrium of the group sufficiently so that help from outside had to be sought. Midway in her pregnancy the patient got very depressed, "limp", "weak", and found herself unable to care for her child. She states, "I found myself groping in a dream world." She pondered all the new duties that would come with the second child and could not see where she would get additional help. When she became seriously disturbed in this fashion, it had widespread repercussions on the whole range of family group members. Her husband had to decrease the amount of time he gave to his work. His mother and father became anxious about the situation—perhaps because they perceived that their son would have to divert some of his giving from them to his wife. The patient's parents had to assume a greater burden in the care of the child. Later when she was hospitalized for a while, the child went to stay with them during that period. A final dramatic phase in this readjustment sequence occurred after the patient had been in the hospital briefly. It was decided that she should stay with her parents for the duration of the pregnancy and that her child would remain at home with her husband. It is at this point that one can see that the patient through her illness has succeeded in restoring the basic group structure that existed before her marriage. Once more she was back with her mother and father in a position to make all kinds of clinging demands upon them. Her husband was at the same time left in the role of being one of the prime givers to the child; of still having to maintain many of his obligations to his parents; and of trying to give her as much support as he could muster.

An example of how such a redistribution of group forces may seriously upset other members of the group and produce new "patients" was provided by the reaction of the patient's mother. The new responsibilities imposed upon her made her feel depressed and inadequate, and she came in for psychiatric consultation. Similarly, the husband became sufficiently disturbed so that he felt the need of some psychotherapeutic help also.

We have attempted to trace the patient's illness in terms of events and patterns in three subgroups that are part of a larger family group structure. We intended this analysis as a rather crude prototype model of how neurotic behavior can be conceptualized in group terms. In order to test the meaningfulness of this model which was derived from data obtained from the separate individuals in the total group, and also as a therapeutic procedure, it was decided to call all of the individuals together for a group meeting and to observe the resulting patterns of interaction. The basic question that was being asked was whether the passivity conflicts and modes of defense against these conflicts which have been described would show themselves in the group interaction process. Would the various family members act out in the group the sorts of roles which it has been assumed they do play. All seven of the group members assembled for an hour and one-half session. The meeting was structured as an opportunity for the various family members to exchange ideas and settle issues, with the intent of helping the patient recover. One of the writers, a psychiatrist, managed the group and structured it. The other acted as an observer, and took down as nearly a verbatim account of the proceedings as possible. Generally, the data obtained confirmed the model of family interrelations we have outlined. The confirming data may be best presented by describing briefly what most characterized each person and subgroup of persons during the session.

To begin with, the patient sat almost completely silent throughout. She contributed nothing to the group discussion and took a pained resigned attitude. She spoke only once near the end of the session. She said, "I don't think the group is getting any place. I don't think anyone knows what's going on. You don't understand me." Her attitude implied that she had nothing to contribute and that she was disappointed in what the others were able to offer to her. Her parents, particularly her mother, took a much more active attitude toward the situation. The mother initially stated in a determined way that she wanted to help her daughter and her son-in-law and that she thought everyone in the group should do their best toward this end. She then systematically tried to analyze some of the difficulties that she felt existed between the patient and the patient's husband and between her side of the family and her son-in-law's side of the family. Her overt role was that of the helper, the solver of problems, the active one. Although her husband was less active verbally, he attempted to make his giving, helpful role clear in two ways. For one thing, he made a definite statement that he had always wanted nothing but the best for his daughter and her husband. Secondly, he took upon himself the job of caring for and supervising the patient's child, who was also present in a play room just outside the room in which the group was meeting. Whenever the child would enter the meeting room, he would reassure him, quiet him, and lead him back to the play room. He made it clear that he was assuming the responsibility for the boy. However, despite this apparent overt helpful role played by the patient's mother and father, their deeper purpose was to disengage themselves from responsibility for their daughter and to recruit others to take up the load. Their pattern of behaviour in the group involved the same compensatory style of denying the passive wishes as was evident in their test data. Their basic passive intent and desire to reject their daughter came out gradually during the course of the session in an increasing number of references to the idea that their daughter and her husband really ought to work out their problems by themselves. They said they wanted to help, but raised the question whether a couple should not be left alone to their own affairs. The mother emphasized that she knew her daughter really wanted to stand on her own two feet and not to take anything from them. Finally, she concluded that the person her daughter most needed help from was her own husband. Her attitude may be paraphrased: "For my daughter's own good we must not interfere in her life by giving her things or doing things for her. I want to do things for her but it just wouldn't be right."

The patient's husband took the most active role in the group interaction. He talked more than anyone else and openly revealed more of his intimate feelings. Much of what was said by the others was directed at him. A large proportion of the statements directed at him were critical and admonished him to change his ways and be more helpful to his wife. The group in general made it clear that his wife was mainly his burden and that she would get better only if he gave more to her. He initially responded in a defensive way to this sort of pressure and vented some of his resentment about his wife's lack of understanding of the necessity for his putting so much time and energy into his work. He complained that his wife was too demanding. But after awhile, his tone changed and he pledged himself to do more for his wife. He responded with acquiescence to the pressure of the other group members that he relieve them of responsibility for his wife. Near the end of the session he made this reassuring comment to his wife: "I know I can help you. You can always depend on me for important things." In an almost inevitable way he found himself assigned by the group to being a giver and a bearer of burdens.

His mother and father were generally quiet and passive throughout the session. This was especially true of his father who only spoke two or three times in the entire period. The few times he did speak it was to defend the position that a man has a right to expect his wife to assume most other family responsibilities if he is preoccupied with his business affairs. He also complained once that his daughter-in-law's family were able to visit more with his son and son's wife and to do more for them because they lived nearer and because they did not own a business which was so time-consuming. He was obviously aware of how little interest he had shown in his son's family and was trying to excuse it. He made no attempts to offer definite advice or help to anyone. His main point was that he did not have any extra time left over to do anything for anyone else. The mother indicated her unwillingness to give much of herself right from the outset. She declared that she did not see who in the group would be able to help her son and daughter-in-law. She emphasized that parents should keep their distance from their children: "If parents mix in too much it's bad." She did imply in various ways that her daughter-in-law should take more responsibility, and she defended her son's inability to give more to his wife because he had to put in so much time in his father's business. In so doing she was obviously defending the demands that she and her husband make upon her son. The other main theme in her remarks had to do with how much her husband neglected her for his work. She indicated that this imposed hardships on her which made it impossible for her to do much for anyone else. Basically, then, both she and her husband made it clear in the group that they have plenty of their own troubles and grievances and that they did not see how they could contribute much to helping their son and his wife. Their position of wanting help rather than being willing to give help was quite open.

We have similar detailed data concerning the two and three generation patterns of interaction of more than 20 families. The analysis of the family we have outlined above has been presented by way of illustration of a conceptual approach which we have found successful in understanding the individual patient as one link in an on-going group process.

REFERENCES

1. ACKERMAN, N. W. 1954. Interpersonal disturbances in the family. *Psychiatry*, 17, 359-368.
2. DOANE, B. K. 1955. Effects of decreased sensory stimulation on visual perception: Notes on experimental work in progress. *Psychol. Abstr.*, 29, 625.
3. ERIKSON, E. 1960. *Childhood and society*. Norton, New York.
4. FISHER, S., and MENDELL, D. The communication of neurotic patterns within family groups. *Psychiatry* (in press).
5. HENRY, J., and WARSON, S. 1951. Family structure and psychic development. *Am. J. Orthopsychiat.*, 21, 59-73. [Reprinted in this collection as No. XIII.]
6. MORRIS, W. S., and NICHOLAS, A. L. 1950. Intrafamilial personality configurations among children with primary behavior disorders and their parents: A Rorschach investigation. *J. clin. Psychol.*, 6, 309-319.
7. PALM, R., and ABRAHMSEN, D. 1954. A Rorschach study of the wives of sex offenders. *J. nerv. ment. Dis.*, 119, 167-172.
8. SPERLINE, M. 1951. The neurotic child and his mother, a psychoanalytic study. *Am. J. Orthopsychiat.*, 21, 351-364.

4

THE MATERIAL CIRCUMSTANCES DIMENSION

This dimension gives an account of the family's material state in the Past, its position in the Present, and what can be predicted about it in the Future.

Of the many elements in a family's material circumstances in the time sequence of Past, Present and Future, the following have been selected for demonstration here:

Material background
Distribution of income
Housing
Hard-core families

XVIII

TIME OF MARRIAGE, MATE SELECTION AND TASK ACCOMPLISHMENT IN NEWLY FORMED COPENHAGEN FAMILIES

KIRSTEN AUKEN

Families live within a material framework, and some of its components are selected here for investigation.

APPROACH AND METHOD

In order to secure adequate information on the conditions of young urban families with children a sequential study of more than 300 families was initiated in February, 1954, and completed in March, 1959.* The material is here analyzed with respect to timing of marriage and social homogamy, housing and work conditions at time of marriage, solutions of basic family tasks, and unsolved problems.

Considering the sequential nature of the study the interview-method was employed despite its costliness with respect to time and money. This method facilitates the task of comprehensive questioning and makes possible—when done in the homes of the families—description of dwelling, environment etc. Ministers of the Church were employed as interviewers.

The families were visited in their homes on four occasions: 1) immediately following the birth of the first-born child, 2) half a year later, 3) around the two years' birthday of the child, and, 4) in connection with the child's third birthday. Both spouses were interviewed together.

A total number of 311 families were asked to participate and only 8

* The members of the research team were: *K. Auken*, M.D., *V. Christensen*, M.D., *O. Krabbe*, D.D., *I. Jørgensen*, Social Worker, and *J. Sørensen*, M.A. An extensive report has been published by these authors: *Familien Lever*, Copenhagen 1962.

Reprinted from ACTA SOCIOLOGICA, Vol. 8, 1964, pp. 128-141.

refused. Due to change of residence, emigration, etc. 28 families had to withdraw from the study after the first visit, but are included in the material concerning mate-selection, timing of marriage and material conditions at time of marriage. The four visits were all completed for 225 families. Yet in the remaining 50 cases the third visit almost coincided with the child's third birthday. Both of the spouses were home together at two-thirds of all the 1078 visits.

In selecting families for the study one wished to concentrate on the "normal", young urban family with children and to contact it immediately following the birth of the first child. So, to qualify for the study the family had to fulfil these three conditions: 1) the child had to be the first child of the couple, 2) it had to be baptized in wedlock, and 3) the baptism had to take place prior to the one year birthday of the child. The motives for choosing baptism as point of departure are twofold: a) 97% of all children in Denmark receive Christian baptism in the People's Church —the official church of Denmark—and b) baptism was found to be an easy and natural way of getting into contact with the young couples.

The families were randomly selected. A certain date was fixed from which all first-born children registered for baptism were to be included in the study. To compensate for the children not receiving Christian baptism a few visits were paid to families—also randomly selected—who only registered the name of their first-born child with the civil authorities. In this manner 184 families were selected in the Greater Copenhagen area and 119 in the suburbs of Copenhagen.

Upon completion of two-thirds of all the visits two of the authors visited 5 % of the families—selected at random—with the purpose of checking the accuracy of the reports. The results of these control visits appeared to agree closely with the information previously obtained through the ordinary visits.

CONDITIONS RELATED TO THE DECISION TO MARRY. TIMING OF MARRIAGE AND SOCIAL HOMOGAMY

1. Decision about Time and Type of Wedding

Out of 303 families 270 have supplied information on what was the *decisive factor in determining the date of wedding*. While 128 (almost 50 %) mentioned pregnancy only, 3 stated completion of husband's education. Approximately 15 %—44 couples—married at the prospect of obtaining independent dwelling. The remaining 95 couples gave a wide range of answers, the most frequent being: had been engaged long enough, knew each other well enough, etc.

Three-fifths—187—of the couples were *married in the church*. About 40 % of these brides were pregnant at the wedding, whereas this applied to more than 50 % of the civilly married brides. 10 % of the spouses married in the church had previously been married against 20 % of the other group.

2. TIME OF MARRIAGE AND PREGNANCY

The average age at marriage in Denmark has steadily been declining for several decades. The reasons are numerous and intricate—the major ones probably being the improved standard of living coupled with an earlier sexual maturity. The average age of the husbands at time of marriage was in 1960 26·3 years and for the wives 22·9.

TABLE 1
DURATION OF MARRIAGE AT THE BIRTH OF THE FIRST CHILD

Duration of marriage	Number of children
The child born before marriage...............	12
Less than 6 months...........................	93
6-9 months...................................	33
9 months-2 years.............................	87
2-6 years....................................	65
More than 6 years............................	13
Total....	303

46 % of the children were premaritally conceived and three-fifths of these before six months prior to marriage.

Yet not all of the "too early" born children were unwanted. Only about one-fourth of all the couples explicitly stated that they had never desired their first child, while another 15 % said that although any thought of the child initially had been disagreeable to them, this was no longer so. The remaining 60 % of the children were both planned and wanted. As was to be expected 90 % of all the undesired children were born too early, but so were 25 % of the wanted and planned children as well.

3. AGE AT MARRIAGE AND PREMARITAL PREGNANCY

TABLE 2
% PREGNANT BRIDES BY AGE OF BRIDE AND BRIDEGROOM

	Age of wife							
	below 18	18-19	20-21	22-24	25-29	30-34	above 34	Total
Age of husband								
18-19	100	67	100	100	100	—	—	82
20-21	100	85	91	33	50	—	—	80
22-24	100	68	34	31	30	50	—	44
25-29	100	33	38	30	8	50	—	31
30-34	—	50	33	—	40	50	—	29
above 34	—	100	—	33	29	100	75	52
Total	100	67	44	30	28	60	38	46

Table 2 shows the great variation in percentage of pregnant brides with age of spouses at marriage. Thus close to all brides were pregnant in couples where both spouses were below 20 at marriage, while in couples where both spouses were 22 and above at marriage, only one-third of the brides were pregnant. Thus there appears to be a fairly close correlation between early marriages and premarital pregnancies.

4. Age at Marriage and Mate-selection vs. Family Background

To get an adequate picture of a child's milieu and its conditions of childhood it is more essential to know with whom it lived and by whom it was brought up than to know the marital status of its parents.

In this study three-fourths of all the spouses lived with both parents during the major part of their childhood. Slightly more than 10 % had in the last part of childhood—i.e. 7-13 years*—been brought up exclusively by one of the parents and in five-sixths of these cases the child stayed with its mother. Only one per cent was brought up in a public institution. Combining this with the information gathered on the marital status of the spouses' parents, one finds that in those marriages that had been dissolved on account of either divorce and judicial separation (37) or decease (34), the child has in 80 % of the cases been brought up by one of the parents.

Table 3 shows the association between age at marriage and parents' marital status, when the spouses were between 7 and 13 years of age.

TABLE 3

AGE AT MARRIAGE BY FAMILY BACKGROUND

| | Marriage of H's parents | | Marriage of W's parents | |
	normal†	not-normal	normal	not-normal
Age at marriage				
Below 18..........	—	—	8	8
18-19.............	8	3	41	11
20-21.............	30	10	51	20
22-24.............	82	23	63	14
25-29.............	53	22	22	10
above 29..........	19	8	8	1
Total....	192	66	192	64
Average age........	24·9	25·3	22·5	21·8

Men with a "not-normal" childhood background apparently married slightly later than those with a "normal" background, whereas the reverse applies to the women from broken homes.

* The rationale behind special investigation of the age 7-14 is that this period is the legal minimum for attending school in Denmark.
† "Normal marriage" refers to the situation where the children have had both parents present. "Not-normal marriage" comprises all other forms of family background—mainly children living alone with their mother.

No tendency for homogamy with respect to "normalcy" of childhood family background was found.

5. AGE AT MARRIAGE AND MATE-SELECTION VS. SOCIAL BACKGROUND

All the parents of the spouses were divided into three—rough—social status groups: 1) small landholders, small shopkeepers and independents in the towns, and unskilled workers, 2) lower executives and skilled workers, and 3) higher executives and independents in the towns and in the countryside. Attempts were then made to detect variations between social status and age at time of marriage.

TABLE 4

AGE AT MARRIAGE AND SOCIAL BACKGROUND

	Social position of H's father				Social position of W's father		
	Group	1	2	3	Group	1	2	3
Age at marriage								
Below 18		—	—	—		9	4	3
18-19		8	1	2		23	20	7
20-21		18	14	6		22	28	18
22-24		35	34	31		22	22	27
25-29		21	24	24		3	11	17
Above 29		12	9	5		3	2	3
Total		94	82	68		82	87	75
Average age		24·8	25·0	25·2		21·1	22·4	23·3

The table reflects the tendency for people from the higher social strata to marry somewhat later than others. This appears especially true of the young women coming from the high status group. It also appears that 50 % of the two extreme social groups were more likely—than would have been the case under complete social mobility—to choose a mate from their own social group than from any other. On the other hand the distribution of the intermediate social group agreed closely with the total distribution.

6. AGE AT MARRIAGE AND MATE-SELECTION VS. EDUCATION

The study established a clear connection between age at marriage and kind and length of education. Spouses with little or no education were heavily represented among the very young families.

Spouses having accomplished a higher education relatively "frequently" choose their mates from the "educated" portion of the opposite sex. Only 35 % of the wives having a degree have married men lacking one, although these constitute 67 % of the total. Despite the fact that women without a degree constitute 72 % of all the women, a mere 47 % of the men having a higher education selected wives without educational degree. But since this correlation equally depends on the entire social background of the spouses, one probably ought to be extremely careful in drawing conclusions on this basis. For one thing there seems to be a fairly close connection between the spouses' educational background and the social position of their fathers.

Whereas 85 % of both men and women coming from the previously mentioned social group 1 did not receive any education whatever, this only applied to 39 % of the spouses from social group 3. And although the spouses from the latter group only accounted for 30 % of the total, they constituted approximately 70 % of all the people having passed matriculation examination, while the remaining 30 % is distributed with ⅔ in social status group 2—and only ⅓ in group 1. It is furthermore instructive to note that there is a gap between male and female education, and that this gap is most salient in status group 3.

Thus, people having completed some higher education tend to select a mate of a similar educational background and to marry relatively late. Yet there also seems to exist a certain connection between social background and education, and between social background, education and mate-selection—and again between social background, education and age at marriage, thus rendering the task of determining the decisive factor in the individual case extremely difficult.

BASIC CONDITIONS AT TIME OF MARRIAGE AND FIRST YEARS OF MARRIAGE

HOUSING AT TIME OF MARRIAGE

The conditions of housing are not only important for the welfare of the young family, they also say something about the conditions under which marriage is entered.

TABLE 5

HOUSING CONDITIONS AT TIME OF MARRIAGE

Nature and type of dwelling	Number of couples
Own (or independent)* dwelling...........	125
Room(s) with parents.....................	69
Room(s) with others.....................	54
Spouses living separated..................	38
Other.................................	13
Not stated.............................	4
Total....	303

Remarkably few of the families possess an independent dwelling at marriage. This furthermore conceals a very uneven distribution over the different age categories. Whereas for instance 38 out of the 55 couples,

* "Independent dwelling" is here defined as a separate dwelling with private kitchen.

where the husband was above 30 years of age when marrying, had independent dwelling at marriage, only 8 out of the 52 couples, where the husband was under 21 years, enjoyed the same privilege. And when keeping in mind that about 80 % of the brides were pregnant at the marriage, this becomes even more outrageous.

Barely ½ of the 170 families who were not in possession of independent dwelling at the marriage had acquired one during the first six months of marriage. And still after one year (or more) ⅓ of this group did not have dwelling of their own. This corresponds to 15 % out of the total number of families. And here again the low "age-at-marriage" groups are heavily over-represented.

FINDINGS RELATED TO THE SOLUTION OF BASIC FAMILY TASKS OVER TIME

1. Housing during the First years of Marriage

The predominant type of residence of our young families is definitely the one of rented flats and apartments. Out of the 225 families having independent dwelling at the first visit, 90 % lived in flats and apartment houses; and 80 % did still do so at the last visit.

TABLE 6

SIZE OF DWELLING AT THE FIRST AND LAST VISIT

Size of dwelling	First visit	Last visit
1 room	27	6
2 rooms	149	146
3 rooms	64	77
4 rooms	24	33
5 or more rooms	7	9
Not stated	4	4
Total....	275	275

In order to increase the size and the quality of their dwellings, the families moved frequently during the investigative period. 50 %—135—moved one or more times.

Table 6 shows that although the many moves have resulted in many improvements of the housing conditions, more than 50 % (152) of the families did not have more than one or two rooms at their disposal even at the end of the study. This is below the average of all families with children, who in turn are worse off than couples without children.

Acquisition of independent dwelling and of more spacious living quarters just barely keeps up with the growth of the families. And the standard of housing* does not undergo any substantial changes during the investigative period. Using "1 person per room" as a minimum criterion of a satisfactory housing situation, only 25 % of all the dwellings

* Measured by density of habitation (i.e. number of persons per room).

—at the last visit—fulfil this basic requirement. This is all shown in table 7.

TABLE 7

DENSITY OF HABITATION AT LAST VISIT*

| | Number of occupants | | | | | |
	2	3	4	5 or more	Not stated	Total
Number of rooms						
1 room	2	3	—	1	—	6
2 rooms	5	74	56	11	—	146
3 rooms	—	36	39	2	—	77
4 rooms	—	16	12	5	—	33
5 or more rooms	—	4	1	4	—	9
Not stated	—	1	—	—	3	4
Total....	7	134	108	23	3	275

2. CONDITIONS OF WORK

When inquiring into the working conditions of the young families the prevailing impression is that the problems in this area are not nearly the size of the ones connected with housing. Stability, for instance, is the main characteristic of the employment of those husbands for whom our information can be considered conclusive. Two-thirds of the husbands have only held one position during the investigative period, while the number of husbands having been employed three or more different places only constitutes 10 % of the total.

The study produced no evidence supporting any correlation between age at marriage and stability of employment; nor was there found any correlation between number of jobs and educational background of the husbands.

The vast majority of the spouses did not consider wife's employment outside home, while children were still small, to be desirable (i.e. 200 out of 270 wives and a similar number of husbands). Almost all of the wives that nevertheless worked outside the home did so out of economic considerations.

TABLE 8

EMPLOYMENT OF WIVES IN THE INVESTIGATED PERIOD

Nature of employment	1 visit	2 visit	3 visit	4 visit	Only one position
Housewife	215	192	186	178	124
Skilled work	20	22	17	16	9
Unskilled work	30	45	55	60	10
Other	10	16	17	21	4
Total....	275	275	275	275	147

* The dwellings (inside the frame) have more occupants than rooms.

Table 8 shows the number of mothers that had no employment out of home during the entire investigative period.

This number (124) is considerably smaller than the number of wives who at the first visit were planning to stay home while the children were small. Adding to this the fact that these mothers probably had several unstated small jobs, it does seem like employment outside the home becomes more attractive as the child grows just a couple of years older. Finally, whereas 50 % of all the wives had not had a second pregnancy by the last interview, this only applied to 14 % of the 124 women that were exclusively working at home.

Around two-thirds of all the wives had a more or less thorough knowledge of the work conditions of their husbands, while the remaining 30 % did not know much of them.

Generally speaking the attitude towards work was one of disinterest. Very few revealed dissatisfaction with their present job, and even fewer were explicitly "happy" about it.

3. CHILD CARE

More than 90 % of the mothers nursed their own babies and 25 % continued beyond the first three months.

TABLE 9

TYPE OF DAY CARE AT VARYING AGE OF CHILD

Type of child care	Age of child			
	½ year	1 year	2 years	3 years
Mother	229	212	210	193
Day nurseries and kindergartens	15	17	21	48
Grandparents	18	19	16	14
Private day nursery	6	12	10	7
Other.....................	7	11	14	10
Not stated	—	4	4	3
Total....	275	275	275	275

Above 80 % of the half-year-old children were, according to table 9, being cared for by their mother during the entire day. At the last interview this number had declined to around 60-70 % or 193 of all the 275 children.

Yet only 150 of these 193 children have been cared for by their mother throughout the entire study; thus only around 50 % of all the children have been exclusively cared for by their mother during the first 3 years of life.

4. FAMILY FINANCIAL SUPPORT

Savings and debts play a very insignificant part in the economy of the families. Only very few families reveal extensive savings, capital and property, nor do very many state any substantial debts. Comparing this fact with the findings on budget-making (cf. p. 427) it seems like the families in general plan their consumption carefully inside the frames of their present income without contracting debts or making any particular savings. Table 10 states the total number of couples in the various income groups both at marriage, first and last visit. This table reflects the serious fluctuations of total income to which the young families are subject during the years around the birth of the first child.

TABLE 10

NUMBER OF COUPLES IN VARIOUS INCOME GROUPS AT MARRIAGE, AND AT
FIRST AND LAST VISIT

	At marriage		At first visit		At last visit	
	Number of couples	Number of W. with independent income	Number of couples	Number of W. with independent income	Number of couples	Number of W. with independent income
*Monthly income**						
Below 800	39	30	47	12	11	4
800-1000	17	14	89	6	41	5
1000-1200	59	58	75	7	79	8
1200-1500	109	109	37	21	57	17
1500-2000	31	31	15	9	46	26
Above 2000	2	2	4	2	12	6
Not stated	18	—	8	—	29	—
	275	244	275	57	275	66

Whereas only 56 families—around 21-22 % of the total—earned less than 1000 kr. a month at the marriage, this group included 51 % of all families shortly after the birth of the first child, where naturally the demands on income increase simultaneously. This income, moreover, is one of current earnings and has not been deflated. The highest income groups, i.e. above 1200 kr., decline correspondingly from 142 (55 % of the total) at marriage to 56 (20 %) at the first interview.

Apparently the majority of the families have at the last interview partly recovered from that decline in income which followed the birth of the child. Now at the last interview only 52 families earned less than 1100 kr. a month, and 46 % had an income exceeding 1200. The families, however, had still not at the last visit restored the "pre-children" standard of living. Firstly, numerous expenditures entered the family budget with the arrival of the child (or children); and secondly, the society as a whole has during the investigative period experienced an unprecedented economic prosperity; and finally, inflation has been quite heavy.

Other findings indicate that ⅔ of all the couples have been subjected to reduction of total income from marriage to first interview, and half of these couples have experienced a considerable decline of more than two steps. At the transition from the first to the last interview less than 10 %

* In Danish Kroner.

had been subject to a decrease in income, and around ⅔ of the couples had raised their income, but only 20 % of them more than two steps.

According to table 10 there quite obviously exists a fairly close correlation between the frequency of "wife-income" and the magnitude of income both at each interview and at the transition from one point to another. Thus the principal reason for the serious fluctuations of income during the years surrounding the birth of the first child appears to be found in the extent to which wives seek employment out of the home.

This study finds a typical pattern of women continuing to work despite the marriage and discontinuing it at the birth of the first child. Thus ⅔ of the women remained in their old jobs after the marriage and another 5 women continued to work but on shorter hours; 7 merely changed place of work. Moreover, 30 out of the 49 women (who stopped working at marriage) were premaritally pregnant; thus the child appears to have been a major motivating factor in several of these cases both for marrying and for the wife quitting her job. Only 60 wives did not stop working out of home by the birth of the first child.

5. ADMINISTRATION OF INCOME

Considerable interest has been attached to the part played by rent and instalment payments in the financial situation of the young families.

At the first interview 154 (out of 275) families spent less than 10 % of their disposable income on monthly rent for their dwelling; and not even 10 % of the families spent more than 20 %. This distribution remained relatively unaltered during the investigative period. Thus at the last visit the majority of the couples still only spent 10 % (or less) on dwelling expenditures, while only 30 couples spent 20 % or more.

There is a rise from approximately 60 % of the families that did not possess anything on deferred payments at the initiation of the study to around 70 % of the total at the last interview. Close to 40 % did not purchase anything in this manner at all during the investigative period. Virtually no correlation was found between the frequency of instalment purchases and size of income, except that the highest income groups tended to make slightly fewer such purchases than the average of the other families.

In extremely few instances the instalments were felt by the couple to be a strain on the financial situation.

Approximately 60 % of the families make up some kind of a budget; around half of the lower income families vs. ⅔ of the remaining families do so.

In half of the families both spouses participated in the administration of the income. 28 % and 21 % stated that this was the prerogative of respectively the husband and the wife. In 50 % of the cases where the husband was responsible for the management of the financial affairs, a budget was never made up, whereas this happened in ⅔ of the rest.

6. Leisure Time and Social Contacts

Concerning leisure the spouses were asked to relate what they had done in the evenings of the week preceding the various interviews. All the spouses had at the first visit spent 91 % of all the 275 by 7 possible evenings at home together and at the last visit 85 %. Only 3 and 6 % respectively had spent time out separately.

Very few of the spouses have actual hobbies such as stamps and photography, etc. Most of the time is spent at listening to the radio, and (at the later visits) at watching T.V., at reading papers and magazines, at making minor reparations in the home, etc.

When out together the couples most frequently visit relatives; but sometimes they will go to a movie. Visits at restaurants, bars and taverns are virtually nonexistent. Social life with friends, neighbors and colleagues is highly limited. When out separately—and neither having evening jobs—the husbands generally attend evening classes, participate in organization work, athletics, etc. The wife very rarely takes part in these kind of activities; probably because the children are small. More than half of the families completely lack neighbor contact. Relations to neighbors are generally very reserved but correct. None of the families meet any problems here.

Eighty per cent of the families stated at all four visits that they spent summer vacation together. At the first interview 15 % stayed at home together during the entire vacation; at the last visit 25 % remained home. Hardly any of the families—the children still being very young—left the country during summer vacation. The majority spent the vacation with relatives (more than 50% of the spouses are born outside Copenhagen).

Relations to the family are generally excellent and characterized by assistance and support from the older generation. Less than 5 % report about friction on this point.

Sunday is the great and comfortable day of rest for the predominant part of the young families. A good number of families state that they "never leave the home on Sundays" nor do they ever invite people over. Not many of the couples are in a habit of steady church-going. Extremely few, though, are decidedly negative in attitude towards the church, but the vast majority is completely indifferent. Fifteen per cent of the couples showed some interest in the church. Yet only a limited number of them attended services regularly and the majority abided by going there at Christmas time. Even spouses who themselves stated that they had been under considerable religious influence during their upbringing did not appear to nourish any greater "churchly" interest than the average. In none of the families did religion cause problems between the spouses. (About ¼ of the couples said a prayer or sang an evening carol with their child).

7. UNSOLVED PROBLEMS

When considering common traits of these young families, we are in many ways confronted with something approaching an almost "bourgeois harmony". They are industrious families attending to their work, carefully planning their finances and building up a home. Apparently one is living at peace with oneself, one's relatives and with one's neighbor, but outgoing activities are very rare.

Yet many families have great problems in a number of areas. Two-thirds do not possess an independent dwelling at marriage, and the dwellings they have or get are below average. One-quarter of the children were unwanted. Only half of the babies are stably being cared for by their mothers during the first three years. The predominant part of the couples are explicitly indifferent to their job, and 10 % have suffered from unemployment periods in the course of the study. Too much work has been a nuisance for still more. Alcoholism is rarely a problem for the young families. But partly due to alcoholism two marriages were dissolved.

A total of 18 marriages—close to 7 %—were dissolved during the investigative period. It seems like a combination of unfortunate environment and childhood, of early marriage, of inferior housing conditions and of lacking support from the older generation has produced difficulties not easily overcome by spouses lacking the necessary physical and mental strength and ability of adaption.

When evaluating the relatively low percentage of divorces one must keep in mind that 1) the study exclusively dealt with couples having small children, and that this group traditionally has the lowest percentage of divorces of all groups, and that 2) the study lasted only 3-4 years.

A FOLLOW-UP STUDY

If the necessary funds can be raised, a follow-up study is scheduled for 1964-65 around the tenth birthday of the child. Prior to the interviews themselves, attempts will be made to predict the success or failure of the individual marriage. The study of the family role distribution will be intensified. Special attention will be given to the condition and development of the child in relation particularly to parents, playmates and school.

XIX

DISTRIBUTION OF INCOME WITHIN
THE FAMILY

MICHAEL YOUNG

*Income is a feature of a family that is easily measured.
Its distribution may not give each family member equal
benefit.*

It is painfully obvious to the student of social policy that growing knowledge about the distribution of the national income between families has
not so far been matched by a growth in knowledge about the distribution
of the family income between its members. In place of knowledge, the
assumption has often been made, though not stated, that the family, while
no longer generally considered a unit for the purposes of earning, can
still be treated as a unit for the purposes of spending. It has been taken
for granted that some members of a family cannot be rich while others are
poor. Most pre-war social surveys postulated, and those responsible for
policy have continued to assume, that "Poverty is a characteristic of a
family, and not of an individual, who is said to be in poverty only because
he happens to be a member of a family which is in poverty."[25] It is my
object to question this assumption by drawing on the available literature,
and my purpose to plead with the Ministry of Labour, in its forthcoming
Budget Enquiry, and with responsible research agencies generally, to
remedy a serious deficiency in our knowledge of our society.

To replace assumption by information is no small venture. The first
task, itself daunting enough, is to discover the ways in which the total
earnings of wage-earning members are divided up between the different
spenders of the family. The second and much more formidable task is to
discover the distribution of actual goods and services between the members of the family. It is not as though there were any neat uniformities in
behaviour. Habits about money vary between parts of the country and

Reprinted from BRITISH JOURNAL OF SOCIOLOGY, Vol. 3, 1952, pp. 305-321.

between social classes—indeed each family has its own little peculiarities. Has it to be concluded that good intentions must bow before the inevitability of ignorance?

It would certainly not be worth assaulting the difficulties at all unless there was some little evidence to suggest the existence of differential poverty within families. In fact, many outstanding social investigators have recorded that the bread-winners are often the meat-eaters. I will cite a few examples chosen from surveys made over the years.

1892   The husband takes 4d. a day for his dinner. Wife and children do not eat much.[1]

1902   "If there's anythink extra to buy," a woman told one of my investigators, "me and the children goes without dinner, or mebbe only 'as a cup o' tea and a bit o' bread; but Jim (her husband) ollers takes 'is dinner to work, and I give it 'im as usual; 'e never knows we go without and I never tells 'im".[19]

1938   It was a matter of daily experience to observe the obvious signs of malnutrition in the appearance of wives of unemployed men with families. They obviously did without things for the sake of their husbands and children, and it was by no means certain that they keep for their own use the "extra nourishment" provided expressly for them in a large number of cases by the Unemployment Assistance Board.[15]

1939   Health Visitors' accounts also speak of the deplorable extent to which the woman will starve herself in order that her children should have a little more or that her labour should be lightened. Nor is this changed even at the times when, for the sake of a coming child as well as for herself, she should be getting a good diet.[23]

1948   Many women admitted that they regularly gave up their butter, egg, and bacon rations to the children.[10]

1948   In one case, out of his £4 10s. wages the husband paid his wife £2 for housekeeping for a family of four, but in practice he got his money back in daily instalments for his cigarettes-and food out.[27]

PRE-WAR INVESTIGATIONS

Half a century ago Rowntree gave a lead to research workers which has never yet been fully followed up. He formulated the concept not only of "primary poverty" but of "secondary poverty". Families were considered to be suffering from the former where their "total earnings are insufficient to obtain the minimum necessaries for the maintenance of merely physical efficiency"; and from the latter where their "total earnings would be sufficient for the maintenance of merely physical efficiency were it not that some portion of it is absorbed by other expenditure, either useful or wasteful".[19] Rowntree noticed, as Booth had noticed before him, that some members of some families with adequate income were yet suffering from acute poverty.

But "primary poverty" had one brilliant advantage: it was statistically measurable. The concept was therefore given a central place, to the exclusion of secondary poverty, in most of the social surveys conducted in the following 40 years. Investigators had first to define "primary poverty" by determining how much money was required to satisfy the minimum needs of men, women and children. (Or, to put it uncharitably, they formulated a middle-class view of what, at any particular time, constituted poverty for working-class people.) Then, having discovered the composition and income of the families in the survey area, they could calculate how many families were living in "primary poverty". Such an approach "assumes that the incomes of all the members of the family are pooled in order that they may be used to the best advantage".[14]

Yet the surveys throw some light into the darkness. For one thing, the family income had to be ascertained, and one method of ascertaining it was to ask the wife. But the wife, it was found, might not know. The Merseyside Survey referred to "the fact that some housewives who were responsible for keeping the budgets would only have knowledge of what was given them to spend, and this sum would not infrequently be less than the aggregate of the family income".[2] The Bristol Survey, commenting on the good relations established between interviewers and families, said that "On several occasions husbands even ran after them to disclose earnings which they had not wanted to reveal in front of their wives."[25] Investigators therefore had to check up with local trade union officials and with employers in order to find out typical wages. In his second survey in 1936, Rowntree gave up the attempt to get information about wages from the wives. "Most of the interviews", he said, "were with women, and frequently a woman only knows what money her husband gives her, not how much he actually receives."[20] He took advantage of his excellent connections in York to obtain the wages of 60 per cent of the wage-earners covered from their employers, and the rest he estimated. In his third survey, he followed the same course, but on this occasion succeeded, with the approval of the trade unions, in getting figures for earnings from employers' wage books for over 95 per cent of the heads of households.[21]

What can be culled from the pre-war social surveys is, therefore, slight but significant. In outlining the methods used to obtain the earnings figures required to calculate "primary poverty", the surveys underlined once again the limitations of the concept itself. If wives did not know what their husbands were earning, it was in the highest degree unlikely that the whole family income was being used to purchase "necessaries".

The Ministry of Labour, in conducting its Working Class Budget Enquiry of 1937-8, ran into just the same difficulty as the social surveys, because its information was normally gathered from wives. It could not plead lack of warning. A Board of Trade Enquiry in 1903 reported that "The wife frequently does not know what the actual earnings of her husband are, but only the weekly sum he gives her for housekeeping."[3] The Ministry took precautions, but however ill or well conceived, they were far from effective in practice. "There are indications, however, in some of the budgets received, that expenditure on tobacco and cigarettes was not in all cases fully stated . . . The experience of previous enquiries into household expenditure has indicated that the particulars given in large-scale collections of family budgets are unlikely to disclose the full amount of expenditure either on tobacco and cigarettes or on alcoholic drink."[13] One part of the explanation was simple enough. Wives filled up the budget forms. They did not know the full extent of their husbands' spending on alcohol and tobacco. They understated this spending and, between them, threw the Ministry's national figures into error. The error can be estimated, by comparing the reported consumption of the Ministry's sample with the estimated total consumption of alcohol and tobacco by working-class people.[9] It would appear that only 14 per cent of the expenditure on drink and 66 per cent of expenditure on tobacco was reported by working-class families."[7] Thus the Budget Enquiry gave backing to the conclusion drawn from the poverty surveys that housewives often did not know either what their husbands earned or how they spent their money.

Pre-war investigators repeatedly emphasized that their results, related as they were to "primary poverty", understated the amount of poverty that actually existed. For their methods led to an understatement of the proportions of women and children living in poverty as compared with their menfolk. Mr. Rowntree puts the matter very clearly in *Poverty and Progress*. "Thus a man may earn 70s. and only give his wife 50s. on which to keep house. If that is less than the sum required to enable the family to live at the minimum standard, the family will *in fact* be living below it, but if 70s. is a figure which would raise the family above the minimum, it is so counted in our statistics."

Two later studies[22, 12] attempted to handle the matter differently. These studies appeared too late to influence the Beveridge Report and perhaps too early, despite their relevance, to influence the Royal Commission on Population. Both studies suggested that husbands not uncommonly kept more for, and spent more on, themselves than they would have done had the income of the family been laid out to the best advantage of all its members. "It is quite unrealistic," said Miss Soutar and her colleagues, "to assume that a man will hand over all his wages for general family use." Miss Soutar and her colleagues claimed that "actual poverty as shown by the housekeeping balance available for food per man is much greater than that shown by the type of measurement usually adopted in social surveys". They found out, from people living on the Kingstanding Estate in Birmingham in 1939, what housekeeping allowances were given by husbands to their wives. The amounts spent on rent, fuel, clothing, etc., included in the minimum standard, and the amounts spent on voluntary insurances and hire purchase, were then deducted from the allowances. This was done because it was found that the housewife usually paid for these things out of her allowance. The final balance was considered available for food. It was found that more than twice as many families were in poverty (as regards food) when measured by this revised standard than when measured by the usual "primary poverty" standard. Most of the families who were above the line according to the "primary poverty" standard, but below according to the housekeeping balance standard, were families with three or more children.

Mr. Madge's enquiry, carried out under the stimulus of Lord Keynes and with the assistance of the late Mr. E. Rothbarth in the early years of the war, was even more illuminating. Madge stated that family earnings are

usually divided into two parts—"Housekeeping money" and "Pocket money" . . . Of the total net earnings in Glasgow, 62 per cent were earned by husbands, 26 per cent by other earners aged more than twenty-two, and 12 per cent by juvenile earners. The husband-wife contract is therefore of key importance to the family standard of living. . . . Of the wife's share of the family income, the far greater part is spent on necessities, i.e. on things which the whole family consumes and uses, and which they cannot do without. The greater part of the earner's pocket money, on the other hand, is spent for the individual benefit of the earner, on things which are not essential for subsistence. The wife must in many cases be hard put to it to extract any pocket money for herself out of her allowance. She is, in fact, the lowest paid, most exploited worker in the country, given a mere subsistence wage, with no limit on hours worked.[12]

It was made clear that the division of income varied not only between families but between parts of the country. The following were the proportions of main earners giving all their earnings to their wives in various towns.[11]*

	Per cent
Slough	5
York	7
Bristol	11
Glasgow	14
Bradford	15
Leeds	24
Blackburn	49

While recognizing the variations in family practice, Mr. Madge was able to generalize his findings and, in effect, come to the same broad conclusion as Miss Soutar and her colleagues about the effect of the intra-family division of income upon the poverty of children. The table below shows how income was divided between husband and wife in Glasgow. The figures for Leeds were similar.

"Over the whole sample", said Mr. Madge, "the extra allowance is 7s. 8d. for the first child; a wife with two children gets 3s. 4d. extra per child; a wife with three children gets 3s. 8d. extra per child." Thus, the

* Such has also been the practice in colliery villages. Cf. Richard Llewellyn in *How Green Was My Valley* (Michael Joseph, 1939). "As soon as the whistle went they put chairs outside their front doors and sat there waiting till the men came up the Hill and home. Then as the men came up to their front doors they threw their wages, sovereign by sovereign, into the shining laps: fathers first and sons or lodgers in a line behind."

TABLE 1

DIVISION OF INCOME BETWEEN HUSBAND AND WIFE

Husband's net earnings in shillings	Percentage of net earnings given by husbands to wives in families with this number of children				
	0	1	2	3	4 or more
Up to 70s.	78	84	86	87	87
70s. to 100s. . . .	75	79	77	81	86
100s. and over . . .	42	65	65	69	72
All families	64	73	72	77	82
Number of families . .	(239)	(148)	(99)	(57)	(43)

husband did raise his allowance to his wife as the number of children increased, but not by as much as the cost of upkeep of the additional children. "The husband's share of the family income does not decrease, with the addition of children to the family, sufficiently to maintain the family standard of living in terms of food, clothes and fuel—the greater part of spending on these items being done by the housewife." And consequently the number of children suffering from poverty was even greater than believed by those who assumed that necessaries had the first claim upon the family income.

It appears that other goods, not conventionally regarded as necessaries, were in fact given priority. Mr. Hajnal and Professor Henderson analysed the data obtained by the 1937-8 Ministry of Labour Budget Enquiry, and showed, in the following table, the weekly expenditure on tobacco for families with different numbers of children.

TABLE 2

EXPENDITURE (PENCE PER WEEK) ON TOBACCO AND CIGARETTES

	Total expenditure 50s. to 60s.	Total expenditure 60s. to 70s.	Total expenditure 70s. to 80s.	Total expenditure 80s. to 90s.
No children	26	28	32	34
One child	25	30	29	36
Two children	21	29	31	36

"It may be seen", say the two authors, "that on average the parents of children spend no less on tobacco than the childless couples, and parents with two children hardly less than those with one child."

Mr. Mark Abrams* collected some data in the course of the enquiries made for the 1950 Hulton Readership Survey which suggest that tobacco was no less a necessity in 1950 than in 1937. The following hitherto unpublished table refers to the cigarettes smoked, and also to beer drinking and expenditure on football pools, all by working-class men.

* My thanks are due to Mr. Abrams, Research Services Ltd., and Hulton Press Ltd., for permission to reproduce the Table.

TABLE 3

MEN'S EXPENDITURE ON CIGARETTES, BEER AND POOLS

Consumption by Men, 1950	Male householders with			
	No children	One child	Two children	Three or more
	%	%	%	%
No. of cigarettes smoked daily :				
None	41	30	27	16
1- 5	7	6	8	8
6-10	20	23	25	25
11-15	12	18	13	18
16-20	12	14	16	20
Over 20	8	9	11	13
	100	100	100	100
Frequency of beer drinking :				
Never	23	21	17	17
Less than once a week	24	30	32	27
Once a week	17	18	23	26
Two or three times a week . . .	22	22	19	23
Every day	14	9	9	7
	100	100	100	100
Weekly expenditure on pools :				
Nothing	57	53	52	51
Less than 2s. 6d.	17	15	15	11
2s. 6d.–4s. 6d.	19	25	25	27
5s. 0d. or more	7	7	8	11
	100	100	100	100

From these figures it looks as though the arrival of children actually pushes the father into heavier smoking, drinking and betting; at least, it does not seem as though men's habits have changed very greatly since 1937. Mr. Abrams points out, however, that two of these sets of figures do not refer to expenditure, and that it is possible that men with larger families smoke more sub-standard cigarettes and drink smaller quantities on each visit to the pub. Moreover, total income of families is probably higher on average where there are more children than where there are fewer; analysis of the 1937-8 Budgets suggests that this was true then, and it is probably still true to-day. Most of the householders with no dependent children are older men, who smoke more pipes and spend less on pools.

The champions of family allowances made a most convincing case on the principal ground that employers did not, and could not be expected to, raise a man's earnings as the number of his dependent children increases. It was therefore inevitable that the "average" standard of life of the members of a family should fall as the size of the family rose; and where the income was low an increase in the number of children plunged the family into ever more acute poverty. The facts produced by the Madge and Soutar surveys showed that the idea of an average family standard of life was misleading. The financial burden of having an extra child was not, they indicated, shared equally by all members of the family, *but fell with especial severity upon the mother and upon previous children.* Some husbands behaved like employers. They did not increase their wives' "wages" as the size of the family increased.* These husbands would often feel the pinch themselves; there would be less for them to consume within the home. But they would still be able to compensate themselves to some extent outside the home if they maintained their own pocket money. The surveys rather strengthened than weakened the case for family allowances, for mothers and children were even worse off than was thought. But their results made crucial one point which was seldom stressed in the discussions on family allowances: that is, the question of who was to receive the allowance, father or mother.

And this became a hotly debated issue when the Family Allowances Bill was discussed in the House of Commons on 8 March, 1945, and M.P.s of all Parties joined together to oppose the Government's decision to make payment to the father. Sir William Jowitt, the Minister of National Insurance, spoke on behalf of the Government. "The conclusion that we have come to in the Bill is that the money should belong to the father but that either parent should be able to encash it. That has this merit, that it enables the normal family to decide for themselves what they want to do, and it really will not matter very much in a happy family what is done. After all, the father is generally the breadwinner. He brings the money and hands it over, or some of it, to the mother. Whether he hands it all over or only some of it, depends, I suppose, on the father, and a bit on the mother too, but the point is that he can, if he likes, only hand over a part and, even if we pay the family allowances to the wife, the husband can, if he is so minded, deduct from the amount that he normally hands over the amount of the allowance, so in that sense the husband has the last word."[6]

Eleanor Rathbone led the all-Party Opposition, and, in so doing, replied to the Minister's argument. "For one man, who is really greedy and unscrupulous", she said, "there are half a dozen who are merely weak, and creatures of habit, who hold on to what is given to them. If the money is given to the mother, and if they know that the law regards it as the child's property, or the mother's property to be spent for the child, that will help them to realize that the State recognizes the status of motherhood. In the majority of cases they will let her have it without decreasing the amount she receives from their income." The day was won: the

* The surveys do not supply any evidence about customs adopted when the size of the dependent family was reduced as the children left school. If housekeeping allowances remained more or less fixed whatever the size of the family, the wife would become much better off in her later life. There would have been much bigger swings for wives than for husbands between the comparative prosperity of the early years of marriage and the later years before retirement and the comparative poverty of the middle years when the number of dependent children was at a maximum.

Government's decision was reversed. But there has been no research since then to find out how family allowances have actually been used and how many husbands, if any, have cut down, or failed to increase, their wives' money because of the Government's allowances.

CHANGES SINCE 1939

How has the distribution of income within the family changed since the early years of the war? The hypothesis put forward is that wives' housekeeping allowances have not increased as much as husbands' earnings.* There is no direct evidence to support this hypothesis: Mr. Madge's enquiries have not been repeated. But there is some circumstantial evidence.

Several of the investigators already mentioned agree that, before the war and in its early years, housekeeping allowances tended to be a higher proportion of smaller, and a lower proportion of larger, incomes. Here, for instance, is Mr. Rowntree in *Poverty and Progress*:

> But it is essential to distinguish between the standard *attainable* and the standard *attained*. The former depends upon the income of the families and it is upon income that the classification of the families is based. But the standard attained depends not only upon income but upon how that income is spent. In the classes below the poverty line there is not a wide margin between these two standards, but that is not true of the classes above the minimum, and it becomes decreasingly so as incomes rise. Up to a certain figure the character of expenditure is determined by necessity; above that figure it is determined by choice. If the head of the household chooses to spend this surplus income on the home and the family, then a rising income implies a rising standard of comfort. But if, on the other hand, he chooses to spend it on himself, either on drink, cigarettes, gambling, or any other purely personal expenditure (which I am not here concerned either to condone or condemn), then, although his income may be comparatively high, the standard of comfort enjoyed by the family as a whole may be very low.

Miss Soutar and colleagues, in *Nutrition and Size of Family*, make much the same statement. "An interesting point about housekeeping money is that in the individual family it tends to remain unchanged however wages or family needs may alter. Many women have said that they've had the same allowance since they were first married. They have to meet the needs of five or six people out of, say, £2 10s. as they had for two." Wives did not necessarily resent this division. " 'You can't expect them to work for nothing' is a remarkably general comment of housewives." Mr. Madge (see Table 1 above) also concurred in stating that, not only did allowances fail to increase in proportion to the cost of upkeep of additional children, but that allowances were a lower proportion of the

---

* Account should also be taken of the changes in allowances given to housewives from subsidiary earners. These may by and large have risen faster than allowances from husbands. But even if they have, this change would not have benefited mothers with children all at school.

larger than of the smaller incomes. The results of these three surveys do suggest that at one time it was customary in working-class families for husbands to give their wives a more or less fixed allowance, whatever the size of the family and whatever the change in their earnings. This practice did not necessarily involve any deceit, and was probably accepted as right by most wives.

Such a custom would mean that the standard of life enjoyed by wives and children would be almost entirely dependent on prices, which would be just as important to them as the level of wages was to their husbands. Working-class earnings always have fluctuated from week to week, owing to short-time and over-time, and when prices were stable, there would be advantages for the wife in getting a guaranteed income. In a deflation, when prices and some wages were falling, wives and children might actually benefit. But in an inflation, when prices and wages were rising, such a custom would cause much suffering if persisted in. The practice suitable to an inflation is something much more flexible. If wives are not to suffer, basic housekeeping allowances should be adjusted upwards at fairly frequent intervals and total amounts spent for the benefit of wives and children out of exceptional bonuses obtained by the husband in addition to his basic wage should be much more variable from week to week. Many younger couples have probably broken away from the traditional custom and adapted themselves to the economic situation by adopting more flexible financial relationships. Many older couples probably continue as before; in such cases the wives need not suffer hardship as long as their children have left school. But there are probably still some families with young children where the old custom prevails.

This was certainly the gist of the observations made by Mr. F. Zweig after the war. "It (housekeeping money) is more often a fixed sum than a percentage of his net income. But even if it is a rough percentage, it is near enough to a fixed sum."[27] The same author in his study of coal-miners said, "I believe that the higher the wage level, the smaller is the percentage given to the housewife. A man who earns about £4 10s., and takes home after stoppages about £3 15s., would give his wife £3, and a man who earns £8 to £9 would rarely give his wife more than £5. He would be more willing to give her a treat from time to time than to raise her 'wages', just because they are guaranteed, lest she should regard the additional payment as a right. 'It is easy to raise them, but it is difficult to lower them if bad times come.' "[28]

A similar story is told by an observer (A. O. Elmhirst) who writes from a Yorkshire mining village in a personal communication. "As to tipping up—our findings are that married manual workers (pit and farm) who are on basic, tip all up and are given pocket money for beer and football and wives buy fags with the shopping. Workers getting higher than basic tend to keep quiet on how much higher and open up packet before going home. They keep out as much as they can without arousing wife's suspicion, and put some by, some of them, and never ask wife for any. Single men up to club and pub entry age tip up all and are given pocket money. After that age they tend to bargain with parents and agree on some for board and lodging and keep the balance."

Some more systematic information was collected by the British Institute of Public Opinion, whose Director, Dr. Durant, kindly included a question on the subject in a poll taken on 29 February 1952. These results suggest that housekeeping allowances have risen less in the poorer than in the richer families, somewhat less in the older than in the younger age groups and less in Southern England than in the rest of Britain.

TABLE 4

VARIATIONS IN HOUSEKEEPING ALLOWANCES

Do you get (give) a housekeeping allowance?
Has this kept pace with any recent increases in your (your husband's) earnings?

	Has kept pace	Has not	No increase	Don't know	Total giving allowance	No allowance given
TOTAL	43	12	17	4	76	24
Men	49	9	16	3	77	23
Women	36	15	18	5	74	26
AGE						
21-29	48	9	19	3	79	21
30-49	46	11	16	4	77	23
50-64	46	13	16	3	78	22
65 and over . . .	19	9	26	2	56	44
CLASS:						
Av + ...	50	10	18	5	83	17
Av	50	12	19	1	82	18
Av –	43	11	16	45	75	25
Very poor . . .	19	13	23	2	57	43
REGION:						
Southern England .	38	13	25	3	79	21
Midlands and Wales	53	9	12	3	77	23
Northern England and Scotland . .	40	12	14	4	70	30

These results and the previous examples provide some backing for the hypothesis expressed at the beginning of this section. There is little or no other information about the division of income. But it may be worthwhile considering the division of expenditure. The total value of housekeeping allowances could be calculated by deducting from total earnings total expenditure on goods bought by husbands. Total earnings are known. Men wage-earners increased their average earnings from £3 9s. 0d. to £8 6s. 0d. between 1938 and 1951. Is anything relevant known about expenditure on goods bought predominantly by men?

The annual White Papers on Income and Expenditure do indicate changes in total expenditure since 1938. One outstanding change is the remarkable increase in the expenditure on tobacco and alcoholic drinks. This increase is not due to an enlarged volume of consumption so much as to the heavy additional taxes imposed. One result is that the price to the consumer of a packet of 10 standard-size cigarettes, for instance, has increased from 6d. in 1938 to 1s. 9½d. in 1952, and for a pint of bitter sold in a Public Bar from 6d. in 1938 to 1s. 5d. in 1952. Total expenditure on tobacco increased from £176 millions to £801 millions and on alcoholic drinks from £285 millions to £788 millions between 1938 and 1951. The total expenditure on tobacco and alcohol has therefore increased from £461 to £1,589 millions, or by nearly four times.[4, 5, 17]* The spectacular rise in taxation on alcohol and tobacco is an outstanding feature of British economic policy since 1939. These taxes are perfect from the point of view of the Chancellor because the commodities taxed are and at the same time are not necessities. First, consumers have behaved as though they were necessities in so far as they have not been deterred from buying them by the higher prices they have had to pay. Working-class men, who might have reacted strongly against sharper income taxes at the lower levels, with harmful effects on incentives to production, have been persuaded to contribute vast sums to the Exchequer in the form of taxes on these goods. Second, drink and tobacco are thought of as luxuries, which carry a taint of immorality, and which, in theory, people can stop buying if they wish. Little public objection is therefore raised to the taxes, even though they are so regressive in their incidence.

In the previous passages on the Ministry of Labour Budget Enquiry of 1937-8, and on the effect on the division of income of an enlargement of the family, it was suggested that husbands usually bought and consumed most of the tobacco and alcohol. Mr. Zweig in *Labour, Life and Poverty*, recorded his impression that habits had not greatly changed.

Out of her allowance the housewife nearly always pays the rent, light and heat, food consumed at home, all school meals, all clothes for herself and the children, and her own and the children's outings. Her husband's pocket money goes on fares, food out, cigarettes, drink, amusements and other pleasures, his own clothes, sometimes also his savings. But, of course, the line of division is not always clearly defined, and there is give and take on both sides.

Some recent figures produced for the Hulton Readership Survey[8]

* Understanding of this remarkable phenomenon has yet to be attained. Economists may welcome it. Psychologists may explain its significance. The superego is defined as the "part of the mind that is soluble in alcohol". Alcohol and nicotine are toxins, says Dr. Fenichel in *The Psychoanalytic Theory of Neurosis* (Routledge, 1946), which "diminish inhibitions, heighten self-esteem and ward off anxiety". Doctors may deplore it. Drs. Doll and Bradford Hill in *Smoking and Carcinoma of the Lung* (B.M.J., 30 Sept., 1950, vol. ii, p. 739) "conclude that smoking is a factor, and an important factor, in carcinoma (cancer) of the lung. . . . The greater prevalence of carcinoma of the lung in men compared with women leads naturally to the suggestion that smoking may be a cause, since smoking is predominantly a male habit." Anthropologists may reassure us that British society is not unique. Dr. Audrey Richards in *Hunger and Work in a Savage Tribe* (Routledge, 1932) has told us, somewhat questionably, "In our own community we do not have to choose between eating our staple food or turning it into beer. But in Bantu society this is so: and such is the longing for excitement after the monotony of village routine that many tribes go short of food in order to drink." By co-operating together, these specialists might help the citizen to understand a major feature of his society.

tend to confirm this impression. It was stated there that in the first quarter of 1949 in the United Kingdom men smoked per week about 3,103 lb. of tobacco (in cigarettes and pipes) as compared with 704 lb. smoked by women: men smoked more than four times as much as women. The same source indicates that beer and spirit drinking is also heavier for men than for women. Thus there were said to be, at the beginning of 1949, 34 per cent of men who drank beer more than once a week, and 43 per cent who drank occasionally, as compared with 6 per cent and 32 per cent respectively for women. Five per cent of men drank spirits more than once a week, and 42 per cent occasionally, as compared with 2½ per cent and 40 per cent respectively for women.

We do not know how much was smoked, and drunk, by married as against unmarried men and women in the post-war, let alone in the pre-war, period so that it is impossible to draw any precise conclusions. But we do know that husbands regarded tobacco and other "luxuries" as being "necessities" of a kind that they would not economize on as their families were enlarged. Have husbands also maintained their consumption of tobacco and alcohol despite the sharp rise in prices? If they have, husbands' expenditure would have risen at the same rate as the national total, by about four times. However, the supposition may be unjustified. Single men and women, particularly juvenile workers, and also married women, may well have increased their consumption at a faster pace than husbands. But it is at any rate likely that spending by husbands on alcohol and tobacco, even if it has not risen by as much as the national total, that is by about four times, has risen faster than the total of husbands' earnings, which have increased less than three times. Thus what is known about tobacco and alcohol consumption makes somewhat more plausible the hypothesis that housekeeping allowances have not risen as fast as earnings.

Indeed, there may be a tendency for wives to suffer, relatively to their husbands, in any period of inflation, and if full employment inevitably means some degree of inflation, in any period of full employment. A period of inflation is a period of rising earnings and of rising prices. Workers organized in strong trade unions can, in such a situation, protect themselves by forcing up their earnings fast enough to preserve their real income. Unorganized workers, in common with all groups with relatively fixed incomes, do less well. Since wives have no unions, each has to reach her own individual arrangement, or bargain, with her husband. Like other unorganized workers, their money income may not advance as fast as prices.

Some wives can, however, safeguard themselves by going out to work. The number of married women in paid work (that is, paid by an employer) is much greater than before the war. "It is a remarkable fact that in the so-called Welfare State there are more married women aged twenty-five to fifty-five at work outside the home than in any peace-time year during the past half-century. Compared with the situation in 1937 the number employed in factories, offices and shops may well have risen by 200 to 300 per cent."[24]

One of the causes has probably been the economic pressure occasioned by inadequate housekeeping allowances. A wife with earnings of her own can afford to spend something on herself.

> Her husband [points out Miss Willoughby] gives her a housekeeping allowance but it is rare in this country for the woman's share in running the common enterprise of home and family to be recognized by a personal allotment from her husband's income. Her personal expenditure has to come out of the housekeeping or she has to ask her husband for the amount she requires for a new dress or hat. The higher the economic and social status of a woman before marriage the more she may resent this situation. She continues to work, in part, for the psychological satisfaction of remaining independent.[26]

Whatever the motives of the mothers, it is clear that the temptation for women to work outside the home will be stronger where their allowances are small.

But what is an economic incentive to some married women may be the exact opposite for some married men. Economists have been no less inclined than doctors[18] to forget that their subjects have families, and that the attitude of workers to their families, expressed in the division of money as in many other ways, is a crucial factor in the workers' attitudes to production. Workers' desire for higher incomes depends upon whether there is a small or large gap between what they already have and what they would like to have. Wherever incomes rise faster than aspirations, the power of monetary incentives will be weakened. But some workers may be more interested in their own individual standard of life than in that of their family. If they retain a large sum for their own pocket money, they may consider they are earning quite enough to satisfy their own aspirations, and may think, from that point on, that leisure is more important than money. Zweig has a suggestive comment to make on this subject. " 'The trouble is,' a miner in Worksop commented to me, 'that wages for the wives have not risen as much as men's wages. They are kept pretty steady.' I believe that is not far off the mark, as the expenses met from pocket money, especially for tobacco and drink, have risen considerably. I think that this factor is to a great extent responsible for the absenteeism of married men."[28]

Greater opportunities for work outside the home have provided one safeguard for wives against a reduction in real income. The other and much more important safeguard has been the Welfare State. To say that inflation reduces the share in money terms of the national income received by wives and children is not to say that their share is necessarily cut down in real terms. It depends in good part upon whether the prices of things bought by men have risen more than the prices of things bought by women. That is just what happened—until 1949, at any rate. Prices of tobacco and drink have risen far more than prices in general, owing to the taxes imposed on them. Men have not consumed much larger quantities. They are no better off. They merely pay more. Prices of food, which bulks large in the housewives' expenditure, have, on the other hand, risen less than the average, owing to subsidies. The Welfare State has benefited wives and children in other ways as well through Family Allowances, School Meals, Milk and Food Supplements, and through the National Health Service. Raising of the school-leaving age has, on the other hand, been paid for largely by mothers who have had to wait longer for the contribution which their children make towards housekeeping expenses when they begin to earn. But in general it is as though the taxes on tobacco and drink had been paid into a family income equalization pool, from which had been drawn the benefits provided by the State.

The effect of Government policy on rents is more complex. Since working-class housewives usually pay the rent out of their portion of the family income, increases in rates (paid with rent) have been borne for the most part by the wives. For the same reason, control over the rents of pre-war accommodation has benefited some housewives. But the high rents of post-war housing have fallen very heavily on the mothers with young children who constitute the overwhelming majority of the tenants of new houses. The state of affairs found by Dr. M'Gonigle in Stockton-on-Tees before the war could be found to-day in many post-war housing estates.

All in all, the Welfare State has undoubtedly been an agency for transferring income from men to women and children. But the benefit has been diminishing. One factor has been the new Interim Index of Retail Prices introduced in 1947. The old Cost of Living Index, based on the Budget Enquiries of 1914 and 1904, gave considerable weight to food and very little to tobacco and drink. Governments deliberately kept low the cost of foodstuffs, so as to prevent a rise in the Index which would have precipitated a rise in wages, and put heavy taxes on drink and tobacco which did not have any appreciable effect on the Index. In order to restrain husbands from demanding wage increases, the Government had to keep down the prices of things bought by their wives. By a curious turn of events, an Index which was the laughing stock of statisticians became the saviour of housewives. Because housewives who took part in Budget Enquiries did not know what their husbands earned and consumed, the Index became a Housewives' Index. Because housewives had been kept short before the first World War, the State came to their rescue in the second.

The new Interim Index, based on the 1937-8 Enquiry, but, unfortunately for the housewives, adjusted to take account of the actual expenditure on drink and tobacco, is much less of a "Housewives Cost of Living Index". From 1947 on, increases in the prices of foodstuffs have had less effect on the new Index than they would have had on the old, and changes in policy on subsidies have not raised the Interim Index so much as they would have raised the old Index. Indeed, a fall in the price of beer (relative to its specific gravity) helped to keep the Interim Index down.

It is clear enough from the Price Indices for food and clothing that housewives have been increasingly hard hit since 1950. The further movement against Britain in the terms of trade since the outbreak of the Korean War and the pegging, and eventual reduction of subsidies,* have sent up prices of housewives' commodities, and depressed the value of their housekeeping allowances, at a faster rate than in any other similar period since 1939.

SUMMING UP

All that I have been trying to do very tentatively in this paper is to illustrate a particular approach to the economics of the family. There are many big gaps. Very little account has, for instance, been taken of the practices in middle-class families or of the influence of subsidiary earners. But I hope that enough has been said, which is not too questionable, to indicate the need to obtain more facts. Now that "primary poverty" has been reduced it would be a tragedy if inflation increased "secondary poverty", and did so partly because no one had any certain knowledge that it was happening.

The difficulties of collecting more facts are only too obvious. But these difficulties, above all the main disadvantage of all previous Budget enquiries—that only the conscientious few supplied reliable information—should not be insuperable. There is a case for five types of enquiry.

(1) Intensive pilot studies of patterns of consumption in a small number of families. Such studies should illuminate the difficulties of ascertaining the distribution of real and money income within the family.

(2) A repetition, on a more ample scale and in the same towns, of the surveys made by Mr. Madge at the beginning of the war. The results might give some direct evidence about changes in the division of family income over the last decade. It would also be worthwhile trying to collect accounts from people who have for their own purposes kept budgets over a period of years, as did the cabinet-maker whose remarkable results for the years from 1850 to 1887 were included in the Board of Trade's 1889 Report.[16]

(3) An enquiry into the actual consumption of specific types of food

---

* The Chancellor of the Exchequer, when stating the reasons for reducing the food subsidies in his Budget Speech on 11 March 1952, appeared to assume once again that the family is a consuming unit. "The subsidies," he said, "conceal from the consumer the real cost of what we have to pay for in exports for the food we import. As a result people tend to spend a large part of their incomes on the non-essentials of life. . . . If they insist on smoking, I shall get the revenue; if not, they will have more to spend on food."

by the different members of the family within the home. Knowledge about the division of money income needs to be supplemented by knowledge about the consumption of food and other goods.

(4) A more complete study of family expenditure than has ever yet been conducted. This is the responsibility of the Ministry of Labour in its forthcoming Budget Enquiry. It is essential that on this occasion facts should be obtained about the spending of husbands, and other earners, as well as housewives. It would be of benefit if the Ministry of Labour would at the same time obtain particulars about incomes, as the Board of Trade did in its 1904 Inquiry. Housewives should be asked for the figures of their allowances, and earners about their total earnings. Such information would provide a very useful comparison with expenditure figures.

(5) A series of sample surveys of family income and expenditure to follow up the large-scale Ministry of Labour Enquiry. These should be undertaken at frequent intervals so that information is continuously available about the economics of the family.

REFERENCES

1. Booth, C. 1892. *Life and labour of the people in London.* Macmillan, London.
2. Caradog Jones, D. (ed.). 1934. *The social survey of Merseyside.* Univ. Press of Liverpool.
3. 1903. *Consumption of food and cost of living of working classes in the United Kingdom and certain foreign countries,* p. 1. Cmd. 1761, H.M.S.O., London.
4. Doll and Bradford Hill. 1950. Smoking and carcinoma of the lung. *Br. med. J.,* ii, 739.
5. Fenichel. 1946. *The psychoanalytic theory of neurosis.* Routledge, London.
6. 1945. *Hansard,* 8 March.
7. Hajnal, J., and Henderson, A. M. 1950. The economic position of the family. Memorandum presented to the Royal Commission on Population. In *Papers of the Royal Commission on Population,* Vol. 5, p. 22. H.M.S.O., London.
8. 1950. *Hulton readership survey. Patterns of British life,* pp. 122-132. Hulton Press, London.
9. 1948. *Industrial relations handbook,* Suppl. No. 2, p. 6. H.M.S.O., London.
10. Instone, S. 1948. The welfare of the housewife. *Lancet,* 4 Dec.
11. Llewellyn, Richard. 1939. *How green was my valley.* Michael Joseph, London.
12. Madge, C. 1943. *War-time pattern of saving and spending.* National Inst. of Econ. and Soc. Research, Cambridge.
13. 1941. *Ministry of Labour Gazette,* Jan.
14. Owen, A. D. K. 1933. *A survey of the standard of living in Sheffield,* p. 20. Sheffield Soc. Survey Committee.
15. Pilgrim Trust. 1938. *Men without work.* Macmillan, London.
16. 1889. *Returns of expenditure by working men.* Cmd. 5861, H.M.S.O., London.
17. Richards, A. 1932. *Hunger and work in a savage tribe.* Routledge, London.
18. Richardson, H. B. 1945. *Patients have families.* Commonwealth Fund, New York.

19. ROWNTREE, B. S. 1902. *Poverty*. Macmillan, London.
20. ROWNTREE, B. S. 1941. *Poverty and progress*, p. 25. Longmans, Green, London.
21. ROWNTREE, B. S., and LAVERS, G. R. 1951. *Poverty and the Welfare State*, p. 7. Longmans, Green, London.
22. SOUTAR, M. S., WILKINS, E. H., and SARGENT, FLORENCE P. 1942. *Nutrition and size of family*. Allen & Unwin, London.
23. SPRING RICE, M. 1939. *Working-class wives*. Penguin Books, London.
24. TITMUSS, R. M. 1951. *Family problems in the Welfare State*.
25. TOUT, H. 1938. *The standard of living in Bristol*, p. 24. Arrowsmith.
26. WILLOUGHBY, G. 1951. The social and economic factors influencing the employment of married women. *Jl. R. sanit. Inst.*, 3 May, 240.
27. ZWEIG, F. 1948. *Labour, life and poverty*. Gollancz, London.
28. ZWEIG, F. 1948. *Men in the pits*, p. 96. Gollancz, London.

XX

HOUSING AS AN ENVIRONMENTAL FACTOR IN MENTAL HEALTH: THE JOHNS HOPKINS LONGITUDINAL STUDY

DANIEL M. WILNER, ROSABELLE PRICE WALKLEY,
JOHN M. SCHRAM, THOMAS C. PINKERTON
AND MATTHEW TAYBACK

*Material circumstances in a materially conscious society
are the easiest to change. Some effects of change due to
improved housing are evaluated.*

A series of reports have described the progress of a longitudinal study of the effects of housing quality on physical morbidity and social-psychological adjustment. The present report is devoted largely to some of the study's preliminary findings in social adjustment and mental health areas. A brief summary of the hypotheses to be tested, the experimental design, and some characteristics of the study population may be a useful preliminary.

STUDY DESIGN AND PREVIOUS FINDINGS

HYPOTHESES TO BE TESTED, EXPERIMENTAL DESIGN, AND MEASUREMENTS MADE

At the outset of the study, a series of hypotheses were formulated in some detail and have previously been reported elsewhere.[1, 2] For present purposes, they may be summarized as follows:

With regard to physical health, the expectation was that the slum environment has a generally deleterious effect and that, in addition, the

---

Reprinted from AMERICAN JOURNAL OF PUBLIC HEALTH, Vol. 50, No. 1, January 1960, pp. 55-63.

incidence of certain specific disease entities may be related to certain specific components of housing quality.

With regard to social psychological adjustment, the expectation was that the slum environment offered inhibitions and restraints upon the development of wholesome family relationships, sociality and neighborliness, and good citizenship in the general community. Finally, slum housing was considered from the point of view of personal psychological development as producing inhibitions and restraints upon realistic aspirations for self and family, upon morale, and upon appropriate solutions of, and points of view towards, life's problems.

Measurements have been made on a test group of approximately 400 Negro families (2,000 persons) and on a control group of approximately 600 Negro families (3,000 persons). Both from interviews with the female head of the household and from public document sources, data have been gathered systematically on housing quality, demographic characteristics, morbidity, social adjustment, health practice and information, dietary habits, school performance of children, and police and juvenile court information.

Initial measures were obtained on both the test and control groups at a time when the test families were living in the slum (the "before" period). Subsequently, the test families moved into a new public housing project, and since that time (the "after" period) we have obtained morbidity data every ten weeks; adjustment data approximately annually.

Previous Findings Summarized

Examination of "before" data reveals close comparability of test and control groups on distributions of all demographic variables examined, for example: family size, age of oldest child, marital status, income, education, and so forth. Although an effort also was made at the outset to match test and control families on initial housing quality, subsequent assembling of individual housing quality items into a weighted index showed that almost 10 per cent more test than control families were to be found in what may be considered "very bad" housing, according to criteria adapted from the American Public Health Association Appraisal Method.

"Before" morbidity data show close initial comparability on medical history (including history of chronic complaints) and incidence of illness in the two months prior to the "before" interview. The first 18 months of the "after" period revealed eventually a small increment for the test group in the direction of the hypothesis. In other words, after a small initial reversal, test illness rates remained slightly lower than control illness rates.[3]

PRELIMINARY SOCIAL ADJUSTMENT FINDINGS

The social adjustment data we are presenting do not take into account certain alterations that had occurred in the test and control groups during the time period under consideration. For example, by the 18-month period some controls had actually moved to public housing projects, but they still appear in the control data. Furthermore, although 5 per cent and 8 per cent of the test and control families, respectively, had dropped out of the study by the same period, they still appear in the "before" data. An analysis of these test and control group losses revealed negligible bias on either demographic variables or "before" measures of adjustment.

ATTITUDES AND EXPERIENCE WITH REGARD TO HOUSING

We know from initial measurements that the "before" housing quality of a majority of test and control groups was in general of poor quality. Later, when test families moved into the housing development, the quality of housing improved markedly for them; former deficiencies such as lack of hot water, sharing of facilities, crowding, lack of central heating, and infestation were wiped out. In general, despite considerable moving about in the first 18 months of the "after" period, control families did not improve their housing quality to the same extent. (The extent to which they did improve it will be discussed in a later section of this report.)

It is of some interest, therefore, to determine whether respondents' reactions to their places of residence correspond to these objective facts. Table 1(a) shows how test and control groups compare at the outset (Wave 1), 18 months later (Wave 7), and, in summary, gives the relative "before"-"after" difference or "gain"* on answers to the question, "How do you like your apartment?" Thus, at the outset, only 13.9 per cent of test respondents, compared to 21.6 per cent of control respondents (reflecting the slightly poorer initial housing quality of the test families) indicated they liked their apartment "a lot." Eighteen months later, 69.2 per cent of the test respondents signified the highest degree of satisfaction with living quarters, a gain of 55.3 per cent. Control respondents also showed some change, from 21.6 per cent to 38.1 per cent, a gain of 16.5 per cent.

Our respondents were also asked to enumerate from a list the places in which their children play. The data, shown in Table 1(b), can be summarized as follows: At Wave 1, approximately 40 per cent of places mentioned by both test and control respondents alike were classified as "not safe" (street, etc.); 18 months later, while the control distribution remained very nearly at the initial level, the test respondents mentioning generally unsafe places dropped to 2.4 per cent.

In formulating the basic hypotheses of the study, it was reasoned that considerations of physical space would loom large in the adjustments of

---

* Although we will be using the concept of "percentage gain", our primary interest in this preliminary report is not in the precise magnitude of the differences; rather, we wish to illustrate the consistency of the test-control picture that has emerged.

test and control families. We know that, while still in the slum, almost half of the test families (and their matched controls) shared some important facility with nonfamily members. We also know that a large proportion—whether sharing facilities or not—lived under crowded conditions, according to prevalent criteria of crowding. The move to the housing project (where such factors are controlled by management regulations) reduced this crowding sharply.

A number of questions were asked about personal and family reactions to the issue of space. On each item, the test gains in the "after" period exceeded those for control families. For example, negative reports of family members being bothered by insufficient space, Table 1(c), showed a test gain of 33.1 per cent, compared to a gain of 12.4 per cent among the controls. An item pertaining to the housewife's opportunities for privacy also showed larger gains among the test than among the control group in the proportions saying they could "very easily" be by themselves somewhere in the apartment if they wanted to, Table 1(d).

TABLE 1

ATTITUDES AND EXPERIENCE WITH REGARD TO HOUSING

| | Wave 1 ("Before") | | Wave 7 ("After") | | Difference† "After" minus "Before" | |
	Test (396)	Control* (633)	Test (377)	Control* (583)	Test	Control
(a) How do you like your apartment?						
"A lot"	13.9%	21.6%	69.2%	38.1%	+55.3%	+16.5%
(b) Safety of places where children play						
Not safe	42.2	39.0	2.4	39.5	−39.8	+ 0.5
(c) Family members bothered by not enough space?‡						
"No"	60.6	72.0	93.7	84.4	+33.1	+12.4
(d) Can you be by yourself in the apartment if you want to?‡						
"Very easily"	23.7	33.7	54.1	44.3	+30.4	+10.6

* Control per cents in Tables 1-4 were adjusted because of the two control families per test family in about half of our matched "pairings." In effect, these double-control families were each given a weight of 0.5.

† A plus (+) indicates "gain" for the specified group between Wave 1 ("before") and the later period ("after"); a minus (−) indicates "loss."

Using the observed variances common to the content areas discussed, a tentative estimate of the standard deviation of the difference of the differences was obtained. A difference of 10 per cent or greater between test gain and control gain over time on a given item may be considered significant at the 0.05 level.

‡ Data were obtained at Wave 5 (after 14 months). N's are 381 and 594 for the test and control groups, respectively.

ACTIVITIES WITHIN THE FAMILY AND RELATIONS WITH NEIGHBORS

One of the study's hypotheses suggested that because of such factors as increased space, intrafamily activities would become more numerous.

Respondents of the appropriate family composition were asked how often members, together, went shopping, sat and talked, went for walks, went to the movies, or listened to the radio or watched TV. Table 2(a) gives the "often" response to only three of these items. For all items in the series, there was somewhat greater increment for the test group than for the control group from the "before" to the "after" period.

TABLE 2

ACTIVITIES WITHIN THE FAMILY AND RELATIONS WITH NEIGHBORS

| | Wave 1 ("Before") | | Wave 7 ("After") | | Difference "After" minus "Before" | |
| | Test (396) | Control* (633) | Test (377) | Control* (583) | Test | Control |
N =						
(a) Family do things together?						
Sit and talk:						
"Often"	62.6%	69.0%	73.7%	70.9%	+11.1%	+ 1.9%
Go for walk:						
"Often"	22.2	24.8	27.1	25.9	+ 4.9	+ 1.1
Go to movies:						
"Often"	15.4	18.2	21.5	19.0	+ 6.1	+ 0.8
(b) You and other women around here help one another out?†						
Picking things up at store:						
"Yes"	31.6	31.8	59.8	38.2	+28.2	+ 6.4
With children:						
"Yes"	49.0	51.2	72.4	56.2	+23.4	+ 5.0
When someone is sick:						
"Yes"	63.9	65.0	75.1	69.3	+11.2	+ 4.3
(c) Where neighborly contacts live?†						
"In building"	27.3	21.0	86.4	17.9	+59.1	− 3.1

The housing development into which the test families moved represented not merely housing free of notable deficiencies; it also constituted housing of a particular architectural pattern. Approximately two-thirds of the families in the project (and in the test sample) live in 11-story buildings with 10 families to a floor. An outside screened corridor runs the length of each floor, connecting all apartments. In the middle of each floor are located the entrances to the two elevators serving the building and a 16 by 30 foot play area.

It might reasonably be expected that such architecture and facilities would have effects on relations among neighbors. Respondents were asked, "How many women around here do you visit back and forth with in the daytime?" Among test families, the percentage having no "visiting" contact with other women decreased 26 per cent; among controls, the decrement was 8 per cent.

In order to obtain information about the nature of these daytime contacts, the respondents were asked, "Do you and other women (around here) help one another out in the daytime in any way like. . . ." (followed

* Control per cents weighted.
  † Data were obtained at Wave 5 (after 14 months). N's are 381 and 594 for the test and control groups, respectively.

by a series of items). The "yes" responses to only three of these items are given in Table 2(b). All items in the series show uniformly greater gain for test than for control families from the "before" to the "after" period.

A further indicator of the role apparently played by architecture in promoting neighborly relations may be seen in the responses to the question, "Where do most of these women live with whom you do things in the daytime?" Table 2(c) shows that in the "before" period, 27.3 per cent of test and 21.0 per cent of control respondents had most of their contacts with women who lived in the same building. For the "after" period, a marked change occurred among the test respondents: 86.4 per cent had main contacts in the same building. For control respondents, main contacts with women in the same buildings are substantially unchanged between the "before" and "after" periods.

SOCIAL STATUS

Is the move into better housing accompanied by a rise in the respondent's estimation of her own status? The test and control groups were asked to classify themselves as to whether they belonged to a group of people going up in the world, going down in the world, or not doing either. Table 3(a) shows negligible and similar gains over time for the two groups, 7.6 per cent and 6.4 per cent for test and controls, respectively, for the "going up" category.

Respondents were also asked to compare their situation (now) to that of "five years ago." The response category "better off" (now) is shown in Table 3(b). Test families gained 19.0 per cent between the "before" and "after" periods compared to a 4.0 per cent gain for the control families.

TABLE 3

SOCIAL STATUS

		Wave 1 ("Before")		Wave 7 ("After")		Difference "After" minus "Before"	
N =		Test (396)	Control* (633)	Test (377)	Control* (583)	Test	Control
(a)	What group belong to? "People going up in world"	67.7%	61.2%	75.3%	67.6%	+ 7.6%	+ 6.4%
(b)	Compared to 5 years ago, how do you feel? "Better off" (now)	55.8	57.6	74.8	61.6	+19.0	+ 4.0

PSYCHOLOGICAL STATE

The basic hypotheses of the study suggested that if housing quality had effects on some of the social and situational variables discussed above, it

* Control per cents weighted.

would probably also have effects ultimately on the inner psychological life of our respondents. Inner psychological variables have been measured by a number of scales constructed especially for this study.* The titles of the scales and a characteristic item from each are shown in a footnote to Table 4.

Each item of a scale has been assigned a "positive" and "negative" direction of response related to the title of the scale. Thus, agreement with the prototype item for "Scale f" is taken to signify the lack of perceived potency (negative); disagreement, the presence of perceived potency (positive). Answers to all items in a scale were summed for each respondent. Table 4 shows how test and control groups distribute themselves over time on the "positive" end of each scale. For all six scales, there is general close similarity in the gains for both groups.

TABLE 4

PSYCHOLOGICAL STATE

Scale‡	N =	Wave 1 ("Before")		Wave 7 ("After")		Difference "After" minus "Before"	
		Test (396)	Control† (633)	Test (377)	Control† (583)	Test	Control
(a) Mood: Positive		37.1%	37.7%	50.7%	48.3%	+13.6%	+10.6%
(b) Adequate emotionality: Positive		42.9	45.2	45.9	40.4	+ 3.0	− 4.8
(c) Optimism-pessimism: Positive		41.9	34.1	50.7	45.3	+ 8.8	+11.2
(d) Satisfaction with status quo: Positive		36.4	36.6	59.7	56.1	+23.3	+19.5
(e) Nervousness: Positive		44.5	42.3	43.5	40.0	− 1.0	− 2.3
(f) Potency: Positive		49.8	39.8	54.7	51.3	+ 4.9	+11.5

* These are unidimensional scales which were constructed and tested on an independent group at the same time that other instruments were being prepared and pretested for the study. The scales met the criterion of 95 per cent reproducibility.

† Control per cents weighted.

‡ Scale a. Mood. Item: "Are you sometimes so blue that you feel there's no use going on?"

Scale b. Adequate emotionality. Item: "Is it often hard for you to control your temper?"

Scale c. Morale—Optimism-pessimism. Item: "If things seem to be going well for a while, there's usually some trouble right around the corner."

Scale d. Morale—Satisfaction with status quo. Item: "I'm really very happy about the way I've been getting along lately."

Scale e. Nervousness. Item: "Are you often so nervous or upset that you can't go on with what you are doing?"

Scale f. Potency—Efficacy of self-help. Item: "When you come right down to it, there's nothing you can do to make things really better for yourself."

DISCUSSION OF THE SOCIAL ADJUSTMENT FINDINGS

The variables reviewed in the preceding section may be looked at as supporting to some extent many of the hypotheses of the study. The test families have without question revealed an awareness of their improved circumstances and in their reports of behavior and attitude have confirmed speculation that space in and of itself is an important factor (Table 1).

More modestly, but consistently, improvement in housing also brings with it increase in activities the family undertakes together; possibly an important finding in a population known more for division than cohesion in family structure, Table 2(a).

Most striking of all is the sharp rise in neighborly interactivity that has accompanied the test move to the project, Table 2(b). The present view is that this rise may be due as much to architecture as to improvement in housing quality; this is a matter to be investigated in subsequent analysis of the data, Table 2(c).

Less confirmation of the basic hypotheses was found in connection with the respondent's self-assignment to a position on the social class hierarchy (Table 3), and in responses to the scales of psychological state (Table 4).

One might reason as follows regarding the contrast between Tables 1, 2 and Tables 3, 4. The issues dealt with in the first two tables are all matters of social reality; those dealt with in the last two tables are matters of personal-psychological import. It is possible that 18 months is enough time to effect differences on the former through housing improvement, but it may take longer to obtain effects, if they are obtained at all, in a person's inner psychological regions. This matter will be illuminated when an evaluation is made of later adjustment data, obtained about 12 months after Wave 7.

Meanwhile, let us turn to an interesting development which suggests that time is not the only factor that needs to be watched carefully if we are to understand completely the influence of housing.

CONTROL "UPWARD" MOVEMENT AND CONSEQUENT SOCIAL ADJUSTMENT GAINS

In the 18 months between Wave 1 and Wave 7, only 8 per cent of the test families moved from the housing project, whereas 56 per cent of the control families moved from their Wave 1 address. Not only was there a high movement rate among the controls, but, in moving, they achieved a marked improvement in housing quality. Thus, at Wave 1, 52 per cent of the controls lived in "very bad" housing (based on criteria adapted from the APHA appraisal scheme); by Wave 7, the proportion had diminished to 28 per cent.

One consequence of this movement among controls to improved housing is of course to reduce the difference in the housing quality of test and control groups in the "after" period, and to that extent such movement makes it more difficult to discern the true effects of housing quality on all dependent variables including the adjustment measures. From preliminary experimenting with various analytic schemes, we have become convinced that analysis of control moves will be an important factor in assessing the role of housing quality in health and adjustment. For, if the housing quality hypothesis is correct, then control families which have improved their housing should show gains from Wave 1 to Wave 7 on the dependent variables of the study precisely as is expected of the test families.

We have, in fact, already obtained data suggesting not only that upward housing quality movement is accompanied by gains in the dependent variable, but also that the size of the housing increment dictates the amount of gain. For example, from a sample of 195 control families which initially occupied some of the worst housing, we distinguished three Wave 1-Wave 7 sub-groups: those which, in moving, made a "large" change, those which made a "moderate" change, and those which made no change in their housing quality. Wave 1-Wave 7 gains were tabulated for each subgroup for the dependent variables.

Table 5 gives the gains for a few selected variables analyzed in this way. On the question, "How do you like your apartment?" the control families which made a large change upward gained 51.9 per cent in the category, "a lot," those which made a moderate change upward gained 22.7 per cent, and those which made no upward movement showed a relatively slight gain. On the question asking respondents to compare their present situation with that of five years ago, similar stepwise but

TABLE 5

SELECTED CONTROLS ONLY: "GAINS" ON SEVERAL DEPENDENT VARIABLES AMONG FAMILIES WITH INITIALLY "BAD" HOUSING WHO MADE "LARGE," "MODERATE," AND "NO" IMPROVEMENT IN HOUSING QUALITY BETWEEN WAVE 1 AND WAVE 7

	Magnitude of Housing Quality Improvement Between Wave 1 and Wave 7		
N =	Large (52)	Moderate (75)	None* (68)
How do you like apartment?			
"A lot"	+51.9%	+22.7%	+10.3%
Compared to 5 years ago, how do you feel?			
"Better off" (now)	+23.1	+13.3	− 1.5
Psychological state			
Optimism-pessimism:			
Positive	+25.0	+16.0	+ 5.9
Satisfaction with status quo:			
Positive	+34.6	+25.4	+14.7
Potency:			
Positive	+26.9	+12.0	+10.3

* Composed of families who moved between Waves 1 and 7 but did not alter housing quality, as well as families who did not move in that period.

more modest gains are apparent. Of even more interest is the distribution of gains in responses to the psychological state scales. On each of the scales shown in Table 5, the greater the housing quality improvement, the greater the gain in the positive end of the scale. It is of interest to compare the latter distributions to those covering the same items in Table 4. This comparison reveals that test gains, even though they might be expected to rank with the gains of "large step" controls, actually fall far short. The key to this puzzle may lie in the analysis we are planning which takes into account the different initial housing quality levels of the matched test families.

Thus it appears that the size of housing quality change is one important consideration in attempting to assess the effect of housing. Another obviously important consideration, mentioned earlier, is the length of residence in the particular dwelling unit. We are only now in process of taking this factor into account by means of an "average weighted housing-quality score" for each control family for the duration of the "after" period of the study.

SUMMARY

We have presented data from the controlled longitudinal study of the effects of the housing environment on social-psychological adjustment. The data confirm some basic study hypotheses concerning attitudes and experience with regard to housing, activities within the family, and relations with neighbors. On many matters covered in these areas, test families showed substantially greater gain in a 14 to 18 month period than did control families. On two important issues having to do with social status and psychological state variables, there seems as yet to be no difference between test and control families.

We also discussed movement to improved housing among control families. Special analysis showed, at least among control families, that size of the "upward" move helps determine the size of the gain on a number of variables, including, even in the relatively short period of the study to date, psychological state variables.

ACKNOWLEDGMENTS

We are indebted to numerous consultants in the fields of social psychology and measurement, especially Professor Isidor Chein, Research Center for Human Relations, New York University; Professor William G. Cochran, Department of Statistics, Harvard University; and Dr. Lee S. Christie, System Development Corporation. Special recognition is due also to the following members of the study staff: Joseph R. Dallas, Mary S. Tyler, and Florence Nolan.

REFERENCES

1. 1954. *Study memorandum BHA-2 : Plan of procedures and analysis of the study of adjustment.*
2. WILNER, D. M., WALKLEY, R. P., and TAYBACK, M. 1956. How does the quality of housing affect health and family adjustment? *Am. J. publ. Hlth,* **46**, 736-744.
3. WILNER, D. M., WALKLEY, R. P., GLASSER, M. N., and TAYBACK, M. 1958. The effects of housing quality on morbidity—Preliminary findings of the Johns Hopkins Longitudinal Study. *Am. J. publ. Hlth,* **48**, 1607-1615.

XXI

THE PSYCHOPATHOGENESIS OF
HARD-CORE FAMILIES

JOHN G. HOWELLS

A family's material circumstances may affect its emotional well-being. The reverse is also true. Emotional instability in the family is often the cause, rather than the product, of its social difficulties.

'All happy families resemble one another; every unhappy family is unhappy in its own way.'—Tolstoy.

Alcoholism, illegitimacy, delinquency, criminality, divorce, suicide, child neglect and unhappiness despite material wealth: these are some of the so called 'social problems'. For these conditions the community attempts explanations.

The community may explain these manifestations as being due to lack of satisfactory material conditions despite the obvious and commonplace disillusionment of those individuals who have achieved material success and still remain unhappy. Secondly, the community tends to suppose that these conditions may indicate some degree of insanity. Statistics show, however, that only a very small section, less than 0·5% of the community, suffer from insanity, while social problems involve a far greater number of people. Thirdly, the community may suggest that these problems spring from some degree of intellectual retardation in some of its members. Careful investigation, however, shows that people at all levels of intellectual endowment are liable to suffer from these social difficulties.

The above explanations ignore the fact that these conditions spring from individual psychopathology, i.e. from the dysfunctioning of the

Based on a paper printed in AMERICAN JOURNAL OF PSYCHIATRY, Vol. 122, 1966, p. 1159.

emotional substratum of the individual. Emotion and emotional disorder are concepts that the public find difficult to grasp, perhaps because emotional matters are inherently subtle or just unfamiliar. Difficulty in grasping emotional phenomena may sometimes lead to ethical prowess being offered as a solution of emotional difficulties. 'Goodness' is offered as a substitute for emotional stability. But experience shows that impeccable ethical precept and practice do not safeguard against emotional illness. There is, however, no contradiction between 'goodness' and stability; these qualities are different entities that can exist together.

The thesis in the investigation to be reported is that many social difficulties are due to emotional causes—to matters of individual psychopathology. Abundant material for study came from an examination of hard-core families, sometimes termed problem or multiply-handicapped families. Social difficulties are a feature of such families. Apathy, delinquency, unemployment, sloth, child neglect, drunkenness, prostitution and broken marriages—all these are familiar aspects of problem families.[4] The problem family is a family that fails to flourish, however advantageous its surrounding circumstances. It is remarkably resistant to improvement, even when much help is offered to it. Hard-core families stand out very clearly in a welfare state. To the advantage of the researcher is the fact that, in the problem family in dire distress, mechanisms which are so unclear in a stable family are thrown into high relief. The main question asked in the investigation was: 'To what extent does psychopathology within the family explain its social difficulties?' This is a preliminary report of the findings.

THE INVESTIGATION

In a town of 120,000 population, 80 problem families are recognized by the official agencies. We have taken a random sample of 30 of these families. The initial sample was reduced to 24 families, due to three families leaving the area and another three families being reclassified as non-problem families. It was accepted that help should go hand in hand with investigation.

The criteria accepted for defining the problem family were those of the agencies in the area. This had the advantage of allowing others to establish the criteria and allowing the investigation to throw light on recognized problems in the area. It carried the disadvantage that the agencies' definition was influenced by what constituted problems in their narrow fields of operation—and within the social groups with which they were concerned. Many problem families are not ascertained by the agencies; thus, in any interpretations of the findings on that sample, it must be borne in mind that the sample is a selected one.

Much has been written about problem families, but, due to the immense difficulties involved, careful studies are few. To collect a representative sample involves working in a geographically limited area. Establishing good reasons for continuous visiting to such families can be very difficult. To obtain cooperation to the point where members of the family will allow intimate study can be even more difficult. Apathy, distrust, belligerence are bars to easy relationships and the keeping of appointments. Psychiatric studies call for the greatest cooperation of all and hence, no doubt, their paucity.

Workers in this study have been collecting data in this area for 16 years. Over the last seven years, due to close cooperation with the agencies concerned, especially the family doctor, it has been possible to arrange for families in the sample to be referred to the Department of Family Psychiatry undertaking the study. Twenty-one out of the 24 families in the sample have been examined, i.e. 87% of the sample. Thus 41 of 42 parents and 142 children were seen; a parent of one family died. It will be noticed that each family was taken on for a full psychiatric evaluation in the same way as other individuals and families attending the Department of Family Psychiatry. Contact was maintained for some years in most of the sample. A special schema of examination, involving more than 500 items, was employed.

RESULTS

Only preliminary findings of the major elements affecting the parents of problem families are reported here.

EMOTIONAL DISORDER IN INDIVIDUAL PARENTS

On a four-point scale of emotional disorder, the findings in 41 parents were the following: The 'very severe' emotional disorder group (15 parents) embraced patients who had persistent, very obvious, severely incapacitating, multiple symptoms and whose condition required the most intensive psychotherapy for a long period and who would be unlikely to respond to it. The patients in the 'severe' group (13 parents) required intensive psychotherapy for a long period to effect amelioration of their condition. Those patients with a 'moderate' degree of emotional disorder (10 parents) also required psychotherapy, but had a good prognosis. One parent was found to be nearly stable, and in two parents psychosis replacing emotional disorder was found.

Very severe emotional disorder	15
Severe emotional disorder	13
Moderate degree of emotional disorder	10
Near stable	1
Psychosis replacing emotional disorder	2
	41 parents

Thus, of 41 parents, 38 required psychotherapy and two were psychotic—a significant and overwhelmingly bad state of mental health.

The overwhelming bad state of mental health in these families is emphasized by comparing this study with other epidemiological studies.

In the United Kingdom, because almost the whole population is on the general practitioner's 'list', it has been possible to undertake research on psychiatric morbidity in the population at large through general practice. Watts[11] reviews ten such studies and concludes that the overall psychiatric morbidity, including all conditions, neurosis, psychosis and psychosomatic disorders, amounts to 30·9%. Thirty per cent is the figure given in an authoritative document by the College of General Practitioners.[2] The incidence of psychiatric morbidity of 30·9% has to be compared with our sample ($N = 41$, and only one near stable individual) where the morbidity rate is 98%.

Shepherd et al.[9] found that the psychiatric morbidity in a sample of adults in general practice was 9% of individuals suffering from 'conspicuous psychiatric disability'. To this they added 5% of the sample who showed 'abnormal personality traits'. Thus 14% could be said to be suffering from severe observable psychiatric disability. That the figure of 14% is a reasonable one can be surmised from Berg's[1] study of families attending a child welfare clinic. Here, 14·2% of parents and children were said to show 'severe' psychiatric problems. This figure of 14% can be compared with the figure in our sample of 69% ($N = 41$, 28 classified) classified as 'severely' or 'very severely' disturbed. Again an overwhelming bad state of mental health in our sample is exposed.

EMOTIONAL DISORDER IN PAIRED PARENTS

On the same four-point scale of degree of emotional disorder, the position for paired parents in the 21 families (41 parents) was as follows:

1 parent with 'very severe' emotional disorder + 1 with 'severe'	5 families
1 parent with 'very severe' emotional disorder + 1 with 'moderate' degree	9 families
1 parent with 'very severe' emotional disorder + 1 near stable	1 family
2 parents with 'severe' emotional disorder	4 families
Families with a 'psychotic' member	2 families
TOTAL	21 families

No family had two parents in the 'very severe' category. To have one such parent was sufficient to be responsible for the plight of the family —even with a 'near stable' partner. Two parents in the 'severe' category were sufficient to handicap the family. The families with psychotic members will be discussed later.

SEX OF PARENTS DIFFERENTIATED

Using the same four-point scale, the position in regard to emotional disorder for 21 mothers and 20 fathers was as follows:

	Mothers	Fathers
In 'very severe' category	13	2
In 'severe' category	4	9
In 'moderate' category	2	8
In 'near stable' category	0	1
In 'psychotic' category	2	0
TOTAL	21 mothers	20 fathers

Thus, for this sample of families, by the criteria adopted, mothers are seen to be significantly more pathogenic than fathers. Most agencies who ascertain problem families are concerned with child neglect. This is more likely to occur if mothers are pathogenic and thus leads to conditions which will cause ascertainment. If 'alcoholism' was the concern of the agencies it is likely that families with pathogenic fathers would be predominant in the sample.

Although the results are probably significant for this sample, it is necessary to add that fathers of these families are more elusive than mothers, and their briefer period of examination may have led to an underestimate of their disabilities.

FAMILIES WITH PSYCHOTIC PARENTS

The definition accepted for psychosis was that of the endogenous, 'process' type; both parents showed the characteristic thought disorder and perceptional difficulties of established schizophrenia.

With such a small sample, inferences must be drawn with caution. Both affected parents were mothers; when child neglect is an important ascertaining feature, families with sick mothers are more likely to be included. In one family, psychosis in the mother was accompanied by a husband in the 'moderate' category of emotional disorder; this was the least handicapped family in the whole sample and has now been upgraded to a non-problem family. The other family, which had a husband in the 'severe' category, was of much concern to the social agencies.

INTELLECTUAL RETARDATION IN PARENTS

In Great Britain, as a general rule, individuals of an intelligence quotient below 70 are said to be 'subnormal', and those below 50 are 'severely subnormal'.

Six parents in five families were subnormal; none was severely subnormal. One family had two subnormal members. In four families with a subnormal parent one parent is also showing a 'very severe' degree of emotional disorder; in one family the two parents are showing a 'severe' degree of emotional disorder. Families with subnormal parents, of whom there must be many in this town of 120,000 population, do not show the characteristic features of problem families; these features are likely to be associated with emotional disorder in the parents. That this is so is suggested by the fact that the most stable parent, the one 'near stable' person, has the lowest I.Q.—53; he could not counterbalance the influence of his 'very severely' disturbed wife.

To date, the intelligence quotients of 28 of the 41 parents have been assessed. The mean I.Q. is 83·6 with a range of I.Q. from 53 to 112. A number of considerations must be borne in mind in interpreting this finding. (a) The agencies who ascertained the families have a disproportionate interest in families of the lower social groups; Savage,[8] who matched a number of problem families with controls from the same economic group, found that his control group contained more members with an I.Q. below average than would be expected in a sample of the whole community. (b) We have found that intelligent parents of problem families are more elusive and less willing to submit to intelligence tests. (c) The sample of 28 parents contained 17 mothers and 11 fathers. Sheridan[10] has shown that mothers of neglected children have a lower I.Q. than average. (d) Parents of problem families live in a disruptive atmosphere which does not allow of continued education, and this tends to lead to a poorer performance on intelligence tests. (e) The emotional disorder in the parents can interfere with performance on intelligence tests. (f) Parents of problem families are often so dishevelled as to give the appearance of being duller than they are.

While children are not the subject of this communication, it may be of interest to report that, of 72 children tested from these families, the mean I.Q. was 90·2 with a range of I.Q. from 59 to 119. The regression to the mean is noted. A complementary study of the intelligence of children of problem families has been reported elsewhere.[5]

SUMMARY OF RESULTS

One of the main results of this investigation is to make clear the high degree of psychopathogenicity that exists in the parents of problem families. It suggests that the definition of the problem family should be widened as follows:

'A problem family is a family showing among its members emotional instability of such a degree that it leads to behaviour which is socially unacceptable.'

This poses the question, 'Do all families suffering from a severe degree of emotional pathogenicity always manifest social difficulties?' The answer may well be 'Yes'. But they will only be ascertained if the agencies are equally interested in social difficulties of all types, and as they manifest themselves in all age, social and intellectual groups.

EMOTIONAL MECHANISMS OF SOCIAL PROBLEMS

This investigation also clarified some of the emotional mechanisms that lead to social difficulties. The emotional basis of social problems can be illustrated by analysing the root causes of three such problems in one of the families investigated.

Firstly, this family displayed the social problem of being heavily in debt. Investigation revealed that this was due to a combination of factors of emotional significance as follows:

1. As the mother cannot mix with strangers, she sends her children to do her shopping, which is therefore less economically carried out, with consequent wasting of finance.

2. Fear of the dark calls for all the lights to be on in the house at night, with resulting heavy electricity bills.

3. The mother's agitated state results in continuous smoking, with more spending of money.

4. The mother's need to expiate guilt, induced by the way she handled her favourite daughter, caused her to buy expensive presents for the child —again depleting resources.

5. As mother panics in public transport, she has to visit friends by taxi—adding further to expenditure higher than her income allows.

Secondly, this mother neglected her children and the following emotional features emerged:

1. The birth of the children was the result of the mother's emotional need to have a baby from which she could have affection.

2. The children were rejected immediately they made demands upon the mother as toddlers.

3. The mother was continually tense and therefore inattentive, irritable, impatient and explosive—with consequent trauma to the children.

4. At other times the mother feels guilty about her own behaviour, and therefore becomes unreasonably over-protective and denies the children beneficial social contacts.

5. She projects on to her own children her unsatisfactory feelings about the maternal grandmother who brought her up.

Thirdly, this family lived in a state of squalor. This resulted from the mother's preoccupation with her own unresolved fears, leading to an apathy and a lack of concentration that made decision and quick action impossible. Accumulated commitments posed tasks too large to tackle and therefore best ignored.

MANAGEMENT OF PROBLEM FAMILIES

To expect social difficulties consequent on emotional disorder to respond to 'reason' is to deny the very nature of the emotions. Emotional ills have their own emotional antidotes. If they are to be successful, solutions cannot ignore the underlying emotional needs. Consider, for example, efforts to enable these families to limit childbearing by adopting birth control measures. These, in problem families, are remarkably ineffective, because they are frustrated by a variety of emotional factors.

1. Some husbands wish their wives to be continually pregnant, because it is only in this way that they can control them.

2. Some mothers wish to be perpetually pregnant, for only by such means do they get emotional satisfaction from the cuddling of small infants.

3. Disturbed people are inefficient—in birth control as in other matters.

4. There is a fatalism about these families; nothing works out in life, so why bother to try.

5. One of the few solaces in the lives of these individuals is sexual pleasure, which they do not wish to deny themselves and which they do not wish to be encumbered by birth control machinery.

This illustration shows the importance of an analysis of the family solution in emotional terms before it is possible to offer effective solutions.

In general, family problems can receive help by three procedures:

Interview therapy

This involves direct individual, dual, group or family group psychotherapy for family members. Unfortunately, its effectiveness is severely limited by the elusiveness of the family members, the lack of facilities and the severe degree of the illness.

Vector therapy

The essential principle in vector therapy* is that, instead of making a direct change in personality by the techniques of psychotherapy, a manipulation occurs which alters the pattern of emotional forces playing on the individual; the aim is to modify adverse, negative emotional influences playing upon individual family members, and to make these forces positive and nurturing. The positive emotional influences operating over time are expected to bring relief to the individual personality. Applying the above principle of *change of forces*, it can be seen that it is possible to fashion entirely new services to alter the emotional climate of the family.

An example of such a manipulation would be to supply day foster care[3] for a child deprived of healthy emotional care by a disturbed parent. This involves the planned separation[6] of young children from depriving mothers, with the cooperation of the parents, and also caring for the child as long as possible during the day within a positive, warm, nourishing, emotional relationship which is supplied by carefully selected substitute parents.

Positive emotional influences spring from contact with stable individuals. The programme must therefore include the deployment of stable individuals at points where they can be of maximum benefit to the unstable. The strong must help the weak.

* See Part One, pp. 101-107, for discussion on Vector Therapy.

A correct assessment of a problem family in emotional terms, followed by the utilization of vector therapy made possible by the skilled personal relationship of a social worker, offers the best remedial help to problem families. New services are required, framed to a family's emotional needs. The results will be partial but worth while. A start with this generation will bring increments with its successors.

Surrounding a family with a health-promoting or salutiferous community

This programme calls for an analysis of every activity, practice and institution, with a subsequent assessment of its emotional value, followed by a decision to encourage those situations which promote the emotional health of the individual, and to remedy those situations which are emotionally unfavourable. It should be possible to replan all the community's activities and practices so that the maximum positive emotional influences are brought to bear on all its members. Although every activity of the community needs to be examined for its emotional effects, one alone is to be selected here for comment. Life in most communities calls for a considerable degree of cooperation between individuals, and this cooperation is not always forthcoming; our highly competitive education system may need to be replanned in order to promote group cooperation.

CONCLUSION

To an unrecognized extent, social difficulties are due to family and individual emotional disorders. This contribution explains how these lead to social difficulties and outlines how they can be modified.

ACKNOWLEDGMENTS

This investigation has called for collaboration with Miss C. M. Whitehead, Miss M. Lawrence and Mrs. P. B. Brooks, three social workers whose able help is acknowledged. My Research Assistant, Mrs. M. L. Osborn, has given invaluable assistance, both in the investigation and the preparation of this report.

REFERENCES

1. BERG, I. 1965. Psychiatric problems in a child welfare clinic. *Med. Offr*, **114**, 315.
2. Council of College of General Practitioners, Working Party report, 1958. *Br. med. J.*, ii, 585.
3. HOWELLS, J. G. 1956. Day foster care and the nursery. *Lancet*, ii, 1254.
4. HOWELLS, J. G. 1956. The psychopathology of a problem family. *R. Soc. Hlth J.*, **76**, 231.

5. Howells, J. G. 1957. The intelligence of children of problem families. *Med. Offr*, **96**, 193.
6. Howells, J. G. 1963. Child-parent separation as a therapeutic procedure. *Am. J. Psychiat.*, **119**, 922. [Reprinted in this collection as No. LI.]
7. Howells, J. G. 1963. *Family psychiatry*. Oliver & Boyd, Edinburgh.
8. Savage, S. W. 1946. Intelligence and infant mortality in problem families. *Br. med. J.*, i, 86.
9. Shepherd, M., *et al.* 1959. Psychiatric morbidity in an urban group practice. *Proc. R. Soc. Med.*, **52**, 269.
10. Sheridan, M. D. 1956. The intelligence of 100 neglectful mothers. *Br. med. J.*, i, 91.
11. Watts, C. A. H. 1956. *Neuroses in general practice*. Second John Matheson Shaw Lecture. Royal College of Physicians, Edinburgh.

5

THE COMMUNITY INTERACTION DIMENSION

This dimension embraces all that is known about interaction at all levels, between the family and the community in the Past, the interaction in the Present and what can be predicted about it in the Future.

Of the many elements of the family-community interaction in the time sequence of Past, Present and Future, the following have been selected for illustration here:

> Extended family
> The school
> Urban society
> The culture

XXII

EXTENDED FAMILY RELATIONS OF DISTURBED AND WELL FAMILIES

NORMAN W. BELL

Nuclear families are part of a greater 'clan' to which they relate. This relationship carries the potential of good or ill for both.

It has long been recognized that the mental health of individuals is related to the family. However, until recently there has been a failure to conceptualize the family *qua* family; studies of individual pathology have usually reduced the family to individual psychodynamic terms.[1] Beginning with Richardson's[2] pioneer attempts to characterize the family as a group with properties in its own right, considerable changes have taken place. Numerous investigators have developed conceptual schemes to describe the subtle and complex processes in families. Such reformulations involve a shift away from the view that mental illness is a characteristic of an individual toward the view that disturbance in one member is a symptom of the functioning of the whole family. Concomitantly, different therapeutic approaches to families as groups[3] or to individuals[4] as family members have been developed.

These reconceptualizations produce a needed corrective to earlier tendencies to overemphasize the significance of an individual's innate tendencies or of isolated segments of relationships in which he may be involved. However, to the family sociologist, there appears a danger that the fallacies of oversimplification and reductionism characteristic of the focus on the individual are being repeated again at the family level. Family psychiatrists seem, by and large, to view the family as a self-contained, invariable unit[5] existing in a social and cultural vacuum. The significance of a grandparent* or an extra-family activity of a parent may

---

* The first volume of *The Psychoanalytic Review* in 1914 includes abstracts of articles on the "grandfather complex" by Jones, Abraham, and Ferenczi.

Reprinted from FAMILY PROCESS, Vol. 1, No. 2, September 1962, pp. 175-192.

be recognized as incorporated in one member's pathology in particular instances. But systematic consideration of the interdependence of the nuclear family and related families of orientation, or of the nuclear family and the surrounding society as a universal structural principle have been lacking.* Both on theoretical[7] and empirical[8,9] grounds it is difficult to find justification for neglecting the frameworks within which families function.

PROBLEM

This paper will explore only one segment of the total web of relationships in which families exist, namely relationships with extended kin. Every society recognizes and patterns the relations of successive generations.[10] The breaking or changing of old ties and the formation of new ties through marriage are always transition points with potential stresses. As Radcliffe-Brown[11] has expressed it "... Marriage is a rearrangement of social structure.... A marriage produces a temporary disequilibrium situation.... The establishment of a new equilibrium after a marriage requires that in certain types of kinship or family structure there is a need felt for emphasizing the separateness of the two connected families.... The principal points of tension created by a marriage are between the wife and the husband's parents and the husband and the wife's parents."[11] (pp. 43-58 passim). The thesis of this paper is that disturbed families are ones in which this "disequilibrium created by marriage" has not been resolved but continues to provoke and maintain conflicts and the underlying discrepancies that cause them, and that well families have achieved some resolution of the problems of ties to extended kin so that these kin are neutral or even positive forces in the resolution of family problems.

Before presenting data relevant to this thesis it may be helpful to review briefly the nature of family processes which lead to individual pathology and some features of the American kinship system, two domains not previously related to one another.

In common with various other family researchers I assume that functional disturbances arise from and are maintained by family interaction, including the emotional dynamics associated with overt behavior. Different researchers have focused upon different aspects of the patterns of interaction, some emphasizing the persistent structural features, others the nature of communication processes, still others the discordance between overt behaviour and inner feelings. Common to all appears to be some conception that, as a group, the family must try to adapt to the discrepancies within and between individuals and reach some equilibrium. Unless the underlying issues are resolved there will be a strong tendency to act out the problems by involving others in biologically, psychologically

* Ackerman[6] is one of the few who have advanced into this area and he puts the stress mainly on the emotional and attitudinal aspects.

or socially inappropriate roles. Such processes lead to disturbances of ego identity. The disturbance, so dysfunctional for the individual, serves positive functions for the family in its efforts to secure or preserve some sort of integration.[12] Removal of, or change in, the disturbed individual upsets the "pathological equilibrium" and leads to changes throughout the system. Much less work has been devoted to well families, but conversely it might be formulated that to cope with discrepancies they adopt mechanisms which actually resolve the discrepancies or at least contain them in ways that are not pathogenic for individual members.

The family processes associated with mental illness or health have been described by others in some detail[13] with focus on the operations within nuclear families. But any nuclear family is part of a larger "family field" and must cope with the establishment and structuring of ties to two families of orientation. Some kinship systems stress the continuity of generations by subordinating the younger generation to the authority of the elder and stress the preference of one lineage over the other. The American kinship system[14] emphasizes the structurally isolated nuclear family and is bilateral. The emphasis on the isolated nuclear family means that there is discontinuity and relative independence of adjacent adult generations. The characteristic of bilaterality means that both the husband's and wife's families are potentially of equal importance in reckoning descent, controlling property, giving support and direction and so on. Since neither side of the family receives a culturally prescribed preference, each family must work out its own balance of the ties to, and independence of, two extended families. This task is further complicated by the tendency to define the maintenance of kinship ties as a feminine rather than masculine role.*

DATA

The data which is to be cited here are drawn from a long-term study of disturbed and well families. The broader project, directed by Drs. John Spiegel and Florence Kluckhohn, is concerned with the interrelation of cultural values, family roles and the mental health of individuals. Details of the population studied have been presented elsewhere[1, 15, 16]; here it is sufficient to note that intact working-class families with at least three generations available for interviewing were studied intensively for periods ranging from two to five years. The families were of varying ethnic backgrounds. Half of them had a functionally disturbed child (here called "disturbed families"); half had no clinically manifest disturbance (called "well families").

Contact with the "sick" families was mainly in the office setting; the

---

* I do not mean to imply that the American kinship system presents more, or more intense, problems than other kinship systems. Other systems engender problems too (e.g. the daughter-in-law in traditional China) but the focal problems are different.

child and both parents, at a minimum, were seen in weekly therapy sessions. Occasionally parents or a parent and child were seen jointly. Family behavior before and after interviews was observed. Eventually all families were visited in their homes on several occasions, and relatives were interviewed where possible or at least were met during visits. With the "well" families there was similarly extended, regular contact by teams of a child psychiatrist, a psychiatric social worker and a sociologist. The bulk of these contacts was in homes. Clearly the meaning of the contact for these well families was different, but we were reasonably satisfied that comparable data were obtained for both groups.

FINDINGS

Four aspects of how extended kin articulate with nuclear families will be discussed. The first two (extended families as countervailing forces and extended families as continuing stimulators of conflict) deal with the dynamics of intergroup relationships. The second two (extended families as screens for the projection of conflicts and extended families as competing objects of support and indulgence) deal more with the social-psychological qualities of the relationships. Distinguishing these four aspects is, of course an analytic device; empirically they are intertwined.

Extended Families as Countervailing Forces

The ability of the nuclear family to contain its conflicts and control the impact of its discrepancies by means of a child is limited. Adult members in particular may experience guilt about the child, particularly when his condition is defined by outside agencies such as schools, courts and neighbors. But even short of this step, parents are capable of experiencing guilt or anxiety through identification with the child, a necessary but often neglected correlate of the child's identification with the parent.

Mr. Costello, for instance, brought his younger son for medical attention when this son began to stutter seriously. The father had suffered from a speech problem himself in childhood. He "understood" his son's stuttering as something learned from an older brother, although it was more closely related to the chronic stool-retention problems this younger child had, the physical symptom for which medical attention was sought. The older son's stuttering had not affected the father deeply; this symptom in the younger son with whom the father was so closely identified was intolerable.

Aging of the child may shift the child's capacity to absorb family tensions so that he is able to escape parental pressures more and get support for himself from the peer group.[17] Maneuvers within the family are not always adequate to restore the pathogenic equilibrium. At such times there may be a resorting to the extended family to shore up crumbling group defenses. Typically this process includes a seeking for support from the natural parents and an attack upon the in-laws. In the full form this becomes reciprocal with the other spouse drawing upon his family for reserves and attacking his in-laws. As the vicious circle progresses, the whole family becomes split. A day in the life of the McGinnis family will illustrate this:

Mr. and Mrs. McGinnis lived in a state of armed truce. Mrs. McGinnis domineered the family in an irrational, active way. Her domination of their oldest son, perceived by herself as maternal devotion, was extreme. Mr. McGinnis had developed set patterns of schizoid withdrawal from the family and persistent needling of the 12-year-old son to grow up before he was drafted into the army or was thrown out of the family to go to work. The bane of Mr. McGinnis' life was his old, unreliable car which in its weaker moments he used to kick and curse. For Mrs. McGinnis and her son this car was the proof of the father's stupidity and the family's low status. Mr. McGinnis was continually harassed to get a new car. One day, independently, he did go out and buy a second-hand station wagon. When Mrs. McGinnis was told of this she conjured up an image of a high, homely, small bus. In the telephone conversations with her family, which quickly followed, this distorted image was elaborated. They soon gathered around to "kid" Mr. McGinnis about running a jitney to New York. Their perverse pleasure was short lived when they saw a quite ordinary station wagon. By this time Mr. McGinnis was bitterly attacking his in-laws and soon after paid a rare visit to his aged mother who was nearly indigent and in a nursing home. His visit reawakened Mrs. McGinnis' suspicions that her mother-in-law had money hidden away which should be given to them. When Mrs. McGinnis' spinster sisters came under fire from Mr. McGinnis, she defended them in exaggerated terms and returned with interest comments about Mr. McGinnis' paranoid sister.

For the McGinnises this schismogenic process was not conscious. Mrs. McGinnis called her various family members every day so there was nothing unusual in her telling them of the "bus" her husband had bought. In other families the process is quite conscious and deliberate. The Manzoni's, for example, knew that visits to their own families made their partners wildly jealous, and knew just at what point to call or visit a relative.

Even children become sensitive to the familial tensions regarding extended families and disappear to visit grandparents, insult visiting relatives, or engage in other operations to crystallize the parents', and eventually, the whole family's, split feelings about in-laws.

The mechanisms by which extended families are brought into conflict situations may be conscious or, at least apparently, unconscious. Frequently the sequence is initiated by what seems to be a casual and innocent conflict. Until we are able directly to observe the initiation of this spreading of conflict, it is difficult to be specific about the mechanisms involved. I feel fairly sure that the process is a subtle one, that no direct reference to conflicts in the nuclear family or direct request for allies has to be made. Rather both or all parties to the relationship are sufficiently sensitized that the spreading process can begin, or flare up, through minimal cues in tone of voice, timing of contacts and so forth. In all, I believe these mechanisms are not different from those observed in the families of schizophrenics, where therapy teams,[18] and hospital staff can become drawn into family conflicts.[19]

In the light of Bott's findings[8] regarding the nature of the social network and intrafamilial role allocation, it is important to inquire into the relationships between the extended families. When they are drawn into family conflicts do they themselves echo those conflicts, as Brodey finds that therapy teams do? None of our families had been geographically mobile to any large extent, so most extended families did have superficial acquaintance with each other. The frequency of active relationships was low, being clearly present in only one out of eleven cases. Since the frequency of active relationships in the general population is unknown, it is difficult to be sure of the significance of this. Of course, in our society the respective parental families stand in no particular relationship to each other and there is no term to denote it.*

Well families also have conflicts, but they differ in several respects. The open conflicts that occur are incidents on a foundation of basic integration, are self-limiting, and do not compromise a wide range of interaction in the future. In striking contrast to the disturbed families, active engagement in disputes was kept within the family by well families. This does not come about by the kin being unaware of the conflicts. Indeed they often seem quite well-informed about them, but these kin groups are not drawn into the pattern of balancing off one side of the nuclear family against the other.

In some well families there was evidence that the extended families not only did not become drawn into and amplify the conflicts, but even acted in benign ways to reduce conflicts and restore family functioning. An interesting example of this occurred in the DiMaggio family:

One summer Mr. DiMaggio's mother wanted to visit a nephew who had recently migrated to Canada from Italy. Over Mrs. DiMaggio's protests it was decided that the grandparents and four of their five sons, including Mr. DiMaggio, would make the trip; Mrs. DiMaggio would stay at home with her youngest child. During the absence of her in-laws, Mrs. DiMaggio became mildly depressed, and developed fantasies that her husband was having a gay time. Though her own family was living nearby, her contact with them did not increase markedly. The night before arriving home, Mr. DiMaggio phoned his wife. Though she did not complain openly, he sensed her state of mind. He felt guilty and when they arrived home, he managed to arrange it so that the rest of the family entered the apartment before he did. In their first contacts the brother-in-law and parents-in-law were attentive to Mrs. DiMaggio. One brother-in-law, a priest, took her aside and talked to her about the obligations of marriage and informed her of how unhappy her husband had been while away. When Mr. DiMaggio did come in, his wife put aside her complaints, brightened up and was genuinely glad to see her husband. Mrs. DiMaggio remained aware of her reactions but resumed a normal, close relationship with her in-laws.

* Other languages do have a term for this relationship, e.g. the Jewish word *Machatenen*.

EXTENDED FAMILIES AS STIMULATORS OF CONFLICT

Extended families are not always passive elements in the situation, and in some instances the initiative for provoking conflict seems to rest with them. Extended families may be responding to discrepancies in their family structure in the same ways, thereby inducing conflicts within the nuclear families we have in focus.

> The Mozzarellas had for some time had the father's unmarried brother living with them and their three children. At one point this brother took or stole a small amount of money from the Mozzarellas. Mrs. Mozzarella was furious and began to fight with her husband. The conflict grew and the brother moved out. Rather than abating, the conflict between husband and wife widened and deepened. Finally Mr. Mozzarella moved out for a few days, but did not stay with his brother. After a few weeks' absence the brother also moved back in with the family.

In all such instances it is likely that the action of the extended family has to fall on prepared grounds in the nuclear family. Often these actions are appropriate—almost uncannily so—to the weak spots in the family organization. In themselves the actions of the extended family may appear innocent enough, but their effects are widespread. Frequently the triggering incident is a gift.*

> Mrs. McGinnis' mother gave her grandson gifts of money just at the times when Mr. McGinnis was berating his son for his failure to earn his own spending money. The money mitigated the economic problem, but increased the father-son conflict and eventually the whole family was at odds.

In some instances the precipitating incident seems to be more genuinely innocent, with the problem being the inability of the family to develop or employ mechanisms for insulating themselves or for controlling conflicts once they have begun.

> Mrs. Manzoni's brother was in an army basic training camp about 40 miles away. He often visited the Manzonis when on leave. His visits were agreeable to the Manzonis who even looked forward to them since their uncontrollable son responded well to direction from this uncle. One weekend, however, he brought a buddy along with him. Mrs. Manzoni tried to be hospitable, but father and son both reacted sharply to this shift. Bitter arguments about the invasions and demands of Mrs. Manzoni's family ensued. Mrs. Manzoni retaliated with accusations that her husband did many favors for his family.

Whether conducted in an innocent or calculated way, extended families frequently do provoke conflicts in the nuclear families. The impact is not always the open conflict described in these examples. Often the impact is at the latent level, exaggerating the discrepancies that already exist.

---

* The gift, as Marcel Mauss has shown,[20] creates an obligation of the receiver to the donor. Normally this cements the social structure. As I shall discuss presently, for conflicted families the assuming and discharging of obligations is problematic and tends to break down the social structure.

At the well end of the continuum extended families do not intervene in their married children's lives in ways which set off the trains of reaction described above. The interventions which do occur do not cut to the bone and are not reacted to in a stereotyped way. To illustrate:

Mr. McNally's brother was a heavy drinker and had served time for theft. Occasionally he would come around to the McNally home, presumably looking for food and money. Mrs. McNally would refuse to let him into the house. Mr. McNally, though he had some interest and sympathy for his brother, supported such responses on the part of his wife. At times he sought out his brother and tried to help him, but these approaches were not timed and carried out so as to reflect on his wife or compensate for her rejection of the brother. On her side, Mrs. McNally did not interfere with her husband's attempts to rehabilitate his brother, though she expected little to come of them. Both husband and wife had mixed feelings about this relative but their attitudes toward him appeared to be appropriate.

Rather than acting as *agents provocateurs*, the extended kin of well families are able to remain neutral and respect the boundaries of the nuclear family. For their part, the well families are not hypersensitive to the actions of kin.

Mrs. Flanagan's parents lived nearby. They were old and somewhat infirm. Periodically heavy demands for help were made on Mrs. Flanagan. Even though the whole family was preoccupied with being cared for and had much physical illness, these demands were accepted as a necessary sacrifice, even by the children. Mr. Flanagan accommodated himself to the demands on his wife by being helpful at home and at his parents-in-law.

EXTENDED FAMILIES AS SCREENS FOR THE PROJECTION OF CONFLICTS

The extended family need not be an active or even potentially active element in the conflict situation. In all cases there was some evidence that the extended family served as a screen onto which a family member could project sentiments which referred more immediately to a spouse, child or parent. This process, which I have labelled the *over-generalization of affect* is mainly of negative sentiments. Positive sentiments are also involved as a reciprocal tendency, though they are not so conspicuous. The over-generalization spreads over social space and time. In the extreme cases an impervious dichotomy of good and bad occurs and rationalizes a wide range of avoidance behavior and expression of dislike.

Mrs. Donovan, in her first therapy sessions, painted a picture of the many deficiencies of her oldest son and her husband. She felt that they were no good and were just like her husband's family, all of whom were no good and never had been any good. Her own father, who died in her adolescence, was completely different, having been intelligent, sensitive, liberal, sophisticated and unprejudiced. Her mother, concerning whom she had more mixed feelings, came in for little comment at this time. Mrs. Donovan had had, since her marriage, minimal contact with her husband's family. Contacts which did occur substantiated her view of her in-laws.

The families in which pathology was highly integrated tended to show a pattern of each spouse directing his or her negative sentiments towards the in-laws and directing positive sentiments toward the natural parents. Reality sometimes makes such splitting difficult. However, grandparents who can in calm moments (or in therapy) be evaluated realistically, tend to be defended when they are criticized by the partner, and part of the defense is an attack upon the partner's side of the family. The reverse picture, of one person directing negative sentiments to his own parents and positive ones to his in-laws seems infrequent. In our cases it was noted only in one family and in this case the tendency was mild.

This sort of conflict involves, naturally enough, parents more than children. Still it is not restricted to them. The children are quite likely to assimilate the parental sentiments and to align with one rather than the other or "slide" between the two.

Jackie McGinnis, for example, could echo all of his mother's feelings and suspicions of his paternal grandmother and condemn the paternal grandfather who had died many years before his birth. At such times he was positive about and in close contact with maternal relatives. To a lesser degree he could reverse the roles if he was in conflict with his mother and wanted to get something from his father.

Again, projection of feelings through space and time need not emerge in overt conflict. The projection may be a stable characteristic of an individual's psychological functioning within the family which magnifies the discrepancies which do exist.

Mrs. McGinnis occasionally used her suspicion that her mother-in-law had money secreted in a Canadian bank in her arguments with her husband, insisting it was money which they had a right to. Even when she was not attacking her husband on this account, it was part of her fantasies about giving her son the education her husband was convinced he should not have and was incapable of getting. Buttressed by this projection, she was able to push her son and herself in directions which took them farther and farther from the father.

I hope that it is clear that there is more to this pattern than the pathological functioning of individuals. Individuals, children as well as parents, utilize the structure of the family and the extended family as arenas in which to express their ambivalent feelings. Reciprocally the schisms of the family and the extended family reinforce and perhaps even stimulate complications in their feelings about parent figures. Individuals who may have been able reasonably well to integrate their ambivalent feelings towards their parents may have difficulty in adapting to the existence of parents *and* parents-in-law.*

Members of well families, as material cited earlier suggests, do not develop such polarized feelings about kin. There certainly were mixed

* Cf. Parsons'[21] proposition that socialization involves the internalization not simply of separate parent figures but also the internalization of the *relationship between* the parents.

feelings and, on occasion, strong negative feelings about kin, but these could be handled and even if not fully expressed, the tendency to split feelings and maintain them in a rigid fashion was not present. This lack of over-generalization of affect was true of positive feelings as well as negative ones. In contrast to Epstein and Westley's[22] normal families, we did not meet the pattern of "adoration" which they observed in the wife-husband relationship. This difference in findings regarding normal families may be a genuine difference in the sample of families studied or may be a function of different methods of investigation used. In our group there was also no "adoration" spreading to the extended families.

EXTENDED FAMILIES AS COMPETING OBJECTS OF SUPPORT AND INDULGENCE

I have chosen to treat separately a theme closely related to all the above. My feeling is that this theme is a central and basic one. It is this: that extended families become competing sources and objects of the support and indulgence for the nuclear family. In American society the norm is for nuclear families to be independent.*

The disturbed families we have seen almost universally presented problems of this sort. When the loyalty and commitment of some members can no longer be implicitly assumed and is called into question, processes are set in motion to generate and amplify conflicts. In some instances the medium of conflict is money, as with Mr. McGinnis:

He had an ambulatory paranoid sister who journeyed about the country taking skilled clerical jobs. Invariably she would develop suspicions that she was being watched and plotted against and quit her job. In desperate financial straits she would wire Mr. McGinnis for money. Though recognizing her as ill, Mr. McGinnis would usually get money somewhere and send it to her. He maintained that he kept this secret from his wife, though she was well aware of what was going on. (Both, incidentally, silently assumed that all this was kept secret from the children, which was also inaccurate.) For Mrs. McGinnis this justified her suspicions that her mother-in-law was holding back and in derivative and half-recognized ways complicated the family fights over money.

The diversion of material goods as well as money to the extended family can be the precipitant of conflicts. For the Manzonis it was the

---

* Legally the situation is confused. Marriage is recognized as a legal union which obligates the husband to support his family, and both parents to support their minor children. Similarly a legal marriage (and even in some circumstances a common-law union) entails the right to pass property onto family members and the right of family members to claim property of a deceased member. At the same time we still have laws, occasionally enforced, that children, even married children, are obligated to support indigent parents.[23] This vagueness of our laws and our mores, together with our bilateral kinship system, presents the possibility of conflict. Family resources—whether they be money, goods, affection or services, are not unlimited. There are always alternative directions in which they may be allocated. Even comfortably situated families may have problems in the allocation of wealth and contain "poverty-stricken" members.[24]

cost of food which was consumed by Mrs. Manzoni's family. Mr. Manzoni felt that the food served his in-laws was better than that served *his* family if they visited, and more of it was consumed.

In other cases the questioned commodity was affection and attention. Mr. McGinnis was preoccupied with the amount of time his wife spent talking to her family on the telephone and compared it to the neglect of his own mother, a neglect of which he himself was guilty. The Manzonis were continually suspicious that the other was seeing his own family and being influenced by them. Children too were perceived as liking one side of the family more, paying more heed to one side, and even of resembling, physically or in personality, one side of the family rather than the other.

In the Costello family such a pattern was developed to the extreme. Their first son was a "mother's boy," the second a "father's boy," and they moved in largely separate interactional spheres. When Mrs. Costello wanted to visit her parents, which she felt obliged to do weekly, her older son would not tolerate being left behind while her younger son protested strongly about going. Each visit was thus a struggle for Mrs. Costello and sufficient proof to Mr. Costello that she should stay at home.

Whatever the resource being contended about, the pattern of real or perceived favoritism for part of the extended family structure can arise. The pattern seems to serve multiple functions; it externalizes the internal conflicts of any given individual and allows him to rationalize his own shortcomings (as with Mr. McGinnis), for his own shortcomings pale into insignificance in the light of the others' misdeeds. At the same time it preserves the conflicts within the family. Being external they are beyond influence of any one person or combination.

Once again well families stand in contrast. They too have problems about the allocation of resources but diverting them to one family of orientation, as the earlier illustration of the Flanigans suggests, does not stimulate feelings of deprivation and resentment. Correspondingly resources from extended families, even when the differential between the contributions of the two sides of the family is considerable, do not become foci of conflict.

To summarize the material presented above, it may be said that disturbed families have difficulties in solving the problems of how to relate to two sets of "parents" and of establishing family boundaries. The absence of boundaries allows family conflicts to spread to extended kin and means a deficit of ability of the nuclear family to insulate itself from the vagueness of the outside world. Thus extended kin are drawn into, or play into the conflicts of the nuclear family so that underlying discrepancies are not resolved but are spread and made more rigid. In this family setting individual members have difficulty in taking roles as representatives of the whole family. *Vis-à-vis* the outside world of kin they act as individuals; what they give to or receive from kin casts them as competitors with other members rather than as collaborators with the whole family. This interpersonal situation appears to foster the awakening and acting out of ambivalent feelings with a consequent circular effect.

IMPLICATIONS

The thesis has been advanced here that the extended families are, or become, involved in family pathology and that different patterns of relationship with extended families are set up by disturbed families than by normal or healthy families. In conclusion I should like to explore some of the implications of such findings for theories of the relationship between family processes and mental illness, and for therapeutic efforts at diagnosis and treatment.

Several years ago Ackerman[25] complained of etiological theories in dynamic psychiatry that they ". . . hypothesize a relation between a piece of the child and a piece of the parent." (p. 182) His evaluation was that these were inadequate and that we had to evolve theories which related to the integrity of the individual to the family as a whole. A great deal of progress in this direction has been made but the question may be raised again with regard to family-centered theories. The point is not that they are incorrect but that they are only part of the picture. Families are seldom, if ever, isolated from kin. If ties to extended families are present and involved in the family processes must we not at some level include this in our theory? The findings presented, though based upon a small and selected population and derived from studies of neurotic children rather than psychotic adults, seem to me to argue in this direction.

The issue can be posed in a more general form. The systems we deal with are not closed, they are always embedded in and to some degree derive their rationale and patterning from, broader systems. For some purposes we may treat them *as if* they were closed but we must never paint them as the whole truth. In this I have tried to look outward from the family system to its kin. One might equally well take cognizance of the fact that the family is involved in many other networks of relationships and that these too may function to stimulate and maintain conflicts or alternatively to contain and correct them.* Ultimately we must refer our finding to the general patterns of values which characterize cultures and subcultures and which have a pervasive influence in shaping personality, family role patterns, and the whole family field extending through space and time, indeed the whole fabric of society. Florence Kluckhohn has devoted her major attention to the analysis of these patterns of value orientations.[26] It is, I believe, possible to show that the type of issue which comes up in this process of re-equilibrating the imbalance associated with marriage, the pathological ways of coping with discrepancies,

---

* For brief comments on how work associates, neighbors and professionals may be assimilated to pathological family patterns see.[4, 12]

and the available alternatives for resolving the issues can be deduced from the variations in value orientations characteristic of different groups.

Our work is vastly complicated by such a theoretical position but I see no alternative to dealing with reality as it is. If a broader range of variables can be dealt with precisely and adequately, we may develop theories with more specificity than our current conceptions. In an earlier era it was popular to attribute mental disturbances to broken homes. I daresay there are 100 papers in the literature reporting such findings. It is only part of the problem of these studies that they report inconsistent findings and that they seldom have adequate control groups. A more serious problem is that broken homes seem to be related to delinquency, neurosis, schizophrenia, and various psychosomatic disorders. An agent so nonspecific is of little help or at best is merely the first step. Most studies of families have also lacked control groups. It is not clear whether the presumably pathogenic processes detected in the families of schizophrenics are really absent in families with less seriously disturbed individuals and perhaps even families without disturbance. Tracing out how pathology is integrated in a broader network than the nuclear family may give some added specificity.

There might also be advantages to paying close attention to the history of families. It is striking that we have not developed models of the developmental processes of families that compare to our models of individual development. For example, in the Donovan family many shifts in group and individual dynamics coincided with changes in the closeness of the nuclear family to the wife's mother.

After their marriage the Donovans lived with the wife's mother, and had a fairly happy marriage. Acute difficulties arose after they moved to their own dwelling; Mrs. Donovan's sentiments about her in-laws became more negative, and Mr. Donovan's contacts with his family, which were more rigidly pursued, became more threatening to the wife. The problems were heightened after Mrs. Donovan's mother remarried. During the course of therapy the two family units jointly purchased a two-family house and lived close to each other again. Many conflicts abated following this move.

If we can learn to listen to the histories patients give, not individual but familial, we can learn much about the dynamics of the group and how the family has got to its present state. Such findings as have been reported may also have implications for our therapeutic endeavors. To the extent that we misplace the causal forces which have led to, and maintain pathology, we may misjudge the potentials for change and how to bring it about. Systematic consideration of patterns of relationships with extended families can give us added leverage in the diagnosis of particular problems with which we are confronted.

Treatment strategies may need rethinking in the light of this view of pathology as a process broader than the individual family. In our research work we saw relatives, not because we had any systematic program or good rationale to intervene therapeutically with them, but in pursuit of our research interests. This was not always readily agreed to by members of the nuclear family but in many cases it had a salutary effect, for the family members, for the relatives, and for their relationships. Relatives were seldom ignorant of the difficulties in the nuclear families or of the involvement with the psychiatric clinic. Nuclear families often preferred to believe that their problems and attempts to get help were unknown to kin, but on close examination, this was another example of "open secrets."

In several cases it was a significant turning-point when the person being seen could allow his relatives to be seen by the therapist.

Mr. Donovan was resistant to therapy in many ways but dead set against his family being seen. After a year with very limited progress (and incidentally some time after the family had moved back into a house shared with Mrs. Donovan's mother), he was able to discuss his discomfort with authority figures unless he could be on close friendly terms with them. A little later, Mr. Donovan offered to take the therapist to visit the rest of his family. Subsequent to this social visit, there took place meaningful discussions of Mr. Donovan's feelings of loyalty to and sympathy with his own family, and his resentment at his wife's depreciation of them, him, and his son.

While such techniques are regarded by many as unorthodox, dangerous and/or unnecessary, I believe a case can be made that there are instances in which therapy fails unless the therapist can understand and involve himself into the fabric of meanings and the network of relationships the patient knows as natural.[4]

As for the relatives, seeing them legitimizes their interest in the nuclear family, but brings this interest under some control. We found they were sometimes able to neutralize their involvement in the nuclear families and get for themselves a broader perspective on the nuclear family. It was also profitable to get, by seeing a relative, a fresh perspective on a case. Just as Brodey sees the advantages of seeing married partners to get a "stereoscopic view" of the relationship, so seeing members of several families offers the advantages of a stereoscopic view of families.

We have not included relatives in therapy on a systematic and regular basis and I can only conjecture about the advantages and problems that "kin group therapy" might bring. There are no logical grounds for stopping at the boundaries of the nuclear family, boundaries which are very permeable and shifting.* At one level, movement in therapy consists of changes in the sentiments about and interaction with extended families. To cite the Donovans once more:

Mrs. Donovan's depreciation of her son, husband and all her husband's family gradually gave way during therapy. In the space of three years, they altered sufficiently to lead her to buy a small Christmas gift for her mother-in-law. Contact of the whole family with her husband's siblings increased. Eventu-

* One wonders what family therapists would do if they attempted to treat matrifocal families such as exist in the south and around the Caribbean.

ally, she visited her mother-in-law and found that she had good qualities as well as bad, and that it was not unpleasant to visit her. As her sentiments were mitigated, her relationship with her husband expanded and changed and shifts even appeared in the whole family constellation.

It is possible that this central process in the whole family might have been speeded up if both partners could have been influenced simultaneously, as indeed we do in treating mother-child pairs.

SUMMARY

This paper has taken up the issue of whether our understanding of functional disturbances can afford to stop at the boundaries of the nuclear family. It has been argued, and some evidence has been presented, that disturbed families are distinguishable from well families in terms of their patterns of relationships with extended families. Disturbed families have a deficiency of family boundaries which leads them to involve extended kin in their conflicts and makes them sensitive to influence from extended kin. Directly or indirectly a considerable segment of kindred systems become part of a pathological drama, until pathology is a characteristic of the system, not of individual persons or families. Such findings require replication with larger samples, but do raise questions about the adequacy of our theories of family pathology and our treatment techniques.

REFERENCES

1. SPIEGEL, John P., and BELL, NORMAN W. 1959. The family of the psychiatric patient. In ARIETI, SILVANO, (ed.) *American handbook of psychiatry*. Basic Books, New York.
2. RICHARDSON, HENRY B. 1945. *Patients have families*. Commonwealth Fund, New York.
3. BELL, JOHN E. 1961. *Family group therapy*. Publ. Hlth Monogr. No. 64. U.S. Dept. of Health, Educ. and Welfare, Washington, D.C.
4. BELL, NORMAN W., TRIESCHMAN, ALBERT, and VOGEL, EZRA, F. 1961. A sociocultural analysis of the resistances of working-class fathers treated in a child psychiatric clinic. *Am. J. Orthopsychiat.*, **31**, 388-405.
5. LEICHTER, HOPE. 1961. Boundaries of the family as an empirical and theoretical unit. In ACKERMAN, NATHAN W., BEATMAN, FRANCES L., and SHERMAN, SANFORD N., (eds.) *Exploring the base for family therapy*. Family Service Assoc. of America, New York.
6. ACKERMAN, NATHAN. 1959. Emotional impact of in-laws and relatives. In LIEBMAN, SAMUEL, (ed.) *Emotional forces in the family*. Lippincott, Philadelphia.
7. BELL, NORMAN W., and VOGEL, EZRA F. 1960. Toward a framework for the functional analysis of family behavior. In BELL, NORMAN W., and VOGEL, EZRA F., (eds.) *A modern introduction to the family*. Free Press, Glencoe, Ill.
8. BOTT, ELIZABETH. 1957. *Family and social network*. Tavistock publications, London.
9. ZIMMERMAN, CARLE, and CERVANTES, LUCIUS. 1960. *Successful American families*. Pageant Press, New York.

10. APPLE, DORRIAN. 1958. The social structure of grandparenthood. *Am. Anthrop.*, **58**, 656-663.
11. RADCLIFFE-BROWN, A. R. 1950. Introduction. In RADCLIFFE-BROWN, A. R., and FORDE, DARYLL, (eds.) *African systems of kinship and marriage*. Oxford Univ. Press, London.
12. VOGEL, EZRA F., and BELL, NORMAN W. 1960. The emotionally disturbed child as a family scapegoat. *Psychoanal. psychoanal. Rev.*, **47**, 21-42.
13. SANUA, VICTOR D. 1961. Sociocultural factors in families of schizophrenics. *Psychiatry*, **24**, 246-265.
14. PARSONS, TALCOTT. 1954. The kinship system of the contemporary United States, in PARSONS, TALCOTT, *Essays in sociological theory*, revised ed. Free Press, Glencoe, Ill.
15. KLUCKHOHN, FLORENCE R. 1958. Variations in the basic values of family systems. *Soc. Casewk*, **39**, 63-72.
16. SPIEGEL, JOHN P. 1959. Some cultural aspects of transference and counter-transference. In MASSERMAN, JULES H., (ed.) *Individual and familial dynamics*. Grune & Stratton, New York.
17. PITTS, JESSE R. 1960. The family and peer groups. In BELL, NORMAN W., and VOGEL, EZRA F., (eds.) *A modern introduction to the family*. Free Press, Glencoe, Ill.
18. BRODEY, W. M., and HAYDEN, M. 1957. The intrateam reactions: Their relation to the conflicts of the family in treatment. *Am. J. Orthopsychiat.*, **27**, 349-355.
19. BOWEN, MURRAY, DYSINGER, R. H., BRODEY, W. M., and BASAMANIA, B. 1957. *Study and treatment of five hospitalized family groups with a psychotic member*. Paper delivered at the American Orthopsychiatric Association Meetings, Chicago.
20. MAUSS, MARCEL. 1950. Essai sur le don. In MAUSS, MARCEL, *Sociologie et Anthropologie*. Presses Universitaires de France, Paris.
21. PARSONS, TALCOTT, and BALES, R. F. 1955. *Family, socialization and interaction process*. Free Press, Glencoe, Ill.
22. EPSTEIN, NATHAN B., and WESTLEY, WILLIAM A. 1960. Grandparents and parents of emotionally healthy adolescents. In MASSERMAN, JULES, (ed.) *Psychoanalysis and human values*. Grune & Stratton, New York.
23. SCHORR, ALVIN L. 1960. *Filial responsibility in the modern American family*. U.S. Dept. of Health, Educ. and Welfare, Washington, D.C.
24. YOUNG, MICHAEL. 1952. Distribution of income within the family. *Br. J. Soc.*, **3**, 305-321. [Reprinted in this collection as No. XIX.]
25. ACKERMAN, NATHAN W., and BEHRENS, M. L. 1955. Child and family psychopathy: Problems of correlation. In HOCH, P. H., and Zubin, J., (eds.) *Psychopathology of childhood*. Grune & Stratton, New York.
26. KLUCKHOHN, FLORENCE R., STRODTBECK, FRED, *et al.* 1961. *Variations in value orientations*. Row, Peterson, Evanston, Ill.

XXIII

THE HUMAN RELATIONS PROGRAM AT THE UNIVERSITY OF IOWA

RALPH H. OJEMANN

A child lives mostly within his own family. But between 5 and 15 years of age he may, in some societies, spend a third of his waking life at school. This experience can be beneficial or hurtful, depending upon the emotional climate of the school.

Some years ago when we were making observations of parental and teacher behavior toward children, it was observed that parents and teachers tended to deal with child behavior as a surface phenomenon instead of taking account of the factors underlying or causing the behavior. Observation also tended to indicate that such an approach to behavior tended to produce conflicts and emotional strains in both adult and child.

For example, if a child attempted to overcome a feeling of inadequacy by "pushing" to be first so often that it interfered with class activity, the teacher who approached this behavior as a surface phenomenon would try to stop it by such methods as reprimanding the child, making him go to the end of the line, or sending him out of the room. She tended to do this without thinking about or inquiring as to the causes of the behavior. Since the feeling of inadequacy remained in spite of the scolding, going to the end of the line, or leaving the room, the child would still be under a strain and would attempt more vigorous action or a different approach. The teacher would soon observe that her attempts to stop the behavior were not successful. She would tend to intensify her attempts to stop the pupil's interfering behavior and the whole round of strains would rise to a new level.

Observation of the behavior of parents toward children tended to reveal a similar situation. Analyses of parental behavior often revealed a

Reprinted from PERSONNEL AND GUIDANCE JOURNAL, Vol. 37, 1958 pp. 198-206.

sequence somewhat as follows. In the early years of the child's life, parents would try to control him by telling him what to do, punishing him, coaxing him, and so on. When these procedures failed after years of trial some parents would give up. This left the child to his own devices for meeting problems and he often failed to find satisfying and cooperative solutions. Other parents would doggedly persist, only to meet with increasing resistance and conflict.

WHAT THE EARLY OBSERVATIONS SUGGESTED

An analysis of such behavior on the part of parents and teachers suggested that if they could extend their insight into and appreciation of the causes of behavior and change from a surface approach to an approach that takes account of the dynamics of behavior, the chances of blocking strong motivations in the child (and also in themselves) would be lessened and the chances for cooperative or mutually satisfying interaction would be increased.

A test of this hypothesis was made in the case of teachers in a study by Wilkinson.[13] Through the use of an experimental and control group it was shown that as the teacher acquired more insight into the backgrounds, ambitions, worries, and concerns of pupils, conflict between teacher and pupil tended to lessen and the pupils' attitudes toward school tended to change in a more favorable direction.

A close examination of the idea that teachers and parents can guide children more effectively and produce less emotional conflict if they approach the child's behavior in dynamic terms suggested that we were dealing with two cases of the larger problem of the relation of one person to another. The reactions of a teacher toward a child or a parent toward a child are essentially reactions of one person toward another. This observation suggested the question, will the hypothesis hold in any human relationship? If we change children to approach behavior dynamically, will that help them in getting along with adults and with their associates?

When we examined the whole problem still more closely we noted another aspect. After a child learns about the factors that underlie behavior, theoretically he could apply this learning not only to the behavior of others but also to his own actions and to the guiding of his own development. For example, if he learned that over-aggressive behavior is often motivated by a feeling of inadequacy, and if he learned something about how feelings of inadequacy develop and how they can be overcome, he would have something to help him interpret his own over-aggressive behavior or his own feelings of inadequacy. The question then became, if we change children so that they appreciate the differences between the surface and dynamic approaches to behavior, will that affect their relationships with others and their relationship to themselves?

This question had two parts. (1) Can children acquire an appreciation of the differences between the surface and dynamic approaches to behavior and apply the dynamic approach in their relations with their parents, teachers, other adults, in their relations with their associates, and in guiding their own development? (2) If they can learn and can be motivated to apply, will that reduce the emotional conflicts and increase the amount of mutually satisfying interaction in these relationships?

This question, with varying emphases on the several aspects, was studied in the investigations by Morgan,[6] McCandless,[5] Bate,[1] and Stiles.[11] In summary, these investigations showed that children in the elementary and secondary grades can learn the beginnings of the dynamics of behavior, that they can learn to apply this knowledge in their relations with others, and that the process of learning about human behavior can be greatly extended on the school level.

THE PLACE OF EDUCATION IN HUMAN RELATIONS IN THE SCHOOL

When it became fairly clear that children can learn to approach behavior in terms of its causes, considerable thought was given to the next problem that suggested itself, namely, how can the material about behavior be inserted into the school curriculum?

Two approaches could be made. One would be to introduce a separate course on human relations. This is perhaps the first suggestion that occurs. When we studied the problem, however, several questions arose.

When we looked over the various "core" areas in the school curriculum we noted several that dealt rather directly with human behavior. Examples are social studies, English (human behavior in literature and writing), home economics (family relationships), and guidance. How did it happen that in spite of these opportunities to study human development people grew up with a surface approach to behavior as in the case of the parents and teachers we had observed? Why is the surface approach so apparent in our culture?

A careful study of this question led to an examination of the content and method of the several subjects as now taught in school, and this revealed an interesting situation. It can perhaps best be described by an example from community civics. When we examine the discussion in the ordinary civics book of such a problem as crime, for example, we find a discussion of how the police force is organized, its function as prescribed by law, methods for detecting and apprehending the criminal, and the system of courts, training schools, and prisons that have been developed. We may find a short discussion of the fact that crime is somewhat associated with economically underprivileged conditions.

But all of this approaches crime as a "surface" phenomenon. We can show this by considering the question we would ask if we approached criminal behavior in terms of its causes. If we do that we would ask such questions as these: Are the ways in which the police and the courts handle a criminal such that after they apprehend him they try to find out what caused the behavior and then take the causes into account in their reactions toward him? Do they try to find out in a given case whether the causes are such that the criminal can be rehabilitated into a self-respecting cooperating citizen and not to be a constant threat to other members of society, or if he cannot be rehabilitated is he then effectively isolated? In other words, do the present systems that society has set up study the criminal to find out the causes of his behavior and base their treatment of him on those findings?

Furthermore, if criminal behavior is caused, then real protection from the criminal requires that the community find out and change those conditions that produced him. Real protection—both in the sense of protection from direct damage to life and property which the criminal may inflict and also in the sense that taking care of criminals is a drain on the other citizens—comes when people in the community are aware of the forces that tend to produce crime and seek to change those forces.

In considering what the forces are we will have to go beyond the observations that poverty and similar conditions are somewhat correlated with crime and ask the more penetrating question—How does it happen that some persons living in a given environment become criminals, while other persons living in the same home and same neighborhood do not? But these questions are not considered in the usual text. The treatment is largely surface in character.

We could give other examples illustrating the same point. In short, much of the treatment of human problems in civics teaches the "surface" approach. What is true for civics also tends to hold true for the other social studies. Stiles,[10] for example, found in analysis of the material on human behavior in 15 social studies readers used in the elementary school that less than one per cent of the selections treated human behavior in the dynamic way. Much of the treatment is of the surface variety.

The question now becomes—Under what arrangement do we have the most effective learning conditions? Do we have it if (a) we have a surface approach to behavior in the usual school subjects and a dynamic approach in a separate course on human behavior, or (b) if we have a dynamic approach wherever human behavior is discussed?

It is well known from studies on learning that changes are made most effectively when that which the child learns is applied consistently in a variety of situations. This suggested to us that we may profitably experiment further with the possibility of changing the content of school subjects from a surface to a dynamic treatment. Accordingly, studies were undertaken to determine how the material on the dynamics of behavior could be integrated into such areas as social studies, English, guidance, home economics, and others. Also, studies were undertaken to see how and to what extent the child could apply the dynamic approach in his relations with his associates and in guiding his own development.

In addition to school influences, there are the home influences. A child learns from the way his parents act toward him. Just as in the case of the teacher, the parent can work with the child using a surface approach or a more causal approach. If he uses principally a surface approach he is demonstrating to the child a non-causal method of working with others which the child will also tend to adopt. We have evidence[7] that children learn early in life a surface approach to behavior.

Such an analysis of the problem indicated to us that if we wanted to develop causally-oriented children, we needed classrooms equipped with teachers who both teach causally-oriented content materials and practise the causal approach in the daily relations with pupils. It would also help if the home environments of these children practised the causal approach at least in some measure. We have attempted to develop such classrooms and homes.

Under our general plan, the program, by arrangement with a school system, provides summer fellowships so that selected teachers can attend an intensive training program. This program is designed to familiarize the teacher-students with the differences between surface and causal approaches, to help them apply the causal approach to the daily activities in the classroom, and to develop skill in teaching causally-oriented materials.

A supervisor of teachers, on the Preventive Psychiatry staff, works with the teachers throughout the year, holding a series of conferences with each. During the summer training program, each teacher assists in the preparation of teaching materials for his own classroom. With the supervisor's help he continues this adaptation of materials for classroom purposes throughout the year. We thus obtain a group of classrooms for our laboratory, each equipped with a causally-oriented teacher and appropriate curricular content.

EXAMPLES OF CURRICULAR EXPERIENCES

To provide a more detailed picture of the integrated program as presently conceived, it may be helpful to examine some of the actual learning experiences that are provided at several age levels. Examples for this purpose will be drawn from two age levels, namely, primary and intermediate.

1. *Examples of experiences at the primary level*

A. *Demonstrations furnished by the teacher's behavior.* At each age level, as has been indicated, the child is influenced by the behavior of the teacher as well as by what he hears or reads. How the teacher handles the day-to-day social situations that arise in the classroom and on the playground, the extent to which the teacher seeks to know the child's ambitions, concerns, and abilities and makes use of this information in planning his program of work and understanding his behavior before dealing with it, are examples of experiences that affect the growth of a causal orientation.

This training of the teacher to practise the causal approach is an important part of the program at all age levels and the primary level is no exception.

Furthermore, as soon as the child has some appreciation of why a situation has to be understood before it can be reacted to logically, the teacher can take the simpler situations that arise and work them out with the class to involve the children in a practical application of a causal orientation. It is important that the teacher choose only the simpler situations at the beginning, for a careful grading as to difficulty is as important in learning human behavior concepts as it is in learning other concepts.

B. *Use of narratives.* To help the primary child develop an appreciation of the differences between the non-causal and causal approaches (at the primary levels the teachers have labeled the approaches the "non-thinking" and "thinking" ways), a variety of materials have been developed which can be read to the child and discussed with him. One type of material consists of stories in which the non-causal and causal procedures are contrasted. Listening to the narratives and discussing them provide vicarious experiences for learning the differences between the two ways of living.

Each narrative describes some behaviour situation. After the situation has been set forth, some character in the story begins to make a surface approach to it, then rethinks his proposed reaction and makes a more causal approach. Some of the ways in which the behavior may have developed come out and one of the characters in the narrative acts in the light of these data. The situation has a reality about it in that someone begins to make a surface approach which children in our culture experience quite frequently. But, it also introduces a new way of living—a way that takes account of the meaning or the causes of behavior instead of its overt form.

For example, in one situation a boy gets into so many fights that something has to be done. The teacher in the story is about to deal with this in the usual way when he recalls that such things do not occur of their own accord. He does a little probing and before long it comes to light that this boy has been teased a great deal because he had to go home immediately after school each day to help take care of his baby sister and didn't have time to play with the other children. When the teacher learns this, he takes measures to work out this basic problem.

To help the child develop a more generalized conception and to prevent him from thinking only of incidents involving himself, situations were developed involving children older and younger than himself and children from quite different environments. There is some observational evidence that situations involving people different from the child tend to be less emotionally charged and therefore less difficult for the child to consider causally in the early discussions.

Each narrative is preceded by a short introduction for use by the teacher. After the reading of the story there is a discussion. The purpose of this discussion is not only to recall the incidents of the story, but also to bring out the differences in procedure when one thinks of causes as contrasted with principal attention to the overt form of behavior. The discussion is also designed to consider alternative ways of meeting situations and some of the probable effects of these alternatives.

It is suggested to the teacher that this material furnish part of the offering in the regular "story period." Under usual school conditions, the material read in the story period deals with various objects and events in the child's environment. Some of it deals with physical objects, some of it deals with people. It is suggested that material dealing with people be heavily weighted with the causally-oriented materials described. The causally-oriented stories are thus part of the primary child's story period content.

C. *Use of expositions to help understand and appreciate the work of the teacher and other persons with whom the child interacts directly.*

An example of this type of material is a leaflet entitled "The Work of the Teacher." This is a simplified discussion contrasting the conception of the teacher as "someone whose main job is to check up on you" with the conception of "a guide to help you learn." This material is designed to be read by the teacher to the class and talked over with them. The logical implications of the "guide to help you" concept are described, including what alternatives are available to the child and their respective probable consequences when he finds his learning experiences not challenging. Included also is a discussion of how it may help the teacher to "tell her when something is worrying you."

The purpose of the material is to help the child gain some understanding of the behavior of the teacher, her feelings, and her methods. It is also designed to help the child begin learning that he has a part in arranging his social environment.

Similar material has been prepared to help the child gain some appreciation of the work of parents and other adults in his social environment.

2. *Examples of experiences at the intermediate level*

A. *The behavior of the teacher.* Since pupils at the intermediate levels can read, syllabi, work sheets and other material to be read by pupils can be prepared. However, at this level as at the primary level, the pupil also learns from what he observes of the behavior of the teacher in the daily interactions with the class. Hence, it is recognized in the integrated program that the teacher's daily behavior is an important part of the learning experience at the intermediate level as well as at the primary level, and the plan includes training of teachers at this level also in practising the causal orientation. A pamphlet prepared for the National Education Association for use by teachers reflects this recognition.* In its full development, the integrated plan expects that all teachers will apply the principles of human development in their daily work in the classroom.

At this level there is also the opportunity to help the pupil take some responsibility for his own development. The discussion of the work of the teacher, referred to in the description of sample materials at the primary level, is extended to include a consideration of how the pupil can help to build up his cumulative record for the school, in what areas he can keep the teacher informed about his attitudes and feelings, and how he can apply what he is learning to his own behavior.

At this level also there is the possibility of using the room council as a laboratory in which the child can apply the causal orientation in a real life situation. Since in the integrated plan the subject matter areas of social studies, health, and reading incorporate material designed to enrich a pupil's conception of the dynamics of behavior, and since he is encouraged to apply the enriched conception to situations arising in the room council, it will be helpful to indicate how the subject matter areas make their contribution before describing the use of the room council in detail.

B. *Teaching causally-oriented social studies*. In elementary social studies each of the major topics can be developed in terms of the basic factors operating in the behavior of the people involved.

The following examples will illustrate this. As an introduction to 5th grade social studies, two teachers† prepared the following introduction:

I. Introduction

to

Fifth Grade Social Studies

This year we are going to try to look at Social Studies in a little different way. In Social Studies we discuss problems about people. It will help us to understand these problems more fully if we know something about why people act as they do.

This little booklet is to be used with your textbook in Social Studies to make it possible for you to learn more about the behavior of people and what the effects of their behavior are.

We will want to find out how situations come about that cause people to act the way they do.

1. What are the needs the people are trying to satisfy?
2. What methods are they using to work out their feelings?
3. What are the effects on other people as a result of the methods chosen to work out those needs or feelings?
4. What might happen if other methods were used?

* Ojemann, Ralph H. Personality adjustment of individual children. No. 5 *What Research Says to the Teacher*, NEA, Oct. 1954.
† Appreciation is expressed to Ann Pavlovsky and Marian Kennedy.

These questions are then developed in the discussion of historical events in subsequent units.

ATTITUDES OF PARTICIPATING TEACHERS

Our program brings up two groups of questions. The first group relates to procedures: How does the plan work? What is the attitude of the teacher toward it? Can teachers be interested in cooperating in such an enterprise? Do the teachers resist training in mental health principles?

Thus far, we have worked with primary, intermediate, and secondary school teachers. At the present writing, we have a group of 15 primary, 15 intermediate, 11 secondary teachers, and 3 counselors drawn from three school systems. They have participated in the summer program and have helped to revise various aspects of the curriculum to develop in the child a sensitivity to the causes and consequences of behavior. For instance, instead of being content with the usual textbook statement that, unlike boundaries between many European countries, the United States-Canadian border has never been fortified, they prepared a discussion, based on available studies of conflict and cooperation, on some of the probable underlying factors in producing the United States-Canadian relationships. The counselors have helped the secondary teachers extend their knowledge of the children in their classes.

The fact that we have had more requests for inclusion in the program than we can accommodate indicates that the teachers on the whole have a positive attitude toward it. Those who have been accepted have cooperated enthusiastically.

Something we learned in our early work may provide a clue to at least part of this cooperation. While most presentations of mental health for teachers today stress the motivating forces operating in the child, little emphasis is given to the problem of how these forces can be expressed constructively under classroom conditions and how the teacher can accept her past mistakes. One of the hypotheses underlying the approach in our program is that much of the resistance appearing in work with teachers arises from the frustration a teacher feels when she learns about a child's needs but does not see how she can meet them under classroom conditions. In our work with teachers we point out these problems early in the program, on the theory that if the teacher realizes we are aware of his problems and are interested in helping him resolve them he will feel less frustrated. As the program has progressed we have found this to be true. Always we attempt to increase the security and self-respect of each individual member of the program by working *with* the teachers rather than telling them.

Can a teacher help children in elementary and secondary schools take a more understandable approach to social situations? If so, what effect does this have on the children? Does it make them more, or less, secure? More, or less, able to develop satisfying relations with others? We have evidence that significant changes have been produced throughout the primary and intermediate grades. This evidence has been reported in several studies.[3, 9, 12]

A typical example may be found in some of the data obtained from our experiments with the 4th, 5th, and 6th grades. At each level a causally-trained teacher was matched with a teacher without such training from a nearby school, who served as a control. The matching was according to sex, age, training, and years of experience. Similarly, the children in the respective classes were equated as to intelligence. The experimental group was like the control group except that the control teacher did not participate in the summer training program and did not use causally-oriented curricular materials.

At the beginning of the school year all the children were given two causal-orientation tests. In one of the tests, the child was presented with a series of social situations to which he was asked to suggest a solution. The possible reactions ranged from arbitrary, judgmental, and punitive, such as: "It serves him right—he should be made to stay in"; to an awareness of possible complexity, such as: "The teacher should find out more about this."

In the second test, another series of social situations was presented, each followed by a series of statements with which the pupil was asked to indicate agreement or disagreement. Some examples are: "It wouldn't make much difference what method the teacher used to make him stop (bothering others) so long as he stopped bothering others." "Since these boys do the same things (described in the situation) they are probably all alike in most ways." "If another boy disobeyed his father the same way, his reason would be the same as Jack's."

The children were given tests again in the spring and the results of the experimental and control classes compared. In all grades a statistically significant change appeared in the experimental group but not in the control group.

Thus it appears that our laboratory, which consists of a teacher trained to be sensitive to the dynamics of behavior and to demonstrate this sensitivity in the daily living in the classroom and using a curriculum which incorporates these principles, is producing a degree of causal orientation among children.

Does the new orientation help causally-oriented children make more satisfying adjustments to their environment? We have various kinds of data to throw light on this question. For example, children from both the experimental and control groups were given the anti-democratic tendency scale test developed by Gough, Harris, Martin, and Edwards.[2] This is essentially a measure of authoritarianism.

A detailed analysis of the results[3] obtained from the experimental and control groups showed a significant difference between the two groups on both scales. The causally-oriented children showed significantly less authoritarianism. It thus appears that as children become more aware of the dynamic complexities of human motivation and behavior, their attitudes toward others begin to change from an authoritarian relationship to a more democratic relationship. In all of the analyses the effects of intelligence were eliminated by various statistical procedures.

ROLE OF CAUSAL ORIENTATION IN MENTAL HEALTH

A great many questions need answering before we can determine what role a causal orientation toward behavior plays in the prevention of mental illness and development of mental health. For example, we want to know what happens in later years to the child oriented causally through his school experiences. We want to know what kinds of behavior disturbances an "inoculation" with a causal orientation will prevent, if any, both during school age and in later years. Already, our laboratory enables us to study the relationships that develop between teachers and pupils in the causally-oriented classroom as compared to the relationships in a non-causally-oriented classroom. It also points the way for a study of a host of questions that arise in the investigations of the causes of emotional breakdowns and the avenues by which mental health in its full measure may be achieved.

ASSUMPTIONS UNDERLYING THE PROGRAM

As we look over the whole program, what are the assumptions that underlie it? It seems that there are two or perhaps three. The first is that we can describe the differences between a surface and a causal approach to behaviour. From the numerous occasions in which we have attempted to communicate the meaning of these concepts, it appears that it is possible to distinguish these approaches in their major aspects. We expect that a gradual refinement in meaning will take place.[4]

A second assumption is that a careful study using methods that can be duplicated and repeated by others so that the results can be checked is the only way in which we will be able to discover what degree of causal orientation can be developed at the various age and intelligence levels and what the effect is when a thorough-going causal orientation appears. It will be noted that we are not assuming that a causal orientation will relieve all mental strains or prevent all mental breakdowns. Rather we are asking the question, to what extent will an "inoculation" with a causal orientation prevent various types of mental illness and increase the amount of emotionally satisfying and creative uses of human energy? In our tests of the effects of the causal orientation, we are interested not only in measuring degree or extent of prevention but we are also interested in measuring degree or extent to which human energies are released in "creative" and "satisfying" achievement.

Finally, in the early stages of our work we had to assume that learning a causal orientation was not so incompatible with the individual goals of the teachers, children, and parents with whom we worked that it produced long-enduring conflict and frustration. Both observation and test results have indicated that this is no longer entirely an assumption but may be considered a generalization that has a degree of support.

Our program, which goes under the title of The Preventive Psychiatry Research Program, is an example of teachers, guidance workers, and other school personnel joining hands with research investigators to study not only whether changes in learners can be made but also what the effects are of these changes in the lives of the learners. Teaching is viewed as a way of creating a new pattern or way of living, the effects of which can then be studied.[8]

REFERENCES

1. Bate, Elsa B. 1948. *The effect of especially prepared materials in a learning program in human growth and development on the tenth grade level.* Unpublished doctoral dissertation, University of Iowa.
2. Gough, H. C., Harris, D. B., Martin, W. E., and Edward, M. 1950. Children's othnic attitudes: I. Relationship to certain personality factors. *Child Dev.*, **21**, 83-91.
3. Levitt, Eugene E. 1955. Effect of 'causal' teacher-training program on authoritarianism and responsibility in grade school children. *Psychol. Rep.*, **1**, 449-458.
4. Levitt, Eugene E., and Ojemann, Ralph H. 1953. The aims of preventive psychiatry and 'causality' as a personality pattern. *J. Psychol.*, **36**, 393-400.
5. McCandless, Boyd. 1941. *A study of selected factors affecting radio listening behavior.* Unpublished doctoral dissertation, University of Iowa.
6. Morgan, Mildred I., and Ojemann, Ralph H. 1942. The effect of a learning program designed to assist youth in an understanding of behavior and its development. *Child Dev.*, **13**, 181-194.
7. Ojemann, Ralph H. 1946. The effect on the child's development of changes in cultural influences. *J. educ. Res.*, **40**, 258-270.
8. Ojemann, Ralph H. 1948. Research in planned learning programs and the science of behavior. *J. educ. Res.*, **42**, 96-104.
9. Ojemann, Ralph H., Levitt, Eugene E., Lyle, William H., Jr., and White-side, Maxine F. 1955. The effects of a 'causal' teacher-training program and certain curricular changes on grade school children. *J. exp. Educ.*, **24**, 95-114.
10. Stiles, Frances S. 1947. *A study of materials and programs for developing an understanding of behavior at the elementary school level.* Doctoral dissertation, University of Iowa.
11. Stiles, Frances S. 1950. Developing an understanding of human behavior at the elementary school level. *J. educ. Res.*, **43**, 516-524.

12. SNIDER, BILL C. F. 1957. Relation of growth in causal orientation to insecurity in elementary school children. *Psychol. Rep.*, 3, 631-634.
13. WILKINSON, FRANCES R., and OJEMANN, RALPH H. 1939. The effect on pupil growth of an increase in teacher's understanding of pupil behavior. *J. exp. Educ.*, 8, 143-147.

XXIV

CHANGING PATTERNS OF PARENT-CHILD RELATIONS IN AN URBAN CULTURE

MARGARET MEAD

Urban communities change—and change the family for ill or good.

It gives me great pleasure to acknowledge the honour of being asked to give the Ernest Jones Lecture for 1957, as a recognition of the long and fruitful cooperation between cultural anthropology and psycho-analysis. Throughout the last thirty years the two approaches to the study of human behaviour have enriched each other in a variety of ways, as psycho-analysis has provided theoretical bases for the interpretation of human behaviour and cultural studies have made it possible to prune psycho-analytic theory of the inevitable provincialisms of theory based on observations made exclusively within the Euro-American tradition.[1] Because both fields are young and growing, they have also been able to take advantage of other developments in the behavioural sciences, such as the approaches of Gestalt psychology,[28] of learning theory,[12,3] of studies in normal child development,[47] as, for instance, those of Piaget in Geneva,[51] and of Gesell and Ilg in the United States.[31,36]. The development of child analysis as a special field also meant a stepping up of the degree of relevance which each discipline found in the other, and the development of modern methods of anthropological field work, particularly in the field called 'culture and personality'—itself a product of earlier cooperation—has meant that more detailed observations in both fields were available for comparative study. The older reliance by anthropologists upon psycho-analytic theory based upon reconstructions from the cases of adult patients and by psycho-analysts upon anthropological reconstructions of the nature of early man and of contemporary primitive man, which stimulated Freud

Reprinted from THE INTERNATIONAL JOURNAL OF PSYCHO-ANALYSIS, Vol. 38, 1957, pp. 369-378.

and his contemporaries, has given place to precise observations of the actual behaviour of children, during childhood, and of actual primitive peoples, carefully observed in their own habitats. The work of Erik Erikson[13] has been the most conspicuous example of a distinguished combination of the results of actual experience of anthropological field work, the practice of child analysis, and the study of normal children.

The years since World War II have brought a series of new behavioural approaches which have given a fresh impetus to these cooperative efforts; I should like to single out especially work on mother-child relationships at delivery and during the first year of life, particularly the work of Bowlby,[9] Spitz,[48] Aubry, [41] Escalona,[14] Jackson,[27] Bakwin,[2] and Mirsky,[37] as well as the earlier work of Margaret Fries[23]; the contributions which have been made to our understanding of circular relationships in human behaviour by the model introduced by cybernetics and general systems theory[6, 15, 16, 17, 18, passim, 20, 56]; the contributions resulting from coordination between the work of the modern ethologists[19, 25, 29, 30, 45, 53, 54, etc.] and psycho-analytic and anthropological studies of behaviour; and the emerging development of a new field of micro-behavioural analysis under the leadership of Bateson and Birdwhistell and their collaborators.[4, 7]

It seemed appropriate to choose as the topic of this lecture a problem which would draw upon both the more traditional and the more recent developments in this long cooperation, that of parent-child relationships, particularly because this would also give me an opportunity to reintroduce some questions relating to human evolution in the light of our newer evolutionary theories of the relationship between evolution and behaviour.[46]

Furthermore, it is in this field that psycho-analysts, anthropologists, and students of child development have been most willing to make recommendations for changes in our own traditional behaviour which might facilitate the development of a more desirable character structure in members of our own culture. Recent developments in practice in children's hospitals, changes in methods of child feeding—'self-demand' or 'self-regulation'—the practice known in the United States as 'rooming in', which permits the new mother to keep her baby with her in the hospital, and the greater role of the father during the early weeks of his child's life, have been the contributions of the last two decades, just as new methods of education in the knowledge of sex, and recognition of the child's ambivalence, of the importance of unconscious factors in the ability to learn, and of the harm that could be done by too restrictive parental practices or by discontinuities within the educative process were the contributions of psycho-analysis and of cultural findings during earlier decades. Because educators, therapists, and the designers of social institutions must always act as quickly as possible for the benefit of the actual living pupils, patients, and populations whom they are attempting to teach, cure, and plan for, there has been a recurrent danger that tentative findings would be put into practice too hurriedly or too uncritically. A continuing obligation of self-review is placed upon those of us who do believe in the relevancy of our work in the preventive and constructive fields of mental health.[34]

Parent-child relationships during the early months have assumed an extra importance as mass methods of education—the radio, television and compulsory early school attendance—all invade the childhood years, even within the home, and as the actual period during which parents have an opportunity to create optimum conditions of growth for their children becomes steadily briefer. Mass methods of obstetrical and pediatric care at birth, especially in the United States but increasingly in other countries as well, were invading the neo-natal period, separating the parturient mother from her husband and other children and from the newborn itself, and enforcing methods of feeding and care which did not take into account the delicate circular relationships between each mother and each child, between the parents, and within the family group. The period of infancy, as a period when irreversible damage could be done and, equally, as a period within which the groundwork of trust could be firmly laid, has, understandably, become a focus of anxiety for parents and practitioners, as fashions have shifted rapidly so that the latest newborn might benefit from the newest theoretical formulation, and the subject of bitter controversy. It is a period also in which violent all-or-none reactions—so familiar to students of the primary process—are likely to cluster, and in which we therefore have a peculiarly difficult task in attempting to introduce our increasing and changing insights in such a way that the corrections will result not in a pendulum swing to the extreme opposite position but in a spiral movement, with the new position retaining the insights while correcting the errors of the earlier one.

In the present context, I am using the word 'urban' to characterize all those parts of the modern world which participate in industrialized society because, although people may still live in the country and raise their own food, the conditions of a modern economy are such that there are essential differences between life in any part of this world and the life of early man, during the many thousands of years when our species-specific behaviour was becoming stabilized. In urban societies people no longer live in small primary groups where the stranger is a rare phenomenon, infants are no longer entirely dependent upon being breast-fed, and men are not bound to their households through their immediate food-getting—as opposed to more remote money-getting—activities. The modern world is one in which many of the day-to-day relationships are with strangers— bus drivers, vendors, clerks—relationships which are segmented and official. As we learn more about the species-specific biological behaviour of man, developed when he lived in small, self-contained, prevailingly monogamous groups, it is important to make use of these new insights in ways which are appropriate to the very different world which man has now built by relying upon his capacity to learn and to transmit what he has learned.

I shall take for special consideration first the establishment of the nurturing relationship in what has been called 'the nursing couple', with all of its variations through the use of wet-nurses, foster parents, artificial feeding, precise nutritional assessments based on assaying the food and the infant's response in weight, and the involvement of the male parent in the actual feeding and associated care of the child.

In order to make this as vivid as possible, I want first to show you a film made, in 1938, by Gregory Bateson and myself among the Iatmul of New Guinea: 'First Five Days in the Life of a New Guinea Baby'.[5] In the film you will see the establishment of a mother-child relationship from the moment immediately after birth, before the cord was cut, and during the next four days. Anthropologists share with psycho-analysts the difficulties which lie in the inaccessibility of their subjects to observation; films and tape recordings are the modern technical devices which can overcome this difficulty both for purposes of immediate communication and as a way of providing materials which can be critically reviewed and restudied in the light of developing theories.

When the film begins, you see the new mother seated in a little wood where sudden birth pains had overtaken her when her husband had sent her hurrying on an errand. The neonate, cord uncut, lies near her, and an old neighbour woman, hastily summoned, has brought water in a bamboo from the river and a shell to cut the cord. The mother ties the cord, cuts it with the shell, places the placenta carefully in an empty coconut shell, and tosses the newborn vertically and horizontally and then over on to an old grass skirt, where he first lies, crying vigorously, stretching and spreading his fingers and toes. The mother stands up while the attending old woman pours the cold river water over her. She then leans down to scrape the blood from her legs. Meanwhile the wet-nurse—another neighbour who has a baby young enough to qualify her as a neo-natal wet-nurse because she is observing the same food taboos—sits holding her own child, smoking a cigar, and brushing insects away from the newborn. Then the wet-nurse gathers up the baby, the mother picks up the placenta, and the procession —new mother, wet-nurse, and the wet-nurse's five-year-old daughter carrying her infant sibling, with her two-year-old brother tagging along, marches into the village, passing the father of the baby, who was debarred from being present at the birth not from rigid religious taboo but by shame, as he sits with his two young siblings, holding his older child, about four. The group settle down under a house (raised high on piles with an upper floor for the wet season), the mother binds her abdomen with bark, and the wet-nurse suckles the newborn. She places her nipple gently in the newborn's mouth and then, while its sucking proceeds vigorously, takes back her own child and jiggles it with one arm while keeping her nipple steady in the mouth of the newborn. The newborn's hands move, search-wise, in the direction of the breast and gradually relax. Then the newborn infant is covered with wet clay by the mother, his nose is shaped with warmed fingers, and he is placed in the hollow formed by her crossed legs. As the women wear only two narrow grass aprons and the infant is unclothed, the whole relationship of the infant to the bodies of mother and wet-nurse is outlined—the baby a pale rose colour against their dark skins.

The film then shows the baby's breast-feeding by his mother on the subsequent four days, and the rhythmic accompaniment to his sucking made by the movement of her great toe. From the first he is handled by being held up and out, away from the mother's body, supported under one armpit and at the side of the head by her thumb and finger. He is stood up on the ground when bathed, and on the fifth day—cord fallen off, breast-feeding established, ready for the cold bath which now replaces the bath of warm swamp water—he is already firmly established in a world in which he will spend the day on his mother's lap or arm.

This situation of a natural birth without complications, in which the mother, with very little help, cares for her own baby and breast-feeds it in happy rhythmic relation to its eager, seeking, sucking behaviour, is the type which has served as a model in the minds of those who are seeking to judge maternal care, filial response and our present institutional care of infants. True, the image of 'natural childbirth' conjured up by those who have never witnessed a birth in a primitive society fails to allow for the already high degree of stylization: the way the cord is tied, the disposal of the placenta, the presence of the wet-nurse, her qualifications decided upon by a system of lactation taboos, the patterned baths of wet clay and of warm and cold water, the bark which the mother bound around her waist, the toss she gave the baby in the air, up and sideways, and the way she shaped its nose with fingers warmed on a leaf laid on a glowing log.

Where ethologists have shown the extreme detail in which some response on the part of the infant evokes a corresponding and appropriate response in the mother, and a chain of interlocking appropriate maternal and filial responses is released and coordinated, anthropologists have documented the enormous variety in the practice of childbirth even among the simplest peoples. But among each people these activities are patterned, and participation in the pattern supplies a culturally predetermined sequence within which the child and the mother *either live or die*. For this is the essence of the primitive situation. Lacking any of the devices and practices of medicine and care, the birth situation among the Iatmul is far closer to that which we must assume for the early ancestors of man, when breast-feeding was the only known method of feeding a child and lactation by some other woman of a group was the first possible supplement to the capacity for lactation of the mother herself.

In judgements of maternal care, a great deal has been heard about 'the rejecting mother' who, because of her own conflicts and anxieties, her rejection of the feminine role or of the sex of her child, etc., 'rejects' her child and so is unable to breast-feed it or even to feed it artificially with sufficient relaxation so that it can trust her and thrive. Anthropologists supplied the information that every primitive woman somehow produced some milk to feed her child, that women who had been so ill with fever that they lost their milk for weeks regained it, and that women who had not had children could, by adopting a vigorously sucking baby, produce milk. All this appeared to reinforce the verdict that the sources of failure in breast-feeding were located in the mother, in defects of psychic functioning, psychosomatic but not somatic in character.

Parallel work by Margaret Fries[23] had focused on the infant in the hospital at birth, and her division of the newborn on the basis of a series of tests, which included suckling behaviour under interruption and frustration, into quiet, too quiet, and active babies placed the emphasis on the innate biological disposition of the infant, to which maternal behaviour should be adjusted. This demand for adjustment on the part of the mother was reiterated in the work of Margaret Ribble,[39] which derived from that of Fries, on 'the rights of infants', again returning the onus of failure to the mother. More recently, Arthur Mirsky[37] has suggested that there are 'rejecting babies'—infants so constituted at birth that they actively reject the feeding situation and arouse reactive rejections in the mother. This shifted the onus back to the infant with the possibility that the source of the failure might lie in the child, but the very phrase 'rejecting baby', although providing a needed corrective for the blanket explanation of the 'rejecting mother', still contained an element of blame.

Detailed studies of maternal-child behaviour in animals, especially the work of Helen Blauvelt[8] and of Mavis Gunther,[24] both stimulated by modern ethological studies, by focusing upon the 'biological adequacy' of the responses of mother and child, within a sequence, have now added a new perspective, if seen within the framework of human evolution. The paradigm for this kind of behaviour is admirably given in the Norwegian film, *Sammi Jaki*.[26] Here we see the reindeer delivering during a period when the herd is pressing towards the sea, where birth would occur under better conditions, nuzzling the infant to get on its own feet, lying down beside it once it is strong enough to suckle, stimulating it to great activity on its feet, and meanwhile listening, restless and anxious, to the sounds of the departing herd. If the infant is strong enough to follow the herd, all is well. But it will avail nothing for the mother to stay with the calf, and so lose the herd with which her survival lies. So she stands, in nicely calculated conflict. Helen Blauvelt's studies of newborn sheep and goats show in detail that the period in which the mother will wait for the infant to get established on its feet is sharply limited; after a given number of hours, during which she has bleated and licked the newborn, she no longer recognizes it as hers. The reindeer film throws into relief the situation for wilder animals where the newborn must move on their own feet or else must selectively be left to die by parents who have no choice. *Turi's Book of Lapland*[55] points the parallel to the human situation.

In primitive human groups, both prehistoric and contemporary, we have to reckon with forms of maternal and filial behaviour in which the concept of biological adequacy has to be related to the conditions of life and of optimum survival. It has been too often assumed that the mother's anxiety, when her infant failed to breast-feed satisfactorily, was a biologically *inadequate* response. A good mother, it has been argued, will respond to the weak, poor feeder with increased attention and love. It would, I believe, be more correct to say that the good *nurse* will so respond. In this situation the nurse, free from the same, precise maternal type of resonation to the child's behaviour, can put all her energies into compensating for the weakness of the child. But I want to advance the hypothesis that the biological mother—to the extent that she is asked to make a biological response, i.e. to provide milk adequate in quantity and quality and to evoke feeding behaviour from her infant, to the extent that her behaviour may be said to have biological roots—has the possibility of *two* 'biologically adequate' responses, one leading to life and the other to death. For the child who sucks well and thrives on her milk, she has more milk and less anxiety. But when a child fails to thrive, her anxiety rises and, as clinical experience has shown, her milk supply falls, the infant receives less food, and a 'vicious circle' is set up. Under primitive conditions, unless culturally patterned practices of wet-nursing and adoption have been set up, such a child will die. So the child whom the mother is able to feed, the child who is able to feed from that mother, will live. The very existence of the lactating-anxiety cycle was a kind of guarantee that in the neo-natal period there would be rigid selection for the most suitable children, without an excessive expenditure of scarce energy on attempting to rear a child with a lesser hold on life. In the same way, genetic defects in maternal behaviour would tend to be held at a minimum. The survival possibilities of a society could be calculated in the numbers of compatible nursing couples in a population, corrected for the presence of supplementary institutions—wet-nurses, the use of artificial foods, and so on.

With each addition to the cultural repertoire for the preservation of infants by means other than lactation by their biological mothers, this primary situation would become less determinative. The mother's anxiety over the child which failed to thrive would be lessened by the knowledge that other means were available, a recourse not open to the animal mother in a domestic herd, who does not know that the shepherd or herdsman may load her stumbling offspring into a cart or sled. The possible relaxation of the deep and, according to this hypothesis, biological anxiety cycle of nursing failure in mother and offspring, whenever alternative methods of feeding the child are available, would explain the seemingly contradictory statistical finding that infant mortality declines with the invention of bottle feeding but that the countries with a very low infant mortality—like Holland—have more breast-feeding and a lower infant death rate than does the United States.

Mavis Gunther,[24] directing research on breast-feeding in the Obstetric Hospital, University College Hospital, London, in which the lactation behaviour of 150 'nursing couples' was studied in detail, believes that she has isolated biologically given elements in the establishment of suckling in human infants comparable to the internal releasing mechanisms of the ethologists: in the response of the infant, first, to a stimulation of the lips, easy to provide, and, second, within three days after birth, to a filling of the 'mouth right to the palate and the dorsum of the tongue' by the nipple, which is dependent upon the length—specifically the protractility—of the nipple and also upon the infant not displaying certain feeding and breathing behaviour which interferes with this stimulation. In her sample of 150 nursing couples, 25 per cent of the mothers had nipples of too little protractility to meet this assumed instinctive need of the infant, and a few of the infants showed innate apathy, breathing difficulties, too small mouths, and so on, which interfered with the establishment of breastfeeding and could not be attributed to any physical defect in the mother's breast. A device has been developed to wear during pregnancy for elongating the mother's nipples.

We have now, in this single situation, illuminated by thirty years of research, a paradigm of the relationships between innate dispositions and the characterological consequences when they are combined with the cultural arrangements of any society. We have recently witnessed attempts to restore more 'natural' parental situations—assumed to be those which are supported by our biological inheritance. Attempts to induce mothers to breast-feed, irrespective of early failure and of failure of the infant to thrive, have produced their own train of new anxieties in which the diminution of the mother's milk, under conditions of anxiety induced by failure, is overlaid by the interpretation of this biologically *adequate* behaviour—seen in terms of evolution and of the need for selective survival under primitive conditions—as a sign of inadequate mothering. In so doing we have failed to take into account the fact that the history of human civilization has been the history of artificially supplementing physical defects, keeping alive the prematurely born and the aged, supplying spectacles, hearing aids, and false teeth, keeping alive the congenitally diabetic with insulin, and so on. With each new advance in medicine or technology, another group of surviving, functioning individuals is added to the population and we come closer to the ideal that every infant who is born shall live, even at the cost of institutionalization of the extreme defectives. It is within this culture, where individual human life is valued and the weakest receive more attention than the strongest, that present-day mothers—and fathers—must function, where defects in their psychodynamic functioning are revealed and do harm to themselves and others. Instead of attempting to return to biological mechanisms which are only too biologically adequate, functioning as they do to ensure the immediate or premature death of large proportions of a population, the task would seem to be to clarify our theories so that we may prevent the release of these ancient biological responses from obscuring the appropriate tasks of twentieth-century parents. At the same time, studies such as those of Mavis Gunther should make it possible for us to compensate for and to supplement, in detailed and specific ways, the specific defects or abnormalities which interfere with a body-dependent function like breastfeeding.

Psycho-analysis has long recognized that man's basic biological equipment is very old and that the processes of education are often heavily at odds with biological propensities. It would seem that the inclusion of an explicit recognition of the extent to which our capacity to save life is at variance with our innate ability to select lives to save would deepen the theoretical discussion of all these problems.

Yet making allowance for the inappropriateness of some of the older biologically given responses need not blind us to possibilities of invoking biological responses which are perhaps far older than our specifically human history. Recent clinical observations have been reported on the capacity of infants a few days old to move a distance as great as fifteen or eighteen inches towards their mother on a flat surface. The method of locomotion is said to be something like that of a worm, involving a twisting of the whole body. These movements have not yet been systematically studied; we do not know what the stimulus is which evoked the movement—whether the odour of the mother's body or the specific odour of the milk, etc. Looked at in biological perspective, this ability of the newborn to orient itself and to move in the direction of the source of food is dramatically illustrated in the definiteness with which newborn turtles, having thrust their way up through the sand, make for the sea,[38] or in the response of young mammals, whose four-legged, handless mothers can only guide them with muzzles and cries. But with the emergence of hands, the mother—ape or human—is able to grasp and manipulate her baby, and the infant's ability to move towards its mother would be of survival value only in the very rare instance where the mother became unconscious after delivery and the infant by moving towards her could rouse her.

The ability of human children to select a balanced diet is another example of a biological capacity very seldom exercised within human history.[11] (The display by caged white rats, exposed to man-synthesized or distilled vitamins and minerals, of a capacity to select constructively among them is a complementary example of a biologically given type of behaviour which could never have been given as full expression in the wild.[40]) Human beings exposed to drinking fountains, one containing and the other lacking an essential and 'tasteless' mineral, will drift towards the mineral one.[40]

The new position of the father in the middle and upper classes in the United States, the United Kingdom, and Northern Europe—with the father's greater care of the young infant arising originally from the absence of servants and spare female relatives and from the restricted housing conditions of the modern, post-World-War-II home—may also exploit a biological given behaviour potential which has not been used for a long time. In very primitive societies it is not unusual to find fathers taking a good deal of care of small infants. So among some Australian aborigines, the father, after his morning hunt has been successful, will carry the young infant while the mother gathers vegetable foods. However, no complex society, so far as I have been able to ascertain, no complicated society with a witten tradition has ever expected the man of stature and education to care for a baby. Mothers, nurses, female relatives, children, even eunuchs, but not fathers, had the physical care of young infants. So it has been possible to say that there seemed to be no instinctive basis for fatherhood comparable to the instinctive bases of maternal behaviour. Fathers were rewarded for caring for their young by the sexual and domestic services of the children's mother; elaborate social sanctions for paternity, expressed in pride, prestige, or the validation of male status, and so on, had to be used, or unmarried men might be refused full citizenship or hunting and fishing licences. But post-World-War-II experience suggests that this new type of paternal behaviour, which is being pursued with such enthusiasm on both continents, may be drawing upon an instinctive response to a small creature—not necessarily identified as own child—of one's own species. Ethology provides us with many instances of the way in which the male, who pays no attention to his own offspring as such, may respond to the cry of distress of any infant of the same species. So, after many thousands of years in which this potential response of the male to handling a small infant—it is apparently necessary for it to be only a few weeks old to establish the effect—has been held in abeyance, possibly wisely, it now emerges at a period when the development of artificial feeding has loosened the dependence of the infant on the mother. It is too early to say what the effects will be—the diminution of that part of male creativity which was complementary to female creativity in childbearing, an alteration in character structure when infants are reared by both sexes, a greater equalization between husband and wife as the husband no longer has to act out, towards his wife, the cherishing behaviour which he learned from his mother but for which he had no other form of expression. But it is an example of the possible use of a biological potential which has been allowed to lie unused through many centuries of civilization.

In a somewhat similar way, the ability of women who have not borne children to lactate if they adopt a sufficiently vigorous infant, which, when I first reported this,[32] was greeted with complete disbelief, has now been well established as occurring in several primitive societies. Although this would provide a way in which an adopting mother could establish a physical tie with her child, the use of any such device at present would collide with our sense of the importance of oral and nutritional satisfaction for developing trust in the young infant. The primitive adopting mother could tolerate the infant's cries, supplemented by milk from other mothers, while she established her milk supply by drinking the juice of many young coconuts; but this would be hard for the psychodynamically oriented pediatrician to tolerate.

Next, I want to come to the question of the kind of early experience that is best for children who, from their earliest days, will encounter strangers. Infants, wherever they have been observed, go through a period when they suddenly discriminate between the known and the un-known person. The Arapesh of New Guinea call this 'the time when human beings appear in the pupils of the child's eyes'. When people lived in small self-contained groups, everyone the child encountered was either a well-known person or else someone whom not only he but also the mother or relative in whose arms he was carried feared and rejected as an enemy. The closeness of his tie to the person in whose arm he was held was both his guarantee of safety and the medium through which he learned how dangerous enemies were.

In Bali, the mother smiles and bows as she greets with surface ex-pressions of respect the stranger or the person of higher caste from another village, but the baby in her arms screams with terror. One can judge from the baby's behaviour how violently it is reacting to a kines-thetically experienced fear which the mother expresses neither verbally nor in her face or posture. When I was in Bali, I read for the first time Miss Freud's *The Ego and the Mechanisms of Defence*,[21] and, going over it in the light of Balinese behaviour around me, I felt that a fourth kind of fear should be added to her list of three: the fear which is communicated kinesthetically to the very young infant. Later, I was delighted to find Miss Freud's descriptions of this kind of fear as experienced by an infant through a parent's fear of bombing.[22]

It is significant that the individual traditionally educated Balinese seldom survived being taken away from Bali, and that even leaving his own village was frightening. But moving in a group—as an orchestra, a dance troop, a whole village going to present tribute to a distant raja—they manage with great ease. In New York, in 1952, the Balinese dancers were reported to 'triple up' three in a chair or a bed, taking comfort from the kinesthetic closeness of the others. On the other hand, Samoans, who have been reared in large families and taken care of by many relatives, with no intense ties to mother or father, adapt easily when they go abroad as individuals.

We have not yet developed a method of bringing up our children so that they can journey easily, alone if necessary, to Hong Kong or Nigeria or the moon, tolerating without fear strangers who look, speak, move, and smell very different. In a situation where the mother must take the child day by day to market, to the clinic, on the bus, on the underground, among strangers, the present tendency to advise very close ties between mother and child is doubtfully the best. Wider experience in the arms of many individuals known in different degrees of intimacy, if possible of different races, may be a much better preparation.

In conclusion, I want to discuss very briefly another aspect of the urban world—the incongruity among all its parts. The house, the motor car, the street, the box the baby's food comes in, the bottle in which the milk is delivered, the book on the table and the pillow on the bed are in shape and colour and design extraordinarily unrelated to each other. In primitive societies, where change is very slow, or among traditional peasant peoples, where costume, crockery, and the shapes of roofs have not changed for generations, each part of the visible and sensible world reinforces each other part. Where the style is kindness, the occasional bad-tempered mother nevertheless lives beneath a kind roof. The shapes of pots, the light of the fire, the tones in other people's voices, the way the road winds around the house, all say to the child, 'You are safe'. The idiosyncrasy or failure of a particular mother or father is muted and made less important; the surrounding environment helps to highlight the moments when they are kind.[33] And each child has a chance to learn from different parts of his experience. Some children will learn more from the shape of the roof, as they lie on their backs looking up at the thatch, others from the feel of the pot in their hands, still others from the cadence of voices, but as these things are all part of a whole, shaped and polished, ground down and tuned up through the generations until they fit and express to the child the particular view of the world within which it is safe and able to mature, there is a great deal more leeway in what can go wrong without doing irrevocable harm. Even extreme psychotic behaviour can be absorbed in such a setting, as people take quick precautions against a man with a spear in his hand, 'who will be all right tomorrow'. An occasional child may bear a scar from such an experience but, by and large, the familiar group seems able to take up the shock because they were all three together, each part supports each other part, nothing is so unexpected, so broken off that it cannot be dealt with.

Just as this is true of the shape of a roof, the shape of a pot, the line of an arrow, so it is also true of the way the child experiences the natural world. Whether the moon is calendrical and tells you when the fish will come over the reef, or whether the marks on the moon are an old woman beating bark cloth or a goddess who has just been swallowed by a demon, whatever the moon is, everyone agrees about it, and the child's experience of the moon and the way in which people see the moon are integrated, so that the child's need to order the natural world through perception is reinforced and supported and given symbolic form by the whole society. As we have reason to believe that the need to perceive the natural world is as deep a human need as is the need for strong, warm, meaningful interpersonal relations, the child in a coherent culture was safer.[10]

But to-day most of our children are growing up in a world where the people who built the urban society believed that it was a violation of what they called 'nature'. 'Nature' is what one's fathers had as opposed to what one's sons invent—I think this is a fair definition. A plough and a sailing ship are natural; a horse and cart was a great deal more natural than an automobile was; at the moment an automobile is more natural than an airplane, and an ordinary airplane is more natural than a jet plane. At present we live in an endless progression of rejection of the next change in energy relationships in the world, and as a result we tend to break and fragment our world and to build in a way that is ugly and forbidding those parts of the world which we regard as unnatural. Different peoples, of course, do this differently. I was very struck, I remember, in World War II with the efforts that post-card makers in Britain made to domesticate tanks. There were some perfectly charming post-cards showing tanks in the middle of wheat fields, with poppies in the field or a lark sitting on the tank, an attempt somehow to absorb into a domestic and meaningful picture this invasive thing that was tearing up the landscape. But by and large we haven't succeeded very well, and our children are growing up in a world where every line, almost every brick, says to them that man is not related to the universe in any reasonable way whatsoever, that he is violating it, exploiting it, extracting from it, and that he is being unnatural. He is eating reinforced bread instead of beautiful, pure, natural bread.

This particular breach in our whole cultural tradition is something our children are experiencing, and the protection that was once given them by the coherence between the landscape and the human manufactured environment is gone. This is a new hazard against which we have to protect them. As we explore further and explore in a variety of ways, as we explore the living world and learn more about the particular detailed propensities of living creatures, particularly of human living creatures, as we learn more about our own origins and the probable conditions under which men once lived and under which we were shaped biologically in the past, as we learn more about the possibilities of life in different sorts of societies, as we learn more from the study of individuals here—both from the study of adult patients to whom something sorrowful has been done and from the study of small children to whom something sorrowful is being done, so that we can study it contemporaneously—and as we learn more in the field of education about the possible needs of the child for the understanding of the universe and for relating his internally perceived reality to the externally perceived reality, we have a continuing task of moulding these new insights and new researches together into a cultural expectation that will use accurately and not unfairly, not making too great demands and not misplacing their potentialities, the biologically given in our nature, as we imaginatively create out of our ability as human beings to build culture those conditions which will supplement and expand and, in many cases, use hitherto unused biological propensities and potentialities of mankind.

REFERENCES

1. ALEXANDER, F., and ROSS, H. (eds.) 1952. *Dynamic psychiatry*. Univ. of Chicago Press, Chicago.
2. BAKWIN, H. 1944. Psychogenic fever in infants. *Am. J. Dis. Child.*, **67**, 176-181.

3. BATESON, G. 1942. Social planning and the concept of deutero learning, in *Science, philosophy and religion : Second symposium*, pp. 81-97. Conference on Science, Philosophy and Religion, New York. Harper, New York.

4. BATESON, G., *et al*. 1958. *The natural history of an interview*. (In preparation.)

5. BATESON, G., and MEAD, M. (n.d.) *First five days in the life of a New Guinea baby*. Film, 2 reels, 22 min., sound. New York Univ. Film Library, New York.

6. BERTALANFFY, L. VON. 1952. *Problems of life*. Wiley, New York.

7. BIRDWHISTELL, RAY E. 1954. *Introduction to kinesics : An annotation system for analysis of body motion and gesture*. Univ. of Louisville, Louisville, Ky.

8. BLAUVELT, HELEN. 1955, 1956, 1957. Contributions to *Group processes*. Cf. SCHAFFNER, B. (ed.).

9. BOWLBY, J. 1951. *Maternal care and mental health*. WHO Monograph No. 2. World Health Organization, Geneva. (Abridged version: *Child care and the growth of love*. Penguin Books, London, 1953.)

10. COBB, E. (n.d.) *Ecology of imagination in childhood*. MS.

11. DAVIS, E. S. 1928. The food consumption of rural school children. *Mass Agric.*, **241**, 97-241.

12. DOLLARD, J., and MILLER, N. E., 1950. *Personality and psychotherapy : An analysis in terms of learning, thinking amd culture*. McGraw-Hill, New York.

13. ERIKSON, ERIK H. 1950. *Childhood and society*. Norton, New York.

14. ESCALONA, S., and LEITCH, M. (n.d.) *Eight infants : Tension manifestations in response to perceptual stimulation*. Film. New York Univ. Film Library, New York.

15. FOERSTER, H. VON, *et al*. (eds.) 1951. *Cybernetics : Transactions of the Seventh Conference*, October 1950, New York. Josiah Macy, Jr. Foundation, New York.

16. FOERSTER, H. VON, *et al*. (eds.) 1952. *Cybernetics : Transactions of the Eighth Conference*, March 1951, New York. Josiah Macy, Jr. Foundation, New York.

17. FOERSTER, H. VON, *et al*. (eds.) 1953. *Cybernetics : Transactions of the Ninth Conference*, March 1952, New York. Josiah Macy, Jr. Foundation, New York.

18. FOERSTER, H. VON, *et al*. (eds.) 1955. *Cybernetics : Transactions of the Tenth Conference*, April 1953, Princeton, N.J. Josiah Macy, Jr. Foundation, New York.

19. FORD, C. S., and BEACH, F. A. 1951. *Patterns of sexual behavior*. Hoeber-Harper, New York.

20. FRANK, L. K., *et al*. 1948. Teleological mechanisms. *Ann. N.Y. Acad. Sci.*, **50**, 178-278.

21. FREUD, A. 1937. *The ego and the mechanisms of defence*. Hogarth Press, London.

22. FREUD, A., and BURLINGHAM, D. T. 1943. *War and children*. Medical War Books, New York.

23. FRIES, M., and WOOLF, P. J. (n.d.) *Series of studies on integrated environment : The interaction between child and environment*. Five films. New York Univ. Film Library, New York.

24. GUNTHER, M. 1955. Instinct and the nursing couple. *Lancet*, 19 March, 575-578.

25. HESS, E. H. 1955. Contributions to *Group processes*. Cf. SCHAFFNER, B. (ed.).

26. HOST, P. (n.d.) *Sammi Jaki*. Film. ABC Films, Oslo.

27. JACKSON, E. G. 1950. Pediatric and psychiatric aspects of the Yale rooming-in project. *Conn. St. med. J.*, **14**, 616.

28. Koffka, K. 1935. *Principles of Gestalt psychology*. Harcourt, Brace, New York.
29. Liddell, H. S. 1955, 1956, 1957. Contributions to *Group processes*. Cf. Schaffner, B. (ed.).
30. Lorenz, K. 1950. The comparative method in studying innate behaviour patterns. In Danielli, J. F., and Brown, R., (eds.) *Physiological mechanisms in animal behaviour*. Proc. Soc. for Exp. Biol. Symposium, No. 4. Cambridge Univ. Press, Cambridge.
31. Mead, M. 1947. On the implications for anthropology of the Gesell-Ilg approach to maturation. *Am. Anthrop.*, **49**, 69-77.
32. Mead, M. 1949. *Male and female*. Morrow, New York.
33. Mead, M. 1953. Introduction. In Collins, R., *The lost and the found*. Woman's Press, New York.
34. Mead, M. 1954. Some theoretical considerations on the problem of mother-child separation. *Am. J. Orthopsychiat.*, **24**, 471-483.
35. Mead, M. 1957. Mother and child. *Lancet*, vi, No. 6, 317.
36. Mead, M., and Macgregor, F. C. 1951. *Growth and culture*. Putnams, New York.
37. Mirsky, I. A., Miller, R., and Stein, M. 1953. Relation of adrenocortical activity and adaptive behavior. *Psychosom. Med.*, **15**, Nov.-Dec.
38. Rank, A. J. 1956. *Among the headhunters*. Film.
39. Ribble, M. 1943. *The rights of infants*. Columbia Univ. Press, New York.
40. Richter, C. P. 1943. The self-selection of diets, in *Essays in honor of Herbert M. Evans*, pp. 499-506. Univ. of California Press, Berkeley and Los Angeles.
41. Roudinesco (Aubrey), J., and Appell, G. (n.d.) *Monique. (Maternal deprivation in young children.)* Film, 2 reels, 22 min., sound. Association pour la Santé de l'Enfance, Paris.
42. Schaffner, B. (ed.) 1955. *Group processes: Transactions of the First Conference*, Sept. 1954, Ithaca, New York. Josiah Macy, Jr. Foundation, New York.
43. Schaffner, B. (ed.) 1956. *Group Processes: Transactions of the Second Conference*, Oct. 1955, Princeton, N.J. Josiah Macy, Jr. Foundation, New York.
44. Schaffner, B. (ed.) 1957. *Group processes: Transactions of the Third Conference*. (In press.)
45. Scott, J. (ed.) 1950. Methodology and techniques for the study of animal societies. *Ann. N.Y. Acad. Sci.*, **51**, Art. 6.
46. Simpson, G., and Roe, A. (n.d.) *Evolution and behavior*. Yale Univ. Press, New Haven. (In press.)
47. Soddy, K. (ed.) 1955. *Mental health and infant development*, 2 vols. Routledge & Kegan Paul, London.
48. Spitz, R., and Wolf, K. A. (n.d.) *Grief—A peril in infancy*. Film, 3 reels, 35 min., silent. New York Univ. Film Library, New York.
49. Spitz, R., and Wolf, K. A. (n.d.) *Mother-child relations*. Film, 2 reels, 22 min., silent. New York Univ. Film Library, New York.
50. Spitz, R., and Wolf, K. A. (n.d.) *The smiling response*. Film, silent. New York Univ. Film Library, New York.
51. Tanner, J., and Inhelder, B. (eds.) 1957. *Discussions on child development: Psycho-biological development of the child*, Vols. I and II. Tavistock Publications, London; International Univ. Press, New York.
52. Tanner, J., and Inhelder, B. (eds.) 1958, 1960. *Discussions on child development: Psycho-biological development of the child*, Vols. III and IV. International Univ. Press, New York.

53. THORPE, W. H. 1956. *Learning and instinct in animals.* Methuen, London.
54. TINBERGEN, N. 1951. *The study of instinct.* Oxford Univ. Press, London and New York.
55. TURI, J. 1931. *Turi's book of Lapland.* Harper, New York and London.
56. WALTER, W. GREY. 1953. *The living brain.* Norton, New York.

XXV

NEUROSIS AND THE MEXICAN FAMILY STRUCTURE

ROGELIO DIAZ-GUERRERO

The culture presses its values on the family, and this carries the possibility for the latter of harmony or disharmony.

In the following description of the Mexican family, I should like to make clear that only the dominant Mexican family pattern is described and that variants are only incidentally touched upon.*

The Mexican family is founded upon two fundamental propositions: (1) the unquestioned and absolute supremacy of the father; and (2) the necessary and absolute self-sacrifice of the mother. The mother's role has from times unknown acquired an adequate qualification in the term "abnegation" which means the denial of any and all possible selfish aims.

These two fundamental propositions in the family derive from more general "existential" value orientations, or better, generalized socio-cultural assumptions which imply an indubitable, biological, and natural superiority of the male. We shall try to demonstrate that the role playing of the members of the Mexican family follows closely—as conclusions follow premises—from the stated socio-cultural propositions.

Even before a Mexican child is born, a set of expectations is already at work. Although in many societies there is a preference for boy babies, in Mexico the stress is greater—it *ought* to be a boy! The birth of a girl, unless it appears after one or two but preferably three boys, is somewhat of an emotional tragedy. In the past, more seriously, and recently more jokingly,

---

* As may be derived from its use in this paper the term "dominant pattern" is used here in a similar but not equivalent manner to F. Kluckhohn's[6] use. Bateson[1] and C. Kluckhohn[5] have also influenced this writer.

Reprinted from AMERICAN JOURNAL OF PSYCHIATRY, Vol. 112, 1955, pp. 411-417.

the virility of a father who gives birth to a girl is considered questionable. Besides this threat, the birth of a girl means: (1) a bad economic break; (2) emotional and physical strain on the family that must compulsively guard her honor which is equivalent to the family's honor. (Actually fundamentally the loss of virginity in a female out of wedlock threatens brutally the fundamental premise of femininity and self-sacrifice in the female); (3) even the best solution through her marriage brings into the family a strange male intruder; (4) if she should not marry she will become a *cotorra*, literally an "old female parrot," an individual with eternal neurotic complaints that are a burden to the family.

One may well ask: why a girl at all? However, after several boys, one girl is desirable in the sense that she will serve her brothers, thus allowing the wife more time to care maternally for the husband.

But let us see now the role expectations for the male child. Above all, he must grow up to fit the dignified role of a male. There must be no dolls or doll houses, but soldiers, guns, military helmets, broomstick horses, swords, titanic yells, imposing screams, panic among the little girls. Any little demonstration of feminine interests will be disapproved by older brothers, uncles, cousins, and the mother herself. Older children discriminate against younger ones on the basis that they are not enough of a male (*machos*) to participate in their games which become progressively more "masculine" (rougher but also implicating a certain dramatically conceded masculinity). Thus the younger children look forward with longing to the attainment of greater virility. Little girls are either avoided or a "steam roller" attitude is taken toward them.

The female child must grow up to her destiny: superlative femininity, the home, maternity. The little girls amuse themselves with dolls and "playing house." They must stay away from the rough games of the boys for, as the educated people explain, it would not be ladylike. This idea is based apparently on variants of the widespread belief that if a girl should run or jump she would become a man. Very early the little girls starts helping her mother in the home chores—an area tabooed for the male child. In order to acquire greater femininity the little girl must start learning delicate feminine activities like embroidery or lace making. Later in life she may learn painting, music, poetry, literature, or philosophy. But even as a little girl she must always dress like a female, keep neat, and be graceful and coquettish. It is interesting to note that one of the postulates under which Mexican public education has labored for years is that one of the main goals of education is to make men more typically male and women more typically female.

During the entire childhood the sign of virility in the male is courage to temerity, aggressiveness, and not to run away from a fight or break a deal (*no rajarse*). But both the boy and the girl must be obedient within the family. Paradoxically a father will feel proud of the child who did not run from a fight in the street, but at home may punish him severely for having disobeyed his orders regarding street fights. This appears to mean that the child must be masculine but not as much as his father.

During adolescence the sign of virility in the male is to talk about or act in the sexual sphere. He who possesses information and/or experience regarding sexual matters is inevitably the leader of the group. The pre-pubescent boys are coldly discriminated from the "seances" of adolescents on the basis that they are not sufficiently male-like to participate. Girls, now instead of being avoided, are the alluring goal of the males. During adolescence there comes into being a peculiar phenomenon. The pursuit of the female unfolds into two aspects. In one of the adolescent searches for the ideal woman—the one he would like to convert into his wife. This one must have all the attributes of the perfect feminine role. She must be chaste, delicate, homey (*hogareña*), sweet, maternal, dreamy, religious, and must not smoke or cross her legs. Her face must be beautiful, especially her eyes—but not necessarily her body. Sexuality takes a very secondary role. In the other aspect the adolescent searches for the sexualized female and with the clear purpose in mind of sexual intercourse. Here the roundness of the lines, and their quantity is a determinant factor. The male Mexican's female ideal implies breasts and hips, particularly hips, far broader and far more quivering than is considered proper in this country. It is even more interesting to note that in every case as soon as the individual has found the woman he may idealize, *ipso facto*, other women become objects for the sexualized search, and tempting objects of seduction.

As adolescence advances into youth and adulthood the extreme differentiation among feminine objects loses some of its momentum. And although the entire expression of sexuality is still only open to lovers or prostitutes, it is also true that the youth or the adult who looks for a woman with matrimonial intentions will, before making his decisions, attend a little more to the quality and quantity of the secondary sexual characteristics of the female. It is well to repeat, however, that even in this case chastity and the other factors of femininity continue to weigh heavily.

From adolescence on and through the entire life of the male, virility will be measured by the sexual potential, and only secondarily in terms of physical strength, courage, or audacity. So much so, that even these other characteristics of behavior as well as still other subtler ones, are believed to be dependent upon the sexual capacity. The accent falls upon the sexual organs and their functions. The size of the penis has its importance. The size of the testicles has more, but more important than the physical size is the "functional" size. It is assumed they are in good functioning when: (1) the individual acts efficiently in sexual activity or speaks or brags convincingly of his multiple seductive successes; (2) when he speaks or actually shows that he is not afraid of death; (3) when the individual is very successful in the fields of intellectuality, science, etc.

In each of these cases the common people, those that Ramos[7] speaks of as putting things crudely, will say, "That guy has plenty of nuts!" (*Muchos huevos*)—or else that he has them very well placed. This socio-cultural proposition of profound depth and breadth seems to embrace in its scope the majority of the Latin American people. A Cuban physician once told me how one of the Cuban presidents had gone alone into a large military post where the commanding general was preparing a *coup d'état*. Man to man, the president made the general confess and made him a prisoner of his former followers. The Cuban physician summed up the story by saying: "Oh! What a man, his testicles are bigger than a cathedral." It is not only the monumental size attributed to the testicles that is amazing in this remark, but the inclusion in one sentence of the two opposing socio-cultural premises: the testicles, virility—the cathedral, the female set of values.

Finally, even the undisputed authority of the male in the home, and in all other functions in relation to the female may be explained by the fact that he has testicles and she does not. Incidents like the following are very common among university students: If one of Mexico's relatively few career women obtains high grades, one or many of the male students will exert himself to express with a serious face and in a loud whisper that he knows from reliable sources that this student has already missed several menstruations. Americans would leap to the conclusion that the girl is pregnant, but in Mexico the implication is that she is becoming a male.

Let us return to the female. After the termination of the grade school, she is returned to the home. It is not feminine to have an advanced education. During adolescence women learn more and more the varied aspects of their roles. Now substituting for, now helping the mother in her care and attention to the males, she irons, washes, cooks, sews buttons, purchases socks and undershorts for her brothers (I was 25 and in the United States before I bought my own underclothes), and is supposed to fulfill the most menial needs of her brothers. The brothers in turn are the faithful custodians of the chastity of the female. On the basis that nothing can happen to the sister if there are no male strangers around, even innocent courtships where well-intentioned gentlemen talk through the railings of a window with girls, are viewed with suspicion. As a consequence, these gentlemen are the subjects of hostility and are seen from the corner of the eye, and the family batteries are ready to shoot in case that such a boy friend may dare to hold the hand of the sister. The precautions are taken to such an extreme that often the friends of the father or brothers are never admitted into the homes—except of course if there is a fiesta, at which time there is a breaking down of most premises. At any rate, it is in this fashion that the girl is prepared to give and give—and receives little or nothing. But it is during adolescence and youth that the Mexican women are going to experience their happiest period. In effect, they will sooner or later be converted into the ideal woman for a given male. Then they will be placed on a pedestal and be highly overevaluated. The girl in this period will receive poems, songs, gallantries, serenades, and all the tenderness of which the Mexican male is capable. Such tokens are numerous, for the male has learned very well in his infancy, through relations with his mother, a very intensive and extensive repertoire for the expression of affection; and, as a part of the maternal ideals, romanticism and idealism dig deep into the mental structure of the Mexican. At any rate, our Cinderella, who has heretofore given all and received nothing in exchange, enters into an ecstatic state as a result of this veneration, this incredible submission—as a slave to a queen—of the imposing, proud, dictatorial and conceited male. Many years later the Mexican female will again experience an ecstasy of the same quality when her children will consider her the dearest being in existence. But this is not surprising—both expressions of sentimentality are only branchings of the same fundamental phenomenon: the set of maternal values.

Soon after the termination of the honeymoon, the husband passes from slave to master and the woman enters the hardest test of her life. The idealism of the male rapidly drops away toward the mother. To make matters worse, the wife cannot be considered as a sexual object in a broad sense. Mexican husbands repeatedly indicate that sex must be practised in one way with the wife and in another with the lover. The most common statement refers to the fear that the wife might become too interested in sex if he introduces her into the subtleties of the pleasure. At other times this fear is expressed in a clearer fashion by saying that the wife might become a prostitute.

The husband must work and provide. He knows nothing, nor does he want to know anything, about what happens in the home. He demands only that all obey him and that his authority be unquestioned. Often after working hours, he joins his friends and along with them proceeds with a life no different from that he practised when unmarried. Toward his children he shows affection but before anything authority. Although he doesn't follow them himself he demands adherence to the "maternal" religious concepts. Often, however, he imposes the authority of his moods and his whims. He is satisfied if his children obey "right or crooked." It is therefore again the premise of the unquestioned authority. The wife submits and, deprived of the previous idealization, must serve him to his satisfaction "the way mother did." Since this is not possible, the husband often becomes cruel and brutal toward the wife.

The Mexican wife enters much before motherhood in the causeway of abnegation—the denial of all of her needs, and the absolute pursuit of the satisfaction of everyone else.

In this frame of reference, we shall describe the aspect that is lacking —the infancy of the Mexican. The Mexican mother is deeply affectionate and tender and overprotective toward the infant. In the beginning the baby gets anything and everything. Infants are deeply loved, fondled, and admired—for the first two years of their existence. In this activity the usually large number of relatives participate. At the same time, slowly in the first two years and then under an intensive pressure, the infant and the child must become well brought up *bien educado*. They must become the model children who will perforce fit into the system of absolute obedience to the parents. This necessary obedience, humility, and respect to the elders and for authority are imposed in a great many ways. Drilling in courtesy and in manners is a prevalent one. Thus, a well-brought-up child may not be yet able to pronounce his name properly, but when asked what it is must invariably follow his answer with *"para servirle"* or *"A sus ordenes"* (To serve you—or at your orders). The Spanish language is saturated with these forms of submission. Actually there are two languages and when two people meet the one in the position of submission refers to the other as *"Usted"* the one in the position of command uses *"iu"* a familiar form of "Usted."

The infant must be well brought up and if words do not suffice, as they often do not, physical punishment is used. The child must learn submission and obedience. In the same fashion he learns in a rigid way the various aspects of the Catholic religion. To end this description, let us say that the mother with her attitude and her affect is the source of all tenderness, sentimentality—and the largest portion of the cultural expressions of the Mexican. The writing, painting, sculpturing, philosophy, and religion are saturated with direct or symbolic allusions to maternity.

In spite of the fact that this is a summarized and incomplete elaboration of the Mexican family pattern, one can easily conclude that the general setting is favorable to the development of neurosis. Also, one is prone to think that the Mexican female would be commonly subject to neurosis. Table 1 seems to substantiate such predictions: 32% plus/minus 2.65 of the male population of Mexico City over 18 years of age are "neurotic" and 44% plus/minus 2.83 of the female population over 18 are "neurotic." The difference is statistically significant to the 0.4% level of confidence.*

At a more specific level one can easily deduce that in the male there should be: (1) problems of submission, conflict, and rebellion in the area of authority; (2) preoccupation and anxiety regarding sexual potency; (3) conflict and ambivalence regarding his double role. He must at times love and generally act maternally and tenderly, and at other times sexually and virily; (4) difficulties in superseding the maternal stage: dependent-

* The data in Tables 1 and 2 are taken from R. Diaz-Guerrero.[3] In this study an effort was made to measure through a 46-question questionnaire the degree of mental health of the Metropolitan Mexican. The data used here are based on the tabulated results from 294 returned questionnaires. The questionnaires were distributed in Mexico City following Cantril's[2] weighted random sample technique. Cooperation was 57%. The importance of dynamic, general psychological and semantic factors as well as the influence of socio-cultural conditionings were taken into account to derive a criterion of "mental health." The study was a preliminary trial.

TABLE 1*

DEGREE OF MENTAL HEALTH

	Males			Females		
	Yes	No	D.K.	Yes	No	D.K.
(1) Are you happier alone than in company?	(12)	82	0	(26)	66	8
(2) Do you get angry frequently?...........	(43)	56	1	(62)	36	2
(3) Do you think life is worth living?.......	77	(12)	11	69	(18)	13
(4) Do you consider yourself a nervous person?...........................	(43)	52	5	(66)	33	1
(5) Are you very sensitive?................	(43)	51	6	(51)	40	9
(6) Do you feel very depressed frequently?...	(34)	64	2	(57)	41	2
(7) Do you like your type of work?.........	68	(27)	5	80	(9)	11
(8) Do you get along better with strangers than with members of your family?......	(29)	66	5	(37)	59	4
(9) Do you believe in trusting people?......	27	(63)	10	13	(77)	10
(10) Do you find it difficult to concentrate?...	(21)	68	11	(24)	58	18
(11) Do you suffer frequently from the bile?..	(28)	66	6	(52)	47	1

feminine individuals; (5) problems before and during marriage: mother's love interferes with the love to another woman (here one should expect an important area of stress where the husband, the wife, and the husband's mother play the dynamics of jealousy); (6) the Oedipus complex, as Freud describes it: almost every aspect of the ideal setting for its development is provided by the premises of the culture and the role playing. Actually areas 2, 3, 4, and 5 above may be considered as partial expressions of the dynamics of the Oedipus complex.

In the female the main area of stress should fall around her variable success in living up to the stiff requirements that the cultural premises demand. Her inability to live up to them should show itself in self-belittlement and depressive trends. Another area of clear disturbance should appear around the "old maid" complex. Finally, the rapid transition of the socio-cultural premises may affect her.

Interestingly enough, even the occasional observer has opportunity to see evidences of mental ill-health in the areas outlined above for the male. My own observation in the practice of psychotherapy has, in many instances, substantiated the expectation that these areas are the most stress producing. In regard to women there is little evidence. Women in Mexico seldom go to the psychiatrist. It is a common observation, however, that more women than men go to the general practitioner with psychosomatic ailments. Table 1 shows that the question dealing with depressive mood is differentially answered in the affirmative by the females, and the only and very carefully selected question regarding psychosomatic ailments, "Do you suffer from the bile?",† shows twice as many women as men suffering from it.

* Translated from R. Diaz-Guerrero.[3] "Neurosis" is defined by the type of answer that has been enclosed in parentheses. These data as well as those reported in Table 2 are based on the tabulated results from 294 returned questionnaires which were distributed in Mexico City following Cantril's weighted random sample technique.

† The "bile" refers to the Mexican tradition that when a person is badly or cruelly frustrated the bile will pour into the blood and will produce all kinds of strange symptoms:

But what seems to be even more commonplace in one degree or another is the existence in the Mexican male of a syndrome for which the common denominator is guilt. The extreme separation between the "female set" of values and the "male set," plus the fact that it is the female who teaches and develops the personality of the child, often provokes in the male guilt regarding deviations from the female pattern. Actually in order to be at ease with the male pattern he must constantly

TABLE 2*

SOCIO-CULTURAL PREMISES (VALUES)

	Males			Females		
	Yes	No	D.K.†	Yes	No	D.K.
(1) Is the mother for you the dearest person in existence?.........................	95	3	2	86	10	4
(2) Do you believe the place for women is the home?..............................	91	6	3	90	7	3
(3) Do you believe that men should "wear the pants in the family"?.................	85	11	4	78	15	7
(4) Do you think that many of your desires are contrary to your moral and religious teachings?...........................	—	—	—	19	72	9
(5) Do you believe it is proper for women to go out alone with men?................	56	35	9	55	34	11
(6) Do you believe that men are more intelligent than women?.....................	44	44	12	23	60	17
(7) Do you believe that the stricter the parents the better the children?.........	41	44	15	40	55	5
(8) Do you think that most married men have lovers?.............................	51	33	16	63	17	20
(9) Do you think it is natural for married men to have lovers?...................	22	67	11	16	74	10
(10) Do you consider yourself to be a well rounded woman?.....................	—	—	—	54	35	11

break with the female one. Perhaps it is not an accident that the main religious symbol is a woman: the Virgin of Guadalupe. From their behavior it appears that the males are caught in a compulsive asking for forgiveness from the same symbol they must betray if they are to be masculine. It is only because a good number succeed in keeping each role distinct and separate, through clear discrimination of the places and situations suitable for the playing of each, that no more or no more serious mental disturbance appears. In many of the male Mexican patients that I have seen there is, to one degree or another, prominent in the picture a battle of "superego" and "id," the former representing the mother set of values and the latter the father set. This is Freudian, metapsychology *à la Mexicain.*

abdominal pains, vomiting, diarrhea, headaches, dizziness, oppression, migraine, etc. Actually almost everything of what is now referred as psychophysiological disorders can be produced.

 * Translated and modified from R. Diaz-Guerrero.[3]

 † The answer "yes" corresponds to the dominant pattern. Exceptions are in questions 4 and 5; here the answer "no" corresponds to the dominant pattern; D.K. "don't know."

From this vantage point one could say that many of the neurosis-provoking conflicts in the Mexican are "inner" conflicts, that is, provoked more by clashes of values rather than by clashes of the individual with reality. That this may be so is further suggested by a study of Gomez Robleda.[4] Searching for the evaluations of the "average Mexican" he found that 34.34% of the people investigated held as their main interest in life "sexuality and erotism" and 17.17% mystical and religious values.

The data in Table 2 seem to substantiate the masculine-feminine socio-cultural dichotomy. The table is self-explanatory in the context of the statements about the main socio-cultural premises. With more adequate polling techniques, one could measure the degree and perhaps the "quality" of the variation from the dominant patterns. For example, there is little variation still in regard to the cultural assumption: "the mother is the dearest person in existence" but there is a tremendous change in regard to "men are superior intellectually to women."

SUMMARY

A presentation is made of the cultural assumptions which it is believed underlie a great deal of the role playing in the Mexican family. Examples are given to demonstrate the effect of the assumptions in actual role playing. Remarks are made regarding (1) the areas where neurotic difficulty would be expected from the assumptions and the role playing, and (2) some evidence which seems to verify such expectations. It is proposed that opinion polls may serve the purpose of identifying the degree of variation of a given group from the dominant pattern.

REFERENCES

1. BATESON, GREGORY. 1944. In HUNT, J. McV., (ed.) *Personality and the behavior disorders*, Vol. 2, pp. 714-735. Ronald Press, New York.
2. CANTRIL, MALCOLM. 1944. *Gauging public opinion*. Princeton Univ. Press, Princeton, N.J.
3. DIAZ-GUERRERO, ROGELIO. 1952. Teoria y resultados preliminares de un ensayo de determinacion del grado de salud mental, personal y social del Mexicano de la ciudad. *Psiquis*, 2, 31.
4. GOMEZ-ROBLEDA, JOSE. 1948. *Imagen del Mexicano*. Secretaria de Educacion Publica, Mexico, D.F.
5. KLUCKHOHN, CLYDE. 1951. In PARSONS, TALCOTT, and SHILS, EDWARD, A., (eds.) *Toward a general theory of action*. Harvard Univ. Press, Cambridge, Mass.
6. KLUCKHOHN, F. R. 1953. In KLUCKHOHN, C., MURRAY, H. A., and SCHNEIDER, D. F., (eds.) *Personality in nature, society and culture*. Knopf, New York.
7. RAMOS, SAMUEL. 1938. *El perfil del hombre y la cultura en Mexico*. Pedro Robredo, Mexico, D.F.

PART THREE

ILLUSTRATIONS OF CLINICAL PRACTICE

Edited by

John G. Howells

1. ORGANISATION
2. THE PRESENTING PATIENT
3. CLINICAL SYNDROMES
4. THERAPY

1

ORGANISATION

Family psychiatry has not only a theoretical basis, but also a system for the practice of psychiatry whereby the family is always the target of the referral service, the procedures of investigation and the processes of therapy.

In two chapters written for this book the following are discussed:

>   Organisation of a service in family psychiatry
>   The psychometric assessment of the family

XXVI

ORGANISATION OF A SERVICE IN FAMILY PSYCHIATRY

JOHN G. HOWELLS

An account is given of the organization of a department of family psychiatry, planned to give a complete psychiatric service for an area to all age groups and clinical categories by an integrated out-patient and in-patient service.

INTRODUCTION

This chapter is concerned with the organisation of a service in family psychiatry. Its content is based upon many years of experience at the first hospital department organised completely for family psychiatry. Starting in 1949, the department developed its concepts by 1957 to the point when family psychiatry was the only clinical approach employed. In this department it is not a side activity or an experimental tool, but a day to day service in family psychiatry for the full range of clinical conditions.

Psychiatric practice taking the adult as the functional unit (adult psychiatry), the child as the functional unit (child psychiatry), or the adolescent as the functional unit (adolescent psychiatry) is obsolete. Individual psychiatry is replaced by a systematic clinical approach which takes the family as the functional unit.

Family psychiatry has not only a theoretical basis to explain the sick family, but also a system for the practice of psychiatry whereby the family is always the target of the referral service, of the procedures of investigation and of the process of therapy. The presenting member, irrespective of age or clinical condition, is regarded merely as an indicator of family psychopathology. Thus, after accepting the presenting member, all the remaining family members are investigated and later treated—the aim is to produce an emotionally healthy family.

There are many points of departure from which to develop a family psychiatric service. Starting with an adult service, with an adolescent service, or with a service devoted to a specific clinical category it is possible in time to arrive at a reformulation in terms of family psychiatry. In the case of the department noted here, development started with a child psychiatric service and ended up with a family psychiatric service embracing all age groups and clinical categories.

Emotional illness (neurosis) is common in the community, and many studies support the view that about 30% of the population require treatment because of it. Family psychiatry is the ideal way to organise a service for emotional illness, and the greater part of the out-patient service will be devoted to it. However, psychosis is much less common, and its incidence in the population is not greater than 0·5%. It is believed by some that family psychopathology may be responsible for the etiology of psychosis—using this term to mean 'process', 'endogenous' or 'true' psychosis, as employed in Europe. Whatever the truth of its etiology, it certainly has repercussions on the family circle. Psychosis is best dealt with by a separate special clinic in the out-patient service of the department of family psychiatry; its own in-patient service should be attached to it, and this is usually large as psychosis tends to require lengthy management.

The account of the organisation of a service in family psychiatry will describe facilities, symptomatology of family dysfunction, referral service, investigation, recording of information, treatment, teaching, research.

FACILITIES

SITING

A department of family psychiatry should be the only psychiatric service of any system of health service. Depending on the structure of the health service, it can be an integral part of district general hospitals, university hospitals, community mental health clinics, or polyclinics. An in-patient service for its patients should be attached, or available to it. The optimum size of population served by a unit should be no more than 250,000, as this permits an intimate knowledge of the community and of its agencies.

OUT-PATIENT SERVICE

The architecture of a department of family psychiatry should be a blend of the domestic and of the functional. This does not necessarily call for a building designed as a house; it is possible to design a hospital building so that it embodies domestic features.

In internal decoration special attention should be paid to the use of colour, so that an atmosphere of warmth, welcome and brightness is created; colours must blend, or otherwise there will be a feeling of restlessness and disharmony. Lighting in the corridors and offices should be bright, but in interview rooms the lighting should be reflected from walls or ceilings, thus giving a more subdued and relaxed atmosphere. Whenever possible, in waiting, interview and staff rooms, there should be curtains, carpets, wooden furniture, flowers and plants to create a general feeling of warmth and relaxation.

The interview rooms, which should be sufficient in number to allocate one to each member of the clinical staff, have normally two functions: that of an office and that of an interview room—the latter being more important than the former. It should be possible to arrange the furniture so that interviewing takes place away from the desk, for instance, round a small side-table on which flowers are placed. Instantaneous tape recording facilities are very helpful, though they call for attention to sound-proofing and ventilation. Some of the interview rooms should be large enough to hold a family group. The work of the clinical psychologist is greatly aided by having a storage room for test materials in addition to his interview room. Most of the interview rooms should have an outside telephone, and communication between staff is facilitated by an internal telephone system. The observation of individual or group sessions becomes possible by the provision of closed circuit television or one-way screens in some of the rooms.

Play rooms are usually on the ground floor. Each room should contain all the facilities required for diagnosis and therapy. In addition to play rooms for individual work, there should be at least one large room suitable for group and club activities. One room should cater for adolescent activities. Further features are ample storage facilities for play materials, and a children's library.

The waiting room, usually sited on the ground floor, should be in two sections: one for adults and adolescents; the other for parents accompanied by children, and in this section should be incorporated a play room or a waiting garden. The main office should contain a switchboard, desks, and facilities for storing records, for duplicating and for photocopying. A staff room suitable for seminars, and a departmental library are essential. A clinical room allows for the storage of drugs, syringe work and urine testing. A small kitchen is necessary for staff requirements and also for club and group activities. Amenities for staff include cloak-rooms, separate toilet accommodation and parking. In addition, there should be a telephone booth for the use of patients. As an integral part of a larger health unit, the department will be able to depend on the larger unit for some facilities, e.g. X-ray, EEG, medical photography, main library, canteen, etc.

Day hospital accommodation is required for children, adolescents and adults. Where the out-patient and in-patient services are fully integrated, this can be supplied with the recreational and therapeutic accommodation for in-patients. Emotionally ill and psychotic patients should not share the same accommodation.

IN-PATIENT SERVICE

Accommodation is required for two categories of patients—the emotionally ill and the psychotic.

For the *emotionally ill*, accommodation is best considered in terms of age groups, there being separate accommodation for children, adolescents, adults and the aged.

For children under 12, a mixed unit for girls and boys should supply two types of care: (a) short term for purposes of diagnosis; (b) long term for purposes of adjusting very disturbed children before return home or placement in hostels, special boarding-schools, cottage homes and foster homes. These latter services are normally supplied by other community agencies. Provision for children is required in the order of 50 beds per million population.

Adolescent units can supply separate provision for males and females, have some facilities in common, or be wholly mixed. There is advantage in having units for early adolescence (12-15 years old), and units for late adolescence (15-18 years old). A small number of beds may be required for emergency cases and for patients posing diagnostic problems. The main task, however, is the long-term adjustment of very disturbed persons. The in-patient units must be supported by after-care hostels, special boarding-schools and foster home placements—again, services arranged by community agencies. Provision for adolescents is required in the order of 100 per million population.

Adult units are mixed, or at least share most of the facilities. Beds are required for emergency care, problems of diagnosis, milieu therapy and intensive psychotherapy. The in-patient units must be supported by after-care hostels and work rehabilitation units. Provision for adults should be in the order of 150 beds per million population.

It is often overlooked that the aged are prone to emotional illness and thus require in-patient care. The reasons for admission are the same as those for adults. The in-patient units must be supported by hostels for the aged and supervised flat accommodation. Provision in the order of 20 beds per million population is needed for the aged.

Accommodation for *psychotic patients* is again conveniently considered in terms of age groups. Admissions should usually be arranged through the special psychosis out-patient clinic of the department of family psychiatry. A diagnostic and emergency unit can handle all age groups except children. The main requirement will be for long-term care. The requirement of beds for psychotic children is small, in the order of 20 beds per million population. Adolescents require rather more provision, in the order of 40 beds per million population. The number of beds required for adults will be dependent on the extent of the service it has to give to the aged and may be as much as 3000 beds per million population. Psychogeriatric units should have well-developed links with the geriatric services.

The in-patient service must be supported by day hospitals, sheltered workshops and an after-care service.

Experience has shown that, in the case of units for children and adolescents, the optimum size should be eight to 12 beds; this allows the staff to create a family atmosphere. Further experience should determine the optimum size of adult units; there is much to suggest that they should be of a similar size. A number of experiments have been concerned with the admission of whole family groups or parts of family groups, e.g. husband and wife, or mother and infant. Flexibility in organisation should make this possible.

The success of in-patient units depends more on staff selection than on any other single factor. Staff are likely to be successful if kindly, tolerant, warm-hearted, unsentimental and with a good sense of humour. These qualities usually go with stability and good relationships with their own parents in childhood and later. The dedicated, the sentimental and the hypermoral are unlikely to be successful.

STAFF

Usually the following clinical staff are employed in the out-patient service —psychiatrists, clinical psychologists, social workers, child therapists. For example: a case load of 350 families embracing over 1000 individuals from a population of 250,000 requires a staff of 16 clinical workers in the out-patient service of the department noted here; there being three psychiatrists, four social workers, three clinical psychologists, five occupational therapists—all full time. This staff is the equivalent of 12 psychiatrists and allied professional workers per million population. Such a staff complement does not allow all the families to receive the full range of treatment, and the number of staff could be larger. There is a complementary staff for research, administration, reception and portering. The in-patient service requires its own clinical and nursing staff.

Staff for a complete in-patient service for a million people requires the minimum of 20 full-time psychiatrists of various grades of seniority, together with complementary staff of allied clinical professions and nursing staff.

Much advantage comes from the same clinical workers remaining responsible for a family, should any of its members pass from the out-patient to the in-patient service, or vice versa. Where the out-patient and in-patient staffs are amalgamated, the total staff should be a minimum of 32 psychiatrists, and complementary staff, per million population. Four departments with integrated out- and in-patient services, serving a population of 250,000 each, are to be preferred, as they can then make links with community facilities with greater ease.

In the recruitment of staff, emphasis should be placed upon the emotional stability of the applicants. Stability in a staff member is rewarding both to himself and to his patient, and even the best analytical therapy is seldom an adequate substitute for it.

Various patterns of co-ordinating the activities of staff members in the out-patient service have been developed. The traditional practice in psychiatry is for all staff members to meet together in a large case conference. But this has certain disadvantages for day to day clinical work —it is time-consuming, tends to promote a committee-patient relationship, often undermines individual responsibility for clinical work, and leads to group dependence. As a teaching medium, however, the value of the large case conference cannot be denied. Another pattern employed is that of the small case conference procedure: the psychiatrist, social worker, clinical psychologist and child psychotherapist concerned with a family meet regularly together. Close collaboration over a period of time allows for many things to go unsaid. Decisions are rapidly arrived at by the team, whilst each individual worker retains responsibility for his own contribution. Formal meetings are supplemented by many informal contacts between workers.

Administrative co-ordination in the out-patient department is also important, and this can be achieved by the complete clinical staff meeting together once a week to co-ordinate appointments and to discuss matters of general interest.

SYMPTOMATOLOGY OF FAMILY DYSFUNCTION

It is fundamental to the doctrine of family psychiatry that psychopathology must always be thought of as an expression of dysfunction in a whole family group. A family can show manifestations, symptoms, of dysfunction at any point in its system. Thus symptoms appear in the five dimensions, as described in Part One of this volume—the individual, the relationship, the group, the material circumstances and the family-community interaction. Almost invariably they appear in all, although this may escape notice except on the closest examination. But the family group will not show manifestations of dysfunction to the same extent through all its aspects, e.g. the second child may show more manifestations than the first, or a girl more than a boy, or its community relations may be more disturbed than its material conditions.

In the *dimension of the individual*, each family member usually shows symptomatology. Naturally, this will not be exposed if examination concentrates on one person alone and overlooks the remainder of the family. But each individual does not show psychopathology of the same kind, nor to the same degree.

The usual classification of individual psychopathology into disease categories is outmoded; such terms as anxiety states, reactive depression, obsessional states, hysterical conditions, neurasthenia highlight one facet only of individual psychopathology—usually the most attention-giving, or the most conspicuous at the moment of examination. But psycho-pathology is never monosymptomatic. In the past, concentration on one symptom only has often led to elevating a symptom into a disease category and to overlooking other equally significant indications of psychopathology in the personality. It is more realistic to accept that personality dysfunction, termed emotional disorder, emotional illness, or neurosis, manifests itself at many points in the personality. It is convenient to classify symptomatology in three main clusters—each cluster indicative of changes in physical state, in affect, or in behaviour. In an individual case, symptoms are usually present in all three clusters. Again, this will be exposed only by a full and detailed examination.

Changes in physical state due to emotional stress (psychosomatic symptoms) occur at all ages and in any body system. Feeding problems in infants, enuresis and encopresis in children, migraine in adolescents, dysmenorrhoea in women, gastric ulceration in men, bronchitis in the aged are just a few symptoms picked at random.

Changes in affect again occur in all age groups. Apathy in infants, timidity in children, anxiety in adolescents, reactive depression in adults, hypochondriasis in the aged are a few of the many manifestations that may be observed.

Changes in behaviour occur also in all age groups. Excessive crying in infants, temper tantrums and destructive behaviour in children, delinquency in adolescents and anti-social acts in adults are again some random examples. Thus, psychopathic states exhibiting anti-social actions belong to the cluster of changes in behaviour; such individuals often exhibit also changes of affect and psychosomatic symptoms, again exhibiting the polysymptomatic nature of emotional disorder.

The emotional *stress* responsible for individual symptomatology frequently arises within the family; sometimes it emanates from emotional sources outside the family. Furthermore, the family may dictate the nature of the symptoms, e.g. aggression is met in children who experience it in the family circle. But community and cultural pressures sometimes dictate choice of symptoms, e.g. gastric ulceration is commoner in Western civilisation than in primitive cultures.

That a *particular* individual in the family comes to the attention of a referral agency may be merely fortuitous. He may be the one with the most attention-giving, or the most awkward symptom, e.g. enuresis; or he may manifest a physical symptom which usually leads to ready attention by the health service; he may be in the age group cared for by the psychiatric service of the area; he may be the only family member under surveillance by community agencies, e.g. a schoolchild ascertained at regular school health inspections; he may be the least disturbed, therefore insightful enough to seek help; he may be the most vulnerable of the family members at that moment, due to gender role, or age, or anniversary reaction, or scapegoating by the family or the interplay of family dynamics.

All that has been said above relates only to emotional disorder. It is believed by many that family psychopathology may be responsible for the etiology of psychosis. There is much to be said for differentiating between 'non-process' and 'process' psychosis. The former, in European psychiatry, would often be regarded as severe emotional disorder, with clear links with family psychopathology and best treated by the methods indicated for emotional disorder. 'Process' psychosis, 'endogenous' psychosis, or 'true' psychosis may also have a less clear link with family psychopathology—although this would be challenged by many. Whatever its etiology, 'process' psychosis has undeniable repercussions on the family circle. Great care should be exercised in diagnosing this uncommon condition. The characteristic symptomatology of 'process' psychosis is different from that of emotional disorder and should not be confused with it.

In the *dimension of the relationships*, each relationship will usually show disharmony. Naturally, this will not be seen unless each relationship is examined, e.g. the mother-child relationship often comes under far greater scrutiny than the father-child relationship; the marital relationship also receives a fair degree of attention—but not always from the psychiatric service. Each relationship will not show psychopathology of the same kind, nor to the same degree.

A disturbed relationship may give rise to any symptom in the three clusters of physical, affective or behaviour change mentioned above, in both individuals of the partnership, e.g. an obsession in the wife and a rash in the husband. Sometimes the symptomatology is shared by both partners, e.g. impotence in both (a psychosomatic reaction); joint depression, suicide or *folie à deux* (affective changes) or overt quarrelling (a change of behaviour). Furthermore, some symptoms tend to be associated with a particular relationship, e.g. a malrelationship between husband and wife is often responsible for ejaculatio praecox, dysparunia, impotence and frigidity.

Here, too, family patterns may dictate choice of symptoms, e.g. in some families open quarrelling is forbidden and its members sulk instead. Cultural pressure may also influence choice of symptom, e.g. sexual taboos increase the incidence of sexual disharmony.

That a *particular* relationship comes to the attention of a referral agency may again be fortuitous. Rows between husband and wife may evoke the attention of friends; the faulty relationship between mother and infant may be picked up by the regular surveillance of a community 'mother and baby' clinic; the relationship most under stress may come to attention, e.g. a marriage, due to the intervention of a third party. That disharmony of relationships comes to attention rather than individual disharmony is equally fortuitous.

Symptomatology in the *group dimension* manifests itself in a pattern common to the whole family. Families may be given to types of physical disability, e.g. accident proneness, stomach disorder, or speech disturbances. They manifest affect changes as a group, e.g. panic may be the group reaction to stress. The family's pattern of behaviour is shared by all its members, e.g. exploitation of neighbours. Choice of family group symptomatology may be influenced by cultural pressure; e.g. culture may dictate that fear be controlled by obsessional ritual.

That group disharmony rather than individual or relationship disharmony comes to the attention of a referral agency is again fortuitous. Usually this is less likely to happen, as few agencies ascertain whole family patterns of dysfunction. It is not inconceivable, however, that in time many more agencies will function as family agencies, e.g. in a number of countries the personal doctor operates more and more as a family physician.

Family dysfunction frequently manifests itself in the *dimension of material circumstances*, e.g. poverty despite an adequate income; sloth resulting from apathy and disinterest; low income due to lack of application; loss of employment as a reaction to family emotional crises. Yet again it is fortuitous that adverse material circumstances are the manifestations that arouse attention in referral agencies, rather than individual, relationship or group disharmony. Most often these manifestations come to the attention of social agencies. But selection factors operate, as an agency may have a special function, e.g. a housing agency may ascertain sloth but overlook employment failure, or an agency may serve lower income groups only, and child neglect may be overlooked in a higher income group.

In the *dimension of family-community interaction* signs of dysfunction may arise at the three points of contact: individual-community interaction, e.g. stealing outside the home by a child; partnership-community interaction, e.g. parents' refusal to send a child to school; or family group-community interaction, e.g. quarrelling with the neighbours. The community influences the family by informal and formal means. Enforcement of the latter is entrusted to agencies with statutory powers, e.g. police, courts, health inspectors, child-care agencies, etc., and these, in addition to enforcement functions, may accept responsibility for ascertainment and management of dysfunction. Usually agencies with statutory powers are likely to observe signs of dysfunction in this dimension of family-community interaction.

REFERRAL

A Referral Service

Emotional stress from within or without the family sets up family psychopathology, which is manifest as the symptomatology discussed above. The family members may be aware of the need for psychiatric help. Frequently, however, the significance of this phenomenon escapes the family, and meaning is given to it only by agencies in close touch with the family. Thus help may be sought directly by the family or indirectly through family agencies. Agencies tend to be selective in their interests, and thus a number are required before a complete ascertainment service is given to the family.

Direct referrals from the family to a psychiatric service carry the advantage of speed. They carry the disadvantage of possible wrong selection of specialist service and by-pass the agencies that can give continuous support, both before and after specialist help. All requirements can be met if the psychiatric service offers direct help in an emergency, but usually families are accepted through agencies only.

Referral agencies can be conveniently divided into medical and social, and the latter into statutory and voluntary bodies. Some of the main medical referral agencies are family doctors, family nurses, polyclinics, hospital departments, departments for the care of the handicapped, and school clinics. Some of the main social referral agencies are child-care agencies, workers attached to legal courts, industrial welfare officers, church workers, moral welfare workers, marriage guidance services, housing departments, school welfare officers, and Government assistance officers.

In some countries medical agencies with associated welfare agencies are ready to offer continuous observation and support of families in what they regard as essentially a medical problem—family psychopathology. Thus, whatever the manifestations of dysfunction, they become the main referral channel to the psychiatric service. The continuous medical coverage is given through a family doctor and the continuous welfare coverage either by a home nursing visitor with experience of physical, emotional and social problems, or by an all-purpose social worker with similar experience. These services are supported by specialist medical and social agencies. A vital condition for success is that the workers offering a continuous service should be trained to see the significance of emotional phenomena.

In other countries medical agencies concern themselves with the more obviously medical problems, e.g. psychosomatic manifestations, neurosis and psychosis, while leaving to social agencies other conditions of social importance, e.g. alcoholism, anti-social behaviour, poor material circumstances and child neglect. There is little doubt that these latter conditions are basically personality problems and arise out of individual and family psychopathology. However, these conditions giving rise to social difficulties do come to the notice of social agencies and may then be referred to the psychiatric service. Thus here there are two main referral channels, medical and social.

A referral usually takes place by letter, more urgently by telephone, and sometimes by a personal visit to the psychiatric department. A community should assure itself that symptomatology in any dimension of a family, in any social class, can readily come to the attention of one or more designated agencies, trained to ascertain psychopathology, and with clear links with the psychiatric service, which will help them with problems beyond their capacity.

In-take Procedure

The request for assistance arrives from the referral agency at the family psychiatric service. It may consist of a request in elucidating a problem that subsequently will be dealt with by the agency itself, or for help in management of a problem, or for both elucidation and management.

Ideally the whole family should be referred from the beginning, and thus there would be no need for clinics with special functions in relation to age groups or clinical categories. Until understanding of family psychopathology is widespread, to insist that nothing less than a whole family will be accepted would lead to severe curtailment of the service. Neither agencies nor families have a high degree of understanding of family psychopathology. Indeed, in general, understanding correlates with the degree of stability. Thus the more disturbed families, in most need of help, would be neglected.

Whatever the family or the agency offers should initially be accepted, whether it be an individual member, the whole family, or part of it. The department of family psychiatry can then itself work to achieve the desired aim of involving the whole family.

Usually a family psychiatric service receives an individual, the presenting member, who is the starting-off point of investigation. In areas accustomed to the traditional individual psychiatric approach, it may be necessary to remind referral agencies that the service accepts individuals of all age groups by establishing in-take clinics for children, adolescents, adults and the aged. These may be just 'clinics on paper', for administrative convenience, and have no separate time or facilities. In large departments it may be convenient for the in-take clinics to actually exist, so that slightly different facilities can be set up for the examination of the presenting patient. Some departments may wish to establish special intake clinics for certain clinical categories of patients, either as a reminder to referral agencies, or out of convenience to itself, e.g. for marital problems, delinquency, psychosis, psychosomatic states, alcoholism, etc. Some departments will have in-take clinics based both on age groups and clinical categories. Whatever the starting point, every in-take clinic leads to the same final aim—involvement of the whole family.

Effective work begins with the establishment of rapport. Thus a pleasant letter should convey to the patient the time and date of the *appointment*. It can be accompanied by a brochure giving information likely to be required before attendance. Care should be taken to see that the right members or member of the family receive the correct appointment. Patients should be received by a welcoming receptionist in the waiting area. It enhances rapport again if contact by telephone is handled by an accommodating, considerate telephonist.

An invaluable institution is that of the *evening clinic*. Patients quite unable to attend regularly during the day may be able to do so in the evening. It has advantages for the mother, who is able to leave her children with her husband. It has obvious advantages to husbands in not interfering with their work programme. Thus members of the family otherwise elusive can be brought into investigation and treatment. It is sometimes the only time when a complete family can easily attend together and is thus a popular time for family group therapy.

A steady flow of referrals keeps the clinical staff at optimum efficiency, and for this a *waiting list* is required. Urgent cases should be seen at once, and the remainder need not wait more than two weeks.

A psychiatric service should give a rapid diagnostic service, or it will hamper the activities of other agencies. If, however, it accepts for prolonged treatment all the cases requiring it, then, with the staff available, a long waiting list will soon accumulate. *Selection* of cases for treatment is essential, as it allows the available staff to be used to the best advantage, prevents the accumulation of a long waiting list and lets patients pass directly from diagnosis to treatment—a highly desirable practice. Accumulating a long waiting list does not allow any more patients to be treated, as treatment is limited by the capacity of the service. Families that cannot be passed from the diagnostic to the treatment service are dealt with by referral back to the referral agency for supportive work.

Other measures which have been found helpful in maintaining a short waiting list are: saving time by the omission of routine case conferences, placing one person in charge of the waiting list, and sending a prepaid postcard with the appointment for the patient to confirm it.

INVESTIGATION

The general aim of the investigation is to obtain a complete picture of the family's functioning and dysfunctioning, assets and liabilities, described under five dimensions. A procedure is followed which starts with the *presenting patient* and then moves to the *whole family*, which is examined by individual, dyadic, or family group interviews, supplemented by *special procedures*. At the end of the investigation a *formulation* is possible which describes family functioning and dysfunctioning and outlines the programme of treatment. Achievement of rapport with individual and family is the golden road to obtaining information.

THE PRESENTING PATIENT

An appointment is fixed, conveyed by letter to the patient, who eventually arrives at the clinic, is welcomed by the hostess or receptionist in the waiting area, and at the time of his appointment is conducted to the psychiatrist's room. The initial step is to establish whether or not he has a mental illness, emotional or psychotic. The following evaluation of the individual is undertaken: (a) a history of the complaint or presenting problem; (b) a systematic exploration for symptomatology following a schema devised for this purpose; (c) a mental examination on another schema devised for the purpose. In schemata for the analysis of symptomatology, in the service noted here, the symptoms are divided into three clusters: (i) symptoms indicating physical change, i.e. psychosomatic symptoms; (ii) symptoms indicative of change of affect; (iii) symptoms indicating a change of behaviour.

Having elucidated the present malfunctioning of the individual, the next step is to build up a picture, following a schema devised for this purpose, of the life experience of the individual from conception to date, including his present personality. Some of the information is collected by questionnaire. Psychometric examinations add to the personality profile.

In a small minority of cases the presenting problem will appear to have a whole or partial organic basis. Thus, at times, there may be need for physical examination, supplemented by pathological, encephalographic, radiological examinations, etc.

Should a child be the presenting patient, much of the information will come from the parents. In addition, the child may undergo play observation or play diagnosis in play rooms equipped for this purpose.

Now it is possible to answer the question, 'Has the presenting patient a mental illness, and if so, is this an emotional illness or psychosis?' A positive diagnosis of an emotional illness leads (a) to the next stage of exploring and describing the family psychopathology of which it is a part, and (b) to the psychiatrist conveying his finding to the referral agency. At times the investigation ends at this point, because it may have revealed a non-psychiatric problem, or because the patient can be dealt with by the referring agency. In the event of a positive diagnosis of 'process psychosis', the patient is transferred to the special clinic for this condition. Depending on the views held for etiology, the procedure may follow that described here.

THE FAMILY PRESENTS

Occasionally the whole family presents itself at the initial interview. More often only one family member does so and the remaining members are gathered in over time as rapport develops; with unco-operative families this may take several months. A few families will never be seen as a whole, but, even with only part of a family, practising family psychiatry to the possible limit will lead to more realistic assessments than individual psychiatry.

A complete family assessment contains information under five dimensions.

1. Description of each *individual* on the lines outlined above for the presenting patient, and including functioning and malfunctioning in the time sequence of past and present. Interview procedures are supplemented by questionnaires, psychometric examinations and play examination of children.

2. Description of all *relationships* in the family, both in the past and in the present. Interview procedures are supplemented by psychometric procedures and by special charts that depict the intimate emotional relationships of each member of the family in his early years.

3. Description of the family's *group properties* in the past and the present.

4. Description of the family's *material circumstances* in the past and the present. Interview procedures are supplemented by questionnaires.

5. Description of *family-community interaction* both past and present.

The information is obtained as the result of interviews with individual family members, dyadic interviews and family group diagnosis. The plan must be flexible enough to use the type of interview most useful at that moment in time and best able to produce the required information. Individual interviews are especially useful with (1), (2) and (4) above, dyadic interviews with (2) above, and family group diagnosis with (2), (3) and (5) above.

Usually the same team of clinical workers should be employed throughout the investigation of one family. The division of labour is as follows. Psychiatrist and social worker undertake the interview procedures with an individual or a family; the areas to be covered are apportioned to each. Questionnaires and charts are the responsibility of the social worker. The clinical psychologist conducts all psychological procedures. Play observation and play diagnosis is the function of the child therapist.

Individual interviews usually last for 50 minutes, dyadic for 90 minutes and family groups for two hours.

All the information obtained is passed into a master file. Each clinical worker in addition keeps *progress notes* on his work with the family.

SPECIAL PROCEDURES

Family Group Diagnosis is a procedure whereby all the members of the family who are meaningful in the family's situation at that moment are interviewed together. This may involve two or three generations. It may include nannies, lodgers, etc., present in the family at that time. The aim of the procedure is to get a first-hand picture of the dynamics of the family. Family group diagnosis is a procedure of such value that it is certain that it will have an established place in psychiatric practice, and, indeed, should rarely be overlooked in the exploration of the family dynamics. The true situation in the family will not usually emerge until a few interviews have passed.

Family group diagnosis should not be confused with family group therapy. Many family groups are termed therapeutic when, in fact, they consist almost exclusively of an exploration of the family dynamics. At the same time, diagnosis may sometimes lead to family therapy. Furthermore, family group diagnosis may be an essential first step in vector therapy and run parallel with it.

Family group diagnosis may be conducted by one clinical worker; it seems that it is easier to establish rapport in this way. Our experience has been that there are more advantages than disadvantages in using one competent worker for family group work. Others maintain that it is better to have a team exploration of the family group. The difficulty that arises in practice is that the loyalty of the family may be fragmented by individuals attaching themselves to different members of the exploring team. Furthermore, communication between members of the exploring team may be faulty, thus there is no unity of decision. A useful procedure is to take the material obtained by one interviewer and subject it to a team analysis.

Play Procedures are utilised for observation and diagnosis with children either as individuals or groups. In this department the work is the responsibility of occupational therapists who have had two years' full-time postgraduate training, and experience both with normal and disturbed children. A schema has been devised for analysing the functioning of the child as the result of play observation. In play diagnosis, by using a variety of play media, the child is encouraged to reveal the dynamics of the family as he sees them.

Psychological Procedures are developing which may give quick and accurate ways of assessing aspects of the family. The Family Relations Indicator (F.R.I.) is already a valuable adjunct to clinical procedures. These techniques are reviewed in the chapter that follows.

Questionnaires are not given immediately at first attendance; they are found to be more effective once rapport has been established. They cover the more historical material and constitute a way by which information can be quickly obtained about dates and events that are unexceptional. The questionnaire can be filled up either at attendance at the department or at home, depending on the circumstances. Sometimes the patient requires the guidance of a secretary. At other times the social worker may find it useful to run through the questionnaire with the patient and thus use it as a controlled interview.

Charts of Relationships give a diagrammatic record of the duration and number of relationships in which a family member was involved in his first 15 years. It includes relationships within and without the child's nuclear family.

In-patient Observation may be required from time to time to establish a diagnosis in an individual family member. It may be profitable, when circumstances permit, to admit a whole family for rapid evaluation.

A regular *consultation service* should be supplied by neurologists, physicians and pediatricians.

FORMULATION

In an ideal exploration time is allowed to achieve a complete description of family functioning. In practice a formulation may have to be made before this point is reached. The formulation describes what is known about the family to date in terms of both its assets and liabilities. The department may be required only to convey this formulation to the referring agency, who may then be able to plan its own treatment programme for the family. Frequently the department alone has the facilities necessary to effective treatment. From the formulation it plans its own treatment programme. Diagnosis may continue parallel with treatment, and information goes on being added to the cumulative master file.

RECORDING INFORMATION

SOURCES OF INFORMATION

There are two main sources:

1. The most meaningful material is likely to come from the individual, dyadic and family group interviews within the department, supplemented by questionnaires, charts, psychometric procedures, play procedures and in-patient observation. Ideally all the information should be complete at the end of the investigation; in practice information continues to be added throughout treatment.

2. Information from the referring agency, or other agencies. This may be spontaneously offered, or come as the result of the department's enquiring by letter, telephone or visit.

All the information, from whatever source, is fed into the master file at the appropriate place.

THE MASTER FILE

One confidential master file for each family is kept in a locked cabinet in the department. Each clinical worker adds to the file, and has access to the information in it.

The material can be *collected* in one of the following ways: (a) On every occasion any member of the family is seen by any clinical worker the master file is at hand, and information obtained as a result of that contact is added in writing to the master file at the appropriate place. (b) Information in the master file is itemised under code numbers. Each paragraph of the interview report is itemised and given the appropriate code number.

Each paragraph is then entered under its code number in the master file by a secretary. (c) An interview can be taped, the material typed, analysed under the coding system and added by the secretary to the master file. (d) Mechanical recording.

The master file *contains* the following: (i) general particulars, e.g. names of family, birth dates, address, referring agency, etc.; (ii) a family profile, either listing the names of the family members or representing the family members in diagrammatic form. The main file consists of a separate account of each dimension of the family which added up gives a complete description of its functioning and malfunctioning in the time sequence of past and present. Hundreds of items are involved, and each item has a code number.

The following *additional* documents are kept with the master file. The data in them will already have been added to the master file. (i) Questionnaires; (ii) charts of relationships of each member of the family; (iii) psychometric report forms; (iv) reports on play observations and play diagnosis; (v) clinical, pathological, X-ray, EEG reports, etc.; (vi) reports of contact with community agencies, e.g. school visit reports, etc.; (viii) miscellaneous material.

The utmost care should be taken to guard the *confidential* nature of case notes, and it is a useful practice for each administrative member of staff on appointment to sign a statement that he has read the warning notice about their confidential nature.

TREATMENT

From investigation the family moves to treatment by the same clinical team and in the same department. By adjusting the treatment case load to what is possible with available resources, the family can pass from investigation to treatment without a waiting period.

Some General Principles

Within family psychiatry the term 'family therapy', treatment of the family, embraces any procedure employed to adjust the family.

Three main procedures are available in family therapy: (a) Psychotherapy by various techniques, which seeks a direct change in the individual, the dyad or the family group. (b) Vector therapy, which seeks to produce a more harmonious interplay of emotional forces within and without the family. (c) Promoting a salutiferous community, which creates the optimum emotional environment for the family.

Sometimes there is emphasis on one, rather than another, but all forms of therapy can exist together; in the ideal case all three forms are in use. The treatment programme must at all times be flexible to meet the ever-changing demands of the family situation. This applies to the choice of individual, dyadic or family group approach in psychotherapy, or whether psychotherapy or vector therapy should be the approach to be employed at that moment.

In view of the attention given to the new technique of family group therapy, it should be emphasised that it is only one of the procedures of psychotherapy, which again is only one section of family therapy; its exclusive use leads to gross limitation of family therapy.

Treatment may have to proceed with part of a family. If the principles of family psychiatry are observed, then, even with a part, the result will be better than if the procedures of individual psychiatry alone were employed.

Diagnosis and therapy run parallel to some extent. From the sending of the initial appointment onwards there is potential for therapy in everything that is undertaken.

PSYCHOTHERAPY

There are three forms of psychotherapy, individual, dyadic and family group. In our experience, the utmost degree of flexibility is required. Sometimes one may start off with family group therapy, later fragment the family into dyadic therapy, or individual therapy, then bring the family together again. In another instance, one may start off with individual therapy and end up with family group therapy. Family therapy is still being undertaken in individual therapy as long as the target is the family psychopathology and the aim to produce a healthy family.

In *individual* psychotherapy the attempt is made to effect an adjustment in the personality of the individual family member. One or more adults or children may be under therapy at one moment. Many techniques can be employed from psychoanalysis to brief therapy. All of them can be encompassed by family psychiatry. In our own practice we use two forms of psychotherapy: (a) supportive therapy, aimed at adjusting the individual and family to stresses and strains in the present; and (b) prolonged psychotherapy which aims at an analysis of the whole life experience of the individual, and interprets it in terms of the real meaning of the emotional events to that person. A close relationship between patient and therapist makes possible the resolution of those adverse situations in the past which are at the root of present disturbance, and so a reintegration of the personality is effected.

Dyadic therapy involves the management of two people together in therapy. The commonest grouping would be that of husband and wife. Other groupings may be father and child, or mother and child, or even two children. The way in which the material is analysed can depend upon the viewpoint of the therapist, and again family psychiatry can encompass any approach.

Family group therapy is a procedure for the therapy of the family as a unit. It is not a procedure for the treatment of an individual through a group experience. The aim is to treat the family through a group experience. Traditional group therapy brings together individuals from a number of families; the aim is to use a group experience to help individuals; this group, unlike a family group, has no group identity, either before or after the interview.

This procedure is a valuable new technique in psychiatry. Nevertheless, it has its limitations, and because as little is known about it as of individual psychotherapy the way is still uncertain. The main principle is that the assets of the family are mobilised in order to overcome its liabilities.

It is one of the dangers in psychiatry to assume that if a group of people meet together to talk, then some good may come of it; it is equally possible for ill to come of it. Thus, if a family group is to meet together for therapy, it should be expected that some new factor is operating. This new factor is the personality of the therapist. The therapist has the task of being the convener of the meeting, its chairman, its catalyst, the representative of community opinion, and of instilling courage that can lead to change. In addition, he introduces the art of psychotherapy, which starts by imparting to the group the significance of emotional events, the significance of its family emotional life now, the significance of the past emotional events that interact with the present events; he then uses the particular strengths of a section of the family, together with his own, to resolve the particular weaknesses of the rest of the family. The therapist has a loyalty to the family as a unit, and this will be tested. He will meet dependence, transference and resistances, old friends from individual psychotherapy.

The family group usually meets in the clinic setting. They can meet informally in a comfortable circle of chairs, or seated around a table. All members of the family of any age group, including infancy, are present. Each family member is allowed equal voice; this is one of the matters that the group members come to learn in time. Less than $1\frac{1}{2}$ hours is unlikely to be worth while, and more than $2\frac{1}{2}$ hours is likely to be exhausting. At first, the picture obtained of the group is false; with time, the true life situations emerge. For some families therapy at home is a natural situation. Others will regard it as more artificial than therapy in a clinic. Usually the latter allows a better utilisation of available therapeutic time.

The following illustrates the need to be flexible in a family group therapy and to allow fragmentation when required. A father, mother and daughter meet together for family group therapy. At one moment father becomes silent, anxious and restless; the group makes no progress. The father then asks that he be allowed to see the therapist alone. When he does so, he relates that some time ago he had an affair with a third party. He ends by wondering whether this information should be imparted to the family group. Discussion may show that two plans should be considered: (i) that the material imparted is of no significance to the family group, and therefore need not be divulged; (ii) that the material is of significance to the wife, who, the patient feels, may suspect the situation. He asks for a meeting between the therapist, the wife and himself, as he feels that the matter needs resolution. Husband, wife and therapist meet —dyadic therapy. Again the couple wonders whether the information should be imparted to the family group. They decide that the event has no significance for the adolescent daughter, and they do not wish to introduce the material to the group. Or they may decide that the daughter may already suspect this relationship, is worried about it, and the matter should be divulged. Thus the therapist, father, mother and daughter meet to discuss the situation. Thereafter, family group therapy continues.

One of the unquestionable advantages of family group therapy is its value as a complementary procedure to vector therapy. A family meets over a number of interviews and develops enough insight to see that a change of emotional influences within or without the family is necessary. With the support of the therapist, it then takes the necessary action to produce a more harmonious interplay of influences.

A complete change, or a complete stabilisation of the family members, may not be required to effect a considerable improvement in a family situation. For example, as the result of free discussion in family group therapy a highly disturbed, rigid, obsessional father, with a highly abnormal attitude toward sexual matters, finds himself able to see that his son should have the freedom to leave the family, and to adopt the values of the community rather than the values of the father. Father's personality is not changed, but, by releasing his son and giving him a dispensation on the matter of sexual values, the son gains immeasurably in his own emotional life.

VECTOR THERAPY

Vector therapy effects a change of the emotional forces within the life space to bring improvement to the individual or family within the life space. Vector therapy can involve: (i) a change in the magnitude of the force, e.g. aggression might be diminished; (ii) a change of direction of the force, e.g. anger may be deflected to someone else; (iii) forces can replace one another, e.g. affection replaces aggression; (iv) a change takes place in the time over which the force operates. Vector therapy can coexist with psychotherapy.

The family member exists in a field of emotional forces within the family. The family group exists in another field of forces outside the group; these forces are directed at individual family members, or at the family as a whole from the community and the culture. Some of these emotional forces within and without the family are disharmonious, destructive and negative. Others are harmonious, constructive and positive. The aim of vector therapy is to change the forces playing on individuals or families, so as to produce a more harmonious set of forces. The change of forces allows constructive work to take place over time, and thus a beneficial change is produced in the life experience of the individual or family.

To be effective, vector therapy is dependent upon the satisfaction of at least three principles. Firstly, that the forces at work on the individual or family have been correctly evaluated. Secondly, that it is possible to deploy facilities that allow of a change of emotional forces. Thirdly, that the individual or family understands the need for the particular manipulation, change, removal, etc. of influences.

Vector therapy is an aspect of family management that calls *par excellence* for the special skills of the social worker. It is she who, given the appraisal of the family from the psychiatric team, is best placed to deploy agencies with facilities that can produce a more harmonious play of forces in the life of the individual or family.

Vector therapy is discussed in more detail in Part I, pp. 101-107, and an example of its application is given in Chapter LI.

A SALUTIFEROUS COMMUNITY

A family is a sub-group in the community and the culture. This subgroup is influenced by its emotional environment. Thus the more harmonious the community, the greater the advantage to the family. In the field of physical medicine every practice, principle, agency, institution in the community has been evaluated for its value to physical health. Where they promote healthy physical living, they have been preserved. Where these elements are damaging to healthy physical living, they have been changed, e.g. clean milk safeguards health. The same exercise needs to be gone through in the emotional field. We must ask ourselves, 'Which practices make for a health-promoting community, a salutiferous community?' Those which promote it should be preserved, and those that are antagonistic to it should be changed. This calls for a vast analysis of community and cultural living. It calls, too, for an awareness on the part of the community that this task needs to be accomplished. Furthermore, before it can be accomplished, there must be, as a result of experimentation and research, exact knowledge of what is harmful and what promotes health; false knowledge can produce wrong massive action that may impede development for many generations.

LIAISON

Treatment, to be effective, calls for liaison with a large number of community agencies. Liaison is also essential at the stages of referral and investigation, and often the same agencies are involved. A family psychiatric service is a special service and does not usually undertake the support of a family for more than a fixed period. Agencies such as family social agencies, family doctors, undertake a continuous service to families. Thus there has to be a referral from them and a handing back to them. Agencies involved in the family are diverse, and include both statutory and voluntary agencies. Maintaining liaison with them and deploying their help throughout the management of the family is one of the important functions of the social worker. Reports from the family psychiatric service are conveyed by letter, by telephone or by personal contact.

SELECTION

Few departments have the staff and resources to meet all the therapeutic demands. Therefore, selection of families for treatment is essential. As an approximate index it can be said of the department noted here that one-third of cases are closed after advice and assessment and the expression of an opinion to the referring agency. A third are accepted for supportive therapy, with co-existing vector therapy. Another third are accepted for prolonged psychotherapy in association with vector therapy. However hard pressed a service, it is of the utmost importance that at least some cases are given the fullest measure of investigation and treatment. It is only in this way that knowledge is accumulated and techniques are improved. Unless intensive work is entered into, work becomes superficial; thus there is no self-improvement. Given good work with a small number of families, the work with the remainder of the families, although it may be curtailed, will never be superficial.

ADDITIONAL THERAPEUTIC PROCEDURES

In addition to the above, any of the following may be employed to assist in achieving the aims of family therapy.

1. *Group therapy*, which may be for groups of children, adolescents, or adults, male or female or mixed. It may be formal in an interview setting, or informal in a club setting.

2. *Play therapy* for children. A young child can communicate only through play; an older child may spontaneously verbalize to the therapist. The play medium appropriate to the child's age, sex and inclination is supplied. Play therapy is used to corroborate information obtained through one medium by that disclosed by another. The first aim is usually to establish rapport, for which much play material is utilized. Thereafter, systematic observation of the child takes place in the play situation; this gives a base-line for comparison later on. Play diagnosis follows. The aim here is to encourage the child to reveal his problems as he knows them, and also to express what he knows about himself and his relationships within the family, the school and the neighbourhood. Play

therapy is the final technique and is employed for one of the following reasons: (a) to support the child while the family is receiving treatment; (b) to support the child when the family environment cannot be changed, or when he cannot be separated from it; (c) to help to separate the child from his family, for either short or lengthy periods; (d) to make a change in the child's personality. The relationship between therapist and child is the most potent therapeutic medium. Within the safety of this relationship, the child expresses his fears, guilt and hate, and, sharing these with the therapist, is encouraged to healthier reactions. With adolescents art therapy is often a useful medium.

3. *Physical methods* are required to supplement the above procedures, e.g. anti-convulsants for an epileptic patient, hypnotics to induce sleep, or sedation to reduce anxiety.

4. *Home therapy*. This may be merely domiciliary visiting, seeking information and giving reassurance, or it may be the base for family group therapy.

5. *A day hospital* programme for children, adolescents or adults. The accommodation can often be shared with in-patients.

6. *Residential care*. This must be supplied for the emotionally ill in all age groups—children, adolescents, adults and the aged. The individual is withdrawn from his traumatic environment and subjected, sometimes for a number of years, to intensive milieu therapy, i.e. a potent form of vector therapy. It is unlikely to be effective unless the remainder of the family group are co-operative; they may need adjustment before the individual member can return to it or agree that on discharge he joins another family group. Thus the family group may need to join the in-patient unit on a day basis, or the whole family be admitted for intensive care. Where after-care is supplied away from home, a whole range of community facilities become necessary—hostels, special boarding-schools, cottage homes, foster homes, work rehabilitation units, supervised accommodation for the aged, etc.

For patients with psychosis, organic and functional, there should be separate accommodation catering for all age groups. Patients are improved by institutional care, but are rarely cured by it. An efficient after-care service can reduce the readmission rate.

7. In some countries severely disturbed families, problem or 'hard-core' families, are housed in *settlements* for which there is a special provision of welfare services.

TEACHING

Professional staff

Time and facilities are essential if effective teaching is to be done. The best teaching affords experience in the whole range of clinical disorders, at the same time allowing the close study of a small number of selected patients. The apprenticeship system, backed by formal instruction in seminars and case conferences, has much to recommend it. Library facilities are essential; they should include not only books and reprints, but also tape recordings of interviews selected for their teaching value.

Related professions

It is also necessary to arouse interest in, and give instruction to, related professions. The best propaganda is a good clinical service. The professions include the following: general practitioner, school medical officer, family health visitor, school nurse, home nurse, midwife, social and welfare worker, staff of children's departments, staff of day nurseries, teacher and hospital nurse.

The public

Experience suggests that it is more effective to concentrate teaching on key personnel, i.e. members of the related professions, than upon members of the public; key personnel in their day to day work can informally influence public opinion.

A department which undertakes much teaching must have considerable extra accommodation, especially rooms for seminars. A large teaching unit needs an auditorium. Teaching staff are additional to the complement of clinical staff, though, of course, staff share teaching and clinical functions. A staff member trained in medical teaching aids is invaluable.

RESEARCH

Systematic investigation into the problems of the family is still in its infancy. Thus every family service should create a research unit, so that it can pose questions and plan systematic enquiry. In a sense, a department of family psychiatry in our present state of knowledge is itself a research endeavour. Much has yet to be understood about individual, family and community dynamics. The ground is common to clinical workers, sociologists and anthropologists.

In a large unit accommodation must be provided for research, administration, research workers, statisticians and medical illustrators. Some units will extend to laboratories for basic research.

REFERENCES

HOWELLS, J. G. 1962, The nuclear family as the functional unit in psychiatry. *J. ment. Sci.*, **108**, 675-684.

HOWELLS, J. G. 1963. *Family psychiatry.* Oliver & Boyd, Edinburgh.

XXVII

THE PSYCHOMETRIC ASSESSMENT OF THE FAMILY

J. R. LICKORISH

Many psychometric techniques are already available for assessing elements in the dimensions of the family. Some have been designed specially for family assessment; others have been adapted for this purpose.

INTRODUCTION

THE NATURE OF PSYCHOMETRIC ASSESSMENT

The term psychometric is used in this chapter in a purely conventional manner. Strictly speaking, it means 'measurement of the psyche, or soul', but it has the derived meaning of 'measurement' of psychological relationships and quantities. The term is an inheritance from the psycho-physics of the early experimental psychologists, and also from the materialistic physics of the nineteenth century. It is true that measurement has a proper place in psychological research and investigation, but it is necessary to remember that the word 'measurement' is used in two different senses. The primary meaning of measurement assumes that there are units in terms of which a given magnitude may be stated. In physics, the familiar units of centimetres, grams and seconds are used, and everything that may be measured physically can be stated in terms of these units. But in psychological measurements, there are no such fundamental units in terms of which psychological relationships and quantities may be stated, with the exception of units of time. Hence, the term 'measurement' in psychology has a secondary meaning and refers to the order, sequence, score, ratio, percentage, or even to the simple absence or presence of a given feature. It is this secondary meaning of the word which is implied by the term 'psychometric', and we must beware of assuming that it pre-supposes the existence of units of measurement, or physical quantity, when, in fact, no such units exist. Most psychological 'measures' are made in terms of numbers which often have an arbitrary relationship to the features which are being measured. The assigning of numbers to psychological features is very useful, because it enables them to be manipulated statistically.

Some psychological reactions are strictly metrical, in the sense that they may be expressed in c.g.s. units. Thus the emotional state of a subject may be expressed in terms of an increased rate of breathing, or a rise in his blood pressure, both of which may be measured in the usual physiological manner. Theoretically it should be possible to use this kind of measure to assess the reaction of a child when confronted with a picture which arouses in him excitement, of either a fearful or a euphoric nature. The difficulties of conducting such an experiment are almost insuperable and, even if they were not, the measurements taken would be physical rather than psychological measures.

It is very important to examine the terms which are so frequently used in psychiatry and psychology in order to obtain a more precise view of their meaning. The various shades of meaning which may be assigned to the word 'psychometric' illustrate the need for doing this. Psychologists are greatly indebted to the linguistic philosophers for their work on the meanings of words, and semantics is a necessary part of psychological discipline.

In this essay the word 'psychometric' will be used to indicate the quality, or intensity, or relative strength of personal relationships for which there are no fundamental units of measurement. If used in this way, the term 'psychometric' is permissible, but it is probably better to avoid the word altogether, since it can easily be replaced by the phrase 'psychological assessment', which does not carry metrical implications.

OBJECTIVITY

It is also necessary to be very careful in using the word 'objective', when speaking of psychometric assessment. There are several definitions of this very difficult word, but, as far as the psychologist is concerned, we may quote English and English (1958) as saying that 'objective' means: 'not dependent upon the judgement or accuracy of the individual observer; free from personal and emotional bias; hence, open to observation by any competent observer'. Another meaning of this term, which is beloved of some psychologists, is 'open to observation by physical instruments'. This latter definition is clearly applicable to the observations of the physicist and others who deal in c.g.s. units. Equally obviously, it cannot apply to the kind of assessment we are discussing in this chapter.

A major aim in the construction of any psychological test is to make it 'objective' in the sense of being 'free from personal and emotional bias.' This aim has been largely achieved in the construction and administration of intelligence tests, but the personal characteristics of the examiner are likely to obtrude themselves when using a rating scale or a projective method of assessment.

It is extremely difficult to eliminate completely the bias of the observer, because, inevitably, the observer is himself part of the observational set-up. This may be illustrated by reference to Fig. 1. If the cube AD represents the total environment within which a person P is being observed, then the total influences bearing upon the person at that time may be represented by the six faces of the cube. Amongst the forces emanating

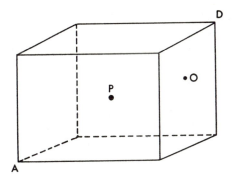

FIG. 1. Diagram to illustrate how the experimenter is involved in the situation that he is observing.

from the faces of the cube is the force due to the observer O. He is 'inside' the situation that he is observing, and so, to some extent, he must exert an influence upon it. This emphasis upon the influence of the observer may appear to be somewhat pedantic, but it is a useful reminder that, in dealing with people, the experimenter is involved in the situation in a way that he is not involved when he deals with inanimate objects.

THE COMPLEXITY OF FAMILY ASSESSMENTS

The psychological assessment of the family appears, at first sight, to be a relatively simple procedure, but we have only to remind ourselves of the complexity of the interpersonal relationships which may exist within the family to realize what a complex undertaking it is to obtain an adequate assessment of the family. Alternatively, the assessment may be concerned with superficial relationships only, or with the relations between a limited number of the members of a family. The complexity of the task may be illustrated by considering the following diagrams.

In Fig. 2 we have a small family of parents and two children. The double-headed arrows connecting F M, C1, C2 indicate the reciprocal relationships existing between them in a normal family. If the family were in a state of psychological equilibrium, there would be six main relationships to be evaluated, and each of these relationships would be of a reciprocal nature. But even a slight change in the relationships between the members of this family group would produce complications. For example, M and C2 might form a sub-group, and thus, not only would

FIG. 2. Diagrammatic representation of normal relationships in a family of four.

they have individual relationships with F and C1, but they might also react to each of them collectively.

If we consider a slightly larger family, as shown in Fig. 3, which includes the maternal grandmother (M.G.M.) either living with the family or being in close proximity to them, then the complexity of the relation-

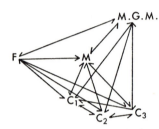

FIG. 3. Relationships in a five-person family together with maternal grandmother.

ships increases enormously, so that there are now at least 15 reciprocal relationships to be evaluated. If the relationship of the M.G.M. is not the same for each of the children, or if there is a distinct difference between her relationship with father and her relationship with mother, then some of these 15 relationships differ in quality and intensity from the others. Also, sub-groups may easily form within the larger group of six people, with consequent further complication of the relationships involved.

Most families have even more complex relationships than those indicated in Fig. 3, since they inevitably have some relationship with the community in which they live and very often with two or more grandparents, together with one or more aunts or uncles, living within the family constellation.

Whilst it is almost impossible at the present time to assess all these relationships by any available psychometric method, attempts have been made, by means of complicated analyses, to amass as much information as possible about the extended family group. Thus, Howells, in an as yet unpublished research, has listed 23 categories and 470 items, in a file of 45 foolscap pages, in order to assess the relationships within the extended family group. In America, the Fels Institute has a similar elaborate method of assessing family relationships. Their schedule extends to 30 quarto sheets, with eight areas of family and personal relationships which are assessed on a ten-point scale.

A large number of questionnaires and rating scales have been constructed to assess family relationships. Many of these questionnaires and scales are devised by individuals conducting specific pieces of research, and, while they may form a model for use in further investigations, there are very few of them which are of universal applicability. We must beware of thinking that we possess a wide range of reliable methods for assessing the various aspects of the family. There are relatively few well tried methods available, partly because the study of the family, as distinct from its individual members, is a relatively recent psychological undertaking. Many of the tests described in this chapter relate to the assessment of the individual members of the family and to intra-family relationships. Relatively few can be used to assess the family as a unit.

PLAN OF THIS CHAPTER

Since the author of this present volume considers the family under five aspects, or 'dimensions', it is convenient to discuss the psychological assessment of the family under the same five heads. The present discussion is *not* a review of the literature on the subject, nor is it concerned with the *results* of investigations into family structure. It simply illustrates the methods by which the 'dimensions' of the family may be assessed, using current psychological tests and procedures. Not all the tests mentioned are available through the test agencies; some are still in the developmental stage and are known only through the published papers which describe them. A few of the procedures mentioned have not, at the time of writing, been described in the journals, and permission to mention them has been sought from the authors. Some aspects of the family are intrinsically difficult to assess, because the necessary data are not readily available. This is particularly true of the past history of the family, since the data consist mainly of personal testimony, with its inevitable omissions and distortions due to the dynamic processes of remembering and recall outlined by Bartlett (1932). Some tests may be used to assess more than one dimension. Thus the Family Relations Indicator, Howells and Lickorish (1962), which assesses the present personal relationships within the family, also by implication, indicates the kind of relationships which have existed over a period of time. For some dimensions there are very few test procedures available, and this deficiency may indicate a profitable field for future research. No test is described under more than one dimension, although, where appropriate, alternative uses for it are mentioned.

THE ASSESSMENT OF THE INDIVIDUAL

Many well-established psychological tests may be used to assess individual members of the family. Amongst these are the Thematic Apperception Test, Symonds Picture Story Test, Rosenzweig Picture Frustration Test, some forms of the Incomplete Sentences and many personality question-naires. Since these tests may also be used to assess personal relationships, they will be described in the next section. In addition to these formal tests, there are other procedures which have been used to assess individual development and personality. Some of these are definite experimental techniques and others employ more sophisticated methods.

Assessment of Pre-natal Behaviour

Several attempts have been made to assess the sensitivity of the unborn foetus and to record its movements in response to sounds and tactile stimuli. Schmeidler (1941) recorded the movements of her own unborn child. She noted the frequency, location and intensity of movements during 42 periods of one hour each, between the fifth and seventh months of pregnancy.

Spelt (1948)* has provided some evidence of the learning ability of the foetus. He used a loud sound as the unconditioned stimulus for the foetus, whilst a tactile conditioned stimulus, in the form of a vibration, was applied to the mother's abdomen. The experiments were performed on foetuses of between 6½ and 8½ months of pre-natal life. He showed that responses could be retained over a period of three weeks and that experimental extinction and spontaneous recovery were also observable.

A correlation between foetal activity and post-natal development has been demonstrated by Richards and Newberry (1938). They compared the mothers' accounts of foetal activity with the developmental level of the infants at the age of six months, which was assessed by using the schedules developed by Gesell (1952). The numbers involved were small but some of the correlations were high.

The Biographical Method

The main events in the life of the developing child are often recorded in a 'baby diary', or 'baby book', by the mother. If this method is carried out by a skilled observer it may conserve valuable information about the person's past life, but in the hands of an unskilled person it is of little scientific value, since it will almost certainly provide a very biased account of the child's early life. Perhaps the best of these biographical accounts was the description by Mrs. Fenton (1925) of the development of her son during his first two years of life. This method has been little used, and more systematic and scientific techniques are now usually employed.

Longitudinal Studies

In this method a given family, or its individual members, are regularly

* Reprinted in this volume as No. IV

assessed at stated intervals, so that after a period of years an account has been compiled of the person's 'past'. This method is employed by the Fels Institute and is described in detail by Baldwin *et al.* (1949).

One *variation of this method*, described by McCord *et al.* (1962), was based on the original data collected in the Cambridge-Somerville Youth Study during the years 1937-39. This data was 'coded', between 1956 and 1958, by a group of workers who had no knowledge of the adult behaviour of the subjects they were assessing. Three 'measures' were adopted: (i) measures of familial environment and parental behaviour, which were assessed by means of rating scales; (ii) measures of the child's behaviour; (iii) measures of the adult behaviour of those who were the subjects of the original study. This last assessment was based upon official community records gathered in 1956. Ratings were made of social deviance in the following areas: criminality, alcoholism and mental illness.

Out of an original 255 boys who had been studied most carefully, 148 were selected for the final analysis. They were chosen on the basis of four measures of the dependent behaviour which they manifested as children. These measures were: (i) striving for adult approval; (ii) relations to peers; (iii) relationship to the counsellor; (iv) their primary reference group, whether their family or a peer group. The following types of dependent behaviour were distinguished: pervasively-dependent; peer-dependent and adult-dependent. This dependent behaviour was correlated with lack of emotional security in the family, with parental rejection and with punishment. In these comparisons a group of 'moderately' dependent boys was used as a control. Six behavioural traits exhibited in the home, school and neighbourhood differentiated the dependent boys from the controls. But there was little difference between the adult behaviour of controls and dependents with respect to criminality, alcoholism or mental illness, although there was a marked tendency for them to succumb to the last-named.

This method involves the accumulation of a vast amount of data by direct observation and its subsequent reduction to a manipulable form by means of rating scales. One special feature of this procedure was the use of data originally collected for a quite different purpose. It is possible that this reduced the amount of bias in the data, so far as the investigation of dependency was concerned.

The Genetic Method is the application of observation techniques over a prolonged period of the child's life, ideally from the time of conception through adolescence to maturity. This is a longitudinal method similar to that employed at the Fels Institute.

A longitudinal statistical study has been made of the indictable offences committed by those who were under 21 years of age during the period 1946 to 1957 and published under the title *Delinquent Generations* (1960). This type of study may be one method of throwing light upon the effects of parental deprivation during a child's early years, since it examines the hypothesis that children born in certain years are more likely to commit offences than others. On the basis of the data presented, the report claims that 'the greatest "crime-proneness" is thus found to be associated with that birth group who passed through their fifth year during the war.'[29]

A similar 'crime-prone' group is said to have been born during the years 1926-28. Children with these birth years would be four and five years old at the worst period of the economic depression. There seems some prima facie evidence for associating 'crime-proneness' with unusually stressful family circumstances when the children are between four and five years old.

This interpretation of the figures has been queried by Williams (1962), who suggests that later environmental factors may be more important than early deprivation.

RECONSTRUCTED DATA

Any method which enables a subject to recall what happened to him in the past may be used in reconstructing his life history.

Questionnaires were used by Radke (1946) to investigate the childhood experiences of parents. The questions were so framed that they covered the relationships between the parents being interviewed and their own parents. The questionnaire consisted of 'short declarative sentences', to which answers were given on a three-point scale.

Hypnosis may occasionally be used with suitable subjects, to enable them to revive memories of their previous life. Lake (1961) has employed LSD with carefully selected subjects, to achieve a similar purpose.

All methods of recall are subject to the distortions described by Bartlett (1932), as well as the processes of repression, selection and inadequate verbalisation. The only adequate safeguard against the falsification of information by these factors is the cross-checking of data derived from several sources.

Interviews and the *case history* approach may be utilised in recovering data about the past dimension. There is a no royal road which leads backwards into the past and no test which will guarantee to reconstruct it. The investigator must use any reliable source of information which is available to him and cross-check it whenever possible.

INFERRED DATA

Many of the projective methods already described usually yield some information about the subject's past life. He may state specifically that his father used to punish him severely, or his description of his present condition may enable the examiner to infer what the conditions of his previous life were like.

THE ASSESSMENT OF RELATIONSHIPS

CLASSIFICATION OF TESTS

Since there are a large number of techniques available for the assessment of personal and family relationships, it is convenient to classify them according to the type of response they require. This is the classification recommended by Rabin and Haworth (1960), although there are, of course, other methods of classifying tests. No method is entirely satisfactory, if only because very few tests assess only one characteristic of the individual. Even an intelligence test, individually administered, discloses much information about the subject's personality and methods of work. Tests of personality and relationships frequently disclose a wide range of information about the person being tested. A test which explores parent-child relationships will almost certainly disclose information about marital and sibling relations. Since no relationship is formed instantaneously, a projective technique which assesses the individual as he now is also discloses, if only by implication, something of the person's past history. In view of the extensive overlap between the types of information given by projective methods, the tests in this section are grouped according to the nature of the responses they elicit.

'ASSOCIATIVE' PROJECTION TECHNIQUES

These tests are so called because the responses made to them depend upon the general principle of 'association of ideas'. The stimuli used in the test are frequently in picture form, and the subject verbalises the ideas and attitudes which he associates with the figures in the pictures.

The Family Relations Indicator is an 'association' method of assessing individual attitudes as well as family relationships (Howells and Lickorish, 1962). This technique employs a series of 33 pictures, drawn to the authors' specifications, showing the following basic family groups: parents; father and child; mother and child (Fig. 4); child alone; sibling group; and child and baby. Each of these situations is replicated three times. There are three introductory cards, showing family groups, which are used to acquaint the child with the test procedure. There is a separate, but parallel, series of cards for boys and girls, the only difference between the two series is the sex of the child in the picture.

The cards are presented informally, and the child is asked to say what he thinks the people are doing, or saying, in the pictures. The child is not asked for a story, but is encouraged simply to make statements about the activities of the figures on the cards. The replication of the scenes has a cumulative effect upon the amount of information provided by the child.

It also provides an internal verification of what he says, since the statements he makes about one of the three replicated cards may be corroborated by those made about the other two.

The replies are 'scored' by selecting from them the items which describe the child's attitude towards other members of the family, or his relationships with them. These items may simply be summarised, or reported more formally, using the following headings to indicate the

FIG. 4. Specimen card from the Family Relations Indicator.

relationships between child and parent: punitive actions; verbal hostility; deprivations; indifference and positive relationship. The child's own attitudes which have been recorded by this technique include: verbal defiance; physical aggression; antisocial activity; guilt feelings; apprehension and jealousy.

The validation study showed that the information given in the responses was supported to a very high degree by the information available from independent psychiatric sources. Although this technique does not disclose all the information about a given family which is theoretically available, what it does disclose has a high degree of validity. The authors stress that the technique should be used in conjunction with other methods of investigation and point out that it is most useful in assessing child-parent relationships. Very little phantasy, or wish-fulfilment, has been found in the responses, and there is no need to interpret the results according to a particular psychological theory. This technique has been developed for use with neurotic children only.

The Test of Family Attitudes by Jackson (1952) consists of eight pictures drawn in black and white with blurred outlines, showing father and mother with one or more children, a child by himself, a father and child, and a mother with a cradle. The child is asked to describe what he sees in the pictures, and there are standard questions which may be asked concerning each picture. The scoring of the test consists in making a general summary of the attitudes and relationships disclosed. The test may be used to discriminate between normal, neurotic and delinquent children (Jackson, 1950).

The Children's Apperception Test (C.A.T.) by Bellak (1950) may be used to explore some family relationships. It consists of ten pictures showing a wide variety of scenes in which animals only are involved. There are five indoor scenes, showing two or more members of a family, which might provide some indication of parent-child relations. A more obvious child-parent card shows two large bears having a tug-of-war, with a small bear helping one of the large bears. The sex of the bears is not indicated. 'Association' responses are required. The test is based upon psychoanalytical theory, and although it should be interpreted in terms of this theory, it will yield useful information if the replies are taken at their face value. Animals are employed in these pictures, because it is said that a child will more readily identify with animal than human figures. Biersdorf and Marcuse (1953) have thrown some doubt on this theory, but it has not been disproved.

The Thematic Apperception Test (T.A.T.) may be used to explore the family relationships of adolescents and adults. It was devised by Murray (1943) and is an 'association' type of test, based on psychoanalytic concepts and designed to give a 'personality picture' in depth. However, 12 of the cards may be used to clarify the following family relationships: father-son; mother-son; mother-daughter; husband-wife; sibling rivalry; and general family relations. When used for this purpose, the responses are evaluated in terms of interpersonal relationships, and the examiner himself must select the relevant statements from the replies without 'interpreting' them.

Symonds Picture Story Test (Symonds, 1948) is suitable for use with adolescents. Of the 20 cards comprising the test, six may be used for elucidating parent-child relationships and five more for investigating boy-girl or sibling relations.

In describing these three tests based upon psychoanalytic theory, we have advocated the dubious procedure of using only a part of the standard test for a rather different purpose from that for which it was originally intended. The justification for this is twofold. First, there are no other picture projective tests for adults and adolescents which provide family scenes, so that one must use what is available. Secondly, there is the purely pragmatic reason that these tests have been found useful for investigating family relationships when used in the manner described.

'LIMITED CHOICE' TECHNIQUES

Some methods of investigating family relationships employ a 'limited choice', or 'forced choice', technique. In this method the subject is presented with a series of questions, or problems, and also with a small number of possible answers to each question, and he must choose his own reply from *one* of these *specified* answers. The number of alternatives from which a choice must be made varies usually from two to five, according to the type of test. A typical example of this method is the questionnaire, with its Yes, No or ? as the possible answer to each item.

The 'Two Houses' Technique. This method has been described by Szyrynski (1963), and a descriptive manual is in preparation. The child is asked to name all the members of his family, including animals, or pets, if he wishes. The names are recorded, and two houses are drawn on a sheet of paper. The child is asked to divide his family between the two houses. He then *invites* members from *the other* house *to his house*. Finally, he *sends away* members from his house to the other house. The child's preferences for the various members of his family may thus be investigated.

The Family Relations Test by Anthony and Bene (1957) is a complex 'forced choice' method. The number of possible replies are determined because they are printed on cards. But all the cards must be allotted to figures representing members of the subject's family. Hence, *what* the subject says about his family is fixed by the statements on the cards. But the subject himself chooses the person *to whom* these statements apply. The material for the test consists of cardboard figures to which are attached little boxes, into which the cards are 'posted'. There is a choice of figures, and the child selects those which he considers represents his own family. He is then presented with the cards, on which are printed statements, such as 'I like this person to cuddle me.' He is asked to put each card into the box attached to the person to whom the statement applies. The method of scoring consists of counting the number of 'outgoing' and 'incoming' positive and negative feelings which exist between the subject and the members of his family. The statements on the cards describe affectionate, hostile and sexual feelings, together with parental over-protection and over-indulgence. Separate sets of cards and record forms are provided for older and younger children. The results may be recorded graphically, thus showing at a glance the main positive and negative feelings between the subject and his family. Whilst it is possible to use this test without interpreting the results according to any particular psychological theory, the F.R.T. is based theoretically upon psychoanalytical concepts.

'COMPLETION' PROJECTIVE TESTS

The 'completion' method is a combination of the 'forced choice' and 'association' techniques, since the words which form the initial stimulus do, to some extent, predetermine the answer, and the reply which is given arises by 'association' with the verbal stimulus.

The Rosenzweig Picture Frustration Test (Rosenzweig, 1948) consists of 24 cartoon-like pictures showing two or three persons, one of whom has made a statement which is enclosed in a balloon. The subject is asked to write an appropriate reply in the blank balloon provided in the same picture. Since many of these pictures show family scenes, it is possible to use them as a means of eliciting relationships between parents, children and siblings. The technique was originally devised to elicit personality traits and characteristics rather than interpersonal relationships. In practice, however, it does disclose a limited number of family relationships very clearly. There are separate forms of the test for adults and children.

The Incomplete Sentences Blank in the form evolved by Rotter and Rafferty (1950) consists of 40 initial phrases, or 'stems', to which the subject adds sufficient words to make complete sentences. Each response is rated on a six-point scale, and the total score indicates the subject's degree of maladjustment. Ten of the 'stems' suggest family or personal relationships, and it should be relatively easy to evolve a blank devoted entirely to eliciting family relationships.

There are many variations of these incomplete sentence blanks, but typical 'stems' for completion are: 'My father is . . .'; 'I am afraid of . . .'; 'The happiest time in my life . . .'. According to Thorne (1955), 'No single form has yet been widely standardised and studied on many clinical populations. Further research is necessary to perfect item structure so as to facilitate projective values.'

Replies to I.S.B. are difficult to handle statistically, because they cannot be reduced easily to a numerical form. Bene (1957) has devised a method of coding them so that other information, besides a simple total score, may be readily extracted from the responses. Briefly, her method is as follows. She uses a code consisting of two-digit numbers. The first of the two digits represents the objects of the responses, which are divided into nine categories denoted by the numbers 0 to 8 inclusive. The second digit represents an attitude towards the object. Here the coding becomes slightly more complex, since the first digits are grouped into four classes and the second digit varies in meaning according to the class of the first digit.

Using this method, a very high level of agreement has been reached between two judges assessing over a thousand items. A statistical analysis of the data revealed that 'the significant differences that were obtained fall into a consistent meaningful pattern. This seems to show that they are not artefacts of the test situation but originate in real differences between the boys' attitudes.'

RATING SCALES

Rating scales are widely used to assess traits and relationships, or any quality which varies in degree or intensity. In assessing family relationships a bipolar scale is frequently employed. Thus the relationship between father and son may be rated on a scale ranging from harshness to kindness.

$$1 \quad 2 \quad 3 \quad 4 \quad 5$$

Kindness |——|——|——|——| Harshness

Some scales use seven or nine points for rating, but for most practical purposes the five-point scale is sufficient. There are literally hundreds of bipolar traits which may be used, so that it is necessary to select the most appropriate scales for assessing the dimension under investigation.

Another common variation of this method is the verbal rating of the frequency of a specific activity. Thus a punishing response could be rated thus:

$$1 \quad\quad\quad 2 \quad\quad\quad 3$$

Smacks   never   sometimes   often

For statistical purposes this verbal rating is easily converted into a three-point scale. These rating scales may be used by any member of the family to record his assessment of any other member, and also by teachers to record their assessment of schoolchildren. Since the answers on these scales may be made directly in terms of numbers, they lend themselves very readily to statistical analysis. Correlations between the ratings of the members of a family may be easily calculated, and a factor analysis may be made of the resulting matrix.

The most extensive application of rating scales to family behaviour has been made by Baldwin, Kalhorn and Breese (1949) at the Fels Research Institute, Yellow Springs, Ohio. This scale is now described in some detail.

Fels Rating Scale

The authors just mentioned have devised a rating scale for recording parent behaviour by the social worker or other person visiting the home. A clinical summary is used in addition to this rating scale, and the records supplement each other. The fundamental assumption underlying the development of these scales is that the central figure in any clinical work is the research worker himself, and a technique which enables the worker to record all the subtleties which he perceives, and which demands all the precision of which he is capable, should increase the value of his opinions. The usefulness of these scales depends upon the conviction that the rating method can be precise and scientific. Whilst the authors have shown that their scales have a high degree of reliability, the scales are not as reliable as well-designed psychometric tests, although they approach them in this respect. There are 30 rating scales altogether, each on a separate sheet, and ten different children may be rated for a single variable on each sheet. The children may be from ten different homes or siblings from several homes, according to convenience. By rating ten different cases on each sheet, the rater is able to use subject-to-subject comparisons for arriving at a rating; and by enforcing the separation of the ratings of different variables on the same child, the tendency to maintain a preconceived relationship between variables is minimised. At the top left-hand side of the sheet is a box for the names and ages of each of the ten children. Below this box are ten vertical, parallel lines, and at the right-hand side of these lines there are simple descriptions of the trait to be rated. The rating is made by placing an X on the vertical rating line, at, or near, the cue which best describes the parent's behaviour towards the child. In addition to the X marking the assessment of the child, two supplementary ratings are made at the same time. The first is called *tolerance* and indicates the 'region of uncertainty' which the rater has concerning his rating. This *tolerance* is marked by a horizontal line both above and below the X. The other supplementary rating is the 'range of variability' of parent behaviour which the observer believes would occur in certain situations. The limits of this range are indicated by a horizontal bracket above and below the X.

The raw score for the ratings is determined by measuring the distance from the bottom of the line to the point X. As a matter of statistical convenience, the raw scores are usually arranged so that they rate from 10 to 99. The position of the rating X is measured to the nearest millimetre. In the Fels programme, about 200 children have been rated every six months, and from these ratings means and standard deviations have been calculated. The raw scores for each child have been transformed into sigma indices which are equivalent to T-scores.

SOCIAL ADJUSTMENT GUIDES

Stott (1958) has produced a series of enquiry forms for assessing the child's relation to school, to the family and to residential care. The enquiry form, or guide, for assessing adjustment within the family provides a series of short statements which are indicative of behaviour and relationships arranged under the following headings: home and family; child's talk about home; parent-child relationship; the mother and father; child's behaviour and ways in the home; health and development and social worker's impression of child. Statements describing the child's behaviour, or attitudes, are underlined and then summarised by transferring the relevant items to headed columns on a 'diagnostic form'. A 'key' is also provided, so that the various items may be arranged in categories like anxious over-concern, hostility-anxiety conflict, estrangement and non-tolerance. The data for use in these guides is gathered by observation and by interviews, and is therefore subject to the errors inherent in these procedures. The use of the forms is an attempt to group items of behaviour in a diagnostically significant manner and, as Stott says, 'to objectify and to quantify phenomena which in the past have mainly been within the preserves of literature, clinical practice and general worldly wisdom'.

MARITAL RELATIONSHIPS

Relationships between husband and wife may be disclosed by several of the projective procedures already described. So far, very few techniques have been devised specifically to assess marital relationships. Some research into methods of assessing marital difficulties is being carried out in America, but little has so far been published. Two methods of investigation may, however, be mentioned.

'Matched Groups' Technique

The well-known method of using a control group and an experimental group has been used by Dicks (1959) to investigate marital breakdowns. He used a sample of 157 disturbed marriages amongst people of relatively high social status and education, and he matched these with those whose marriages were undisturbed.

The Colour Matching Technique

This method was devised by Goodrich and Boomer (1963) as 'a brief experimental technique for studying the coping behaviour of husband and wife when they attempt to resolve a marital conflict'. The procedure has been applied to 50 marital pairs and is reported to have produced 'meaningful differences' in the methods of resolving interpersonal conflicts.

Husband and wife are seated opposite to each other, with a large two-sided easel between them. Neither can see the other, but both can see the examiner. In front of each subject, on the easel, are five columns of coloured squares. In each column are six squares which are different shades of the same colour. The squares are numbered, and the columns are labelled with the name of the basic colour.

The examiner presents a colour, and husband and wife match it with the colours in front of them. When they have each *independently* made the colour match, they discuss it with each other. The colours are so arranged that disagreement is certain to arise over the matching, at irregular intervals. Behavioural difficulties are disclosed as the discussions about the colour matchings proceed.

PARENTAL ATTITUDES

The attitude of parents towards their children may be assessed by means of a suitable picture projective technique and by some of the other methods already mentioned. There are also a few methods, specifically devised to measure parent-child attitudes and relationships, which have made use of questionnaires, rating scales and even films.

The Parental Attitude Research Instrument (P.A.R.I.) is a series of scales for assessing parental attitudes towards child-rearing and has been developed by Schaefer and Bell (1958). This instrument is a questionnaire of 115 items and measures 23 variables. Each variable is represented by five items, and its reliability is adequate only for the comparison of group results. The authors suggest that the instrument should be used to make a preliminary survey of a new field of investigation, using fairly large samples. Then, if some of the variables are found to discriminate between the attitudes being tested, these variables should be used alone, with a larger number of items, so that a greater reliability may be obtained. Thus perhaps only four or five scales would be employed, instead of the 23 in the original Parental Attitude Research Instrument. As at present constituted, the P.A.R.I. is what Cronbach has described as a 'broad band-width' instrument, and its authors point out that in this type of assessment a choice must be made between 'comprehensiveness of coverage and precision of measurement'. The instrument should be administered individually, or in closely supervised, small groups. Each item is answered by one of four categories: strong or mildly agree; or mildly or strongly disagree. These replies are rated on a four-point scale, and the score for each variable is the sum of the ratings thus obtained. The 23 scales include the following, encouraging verbalisation: breaking the will; marital conflict; strictness; irritability; deification (i.e. regarding the parents as *absolute* authorities); suppression of sexuality and of aggression; ascendancy and dependency of the mother.

The original P.A.R.I. was designed for assessing mother-child attitudes, but a form for fathers has also been developed, using 30 variables (or scales) with eight items in each. Some of the variables included in the father form, but not in the mother form of P.A.R.I., are: harsh punishment; deception; inconsiderateness of wife; autonomy of child; and suppression of affection.

The authors of the P.A.R.I. review recent work on the study of parent-child relationships in the paper already cited and point out some of the weaknesses in the research methods adopted. They also provide the full list of items used in their scale, which they permit to be reproduced when suitably acknowledged.

Situational responses were employed by Jackson (1956), who devised a series of questions about situations which might occur in the home. Parents were asked how they would react to these situations. Their replies were recorded on a bipolar scale ranging from 'little pressure toward conformity' to 'great pressure toward conformity'. Eleven situations were described, like 'taking money from your purse' or 'glancing into your bedroom'.

A projective puppet film has been devised by Haworth and Woltmann (1959), which may be used to detect sibling rivalry and aggression towards parents as well as personality traits. The film depicts a boy who is jealous of his baby sister. A witch helps him to get rid of the baby, who is rushed to hospital desperately ill. The boy is filled with remorse; he recalls and kills the witch. The baby recovers, and the parents demonstrate their love for the little boy. The film is shown to a group of 10-15 children. Half-way through the showing, the film is stopped and the children are asked to complete the story. At the end of the film each child is asked, individually, a set of standard questions centring upon the boy in the story. (Haworth, 1961.)

Films have also been employed in a variation of the picture projective method devised by Eiserer (1949). He presented both still and motion pictures to adolescents, in order to elicit stories about adolescent-parent relationships. A series of 15 pictures was used; and they were divided into those with a positive tone, a negative tone and a neutral tone. The responses to them were rated as: (i) descriptive only; (ii) descriptive with feelings and attitudes; (iii) feelings, attitudes and desires mainly, with a few descriptions; and (iv) feelings, desires and attitudes only. The results were evaluated by an Analysis of Variance. Eiserer found that the motion pictures tended to produce more verbalisation than the still pictures, but those that were effective motion pictures were effective still ones. There was not sufficient evidence to warrant the production of a motion picture series, since the information produced by the motion pictures was not so much greater than that produced by the stills.

A 'multi-dimensional' study of the effects of parental attitudes was carried out by Radke (1937). Parents first completed extensive questionnaires and afterwards were interviewed about their attitudes and practices of child rearing. Data concerning the children's behaviour was obtained by interviewing the children, collecting ratings from their teachers and by projective techniques, including doll play.

A further interesting assessment made by Radke was the attempt to correlate certain kinds of behaviour with certain types of home.

FATHER-CHILD RELATIONSHIPS

There are relatively few techniques specifically designed to evaluate the relationship between father and child. This may be due to a cultural bias, which regards the care of the child as almost exclusively the concern of mother. It may also be due to the failure to consider the value of 'parenting', as opposed to 'mothering', suggested by Howells (1962).

Father's attitude may be assessed by projective techniques, but the absence of father from home for prolonged periods during World War II provided a natural, experimental situation for comparing 'families with father' and 'families without father'.

Doll play was used by Bach (1946) to investigate the effect of father's prolonged absence from home upon American children between eight and ten years of age. Using a standardised doll play situation, he compared the phantasies produced by 20 children whose fathers had been away from home with a similar number whose fathers had not been absent.

MOTHER-CHILD RELATIONSHIPS

Methods of assessing the influence of the mother upon the child are difficult to devise. It is almost impossible to create an experimental situation to test out this variable, but some naturally occurring situations have been utilised for this purpose. Howells and Layng (1955), in studying the effects of the separation of the child from its mother, compared a neurotic group of children attending a psychiatric clinic with a control group of mentally healthy children. The mean age of each group was 6.9 years and 6.5 years, respectively. They found that separation caused no harm to the children, and that some of them enjoyed and benefited from it. Heinicke (1956) studied the effects of the extent of separation by comparing the children in a day nursery with those in a residential nursery. The two groups were standardised as far as possible, so that the amount of separation was the major variable.

Spitz (1945) compared two groups of institutionalised children with respect to retardation. One group was in a nursery attached to a women's prison and so their mothers had access to them, whilst the members of the other group were not visited by their mothers.

An experimental approach to the effects of the mother on the child was devised by Rheingold (1956). He arranged for one person to have the care of eight babies and for them to be given as much individual care as possible. The control group was cared for by several people according to institutional routine. The dependent variable was the amount of social responsiveness manifested by the child.

These studies indicate the manner in which the assessment of the mother-child relationship may be attempted. For ethical reasons, the field of true experiment is very restricted, and the most promising studies are those undertaken in conditions which naturally lend themselves to experimental manipulation.

An observational method was employed by Merrill (1946) to investigate mother-child interaction. She observed mother and child through a one-way screen and recorded her observations, using a system of notation. Thirty-two behavioural categories were employed in recording the observations, which were made at very short intervals. The record was subsequently analysed under 11 variables, as follows: lack of contact; structurising; structuring the change in activity; helping; criticising; non-cooperation; teaching; interactive play; directing; interfering; and co-operation.

A standard play situation was also devised by Merrill (1946) as a more objective means of assessing mother-child interaction. The standard play situation was set up, and mother and child were introduced into it. The interactions of the couple were observed through a one-way screen for two periods of 30 minutes each. Before the second session took place, each mother was told that the child's play during the first session had not demonstrated its capacities to the full. This criticism tended to increase the mother's direction of her child's activities.

A less artificial observational method was used by Tucker, as reported by Thompson (1952). In this investigation, Tucker compared the behaviour of mothers towards their own children with their behaviour towards other children. This was carried out in a home nursery school, in which each mother was, in turn, an assistant teacher. Her responses and attitudes towards both her own children and the others were recorded by an observer.

A rating scale was used by Shohen (1949) to measure mother-child relationships. The scale consisted of 85 items classified into the following categories: dominant; possessive; ignoring; miscellaneous. The items were indicative of parental attitudes towards children, and there was evidence to show that the scales differentiated between the mothers of 'problem' and 'non-problem' children.

SIBLING RELATIONSHIPS

The rating of matched groups of siblings was undertaken by Koch (1955), who chose her subjects so that each child in the sample had one sibling differing from him in age by anything from 25 to 48 months. There were 128 children aged 5 or 6 years in the sample, and they were rated by their teachers on 58 traits. Of these traits, 24 were taken from the Fels Child Behavior Scales and 34 from the California Behavior Inventory for Nursery School Children. The ratings were converted to nine-point scales, which were then normalised. The sample was divided into eight groups, according to sex and to whether the siblings were older or younger than the members of the group. Groups were matched for age, occupation of father and the character of the neighbourhood in which the subjects lived.

The analysis of the data consisted in comparing the ordinal position and the sex of subject and sibling in order to ascertain if these were correlated with the traits of the children in the sample.

Interaction in pairs was a method used by Jack (1934) to assess the dominance of one child over another, during the pre-school period, and it has been summarised by Thompson (1952). Jack placed children in pairs in a potentially competitive situation and observed them through a one-way screen for periods of five minutes at a time. Ascendant responses were credited to the child who: (i) verbally or forcefully attempted to secure the play material; (ii) succeeded in securing the materials, or defended them, or snatched them back; (iii) directed and secured the compliance of his companion, or verbally attempted to do so; (iv) forbade or criticised his companion; (v) provided a pattern which his companion imitated.

Whilst this method was designed to test children in a peer group, it could be adapted to assess sibling rivalry, if the age difference between the sibs was small.

THE ASSESSMENT OF THE FAMILY GROUP

FEATURES OF FAMILY GROUPS

The family group possesses many characteristics which are similar to other groups and may, therefore, to that extent be treated like them (Moreno, 1934). But, as Hoffman and Lippitt (1960) have pointed out, there are important differences between the family and other groups. Each member of the family group has a status based on sex and age, and there is a marked division between the parents and the child. The family group in Western society is necessarily small, and each member has a unique significance. The family group also has a 'natural' biological history which is not possessed by other groups. The family group has standards of conduct and behaviour patterns which are peculiar to itself. They have been built up over the years, and the family's behaviour must be interpreted in the light of these traditions. The family group also varies considerably in size and duration. Membership of the group cannot be acquired, since it is bestowed by the parents.

When comparative studies are being undertaken, it is very important to ensure that the families under consideration are strictly comparable, especially as the sample numbers employed are usually, of necessity, quite small. If only some members of a family are being compared with corresponding members in another family, it is still important to ensure that the families as a whole are strictly comparable. The relationships between the sibs in a five-member family are likely to be different from those in a seven-member family, even if their ages are the same.

Family interviews, in which all the family members are seen together by the investigator, are becoming increasingly popular for diagnostic and therapeutic purposes. This method should be treated with care, for, whilst it may produce reliable information about family dynamics, it may result in the production of artefacts. The members are in a highly artificial situation, and may over-respond or 'play to the gallery' during the interview. To quote Hoffman and Lippitt (1960) again, 'revealing behavioural units do not occur frequently, nor at predictable times, and they may not occur at all in front of an observer.' Some of the methods described in this chapter attempt to overcome these objections, by confronting the family group with disagreements between the members and so producing a vigorous discussion, or by leaving the group to themselves and recording their activities with or without their knowledge.

The family interview method may at present be regarded as potentially useful, but its usefulness is unproven and there appears to be no evidence to show that this group approach is superior to the method of individual therapy.

Interaction between the members of the family is usually assessed by projection, questionnaire or rating scale methods. Besides the one-to-one relationships between family members, there are relationships between the sub-groups within the family to be considered. The larger the family, the greater the possibility of the development of sub-groups within it. When the family is extended to include the in-laws, the number of possible constellations becomes very large. The *individual* attitudes and characteristics of the family members may be assessed by the usual standard tests, but we are concerned in this section with the reaction *between* family members.

The method of 'revealed differences', devised by Strodtbeck (1951), is applied by Titchener (1962) to the family as a whole in the following way: The whole family is invited to attend the clinic, and upon their arrival each member is given a questionnaire with 15 items calling for opinions on various aspects of family life. They are asked to complete these questionnaires independently of the rest of the family, and this usually occupies about 15 minutes. The questionnaires are then collected, and the replies of each of the other members of the family are recorded on each member's questionnaire. The papers are then returned to the various members. The family group is then invited into the conference room with a one-way screen and sound recording apparatus. This equipment is in full view of the family. They are then told that they were not expected to agree on all the items in the questionnaire, and, by looking at the answers which other members of the family have given, they can see for themselves the difference between their own opinion and the opinions of the rest of the family. The group is then asked to make a thorough and freely spoken attempt to reconcile the differences which have been revealed. The experimenter leaves the room and observes the ensuing discussion through the one-way screen, and the whole proceeding is filmed and recorded. An analysis of the results obtained in this way has isolated and demonstrated many very important mechanisms which the family develops as a result of years of living together.

The interaction method of assessing the family, according to Haley (1959), consists of considering the family in relation to the ways in which its members may communicate with one another. To do this, it is necessary to have the family together in one group and to observe the ways in which they act and react with each other along the following lines.

1. Whatever the family does when it is together is equivalent to some kind of action between its members. To every person's word or action, a reply will be made by one or more of the other members. Even when one person appears to 'do nothing' this is in fact a reaction to the situation.

2. Action of some kind is inevitable within the group. This may take the form of bodily activity, speech, gestures or refusal to speak.

3. Whatever is said or done by one member of the group will be qualified in some way by the others. They may object, or twist the statements, or deprecate what the other person has said.

4. The actions and statements of an individual may or may not be congruent with each other. Thus, the tone of voice in which a statement is uttered may or may not match the content of the statement. This incongruency is not the same as contradiction, but it is rather a suggestion that the statement made is not to be taken too seriously.

5. Within a group some kind of leadership will nearly always emerge, at least over a period of time. In the family group, father or mother may try to dominate the scene, or each of them or both may give way to an aggressive child.

6. Even within a small group of three people it is possible for two sub-groups to be formed. Thus, mother and daughter may combine against father, or father and mother may agree in rejecting the child.

7. The way in which blame is handled by the group is also instructive. There may be a scapegoat, and the mechanism of projection may come into play, or, in a more reasonable group, blame will be apportioned and accepted in a rational manner.

These are some of the many features which may be observed within a three-person system of interaction. But it is difficult to devise a satisfactory scheme by which such interaction may be recorded in a reasonably objective and statistically manipulable manner.

The family group interview is a complex affair, and some method of analysing the discussion and making it amenable to assessment and interpretation is needed. Clearly, a whole mass of verbal responses given in such an interview is quite unmanageable in the raw state. Jackson, Riskin and Satir (1961) have described the following method of analysing a family interview.

The interview is recorded on a tape and its content is analysed under two main headings: interactional dynamics, and communication. These analyses are arranged in columns parallel to the items in the transcript, as follows:

Transcript	Interactional Dynamics Analysis	Communication Analysis

In addition to the actual text of the responses, the transcript column contains descriptive comments about the tone of voice, pauses, laughter, mimicking and other expressive items.

The interactional dynamics analysis concentrates on three perceptions: (i) the subject's perception of the self; (ii) his perception of the other; and (iii) the perception of the other in relation to the subject's own self (i.e. 'How I see you seeing me'). These perceptions form the basis of three types of inferences about the motives underlying them. One type of inference answers the question, what is the subject implying about his relationships by the kind of statements he makes? Another inference attempts to reconstruct the early life experience of the subject, 'on the assumption that earlier experiences with parental figures affect the ways that one later perceives one's self and others. . . .' The third type of inference attempts to indicate how the children are related to the marital partnership. The inferences are placed in the interactional column, along with any necessary quotation from the transcript. Parentheses and italics are used to distinguish between statements of a low and high inferential nature.

The communication analysis distinguishes between 'symmetrical' and 'complementary' statements. The former type of statement 'is a comment on the equality of some aspect of a relationship.' A simple example of this comment would be discussion between peers of their relative prowess in some skill. The 'complementary' statement is one that 'asks' or 'offers'. By a convention, the statement that 'asks' is called the 'complementary one-down position', or CD, and the statement which 'offers' is termed the 'complementary one-up position', or CU.

The communications between persons may also be analysed in terms of the way in which one 'message' in the communication 'qualifies' another, by either reinforcing or contradicting it. If one message contradicts another, it is labelled a 'disqualification', which may be either 'sequential' or 'incongruent'. A 'sequential disqualification' is a 'verbal contradiction', like the phrase 'go away closer'. An 'incongruent disqualification' occurs when there is a discrepancy (i) between the statement and the affective manner in which it is made, or (ii) between the statement and its context. The term 'message' is not synonymous with 'communication', since the latter may contain more than one of the former. Thus words, gesture and tone of voice may give three (different) messages in one communication.

If there are frequent disqualifications in the conversation of the family, then there are likely to be many 'incomplete transactions'. These arise because one member does not make his meaning clear to another.

No attempt has been made to 'code' the analysed interview any further. The analysis is presented in parallel columns with the appropriate comments added in parentheses.

Interaction between husband and wife has been assessed by using a questionnaire devised by Herbst and called the Day-at-Home Measure (Mussen, 1960). It consists of 33 items about simple household tasks, and each item is followed by a list of family members. The replies indicate the member who *does* or *should do* the task, the one who *may* do it, and those who *never do* it. The subject also indicates who makes the *decisions* concerning the various tasks. Herbst chose the items to represent household duties, child care and control, social activities and economic activities.

This questionnaire was originally intended for use with children, and there are many variations of the basic procedure. Hoffman scored the *doing of* and the *deciding about* items separately. Others distinguished between the joint activities of husband and wife and the individual performance of items, and also the *frequency* of each activity by each parent. The answers have also been scored to assess sex role, reversal, and the amount and type of participation.

Doll play is another method which may be used to investigate the present relationships between the members of a family, as described by Levin and Wardwell (1962).

The child is presented with a set of dolls representing its family, and is allowed to manipulate them, as it pleases, and also to talk about what is happening to the dolls at the same time. A doll's house without a roof may be provided, or the child may be given material out of which he may construct an indoor or outdoor scene. Usually pre-school children are chosen for this type of investigation, but several studies have been reported with children up to the age of ten years. Both boys and girls are usually willing to engage in this form of play.

It is not essential for the child to make up a story about what he is doing, but there is always some 'interaction' between the child and the investigator. This interaction may be reduced to the bare minimum, or restricted to levels laid down by Pintler (1945). Alternatively, the experimenter may adopt a constant attitude of permissiveness, without interfering with the child's play. The sessions may last for a predetermined period, or the child may be allowed to play as long as he wishes.

Variations of the doll play technique include: (a) A definite set-up is arranged for the child, and its reactions to this are noted. (b) The dolls may be used simply as a means of gaining the child's interest, so that he will talk more readily to the examiner. (c) The child may be asked to complete a story on the basis of a particular scene in the doll play.

A structured doll play test (S.D.P.T.) has been devised by Lynn (1959), in which ten specified situations are presented to the child in a given order. This is an attempt to standardise the procedure and hence to make the results of the doll play comparable in terms of scores.

Although this is desirable from one point of view, an important feature of doll play is its extreme flexibility with regard to the number and type of figures and their setting. There is some evidence to suggest that elaborate material is no more productive than crude material, and that a doll family which duplicates the child's own family is more productive than a standard set of dolls. The house setting for doll play may produce more conventional reactions on the part of the child than does a less structured setting. More, rather than less, interaction between child and experimenter tends to produce a large number of non-stereotyped responses, more aggression and more changes of theme. The responses are also influenced by the sex of the experimenter.

The reliability of the doll play sessions may be assessed by correlating the responses in two consecutive sessions, or between the former and the latter half of the same session.. Coefficients of the order of 0.70 have been claimed for both these methods.

The validity of the results of play sessions is very difficult to establish, because of the phantasy and released aggression which are manifested in them. There is a wide disagreement between reported results, but two authors claim that probably 75% of the child's responses replicate his experiences.

Aggression has been throughly explored by means of doll play, and this is clearly of immense importance in family relationships. Other family topics amenable to this method of investigation are phantasies of father, parental roles, sibling rivalry, hostility, sex differences, separation from parents, and the preferred parent.

Relationship between peers

A 'peer' is defined by English and English (1958) as 'a person deemed an equal for the purpose in hand', or 'a companion or associate on roughly the same level of age or endowment'. The latter definition is preferable in the present context. Relationships between peers exist within the class-room and between children and their playmates and associates. A 'peer group' may be formed of children (or adults) on the basis of physical propinquity, mutual acquaintances, or common interests. The relationships that exist within these peer groups may be assessed by sociometric techniques which were first described by Moreno (1934).

A simple sociometric assessment may be carried out by asking each child in the peer group to name which member of the group he would like for a partner in some specified activity. In a small group of seven children the results of these choices might be represented by the diagram in Fig. 5.

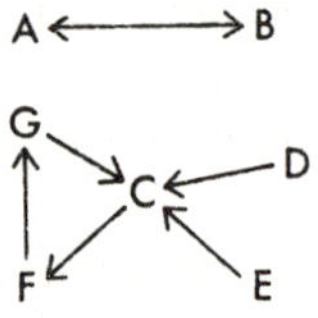

Fig. 5. Sociometric diagram showing choices made by seven children in a peer group.

The choices are represented by the arrows. A and B have chosen each other. D, E and G have chosen C, F has chosen G, whilst C has chosen F. If second choices are also called for, then the connections become more complex. In this group, A and B form a sub-group, D and E are isolates (i.e. they are not chosen by anyone), and C is clearly the most popular member of the group. This method discloses only those children who are liked by their peers and gives no indication of the extent to which some children are positively rejected by others.

In order to gain information about how children were *disliked* by their peers, Thompson and Powell (1951) devised a series of seven-point rating scales on which every child in the peer group rated every other child on a bipolar scale of 'acceptance-rejection'. These ratings indicate the socially popular children, and differentiate between the social non-entities and the socially rejected.

The paired comparisons technique is a more elaborate sociometric method, which requires each member of the group to make a choice between every possible pair in the group. It is a laborious procedure, but it is more reliable than those previously mentioned. It has been used extensively by Koch (1946), and the technique is described by Guilford (1936).

The amount of interaction between the members of a family, and the concomitant stresses, strains and frustrations may be related to what Bossard (1951) has called a Spatial Index for Family Interaction. This index takes account of the number of persons in the household and the consequent number of interrelations between them, together with the area of floor space in the living quarters.

ASSESSING THE MATERIAL DIMENSION

The material dimension of the family may be described in terms of income, social class, occupation, size and nature of house, neighbourhood, or geographical area. The criterion employed varies according to the research which is being undertaken. Some methods of assessment combine two or more of the above criteria into one index, others use a single criterion like occupation, which is probably the best single index available.

SOCIAL STATUS

There is no generally agreed method of defining social status, and different investigators define it in different ways. Some regard it as essentially a 'way of life', others as the possession of power over people, or possessions. Some research workers prefer to use a continuous ranking system, rather than discrete classes, thus there are 'almost as many positions as there are families to be classified' (Mussen, 1960). Different authorities have used the following criteria for assessing social status: occupation (Marx); consumption patterns (Veblem); 'other people's judgements of a family's prestige and esteem' (Warner and Lunt); and the subject's self judgement (Centers).

The British Registrar General's report defines five social classes which are used as a broad classification for the census returns. Detailed lists are provided of the various occupations included in each of these classes. For most research purposes it is sufficient to place the family within one of these five categories.

It should be remembered, however, that social status by itself is not sufficiently meaningful, and some indication of the community in which a particular family lives should also be given.

The stratified sampling method may be used to give added meaning to a given social class, since the class is then related to the ethnic and geographical environment in which the family lives. This method was used by Wechsler (1955) to specify the sample population used in the standardisation of the Wechsler Adult Intelligence Scale. He employed 13 occupational classes and also four main geographical areas. In addition, there was the usual classification by age and sex, and also further categories of urban or rural residence, length of schooling and race. The location of an individual or family within these various categories is a more precise method of stating the material dimension to which they belong than simply assigning them to an occupational class alone. The type of research which is undertaken will determine whether or not this elaborate classification is justified.

Occupational indices have been widely used to assess the material dimension of the family. Kahl and Davies (1955) made a study of 19 class indices, and concluded that the occupation of the bread-winner was, for most practical purposes, a sufficiently accurate indication of the family's social status.

The Index of Status Characteristics was developed by Warner, Meeker and Eells (1949). They combined the criteria of occupation, dwelling area, type of house and source of income.

The Index of Social Position devised by Hollingshead and Redlich (1958) uses simply occupation, dwelling area and education as its criteria.

Haer (1957) made a study of the ability of several indices to predict attitudes and behaviour. He concluded that Warner's Index of Status Characteristics has the greatest predictive power. It is worth pointing out that there is an advantage in using a well recognised method of social classification, like occupational status, since this more readily enables comparisons to be made between different studies based upon the material dimension.

THE ASSESSMENT OF FAMILY-COMMUNITY INTERACTION

The interaction of the family with the community may be assessed in four different ways: (i) The relationship of the family as a whole with the community may be described in broad caregories like political, educational, religious, and leisure time affiliations. (ii) The relation between individual members of the family and the community may be tabulated. (iii) It is also possible to take a *cross-section* of the activity of the family at any given time, using a 'time sampling' method. (iv) The relations of the family to the community may be studied over a period of years, thus giving a longitudinal survey of its community relationships.

The first type of interaction requires no specific test for its evaluation. It is sufficient to state the relevant category and the members of the family who are included in it. It is essential to make this assessment when matched pairs, or groups of families, are being investigated with respect to a given variable.

The second type of interaction may be assessed by recording the length of time each member of the family spends in activities outside the home. A sample analysis of the interaction between the community and a family of three people is shown in Table 1. This analysis also records the amount of time each member of the family spends at home. The activities for a whole week are grouped under 12 heads. Six of these groups relate to time spent at home, and six record non-domestic activity. The groups can be made as numerous as necessary, but most activities fall into one or other of the categories shown in Table 1. The information must be collected by interviewing the people concerned and asking them what they were doing during each half-hour period of the day. If the day is typical, then the hours spent in each activity may be multiplied by five, and to these totals are added the hours spent in each activity during Saturday and Sunday. Once the categories of activities are determined and the appropriate hours are allotted to them, the tabulated results lend themselves very readily to statistical comparison and manipulation. Of course, this method of assessing community interaction is not a 'test', nor is a formal test required. The requirements are a careful analysis of the family's activities under appropriate heads, together with a meticulous recording of how the family spends its week.

There are a number of possible errors which must be avoided in making these assessments, if they are to be compared with one another. The week must be 'typical' of the family's activities. All assessments must be made for the same week. The families must be comparable in social status, ages and numbers of children, and other variables.

Various indices could be compiled from the tabulated figures, e.g.

$$\frac{\text{time at home}}{\text{time away from home}} \qquad \frac{\text{time given to children}}{\text{total leisure time}}$$

It might well be found that there were correlations between one or more of these indices and various types of behavioural disorders.

The third method of assessing community interaction consists, fundamentally, of securing answers to the questions: 'Where were you?', or 'What were you doing?', at a certain time on a certain day. The replies are classified according to the interaction they denote, and if they are to be treated statistically they must be coded in some way.

This method is obviously subject to all the difficulties involved in accurate recall and the possible falsification of replies by the subject. If accurately carried out, it would give similar results to the second method, but it would give much less detail. It is much quicker to apply and can be used to sample certain aspects of family-community interaction. Method two is always to be preferred, although the number of families in the

TABLE 1

TABULATION OF MAJOR ACTIVITIES OF A FAMILY OF THREE DURING A SAMPLE WEEK OF 112 WAKING HOURS

Activities During a Week of 112 Hours (7 ×16)

Subject	At Home							Away From Home						
	Pers.	Hobby	Cult.	Child.	Relax.	Dom.	Total	Travel	Work	Club	Sport	Social	Other	Total
Father	8	12	6	15	6	5	52	5	45	2	5	3	—	60
Mother	12	—	7	15	5	45	84	1	10	Assoc. 2	—	10	shop 5	28
C1 (12)	7	8	Home'k 10	—		5	30	5	Sch. 35	Org. 3	5	2	—	50
C2														

sample will usually be much smaller than those subjected to method three.

The fourth method is the longitudinal one. This has already been described in relation to individuals, and its application to the family employs the same principles. Its contents includes the changing relationships of the individual members of the family to the community, as well as the relationships of the family *en masse* to the society in which it lives.

The interaction of the family with the surrounding community has received little formal study, although there have been many descriptive accounts of the relation of the family to society, like those of Folsom (1948). Perhaps the concept of 'situational determinants' outlined by Thorne (1955) might be a starting point for future formal research.

REFERENCES

1. ANTHONY, E. J., and BENE, E. 1957. A technique for the objective assessment of the child's family relationships. *J. ment. Sci.*, **103**, 541-555.
2. BACH, G. R. 1946. Father-fantasies and father-typing in father-separated children. *Child Dev.*, **17**, 63-80.
3. BALDWIN, A. L., KALHORN, J., and BREESE, F. H. 1949. The appraisal of parent behaviour. *Psychol. Monogr.*, **63**, 4.
4. BARTLETT, SIR FREDERIC C. 1932. *Remembering.* Cambridge Univ. Press, London.
5. BELLAK, L. 1950. *Children's apperception test*, 2nd rev. ed. Australian Council for Educ. Research, Melbourne.
6. BENE, E. 1957. The objective use of a projective technique. *Br. J. educ. Psychol.*, **27**, 89-100.
7. BIERSDORF, K. R., and MARCUSE, F. L. 1953. Responses of children to human and to animal pictures. *J. project. Tech.*, **17**, 455-459.
8. BLUM, G. 1950. *The Blacky pictures.* Psychological Corporation, New York.
9. BOSSARD, J. H. S. 1951. A spatial index for family interaction. *Am. sociol. Rev.*, **16**, 243-246.
10. DICKS, H. V. 1959. Marital breakdown. *Br. med. J.*, ii, 567.
11. *Delinquent generations 1960.* A Home Office Research Unit Report. H.M.S.O. London.
12. EISERER, P. E. 1949. The relative effectiveness of motion and still pictures as stimuli for eliciting phantasy stories about adolescent-parent relationships. *Genet. Psychol. Monogr.*, **39**, 205-278.
13. ENGLISH, H. B. and A. C. 1958. *A comprehensive dictionary of psychological and psychoanalytical terms.* Longmans, Green, London.
14. FENTON, J. C. 1925. *A practical psychology of babyhood.* Houghton Mifflin, Boston.
15. FOLSOM, J. K. 1948. *The family and democratic society.* Routledge & Kegan Paul, London.
16. GESELL, A., and AMATRUDA, C. S. 1952. *Developmental diagnosis.* Hoeber, New York.
17. GOODRICH, W., and BOOMER, D. S. 1963. Experimental assessment of marital modes of conflict resolution. *Family Process*, Spring 1963.
18. GUILFORD, J. P. 1936. *Psychometric methods.* McGraw-Hill, New York.
19. HAER, J. L. 1957. Predictive utility of five indices of social stratification. *Am. sociol. Rev.*, **22**, 541-546.

20. HALEY, J. 1959. The family of the schizophrenic: A model system. *J. nerv. ment. Dis.*, **129**, 357-374.

21. HAWORTH, M. R. 1961. Repeat study with a projective film for children. *J. consult. Psychol.*, **25**, 78-83.

22. HAWORTH, M. R., and WOLTMANN, A. G. 1959. *Rock-a-bye baby : A group projective test for children.* Psychological Cinema Register, University Park, Pa.

23. HOFFMAN, L. W., and LIPPITT, R. 1960. The measurement of family life variables. In MUSSEN, P. H. (ed.) *Handbook of research methods in child development.* Wiley, New York.

24. HEINICKE, C. M. 1956. Some effects of separating two-year-old children from their parents: A comparative study. *Hum. Relat.*, **9**, 106-176.

25. HOLLINGSHEAD, A. B., and REDLICH, F. C. 1958. *Social class and mental illness. A community study.* Wiley, New York.

26. HOWELLS, J. G. 1962. The nuclear family as the functional unit in psychiatry. *J. ment. Sci.*, **108**, 675-684.

27. HOWELLS, J. G., and LAYING, J. 1955. Separation experiences and mental health. *Lancet*, ii, 285-288.

28. HOWELLS, J. G., and LICKORISH, J. R. 1967. *The family relations indicator.* Oliver & Boyd, Ltd: Edinburgh.

29. JACK, L. M. 1934. An experimental study of ascendant behaviour in pre-school children. *Univ. Iowa Stud. Child Welf.*, **9**, No. 3.

30. JACKSON, L. 1950. Emotional attitudes towards the family of normal, neurotic and delinquent children. *Br. J. Psychol.*, **41**, 35-51.

31. JACKSON, L. 1952. *A test of family attitudes.* Methuen, London.

32. JACKSON, P. W. 1956. Verbal solutions to parent-child problems. *Child Dev.*, **27**, 339-351.

33. JACKSON, D. D., RISKIN, J., and SATIR, V. 1961. A method of analysis of a family interview. *Archs gen. Psychiat.*, **5**, 321-339.

34. KAHL, J. A., and DAVIS, J. A. 1955. A comparison of indexes of socio-economic status. *Am. sociol. Rev.*, **20**, 317-325.

35. KOCH, H. L. 1946. The social distance between certain racial, nationality and skin-pigmentation groups in selected populations of American school children. *J. genet. Psychol.*, **68**, 63-95.

36. KOCH, H. L. 1955. Some personality correlates of sex, sibling position and sex of sibling among five- and six-year-old children. *Genet. Psychol. Monogr.*, **52**, 3-50.

37. LAKE, F. 1961. Appendix on LSD. In DUCKER, E. N. *A Christian therapy for a neurotic world.* Allen & Unwin, London.

38. LEVIN, H., and WARDWELL, E. 1962. The research uses of doll play. *Psychol. Bull.*, **59**, 27-56.

39. LYNN, D. B. and R. 1959. The structured doll play test as a projective technique for use with children. *J. project. Tech.*, **23**, 335-344.

40. McCORD, W. and J., and VERDEN, P. 1962. Familial and behavioural correlates of dependency in male children. *Child Dev.*, **33**, 313-326.

41. MERRILL, B. 1946. A measurement of mother-child interaction. *J. abnorm. soc. Psychol.*, **41**, 37-49.

42. MORENO, J. L. 1934. *Who shall survive?* Rev. ed. 1955. Nervous & Mental Disorders Publ. Co., Washington, D.C.

43. MURRAY, H. A. 1943. *Thematic apperception test.* Harvard Univ. Press, Cambridge, Mass.

44. MUSSEN, P. H. (ed.) 1960. *Handbook of research methods in child development.* Wiley, New York.

45. PINTLER, M. H. 1945. Doll play as a function of experimenter-child inter-action and initial organisation of materials. *Child Dev.*, **16**, 145-166.
46. RABIN, A. I., and HAWORTH, M. R. 1960. *Projective techniques with children.* Grune & Stratton, New York.
47. RADKE, M. J. 1937. The relation of parental authority to children's behaviour and attitudes. *Univ. Minn. Child Welf. Monogr.*, No. 22.
48. RADKE, M. J. 1946. The relation of parental authority to children's behaviour and attitudes. *Inst. Child Welf. Monogr.*, No. 22.
49. RHEINGOLD, H. L. 1956. The modification of social responsiveness in insti-tutional babies. *Monogr. Soc. Res. Child Dev.*, **31**, 2.
50. RICHARDS, T. W., and NEWBERRY, H. 1938. Studies in fetal behaviour III. *Child Dev.*, **9**, 79-86.
51. ROSENZWEIG, S. and L. 1948. *The children's form of the Rosenzweig picture-frustration study.* St. Louis.
52. ROTTER, J. B., and RAFFERTY, J. E. 1950. *The Rotter incomplete sentences blank.* Psychological Corporation, New York.
53. SCHAEFER, E. S., and BELL, R. Q. 1958. Development of a parental attitude research instrument. *Child Dev.*, **29**, 3.
54. SCHMEIDLER, G. R. 1941. The relation of fetal activity to the activity of the mother. *Child Dev.*, **12**, 63-68.
55. SHOBEN, E. J., Jr. 1949. The assessment of parental attitudes in relation to child adjustment. *Genet. Psychol. Monogr.*, **39**, 101-148.
56. SPELT, D. K. 1948. The conditioning of the human fetus *in utero*. *J. exp. Psychol.*, **38**, 338-345. [Reprinted in this collection as No. IV.]
57. SPITZ, R. A. 1945. Hospitalism. In *Psychoanalytic study of the child*, Vol. I. International Univ. Press, New York.
58. STOTT, D. H. 1958. *The social adjustment of children.* Univ. of London Press, London.
59. STRODTBECK, F. L. 1951. Husband-wife interaction over revealed differences. *Am. sociol. Rev.*, **16**, 468-473.
60. SYMONDS, P. M. 1948. *Manual for Symonds picture story test.* Teachers College, Columbia Univ., New York.
61. SZYRYNSKI, V. 1963. The 'two-houses' technique. *Can. psychiat. Ass. J.*, April.
62. THOMPSON, G. G., and POWELL, M. 1951. An investigation of the rating-scale approach to the measurement of social status. *Educ. psychol. Measur.*, **11**, 440-455.
63. THOMPSON, G. G. 1952. *Child psychology.* Houghton Mifflin, Boston.
64. THORNE, F. C. 1955. Principles of psychological examining. *J. clin. Psychol.*
65. TITCHENER, J. L. 1962. Summary of a paper read at the Annual Meeting of the American Psychiatric Association. *Quoted by kind permission of the author.*
66. VIDICH, A. J. 1956. Methodological problems in the observation of husband-wife Interaction. *Marriage family Living*, **18**, 234-239.
67. WARNER, W. L., MEEKER, M., and EELLS, K. 1949. *Social class in America.* Science Res. Associates, Chicago.
68. WECHSLER, D. 1955. *Manual for the Wechsler adult intelligence scale.* Psycho-logical Corporation, New York.
69. WILLIAMS, G. P. 1962. *Patterns of teenage delinquency.* Christian Econ. and Soc. Res. Foundation, London.

2

THE PRESENTING PATIENT

Psychopathology in a family member is an expression of dysfunction in the whole family group. Special factors may be operating to cause a particular member of the family to be under greater stress at one period in time, and so determine the referral of this member. Those factors illustrated here are:

> Birth order
> Sex of sibling
> Scapegoating
> Anniversary reaction
> Communication insanity

XXVIII

PARENT BEHAVIOR TOWARD FIRST AND SECOND CHILDREN

JOAN KALHORN LASKO

Parent behaviour may be different towards first as contrasted with second child. The age span between siblings is a related factor.

INTRODUCTION

Understanding of the developing personality of the child demands greater and greater knowledge of the meaningful psychological stimuli to which the child is reacting and from which he is learning modes of behavior. The vague concept "home environment" has been used to indicate recognition of the framework within which the child's earliest learnings occur. But first approaches to description of this environment were limited to a sterile appraisal of the physical assets or limitations of the home—family income, number of books and magazines available, cubic footage per family resident, etc. In fact, in their determination to objectify appraisal of the home, research workers expended great effort in constructing scales which would reliably classify the so-called economic assets of a residence—for example, Chapin's *Scale for rating living room equipment*.[9]

Quick recognition, however, of the inadequacy of this approach is indicated by Baldwin *et al.*[5] writing in 1930. They state in *Farm Children*, the report of a sizable research project undertaken by members of the staff of the Iowa Child Welfare Research Station and of the State University of Iowa:

Contacts made through visiting and staying in rural homes such as are pictured here, emphasized the conviction that the material possession of a home are not its most significant assets. In this study, however, homes were measured by their physical aspects. Eventually this was seen to be a shortcoming. The lack of detailed material on specific points concerning the personalities of parents and

Reprinted from GENETIC PSYCHOLOGY MONOGRAPHS, Vol. 49, 1954, pp. 97-137.

their attitudes toward the child hinders the interpretation of home life that would contribute greatly to a study of the development of the rural child (p. 42).

The heredity-environment controversy, particularly in the realm of the child's intellectual endowment, precipitated a search for aspects of the home environment to which developmental data might meaningfully be related. Obvious parental characteristics such as education,[13] occupation,[14] were explored as potential leads to unraveling the mental growth of children; the data, incidentally, being used as happily and readily by hereditarians as by environmentalists. However, by 1936, Coffey and Wellman[10] were concluding:

> In general, these findings indicate that cultural status, as measured by occupation of father and educational level of the parents, while related to the intelligence of the children on entering preschool, was not a significant factor in the changes in intelligence of children while attending the preschools (p. 202).

During the 1930's, impetus came from the clinical fields for a more psychological description of the parent-child relationship. Symonds,[21] writing in 1939, gives David Levy, a psychiatrist, credit for bringing such concepts as rejection, overprotection, aggression, dominance, etc., into clear relief as dynamic constituents of parental emotions toward the child and, of course, as an equally important aspect of the child's perception of himself and of the world.

In spite of these new insights, progress in untangling an admittedly complex problem, has not been rapid. Fifteen years later Radke,[18] reviewing the literature on parent-child relationships, says:

> . . . (this) leaves no room to doubt that some variations of personality are related to variations within the home. The nature of these interactions, however, has not emerged with any degree of clarity. . . . Part of the difficulty that studies in this area have encountered is due to the fact that the investigators have been content with unanalyzed, generalized, stereotyped descriptions of the home. The result is a seemingly hopeless confusion of generalizations in the reported findings. . . . Understanding can be attained only as the home is perceived and studied in terms of the areas of stimulation, of freedom and restraint, of security and insecurity, of tension and satisfaction which it offers the individual child (p. 13).

The Fels Research Institute, in its longitudinal study of human development, has utilized ratings of parent-behavior, based on observations of the mother-child interaction during home visits, as a means of measurement of certain aspects of the child's psychological environment. The battery of rating scales was developed by Champney,[7,8] and represents an effort to sample significant dimensions of the parent-child relation. Research demonstrating the reliability and validity of the scales has been reported in detail elsewhere[3] and will not be repeated here. Use of the scales at Fels has permitted the description of patterns of parent behavior,[4] which, it was found, differentiated one home from another both in terms of the emotional relationship between parent and child and in terms of parental policies in handling the child. The present study was undertaken to explore intra-family dynamics by examining the consist-encies and changes in parent behavior toward first and second (representing subsequent) children.

The presumptive relation between ordinal position and certain per-sonality characteristics has long been a source of speculation and research. Adler[2] attributes definite syndromes to first, second, and third children, on the basis of his clinical experience. He says:

> The oldest child feels dethroned by the coming of his brother and wants to restore his place by fighting. Unless he can overcome in the struggle for supremacy in his universe he is apt to become depressed, peevish, more or less hopeless, and will show his hopelessness later in life if confronted by problems. He is very likely to be conservative, to understand power and to agree with it. If he is strong enough he becomes a fighting child.
>
> As for the second child, he is never alone, but is always confronted by the older child. This constant picture before him of an older and bigger child begets in him a sense of rivalry. If successful, he is an excellent type, but if defeated, for instance, if he is not able to compete successfully with the older child in work and in play, he loses hope, becomes depressed and has a bad time of it.
>
> The third child has to fight for a place in the sun, but he has no successor. This gives him a great sense of power, and if he is capable he often overcomes the older children in the family by his sense of importance. If he is not capable, he perhaps hides behind the fact of being spoiled, and becomes lazy, escaping from tasks, wasting time and making excuses (p. 14 and p. 52).

Writing in 1933, Jones[15] lists almost a hundred research articles on order of birth and its relation to other factors about the individual. Galton[12] found, for example, a disproportionate number of eldest sons among the eminent men of English science. Terman's data[22] on gifted children and Cattell's figures[6] for American men of science are in essential agreement with Galton. Other studies have attempted to relate birth order with varying personality characteristics or levels of adjustment, only to report contradictory or inconclusive findings. For example, Stagner and Katzoff[20] administered the Bernreuter to 430 male college students and report there were no significant differences in scores related to birth order. Krout,[16] on the other hand, using a schedule requiring verbal replies, lists a number of findings of statistical relationships between personality traits and ordinal position. And Abernethy,[1] using the Bernreuter and the Bell Inventories on a group of college women, declares that the oldest child is more aggressive, less neurotic, and better adjusted than later born in-dividuals.

Dean,[11] however, in a study where mothers were asked to do paired comparisons of their two children (like-sexed siblings, in this instance, under seven years of age) found rather consistent personality differences ascribed to the two children. The first child was described as more worried, sensitive, and excitable, and more dependent on adults, while the second child was more affectionate, independent, and physically aggressive toward peers. It appears, then, that the adult in close relation to the two children perceives them as possessing differing syndromes of personality characteristics.

An effort to systematize psychological environmental influences and relate them to the needs of children may be found in the growth study conducted under the auspices of various departments of Harvard University by Sanford and associates.[19]

Here, from intensive clinical interviews with parents (primarily mothers), judgments of "environmental press" were made according to the Murray variables.[17] "Family position" was considered one such press, combining Murray's variables, p Rival and p Birth of Sibling. The needs of the children themselves had been assessed, by a variety of techniques, and were also expressed in the Murray framework. Tabulations were then made of the number of eldest, middle, or youngest children appearing in the "high" or "low" groups on a given need. These findings will not be reported in detail, since the small number of cases involved did not permit the relating of any press other than the simple one of family position to the children's needs. That is, no attempt was made to relate the parent behavior (expressed as syndromes of press) to the need systems of the oldest or youngest child. However, the authors hypothesize:

> In an attempt to simplify the meaning of these positions in the family, we may say that in general the eldest child is reacting passively to over-training on the one hand and to a loss, through the birth of siblings, of prestige, love and attention on the other. The middle child never having monopolized affection has nothing to lose and everything to gain through organized activity, as has the youngest child. But the probable virtue in the position of the youngest lies in the fact that his self-confidence has never been jolted by competition with a newly arrived sibling (p. 348).

It is regrettable that their available data as to the general constellations of parental behavior were not used to examine the theory that parents show, for instance, certain behaviors more readily to first or to youngest children than to others. Findings from this study also offer limited generalizations since the group was quite small and was selected from a highly-advantaged private school population.

In the studies just reported, evidence is conspicuously lacking regarding the environmental setting in which ordinal position differences come about. Beyond *a priori* statements as to the parents' reactions to first, middle, youngest, or only children, statements usually based on clinical experience rather than research demonstration, little can be found which clarifies the picture of home influences contributing to systematic typologies among the children. If there is meaning to such a descriptive concept as Adler's "the oldest child personality," there must, of necessity, be certain likenesses from parent to parent in mode of dealing with the first as distinguished from the later children.

The existence of a "first child personality" implies that there are universalities of experience which first children undergo. This, in turn, leads us to search for common variables in the situation of being a parent a first time that are important enough to transcend the myriad idiosyncratic needs each parent brings to the situation. Analysis of the group situation into which the child is born can give us some clues as to the common experience to which all first parents may be reacting. The first child enters a situation that is adult-oriented; two people, presumably mature, have established a relationship to each other. Now, that small group must effectively integrate a new member whose capacities, assets, and limitations are in almost every way different from theirs. Whatever the balance of dominance-submission, interdependency, and so on that the two adults have contrived as a working basis for themselves, they must now form a relationship with a completely dependent third party. And they must take responsibility for the guidance and control of the child's behavior to a degree seldom required in an adult relationship. Whatever the emotional readiness, even eagerness, of the parents in their attitude toward the first child, the adjustment process is one full of new learnings, and the situation elicits in all probability needs and responses in them formerly dormant. Moreover, many adults in our present-day world have had no experience as such with children, with the details of their physical care and management, with their unpredictable needs and frustrations. The parent may find himself helpless and insecure as to what it is he should do for and to the child.

Evidence for such generalizations is readily garnered from parents themselves as they verbalize about their anxieties, their ignorance, their frustrations in caring for the first child. "Once she could talk, I felt all right about her—I knew what she needed. But it used to drive me crazy to have her cry and not have any way of knowing what was wrong." Or, "I didn't know much about children; I didn't want *my* child to be a spoiled brat that other people didn't like, so I was pretty strict about what he could or couldn't do." Or, "I *learned* on my oldest child—the others are getting the benefit of what I found I did wrong—but it was awfully hard on him."

From these commonplace remarks, certain clinical deductions seem reasonable. It appears likely that the adjustment problems the first child occasions the parent, and especially the mother, would contribute heavily to emotional ambivalence. Furthermore, when she perceives herself as committing "errors" in her handling of the child, whether from inexperience or misconceptions about child development, the guilt engendered is likely to produce hostility in its turn. With or without such hostility, however, there is the likelihood that the mother is less spontaneous and consistent in her expression of warmth to the first child than she is in her attitude toward subsequent children.

Apart from the emotional relationship between parent and child, one might conjecture that certain changes in standards and expectations occur as the parent becomes familiar with children's capacities and limitations.

Adults accustomed to verbal methods of problem solution, rational discussion of difficulties, the postponement of reward or satisfaction when necessary, are seldom geared to either understanding or acceptance of the child's non-verbal, non-rational, emotionally insistent behavior. In all probability, this disparity between adult expectations and habits and the child's mode of response is most acutely present in the parent-first child constellation. Methods of handling the child will, of course, reflect parental goals and in this situation may be designed to influence him toward conformity with adult stereotypes to an unrealistic degree.

It also seems possible that, in contrast to this tendency to accelerate the child and expect too much of him, the mother, through ignorance of his general abilities, might baby and overprotect the child in many areas. Mothers themselves verbalize considerable anxiety about the task of motherhood and their responsibilities, and it seems reasonable to assume that one mechanism with which the anxiety can be handled is that of overprotecting the child so that no harm can befall him. Here again it might be argued that increased experience and familiarity with children's own resiliency would alleviate anxiety and reduce the necessity for such great solicitude with later born children. There is, too, the realistic fact that the average mother, with little or no domestic help, has less time to lavish on later children, whether to accelerate their development or to protect them from environmental hazards.

The general theoretical framework just described permits the formulation of certain questions regarding the parental behavior as directed toward first and later born children. The following specific hypotheses are raised: (a) that parent behavior toward the second child, representing later born children, is warmer than toward the first. "Warmth" is defined in terms of ratings on five variables of the Fels Parent Behavior Rating Scales: "Child-centeredness of the home," "Acceptance of the child," "Affectionateness toward the child," "Approval of the child," and "Rapport between parent and child." A sixth variable, "Intensity of contact with the child," has been added to supplement the picture of the parent's emotional relationship to the child. A corollary of this first hypothesis is that there is more parent-child friction between the mother and the first child and that she is more emotional in her behavior toward him. The scales "Disciplinary friction" and "Emotionality to the child" are used to test this assumption. (b) That the parent is less anxious about and protective toward the second child than the first. Ratings on three scales, "Babying," "Protectiveness," and "Solicitousness" are pertinent. (c) That the parent interferes less, so to speak, with the second child. "Interference" is thought of here as a conscious attempt to manipulate the child. This is tested by comparing ratings on the scales "Quantity of suggestion," "Readiness of criticism," "Accelerational attempt," and "Readiness of explanation." (d) That the parent is more permissive toward the second child. The scales relating to this concept are: "Justification of policy,"

"Democracy of policy," "Restrictiveness of regulations," "Coerciveness of suggestions," and "Readiness of enforcement."

As important as the demonstration of differences in parent behavior toward first and later born children is the determination of whether or not these differences are persistent through a period of years in the lives of the children or are of relatively short duration. Are there discernible age trends in the mother's behavior toward the two growing children? Is one child subjected to fluctuating or inconsistent treatment while the other benefits from more stable policies and attitudes? Analysis of serial data provides information on this point.

Of equal interest is the question as to whether or not these differences are characteristic only of the mother's relation to the first two children. Does the mother continue to change in a systematic and predictable manner as she continues to have children? A test of the hypothesis that the major changes do occur after the first child is a comparison of ratings on a sub-group of second children matched with their next younger siblings. Similarly, a comparison of second children who remain youngest in the family, with the special role so created, with those who have been displaced by a third child has bearing on this problem.

METHODOLOGY AND RESULTS

A. Description of the Group

Individuals gain membership in the Fels study through the mother's own application for admission during her pregnancy. Primary selective criterion for the Institute's acceptance of an applicant is the likelihood that the family will be permanent in this area. Fels parents as a group are above national average in intelligence, economic status, and educational experience but a wide range is, nonetheless, represented. Both rural and urban families are included, the latter coming primarily from villages and small towns rather than large industrial centers.

Within the total Fels group, 46 pairs of siblings were available who were the first and second children in their respective families. Home visits had routinely been made to these families at about an interval of every six months; the behavior of the mother toward each of her children had then been separately rated on the full battery of the Fels Parent Behavior Rating Scales.* Successive visits and ratings, therefore, permitted a matching procedure which allowed comparison of the mother's behavior toward the two children when they were the same chronological age. Thus, whatever the absolute age differences between the siblings might be, all data reported here concern ratings of the mother's attitudes and interactions with the children when they were both three or both six or both

* In all, the ratings of six home visitors comprise the data used in the study. Table 15 indicates the proportion of ratings done by the author as compared with those contributed by the five other home visitors.

ninc. Also, since a series of such ratings was available, it was possible to make successive matchings of the pairs at various age levels; Table 13 presents an inventory of the 46 pairs of cases and shows at what age levels any given pair was represented. Table 8 presents data as to the sex of the pairs of siblings studied; Table 10 is a frequency distribution of the absolute age difference between the pairs of siblings.

B. Parent Behavior Toward First and Second Children

Forty pairs of first and second children, matched as to their chronological age at the time the mother's behavior toward them was rated, were compared on 21 variables of parent-behavior. Table 1 names the individual scales and lists cue-words for the ends of the dimensions to assist the reader in differentiating the variables. Reproductions of these and the other scales of the Fels battery may be found in an earlier publication.[3] (Nine scales of the total battery were omitted either because it was felt they were not relevant to the particular problem or because ratings on them have low reliability, e.g., "Severity of Punishment.")

The total N of 46 pairs was reduced to 40 by eliminating any pairs in

TABLE 1

THE VARIABLES OF PARENT BEHAVIOR

Scale No.	Variable	Low score	High score
1.91	Child-Centeredness of Home:	Child-Subordinating	Child-Centered
5.2	Direction of Criticism:	Disapproval	Approval
7.2	Acceptance of Child:	Rejection	Devotion
8.3	Affectionateness:	Hostile	Affectionate
8.4	Rapport Between Parent and Child:	Isolation	Close Rapport
2.12	Intensity of Contact:	Inert	Vigorous
4.1	General Babying:	Refuses to Help	Over-Helps
4.2	General Protectiveness:	Exposing	Sheltering
7.1	Solicitousness for Child's Welfare:	Nonchalant	Anxious
3.3	Accelerational Attempt:	Retardatory	Acceleratory
6.1	Readiness of Explanation:	Thwarts Curiosity	Satisfies Curiosity
8.1	Understanding:	Obtuse	Keen
3.21	Quantity of Suggestion:	Non-Suggesting	Suggesting
5.1	Readiness of Criticism:	Uncritical	Critical
3.11	Restrictiveness of Regulations:	Freedom	Restrictiveness
3.22	Coerciveness of Suggestion:	Optional	Mandatory
3.12	Readiness of Enforcement:	Lax	Vigilant
3.14	Justification of Disciplinary Policy as presented to the child	Arbitrary	Rational
3.15	Democracy of Regulation and Enforcement Policy	Dictatorial	Democratic
3.18	Disciplinary Friction	Concordant	Contentious
8.2	Emotionality	Objective	Emotional

which a rating on one scale or another had been omitted and by discarding randomly selected pairs. It was desirable to have 40 rather than 46 pairs so that each cell in the analysis of variance design to be described later would have equal entries. Where more than one pair of ratings were available for the sibling pairs, selection of the sets to be used was randomized according to a predetermined system which insured that pairs of all ages would be equally represented.

An analysis of variance design was used to compare the scores of the two groups of children. The design was laid out as follows:

Source of variance	df
Between groups	1
Between families	39
Residual error	39
Total	79

The residual error term was obtained by subtracting from the total sums of squares the "between families" and the "between groups" sums of squares. Table 2 presents the scores for the two groups of children expressed as means.* As can be seen, on only two variables do the groups differ at the .05 level of confidence, a finding which might occur by chance alone when so many comparisons are made. However, inspection of the direction of the difference scores indicates the following: (a) differences on all the "warmth" variables, with the exception of child-centeredness of the home, favor the second child; (b) differences on the "control" variables (restrictiveness, coerciveness, justification of policy, etc.) also favor the second child, indicating that he is more permissively treated; (c) differences on the "anxiety" variables, babying, protectiveness, and solicitousness, are counter to the original hypothesis that the mother worried about and was protective of the first child. The hypothesis that the mother interfered with the first child more, in the sense of accelerating, suggesting, and criticizing, is not upheld by these data; the differences between the two groups are very small and the direction of the difference shifts from one variable to another.

Pearson product-moment correlations were computed on these same 40 pairs. The correlations and the confidence level are also reported in Table 2. The findings here indicate quite dramatically that there is significant consistency in the mother's policies and techniques of managing her two children but that the quality of her emotional relationships cannot be predicted from one child to the other. For none of the "warmth" variables, which we have used to define the emotional relationship of the parent to the child, was there a significant correlation between the mother's behavior toward the first and toward the second child. Nor was the correlation for "disciplinary friction" significant, indicating that she may get

* Ratings are scored, using a millimeter scale, from 10 to 99; after a six-month period, when the visitor has rated each mother in relation to each child in the study, the raw ratings are normed and converted into T-scores with a mean of 50 and a standard deviation of 10. (Cf. Baldwin et al.[3] pp. 35-36.)

TABLE 2

PARENT BEHAVIOR TOWARD FIRST AND SECOND CHILDREN

Variable	Mean		MD	p	r	p
	1st	2nd				
Child-centeredness	50.2	49.4	0.8		.23	
Approval	47.6	51.9	− 4.3	.05	.25	
Acceptance	48.8	50.2	− 1.4		.22	
Affectionateness	49.1	52.3	− 3.2		.30	
Rapport	49.3	51.1	− 1.8		.08	
Intensity of Contact	51.4	52.6	− 1.2		− .02	
Babying	47.4	51.3	− 3.9	.05	.37	.02
Protectiveness	47.5	49.8	− 2.3		.54	.01
Solicitousness	49.2	50.8	− 1.6		.29	
Accelerational Attempt	52.9	51.8	1.1		.43	.01
Readiness of Explanation	52.1	52.4	− 0.3		.56	.01
Understanding	51.3	51.6	− 0.3		.32	.05
Quantity of Suggestion	50.0	50.6	− 0.6		.68	.01
Readiness of Criticism	51.4	50.9	0.5		.31	
Restrictiveness	49.6	47.9	1.7		.65	.01
Coerciveness	50.2	48.3	1.9		.47	.01
Readiness of Enforcement	51.5	49.1	2.4		.50	.01
Justification of Policy	49.5	51.5	− 2.0		.70	.01
Democracy of Policy	50.2	50.4	− 0.2		.57	.01
Disciplinary Friction	52.7	49.9	2.8		.20	
Emotionality to Child	49.7	49.8	− 0.1		.56	.01

N equals 40 for each group. Age-matched sibling pairs were used, the pairs ranging from two years to 10 years at the time the mothers' behavior was rated.

along smoothly with one child at the same time that relations with another are discordant. However, in almost every case, the variables relating to policies of child management correlate significantly. It is safer, in other words, to predict a mother's arbitrariness or rationality in managing a child from seeing her with one of her children than to predict her acceptance of or affectionateness toward the unseen child.

On the supposition that the absolute age difference between the children or the sex of the pairs might be substantial contributors to the way in which the mother treated them, it was decided to compare the ratings of mothers' behavior toward like-sexed pairs of children with those of mothers of different-sexed children. Unfortunately, the small N did not justify a further breakdown into boy pairs, girl pairs, boy-older and girl-older pairs, though there is good reason clinically to presume these would be important in family dynamics. It was possible at the same time to compare the variability attributable to the fact the pairs were close together in age or widely spaced.* The pairings then looked as given in Table 3.

* The age ranges referred to consist of the actual chronological difference between the first two children. Matched ratings were used in this study as in the others.

TABLE 3

	Like-sexed pairs	Unlike-sexed pairs
Small age Difference	Range 18 mos.- 28 mos.	Range 13 mos.- 30 mos.
Large age Difference	Range 32 mos.- 68 mos.	Range 31 mos.- 65 mos.

Ten pairs of children were included in each of these cells. The analysis of variance design for this part of the study was set up as given in Table 4. The results of this portion of the analysis were, unfortunately, not clear cut and are, therefore, difficult to interpret. Listed in Table 5 are the findings which reached a confidence level of .05 or better.

TABLE 4

Source of variation	df	
Between families	39	
Sex of pairs		1
(Like sex vs. unlike)		
Age difference of pairs		1
(Large age diff. vs. small)		
Sex x Age		1
Residual		36
Within families	40	
Ordinal Position		1
Ordinal Positon x Family		39
Ordinal Position x Sex of Pairs		1
Ordinal Position x Age diff.		1
Ordinal Position x Sex x Age		1
Ordinal Position x Residual		36
Total	79	

It would seem that the absolute age difference between the pairs is an important factor in determining how the mother treats the children; moreover, benefits seem to be weighted in the direction of closely spaced children. That is, the mother of children close together in age tends to treat them more rationally, democratically, and with more understanding than does the mother whose children are more widely spaced. One can only theorize as to the selective factors which might be operant; it may be that mothers who subscribe to modern tenets of child care also tend to have children closer together than do the so-called old-fashioned mothers. Or, it may be that two children close together in age are more satisfactorily handled by these methods because of the similarity of their general developmental stage needs, etc. In any case, the finding is not in accord with the lay notion that two children close together in age are disruptive and difficult for the mother to handle. (However, somewhat contradictory results emerge from a differently designed analysis to be discussed later in this chapter.) The separate findings are provocative and are an indication that further research into intra-family dynamics should scrutinize the influence of age difference between sibling pairs.

TABLE 5

Variable	Contributing factor	Level of confidence
Justification of policy	Age difference (Small age difference higher)	beyond .01
Democracy of policy	Age difference (Small age difference higher)	.05-.01
Readiness of explanation	Age difference (Small age difference higher)	.05-.01
Understanding	Age difference (Small age difference higher)	.05-.01
Accelerational attempt	Ordinal position x Age (More acceleration for small age diff.; especially for second children)	.05-.01
Babying	Sex of pairs x age difference (Small age diff., like-sexed pairs Large age diff., unlike pairs tended to receive higher scores)	.05-.01
Rapport	Ordinal position x Age (1st child, small age difference 2nd child, large age difference tended to receive higher scores)	.05-.01

C. ANALYSIS OF AGE TRENDS IN PARENT BEHAVIOR

A description has been given earlier of the series of ratings available on the pairs of siblings and of the method of matching these ratings so that the mother's behavior was rated when each of the children was the same age. For the analysis of shifts in the mother's behavior as the two children grew older, the ratings were separated into nine groups, composed as given in Table 6.

It can be seen that the group number corresponds roughly to the average age of the pairs of children when the mother was rated, with the exception of Group 9 where nine- and ten-year-old pairs were combined to increase the N. The matchings were gratifyingly close, as shown by the mean age difference when the pairs were rated. In no pairing was the age difference larger than six months and for the pairings of the very young children in Group 1 only one set had a difference as large as three months. It should be emphasized that these nine groups had a high percentage of overlapping membership from one age level to another; for example 16 of the 18 pairs in Group 1 also appear in Group 2, while Groups 2 and 3 have 25 pairs in common.* However, in all instances different sets of ratings constitute the data used. The overlap was not consistent enough, and thus the N was insufficient, to work simply with difference scores for the same pairs of children throughout the age range. Therefore, the findings reported are means for the first and the second children in each group.

* Reference to Table 13 will make evident the nature of the groupings and the amount of overlap of individual pairs of cases.

TABLE 6

Group	N (Pairs)	Mean age 1st	2nd	Age range (Mo.) within group	Mean diff. 1st 2nd
1	18	20.4	20.5	15-24	1.4 mos.
2	28	30.1	30.1	24-38	1.6 mos.
3	28	41.0	40.5	31-47	1.6 mos.
4	27	53.7	53.9	46-59	1.3 mos.
5	24	65.3	65.5	58-72	2.2 mos.
6	22	76.3	75.7	69-86	2.0 mos.
7	20	90.5	90.9	80-98	2.0 mos.
8	20	102.2	101.5	96-108	2.2 mos.
9	19	119.3	119.0	111-128	1.3 mos.

Table 7 presents the obtained means and standard deviations for these nine age groups on the 21 parent behavior variables. Table 8 shows the differences between the means for the first child and second child groups and indicates the level of confidence with which these differences can be viewed. The means for the second children were subtracted from those for the first children; thus, a negative difference score indicates that the group of second children scored higher on that particular variable. The formula for the standard error of the difference between means was corrected for correlation of the measures.

The picture given by these data seems as follows: at a very young age the first child enjoys a markedly child-centered environment characterized by accelerational attempts of a verbal-intellectual kind (evidenced by the scores on 3.3, "Accelerational Attempt" and 6.1, "Readiness of Explana-

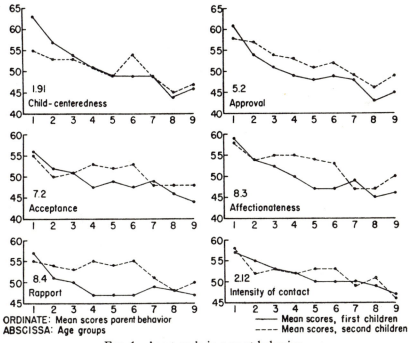

ORDINATE: Mean scores parent behavior   —— Mean scores, first children
ABSCISSA: Age groups   ---- Mean scores, second children

FIG. 1. Age trends in parent behavior.

TABLE 7

AGE TRENDS IN PARENT BEHAVIOR TOWARD FIRST AND SECOND CHILDREN*

Variable	Groups																	
	1		2		3		4		5		6		7		8		9	
	M	SD	M	SD	M	SD	M	SD	M	SD	M	SD	M	SD	M	SD	M	SD
Child-centeredness	63	7.5	57	8.5	54	10.4	51	11.5	49	7.7	49	9.7	49	7.9	44	5.5	46	6.0
	55	5.4	53	8.7	53	7.9	51	10.4	49	7.2	54	8.2	49	7.8	45	7.4	47	7.6
Approval	61	10.2	54	10.9	51	12.3	49	10.1	48	9.2	49	11.7	48	11.4	43	8.4	45	6.7
	58	9.1	57	8.3	54	9.0	53	8.6	51	7.3	52	7.8	49	8.3	46	7.8	49	7.0
Acceptance	56	5.6	52	7.8	51	10.7	48	9.7	49	8.1	49	9.9	49	9.2	46	7.5	44	7.8
	55	7.6	50	7.4	51	9.1	53	9.0	52	7.5	48	5.3	48	7.6	48	7.9	48	8.2
Affectionateness	59	6.5	54	9.1	52	9.6	50	10.2	47	9.2	47	10.8	49	9.7	46	7.8	46	5.5
	58	7.4	54	8.3	55	8.2	55	7.4	54	5.6	53	6.9	47	6.8	50	9.0	50	8.4
Rapport	57	3.8	51	9.0	50	10.2	47	9.5	47	8.3	47	11.2	49	9.6	48	7.4	47	7.5
	55	6.9	54	8.2	53	8.1	55	7.7	54	7.0	53	6.0	51	6.3	48	9.4	50	7.8
Intensity of Contact	57	7.0	55	7.7	53	9.1	52	9.7	50	9.2	50	11.7	50	11.1	49	10.3	47	5.8
	58	8.2	52	9.6	53	7.0	52	10.3	53	9.6	53	8.0	49	7.2	51	9.3	46	7.2
Babying	57	10.6	56	8.7	53	10.3	50	9.8	49	8.7	46	9.0	45	10.3	45	9.9	44	6.4
	56	9.0	54	10.2	55	9.3	54	9.3	50	7.2	50	8.9	47	7.9	47	9.8	48	10.6
Protectiveness	57	9.5	53	9.3	52	9.2	50	10.6	47	10.0	48	10.4	45	11.1	45	10.0	46	9.0
	56	8.9	51	11.4	52	9.7	52	9.4	50	9.0	50	8.1	46	9.9	46	10.8	49	10.4
Solicitousness	55	7.4	51	9.4	53	9.0	48	10.9	51	9.6	50	10.5	46	10.2	46	8.9	46	9.2
	53	11.0	49	11.0	50	8.1	50	11.1	50	7.9	44	8.6	45	9.2	45	11.2	50	11.0
Accelerational Attempt	56	10.0	51	9.6	50	9.6	51	10.4	56	8.2	52	11.1	50	10.3	50	10.1	50	8.7
	50	9.6	49	11.2	47	10.1	49	11.1	51	9.4	53	7.3	50	8.1	50	8.8	51	8.3
Readiness of Explanation			55	8.7	51	8.8	53	8.6	52	9.8	51	11.9	52	10.3	52	9.3	49	7.7
			48	10.0	49	10.6	48	10.7	53	9.8	53	8.5	47	7.2	47	8.5	49	7.2
Understanding	54	9.1	53	9.3	51	8.7	50	9.7	52	8.5	51	10.1	52	9.5	50	9.6	50	7.1
	52	11.0	52	9.4	52	9.0	52	9.5	53	10.8	56	6.7	48	7.8	49	8.4	49	5.4
Quantity of Suggestion	58	8.5	53	9.4	54	9.2	50	9.1	48	8.4	49	9.2	48	9.6	48	7.5	45	5.7
	54	10.2	50	8.4	49	9.9	50	10.0	47	9.7	50	9.8	44	6.5	52	8.4	50	10.5
Readiness of Criticism	51	11.0	50	10.3	51	9.2	51	10.5	54	7.5	52	9.3	51	8.5	52	9.7	50	8.1
	55	8.9	51	8.0	53	8.7	53	8.7	49	9.3	51	7.9	49	10.1	55	8.7	48	9.9

TABLE 7 (Continued)

Variable	Groups																	
	1		2		3		4		5		6		7		8		9	
	M	SD	M	SD	M	SD	M	SD	M	SD	M	SD	M	SD	M	SD	M	SD
Restrictiveness	47	8.6	48	10.0	50	9.3	49	10.2	49	8.6	49	9.8	48	11.7	48	11.3	51	11.8
	50	6.6	48	9.9	47	9.8	48	9.8	48	9.3	46	9.8	52	10.7	52	10.6	51	7.9
Coerciveness	42	7.7	46	10.2	48	10.4	50	10.6	50	10.6	48	9.0	48	11.1	52	10.1	52	9.4
	48	10.0	47	8.0	50	9.9	49	9.6	47	9.6	49	9.7	50	9.7	52	10.0	51	10.0
Readiness of Enforcement	48	9.7	47	8.5	49	10.1	51	11.3	52	8.3	50	10.6	51	8.2	51	10.0	54	6.8
	49	7.2	45	7.7	48	8.2	51	8.8	48	7.7	50	8.7	53	7.4	53	7.4	51	9.9
Justification of Policy			54	9.7	51	9.9	51	10.4	53	10.1	53	9.2	49	10.4	49	10.0	48	9.8
			51	10.2	49	9.8	51	8.8	53	9.0	52	8.4	47	10.5	47	10.8	49	7.8
Democracy of Policy			54	7.3	51	8.8	48	8.9	50	11.2	54	10.2	51	10.0	51	10.0	50	9.1
			52	8.4	48	10.0	49	9.9	53	9.2	53	7.5	47	9.4	47	10.7	51	9.1
Disciplinary Friction	47	9.0	52	10.2	53	10.6	54	9.3	55	6.8	50	8.3	54	9.1	54	10.6	51	8.3
	49	7.9	47	10.5	50	8.5	50	9.7	48	6.8	49	7.4	55	8.8	55	9.0	50	6.4
Emotionality to Child	49	10.1	50	11.4	52	10.0	48	9.6	49	8.9	48	9.8	50	9.8	50	9.6	48	9.1
	53	11.6	48	11.5	52	10.3	51	9.3	47	8.1	45	8.3	48	10.3	48	9.3	51	7.9

* The first row in each pair of scores gives means and standard deviations for the group of first children. Scores for the second children appear in the second row.

TABLE 8

MEAN DIFFERENCE SCORE,* PARENT BEHAVIOR TOWARD FIRST AND SECOND CHILDREN

Variable	Groups																	
	1		2		3		4		5		6		7		8		9	
	MD	P	MD	P	MD	P	MD	P	MD	P	MD	P	MD	P	MD	P	MD	P
Child-centeredness	7.7	.001	3.8	.10	0.6		0.7	.10	0.0	.10	-5.1	.05	-0.1		-1.5		-1.1	
Approval	3.1		-2.4		-2.2		-4.1	.01	-3.5	.05	-3.2		-0.6		-3.4		-4.2	.10
Acceptance	0.5		1.9		0.3		-4.9	.05	-3.7	.001	-5.1	.05	0.9		-1.3		-3.9	.10
Affectionateness	1.6		-0.5		-3.5	.05	-4.2	.001	-6.8	.001	-6.0	.05	1.3		-2.0		-4.3	.10
Rapport	1.7		-3.4	.10	-2.8		-7.2		-7.1		-7.8	.001	-2.4		-0.2		-3.0	
Intensity of Contact	-0.1		2.8		0.4		-0.2		-3.5	.10	-2.7		0.7		-1.4		0.8	
Babying	1.1		1.4		-1.4		-4.5	.10	-0.5		-3.9	.10	0.3		-1.9		-4.2	
Protectiveness	0.7		2.2		0.3		-1.2		-3.5		-2.4	.10	-1.4		-0.4		-3.8	.05
Solicitousness	2.2		2.3		2.9		-2.0		1.0		5.2	.05	-1.2		1.0		-4.1	.05
Accelerational Attempt	5.7	.10	2.0		3.0		1.9	.02	5.6	.01	-1.0		0.5		0.0		-1.3	
Readiness of Explanation			6.2	.01	2.0		4.1		-0.4		-2.2	.10	-1.8		5.2	.02	-0.1	
Understanding	2.1		0.8		-0.4		-1.9		-1.0		-5.0		2.2		4.7	.05	0.5	
Quantity of Suggestion	3.9		3.5		4.6	.05	-0.3		1.3	.05	-1.0		4.8	.10	-4.1	.10	-4.9	.10
Readiness of Criticism	-3.3		-0.6		-0.7		-1.4		5.3		1.0		2.1		-2.3		1.1	
Restrictiveness	-3.2		-0.1		3.1	.10	1.1		0.9		1.3		2.1		-3.5	.10	-0.8	
Coerciveness	-5.7	.05	-1.3		-1.9		1.5		3.4		-0.8		-1.4		-0.1		0.7	
Readiness of Enforcement	-0.3		1.6		0.9		1.8		3.3		-0.4		1.2		-1.8		3.0	
Justification of Policy			3.1	.10	1.8	.02	0.0		-0.2		1.1		2.0		2.6		-1.2	
Democracy of Policy	3.1	.10	1.9		3.3		-1.5		-3.0		-0.1		0.5		4.4	.10	-1.0	
Disciplinary Friction	-1.6		4.5	.10	3.6	.10	3.6		7.8	.001	2.3		0.4		-0.9		1.5	
Emotionality to Child	-4.4	.01	2.5		-0.1		-2.9		2.6		1.2		0.8		2.0		-2.6	

* The mean score for the group of second children has been subtracted from the mean score for the group of first children.

TABLE 9

Correlation of Parent Behavior Toward Age-Matched Sibling Pairs of First and Second Children

| | Groups | | | | | | | | | | | | | | | | |
| Variable | 1 | | 2 | | 3 | | 4 | | 5 | | 6 | | 7 | | 8 | | 9 | |
	r	P	r	P	r	P	r	P	r	P	r	P	r	P	r	P	r	P
Child-centeredness	.31	.01	.20		.19		.57	.01	.40		.14		.22		.64	.01	.24	.01
Approval	.10	.05	.29		.53	.01	.30		.28		.44	.05	-.02		.09		-.06	
Acceptance	.32	.05	.61	.01	.33		.66	.01	.40		.34		.19		.32		.17	
Affectionateness	.37		.60	.01	.60	.01	.51	.01	.37		.32		-.09		.54	.02	.08	
Rapport	-.30		.44	.02	.44	.02	.47	.02	.34		.09		-.33		.54	.02	-.19	
Intensity of Contact	.31	.02	.05		.15		.33		.43		.22		-.07		.00		.46	
Babying	.66	.01	.43	.05	.43	.05	.23		-.01		.42		.23		.57	.01	.40	.01
Protectiveness	.53	.05	.11		.32		.20		.47	.05	.31		.51	.05	.78	.01	.77	.01
Solicitousness	.50	.05	.13		.23		.28		.43	.05	.40		.67	.01	.56	.01	.72	
Accelerational Attempt	.29		.62	.01	.43	.05	.64	.01	.65	.01	.42		.55	.02	.45	.05	.22	
Readiness of Explanation			.70	.01	.59	.01	.63	.01	.68	.01	.67	.01	.60	.01	.56	.01	.64	.01
Understanding	.48	.05	.40	.05	.66	.01	.53	.01	.54	.01	.27		.13		.39		.32	
Quantity of Suggestion	.11		.05		.43	.05	.35		-.17		.42		.49	.05	-.05		.16	
Readiness of Criticism	.57	.02	-.23		.36		.37		.21		.72	.01	.78	.01	.03		.23	
Restrictiveness	.36	.05	.20		.61	.01	.36		.22		.39		.68	.01	.74	.01	.66	.01
Coerciveness	.52		.32		.70	.01	.23		.53	.01	.30		.50	.05	.47	.05	.70	.01
Readiness of Enforcement	.41		.10		.48	.01	.45	.02	.24		.31		.70	.01	.39		.40	
Justification of Policy			.60	.01	.66	.01	.60	.01	.52	.01	.30		.58	.01	.59	.01	.54	.02
Democracy of Policy			.53	.02	.76	.01	.58	.01	.42	.05	.59	.01	.59	.01	.49	.05	.44	
Disciplinary Friction	.12		.07		.33		.10		.26		.53	.02	.40		.29		.41	.02
Emotionality to Child	.85	.01	.27		.60	.01	.32		.25		.57	.01	.62	.01	.56	.02	.54	

tion"). By age three or four, however, the home no longer revolves around him and, starting from a much more favored position in the beginning, he is less warmly treated than is his younger sibling at a similar age. Figures 1 and 2 make especially clear the rather dramatic contrast in the treatment of the two children as they grow older. It is interesting, moreover, that the discrepancy is much less marked once the second child reaches school age. It may well be, as has been clinically noticed, that

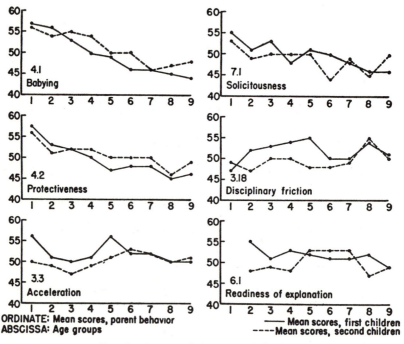

ORDINATE: Mean scores, parent behavior
ABSCISSA: Age groups

——— Mean scores, first children
- - - -Mean scores, second children

FIG. 2. Age trends in parent behavior.

mothers change attitudes and behavior somewhat radically when they perceive the necessity, real or imagined, of fitting the child to the school society. Whatever the reason, the curves for most of the variables become strikingly similar once the two children are six or seven years of age.

The hypothesis that the mother is more babying and protective of and more anxious about the first child does not seem borne out with any consistency by these data. By and large the difference scores do not reach a level of statistical significance, and in the isolated instances where the level of confidence is .05 or better the findings are likely to be contradictory from one year level to the next. It is true that mothers tend to verbalize anxiety about the routines of caring for their first child more than is evident later, but it should be remembered that these scales have been rather carefully designed to consider as evidence only overt behavior thought to have direct impact on the child. On this level, apparently, the visitors felt that the mothers did not betray their trepidations nor allow them to intrude on policies about the care of the child. Figure 2 illustrates that it is the second child rather than the first towards whom the mother is babying and protective.

The hypothesis that the mother is more permissive with the second child is not borne out, at least at the younger ages when she appears to be critical and coercive of the second child whereas she inclined to be more democratic in her policies and rational in her techniques with the oldest child at these ages. (This may well reflect some skew in the Fels population where a number of "child development" trained mothers try out "book techniques" on the first child and then modify their behavior into a more personally satisfying approach with subsequent children.) Disciplinary friction, however, is, at almost all age levels, more marked between the mother and the first child than with his sibling. The friction becomes most pronounced at age five, a period when warmth toward the first child is also at low ebb, and when disciplinary policies seem to tighten up as well. The fact, however, that these nine age levels represent neither independent samplings of first and second children nor sequential curves for identical children must be kept in mind as a limitation on the interpretation of these trends. Repeated representation of certain pairs of cases at the various age levels, while other pairs may appear only once or twice, introduces a possibility of bias that cannot be assessed.

However, a further element to be considered is the interpretation of mean trends and mean difference scores is the likelihood that certain facets of the mother's behaviour would be, in a sense, central to her own personality and would, therefore, be characteristic of her treatment of both children throughout this age range. Less central characteristics would be expected to fluctuate with the age of the child or as she reacted to the differing personalities of the two children; inconsistent or low correlations would be expected in such instances. Accordingly, Pearson product-moment correlations were computed for each variable at each age level.* Referring to Table 9, it is immediately evident that the highest and most consistent correlations appear on the variables concerned with broad policies of child management. "Democracy" and "Justification of Policy" are consistently high, as are "Accelerational attempts," "Readiness of explanation" and, to a somewhat lesser extent, "Understanding." "Emotionality" also is rather consistently high; the level of objectivity or emotionality displayed toward the child is probably a fairly stable characteristic of the parent. It is interesting to note that the high correlations among the "warmth" variables tend to mass around the two, three, and four-year-old age levels; it may be that the rather more limited range of

* It was not possible to compute means of correlations on Variables 3.14 Justification of policy, 3.15 Democracy of policy, or 6.1 Readiness of Explanation for Group 1 because of the number of cases where ratings had been omitted. It is especially difficult to garner evidence for these particular variables in the mother's handling of the very young child.

child behavior at these early ages elicits similar emotional response to both children from the mother. Again, caution must be exerted in interpretation, however, both because of the overlapping membership in the groups at the various age levels and because of the high intercorrelations of the variables themselves.

"Babying," "Protectiveness," and "Solicitousness" seem stable characteristics of the mother in her behavior toward very young children and again toward the school-age child. It is quite possible that the hazards to which the very young child is liable and those represented by having the child move out of the home and into society activate similar behavior and attitudes in the mother.

As has been indicated, however, neither the changes in mean scores with age nor the magnitude of the correlation coefficients can provide a definitive answer to the question whether the mother shifts more or less in her treatment of the first child than she does with the second. Accordingly, it was decided to eliminate all overlap among the cases and test directly the correlations with age.* Since most of the pairs of siblings had more than one set of ratings available, it was necessary to randomize the selection of the set by which each pair would be represented. One pair, selected at random, was omitted from the computations in order to allow equal representation by five pairs at each of the nine age levels. Table 10 presents the results of these correlations.

Six variables are significantly correlated with age in a negative direction for first children; no variable reaches a confidence level of .05 among the second children correlations. A unifying theme is immediately evident among these six variables, "Child-centeredness of the home," "Babying," "Protectiveness," "Solicitousness," "Intensity of Contact," and "Quantity of Suggestion." It appears that the most important change in the parent-child relationship here is one of diminished interaction. Indeed, the diminishing affectionateness and rapport reflected in the mean changes discussed earlier may be as much decreased interchange between parent and child as loss of warm feeling. The second child, on the other hand, has a more stable environment, the fluctuations in no instance being of a high order.

D. Analysis of the Role of the Second Child

In the next analysis, an attempt was made to determine to what extent the second child's favorable position was related to his being the youngest in the family, or, alternatively, his not yet being displaced. The second children among the three- and four-year-old groups already analyzed were divided into two sections, according to whether or not a third child had

---

* Appropriate tests of linearity were computed for all variables for first and second children. Variable 3.18, in the first-child group, did not meet the requirements and was, therefore, omitted.

already been born into the family. For the three-year-olds there were eight children who had been "displaced," 16 who had not been. (Instances in which the mother was pregnant at the time the second child had been rated were discarded in order to give a more clear cut contrast.) Among the four-year-old second children, 13 had a younger sibling and 13 did not.

TABLE 10

CORRELATION OF PARENT BEHAVIOR SCORES WITH AGE OF CHILD

Variable	1st children			2nd children		
	N	r	P	N	r	P
Child-centeredness	45	−.54	.01	45	−.17	
Approval	45	−.26		45	−.15	
Acceptance	45	−.17		45	.07	
Affectionateness	45	−.26		45	−.01	
Rapport	45	−.18		45	.05	
Intensity of Contact	45	−.38	.01	45	.08	
Babying	45	−.39	.01	45	−.15	
Protectiveness	45	−.42	.01	45	−.12	
Solicitousness	45	−.47	.01	45	−.01	
Accelerational Attempt	45	−.03		45	.14	
Readiness of Explanation	42	−.26		43	−.02	
Understanding	45	−.10		45	.00	
Quantity of Suggestion	45	−.35	.05	44	.05	
Readiness of Criticism	45	.00		45	−.04	
Restrictiveness	45	.22		45	.04	
Coerciveness	44	.21		44	.25	
Readiness of Enforcement	45	.21		45	.10	
Justification of Policy	43	−.19		45	−.05	
Democracy of Policy	42	−.01		45	.08	
Disciplinary Friction*				45	.06	
Emotionality to Child	45	−.13		45	−.12	

Inspection of Table 11 reveals that the mother's behavior toward her second child is radically altered if, at three, he has a younger sibling, whereas at four none of the differences between the "displaced" and the "nondisplaced" second children is significant. This seems reasonable when one thinks of how much more "civilized" and manageable the four-year-old child is than the three-year-old. The demands and needs of a three-year-old would be much easier to meet, and possibly seem more reasonable, when a younger child is not usurping, and needing, the mother's time. Accordingly, a great deal less warmth is accorded the "displaced" three-year-old; he is accorded less attention and understanding; and disciplinary friction is marked. One might say that mother and child handle "displacement" with more equanimity when the child is four.

* This correlation was not computed for the first-children group as assumptions of linearity could not be met.

TABLE 11

COMPARISONS OF PARENT BEHAVIOR SCORES FOR "DISPLACED" AND "NONDISPLACED" SECOND CHILDREN*

Variable	Three-year-olds Mean diff.	P	Four-year-olds Mean diff.	P	Matched cases Mean diff.	P
Child-centeredness	−6.6	.10	−2.2		−2.9	
Approval	−11.9	.01	−4.2		3.1	
Acceptance	−8.9	.05	−3.1		−2.2	
Affectionateness	−9.8	.01	1.0		−0.8	
Rapport	−10.4	.001	−1.2		−1.9	
Intensity of Contact	−5.0	.10	−5.1		−0.4	
Babying	3.4		−5.4		−3.0	
Protectiveness	−4.0		−0.7		−2.4	
Solicitousness	−0.3		−2.1		−1.0	
Accelerational Attempt	−2.6		−0.1		−3.4	
Readiness of Explanation	−6.3		2.1		0.1	
Understanding	−7.4	.05	−0.9		2.1	
Quantity of Suggestion	1.1		−3.1		−6.9	.05
Readiness of Criticism	−0.6		−1.8		−4.6	.10
Restrictiveness	2.6		−1.6		−7.0	.05
Coerciveness	3.4		0.5		−8.6	.01
Readiness of Enforcement	−1.0		−5.2		−5.1	.05
Justification of Policy	−6.1		1.4		0.9	
Democracy of Policy	−7.4	.05	3.1		6.1	.10
Disciplinary Friction	9.9	.02	1.5		−1.9	
Emotionality to Child	7.4	.10	−0.7		−1.1	

The final group in this table was chosen to test further the role of the second child when he is the permanent youngest member of the family. There were 14 two-child families among the original 46 families in this research group. (These were considered "permanent" two-child families if both children were of school age, or if the mother had expressed determination to have no more children, etc.) To refine the analysis, a matching technique was used. The second child from each of these families was paired, as closely as possible, with a second child from larger families according to age, the sex of the first two children in the family, and rough socio-economic criteria (e.g., an attempt was made, not always successfully, to match a farm child with a farm child, etc.). Mean age of the two groups was around 60 months, a year and two years older, respectively, than the groups described above. Again, as in the four-year-olds, no striking differences emerged in the warmth with which "displaced" second children were treated. However, an unexpected finding was the discovery

* Difference score computed by subtracting the mean of the "nondisplaced" group from the mean of the "displaced" group. N for three-year-olds, 8 "displaced," 16 "nondisplaced." For four-year-olds, 13 in each group. Fourteen in each group of the "matched" cases. (Cf. text for details of matching.)

that the second child who is youngest in the family is treated much more restrictively and coercively than is the "displaced" second child. This restrictiveness, combined with accelerational attempts, might well stem from the mother's desire to have the youngest child behave with as much maturity and/or conformity as his older sibling. This seems especially understandable at the age level considered here, the five-year-old, when the mother of two children is close to regaining her freedom from the confining demands of the young child. The mother who has children younger than five may be less inclined to accelerate the five-year-old or to impose overly mature standards upon him, since the younger children are still demanding her time.

E. Comparison of Parent Behavior Toward Second and Third Children

In a further effort to determine the nature of the shifts in parent behavior a comparison was made of siblings who were second and third children in

TABLE 12

COMPARISON OF PARENT BEHAVIOR TOWARD AGE-MATCHED SIBLING PAIRS OF SECOND AND THIRD CHILDREN

Variable	Mean diff. (2nd - 3rd)	P	r	P
Child-centeredness	−0.1		.31	
Approval	−3.4		.24	
Acceptance	−0.8		.08	
Affectionateness	−0.7		.45	
Rapport	−3.0		−.14	
Intensity of Contact	−1.0		.38	
Babying	−0.3		.31	
Protectiveness	−2.6		.67	.01
Solicitousness	1.9		.52	.05
Accelerational Attempt	4.4	.05	.49	
Readiness of Explanation	0.8		.53	.05
Understanding	−0.5		.34	
Quantity of Suggestion	−2.4		.02	
Readiness of Criticism	1.0		.37	
Restrictiveness	−5.7	.05	.40	
Coerciveness	−0.7		.58	.05
Readiness of Enforcement	−0.9		.09	
Justification of Policy	1.7		.63	.01
Democracy of Policy	5.6	.05	.25	
Disciplinary Friction	−1.1		.14	
Emotionality to Child	−0.5		.34	

N equals 16 pairs for all variables except "Intensity of Contact" for which 15 pairs were used.

their respective families. Sixteen such pairs were matched, with chronological age held constant as in the earlier comparisons; the mean age of the pairs was four-and-a-half years. Table 12 presents the mean differences, scores of third children having been subtracted from those of second children, and the correlations for this group of children. Although most of the differences do not reach a statistically significant level, it can be seen that the warmth scores are higher for the third children. However, this group is handled more restrictively and more arbitrarily than are second children, is protected more and accelerated less. It would appear that the mother develops an attitude of warmth combined with strictness as she has more children. Whether this is an outgrowth of more experience in the maternal role or reflects her increasing load of responsibility is not differentiable. Nevertheless, this is further evidence that there are systematic changes in the way a parent behaves to children in various positions in the family. As we have seen from earlier comparisons, the age difference between the siblings, to some extent the sex of the siblings, and the age at which the comparisons are made all have bearing on the picture of parental behavior obtained.

In general, the correlational pattern is similar to that obtained between first and second children. Since the N is so much reduced in the second-third child comparison, most of the correlations do not reach a statistical level of significance but the general agreement in level and direction is marked. Again, it is in the area of parental policies and methods that the higher correlations are found, with the variables related to the warmth of the parent-child relationship not significantly correlated.

SUMMARY AND CONCLUSIONS

Interest in the problem of whether certain physical or personality characteristics might be associated with the individual's position within the family structure has a long philosophical history. Varieties of research studies have given support to much speculation about the correlates of ordinal position, but the findings are often contradictory and inconclusive. However, discarding for the moment any hereditarian biases, little theorizing has been done as to the specific environmental factors to which the presumed typologies associated with ordinal position might be attributed. Research on this aspect of the problem has been notably lacking, supplanted, for example, by *a priori* assumptions about parental behavior to the only, the oldest, or the youngest child.

The hypotheses tested in the present study were an outgrowth of an analysis of the group structure into which the first child must necessarily be integrated. The adjustment problems faced by the adults as they make room in their relationship for a dependent, non-rational, demanding individual for whom they have sole responsibility might lead, it was felt, to a certain amount of emotional ambivalence, whatever the conscious attitudes the adults might hold toward parenthood. Such ambivalence would produce behavior toward the first child which was less warm and less consistent than that exhibited to later children when the adults were more experienced and comfortable in the parental role.

It was further hypothesized that, in present-day society, adults lack knowledge about and understanding of children and that this lack of experience makes them prone to expect both too much and too little. These contradictory expectations would take the form of accelerational attempts, restrictiveness designed to elicit early conformity to societal standards, and babying and protectiveness to ward off environmental hazards. It might be expected that conflicting emotional attitudes coupled with lack of experience and skills in the area of child care would produce anxiety in the parent as well. Effort to control this anxiety would also lead to policies of restrictiveness and protectiveness. It was felt that experience with the first child would bring greater realism into the parental attitudes and policies with subsequent changes of behavior toward later children.

The study reported here compared mothers' behavior toward their first and second children when the siblings were the same chronological age. Forty-six pairs of children whose mothers had been rated on the Fels Parent Behavior Rating Scales were the subjects of the analysis. The ratings had been performed over a period of years by trained psychologists on the basis of their observations of mother-child interaction in the home. The families studied had been members of the longitudinal program of the Fels Research Institute for the Study of Human Development since before the birth of the children.

The fact that routine home visits had been made over a number of years permitted the matching of ratings of the mother's behavior to her two children when they were the same chronological age. Moreover, for many of the children, several such pairings were possible at successive age levels. Ratings contributed by six home visitors, of whom the author was one, comprise the data used in the study. The reliability and validity of the scales have been reported in detail previously.

The first hypotheses tested had to do with over-all differences in parental treatment of first and second children. It was theorized that the parental handling of first children would be marked by less warmth, more anxiety, more interference, and more restrictiveness than would the handling of second children. An analysis of variance design was used to compare 40 pairs of siblings, matched for age, the pairs ranging from two to 10 years. The scores on 21 variables of the Fels battery of rating scales were utilized as measures of parent-child relationship. It was found that, while few of the differences between the mean scores for the two groups were statistically significant, the trend was in the predicted direction for the warmth variables and for the variables related to parental control and disciplinary policies. However, the parent did tend to baby, protect, and be solicitous of the second child to a greater extent than the first, whereas the converse had been hypothesized. Scores on the so-called "interference" variables did not differ significantly between the two groups and the direction of the difference tended to shift from one variable to another.

The analysis of shifts in parent behavior as the two children grow older casts some light on the nature of the differences in treatment of the siblings and to some extent is explanatory of the lack of conclusive findings in the over-all comparison. With different ratings being used each time, the scores for nine different age groups of sibling pairs were analyzed. Here it was found that the first child experienced an early environment which was extremely warm and child-centered but that this preferment was soon lost. The second child started at a less extreme level but maintained his position in the family's affectional structure more effectively. These differences were most marked in the pre-school ages; from ages six to 10, the discrepancies in the treatment of the two children were very slight on most variables. Since the over-all comparison of behavior toward first and second children included pairs ranging from two to 10 years of age, it is probable that the differences present in the earlier years were obscured by the similarity of scores for the older pairs of children. Thus, the age trend analysis presents a richer picture of the shifts in parental policies and attitudes than does the cross-sectional diagnosis. Interpretation of the age trend data, however, is complicated by the overlapping cases which appear at various age levels.

The age trend analysis indicates that the first child, in the pre-school years, is subjected to a great deal of verbal stimulation and acceleration. Special accelerative attempts seem to occur before the first child is two and again when he is five; these scores probably represent parental emphasis on skill-acquisition (language, toilet training, etc.) for the very young child and school readiness for the five-year-old. The second child is also subjected to acceleratory pressures by the time he is school age but escapes the earlier efforts to speed up his development.

As in the cross-sectional analysis, evidence from the longitudinal data indicates that it is the second child who receives more babying and protection from the parent. The curves describing parental solicitude toward the two children are erratic and do not lend themselves to interpretation. Though mothers frequently verbalize that they worried more about their first child and took greater precautions for his safety and well-being, the ratings do not bear out this memory. It may be that the mothers coped with their anxieties better and exhibited more competent behavior than they realize or remember, or which is more likely, it may be that the visitor was unable to detect the subtle nuances by which these internal feelings might have been conveyed to the child.

The age trend analysis showed no consistent difference in the permissiveness with which first and second children were treated, but there was a marked and fairly consistent tendency for disciplinary friction to be higher in the mother's interaction with her oldest child. This is particularly true of the siblings when they are five.

Two types of correlational analyses were performed to discover whether certain facets of parental behavior seemed central to the mother's own personality and therefore characteristic of her treatment of both children. Correlations performed on the cross-sectional sample of 40 pairs of children indicated that almost every variable reflecting the mother's policies toward the children and methods of handling them was significantly correlated. For example, the tendency to be rational or to be arbitrary toward the child seems a fundamental and persistent part of the mother's technique of managing the child. However, variables describing the emotional relationship of the parent to the child—e.g., acceptance, affectionateness, rapport—were in no instance significantly correlated. From the correlations computed at the various age levels, though, we find that the mother's tendency to be anxious and to baby the child appears most marked at the youngest age level and again when the two children are school age; that is, she reacts similarly to both her children at these age levels. Warmth, or its lack, seems to be a more stable characteristic of the mother in her dealings with the two children when they are preschool age; later, she seems to react to them more as separate personalities.

Difficulty in interpreting the age trend data, because of the overlapping membership in the groups, led to still another correlational analysis to determine whether the mother shifted significantly in her treatment of either of the two children as they grew older. Pearson product-moment correlations were run for 45 first and 45 second children between parent behavior scores and the child's age when the mother was rated. No significant relation was found between parent behavior and age for the second children; however, six of the 21 variables were significantly correlated in the group of first children. In each case the correlation was negative. Lowered interaction between parent and child appeared to be the underlying dynamic; the home was less child-centered, contact with the mother less vigorous, and there was a reduction in babying, protectiveness, quantity of suggestions, and parental solicitude. The fact that no variable correlated significantly for the second children might be taken to indicate greater stability of parental policies; that is, the mother makes no systematic change in attitude or techniques of management merely on the score of the child's age.

An analysis of variance design was utilized to determine whether or not the age difference between the pairs of siblings or the sex of the pairs was an important contributor to variation in parental handling. Findings from this analysis were somewhat obscure, but a number of differences seemed to be attributable to the age difference between pairs. Children close together in chronological age benefited from more rational and understanding treatment than did widely spread sibling pairs.

616   CLINICAL PRACTICE

In an effort to determine the nature of the second child's role in the family and to assess the amount to which the mother continues to change her policies and attitudes toward later born children, a number of comparisons were made of subgroups. In comparing three-year-old and four-year-old displaced second children with three- and four-year-old second children who were youngest in the family, it was again found that age difference between children was an important contributor to the way in which the mother changed. Second children already having a younger sibling when they were three were at a marked disadvantage when contrasted with three-year-olds who remained the youngest in the family; they were treated less warmly, more restrictively, and encountered more friction in contact with the mother. However, the four-year-old groups were treated alike by the mother, whether or not a younger sibling had been born. These findings were interpreted to indicate that it is easier for the mother to meet the needs of the different children if they are more widely spaced. Comparison of five-year-old children who were permanently the youngest in the family with those who had younger siblings brought out still other facets of family interaction. It appears that the mother treats the five-year-old who is youngest in an acceleratory, restrictive, and coercive manner as if expecting him to live up to the requirements imposed on his older sibling. It may be that mothers who have younger children continue to *gauge* each child's development more realistically. Comparison of second children with the next younger sibling revealed that the changes found in the first child-second child comparison continue, though in modified form. The third child is treated slightly more warmly and indulgently than is the second, though few of the differences reached statistical significance.

To summarize the major findings:

1. Parent behavior toward first children as contrasted to second is on the average less warm emotionally and more restrictive and coercive. These differences are more apparent in the pre-school years than later. A similar differential exists between second and third children, though on a less distinct level.

2. Parent behavior toward second children does not tend to change systematically as the child grows older. Systematic changes do occur in the treatment of first children, mainly in the direction of reduced parent-child interaction.

3. Parents tend to be consistent in their methods of handling children and in their policies of child-rearing as revealed by the correlations between the treatment of first and second children. However, the nature of the emotional relationship between parent and child is less predictable from one sibling to another.

4. The age difference between the siblings is an important contributor to the variation in parent behavior toward the two children. It appears that closely spaced children are, in certain respects, more advantageously

treated than are widely spaced children. However, comparisons of children displaced when they were three and those displaced when four indicated that the former suffered greater loss of warmth and attentiveness from the mother.

APPENDIX

TABLE 13

INVENTORY OF CASES (PAIRS) USED IN AGE TREND ANALYSIS

Pair No.	Groups 1	2	3	4	5	6	7	8	9	Times used
1	x	x	x	x	x	x				6
2	x	x	x	x	x	x				6
3	x	x	x	x	x	x				6
4	x	x	x	x	x	x	x	x		8
5	x	x								2
6								x	x	2
7		x	x	x	x	x	x			6
8		x	x	x	x					4
9					x					1
10	x	x	x	x		x				5
11		x	x	x						3
12								x	x	2
13	x	x	x							3
14	x	x								2
15	x	x	x	x	x	x	x			7
16								x	x	2
17							x	x	x	3
18		x	x	x	x	x	x	x		7
19	x	x	x	x						4
20		x	x	x						3
21								x	x	2
22							x	x	x	3
23	x	x								2
24			x	x	x	x	x	x	x	7
25									x	1
26	x	x	x	x	x	x	x			7
27		x	x	x	x	x		x		6
28				x	x	x	x		x	4
29		x	x	x	x					4
30	x	x	x	x	x		x			6
31							x	x	x	3
32				x	x	x	x	x	x	5
33		x	x							2
34					x	x				2
35				x	x	x	x	x	x	6
36	x									1
37		x	x	x						3
38	x		x	x						3
39	x	x	x	x	x	x	x	x	x	9
40		x	x	x	x	x	x	x	x	7
41							x	x	x	3
42		x	x	x	x	x	x	x	x	8
43		x	x	x	x					4
44		x	x	x	x	x	x	x	x	8
45	x	x	x	x	x	x	x	x	x	9
46	x	x	x	x	x	x	x	x	x	9
N equals	18	28	28	27	24	22	20	20	19	

TABLE 14

SEX OF PAIRS IN AGE TREND ANALYSIS

	1	2	3	4	5	6	7	8	9
Like Sex Pairs	56%	54%	50%	52%	62%	55%	60%	50%	53%
Boys	33%	25%	21%	26%	33%	32%	30%	25%	21%
Girls	22%	29%	29%	26%	29%	23%	30%	25%	32%
Unlike Pairs	44%	46%	50%	48%	38%	45%	40%	50%	47%
Boy Older	28%	29%	25%	26%	25%	32%	25%	20%	21%
Girl Older	17%	18%	25%	22%	13%	14%	15%	30%	26%

TABLE 15

AUTHOR'S RATINGS USED IN AGE TREND ANALYSIS

	1	2	3	4	5	6	7	8	9
Author Rated									
1st Child	28%	32%	32%	33%	17%	27%	30%	20%	16%
2nd Child	33%	32%	25%	26%	17%	14%	35%	20%	37%
Both	6%	11%	11%	22%	25%	18%	10%	15%	16%
Other Raters	33%	25%	32%	19%	42%	41%	25%	45%	32%

TABLE 16

FREQUENCY DISTRIBUTION: ABSOLUTE AGE DIFFERENCE IN MONTHS OF SIBLING PAIRS USED IN AGE TREND ANALYSIS

Age Difference		1	2	3	4	5	6	7	8	9
12-17						1	1	1	2	2
18-23		2	4	5	6	8	7	6	5	5
24-29		4	6	4	4	3	3	4	2	2
30-35		4	7	8	8	7	6	6	7	6
36-41		1	2	2	1					
42-47		3	4	3	3	3	3	2	2	2
48-54		2	2	3	3	2	1	1		
55-		2	3	3	2		1		2	2
	Mean	37	37	37	35	30	31	29	31	32
	Meridian	33	32	33	32	29	30	27	31	30

ACKNOWLEDGMENTS

The present study was executed under the joint auspices of the Fels Research Institute and the Department of Psychology of Ohio State University. The author wishes to acknowledge deep indebtedness to the Fels Fund and to Dr. L. W. Sontag, Director of the Institute, for the facilitation of the project. Sincere appreciation is due Dr. John I. Lacey, of the Institute, and Dr. Boyd R. McCandless, then of Ohio State University, who provided guidance and assistance throughout the course of the study.

REFERENCES

1. ABERNETHY, E. M. 1940. Data on personality and family position. *J. Psychol.*, **10**, 303-307.
2. ADLER, A. 1928. Characteristics of the first, second, third child. *Children*, **3**, 14 and 52.
3. BALDWIN, A. L., KALHORN, J., and BREESE, F. H. 1949. The appraisal of parent behavior. *Psychol. Monogr.*, **63**, No. 4.
4. BALDWIN, A. L., KALHORN, J., and BREESE, F. H. 1945. Patterns of parent behavior. *Psychol. Monogr.*, **58**, No. 3.
5. BALDWIN, B. T., FILLMORE, E. A., and HADLEY, L. 1930. *Farm children.* Appleton, New York.
6. CATTELL, J. McK. 1927. *American men of science.* Science Press, Garrison, N.Y.
7. CHAMPNEY, H. 1941. The measurement of parent behavior. *Child Dev.*, **12**, 131-166.
8. CHAMPNEY, H. 1941. The variables of parent behavior. *J. abnorm. soc. Psychol.*, **36**, 525-542.
9. CHAPIN, F. S. 1930. *Scale for rating living room equipment*, p. 4. Univ. Minn. Inst. Child Welf., Minneapolis.
10. COFFEY, H. S., and WELLMAN, B. L. 1935. The role of cultural status in intelligence changes of pre-school children. *J. exp. Educ.*, **4**, 191-202.
11. DEAN, D. 1947. *Relation of ordinal position to personality in young children.* Unpublished Master's thesis, State University of Iowa.
12. GALTON, F. 1874. *English men of science : Their nature and nurture.* Macmillan, London.
13. GOODENOUGH, F. L. 1927. The relationship of the intelligence of pre-school children to the education of their parents. *Sch. Soc.*, **26**, 54-56.
14. GOODENOUGH, F. L. 1929. The relation of the intelligence of pre-school children to the occupation of their fathers. *Am. J. Psychol.*, **40**, 284-294.
15. JONES, H. E. 1933. Order of birth. In MURCHISON, C. (ed.) *Handbook of child psychology.* Clark Univ. Press, Worcester, Mass.
16. KROUT, M. H. 1939. Typical behavior patterns in twenty-six ordinal positions. *J. genet. Psychol.*, **55**, 3-30.
17. MURRAY, H. A., *et al.* 1938. *Explorations in personality : A clinical and experimental study of fifty men of college age.* Oxford Univ. Press, New York.
18. RADKE, M. 1946. The relation of parental authority to children's behavior and attitudes. *Univ. Minn. Child Welf. Monogr.*, No. 22.
19. SANFORD, R. N., *et al.* 1943. Physique, personality, and scholarship. *Monogr. Soc. Res. Child Dev.*, **8**, No. 1.
20. STAGNER, R., and KATZOFF, E. T. 1936. Personality as related to birth order and family size. *J. appl. Psychol.*, **20**, 340-346.
21. SYMONDS, P. M. 1939. *The psychology of parent-child relationships.* Appleton-Century, New York.
22. TERMAN, L. M., *et al.* 1925. *Genetic studies of genius :* Vol. 1. *The mental and physical traits of a thousand gifted children.* Stanford Univ. Press, Stanford, Calif.

XXIX

SEX OF SIBLING, BIRTH ORDER POSITION, AND FEMALE DISPOSITIONS TO CONFORM IN TWO-CHILD FAMILIES*

RICHARD SCHMUCK

The sex of a child may influence parental behaviour. Similarly, the sex of its sibling may influence a child's behaviour.

Adler's classical speculations[1] as well as recent empirical findings reported by Schachter[6] and Sampson[5] suggest the importance of birth order position as an independent variable in the study of personality development. While Adler's insights lack systematic continuity and empirical verification, those of Schachter and Sampson are derived from theory and supported by research. One of Schachter's hypotheses suggests that first born individuals are more anxious and affiliatively dependent than later born persons. Indeed, among the findings he reports, Schachter describes a study in which first born males were found to be less resistant to change in a social influence situation than later born males. In three small studies, Sampson carries Schachter's research further while investigating the inter-relations among birth order position, sex differences, motivation, and conformity. Briefly, Sampson reports that first born persons have a stronger achievement motive than later born persons; first-born females exhibit greater resistance to influence than later born females; and first born males exhibit less resistance to influence than later born males. Thus, Sampson's research suggests that Schachter's findings concerning the first born being more conforming applies only to males.

None of this previous work concerning birth order position, motiva-

* The author wishes to express his gratitude to J. Adelson, R. Cutler, G. Desautels, and B. Forrin for their help with this study.

Reprinted from CHILD DEVELOPMENT, Vol. 34, 1963, pp. 913-918.
© 1963, Society for Research in Child Development, Inc.

tion, and conformity has incorporated sex of sibling as an independent variable. The study reported here was done in order to investigate the respective influences of sex of sibling and birth order position on personal dispositions to comply or defy. We assume that sex of sibling is an important conditioner of personality especially in the area of conformity because of the theoretical speculations of Parsons and Bales.[4] Parsons and Bales argue that the family as a micro social system can be understood through combining some of the principles of group dynamics and functional sociology. One of their major postulates concerns the designation of genotypic roles in the "ideal-typical" family. Briefly, they describe the primary role of father and mother as instrumental (task) and expressive (social-emotional) respectively, those of son and daughter as instrumental inferior and expressive inferior. Parsons and Bales argue also that familial stability is maintained only when each of these roles is appropriately dovetailed. As one or more of these roles is deleted, certain system alterations as well as individual role performer changes take place in maintaining system stability. Thus, it is our inference that families with two sons or two daughters should differ systematically from families with one son and one daughter.

This study is designed to include sex of sibling as a possible independent variable of importance in the study of personality development. From the Parsons-Bales theory, we would hypothesize that boys insofar as they are to solve the externally given problems which challenge the family should tend to be more nonconforming, while girls in solving familial problems of smooth operation and interpersonal emotion should be more conforming in the "ideal-typical" family. However, in families with two boys or two girls, one of the boys should tend to be more conforming (more expressive inferior) than his brother, while one of the girls should tend to be less conforming (less expressive inferior) than her sister.

Two other approaches challenge this Parsons-Bales theory. The first of these involves the process of modeling. The argument here is that the second born models much of his behavior after that of the first born regardless of the sex. Thus, second-born girls with a sister should tend to be more conforming and second-born girls with a brother less conforming, etc. The second follows from Sampson's research which gives us the prediction that first-born boys should be more conforming than second born boys and that first-born girls should be less conforming than second born girls.

METHOD

SUBJECTS

Seventy-five female students from the University of Michigan volunteered as subjects. Only those girls were selected who were characterized by being from one of the following: (1) two-child families with (a) a younger brother, or (b) a younger sister, or (c) an older brother, or (d) an older sister; or (2) one-child families. Each of the girls in the two-child families differed from their siblings in age from 2 to 5 years. Fifty-one students were selected for the study. This population of subjects was distributed as shown in Table 1.

TABLE 1

CATEGORIES OF SUBJECTS*

Category	N
Only child	15
Subject with younger brother	9
Subject with younger sister	9
Subject with older brother	9
Subject with older sister	9

INSTRUMENT AND PROCEDURE

The personal disposition to conform was measured by a short projective instrument consisting of three pictures designed by Davis.[3] According to Davis's work, these pictures are related to compliant-defiant derivatives of the anal complex in psychoanalytic theory and were validated with Blum's Blacky Test.[2] The Davis instrument includes:

Picture 1—A girl sitting in the midst of a messy room. This picture relates to a personal dimension involving orderliness-disorderliness.

Picture 2—A girl sitting at a large table, on top of which is a piggy bank, and scattered piles of coins. This picture relates to a personal dimension involving frugality-impulsiveness.

Picture 3—A woman standing in a bathroom looking at a child seated on a toilet. This picture relates to a personal dimension involving compliant-defiant attitudes toward the toilet training situation.

This instrument was administered to all subjects by projecting the pictures on a screen. For each picture the subjects were requested to compose a short story, telling what the situation is, what led up to the situation, what the people are thinking and feeling, and what they will do. The subjects were allowed 5 minutes to write their story for each picture.

RESULTS AND DISCUSSION

Each story written by the subjects was scored as indicating either a personal tendency to conform or defy. The criterion used for these scoring designations was the global content analysis method proposed and validated by Davis. The stories were placed into one of the two coding categories by two judges with 96 per cent agreement. On the remaining stories, the judges agreed on the appropriate category after discussion. In

---

* 2- to 5-year age difference between siblings.

order for a subject to be classified as having a tendency to conform, she had to score "conforming" on at least two of the three pictures. And conversely, for her to be classified as having a tendency to defy, she had to score "nonconforming" on at least two of the three pictures. Table 2 shows the results of this analysis.

TABLE 2
CLASSIFICATION OF SUBJECTS INTO COMPLIANT OR DEFIANT CATEGORIES

	Defiant	Compliant
Only child	7	8
Subject with younger brother	2	7
Subject with younger sister	6	3
Subject with older brother	4	5
Subject with older sister	8	1

Only children were included in the study as controls. Our expectation was that only children would have scores comparable to a general population of college girls. The results in Table 3 indicate that for only children the ratio is two to one in favor of a tendency to defy on picture 1 and approximately one to one on both picture 2 and picture 3. These results are in accord with those proportions reported by Davis. The results, picture by picture, are shown in Table 3.

TABLE 3
COMPLIANT AND DEFIANT STORIES RELATED TO INDIVIDUAL PICTURES

	PICTURE 1 D*	C	PICTURE 2 D	C	PICTURE 3 D	C	TOTALS D	C
Only child	10	5	7	8	8	7	25	20
Subject with younger brother	5	4	1	8	3	6	9	18
Subject with younger sister	6	3	2	7	8	1	16	11
Subject with older brother	7	2	2	7	4	5	13	14
Subject with older sister	8	1	5	4	7	2	20	7

An analysis of variance of the two variables, sex of sibling and birth order position, indicates that a significant difference exists for determining personal tendencies to conform or defy due only to the sex of sibling variable. The difference as shown in Table 4 is such that those subjects with female siblings show less of a tendency to conform than those with a male sibling. The data in Table 3 indicate that picture 3 is highly important in determining this difference.

This finding supports the familial social system-balance speculation of Parsons and Bales. Their theory predicts indirectly that a higher probability exists that girls with a brother will tend to develop more feminine characteristics, in this case tendencies to conform, than girls with a sister. While, on the other hand, there is a higher probability that girls with a sister will develop more masculine characteristics, tendencies to defy. The

* D = defiant; C = compliant.

TABLE 4

SUMMARY OF ANALYSIS OF VARIANCE:
DIFFERENCES IN COMPLIANCE-DEFIANCE DUE TO SEX AND BIRTH ORDER

	df	MS	F
Sex of Sibling.....................	1	5·445	8.17*
Birth Order......................	1	1.778	2.67
Interaction.......................	1	.000	.00
Within Cells	32	.667	
Total...........................	35		

finding does not support either the modeling speculation which argues that second-born siblings will resemble the first born more often than not, regardless of sex differences, or Sampson's finding that first-born girls are less conforming than later born girls.

An alternative explanation for our finding can be presented directly from psychoanalytic theory. During the Oedipal phase, a girl becomes affectively attached to her father and a boy to his mother. According to psychoanalytic theory, sexual identity is learned during the resolution of the interpersonal conflicts arising in this situation. In families with two female children, both competing for the affect of their father, more conflict and hostility is probable between the two girls than in the family with one boy and one girl. For in the latter "balanced-family," the female child would not have to share affective investment in her father with anyone except her mother. Conversely, the same applies to the male child. Hostilities created in the family with two girls might be directed at three objects: (a) the sister since she takes too much affect from the father, (b) the mother since she takes too much affect from the father, or (c) the father because he shares his affect with sister and mother. In the latter two cases, the siblings are directing hostilities and defiance toward authoritarian and disciplinarian figures representing the adult community and societal standards. These speculations are partially supported by the importance of picture 3 in determining which girls had tendencies to conform or defy. Picture 3, the toilet training scene, is the only picture which directly confronts the subject with an interpersonal situation involving adult and child in an authoritarian-follower relation.

It is impossible to say whether an explanation presented by the Parsons-Bales social system formulation, the Freudian psychoanalytic formulation, a combination of the two, or some other is appropriate here. Our finding is explicit, however, in indicating a need for further elaboration on the findings already presented in research on sibling constellations. Our research indicates that sex of sibling must be considered as an important independent variable in understanding the development of personal tendencies to conform or defy. It also indicates that the work relating sibling position to motivation and conformity is limited in scope. Our

* $p < .01$ level.

finding emphasizes the necessity for multivariable research designs in studying the possible ramifications of sibling constellations.

SUMMARY

This study explores the effect of two dimensions of sibling constellations, birth order position and sex of sibling, on the development of personal tendencies to conform in girls. A three-picture projective test measuring personal tendencies to comply or defy was administered to 51 female students at the University of Michigan. Only girls participated in the study who were characterized by being from one of the following: (1) two-child families with (a) a younger brother, or (b) a younger sister, or (c) an older brother, or (d) an older sister; or (2) one-child families. Each of the girls in the two-child families differed from their siblings by from 2 to 5 years of age. An analysis of variance indicates that sex of sibling is the only significant variable ($p<.01$). No interaction between birth order position and sex of sibling was indicated by the data. The results show that girls with a sister more often have personal tendencies to defy than girls with a brother. Two theoretical explanations, a Parsons-Bales social system-balance speculation and a Freudian psychoanalytic speculation, appear appropriate for the finding. This work indicates that multivariable research designs linking dimensions of sibling constellations to personality characteristics are appropriate next studies in this area.

REFERENCES

1. ADLER, A. (LINTON, J., and VAUGHAN, R., trans.) 1945. *Social interest: A challenge to mankind.* Faber & Faber, London.
2. BLUM, G. S. 1949. A study of the psychoanalytic theory of psychosexual development. *Genet. Psychol. Monogr.*, **39**, 3-99.
3. DAVIS, M. C. 1954. *An empirical investigation of differences in fantasy associated with compliant and defiant dimensions of character.* Unpublished thesis, Bennington College.
4. PARSONS, T., and BALES, R. F. 1955. *Family, socialization and interaction process.* Free Press, Glencoe, Ill.
5. SAMPSON, E. E. 1962. Birth order, need achievement, and conformity. *J. abnorm. soc. Psychol.*, **64**, 155-159.
6. SCHACHTER, S. 1959. *The psychology of affiliation.* Stanford Univ. Press, Stanford, Calif.

XXX

PREJUDICIAL SCAPEGOATING AND NEUTRALIZING FORCES IN THE FAMILY GROUP, WITH SPECIAL REFERENCE TO THE ROLE OF "FAMILY HEALER"

NATHAN W. ACKERMAN

Coping mechanisms for anxiety and conflict in the family include a shift of alignments and splits within the group, with prejudicial scapegoating of one part by another. The process requires a persecuter, a victim and a 'healer'. It can have significance for the emotional health or ill-health of the family members.

A long-time objective of family study is the development of a family typology, a classification of families according to their psychosocial organization and mental health functioning. Of special interest is the correlation of structure, function and developmental stage of the family with the emotional destiny of its individual members. This is an undertaking of huge dimensions. Present limitations of knowledge make a frontal attack on the problem in its entirety hardly feasible; we must be satisfied with a piecemeal approach. We are engaged, therefore, in a series of limited, exploratory studies, hoping to move, stage by stage, toward the ultimate goal of a systematic family classification. In so doing, we are building stepping-stones toward an integrated, conceptual framework for understanding the relations of family dynamics and health. Toward this end, we accumulate data in the following areas: (1) the harmonizing and balancing of essential family functions, epitomizing in a general way the

Reprinted from THE INTERNATIONAL JOURNAL OF SOCIAL PSYCHIATRY, CONGRESS ISSUE 1964.

potentials of unity, stability and growth of the family group; (2) the dominant and competing representations of family identity, goals and values: the identity associations of individual and family; (3) the characteristic alliances and splits within the family rôle relationships and characteristic patterns of complementarity; (4) the core conflicts of the family unit and the methods of coping: the dynamic interrelations of interpersonal and intrapersonal conflict, the interplay of family defence of the integrity and continuity of family functions, and individual defence against conflict and anxiety: the special function as defence of a change of alignments and splits within the group and the prejudicial scapegoating of one part by another; (5) the relations between selective idiosyncratic features of family structure and function and the susceptibility of its members to emotional breakdown.

For the gathering of data and insights in these several areas, we pursue a series of focused studies on one or another special aspect of family development and adaptation. For these purposes, we use our library of sound moving pictures of families in treatment. We now have 120 hours of films of family treatment interviews, covering more than thirty-five different families. From such data, we hope to uncover some of the connections between family dynamics and mental health, and thereby identify criteria by which to distinguish the family types which breed a psychotic member from those others which produce neurotic members, acting-out types of character disorder, or learning failures with associated behavior deviations.

Central to the whole problem of family dynamics and health are the relations of conflict and coping within the matrix of changing patterns of interaction. The outcome of the struggle with conflict may be broadly stated in the following alternatives: (1) The conflict is correctly perceived and an early and rational solution is found. (2) The conflict is correctly perceived and is effectively contained, while a solution, not immediately available, is being sought. (3) The conflict is misperceived and distorted; it is not effectively contained, nor is it appropriately solved; it is not adequately compromised or compensated; it spills out into irrational "acting-out". (4) The control of conflict fails, resulting in progressive disorganization of family relations and impairment of family functions.

The range of mechanisms for coping with conflict and anxiety in a family may be tentatively stated as follows: (1) Enhancement of the bond of love, sharing and identification. (2) "Repeopling" of the group—the elimination of a member or the addition of a new member. (3) A change in the external environment of the family unit. (4) A change in the configuration of family rôle relationships brought about through a variety of devices: (a) shared solution of conflict and the attainment of an improved level of complementarity; (b) the reduction of intensity of conflict through manipulation, coercion, compromise compensation, denial or escape; (c) making rôles more rigid; (d) making rôles more fluid; (e) a shift in alignments and splits within the group and prejudicial scapegoating of one part by another.

It is the last of these, prejudicial scapegoating, to which we now turn our attention. In the course of our clinical explorations, we have been impressed with the emergence of a special set of emotional mechanisms which we characterize as "prejudicial scapegoating and neutralizing forces in the family group". Recurrently we observe certain constellations of family interaction which we have epitomized as a pattern of interdependent rôles, those of the destroyer or persecutor, the victim of the scapegoating attack, and the "family healer" or the "family doctor". We constructed a theoretical model to represent this cluster of interrelated rôles. Stated in simplified terms, the destroyer or persecutor uses a special prejudice as the vehicle of his attack. Another member of the family becomes the object of this attack, the victim of scapegoating; he sustains an emotional injury which renders him susceptible to breakdown. The "family healer" or "doctor" intervenes to neutralize the destructive powers of this attack and thereby, in some measure, rescues the victim. The enactment of these reciprocal rôle behaviors may be overt, covert; simple or complex; sharply outlined or relatively amorphous. These processes may occur at multiple levels of family interaction. They may change as the family moves from one stage of adaptation to another, or otherwise undergoes change in its organization. We now test the theory that a specific patterning of these emotional mechanisms offers a useful diagnostic clue to the psychosocial identity and emotional health of a given family.

Close study of family interaction suggests specific kinds of prejudicial scapegoating are characteristic of a given family and become organized in an irrational way around special meanings that are attached to differences among the family members. Prejudice of this kind is of a distinct and private nature. It differs from the common stereotypes of prejudice in the wider community. Insofar as it is a recurrent and predictable manifestation of the idiosyncratic quality of family life, it provides a specific diagnostic clue to the emotional organization and functioning of a special kind of family.

From this hypothesis arise several questions. (1) What is the special rôle of prejudicial scapegoating in the life history of a given family? (2) How are the rôle functions of attacker, victim and healer organized within such a family? (3) What is the significance of these processes for the emotional health of the family and its members? (4) What is the relation between this kind of social disorder and the susceptibility to specific mental disorder?

Before amplifying these questions, we must first make clear our conception of the phenomenon of family prejudice. We distinguish here two categories of prejudice, private and public. They are different and yet interdependent. Prejudice within the private life of the family assumes a form manifestly unlike that encountered in public life, i.e. the familiar antagonisms based on differences of color, religion, ethnic origin, etc. Private intrafamilial prejudice is of another kind, so subtly different that it is often not recognized as prejudice at all, yet it is there just the same—real, abundant, intense, far-reaching in its effects. It attaches to differences, the real and unreal, among family members. Private prejudice may become displaced and translated into public forms of prejudice. Public forms of prejudice may in circular fashion aggravate the tendency to private prejudice.

In a basic sense the members of one family may be viewed as being the same kind of people. They are, in fact, related by blood. They resemble one another; they have much in common; they share the same way of life. In view of this sameness, one might expect an absence of prejudice among the insiders and the concentration of prejudice against outsiders. This is not the case, however. Among members of the same family group, there are elements of differences as well as sameness, differences in appearance, attitudes, traits, strivings and values. Depending on the idiosyncratic emotional structure of a particular family, symbolic meanings are attached to these differences which are then subjectively felt by one or another part of the family as a distinct danger. The person showing the difference is felt to be the alien, the invasive stranger who threatens the security, the needs and values of other members of the group. Sharing this sense of threat, several or most members of the family form an alliance to attack the source of the difference.

In the inner life of the family, such prejudice becomes organized around a range of differences: the battle between the sexes—male or female, or vice versa; youth against grown-ups or vice versa; brain against brawn or vice versa; money and power *vs.* a passive way of life; control *vs.* spontaneity and pleasure; a liberal *vs.* a conservative political ideology. At other levels, prejudice becomes attached to such qualities as fat or skinny, tall or short, smart or stupid, light or dark skin, smooth or hairy skin. Still other prejudices of this kind attach to such matters as habits of eating and dressing or cleanliness and orderliness.

A question may promptly be raised: Why do we call this prejudice? Are there not valid reactions to difference, legitimate likes and dislikes, preferences and aversions that may not constitute true prejudice? Certainly it is so that people who achieve sound health have a full measure of likes and dislikes, attractions and repulsions. Such attitudes become transformed into true prejudice, however, to whatever extent they become rigid, fixed or automatized and walled off from the corrective influence of the prevailing realities. Furthermore, such prejudice may be mild or intense, benign or malignant. In its benign form, such prejudice need not extend to the compulsive urge to hold the self together by breaking someone else down. In point of fact, however, the more disturbed the family becomes, the more do the members lean toward organization of malignant forms of prejudice. The significant feature is its very contagion.

Some, or even all, members of the family become bound in its organization. While contagious, it is also selective in its influence. It aggravates prejudice in some members, while fortifying the immunity of others against it.

Prejudice and mental illness have something in common. Both have to do with human relations and are affected by the struggle to reconcile human differences. Both impair a person's ability to perform his tasks in life, especially that of getting along with other people. The ultimate source of both conditions is the intimate emotional exchange within the family group, which is the prime training ground for learning to get along with other people. It is exactly the striving within the family to establish one's position and to win the reward of affection and respect for one's unique quality, that affects the proneness to prejudice as well as to mental illness.

Nevertheless, in some crucial respects, the two forms of behavior are distinct. They evidence themselves in a different life context, and yet between them there is a significant dynamic connection. People moving toward an emotional breakdown frequently lean on prejudice as defence. To save themselves, to stave off the threat of their own breakdown, they are motivated to break down another member of the family. There is convincing force to such remarks as "My mother is driving me crazy" and "She'll be the death of me yet".

Our immediate concern is with these private family prejudices, both as individual defence against the fright of dangerous exposure and as family defence of the continuity of family functions. To the degree to which an individual feels incomplete, weak, exposed and vulnerable, the difference of another can become magnified, symbolically, to the dimensions of penetrating threat. In analogous fashion, to the degree to which the family as a group fails to integrate an effective identity and value orientation, or suffers a split of identity, the assertion of difference in one part of the family may be felt as a menace to the unity and continuity of the family as a whole.

To return to the questions posed earlier, when a clinician trains his eye on a troubled family, he is immediately struck by the division of the group into competing emotional alliances. Each member identifies with particular component representations of family identity, expressed in terms of what he or she wants the family to be or do. A competing faction wages its battle around the felt threat of these differences. Around these differences, there is the patterning of specific family prejudices. In the unfolding of such emotional mechanisms, we believe we can identify the three main patterns already mentioned, the rôle of the attacker, the victim and the healer. At a given point in time, these rôles are fulfilled by particular members and with the passage of time by other members. Each of these is selected for his respective rôle by shared unconscious emotional processes within the group. The family destroyer punishes the member whose difference is felt as an offence and as a menace to family continuity. The member who is chosen as scapegoat suffers an emotional injury and is thus rendered vulnerable to the danger of mental breakdown. Still another family member enters the rôle of peace-maker, protector, healer, or if you like, family doctor, rising to the rescue of the victim of the punishing attack. To the degree to which the rescuing member holds the capacity to neutralize the destructive force of the prejudicial assault, he offers to the scapegoating victim some immunity against breakdown. At times, the member who starts out as the rôle of persecutor or destroyer may shift into the rôle of victim or healer, or vice versa. Each of these functional rôles may be fulfilled at various times by members of the nuclear family or by a relative, a delegate of the extended family. Again it is to be emphasized that this is a theoretical model rather than an actuality and in the clinical observation of family life these patterns may be complex, disguised and difficult to identify.

Further developments are involved. In the unfolding of critical family conflict, a primary prejudice attaching to the conspicuous and threatening difference of one member may evoke a counter-prejudice. In this case, the emotional sequence is attack, defence and counter-attack. Thus the emergence of one pattern of scapegoating evokes the emergence of an opposite pattern of attack and scapegoating. Ultimately, reciprocal patterns of attack and scapegoating appear on the scene. The rôle of family healer then becomes progressively more complicated and may be fulfilled in sequence by different members of the group. In this context, one direction of scapegoating may be counterbalanced by another. The scapegoating may occur also at multiple levels and in a circular pattern. A pair of parents may scapegoat a teenager, the teenager may scapegoat a sibling. All of them together may then scapegoat a grandparent. Or the scapegoating theme may unfold in a different way. In a conflict between a pair of parents, the teenager may at one point in time enter the rôle of healer of the war between the parents and at a later stage turn into destroyer.

Temporarily this process may serve to bind the family closer together. At another stage it may be critically divisive in its effects. The less rational the prejudice, the more does it lead to progressive distortion of family rôle relationships and impairment of essential family functions. Although it may temporarily serve as a means of support for one or another partial family alliance and corresponding family identity and value orientation, at its core this process becomes progressively less rational, fragments family relationships and alienates its members.

In this concatenation of events, several other developments are possible, contingent on the emotional condition of the family. If the condition favors it, there may be a movement toward resolution of the primary prejudice and, with this, an easing of the scapegoating assault; or, if the emotional matrix so disposes, a counter-prejudice may emerge. Beyond that a range of efforts unfold, the intent of which is to neutralize and assuage the harm inflicted upon the victim of family scapegoating.

If the movement is towards the resolution of the primary prejudice, and the pressure towards splitting the family and the setting up of competing alliances is reduced, the family members reach out for an improved quality of union and love. On the other hand, if this is blocked, the primary prejudice evokes a counter-prejudice and the function of family healer is stirred to action; it becomes, in fact, an urgent necessity.

But one must bear other alternatives in mind. The prejudicial attack may shift from its original object to another member of the family. One prejudice may be substituted for another. The attack may be displaced from the family scapegoat to a new target outside the family.

The vicissitudes of control of intrafamilial prejudice are the paths along which the emotional split of the family group achieves a specific pattern; one part of the family pits itself against another. Therefore, prejudice and counter-prejudice formations need to be correlated with the split of the family into warring segments, with a conflict over differences, the method of coping, and with the unconscious selection of particular family members as scapegoats and others as rescuers or healers.

If, on occasion, a member tries to avoid being sucked into the family conflict, and for his own safety seeks to remain unaligned, he achieves, at best, merely a temporary and precarious protection. Over the stretch of time, such an attempt at non-involvement is short-lived and must fail. Often such a gesture at non-involvement is patently false; in fact, it conceals an entry into a compensatory alliance with some other part of the nuclear family or extended family, or reflects a flight for protection into alliance with a peer group. It is of the very essence of the emotional life of the family that there is no such thing as non-intervention. At the very most it is a protest, a dramatic gesture. Even so, it cannot be sustained because it disconnects the member's feeding line to the family and ultimately ends in alienation. What it really cloaks is a hidden tendency to fickleness and betrayal and the urge to find compensatory belongingness and protection elsewhere. A member of the family behaving in this way may erratically juggle his alliances from one side of the family to another. In such a setting, "acting-out" becomes not merely a unit of experience in which one member lives out the unconscious urges of another, but also the vehicle for the discharge of shared aggression as one part of the family does battle with another.

It is, therefore, of the essence to identify specific forms of family prejudice, the rôles of persecutor, scapegoat and healer, the competing family alliances, the specific conflicts around which the battle rages, and the type of family group and individual defence that are mobilized to neutralize the destructive results of scapegoating.

SUMMARY OF RELEVANT HYPOTHESES

(1) Disturbed families tend to break up into warring factions: (*a*) each member allies himself with one or another faction; (*b*) each faction com-

petes for the dominant position; (*c*) each faction asserts a preferred family identity and value orientation representing a preferred set of goals, rôle expectations and rôle complementarity; (*d*) each faction attaches a specific meaning to individual difference and organizes around this specific device of prejudicial scapegoating.

(2) A leader emerges in each faction: (*a*) each leader personifies the family identity and values of his faction.

(3) A particular member of the family is chosen as a victim of prejudicial attack: (*a*) an idiosyncratic quality of this member becomes a symbolic representation of the perceived threat to the dominant family identity.

(4) A defensive counter-attack is mobilized: (*a*) the scapegoat allies himself with another part of the family and asserts an opposed form of prejudice; (*b*) to the extent that this defensive alliance succeeds, the primary scapegoat minimizes his own injury at the expense of another. He may shift from the rôle of scapegoat to that of persecutor; (*c*) to the extent that this defensive alliance fails, the primary scapegoat finds himself undefended and alone; he becomes progressively more vulnerable and may suffer a breakdown; he denies that he is in the scapegoated position and pretends the victim is another member of the group; he shifts to the rôle of healer; if this succeeds, he may reduce or nullify his vulnerability.

(5) A member is unconsciously selected as the "healer" or "family doctor": (*a*) he provides the emotional antidote to the destructive effects of the prejudicial assault; (*b*) he may be motivated to accept this rôle in order to turn the attack away from himself, or he merely pretends to be the healer, while being secretly absorbed only with his own security.

(6) The health–sickness continuum is influenced by the shifting balance of the effective struggle between the factions toward: (*a*) entrenchment of valid values of family identity and appropriate balancing of family functions which enhance love, loyalty, sharing, identification and growth; (*b*) entrenchment of a progressive trend towards the organization of competing prejudices, rigidifying the family organization and constricting the rôles or pathologically loosening them in a way that reduces emotional nourishment for all members; (*c*) the relation of these processes to emotional health of the family group and its individual members may be examined at the following levels: (i) the preservation and enhancement of the unity of one part of the family at the expense of another—some aspects of family unity are protected and other aspects sacrificed; (ii) some essential functions are maintained and other functions are impaired or lost; (iii) in a selective manner some levels of family relationship complementarity are protected, while others are reduced, distorted or lost; (iv) some levels of coping are effective and other levels fail. This can be traced to specific patterns of interplay between family group defence and individual defence against anxiety.

These processes are reflected in a shift of equilibrium as between health-maintaining and sickness-inducing tendencies in the family with a corresponding effect on the potentials of growth for the family as a unit and for its members, and, at the opposite pole, contribute to the precipitation of mental illness in one or another member.

XXXI

ANNIVERSARIES IN MENTAL ILLNESS*

JOSEPHINE R. HILGARD and MARTHA F. NEWMAN

*A breakdown in health at a moment in time may have
been determined by it being the anniversary of a significant
event in the past life of the individual. Parent loss is
one of these events.*

This paper reports the first results of a systematic search for cases of
anniversary reactions among hospitalized patients—that is, cases in which,
after becoming a parent, the patient developed a psychosis, or neurosis
severe enough to need hospitalization, which seemed to represent an
anniversary or re-enactment of significant events in his own childhood,
particularly the loss of his father or mother. In other words, a central
problem involves the way in which the presence of children influences
adult functioning, especially in relation to the adult's own unresolved
problems from childhood. The study reported here is a more extensive
and systematic examination of the hypotheses presented in an earlier
paper which described anniversary reactions in two patients who had lost
parents in childhood.[3]

While in many patients who are less ill, one may catch glimpses of this
same process, there is an overlay of more-or-less successful defenses,
which can obscure the clear delineation of the anniversary syndrome.
Thus we have concentrated upon psychotic material, which offers more
potentially identifiable cases. We have also confined our study to patients
whose reality testing was relatively intact until after marriage and parenthood. In our investigation, we are attempting to afford a more concise

* We wish to express our appreciation of Mrs. Charlotte von Witzleben, who was a
valued staff member on this project from 1954 until her untimely death in January, 1956.

picture of the anniversary process and its frequency, to contribute to the study of identifications and integration, and to learn more about the impact of children upon parents and upon the marital relationship.

In the search for cases fitting the general specifications of potential anniversary material, we turned to sources with a large number of admissions of psychotic patients, where historical background material was available and where there was access to the patients for exploratory psychotherapy. Agreements were worked out with the Veterans Administration Hospital in Palo Alto and with Agnews State Hospital for the review of all cases and the use of those meeting the criteria of the study. As the investigation proceeded, the preponderance of female cases meeting our criteria meant that it was not economical of time to continue our work at the Veterans Administration Hospital; thus the remainder of our work centered exclusively at Agnews State Hospital, and our quantitative data are based exclusively on patients at this Hospital. One of the two illustrative cases reported in this paper is, however, from the Veterans Administration Hospital.

What criteria did we set for potential anniversary cases, from among the large initial group? We decided to investigate all instances in which the patient had, between the ages of 2 and 18 inclusive, lost a parent, and in which the patient had not been hospitalized for mental illness until after marriage and parenthood. We could then attempt to correlate dates of childhood loss with dates of first hospitalization.

It was postulated that psychotic symptoms might be aroused either when the patient neared the age of the parent at death, or when the patient's child reached the age that the patient had been when the parent died. Thus the onset might represent a *coincidence with the parent's age*, if, for example, the patient's mother had died at 28 and the patient's initial hospitalization or mental illness occurred when she was 28 or within one year of this age. Or the onset might represent a *coincidence with the child's age*, if, for example, the parent had died when the patient was 8 years old and, at the time of the patient's first admission, a child in the family was 8 years old, or within one year of this age. A double coincidence might occur if the patient had reached the parent's age at death and also had a child the same age he was at the parent's death.

Our criteria for selection also included the following restrictions: All patients were to be white, American-born, under 50 years of age, with a diagnosis of psychosis or neurosis severe enough for treatment in a mental hospital, excluding alcoholism and psychopathic personality.

Of the 3,909 admissions to Agnews State Hospital in a sampling of nine months in 1954 and nine months in 1955, 122 cases met the above criteria. These 122 cases then became the active experimental sample. Of these, 104 were women and 18 were men. The 18 men in the experimental sample represented 1 per cent of total men admitted; the 104 women represented 5.5 per cent of total women admitted. This discrepancy, far above chance expectation, is being investigated in a separate study. Because of the small number of men, only women who had lost parents were used for statistical purposes.

Women who had lost mothers in childhood totaled 43 cases and women who had lost fathers totaled 54. An additional 7 women had lost both. The two groups of mother-loss and father-loss were treated separately because, at least in these small samples, the syndrome appeared much more frequently among women who had lost mothers. In the women who had lost mothers, approximately one-third of the cases showed age coincidences, while only one-ninth of women who had lost fathers showed such coincidence.

A statistical method was used to determine whether or not these coincidences were beyond chance expectations. While we shall not go into detail here, the logic was as follows: We pooled all of the *childhood loss dates* in one group and all of the *first hospitalization dates* in a second group, and then determined how often they would correspond by chance. In other words, we tried to determine whether a patient's own anniversary dates were any better targets for her onset of illness than anniversary dates borrowed from other patients in the sample. This procedure is more valid than attempting to match some outside control group to this highly specialized sample of patients. Analysis is not yet complete, because we are accumulating more data, but the results so far suggest that the number of coincidences in women who had lost mothers is probably beyond chance expectation.

At best, a statistical test can show only that anniversaries are important. For the findings to be significant in understanding and treating mental illness, detailed information from individual cases is needed. We shall here present clinical material from two of our cases to indicate the kind of data with which we are dealing.

LAURA H—A CASE OF FATHER-LOSS

Laura H had been hospitalized at the age of 30 for the first time, with the symptoms of catatonic schizophrenia. This had happened two years before we saw her. She fitted our sample because she had lost a parent in childhood; her father had been shot to death when she was 6 years old. At the time of her first hospitalization her only child, a daughter, was 6 years old.

Laura was the oldest of three children, the only girl, a favorite of the father. He had been quite indulgent, babied her, and brought her presents. At first in treatment she portrayed an ideal picture of him, but later on she recalled her resentment over his repeatedly leaving her in the parked car while he visited a woman during the year or two before his death. At a party the night before the fatal shooting, the father had put his arm around the wife of the man who shot him the next morning.

Laura saw her father's death from the window. She expressed guilt because she had seen the gun in the man's hand as he came through the house looking for her father, and she had not called for help.

Following her father's death, Laura was nervous, had difficulty eating, and did poorly in school. She also had a few seizures characterized by the following symptoms: staring glassily, walking in a daze like a sleepwalker, falling down and fainting, setting her jaws and clenching her teeth as in a convulsion. The seizures were precipitated, for instance, when she saw a fight, saw the school building on fire, and saw an accident happen to her younger brother. These attacks, though infrequent, recurred for a year after her father's death. After she was placed in a special boarding school away from home, they stopped.

In the school, where she remained for a year, she was given special attention and care, and she afterwards recalled members of the staff with affection. One event appeared to have made a lasting impression upon her. About three months after she arrived at the school, she had an appendectomy, to which she reacted with terror. Since this occurred on December 21, she was unable to participate in the Christmas play. At about this time, she became religious; although neither parent had stressed this at home, the atmosphere of the school was a strongly religious one.

The mother's reaction to the tragedy of the father's death had its impact on Laura, who remembered her as depressed, choked and crying, with a continuing unhappiness. The mother, who was a schoolteacher, went back to college to get more training and then continued teaching in order to support the family. When one of the authors saw the mother, she seemed dominating, aggressive, and very talkative, in contrast to Laura, whose usual personality was timid and unaggressive.

Between the ages of 9 and 11, Laura rejoined the family, her grandmother looking after the home and children while the mother taught. The grandmother was described as an ardent churchwoman, stubborn, and strong willed. When Laura was 11 she went to live with an aunt and uncle in the country, remaining there for two years. The mother then remarried, and Laura returned home, but life with her stepfather was not happy for her. She described him as an old-country disciplinarian who understood boys much better. He was seductive at times toward her and her girl friends. The patient said that she thought her mother was jealous of her with the stepfather, and she guessed that she was jealous of her stepfather's place with her mother. The mother said that she thought the stepfather was jealous of the closeness between Laura and herself.

Laura graduated from high school with mediocre grades. She obtained a job as a skilled factory worker, the same type of work that her father had done. She was restless, and, after a short period in the factory, joined the WAC's. There she met her husband, who was an engineer, and after a brief courtship they were married. He was 15 years older than she, an only child and still quite attached to his mother, dependent, passive and a steady worker.

The couple took precautions against pregnancy only for the first few weeks of marriage, for Laura felt an intense desire for a child. After the birth of their daughter the next year, her personality began slowly to change. Her husband said that earlier she had been slender, happy, artistic, musical, and excellent company, with but one outstanding fault—she was usually very late. After Sue's birth she began to gain weight, with an increase of 50 pounds in the next six years. When Sue was a baby, the patient was very affectionate with her, and during Sue's early childhood there was a fairly good relationship, although the child was thin and an eating problem. The husband would sometimes find the two romping together, but this stopped some months before the patient's breakdown.

Also near the time of the breakdown, Laura developed the conviction that her husband was having an affair with another woman and was taking their daughter along when he went to see her.

Laura began having seizures, which her husband described as epileptic, during the six months prior to her first hospitalization. Her eyes would become staring and glassy, her body would become rigid, and she would faint. Laura's mother, who was extremely exercised at these seizures' being termed epileptic, said that the description of them tallied exactly with the "trances" which had occurred 25 years before, following the father's death, and which had not recurred since. It was during the longest of these episodes, which lasted six days, that Laura was first hospitalized and diagnosed as catatonic. Laura was then 30 and her daughter 6.

After the patient returned home from this first brief hospitalization, she encircled December 21 on her calendar, according to her husband—the same date on which the frightening appendectomy had occurred. When December 21 came, she had a luminous vision of an angel. While prior to this vision her reading had been mainly confined to books and magazines on romance, the stage, and the screen, now she abruptly changed to Bibles, big and little, Catholic and Jewish.

The major repetitions which appear in this case are as follows: When the patient was hospitalized, she was the same age that her father had been at his death, and the daughter was the same age that the patient had been when he died. The seizures which preceded the first hospitalization were apparently like those which she had had following her father's death. The resurgence of religious interest also presented a parallel; just as she had turned to religion with the crisis of the childhood appendectomy, in the religious atmosphere of the school, so she apparently turned to religion during this reliving experience, in approximately the same time sequence. In treatment she commented, "I had religion after my father's death. Before that I had my father." Another parallel was the patient's conviction about her husband's unfaithfulness and their daughter's accompanying him.

Thus there appear to be enough repetitions to support the interpretation that the anniversary was more than a chance coincidence. What is the dynamic interpretation? The problem in these cases almost always turns out to involve complex identifications and shifts of identifications with environmental events, such as the birth of the child or the reaching of anniversaries. It appears that as long as Laura's father was alive, she had an image of herself as the loved daughter who in some ways successfully replaced the mother. She was then punished for this by the death of her father and the prolonged mourning of her mother. The familiar Oedipal conflict could not be resolved because of the father's death and the repressive influence of guilt. This leads to the assumption that there was a fixation primarily at the Oedipal level.

While this patient showed more childhood disturbance than any other in our sample, she weathered the crisis sufficiently to graduate from high school, work, and marry. The choice of a spouse was a key one—and is likely to be in anniversary symptomatology, where one is dealing with re-enactments and must be alert to what happens at the time of major life choices, such as the choice of occupation and the choice of a mate. Thus Laura's choice of an older man who was parental toward her was a key factor in subsequent developments. In marriage, she tried to recapture her role as a daughter, which was successful until she was replaced by her own daughter. It was with the advent of the child that her adult symptomatology began. Laura's mother was aware of the parallelism in the two generations and expressed it cogently:

> Have you seen Laura's daughter and her father? Well, Laura's relation to *her* father was exactly the same. Sue has every mannerism her mother had at that age, and she's a diplomat too. She is my Laura all over. . . . Laura was "Daddy's only girl" and the first born. He made over her plenty. Martin is an old bachelor who fell in love with a young wife and has a beautiful daughter who is the apple of his eye.

This case deviates in one way markedly from other cases of father-loss in our statistical sample. Laura's age coincided with her father's age at death, and her child's age coincided with her own age at his death. In the six other cases, the age coincidences were only with the child's age; a first or second child in the family was now the age the patient had been at the time of the loss. Of these six cases, two were hospitalized shortly after giving birth to an infant, and this factor was probably an important one in the timing.

ELEANOR M—A CASE OF MOTHER-LOSS

Eleanor M was first hospitalized at the age of 33, with a diagnosis of paranoid schizophrenia. She fitted into our sample because she was then the mother of two boys, aged 9 and 7, and she had lost her own mother when she was 8; and because her mother had been 34 at death.

The mother had had an operation at the age of 32 and had died two years later of uterine cancer. The patient, who was 6 at the time of the operation, remembered this period vividly. She recalled her mother's increasing weakness and back pain, which had started about a year before her death, and the fact that her mother's left leg was swollen and painful—probably because of abdominal obstructions of the leg vessels. About two months before her death, the mother had become bedridden.

The patient expressed unhappiness and guilt because she had not been a better daughter to her mother—because of her childhood naughtiness and her inability to express her feelings for her mother. She had been full of the "Old Nick"; for instance, when her mother was in the hospital, she and her brother had given their teddy bear an enema, which was wrong. She and her brother had often fought, and she, two years older, bore the responsibility. Their mother would say in distress, "Oh, if you two wouldn't fight so much."

Eleanor's inability to express feeling for her mother was highlighted by the contrast with her brother: "My brother was the kind who could show affection, and I couldn't. He could love my mother and show it, where I loved her and couldn't show it." When the mother died, Eleanor did not cry, and her grandmother told her that this was strange. The patient also said, verbalizing jealousy and resentment of her brother, "Grandmother rubbed it in that Bobby was sweet with mother when she was sick and I'd just stand there, because I wasn't that type of child."

Eleanor, who was named for her mother, had an idealized image of her mother as having been very popular, liking people, bringing party favors home for her, making her pretty clothes, and being a good housekeeper and cook. The father, a successful business man, was away from home a good deal. For years he suffered from peptic ulcers, finally undergoing an operation. The patient had an idealized picture of him, also; and her husband, even though he was not given to psychological explanations, said that she had a "father fixation." Although she had seen little of her father since her marriage, as their homes were in different parts of the country, she spoke of him with great attachment, and when she was troubled during her illness, she would say, "I want my Daddy."

A year after the mother's death, the father remarried, and there was a half sibling by this marriage. The patient, who had long been a problem to her own mother, found her situation with her perfectionistic stepmother impossible, and all her hostility was channeled against her, as the "bad parent." Within two years, Eleanor was sent to live with her grandmother, where she remained until she was 15, when the grandmother died of cancer. The patient expressed guilt toward this grandmother, feeling that she had done too little for her, particularly when she was dying, although she also spoke of not liking many of the grandmother's characteristics.

After graduation from college, where she majored in her father's field, Eleanor worked for a year, and then married. The husband, when one of the authors talked to him, appeared to be a cold, rather distant person. He earned a modest salary in a government position. The marriage had never been really happy but it deteriorated markedly in the two years preceding her hospitalization. Most of the patient's hostility was channeled against him; she would speak angrily of him and then mention her devotion to her father. Thus the husband was the "bad parent" of the past.

Eleanor considered her two boys to be like herself and her brother in personality. The older one was like her—he could not display affection, but showed how he cared by misbehaving; while the younger boy was like the brother in his friendliness and loving interest. The husband gave the same contrast but said that the patient's attitude toward the two boys was the important factor; she had always been distant toward the older boy who was much like her, and she showered affection on the younger one, often calling him "lover." When the older boy was born, she had wanted a girl, of course, which would have recapitulated her own position.

Eleanor had complained of a weak back and chronic low back pain ever since her marriage, and particularly since the birth of the children. Her husband observed that she had insisted on lifting heavy furniture when it was quite unnecessary, and he felt that this was largely responsible for the acute back condition.

At the age of 32, the same age as her mother had been at the time of operation, Eleanor had an operation on her back. Following the operation, which was not a serious one, she was convinced that she had really been operated on for cancer and that she had not been told the truth. She thought that she should be getting intravenous feeding—which may well have been the way her mother had been fed after the abdominal operation—and she felt that nothing the doctors did helped her. She also complained of pain in her left leg and hip. Later she spontaneously compared this period to the period of her mother's operation, and commented that her boys had to endure in her illness what she had had to endure in her mother's.

A month before she was hospitalized for the mental condition, she told her husband that a voice had called, "Eleanor, Eleanor," while she was working; when she was later asked what she thought this was, she said, "I guess it was my conscience." She began to believe that her minister had occult powers, and, when she listened to sermons, that he was preaching to her. She also made references to a "prickly conscience."

The first hospitalization was relatively short, and she managed on a barely ambulatory basis for the next year. Gradually she began to remain in bed for longer and longer periods, and finally she did not get up at all and became delusional. She was rehospitalized, at which time one of the authors saw her in treatment. In telling about her mother's having remained in bed after a particular date, she was surprised to find that this was the exact month and day when she herself had taken to her bed. Here was a fact, well known to the patient for many years, which she "forgot" as she embarked on the reliving experience.

Similarly, she had earlier mentioned the date, during her mother's thirty-fourth year, when she had died, but when this anniversay occurred, while Eleanor was in her own thirty-fourth year and in the hospital, she did not recall it until the psychiatrist later talked to her about it. At this time, however, she became more confused than she had been for a good while, and the material centered on survival. She also had amnesia for her younger son's eighth birthday, which had occurred a few months before her rehospitalization. "He had a birthday and I remember nothing about it. It was the one when he was 8." Other people told her that she had made extensive preparations for it, but she still could recall nothing.

Here again, there are a number of striking parallels which suggest an anniversary or reliving experience. How may this material be interpreted dynamically? Guilt was a strong motif in the patient's psychotic productions, with a number of references to conscience. Was it that a death should be punished by death? And was this accomplished symbolically through the reliving in the psychosis?

To the patient, people were either very good, or they were bad; and she saw herself as having been the bad child, antagonistic to her mother during her mother's life, antagonistic to her stepmother and grandmother—in short, to the significant women. Her continued negativism with its denial of dependence on mothers suggested an unresolved dependence at a pre-Oedipal level and a fixation primarily at this level.

As the only daughter, she had a special position with her father, and one may speculate that a part of her guilt arose from the rivalry with the mother for the father. After her mother's death, he was her only support, and she was unable to face her disappointment in him when he remarried; instead, more of her hostility was placed on the rival stepmother. A second basis for guilt over the mother's death was her jealousy of the younger brother's favored position with the mother and her deep anger at the mother over such favoritism.

The re-enactment of these emotions appeared in her favoritism toward the son who was in the same position as the favored brother. In a curious, roundabout way this is similar to identification with the aggressor. Did the favored son, toward whom she was able to express affection, also represent the old affectional tie, displaced from her father? In those cases in which the bond to the father is not resolved, is it reflected in this acting out toward a favored son?

This patient may be seen as a person in whom 'discordant' or negative characteristics developed. She was not loved for her positive traits as much as she was given attention for her misbehavior. She felt unloved except by her father, who was away from home much of the time. This made positive identifications difficult. The death of the grandmother in the patient's adolescence again meant a severing of ties rather than a growth in them and beyond them. Thus her life was a series of discrete, broken identifications with little opportunity for integration—which would be another factor in the reliving experience. That is, she relived a series of identifications, of which the one with her mother was the most important.

SOME IMPLICATIONS OF THE ANNIVERSARY HYPOTHESIS

Although we are presenting in this paper only two cases, much that we wish to say about the implications of the anniversary hypothesis is based on data shown by the wider group of patients in our sample. One of the advantages of our method is that we are dealing with a much larger sample of cases than ordinarily comes into clinical practice.

Our hope is to move from the plausible explanation of a single case to a statistical demonstration that the events being considered are related beyond chance expectation. The 14 age coincidences in our sample of 43 cases in which the patient had lost a mother in childhood turn out to be about double what one would expect by chance. One important advantage of a comparatively large sample is the avoidance of generalization from a dramatic individual case. For example, one of our earliest and clearest cases of anniversary reaction was in a male patient; thus we began our study in a Veterans Administration hosital, only to find, as the study progressed, that the condition is rare among men.

Thus while the statistical approach has the disadvantage of the loss of richness of the individual case, it has the advantage of clarifying principles of wider generality. The criticism that a statistical method will prove to be superficial can be answered if the cases selected statistically are followed up clinically and use is made of the insights gained from individual psychoanalytic experiences. Thus the statistical and the individual methods for the study of data are complementary.

While this study has been confined to psychotic manifestations in parents related to loss of a parent of their own in childhood, we wish to call attention to a few of the wider implications of the anniversary hypothesis. The specific problem of parent loss has formative influences upon personality which, when they are searched for, can be noted among the neurotic population as well as among psychotics. In addition, the death of a loved one is not the only event having anniversary significance. For example, a mother who had a disturbed adolescence may become disturbed when her daughter reaches adolescence. Recurrent anniversaries need not be tied to age; they may be related to the time of year or to festivals, such as Christmas, birthdays, and Sundays, or to other periodicities.

We are investigating the possibility of common factors among anniversaries of different kinds.

We are also in the process of exploring many questions raised by the data in this study. For exmple, the obvious question intrudes: Why do some adults who have lost parents in childhood become psychotic when they have children, while most escape? While the factors are complex, our data suggest that *the stage of the child's development* at which the parent is lost may be decisive. Our sampling included mother-loss up to the age of 19; however, in most of the cases showing anniversaries, the mother-loss occurred at or before the age of 12, with a greater proportion in the age range of 7 to 12. While this latter range is chronologically appropriate to the period of latency, the case material suggested an arrested development prior to the mother-loss, so that a fixation at the pre-Oedipal period may have been one of the factors causing greater trauma when the mother died.

In addition, ameliorative factors which cushion the shock may be responsible in many cases in which psychosis does not result. Here the intrapsychic and the social show a complex interplay. When care falls to a warm grandmother, with whom a good relationship has already been established, the blow may not be as severe as when the father marries a woman little prepared for parenthood, or when the child has no substitute mother to whom to relate.

Thus a fixation at the developmental age at the time of loss, plus an interference with normal identifications, appear to help set the stage for relieving and the reaction to reliving. Because of the fixation, the now adult patient reacts as though she were still a member of her childhood family of orientation rather than a member of a present family of procreation. The patient still needs to be the child, but, through motherhood, she is catapulted into the parental role. The fixation, therefore, as a solution to her earlier developmental problem, is upset by the birth of the child. The old defenses are broken, and the repetition compulsion begins to operate; she reacts to husband and child in a way which reinstates her childhood. In a number of our patients there is the incorporated image of the mother as a sick person. If this were carried to the conclusion which occurred in childhood, the patient would have to die. At this point the psychosis intervenes, which acts out the loss and preserves the relation in fantasy.

A second question arose unexpectedly from the quantitative findings: Why are there in our sample so few men who have lost parents in childhood, and why did we find few instances of anniversaries in men? Since just as many boys as girls lose their parents, later psychoses in men must be less commonly an outcome of childhood parent-loss. The outcome in men, is, we suggest, probably to be found in another group—the alcoholics, whom we excluded from our experimental sample, because we felt that this symptom favored chronic processes which would tend to obscure the distinct timing and symptomatology of the anniversary. When we investigated the alcoholics at the hospital where we did most of our study, we found that those who had entered for the first time after parenthood included a disproportionate number of men; and, more important, that there was a higher proportion of parent-loss in childhood among the men alcoholics than among the women alcoholics. If, among the men who had lost parents in childhood, one totals the two groups of psychotics and alcoholics, this approximates the total women who fall into the same two groups. In other words, in those who had lost parents in childhood, the men include a small number of psychoses and a large number of cases of alcoholic addiction; while among the women there is a larger number of psychotic reactions and a correspondingly small number of alcoholics. This leads to the conjecture that, for men, alcoholism may be in some cases an alternative to the psychotic break.

That this is more than a statistical coincidence is suggested by a few cases of clear anniversary reactions which we have seen among men alcoholics. For example, the history of a patient whom we shall call Mr. X suggested the reliving phenomena so characteristic of the anniversary. Mr. X was fifth in a sibship of five children, the youngest by 10 years. When he was 6 years old, his parents separated, and when he was 12 his father died. The patient married, had five children, and named the fifth and last child for himself. When this child was 6 years of age, the patient separated from his family, and when the child was 12, the patient was hospitalized for alcoholic intoxication with hallucinosis. He said that he had never really understood why he had left his family six years before. The patient's mother wrote us about the impact of the loss when the patient was 12: "Charlie got along in school till he was 12 years old. His father died that year. He didn't like to go to school after that." It was as though, with the death of his father, a part of time had stopped for him.

The third question concerns the difference in impact between the loss of a mother and the loss of a father. For the reasons just indicated, we have more data on women who have lost mothers and fathers than we have for men. For women, father-loss does not tend to produce anniversaries reflecting the father's age at death. Instead, two other circumstances are prominent: There are many cases of psychoses following childbirth; and there are cases in which the timing of the psychosis corresponds to the age of the mother at the time the father died. If this second precipitating occasion turns out to be more typical, the dynamics may be consonant with those of mother-loss, reflecting the complex problems of pre-Oedipal and Oedipal fixation, unresolved because of the trauma suffered by both the child and the grieving mother.

We have been interested in the extent to which our patients as children could grieve openly for their parents at the time of death. In neither of the cases reported in this paper were we able to find evidence of adequate mourning in the patient, but in both cases the patient as a child was subjected to intense or long-continued mourning on the part of close adults. Laura's mother was depressed for a long period, and Eleanor recalled her grandmother's grief and her stories about the mother's illness, which continued for years. The child's reaction and the parent's reaction at the time of a loss, with details of their interaction, need further study.

Berliner and Bressler have reported the anniversary syndrome in cases of ulcerative colitis.[1,2] In Berliner's case, the loss of the mother was through death, and in Bressler's the loss occurred through psychosis. Scott has published a report of a case of agitated depression in an older man when he approached his grandfather's age at death.[4] In addition, a number of unpublished cases have come to our attention. Answers to the questions which have been raised in this paper—why some people react to parental loss while others do not, why men differ from women in their choice of symptoms, and what the difference is in impact of father-loss and mother-loss—can come only from the publication of additional cases, as well as from planned, long-range investigations.

REFERENCES

1. BERLINER, R. 1938. The psychogenesis of a fatal organic disease. *Psychoanal. Q.*, **7**, 368-379.
2. BRESSLER, B. 1956. Ulcerative colitis as an anniversary symptom. *Psychoanal. Rev.*, **43**, 381-387.
3. HILGARD, J. R. 1953. Anniversary reactions in parents precipitated by children. *Psychiatry*, **16**, 73-80.
4. SCOTT, W. C. M. 1955. A psychoanalytic concept of the origin of depressions. In KLEIN, M., HEIMAN, P., and MONEY-KYRLE, R. (eds.) *New directions in psychoanalysis*. Basic Books, New York.

XXXII

A PSYCHOTIC FAMILY—FOLIE À DOUZE

HERBERT WALTZER

*Attitudes communicated to other family members may
have the force of an illness. Persecutory delusions are a
common shared manifestation. Such shared manisfestations
will emerge only on examination of the whole family—as
only one member commonly presents to a psychiatric service.*

The term *folie à deux*, coined by Lasegue and Falret in 1877, is an interesting entity that has received much study in the past century. Although relatively few cases have been reported, its incidence would seem to be much greater. As with the family that is the subject of this account, these cases are accidentally uncovered. Gralnick,[7] in his excellent review of the literature, speaks of a "psychosis of association" and defines it as "the transference of delusional ideas and/or abnormal behavior from one person to one or more others, related or unrelated, who have been in close association with the primarily affected person." To complete this definition, one would add that it is not subject to correction. It has been variously called "infectiousness of insanity" (Ideler, 1838); "psychic infection" (Hoffbauer, 1846), "contagious insanity" (Parsons, 1883), "collective insanity" (Ireland, 1886), "double insanity" (Tuke, 1887), "influenced psychoses" (Gordon, 1925) and "mystic paranoia" (Pike, 1933).

The French workers in this field studied and described the various sub-forms of folie à deux in the middle and latter part of the nineteenth century. Such terms as *folie imposée* (imposed psychosis), *folie communiqué* (communicated psychosis), *folie simultanée* (simultaneous psychosis) and *folie induite* (induced psychosis) were introduced into the literature. Zabarenko[19] and Gralnick[7] described these sub-forms and cited examples.

Reprinted from THE JOURNAL OF NERVOUS AND MENTAL DISEASE, Vol. 137, No. 1, July 1963, pp. 67-75.

The term "psychosis of association" has more or less replaced these older forms in present psychiatric literature. It is certainly difficult to conceive of a delusional psychosis appearing simultaneously in two or more individuals. The dividing line differentiating these sub-forms is not always sharp, nor does it permit a better understanding of this entity.

ETIOLOGY

Kallman[10, 11] and Mickey[10] stressed the factor of inheritance in consanguinous cases of folie à deux, and suggested that environmental factors are not sufficient in themselves to precipitate a psychosis in a family unit. Craike and Slater[4] reported a case of folie à deux in monozygotic twin sisters who shared similar paranoid delusions, although they had been living apart since the age of nine months. Adler and Magruder[1] and Oatman[14] described cases of psychosis of association in identical twins which were precipitated by environmental stresses, although a constitutional predisposition to schizophrenia was present. Dewhurst and Todd[6] said that most authorities agree that both environmental and hereditary factors play a part in precipitating a psychosis of association in consanguinous partners. The highest incidence of psychosis of association is found in sister-sister combinations. The above authors felt that a diagnosis of folie à deux should not be made unless the following criteria have been fulfilled:

1) there must be present positive evidence that the partners have been intimately associated;

2) there must be present a high degree of similarity in the general motif and delusional content of the partner's psychosis;

3) there must be present unequivocal evidence that the partners accept support and share each other's delusional ideas.

All these criteria are present in the psychotic family reported here, and it is submitted that the term folie à deux (*folie à douze*) is fully justified. Folie à douze is used here since the family consists of 12 members, each possessing the same delusional ideas. This expression is also used to indicate the relative ease in which delusional ideas can become incorporated into the psychic life of exposed individuals.

Psychosis of association is not limited to members of a family but has been observed in larger groups, including entire cultures and societies. Brussel and Oatman used the respective terms "folie à beaucoup" and "folie collective." Bender and Yarrell[2] described 18 psychotic disciples of Father Devine who were all admitted to the same mental hospital with very similar delusions (contagious insanity). Montague[13] mentions the "diabolical, hostile, paranoid Dobuans of northwestern Melanesia who make a virtue of treachery and ill-will." Sarvis[17] suggests that a paranoid reaction is among the most primitive and potentially most nearly universal of all human reactions. A paranoid attitude or a delusional idea can be subsequently communicated from parent to child and from generation to generation. Delusion formation is a process that starts with the individual and, like an infection, can ultimately encompass an entire society.

CASE REPORT

Both parents and their 13-year-old son, L., were remanded to the Psychiatric Division of Kings County Hospital for observation. The court remand indicated that the parents were not proper guardians because they were mentally disturbed. The parents expressed their view to the court that they were being persecuted by neighbors, school authorities, public officials, gamblers and bookies, Negroes, Puerto Ricans and Jews. Mr. C. had not left his home for at least five years because of his fears. The parents communicated these fears to their children, who were not permitted to play or associate with other neighborhood children. In school the children kept to themselves and did not participate in any extra-curricular activities.

The family lived in a four-story ten-room brownstone house in a racially mixed section of Brooklyn. The home was kept immaculately clean but was cluttered with old furniture. Until 1952, the family had been using the basement and parlor floors for a restaurant and the two upper floors for living quarters. They subsequently closed the restaurant and no longer made use of that area.

The mother, Mrs. C., is 37. She was born to orthodox Jewish parents, the second of three children, and spent her entire childhood in Brooklyn. She described her childhood as very pleasant and added that financial problems never existed. She felt there was a good relationship between her parents. The patient's father, a lawyer, totally blind since she was a year old, had been married twice previously. Her mother, who had worked at removing chicken feathers in a kosher butcher store, had also been previously married. Her father died at 72 and her mother at 65 when the patient was 12 and 23 years respectively. She mentioned her 36-year-old brother, who is single and a letter carrier, but said that she had no contact with him or with any other relative.

She was graduated from high school and subsequently attended the New York School of Dietetics for one year, where she met her husband, a Chinese. He was her first date and she knew him about a year prior to their marriage. They eloped and were married in Maryland in 1944. Mrs. C. stated that her family was prejudiced towards minority groups. Nonetheless, she felt that her mother approved of her marriage to Mr. C. Mrs. C. functioned as a housewife while her husband operated a Chinese-American restaurant until 1952. Then, she alleged, they had to close the establishment because of the harassment they received from bookies, gamblers, Jews and Negroes. The family has since become dependent upon public welfare for its subsistence.

Mr. C., now 72, was born in Hong Kong and came to the United States in 1917. He has never applied for American citizenship. He was graduated from high school and then attended Trinity College in England for two years. Mr. C. refused to discuss his childhood or his family but spontaneously reported that his brother had been murdered.

PSYCHIATRIC EXAMINATIONS

PARENTS

Mrs. C., the mother, is a very obese woman who appeared much older than her 37 years. Hirsutism was noted and was particularly pronounced about the upper lip. Although superficially cooperative during the interview, she nonetheless reacted with suspicion to the examiner. She was oriented as to time, place and person, and manifested no evidence of an organic brain syndrome. Her speech was coherent, but irrelevant and circumstantial. Her affect was intense, labile and generally appropriate to her expressed ideation, but not to the interview situation. Both auditory and visual hallucinations were elicited. She stated that the Welfare Department was in league with the bookies and gangsters in their attempt to eject her family from their home. She insisted that the welfare department supervisor, who is Jewish, was trying to mislead 36,000 children. She indicated that the gangsters, bookies, police and teachers were trying to ruin her family and murder her husband. She feared that the Negro children and Jewish teachers were trying to contaminate the minds of her children. She accused the school principal of having sexual relations with her daughter P., 15, because the zipper of his trousers was open. Diagnostic impression: schizophrenic reaction, paranoid type. Mrs. C. was committed in April, 1961, to Kings Park State Hospital.

Mr. C. appeared at least ten to 15 years younger than his 72 years. He had an excellent command of the English language and obviously was well read. He was oriented as to time, place and person. His speech was coherent, though often circumstantial and irrelevant, and also displayed a loss of goal direction in his thinking. In manner he was extremely grandiose. His affect was intense, constricted and generally appropriate to the expressed ideation but not to the interview situation. He carried in his pockets many old notebooks, containing names and places, as well as newspapers. He stated that he had not left his home in five years because the Jews, bookies and gangsters, Negroes, Puerto Ricans and "poor whites" were plotting against him. He felt that even the police were involved in the plot to take his life. He had his children rotate guard duty in order to prevent any would-be assailant from entering his home. Auditory and visual hallucinations were noted. The following is a letter written by Mr. C. to his children:

"I am sorry that the Jew bookies and gangsters had us framed up and forced into this crazy ward. I enclose you two four-cent stamps if you want to write

Mama and me. Yesterday Mama was taken away to another crazy hospital. Remember these Jew gangsters did it to us and the Chinese race."

Diagnostic impression: schizophrenic reaction, paranoid type. Mr. C. was committed in April, 1961, to Kings Park State Hospital.

CHILDREN

The 15-year-old daughter, P., was interviewed at Caligy Hall, a girl's residential treatment center. An obese girl of Eurasian appearance, she expressed essentially the same delusional statements as her parents, but they were lacking bizarre elements. Her speech was coherent, relevant and goal directed. Her affect was intense and appropriate to the expressed ideation. The girl did not admit any hallucinatory experiences; there was no evidence of psychotic disorganization. Diagnostic impression: paranoid reaction in a girl undergoing adolescent adjustments.

The 14-year-old boy, D., was interviewed at the Children's Shelter of

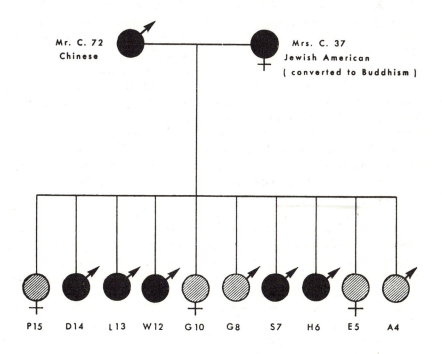

FIG. 1. Diagram of family structure.

New York City. He did not manifest any disturbances in his sensorium. His speech was coherent but often irrelevant and without appropriate goal direction. The boy's affect was consistent with his ideation but inappropriate to the interview situation. He expressed the same delusional ideas but with great elaboration. He told of seeing the gangsters kill cats and of throwing them into his backyard. In addition, he stated that he had seen people murdered in the adjacent bar and grill. Auditory hallucinations were also present. Diagnostic impression: schizophrenic reaction, paranoid type.

L., a 13-year-old boy, was hospitalized at King's County Psychiatric Hospital. L. was extremely guarded and evasive during the interview. His speech was coherent but irrelevant and without goal direction. He was oriented as to time, place and person. His affective display was blunted and inappropriate. Auditory hallucinations, in the form of gangsters' voices threatening to kill him, were present. Visual hallucinations were also present; he 'had seen a woman murdered by gangsters.' He felt the teachers were against him because he is Chinese, and that he was sent to the crazy hospital because he accused the principal of wanting to have sexual relations with his sister. He repeatedly insisted the principal had such intentions. Diagnostic impression: schizophrenic reaction, paranoid type. L. was committed to a state hospital.

W., a 12-year-old boy, was interviewed at the Children's Shelter in New York City. W. manifested a clear sensorium in the presence of marked delusional ideation. He stated that the children were against him because he is Chinese, and that the principal wanted to poison him. He reported that the school principal had accused him of throwing peaches on the classroom floor at 4:00 A.M. He stated that he had seen the principal cut off a cat's tail and throw it down a drain. Auditory hallucinations were also present. Diagnostic impression: schizophrenic reaction, paranoid type.

The 10-year-old girl, G., was interviewed at Caligy Hall. She seemed the least disturbed of the older children. G. related in a warm and friendly manner to the examiner, and her delusional ideas were expressed in the presence of a clear sensorium. There were no bizarre features to the delusions elicited, nor was there evidence of any hallucinatory experiences. Diagnostic impression: paranoid reaction.

G., an eight-year-old boy, was seen at the Children's Shelter. He was found to be both physically and emotionally immature for an eight-year-old. His sensorium was found to be intact. The same order of delusions was expressed. No hallucinations or other manifestations of psychosis were elicited. Diagnostic impression: paranoid reaction.

S., a 7-year-old boy, was also seen at Children's Shelter. Both auditory and visual hallucinations were elicited in the presence of a clear sensorium. His affect was inappropriate to the ideation and to the interview situation. His speech was extremely poor, and his thought processes indicated a distinct loosening of associations with loss of goal direction. Diagnostic impression: schizophrenic reaction, paranoid type.

H., a 6-year-old boy, when seen at Children's Shelter, spoke of having witnessed the gangsters almost kill his father. He stated that he observed a mouse bite the toe of one of the gangsters. In addition, auditory hallucinations were found in the presence of a clear sensorium. His affect was appropriate to the ideation but inappropriate to the interview situation. Diagnostic impression: schizophrenic reaction, paranoid type.

E., a 5-year-old girl, was also seen at Children's Shelter. The child's sensorium was found intact. The same delusions were expressed but were lacking in the bizarre quality found in most of the family members. No hallucinations or other evidence of psychosis was elicited. The child related well to the examiner. Diagnostic impression: paranoid reaction.

The same delusional ideation was elicited from the four-year-old boy, A. No hallucinations or other evidence of psychosis was noted. His sensorium was found to be clear, and he related very well to the examiner. His affect was appropriate to both the ideation and to the interview situation. Diagnostic impression: paranoid reaction.

COMMENTS

Each family member was interviewed by the writer. Initially, there was some reservation in designating the children as paranoid, particularly the two youngest. This was finally justified, however, because their reported behavior both at school and at home was in accord with the delusional ideation. With the exception of the two youngest, the delusions appeared firmly entrenched and ego-syntonic. The two youngest reproduced parental statements without any obvious conviction. The older children spoke with conviction and some of them introduced new delusional details not expressed by the parents or by other siblings. The non-schizophrenic children did not manifest the ego disorganization and secondary symptoms observable in the schizophrenic children. All the children made use of projection as a defense mechanism in dealing with their conflicts. Cognizance, however, was taken of the relative immaturity of ego-functioning, particularly in the area of reality testing. The psychic stress or conflict impinged upon and caused decompensation of the autonomous ego-functions in the sicker children. The children with poorer ego development became more disorganized in their thinking and behavior. To achieve a new equilibrium or homeostasis, delusion formation had seemingly become necessary.

L., 13, was the most seriously disturbed of all the children. Five of the ten siblings manifested a paranoid schizophrenic psychosis, whereas the remaining five children were diagnosed as having a paranoid reaction. Interestingly enough, none of the female siblings were diagnosed as schizophrenic. The question arises as to the presence of sex-linked genetic factors. In Kallman's survey,[9] the probability of schizophrenia in the children of two schizophrenic parents is reported to be 68.1 per cent. The cross-breeding proportion of one schizophrenic and one non-schizophrenic parent yields expectancy figures of 14.8 per cent to 23.9 per cent. The incidence of schizophrenia in the children of schizophrenic parents in this family was 50 per cent. Nothing is known of the incidence of schizophrenia in the families of the parents. Gregory[8] pointed out that schizophrenia had been extensively studied by means of twin and family data, but the extent and nature of possible genetic factors in the syndrome remain uncertain. His conclusion was that there was no monogenic hypothesis compatible with the findings, and suggested three alternatives: 1) predominantly environmental factors, 2) genetic heterogeneity, 3) polygenic inheritance.

Although genetic factors probably play a role, one cannot minimize in its etiological significance the presence of noxious agents, namely the parents and the disturbed environment which was relatively constant and identical for all the children, in the precipitation of delusional thinking. Since this is felt to be of important etiological significance, one might anticipate the gradual diminution or ultimate disappearance of delusional thinking in the children if they were removed from these noxious stimuli for an extended period. A relationship appears to exist between the tenacity and ego-syntonicity with which the delusions are held and the duration of exposure to these noxious stimuli.

The mother was the more disturbed, whereas the father was the primary agent. In folie à deux, Dewhurst and Todd[6] have stated that the dominant partner's delusions are continually reinforced by a kind of feedback mechanism due to the incessant echoing of his beliefs by the weaker member. These authors feel the important factors which enable one individual to obtain dominance over another one: superiority in age, intelligence, education and "drive" (aggressiveness). These factors certainly apply to Mr. C., who must be viewed as the dominant figure.

Mr. C. projected all his difficulties initially on to the Jewish people and subsequently on to other minority groups, whom he had seen as persecutors of the Chinese (himself). Mrs. C., being originally of the Jewish faith, was identified by Mr. C. with the persecutors. He ultimately convinced or brainwashed Mrs. C., who then accepted his ideas. Thus Mrs. C. identified with Mr. C., the aggressor, became converted to Buddhism and then directed her hostility and aggressivity toward the Jews. Mr. C.'s ambivalent feelings towards himself are reflected in his discussion of the Chinese (himself). In order to defend against feelings of inadequacy and inferiority, he then projected these feelings onto others who become persecutors of the Chinese (himself). His persecutors are of "lower" social position, namely the Jews, Puerto Ricans, Negroes, bookies and gangsters. One might speculate that Mr. C. was beginning to experience potency difficulties, or the awakening of latent homosexual feelings, which are frequently seen in the paranoid individual. This, however, could not be ascertained from the clinical examination. His aggressive impulses manifested themselves in the form of emotional outbursts and threats. His ego unconsciously attempted to resolve the conflict and restore psychic equilibrium through use of projection and delusion formation as a means of controlling undesirable thoughts, feelings and impulses.

Because of a more fragile ego structure, Mrs. C. manifested greater disorganization in her thinking and delusional content was more bizarre. The maintenance of relative social isolation in the presence of a constant monoideational stimulus in the form of a delusion impinging on immature ego structures, resulted in the incorporation of this delusion in the psychic life of the children. The children identified with their pscyhotic parents. Reality testing, a vital ego function, suffered as a result of social isolation and decompensation followed.

Pulver and Brunt[16] reviewed the psychodynamic explanation of folie à deux. Deutsch[5] pointed out that the delusion is an attempt to rescue the object through identification with it or its delusional systems. She also indicated that the recipient never accepts ego-alien material and the delusional ideation must be similar to the unconscious fantasies, and fit the defense mechanisms of the secondary partner.

Lidz et al.[12] found that family life was distorted by a skew in the marital relationship in size of the 14 marriages studied. They stated that the serious psychopathology of one marital partner dominated the home. In some families, they found that the distorted ideation of one partner was accepted or shared by the others, thus creating an atmosphere of folie à deux or even a folie à famille where the family shared the aberrant conceptualizations. They further stated that in all of these families, one partner who was extremely dependent or masochistic had married a spouse who had appeared to be a strong and protecting parental figure. They felt it to be significant that no member of these six marriages had intense emotional bonds to the parental family, and it is possible that the absence of alternative sources of gratification tended to hold the spouses together. This observation was supported in the present study. Neither Mr. nor Mrs. C. mentioned having any emotional bonds with their parents during their adult lives.

DISCUSSION

The tendency towards psychotic disorganization, including paranoid symptom formation, in individuals whose sensory stimulation is impaired, i.e., blind and deaf individuals as well as persons immoblized in an artificial lung or body cast, is well known. The reaction to the stress of relative sensory deprivation is determined by the ego strengths and weaknesses of the individual. Solomon[18] reported the common features in cases of sensory deprivation as "intense desire for extrinsic sensory stimuli and bodily motion, increased suggestibility, impairment of organized thinking, oppression and depression, and in extreme cases hallucinations, delusions and confusion." Sarvis[17] suggested that sensory deprivation, sensory overload and sensory distortion all tend to produce disorganization of secondary thought processes. When the external frame of reference is deficient, overwhelming or distorted, the individual subject tries to maintain a stable sense of identity and intact ego by internal frames of reference and by his own typical methods of defense.

There are marked similarities between what transpires in the development of a folie à deux and the process of brainwashing. Three phases are present in both. The first phase may be viewed as the "disorganizing or regressive phase" and consists of the breakdown of existing defenses and resistances. In brainwashing and folie à deux, this is accomplished through social isolation, sensory and ideational deprivation. During the second phase identification with the aggressor, who is viewed as the rescuer, takes place. The submissive individual identifies with the dominant person who is consciously or unconsciously carrying out the operation. The brainwashee is exposed to kindness and consideration during this phase. The third phase is the reindoctrination period. Constant monoideational stimulation is maintained until the ideas are incorporated by the individual who is in a submissive role. The second and third phases are only possible after the first has been successful.

Dewhurst and Todd[6] stressed the importance of an intimate rapport between persons for the development of folie à deux. Cameron[3] pointed out that a pseudo-community is formed, and that these individuals isolate themselves not only from the greater community but even from their own neighbors. This distrust of mankind often then degenerates into a paranoid psychosis. Dewhurst and Todd stated, "this withdrawal from normal social intercourse greatly favors the domination of the weaker partner by the stronger, as the former is then cut off from counterbalancing influences. In many cases, there is evidence that a leader, follower relationship existed between the partners before the dominant member became psychotic."

Dewhurst and Todd pointed out the similarity to hypnosis. They remarked that "hypnosis is dependent on the establishment of a degree of dominance by the exponent over the subject. Under these circumstances, the former can induce the latter to accept suggestion without critical appraisal of its validity. In psychosis of association, the submissive partner is being induced by the process of suggestion to accept the delusional ideas of the dominant one." In hypnotic induction, a constant single stimulus (voice, sound, object) is maintained in conjunction with a relative deprivation of other stimuli. The same similarity exists between hypnosis and brainwashing, namely the physical or social isolation, the ideational deprivation, in the presence of constant monoideational stimulation.

Orne[15] stated that in hypnosis, the therapist enters a folie à deux with the patient. He states, "one requirement of successful hypnosis is that the patient should be able to ascribe magical powers to the therapist. It is necessary for the therapist employing hypnosis to enter into this relationship, act out and participate in the folie à deux while maintaining sufficient objectivity to recognize that he does not acquire the power the patient ascribes to him." He felt that there may be an analogy drawn between the psychotherapeutic process and the hypnotic state.

In spite of the many major differences, there are certain features in common to psychotherapy and brainwashing. Therapy may be viewed as consisting of three phases. The first consists of the breakdown of the resistances and defenses. During the second phase identification with the therapist and a positive transference relationship develops. And during the third phase, the development of insight and the modification of pathological mechanisms takes place. This explanation, however, is certainly an oversimplification of the psychotherapeutic process.

Folie à deux would appear to occur more frequently than is reported in the literature. This diagnosis can only be made when all the individuals who have been in intimate contact with the patient have undergone psychiatric examination. The sickest family member may not be the primary agent nor necessarily undergo psychiatric hospitalization. Delusion formation *per se* may exist in other family members without being grossly disruptive to ego-functioning. For example, if the delusions are of a benign grandiose nature, the individual may never come under psychiatric examination.

QUESTIONS

Will separation of the children from their parents, in actuality, modify the tenacity or ego-syntonicity with which the delusions are held? Did the difference in racial backgrounds of the parents significantly contribute to the formation of a folie à deux? It would certainly appear to have complicated the process of identification occurring in the children. Will some of the non-schizophrenic children, under future stress, decompensate and manifest a schizophrenic psychosis? A follow-up of this family would help answer some of these questions.

THERAPEUTIC CONSIDERATIONS

Separation from the noxious stimuli in addition to supportive counterbalancing psychotherapeutic measures appear necessary for the reestablishment of psychic health. The supportive measures would consist of increasing the socialization process as well as assisting in strengthening of the reality-testing function of the ego.

Similarly, such measures as the free exchange of peoples, ideas and flow of communications would serve to diminish international tensions resulting from suspicion. Removal of the social and ideational deprivation strengthens the reality-testing abilities and reduces the paranoid tendencies.

SUMMARY

A case of folie à deux (folie à douze) was presented in which all family members possessed the same persecutory delusions. The etiological importance of noxious environmental stimuli is stressed. Sensory isolation and ideational deprivation are seen as important factors in achieving an hypothesized first phase, the disorganizing or regressive phase. During the second phase identification with the aggressor takes place. The third phase is the reindoctrination period during which incorporation of the delusional ideas take place. There are similarities with regard to what transpires in folie à deux and in brainwashing, hypnosis and psychotherapy. Therapeutic maneuvers must be designed to increase the socialization process and to strengthen the reality-testing function of the ego.

Since a paranoid reaction is among the most primitive and potentially most nearly universal of all human reactions, one would expect the incidence of folie à deux to be much greater than is generally appreciated.

REFERENCES

1. ADLER, A., and MAGRUDER, W. W. 1946. Folie à deux in identical twins treated with EST. *J. nerv. ment. Dis.*, **103**, 181-186.
2. BENDER, L., and YARRELL, Z. 1938. Psychoses among followers of Father Divine. *J. nerv. ment. Dis.*, **87**, 418-449.
3. CAMERON, N. 1959. Paranoid conditions and paranoia. In ARIETI, S. (ed.) *American handbook of psychiatry*, pp. 508-539. Basic Books, New York.
4. CRAIKE, W. H., and SLATER, E. 1945. Folie à deux in uniovular twins reared apart. *Brain*, **68**, 213-221.
5. DEUTSCH, H. 1938. Folie à deux. *Psychoanal. Q.*, **7**, 307-318.
6. DEWHURST, K., and TODD, J. 1956. The psychosis of association—Folie à deux. *J. nerv. ment. Dis.*, **124**, 451-459.
7. GRALNICK, A. 1942. Folie à deux. *Psychiat. Q.*, **16**, 230-263.
8. GREGORY, I. 1960. Genetic factors in schizophrenia. *Am. J. Psychiat.*, **116**, 961-972.
9. KALLMAN, F. J. 1938. *The genetics of schizophrenia*, pp. 143-164. Augustin, New York.
10. KALLMAN, F. J., and MICKEY, J. S. 1946. Genetic concepts of folie à deux —Re-examination of induced insanity in family units. *J. Hered.*, **37**, 298-306.
11. KALLMAN, F. J. 1946. The concept of induced insanity in family units. *J. nerv. ment. Dis.*, **104**, 303-315.

12. LIDZ, T., CORNELISON, A. R., FLECK, S., and TERRY, D. 1957. The intra-familial environment of schizophrenic patients: II. Marital schism and marital skew. *Am. J. Psychiat.*, **114**, 241-248.

13. MONTAGUE, A. 1961. Culture and mental illness. *Am. J. Psychiat.*, **118**, 15-23.

14. OATMAN, J. G. 1942. Folie à deux—Report of a case in identical twins. *Am. J. Psychiat.*, **98**, 842-845.

15. ORNE, M. T. 1962. Implications for psychotherapy derived from current research on the nature of hypnosis. *Am. J. Psychiat.*, **118**, 1097-1103.

16. PULVER, S. E., and BRUNT, M. Y. 1961. Deflection of hostility in folie à deux. *Archs gen. Psychiat.*, **5**, 257-265.

17. SARVIS, M. A. 1962. Paranoid reactions. *Archs gen. Psychiat.*, **6**, 157-162.

18. SOLOMON, P., LEIDERMAN, P. H., MENDELSON, J., and WEXLER, D. 1957. Sensory deprivation: A review. *Am. J. Psychiat.*, **114**, 357-363.

19. ZABARENKO, R., and JOHNSON, J. A. 1950. The psychosis of association—Folie à deux. *Psychiat. Q.*, **24**, 338-344.

3

CLINICAL SYNDROMES

Every clinical symptom and category can be regarded as an expression of family dysfunction. Selected for discussion here as products of family dysfunctioning are:

> The symptom
> Physical illness
> Brain damage
> Gilles de la Tourette's Syndrome
> Psychosomatic disorder
> Suicide
> Homicide
> Schizophrenia
> Manic-depressive psychosis
> Retardation

XXXIII

SYMPTOMATOLOGY: A FAMILY PRODUCTION

Its Relevance to Psychotherapy

VIRGINIA M. SATIR

To understand a symptom, the family system of the symptom bearer must be understood. Research continues to delineate family systems and their related symptoms.

The main premise underlying the idea that symptoms are a family production is the notion that all families operate as systems. A past and currently held view of symptoms is that they are a product of organicity or internal psychodynamics. It would follow, then, that therapy of the individual would be logical. There now is some evidence to suggest that symptoms can also be the product of a family system which then makes therapy of the total family unit logical.

There is some further evidence to suggest that the system may well be the overriding factor in the use of one's internal dynamics, and the use of the current context and situation at any given point in time. Further, it may well be that the system is the primary means by which internal dynamics gets developed.

One characteristic of any system is that it appears to have an order and sequence of its essential parts, and has a beginning which then becomes repetitive and predictable; a family system would be no exception. The order and sequence of the family system can be referred to as 'family rules'. These rules are derived from the initial evolvement of the system and, in turn, then become the essential basis for its operation and perpetuation. These rules are largely out of the awareness of the persons whom they govern.

It does seem, from observation of families in which there are symptoms, that the rules of the family system do not fit the total growth needs (physical, emotional, social, intellectual—in terms of survival, intimacy,

---

productivity, and making sense and order) of all the individuals who are a part of that system. They may be partial for each individual or leave out some all together.

The premises underlying the idea that symptoms are a family production grew out of the Bateson Project as one of several early investigations of the schizophrenic family.

Order and sequence in a family could be seen in the decision-making process which is made by negotiation or power (who initiates and who finalises) and in the communication picture. Literally, this picture can be observed by looking at three factors: (i) who speaks; (ii) who speaks for whom; (iii) who speaks attributing blame or credit to another.

From this point of view, the behaviour of any family member is entirely appropriate and understandable in terms of the rules of his family system. That is, the behaviour of an individual may not fit his own growth needs nor the expectations in the awareness of other family members, but it does fit the rules of the family system—and the context in which he is behaving. To understand a symptom, then, one must understand the family system of which the symptom-bearer, or identified patient, is a member.

In general, then, a family system which does not (a) accommodate the growth needs of each family member, (b) does not include methods for achieving satisfactory joint outcomes and (c) does not include ways for using the outside world to expand and change itself can be potentially a 'dysfunctional' family system. When a family with a dysfunctional family system encounters undue stress, symptoms may appear in one or more family members. The kind of symptom which appears and the person in whom it appears both give clues to the nature of the family system.

Many of the initial observations which suggested this approach to symptoms were made during therapy and research involving families with a schizophrenic member. Parents of schizophrenic children typically report that things are pretty perfect between them: it is only their crazy son or daughter who makes life difficult. If one tries to discover more facets of the husband-wife relationship, one finds evidence of personal inadequacy, frustration and disappointment in this relationship. Improvement in the 'sick' child, however, seems to bring out this difficulty rather than make it better; as the patient gets better, the marriage seems to get worse.

The important aspect of this observation is not that 'inadequate' parents produce 'crazy' children, but that by acting crazy the child appears to serve an important function in the family. By behaving in the way that he does, he appears to keep the marriage and family intact. Thus no one individual in the family is sick; it is the whole pattern of relationships which is 'pathological'; and it is this pattern which must be studied, if we are to really understand the symptom which the system produces.

Research began by Gregory Bateson and others opened a whole new area of thought about these relationships between individual behaviour and the family. The initial project involved simply looking at the communication patterns in families with one schizophrenic member. This work led to the double-bind theory. The formal aspects of this theory are beyond the scope of this paper, but the basic notion of the double-bind is quite important and relatively simple. The double-bind theory asserts that the schizophrenic child learns his behavioural, or communicational, patterns through the repeated exposure to the double-bind situation.

The conditions for a double-bind situation are as follows. The person being 'bound' receives strong conflicting messages from a survival figure (from someone on whom he is physically and/or emotionally dependent). That is, he receives one message at one level of communication (say, for example, at the verbal level) and a simultaneous but contradictory message at another level (for example, through body position or gesture). And, in addition to receiving these two mutually exclusive messages, he is, for some reason, unable either to leave the entire situation altogether or to comment on the discrepancy between the two messages.

For example, a mother may say to her young child: 'Come close to Mother, Johnny, if you love her,' while simultaneously expressing rigidity through her gestures. The child cannot *not* respond to these two conflicting injunctions ('come close' and 'go away'). The presumption is that family rules prevent this making a comment on the discrepancy between these two commands which his mother has given him. His survival is obviously tied up with his mother. The double-bind theory asserts that repeated exposure to this sort of situation will significantly reduce the child's ability to judge the meaning of, and respond to, any remark by appropriately using the context in which it is made. This, then, gets evolved into a rule by him about how he should be, and what he should expect from others. If this rule assaults his growth, he becomes a potential symptom-bearer.

There are many possible variations of the double-bind situation, and quite a few subtle facets of the problem it presents to both the 'binder' and the 'victim'. Its important implication here, however, is that bizarre, seemingly meaningless behaviour may indeed be appropriate reactions to this sort of situation. In his universe—that is, in his family—the schizophrenic may thus be behaving in quite an appropriate way. And the reason that this behaviour is appropriate may be closely tied to the family's patterns of communication, which, in my opinion, are, for the most part, outside of the family's awareness.

Workers have also noted that in families with schizophrenic members there is little use of personal pronouns or of first names. Family members rarely look directly at the person to whom they are speaking, and often the way they sound or look is incongruent with what they say. In all, it seems that they have few ways of insuring that they clearly understand each other's meaning.

Thus two important ideas which came out of the early work with schizophrenics and their families are (i) the family operates as a system, and the symptoms of any family member are signs that the system is dysfunctional; and (ii) the significant rules of the system concern the way in which family members communicate with each other. That is, the family behaves as if it has rules about communication, and it is the rigidity or restrictions of these rules and the consequent distortions which ultimately create the need for symptoms.

These two ideas have many implications for theories of aetiology and the treatment of symptoms. However, they clearly are still working hypotheses rather than scientific theories, and thus we have studied and are studying the underlying assumptions of this point of view. We are studying normal and 'pathological' families in an effort to demonstrate the validity of the idea that families operate as systems. And we are also comparing different kinds of families—families with delinquent members, under-achievers, or individuals with ulcerative colitis, for example—in an effort to find relationships between communication patterns and types of symptoms. Presumably, different kinds of dysfunctional systems lead to different sorts of symptoms.

At the clinical and sometimes somewhat impressionistic level, we have made the following observations. The male and female adults who started the family are, of course, its initial architects. They, too, come out of a previous family system. The system of any family thus began when courtship took place, and was developed and modified as the marriage went along, and as children were integrated into the family. When one is interviewing a family, one can use the investigation of these stages and events to shed light on the present system. The connection appears quite obvious. When one is trying to find out the meaning of present behaviour, however, the important thing to discover is what are the rules *now* in this family—who may do what, under what conditions? Who may comment, and on what may he comment?

We have found that families who have symptom-bearers have certain characteristic restrictions and certain kinds of rules. Their rules do not clearly allow for recognition of the uniqueness and separateness of each person in the family. They seem to require that decisions be made in terms of a power struggle rather than through negotiation, and in terms of appropriateness to objective reality. The rules seem to forbid family members from expressing differences from each other: differences between people seem to represent assault or criticism to the family members.

Particularly in looking at families with children who are the symptom-bearers, we have learned to view the symptom as a sign that these family rules somehow conflict with requirements of human life. All human beings must survive, grow, get close to others, and produce; and family rules must provide ways for these events to occur, or individuals will display symptoms. In this sense, a symptom is seen as a comment on the discrepancy between the family rules and the growth needs of individual family members.

Each child in a family needs to grow; and in growing he must struggle with the following questions:

1. How can he be a powerful person in a situation in which there are already labelled powerful people? Is there room for one more?

2. How can he become independent in the human situation in which interdependency is also required? And, if others seem to require that he choose between these two aspects of life, which one should he pick? And how should he pick?

3. How can he become sexually delineated when the genital differences are shrouded in secrecy?

4. How may he produce without his production becoming the primary measure of his own worth?

5. How may he report what he sees, hears, feels and thinks about himself and other people in the presence of others, without anyone 'dropping dead'—that is, without anyone manifesting anger or pain that has only an implication of death or destruction?

The way in which a child struggles with these questions will, in a large part, be determined by what kind of question he is allowed to ask and in what way he might ask it. We assume that a sympton of a child is a sign that some effort of growth in one or more of these areas has been unsuccessful, and, furthermore, that he is able to express this frustration in his growth only indirectly; that is, through a symptom rather than through direct report of the problem.

Thus, when we are confronted with a family member with a symptom, we look at three things. First, who labelled what behaviour as a symptom, and what was actually seen or heard which led to calling this behaviour a 'symptom'? Second, what does the symptom say about a prohibition of growth for the person wearing the symptom? That is, what does the symptom suggest about a discrepancy between the rules of the family system and requirements for individual growth? And, finally, we ask, how does this lack of growth therefore help to maintain the survival of individuals in the family and to maintain relationships between other family members? Turned around, this last question becomes: How does the symptom indicate the presence of pain, trouble or confusion in the adults in the family?

Viewing the symptom as an appropriate behavioural manifestation to an inappropriate system obviously has implications for therapeutic management and direction.

First, it suggests that the whole family unit should be seen together at one time in one place. This is in contrast to seeing only the 'afflicted individual'. It further suggests that the initial explorations centre around understanding and making explicit the currently operating system. This is in contrast to the pathology of the individual. The place in growth of every member in the family can then better be seen against the back-drop of the family system. Consequently, then, each person's behaviour becomes understandable. This shifts treatment emphasis from the 'disease' model to the 'growth' model.

Additional early explorations centre around the understanding and explicit manifestations of the rules for operating the current system, and how each person reacts to others and uses these rules for himself.

Another connection that gets made early is the appropriateness of any behaviour by anyone, given the rules of the system in which he operates.

Then comes the job of changing the system, which is done by changing the rules, which in turn changes the system.

One can expect that in dysfunctional families that the 'rules' will be some form of inhibition, distortion, or assault on growth. The rules need to be changed to growth inducing and producing for each and every member. This calls for the therapist to perceive and behave differently. He needs to be concerned with process rather than outcome. He needs to be concerned with what meaning is invested by the sender and what meaning is invested by the receiver—no matter what the content, he needs to see how the behaviour fits the expectation of each member in terms of the context, the commitment and contract between the members, and how it is used by each. In other words, to discover the system below the apparent behaviour.

This, then, suggests different data that the therapist pays attention to, new techniques for its use, and new uses for the self of the therapist.

Clearly, one of the problems in analysing an individual's behaviour, using the systems and communication approach, is that we lack clear and universal terms in which to describe family systems and family rules.

In an effort to learn more about how we can describe, identify and analyse family interaction, we have constructed a structured interview. Other researchers in the field have constructed similar ones. This interview makes it possible to observe families in action, thus giving clues to internal dynamics, their actions and reactions to one another, through their communication patterns. The rules of the family system can be more easily inferred. This interview is given to each family which participates in any of our research projects. (This includes quite a few 'normal' families drawn from the community around the research institute.) Families with symptoms include families who have schizophrenic, delinquent, asthmatic and chronically unemployed members, as well as families in which there are under-achievers or individuals with ulcerative colitis.

We are now using this structured interview in six major ways.

1. We are using it as a method for structuring family behaviour and thus developing ways of classifying family behaviour. That is, we use it

to provide raw data on family behaviour, which will hopefully lead to the formulation of appropriate units and concepts in which we can describe families.

2. We are using it to compare different families task by task.

3. We also use the interview to compare families with themselves, by giving it at the end of treatment as well as before treatment.

4. We use the interview to compare the type of information which this procedure reveals to the type of insight and information which therapy brings out.

5. We also use it as a diagnostic tool—that is, we are developing it as a method for providing the therapist with important and useful information about the family, and thus also with guide-lines for treatment.

6. Finally, we use the interview as part of treatment itself, because it gives a new and sometimes therapeutic experience to the family. By performing some of the tasks, they frequently break some of their dysfunctional rules (growth inhibiting, distorting or assaulting). Observing that catastrophe does not follow this event is an important experience for the family members.

Several workers are using the interview in the first way described, that is, as raw data for the development of ways to describe and classify interaction. Dr. Jules Riskin,* for example, is working on a set of scales to describe family interaction. These scales involve concepts such as clarity versus incongruency—that is, the degree to which verbal content matches the delivery of a speech, topic change or same topic, commitment versus avoid commitment, agree or disagree, and increased intensity or decreased intensity. In general, his results suggest that these scales do isolate meaningful and significant variables of interaction, and may provide a valid and reliable method for both differentiating and describing families.

Another investigator, Jay Haley,† is trying to develop a more mechanical method for differentiating families and measuring interaction. He uses a four-minute sequence of a three-person interchange (father, mother and one child) and records simply the order of speaking. The pattern of 'who speaks after whom' is significantly different in disturbed families; it is more rigid. One of the basic implications of his research is that the family does show patterns, and does not behave randomly—which, of course, supports our thesis that the family is a system.

And, in our therapeutic efforts, we continue to look at the family as a system, and try to change the system which we think changes the need of the individual to have a symptom. Successful treatment produces a new system which allows openly for growth for all.

Learning to describe, identify, interpret and then use the family system for the growth of all family members is thus our general goal, both in treatment and research. We think that we have come some of the

* Associate Director, Mental Research Institute, Palo Alto, California.
† Research Associate, Mental Research Institute, Palo Alto, California.

way; but there is still a long way to go. The results so far suggest that we are, at least, on a promising path.

BIBLIOGRAPHY

1. ACKERMAN, N. W., BEATMAN, F. L., and SHERMAN, S. N. (eds.) 1961. *Exploring the base for family therapy*. Family Service Assoc. of America, New York.
2. HALEY, J. 1964. Research on family patterns: An instrument measurement. *Family Process*, 1, 41-65.
3. JACKSON, D. D. (ed.) 1960. *Etiology of schizophrenia*. Basic Books, New York.
4. JACKSON, D. D., RISKIN, J. H., SATIR, VIRGINIA M. (with comments by WYNNE, L.). 1961. A communication analysis of a segment of family interaction. *Archs gen. Psychiat.*, Oct.
5. LAING, R. D. 1961. *The self and others*. Tavistock Publications, London.
6. RISKIN, J. 1963. Methodology for studying family interaction. *Archs gen. Psychiat.*, 8, 343-348.
7. RISKIN, J. 1964. Family interaction scales: A preliminary report. *Archs gen. Psychiat.*, 11, 484-494.
8. SATIR, VIRGINIA M. 1964. *Conjoint family therapy*. Science and Behavior Books, Palo Alto, Calif.
9. WATZLAWICK, PAUL. 1963. *An anthology of human communication*. Science and Behaviour Books, Palo Alto, Calif.

XXXIV

STREPTOCOCCAL INFECTIONS IN FAMILIES

ROGER J. MEYER AND ROBERT J. HAGGERTY
With Technical Assistance of
NANCY LOMBARDI AND ROBERT PERKINS

Some individuals are susceptible to streptococcal infection.
One of the factors in susceptibility is family stress.

There is little precise data to explain why one person becomes ill with an infecting agent and another not. Stress, in the form of immersion in cold water, many years ago, by Pasteur,[1] was shown to increase the susceptibility of chickens to anthrax. In humans such experimental data is difficult to obtain, but it is clear that for many common infections (such as those with beta hemolytic streptococci) commensalism, or peaceful-coexistence between this organism and its human host, is the rule, while disease is the exception. Cornfeld *et al.*[2,3] found that as many as 29.8% of well school children harbored this agent, but Mozziconacci *et al.*[4] showed that the risk of being colonized by streptococci was not a random one, for in some individuals the rate was higher than expected. Despite intimate exposure between husbands and wives, both rarely carry the same organism at the same time.[5]

Once an individual is colonized with streptococci, his risk of developing illness varies, widely, being reported as high as 43%[6] to as low as 20%.[2] Breese and Disney,[7] Brimblecombe *et al.*,[8] and others have also shown that susceptible individuals vary in their rate of acquisition and illness when exposed to other persons carrying hemolytic streptococci.

The present study was designed to study some of the factors responsible for this variability in individual susceptibility to beta hemolytic streptococcal acquisition and illness.

Reprinted from PEDIATRICS, Vol. 29, No. 4, April 1962, pp. 539-549.

METHODS

Sixteen lower-middle class families, comprising 100 persons who were being followed in a comprehensive family health care program, were systematically investigated for a 12-month period from April, 1960, through March, 1961. They were selected if they had two or more children and would co-operate in the study. All but one family had at least one child of school age. In the hope of obtaining wide variation in the rates of infection, two groups of eight families each were chosen on the basis of their previous history of frequent or infrequent respiratory infections.

Throat cultures were made on all family members every three weeks and at times of acute illness, by vigorous swabbing of both tonsils or tonsillar fossae. These swabs were promptly inoculated on the surface of 5% defibrinated horse-blood agar plates, and a stab was made through the streaked material to study hemolysin production by subsurface colony growth. After incubation at 37°C for 18 to 24 hours, representative beta-hemolytic colonies were isolated in pure subculture on 5% defibrinated sheep-blood agar, and identified by Gram-stained smear, grouped by the bacitracin disk method[9] and grouped and typed by Lancefield's method.[10] Specific typing sera against 39 different serologic types were supplied by the Communicable Disease Center of the United States Public Health Service at Chamblee, Georgia. Sera for anti-streptolysin 0 titers were drawn approximately every four months and measured by standard methods.[11] A difference of two dilution increments was considered a significant increase.

Acquisition was defined as the detection of a new type of Group A beta-hemolytic streptococcus or the reappearance of the same type after at least eight weeks with negative cultures. *Streptococcal illness* was defined as the appearance, in association with a positive culture for beta-hemolytic streptococcus, of one or more of the following: a red, sore throat with or without exudate or cervical adenopathy; coryza; epistaxis; moderate or marked pharyngeal exudate; cough; otitis media; and scarlatina-form rash.

Diagnosis and treatment of respiratory infections deemed serious enough by the parents to warrant a call to their physician were carried out as usual by the family's assigned pediatric house officer or medical student under the supervision of the authors. Diagnoses were made on the basis of anatomic findings, symptoms, or both, and conformed to the usually accepted diagnostic terms.

Serial interviews were conducted by the authors with the families about past and current medical and social factors that might influence the incidence of illness; each family kept, in addition, a diary of illness, therapy, and life events. Since this was an exploratory study, attempts were made to record many factors considered by other authors or by the families to be responsible for the development of infections, with the goal of a detailed study of a few families for fruitful leads, rather than a definitive study of only a few variables. The independent variables recorded were streptococcal acquisitions and illness rates, prolonged carrier states (defined as over one month), and antistreptolysin O titer rises. Table 1 indicates the dependent variables studied, grouped under host, agent, and environmental categories.

TABLE 1

BETA-STREPTOCOCCAL INFECTIONS IN FAMILIES:*
FACTORS STUDIED

Host	*Agent*
Age	Colony count
Sex	Group type
Family history	
Antibody response	
Tonsillectomy	

Environmental Factors	
Season	Sleeping arrangements
Weather	Acute stress
Housing	Chronic stress
Family size	Therapy

RESULTS

Of the 1,639 cultures obtained, 248 (20.6%) were positive for beta-hemolytic streptococci (Table 2), 22.4% of which did not belong to Group A. Twenty-four per cent of *all* recorded illnesses in the families were associated with an isolation of beta-hemolytic streptococci, but 52.5% of all acquisitions were not associated with any illness. The overall streptococcal illness rate was 0.9 per person year.

AGENT FACTORS

Surprisingly, no significant differences were found between illness rates associated with the acquisition of Group A as compared to non-Group A streptococci (Table 3), nor with the various specific types of Group A streptococci. Of the Group A strains nontypable ones were isolated 99 times (40%), A-1 and A-12 31 times each (each 12%); types 4, 5, 13, and 28 accounted for all the others (48%) seen. Persons with greater numbers of streptococci on a blood agar plate also were no more likely to be ill than those who had small numbers of colonies (Table 4).

While quantitation of the number of colonies per blood agar plate is not an infallible method of determining the number of organisms in

* 100 persons, 16 families, 12 months.

patients, carefully standardized techniques of swabbing, culturing, and reading by the same experienced technician were carried out to minimize these variations.

TABLE 2

BETA-STREPTOCOCCAL INFECTIONS IN FAMILIES*

Age (yr)	Persons (no.)	Person-months	Cultures (no.)	Positive Cultures (no.)	Positive Cultures per Person-month
<2	16	192	228	11	0.057
2-5	28	360	563	98	0.272
2-15	22	252	386	99	0.392
16+	34	396	462	40	0.103
	100	1,200	1,639	248	0.206

This lack of correlation between illness and the two agent factors—streptococcal group and type, and number of colonies—may have been because most of the illnesses recorded were not caused by the streptococci isolated.

The low rate of antistreptolysin O increase observed following beta-hemolytic streptococcal acquisitions (28%) may be partially explained by the predominance of younger patients less likely to develop antibodies in response to streptococcal infection; a number of young children sustained quite elevated titers during the study, however. Another factor may be that the interval between samples was prolonged, although Rantz et al.[12] reported persistence of elevated titers over a considerable period of time, varying with age, reinfection and other factors. The relatively high rate of reinfection in the present study tends to diminish the disadvantage of the prolonged interval between antistreptolysin O titers, despite the desirability of a shorter interval. Even in those illnesses in association with beta-hemolytic streptococci and followed by antistreptolysin O increase, there was no significant difference between antibody increase associated with non-Group A (21.9%) and Group A (29.0%) strains. When more than half the colonies in the original agar plate were streptococci, 38% of these patients had a subsequent antibody increase, while only 21% with plates with under 50% streptococci developed such an increase (p less than 0.01).

Thus, differences in the group and type of streptococci, and the number of colonies isolated, while undoubtedly of some importance in the pathogenesis of illness, did not seem to play a crucial role in determining acquisition, illness rates, or immune response. Increased predominance of streptococci on culture was associated with a significantly higher frequency of antibody increases, but neither were consistent indicators of clinical disease.

* 12 months, 16 families.

TABLE 3

BETA-HEMOLYTIC-STREPTOCOCCAL INFECTIONS IN FAMILIES:
RELATION OF ILLNESS TO STREPTOCOCCAL GROUP

Group	Cultures				Acquisitions			
	Ill		Not Ill		Ill		Not Ill	
	No.	%	No.	%	No.	%	No.	%
A	68	34.4	129	65.6	48	43.2	63	56.8
Non-A	21	36.8	36	63.2	8	38.0	13	62.0

HOST FACTORS

Age was certainly one important factor responsible for differences in colonization rates, with school children having the highest, two- to five-year-olds the second highest, adults the next, and infants under two years old the lowest rates of acquisition (Table 2). Once colonized, the chance of an individual becoming ill varied little between different age groups (Table 5), but the type of illness was quite different in these different age groups (Table 6), a point clearly documented by Rantz et al.[13] and others. In spite of these differences in the symptoms and signs of infection, there was little difference in severity by age.

TABLE 4

BETA-STREPTOCOCCAL INFECTIONS IN FAMILIES:
RELATION OF NUMBER OF COLONIES TO ILLNESS

Quantity of Colonies	Positive Cultures (%)	
	Ill	Not Ill
<25%	23.5	27.6
25-50%	42.4	38.3
>50%	28.2	31.1
Unknown	5.9	2.9
	100.0	99.9

Only 28% of all streptococcal acquisitions were followed by an antistreptolysin O elevation. This was far more likely to occur after an illness (49%) than after an asymptomatic colonization (16%), and it occurred more frequently in school-age groups than in either younger children or adults (although the numbers for each group are too small to permit significance testing).

There was no significant association of streptococcal illness or antibody increase with sex, family history of repeated respiratory infections, strong personal allergic history, or the presence or absence of tonsils. There was a slightly higher chronic carrier rate among individuals still possessing their tonsils. Mothers were more likely to become colonized and ill than fathers.

ENVIRONMENTAL FACTORS

Physical Environment

The largest number of cultures positive for beta-hemolytic streptococci occurred in March and April, but a great deal of variation in both colonization and illness was observed from month to month, with several other months almost equalling the spring months. The late summer and fall months were characterized by the isolation of a much higher proportion of non-Group A strains, however. In spite of this general correlation with the seasons, no consistent relation of colonization or illness rates to specific weather characteristics could be determined; no relation could be found between the rates of streptococcal acquisition or illness and humidity, temperature level and change, or type or amount of precipitation. Housing was generally adequate for all these families, and there was no correlation between acquisition or illness rates and number of rooms, type of heating, or type of house.

TABLE 5

BETA-STREPTOCOCCAL INFECTIONS IN FAMILIES*

Age (yr)	Persons in Study (no.)	Persons with Positive Culture during Year (no.)	Individual Beta-streptococcal Acquisitions	
			Total Number	With Illness
<2	16	7	9	4
2-5	28	26	53	31
6-15	22	20	48	25
16+	34	19	29	13
Individuals	100	72	139	73
Total Family Episodes	..	..	47	33

Surprisingly, there was also no consistent relation between family size and number of acquisitions or illness. For example, the greatest number of individual acquisitions occurred in a family of only two children, while another family with seven children had one of the lowest rates. All families had about the same potential contact with streptococci, as judged by the number of school age children, the degree of neighborhood crowding, and other types of non-home contacts, including the fathers' working environment.

Family sleeping patterns appeared to be the only physical factor related to acquisition or illness; when one family member acquired a beta-hemolytic streptococcus he was twice as likely to spread it to another family member occupying the same bedroom as to the other family members sleeping in separate rooms.

* All 16 families were positive at sometime during the 12 months observation.

TABLE 6

BETA-STREPTOCOCCAL INFECTIONS IN FAMILIES

Age (yr)	Persons (no.)	Illness Rates Per Person-year (associated with beta-streptococci)*			
		Undifferentiated Upper Respiratory	Pharyngitis & Tonsillitis	Otitis Media	All Other
< 2	16	1.68(0.31)	0.31 (0)	0.69 (0.18)	0.56 (0)
2-5	28	2.52 (0.53)	0.68 (0.43)	0.43 (0.14)	1.80 (0.14)
6-15	22	2.18 (0.81)	0.46 (0.27)	0.05 (0)	1.41 (0.31)
16 +	34	0.97 (01.7)	0.56 (0.24)	0 (0)	0.76 (0.12)

Human Environment

Throughout the year parents frequently commented on the relation of acute family crises to the onset of illness. Figure 1 illustrates such an example in a family who otherwise had no streptococcal acquisitions during the entire year. As far as can be determined, exposure of all family members to beta-hemolytic streptococcus occurred on May 1, but only the child who was subjected to increasing pressure during the week to learn her catechism before confirmation, became colonized and ill. This was not an isolated coincidence; similar circumstances were seen in other families. By means of the interview and diaries, life events that disrupted family or personal life and caused excess anxiety, and other evidences of disorganization were independently recorded.

About one quarter of the streptococcal acquisitions and illnesses followed such acute family crises, and there was an even clearer relation between both acquisitions and illness and these acute crises when the period two weeks before and two weeks after acquisitions or illness was compared. Table 7 documents this relation and shows that streptococcal acquisition and illness, as well as non-streptococcal respiratory infections,

TABLE 7

RESPIRATORY INFECTIONS IN FAMILIES: RELATION TO ACUTE STRESS

Type Episode	Episodes of Acute Stress (no.)		Infections	
	Two Weeks before	Two Weeks after	Total Number	Associated with Stress (%)
Beta-strep illness	17	3	56	35.7
Beta-strep acquisitions without illness	12	3	76	19.5
Non-strep respiratory infections	17	4	201	10.5
Totals	46	10	333	17.0

* Beta streptococcal illness rate per person-year, 0.9; 24.1% of all illness associated with beta streptococci 52.5% of all acquisitions not associated with illness.

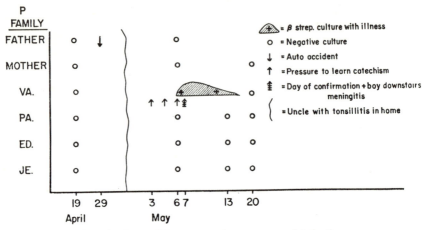

FIG. 1. Acute life stress and streptococcal infection.

were about four times as likely to be preceded as to be followed by acute
stress. While this difference is statistically quite significant, the causal
role and the precise mechanisms are far from clear. The types of acute
crises seen in the 29 episodes occurring in the two weeks before acquisition
of streptococci are listed in Table 8. Exposure of child to wet and cold
often occurred during the study but was rarely associated with such
acquisitions unless fatigue was also present.

An equally useful dependent variable was the level of chronic stress
found in each family. The level of chronic stress was determined by a

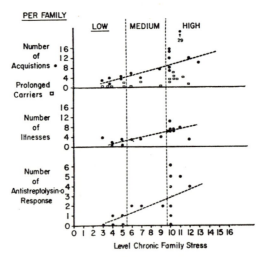

FIG. 2. Beta-streptococcal infections in
families—relation to chronic stress. The
dotted line represents a visual mean for each
of the independent variables.

TABLE 8
ACUTE FAMILY STRESS AND RESPIRATORY INFECTIONS

Type of Stress	Episodes (no.)
Loss of family member	6
Death of grandmother (3)	
Serious illness in family	3
Pneumonia, amputation, nephritis	
Minor illness: serious implications	6
Broken leg, birth, breast lump removal	
Family crisis: non-medical	8
Aunt divorced, burned out, confirmation, father lost job, all tired and wet	
Non-family crisis: impact on members	4
Witness to violent death	
Multiple family stresses	2
Total	**29**

rating scale based upon four general indices of family functioning as judged independently by two observers (physician and bacteriology technician) and occasionally by other members of the health team (Table 9). This rating scale was designed to measure family functioning as described

TABLE 9
RESPIRATORY INFECTIONS IN FAMILIES: CHRONIC FAMILY STRESS RATING SCALE

Family Function	Scale		
	Smoothly Functioning	→	Disorganized
External relations	0	→	4
Arrangement for outside activity			
Ability to use non-family members in emergency			
Ability to use community resources			
Network of relations-friends and neighbors			
Relations to legal institutions			
Internal relations	0	→	4
Child-rearing values consistent with children's needs			
Parental and family responsibility for each other			
Realistic care of ill member			
Parents' relations to each other			
Emotional adjustment of family members			
Medical care	0	→	4
Plan for preventive services			
Realistic ability to detect and seek help for individual ills			
Capacity to relate to medical resources			
History of handling of previous medical stresses			
Environmental and economic	0	→	4
Suitability and organization of home			
Income adequacy-cost in parents' energy			
Ability to meet medical and other needs			
Total	**0**	→	**16**

by Bell and Vogel[14] and others. Total scores could range from 0 to 16, with higher numbers indicating greater degrees of disorganization and chronic stress.

When all four independent variables (acquisition rates, prolonged carrier states, streptococcal illness rates, and antistreptolysin O responses) were compared, there is a definite increase of all these variables as chronic stress scores increased (Fig. 2). Table 10 indicates the number of streptococcal acquisitions followed by an increase of antibodies in the low compared to the moderate and high stress families. After an acquisition of streptococci, antistreptolysin O increases were seen in only 21% of the patients in the low stress families, compared to 49% of those patients in the moderate-high stress families, a statistically significant difference (p = 0.01).

As part of the initial interview with these families, they were asked which of their children was most likely to become ill. All had a ready answer, sometimes modifying this by saying that although one was more likely to become ill, another was more likely to become seriously ill if he became sick at all. It is interesting that the parents were able to predict correctly which child was more likely to become ill in 11 of the 16 families.

THERAPY

Adequate penicillin therapy for streptococcal infections has been shown to eradicate the organism[15,16] and also to suppress antibody responses[17,18] in the majority of instances. As seen in Table 11 patients adequately treated with penicillin were less likely to have an antibody increase following acquisition of a beta-hemolytic streptococcus than those not treated. A larger number of patients would be required before antibody response could be correlated significantly with the time therapy was begun, however.

Adequate treatment was followed by reappearance of the same type of streptococcus in a few families, confirming previous reports.[17] In three families these recurrences ceased only after prolonged carrier states had been allowed to exist until antistreptolysin O rises occurred.

TABLE 10

BETA-STREPTOCOCCAL INFECTIONS IN FAMILIES*

| Level of Chronic Family Stress | Antistreptolysis O Response† | | | No Strep Acquisitions |
| | Episodes Group A Acquisition | | | |
	ASO Rise	No Rise	Total	
Low	3	11	14	19
Moderate-high	34	36	70	9

* 100 persons, 16 families, 12 months.
† Two or more tubes.   (P<0.05.)

Thirty per cent of acquisitions treated with penicillin were followed by the appearance of penicillin resistant staphylococci in the throat, compared to only 19% in those patients who received no therapy. In two patients the presence of these penicillinase-producing organisms was associated with failure of penicillin treatment to eradicate the streptococcus.

TABLE 11

BETA-STREPTOCOCCAL INFECTIONS IN FAMILIES*

Therapy	Antistreptolysin O Response† to Separate Acquisitions		
	Rise	No Rise	Total
Penicillin	11	33	44
No therapy	22	12	34
	33	45	78

COMMENT

It is clear that there are few solid data to explain why one child becomes sick or colonized, while another does not, with such a common organism as the beta-hemolytic streptococcus. From the clinician's point of view it has become exceedingly difficult to decide who should be treated, a paradoxical situation since there are few other infections for which such safe and effective therapy is available. The clinical diagnosis of streptococcal infection cannot be expected to be much better than 75% correct[19] even if "syndromes of symptoms and signs" are used[20] rather than single findings. On the other hand, streptococci are so often found in healthy children that their presence in children with acute respiratory infections does not, *per se*, indicate a significant streptococcal infection. Thus throat cultures, while helpful, cannot be used alone to decide which person requires therapy. Since therapy does not reduce the duration of acute symptoms[21] or lower the carrier rate in schools,[2,22] there are only two general reasons to treat streptococcal disease: (1) the presence of suppurative complications, or (2) the risk of non-suppurative complications. The patient with suppurative complications presents only a minor problem; all would agree that he must be treated. But not until more satisfactory criteria are available for deciding who is most likely to develop the non-suppurative complications can more rational treatment be given. The fact that adequate penicillin therapy will reduce the antistreptolysin O response to a given infection has been shown before[17,18] and is confirmed in our data. Such treatment for illness does not depress the individual's

* 100 persons, 16 families, 12 months.
† Two or more tubes.

eventual production of antibodies, which may well be the response to a large number of asymptomatic infections ultimately giving rise to antibody responses, as shown by Breese *et al.*[23] Although type-specific streptococcal immunity does not prevent colonization, it does inhibit type-specific illness, which bears out the importance of such acquired immunity.[24] If, as seems likely, it is useful for an individual to develop antibodies, the least risk of non-suppurative complications probably follows such asymptomatic infections. Thus, in general, carrier states may be left untreated with very little risk.

Indeed, in occasional patients penicillin therapy seems to exert an adverse influence either by suppressing the formation of protective antibody or by promoting the growth of penicillinase producing staphylococci that may interfere with the action of penicillin against streptococci.

The purpose of this investigation was to study the factors that predispose to respiratory infections, with the ultimate hope that one might gain some clinically useful data as to which individuals in family groups would be more likely to acquire such infections. The agent factors investigated did not yield much useful information; neither group, type nor number of colonies were very reliable indicators of who had significant infection. Although only Group A streptococci are generally credited with responsibility for non-suppurative complications, Packer *et al.*[25] also reported that non-Group A organisms were capable of producing both illness and antibody response.

Age was an important factor in host susceptibility to streptococcal illness. (School-aged children were most susceptible, followed by two- to five-year-olds.) Weather played only a minor seasonal role, for while infection increased during the late winter and spring, precise types of weather or weather changes could not be shown to be associated with higher rates of infection in this small study group, as had previously been shown for influenza.[26] Close contact with other family members ill with proven streptococcal disease, particularly through sharing a bedroom, increased the likelihood of significant disease.

When acute life stress or chronic family disorganization is considered in addition to these other factors, there seems to be an additional criterion for selecting the more susceptible individual or family. Not only are higher acquisition and illness rates associated with acute and chronic stress situations, but also the proportion of persons in whom there is a significant rise of antistreptolysin O following the acquisition of streptococci increases with increasing stress. While this does not prove that such persons are more likely to have non-suppurative complications—only a very large study could show this—it does suggest that this may be one explanation for the well-known increased risk of rheumatic fever among lower socio economic groups.[27, 28] It remains to be determined whether stress is higher or significantly different in lower socioeconomic groups.

Certain emotional states have been shown to be associated with the onset of certain illnesses[29] and with the occurrence of beta-hemolytic streptococcal colonization.[30] Neither the precise emotional states that might predispose to increased rates of infection, nor the pathophysiologic mechanisms by which such changes could be mediated are known.

Stress is generally credited with increasing the output of adrenal corticosteroids, but beyond isolated examples in patients with tuberculosis[31,32] and varicella,[33] few data exist to support such a mechanism as being responsible for increased risk in acute infections. While a great many studies have been performed in animals in an attempt to elucidate some of these factors responsible for resistance and susceptibility[34-39] it is difficult to translate these findings to man. Studies aimed at linking changes in the host's internal environment as measured by hormones, antibodies and leukocytes, with external environmental changes of weather, housing, nutrition, family living, fatigue, medical therapy, and life stress are clearly the next step. Only in this way can meaningful relations with sound therapeutic and preventive implications be found. From our data it seems likely that no one cause will be found, for beta-hemolytic streptococcal infections seem to be another example of "multiple causation" of disease.

SUMMARY

Sixteen lower-middle-class families, comprising 100 persons, were intensively studied for one year, with systematic throat cultures for beta-hemolytic streptococci, periodic measurements of antistreptolysin O titer, and clinical evaluation of all illnesses; the results of those observations were compared to certain dependent variables of host, agent, and environment. The factors that seemed to play an important part in determining whether a given person acquired a streptococcus, became ill with this acquisition, or developed a subsequent increase in antistreptolysin O were age, season, closeness of contact with an infected person as measured by sleeping arrangements, acute or chronic family stress, and penicillin treatment. No relationship was found between streptococcal episodes and the number or type of streptococci present, sex of the patient, the presence or absence of tonsils, an allergic history, changes in weather, type of housing, or family size. Further evidence for the multiple causation of beta-hemolytic streptococcal disease has been obtained, although the mechanisms through which these factors exert their influence are not clear.

ACKNOWLEDGMENT

The authors wish to express their appreciation for the professional advice of Dr. Benedict Massell in carrying out this study, and to the families whose cooperation made the study possible.

REFERENCES

1. PASTEUR, L., JOUBERT, J., and CHAMBERLAND. 1878. Le charbon des poules. *Compt. Rend. Acad. Sci.*, **87**, 47. (Cited by PERLA, D., and MARMORSTON, J. 1941. *Natural resistance and clinical medicine.* Little, Brown & Co., Boston.)

2. CORNFELD, D., and HUBBARD, J. P. 1961. A four-year study of the occurrence of beta-hemolytic streptococci in 64 school children. *New Engl. J. Med.*, **264**, 211.

3. CORNFELD, D., *et al.* 1961. Epidemiologic studies of streptococcal infection in school children. *Am. J. publ. Hlth*, **51**, 242.

4. MOZZICONACCI, *et al.* 1961. A study group of A hemolytic streptococcus carriers among school children: II. Significance of the findings. *Acta pediat.*, **50**, 33.

5. HARVEY, H. S., and DUNLAP, M. D. 1960. Upper respiratory flora of husbands and wives: A comparison. *New Engl. J. Med.*, **262**, 976.

6. JAMES, W. E. S., BADGER, G. F., and DINGLE, J. H. 1960. A study of illness in a group of Cleveland families: XIX. The epidemiology of the acquisition of group A streptococci and of associated illness. *New Engl. J. Med.*, **262**, 687.

7. BREESE, B. B., and DISNEY, F. A. 1956. The spread of streptococcal infections in family groups. *Pediatrics*, **17**, 834.

8. BRIMBLECOMBE, F. S. W., *et al.* 1958. Family studies of respiratory infections. *Br. med. J.*, i, 119.

9. MAXTED, W. R. 1953. The use of bacitracin for identifying group A hemolytic streptococci. *J. clin. Path.*, **6**, 224.

10. SWIFT, H. F., WILSON, A. T., and LANCEFIELD, R. C. 1943. Typing group A streptococci by micro precipitation in capillary pipettes. *J. exp. Med.*, **78**, 127.

11. HODGE, B. E., and SWIFT, H. F. 1933. Varying hemolytic and constant combining capacity of streptolysins: Influence on testing for antistreptolysins. (MASSELL, B.: Modification of this method.) *J. exp. Med.*, **58**, 277.

12. RANTZ, L. A., MARONEY, M., and DiCAPRIO, J. M. 1951. Antistreptolysin O response following hemolytic streptococcus infection in early childhood. *Archs intern. Med.*, **87**, 360.

13. RANTZ, L. A., MARONEY, M., and DiCAPRIO, J. M. 1953. Hemolytic streptococcal infection in childhood. *Pediatrics*, **12**, 498.

14. BELL, N. W., and VOGEL, E. F. (eds.) 1960. Introductory essays. In *A modern introduction to the family.* Free Press, Glencoe, Ill.

15. CHAMOVITZ, R., *et al.* 1954. Prevention of rheumatic fever by treatment of previous streptococcal infections. *New Engl. J. Med.*, **251**, 466.

16. BREESE, B. B., and DISNEY, F. A. 1958. Penicillin in the treatment of streptococcal infections: A comparison of effectiveness of five different oral and one parenteral form. *New Engl. J. Med.*, **259**, 57.

17. BROCK, L. L., and SIEGEL, A. C. 1953. Studies on prevention of rheumatic fever: Effect of time of initiation of treatment of streptococcal infections on immune response of host. *J. clin. Invest.*, **32**, 630.

18. LANCEFIELD, R. C. 1959. Persistence of type specific antibodies in man following infection with group A streptococci. *J. exp. Med.*, **110**, 271.

19. BREESE, B. B., and DISNEY, F. A. 1954. The accuracy of diagnosis of beta streptococcal infections on clinical grounds. *J. Pediat.*, **44**, 670.

20. STILLERMAN, M., and BERNSTEIN, S. H. 1961. Streptococcal pharyngitis: Evaluation of clinical syndromes in diagnosis. *Am. J. Dis. Child.*, **101**, 476.

21. BRUMFITT, W., O'GRADY, F., and SLATER, J. D. H. 1959. Benign strepto-coccal sore throat. *Lancet*, ii, 419.

22. PHIBBS, B., *et al.* 1958. The Casper Project—An enforced mass-culture streptococci control program. *J. Am. med. Ass.*, 166, 1113.

23. BREESE, B. B., DISNEY, F. A., and TALPEY, W. B. 1960. The prevention of type specific immunity to streptococcal infections due to the therapeutic use of penicillin. *Am. J. Dis. Child.*, 100, 353.

24. WANNAMAKER, L. W., *et al.* 1953. Studies on immunity to streptococcal in-fection in man. *Am. J. Dis. Child.*, 86, 347.

25. PACKER, H., ARNOULT, M. B., and SPRUNT, D. H. 1956. A study of hemo-lytic streptococcal infections in relation to antistreptolysin O titer changes in orphanage children. *J. Pediat.*, 48, 545.

26. KINGDON, K. H. 1960. Relative humidity and airborne infections. *Am. Rev. resp. Dis.*, 81, 504.

27. KNOWNELDEN, J. 1949. Mortality from rheumatic heart disease in children and young adults in England and Wales. *Br. J. prev. soc. Med.*, 3, 29.

28. QUINN, R. W., and QUINN, J. P. 1951. Mortality due to rheumatic heart disease in the socio-economic districts of New Haven, Connecticut. *Yale J. Biol. Med.*, 24, 15.

29. SCHMALE, A. H., Jr. 1958. Relationship of separation and depression to disease: A report on a hospitalized medical population. *Psychosom. Med.*, 20, 259.

30. KAPLAN, S. M., GOTTSHALK, L. A., and FLEMING, D. E. 1957. Modifications of oropharyngeal bacteria with changes in the psychodynamic state. *Archs Neurol. Psychiat.*, 78, 656.

31. LURIE, M. B. 1960. The reticuloendothelial system: Cortisone and thyroid function: Their relation to native resistance and to infection. *Ann. N.Y. Acad. Sci.*, 88, 83.

32. HOLMES, T. H., *et al.* 1957. Psychosocial and psychophysiologic studies of tuberculosis. *Psychosom. Med.*, 19, 134.

33. HAGGERTY, R. J., and ELEY, R. C. 1956. Varicella and cortisone. *Pediatrics*, 18, 160.

34. DUBOS, R. J., and SCHAEDLER, R. W. 1959. Nutrition and infection. *J. Pediat.*, 55, 1.

35. EVANS, D. G., MILES, A. H., and NIVEN, J. S. F. 1948. The enhancement of bacterial infections by adrenaline. *Brit. J. exp. Path.*, 29, 20.

36. HAYASHIDA, T. 1957. Effect of pituitaryadrenocorticotropic and growth hormone on the resistance of rats infected with pasteurella pestis. *J. exp. Med.*, 106, 127.

37. TEODORU, C. V., and SHWARTZMAN, G. 1956. Endocrine factors in patho-genesis of experimental poliomyelitis in hamsters: Role of inoculatory and environmental stress. *Proc. Soc. exp. Biol. Med.*, 91, 181.

38. SPRUNT, D. H., and FLANIGAN, C. C. 1956. The effect of malnutrition on the susceptibility of the host to viral infection. *J. exp. Med.*, 104, 687.

39. RASMUSSEN, A. F., Jr., MARSH, J. T., and BRILL, N. Q. 1957. Increased sus-ceptibility to herpes simplex in mice subjected to avoidance—Learning stress or restraint. *Proc. Soc. exp. Biol. Med.*, 96, 183.

XXXV

FAMILY THERAPY IN THE TREATMENT
OF THE BRAIN DAMAGED CHILD

ALBERTO C. SERRANO AND NORMAN J. WILSON

*The brain-damaged child reacts to the family pattern of
behaviour. Understanding this enhances diagnosis and
management.*

The brain damaged child with associated behavioral disorders presents a problem of evaluation and disposition of considerable magnitude in child psychiatry and in pediatrics. In our recent experience, approximately one out of each ten patients seen in the Division of Child Psychiatry is given a primary diagnosis of chronic brain syndrome with behavior disorder and frequently with some degree of mental retardation as well.

These patients traditionally have been approached primarily from the standpoint of psychological and neurological examination. However, we find that the diagnosis and treatment of the brain damaged child is facilitated by a clear understanding of the family group in addition to the usual psychiatric, neurological, and psychological approaches.

There are many references in the literature describing the signs and symptoms that make up the brain damage behavior syndrome.[1-5] These include hyperkinesis, low frustration tolerance, short attention span and distractibility, perseveration, emotional lability, overwhelming anxiety, scattered deficits in intellectual functioning, impulsivity, and antisocial behavior. It should be emphasized that although these findings are seen together most frequently in brain damaged children, they are not pathognomonic of organicity and occur in children with functional behavior disorders as well. A given child has his own particular cluster from the constellation.

Reprinted from DISEASES OF THE NERVOUS SYSTEM, Vol. 24, No. 12, December 1963.

Formerly most workers tried to define causality of all such disturbed behavior in either psychological or organic terms alone but in recent years a trend has developed toward a more eclectic attempt to integrate the psychodynamic and the organic. At this stage in our knowledge this may represent the more realistic approach. A minimally brain damaged child may show a more severe disturbance of behavior than a child with more extensive injury. Thus, the disturbed behavior cannot be explained solely on the basis of anatomic impairment. On the other hand, specific environmental data are relatively easier to obtain than neuropathologic data, and it is often tempting to build an etiologic case out of dynamic factors alone when many of them may in themselves be secondary to the organic. The child as a psychobiological unit is subject to biological and social influences, and has a psychological continuity of his own. The outcome of brain injury is the end result of factors influencing all these three spheres.[6]

While biological damage cannot ordinarily be altered or removed, the brain damaged child has other resources and potentials highly sensitive to social influences, no one more important than the impact of the family. His family makes up the solid background of his environment. Their attitude in accepting and supporting, or in rejecting the handicapped child along with his basic personality resources, has more to do with his general adjustment than do the presence of organic factors alone.[7]

In reviewing the recent experience of the Division of Child Psychiatry, we have found 34 cases of organic brain syndromes with behavior disorders. These were mostly minimally and mildy brain damaged children. The more severely organic children have gross neurological, physical, and intellectual handicaps and are more commonly seen by pediatricians and neurologists. Contrary to the usual large margin of predominance of males to females by most investigators, our cases were nearly equally distributed between the sexes, with 19 males and 15 females. (They ranged in age from 4 to 17 years at the time of initial contact, with a median age of 11.) The diagnostic evaluation included: (1) a detailed history, (2) a physical and neurological examination, (3) psychological testing, (4) an electroencephalogram, and (5) interviewing of the child and the family.

The history placed special emphasis on prenatal, neonatal, and developmental history as well as a careful investigation of childhood illnesses. The physical and neurological findings in brain damaged children have been well described by Strauss, Bender, Clements, and others.[1-4, 7] These need not be enumerated here save to re-emphasize the subtlety of the "soft" neurological signs: the equivocal deficits or asymmetries of complex integrated behavior such as postural reflexes, fine motor coordination, perceptual motor tasks, laterality, speech, and so forth. The psychological testing included the Wechsler Intelligence Scale for Children (WISC), Bender-Gestalt, Draw-A-Person, various reading scales, and some projective testing. Scatter was the most common finding in the

WISC, as well as verbal scale exceeding performance I.Q. In the Bender-Gestalt the most common abnormalities were rotation, "dog ears," perseveration, and a disorganized pattern. The presence of abnormalities in the electroencephalogram, the most common being scattered slow spike activity, lent helpful corroborative evidence to the case of organicity.

In interviewing the child and the family, a multiple disciplinary team containing one or two psychiatrists, a clinical psychologist, and a psychiatric social worker, had the chance to observe the various patterns of family interaction and dynamics in both individual and group situations, especially as they related to the nominal patient. In addition, behavioral and academic data from school reports were valuable in the evaluation.

The addition of a family centered approach to the diagnosis and treatment of the brain damaged child was based not only on the traditional child guidance clinic procedure but more so on the experience of the authors working with emotionally disturbed adolescents and their families, using a brief intensive psychotherapy program called Multiple Impact Therapy.[8-11] Starting with a team-family conference, it proceeds through a series of different combinations of the people involved. It includes multiple therapist situations, individual interviews, and group therapy interspersed with brief staff conferences. That study yielded an understanding of the various stabilizing factors utilized by families to maintain what has been labeled family homeostasis. It was noticed that a disturbed child seemed in many cases to serve as a stabilizing factor as if his symptoms helped to drain off chronic unexpressed family tensions.[12] The child's individual potentials and emotional growth had become subservient to that role. It was also found that the child with a physical handicap often became a natural target for the unresolved childhood problems of the parents.

In the experience reported in this paper, there were cases where an obviously brain damaged retarded child was pressured for high scholastic achievement, his handicap known to the parents but unwittingly denied. Conversely, cases of minimal brain damage with infantile behavior secondary to severe overprotection were not rare. These findings and the irregular results obtained by utilizing unidimensional approaches made for our increasing interest in exploring the family as a key dimension in the correct diagnosis and treatment of this problem.

The treatment program must be tailored to the data that are obtained in each case. Drug therapy is frequently most useful, especially in controlling the hyperkinesia and seizures where the latter is a problem. Captodiamine, dextro-amphetamine, deanol, diphenylhydantoin, meprobamate, phenobarbital, chlorpromazine, thioridazine, and trifluoperazine are among the drugs that we have found to be helpful in individual cases, but it must be said that individual responses to different dosages of these medications is highly variable.

The following case will serve as an illustration:

A.R., age nine was referred to our clinic during the summer of 1961. He was hyperactive, soiled his pants, and had not yet been able to pass the first grade. His parents related that the patient had always been a "problem child" as compared to his brother, one year older. He was loud and impulsive and was never able to play with children his own age. A physician who was consulted suggested that A. might have a mild degree of brain damage, but no recommendations were made nor was treatment instituted. When he started school, teachers noticed that the patient was asocial and hyperactive. He could not sit still in class or concentrate on his work. The parents were ashamed of his behavior but seemed to be unable to face the problem.

He repeated the first grade and the same difficulties occurred. He was then taken to a psychologist. A series of tests showed that he was performing below the normal level of intelligence. A physician then placed the patient on dextroamphetamine, which made him more hyperactive. Barbiturates and meprobamate were later used without improvement. He was kept in the first grade for three years, after which he was promoted to the second grade because of his size.

The family also complained of the patient's bowel habits. He would defecate a small amount in his pants, ignoring this and running around soiled until his family brought him to the toilet. His mother related that earlier in his life he had always been very constipated and that she gave him enemas every day or so.

The patient had been a full term infant, the prenatal and neonatal periods uncomplicated. He had no serious illness or accidents. His early physical development was remarkable only in that his growth pattern was slower than his older brother's. The parents noticed early that he preferred to play with children two or three years younger. He would dominate the play and "throw frequent temper tantrums."

The father is a college graduate. He saw himself as having no personal nor marital problems. His wife related that she had had a great deal of difficulty early in her life. She was a second child and always had felt neglected by her family in favor of her older sister. When the nominal patient was born she had special feelings for his being a second born and always protected him accordingly. She blamed herself for his behavior, assuming that it was caused by her overprotective attitude.

The family as a group, with the three children, was interviewed by the team. The referred patient was very hyperactive, wandering around the room banging ash trays, moving chairs and investigating papers on the desk. The younger brother, age five, followed him as a leader. The older brother sat rather meekly in a chair and watched. The embarrassed parents commented that the patient's brothers knew nothing about his "illness," and wondered about their being present. This was rapidly refuted as they admitted having made many exceptions for the patient's misbehavior which they had not made for his brothers (who had many times complained of the unfairness). The open discussion of the problem was encouraged, the father voiced his guilt for feeling angry at and frustrated by the boy, as well as resenting his wife's overprotective attitude. His wife expressed guilt for her closeness to the child and her impatience with his bowel difficulties.

A battery of psychological tests and an interview with the patient showed poor impulse control, reading reversals, poor visual-motor coordination, spatial visualization difficulties, short attention span, distractability, and speech difficulties. He was functioning at a Full Scale WISC of 72, the Verbal Scale 72, and Performance 76. An EEG revealed "occasional sporadic high voltage slow spikes in all leads." The neurological examination demonstrated awkwardness and confused laterality in addition to the previously described signs. It was felt that the patient had a mild degree of brain damage. It was also felt that he had been overprotected and not dealt with consistently. The mother seemed to have placed her second son in her own position as a second sibling from the start. She also seemed to be of less intellectual capacity than her husband. Both parents placed high emphasis on academic achievement and perfection.

The treatment program outlined included deanol 300 mg. daily and recommendations for special education classes. As there were no such facilities in their town, the family had to take the problem to the local educational authorities, this being almost a routine procedure to start such classes in Texas and something they had to initiate themselves. The family was counseled on the need to establish a consistent set of rules encouraging the child to assume more responsibilities, particularly regarding his bowel troubles. The findings were discussed with individual family members as they related to their own personal involvement and their projected feelings. Regular follow-ups were held monthly for a while, and spaced less frequently as the need for continuous assistance diminished. There has been slow but substantial improvement in most areas. He has attended special education classes for the past year, learning to read and write at a level appropriate to the first grade. While his behavior has still been impulsive and his frustration tolerance low, it has improved to the extent of his participating in various activities with peers, instead of being so isolated. His older brother seems to accept him better since he understands the nature of the problem, and he himself has been acting "more relaxed." The family reports that very few accidents of encopresis occur now. In the clinic, the patient shows better coordination. His speech is normal, and he shows considerable pride in his achievements. His parents have needed further assistance in understanding the limitations of their son, particularly insofar as education. Both parents have uncovered the feeling that it was unbearable for them to accept what appears to be the externalization of their own inferiorities. The parents have now reduced the amount of attention given to their "sick" child and have been able to enjoy more adult interests, particularly in community activities and the like.

SUMMARY

Our experience in the diagnosis and treatment of the minimally and mildly brain damaged children has included the evaluation of the total family constellation, in addition to the more traditional physical and psychological studies of the problem child. The disturbance of the child seems to be the end result of a combination of at least three factors: soma, psyche, and family. Each aspect is studied by a team of psychiatrists, psychologist, and social worker. The result is a multidimensional diagnosis that we have found to be of important therapeutic value. The treatment plan aims at facilitating a better utilization of potentials, by means of drugs, psychotherapy, school placement, and recommendations for a regulated life, depending on the degree of pathology present in each of the various aspects studied in child and family.

REFERENCES

1. STRAUSS, A. A., and LEHTINEN, L. K. 1947. *Psychopathology and education of the brain-injured child.* Grune & Stratton, New York.

2. STRAUSS, A. A., and KEPHART, N. C. 1955. *Psychopathology and education of the brain-injured child*, Vol. 2. Grune & Stratton, New York.
3. BAER, P. E. 1961. Problems in the differential diagnosis of brain damaged childhood and schizophrenia. *Am. J. Orthopsychiat.*, 31, 78.
4. CLEMENTS, S. D., and PETERS, J. E. 1962. Minimal brain damage in the school-age child. *Archs gen. Psychiat.*, 6, 185.
5. KNOBEL, M. 1962. Psychopharmacology of the hyperkinetic child. *Archs gen. Psychiat.*, 6, 198.
6. EISENBERG, L. 1957. Psychiatric implications of the brain damaged child, *Psychiat. Q.*, 31, 72.
8. RITCHIE, A. 1960. Multiple impact therapy: An experiment. *Social Work*, 5, 16.
9. MACGREGOR, R. 1962. Multiple impact psychotherapy with families. *Family Process*, 1, 15. [Reprinted in this collection as No. XLIX.]
10. SERRANO, A. C., McDANALD, E. C., *et al*. 1962. Adolescent maladjustment and family dynamics. *Am. J. Psychiat.*, 118, 10. [Reprinted in this collection as No. VII.]
11. GOOLISHIAN, H. A. 1962. A brief psychotherapy program for disturbed adolescents. *Am. J. Orthopsychiat.*, 32, 142.
12. VOGEL, E. F., and BELL, N. W. 1960. The emotionally disturbed child as a family scapegoat. *Psychoanal. psychoanal. Rev.*, 47.

XXXVI

FAMILY DYNAMICS IN A CASE OF GILLES DE LA TOURETTE'S SYNDROME

ROBERT W. DOWNING, NATHAN L. COMER
AND JOHN N. EBERT

In addition to an organic factor, psychodynamic factors play a part in the aetiology of Gilles de la Tourette's syndrome. The sources of the latter in the family are discussed as they relate to an unmarried female patient.

In 1885 Gilles de la Tourette[5] described a clinical syndrome which was characterized by "motor incoordination" (multiple tics), coprolalia and, less consistently, echolalia and echokinesis.

According to Eisenberg *et al.*,[4] the typical case history reveals the following course: the illness begins in childhood, usually before the age of ten years, with tics of the upper part of the body, face, shoulder or arm. The tics are explosive in nature, initially transient, and noted to be worse at times of stress, fatigue or excitement. As the disease progresses, intervals of relative freedom from the tics become less frequent and the tics spread to the trunk and legs. At some stage, inarticulate cries, which may resemble throat rasping, barking, or quacking accompany the convulsive movement. The cries then become articulate and consist of single words or phrases, often echolalic. The final feature, the appearance of which is pathognomonic for the syndrome, is coprolalia, the sudden uncontrolled and repetitive utterance of obscenities.

While an organic factor in etiology is often mentioned and may indeed contribute a diathesis,[6, 8, 12] major emphasis has more recently been placed upon the role played by psychodynamic factors in the development of the syndrome.

Reprinted from THE JOURNAL OF NERVOUS AND MENTAL DISEASES, Vol. 138, No. 6, June 1964, pp. 548-557.

Conflicting feelings toward parental and authority figures seem to be centrally involved in the pattern of symptomatology. Ascher[1] found that symptoms of echolalia and coprolalia appeared when the patient developed unacceptable feelings and attitudes toward one or both parents and attempted to suppress them. Dunlap[3] felt that the compulsive sounds and movements of the patient he studied were related to feelings of guilt and hostility directed toward authority figures. The pattern of strict parental domination and a struggle between the suppression and expression of explosive hostility appears in many case histories.[1, 2, 6, 8, 11]

A wide range of symptom clusters is associated with *maladie des tics* in the literature. Ascher[1] reported that all of the five patients he studied had obsessive personalities. Mahler[9] referred to the anal and markedly narcissistic character structures of maladie des tics patients. In the same vein, Bochner stated, "The majority of the cases described in the literature have had factors of an obsessive-compulsive neurosis".[2] Hysterical patterns are noted, however, in cases described by Schneck.[10] Hollander[6] stated that maladie des tics is characterized by severe ego defects and narcissistic orientation. Finally, Ascher[1] found considerable resemblance, particularly in the case of stereotyped mannerisms and speech, between the features of the syndrome and the symptomatology of schizophrenia. Bochner[2] reported that four of 15 cases he noted in a survey of relevant literature terminated in schizophrenia.

The present paper reports a case of Gilles de la Tourette's disease in which all the members of the family were interviewed and psychologically tested. The family consisted of the patient, her parents and her two siblings. It is the writers' intent to describe the patterns of interaction between family members and to relate these to the psychopathology seen in the patient and others in the group.

CASE HISTORY OF PATIENT

The patient, Patricia, was a 24-year-old, attractive, single white female who, when originally seen, was attired in a skin-tight dress which displayed a rather voluptuous figure. She had been referred because of uncontrolled repetitive shouting of "Shit," "Fuck you," and, in the presence of Negroes, "Nigger! Nigger!" Associated with this shouting was "twitching" of the right side of her face and neck.

The onset of the illness occurred when the patient, then eight years old, attended her paternal grandmother's wake. At that time, she began screaming and "shaking all over." After several hours she recovered but then had nightmares about her grandmother's burial for two weeks. Six months after the wake, the patient began to "twitch" involuntarily. This involved flexion of her right arm and turning her head to the right.

At age ten, Patricia began imitating animal sounds and actions. Not long afterward, she started repetitively to blurt out various obscene phrases. Her tic and coprolalia were worse at bedtime, prior to menstrual periods and during periods of anger. The symptoms were relatively well controlled during the day.

The father's rigid controllingness emerged quite blatantly during the patient's teens. It was reported that, when Patricia was 13 and wanted to attend art school, her father forbade it because the school was integrated. At 16 the patient was offered a modeling job in Florida which her father prohibited her from accepting because she would "become a bum." Patricia was offered a job dancing in New York when she was 18 but her father said he would "cripple" her if she went there. The patient ate heavily at these times to get revenge and her symptoms worsened. Her retaliative anger may also be seen in her reaction to a fatal fall of her grandmother when the patient was 17. This reaction took the form of a fear that her parents would die in their sleep.

Despite her symptoms, Patricia did well in school and graduated from high school at 17. She felt she was unpopular in school and had no male friends because her father frightened them away. Following her graduation, she worked as a typist and was able to keep a steady job until just prior to her referral for treatment. Her typing was always "just so" and never had any errors. She was discharged, however, because her outbursts had become so disturbing to her co-workers that they could not do their work.

Patricia was a member of several social clubs where she was popular but known as a "lady." She has never had intercourse and was "mortified" by all the things related to sex until she had a sisterly relationship with an older man. Her symptoms worsened when this man dropped her for another girl, a friend of both. Recently the patient has bleached her black hair to an extremely light tint and the hair color stands in pointed contrast to her somewhat swarthy complexion.

As far as family relationships were concerned, the patient's mother was described by her as a perfectionist who has had episodes of exhaustion, depression and spasms in her legs requiring intermittent medical care. The mother was employed as a seamstress while the patient was cared for by her maternal grandmother. The patient did not get along with Marsha, a sister six years her senior. Patricia felt that she was prettier than her sister and believed that her sister was, consequently, jealous of her. She liked Arthur, a brother five years her junior because he was quiet, slow, sickly and a "good boy." The father has worked as a tailor at home, saying that he couldn't stand his colleague's sloppy work. He has a twitch on the right side of his neck. The mother's sister lives nearby and has a similar twitch. According to the patient's report, the father stopped being affectionate toward the children about the time they reached age four. This upset the patient, who says she was beaten when she tried to embrace him. She felt he acted this way because her mother was not affectionate toward him.

Physical examination and laboratory data, including an EEG, were all within normal limits. Pharmacologic treatment was attempted with a wide range of medications: meprobamate (400 mgm q.i.d.) and Stelazine (5-10 mgm q.i.d.) for six weeks, Tofranil (50 mgm t.i.d.) for two weeks (discontinued when symptoms became aggravated), amphetamine (20-30 mgm) for three weeks, Nardil (15 mgm t.i.d.) for one month and Librium (25 mgm q.i.d.) for one month. None of these produced any improvement. Twenty CO_2 treatments also failed to effect any change. The patient has been seen in psychotherapy two to four times per week for a three-year period with little contribution toward symptomatic relief.

METHOD OF TEST ADMINISTRATION

All members of the family were seen individually by one of the authors (RWD) and given the following psychological tests: 1) The Wechsler Adult Intelligence Scale (Information, Comprehension, Similarities, Digit Span, Digit Symbol, Picture Completion, Block Design and Picture Arrangement subtests); 2) The Rorschach; 3) The Thematic Appercep-tion Test (ten cards, with all family members, receiving cards 1, 2, 3BM, 4, 12MF, 10, 16, 9GF; the males receiving in addition, 6BM and 7BM; the females, 6GF and 7GF); 4) A Word Association Test; and a Sentence Completion Test.* One of us (JNE) visited the family in the home and administered the Leary Interpersonal Check List[7] in a family group set-ting—a context which it was felt might bring out the conscious evaluations of each other by the family members. Each family member was asked to fill out a Check List to describe himself and one to describe each of the other family members. With mother, father, the patient and her two siblings participating, this provided 25 Interpersonal Check List protocols in all. Data from the Interpersonal Check List can be summarized as scores in eight areas identified as follows:

AP Managerial-Autocratic
BC Competitive-Narcissistic
DE Aggressive-Sadistic
FG Rebellious-Distrustful
HI Self-Effacing-Masochistic
JK Docile-Dependent
LM Cooperative-Over-conventional
NO Responsible-Hypernormal

Moderate scores in each area are thought to represent the normal scores of the traits first appearing in each item of the above list. High scores are considered indicative of the pathological exaggerations identified by the second adjective appearing in each item. The traits are usually represented

* These tests have been constructed or modified in this setting for use with our patient population.

in a circular configuration with the apposition of BC and AP forming the closed circle. Traits closest to each other in this circle are thought of as most similar. Those separated by four positions are their opposites (*e.g.*, AP Managerial-Autocratic and HI Self-Effacing-Masochistic). Data quantifying each family member's ratings of himself or herself and of all other family members are presented in Table 1. Scores in each area may range from 0 (low) to 16 (high).

The following section represents an integration of findings from all tests with some additional material from interviews with the patient or other family members.

PATTERNS OF FAMILY INTERACTION

In discussing these data and their interpretation, the pattern of interaction between the mother and father will first be described. Next the manner in which the parental interaction seems to have been responsible for engendering conflicts in the siblings of the family other than the patient will be discussed, and finally comments will be made about the unique way the patient's tic seems to have served defensive functions in this family setting.

The relationship between mother and father appears to have maintained itself through a kind of symbiosis of interlocking patterns of pathology. The father is a man with great dependency needs and grave doubts concerning his adequacy as a male. Thus, five of the seven instances of stimulus word repetition, one type of conflict indicator on the Word Association Test occur with the stimulus words "breast," "mouth," "suck," "nipple" and "bite." His response to the stimulus word "hungry" is "starved." His story to Card 1 of the TAT deals with "a kid . . . looking at the violin, wondering if he could make it, wondering if he would be good enough." After much doubt expressed concerning the sex of the figure on Card 3BM, he decided it was a woman because he could see no pants legs. His history, as well as several Sentence Completion responses indicate that, rather than risk the devastating possibility of failure which might come through an earnest effort to achieve, and rather than chance an exposure to direct competition; he has chosen never to attempt to function at an occupational level commensurate with his intelligence (Wechsler Full Scale I.Q., 120). Within recent years, he has renounced almost entirely the responsibility of working. His uncertainties about himself leave him angry, envious, but afraid of giving vent to feelings in situations where there is any chance of dangerous retaliation. His Sentence Completion Test responses emphasize the importance he attaches to "popularity" and his tendency to respond to aggression by "backing down." Yet he is rated on the Leary Interpersonal Check List by all family members as the most dominant and least loving member of the family group (*cf.* Table 1). Consequently, it seems likely that his behavior has been meek and retiring outside the family circle, but domineering and aggressive in interaction with other members of the family. In responding to a Sentence Completion Test item concerning sexual desires he states *"I used to look at a girl and want it."* His Rorschach reflects extreme sexual preoccupation, and feelings of sexual attraction toward someone other than the marital partner is a recurring theme in TAT stories. The pattern of schizoid personality into which the behavioral orientation of the father should be fit is thus also probably accompanied by an intensification of sexual drive and an awareness of sexual feelings toward all the female members of the family.

Many of the mother's traits contribute to the generation and maintenance of a symbiotic relationship. Her limited intelligence (Wechsler Full Scale I.Q., 81) minimizes the threat of competition with the father. The subservience reflected in her test protocols is more apparent than real, since history material indicates that she manages to gratify her narcissistic

TABLE 1

RATINGS OF SELF AND EACH OTHER FAMILY MEMBER BY PATRICIA AND THE OTHER MEMBERS OF HER IMMEDIATE FAMILY

	AP*	NO	LM	JK	HI	FG	DE	BC
Rating of Patricia								
By: Patricia	9	16	15	13	12	7	5	3
„ Mother	9	15	14	13	12	9	7	6
„ Father	7	14	14	8	8	11	12	7
„ Marsha	5	10	12	5	8	3	3	2
„ Arthur	7	3	9	5	6	8	6	6
Rating of Mother								
By: Patricia	8	16	16	11	11	5	2	2
„ Mother	8	16	15	13	13	5	4	7
„ Father	4	14	11	8	7	7	9	6
„ Marsha	4	12	12	7	5	5	1	4
„ Arthur	3	14	12	8	13	7	10	1
Rating of Father								
By: Patricia	11	12	9	4	4	4	7	8
„ Mother	7	6	7	6	3	9	9	9
„ Father	6	14	12	4	5	6	10	8
„ Marsha	9	5	3	1	1	7	8	6
„ Arthur	13	7	13	3	3	11	7	8
Rating of Marsha								
By: Patricia	10	14	12	5	6	1	5	6
„ Mother	9	15	13	8	7	4	8	8
„ Father	11	15	12	6	5	11	9	10
„ Marsha	6	8	9	4	4	6	10	3
„ Arthur	9	3	9	1	3	8	9	4
Rating of Arthur								
By: Patricia	8	12	11	6	5	2	4	9
„ Mother	11	15	14	12	8	4	5	9
„ Father	5	11	9	5	2	2	5	6
„ Marsha	6	6	9	7	6	2	3	6
„ Arthur	8	10	12	4	5	5	6	9

* See text for a key to interpretation of these symbols.

wishes for having her own way by using illness to maintain an absolute control over the family. Her control is coupled with a genuinely responsible attitude toward the family which is recognized by the high Leary Interpersonal Check List ratings in sector NO, responsibility, which she is given by all family members. From the Interpersonal Check List data, it appears that the father is able consciously to acknowledge the mother's responsibility and cooperativeness, but is also aware of her aggressiveness; however, he cannot see or consciously admit to the extent of her controllingness. It might be inferred, then, that her capacity to dominate by indirection thus provide some security for the father, but lets him express some hostility and perhaps appear to keep the upper hand without fear of retaliation. The mother's picture of the father as hostile and unloving (*cf.* Table 1) may leave him feeling hurt and superficially disgruntled. Since she does not seem overtly to recognize his deep feelings of dependency (her Interpersonal Check List ratings attribute to him moderate amounts of aggressivity and competitiveness) the more far reaching effect here is most likely one of bolstering his all too uncertain feelings of masculinity. The mother possesses a hysterical orientation toward sex, finding sexual relations with her husband distasteful, but probably finding enjoyment in romantic sexual fantasies. (For example, the following two Sentence Completion Test responses: *When it comes to sexual relations she prefers "not to bother." She daydreams about "her boyfriends."*) While this state of affairs leaves the father vociferously dissatisfied* and preoccupied with his sexual impulses toward a wide range of women, it probably also is a relief for him in that it makes it unnecessary for him to put his masculinity to very frequent test.

It seems quite likely, however, that the parents' mode of interaction also maintains a high intrafamily level of tension. The father's dependency needs are sufficiently strong and have enough of an element of primitive oral deprivation that he constantly feels frustrated and reacts with anger. The combination of poor impulse control and fear of a complete breakdown in the control functioning probably results in a pattern of behavior erratically shifting between impulsive, aggressive displays and withdrawal and apathy. As his family has grown, his dependency needs, no doubt, have become even more frustrated and he has come to regard himself as a kind of sibling in the family. This situation seems well reflected in the following Sentence Completion items: *His family treats him as "I wouldn't know that . . . as a lovable child." He feels that his family don't "love him any more." He got sore when "love and affection was shown to the other children."* As previously stated, his situation with regard to sexual gratification has the advantage of enabling him to avoid any rigorous

---

* The following examples from the Sentence Completion Test seems relevant here: *Most women "are bad." Most women should "be seen and not heard."* His greatest sexual difficulty is that *"a wife would be frigid."* TAT stories included a wife who was spying on her husband; a wife who is "no good," "found out" and strangled by a husband.

test of his masculinity but it is chronically frustrating, it leaves him extremely angry at women, and it contributes to the generation of fantasies which mobilize further fear of loss of control and great quantities of guilt. He attempts to bolster his male self-respect by viewing himself as an attractive, virile person who takes adversity "like a man." Emphasizing respectability and control in his children may represent a further means of strengthening his own control. Finally, his envy of those who have been more successful than he is projected onto them, so that he sees others as envious of him. Consequently, he tends to be uneasy and suspicious of others. In responding to a Sentence Completion item, he reports that it makes him nervous when *"They whisper behind his back."* At another point, he reports that he is afraid "of the law."

The marital relationship has had its frustrating aspects for the mother also. Her history reveals that she brought to marriage a resentment toward men, originating in her feelings toward an alcoholic father. Interview material indicates that she found it extremely disturbing that she could not respect her husband and found herself receiving from him the same rejection which she had received from her father. During the earlier phases of her life, she found it hard to maintain the "respectability" which had become of central importance to her. Furthermore, the martyr-like sense of duty with which she undertook motherhood provided little compensation for a family situation in which husband and children demanded much but gave little. Projective test protocols indicate that she finds the attention which she gains through her hypochondriasis a poor substitute for the attention which she desires and which she finds, most likely, in her hysterical fantasies. Both mother and father suffer from chronic, mild depressive tendencies.

The interacting psychopathology of mother and father may be readily seen emerging in the personality organization of all of the siblings. Marsha, the oldest daughter, might be described as an "angry rabbit." She and, as will be pointed out later, her brother, seem to have reacted to the father's unpredictable angry displays by developing a yielding and appeasing outward orientation toward authority, but inner aggressiveness and rebelliousness. After seeing two buffaloes fighting on Rorschach Card 2, she sees a "rabbit standing up." In her Sentence Completion items, she describes her personality as "pleasant," says that when she is with a group of people "she tries to be pleasant," and states that *when her friend becomes angry at her "she tries to please him."* Marsha seems to have sought further self-protection by minimizing her feeling investment in other family members. This may be seen, for example, in the low ratings which she applies to most family members on all of the traits of the Leary Interpersonal Check List (*cf.* Table 1). The father reacts to her with an ambivalence which seems to be typical of his feeling toward all members of the family except his son (see below). He depicts her on the Leary Interpersonal Check List as responsible but rebellious and sees both loving and aggressive traits as significant to her personality. Her appeasing manner seems to have fooled none of the family members since they all attribute to her a more than average amount of controlling tendency (Table 1).

Marsha herself seems to recognize the "pleasing and nice manner" which she affects as a facade. Although resenting the domination and over-control of her parents, she takes some of her anger out on her own children by dominating and over-controlling them. She is extremely guilty about her punitive maternal behavior. Many aspects of this situation are to be seen in her story to Card 16 of the TAT (the blank card).

"I see children playing with bicycles and dolls. They are happy children but sometimes they cry a lot. Not too easily pleased, at times, with their toys. It makes the mother feel very miserable. She tries to help. She scolds them and tries to help them and have patience with them, and then they quiet down."

An unresolved Oedipal complex leaves her with many sexual problems. Her Rorschach protocol indicates that she perceives men as animalian, phallic creatures. Such a view of the male may well be a reaction to her father's sexuality. Unconsciously, she seems to regard the mother as an ever-watchful custodian to her morality. Pervasive fantasies in her TAT stories about extramarital affairs seem to reflect both her attachment to the father and her assimilation of the parental tendency to be dissatisfied with one's marital partner and to seek satisfaction outside marriage, in fantasy, if not in behavior. For Marsha, neurotic defenses appear to be holding the line against a potential for schizophrenia seen in occasional cognitive lapses and hints at primitive experiencing of oral need. Her major defenses include obsessive worrying and denial of her problems and unhappiness.

Arthur, the next oldest child, is currently at a stage where he is striving for success in the quite competitive field of commercial art. He is extremely insecure, uncertain of his abilities, and seems to fear that he will never be the man his father was. Among his Rorschach responses are included: a beast of prey, Dracula, horses on the edge of a cliff, a fire and an atomic explosion. Card 1 of the TAT indicates some of his reactions to his father:

"Well, I think it seems like he is grieving over the fact that he would like to play the violin. Maybe it was his father's and he wishes he could play it. He would like to learn how to play, but he don't know how." [What happened?] "We'll give it a happy ending. He studies and he learns how to play, but nothing great happens."

Arthur seems afraid that the father will resent his not following the father's trade. He may be somehow sensing that he, by going into a semi-professional area, is coming closer to functioning at his capacity level (Full Scale Wechsler Adult Intelligence Scale I.Q., 119) than did the father. To a Sentence Completion Test item, he responds: Many fathers "try to teach their sons their own profession so they could take pride in saying 'This is my son'."

Arthur's obvious tendencies to overestimate the power and achievements of the father seem intimately related to the Oedipal conflict within which he still finds himself embroiled. He is quite attached to the mother, like his father, needing very much to depend upon her. Arthur's conscious picture of the mother, as reflected in the Leary Interpersonal Check List, emphasizes her tendency to be at once responsible and self-effacing. While consciously he does not view her as a controlling person, still he does not see in her the docility which she manages to see in herself. At a deeper level, he resents the manipulative control which grows from her overprotectiveness. His combined dependency and resentment toward the mother may be reflected in his Sentence Completion Test response: *His mother always used to "tell him 'It's going to rain today, so take your umbrella'."*

Still, Arthur idealizes her and is seeking a mother figure to marry. Consequently, none of the girls whom he has encountered come up to his perfectionistic standards. He is very much afraid of the father's resentment over his attachment to the mother and seems to experience something quite akin to castration fears in a manner vivid, direct and primitive. On Card 2 of the Rorschach he sees: "blood . . . bleeding . . . pouring out . . . a deep cut with blood spurting out." His fears of the father's retaliative anger seem more a reflection of his own guilt than an accurate perception of his father's feelings. Actually, the father's reaction to his son seems to lack both the emotional intensity and the ambivalence that color his reaction to other family members. Inspection of Table 1 reveals that the father's highest ratings of Arthur are in the areas of responsibility and cooperativeness. This predominantly positive evaluation of his son may result partly from the fact that his son does not arouse the same type of sexual conflict generated by his two daughters, partly from the fact that he does not feel his son to be as controlling as he senses his two daughters to be. Also, the father's schizoid orientation may permit him to be less ambivalent only toward those in whom his feelings are less intensely invested.

Uncertain of his masculinity (a trait which could result from identification with either parent), Arthur rejects his own dependency and childishness and is full of seething rebellion. Still, his fears have caused him to strive to fit in and to behave in a "correct" manner. He seems to hold his hostile feelings in check by means of obsessive ruminations about the virtues of conciliation and appeasement and through the repeated inner rehearsal of standards of "right" behavior. His Sentence Completion Test responses were so long and involved that there was barely sufficient room to record them. The state of affairs here under discussion, resulting as it does in the accumulation of considerable unexpressed impulse, leaves Arthur anxious, afraid of loss of control and beset by bouts of cognitive fluidity. He seems convinced of his own evil.

While the defense mechanisms adapted by Patricia, the patient, to deal with the conflicting forces in the family interaction resemble those of the mother in some ways, they differ in most repects quite radically from those employed by any member of the family. Like the mother, Patricia overemphasizes the positive attributes of the other members of the family and tends to minimize their negative aspects (*cf.* Table 1). While this tendency to avoid the annoying and aggravating aspects of other family members seems to have pushed the mother toward a martyr syndrome and domination through a hypochondriacal orientation, the nature of Patricia's tic seems to provide her with an opportunity for discharge of hostility without having to recognize the hostile implications of her behavior and without directly communicating its hostile nature to those against whom it is directed. It seems also quite likely that it is this advantageous pattern of defense which, in the present family constellation, saves her from the self-contempt which arises from the mixture of outward appeasement and inner aggression which characterizes her brother and sister.

The opportunities for hostile expression provided by her symptom appear quite numerous. The shouting of obscenities violates the code of respectability which both parents would like to maintain and makes them both acutely uncomfortable. The sexual content which the symptom involves has led the father to tell his daughter that she has a "dirty mind" and "needs a man." The sexual stimulation which her symptom provides, no doubt, generates considerable threat for him, particularly since impulse control is something which he experiences as a problem. Again, since through her symptom the patient manages to give voice to the rebellion and aggression felt but unexpressed by her brother and sister, she both threatens and angers them. It may be precisely because the father's intimidating manner has not been able to induce in Patricia the "scared rabbit" behavior seen with Arthur and Marsha that the father is more ready to recognize the hostile element in Patricia than in her brother and sister. As seen in Table 1, the father's aggressiveness rating for Patricia is much higher than that for Arthur or Marsha. The patient's tendency to shout "Nigger!" and "Jew!" when in the presence of the people who would be most affected by these vocalizations seems also to point toward the hostility-releasing function of her symptom.

In interview, the patient reports that sometimes she feels that she must shout particular words and feels that she is forced to do so despite her efforts to the contrary. This issue arises when she enters a hospital unit where there are a number of Negro patients and Negro staff members and feels obliged to shout "Nigger!" It also seems to have been playing a role in the manner in which words such as "penis" (from the Word Association Test) began to enter her shouted verbalizations after they had been presented to her as test stimuli.

The attention-getting and sexually provocative aspects of the patient's symptoms seem more closely related to hysterical elements in her behavior, such as the tendency toward romantic daydreaming which she shares with her mother. Her story to the blank card of the TAT (Card 16) well illustrates her orientation here.

"This is the hard one. Well, let's say there was a pretty girl all dressed up in her best clothes. She was very pretty, well-liked, everybody loved her, especially the men. And what she wanted to do in life was to become a great actress. She went away and started to study and finally she became one of the best actresses in the world."

The following quotation from Card 13MF of the TAT is perhaps of more explicit hysterical flavor: "A woman can really tease a man, you know, I've heard many stories about it. She probably teased him so much and would not give him anything. He attacked her and killed her." Possibly arising from identification with the mother figure (the patient seems to be the sibling closest to her) her hysterical personality orientation strongly colors her relationship with a seductive but guilty father (see above) and points to the unresolved Oedipal conflict which she shares with her siblings.

It may be that the effectiveness of the patient's symptoms for expressing impulse without awareness has minimized for her not only the tendency toward hypochondriasis and martyrdom seen in the mother and towards stultifying self-contempt seen in the brother and sister, but also the inclination toward schizophrenic-like distortions in cognitive processes and the fears of loss of impulse control seen in all family members except the patient and her mother.

DISCUSSION

The tics present in the behavior of Patricia's father and of her aunt would seem to suggest some hereditary predisposition for her illness. The stress of the grandmother's wake probably provided the precipitating factor which converted a potential symptom pattern into actuality. The early transient nature of tics and the progress of her vocalizations from inarticulate cries to articulated obscenities seem to follow the pattern of development of the syndrome noted by others.

The tendency toward rigid control and emphasis upon correct behavior upon the part of the parents appears to have produced in all siblings the form of ambivalence toward parental and authority feelings noted by Ascher[1] and Dunlap.[3] It is interesting to note that the symptom has probably enabled the patient to experience less intensely a conflict identical to that disturbing her siblings. The effectiveness of this mode of conflict resolution in the present family setting no doubt represents one factor contributing to the persistence of this form of symptomatology through three years of psychotherapy.

It seems also worthy of emphasis that strong elements of obsessive-compulsive, hysteric and schizophrenic-like psychopathology are noted in the family and that the patient's symptoms and behavior appear to combine elements of the former two, but not the third set of symptom patterns. It might be speculated that, should the patient's current modes of defense somehow become unavailable to her, or should psychotherapy facilitate her abandoning them, her reality testing might deteriorate to the fluid level seen in most of the other family members and an actual schizophrenic psychosis might make its appearance.

SUMMARY

A battery of psychological tests, including the Wechsler Adult Intelligence Scale, the Rorschach, the Leary Interpersonal Check List, the TAT and a Word Association and Sentence Completion Test, were administered to a 24-year-old white female maladie des tics patient, her parents and the male and female siblings who make up her immediate family. The types of conflicts engendered in the family group as a result of the conflicts of the parents and the mode of interaction between them were discussed. The modes of dealing with these conflicts utilized by the patient and her two siblings were compared and contrasted. The effectiveness of the patient's symptoms in allowing her to express her rebelliousness, hostility and sexuality in the family setting in such a way as to avoid the demeaned self-concept seen in the other siblings, who feel rebellious but act subserviently, has been emphasized. Elements of obsessive-compulsive, hysterical and schizophrenic-like behavior in the family atmosphere were considered in relation to the way they have affected the patient's defensive behavior.

REFERENCES

1. ASCHER, E. 1948. Psychodynamic considerations in Gilles de la Tourette's disease (maladie des tics). *Am. J. Psychiat.*, **105**, 267-276.
2. BOCHNER, S. 1959. Gilles de la Tourette's disease. *J. ment. Sci.*, **105**, 1078-1081.
3. DUNLAP, J. R. 1960. A case of Gilles de la Tourette's disease (maladie des tics): A study of the intrafamily dynamics. *J. nerv. ment. Dis.*, **130**, 340-344.
4. EISENBERG, L., ASCHER, E., and KANNER, L. 1959. A clinical study of Gilles de la Tourette's disease (maladie des tics) in children. *Am. J. Psychiat.*, **115**, 715-723.
5. GILLES DE LA TOURETTE, G. 1885. Étude sur une affection nerveuse caractérisée par de l'incoordination motrice accompagnée d'echolalie et de copralalie. *Archs Neurol.*, **9**, 17-42, 158-200.
6. HOLLANDER, R. 1960. Compulsive cursing. *Psychiat. Q.*, **34**, 599-622.
7. LEARY, T. 1957. *Interpersonal diagnosis of personality*. Ronald Press, New York.
8. MacDONALD, I. 1963. A case of Gilles de la Tourette syndrome with some etiological observations. *Br. J. Psychol.*, **109**, 206-210.

9. MAHLER, M., and RANGELL, L. 1943. A psychosomatic study of maladie des tics. *Psychiat. Q.*, **17**, 579-603.
10. SCHNECK, J. M. 1960. Gilles de la Tourette's disease. *Am. J. Psychiat.*, **117**, 78.
11. SLAP, J. W. 1957. Psychotherapy with a case of maladie des tics. *J. Hillside Hosp.*, **6**, 43-54.
12. WECHSLER, I. S. 1952. *Clinical neurology*, 7th ed. Saunders, Philadelphia.

XXXVII

THE FAMILY IN PSYCHOSOMATIC PROCESS
A Case Report Illustrating a Method of Pychosomatic Research

JAMES L. TITCHENER, JULES RISKIN
AND RICHARD EMERSON

Ulcerative colitis, a psychosomatic process, can be the product of a mother-child relationship, itself dictated by family dynamics

This paper is the report of a study of an entire family in which one son developed ulcerative colitis. It has been written to point out a method by which one of the conditions specific to the etiology of psychosomatic processes may be further understood. In setting forth this method we propose an expansion of current hypotheses regarding the object relations factors in the causes of and predisposition to psychosomatic illness.

In his thorough review of the ulcerative colitis syndrome Dr. George Engel writes: "Elucidation of the specific aspects of the object relations constitutes a most important problem for further research."[1] This comment seems appropriate for the whole field of psychosomatic investigation. From his own research and from his extensive review of the work of others, Engel has formulated the recurrent patterns of significant relationships in ulcerative colitic patients and he has pointed out how these rigid and confining patterns predispose these individuals to psychosomatic illness. This formulation is part of a theory of the etiology of ulcerative colitis.

Dr. Engel views ulcerative colitis as a response of the whole organism a particular locus in the lining of the large bowel. The effective and

Reprinted from PSYCHOSOMATIC MEDICINE, Vol. 22, No. 2, March-April 1960, pp. 127-142.

healthy bowel lining serves as a selective barrier against penetration of organisms and other substances from the "outside," i.e., the lumen of the colon. In ulcerative colitis the physiologic function of the bowel lining quite probably becomes affected in such a way that organisms in the lumen can penetrate and are, thereafter, no longer innocuous, but pathogenic. It is considered likely that a constitutional predisposition is necessary for this situation. Among the other possible factors, some still unknown, is the psychophysiologic factor; there is imposing clinical evidence to support the significance of a psychosomatic relationship.

The reports of Engel and others reviewed by him are persuasive that the essential psychological condition operating with somatic factors towards the onset of ulcerative colitis is an affective state characterized by helplessness and despair arising from a deep disturbance in a key object relation which is lost or threatened, or whose loss is imagined. The ulcerative colitis patient is unable to accomplish the grief work nor any other adjustment to object loss and so suffers a deep disruption of previous adaptation, with consequent development of a state of helplessness. It is probable that this drastic change in psychological systems breaks through to affect the operation of somatic systems, particularly if they are predisposed to dysfunction.

This unfortunate lack of adaptive capacity, combined with incessant need, develops, in Engel's view, from the early, very much prolonged symbiosis between mother and child. In very brief summary, the mother-infant and mother-child relationship are conditional ones in which mother will give love if she can control. The necessary submission of the child lays the groundwork for uninterrupted need for similar relationships throughout life. Such relationships in adolescence and adulthood, when society rules against the maintenance of a symbiosis with mother, are very difficult to find and to maintain with potential substitutes. Usually the patient-to-be manages to find someone who will fill the bill at least partially. But almost always this chosen person, who perhaps unwittingly finds himself or herself a "key" person, cannot stand the strain and the interpersonal needs of the potential patient are frustrated or threatened. Such individuals are so sensitive to the vicissitudes of the mutually controlling relationship that almost any occurrence may upset the tenuous equilibrium.

THE FAMILY IN A PSYCHOSOMATIC PROCESS

In launching our study we have assumed the conditions for the onset of ulcerative colitis as Engel has hypothesized them. Our contribution toward a new look at this hypothesis is confined to the object relation aspects of the formulation.

Our investigative approach may be likened to the one used by cultural anthropologists who, if interested in the psychodynamics of a relationship in a culture would study not one but both persons involved and, further, would seek any others who could offer intimate observations upon the relationship in question.

Our methods of study of whole families provide us with corroborating and contrasting observations by each family member, including comments upon individual feelings, upon the feelings and behavior of others, and upon their own and other relationships. We are enabled to derive a stereoscopic view of the family as a field and of the individuals' functions in this field. In addition, we can develop concepts of the family's working as a whole system—a social unit with a structure and a dynamic pattern.

We assume that, as with personality, there are patterns of adaptation for a family too. A particular person or a particular relationship—for example, mother and child—are involved continually in mutually influencing transactions with the whole family, as a social system. Let us now return to Engel's hypotheses about the prolonged mother-child symbiosis which becomes a mutually controlling relationship, pathogenic, in some cases, of ulcerative colitis. We would add that this relationship is, from the beginning and during its later vicissitudes, conditioned by the milieu in which it exists—the family. The mother-child axis turns in a social field of which the family constitutes a large and important segment.

To put our case more strongly, our approach would seem to obviate a concept of a colitigenic mother, as it would also the schizophrenogenic mother, for the relationship is not one in which the mother *per se* forces herself in a pathogenic way upon a child, but one made by the mother and conditioned by the dynamics of the family in which she and her child live. The significant element is not simply the mother's personality, but the way she acts in the particular relationship with the particular child in a particular period—all in the context of the *whole* family's psychodynamic patterns.

Let us imagine a study in which personality assessments of 20,000 mothers of ulcerative colitis patients were compared with those of 20,000 mothers of children without colitis. We would surmise that, though there would be a contrast in the groups, the correlation of colitis patients with mothers having certain traits of personality at the time of assessment would *not* be especially high. We are of the opinion that colitigenic mothers are not born nor even made in their own childhood. Their ways of relating to their children come into being *in a family situation* and their special relationships with future ulcerative colitis patients are largely determined by the dynamics of the family environment. The figure of the mother obtained in the anamnestic data from the patient is not reality, nor totally a mythical figment of the patient's psychopathology. Truly, the mother figure, like other figures in the family, is largely *a family legend* created by the relationships of *all* the individuals in the family with a central figure. The patient, then, presents us this image compounded of reality, of his own distortions, and of the family's idea of mother. One thing is probably true, however: Whatever the mother "really" is beneath the figure and the role and the image represented in the family, she is this way most of all with the patient. We can speculate that the deeper, intrapsychic conflicts, emerge most strongly in the relationship with the patient-to-be. This selection of the patient for the focus of family conflict is determined by a number of factors—environmental, individual, and constitutional. For a real understanding of the forces which motivate object choice and which bring about sensitivity to object loss we need to examine early and late object relations from this multidimensional point of view, rather than being concerned only with the binary relationship in a vacuum.

A study correlating mothers' personalities with a psychosomatic illness is, in our theory, likely to produce unimpressive results because of the existence of so many other factors crucial in the moulding of the object relations which are the really essential aspects of pathogenesis. More important, studies of this kind fail to provide us with much information about *how* the mother's relations with a patient have influenced him.

In the following case study we wish to demonstrate how object relations can be seen in depth. We shall attempt to illustrate our opinion that the mother's attitudes and behavior alone are not etiologically responsible for the predisposition and onset of the illness. If her characteristics were so responsible, might she not have started a small epidemic of ulcerative colitis in this family? Instead, the theoretically pathogenic object relations are moulded by the whole interlocking set of relations, although the mother is a central figure. We shall further try to demonstrate how the affected member of the family becomes a focus of conflict for the parents and his siblings.

The case report was assembled as part of a larger and more general research on family dynamics,[2] which is related to the expanding interest in the dynamics of the individual and his family. Ackerman,[3] Chance,[4] and Kluckhohn and Spiegel[5] have provided extensive review and bibilography in this area.

The methods of our research included an observed interaction session including all family members, a number of interviews with each member individually, and a family relations inventory designed by our research team. For the purposes of this report we shall include only the individual interviews, although we learned about some aspects of the family inadvertently in some informal sessions with several of the family members. The individual interviews have a sequence which lends them some extra value. One member (J. T.) of the research team does all of the interviewing with a family, seeing its members in sequence. Then, when a series has been completed, it is repeated. In the family studied, the series was repeated four times with the exception of the patient's brother who could be interviewed only once for somewhat more than an hour. In this case we also have notes from a course of psychotherapy undergone by the patient. The interlocking or revolving sequence of interviewing tends to bring out some aspects of a family's characteristic transactions. The interviewer's ear soon becomes very sensitively tuned to the communication of the family group he is seeing, and the material covered in the associative anamnesis interviewing is directed somewhat by what the interviewer hears from all the family members. For example, in this family there was a surprising tendency for all to comment upon some early memories first reported by the patient. This tendency was encouraged by the interviewer. The fact that several people involved in a fairly intimate situation comment upon the same current issues is also extremely helpful in seeing, almost *in vivo*, what characteristically transpires in a family.

CASE HISTORY

Our acquaintance with the Neal family (pseudonym) began in early 1957 when Bob, Jr. was admitted to our psychosomatic study service upon the urgent recommendation of an internist and a psychiatric consultant. By that time Bob had lived through more than 12 months of discouraging battle with his ulcerative colitis. The anniversary of onset had passed just before Christmas without signs of improvement and, in fact, it had seemed to be marked by a moderate relapse. His self-respect had suffered with the suggestion of psychiatric treatment and his reluctant agreement to the hospital admission had carried some degree of last-resort submission on his part.

As far as we know, the illness began about the middle of December 1955 with twelve watery and bloody stools per day, diffuse abdominal pain, and nausea. Through December and January 1955-6 the diagnosis of ulcerative colitis was confirmed by proctosigmoidoscope and x-ray. He improved slowly with antibiotics and supportive care although there was a gradual decline in weight from his original 170 lb., and an anemia that stabilized at medium-low levels. A psychiatrist had one brief contact in February 1956, but his interview and the suggestion of hospitalization in a Veterans Administration psychiatric service resulted only in a petulant change of physicians. After Bob left the hospital, his condition improved a little, then relapsed a little, each setback shaking further his hope of final relief. By the fall of 1956 the relapses were more severe and enduring than the remissions, while home medical care became less effective and less resourceful.

When we first met him, Bob was a long, thin young man of 24, usually huddled and curled in his bed with a stool-chair close by. He weighed about 115 lb. Any conversation of more than 10 minutes had to be interrupted by a rush from the bed and a burst of diarrhea. He had long, dark-blond hair falling over a pale, strained, and thin face. Talking with others was painful for him, not so much because it was fatiguing and he was ill, but more because it was emotionally difficult. Medically he was toxic and psychiatrically he was helpless and hopeless. The alternate sides of Bob's character can, even at this point, be illustrated by the contrasting picture of him 12 months later, after treatment, surgery, and steroids. Then we see him standing, emerged from the cocoon of bedclothes and psychic withdrawal, with a full, heavy face and an air of complacent, assured stiffness.

Mrs. Neal was seen the day of admission. She is a moderately obese woman of slightly more than average height. She seemed relaxed, accessible, and poised. She talked easily, gave quick assurance of understanding our methods, and promised cooperation. She appeared to be empathic towards her son's recent ordeal, although first impressions could have been mistaken. She never showed much tension in response to the course of Bob's illness. Nevertheless, even a researcher oriented to the subtleties of family dynamics was surprised by the occurrence that took place immediately after this first interview, when the mother went from the office to her son's room and burst in saying, "Your father is in an agony of stomach pain from worrying about you." This drastic double-bind[6] and conflictful expression of common family problems, which will be explained more completely below, expresses the divided pity of the mother and forces Bob, in a loving way, to accept the responsibility for the father's illness. It would be impossible to say whether the occurrence had a physiological effect, since the bowel was already operating at near maximum speed of contraction, secretion, and hemorrhage. Soon thereafter, Bob was seen in his room. He was tightly huddled, sometimes trembling and almost unable to talk except to emit short bursts of anger at his father for not taking care of himself and his stomach. The conversation was strategically directed towards introductory small-talk. A little anxious himself, the interviewer strayed to the window and there spoke aimlessly of promises to bring magazines and of the hospital's need for new buildings to replace the old, dreary ones. While the interviewer was looking away, the patient hurried from his bed and had a torrential bowel movement. With the decision, then, that the patient needed a nurse more than a doctor, the interviewer ended the first contact.

Mr. Neal (Bob, Sr.) is a stout, full-faced man of about 50, with silver hair and moustache. He leaned back in his chair in a posture of confidence, but sometimes would tilt forward on his elbows to make a point. With a few exceptions his manner was that of a man of straightforward half sincerity. He exuded a confidential and friendly air which is useful in business and was usual in his interviews, although he spoke meaningfully of personal feelings and of his observations of others in the family. Several brief times in each interview the impact of events would change his voice a little to an imploring tone.

There were three other children: Doris, 29, and Dottie, 22, were not available, although we know something of them. Ken, 27, is a trim air force officer with a quiet, friendly, but noncommittal manner.

PRECIPITATION OF THE ILLNESS

The precipitating events of a serious illness seem to gather in one period linking and joining forces to upset a psychosomatic equilibrium. Bob Neal's difficulties were preceded by a set of associated occurrences, some of which were probably not truly separate precipitating factors, but rather representations or subordinates of the more significant ones.

By the fall of 1955 Bob was out of the Navy two years and in a business college, where his work was deteriorating. He seemed distracted, while his parents were urging him on and demanding to know why he could not do better. He partially supported himself, feeling a little angry that he had to but, at the same time, ashamed and guilty that he was being helped by his parents. It was impossible for him to know whether it was proper to be dependent upon his father while attending college, since it was never decided whether he appreciated the financial strain on his parents. His younger sister was being sent to the same college at the same time; was this reason to pay his own way or justification for expecting more?

These circumstances further affected object relations. The mother, by her own report and from those of others, had entered menopause in early 1955. She seemed less attracted by previous interests, was more likely to be irritated, and withdrew from her previous maternal attitudes. She was subject to crying spells, manifesting less energy, more complaints, and increased expectations of others.

About the same time (and also related to the uncertainties regarding college) Bob became puritanically angry at his younger sister, although they had previously had a close and sympathetic relationship. He felt she was "running with the wrong crowd," that she had involved herself with the "wrong man" and, worst of all, was behaving in a disrespectful, irresponsible, and impudent manner. He knew, and said, that he could not have escaped censure had he acted that way. But, most important, his criticism and bitterness, openly expressed, brought about resentful quarrels and a subsequent break with his sister. Coincident with Bob's near failure in college and the financial complications arising from his attendance, his father began to show, in the form of gastrointestinal symptoms, the effects of strain. However, these symptoms did not deter him from his exhausting work, but rather forced an even more frenzied and hard-driving application to business interests. The father's response to the mother's emotional change was that of strenuous work over long hours while, as an executive, he took on complex tasks that promised one crisis after another. Mother and son shared the worry over the father's alleged foolhardiness; in Bob's case it turned to exasperation. Perhaps realistically, he wondered how necessary it was for his father to exert and punish himself so much when the return of a peptic ulcer threatened. The father's ways of dealing with his illness affected Bob's relations with both parents, adding to his problems of self-respect and feelings of inadequacy. While the father strove mightily and while he obviously had pain, he urged his son as he always had, to fear not and to perform better—At what price? the son might ask. Bob must have known the frustrations his father suffered in his self-incurred struggles. Perhaps as a parable of his attitudes to his father, Bob reported an incident that occurred in the fall of 1955 and involved his relations with a part-time employer. As assistant to a bartender, he was caused anguish by the demands of the latter that he have the courage to throw out unruly customers. Bob knew that at the same time this same man was stealing from the cash drawer.

For several years Bob had been courting a girl, with whom there was an informal understanding about marriage. This girl, named Dottie, as was his younger sister, we know little about, except that the state of his relationship with her heavily affected our patient's equilibrium. In very gross summary it seems to be true that by the fall of 1955 the courtship had gotten to the point where he felt pressed to commit himself, yet he did not feel secure enough to set a date for marriage. In early 1955, he thought he was involved in a pregnancy case as a result of a presumed interval of dalliance with another girl. The latter had married by that time out of malice toward Bob, but claimed to be pregnant by him. This episode threatened scandal, but proved a false alarm and taught him a stern lesson in fidelity. Bob thought he wanted to marry late in 1955, while his father, particularly, thought it a good idea that Bob become a "family man" and show his independence. The couple tacitly agreed upon the spring of 1956. In the midst of this excitement and during some celebrating at college, where he had very recently acquired the habit of taking some alcohol every night, he found himself on edge about the coming holidays and the trip home. He vaguely remembers having some diarrhea before the vacation, but this symptom dims in importance relative to the acute onset of his illness soon after coming home for Christmas.

From this account three main currents stand out, yet even these cannot be clearly disentangled.

First, there is evidence concerning the change in Bob's mother in the direction of withdrawal, depression, irritability, and less maternal dependability.

Secondly, perhaps as consequence of the change in Mrs. Neal, the father began to manifest a recurrence of his gastrointestinal illness and, at the same time, an increase in the over-compensating drive expressed through the search for business crises. He doubted more the advantages of supporting his son in college, urging better performance and more independence upon him, and advising incessantly that fear of the future should be shunned. Meanwhile, Bob did poorly in school and became dreadfully uncertain that he would have the funds to finish.

Thirdly, there was the commitment to marry, which seemed something thrust upon him rather than being sought and desired. He wondered whether he had dealt with another girl cruelly, and was partially relieved to find that he had not. In spite of insecurity about marriage, he felt that he was obliged to marry and hoped that he would find someone dependable. His troubles with his sister seem to represent the conflicts involving his fiancee and his mother, as well as the malice of an old rivalry that added to his guilt and shame. He felt an ambivalence involving anger and a wish to break from all three of these women, but this wish was opposed by his continuing needs. We know from both Bob and his mother that very shortly after the onset of the disease the older brother and sister petitioned the mother by letter (since Bob was then home and ill) that she not "baby" him as she always had.

The force of these trends in the year that preceded the onset of the illness is made more evident from what we learned about the patient's life history and from his reactions during the months of psychotherapy that followed admission.

FAMILY HISTORY

The Neal family had two children by 1932. The father tells us that he left home early in his life and fought hard to protect his family during the depression. Though the Neals always had an income, the father's early experience warned him that he must be industrious if poverty were not to overtake him. The arrival of Bob, Jr., in the depth of the depression in 1932 undoubtedly posed some threat to the family security, although we have no way of really knowing how much. The Neals tell a story about Bob's birth that may reflect upon the significance to them of his arrival in the family. Mr. Neal tells it most dramatically: "But Bob was a little bit different than the rest of them. Did she tell you the way he was born? Well the children had the mumps when she was carrying Bob—or the whooping cough, that's what it was. So I took them up to my folks and left them and I went up to see them one night a week. When I got back, my gosh, the police was swarming all over the place. I went in there thinking, 'What in the world is wrong!' Well, her and this woman were sitting out on the front porch and my wife got up to go in the house to do something and a nigger came running out of the bedroom around the bed and jumped out the window. It liked to scare her to death. So she run out—we didn't have a telephone—she ran out the front door and started over to the neighbors and the neighbor's dog jumped off the porch and scared her. She was a nervous wreck! Well, the next morning Bob was born. That was on a Friday night 'cause Saturday I had to get the payroll out. I don't know whether that could affect a child or whether it would have made her feel any different towards him, but he was a good child, he slept good, and had very little sickness or anything else."

We have little doubt of the truth of this story with respect to the essentials of its plot. We have interpreted the story for its current significance as a kind of family legend to explain to the rest of the family why Bob is "different." The way that the parents tell the tale and the portentous meaning they attach to it make this episode a family legend with symbolic significance. They seem to speak of the anxiety Bob's birth signified. Each parent attributes the main fright to the other. Most evident is the indication of an intruder entering the home. Several times we have been asked for our opinion on the effect of this incident upon Bob's later development. In other words, they ask what effect their feelings had upon the intruder.

We know from the comments of everyone in the family that this child, with his father's name, was given extra care and protection by the mother. The mother admits to some of it, but denies that the term baby is descriptive of her attitudes. She claims to have sensed that this boy needed more, particularly in rivalrous situations with his siblings.

Some of Bob's memories constitute comments upon the effects of early childhood. He recalls the financial strain of buying a new house shortly after the birth of his younger sister, and that this house was endangered by the flooding river. The mother comments that actually the new house had been a step forward for the family, and that this same house was one of those most safe from the floods threatening their community. This memory at once depreciates the father and adopts his feeling of threat and insecurity. Bob relates another memory of childhood as though it were an episode of childish rebellion. He recalls collecting Christmas trees from the neighborhood and piling them in the driveway to the extent that they blocked the father's entrance to the garage. Mother tells of the incident as though it was a bit of sportive behavior on the part of her son. Bob also tells—with some of the original terror—of being cornered in the back yard by rats and of being rescued by his mother. No one else remembers this incident, but here is little wonder that his mother felt he needed help in relations with his siblings. We know little of his later childhood, except that after the age of five or six, Bob was an appealing and outgoing boy according to the reports of both parents. By the time he entered high school he had acquired a severe form of examination anxiety, although he did his best to conceal his fear. This hiding was reinforced by his father's incessant and particular advice to stifle all recognition and expression of anxiety. "When it came to butting his head against a wall, when he *had* to do something, he had a psychological fear of it," his father said.

Nevertheless, Bob became a reasonably successful athlete as a high school varsity football and basketball player. This activity has his mother's enthusiastic sponsorship, an attitude she had acquired from her brothers. She was a spectator at all of his games, although the father never could find the time to attend even one of them. Although he had been more successful in these activities than in anything else in his life, Bob never talked of his athletic experience with any pride or pleasure.

He finished high school at the start of the Korean conflict and, managing to overcome his mother's stout resistance, entered the Navy, as had his brother before him. His recollection of the service career is characterized by a feeling of isolation and loneliness in relation to his fellow sailors. He recoiled from the language commonly used by the others, but he felt ashamed when he found himself speaking it. His ship was hit off the Korean coast by shore batteries. When his mother read the news, she became distraught, expecting to receive the announcement of his death. Bob was disgusted when he heard of his mother's reaction. This event had none of the terror for him that he felt when caught with a soiled uniform during an admiral's inspection.

THERAPY

It can be appreciated that the doctor (J. R.) responsible for the psychotherapeutic part of the total treatment faced some difficult tasks. However, anyone experienced in such matters will know that the coordination and balance of the three methods of treatment (psychiatric, medical, and surgical) in a complicated case is difficult to maintain. Try as the psychotherapist may to coordinate the efforts of the internist and the surgeon with his own work, at times the collaboration becomes imperfect. Occasionally the psychiatrist will find himself making surgical and medical decisions certain to influence his relationship with the patient; at other times he will find that a decision has been made without his consultation and with which he would not have agreed. His treatment goals, his comprehension, his therapeutic anxieties, and his countertransference are all complicated by the delicate imbalances inevitably occurring in a three-way collaborative treatment. Although these were factors influencing the treatment of Bob Neal, they never completely upset his progress. Over the approximately 16 months of Bob's treatment on our service, his principal therapies consisted of steroids, two operations (an ileostomy and a colectomy, 10 and 13 months after hospital admission), and his work with the psychotherapist. To describe the nuances of the interactions between these approaches would require another study. In fact, it will be necessary to be cautious in interpreting the occurrences of relapse and remission as responses to psychotherapy. In this study we can hope only to learn more about the patient's conflicts and defenses, leaving aside the question of the absolute value of psychotherapy for ulcerative colitis.

Analysis of the purely verbal interaction of the first month of psychotherapy is of little use. In the interviews there was a halting and stereotyped expression of thought and feeling. He really doubted the value of this work, but tried to conform. Certainly, the acute phase of his physical illness affected his participation, and he slowly made some adjustment to the ward, the nurses, and other patients. Rorschach tests done shortly after admission and then repeated a month later show some change. In the beginning he was seen as an outwardly adjusted and conforming person with underlying detached and depreciative attitudes toward others. At a still deeper level there was evidence of angry frustration—of an individual who wanted much but expected only husks of things or token gratifications. He seemed regressed to an infantile level, but even there he was depressed. A month later, after improvement on steroids, Rorschach tests found him much the same, although there were increased indications of hostility and other signs of an enhanced willingness for emotional expression.

After this very halting, difficult beginning, Bob began to express some material relevant to his suspicion of the frightening power of his needs and feelings. He noted that he was worse when home on pass or when the psychotherapist was away. A struggle for power and control began to emerge as a feature of his relationship with his fiancée: "She is the one who can relax me." However, it was necessary that she be there at the right time and do the right things or she would disturb him more than anyone else. Meanwhile, he worried about the drain of the hospital expenses upon his father. Following one interview in which these problems with father and fiancée became associated, he suddenly acquired a sensitivity to one of his medicines and developed a distressing and massive urticaria. "Amazingly," the observer's notes state, the diarrhea and cramps disappeared for the duration of his skin disorder. Prior to this anxiety occurrence the therapist had decided to facilitate the relationship through a bit of role playing in which he became the "good doctor," on the patient's side, against the "bad doctors" who unfeelingly prescribed things to make him uncomfortable. We cannot say whether this maneuver was necessary, but it appeared to raise the question of the trust the patient could have in the relationship. He first doubted the therapist's reliability, then relaxed with him and hinted, shamefully, that he found himself at the apex of a triangle involving his doctor and the head nurse. However, at the same time, the therapist's role of siding with the patient led to expressions indicating that the doctor would bend to the patient's will, which produced tension in both Bob and the therapist. Bob could not find the relationship really gratifying and the doctor found Bob "demanding" and "oral-aggressive"—both irritating qualities. But then, for reasons no longer manifest, the psychotherapist began to take control enough to balance some of the patient's drives and, at that point, Bob seemed more a master of his own feelings and less fearful of abandonment. The therapy could by no means settle on this plateau, for there were other forces to contend with: problems with the family and fiancée, and difficult issues concerning the ulcerative colitis. However, Bob tried to hold the relationship at this mutually controlled level. He feared the anger that might break it and he resented the therapist when a decrease in his defensiveness was urged. He wondered how much was demanded of him in terms of psychiatric performance in therapy. The latter has a realistic basis, since it appeared that with physiological improvement the expectations of everyone—therapist, family, fiancee, and nurses—increased.

These trends in therapy brought from him memories of submission to his mother's urging during the year of illness before admission to our hospital. She would cheerfully suggest that he "go out" and enjoy himself to prove his strength, and that he widen his shrinking perspective. Although he had no enthusiasm at all for such activity, he would be afraid not to humor her. He also submitted, despite his own opinions, to her repeated suggestion that he ignore the doctor's advice and eat foods not on his prescribed diet. In fact, he was not tempted by these foods, but his mother thought he should be. Her urging seemed to say: "I am offering you signs of love, but you won't accept them." He felt guilty about resisting the foods that he thought it wrong to eat. These memories were associated with a description of the tenseness that had been present in the relationship with the mother since his return from the service. The "change of life" previously noted required more energy and more appeasement from the patient in order to maintain the old equilibrium. His father had warned that the mother had changed while Bob was away. He recalled ruefully in the same interview the closeness with his mother when he had been a successful athlete. It is possible that he longed for the days when the mother-son relationship had been mutually most gratifying.

Meanwhile, there seemed to be little chance for relaxation in the psychotherapy. This was never a relationship which permitted some quiet and rewarding reflection upon thoughts and feelings. There was a tautness, difficult to analyze at the time, which represented a push and pull in the interaction between doctor and patient. There could be no sharing, no peaceful discussion. Remarks had to be expressed or shamefully withheld while the patient expected to be pushed and pulled in the same manner. He tested repeatedly to see what would be required from him and what he could safely resist without the danger of severing the relationship. It was difficult as a therapist to see beyond the patient's stubbornness and his tendency to deal with every event in strictly literal terms. Although we see now that he wanted a dependent relation with the therapist, he wanted it to be without intrusion into emotions on the verbal level and without danger of anything unexpected. He said once, "You're just like my mother: you asked me if I wanted another appointment; I said, 'No,' and you came away." He went on to say that he could not understand why the therapy had to concern itself with such irritating matters as his worry over finances (father), dreams, and the idea "that I'm trying to hang on to some feelings." He could talk somewhat about his irritation towards his mother, since he felt at fault for that.

Thereafter, the more open hostility towards the therapist increased until headaches replaced bowel symptoms. This phase, in which the therapist was becoming pessimistic and shifting to the viewpoint that the patient needed surgery, seemed to be preparation for the next phase in the treatment. A more frankly dependent move occurred in which, in Bob's mind, the therapist became a clearly reliable person who made decisions, commiserated with the patient over his need for surgery and, in general, had taken or had been given the control of the relationship. Most likely this mutually controlled relationship repeated in an assuring way the early mother-child relationship. With very little trouble Bob provoked his fiancee to defy him and this to give him reason for breaking the engagement. His reaction to this break was not intense. It seemed to have meaning only in the context of his new and more reliable symbiosis. He could afford to give up the fiancee at this point.

However, by this time surgery did seem indicated. The patient had had steroids so long and in such doses that it did not seem that he could soon relinquish them. Hence, rather than serving as a start for a long process of psychiatric treatment, the relationship was instead an aid in helping the patient through surgery.

For the purposes of this study the events in psychotherapy demonstrate for us the type of object relations our patient tends to form. We can see the push and pull, arduous for both Bob and his therapist, and how the interaction finally settled to some form of equilibrium in which the stronger member of the symbiosis has control but is also controlled.

In the following section, the causes of Bob's need for this kind of situation are sought in the milieu in which such habits were made necessary the network of relationships within which Bob's personality developed —his family.

THE NEAL FAMILY

Throughout the worst of Bob's illness, Mrs. Neal had been his faithful, though often insistent, nurse. During some of the most difficult times at home Bob was close to morphine addiction, and the prevention of this was arduous for mother and son. His sleep pattern reversed, and his mother sat with Bob through the hours from midnight to day talking endlessly of his childhood days. She commented: "I think it's been rough on me, since on top of it I'm going through the change of life. I said to a friend that maybe it's been a blessing in disguise, since maybe I would have given up to my own feelings had I not had him to worry about this year." In discussing this remark she explains at length that she "swallowed my own feelings." Anger, her disappointment regarding the lack of financial and social success, and depression were diverted into maternal care, pity, and worry over the adversities of another. Bob's illness revived, in many of its essentials, the guilt-appeasing, controlling, emotionally expensive symbiotic relationship of earlier days—but not quite!

In talking of herself Mrs. Neal was the most guarded of all. Although immensely voluble and indirect in telling of her life, she dealt with her own feelings and her personal history on a chatty and bland level. She was an only girl with three brothers, one of whom—the youngest—died when she was about seven. She had no memory of feelings about his death. She recalls a tiny and sickly mother, some kindly brothers, and a strong, authoritarian, and distant father. Family solidarity and respectability, without sign of emotional disturbance, was her ideal and a treasured memory of her childhood experience. She revealed slightly the feelings of insecurity imparted by her husband and reinforced by the realities of the economic depression, but these emotions were not nearly as intense as her perception of others' needs, particularly those of her husband and her third child, Bob. As mentioned above, she has no doubt that Bob required her special attention during childhood; she also knows that her husband has always disagreed and even resented this tendency. She said that the rest of the family thought she "favored" the third child, but she knows that it was simply that he needed her more.

Mr. Neal (Bob, Sr.) was far more open in talking of himself, at least in so far as he reveals his character. We see more clearly in him the nature of the equilibrium between needs and reactions to them, and between conflicts and adaptive techniques to quiet the anxiety arising from them.

In addition, Mr. Neal's personality stands out in his relations with Bob, Jr. He spoke first, and with effect, of his perception of an inability to speak effectively and comfortably to his children and particularly to the one who bore his name. He could see that his lifelong absorption in his work, and his consistently long hours had deprived him of the feelings of closeness and other gratifications his family might have afforded him. But, more selfrighteously, he repeatedly told of how he had tried to convey a belief in fearlessness and independent strength. He felt he had demonstrated to his son what hard work could do for a man, and he emphasized hard work because he had known poverty in a large family as a boy, because it had been necessary that he support himself when he was 16, and because his mother had died shortly before he left home. The evidence is clear that the hard driving suited his angry fight against material insecurity, that it helped withdraw him from his need for love, that it reassured him that he could overcome his difficulties—in a word, overcompensation. In later years when economic adversity was not so threatening, Mr. Neal sought out and obtained executive positions which were not so financially rewarding as they were filled with unending crises and laced with complicated troubles. He is known in his business circles as one whom employers have given the thankless, troublesome tasks that require much worry and a 70-hour week. Mr. Neal enjoyed voicing his unconvincing complaints and he was genuinely proud that he had almost never had a vacation except for sick leaves.

The woman he left at home through all this—Mrs. Neal—was allowed to respond to his wishes for loving care only when he was troubled by his ulcer. He knew that he was usually too tired, too headachy, and too preoccupied to ask from her or give to her. When he wanted to yield a bit to his needs he had to "shove off" his wife's sympathy and affection. Currently he sometimes feels that even when he is ill his wife has lost her ways of approaching him, presumably because she had been held off so often.

There are indications that Mr. Neal permitted some warmth between himself and his older son and two daughters; but he was alienated from Bob somehow. He thinks that perhaps it was because of the protectiveness Mrs. Neal lavished on the boy, making it necessary for him to strengthen the child by the opposite treatment; it also seems that the special attitude of the mother towards Bob may further have shut out the father. The latter idea neatly rationalizes the father's own participation in frustration of his own needs.

He explains his conviction that his son needed to cultivate independence and fearlessness with an incident from Bob's boyhood: One evening, Bob was out when supper was served. His father went to fetch him and, finding him, called his name. The boy retreated further into the shadows. The father called again and walked towards him, but Bob ran again. Ignominiously he called and called into the silence, but had to go back without his son. He was deeply hurt and the question he never could face was, had he, the father, caused fear in his son? From that time he sought often to extinguish signs of anxiety in Bob and, in doing so, warned him repeatedly of the things feared by himself. His rivalry with his namesake could not help but emerge. When the mother was overprotective, father was "rough." It was this offspring who had to do the most to get his college education. It was Bob who, by implication, was the greatest drain on finances even before his illness. When young Bob was home long his father forcefully suggested marriage and a job elsewhere. When the mother worried about the son's illness, the father reassured her that death too could be tolerated; for, after all, he had known the death of both parents and two siblings.

Mr. Neal had a recurrence of his ulcer just before Bob's admission to our hospital. Then, when the events in the hospital were most acute, Mr. Neal decided that, for the first time in more than 10 years, a vacation and rest were in order. Mrs. Neal agreed that her husband needed this trip with her; for once he seemed to be submitting to her wish to care for him. Near the end of Bob's hospitalization, when plans were being made, Mr. Neal again put forth his idea that his son would be better alone in a distant city. As we reflect on the problem the father, of course, seems to be wrong—but he was also right.

Ken Neal, 27, and Bob's older brother is, in many respects, a model of his father. He has the self-assurance and complacent ease, but his exterior is not quite so brittle. He has rather successfully adopted the themes of independence and strength and he does not find it necessary to struggle quite so much to compensate for his need for some emotional attachment. He is a successful career officer in the Air Force, risen from the ranks. He moved from post to post, always seeking another technical school and cheerfully taking the distant assignment, claiming he needed no place to "light." In his relationships he was outwardly noncommittal and nonchalant. He was matter-of-fact about his mother's forceful attitudes. He recognized her needs and put distance between himself and her. He was sympathetic, but not especially worried or stirred emotionally by his brother's illness. In fact, he seemed not at all surprised that an illness would bind his mother and brother. He agreed with the father's idea that Bob should depart from his parents' home. In our contacts with Ken he revealed the conflictual side of himself in only two ways; one of these was characteristic, the other a surprise. First, he told us with little affect that he had been twice engaged. He had drifted rather easily from the first relationship and the second was near a break at the time of our interviews. About a week before, he had planned a marriage after his fiancee had proposed it; a lawsuit involving the girl had then intervened. He rather dispassionately accepted the interruption and seemed little concerned whether the marriage would ever take place.

Near the end of our last talk, Ken was asked if he had any questions. Without change in facial expression he said, "Well, I get lonely sometimes." Then he halted and floundered a little before adding, "I have one thing that bothers me. I can't express my emotion. I have a terrible time with it. I want to stay just as far away from emotion as I can. I hate to get emotionally involved, even with my family. It hurts me . . . it hurts them sometimes, I know." This sudden expression is surprising from a taciturn young man who joins the rest of his family in the unity of dampening feeling, and in upholding the family ideal that emotional quiet and a respectable calm must be maintained in family life.

We are not at all certain of our data concerning the two sisters, since we have not seen them. However, from the corroborating comments of the others we have strong hints that Doris, 29, the oldest, is a slightly more rigid and imperious version of her mother. Dottie, 22, must have been—in the view of this family—"spoiled," since she is more truly independent and boisterous than the rest. She was obviously a rugged competitor with her brother.

AN ATTEMPT AT FAMILY ANALYSIS

Remaining is the goal of demonstrating from the above account that, in Bob's case, the rigid and confining patterns of object relations were not only formed in the binary mother-child symbiosis, but were conditioned by the multidimensional matrix of object relations constituting the field in which his personality developed. When we attempt, in studies of human behavior, to analyze events occurring in multidimensional fields rather than in simple binary systems, we compound our difficulties. However it is the argument of this paper that the ways of forming and selecting object relations are shaped in a complex system such as the family.

We have chosen to simplify this task for ourselves and the reader in the following paragraphs by describing a number of interpersonal cycles which, in time, fixed the type of interpersonal relations Bob would have to make in adolescence and maturity. These cycles are conceptually designed to depict the flow of feelings and conflicts among family members. It is possible to construct an almost endless number of these cycles. Their schematic nature allows only a summary of the complexity of incessantly interacting systems. We hypothesize that most of these cycles operate simultaneously, and that the one on which we concentrate at any moment is determined by our point of view at the time. However, one or more may predominate in particular aspects of the family transactions and also at one time in the family's history. It is our thesis that the whole field —that is, all the individuals—is involved and influenced by each of the cycles. For the sake of convenience and simplicity in this paper the field will be limited to the mother, father, and patient—a system complex enough for a first attempt. The others, nevertheless, influence this three-person system in many ways.*

The basic cycle operating in the relationship of these three began before Bob was born. It had its overt impact briefly and then was deeply buried, although it made the succeeding family adaptations necessary. The following is a graphic representation of the cycle (Fig. 1).

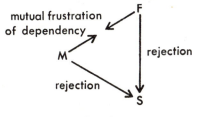

FIG. 1

In this and subsequent representations, M, F, and S signify mother, father, and son, respectively.

The mutual frustration of dependency needs in a mother who needed more than she seemed and a father who, for a long time greatly feared poverty, led to the unconscious wish that they could exclude an additional burden from their family and home. Maintenance of equilibrium in a system functioning like this cycle is impossible. It is potentially explosive, and each of the three family members must be driven off.

Hence, two more cycles come into almost immediate operation (Fig. 2).

* Lindemann[7] has used a similar conceptual scheme in the explanation of his hypotheses concerning the key object relation in the pathogenesis of ulcerative colitis.

In the first of these two cycles the mother compensates partially for her dependency needs and counteracts her guilt by maternalizing the new son. In a sense, the mother obtains an opportunity for expression of her own needs, but the father gets only a rival. Later, the son adopts the style

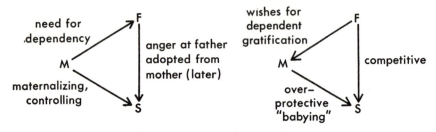

FIG. 2

of his mother's angry feelings towards the husband and father. In the second cycle the mother's "babying" of her son intensifies the father's competitive feelings.

The father's defensiveness is the main impetus for another set of cycles in which we can use the almost identical terms given us by father and son for their feelings towards the mother: shoving her off when they perceive any need for her (Fig. 3).

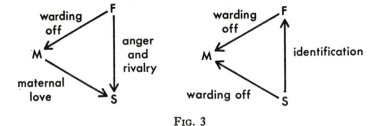

FIG. 3

Father has to ward off mother as part of his overcompensation, but still feels the rivalry towards his son as the mother is pushed into expressing maternal love to him. However, to help balance the system, the son identifies with the father, and does his own warding off.

The situation which most probably was significant in the precipitation of Bob's illness is as follows (Fig. 4).

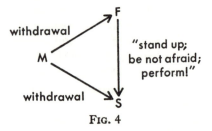

FIG. 4

Essentially the above cycle is initiated by the mother's withdrawal from both father and son as a result of a menopausal depression. The father reacts in his usual manner (with overcompensation) and competitively demands that his son show the same alleged courage. But Bob's defenses are not so well developed, and thus his father's attitudes towards him only intensify the reactions to the relative loss of the mother. An attempt at renewal of the old symbiosis leads to a cycle which involves the whole family (Fig. 5).

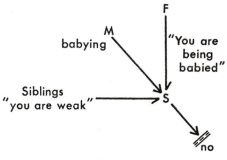

FIG. 5

The siblings' and father's feelings in response to the mother's withdrawal stimulates rivalry toward the one who has supposedly enjoyed the most maternalizing in this family. There are not many possibilities for achieving an equilibrium in this cycle unless the illness causes a major shift in the total family adaptation. An escape was needed, and it was most likely that this would involve sickness.

Several other reconstructions are possible to conceptualize the dynamics of this family as a history and as a factor in the precipitation of our patient's ulcerative colitis. Our motive is primarily illustrative: to show that reconstructions can be made—by our schematic cycles or by some other evaluative system which attempts to span the entire field of family relations.

The family's adaptation involved resolution of a conflict between frustrated needs for dependency and the family ideal of independence, respectability, and avoidance of allegedly selfish desires. To do this, the members of the family must remain, for as long as possible, deeply committed to each other. In the process of this devotion to common needs there must be no overt demonstration of individual needs, since such an eruption would compromise the family ideals. There cannot be the slightest hint of the emotions which arise from frustration of needs. Our methods of study of this family revealed that, to accomplish this resolution, a definite organization of family life is required. Essentially, the organization in the Neal family consists of the maintenance of a rigid system from which the unexpected and the uncertain are eliminated. Roles within this organization are carefully prescribed and rigidly adhered to. For the maintenance of emotional tranquillity this family requires that communication be confined largely to the matter-of-fact; vagueness, excitement, or disturbance are shunned. Nevertheless, there must be some break-through and when this occurs it can be extreme. The stereotyped form of communication cannot permit much perception of another's inner feelings. In our summarizing phrase—anxious cohesion—for a family of this kind, we refer to a quality of family life in which the individuals maintain almost desperately their cohesions as a group at the high cost of *underlying* anxiety.

SUMMARY

1. We have suggested in this case study that the object relations aspects of psychosomatic hypotheses may be more comprehensively investigated by inquiry into the patterns of interlocking relationships in the family. Use of the field study method of the anthropologist in observing the whole family provides a view in depth of important relationships, instead of reports from the individual patient.

2. We have proposed an expansion of current hypotheses concerning the object relations aspects of predisposition and etiology in psychosomatic research. In the case discussed we have attempted to show that the patient's adaptation was conditioned by an interlocking set of relationships within the family. The crucial mother-child relationship was itself conditioned by the family setting as a transacting field of object relations between its members. In our opinion it is not the *mother* who affects the child, but the *fam ly's mother*, whose relationship with the child is a product of the dynamics operating within the family as a social system.

REFERENCES

1. ENGEL, G. L. 1955. Studies of ulcerative colitis: III. The nature of the psychological processes. *Am. J. Med.*, **19**, 231.
2. TITCHENER, J., and EMERSON, R. 1958. Some methods for the study of family interaction in personality development. *Psychiat. Res. Rep.*, **10**, 72.
3. ACKERMAN, N. W. 1958. *The psychodynamics of family life.* Basic Books, New York.
4. CHANCE, E. 1959. *Families in treatment.* Basic Books, New York.
5. KLUCKHOHN, F., and SPIEGEL, J. (eds) 1954. Integration and conflict in family behavior: A report of the Committee of the Group for the Advancement of Psychiatry. Report No. 27.
6. BATESON, G., JACKSON, D. D., HALEY, J., and WEAKLAND, J. 1956. Toward a theory of schizophrenia. *Behl Sci.*, **1**, 4. [Reprinted in this collection as No. XL.]
7. LINDEMANN, E. 1950. Modifications in the course of ulcerative colitis in relationship to changes in life situations and reaction patterns. Life stress and bodily disease. *Proc. Ass. Res. nerv. ment. Dis.*, **29**, 706.

XXXVIII

ATTEMPTED SUICIDE AND FAMILY DISORGANIZATION

JACOB TUCKMAN AND WILLIAM F. YOUNGMAN

The amount of help sought from community agencies is an index of family disorganisation. This disorganisation was found to be characteristic of families where children, adolescents or adults attempted suicide.

INTRODUCTION

The interrelation of attempted suicide, family disorganization, and delinquency has been demonstrated in a sample of 100 children and adolescents under 18 years of age.[6] Family disorganization was defined operationally as contact, by the adolescent making the suicide attempt or by a member of his family, with one or more community agencies providing health and welfare services. Such a definition seems to have considerable validity because contacts with community agencies indicate that the family has a problem of such magnitude that it cannot cope with it through its own resources and requires help from specialized community facilities; moreover, it is a more objective measure of family disorganization than judgments based on retrospective accounts obtained through interview. The amount of agency contact, by children and adolescents attempting suicide or by members of their families, ranged from 17 per cent for agencies providing psychiatric services to 51 per cent for agencies concerned with delinquency. Without regard to the type of agency, 75 per cent of the sample had been known to one or more agencies.

The purpose of this study is to test whether the interrelationship of attempted suicide, family disorganization, and delinquency previously found for children and adolescents applies to adults (18 years of age and older).

Reprinted from THE JOURNAL OF GENETIC PSYCHOLOGY, Vol. 105, 1964, pp. 187-193.

SAMPLE AND PROCEDURE

From a study of 1,112 consecutive attempted suicides coming to the attention of the Philadelphia Police Department during the two-year period April, 1959, to April, 1961,[7] a 20 per cent random sample of 223 individuals was drawn for the present investigation. As in the study of children and adolescents, information concerning agency contacts was obtained through the Social Service Exchange, the clearing house in the community for registration of persons known to health and welfare agencies. Information was sought not only for the person making the attempt, but also for his spouse, parents, children, and siblings; but no information was sought for grandparents, aunts, uncles, relatives of the spouse, or relatives of the siblings (except for parents). Only contacts before the date of the attempt were used.

In 186 of the 223 cases, the Social Service Exchange was able to determine whether the person making the attempt or members of his family had been known to any agencies in the community. In 21 cases the identifying information (i.e., age, race, address, etc.) was not sufficient for the Social Service Exchange to determine whether the individual had had any agency contact. In 16 cases it was possible that the individual had had contacts, but no definite determination could be made with the available information. The study therefore was limited to the 186 cases who could be identified. Of these 186 cases, 69 per cent were female and 31 per cent were male; 75 per cent were white and 25 per cent were non-white. The age distribution showed 24 per cent between the ages of 18 and 24, 33 per cent between 25 and 34, and 43 per cent were 35 years of age or over.

In the earlier study, each agency to which the adolescent or his family had been known was asked for more detailed information about the nature of its contact with the family, with particular emphasis on relevant background factors. However, in general, the data obtained in that way yielded little information not already available from a knowledge of the functions of the agencies. Therefore, this procedure was not followed in the present study.

The health and welfare agencies were classified into the following categories, according to the system used in the earlier study:

1. Health: in or outpatient care at hospital or clinic for a physical condition.
2. Psychiatric: in or outpatient care.
3. Economic: public assistance.
4. Protective: care and placement of neglected children.
5. Delinquency: police, court, correctional institution, probation.
6. Domestic relations: Municipal Court for Domestic Relations.
7. Counseling: family, school, marriage clinic.
8. Other: Red Cross, legal aid, day care center, etc.

FINDINGS

Fifty-one per cent of the families had been known to one or more health and welfare agencies; this is an underestimation because only contacts by the person making the attempt, spouse, parents, children, and siblings were considered. Although data are not available regarding the extent to which the general population requires the services of community agencies, it seems reasonable to say that the families in this study have had greater contact than most families.

The number of agency contacts ranged from 0 to 22. Forty-nine per cent of the families had had no contact, 35 per cent had had from one to five contacts, 11 per cent had had from six to 10, two per cent had had from 11 to 15, three per cent had had from 16 to 20, and one per cent had had more than 20. The total number of agency contacts was 476, distributed by type as follows: domestic relations, 23 per cent; protective, 21 per cent; health, 17 per cent; delinquency, 15 per cent; economic, 13 per cent; counseling, 6 per cent; psychiatric, 3 per cent; and other agencies, 3 per cent. Five per cent of the families accounted for 32 per cent of all contacts; 10 per cent of the families, for 50 per cent of all contacts.

A comparison of cases known to health and welfare agencies with those not known to any agency showed no significant difference between the two groups with respect to race, sex, age, marital status, method, type of poison (when poison was the method), time of day of the attempt, police description of the person's condition when he was found, circumstances precipitating the attempt (reported by the person making the attempt or by another respondent), time interval between attempt and discovery, physical health, mental health, previous threats or attempts, and presence of a suicide note.

The distribution of contacts by type of agency and by family composition is shown in Table 1. Because a small number of families had a disproportionate number of contacts, this effect was controlled in the following manner. Duplication was eliminated for number of contacts, under each type of agency. For example, contacts with five different health agencies by an individual were considered as only one contact with a health agency. In Table 1, such contacts are shown for each type of agency for each family member, but the overrepresentation of a small number of families was minimized further by eliminating duplication for (a) type of agency—e.g., contacts with eight different types of agencies were shown as only one contact with any agency; and (b) family composition—e.g., contact with health agencies by the person making the attempt, and by any or all of the other family members (i.e., spouse, parents, children, and siblings) were shown as only one family contact.

The data in Table 1 clearly indicate that family breakdown or family disorganization characterizes the life experience of persons attempting

TABLE 1

PER CENT OF UNDUPLICATED HEALTH AND WELFARE AGENCY CONTACTS (BY TYPE OF AGENCY AND FAMILY COMPOSITION) FOR 186 ATTEMPTED SUICIDES

Family composition	Type of agency								Contact with any agency*
	Domestic relations	Health	Protective	Delinquency	Economic	Counseling	Psychiatric	Other	
Person attempting suicide	20	9	10	12	8	5	2	2	41
Spouse	1	1	6	2	1	1	2	1	11
Parents	15	9	3	4	10	2	2	0	24
Children	3	4	4	4	2	2	0	2	13
Siblings	12	9	8	7	6	4	2	3	21
Families†	34	23	21	20	19	12	6	6	51

* Contacts with more than one agency were counted as only one contact.
† Includes person making the attempt, spouse, parents, children or siblings, but counted only once as a family.

suicide. For problems in domestic relations, 34 per cent of the families had contact with the Municipal Court. The nature of the contacts varied. Most frequently, they involved court action against the father for failure to support his family or his illegitimate children; less frequently, marital conflict was so great as to force one of the partners, usually the wife, to take action against the other. Twenty-one per cent of the families had contacts with agencies providing protective services for children, usually the Society to Protect Children from Cruelty, suggesting a home situation so detrimental to the welfare of children that intervention was necessary. In most of these cases, the children were removed from the home and placed in institutions or in foster homes. Nineteen per cent of the families had had contacts with agencies providing economic assistance; and 23 per cent, with health agencies for in- or outpatient physical care. Of course, there is overlap between the two because families unable to maintain themselves financially are not able to meet in part or in full the cost of medical care.

Twenty per cent of the families had a history of delinquency. Most of the contacts involved delinquent behavior in childhood and in adolescence and, in a few cases, criminal activities in adulthood. Twelve per cent of the families had been known to counseling agencies and six per cent to psychiatric facilities, usually outpatient clinics. Most of the counseling and psychiatric contacts, initiated by school or police rather than by the family, involved children presenting behavior difficulties in school, often a precursor of delinquency.

The data in Table 1 clearly indicate the pervasiveness of family breakdown, as shown by the involvement of its members in independent agency contacts. The differences in involvement among family members must be accepted with considerable caution. In some cases, the differences are a function of age and life experience. For example, it would hardly be expected that any significant number of children would have had domestic relations contacts because the median age of their parents (the persons attempting suicide) was only 32.5 years. In time, as more of the children reach adulthood, more may be involved in such contacts. In most cases, the differences among family members are a function of the way agency contacts are classified. For example, contacts for domestic relations were arbitrarily shown only for the person making the attempt even though the spouse was also involved. Agency contacts for economic assistance were arbitrarily shown only for the person making the attempt even though spouse and children were also involved. By contrast, contacts for protective services were arbitrarily shown only for the child. Such contacts shown for other family members refer to the need for protective services when they were children. Although the method of classifying agency contacts minimizes the involvement of family members, the pervasiveness of family breakdown is evident. Forty-one per cent of the persons making the attempt were involved in a contact with some type of agency; 24 per cent of parents, 21 per cent of siblings, 13 per cent of children, and 11 per cent of spouses were also involved in independent contacts. Further analysis shows that the contacts tended to be by individuals within the same family unit rather than by unrelated persons. In 63 per cent of the families with any agency contact, two or more members were involved in independent contacts; in 53 per cent, two or three generations were involved.

DISCUSSION AND CONCLUSIONS

There are differences between the present study and that of attempted suicide by children and adolescents. Family breakdown, as measured by contacts with health or welfare agencies, was more prevalent among children and adolescents (75 per cent of the families) than among adults (51 per cent). Furthermore, the distribution of the areas of breakdown showed that delinquency was relatively more important among children and adolescents, while domestic relations problems were relatively more important among adults. One explanation for the differences may be that the younger the person making the attempt, the greater the amount of family disorganization, but this inference does not appear to be valid, as no differences were found between age and family disorganization in the adults sample. A more reasonable explanation for the differences may be (a) the tendency in recent years to focus more sharply upon multiproblem families, in which delinquency is an important aspect, and (b) the fact that 17 per cent of the adult sample lacked sufficient identifying information to determine whether they had been known to a health and welfare agency, whereas in the sample of children and adolescents all cases could be identified.

Whether or not the differences are real, it is clear (from the two studies) that family disorganization is characteristic of persons attempting suicide. This finding is consistent with those of other studies using different criteria of family breakdown: e.g., loss of parent through death of one or both parents, or absence of one or both parents due to separation, divorce, desertion, or illegitimacy[2, 3, 4]; or broken home, based on factors such as parental rejection, emotional deprivation, parental quarreling, and alcoholism.[1, 5] Although delinquency may be a more important aspect of suicidal behavior in children and adolescents than in adults, the pervasiveness of family disorganization (as seen in the involvement of different members of the family)—frequently over a period of two or three generations—emphasizes the complexity of the problem and the difficulty in separating cause and effect. This suggests the importance of other factors (e.g., marital discord, parental neglect, and emotional deprivation in childhood, physical illness, mental illness, economic dependency, and difficulty in interpersonal relations, as well as delinquency) in the association of family disorganization and attempted suicide. The particular area of breakdown emerging in any study of attempted suicide may be a function in part of the age and life experience of the members of the sample and in part of the kinds of social problems receiving most community attention.

REFERENCES

1. BATCHELOR, I. R. C., and NAPIER, M. B. 1953. Broken homes and attempted suicide. *Br. J. Delinq.*, **4**, 99-108.
2. PALMER, D. M. 1941. Factors in suicidal attempts: A review of 25 consecutive cases. *J. nerv. ment. Dis.*, **93**, 421-442.
3. REITMAN, F. 1942. On the predictability of suicide. *J. ment. Sci.*, **88**, 580-582.
4. ROBINS, E., SCHMIDT, E. H., and O'NEAL, P. 1957. Some interrelations of social factors and clinical diagnosis in attempted suicide: A study of 109 patients. *Am. J. Psychiat.*, **114**, 221-231.
5. SIMON, W. 1950. Attempted suicide among veterans: A comparative study of 50 cases. *J. nerv. ment. Dis.*, **111**, 451-468.
6. TUCKMAN, J., and CONNON, H. E. 1962. Attempted suicide in adolescents. *Am. J. Psychiat.*, **119**, 228-232.
7. TUCKMAN, J., YOUNGMAN, W. F., and BLEIBERG, B. M. 1962. Attempted suicide by adults. *Publ. Hlth Rep.*, **77**, 605-614.

XXXIX

CHILDREN WHO KILL—A FAMILY CONSPIRACY?

DOUGLAS SARGENT

A homicidal child may be acting as the unwitting agent of an adult in the family with whom he may have a special emotional bond.

Why dois your brand sae drap wi bluid,
　　　　　Edward, Edward,
Why dois your brand sae drap wi bluid,
　　and why sae sad gang ye O?
　　　. . . . .
I hae killed my Fadir dier,
　　　　　Mither, Mither,
I hae killed my Fadir dier,
　　alas and wae is mee　　　O!
　　　. . . . .
And what wul ye leive to your ain
　　Mither dier,
　　　　　Edward, Edward?
And what wul ye leive to your ain
　　Mither dier,
　　my dier son now tell me O?
The curse of hell frae me sall ye bier,
　　　　　Mither, Mither,
The curse of hell frae me sall ye bier,
　　sic counsiels ye gave to me O!
　　　　—EDWARD (old Scottish ballad)

Homicide committed by children is not rare. The murder of Abel was the first crime recorded in the Old Testament, and the biblical description of Cain's crime provides a motive which most clinicians today would

Reprinted from SOCIAL WORK, Vol. 7, No. 1, January 1962, pp. 35-42.
Reproduced with permission of National Association of Social Workers, 95 Madison Avenue, New York 16, N. Y.

accept with equanimity—rejection and rivalry with a preferred sibling.

Nine child homicide cases were referred to the Juvenile Court in Wayne County last year. Out of the study of these children who have killed, and of similar children whom the writer has elsewhere examined, has emerged an interesting cluster of phenomena. This paper will discuss those phenomena and present some speculative remarks on the motivation of children who kill.

The hypothesis it attempts to support is that sometimes the child who kills is acting as the unwitting lethal agent of an adult (usually a parent) who unconsciously prompts the child to kill so that he can vicariously enjoy the benefits of the act. There are two corollaries to this hypothesis: first, that the adult plays upon the latent currents of hostility the child feels toward the victim—hostility which, without the adult's provocation and the child's special susceptibility to it, probably would remain inoperative and under the control of the child's ego; and second, that the child's susceptibility to, and readiness to act upon, the unconscious prompting of the adult rests upon the immaturity of the child's ego and the presence of a special emotional bond between the child and the adult.*

The following five cases, greatly condensed, demonstrate with varying degrees of clarity the relationship between a child's homicide and an adult's (unconscious) desire for the results of that crime.

CASE NO. 1

Eight-year-old Art, with the help of his 7-year-old brother, shot and killed his father while the parent sat reading the Bible in his cabin in the woods. The father, an eccentric recluse, had been divorced from the boys' mother for several years. The boys lived with their mother and stepfather in town; during summer vacations, the father often "borrowed" them for weekends. These weekends were not vacations for the children. Rather, under their father's heavy hand, they were forced to clean up his cabin, prepare his meals and, in short, obey his every whim. All the while he threatened them with beatings if they disobeyed him. From time to time he carried out these threats.

Returning from Army service deeply disturbed mentally, the father had developed the delusion that he was Jesus Christ. He wore ragged clothes and affected a beard, which he fancied made him resemble Jesus. He had the fixed idea that he would die at the hands of his children when he was $33\frac{1}{2}$ years old. (He thought this to be the age of Jesus when He was crucified.) Despite her ex-husband's obvious aberration, and over her sons' strong protests, Art's mother made her children continue the visits to their father.

* The hypothesis and corollaries are derived from the work of Adelaide Johnson, M.D., and others. *See* "Sanctions for Superego Lacunae of Adolescents," in K. R. Eissler, M.D., ed., *Searchlights on Delinquency* (New York: International Universities Press, 1949).

The day before his death, the father behaved in an even more peculiar fashion than was his habit: he commanded his sons not to come near him or touch him. When, by accident, one of the boys brushed against him at dinner that evening, he threatened that the next morning he would beat them both. Ordering them to go outside and play, he sat down in the cabin with his back to the door to read his Bible.

For a while the boys amused themselves taking turns tying each other to a tree. Wearying of this game, Art suggested that they go and get their father's gun from the glove compartment of the car; he further suggested that they load it and shoot him. They did just that. Art, firing from a distance of about thirty feet, fatally wounded his father—who died at exactly $33\frac{1}{2}$ years of age.

The story came to light when the boys were referred to a child guidance clinic because of failure in school (despite good intelligence), unruly, defiant behavior, and threats that they would kill any teacher who attempted to make them behave differently. When they appeared at the clinic, both of them—but especially Art—were markedly depressed, apathetic, and showed a profound inhibition of aggression. The events just described were revealed by them and their mother.

The mother's story provided some additional facts of interest. She said that if Art had not killed her ex-husband, she "would be sitting up in jail right now." When questioned about this she replied that she hated her ex-husband so much that she had often thought of killing him herself. When the writer expressed doubts of an 8-year-old boy's ability to fire a gun accurately enough to kill, even though he might wish to do so, she countered with the statement that her husband had taught both children and herself to shoot well, and that Art was an expert shot. She added that four years earlier, when the boys were living temporarily with their father, Art had asked her, "Mommy, when will we come to live with you all the time?" She remembered replying, "Not as long as your father is alive."

It is suggested that Art's father, in order to fulfill the requirements of his religious delusion, managed to commit suicide by provoking his children to kill him. It is further suggested that Art's mother planted the idea in Art's mind that she would not be unhappy if his father were dead.

CASE NO. 2

Bob, age 16, killed his stepfather with a single blast of a shotgun when the latter, in a drunken rage, dared him to try and stop him from beating Bob's mother. The stepfather, an unemployed alcoholic, had been a burden to the family for several years. Bob's mother increasingly shifted the responsibility for the family from her husband to her son, who worked in a drugstore in addition to attending school. She informed both her son and her husband in various ways that she considered the husband a superfluous nuisance and that the family would be better off without him. For several weeks the husband became progressively depressed and, in his despondency, drank all the more. On the day of his death, he took out his collection of guns and "played with them" on the living-room floor. A quarrel broke out, and the husband threatened to hit his wife. She turned to her son for protection. He picked up a shotgun and told his stepfather to stop. The stepfather advanced on the boy, daring him to shoot. Bob complied, with fatal results.

After the shooting Bob was confined in the Detention Home for a short time, then was placed in a home for boys for about a year. He became very depressed and, despite good intelligence, developed a marked learning inhibition. In addition he developed a peptic ulcer and glycosuria. During psychotherapy these symptoms were seen in part to be self-inflicted punishments for the murder.

When he returned home a year later, Bob became even more slavishly obedient to his mother than he had been before his stepfather's death, feeling that since he had killed her husband he must now take his place. It was only with great difficulty that he was able to understand and consciously feel the hostility he had toward his mother for having pushed him into the role of murderer. On the other hand, Bob's mother made it very clear that the home was a much better place without her deceased husband.

CASE NO. 3

Charles, age 15, listened in on a telephone conversation between his mother and her lover, then "saw red and didn't know what I did." Although it was not possible to learn the content of the telephone conversation that so enraged him, what he "did" was to take his rifle, track down his mother's lover, and kill him. Then he called an aunt and told her to inform his mother that he "did that errand for her."

Charles's mother had been carrying on an open love affair with the victim over a period of several months. Three years earlier she had had another love affair with the same man, a fact known to her husband and son. Upon first learning of his wife's infidelity, Charles's father had become so depressed that he required psychiatric treatment. As a concession to her husband's illness, she temporarily relinquished her lover. Following the resumption of the affair, Charles, at his father's request, went to work after school in his father's bar, washing dishes and "just helping out and hanging around." Charles said that he wanted to be near his father in order to help protect him should anyone try to harm him. On several occasions the lover came to the bar, taunting Charles's father in front of his son and customers with details of the love affair. When the father passively accepted this ridicule, Charles was so crushed by his failure to defend himself that he silently vowed to avenge the family honor.

His father was aware of his son's feelings, but did nothing to discourage him from becoming involved in the sordid affair. Charles said in court that he shot the man because he did not want his father to get sick again. The most revealing aspect of this case—one that lends credence to the view that Charles's motive for killing his mother's lover was, at least in part, borrowed from someone else—was his father's statement in court, delivered with great feeling: "That boy is my right arm." He went on to say that Charles was on the high-school rifle team and was an expert marksman. He had developed his son's interest in guns from an early age, starting with a BB gun and progressing through pellet guns, .22 rifles, and shotguns. He felt this to be a natural part of his educational duty toward his son.

For Charles, humiliated by his father's passivity and enraged by his mother's flagrant infidelity, the lover was the perfect target upon whom to vent his pent-up rage. By responding to the unconscious provocation of his father to kill this man, he could reinforce his own reaction formation against the hostility he felt toward his own father and at the same time give expression to his anger. In interviews with the clinic social worker Charles's mother gave further evidence of being a seductive psychopath who enjoyed pitting men against each other. The possibility that she also played some part in stimulating the boy to murder her lover is not remote.

CASE NO. 4

David, age 14, observed his intoxicated father abusing his mother and attempted to intervene. His mother picked up a paring knife and a belt, either to defend herself with or to frighten off her husband. When her husband wrenched the belt from her hand and began to beat her with it, she called to David to get his rifle and put a bullet in it. (Later she claimed that she only wanted her son to threaten her husband in the hope that he would leave the house.)

David ran upstairs to his room with his father in pursuit. After attempting to warn his father away, David pulled the trigger. His father died several hours later in the hospital. For many weeks afterward both David and his mother were very depressed, the mother's depression bordering on psychosis. For his part, David tried to deny his father's death, repeating, like a broken record, "the hole was so small, there was no blood, why did he die?"

The victim of this tragedy was a chronic alcoholic who in life was a burden to the whole family, especially to his wife. She had many complaints about her husband—laziness, lack of ambition, drinking, alternating these with wistful comments about her own thwarted social and educational ambitions. (She had many literary aspirations, of which she was mildly ashamed, and which her husband ridiculed.) The mother reflected on the failure of her attempts to push and encourage her husband to better achievement. These self-accusations were interspersed with bitter complaints about her husband's shortcomings and the mistake she had made in marrying him. She mentioned, however, that David alone seemed to feel affection for his father—affection the father reciprocated when sober. The morning of the killing, however, her husband had struck David, who ran crying from the house.

David was an intelligent boy with a severe reading disability which seemed related to his mother's exaggerated ambitions for his scholastic achievement. He remembered that his mother once said that she would like to "split his [father's] head open."

A clearer picture of this conflicted woman's role in her husband's death is obtained when one studies her background. The oldest of seven siblings, her mother's death left her, at age 13, in charge of the family. Her father expected her to play the role of mother to her siblings. She remembers bitterly that she found the care of the youngest child, a brother, especially onerous. She remembered her father as a cold, harsh, slave-driving man who gave her the impression that anything enjoyable was taboo: "With him it was work, work, nothing but work!" She seemed to blame her father for her own failure to make a more enjoyable life for herself, and felt that had she not wanted to get away from home she would never have married her husband. She complained that her husband only added to her burdens by acting "like another child."

The writer suggests that this disappointed and overworked woman unconsciously responded to her husband and her youngest son, David, as if they were the demanding siblings of her truncated childhood, unleashing upon them the fury she must have felt toward her siblings when, as a child, she was given responsibilities beyond her years. In selecting her youngest child as the trigger man she may have been revenging herself on him as well as using him. (She thought that he would probably be confined.)

The murdered husband had also inflamed the situation by his own suicidal tendencies. He became an alcoholic at about age 25, shortly after his own father committed suicide. During his drinking bouts he often challenged several men to a fight simultaneously, and received numerous severe beatings. This suggests a masochistic orientation. Could he have felt responsible for his father's death and provoked his own son to kill him, talion fashion? It would appear that David's affection for his father was not strong enough to withstand the onslaught of his father's direct attack on him, his mother's own murderous provocation, and his father's (tentatively assumed) suicidal wishes.

CASE NO. 5

Ernest, age 3½, was referred to a child guidance clinic with the chief complaint that his mother was afraid he would kill someone. (While this case has—as yet—no fatal outcome, it is included because it illustrates especially clearly the degree to which a mother was able to get her son to act out for her, her own unconscious hostile impulses.) The mother's description of Ernest's behavior seemed to lend support to her fears:

He fractured his 8-year-old brother's skull by hitting him with a coke bottle and a pair of pliers; set fire to the baby's crib; put poison in the baby's bottle of milk; threw a butcher's knife at his brother and told his mother he was going to kill him; beat a neighbor's child over the head with a baseball bat; urinated in his sister's face; broke a puppy's leg because he was angry at it; killed or tortured other animals; stole from a local grocery store; ingested his brother's "heart medicine"; left the house at dawn in his bare feet in midwinter and walked down to a nearby river; and so forth. His parents were so helpless to control him that, in desperation, they sometimes tied this very young child to a tree in the front yard.

When the writer saw this boy for evaluation, his behavior was so alarming that he was immediately referred to a children's psychiatric hospital, where he was admitted for residential treatment. The staff was alerted for extreme aggression. To everyone's surprise, however, after an initial period of testing the ability of the hospital staff to withstand and control his aggression, Ernest soon settled down. Once his attempts at aggressive control and threats were met with calm, firm, consistent debunking, he readily relinquished his aggression. He was, in the words of his ward physician, "probably less of a behavior problem during his stay in the hospital than any other patient we have ever had."

How can the wide discrepancy between this child's behavior at home and his benign adjustment at the hospital be explained? That he was being stimulated toward aggressive behavior at home, and that his parents were unable to exert any controls on him, was quite apparent. Obviously, more information was needed about the nature and source of the stimulus —and it was discovered in his mother's background.

Ernest's mother, a 24-year-old woman of limited intelligence with a passive-dependent personality orientation, was reared in a very strict, puritanical home. She was not allowed to date boys. In rebellion, at age 15, she sneaked out of the house to meet a lover; subsequently, she became pregnant. Her parents refused to let her marry her willing paramour, but insisted instead, that she bear the child and rear him. (This illegitimate child is the 8-year-old boy who later became the most frequent target of Ernest's violent attacks.) The child was born with a heart defect and suffered from asthma as an infant. He demanded a great deal of attention from his mother, who felt overwhelmed by his demands. She remembered that during her own childhood her parents had often talked about death, and after the birth of her child she herself became preoccupied with fears that the child would die, or that she or her parents would die. When she met and married her husband these fears subsided. He assured her of his interest in her child and his wish to adopt him. As children were born into this union, however, adoption was no longer mentioned. While her husband verbalized warm and affectionate concern for his wife's illegitimate child, this seemed to be only a façade. (The husband impressed the social worker and the psychiatrist who saw him as a shallow, apathetic, emotionally withdrawn man.) With the increased burden of caring for more children, and the progressive deterioration in her oldest child's health, requiring hospital care, Ernest's mother again became "nervous and fearful." It was during this time that Ernest began his uncontrolled aggressive activity.

It is suggested that this illegitimate boy represented to his mother the symbol of her shame and her parents' narrow, punitive behavior toward her. Her fears for his safety and that of her parents, then, represented a reaction formation against her own death wishes toward both child and parents. When she married the fears disappeared; she felt supported by her husband and the burden for the care of her child was lessened, reducing the hostility she felt toward him because of her predicament. At the same time, her husband served as a symbolic protection against an outbreak of her own dangerous impulses. As other children were born and added to her burdens, however, and as her sickly eldest child required more and more medical care (while simultaneously her husband failed to make good his promise to adopt him) she again experienced anxiety—the outward sign of an upsurging unconscious wish that this troublesome child would die. It is this wish that Ernest undoubtedly perceived and responded to, and that lay at the bottom of his mother's inability to control his unbridled aggression.

Interestingly enough, Ernest was admitted to the psychiatric unit at the same time that his brother was admitted to the pediatric service for cardiac surgery. Although Ernest's parents were most convincing in their pleas for help and eloquent in their description of his desperate need for hospital care, once he was admitted to the psychiatric service they began to violate visiting rules and press for his discharge. Within three weeks (and before the cardiac patient's release) they removed Ernest against medical advice, rejecting all attempts by the hospital and guidance clinic to follow the case.

IS CHILD AGENT OF ADULT?

The *hypothesis* set forth in the introduction is threefold: First, does the child who kills act as the agent of an adult, and, if so, is he unaware of the adult's provocation? None of the children in this series were aware that their acts were anything but their own doing, and all of them were quite willing to accept full responsibility for these acts. However, all except Charles, who killed his mother's lover, denied any actual murderous intent; two of them expressed stunned disbelief that their victims died. There was no tendency to project the blame onto anyone else, nor were they able to see any connection between the behavior of the surviving provocative parent and their own actions. Curiously, each child had a strong protective attitude toward the parent who provoked the killing, and even toward the victim (a quite natural reaction, incidentally). It is entirely possible that the mothers unconsciously exploited their son's protective attitudes and provoked their husbands to assault them at a time when the sons were present.

Second, was the provoking parent unconscious of his (usually "her") death wish and provocation of the child? Although all surviving parents were questioned closely, none of them were able to admit any conscious wish that the victim die or that the child even harm the victim. (This is to be expected—but their replies did have the ring of truth.) On the other hand, they all were able to admit that they had consciously wished that the victims were "somehow out of the way." They all felt guilty that their children had become involved in their marital problems. Most of them reacted to the killings with sufficient guilt to suggest that in some vague, indirect way, they felt responsible for the deaths of the victims.

Third, in all the "fatal" cases the surviving parents—despite feelings of guilt—acted as though the deaths of their spouses had relieved them of a burden. The bulk of the clinical material, then, seems to support the hypothesis.

The *first corollary* suggests that the stimulating adult accomplishes his goal by inflaming in the child latent hostile feelings toward the victim. The writer suggests that the child has his own unconscious motive, distinct from that of the provoking adult—a motive which is acted upon and spurred into open expression by the provocation of the adult. This can only be inferred from the material, and cannot be proved. However, two sources of hostility in the child are pointed to by the material. In the first four cases, statements made to the child either by the mother or father suggest that the child's Oedipal attachment to his mother and rivalry with his father (or surrogate) were a source of hostility toward the victim. For example, in Case 2 it became clear during psychotherapy that Bob had reacted to the acquisition of a stepfather at age $2\frac{1}{2}$ as though a foreign interloper and rival had come. His dreams and fantasies after the killing showed that his willingness to accept full responsibility for his stepfather's death was based on this earlier death wish, as though he had killed the Oedipal rival of his childhood. In Case 5, the generalization of Ernest's aggression onto other siblings offers sibling rivalry as another source of hostility.

The *second corollary* suggests that the child's susceptibility to the unconscious stimulation of the parent or adult rested upon both the immaturity of the child's ego and the presence of a special bond between stimulating adult and child. The ego's task of mastering impulses is difficult enough for all children, but is even more so when the adult who should help the child in this task hinders him instead. None of the children in this series (with the exception of Ernest) had a history of disobedient or delinquent behavior. It can be assumed, then, that they were tractable and obedient to their parents' wishes. Might not this also include obedience to the parents' unconscious command to kill?

In this connection it might be worth while to comment on the concept of superego lacunae as it applies to the five cases. The writer does not believe that this material points to the presence of discrete areas of superego defect. It is difficult to imagine that these children had no internalized taboo against murder, considering that they all felt guilty and depressed about their acts. Their behavior and emotional state after the murder, rather, suggest the presence of a strict and punitive superego, but one whose effect was temporarily suspended. The writer contends that in all five cases the child's superego would have been adequate to keep murderous impulses at bay—providing it were acting on its own. But, being immature, the superego was still under the sway of the parents and susceptible to parental commands. Under the influence of parental promptings, it was temporarily put out of action, much as a junior officer is temporarily relieved of command when a senior officer appears on the scene. After the event, however, the child's superego was still able to produce guilt, shame, and depression. The defect, then, is in the ego.

In addition to the usual bond between parent and child, the material suggests that in most instances there was a special emotional tie binding the child-murderer to the provocative adult. This bond seems to have played an important part in the murder. In Case 1, for example, there was a special bond between Art and his brother and their suicidal, delusional father, at least in the father's mind. He needed the boys to fulfill his grandiose delusion that he was Jesus Christ and would die at the hands of his children. In Case 2 it was clear that Bob's mother looked upon him as a better provider than her husband, and a preferable "head of the family" than the man to whom she was married. Charles (Case 3) was, in his father's eyes, his "right arm," and had been cultivated in the role of his father's protector and avenger from early boyhood. David (Case 4) was the youngest child in the family. His mother had a particularly strong hostile feeling toward her own youngest sibling, which may explain in part why David was the one chosen to be his mother's avenger. A special bond between Ernest (Case 5) and his mother is not apparent. However, he was the only child old enough and strong enough to carry out his mother's "unconscious commands." (In addition, Ernest claimed that he was his father's favorite child and added, in that connection, that his father did not like his older brother.)

IMPLICATIONS FOR TREATMENT OR PREVENTION

Granting that the material presented so far is highly speculative and perhaps only of theoretical interest, does it have any implications either for treatment or prevention of murder? This cannot be answered with any certainty and must remain the subject of further investigation. Two suggestions might be in order, however. First, if in the events which led to a child's act of homicide, there can be discerned strong evidence that he was acting upon the provocation of an adult whose influence he was unable to resist, this knowledge should be communicated to the child in such a way as to relieve him of an excessive load of guilt. It may also be used as evidence of extenuating circumstances in the child's behalf before the court. In adopting this approach, the professional person must consider to what extent the guilt feelings serve to protect the child from further impulsive action, weighing the protective benefits accruing to the child and to society from the total inhibition of his aggression against those which may result from liberating other energies which the child's depression inhibits. The one child in this series treated by the writer— Ernest (Case 5)—seemed to benefit from the relief of guilt without showing any tendency toward blatant, uncontrolled aggression.

Second, if one can identify in the parents strong hostile feelings toward some member of the family, as well as a tendency for a child to act out one or both parents' unconscious impulses, or for the parent to select the child as the vehicle of expression for his own unconscious wishes— then it is necessary to be alert to potential danger. There should at least be consideration as to the possible need for vigorous therapeutic intervention with both child and parents—perhaps even removal of the child from his home if treatment is not possible. Of course, the cases presented reinforce the conviction that no psychiatric evaluation of a child is complete without a simultaneous evaluation of his parents and whatever other studies are required to arrive at a comprehensive and dynamic understanding of the family unit. (The obvious conclusion is that no single undercurrent of provocation is sufficient to impel a child to murder; rather, it seems to require severe provocative trends acting in concert.)

Finally, both the process by which a parent selects a particular child as the agent of expression for his unconscious aggression, and the process of communication of these impulses between child and parent, would seem to offer the investigator fruitful fields of study. This would involve a multifaceted inquiry into the dynamic interaction between both parents and child, including psychotherapy for each individual.

If the material presented is convincing enough to support the theory that some children who kill are simultaneously victims of an unconscious family conspiracy, then there is justification in adding their names to the long roster of children whom Ruth Eissler has called the "scapegoats of society."*

* *See* Ruth Eissler, M.D. Scapegoats of society, in *Searchlights on delinquency, op. cit.*

XL

TOWARD A THEORY OF SCHIZOPHRENIA

GREGORY BATESON, DON D. JACKSON, JAY HALEY
AND JOHN WEAKLAND

The theory of schizophrenia presented here is based on communications analysis, and specifically on the Theory of Logical Types. From this theory and from observations of schizophrenic patients is derived a description and the necessary conditions for a situation called the 'double bind' —a situation in which no matter what a person does, he 'can't win'. It is hypothesised that a person caught in the double bind may develop schizophrenic symptoms. How and why the double bind may arise in a family situation is discussed, together with illustrations from clinical and experimental data.

This is a report* on a research project which has been formulating and testing a broad, systematic view of the nature, etiology, and therapy of schizophrenia. Our research in this field has proceeded by discussion of a varied body of data and ideas, with all of us contributing according to our varied experience in anthropology, communications analysis, psychotherapy, psychiatry, and psychoanalysis. We have now reached common

* This paper derives from hypotheses first developed in a research project financed by the Rockefeller Foundation from 1952-54 administered by the Department of Sociology and Anthropology at Stanford University and directed by Gregory Bateson. Since 1954 the project has continued, financed by the Josiah Macy, Jr. Foundation. To Jay Haley is due credit for recognizing that the symptoms of schizophrenia are suggestive of an inability to discriminate the Logical Types, and this was amplified by Bateson who added the notion that the symptoms and etiology could be formally described in terms of a double bind hypothesis. The hypothesis was communicated to D. D. Jackson and found to fit closely with his ideas of family homeostasis. Since then Dr. Jackson has worked closely with the project. The study of the formal analogies between hypnosis and schizophrenia has been the work of John J. Weakland and Jay Haley.

Reprinted from BEHAVIORAL SCIENCE, Vol. 1, No. 4, October 1956, pp. 251-264.

agreement on the broad outlines of a communicational theory of the origin and nature of schizophrenia; this paper is a preliminary report on our continuing research.

THE BASE IN COMMUNICATIONS THEORY

Our approach is based on that part of communications theory which Russell has called the Theory of Logical Types.[17] The central thesis of this theory is that there is a discontinuity between a class and its members. The class cannot be a member of itself nor can one of the members *be* the class, since the term used for the class is of a *different level of abstraction*—a different Logical Type—from terms used for members. Although in formal logic there is an attempt to maintain this discontinuity between a class and its members, we argue that in the psychology of real communications this discontinuity is continually and inevitably breached,[2] and that a priori we must expect a pathology to occur in the human organism when certain formal patterns of the breaching occur in the communication between mother and child. We shall argue that this pathology at its extreme will have symptoms whose formal characteristics would lead the pathology to be classified as a schizophrenia.

Illustrations of how human beings handle communication involving multiple Logical Types can be derived from the following fields:

1. *The use of various communicational modes in human communication.* Examples are play, non-play, fantasy, sacrament, metaphor, etc. Even among the lower mammals there appears to be an exchange of signals which identify certain meaningful behavior as "play," etc.* These signals are evidently of higher Logical Type than the messages they classify. Among human beings this framing and labeling of messages and meaningful actions reaches considerable complexity, with the peculiarity that our vocabulary for such discrimination is still very poorly developed, and we rely preponderantly upon nonverbal media of posture, gesture, facial expression, intonation, and the context for the communication of these highly abstract, but vitally important, labels.

2. *Humor.* This seems to be a method of exploring the implicit themes in thought or in a relationship. The method of exploration involves the use of messages which are characterized by a condensation of Logical Types or communicational modes. A discovery, for example, occurs when it suddenly becomes plain that a message was not only metaphoric but also more literal, or vice versa. That is to say, the explosive moment in humor is the moment when the labeling of the mode undergoes a dissolution and re-synthesis. Commonly, the punch line compels a re-evaluation of earlier signals which ascribed to certain messages a particular mode (e.g., literalness or fantasy). This has the peculiar effect of attri-

---

* A film prepared by this project, "The Nature of Play; Part I, River Otters," is available.

buting *mode* to those signals which had previously the status of that higher Logical Type which classifies the modes.

3. *The falsification of mode-identifying signals.* Among human beings mode identifiers can be falsified, and we have the artificial laugh, the manipulative simulation of friendliness, the confidence trick, kidding, and the like. Similar falsifications have been recorded among mammals.[3, 13] Among human beings we meet with a strange phenomenon—the unconscious falsification of these signals. This may occur within the self— the subject may conceal from himself his own real hostility under the guide of metaphoric play—or it may occur as an unconscious falsification of the subject's understanding of the other person's mode-identifying signals. He may mistake shyness for contempt, etc. Indeed most of the errors of self-reference fall under this head.

4. *Learning.* The simplest level of this phenomenon is exemplified by a situation in which a subject receives a message and acts appropriately on it: "I heard the clock strike and knew it was time for lunch. So I went to the table." In learning experiments the analogue of this sequence of events is observed by the experimenter and commonly treated as a single message of a higher type. When the dog salivates between buzzer and meat powder, this sequence is accepted by the experimenter as a message indicating that "the dog has *learned* that buzzer means meat powder." But this is not the end of the hierarchy of types involved. The experimental subject may become more skilled in learning. He may *learn to learn*,[1, 7, 9] and it is not inconceivable that still higher orders of learning may occur in human beings.

5. *Multiple levels of learning and the Logical Typing of signals.* These are two inseparable sets of phenomena—inseparable because the ability to handle the multiple types of signals is itself a *learned* skill and therefore a function of the multiple levels of learning.

According to our hypothesis, the term "ego function" (as this term is used when a schizophrenic is described as having "weak ego function") is precisely *the process of discriminating communicational modes either within the self or between the self and others.* The schizophrenic exhibits weakness in three areas of such function: (*a*) He has difficulty in assigning the correct communicational mode to the messages he receives from other persons. (*b*) He has difficulty in assigning the correct communicational mode to those messages which he himself utters or emits nonverbally. (*c*) He has difficulty in assigning the correct communicational mode to his own thoughts, sensations, and percepts.

At this point it is appropriate to compare what was said in the previous paragraph with von Domarus'[16] approach to the systematic description of schizophrenic utterance. He suggests that the messages (and thought) of the schizophrenic are deviant in syllogistic structure. In place of structures which derive from the syllogism, Barbara, the schizophrenic, according to this theory, uses structures which identify predicates. An example of such a distorted syllogism is:

Men die.

Grass dies.

Men are grass.

But as we see it, von Domarus' formulation is only a more precise—and therefore valuable—way of saying that schizophrenic utterance is rich in metaphor. With that generalization we agree. But metaphor is an indispensable tool of thought and expression—a characteristic of all human communication, even of that of the scientist. The conceptual models of cybernetics and the energy theories of psychoanalysis are, after all, only labeled metaphors. The peculiarity of the schizophrenic is not that he uses metaphors, but that he uses *unlabeled* metaphors. He has special difficulty in handling signals of that class whose members assign Logical Types to other signals.

If our formal summary of the symptomatology is correct and if the schizophrenia of our hypothesis is essentially a result of family interaction, it should be possible to arrive a priori at a formal description of these sequences of experience which would induce such a symptomatology. What is known of learning theory combines with the evident fact that human beings use *context* as a guide for mode discrimination. Therefore, we must look not for some specific traumatic experience in the infantile etiology but rather for characteristic sequential patterns. The specificity for which we search is to be at an abstract or formal level. The sequences must have this characteristic: that from them the patient will acquire the mental habits which are exemplified in schizophrenic communication. That is to say, *he must live in a universe where the sequences of events are such that his unconventional communicational habits will be in some sense appropriate.* The hypothesis which we offer is that sequences of this kind in the external experience of the patient are responsible for the inner conflicts of Logical Typing. For such unresolvable sequences of experiences, we use the term "double bind."

THE DOUBLE BIND

The necessary ingredients for a double bind situation, as we see it, are:

1. *Two or more persons.* Of these, we designate one, for purposes of our definition, as the "victim." We do not assume that the double bind is inflicted by the mother alone, but that it may be done either by mother alone or by some combination of mother, father, and/or siblings.

2. *Repeated experience.* We assume that the double bind is a recurrent theme in the experience of the victim. Our hypothesis does not invoke a single traumatic experience, but such repeated experience that the double bind structure comes to be an habitual expectation.

3. *A primary negative injunction.* This may have either of two forms:

(a) "Do not do so and so, or I will punish you," or (b) "If you do not do so and so, I will punish you." Here we select a context of learning based on avoidance of punishment rather than a context of reward seeking. There is perhaps no formal reason for this selection. We assume that the punishment may be either the withdrawal of love or the expression of hate or anger—or most devastating—the kind of abandonment that results from the parent's expression of extreme helplessness.*

4. *A secondary injunction conflicting with the first at a more abstract level, and like the first enforced by punishments or signals which threaten survival.* This secondary injunction is more difficult to describe than the primary for two reasons. First, the secondary injunction is commonly communicated to the child by nonverbal means. Posture, gesture, tone of voice, meaningful action, and the implications concealed in verbal comment may all be used to convey this more abstract message. Second, the secondary injunction may impinge upon any element of the primary prohibition. Verbalization of the secondary injunction may, therefore, include a wide variety of forms; for example, "Do not see this as punishment"; "Do not see me as the punishing agent"; "Do not submit to my prohibitions"; "Do not think of what you must not do"; "Do not question my love of which the primary prohibition is (or is not) an example"; and so on. Other examples become possible when the double bind is inflicted not by one individual but by two. For example, one parent may negate at a more abstract level the injunctions of the other.

5. *A tertiary negative injunction prohibiting the victim from escaping from the field.* In a formal sense it is perhaps unnecessary to list this injunction as a separate item since the reinforcement at the other two levels involves a threat to survival, and if the double binds are imposed during infancy, escape is naturally impossible. However, it seems that in some cases the escape from the field is made impossible by certain devices which are not purely negative, e.g., capricious promises of love, and the like.

6. Finally, the complete set of ingredients is no longer necessary when the victim has learned to perceive his universe in double bind patterns. Almost any part of a double bind sequence may then be sufficient to precipitate panic or rage. The pattern of conflicting injunctions may even be taken over by hallucinatory voices.[14]

The Effect of the Double Bind

In the Eastern religion, Zen Buddhism, the goal is to achieve Enlightenment. The Zen Master attempts to bring about enlightenment in his pupil in various ways. One of the things he does is to hold a stick over the pupil's head and say fiercely, "If you say this stick is real, I will strike

---

* Our concept of punishment is being refined at present. It appears to us to involve perceptual experience in a way that cannot be encompassed by the notion of "trauma."

you with it. If you say this stick is not real, I will strike you with it. If you don't say anything, I will strike you with it." We feel that the schizophrenic finds himself continually in the same situation as the pupil, but he achieves something like disorientation rather than enlightenment. The Zen pupil might reach up and take the stick away from the Master—who might accept this response, but the schizophrenic has no such choice since with him there is no not caring about the relationship, and his mother's aims and awareness are not like the Master's.

We hypothesize that there will be a breakdown in any individual's ability to discriminate between Logical Types whenever a double bind situation occurs. The general characteristics of this situation are the following:

1. When the individual is involved in an intense relationship; that is, a relationship in which he feels it is vitally important that he discriminate accurately what sort of message is being communicated so that he may respond appropriately.

2. And, the individual is caught in a situation in which the other person in the relationship is expressing two orders of message and one of these denies the other.

3. And, the individual is unable to comment on the messages being expressed to correct his discrimination of what order of message to respond to, i.e., he cannot make a metacommunicative statement.

We have suggested that this is the sort of situation which occurs between the pre-schizophrenic and his mother, but it also occurs in normal relationships. When a person is caught in a double bind situation, he will respond defensively in a manner similar to the schizophrenic. An individual will take a metaphorical statement literally when he is in a situation where he must respond, where he is faced with contradictory messages, and when he is unable to comment on the contradictions. For example, one day an employee went home during office hours. A fellow employee called him at his home, and said lightly, "Well, how did you get *there*?" The employee replied, "By automobile." He responded literally because he was faced with a message which asked him what he was doing at home when he should have been at the office, but which denied that this question was being asked by the way it was phrased. (Since the speaker felt it wasn't really his business, he spoke metaphorically.) The relationship was intense enough so that the victim was in doubt how the information would be used, and he therefore responded literally. This is characteristic of anyone who feels "on the spot," as demonstrated by the careful literal replies of a witness on the stand in a court trial. The schizophrenic feels so terribly on the spot at all times that he habitually responds with a defensive insistence on the literal level when it is quite inappropriate, e.g., when someone is joking.

Schizophrenics also confuse the literal and metaphoric in their own utterance when they feel themselves caught in a double bind. For example, a patient may wish to criticize his therapist for being late for an appointment, but he may be unsure what sort of a message that act of being late was—particularly if the therapist has anticipated the patient's reaction and apologized for the event. The patient cannot say, "Why were you late? Is it because you don't want to see me today?" This would be an accusation, and so he shifts to a metaphorical statement. He may then say, "I knew a fellow once who missed a boat, his name was Sam and the boat almost sunk, . . . etc." Thus he develops a metaphorical story and the therapist may or may not discover in it a comment on his being late. The convenient thing about a metaphor is that it leaves it up to the therapist (or mother) to see an accusation in the statement if he chooses, or to ignore it if he chooses. Should the therapist accept the accusation in the metaphor, then the patient can accept the statement he has made about Sam as metaphorical. If the therapist points out that this doesn't sound like a true statement about Sam, as a way of avoiding the accusation in the story, the patient can argue that there really was a man named Sam. As an answer to the double bind situation, a shift to a metaphorical statement brings safety. However, it also prevents the patient from making the accusation he wants to make. But instead of getting over his accusation by indicating that this is a metaphor, the schizophrenic patient seems to try to get over the fact that it is a metaphor by making it more fantastic. If the therapist should ignore the accusation in the story about Sam, the schizophrenic may then tell a story about going to Mars in a rocket ship as a way of putting over his accusation. The indication that it is a metaphorical statement lies in the fantastic aspect of the metaphor, not in the signals which usually accompany metaphors to tell the listener that a metaphor is being used.

It is not only safer for the victim of a double bind to shift to a metaphorical order of message, but in an impossible situation it is better to shift and become somebody else, or shift and insist that he is somewhere else. Then the double bind cannot work on the victim, because it isn't he and besides he is in a different place. In other words, the statements which show that a patient is disoriented can be interpreted as ways of defending himself against the situation he is in. The pathology enters when the victim himself either does not know that his responses are metaphorical or cannot say so. To recognize that he was speaking metaphorically he would need to be aware that he was defending himself and therefore was afraid of the other person. To him such an awareness would be an indictment of the other person and therefore provoke disaster.

If an individual has spent his life in the kind of double bind relationship described here, his way of relating to people after a psychotic break would have a systematic pattern. First, he would not share with normal people those signals which accompany messages to indicate what a person means. His metacommunicative system—the communications about communication—would have broken down, and he would not know what kind of message a message was. If a person said to him, "what would you like to do today?" he would be unable to judge accurately by the context or by the tone of voice or gesture whether he was being condemned for what he did yesterday, or being offered a sexual invitation, or just what was meant. Given this inability to judge accurately what a person really means and an excessive concern with what is really meant, an individual might defend himself by choosing one or more of several alternatives. He might, for example, assume that behind every statement there is a concealed meaning which is detrimental to his welfare. He would then be excessively concerned with hidden meanings and determined to demonstrate that he could not be deceived—as he had been all his life. If he chooses this alternative, he will be continually searching for meanings behind what people say and behind chance occurrences in the environment, and he will be characteristically suspicious and defiant.

He might choose another alternative, and tend to accept literally everything people say to him; when their tone or gesture or context contradicted what they said, he might establish a pattern of laughing off these metacommunicative signals. He would give up trying to discriminate between levels of messages and treat all messages as unimportant or to be laughed at.

If he didn't become suspicious of metacommunicative messages or attempt to laugh them off, he might choose to try to ignore them. Then he would find it necessary to see and hear less and less of what went on around him, and do his utmost to avoid provoking a response in his environment. He would try to detach his interest from the external world and concentrate on his own internal processes and, therefore, give the appearance of being a withdrawn, perhaps mute, individual.

This is another way of saying that if an individual doesn't know what sort of message a message is, he may defend himself in ways which have been described as paranoid, hebephrenic, or catatonic. These three alternatives are not the only ones. The point is that he cannot choose the one alternative which would help him to discover what people mean; he cannot, without considerable help, discuss the messages of others. Without being able to do that, the human being is like any self-correcting system which has lost its governor; it spirals into never-ending, but always systematic, distortions.

A DESCRIPTION OF THE FAMILY SITUATION

The theoretical possibility of double bind situations stimulated us to look for such communication sequences in the schizophrenic patient and in his family situation. Toward this end we have studied the written and verbal reports of psychotherapists who have treated such patients intensively; we have studied tape recordings of psychotherapeutic interviews, both of our own patients and others; we have interviewed and taped parents of schizophrenics; we have had two mothers and one father participate in intensive psychotherapy; and we have interviewed and taped parents and patients seen conjointly.

On the basis of these data we have developed a hypothesis about the family situation which ultimately leads us to an individual suffering from schizophrenia. This hypothesis has not been statistically tested; it selects and emphasizes a rather simple set of interactional phenomena and does not attempt to describe comprehensively the extraordinary complexity of a family relationship.

We hypothesize that the family situation of the schizophrenic has the following general characteristics:

1. A child whose mother becomes anxious and withdraws if the child responds to her as a loving mother. That is, the child's very existence has a special meaning to the other which arouses her anxiety and hostility when she is in danger of intimate contact with the child.

2. A mother to whom feelings of anxiety and hostility toward the child are not acceptable, and whose way of denying them is to express overt loving behavior to persuade the child to respond to her as a loving mother and to withdraw from him if he does not. "Loving behavior" does not necessarily imply "affection"; it can, for example, be set in a framework of doing the proper thing, instilling "goodness," and the like.

3. The absence of anyone in the family, such as a strong and insightful father, who can intervene in the relationship between the mother and child and support the child in the face of the contradictions involved.

Since this is a formal description we are not specifically concerned with why the mother feels this way about the child, but we suggest that she could feel this way for various reasons. It may be that merely having a child arouses anxiety about herself and her relationships to her own family; or it may be important to her that the child is a boy or a girl, or that the child was born on the anniversary of one of her own siblings,[8] or the child may be in the same sibling position in the family that she was, or the child may be special to her for other reasons related to her own emotional problems.

Given a situation with these characteristics, we hypothesize that the mother of a schizophrenic will be simultaneously expressing at least two orders of message. (For simplicity in this presentation we shall confine ourselves to two orders.) These orders of message can be roughly characterized as (a) hostile or withdrawing behavior which is aroused whenever the child approaches her, and (b) simulated loving or approaching behavior which is aroused when the child responds to her hostile and withdrawing behavior, as a way of denying that she is withdrawing. Her problem is to control her anxiety by controlling the closeness and distance between herself and her child. To put this another way, if the mother begins to feel affectionate and close to her child, she begins to feel endangered and must withdraw from him; but she cannot accept this hostile act and to deny it must simulate affection and closeness with her child. The important point is that her loving behavior is then a comment on (since it is compensatory for) her hostile behavior and consequently it is of a different *order* of message than the hostile behavior—it is a message about a sequence of messages. Yet by its nature it denies the existence of those messages which it is about, i.e., the hostile withdrawal.

The mother uses the child's responses to affirm that her behavior is loving, and since the loving behavior is simulated, the child is placed in a position where he must not accurately interpret her communication if he is to maintain his relationship with her. In other words, he must not discriminate accurately between orders of message, in this case the difference between the expression of simulated feelings (one Logical Type) and real feelings (another Logical Type). As a result the child must systematically distort his perception of metacommunicative signals. For example, if mother begins to feel hostile (or affectionate) toward her child and also feels compelled to withdraw from him, she might say, "Go to bed, you're very tired and I want you to get your sleep." This overtly loving statement is intended to deny a feeling which could be verbalized as "Get out of my sight because I'm sick of you." If the child correctly discriminates her metacommunicative signals, he would have to face the fact that she both doesn't want him and is deceiving him by her loving behavior. He would be "punished" for learning to discriminate orders of messages accurately. He therefore would tend to accept the idea that he is tired rather than recognize his mother's deception. This means that he must deceive himself about his own internal state in order to support mother in her deception. To survive with her he must falsely discriminate his own internal messages as well as falsely discriminate the messages of others.

The problem is compounded for the child because the mother is "benevolently" defining for him how he feels; she is expressing overt maternal concern over the fact that he is tired. To put it another way, the mother is controlling the child's definitions of his own messages, as well as the definition of his responses to her (e.g. by saying, "You don't really mean to say that," if he should criticize her) by insisting that she is not concerned about herself but only about him. Consequently, the easiest path for the child is to accept mother's simulated loving behavior as real, and his desires to interpret what is going on are undermined. Yet the result is that the mother is withdrawing from him and defining this withdrawal as the way a loving relationship should be.

However, accepting mother's simulated loving behavior as real also is no solution for the child. Should he make this false discrimination, he would approach her; this move toward closeness would provoke in her feelings of fear and helplessness, and she would be compelled to withdraw. But if he then withdrew from her, she would take his withdrawal as a statement that she was not a loving mother and would either punish him for withdrawing or approach him to bring him closer. If he then approached, she would respond by putting him at a distance. *The child is punished for discriminating accurately what she is expressing, and he is punished for discriminating inaccurately—he is caught in a double bind.*

The child might try various means of escaping from this situation. He might, for example, try to lean on his father or some other member of the family. However, from our preliminary observations we think it is likely that the fathers of schizophrenics are not substantial enough to lean on. They are also in the awkward position where if they agreed with the child about the nature of mother's deceptions, they would need to recognize the nature of their own relationships to the mother, which they could not do and remain attached to her in the *modus operandi* they have worked out.

The need of the mother to be wanted and loved also prevents the child from gaining support from some other person in the environment, a teacher, for example. A mother with these characteristics would feel threatened by any other attachment of the child and would break it up and bring the child back closer to her with consequent anxiety when the child became dependent on her.

The only way the child can really escape from the situation is to comment on the contradictory position his mother has put him in. However, if he did so, the mother would take this as an accusation that she is unloving and both punish him and insist that his perception of the situation is distorted. By preventing the child from talking about the situation, the mother forbids him using the metacommunicative level—the level we use to correct our perception of communicative behavior. The ability to communicate about communication, to comment upon the meaningful actions of oneself and others, is essential for successful social intercourse. In any normal relationship there is a constant interchange of metacommunicative messages such as "What do you mean?" or "Why did you do that?" or "Are you kidding me?" and so on. To discriminate accurately what people are really expressing we must be able to comment directly or indirectly on that expression. This metacommunicative level the schizophrenic seems unable to use successfully.[2] Given these characteristics of the mother, it is apparent why. If she is denying one order of message, then any statement about her statements endangers her and she must forbid it. Therefore, the child grows up unskilled in his ability to communicate about communication and, as a result, unskilled in determining what people really mean and unskilled in expressing what he really means, which is essential for normal relationships.

In summary, then, we suggest that the double bind nature of the family situation of a schizophrenic results in placing the child in a position where if he responds to his mother's simulated affection her anxiety will be aroused and she will punish him (or insist, to protect herself, that *his* overtures are simulated, thus confusing him about the nature of his own messages) to defend herself from closeness with him. Thus the child is blocked off from intimate and secure associations with his mother. However, if he does not make overtures of affection, she will feel that this means she is not a loving mother and her anxiety will be aroused. Therefore, she will either punish him for withdrawing or make overtures toward the child to insist that he demonstrate that he loves her. If he then responds and shows her affection, she will not only feel endangered again, but she may resent the fact that she had to force him to respond. In either case in a relationship, the most important in his life and the model for all others, he is punished if he indicates love and affection and punished if he does not; and his escape routes from the situation, such as gaining support from others, are cut off. This is the basic nature of the double bind relationship between mother and child. This description has not depicted, of course, the more complicated interlocking gestalt that is the "family" of which the "mother" is one important part.[11, 12]

ILLUSTRATIONS FROM CLINICAL DATA

An analysis of an incident occurring between a schizophrenic patient and his mother illustrates the "double bind" situation. A young man who had fairly well recovered from an acute schizophrenic episode was visited in the hospital by his mother. He was glad to see her and impulsively put his arm around her shoulders, whereupon she stiffened. He withdrew his arm and she asked, "Don't you love me any more?" He then blushed, and she said, "Dear, you must not be so easily embarrassed and afraid of your feelings." The patient was able to stay with her only a few minutes more and following her departure he assaulted an aide and was put in the tubs.

Obviously, this result could have been avoided if the young man had been able to say, "Mother, it is obvious that you become uncomfortable when I put my arm around you, and that you have difficulty accepting a gesture of affection from me." However, the schizophrenic patient doesn't have this possibility open to him. His intense dependency and training prevents him from commenting upon his mother's communicative behavior, though she comments on his and forces him to accept and to attempt to deal with the complicated sequence. The complications for the patient include the following:

1. The mother's reaction of not accepting her son's affectionate gesture is masterfully covered up by her condemnation of him for withdrawing, and the patient denies his perception of the situation by accepting her condemnation.

2. The statement "don't you love me any more" in this context seems to imply:

(a) "I am lovable."

(b) "You should love me and if you don't you are bad or at fault."

(*c*) "Whereas you did love me previously you don't any longer," and thus focus is shifted from his expressing affection to his inability to be affectionate. Since the patient has also hated her, she is on good ground here, and he responds appropriately with guilt, which she then attacks.

(*d*) "What you just expressed *was not* affection," and in order to accept this statement the patient must deny what she and the culture have taught him about how one expresses affection. He must also question the times with her, and with others, when he thought he was experiencing affection and when they *seemed* to treat the situation as if he had. He experiences here loss-of-support phenomena and is put in doubt about the reliability of past experience.

3. The statement, "You must not be so easily embarrassed and afraid of your feelings," seems to imply:

(*a*) "You are not like me and are different from other nice or normal people because we express our feelings."

(*b*) "The feelings you express are all right, it's only that *you* can't accept them." However, if the stiffening on her part had indicated "these are unacceptable feelings," then the boy is told that he should not be embarrassed by unacceptable feelings. Since he has had a long training in what is and is not acceptable to both her and society, he again comes into conflict with the past. If he is unafraid of his own feelings (which mother implies is good), he should be unafraid of his affection and would then notice it was she who was afraid, but he must not notice that because her whole approach is aimed at covering up this shortcoming in herself.

The impossible dilemma thus becomes: "If I am to keep my tie to mother I must not show her that I love her, but if I do not show her that I love her, then I will lose her."

The importance to the mother of her special method of control is strikingly illustrated by the interfamily situation of a young woman schizophrenic who greeted the therapist on their first meeting with the remark, "Mother had to get married and now I'm here." This statement meant to the therapist that:

1. The patient was the result of an illegitimate pregnancy.

2. This fact was related to her present psychosis (in her opinion).

3. "Here" referred to the psychiatrist's office and to the patient's presence on earth for which she had to be eternally indebted to her mother, especially since her mother had sinned and suffered in order to bring her into the world.

4. "Had to get married" referred to the shot-gun nature of mother's wedding and to the mother's response to pressure that she must marry, and the reciprocal, that she resented the forced nature of the situation and blamed the patient for it.

Actually, all these suppositions subsequently proved to be factually correct and were corroborated by the mother during an abortive attempt at psychotherapy. The flavor of the mother's communications to the patient seemed essentially this: "I am lovable, loving and satisfied with myself. You are lovable when you are like me and when you do what I say." At the same time the other indicated to the daughter both by words and behavior: "You are physically delicate, unintelligent, and different from me ('not normal'). You need me and me alone because of these handicaps, and I will take care of you and love you." Thus the patient's life was a series of beginnings, of attempts at experience, which would result in failure and withdrawal back to the maternal hearth and bosom because of the collusion between her and her mother.

It was noted in collaborative therapy that certain areas important to the mother's self-esteem were especially conflictual situations for the patient. For example, the mother needed the fiction that she was close to her family and that a deep love existed between her and her own mother. By analogy the relationship to the grandmother served as the prototype for the mother's relationship to her own daughter. On one occasion when the daughter was seven or eight years old the grandmother in a rage threw a knife which barely missed the little girl. The mother said nothing to the grandmother but hurried the little girl from the room with the words, "Grandmommy really loves you." It is significant that the grandmother took the attitude toward the patient that she was not well enough controlled, and she used to chide her daughter for being too easy on the child. The grandmother was living in the house during one of the patient's psychotic episodes, and the girl took great delight in throwing various objects at the mother and grandmother while they cowered in fear.

Mother felt herself very attractive as a girl, and she felt that her daughter resembled her rather closely, although by damning with faint praise it was obvious that she felt the daughter definitely ran second. One of the daughter's first acts during a psychotic period was to announce to her mother that she was going to cut off all her hair. She proceeded to do this while the mother pleaded with her to stop. Subsequently the mother would show a picture of *herself* as a girl and explain to people how the patient would look if she only had her beautiful hair.

The mother, apparently without awareness of the significance of what she was doing, would equate the daughter's illness with not being very bright and with some sort of organic brain difficulty. She would invariably contrast this with her own intelligence as demonstrated by her *own* scholastic record. She treated her daughter with a completely patronizing and placating manner which was insincere. For example, in the psychiatrist's presence she promised her daughter that she would not allow her to have further shock treatments, and as soon as the girl was out of the room she asked the doctor if he didn't feel she should be hospitalized and given electric shock treatments. One clue to this deceptive behavior arose during the mother's therapy. Although the daughter had had three previous hospitalizations the mother had never mentioned to the doctors that she herself had had a psychotic episode when she discovered that she was pregnant. The family whisked her away to a small sanitarium in a nearby town, and she was, according to her own statement, strapped to a bed for six weeks. Her family did not visit her during this time, and no one except her parents and her sister knew that she was hospitalized.

There were two times during therapy when the mother showed intense emotion. One was in relating her own psychotic experience; the other was on the occasion of her last visit when she accused the therapist of trying to drive her crazy by forcing her to choose between her daughter and her husband. Against medical advice, she took her daughter out of therapy.

The father was as involved in the homeostatic aspects of the intra-family situation as the mother. For example, he stated that he had to quit his position as an important attorney in order to bring his daughter to an area where competent psychiatric help was available. Subsequently, acting on cues from the patient (e.g., she frequently referred to a character named "Nervous Ned") the therapist was able to elicit from him that he had hated his job and for years had been trying to "get out from under." However, the daughter was made to feel that the move was initiated for her.

On the basis of our examination of the clinical data, we have been impressed by a number of observations including:

1. The helplessness, fear, exasperation, and rage which a double bind situation provokes in the patient, but which the mother may serenely and un-understandingly pass over. We have noted reactions in the father that both create double bind situations, or extend and amplify those created by the mother, and we have seen the father passive and outraged, but helpless, become ensnared in a similar manner to the patient.

2. The psychosis seems, in part, a way of dealing with double bind situations to overcome their inhibiting and controlling effect. The psychotic patient may make astute, pithy, often metaphorical remarks that reveal an insight into the forces binding him. Contrariwise, he may become rather expert in setting double bind situations himself.

3. According to our theory, the communication situation described is essential to the mother's security, and by inference to the family homeostasis. If this be so, then when psychotherapy of the patient helps him become less vulnerable to mother's attempts at control, anxiety will be produced in the mother. Similarly, if the therapist interprets to the mother the dynamics of the situation she is setting up with the patient, this should produce an anxiety response in her. Our impression is that when there is a perduring contact between patient and family (especially when the patient lives at home during psychotherapy), this leads to a disturbance (often severe) in the mother and sometimes in both mother and father and other siblings.[10, 11]

CURRENT POSITION AND FUTURE PROSPECTS

Many writers have treated schizophrenia in terms of the most extreme contrast with any other form of human thinking and behavior. While it is an isolable phenomenon, so much emphasis on the differences from the normal—rather like the fearful physical segregation of psychotics—does not help in understanding the problems. In our approach we assume that schizophrenia involves general principles which are important in all communication and therefore many informative similarities can be found in "normal" communication situations.

We have been particularly interested in various sorts of communication which involve both emotional significance and the necessity of discriminating between orders of message. Such situations include play, humor, ritual, poetry, and fiction. Play, especially among animals, we have studied at some length.[3] It is a situation which strikingly illustrates the occurrence of metamessages whose correct discrimination is vital to the cooperation of the individuals involved; for example, false discrimination could easily lead to combat. Rather closely related to play is humor, a continuing subject of our research. It involves sudden shifts in Logical Types as well as discrimination of those shifts. Ritual is a field in which unusually real or literal ascriptions of Logical Type are made and defended as vigorously as the schizophrenic defends the "reality" of his delusions. Poetry exemplifies the communicative power of metaphor—even very unusual metaphor—when labeled as such by various signs, as contrasted to the obscurity of unlabeled schizophrenic metaphor. The entire field of fictional communication, defined as the narration or depiction of a series of events with more or less of a label of actuality, is most relevant to the investigation of schizophrenia. We are not so much concerned with the content interpretation of fiction—although analysis of oral and destructive themes is illuminating to the student of schizophrenia —as with the formal problems involved in simultaneous existence of multiple levels of message in the fictional presentation of "reality." The drama is especially interesting in this respect, with both performers and spectators responding to messages about both the actual and the theatrical reality.

We are giving extensive attention to hypnosis. A great array of phenomena that occur as schizophrenic symptoms—hallucinations, delusions, alterations of personality, amnesias, and so on—can be produced temporarily in normal subjects with hypnosis. These need not be directly suggested as specific phenomena, but can be the "spontaneous" result of an arranged communication sequence. For example, Erickson[4] will produce a hallucination by first inducing catalepsy in a subject's hand and then saying, "There is no conceivable way in which your hand can move, yet when I give the signal, it must move." That is, he tells the subject his hand will remain in place, yet it will move, and in no way the subject can consciously conceive. When Erickson gives the signal, the subject hallucinates the hand moved, or hallucinates himself in a different place and therefore the hand moves. This use of hallucination to resolve a problem posed by contradictory commands which cannot be discussed seems to us to illustrate the solution of a double bind situation via a shift in Logical Types. Hypnotic responses to direct suggestions or statements also commonly involve shifts in type, as in accepting the words "Here's a glass of water" or "You feel tired" as external or internal reality, or in literal response to metaphorical statements, much like schizophrenics. We hope that further study of hypnotic induction, phenomena, and waking will, in this controllable situation, help sharpen our views of the essential communicational sequences which produce phenomena like those of schizophrenia.

Another Erickson experiment[12] seems to isolate a double bind communicational sequence without the specific use of hypnosis. Erickson arranged a seminar so as to have a young chain smoker sit next to him and to be without cigarettes; other participants were briefed on what to do. All was ordered so that Erickson repeatedly turned to offer the young man a cigarette, but was always interrupted by a question from someone so that he turned away, "inadvertently" withdrawing the cigarettes from the young man's reach. Later another participant asked this young man if he had received the cigarette from Dr. Erickson. He replied, "What cigarette?", showed clearly that he had forgotten the whole sequence, and even refused a cigarette offered by another member, saying that he was too interested in the seminar discussion to smoke. This young man seems to us to be in an experimental situation paralleling the schizophrenic's double bind situation with mother: An important relationship, contradictory messages (here of giving and taking away), and comment blocked—because there was a seminar going on, and anyway it was all "inadvertent." And note the similar outcome: Amnesia for the double bind sequence and reversal from "He doesn't give" to "I don't want."

Although we have been led into these collateral areas, our main field of observation has been schizophrenia itself. All of us have worked directly with schizophrenic patients and much of this case material has been recorded on tape for detailed study. In addition, we are recording interviews held jointly with patients and their families, and we are taking sound motion pictures of mothers and disturbed, presumably preschizophrenic, children. Our hope is that these operations will provide a clearly evident record of the continuing, repetitive double binding which we hypothesize goes on steadily from infantile beginnings in the family situation of individuals who become schizophrenic. This basic family situation, and the overtly communicational characteristics of schizophrenia, have been the major focus of this paper. However, we expect our concepts and some of these data will also be useful in future work on other problems of schizophrenia, such as the variety of other symptoms,

the character of the "adjusted state" before schizophrenia becomes manifest, and the nature and circumstances of the psychotic break.

THERAPEUTIC IMPLICATIONS OF THIS HYPOTHESIS

Psychotherapy itself is a context of multilevel communication, with exploration of the ambiguous lines between the literal and metaphoric, or
reality and fantasy, and indeed, various forms of play, drama, and hypnosis have been used extensively in therapy. We have been interested in
therapy, and in addition to our own data we have been collecting and
examining recordings, verbatim transcripts, and personal accounts of
therapy from other therapists. In this we prefer exact records since we
believe that how a schizophrenic talks depends greatly, though often
subtly, on how another persons talks to him; it is most difficult to estimate
what was really occurring in a therapeutic interview if one has only a
description of it, especially if the description is already in theoretical terms.

Except for a few general remarks and some speculation, however, we
are not yet prepared to comment on the relation of the double bind to
psychotherapy. At present we can only note:

1. Double bind situations are created by and within the psychotherapeutic setting and the hospital milieu. From the point of view of
this hypothesis we wonder about the effect of medical "benevolence" on
the schizophrenic patient. Since hospitals exist for the benefit of personnel as well as—as much as—more than—for the patient's benefit, there
will be contradictions at times in sequences where actions are taken
"benevolently" for the patient when actually they are intended to keep
the staff more comfortable. We would assume that whenever the system
is organized for hospital purposes and it is announced to the patient that
the actions are for *his* benefit, then the schizophrenogenic situation is
being perpetuated. This kind of deception will provoke the patient to
respond to it as a double bind situation, and his response will be "schizophrenic" in the sense that it will be indirect and the patient will be unable
to comment on the fact that he feels that he is being deceived. One
vignette, fortunately amusing, illustrates such a response. On a ward with
a dedicated and "benevolent" physician in charge there was a sign on the
physician's door which said "Doctor's Office. Please Knock." The
doctor was driven to distraction and finally capitulation by the obedient
patient who carefully knocked every time he passed the door.

2. The understanding of the double bind and its communicative
aspects may lead to innovations in therapeutic technique. Just what these
innovations may be is difficult to say, but on the basis of our investigation
we are assuming that double bind situations occur consistently in psychotherapy. At times these are inadvertent in the sense that the therapist is
imposing a double bind situation similar to that in the patient's history,

or the patient is imposing a double bind situation on the therapist. At other times therapists seem to impose double binds, either deliberately or intuitively, which force the patient to respond differently than he has in the past.

An incident from the experience of a gifted psychotherapist illustrates the intuitive understanding of a double bind communicational sequence. Dr. Frieda Fromm-Reichmann[5] was treating a young woman who from the age of seven had built a highly complex religion of her own replete with powerful Gods. She was very schizophrenic and quite hesitant about entering into a therapeutic situation. At the beginning of the treatment she said, "God R says I shouldn't talk with you." Dr. Fromm-Reichmann replied, "Look, let's get something into the record. To me God R doesn't exist, and that whole world of yours doesn't exist. To you it does, and far be it from me to think that I can take that away from you, I have no idea what it means. So I'm willing to talk with you in terms of that world, if only you know I do it so that we have an understanding that it doesn't exist for me. Now go to God R and tell him that we have to talk and he should give you permission. Also you must tell him that I am a doctor and that you have lived with him in his kingdom now from seven to sixteen—that's nine years—and he hasn't helped you. So now he must permit me to try and see whether you and I can do that job. Tell him that I am a doctor and this is what I want to try."

The therapist has her patient in a "therapeutic double bind." If the patient is rendered doubtful about her belief in her god then she is agreeing with Dr. Fromm-Reichmann, and is admitting her attachment to therapy. If she insists that God R is real, then she must tell him that Dr. Fromm-Reichmann is "more powerful" than he—again admitting her involvement with the therapist.

The difference between the therapeutic bind and the original double bind situation is in part the fact that the therapist is not involved in a life and death struggle himself. He can therefore set up relatively benevolent binds and gradually aid the patient in his emancipation from them. Many of the uniquely appropriate therapeutic gambits arranged by therapists seem to be intuitive. We share the goal of most psychotherapists who strive toward the day when such strokes of genius will be well enough understood to be systematic and commonplace.

REFERENCES

1. BATESON, G. 1942. Social planning and the concept of 'deutero learning'. *Science, philosophy and religion : Second symposium.* Conference on Science, Philosophy and Religion. Harper, New York.
2. BATESON, G. 1955. A theory of play and fantasy. *Psychiat. Res. Rep.,* **2,** 39-51.
3. CARPENTER, C. R. 1934. A field study of the behavior and social relations of howling monkeys. *Comp. Psychol. Monogr.,* **10,** 1-168.

4. ERICKSON, M. H. 1955. Personal communication.
5. FROMM-REICHMANN, F. 1956. Personal communication.
6. HALEY, J. 1955. Paradoxes in play, fantasy, and psychotherapy. *Psychiat. Res. Rep.*, **2**, 52-58.
7. HARLOW, H. F. 1949. The formation of learning sets. *Psychol. Rev.*, **56**, 51-65.
8. HILGARD, J. R. 1953. Anniversary reactions in parents precipitated by children. *Psychiatry*, **16**, 73-80.
9. HULL, C. L., *et al.* 1940. *Mathematico-deductive theory of rote learning.* Yale Univ. Press, New Haven.
10. JACKSON, D. D. 1954. An episode of sleepwalking. *J. Am. psychoanal. Ass.*, **2**, 503-508.
11. JACKSON, D. D. 1954. Some factors influencing the Oedipus complex. *Psychoanal. Q.*, **23**, 566-581.
12. JACKSON, D. D. 1954. *The question of family homeostasis.* Presented at the American Psychiatric Association meeting, St. Louis, May 7.
13. LORENZ, K. Z. 1952. *King Solomon's ring.* Crowell, New York.
14. PERCEVAL, J. 1836. *A narrative of the treatment experienced by a gentleman during a state of mental derangement, designed to explain the causes and nature of insanity, etc.* Effingham Wilson, London.
15. RUESCH, J., and BATESON, G. 1951. *Communication: The social matrix of psychiatry.* Norton, New York.
16. VON DOMARUS, E. 1944. The specific laws of logic in schizophrenia. In KASANIN, J. S. (ed.) *Language and thought in schizophrenia.* Univ. of California Press, Berkeley and Los Angeles.
17. WHITEHEAD, A. N., and RUSSELL, B. 1910. *Principia mathematica.* Cambridge Univ. Press, Cambridge.

XLI

A REVIEW OF THE DOUBLE BIND THEORY

PAUL WATZLAWICK

The 'double bind' theory is reassessed, reviewed, and brought up to date.

In 1956, Bateson, Jackson, Haley, and Weakland reported on a research project which they had undertaken to formulate and test a new view on the nature of schizophrenic communication. This report was entitled "Toward a Theory of Schizophrenia",[97]* and postulates the concept of the *double bind*.

The present paper has the purpose of reviewing the literature of the last five years (1957-1961 inclusive) and assessing the attention the concept has found in psychiatric thinking.

This review is based on a search of 37 American and European periodicals and of other pertinent publications in the field of psychiatry and of the behavioral sciences in general. It should, therefore, be reasonably comprehensive.

At the outset it may be useful to state once more the definition of a double bind, as contained in the original paper:

The necessary ingredients for a double bind situation, as we see it, are:

1. *Two or more persons.* Of these, we designate one, for purposes of our definition, as the "victim." We do not assume that the double bind is inflicted by the mother alone, but that it may be done either by mother alone or by some combination of mother, father, and/or siblings.

2. *Repeated experience.* We assume that the double bind is a recurrent theme in the experience of the victim. Our hypothesis does not invoke a single traumatic experience, but such repeated experience that the double bind structure comes to be an habitual expectation.

3. *A primary negative injunction.* This may have either of two forms: (a) "Do

* Reprinted in this volume as No. XL.

Reprinted from FAMILY PROCESS, Vol. 2, No. 1, March 1963, pp. 132-153.

not do so and so, or I will punish you," (b) "If you do not do so and so, I will punish you." Here we select a context of learning based on avoidance of punishment rather than a context of reward seeking. There is perhaps no formal reason for this selection. We assume that the punishment may be either the withdrawal of love or the expression of hate or anger—or most devastating—the kind of abandonment that results from the parent's expression of extreme helplessness. (Our concept of punishment is being refined at present. It appears to us to involve perceptual experience in a way that cannot be encompassed by the notion of "trauma.")

4. *A secondary injunction conflicting with the first at a more abstract level, and like the first enforced by punishments or signals which threaten survival.* This secondary injunction is more difficult to describe than the primary for two reasons. First, the secondary injunction is commonly communicated to the child by nonverbal means. Posture, gesture, tone of voice, meaningful action, and the implications concealed in verbal comment may all be used to convey this more abstract message. Second, the secondary injunction may impinge upon any element of the primary prohibition. Verbalization of the secondary injunction may, therefore, include a wide variety of forms; for example, "Do not see this as punishment"; "Do not see me as the punishing agent"; "Do not submit to my prohibitions"; "Do not think of what you must not do"; "Do not question my love of which the primary prohibition is (or is not) an example"; and so on. Other examples become possible when the double bind is inflicted not by one individual but by two. For example, one parent may negate at a more abstract level the injunctions of the other.

5. *A tertiary negative injunction prohibiting the victim from escaping from the field.* In a formal sense it is perhaps unnecessary to list this injunction as a separate item since the reinforcement at the other two levels involves a threat to survival, and if the double binds are imposed during infancy, escape is naturally impossible. However, it seems that in some cases the escape from the field is made impossible by certain devices which are not purely negative, e.g., capricious promises of love, and the like.

6. Finally, the complete set of ingredients is no longer necessary when the victim has learned to perceive his universe in double bind patterns. Almost any part of a double bind sequence may then be sufficient to precipitate panic or rage. The pattern of conflicting injunctions may even be taken over by hallucinatory voices.[11a]

References to the *theoretical* aspects of the double bind are relatively few in number. Two brief references can be found in the *American Handbook of Psychiatry*; one by Ruesch[66] in his contribution to the "General Theory of Communication in Psychiatry," and the second by Cobb[22] in the chapter on Neurology. Cobb points to the fact that nervous and mental disorders are phenomena of such complexity that different conceptual frameworks can be used for their study without necessarily conflicting with one another. One of the examples he uses in support of this fact is schizophrenia which, according to the approach chosen, can be viewed as genogenic, histogenic, chemogenic, or psychogenic. As an explanatory principle for this latter category he mentions the double bind theory.

The general attitude towards the communicational approach to the problems of mental illness is well summarized by Mora[56] in his contribution to the *American Handbook of Psychiatry*, even though he does not specifically refer in it to the double bind theory:

> Outside the realm of psychoanalysis, but more in line with the American emphasis on the value of symbolic logic, of language, of interactional systems and the like, are the theoretical formulations by Jurgen Ruesch and Gregory Bateson of communication as the "social matrix of psychiatry." Although these formulations are still too recent to allow any historical judgment, they seem to be an expression of the "operationalistic" tendencies largely diffused in psychological quarters. As such, they are subjected to the same type of criticism leveled against conditioned reflex theory—namely, a lack of understanding of the basic inner condition of the patient. So far, they have met, if not open resistance, an attitude of caution.

Very few of the references to the double bind theory deal with what its originators consider the essential concept, i.e., the *Theory of Logical Types*. The reason for this is not clear. In the first place, it would appear that it is due to a rather widely though tacitly shared belief that a basic science like logic has no place in the behavioral sciences. Logic is not infrequently thought of as a dry abstraction too remote from the complexities of life to be of any help. Another possible reason is that rather unusual subjective difficulties oppose themselves to an awareness of the complex structure of the logical types. This is not too surprising once it is realized that one of the primary functions of the ego is to avoid a confustion of logical levels in all its dealings with outer and inner reality, and to protect the mind from the potential dangers of this confusion. Not unlike the resistance to the lifting into consciousness of unconscious emotional material, attempts at gaining introspection into the vital ego-function which normally guarantees proper dealing with the complexities and paradoxes of logical typing in everyday life and especially human communication, are likely to encounter similar difficulties. Anybody who has tried to tamper with the Pandora box of logical levels can attest to these formidable resistances. It is, therefore, difficult to appreciate Ostow's[58] sweeping statement that the double bind theory is "an example of . . . mathematico-logical pseudo-psychologizing." He goes on to say:

> In the journal *Behavior* (sic) one can find many attempts to apply . . . general systems theory to psychologic and psychiatric problems. I have yet to see such an attempt which has made a real contribution to our understanding. The reason for this failure is not that the theory is incorrect, nor even that it is essentially inapplicable to human behavior. In my opinion, the reason is that those who try to apply the theory, in general, refuse to deal with the ultimate variables of human behavior, as expressed in psychoanalytic metapsychology, and postulate their own variables based solely on naive, *a priori*, and invalid assumptions. Such assumptions, no matter how elegant the theory applied to them, can yield only naive and invalid conclusions.

Even an otherwise sympathetic reviewer of the double bind theory like Laing[47] has evident difficulty in seeing why the Theory of Logical Types should be invoked. "The authors," he writes

seem in doubt about what "frames of reference" to employ or develop in casting
their theory. They use the potentially fruitful though at present vague expression
"modes of communication," but they try to develop this formulation in terms of
Logical Types. But it is doubtful if the Logical Type theory they employ is any
longer viable.

The author does not elaborate further on the reasons for his doubt.

Again, it may be helpful to quote here from the original paper:

We hypothesize that there will be a breakdown in any individual's ability to
discriminate between Logical Types whenever a double bind situation occurs.
The general characteristics of this situation are the following:

1. When the individual is involved in an intense relationship; that is, a relationship in which he feels it is vitally important that he discriminate accurately
what sort of message is being communicated so that he may respond appropriately.

2. And, the individual is caught in a situation in which the other person in the
relationship is expressing two orders of message and one of these denies the other.

3. And, the individual is unable to comment on the messages being expressed
to correct his discrimination of what order of message to respond to, i.e., he
cannot make a metacommunicative statement.

Specific mention of Russell and Whitehead's Theory of Logical Types
and its application to the double bind theory is made by Szasz[82] in connection with his game-playing model of human behavior:

... It was not until 1922, however, that Russell explicitly applied the principles
of the theory of types to the logic of languages. This led to establishing hitherto
unexpected connections between mathematics, logic, linguistics, philosophy, and
finally psychiatry and the study of social behaviour ... I believe Bateson[94] was
the first to call attention to the significance of Russell's theory of types for psychiatry. Defining psychiatry as the study of (human) behaviour, he emphasized
the need to distinguish various levels of communications (i.e., communication
and metacommunication). In a recent essay, Bateson et al.[97] again made use of
Russell's theory of logical types, applying it to the elucidation of the communications which the schizophrenic patient and his significant objects characteristically
exchange with one another.

Logical typing of signals and multiple levels of learning were considered
in the original paper inseparable sets of phenomena—"inseparable because
the ability to handle the multiple types of signals is itself a *learned* skill
and therefore a function of the multiple levels of learning." As ten
thousands of pages of psychological journals bear evidence, learning
theory and learning experiments have received more attention than
probably any other psychological phenomenon. However, while the
vast majority of these papers are traditionally concerned with the acquisition of a single and isolated skill only, the learning theory approach
proposed here differs from them by taking into account the complexities
of discontinuous and multiple levels of learning.* During the period
under review at least two papers were published which deal with schizo-

---

* The postulation of these levels of learning preceded the double bind theory by
many years and was independently investigated by Hull et al.[46] in 1940, by Bateson[93] in
1942 and by Harlow[40] in 1949.

phrenia and learning theory and also refer to the double bind concept. One is by Mednik[54] who acknowledges the double bind concept as a theoretical explanation of the schizophrenic thinking disorder, but does so within a framework of escalating drive and anxiety patterns.

The other paper is by Rashkis and Singer[62] and is paradigmatic of a frequent misunderstanding of the double bind theory. In the part of their paper dealing with learning theory, these authors state:

Liddell has described an experiment in which a hungry rat is fed when he sees a circle but not when he sees an ellipse. The ellipse is then gradually made more circular and the circle more elliptical until the rat can no longer differentiate between them. This type of learning is usually referred to as DR, or "discrimination response," and in the experiment described by Liddell is seen the breakdown of such a learned reaction. Here, as the discrimination is made successively more difficult, there is, to be sure, at first an improved differentiation, but this then levels off, becomes worse, and finally disappears altogether; the rat no longer acts as though he could distinguish circles from ellipses. The outcome is what has been referred to as an experimental neurosis, or, better, psychosis.

What Bateson has called the "double bind," and what in Lewinian terms we have called a conflict of avoidances, may now be seen more sharply in terms of a failure in discrimination.

We hold that this conclusion is erroneous. The double bind is *not* a failure in discrimination, nor is this experiment itself conclusive of such a phenomenon. Weakland and Jackson[102] pointed out the non-Pavlovian aspects of these discrimination experiments and recently Bateson[98] has stated:

In the well-known experiments in which an animal subject is reduced to psychotic behavior by first training the subject to discriminate e.g. between an ellipse and a circle and then making the discrimination impossible, the "trauma" is not as is commonly stated, the "breakdown of discrimination" but is the breakdown of that pattern of complex contingencies which the experimenter had previously taught to the animal. As I see it, what happens at the climax of the experiment is that the animal is penalized for following a deeply unconscious and abstract pattern which the psychologist previously rewarded. It is not that the animal cannot discriminate, it is that the animal is put in error when he thinks that this is a context for discrimination.*

* Animal experiments have also shown that an untrained animal, exposed from the very beginning to a universe in which discrimination is impossible because all events are made by the experimenter to occur at random, will adapt to this kind of contingency pattern and will not exhibit the specific pathology described above.
It would appear, however, that not any breaking of a previously established contingency pattern leads to pathology. In the course of his life an individual is again and again confronted with situations for which neither past experience nor the present context offer an adequate explanation. These situations can be extremely stressful and anxiety-producing, but are certainly not pathogenic *per se*. After all, millions of people grow up, resolve the problem of becoming independent while still remaining emotionally attached to their parents, adapt to different cultural patterns and somehow bridge similar paradoxes without turning schizophrenic. But in most of these typical situations, the individual can either remove himself physically, comment on the inconsistency of the injunctions imposed upon him, reject or modify them, leave the field in some other way or —most important of all—maintain his basic premises and at the same time expand them

There is considerable discrepancy of opinion as to the *pathogenicity* of the double bind. In this connection it may be helpful to repeat here the view of the authors expressed in their original paper:

> If our formal summary of the symptomatology is correct and if the schizophrenia of our hypothesis is essentially a result of family interaction, it should be possible to arrive *a priori* at a formal description of these sequences of experience which would induce such a symptomatology. What is known of learning theory combines with the evident fact that human beings use *context* as a guide for mode discrimination. Therefore, we must look not for some specific traumatic experience in the infantile etiology but rather for characteristic sequential patterns. The specificity for which we search is to be at an abstract or formal level. The sequences must have this characteristic: that from them the patient will acquire the mental habits which are exemplified in schizophrenic communications. That is to say, *he must live in a universe where the sequences of events are such that his unconventional communicational habits will be in some sense appropriate.* The hypothesis which we offer is that sequences of this kind in the external experience of the patient are responsible for the inner conflicts of logical typing. For such unresolvable sequences of experiences, we use the term "double bind."

The existence of these sequential patterns in schizophrenia is denied by Singer[76] and Sanua[68] in very brief references. It must be reiterated, however, that these patterns occur on an abstract level and are usually of a very subtle nature.* Arieti,[7, 8] Ackerman,[2, 3] and Bruch,[14, 16] while validating the usefulness of the double bind concept, question the pathogenicity on different grounds, and seem to overlook what in the original paper was defined as the *tertiary negative injunction prohibiting the victim from escaping from the field.* Arieti, for instance, points out that

> ... all of us would agree that our schizophrenic patients have been repeatedly exposed to this double-bind situation. But I think we would also agree that many neurotics were exposed, and many normal people, and we, too.

However, while this is undoubtedly correct, the long-lasting exposure to double binds which is part and parcel of the family life of schizophrenics or of other schizophrenogenic life situations, and the impossibility of the victim's leaving the field and seeking corrective experiences and identifications outside the family, is not sufficiently accounted for by these authors. As Foudraine,[36] in taking issue with Arieti's view, points out:

> so as to include the new contingencies. This is not to imply that we are blind to the high incidence of schizophrenia in all phases of life involving the breaking-up of an old pattern. But we do suggest that the individuals who cannot master these situations are the ones who in their early experiences were threatened with punishment if they tried to leave the field or even showed that they were aware of the paradox imposed upon them— in other words: who had been double-bound. (Cf. in this context also Leder,[48] Stierlin[79] and Lu.[52]) It is on these grounds that we doubt the specificity of Devereux's Sociological Theory of Schizophrenia,[28] proposed in 1939, of which—according to him[29]—the double bind theory is an independent rediscovery.

> * May it here suffice to point out that specific double bind sequences have been unfailingly present in the approximately 50 families so far studied both by the Bateson Group (Project for the Study of Schizophrenic Communication) and the staff of the Mental Research Institute. An Anthology tape of typical interchanges is being prepared and should be available in the not too distant future.

This double-bind hypothesis, attempting to explain in terms of a learning-theory, the serious communicational disorders of the schizophrenic patient which drive him to a state of progressive isolation, is certainly very fascinating. Arieti, in a critical comment, considers the mechanisms of the double-bind non-specific for schizophrenia or neurosis. According to him human beings are constantly exposed to these double or multiple-bind situations. He compares the situation with that of divided loyalty and believes that the mechanism is not pathological in itself, but rather in the way the parents make use of it. I doubt whether Arieti does justice to the double-bind theory.*

Laing[47] refers to the same phenomenon by stating:

The situation is sealed off for the "victim" by a further unavowed injunction for-bidding him or her to get out of the situation, or to dissolve it by commenting on it. The "victim" is thus in an "untenable" position. He cannot make a single move without evoking a threatened catastrophe. . . .

and Schwartz[72] by pointing to "the distortion or absence of a social en-vironment which facilitates appropriate discriminative responses." Alanen[4] also emphasizes "the intensive and enduring 'pseudo-mutuality' in the family relations of many schizophrenics, described by Wynne et al., as well as the double bind situation. . . ." Symonds[81] sees in the double bind situation one of the sources of the schizophrenic process but does not believe that it accounts for the entire disorder. Also, Rosenthal,[65] in a study on identity confusion in twins, refers to the double bind concept as one of the patterns of mother-child relationship leading to this con-fusion. Clausen and Kohn,[21] Rioch,[63] Meyers and Goldfarb,[55] Goldfarb,[38] Varley,[85] and Spiegen and Bell[78] concur in the specificity of the double bind situation in the families of schizophrenics.

With regard to the effect of a double bind on the victim, the original paper suggests that

. . . he must deceive himself about his own internal state in order to support mother in her deception. To survive with her, he must falsely discriminate his own internal messages as well as falsely discriminate the messages of others.

While this point seems to have been overlooked by Symonds,[81] it is emphasized by Bruch,[13, 14] McReynolds,[53] and Weigert.[88]

References to the *specific family structure* which is conducive to double bind situations are relatively numerous, though brief.[1, 10, 12, 21, 35, 37, 39, 45, 50, 61, 64, 83, 85, 89, 90, 91, 92] By and large, these authors agree that the mother is the dominant parent whose pathological influence on the child is not sufficiently counteracted by the typically rather weak or withdrawn father.

The *role of the mother* is treated in the original paper in detail and the repercussions of the patient's improvement either on the mother or on other family members (e.g. a sibling) are discussed. Bruch[13] concurs with this aspect of the mother-patient relationship and states:

* However, in the *American Handbook of Psychiatry*, Arieti[6] does suggest a higher frequency of double bind situations in the childhood of schizophrenics than of other people and sees in it one of the possible factors responsible for the general state of anxiety that eventually leads to the disorder.

It is also in line with the observation that the mother, or some other person, who was interacting with the patient in this [i.e. a double bind] pattern may become severely disturbed when the patient no longer responds in the accustomed way.

However, what the original paper omitted to mention more specifically (but what has since been dealt with in detail by Weakland[103]) is the fact that a double bind always binds *both* parties and that, strictly speaking, there is no "binder" and "bound," but rather *two* victims. This fact is most clearly stated by Laing[47]:

> ... One must constantly remember, of course, that the child from babyhood may put his parents into untenable positions. This may occur in the early baby-mother interaction where the baby cannot be satisfied. It cries "for" the breast. It cries when the breast is presented. Its crying is intensified when the breast is withdrawn. A mother unable to "click with" or "get through" to such a baby may become intensely anxious, and feel hopeless as a mother. She then withdraws from the baby in one sense, while becoming over-solicitous in another sense. Double binds are usually mutual.

The mutuality of the interaction between mother and child and especially the child's reaction to the mother is seen somewhat differently by Searles[73, 74, 75] who criticizes the purely negative role ascribed to the mother in the original paper. He claims that

> ... an even more powerful reason for the continuance of the symbiosis into the offspring's chronological adulthood, resides in his basically loving and loyal sacrifice of his own individuality in order to preserve the mother's unstable personality-equilibrium. He senses that his own sick personality-functioning dovetails with hers in such a way as to keep her head above water.[75]

Searles further draws attention to the playful quality which according to him exists in this interaction:

> Moreover, while Bateson et al. brilliantly describe the complexity of the incessant jockeying for position that goes on between patient and mother, they seem unaware that this jockeying can involve an element of covert, but intensely and mutually pleasurable, playfulness with this endlessly fascinating, complex "game," as I have repeatedly discovered with my patients, relatively late in the course of therapy. The authors dwell upon this as being solely in the nature of anguished, conflictual, desperate relatedness.[73]

However, from the above it is not quite clear whether Searles refers here to the actual mother-child interaction *in* a double bind situation, or to the particular game-like quality of that later stage of a successful psychotherapy of a schizophrenic which is, for instance, described by Scheflen[71] in his extensive report on John Rosen's direct analysis and the deliberate use of therapeutic double binds by that therapist. In another paper Scheflen[70] refers to the occurrence of double binds in regressive one-to-one relationships in general and not only in the classic mother-child symbiosis. The mutuality of double-binding is also recognized by Ackerman,[2] Perr,[60] and Boszormenyi-Nagy,[9] whereas Hoffer and Callbeck[43] question the validity of the double bind theory on the assumption that the

. . . basic fault may be within the illness and not be a result of faulty transmission. The error may be a faulty receiver. It is difficult to understand why a schizophrenic person should be so perceptive of mother's faulty signals and be so unaware of his own.

The authors, unfortunately, do not elaborate, and especially their statement about the patient's unawareness remains unclear. How skilled the schizophrenic usually is in manipulating his environment is, on the other hand, borne out by Arieti[7]: "At times the psychotic masters the situation by shifting to the metaphoric field; more often, he becomes an expert in setting double bind situations."

What is the relationship of the double bind theory to the classic concept of *ambivalence*? It will be remembered that ambivalence in Bleuler's sense is the simultaneous presence of mutually contradictory "psychisms" —in particular love and hate (emotional ambivalence)—and that Bleuler thinks of it as a *manifestation* of schizophrenia and not as a *pathogenic* factor. Furthermore, it is described as a purely intrapsychic phenomenon and not as an interactional pattern. Arieti[7] considers the double bind "a special ambivalence, inasmuch as it is not merely indecision between possible alternatives, but a circular process, or a feedback mechanism." Cornelison[25] feels that the reader might consider the double bind concept "as a warmed-over version of ambivalence," while the original paper presents it as a communicational experience which, Cornelison suggests, is "an added dimension to the idea of ambivalence." However, once the idea of the multiplicity of levels in human communication is accepted, it will be seen that feelings like love and hate, hope and fear, wanting and not wanting, can share the same more abstract premises and do not, therefore, necessarily contradict each other at that (meta-) level.

It is suggested in the original paper that anybody caught in a double bind situation will feel "on the spot" and that his ability for correct discrimination of logical types will be impaired. It is also pointed out that the schizophrenic feels so terribly on the spot at all times that he habitually responds with defensive maneuvers involving shifts in the levels of communication, e.g. between the literal and the metaphorical. As the original paper puts it:

His (the schizophrenic's) metacommunicative system—the communications about communication—would have broken down, and he would not know what kind of message a message was. If a person said to him, "what would you like to do today?" he would be unable to judge accurately by the context or by the tone of voice or gesture whether he was being condemned for what he did yesterday, or being offered a sexual invitation, or just what was meant.

The defensive maneuvers employed by the schizophrenic in this area, i.e. his shifts between the literal and the metaphorical, the use of unlabelled metaphor, disqualifications of self and others, the continuous incongruity between what is said and how it is qualified, the blocking of spontaneous comments, the phenomenon of symbolic language—

these typically schizophrenic ways of communicating are referred to in more or less detail by several authors in relation to the double bind theory.[7, 11, 13, 20, 30, 36, 75, 81] In particular Ferreira[32] has examined the characteristics of schizophrenic language in terms of the basic assumptions of the theory.

Turning now to the double bind and its *relation to the therapy of schizophrenia*, mention should first be made of an interesting contribution by Urquhart and Forrest[84] to the old controversy of biochemical versus psychological therapy. They report on an unsuccessful clinical trial of acetylpromazine and promazine hydrochloride in chronic schizophrenics. In the course of this trial, however, they noticed that the patients responded to the intensified attention they received from the doctors, and they suggest:

> The apparent benefit derived from weekly interviews, though based on a small number of patients, seems to be the most significant observation of this trial. From the historical standpoint we are in process of rediscovering what was known 150 years ago, namely that chronic patients are responsive to friendly interest and encouragement. But to be effective such interest must be directed within a conceptual framework regarding the nature of schizophrenia itself. If we believe in the psychogenesis of schizophrenia then clearly a psychotherapeutic approach is appropriate, though not necessarily effective. Such work has been reported by Bateson and his co-workers at Palo Alto (1956).

Several papers[2, 19, 59, 64] dealing with the treatment of the family as a unit, contain specific references to the double bind theory and its relevance in this type of therapeutic approach to psychosis.

J. H. Smith,[77] Hora[44] and Savage[69] warn of the subtle and yet very real danger of a double bind which the therapist may unwittingly impose on his psychotic patients. Savage, in particular, points out that:

> The inordinate investment of time and energy coupled with the scant return often reinforce the analyst's tendency to obtain narcissistic gratification at the patient's expense, by reason of the patient's helpless dependence on him; he may unconsciously need the patient to remain sick, and, while *consciously* enjoining him to growth and development, may, *unconsciously*, not welcome it at all. These conflicting conscious and unconscious messages to the patient that he both grow up and remain a child at the same time place the patient in the pathogenic "double-bind" situation described by Bateson, Jackson et al.

The problem of the *resolution of a pathogenic double bind* and of the use of *therapeutic double binds* has been dealt with by a number of authors. Reference must here again be made to Scheflen's rather extensive treatment of the subject.[70] Pointing out that John Rosen uses double-binding techniques in a highly intuitive and often not conscious way, the author states:

> The schizophrenic problems of symbiosis and the symbolic defect are probably related in mutual simultaneous causation. The fear of dying cements the symbiotic dependency and the training to remain symbiotic makes abstraction im-

possible. Theoretically, then, psychotic episodes of schizophrenia might be terminated by the formation of apparent symbiosis. Possibly this is a first stage in all successful interpersonal methods. Modification of schizophrenia itself, however, would require the repudiation of the infantile one-to-one phantasy or at least of the literal expectation of living in symbiosis.

The matter could be formulated in the language of the "double bind" by postulating that the basic implicit instruction of the schizophrenogenic parent is: "Remain symbiotically related to me." The explicit instruction, "Move away," is the aspect of parental rejection which Rosen and others have thought to be the whole communication. Rosen's portrayal and cues to non-literality are out-of-awareness just as were the parental instructions to remain attached. He thus tries to supply the missing metacommunication about the literality of remaining attached to a parent.

Some observations seem to strengthen these speculations. Those patients who appeared to comprehend that the idealizations were not to be taken literally, often showed rapid clinical improvement of psychosis. The "maturational spurts" mentioned above often accompanied Rosen's role-playing in which he contrasted sexual and parental roles and in which he offered evident metacommunications about their literality. Such patients developed a humorous, playful, game-like relationship with Rosen and at the same time they began to show pleasure, affection, and reduced anxiety. Such patients kidded with Rosen about faithfulness, sexuality, dependency and his professed maternalness. They teased him about his "trickery and deception" as if they understood it was somehow for their benefit. On the other hand the two patients who had the poorest result took every interchange with complete and serious literality. The suggestion that these simultaneous occurrences may be causally related is sufficient to warrant further study.

In another report from the Institute of Direct Analysis, English[31] reviews the double bind concept, but both his examples and his conclusions seem to miss the essential problem of a double bind. The boy who is *able* to convey to his mother the message that he had to go fishing without telling her, because otherwise he would have had to submit to her disapproval and stay home or defy her disapproval and feel guilty, is precisely *not* in a double bind. Similarly, in the example chosen by English from a therapy session, Rosen simply confronts the patient with the painful fact that the patient's family does not care for her, but nowhere in this interchange does Rosen resort to therapeutic double-binding techniques. Burton,[18] Hayward[41] and Hill[42] have presented extensive clinical case descriptions in the light of the double binds involved and the author's attempts at their resolution. They concur that the double bind theory opens up a new dimension to the understanding of schizophrenic behavior.

It may seem from the foregoing that it is sometimes extremely difficult to decide where the line between pathogenic and therapeutic double binds is to be drawn. While it is certainly true that "for successful psychotherapy, communication between therapist and patient must be clear and congruent" (Fine,[34]), or that successful teachers of emotionally disturbed children create an atmosphere which "appears to be singularly free from 'double bind' entanglements" (Bruch and Rosenkotter[15]), the use of a therapeutic double bind always implies a certain element of trickery.

Haley has shown that any kind of trance induction is a double bind phenomenon,[101] and the double binds inherent in humor, play, fantasy, etc. have been investigated by Bateson,[95, 96] Haley[100] and Fry.[99] Indeed, it would be impossible to imagine any emotional involvement, such as for instance courtship, in which double-binding does not constitute a core element.

Still on the subject of the resolution of double-binds in the treatment situation, mention must be made to various articles briefly dealing with different aspects of the problem, i.e. Novey,[57] Cohen,[23] Varley,[85] Lichtenberg and Pao,[49] and Ruesch.[67]

In a paper on *delinquency* and the rather suggestive similarities between the dynamics of schizophrenic and delinquent families, Ferreira[33] postulates the "split double-bind" as a characteristic pattern of interaction. According to him, the source of the messages is split and the victim is caught in a *bipolar* message emanating from father and mother separately. Furthermore, Ferreira claims, there is no tertiary negative injunction in the split double-bind, i.e., the victim can not only leave the field, but is often actually "pushed" out of it. The concept of the split double-bind is taken up by Coodley[24] in a paper on delinquency and addiction.

Brief references to double binds observable in *psychiatric training* can be found with Appel et al.,[5] Curran[27] and especially Coser[26] who deals with the plight of the psychiatric resident who must assume the role of a student with his seniors and a professional, non-student role with his patients.

Further extensions of the theory to non-schizophrenogenic stress situations are suggested by Arieti[7] with regard to loyalty problems, and the field of art and esthetics in general. The specific double bind situation inherent in an individual's position *vis-à-vis* society is formulated by Watts[87, cf. also 86]:

> Here, then, is a major contradiction in the rules of the social game. The members of the game are to play *as if* they were independent agents, but they are not to *know* that they are just playing as if! It is explicit in the rules that the individual is self-determining, but implicit that he is so only by virtue of the rules. Furthermore, while he is defined as an independent agent, he must not be so independent as not to submit to the rules which define him. Thus he is defined as an agent in order to be held responsible to the group for "his" actions. The rules of the game confer independence and take it away at the same time, without revealing the contradiction.

An appraisal of the double bind theory in the light of existentialism is presented by Burton[17] who contends

> ... that the problem of schizophrenia mirrors the problems of all people—that it represents one mode of existence among the many that can be chosen. It is one way of eluding the Absurd—that is, reality. The problem of schizophrenia has been called nothing more and nothing less than the problem of reality. The hypothesis of the "double bind," if removed from the limiting and situational context in which its authors place it, seems to be the problem of Absurd in the

larger sense. The Absurd is the double bind par excellence and the model for all others.

Except for the United Kingdom, the double bind theory seems to have found little attention in Europe.* This is not surprising when one bears in mind that psychiatric thinking in Europe is traditionally oriented either along strictly organistic lines or else has an intrapsychic orientation based on the principles of *monadic*, but not interactional psychology. Incidentally, even the translation of the term "double bind" into other languages is difficult. Thus, the best translation a bilingual author like Stierlin[80] has come up with in German is "Beziehungsfalle" (relationship trap). The German author Loch,[51] in a report on the pathogenesis and metapsychology of a case of schizophrenia, translates the term with "Zwickmühle," i.e. double mill.

REFERENCES

1. ACKERMAN, N. W. 1958. *The psychodynamics of family life*. Basic Books, New York.
2. ACKERMAN, N. W. 1960. Family-focused therapy of schizophrenia. In SHER, S. C., and DAVIS, H. R. (eds.) *The out-patient treatment of schizophrenia*. Grune & Stratton, New York.
2a. ACKERMAN, N. W. 1961. The schizophrenic patient and his family relationships: A conceptual basis for family focused therapy of schizophrenia. In GREENBLATT, M., LEVINSON, D. J., and KLERMAN, G. L. (eds.) *Mental patients in transition: Steps in hospital-community rehabilitation*. Thomas, Springfield, Ill.
3. ACKERMAN, N. W. 1960. Discussion of Hasting's paper 'Professional staff morale'. In SHER, S. C., and DAVIS, H. R. (eds.) *The out-patient treatment of schizophrenia*. Grune & Stratton, New York.
4. ALANEN, Y. 1960. Some thoughts on schizophrenia and ego development in the light of family investigations. *Archs gen. Psychiat.*, **3**, 650-656.
5. APPEL, K. E., GOODWIN, H. M., WOOD, H. P., and ASKREN, E. L. 1961. Training in psychotherapy: The use of marriage counseling in a university teaching clinic. *Am. J. Psychiat.*, **117**, 709-711.
6. ARIETI, S. 1959. Schizophrenia: The manifest symptomatology, the psychodynamic and formal mechanisms. *American handbook of psychiatry*, Chap. 23. Basic Books, New York.
7. ARIETI, S. 1960. Recent conceptions and misconceptions of schizophrenia. *Am. J. Psychother.*, **14**, 3-29.
8. ARIETI, S. 1960. Discussion of Ackerman's paper 'Family-focused therapy of schizophrenia.' In SHER, S. C., and DAVIS, H. R. (eds.) *The out-patient treatment of schizophrenia*. Grune & Stratton, New York.
9. BOSZORMENYI-NAGY, I. 1962. The concept of schizophrenia from the perspective of family treatment. *Family Process*, **1**, 103-113.
10. BOWEN, M. 1960. A family concept of schizophrenia. In JACKSON, D. D. (ed.) *The etiology of schizophrenia*. Basic Books, New York.
11. BRADY, J. P. 1958. Language in schizophrenia. *Am. J. Psychother.*, **12**, 473-487.

* It was introduced in the European literature by Bruch.[13]

12. BRODY, E. B. 1961. Social conflict and schizophrenic behavior in young adult negro males. *Psychiatry*, **24**, 337-346.
13. BRUCH, H. 1959. Studies in schizophrenia: Psychotherapy with schizophrenics. *Acta psychiat. scand.*, **34** (Suppl. 130), 28-48.
14. BRUCH, H. 1961. Transformation of oral impulses in eating disorders: A conceptual approach. *Psychiat. Q.*, **35**, 458-481.
15. BRUCH, H., and ROSENKOTTER, L. 1960. Psychotherapeutic aspects of teaching emotionally disturbed children. *Psychiat. Q.*, **34**, 648-657.
16. BRUCH, H., and PALOMBO, S. 1961. Conceptual problems in schizophrenia. *J. nerv. ment. Dis.*, **132**, 114-117.
17. BURTON, A. 1960. Schizophrenia and existence. *Psychiatry*, **23**, 385-394.
18. BURTON, A. 1960. The quest for the golden mean: A study in schizophrenia, in BURTON, A. (ed.) *Psychotherapy of the psychoses*. Basic Books, New York.
19. CARROLL, E. J. 1960. Treatment of the family as a unit. *Penn. med. J.*, **63**, 57-62.
20. CHAPMAN, L. J. 1960. Confusion of figurative and literal usages of words by schizophrenics and brain-damaged patients. *J. abnorm. soc. Psychol.*, **60**, 412-416.
21. CLAUSEN, J., and KOHN, M. L. 1960. Social relations and schizophrenia: A research report and a perspective. In JACKSON, D. D. (ed.) *The etiology of schizophrenia*. Basic Books, New York.
22. COBB, S. 1959. Neurology. In ARIETI, S. (ed.) *American handbook of psychiatry*, Pt. 12, Chap. 81. Basic Books, New York.
23. COHEN, R. A. 1958. The hospital as a therapeutic instrument. *Psychiatry*, **21**, 29-35.
24. COODLEY, A. E. 1961. Current aspects of delinquency and addiction. *Archs gen. Psychiat.*, **4**, 632-640.
25. CORNELISON, F. S. 1959. Review of WHITACKER, C. (ed.) 'Psychotherapy with chronic schizophrenics,' in *Psychosom., Med.*, **21**, 84-85.
26. COSER, R. L. 1960. Laughter among colleagues. *Psychiatry*, **23**, 81-95.
27. CURRAN, C. A. 1961. Counseling skills adapted to the learning of foreign languages. *Bull. Menninger Clin.*, **25**, 78-93.
28. DEVEREUX, G. 1939. A sociological theory of schizophrenia. *Psychoanal. Rev.*, **26**, 315-234.
29. DEVEREUX, G. 1959. The nature of the bizarre: A study of a schizophrenic's pseudo slip of the tongue. *J. Hillside Hosp.*, 8, 266-278.
30. DITTMANN, A. D., and WYNNE, L. C. 1961. Linguistic techniques and the analysis of emotionality in interviews. *J. abnorm. soc. Psychol.*, **63**, 201-204.
31. ENGLISH, O. S. 1961. Clinical observations on direct analysis. In ENGLISH, O.S., *et al.* (eds.) *Direct analysis and schizophrenia: Clinical observations and evaluations*. Grune & Stratton, New York.
32. FERREIRA, A. J. 1960. The semantics and the context of the schizophrenic's language. *Archs gen. Psychiat.*, **3**, 128-138.
33. FERREIRA, A. J. 1960. The 'double-bind' and delinquent behavior. *Archs gen. Psychiat.*, **3**, 359-367.
34. FINE, L. J. 1959. Nonverbal aspects of psychodrama. In MASSERMAN, J. M., and MORENO, J. L. (eds.) *Progress in psychotherapy*. Grune & Stratton, New York.
35. FLECK, S. 1960. Family dynamics and origin of schizophrenia. *Psychosom. Med.*, **22**, 333-344.
36. FOUDRAINE, J. 1961. Schizophrenia and the family: A survey of the literature 1956-1960 on the etiology of schizophrenia. *Acta psychother.*, **9**, 82-110.
37. GARMEZY, N., CLARKE, A. R., and STOCKNER, C. 1961. Child rearing atti-

tudes of mothers and fathers as reported by schizophrenic and normal parents. *J. abnorm. soc. Psychol.*, **63**, 178-182.

38. GOLDFARB, W. 1961. The mutual impact of mother and child in childhood schizophrenia. *Am. J. Orthopsychiat.*, **31**, 738-747.

39. GROTJAHN, M. 1960. Trends in contemporary psychotherapy and the future of mental health. *Br. J. med. Psychol.*, **33**, 263-267.

40. HARLOW, H. F. 1949. The formation of learning sets. *Psychol. Rev.*, **56**, 51-65.

41. HAYWARD, M. L. 1960. Schizophrenia and the 'double-bind'. *Psychiat. Q.*, **34**, 89-91.

42. HILL, L. B. 1957. Psychotherapy of a schizophrenic. *Am. J. Psychoanal.*, **17**, 99-109.

43. HOFFER, A., and CALLBECK, M. J. 1960. Drug-induced schizophrenia. *J. ment. Sci.*, **106**, 138-159.

44. HORA, T. 1959. Epistemological aspects of existence and psychotherapy. *J. indiv. Psychol.*, **15**, 166-173.

45. HORA, T. 1959. Ontic perspectives in psychoanalysis. *Am. J. Psychother.*, **19**, 134-142.

46. HULL, C. L., HOVLAND, C. L., ROSS, R. T., *et al.* 1940. *Mathematico-deductive theory of rote learning : A study in scientific methodology.* Yale Univ. Press, New Haven.

47. LAING, R. D. 1961. *The self and others. Further studies in sanity and madness.* Tavistock Publications, London.

48. LEDER, H. H. 1959. *Acculturation and the 'double-bind'.* M.A. thesis, Dept. of Anthropology, Stanford University.

49. LICHTENBERG, J. D., and PAO, PING-NIE. 1960. The prognostic and therapeutic significance of the husband-wife relationship for hospitalized schizophrenic women. *Psychiatry*, **23**, 209-213.

50. LIDZ, T., CORNELISON, A., TERRY, D., and FLECK, S. 1958. Intrafamilial environment of the schizophrenic patient: VI. The transmission of irrationality. *Archs neurol. Psychiat.*, **79**, 305-316.

51. LOCH, W. 1961. Anmerkungen zur Pathogenese und Metapsychologie einer schizophrenen Psychose. *Psyche, Berl.*, **15**, 684-720.

52. LU, Y. C. 1962. Contradictory parental expectations in schizophrenia. *Archs gen. Psychiat.*, **6**, 219-234.

53. McREYNOLDS, P. 1960. Anxiety, perception and schizophrenia. In JACKSON, D. D. (ed.) *The etiology of schizophrenia.* Basic Books, New York.

54. MEDNIK, S. A. 1958. A learning theory approach to research in schizophrenia. *Psychol. Bull.*, **55**, 316-327.

55. MEYERS, D. I., and GOLDFARB, W. 1961. Studies of perplexity in mothers of schizophrenic children. *Am. J. Orthopsychiat.*, **31**, 551-564.

56. MORA, G. 1959. Recent American psychiatric developments (since 1939). In ARIETI, S. (ed.) *American handbook of psychiatry.* Basic Books, New York.

57. NOVEY, S. 1960. The outpatient treatment of borderline paranoid states, *Psychiatry*, **23**, 357-364.

58. OSTOW, M. 1960. Discussion of ARIETI's 'Recent conceptions and misconceptions of schizophrenia'. *Am. J. Psychother.*, **14**, 23-29.

59. PARLOFF, M. B. 1961. The family in psychotherapy. *Archs gen. Psychiat.*, **4**, 445-451.

60. PERR, H. M. 1958. Criteria distinguishing parents of schizophrenic and normal children. *Archs Neurol. Psychiat.*, **79**, 217-224.

61. QUERY, J. M. N. 1961. Pre-morbid adjustment and family structure: A

comparison of selected rural and urban men. *J. nerv. ment. Dis.*, **133**, 333-338.

62. RASHKIS, H. A., and SINGER, R. D. 1959. The psychology of schizophrenia. *Archs gen. Psychiat.*, **1**, 406-416.

63. RIOCH, D. McK. 1961. The sense and the noise. *Psychiatry*, **24**, 7-18, (Suppl. to No. 2).

64. ROSENBAUM, C. P. 1961. Patient-family similarities in schizophrenia. *Archs gen. Psychiat.*, **5**, 120-126.

65. ROSENTHAL, D. 1960. Confusion of identity and the frequency of schizophrenia in twins. *Archs gen. Psychiat.*, **3**, 297-304.

66. RUESCH, J. 1959. General theory of communication in psychiatry. In ARIETI, S. (ed.) *American handbook of psychiatry.* Basic Books, New York.

67. RUESCH, J. 1961. *Therapeutic communications.* Norton, New York.

68. SANUA, VICTOR D. 1961. Sociocultural factors in families of schizophrenics: A review of the literature. *Psychiatry*, **24**, 246-265.

69. SAVAGE, C. 1961. Countertransference in the therapy of schizophrenics. *Psychiatry*, **24**, 53-60.

70. SCHEFLEN, A. E. 1960. Regressive one-to-one relationships. *Psychiat. Q.*, **34**, 692-709.

71. SCHEFLEN, A. E. 1961. *A psychotherapy of schizophrenia: Direct analysis.* Thomas, Springfield, Ill.

72. SCHWARTZ, D. P. 1959. The integrative effect of participation. *Psychiatry*, **22**, 81-86.

73. SEARLES, H. F. 1958. Positive feelings in the relationship between the schizophrenic and his mother. *Int. J. Psychoanal.*, **39**, 569-586.

74. SEARLES, H. F. 1959. The effort to drive the other person crazy—An element in the aetiology and psychotherapy of schizophrenia. *Br. J. med. Psychol.*, **32**, 1-18.

75. SEARLES, H. F. 1959. Integration and differentiation in schizophrenia: An over-all view. *Br. J. med. Psychol.*, **32**, 261-281.

76. SINGER, R. D. 1960. Organization as a unifying concept in schizophrenia. *Archs gen. Psychiat.*, **2**, 61-74.

77. SMITH, J. H. 1960. The metaphor of the manic-depressive. *Psychiatry*, **23**, 375-383.

78. SPIEGEL, J. P., and BELL, N. W. 1959. The family of the psychiatric patient. In ARIETI, S. (ed.) *American handbook of psychiatry.* Basic Books, New York.

79. STIERLIN, H. 1959. The adaptation to the 'stronger' person's reality: Some aspects of the symbiotic relationship of the schizophrenic. *Psychiatry*, **22**, 143-152.

80. STIERLIN, H. 1959/60. Report on the Hawaiian Divisional Meeting of the American Psychiatric Association, May 1958. *Psyche, Berl.*, **13**, 843-845.

81. SYMONDS, A. 1960. Discussion of ARIETI's 'Recent conceptions and misconceptions of schizophrenia'. *Am. J. Psychother.*, **14**, 21-23.

82. SZASZ, T. S. 1961. *The myth of mental illness: Foundations of a theory of personal conduct.* Hoeber-Harper, New York.

83. TITCHENER, J., and EMERSON, R. 1958. Some methods for the study of family interaction in personality development. *Psychiat. Res. Rep.*, No. 10, 72-88.

84. URQUHART, R., and FORREST, A. D. 1959. Clinical trial of promazine hydrochloride and acetylpromazine in chronic schizophrenic patients. *J. ment. Sci.*, **105**, 260-264.

85. VARLEY, B. K. 1959. 'Reaching out' therapy with schizophrenic patients. *Am. J. Orthopsychiat.*, **29**, 407-416.

86. WATTS, A. W. 1958. *Nature, man and woman.* Pantheon Books, New York.
87. WATTS, A. W. 1961. *Psychotherapy east and west.* Pantheon Books, New York.
88. WEIGERT, E. 1960. Loneliness and trust—Basic factors of human existence. *Psychiatry*, **23**, 121-131.
89. WHITE, R. B. 1961. The mother-conflict in Schreber's psychosis. *Int. J. Psychoanal.*, **42**, 55-73.
90. WILL, O. A. 1959. Human relatedness and the schizophrenic reaction. *Psychiatry*, **22**, 205-223.
91. WOLMAN, B. B. 1961. The fathers of schizophrenic patients. *Acta psychother.*, **9**, 193-210.
92. WYNNE, L. C., RYCKOFF, I. M., DAY, J., and HIRSCH, S. I. 1958. Pseudo-mutuality in the family relations of schizophrenics. *Psychiatry*, **21**, 205-220.
93. BATESON, G. 1942. Social planning and the concept of 'deutero-learning,' *Science, philosophy, and religion : Second symposium.* Conference on Science, Philosophy and Religion. Harper, New York.
94. BATESON, G., and RUESCH, J. 1951. *Communication : The social matrix of psychiatry.* Norton, New York.
95. BATESON, G. 1955. A theory of play and fantasy. *Psychiat. Res. Rep.*, No. 2, 39-51.
96. BATESON, G. 1956. The message 'This is play', in *Second Conference on Group Processes.* Josiah Macy, Jr. Foundation, New York.
97. BATESON, G., JACKSON, D. D., HALEY, J., and WEAKLAND, J. H. 1956. Toward a theory of schizophrenia. *Behavl Sci.*, **1**, 251-264. [Reprinted in this collection as No. XL.]
98. BATESON, G. 1962. Exchange of information about patterns of human behavior. *Symposium on information storage and neural control*, Houston, Texas. (To be published.)
98a. BATESON, G. (ed.). 1961. *Perceval's narrative. A patient's account of his psychosis, 1830-1832.* Stanford Univ. Press, Stanford, Calif.
99. FRY, W. F. *Sweet madness : A study of humor.* Pacific Books, Palo Alto, Calif. (In press.)
100. HALEY, J. 1955. Paradoxes in play, fantasy, and psychotherapy. *Psychiat. Res. Rep.*, No. 2, 52-58.
101. HALEY, J. 1958. An interactional explanation of hypnosis. *Am. J. clin. Hyp.*, **1**, 41-57.
102. WEAKLAND, J. H., and JACKSON, D. D. 1958. Patient and therapist observations on the circumstances of a schizophrenic episode. *Archs Neurol. Psychiat.*, **79**, 554-574.
103. WEAKLAND, J. H. 1960. The double-bind hypothesis of schizophrenia and three-party interaction. In JACKSON, D. D. (ed.) *The etiology of schizophrenia.* Basic Books, New York.

XLII

SCHIZOPHRENIC PATIENTS AND THEIR SIBLINGS

THEODORE LIDZ, STEPHEN FLECK, YRJÖ O. ALANEN
AND ALICE CORNELISON

The Yale group of workers have made a significant contribution to the understanding of the intrafamilial environment of schizophrenics. Factors in the parents lead to deviant perception of himself in the child and are conducive to the production of schizophrenia.

A number of studies carried out by ourselves and others have demonstrated that schizophrenic patients virtually always grow up in seriously disturbed homes.[1,3,4,6,15,16,32] Since the finding provides one of the most consistent leads concerning the etiology of schizophrenia, we have been seeking to describe the characteristics of these families and to isolate factors that may be specific to the genesis of schizophrenia. The question has been raised repeatedly: If the family milieu is critical to the production of schizophrenia in a particular offspring, if it exerts a serious pathogenic influence upon this child, what about the siblings? Why are they not affected?

We designed our entire intensive study of the families of patients around this question, selecting only families in which the schizophrenic child had at least one sibling who could be studied. This permitted a comparison of the patients with persons who were not schizophrenic but who had been raised by the same parents and exposed to many similar intrafamilial influences. The siblings rather than some other arbitrarily selected persons form a comparative group—and we are pointedly avoiding

Reprinted by special permission of The William Alanson White Psychiatric Foundation, Inc., from PSYCHIATRY: JOURNAL FOR THE STUDY OF INTERPERSONAL PROCESSES, Vol. 26, No. 1, February 1963.

the term *controls*, since we do not believe that a true control series can be established in this type of study.

Of course, we do not aspire to a definitive answer, for if the question of why one child in a family rather than another becomes schizophrenic could be answered, the cause of schizophrenia would be virtually found. Genetic investigations, despite the impressive findings of twin studies, have thus far failed to produce evidence for either a dominant or a recessive trait.[14, 27, 29] Their failure may be due to primary reliance upon hospital records and the incidence of overt and flagrant schizophrenia. The contribution of the various genetic studies has recently been reviewed by Jackson, and currently Rosenthal is carefully examining their methodologies and findings.[13, 24, 26, 27] The evidence indicates that extragenetic influences play a very significant role. The scrutiny of our data can help clarify the problem, particularly along two lines: First, by noting the incidence of serious psychopathological conditions among the siblings. Second, by examining the differences in the intrafamilial influences impinging upon the siblings within a family with particular reference to (a) the changes in family circumstances and intrafamilial role relationships that alter the conditions under which siblings are raised; (b) the mother's capacities to provide affectionate nurturant care to the various siblings during infancy; (c) the different role allocations and role assumptions of the children in the family dynamics; (d) how the parental personalities and the configuration of their relationship lead children of one sex to be confronted by greater developmental problems than children of the opposite sex; (e) idiosyncratic problems; and (f) the influence of the siblings upon one another.

The findings to be presented are based upon the intensive study of sixteen families who had an adolescent or young adult offspring hospitalized in the Yale Psychiatric Institute. Inclusion in the series was based upon the availability of the mother and at least one sibling for repeated interviews, projective testing, and observation. In all except two families, the father was living and was included in the study, creating a bias toward unbroken families. With the exception of two upwardly mobile lower-middle-class families, all were upper-middle-class and upper-class families capable of supporting an offspring in a private hospital for prolonged periods. The distinct bias toward families with some degree of prestige in their communities was welcomed to minimize the potential effects of poor extrafamilial socioeconomic environments. The basic means of gaining information were repeated interviewing of all family members by the same social worker and by psychiatrists—the latter interviewing in some instances becoming synonymous with fairly intensive psychotherapy;[5] observing the interaction of family members with each other and hospital staff;[7] and projective testing of all family members.[29] Diaries, family friends, former teachers, and nursemaids were drawn into the study whenever feasible, and home visits were made in most cases.

Families were studied for periods ranging from six months to six years, and, except for the first three cases, all were actively studied for more than a year. Any attempt to reconstruct a family environment as it existed over a period of fifteen to thirty years will have grave deficiencies, but, with a few exceptions, these families are probably known more intimately than any series of families that have been studied for any purpose.

All of the families were seriously disturbed. The difficulties pervaded the entire family interaction and could not be encompassed by focusing upon isolated segments of the data alone, even though in a series of papers we have sought to focus on differing aspects of the family milieu and to analyze the family transactions from various perspectives. We have noted the severe psychopathology of the fathers as well as of the mothers,[17, 21] and we have found that these families were either schismatic—that is, dividing into two antagonistic and competing factions—or were "skewed" in that the serious personality disturbance of one parent set the pattern of family interaction.[18] We have described the irrational and paralogical modes of thinking and communicating that prevailed in these families, suggesting that the children received a very faulty training in reality testing.[19, 20, 22] We have also discovered that the parents commonly struggled with incestuous and homosexual tendencies themselves, and that the ensuing difficulties, together with the faulty family dynamics, left the schizophrenic offspring unable to resolve his Oedipal problems and gain a secure identity as a member of his or her sex.[8, 19] Our findings, though at times expressed in different terms, are very much in accord with those of Bateson and Jackson, Weakland, Wynne, Bowen, Brodey, Alanen, and others who have studied families of schizophrenic patients.[1, 2, 3, 4, 11, 30, 32] To summarize, we do not consider it likely that any single factor such as a faulty mother-infant relationship will prove to be responsible in itself for causing schizophrenia, but we have found that the structure and interaction of these families are highly detrimental to the ego development of children raised in them.

Studying these families has led to a search for the fundamentals in the organization of the family that are requisite for reasonably stable development of its offspring. We find that these parents fail to provide a satisfactory family milieu because they cannot form a coalition as members of the parental generation, maintaining their appropriate sex-linked roles, or transmit instrumentally valid ways of thinking, feeling, and communicating suited to the society into which the child must emerge. The child who grows up in a family lacking in these fundamentals has confused and confusing models for identification, has difficulty in achieving a sex-linked identity, in overcoming his incestuous attachments, and in finding meaningful and consistent guides for relating to others because of the deviant perception and cognition of himself and the world which he has acquired in his family.

Comparing the intrafamilial factors influencing the schizophrenic patient with those affecting his siblings obviously presents difficulties. The investigators are aware of the bias that can arise from the knowledge that one sibling is schizophrenic and another is not. As the difficulty is inherent in the study, nothing could be done except to take it into account. Another problem is that an intensive study including all family members could not encompass a large sample, and unless the study was intensive, it could not expect to gain meaningful answers. In the sixteen families the various combinations and sequences of brothers and sisters were limited, and some factors of potential pertinence require study of various permutations of gender and sequential placement within the family. Another limitation arises in presenting the material: It is difficult to compare the developmental situations of the siblings briefly, for the material is inordinately complex and properly would require a thorough exposition of each family.

The 'Normal' Sibling

Any intent to compare the development of the schizophrenic patient with that of 'normal' siblings had to be modified greatly for the simple but incontrovertible reason that only a small minority of the siblings could be considered reasonably well adjusted. While normality cannot be readily defined, everyone who has examined the material has been struck by the serious personality problems of the siblings as a group. The sixteen patients have a total of twenty-four siblings. Only five or six of the siblings are making reasonably adequate adjustments, and of these only three are considered well adjusted, even if the assessments are slanted favorably.* Examining the siblings for the presence of serious psychopathology, we find that three are clinically schizophrenic and another six or seven, including one who is a severe psychopathic personality, are making borderline and very tenuous adjustments. The remaining eight or nine siblings suffer from a variety of clinical neuroses, acting-out tendencies, and psychosomatic ailments, alone or in combination, for which four had required psychiatric treatment prior to the time of study (see Fig. 1).

The listing of psychiatric diagnoses for the siblings would serve little. The range and severity of their problems can be illustrated by citing the problems of the children in the two families with the largest number of siblings. By chance, one contained four sons and the other four daughters. In the Schwartz family,† the youngest son was the patient, a paranoid schizophrenic with delusions that people were against him, accusing him of homosexuality. His oldest brother was a severe sociopath, an em-

* Margaret Thaler Singer, in an unpublished investigation, estimated the stability of fourteen siblings of eleven schizophrenic patients through a study of their projective tests. She considered four to be constricted normals, five as moderately or severely neurotic, and five as clearly schizoid or latently schizophrenic.

† All names are fictitious.

bezzler, forger, and gambler. The second son had been disturbed in adolescence and may have been transiently delusional in early adult life, but had become a successful mathematician and had moved far away from the family and its problems. The third son was seriously phobic, suffered from anxiety, and was unable to practice his profession, although he managed to hold a routine job and to marry, living with his wife in the parental home.

The second daughter in the Thomas family had been schizophrenic for many years, the most chronic and withdrawn patient in the series. Her older sister had been in analysis for several years because of serious and diffuse emotional and marital difficulties. The third daughter, who also was in psychiatric treatment, had severe marital problems, had a

Well Adjusted	Adequately Adjusted	Emotionally Disturbed	Borderline	Schizophrenic
3	3	8	7	3

FIG. 1. Range of adjustment of 24 siblings of schizophrenic patients.

violent temper, and felt chronically frustrated, tending to be highly suspicious of the motives of others. The youngest sister had withdrawn from the family and had married. She refused to use her inherited wealth, tying herself down to her housework and children in a bizarre, obsessive manner, maintaining a very precarious balance. She is a borderline or ambulatory schizophrenic.

While the nonschizophrenic personality disorders of the siblings may be of little interest to those who consider schizophrenia to be a clearly circumscribed disease entity, or to those seeking a predominantly genetic etiology, these disorders have pertinence to psychiatrists who entertain the hypothesis that schizophrenia is related to deviant personality development. If the intrafamilial transactions play a major role in shaping the personality of the offspring raised within the family, each child in these seriously disturbed families may well be affected in different ways and to differing degrees, and not all need reach the extreme of a schizophrenic reaction.

The personality problems of the siblings will receive further scrutiny during the discussion of the influences affecting their development within their families. However, two defensive maneuvers, marked constriction and flight from the family, require special comment because they were strikingly characteristic, particularly of the siblings who had made reasonably good adaptations.

Of the four best adjusted siblings, only one, a girl who had two psychotic brothers, seemed reasonably free and imaginative. The other three, as well as many of the more disturbed siblings, suffered from marked constriction of their personalities with notable limitations in their range of emotional maturity, their perceptiveness, and the use of their intellectual resources.* A sibling may, for example, successfully pursue a scientific career that requires minimal interpersonal awareness and remain relatively impoverished in other areas. The constricted personality usually utilizes the defense of isolation to prevent recognition of the extent of the intrafamilial difficulties, for facing the total situation would be shattering. In some, whole periods of the past have been completely repressed and particularly traumatic experiences have produced amnesias. In the investigation, where intensive therapy could not be offered the siblings, such defenses had to be respected as essential to the sibling's ego integrity.

A sister of a young schizophrenic woman had managed to avoid involvement in the parental conflict in which her sister had been enmeshed, carefully placating both parents. She was a relatively poor informant about the family, insisting that she could remember very little about her childhood, or even about many recent occurrences. She went on to exlain that life in her family had been so painful that she had taught herself very early in childhood to think as little as possible about the family quarrels, never letting herself review a day's happenings. She tried to concentrate upon avoiding trouble, pleasing her parents, and doing well at school until she could leave for college and lead her own life. She did not consciously know how she felt about her strange and difficult parents. While we have counted this young woman among the more stable siblings —indeed the most stable sibling of the same sex as the patient—Margaret Thaler Singer, who interpreted the projective tests of the members of this family without any knowledge about them, wrote the following excerpt:[12, 28, 29]

To coin a phrase, this girl is "her parents' child." One can see the impact of their communication styles upon her. She uses fragmented remarks, tells a story [on the TAT], then takes it back saying that she didn't find a meaning! Nothing gets validated and confirmed. She often describes interactions as rather pointless, fragmented affairs which she then denies . . . people are not responsible for their own wrongdoings . . . children might need their attention brought back to concrete realities—they are seen as inattentive and drifting—people in general are not good, and interactions hardly ever lead to anything pleasant. She is more than willing to leave crazily incompatible acts hanging together as if they made sense or were sequitors. . . . Men are seen in very poor light. . . . Mother is not seen in a positive way at all. On one card she told no story at all where a mother is usually seen. On another two stories the wife poisons the husband. . . .

Thus the projective tests bore out the clinical impression that this woman had managed to deal with potentially serious disturbance by constriction, isolation, and denial.

* Margaret Thaler Singer has also emphasized personality constriction as a major defense of siblings of schizophrenic patients from her unpublished study of the projective tests of a series investigated at the National Institute of Mental Health by Lyman Wynne and his co-workers.

One of the most successful siblings, the brother of a schizophrenic girl, had knowingly or unknowingly gratified his parents' ambitions for him by choosing a wealthy spouse and becoming a capable physician. He was pleasant and affable, but communicated little of pertinence. Singer, again without knowledge of the subject, stated, on the basis of the projective tests:

> He is obsessive. He has learned from his father to take an intellectual position and try to seem detached. On the Sentence Completion Test he talks of viruses, chemistry, Beethoven, pharmaceutics, and politics. He senses he is nonrevealing and unimaginative... He is repudiating imagination and fantasy... particularly on the TAT where he says things are a... matter of course... innocuous ... status quo... nothing drastic... just a passing thing... no outcome... just simply another thing, etc. He has learned the Pollyanna-like style both his parents have....

Although personality constriction was prominent in the siblings in this study, we know that some siblings of schizophrenic patients are reasonably stable and also highly sensitive and productive. A number of outstanding authors have had schizophrenic siblings, and some have apparently abreacted their traumatic lives in their artistic productions. Psychiatrists with schizophrenic siblings have sensitively used the insights gained within their own families to understand and treat schizophrenic patients.

Some siblings realize that they must flee from the disturbing family environment as soon as possible in order not to be overwhelmed. Several of them recounted how they had maintained an emotional aloofness for several years until they could get away; in others, the predicament of the schizophrenic sibling became so intolerable and frightening that they impulsively left home, as did a character in *The Glass Menagerie*.[31] In leaving the home, they are apt to try to block out the past and disengage themselves from their families. Of course, these siblings are often more able to leave the parental attachments and survive on their own than are the patients, in whom such attempts at disengagement may precipitate an acute psychotic break. The sister whose constriction has just been noted had no intention of returning home after finishing college and married promptly upon being graduated. In another instance, a college girl became bedridden soon after her brother was hospitalized, and then with the support of her psychiatrist moved away from the home and severed contact with her mother; even many years later she continued to avoid her parents, and she visited her brother, who was hospitalized very close to her home, only two or three times in four years. The brother of a male patient kept away from his mother—who was schizophrenic, divorced, and pathetically lonely—because, in his frenzy at her engulfing ways, he found himself planning ways of murdering her. The most stable of the four Schwartz brothers was the only one who had left the family; he lived at a great distance and kept himself absorbed in his mathematics. One sister in the Thomas family, but not the best adjusted, had made a complete break with her family, not only avoiding contact, with them but also consciously seeking to lead a totally different type of life.

DIVERGENT INFLUENCES UPON THE OFFSPRING WITHIN A FAMILY

THE EFFECTS OF CHANGING FAMILY CIRCUMSTANCES

The family is not static but is an organization with a dynamic configuration in which role relationships change constantly. Time is a factor in these changes, as children enter new developmental phases and parents grow older. Sometimes marked shifts in the family occur, leading to a loss of equilibrium or to deleterious defensive measures to maintain a semblance of role reciprocity between members. In some instances the family situation and the parental attitudes altered so markedly that the patient was raised altogether differently from his siblings, and a similar outcome of the developmental process could not be expected. The Forel family offers a clear example.

The Forel marriage had never been compatible. The father, a weak man, had struggled ineffectually against the domination of the family by his wife, who was abetted by her two older sisters. All three sisters were contemptuous of men, and the oldest was a virago who despised and sought to control men. Mrs. Forel was cold, highly narcissistic, and a teasing flirt. She refused to move away from the neighborhood where her mother and sisters lived, and each summer abandoned her husband to vacation with them for two months. The marriage became increasingly schismatic, with Mr. Forel feeling himself an outcast in his own home, his opinions devalued, and his wishes ignored. His frequent tantrums increased his wife's contempt for him.

There were three children; the patient, a boy, was the youngest child, with a sister thirteen years older and a brother eleven years older. All of the children suffered from the family atmosphere. The older brother considered his childhood to have been abysmal, but far better than the patient's. For the two older children the parental influences had been modified by close contact with the extended families of both parents. The older son had been a favorite of his grandparents and aunts, gaining their admiration and praise by ingratiating himself in an obsequious fashion that enraged his father. He became highly neurotic, terrified of male authorities. He believed that he had escaped very serious disorganization by, first, his attachment to a male teacher, identifying himself with him and trying to follow in his footsteps, and then by developing a psychogenic dermatitis that led him into intensive psychotherapy. The sister became a seriously constricted and anxious woman.

Shortly before the conception of the patient, the parents had verged upon the separation they had often considered. Mr. Forel had been offered an opportunity to establish a business in another state, but his wife refused to move away from her sisters. When Mr. Forel issued an ultimatum and threatened divorce, his wife capitulated and agreed to move, and also agreed to resume the sexual relationship she had terminated eleven years before. The patient was a product of the brief reconciliation. Finding herself pregnant, Mrs. Forel became enraged at her husband and sought unsuccessfully to terminate the pregnancy. After the child was born, she paid little attention to him, and, feeling lost without her sisters, upon whom she had always been dependent, she began to drink heavily and to entertain male friends. During the patient's childhood, both parents were frequently intoxicated, and the older children reported that the father often carried his wife home dead drunk. The older siblings and the father tried to fill a mothering role toward the patient. Then, when the patient was six, Mrs. Forel was seriously disfigured in an auto accident which occurred when her husband fell asleep while driving. She became depressed and refused to leave her room until her appearance could be restored surgically, more than a year later. Feeling guilty, the father sought to make amends by becoming subservient to her, and was treated more contemptuously than ever. Then in rapid succession, the brother left for college, the sister married, and the father failed in his business. The family moved again, and shortly thereafter the father developed a malignancy. As he went downhill, his wife totally neglected him, fearing that she might catch cancer from him. The father died when the patient was eleven, and from then on the boy never had a real home. They lived with his married sister for a time; and then his mother moved in with the oldest sister. This aunt hated the patient, who was defiant toward her, and refused to permit him to live in her house. He boarded in the neighborhood, visiting his mother when his aunt was not at home.

In at least half of the families, the sequential position of the offspring formed a significant differentiating influence because of changing family circumstances, although the changes were less dramatic in the other cases than in the one described above. The children's position in a family can, however, make considerable difference in the parents' attitudes toward them even when they are of the same sex and closely proximate in age because of the places they fill in the dynamic equilibrium of the family. We have considered two of the most difficult problems of differentiation in our series in previous papers: The differing role and identity assignments of a set of identical twins,[19] and the very different situations confronting two sisters born less than two years apart, the older of whom is schizophrenic and the younger reasonably well adjusted.[21] The mother of the twins had selected the older twin to live out her masculine fantasies of the life denied her because she was a woman and was herself a less favored younger twin, while she identified the younger of the twins with her feminine, passive, and masochistic self. In the other case, the older of the sisters had become the focal point and scapegoat in a conflict between her parents that had antedated her birth and had been brought to a crisis by her conception, whereas the younger sister had remained relatively peripheral to the continuing parental quarrel.

THE MOTHER'S CAPACITY TO PROVIDE NURTURANT CARE DURING THE PATIENT'S INFANCY

In half of the cases studied, a clear disturbance was found to have existed in the relationship of the mother with the patient as an infant—a disturbance that was not present, or at least not to the same degree, in her relationship with her other children. This is in keeping with theories of the importance of infantile deprivation and maternal rejection in the genesis of schizophrenia. Three mothers had been physically incapacitated for many months following the patient's birth, disabilities that had been aggravated by their emotional problems at the time. One mother had been fearful of handling her oldest child, particularly of bathing him, a task which the father had to carry out. The mother of the two schizophrenic Robb sisters had been too insecure to take care of her oldest daughter and had turned her care, as an infant and small child, over to a nurse; when her son was born, three years later, she had cared for him herself; but when the younger daughter was born, she paid little attention to her, for she was preoccupied with hostility toward her unfaithful husband, had started an affair, and was considering divorce. Another mother of two daughters had suffered "gloomy thoughts" following the birth of the younger girl, who became the patient, whereas the birth of the older child had been a joyous occasion—and a clear preference for the older child continued during the ensuing years. Mrs. Forel, already referred to, had sought to abort her youngest child, who became the patient, and had been emotionally withdrawn from him during his infancy, as well as during his later years. At least one other mother's efforts at mothering were seriously impeded by her husband's extreme jealousy of any attention she sought to give her son, a situation that did not recur after the birth of a daughter. In several other instances, the mother had difficulty in providing proper nurturant care for her children as infants, but notable differences in the care provided the patient and the siblings were not apparent.

It is difficult properly to assess such influences in the first year of the patient's life. The problem is partly one of retrospective assessment, but even more one of sorting out what is pertinent and decisive in families where serious difficulties had existed prior to the patient's birth and then continued throughout his developmental years. Two things are apparent: That these difficulties in nurturing the infant did not occur in all cases, and that this problem was but one among many parent-child difficulties. However, such deprivation may be important in predisposing the child to schizophrenia. It may also indicate the start of a chronically faulty mother-child relationship, and such unsatisfactory parent-infant interaction may set a pattern aggravated by constant feedback from child to mother, mother to child, and one parent to the other, involving the sibling relationships as well.

The Child's Role in the Family Dynamics

The child and parental conflicts

In those families that we have designated as "schismatic," the parents were in open conflict, trying to coerce each other, each encountering from the other either defiance or, at best, a temporary hostile and resentful submission. Each undercut the worth and self-esteem of the other and divided the family, the mother wooing the children to side with her, and the father wooing them to side with him in the conflict, each parent fostering distrust and devaluation of the other. In many cases a constant threat of family dissolution hung over the children. The parents were preoccupied with their marital problems, and, in the absence of affection and support from each other, turned to a child to fill their emotional needs. In our experience, the child who becomes schizophrenic is caught in the schism to a greater degree than are the others in a variety of ways: First, he may fill the role of the "scapegoat" whose difficulties preoccupy the parents and mask their basic unhappiness with one another. Second, he may insert himself into the split, seeking to widen the gap between them to gain one parent for himself. Third, he may devote his energies and attention to bridging the gap between the parents. He straddles issues, divides his loyalties, and seeks to become a different person for each parent in order to fill the emotional needs of both, consuming his energies in preserving the parents' marriage and in salvaging their lives, rather than in the interests of his own independent ego development. Fourth, he may be caught in a bind in which loyalty to one parent means rejection by the other; because of their opposing standards and needs, he cannot satisfy and feel accepted by one without arousing dissatisfaction or hostility in the other. The widely discrepant attitudes and directives of the parents cannot be integrated within the single child—the irreconcilable parents become irreconcilable introjects.[8, 9, 30]

The reasons why one offspring rather than another becomes most intensively involved are diverse: The sequential position, the child's sex, changes in the family situation, childhood illnesses, and others not so readily categorized. However, the patient's involvement commonly relieves the other children of much of the burden. The following case excerpts illustrate how one child became more caught up in the family schism than the siblings.

In the Nussbaum family, the parents, preoccupied with their own problems, could invest little in their daughter from the time she was born, resenting her because her birth had prevented the divorce which they had considered. The baby became irritable and difficult and filled the role of scapegoat, diverting attention from the parents' dissension, and eventually she widened the gulf between the parents by displacing the mother in the father's affections to the extent of near incestuous involvement.

Mrs. Nussbaum had been delighted with her first-born son and very proud of him. When the daughter was born three years later, the mother was unable to care for the infant, supposedly because of a back injury that she blamed on her husband's neglect during the pregnancy. During the year before the daughter's birth, the couple had had a severe disagreement as a consequence of a feud between their parental families. The couple never became reconciled and lived together in an atmosphere of resentment, at times not speaking to one another for weeks. Mrs. Nussbaum felt trapped in an intolerable marriage, grew increasingly sullen and caustic, and eventually became severely disturbed. Although she could not act warmly toward her daughter, she continued to find solace and pleasure in her son.

Mr. Naussbaum remained away from home as much as possible, and turned to his daughter for the affection and admiration he could not gain from his wife. At times, he seemed to be spiting his wife by the alliance with the girl. He became very seductive toward his daughter, sleeping with her when she became anxious at night and cuddling her to sleep until she began, during adolescence, to express fears of becoming pregnant. The child's problems became a major concern to both parents, but also a source of mutual recrimination. The mother sought to devote herself to her daughter's care when she became increasingly difficult during adolescence, but would lose patience and go into rages in which she would tell the girl that she wished she were dead. The mother, fairly typically, lacked empathy for her daughter, and because of her inconsistent behavior and the father's devaluation of her formed an unacceptable model, while the father seductively substituted the daughter for his wife. Thus the patient was at times a scapegoat and at other times a divisive influence. In contrast, the son received affection from both parents, for his father was very much interested in him, and although he was affected by the parental conflict, he was never in the center of it and was two years old before it arose. Further, his father as a professional man provided an excellent career model for him, even in his mother's eyes.

The older of the two daughters in the Grau family was caught in a particularly difficult bind because of the parents' dissensions that antedated her birth and their irreconcilable ideas about religion, which focused upon how the child should be raised. Her Protestant father refused to permit her to be baptized into Catholicism despite his written promise, he constantly condemned Catholicism and all Catholics, and he later refused to permit her to go with Catholic boys. Her Catholic mother fought back, sought to woo the girl to Catholicism, and secretly circumvented her husband. She was constantly anxious about her unbaptized child, and eventually had her baptized without her husband's knowledge. The parents' religious quarrels were but symptomatic of many areas of discord.

The patient struggled with these irreconcilable introjects until she finally defiantly sided with her paranoid father and sought to win him away from her mother. The younger daughter, while also subjected to the conflict, never became the focus of it. To some extent, the father relinquished her to his wife; since the older sister preempted the father's attention and affection, the younger could form an alliance with her mother. As we shall note later in the paper, the sister learned at an early age to sidestep the difficulties in which the patient became involved.

In the Benjamin family the son who became schizophrenic sought to satisfy the disparate ambitions his parents held for him, to fill their unmet needs, and to keep them from separating. When they were at odds, he would become frightened by their seductiveness toward him; yet he would become jealous and more disturbed whenever they became more compatible. Both parents used the son's indications of affection and his criticisms of the other parent as a vindication of themselves, wooing him as an ally. At the same time, the father could not permit his son to gain a better education than he himself had obtained, and he unconsciously sabotaged his wife's hopes and the boy's ambitions. The confusions in the sexual sphere were even greater, with both parents behaving seductively toward their son. The patient's older sister could simply side with her father and did not seek to hold the parents together. She was not threatened by seduction from the mother, and her father was less physically seductive toward her than toward his son. Less involved in the parents' difficulties and hence less burdened by guilt, she could also exploit the parents' disagreements to gain goals of her own which her brother could not do.

The child's role in "skewed" families

Not all of the parents were in overt conflict. In the families that we have termed "skewed"—predominantly families with male schizophrenic offspring[9]—the serious personality problems and deviant ways of the dominant parent were not countered by the spouse. The patient, in contrast to his siblings, is the object of a particular intrusiveness by the dominant parent, usually the mother, which blurs the ego boundaries between parent and child and ties the patient to satisfying the parent's needs and to continuing a primary relatedness with her. The boy's differentiation from the initial symbiotic bond to his mother and the development of identification with his passive father are impeded. The symbiotic attachment leads to confusion of sexual identity, incestuous concerns, and a greater assimilation of the disturbed parent's deviant and paralogical ways. The siblings may resent the patient's special relationship with the mother, but they are freer to develop into independent persons. The oldest child may be selected as the object of this intrusive relationship, but in some instances the mother holds on to the youngest child as the older children grow away from her.

In the family with identical twins, the mother never established ego boundaries between herself and her twins. From the time of their birth, her entire life was wrapped up in these phallic extensions of herself. The older brother of the twins, together with the father, became outcasts. The mother banished the father from her room and bed, and she considered the older son to be uncouth and unimportant. The older brother hated the twins, envied them, and suffered; and he became accident-prone, seriously unstable, and given to acting-out tendencies. Yet he could identify with his father, who, despite his wife's contempt and ridicule, was a far more stable person than she. The older brother did not need to struggle to differentiate himself from his mother or to escape her bizarre demands; and eventually he felt very free to leave home and seek fulfillment elsewhere.

The Siblings' Gender

While most of the siblings were emotionally unstable, our data indicate that the most generalized and consistent factor related to the severity of the disturbance was the sex of the sibling. This factor is complex; since it is a function of the parental personalities and their interrelationships, its origins can antedate the birth of any of the children.[9] The significant finding is that siblings of the same sex as the schizophrenic patients were, as a group, clearly more disturbed than siblings of the opposite sex. The developmental tasks confronting children of opposite sexes in a particular family were very different. While the sample in this series is small and unsuited for statistical analysis, the finding is in accord with the studies of concordance rates for schizophrenia in dizygotic twins, with studies of *folie à deux*, and with the findings of Penrose and others concerning concordance rates for schizophrenia in siblings of schizophrenic pa-

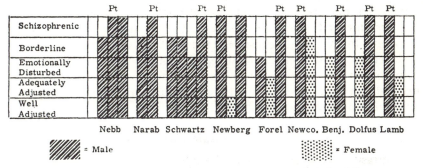

FIG. 2. Estimated adjustments of male patients and their siblings.

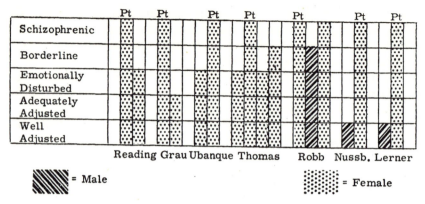

FIG. 3. Estimated adjustments of female patients and their siblings.

tients.[10, 14, 23, 25, 27] Such findings have led to the consideration of a sex-linked genetic factor, but Rosenthal's recent analysis of the collective data from the various studies shows that the gender-linkage within the more extended family does not appear to follow genetic lines.[25, 27]

As shown in Fig. 2, the nine male patients in our series had fourteen siblings—eight brothers and six sisters. Three had only brothers, two had a brother and sister, and four only a sister.

Fig. 3 shows the female patients and their siblings. The seven female patients had a total of ten siblings—seven sisters and three brothers. The paucity of brothers is unfortunate and limits the usefulness of the data. Four of the female patients had only sisters; one had a brother and a sister; and two had only a brother.

The sisters of male schizophrenics

The only sibling of a male schizophrenic who could be considered emotionally healthy and well adjusted is a sister. One other sister, now a young adolescent, may attain reasonable stability despite some acting-out tendencies. Two other sisters of male schizophrenics are living reasonably satisfying lives despite fairly serious personality problems; one is seriously constricted and insecure in her marital relationship, and the other has psychopathic traits that have thus far not led to serious difficulties. The remaining two women, the sisters of the most chronic male patients, were both seriously disturbed at one time, and both sought psychotherapeutic help; one is now pursuing a profession effectively, and the other has married and is raising a family, but is seriously constricted and insecure and is making a tenuous adjustment.

The brothers of male schizophrenics

In contrast to the sisters, none of the eight brothers can be considered to have remained reasonably stable. Two have been psychotic; one became paranoid in childhood, and the other, an identical twin of a patient, has been a transvestite with bizarre fantasies and thought processes.[19] Another brother is a criminal sociopath; a fourth is making a tenuous borderline adjustment and shows many schizophrenic features on his projective tests. The fifth, the older brother of the identical twins, is accident-prone and severely obsessive, and has many other disrupting personality problems. The sixth is phobic and limited, and has serious career and marital problems. The two remaining male siblings are now doing fairly well, but both went through many years of serious turmoil: one may have been transiently delusional in adolescence, and the other suffered from a severe neurodermatitis, had serious concerns over his masculinity, and at times was incapacitated by anxiety, but he worked out his major problems in psychotherapy.

The brothers of female schizophrenics

Two of the three brothers have successfully pursued professions and have remained emotionally stable, although they are both limited by constriction of their personalities. The third brother, a man with two chronically schizophrenic sisters, has had considerable difficulty in both work and marriage and is rather schizoid.

The sisters of female schizophrenics

Only one of the seven sisters of the female patients has made a reasonably stable adjustment, and her limitations have already been mentioned. Her skillful avoidance of crippling involvement in a very bad family situation has been discussed in detail in another paper.[21] One sister is chronically schizophrenic, and another, who completely withdrew from her family, is making a borderline schizophrenic adjustment. The remaining four sisters are rather seriously unstable, but the extent of the disabilities of two could not be clearly determined because of their fear of involvement and avoidance of frequent contact with the investigators. One of them had left home precipitately soon after her sister was hospitalized.

Two illustrations of the factor of gender

The indications that certain family constellations and interaction patterns create greater vulnerability to the development of schizophrenia for offspring of one sex than for the opposite sex[9] are highlighted by the two families with alternate gender sequence of their three children. In one, two sons were separated by a daughter, and, in the other, two daughters were separated by a son. In both families the oldest and youngest children were schizophrenic, while the middle child of the opposite sex was not. While this finding probably is partly a matter of chance, the family situations will be presented briefly to illustrate how the family configurations created very different developmental tasks for the boys and girls within these families.

In the Newberg family the oldest son became acutely schizophrenic at the age of fifteen. The daughter, who was thirteen at the time, has remained well and is probably the most stable and adaptable of any of the siblings in our series. The third child, a boy who was then nine years old, suffered from night terrors and paralyzing separation problems, and soon after his brother's hospitalization developed delusional beliefs about his teachers and schoolmates.

The Newberg marriage had been filled with mutual recrimination and frequent threats of separation almost from its inception, with most of the quarrels focusing on the intense attachment of both spouses to their natal families. Mr. Newberg was the most poorly organized father of any of the male patients. Raised in a disorganized family abandoned by the father, he had at an early age assumed responsibility for the support of his mother. He remained intensely attached to her, was jealous of his brothers, and spent much of his spare time in his mother's home. He was equally rivalrous with his sons, behaving in many ways like another child in the family. He talked incessantly, in a driven way that the interviewers found difficult to endure for even an hour at a time. He was scattered, pursuing one fixed idea after another. Although a steady provider, he was caught between his ambitions and his needs for security, and he constantly threatened to leave his job to pursue some hare-brained scheme. In his free time he worked upon a sequence of inventions that never materialized or a succession of hobbies each of which he was going to turn into a business. He talked constantly of his great abilities but accomplished little, and he created great confusion when at home.

Mrs. Newberg, in contrast, was one of the most stable mothers in our series. She depended greatly upon her older son, and sought compensation for her unhappy marriage in her children. Although she was oversolicitous, she maintained a reserve that probably impeded her relationships with them. She was firmly attached to her three sisters and refused to move away from the street on which they all lived, which caused her husband great inconvenience. While she justified this, in part correctly, by her husband's unreliability and her need for companionship and help in raising the children, her husband resented her lack of confidence in him. Mrs. Newberg's sisters intruded themselves into the affairs of the Newberg household, and one in particular was openly hostile and contemptuous of Mr. Newberg, constantly belittling him even in the presence of his children.

In this family, the sons had a very faulty paternal model in a man who boasted much and achieved little, who was highly inconsistent and given to suspiciousness, and who was more of a rival to them than a father. The mother and her sisters constantly denigrated him and placed little trust in him, conveying to the boys that they must not resemble him.

They lived in an atmosphere where women dominated the extended family and were highly critical of men. For a son to become like the father meant becoming virtually psychotic, subject to constant hostile criticism and contempt, and almost intolerable to the mother whose love they sought.

The daughter's situation was very different. Surrounded by women who were mutually supportive, she had a number of positive feminine models. Although her father was frequently angry with her mother, he also expressed considerable admiration for her. The daughter was clearly her father's favorite, and her mother was not jealous or rivalrous. Further, the daughter did not need to fill the place in her mother's life that her father had left unsatisfied; she did not have to achieve as a man in a world in which her grandiose father could accomplish little; nor did she have to face the issue, which confronted her brothers, of how a man could satisfy and be lovable to a woman when the father was so unsatisfactory to their mother and aunts.

The Robb family, in which two chronically schizophrenic daughters were separated by a son who, despite serious difficulties and several bad starts, has managed to achieve a career and marry, presents an analogous situation. Mr. Robb, a professor of education, married a troubled heiress who was seriously lacking in self-esteem. The couple had very different ideas of family life, child rearing, and the types of people with whom they wished to associate. Mrs. Robb accepted her dominating husband's decisions and choice of friends and quietly suffered in associating with people whom she despised. When, however, her husband started a series of sexual liaisons, she followed suit to vent her anger and gain quiet vengeance. Then Mr. Robb invited female exchange students from abroad to live with the family, ignoring his wife's protests. Soon he was spending evenings talking with them and ignoring his wife, and he turned to one of these, who was a teacher doing advanced study, for guidance in raising the children. For many years Mrs. Robb had had little authority in her own home, but now her inadequate self-esteem and confidence fell markedly as her opinions were pointedly ignored and belittled. Deeply resentful and preoccupied with her unhappiness, she could invest little in her children.

The oldest daughter was cared for by a nursemaid during her infancy, but when the son was born the nurse was discharged, and the mother gained considerable satisfaction from caring for him. However, it was soon after the second daughter was born that the mother discovered that her husband was having an affair and in revenge also started an affair. From then on she gave little thought or attention to her children. Even though the situation has been presented only in barest outline, one can note that the daughters were uncherished by their mother and that they gained a strange view of the worth and role of a woman, since she was unempathic as a mother, and consistently devalued and held in contempt as a wife. The girls could readily feel that they could not satisfy or gain the affection of their oversolicitous and seductive father by growing up to resemble their mother. The son, who also developed rather serious problems, had at least received maternal affection and attention during his infancy and early childhood; and he had a successful and renowned father who provided a model—and whose example he eventually followed by marrying a wealthy woman from an unstable family.

When the families with schizophrenic sons and those with schizophrenic daughters were examined as separate series, notable differences in their configurations became apparent. Because of the parental personalities and the nature of their interactions, the families with schizophrenic sons presented more serious impediments to the integrated ego development of boys than of girls, and the opposite was true for the families with schizophrenic daughters, although a few families were probably equally noxious to children of both sexes.

The parent of the same sex as the patient—the fathers of sons and the mothers of daughters—formed a very poor model for the patient to internalize in order to gain identity as a man or woman because of the parent's serious psychopathology, because of the parent's attitudes toward the child, or because of the spouse's derogatory and undermining behavior toward this parent, and commonly for all three reasons. To maintain the approval and affection of the parent of the opposite sex, the child sought to differentiate himself from, rather than identify himself with, the parent of the same sex, and thus lacked a positive sex-linked model to follow in order to gain maturity as a man or a woman. The situation was aggravated because the parent of the opposite sex from the child seductively used the child as a replacement for the unsatisfactory spouse in filling his own emotional needs and thus interfered with the child's development into an independent person. Although the case illustrations have emphasized the child's difficulty in achieving identity as a member of his own sex, the problems created for his development go far beyond this. The resolution of the Oedipal ties is impeded, and incestuous wishes remain conscious into adolescence; fears of vindictiveness by the parent of the same sex are heightened by the realistic rivalries existing in the family; and narcissistic and homosexual proclivities are fostered by the confused and confusing sexual identities of the parents.[8]

The case material reveals that with but rare exception the mother of the male patient is engulfing the son, seeking to maintain a symbiotic closeness with him, while the father is distant and rivalrous toward the son or is himself but a weak, emasculated appendage of his wife. In contrast, the mother of the female patient is aloof and distant from her, either because she is unable to accept in a daughter the femininity she rejects in herself or because she seeks to ward off homosexual impulses, while the father tends to be derogatory of women in general but seductive of the daughter, whose admiration he needs to bolster his insecure masculinity and narcissism. A more detailed examination of these differences in another paper suggests that satisfactory ego development and integration in boys and girls depends upon different requisities in the family structure and interaction.[9] A boy's ego development will be injured more seriously than a girl's by a mother who cannot establish clear ego boundaries between herself and the child, since to achieve a firm masculine identity he must break away from the initial mother-child symbiosis more completely than a daughter needs to. In addition, a father who fails to fill a masculine instrumental role in the family will be more detrimental to a boy, who needs to learn this role, than to a girl. Conversely, a girl will be harmed more seriously by a cold and aloof mother, for the attainment of maternal affectional characteristics through empathic absorption of maternal feelings is more critical to a girl's development than to a boy's; and a father who dominates and derogates the mother and tends to be antagonistic and belittling toward all women will affect a girl's development more deleteriously than a boy's. The exposition of the different developmental tasks confronting boys and girls and how they are furthered or impeded by the family configuration goes beyond the purposes of this paper; here we are seeking only to indicate why a child of one sex may be more vulnerable to personality disorganization within a given family than a child of the opposite sex.

IDIOSYNCRATIC PROBLEMS IN THE PARENTS' RELATIONSHIP TO THE SCHIZOPHRENIC OFFSPRING

The comparison of some of the patients with their siblings must take into account certain special problems related to unique circumstances. Expectations before birth as well as many circumstances at and following confinement can set the stage for certain interaction patterns in the family or certain attitudes toward a particular infant. For example, differences in temperament present at birth may influence the ensuing child-parent relationship and interaction, although this, like many other such influences, is difficult to assess retrospectively.

The Nebb twins, one of whom was overtly schizophrenic and the other a transvestite who might also be considered schizophrenic, were, in contrast to their older brother, placed at birth in a special and unusual situation because their mother had been competing with her own twin sister to see which of them could produce twins. The birth of the twin sons was a major triumph for Mrs. Nebb, who had been the deformed and neglected member of her family, and they were to be her means of achieving prestige and dominance.[19]

In another family, the daughter who became the patient had manifested artistic talent to an unusual degree by the age of three. Two relatives in the maternal line who had been similarly gifted from earliest childhood had become psychotic. The patient's mother had been directed away from developing a similar talent lest it lead to insanity, but the patient's unusual ability could not be suppressed. The mother was naturally ambivalent about the patient's dominant activity and vacillated between encouraging it and seeking to guide the girl into more conventional channels. The bright but untalented older brother had not been subjected to such ambivalent guidance, nor to an a priori expectation of great vulnerability to psychosis.

It must be noted, however, that there were other problems in both families that were just as serious as in the other families in the series.

THE INTERACTION BETWEEN THE SIBLINGS

In our scrutiny of the divergent influences upon the siblings within a family, we must also note the effects of the interaction between the siblings themselves, although this topic extends beyond the limits and purposes of this paper. In the Narab family, the overtly schizophrenic mother considered both of her sons to be geniuses—even, at times, Messiahs—and her extreme intrusiveness into the lives of both was not countered by the father. The younger son became schizophrenic while the older traversed a narrow path, skirting overt psychosis. He was filled with venom toward his mother and feared that he might act out his homicidal fantasies about her if he remained near her; and, at times, he was almost equally hostile toward his younger brother. While ex post facto analysis is particularly hazardous in this instance, several factors seem important. Mrs. Narab had been smotheringly dominant of her first-born, but with the birth of the second son she turned her major energies toward him; and as the older son began to move away from her, she clung all the more tenaciously to the younger. The first-born could express his jealousy and anger toward his brother, dominating him and forcing him into a passive and masochistic position—one might say into developing a more Messiah-like personality and possibly emulating his father, whom both sons considered homosexual. The absorption of the mother's needs by the younger son appears to have provided greater freedom for the older.

Illness in one offspring—whether the schizophrenic patient or the nonschizophrenic sibling—affects the siblings differentially. At least three of our patients experienced comparative neglect when the prolonged illness of older siblings—rheumatic fever in one instance—required a great deal of the mother's attention. In the Schwartz family, the severe psychopathy of the oldest brother preempted the economic and emotional resources, as has already been noted. It was the youngest son who became psychotic. Not only had his father become ineffectual as a husband and father shortly after his birth, but his mother's attention had become absorbed by the oldest son's markedly antisocial and delinquent behavior. The family lived in a "tough" neighborhood, and the next older brother had protected the patient, as the baby of the family, and fought his battles for him—abetting his development as a passive, dependent child who was very insecure of his masculinity.

In the Grau family, the patient's difficulties throughout her childhood had had a very different impact on the younger sister. She explained that her older sister had borne the brunt of her mother's insecurity in raising children; the mother had relied on' books with her first child but raised the second daughter according to less rigid directions. Moreover, the second daughter had avoided involvement in the parental conflicts by noting how her sister became embroiled with one or the other parent at each phase of development, and her major guide in life had been side-stepping situations that had caused difficulties for her sister. It also became clear that her antagonism to her older sister who created so much difficulty had led her to side with her mother rather than to seek the affection of her paranoid father.

The influences of the siblings upon one another may be diverse, but the child who becomes schizophrenic often lessens the impact of the parental pathology upon the siblings by serving as a target of the parents' intrusiveness, as a scapegoat, or as an example for the siblings of what not to do.

This comparison of sixteen schizophrenic patients with their twenty-four siblings, in an effort to clarify why the patient rather than his siblings became schizophrenic, has presented only a general survey of the problems, for any careful scrutiny from a genetic-dynamic orientation would require a separate article, if not a monograph, for each family. Several general findings that warrant attention have emerged from the study. One of these is that the question of why one child within a family becomes schizophrenic while the others remain 'well' or 'normal' requires re-statement. As many siblings were psychotic as reasonably well integrated, and all except five or six of the twenty-four siblings suffered from serious personality disorders.

A definite gender-linkage was found in the occurrence and severity of the psychiatric disturbances in the siblings. The brothers of the male schizophrenic patients were clearly more disturbed than the sisters; and the sisters of schizophrenic females were sicker than the brothers, although the value of this finding is limited by the paucity of brothers of female patients in our series. Only one sibling of the same sex as the patient was considered to be reasonably stable; and no sibling of the opposite sex from the patient was overtly psychotic.

The influence of the parents and of their interaction with one another upon sons and daughters differed. In general, different configurations of parental personalities existed in the families with male and female schizophrenic offspring.

Other differentiating influences upon the development of the children occurred with varying frequencies and in various combinations. In half of the cases, the mother had been either physically incapacitated, too intensely preoccupied with her marital problems, or too anxious and insecure to provide nurturant mothering care during the patient's infancy, while such conditions did not apply during the infancy of the siblings. In half of the families the patient was raised under conditions that were different from those under which the siblings were brought up; in a few families the difference was very marked.

When the siblings were close in age—and even when they were identical twins—they were also subjected to very different intrafamilial influences. The child who becomes schizophrenic may become a pawn or scapegoat in the parental conflict; he may be caught in a bind between the conflicting needs and wishes of the parents, who become irreconcilable introjects; he may invest his energies in seeking to salvage the parents' marriage and to satisfy the needs of both; he may insert himself into the split between the parents, and become a needed complement to one parent. The patients' energies during their developmental years were deflected from developing an integrated independent ego, and failure of closure of their Oedipal attachments left them prone to incestuous conflicts during adolescence. The influence of the siblings upon one another may create more or less precarious circumstances and greater or lesser vulnerability.

We have not, of course, included all of the factors that may have been conducive to the production of schizophrenia. Little attention has been given to family characteristics that were reasonably similar for all of the siblings, particularly the paralogic modes of thinking and communicating of one or both parents that were present in all the families.

Although any reconstruction of the intrafamilial circumstances that influenced the development of these patients and their siblings cannot be fully satisfactory, the material offers clear and reasonable grounds for the understanding of why one child rather than another in a family becomes schizophrenic. The data support rather than refute the hypothesis that the intrafamilial environment plays a critical role in the etiology of schizophrenia.

REFERENCES

1. ALANEN, Y. O. 1958. The mothers of schizophrenic patients. *Acta psychiat. neurol. sand.*, **33**, Suppl. 124.
2. BATESON, G., JACKSON, D. D., HALEY, J., and WEAKLAND, J. H. 1956. Toward a theory of schizophrenia. *Behavl Sci.*, **1**, 251-264. [Reprinted in this collection as No. XL.]
3. BOWEN, M. 1961. The family as the unit of study and treatment: I. Family psychotherapy. *Am. J. Orthopsychiat.*, **31**, 40-60. [Reprinted in this collection as No. XLVI.]

4. BRODEY, W. M. 1961. The family as the unit of study and treatment: 3. Image, object and narcissistic relationships. *Am. J. Orthopsychiat.*, **31**, 69-73.

5. CORNELISON, A. R. 1960. Casework interviewing as a research technique in a study of families of schizophrenic patients. *Ment. Hyg.*, **44**, 551-559.

6. FLECK, S. 1960. Family dynamics and origin of schizophrenia. *Psychosom. Med.*, **22**, 333-344.

7. FLECK, S., CORNELISON, A. R., NORTON, N., and LIDZ, T. 1957. The intrafamilial environment of the schizophrenic patient: II. Interaction between hospital staff and families. *Psychiatry*, **20**, 343-350.

8. FLECK, S., CORNELISON, A. R., SCHAFER, S., TERRY, D., and LIDZ, T. 1959. The intrafamilial environment of the schizophrenic patient: Incestuous and homosexual problems. In MASSERMAN, J. H. (ed.) *Science and psychoanalysis*, Vol. II: *Individual and familial dyanimcs*, pp. 142-159. Grune & Stratton, New York.

9. FLECK, S., LIDZ, T., and CORNELISON, A. R. 1963. Comparison of parent-child relationships of male and female schizophrenic patients. *Archs gen. Psychiat.*, **8**, 1-7.

10. GREENBERG, H. P. *Folie à deux: An historical and clinical study*. Unpublished thesis.

11. HALEY, J. 1959. The family of the schizophrenic: A model system. *J. nerv. ment. Dis.*, **129**, 357-374.

12. HOLZBERG, J. D. Unpublished notes.

13. JACKSON, D. D. (ed). 1960. *The etiology of schizophrenia*. Basic Books, New York.

14. KALLMANN, F. J. 1953. *Heredity in health and mental disorder*. Norton, New York.

15. LIDZ., R. W., and LIDZ, T. 1949. The family environment of schizophrenic patients. *Am. J. Psychiat.*, **106**, 332-345.

16. LIDZ, T. 1958. Schizophrenia and the family. *Psychiatry*, **21**, 21-27.

17. LIDZ, T., CORNELISON, A. R., FLECK, S., and TERRY, D. 1957. The intrafamilial environment of the schizophrenic patient: I. The father. *Psychiatry*, **20**, 329-342.

18. LIDZ, T., CORNELISON, A. R., FLECK, S., and TERRY, D. 1957. The intrafamilial environment of the schizophrenic patient: II. Marital schism and marital skew. *Am. J. Psychiat.*, **114**, 241-248.

19. LIDZ, T., CORNELISON, A. R., SCHAFER, S., TERRY, D., and FLECK, S. 1962. Ego differentiation and schizophrenic symptom formation in identical twins. *J. Am. psychoanal. Ass.*, **10**, 74-90.

20. LIDZ, T., CORNELISON, A. R., TERRY, D., and FLECK, S. 1958. The intrafamilial environment of the schizophrenic patient: VI. The transmission of irrationality. *Archs Neurol. Psychiat.*, **79**, 305-316.

21. LIDZ, T., FLECK, S., CORNELISON, A. R., and TERRY, D. 1958. The intrafamilial environment of the schizophrenic patient: IV. Parental personalities and family interaction. *Am. J. Orthopsychiat.*, **28**, 764-776.

22. LIDZ, T., WILD, C., SCHAFER, S., and FLECK, S. 1961. *The thought disorders of parents of schizophrenic patients*. Paper presented at the Third World Congress of Psychiatry, Montreal.

23. PENROSE, L. S. 1945. Survey of cases of familial mental illness. *Dig. Neurol. Psychiat.*, Series 13, 644.

24. ROSENTHAL, D. Unpublished data.

25. ROSENTHAL, D. Unpublished data on studies of concordance rates for schizophrenia in dizygotic twins.

26. ROSENTHAL, D. 1959. Some factors associated with concordance and dis-

cordance with respect to schizophrenia in monozygotic twins. *J. nerv. ment. Dis.*, **129**, 1-10.

27. ROSENTHAL, D. 1960. Confusion of identity and the frequency of schizophrenia in twins. *Archs gen. Psychiat.*, **3**, 297-304.

28. SINGER, M. T. Unpublished data.

29. SOHLER, D. T., HOLZBERG, J. D., FLECK, S., CORNELISON, A. R., KAY, E., and LIDZ, T. 1957. The prediction of family interaction from a battery of projective tests. *J. project. Tech.*, **21**, 199-208.

30. WEAKLAND, J. H. 1960. The 'double bind' hypothesis of schizophrenia and three-party interaction. In JACKSON, D. D. (ed.) *The etiology of schizophrenia*, Chap. 13. Basic Books, New York.

31. WILLIAMS, T. 1955. *The glass menagerie.* Hawthorne, New York.

32. WYNNE, L. C., RYCKOFF, I. M., DAY, J., and HIRSCH, S. I. 1958. Pseudomutuality in the family relations of schizophrenics. *Psychiatry*, **21**, 205-220.

XLIII

THOUGHT DISORDERS AND FAMILY RELATIONS OF SCHIZOPHRENICS

LYMAN C. WYNNE AND MARGARET THALER SINGER

Research in schizophrenia is described from the National Institute of Mental Health, in which the focus is upon links between family patterns and structural aspects of schizophrenic impairment, especially upon thought disorder.

INTRODUCTION

In this paper we shall describe a strategy for research on schizophrenia in which the focus is upon links between family patterns and structural aspects of schizophrenic impairment, especially upon thought disorder. This orientation has now been successfully used in a series of systematic studies in which individual forms of thinking have been specifically deduced ("predicted") from the forms of perceiving, relating, and communicating found in the family in which the individual has developed.

Preliminary to publications on this research by our colleagues and us, we shall outline here the clinical and conceptual basis for this research strategy. Some of the limitations of past studies of the family relations of schizophrenics will be discussed. We shall suggest that more specific attention to the issue of structural ego impairment in schizophrenia can heighten the significance and fruitfulness of family studies. Next, we shall describe the clinical setting and the kinds of research data which have thus far been available in our program. Finally, we shall review some of the clinical observations which have helped us spell out our hunch that a focus upon thought disorder is strategic for systematic family studies of young adult schizophrenics.

Reprinted from the ARCHIVES OF GENERAL PSYCHIATRY, Vol. 9, September 1963, pp. 191-198.

FAMILY STUDIES

We and our collaborators at the National Institute of Mental Health assume that personality development, both normal and psychopathological, is determined by the constant dynamic interaction of both experiential factors and innate maturational factors. Although experiential factors are generally acknowledged as crucial determinants in the neuroses, there is much less agreement about the extent to which experience with the environment shapes psychoses, including schizophrenia. A tacit traditional tendency has been to relate the core, primary symptoms of schizophrenia, such as formal thinking disorders, to biological determinants and to link secondary features, such as delusional content and social withdrawal, to environmental influences. The work presented here departs from this tradition by investigating possible relationships between thinking disorders of young adult schizophrenics and the family environment in which they have been reared.

A number of clinical and sociopsychological studies of the families of schizophrenics have been made over the years. Early attention turned to important but nonspecific family disturbances such as "broken homes." Other studies were concerned with the content of parental attitudes such as over-protection, dominance, weakness, and passivity. The particular aspects of individual schizophrenic illness to which these attitudes might be linked were either left unspecified or a relationship to certain secondary features of schizophrenia, particularly withdrawal symptoms, was implied. The core features of schizophrenia, especially the formal thinking disorder and the affective and volitional disturbances, have generally been ignored in the attitudinal studies. These studies have not provided specific hypotheses to account for the structural or formal ego-defects found in individual schizophrenics.

More recently, psychotherapy and case work with the families of schizophrenics have brought under study another level of functioning in these families, namely, the forms of thinking and communicating in family transactions and the emotional dynamics of family organization. Furthermore, the over-all role structure and subculture of the family have been linked hypothetically to psychological processes and structures in the individual patient-offspring. In 1958 Wynne et al.[1] formulated a hypothesis pertinent to thinking disturbances:

The fragmentation of experience, the identity diffusion, the disturbed modes of perception and communication, and certain other characteristics of the acute reactive schizophrenic's personality structure are to a significant extent derived, by processes of internalization, from characteristics of the family social organization . . . Also internalized are the ways of thinking and of deriving meaning, the points of anxiety, and the irrationality, confusion, and ambiguity that were expressed in the shared mechanisms of the family social organization.

About the same time one of the papers by Lidz et al.[2] focused upon the "transmission of irrationality" in the families of schizophrenics. More recently, Rosenbaum,[3] reviewing observations at the National Institute of Mental Health and the Palo Alto Mental Research Institute, and Schaffer et al.,[4] discussing observations made by therapists seeing families in conjoint psychotherapy, have discussed possible connections of family patterns to thinking disorders in offspring.

However, these exploratory clinical studies, invaluable in the construction of fresh and meaningful hypotheses, were not intended to evaluate hypotheses systematically. None of the intensive clinical studies of the families of schizophrenics have thus far reported comparisons with families of nonschizophrenic individuals studied in the same way. Usually the investigators themselves have been quite convinced that the families of schizophrenics are indeed distinctive, but it must be granted that such an impression has remained less than convincing to others who have not engaged personally in intensive work with such families.

It also must be conceded that the studies of the families of schizophrenics thus far have referred to individual schizophrenic processes in rather global and unitary terms, without distinguishing different forms of individual schizophrenic disorder to which family patterns may be linked. Despite accumulating evidence that so-called process and reactive schizophrenics and schizophrenics with "good" and "bad" premorbid histories differ significantly in many respects, the kind of schizophrenics found in the families studied have by and large not been discriminated in family research.

In addition, cultural and social class variations have not been empirically examined in relation to family patterns on the one hand and structural ego impairment on the other. An important issue is whether particular kinds of family (or family-substitute) patterns are in fact universally relevant to schizophrenic illness wherever such illness occurs and thereby possibly significant etiologically, or are merely relevant idiosyncratically within the culture and class setting of each study.[5]

Finally, little attention has been given to the problems posed by the longitudinal development of schizophrenia, including the possibility that some of the familial characteristics might be secondary results, caused by the presence of a sick offspring in the family.

This paper begins a series of reports of empirical, systematic studies in which we shall gradually try to cope with these very formidable, conceptual, and methodologic problems. These problems have by no means been all solved. However, we do feel we have evolved certain principles which may facilitate progress in this important research area.

CLINICAL SETTING FOR NIMH FAMILY STUDIES

When the clinical research and treatment program of the Family Studies Section of the National Institute of Mental Health (NIMH) was initiated in 1954, each member of the families of young adult schizophrenics was seen in individual psychotherapeutic or social work relationships.* The regularity with which relationships in these families were found to be severely disturbed—even though almost none of the parents had been hospitalized or treated for overt psychiatric disorders—led to a series of hypotheses about the characteristics of these families and about some of the internalization processes by which family pattern and illness in an offspring might be related.[1,4] These hypotheses conceived of the family as a social organization, or, in sociological terms, a social subsystem,[6] calling for special scrutiny of the role structure within the family.[7] In other words, the organization and transactions of the family as a whole were regarded as significant in their own right, in addition to the importance of the one-to-one relations between each parent and each child.

In accord with these considerations the treatment program has since 1957 included conjoint family psychotherapy[3,4] in which all the members of each family meet together as a unit: both parents, hospitalized late adolescent or young adult patient, and those siblings who live in the parental household. In these sessions, ordinarily held twice weekly with two therapists, the treatment has focused on family transactions rather than on the individual patient. Excerpts selected from tape recordings of the family therapy have provided data for a systematic study of parental communication.[8] Individual diagnostic interviews are routine and usually individual psychotherapy with one or more family members is carried out concomitantly with the family therapy. Home visits and family art therapy sessions[9] are also a regular part of the program, in addition to the use of the treatment resources of the hospital ward in which the young adult patient is hospitalized.

Two other major new phases of the program was also initiated in 1957: treatment and study of matched comparison families and psychological testing with each member of both the schizophrenic and the comparison families. The tests used are the Rorschach, Thematic Apperception, Draw-A-Person, Sentence Completion, Minnesota Multiphasic Personality Inventory, the Proverbs Test and, somewhat later, the Object Sorting Test. More recently, certain standardized evaluation procedures given to family members together have been introduced, especially the Revealed Difference Technique[10] and the Family Rorschach.[11]

COMPARISON SAMPLES

The comparison studies were with families of psychiatrically disturbed but nonschizophrenic late adolescent and young adult patients, mainly suffering from obsessional, depressive, and acting-out disorders. All of these patients with neuroses and characterologic disorders, like their

* Among a considerable number of colleagues who have participated in the clinical work and contributed to the conceptualization, we wish especially to note those whose collaboration has been most prolonged: Drs. Juliana Day, Alexander Halperin, Irving M. Ryckoff, Leslie Schaffer, and Mrs. Hanna Kwiatkowska, Mr. Stanley Hirsch, and Miss Carol Hoover.

schizophrenic counterparts, were sufficiently impaired to be hospitalized for psychiatric reasons. Of about 50 families of late adolescent or young adult patients who have been studied for at least two months (up to five years), about one third have had a disturbed, neurotic offspring and two thirds have had schizophrenic offspring. This variety of patients has enabled us to compare the families of the schizophrenics with the families of other kinds of psychiatrically disturbed patients studied in the same fashion. Currently, similar cross-cultural family studies are being initiated.

In addition, psychological tests have been studied from 80 carefully matched pairs of parents of child patients—20 autistic schizophrenic children, 10 withdrawn neurotic children, 10 aggressive, acting-out children, 20 asthmatic children, and 20 chronically, medically ill children.

We feel that an essential feature of comparison studies of families is the constant factor of a sick offspring, disturbed and disturbing. Families with normal offspring may be differently motivated to take part in a program of testing and clinical interviewing. Also, such families have not had to develop means of coping somehow or other with the presence of a sick offspring. Thus, we have not merely compared disturbed and non-disturbed families but families with different *varieties* of disturbance.

It should be noted that we have tried to select families for study in which some degree of interaction between patient and family has continued and in which the children have been raised by their own parents. Patients who have been both chronically hospitalized and have long ago lost all contact with their families have not been included because of the difficulties of evaluating the secondary consequences of the hospitalization itself.

The recognition of major disturbance and hospitalization of the selected patients had occurred in most instances relatively recently, generally less than two years before entering our research program. This facilitated the collection of historical data about earlier phases of the family life and the patient's disturbance. The historical data have provided valuable leads and hypotheses but have not been relied upon for systematic comparisons.

Thus far, we have compared families only after pathology has developed in an offspring. Ultimately, predictive longitudinal studies will be needed to evaluate more fully earlier developmental phases. Meanwhile, however, our research findings in which patients and their families are differentiated blindly may help reduce the range of reasonable alternative hypotheses about etiology and pathogenesis. We hope that this work will help specify dimensions and details which will be especially important to consider in longitudinal studies.

CLINICAL FORMULATIONS

Observations in both the testing program and the conjoint family therapy strengthened our hunch that a fruitful strategy for systematic studies would focus upon possible links between family transactions and types of thinking disorders in offspring. Observations that have been particularly imporant are concerned with the styles of focusing attention and communicating in these families which may have a disorganizing, complementary impact, or may provide models which are internalized in the same form into the ego structure of the growing offspring.

TRANSACTIONAL "THOUGHT DISORDER"

Characteristically, in the families of the young schizophrenics, the degree of disturbance in family transactions is greater and qualitatively different from that found in the contributions of any individual family member. The fragmentation, disjunctive quality, and blurring of attention and meaning found in *sequences* of family transactions cannot be adequately described by mechanically adding up the degree of disturbance of individuals out of context. Rather, these individuals must be seen or imagined as part of a relationship system in order to grasp the potential impact of the family as a whole. It may then become apparent that focus and direction to family transactions are apt to become lost or never achieved, with meaning and point emerging at only the most nebulous levels. Although the *isolated* statements of individuals may even appear "normal," nevertheless, viewed from beginning to end, the over-all transactional disorder in a family's communication sequences may be comparable stylistically to that found in the vagueness or fragmentation of a severely impaired schizophrenic. That is, the form or structure of these family-wide transactions is comparable to that of individual schizophrenic thought disorder. In a very loose analogy, one can speak of a "thought disorder" of a particular variety and intensity in the family social system.

Consider the following brief example from a family therapy session:

Daughter (presenting patient), complainingly: Nobody will listen to me. Everybody is trying to still me.
Mother: Nobody wants to kill you.
Father: If you're going to associate with intellectual people, you're going to have to remember that still is a noun and not a verb.

The impact of fragmented communication builds up over time and is hard to convey by brief examples. Some illustrations have been provided elsewhere.[3, 4, 8, 11a, 15] A further verbatim example, with a partial hint of the impact upon the patient, is as follows from tape-recorded interaction while a family was alone in a room waiting for a family interview to begin:

F: Well those . . .
M: One minute it's . . .
F: . . . shoes are . . .
M: . . . rainin', and the next . . .

F: ... the shoes fit ...

M: ... minute it's—the sun is shinin'.

F: Well those shoes fit much better, don't they?

Daughter (patient): What shoes?

F: The ones you're wearin'. [pause] Those shoes are ...

D: They're nice.

F: ... a bet- ...

D: Yeah.

F: ... a good fit.

D: Unh.

M: I guess [occupational therapist] is on a holiday, hunh? Mary? [pause] She was going up to Maine.

F: Was talking with Uncle Jack on the phone the other night. He's all uh pepped up about his coming marriage in July.

D: Well I guess so. [faintly disinterested tone]

F: He is!

M: Eighth of July ...

F: Uh yeah.

M: ... he's gonna get married. And, Mary, she's one of seven girls. Isn't that sumpin'. Hanh? [pause] Aren't you happy? Ah ...

D: Oh yes, I'm just biz ...

M: ... about Uncle Jack gettin' ...

D: ... bubbling over. [faint half-laugh; sarcastic tone]

M: Hanh?

D: Just bubbling over.

M: [protestingly] Well, I think it's nice! He's fifty years old! [pause]

F: I told him he was old enough. Uncle Harry says he [half-laughs] waits until he's sure that they're ...

M: Do you think he's ...

F: ... ripe. [half-laugh]

M: ... old enough, Mary.

F: [half-laugh]

M: Hanh? [cackles]

F: Uncle Harry says, "Your brother waited until he's sure they're ripe before he picks 'em."

M: [cackles] O-o-o-o Jim-im-y! [laughingly]

F: [laughs]

M: Uncle Harry said that. [amused tone] Isn't he funny?

D: [dryly] Hilarious.

F: He says ...

D: I mean ...

M: [cackling]

D: ... it's the ...

F: Ah ...

D: ... funniest thing in the world. [weak half-laugh]

F: He says Uncle Herbie and Unc ... and Jack wait until they're ripe.

D: Tell me when to stop laughing. [pause]

M: [sighs] [wan half-laugh] [25 sec.]

F: You got a problem today, Mary? Or what?

D: [deep sigh]

M: Hmm?

F: Do yuh, Mary?

D: [angrily and sarcastically] No, I just ache all over, that's all.

F: Oh, you got ... you think you got the ...

D: Yes.

F: . . . flu?

D: My wound is i-in pain and my arms hurt and everything. That's all!

F: What wound? Un hunh? What wound? You won't get a wound except in battle.

D: No. Yeah. I guess not. Wait'll somebody locks you up for almost a year and tells yuh to get the mop when you're [slightly tearful] practically . . . It's very hilarious, isn't it? It's quite funny!

Clinical observations of family transactions over a period of years have been suggested that the degree and quality of thinking disturbance in an offspring can perhaps be predicted more adequately from the way family members "fit together" than from looking at the parents only as individuals. The family style of "fitting together," or failing to do so, can be examined at the level of transactional sequences, as found in family therapy interviews[8] and in relatively standardized procedures such as the Family Rorschach.[11] On another level of conceptualization, the over-all family patterning can also be examined in terms of the concept of the family role-structure, or the social subsystem of the family.[1, 5, 5a]

These formulations of over-all family patterning have been central both in the predictive family studies we have now completed and in research currently being planned. The use of these complex but significant concepts in a predictive effort is strategic, as Benjamin has suggested in discussing prediction as a method, not only as a contribution to evaluating specific propositions, but because of "the necessity all predictions impose for greater precision and differentiation in defining concepts."[11b]

INDIVIDUAL FORMS OF THINKING

Disturbed thinking in individual family members may be difficult to detect in emotionally protected or constricted, role-structured relationships but nevertheless be blatant when the family members talk to each other, in unstructured test situations, and in freewheeling psychotherapeutic relationships. In anxiety-arousing situations, especially when intimacy, on the one hand, or separation and loss, on the other hand, threaten to emerge, some individuals show loosened forms of schizophrenic thinking which may not be apparent in fact-oriented, history-taking individual interviews or in the occupational activity of the father.

Other members of the families of schizophrenics are highly constricted in their thinking and react to threatening situations in a highly literal ("concrete") fashion. These concrete, reductionistic responses tend to have a fragmenting effect on the communication of the *rest* of the group. Their cognitive styles are over-focused and constricted and are associated with emotional detachment. These tendencies seem especially common among the "well" siblings of schizophrenics and in parents who often have the reputation within the family and the community of being emotionally impervious but otherwise "normal." These persons, while not showing an individual thought disorder in the usual sense, nevertheless contribute to disjunctive family transactions and may evoke blurred, fragmented, or confused experience and thinking in persons who are trying to relate emotionally to them.

SUBJECTIVE EXPERIENCE OF THERAPISTS

The transactions of these families have a characteristic impact upon the subjective experience and behavior of family therapists who try to interact with these families intensively in long-term conjoint therapy.[4] If they succeed in participating emotionally with these families, the therapists sometimes experience a form of subjective blurring or fragmentation of meanings, from which skilled therapists hopefully can step back in order to reflect and comment, not simply to ward off the experience. Alternatively, other therapists defend themselves against such experience so thoroughly that they end up as totally detached as the "well" siblings and parents described above. Such detachment is achieved at the price of not grasping the depth of the transactional disorder in these families. These forms of experience occur most strikingly in response to transactions of the family as a whole; indeed, they are often less prominent in response to the presenting schizophrenic patient than to the rest of the family.

SIBLING DIFFERENCES AND SIMILARITIES

It is our tentative impression, from the study of the structure of the families of schizophrenics at the time the patients have reached young adulthood or late adolescence, that differences and similarities between the patients and their siblings can be accounted for by the interaction of the same two main sets of factors operative in nonschizophrenic families: first, biologic variation which is nonspecific for schizophrenia, and, second, differences in the role of the offspring within the family social structure and emotional organization.

All families make use of biologic differences in sex, age, and birth order as starting points for intrafamilial role differentiation. In addition, neonatal characteristics, especially activity patterns and responsivity to environmental stimuli, which may have a biological basis, but at present seem nonspecific for any particular form of psychopathology, apparently arouse quite different emotional reactions in different parents and set in motion diverse role-expectations depending on the meaning attached to these characteristics. For example, a quiet, unresponsive baby may be satisfying to one mother but anxiety-provoking and frustrating to another.

Still other role differences seem to evolve out of the meanings attached in a particular family to objectively trivial physical features and to physical ailments which in themselves are nonspecific but may lead to a particular child becoming a focus of anxiety or special handling.

Other differences in the family role-expectation toward the various offspring arise out of the vicissitudes of parental emotional or physical states. For example, a child born when the mother is depressed over the death of her own mother will have a different meaning for the mother than children born several years sooner or later.

Thus, it is inappropriate to expect that siblings will experience the same psychological environment just because they grow up in the same family. Certain family patterns may nevertheless affect all the offspring, and contribute to some similarities. For example, those families in which all roles are poorly delineated, or are defined in contradictory and inconsistent ways, will provide a different kind of experience for offspring from that in families with relatively clear, consistent, and developmentally appropriate role-expectations.

By examining the developmental *interplay* of these biological variations and family role-expectations, together with role-expectations from the broader culture, we have been able to make reasonable reconstructions of the differences, and similarities, between schizophrenics and their siblings.

In disturbed families this interplay often involves distortions of obvious biological characteristics. For example, confused sex and generation roles and stereotyped roles which remain unchanged as the child grows older,[7] may lead to bizarre difficulties in the child's emerging sense of identity. In two families studied at NIMH in which the schizophrenic offspring were genetically identical, in one instance, quadruplets, and in the other, triplets, a sibling hierarchy was established which would have been appropriate for siblings of different ages but was strange indeed for siblings born a few minutes apart: the first-born of each of these sets of siblings was regarded as the leader, expected to guide and look after the others from a very early age.[12]

It is our impression that offspring who become overtly schizophrenic characteristically have had family roles in which they are more deeply enmeshed in the family's emotional life than are their nonschizophrenic siblings. The schizophrenic offspring usually fill conflicted roles in which they are greatly needed, for example, to mediate between the parents, to live out an externalized representation of dissociated aspects of one or both parents' personalities, etc. The less overtly disturbed siblings, in contrast, characteristically have less subjective conflict, have not been so participant in the family struggles and have often been able to move out of the family emotionally at an early age. Sometimes they have achieved considerable personal growth from extrafamilial experience which seems much less common among the schizophrenic offspring. Nevertheless, on closer study of the so-called well siblings, it appears that their psychological intactness has commonly been achieved at the cost of an emotional shallowness and cognitive constriction, so that they notice and experience less than their more disturbed siblings. The nonschizophrenic offspring in the families of schizophrenics often appear quite well integrated in situations which are highly structured, but they become very much more disorganized when the environment does not provide structure and they must rely on their own inner experience. Their performance then is much more like that of their schizophrenic siblings. Some of these observations about sibling differences have been discussed and exemplified by Day and Kwiatkowska in a paper from this research program.[13]*

SUMMARY

In summary, comprehensive clinical studies comparing families of schizophrenics with families of nonschizophrenic psychiatric patients and comparing patients with their siblings have been conducted for some years at the National Institute of Mental Health. These studies have suggested that intrafamilial communication and relationship patterns can be linked in considerable detail to forms of personality organization, including styles of thinking, in offspring who have grown up in these families. A series of systematic studies will be reported in companion papers to verify and extend these clinical formulations.

* A very impressive study of the significance of intrafamilial role differences in schizophrenia has recently been reported by Caudill.[14] He has found that eldest sons and youngest daughters of traditional middle-class Japanese families are overrepresented, when compared with siblings in the schizophrenic population of four Japanese hospitals. This statistically significant tendency was not found in new middle-class ("salary man") families. These findings appear consistent with distinctively conflictual roles commonly found in Japanese families who are attempting to retain the traditional Japanese family role-structure.

REFERENCES

1. WYNNE, L., RYCKOFF, I., DAY, J., and HIRSCH, S. 1958. Pseudo-mutuality in the family relations of schizophrenics. *Psychiatry*, 21, 205-220.
2. LIDZ, T., CORNELISON, A., TERRY, D., and FLECK, S. 1958. Intrafamilial environment of the schizophrenic patient: VI. The transmission of irrationality. *Archs Neurol. Psychiat.*, 79, 305-316.
3. ROSENBAUM, C. P. 1961. Patient-family similarities in schizophrenia. *Archs gen. Psychiat.*, 5, 120-126.
4. SCHAFFER, L., WYNNE, L., DAY, J., RYCKOFF, I., HALPERIN, A. 1962. On the nature and sources of the psychiatrists' experience with the family of the schizophrenic. *Psychiatry*, 25, 32-45.
4a. WYNNE, L. C., and SINGER, M. T. 1963. Thought disorder and the family relations of schizophrenics: II. A classification of forms of thinking. *Archs gen. Psychiat.*, 9, 199-206.
5. WYNNE, L. C., and SINGER, M. T. 1963. *The transcultural study of schizophrenics and their families.* Presented at the joint meeting of the American Psychiatric Association and the Japanese Society of Psychiatry and Neurology, Tokyo, May.
5a. SINGER, M. T., and WYNNE, L. C. 1965. Thought disorder, and the family relations of schizophrenics: IV. Results and implications. *Archs gen. Psychiat.*, 12, 201.

6. PARSONS, T., and BALES, R. 1955. *Family, socialization and interaction process.* Free Press, Glencoe, Ill.

7. RYCKOFF, I., DAY, J., and WYNNE, L. C. 1959. Maintenance of stereotyped roles in the families of schizophrenics. *Archs gen. Psychiat.,* **1,** 93-98.

8. MORRIS, G., and WYNNE, L. C. Characteristic styles of communication of families of amorphous and fragmented schizophrenics. To be published.

9. KWIATKOWSKA, H. 1962. Family art therapy: Experiments with a new technique. *Bull. Art Therapy,* Spring, 3-15.

9a. SINGER, M. T., and WYNNE, L. C. 1965. Thought disorder and the family relations of schizophrenics: III. Projective test methodology. *Archs gen. Psychiat.,* **12,** 187.

10. STRODTBECK, F. 1951. Husband-wife interaction over revealed differences. *Am. sociol. Rev.,* **16,** 468-473.

11. LOVELAND, N., and WYNNE, L. 1963. The family Rorschach: A new method for studying family interaction. *Family Process,* Sept.

11a. WYNNE, L. C. 1961. The study of intrafamilial alignments and splits in exploratory family therapy. In ACKERMAN, N. W., BEATMAN, F. L., and SHERMAN, S. N. (eds.) *Exploring the base for family therapy.* Family Service Assoc. of America, New York.

11b. BENJAMIN, J. 1959. Prediction and psychopathological theory. In JESSNER, L., and PAVENSTEDT, E. (eds.) *Dynamic psychopathology in childhood,* pp. 6-77. Grune & Stratton, New York.

12. WYNNE, L. C., DAY, J., HIRSCH, S., and RYCKOFF, I. 1957. The family relations of a set of monozygotic quadruplet schizophrenics. *Report of the Second International Congress of Psychiatry,* Vol. 2. Zurich, Switzerland, Sept.

13. DAY, J., and KWIATKOWSKA, H. 1962. The psychiatric patient and his 'well' sibling: A comparison through their art production. *Bull. Art Therapy,* Winter, 51-66.

14. CAUDILL, W. 1963. *Sibling rank and psychiatric patients.* Paper prepared for Second Conference on Modernization of Japan (held under auspices of Association for Asian Studies), Bermuda, January.

XLIV

THE RELATION OF THE FAMILY TO
MANIC-DEPRESSIVE PSYCHOSIS

CECILE BOLTON FINLEY AND DAVID C. WILSON

An environmental aetiology has been suggested for manic-depressive psychosis. From this study it is postulated that the hostility of the family pattern leads to an attitude of depression in a family member, or to an outward explosion which appears as mania.

No definite cause for manic-depressive psychosis is known but many writers are convinced that there is a hereditary factor. Undoubtedly there are certain intra-personality configurations that are common to persons developing the disease. These characteristics are thought by many to be produced by the culture medium within which the person is nurtured. The common view is expressed by Myerson: "It is not doubted at the present time that the fundamental basis of manic-depressive psychosis is in an inherited constitution. The vast literature on this subject is practically unanimous, although it also appears from certain studies that there probably is an environmental root to the development of this psychosis although what that environmental root may be no one knows."[1] It is to find this unknown environmental root that this study is made.

The social status of persons developing this condition is well established. Landis, Carney and Page have this to say about the matter: "The social status of manic-depressive patients is well above that of all the organic psychoses and of dementia praecox. Comparatively few manic-depressive patients come from either the low educational or economic levels. A large number have attended high school and college. The economic status of those admitted to state hospitals is not the highest, but this may

Reprinted from DISEASES OF THE NERVOUS SYSTEM, Vol. 12, 1951, pp, 39-43.

be due to the fact that the wealthier manic-depressives go to private institutions. This disease is responsible for 16.7% of first admissions to private hospitals and for only 12.9% of first admissions to state mental hospitals."[2] It is the family of the American middle class that supplies the majority of the patients of the manic-depressive group. In a German psychiatric clinic to which patients are admitted irrespective of social position, Luxemberger found manic-depressive psychosis to be nearly three times as frequent in the highest social class and four times as frequent in the professional class as in the general population.[3] The influence of Western European culture is very similar to that found to prevail in the United States.

This Western European culture which has passed over the seas to develop in a more rigid form in the United States was based on family formation. The family unit as it has developed in its strict form is stronger than its parts, and the individual often has to bend to fit the mold constructed by family tradition. Individuals ceased to move freely at their own initiative but bowed to family dominance. Frequently the father or the mother is dominant in the group but more often there is a multi-

TABLE 1

AVERAGE RATES OF MANIC DEPRESSIVE PSYCHOSIS
TOTAL FIRST ADMISSIONS—NORTH, SOUTH, MIDWEST, WEST

NORTH
Male: 6 Vary from Average. More Than One Fourth Average.
Female: 14 Vary from Average. More Than One Fourth Average.

NEW ENGLAND

	Male	Female
Maine	10%	23%
New Hampshire	6%	5%
Vermont	7%	17%
Massachusetts	3%	8%
Rhode Island	8%	19%
Connecticut	4%	8%

MID-ATLANTIC

New Jersey	6%	12%
Pennsylvania	6%	12%
New York	3%	5%

EAST NORTH CENTRAL

Ohio	6%	10%
Indiana	5%	13%
Illinois	3%	7%
		(Average 10%)

SOUTH ATLANTIC

Delaware	7%	22%
Maryland	2%	4%
District of Columbia	6%	5%
West Virginia	6%	16%

NORTH CENTRAL

Michigan	5%	7%
Wisconsin	13%	21%
AVERAGE	6%	12%

phasic dominance resting now on the father, now on the mother, or the older brothers, while all the time the family is the influence that controls behavior.[4]

Margaret Mead in the discussion of Ruth Benedict's paper regarding the effect of swaddling of infants suggests that the way the swaddling is done, not the act itself, is what influences the after-life of the child. The meaning to the family of swaddling is translated in non-verbal emotional language to the child so that the development of the Pole, the Jew and the Russian is differentiated not by similar act, but by the dissimilar meaning.[5] It is not what the family does, but what the meaning is behind the behavior that shapes the child.

Spurgeon English in reporting on observation of trends in manic-depressive psychosis states that "The manic-depressive with his lack of love in early life feels a greater need for love expressed on a childish level than the average." Frieda Fromn Reichmann in discussing English's

TABLE 2

SOUTH

	Male	Female
Kentucky	7%	16%
Tennessee	9%	28%
Alabama	19%	29%
Mississippi	8%	12%
Virginia	12%	27%
North Carolina	16%	29%
South Carolina	13%	16%
Georgia	12%	12%
Florida	7%	29%
AVERAGE	11%	22%

MID-WEST

	Male	Female
Minnesota	8%	13%
Iowa	7%	12%
Missouri	6%	17%
Arkansas	8%	14%
Louisiana	4%	8%
North Dakota	8%	8%
South Dakota	8%	13%
Nebraska	3%	2%
Kansas	12%	19%
Oklahoma	6%	13%
Texas	9%	21%
AVERAGE	7%	13%

WEST

	Male	Female
Montana	8%	13%
Wyoming	7%	17%
New Mexico	(No Figures)	
Idaho	8%	8%
Utah	9%	16%
Arizona	11%	17%
Nevada	3%	8%
Washington	9%	18%
Oregon	8%	15%
California	6%	19%
AVERAGE	7%	14%

Table 3

"Q" Family Tree
Grandfather—John Rhodes Q. (Baptist Minister) married Emma — Paternal Side
Six Sibs

John R. (Dead)	Connie m.—J.O.	Bertie m. Millard	Charles m. Carrie	Frederic H. m. Ida	John R. m. Jo Ann
	1 Sib—Leslie m. Russell E.	6 Sibs	6 Sibs	4 Sibs	2 Sibs
		1. Harry m. Gretchen No Sibs	1. Lawrence R. m. Ella N.	1. Frederic H.* m.	1. Lois (Dead)
		2. Virginia* m. James	2. Guilford m. Ethel K.	2. Dean* m. Louise No Sibs	2. Sarah Louise 1 Sib—Fred, Jr.
		3. Phillip m. & Sibs	3. Velma m. S. H.	3. Payne* m. Louise No Sibs	
		4. John m. & Sibs	4. Marjorie m. Clarence E.	4. Willard (Dead) m. Dorothy 1 Sib—Dorothy	
		5. Alfred Unmarried	5. Vernon m. Agnes		
		6. Elizabeth Unmarried	6. Charles Unmarried		

* Persons with affective disorder.

TABLE 4

"Q" FAMILY TREE

MATERNAL SIDE

GRANDFATHER JOHN P. (METHODIST MINISTER) MARRIED ELLEN CUSHEN

TEN SIBS

JOHN T. (Dead)	FRANK m.	THOMAS E. m.

IDA DORSEY m. FREDERIC H. Q. 4 SIBS	CARRIE m. CHARLES Q. 6 SIBS

MORRIS (Dead)	LIL m. BAKE B. WOODSON 1 SIB	NELL* m. HALE CONNOLLY No SIBS	PEARL (Dead)

INDA m. WALTER F. CLARK

I

1. Frederic H.*
   m. Lois
   2nd Sarah
   1 Sib
2. Dean*
   m. Louise
3. Payne*
   m. Louise
4. Willard (Dead)
   m. Dorothy
   1 Sib

II

1. Lawrence R. m. Elle Nancy
   2 Sibs–Girls
2. Guilford m. Ethel
   3 Sibs–Girls
3. Velma m. S. H.
   1 Sib–Girl
4. Marjorie m. C. E.
   2 Sibs–Girls
5. Vernon m. Agnes
   2 Sibs–Girls
6. Charles
   Unmarried

* Persons with affective disorder.

paper makes a contribution from her biographical data. She says: "I wish to elaborate on Dr. English's statement that 'this is due to faulty handling of love and hatred in early childhood.'[6] From the childhood history of our patients they come as a rule from families with multiple family figures. Moreover, there is usually no one who is interested in the welfare of the child in his own right. The relatedness of the grown-ups

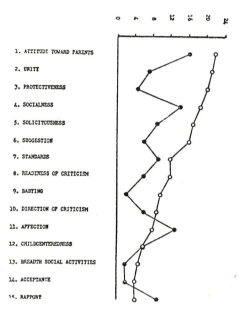

1. ATTITUDE TOWARD PARENTS
2. UNITY
3. PROTECTIVENESS
4. SOCIALNESS
5. SOLICITOUSNESS
6. SUGGESTION
7. STANDARDS
8. READINESS OF CRITICISM
9. BABYING
10. DIRECTION OF CRITICISM
11. AFFECTION
12. CHILDCENTEREDNESS
13. BREADTH SOCIAL ACTIVITIES
14. ACCEPTANCE
15. RAPPORT

FIG. 1. Comparison of scores of manic depressive patients with scores of normal controls on Fels Traits indicated. Positive scores represent extremes of pressure.

to the child is determined by the purpose for which it is needed and by the role into which it is cast according to the need of the family. . . . They (these families) accomplish these necessities by eagerly cultivating their part in a closely knit group unity and by adhering and teaching their young to adhere to their conventionalized group values. . . . Manic-depressives can only be treated successfully if the therapist is able to help them break through their clinging dependence upon the family and its substitutes and to revaluate the conventional group values of the family."[7]

These writers believe that manic-depressive psychosis is a disease of the upper economic bracket and also of families of the better social standing. There is a distinct feeling that in the environment there is some causative factor. Since the disease is apparently a family affair, it is well to look into the families of persons who suffer from the disease to see how they differ from families in which the disease does not develop.

A typical American family is supposed to be an Anglo-Saxon middle-class family of Protestant faith. This typical family is found in its most static form along parts of the Eastern Seaboard and in the Southern States.[8] It is interesting to find that studies by the U.S. Department of Commerce Bureau of Census published in 1948 in their Bulletin regarding patients in mental institutions of 1916 show that the percentage of first admissions that are diagnosed as having manic-depressive psychosis average at least one-third more in the Southern states than in any Northern

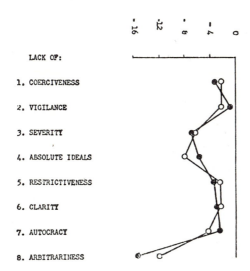

LACK OF:

1. COERCIVENESS
2. VIGILANCE
3. SEVERITY
4. ABSOLUTE IDEALS
5. RESTRICTIVENESS
6. CLARITY
7. AUTOCRACY
8. ARBITRARINESS

FIG. 2. Scores of families of manic depressive patients and normal controls on Fels discipline rating. Positive scores represent extremes of pressure.

or Western states, other than Maine in the Northeast and Wisconsin in the North Central district, a finding that suggests again the family relationship to the disease.[9]

From these data it was thought worthwhile to study the relationship of the family organization in the South in relation to this disorder. Immediately a remarkable family was unearthed where two brothers had married two sisters. The older couple had four children. Three of these developed manic-depressive psychosis. The younger couple had six children, none of whom developed any signs of the disease. It was apparent that if there was an environmental factor at work in the family organization, it would be evident in this setting. Ida P and Carrie P were sisters. Ida was the older and more dominant. Fred Q and Charlie Q were brothers. Fred was the older but very passive, easy-going and submissive, while Charlie, the younger, was more self-assertive. Charlie and Carrie made a better team than did Fred and Ida.

Investigation of the two families showed that although they lived and developed within a mile of each other, the intra-family setting was entirely different. Family "Q I" was very close and a dominant mother held the group together as a unit so that even in adult life her four sons were controlled by family pressures, while in the other family the discipline

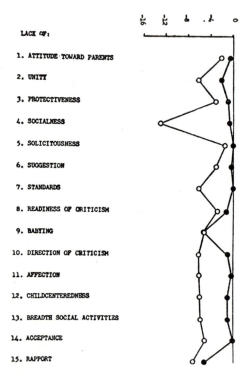

LACK OF:

1. ATTITUDE TOWARD PARENTS
2. UNITY
3. PROTECTIVENESS
4. SOCIALNESS
5. SOLICITOUSNESS
6. SUGGESTION
7. STANDARDS
8. READINESS OF CRITICISM
9. BABYING
10. DIRECTION OF CRITICISM
11. AFFECTION
12. CHILDCENTEREDNESS
13. BREADTH SOCIAL ACTIVITIES
14. ACCEPTANCE
15. RAPPORT

FIG. 3. Comparison of scores of families of manic depressive patients with scores of normal controls on Fels Traits indicated. Negative scores represent extremes of freedom.

was stern but each member was permitted to follow his own inclinations as an individual. The desires of the individual were fostered by the parents for the greater good of the child rather than from the standpoint of family unity or welfare of the group. The occurrence of severe crippling illness and the tragedies that went with it obscured the picture of the development of Family "Q II," and even today, after the mother and father are gone, the thinking of the surviving members is first of the family. Their property belongs to the group rather than to individuals.

The investigation of this family has led to selection of ten families in which manic-depressive disorders have occurred, and ten families of similar economic status as well as size in which there has been no evidence of the condition. It is planned to study the groups by means of a questionnaire and by means of individual interviews until a picture of the family can be drawn. This study is still under way, and to date only five families have had a thorough study. From these studies a concept is forming, but presentation of this concept of the family setting characteristic of the affective disorders will have to wait further examination before

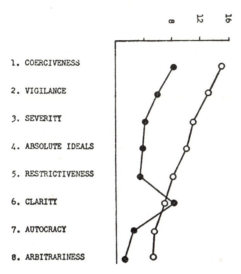

Fig. 4. Scores of families of manic depressive patients and normal controls on Fels discipline rating. Negative scores represent extremes of freedom.

it can be expressed. However, interesting data has been compiled. A modified family opinnionaire intended to show patterns of parent behavior was employed. This Fels Rating Scale was originated by the Fels Research Institute.[10] It studies the opinion of the members of the family regarding the family organization and the parental discipline. The opinion of the member is gauged by degrees above or below the culture norm. The degrees positive or above the norm denote family pressure in certain traits, while degrees negative denote freedom from coercion in these traits. Fifteen opinionnaires of members of manic-depressive families were graded and thirty opinionnaires from adult college students in whose families there was no known disease were contrasted with the fifteen. The figures 1-4 show graphically the differences between the manic-depressive and the normal controls.

Although the number of opinionnaires examined is limited and the families studied still very few, already a definite difference has been demonstrated. There is something in the family setting that is of significance in the construction of manic-depressive psychosis. The setting of a family pattern by a dominant mother, a dominant father or by dominant siblings constructs a walled-in existence for family members which frustrates individual initiative and makes weaker members feel guilty because of the ensuing hostility. This hostility to their fixed life leads to an attitude which causes depression, or an explosion outward which appears as mania.

SUMMARY

This paper seeks to demonstrate that manic-depressive psychosis is most frequently found among members of families with traditions of the more intellectual and better established groups. The disease is more common in the South. Detailed studies of five Southern families indicate that there is a different pattern of organization and discipline in families prone to the disease. A contrast of opinionnaires filled out by members of such families with members of supposedly sound families substantiates this difference.

REFERENCES

1. Myerson, Abraham, and Boyle, D. Rosalie. 1941. The incidence of manic-depressive psychosis in certain socially important families, preliminary report. *Am. J. Psychiat.*, **98**, 12.
2. Landis, Carney, and Page, James D. 1948. *Modern society and mental disease*, pp. 64-65. Farrar & Rinehart, New York.
3. Noyes, Arthur P. 1949. *Modern clinical psychiatry*, 3rd ed., p. 328. Saunders, Philadelphia.
4. Kluckhohn, Clyde. 1949. *Mirror for man: The relation of anthropology to modern life*, pp. 200-203. McGraw-Hill, New York.
5. Child rearing in certain European countries—Discussion. *Am. J. Orthopsychiat.*, **19**, 349-350.
6. English, O. Spurgeon. 1949. Observations of trends in manic-depressive psychosis. *Psychiatry*, **12**, 125.
7. Reichmann, Frieda Fromn. Discussion of above. *Psychiatry*, **12**, 133-134.
8. *Mirror for man.* (See above.)
9. *Sociological data, patients in mental hospitals*, p. 16. U.S. Dept. Commerce. U.S. Government Printing Office.
10. *Pattern of parent behavior. Psychological monograph*, 1948, Nos. 58, 3. American Psychiatric Assoc., Northwestern University, Evanston, Ill.

XLV

THE FAMILIES OF DULL CHILDREN
A Classification for Predicting Careers

ZENA STEIN AND MERVYN SUSSER

*Family analysis has identified a group of dysmorphic
families. Educational subnormal children from such
families are found to be at a disadvantage in terms of
domestic stability, employment records and contact with
the law. They are vulnerable to institutional admission.*

Under the Education Act of 1944, children who are backward at school
may be referred for a special medical examination and officially "ascertained" as educationally subnormal (E.S.N.). On leaving school, they
may be notified to the Local Health Authority and placed under the
supervision of the mental health service. Some authorities, believing that
these young people are able to manage their own affairs, take no action
in such cases, whereas others place nearly all of them under statutory
supervision and thus give them the legal status of mental defectives.

The absence of uniformity in dealing with them prompted the present
investigation, the purpose of which was to discover whether a grouping
of E.S.N. subjects by family circumstances might indicate their real needs.

METHOD

It was decided to follow up a group of subjects who had been ascertained
as E.S.N. during their schooldays, and to interview both them and their
parents. Additional information was sought from other sources, such as
School Welfare Departments, the National Society for the Prevention of

Reprinted from BRITISH JOURNAL OF PREVENTATIVE AND SOCIAL
MEDICINE, Vol. 14, 1960, pp. 83-88.

Cruelty to Children (N.S.P.C.C.), Children's Departments, Health Departments, Probation Officers, and voluntary agencies.

In the cohort of children born between 1933 and 1937, 319 subjects had been ascertained as E.S.N. in Salford City and Lancashire County. From these individuals, who were aged between 20 and 24 years at the time of the study, a group of 106 was selected at random for investigation. Adequate records were not available for earlier cohorts. Interviews were successfully completed with the parents of all save seven of the subjects. Sufficient information was obtained about all the 106 cases to enable each to be placed in one of the three family groups described below.

FAMILY GROUPS

In making this classification attention was focused on two functions of the elementary family. The first of these is the provision of a set of enduring human relationships and the second the provision by the adult members of basic standards of care for the children.

It was assumed that the first function had been fulfilled if the subject's elementary family group had always included at least one parent or substitute parent until he had reached the age of 10 years. The second function was taken as fulfilled if the family had not been prosecuted by any of three social agencies: the School Welfare and Attendance Office, the N.S.P.C.C., and the Children's Department.

By our criteria, both functions had been fulfilled in 74 families (termed "functioning"), ten families (termed "deviant") had been dealt with by at least one of the three social agencies, and 22 families (termed "dysmorphic") had failed to provide enduring relationships.

RESULTS

1. AT THE TIME OF ASCERTAINMENT

The Subjects

Sex and I.Q. Scores.—There were 68 boys and 38 girls in the survey group. Their I.Q. scores, assessed at school on the Terman Merrill test, ranged from 44 to 86, the average for boys being 72 and for girls 64.

When the subjects were divided into the three family categories, the sex and I.Q. distributions of the functioning and deviant groups were found to be alike and to differ from those of the dysmorphic group. Thus in the functioning and deviant groups there were more than twice as many males as females (58 to 26), but in the dysmorphic group females outnumbered males (12 to 10). The average I.Q. for the boys was roughly the same in all three family groups, but for girls it was slightly lower in the functioning and deviant groups than in the dysmorphic group (64 and 68 respectively).

The Families

Social Class (Table 1).—In the present series there were no cases from Social Class I and only four from Social Class II. This distribution accords with hospital and other statistics on the feeble-minded (Registrar General, 1958) and on backward children (Burt, 1950). There were fewer fathers in Social Class III than expected, and only three of these were in non-manual occupations.

TABLE 1

SOCIAL CLASS AT THE TIME OF ASCERTAINMENT OF THREE FAMILY TYPES
(106 Subjects)

Social Class*		Type of Family			
		Functioning	Deviant	Dysmorphic	Total
I	...	0	0	0	0
II	...	3	0	1	4
III	...	15	1	3	19
IV	...	6	1	0	7
V { Regular Work	...	47	6	5	58
Casual or Irregular Labourers ...	...	3	2	12	17
Unknown	...	0	0	1	1
Total Males ...	...	50	8	10	68
Females	...	24	2	12	38
Grand Total ...	...	74	10	22	106

Only 4 per cent. of fathers of functioning families were casual or irregular labourers, but the dysmorphic families were weighted in favour of such occupations (55 per cent.). The fathers of deviant families were intermediate between these.

All the families, including those in Social Class II, belonged to working class cultures, and almost all the fathers were in urban employment.

After the time of ascertainment, one deviant family in Social Class III moved down to Class V, and two functioning families moved up to Social Class II from Social Classes III and IV respectively.

Structure (Table 2).—67 (90 per cent.) of the children from functioning families and all those from deviant families had always lived with both parents till they reached the age of 10 years.

By definition, no cases from dysmorphic families had lived with parents throughout the whole of this period; eight did so until they reached 5 years of age and a further three until they were 2 years old, and in eleven cases the elementary family was never established. After an initial break-up of family life, seven later lived with a parent or with other relatives for short periods, but fifteen failed to find support from relatives. It was characteristic of the group as a whole that the subjects had experi-

* For seven illegitimate subjects, the maternal grandfather's occupation has been used as the index.

TABLE 2

ELEMENTARY FAMILY STRUCTURE* DURING THE FIRST 10 YEARS OF LIFE
(106 Subjects)

Period with Both Parents (yrs)	Type of Family			
	Functioning	Deviant	Dysmorphic	Total
Never	0	0	11	11
Up to 2	2	0	3	5
Up to 5	2	0	7	9
Up to 9	3	0	1	4
10 and over ...	67 +	10 +	0	77
Total	74	10	22	106

enced numerous changes of foster homes or institutions during their childhood.

Only one of the ten illegitimate subjects was born into a family classed as functioning and the remaining nine were born into families classed as dysmorphic.

Desertion by one or both parents accounted for the disruption of eight families and early death of a mother for two. In three other cases the children were removed from their homes after the parents had been prosecuted for neglect. Early death of a father had occurred in two families which nevertheless continued to function.

Agency Contacts (Table 3).—Three of the 74 functioning families were visited by the School Attendance Officer, in each case for truancy, which required only one visit and no prosecution.

Two functioning families appeared in the records of the N.S.P.C.C., each with single contacts to press for attendance at school medical clinics. In accord with our definition, five of six deviant families on the list of the School Attendance Officers had been prosecuted and five deviant families had been cautioned or prosecuted by the N.S.P.C.C. The Children's

TABLE 3

AGENCY CONTACTS OF 84 DEVIANT AND FUNCTIONING FAMILIES

Agency	Type of Family		
	Deviant	Functioning	Total
School Welfare	6	3	9
N.S.P.C.C	5	2	7
Children's Department	5	0	5
Known to None of These Agencies	0	69	69
Total Number of Contacts ...	16	5	21
Total Number of Families ...	10	74	84

* In twenty of these families, the father was away for various periods on war service. In a further seven the subject spent periods in hosital, and in three others he was evacuated.

Department had records of five deviant families, and in four of these the subject had been taken into temporary care.

For the functioning families, the average number of contacts with a wide range of social agencies was one; for deviant families it was three.

II. At the Time of Follow-up

Domestic Unit.—At the time of follow-up, twelve of the young women from functioning and two from dysmorphic families were married; eight of the young men from functioning, two from dysmorphic, and one from deviant families were also married. 81 (96 per cent.) of the subjects from functioning and deviant families were living either with parents or spouses at the time of follow-up. Against this, only ten (45 per cent.) of the subjects from dysmorphic families were living with kin. By this time, seven cases, one from a functioning family and six from dysmorphic families, were in mental deficiency hospitals. All had been admitted on emergency applications soon after leaving school, following misdemeanours which were sometimes multiple but always minor (petty theft, two cases; "found wandering" and the suspicion of immorality, two cases; impudence to an employer, one case; "out of control" at home or school, two cases). No child was in a mental deficiency institution at 10 years of age and Table 4 shows that, for E.S.N. groups, admission is a specific hazard of adolescents who have no support from kin.

Employment Records.—There was little unemployment in the area during the relevant period and only those subjects who were later admitted to institutions had had difficulty in finding jobs. There was, however, a high proportion of unstable job histories in the dysmorphic group.

Table 4

Present Home of 106 Subjects, by Family Type and Sex

Home		Type of Family			
		Functioning	Deviant	Dysmorphic	Total
With Kindred	With family of origin ...	52	8	3	63
	With spouse alone ...	13	1	3	17
	With spouse and parents	5	0	0	5
	With spouse and spouse's parents	2	0	1	3
	With other relatives ...	0	0	3	3
With Strangers	In Lodgings	0	1	3	4
	No fixed abode ...	0	0	1	1
Institution	Mental deficiency colony	1	0	6	7
	Other medical institution	0	0	1	1
	Private or church institution	1	0	1	2
Total		74	10	22	106

Thus, the average duration of each job in the dysmorphic group was less than 20 months compared with more than 30 months in the other two groups. Similar differences were detected when aspects of work were considered: *e.g.* longest period in any one job, total number of jobs, number of short term jobs, and number of persons with stable jobs within a year of leaving school. Calculations taking into account the duration of the period of possible employment and thus adjusted for age at leaving school, for time spent in the forces or in institutions, and for marriage in women yielded differences that are unlikely to be due to chance ($P = 0\cdot01$ for the men, $P = 0\cdot03$ for the women). As the distributions were not normal, probabilities were calculated by a distribution-free test (Mood, 1950).

Legal Offences.—The 68 male subjects included eleven who had had one legal charge preferred against them and eighteen who had been charged more than once. The family group distribution of these offenders was as follows:

Legal Charges (males only)	Family Group			
	Functioning	Deviant	Dysmorphic	Total
None	33	3	3	39
One	6	1	4	11
More than One ...	11	4	3	18
Total at risk ...	50	8	10	68

It is clear from these figures that relative to the numbers "at risk", single and multiple offences featured most often in the dysmorphic group. Deviant families were intermediate.

Only three females, two from dysmorphic and one from a functioning family, had had legal charges preferred against them.

Illegitimate Births.—Two women, one from a functioning and one from a dysmorphic family, had had babies out of wedlock.

DISCUSSION

Objective Classification of Family Function

Important functions of a family are to provide a home with a set of enduring human relationships, and basic standards of care for its dependent members.

Satisfactory function depends largely on the intact structure of the family. Structure is based on kinship and marriage and in our society the typical unit is the elementary family, composed of father, mother, and children, who share a common home until the children are old enough to marry or earn their own living. In the present study relationships were regarded as enduring if at least one parent or parent-substitute had lived with the child until he reached the age of 10. In some cases, family function was maintained in spite of departures from the typical structure of the elementary family, as Table 2 shows. As the results for subjects from these families were similar to those from typical functioning families, it was thought unnecessary to categorize them separately. Thus the following variations in structure satisfied the criterion of enduring relationships:

1. Substitution of other kin for parents, *e.g.* grandmother (2 cases).

2. One parent fulfilling the functions of both mother and father, *e.g.* widowed mother able to rear her children without breaking up the family (2 cases).

3. Temporarily incomplete families, *e.g.* a father on war service (17 cases), away on distant work (1 case), or a parent in hospital (2 cases).

4. Families with a child temporarily removed but persisting as a unit and maintaining contact with the child, *e.g.* 3 cases evacuated and 7 cases admitted to hospital for more than 3 months.

Other variants, such as adoption, might have been allowed in the category of functioning families but did not in fact occur.

In dysmorphic families, structure was so damaged that they were unable to provide the child with enduring relationships. This arose usually in situations which were already precarious because of poverty, irregular employment, isolation from kin, or physical and mental handicaps, and the immediate factors were usually parental death or desertion, separation or divorce, or an illegitimate birth following a casual union. As a result, all 22 cases in this group had been in supportive institutions at some time before the age of 10. This is a high proportion of the total as compared with a national sample of children born in 1946 (Douglas and Blomfield, 1958). At 5 years of age, only 0·07 per cent. in the national sample had been separated from their parents; taking the same age and the same criteria for separation, 13·5 per cent. of our sample would have suffered separation.

Basic standards of care were regarded as maintained if the child had been given economic and social support at a level not in conflict either with norms accepted at all levels of society or with local social norms. Social norms may be taken as "people's ideas about what behaviour is customary and what behaviour is right and proper in their social class" (Bott, 1956).

The chosen criterion of deviation from these norms was prosecution or cautioning by three social agencies concerned with child care which have the power to invoke legal sanctions. We chose this criterion because contacts with these agencies arose from conflicts with general and local norms. Child care that was considered inadequate by neighbourhood standards had sometimes provoked reports to the agencies. In other cases failure to attend school, a general obligation enforced by law, had initiated action by education authorities. In addition, social workers in these and other agencies, influenced in turn by their own notions and standards, ultimately determined whether the agencies acted and how they acted. The families in this group had usually failed to provide adequate shelter, food, clothing, or schooling, and they belonged to the category of so-called "problem families".

Intervention by an agency which could invoke legal sanctions had usually meant that a host of other agencies, voluntary and statutory, had also intervened at some stage. The nature as well as the number of contacts which functioning families had with social agencies differed from those of the deviant families. Deviant families tended to attract disciplinary action, as opposed to functioning families for whom the contact was more often voluntary, as with child guidance clinics.

The parents of most of the deviant families were native to the districts in which they now lived and had numerous social contacts with their relatives. Although these connexions might have helped to maintain the cohesion of the family, they did not screen its members from contact with the social agencies. Support from relatives, however, might have prevented admissions to supportive institutions.

FAMILY CLASSIFICATION AND CAREER

E.S.N. subjects, grouped by objective criteria according to the function of their family of origin, have careers with distinctive patterns.

The great majority of subjects from functioning families were holding steady jobs, living with their parents or spouses, and leading stable social lives. The social adjustment of subjects from deviant families, as judged by dwelling place, admissions to institutions, employment, though not contact with the law, were similar to those from functioning families. At the time of follow-up most of the subjects had yet to experience child-bearing and child-rearing, the phase of the family cycle during which agency attention is most often attracted to the deviant family.

For those from dysmorphic families, the follow-up situation was markedly different. More than half of the cases from these families were living either alone in lodgings or in institutions, their work records were poor, and their police records tarnished.

SELECTION FOR ASCERTAINMENT

As in previous surveys of ascertained E.S.N. youths, a disproportionate number of subjects from "broken homes" was found (Ramer, 1946; Reeves-Kennedy, 1948; Graham, 1958; Ferguson and Kerr, 1958). This excess might arise because more subjects of a given intelligence are ascertained from broken families than from intact families, or because in some way broken families produce more backward children than intact families. According to a study in Derby, boys with intelligence quotients below 80 came from broken homes no more often than matched controls with intelligence quotients in the range 94 to 106 (O'Connor and Loos,

1951). This suggests that, given the same intelligence, children from dysmorphic families are more liable to be ascertained as educationally subnormal than are those from functioning families. This may also apply to deviant families, whose members tend to fail in school and to attract the attention of teachers and of the school health service. Other evidence from this investigation suggests that selection by social factors occurs to a marked degree in ascertainment and probably accounts for the I.Q. difference between the two sexes.

The higher average test score for boys (P 0·001–0·002) is consistent with the larger proportion of boys ascertained in our sample and also throughout the country (Ministry of Education, 1956). As the distribution of intelligence between the sexes is similar, it follows that the threshold of intelligence for ascertainment is higher for boys than for girls. Thus factors beyond intelligence, such as social and classroom behaviour, must influence the selection of boys rather than of girls for ascertainment.

This sex difference occurred only in functioning and deviant families, from which boys came more than twice as often as girls, and not in dysmorphic families, from which they came in approximately equal numbers. Evidently the disturbances arising from dysmorphic situations were so severe that they overrode the usual sex bias, or else girls were considered to be more in need of special education in these situations.

Admissions to Mental Deficiency Hospitals

The present survey has shown that, on leaving school, ascertained children from dysmorphic families are more liable to be admitted to mental deficiency institutions, than are those from intact families. Admissions tend to follow a typical pattern. At 18 years of age these children are discharged from the care and the institutions of the Children's Departments to fend for themselves. During adolescence, behaviour difficulties, frequent job changing and homelessness, or the prospect of such problems, exert a cumulative effect on those concerned with the care of these dull children, until finally admission is precipitated by some trivial offence.

Subjects from functioning families make social adjustments which are probably normal in their social groups and they are rarely admitted to mental deficiency hospitals. It follows that, just as the children who are officially recognized as educationally subnormal are not a true cross-section of mentally-retarded children, neither are the inmates of mental deficiency institutions a true cross-section of mentally-retarded adults. These institutions include an unduly high proportion of individuals from dysmorphic families, with the result that assessments of their social competence, intelligence, or personality cannot be relied upon to indicate the social consequences of mental retardation as such. Thus the present investigation suggests that the high delinquency rates and poor employment records of the subnormal in the community and especially in hospital may be largely a consequence of family disruption and homelessness. Several previous studies may need re-evaluation in the light of these findings.

Family analysis has identified a group of dysmorphic families among the educationally subnormal, which is vulnerable irrespective of intelligence quotient. In most cases they need homes, counselling, and therapy continuously from the onset of disaster until they become settled in the community.

SUMMARY

1. A classification of families, based on their provision of a set of enduring human relationships and basic social needs, is described. These groups are: functioning, deviant, and dysmorphic.

2. The relationship between type of family and the eventual adjustment of 106 subjects, ascertained subnormal at school, has been studied at a follow-up made when they were between 20 and 24 years of age.

3. In terms of domestic stability, employment records, and contacts with the law, subjects from dysmorphic families are shown to be at a disadvantage compared with those from functioning and even from deviant families. In their early 20s, subjects from deviant families resemble those from functioning families in social performance.

4. Ascertained young people from dysmorphic families are shown to be a vulnerable group; more than a quarter of them had been admitted to mental deficiency institutions after leaving school, although they were no less intelligent than the ascertained children from intact families, who were very rarely admitted.

5. Intelligence did not account for the observed differences in social performance in the three family types.

6. Boys are more likely to be ascertained than girls of the same intelligence, although this does not hold for subjects from dysmorphic families.

ACKNOWLEDGEMENTS

We were assisted by Medical Officers of Health and social workers from many authorities and we are grateful for their help.

Dr. N. O'Connor, Dr. M. Carstairs, and Dr. J. Tizard of the Social Psychiatry Unit, Maudsley Hospital, and Drs. Ann and Alan Clarke of the Manor, Epsom, have made valuable criticisms, and Dr. M. Bulmer has assisted us in the statistical analysis. We thank particularly our field workers, Mrs. Godsell and the Misses Edwards, Melsher, Normanton, Perryer, and Sherman, and our technical assistant, Mrs. Pendred. We thank Dr. J. L. Burn and Dr. S. C. Gawne for their help, and Professor C. Fraser Brockington for his interest and encouragement. We have profited greatly from discussions with Dr. W. Watson of the Department of Social Anthropology, Manchester University.

REFERENCES

BOTT, E. 1956. *Hum. Relat.*, **9**, 325.

BURT, C. L. 1950. *The backward child*, 3rd ed. Univ. London Press, London.

DOUGLAS, J. W. B., and BLOMFIELD, J. M. 1958. *Children under five*. Allen & Unwin, London.

FERGUSON, T., and KERR, A. W. 1958. *Scot. med. J.*, **3**, 31.

GRAHAM, J. A. G. 1958. *Med. Offr.*, **99**, 191.

Ministry of Education. 1956. The health of the school child. *Report of the Chief Medical Officer of the Ministry of Education for 1954 and 1955.* H.M.S.O., London.

MOOD, A. M. 1950. *Introduction to the theory of statistics.* McGraw-Hill, New York.

O'CONNOR, N., and LOOS, F. M. 1951. Occupational record of backward boys: The relation between intelligence, family size, and job history. *Report for the Medical Research Council* (Unpublished).

RAMER, T. 1946. The prognosis of mentally-retarded children. *Acta psychiat. scand.*, Suppl. 41.

REEVES-KENNEDY, R. J. 1948. *The social adjustment of morons in a Connecticut city.* Mansfield-Southbury Training Schools (Social Service Department, State Office building), Hartford.

Registrar-General. 1958. *Statistical review of England and Wales for the two years, 1952-1953. Supplement on Mental Health.* H.M.S.O., London.

4

THERAPY

The management of family psychopathology embraces many techniques—some traditional and some devised for the purpose. Illustrated here are the following procedures:

Family Group Therapy
Family therapy at home
Multiple Impact Therapy
Management of the marital partner
Vector therapy
Inpatient care

XLVI

FAMILY PSYCHOTHERAPY

MURRAY BOWEN

This account by a pioneer in the field of family research in schizophrenia outlines psychotherapy based on the family unit; in a number of instances entire families were admitted to hospital for therapy.

THE RESEARCH PROJECT

The resource material for this workshop comes from a research project in which normal parents and their adult schizophrenic offspring lived together on a psychiatric ward of a research center in a continuing "in residence" observation and treatment situation. The theoretical orientation "the family as the unit of illness" regarded the psychosis in the patient as a symptom of an active process that involved the entire family. The treatment approach "the family as the unit of treatment" was a method of psychotherapy in which all family members attended all the psychotherapy hours together.

Certain important background information about the project will be summarized briefly in this introduction. The project was started in 1954 and terminated at the end of 1958. The study was first focused on the mother-patient relationship. Three mothers lived on the ward with the patients. Each mother and each patient had individual psychotherapy. The "living together" situation provided a new area of observational data that had not been anticipated from previous work with mothers and patients individually. This data led to the formulation of the "family unit" hypothesis which was instituted at the end of the first year. The psychosis in the patient was then seen as a single manifestation of the total family problem. The research plan was changed to admit families so that the entire family unit could live together on the ward. The psycho-

Reprinted from THE AMERICAN JOURNAL OF ORTHOPSYCHIATRY, Vol. 31, No. 1, January 1961, pp. 40-60.

therapy was then directed at the family unit, rather than to individuals in the family.

A total of 18 families participated in the study. This included the 3 mother-patient families from the individual phase. Two of the mother-patient families continued to participate after the change to the "family unit" orientation. One of the mother-patient families lived on the ward for 25 months and the other for 35 months. There were 7 families with fathers, mothers, patients and normal siblings who lived "in residence" as long as 33 months and whose averaging participation was a few days under 12 months. These 7 families were the center point of the project. They provided observational data which made it possible to further define the hypothesis, and the psychotherapeutic data which made it possible to work out details of family psychotherapy. After the family psychotherapy was defined as a workable structure, there were 8 families with fathers, mothers and psychotic patients who were treated in outpatient family psychotherapy for periods as long as 30 months. An additional 12 families were studied in detailed outpatient evaluations. These families provided valuable supplemental data, but since they were not part of the family psychotherapy effort, they were not included in the research study.

A number of practical changes were involved in adapting the "family unit" operation to the ward setting. The ward could accommodate two or three families at a time, depending on the size of the families. Small families were chosen in order to accommodate as many as possible. The ward milieu was structured so that crucial elements of the family unit could be maintained in the living-together situation. The parents were required to assume the principal responsibility for the care of their psychotic offspring. The nursing staff functioned more to help the parents than to assume direct responsibility for the patients. One parent was free to continue regular employment as long as the other parent remained with the patient and both parents could attend the daily family psychotherapy hours. Both parents could leave together by making arrangements with the nursing staff to "sit" with the patient. Parents could take the patients on outside trips provided they could handle the situation responsibly.

This long-term view of the families as they lived, ate, worked and played together through periods of calmness and crisis, periods of family success and family failure, and periods of serious family illness provided a "talking and action" view of the family that has not been equaled by any other situation in our experience. Also to be stressed is the fact that the staff was in a therapeutic position to the families. The psychotherapist, in a helping relationship, had access to an area of communication and data that is not available to the "objective observer" relationship.

FAMILY PSYCHOTHERAPY

The family psychotherapy for this research project was developed directly from the theoretical premise "the family as the unit of illness." Some knowledge of the theoretical premise is crucial to a clear understanding of the therapeutic approach. I shall deal first with the theoretical premise "the family as the unit of illness," and then with the psychotherapeutic approach "the family as the unit of treatment."

The development of the theoretical premise, presented in detail in other papers,[1,2,3] will be summarized briefly. The first working hypothesis for the project was developed from previous experience in psychoanalytic psychotherapy with schizophrenic patients and with their parents. Improvement had been more consistent in the patients whose parents were also in psychotherapeutic relationships. Schizophrenia was regarded as a psychopathological entity within the person of the patient, which had been influenced to a principal degree by the child's early relationship with the mother. The basic character problem, on which psychotic symptoms were later superimposed, was considered to be an unresolved symbiotic attachment to the mother. The symbiotic attachment was regarded as an arrest in the normal psychological growth process between mother and child, which was initiated by the infant's response to the emotional immaturity of the mother, which neither wanted and against which both had struggled unsuccessfully over the years. This latter point was important. When the hypothesis avoided "blaming" the mothers, new theoretical and clinical flexibilities became possible. I believe "blaming" is inherently present, no matter how much it is toned down or denied, in any theory that views one person as "causal" to the problem in another. The hypothesis further postulated that mother and patient could begin to grow toward differentiation from each other with individual psychotherapy for both.

The research plan in the first year provided for mothers and patients to live together on the ward, for staff persons to interfere as little as possible in the relationship problems between the two, and for each to have psychotherapy. The working hypothesis, formulated from experience with mothers and patients individually, had accurately predicted the way each would relate to the other as individuals. It did not predict, nor even consider, a large area of observations, that emerged from the living-together situation. The "emotional oneness" between mother and patient was more intense than expected. The oneness was so close that each could accurately know the other's feelings, thoughts and dreams. In a sense they could "feel for each other," or even "be for each other." There were definite characteristics to the way the "oneness" related to fathers or other outside figures. This emotional oneness is quite different from the emotional separateness between the mothers and their normal children. There were repeated observations to suggest that the mother-patient oneness extended beyond the mother and patient to involve the father and other family members. The mothers and patients used individual psychotherapy more to restore harmony to the oneness than to differentiate from each other.

With the change to the family unit hypothesis, the focus was on the "family oneness" rather than on individuals. At that point we could have kept the familiar individual orientation and focused on characteristics of individual relationships, but we had the research facility to make an exploration into the different way of thinking, and there were observations to support the "family unit" hypothesis as a profitable way to approach the problem. The hypothesis was changed to regard the psychosis as a symptom of an active process that involved the entire family. Just as a generalized physical illness can focus in one organ, so schizophrenia was seen as a generalized family problem which disabled one member of the family organism. The research plan was changed to admit new families in which fathers, mothers, patients and normal siblings could live together on the ward. The research design was adapted to the family unit instead of the individual. For instance, the ward milieu was adapted for family activity rather than individual activity, and the staff attempted to think in terms of the family unit rather than the individual. The psychotherapy was changed to "the family as the unit of treatment" approach.

The theoretical concept "the family as the unit of illness" is basic to every aspect of the research and clinical operation. It is the theoretical foundation from which family psychotherapy was developed as a logical orderly system. The terms "family as a unit" and "family unit" are used as short forms of "the family as the unit of illness." On one level this concept appears so simple and obvious that it hardly deserves second mention. On another level, the concept is subtle and complex, with far-reaching implications that involve a major shift in the way man thinks about himself and illness, and in the theory and practice of medicine. In an effort to communicate as clearly as possible about the concept, I shall describe some of the experiences of the staff in shifting from the individual to the family unit orientation.

The staff experienced three main levels of awareness of the family unit concept. The first was the level of *intellectual awareness*. It was relatively easy to understand the concept intellectually.

The second was the level of *clinical awareness*. It was infinitely more complex to put the concept into clinical operation than to understand it intellectually. First it was necessary to further clarify and define our own thinking. All existing theories, terminology, literature, teaching, the rules of society that deal with sick people, and the rules and principles that deal with the practice of medicine, are based on the familiar individual orientation. It was hard for the staff to give up this "second nature" way of thinking. Then came the problem of operating in a medical center which regarded "the individual as the unit of illness." The individual orientation in medicine is strict. It requires that the individual be called "patient" and that individual pathology be defined with tests and labeled with a "diagnosis." Failure to focus on the individual can be regarded as medical irresponsibility. Our problem was to find a way to operate a "family unit" project in an institution with an individual orientation. Our research center permitted certain flexibilities not possible in a strict clinical setting. For instance, the center permitted a "For Research Study Only" diagnostic label. In general, the minimal individual requirements of the center were met, but within the research ward the use of "diagnoses" and the term "patient" was avoided. The same problem has come up in our writing. It becomes so complicated to avoid terms such as "patient" and "schizophrenia" that we have temporarily resolved the dilemma by sparing use of familiar terms. In the course of implementing the family unit concept into the clinical operation, we came to "know" the concept in a way that was quite different from the intellectual awareness.

The third level was that of *emotional awareness*. There was a definite process in changing from emotional identifications with the individual to an emotional awareness of the family unit. The first emotional reaction in a new staff member was usually overidentification with one family member, usually the patient, and anger at the family members most involved with the patient, usually the mother. Family members work constantly to get staff members to support their individual viewpoints. The second emotional reaction was usually that of alternating overinvolvements, first with one, and then with another family member. Gradually there would come an emotional detachment from the stressful overinvolvements and a beginning capacity to become aware of the over-all family problem.

As I see it, the theoretical focus on the family unit, plus the constant daily contact with the living together situation, set the stage for this automatic detachment from the individual and the growing emotional awareness of the family. The detachment proceeded most rapidly in those who had the best control over countertransference overinvolvement. Some staff members were never free of overinvolvements with one family member and angers at other family members. It is essential that the family psychotherapist relate himself to the family and that he avoid overinvolvement with the individual. There are constant forces within the family and within himself to cause him to revert to the familiar individual orientation. When anxiety is high, the family members exert more pressure for individual relationships. When the therapist is anxious, he is more likely to respond with his second nature individual orientation that "feels right." I found that the use of terms associated with the individual orientation was sufficient stimulus to cause me to revert to individual thinking. I was responsible for the family psychotherapy. In an effort to maintain a family unit orientation, I avoided the use of many familiar psychiatric terms associated with the individual and forced myself to use simple descriptive terms. Other staff members have been freer to use familiar terms.

Early in the study we used a term which was discarded because it has certain inaccuracies, but it does convey a fairly clear notion of the hypothesized psychological unity in the family. The term *undifferentiated family ego mass* suggests a central family oneness. Some siblings are able to achieve almost complete differentiation from the family while others achieve less. The one who becomes psychotic is an example of one who achieves little differentiation. On one level each family member is an individual, but on a deeper level the central family group is as one. Our study was directed at the "undifferentiated family ego mass" beneath the individuals. In the literature the concept that appears to be closest to our family unit idea was presented by Richardson in *Patients Have Families.*[4] He did not develop his concept as specifically as we have done, but one section of his book is headed "The Family as the Unit of Illness" and another "The Family as the Unit of Treatment." With the increasing number of family research studies, terms such as "family unit" and "family as a unit" have become commonplace. Most investigators have used theoretical thinking based on individual theory, and "family unit" terms that refer in a nonspecific way to a group of individual family members. According to our hypothesis this would be a "family group" rather than a "family unit." The term "family psychotherapy" is also used frequently. We have used the term to refer to psychotherapy directed at the hypothesized emotional oneness within the family. According to our hypothesis, a psychotherapy based on individual theory and directed to a group of individuals in the same family would be "family group psychotherapy," which is quite different from the method "family psychotherapy" as presented here.

In an effort to remove the psychotherapy from the status of an empirical trial-and-error method, it was incorporated into the research hypothesis so that the hypothesis determined the course of the psychotherapy and psychotherapy observations could be used to change the hypothesis. There were three main steps in adapting the hypothesis to the clinical operation. Each step had its own unique resistances. The first was to *think* in terms of the family unit rather than the individual. This step was incorporated into the hypothesis. Resistance to this was within the staff. It was difficult to give up "second nature" individual thinking. The second step was to *relate* to the family unit rather than to individuals. This step was incorporated into the research design. Resistance was both in the staff and in the families. In periods of high anxiety, the tendency to revert to the individual orientation was present both in the families and in the staff. The third step was to *treat* the family psychotherapeutically as a single organism. This step was incorporated into the research as "family psychotherapy." Obviously it was necessary to first *think* of the family as a unit and to be reasonably successful at *relating* to the family unit before it was possible to *treat* the family as a unit.

Now to a consideration of the way the family psychotherapy was integrated into the total research plan. The first step was to state the hypothesis in great detail.* Every possible clinical situation was antici-

---

* The detailed hypothesis has been presented in other papers.[1, 2, 3]

pated, explained according to the hypothesis, and recorded as predictions to be checked against clinical observations. The working hypothesis was thus a theoretical blueprint which postulated the origin, development and clinical characteristics of the family problem, which served as a basis for knowing the clinical management before a clinical situation arose, and which predicted clinical response in family psychotherapy. This corresponds to the *thinking* step outlined above. The second step was the development of a research design through which the working hypothesis could be put into clinical operation. The ward milieu was changed to fit the hypothesis as nearly as possible. For example, occupational therapy was planned for the family unit instead of the individual. This step corresponded to the *relating* step outlined above. The third step was the development of a psychotherapy consistent with the hypothesis.

Thus the entire operation came under the direction of the working hypothesis. Clinical predictions came to have great use. There were constant checks between predictions and actual observations. There were areas in which the predictions were amazingly accurate, and others with great inconsistency. The areas of inconsistency then became areas for special study. Eventually, when there were sufficient clinical observations to support a change, the working hypothesis was reformulated, the research design and the psychotherapy modified to conform to the reformulated hypothesis, and new predictions made. In this way the psychotherapy was linked point by point with the hypothesis, and observations that recurred consistently in psychotherapy could eventually become the basis of a change in the hypothesis. It was possible at any time to make changes in the psychotherapy but only *after* it was possible to reformulate the hypothesis and to *make the changes on the basis of theory*, rather than make changes in clinical emergencies that were based on "clinical judgment" or "feelings." The working hypothesis, which is also our current theoretical concept of schizophrenia, has been presented in detail in another paper.[3]

There is a wealth of dramatic clinical observations in a project such as this. The main problem is selecting and classifying data. I have focused on broad patterns of behavior rather than detail, and specifically on broad patterns present in all the families. There are a number of these which have been incorporated into the working hypothesis, which then served as the basis for modification of the psychotherapy. These relationship patterns have been described in other papers,[3,5,6] but they have played such an important part in the development of the psychotherapy that it is necessary to summarize some of them here.

Family members are quite different in their outside business and social relationships than in those within the family. It is striking to see a father who functions successfully and decisively in business but who, in relation to the mother, becomes unsure, compromising and paralyzed by indecision. In all the families there has been emotional distance between the parents which we have called the "emotional divorce." At one extreme were the parents with a calm controlled distance from each other. The parents had few overt disagreements and they saw the marriage as ideal. The marriages had the *form* and *content* of closeness in that they went through the actions of closeness and used terms of endearment associated with closeness, but *emotion* was obliterated. Neither husband nor wife could communicate inner thoughts, fantasies or feelings to each other, although both could communicate thoughts and feelings to others. At the other extreme were parents who fought and argued in their brief periods of closeness and who spent most of their time in a "cold war" distance from each other. Most of the parents maintained the distance with varying combinations of calm control and overt disagreement.

Both parents are equally immature. In outside relationships, both could cover up the immaturity with façades of maturity. In their relationship with each other, especially when they attempted to function together as a team, one would immediately become the adequate or overstrong one and the other the inadequate or helpless one. Neither could function in the midground between these two extremes. Either could function in either position, depending on the situation. Overadequate fathers were cruel and authoritative and inadequate mothers were helpless and complaining. Overadequate mothers were dominating and bossy and inadequate fathers were passive and compliant. We have called this the "overadequate-inadequate reciprocity." The one who makes a decision for the two of them immediately becomes the overadequate one who is seen as "dominating" the other, who is "forced into submission." When neither will immediately "give in" they fight and argue. Neither wants the responsibility of "dominating," the anxiety of "submitting," nor the discomfort of fighting. The emotional divorce is a mechanism to make the relationship more comfortable. They keep the distance, avoid teamwork decisions, seek individual activities and share inner thoughts and feelings with relatives, friends, children or other outside figures. As the years pass, the parents tend to develop fixed patterns in which one is usually overadequate and the other inadequate. The overadequate-inadequate reciprocity and the decision paralysis create a state of extreme *functional helplessness* in the family.

There is an intense interdependence between father, mother and patient which we have called the "interdependent triad." It is usual for normal siblings to become rather involved in the family problem, but not so deeply that they cannot separate themselves from the triad, leaving the father, mother and patient interlocked in the family oneness. There are constant patterns of functioning within the triad. Either parent can have a close relationship with the patient, provided the other parent permits it. The parents, separated from each other by the emotional divorce, share the patient much as divorced parents share their children. The most familiar pattern is one in which the mother, in an extreme overadequate position to the helpless patient, has the "custody" of the patient, while the father is distant and passive. There are situations in which the mother-patient relationship is disrupted, following which the father then functions very much as does the mother in the close attachment to the patient.

The parents hold strong opposing viewpoints about many levels of issues in their lives together. The one issue about which there is strongest disagreement is the management of the patient. A father and mother with a high level of overt disagreement said, "We agree on everything but politics. Isn't that strange?" Other parents with a low level of overt disagreement said, "We agree on everything except how to raise children, and how to raise parakeets." It is important for the psychotherapist to know that the parents hold these opposite viewpoints about the patient, even though the opposing viewpoint is not expressed. Opposing viewpoints appear to be related more to opposing the other than to real strength of conviction. There have been exchanges of viewpoints in which each parent comes to argue the viewpoint formerly used by the other. The opposing viewpoints seem to function in the service of maintaining identity. For instance, the ones who "give in" have described a "loss of identity," "loss of part of myself," and "inability to know what I think and believe." "Speaking up" seems to be a way of maintaining identity. The "differences" constitute a pressing daily problem for the parents. To them, the answer lies in reaching an agreement and "... that is impossible." Actually, their own effort to talk out the difference results in greater difference! The more clearly one states a viewpoint, the more vigorously the other raises the opposition.

Some definite *principles, rules and techniques* of family psychotherapy have been developed. The principles are derived directly from the working hypothesis. The rules establish the structure for adapting principles to the psychotherapy operation. The techniques are devices used by the therapist to implement the rules. For instance, one of the principles considers the family as a psychological unit. The rule requires the family to participate as a unit in the family psychotherapy. The techniques are devices used by the therapist to implement the rules. In this paper I shall focus on the more simple structure of a single family in family psychotherapy with one therapist, and avoid the more complex situations with multiple therapists and atypical family groups.

The initial goal is to get the family unit into a continuing relationship with the therapist in which family members attempt to "work together" in the hour to discuss and define their own problems. The therapist works toward a position of unbiased detachment, from which position he is able to analyze intrafamily forces. If we think of the family as a single organism, the situation has certain analogies to the structure of psychoanalysis. The family "working together" is similar to the patient who attempts to free associate. The therapeutic effort is to analyze existing intrafamily relationships *in situ*, rather than to analyze the transference relationship between patient and analyst. When the therapist is successful in relating to the family unit and in avoiding individual relationships, the family unit develops a dependence on the therapist similar to neurotic transference, which is quite unlike the intense primitive attachment of psychotic patient to therapist.

We begin the psychotherapy with a simple explanation of the theoretical premise of the project and of the "working together" structure in the hours. The working together may appear simple on the surface but it is directed at the heart of the problem. The "emotional divorce," the "overadequate-inadequate reciprocity" and the problems of the "interdependent triad" stand in the way. The structure demands that one member functions as leader and start the hour. When the family is able to start, deep anxiety is stirred up. There are definite mechanisms (equivalent to resistance in individual psychotherapy) by which the family avoids the anxiety of working together. When anxiety mounts, the family effort can become blocked. As I see it at this point, one of my main functions is that of an "enabler" who helps them get started at working together, who follows along when they can work together, and who helps them start again when there is a block.

A family with a psychotic family member is a functionally helpless organism, without a leader, and with a high level of overt anxiety. It has dealt helplessly and noneffectively with life, it has become dependent on outside experts for advice and guidance, and its most positive decisions are made in the service of relieving the anxiety of the moment, no matter how many complications this may cause tomorrow. How does the therapist help this kind of family into a working-together relationship? Some of our most important principles and rules are directed at this area. In broad terms, the goal is to find a leader in the leaderless family, to respect the family leader when there is a functioning leader, and to find ways to avoid individual relationships and the position of omnipotence into which the family attempts to place the therapist. A review of the research families will illustrate some of the problems with family leaders.

In the 15 families with fathers, there were 8 in which the mothers functioned clearly as the overadequate ones in relation to helpless patients and as decision-makers for the family. The fathers were distant, passive, resisting critics of the mothers' activities. Even though the fathers did not express it openly, their thoughts focused on what the mothers were doing wrong and on what the *mothers* should do to correct it, but not on any initiative or action for themselves. These mothers could motivate the family effort, overcome the fathers' and patients' resistance to coming to the hours and initiate the "working together." These families have done best in family psychotherapy.

There were four families in which the fathers functioned as spokesmen for the mothers, who remained behind the scenes. A parody of this situation might go as follows: The mother tells the father that he has to decide